PHL
KT-175-573

ENCYCLOPEDIA OF
Asian Culture

ENCYCLOPEDIA OF

Asian Culture

Editors

P. N. CHOPRA ▪ PRABHA CHOPRA

VISION BOOKS

(Incorporating Orient Paperbacks)

New Delhi • Bombay • Hyderabad

ISBN 81-7094-306-X

Published in 1999 by
Vision Books Pvt. Ltd.
(Incorporating Orient Paperbacks & CARING imprint)
24 Feroze Gandhi Road, Lajpat Nagar III,
New Delhi-110024 (India)
Phone: (+91-11) 6836470/80
Fax: (+91-11) 6836490
e-mail: visionbk@del2.vsnl.net.in

Printed at
Rashtra Rachna Printers
C-88 Ganesh Nagar Complex, Pandav Nagar,
Delhi 110092, India

Contents

Part 7: Puppet Theatre

Part 8: Cinema in Asia

Part 9: The Ramayana in Asia

Part 10: Games and Pastimes

Part 11: Embroidery, Textiles and Batik

List of Illustrations

Introduction

Culture, a nebulously defined identity manifests itself best through the medium of art. Whenever and wherever two or more artistically well-developed civilizations come across each other, there is a mutual give and take between the respective art-forms belonging to such civilizations and indeed the impact of such a merger or assimilation is clearly felt. Even where there is no such fusion, merger or complete assimilation, the impact of one art on the other is easily perceptible. Thus, through the vicissitudes of history the art-forms pertaining to one culture have not always been a total product of one nation alone. In fact, the art-forms of any nation or a civilization have in them, as in the case of people, numerous traits and strains not belonging to the indigenous character.

Whether it be a Gothic arch, a Pathan arch or a Hindu *Shikhar,* a mutual give and take is always discernible. This reciprocal impact has been a source of further development and enrichment of all art-forms in the world. Indeed, the hope for survival of the cultural heritage of mankind — and ultimately for enduring peace — lies in the mutual appreciation of art-forms of various nations.

The first influential notion of culture in its more recent sense can be marked, interestingly, by an exact date, 1871. It was only then, says a scholar, that the Englishman, Edward B. Taylor, offered in the first sentence of the first page of his famous *Primitive Culture* the one definition that has doubtless been quoted more often than all others combined. "Culture or civilization," said Taylor, "is that complex whole of which includes knowledge, belief, art, morals, law, custom and any other capabilities and habits acquired by man as a member of society." Culture is the universal characteristic of human societies. Thus, even as civilizations are born, bloom and even die as did the ancient Greek and Egyptian civilizations, the essence of a culture lives on in the heart of man. No human groups have ever been known that did not have language, traditions, customs and institutions.

There are numerous examples, in the long history of man, of cultural interactions which have fused not only customs and habits but the different races of man, so that most cultures have become composite.

In this way, certain cultures like the Indian, Malaysian, Philippines, Thai and others tend to be one-world cultures. Obviously, our present civilization is the product of prolonged fusion of countless ethnic units and different mental and social habits which have mixed so completely that they have lost their alien character.

In studying the interconnections of Asian cultures dating back to thousands years before Christ, we find that despite long distances between various countries, the operation of trade routes, the comings and goings of soldiers and consequent inter-marriages, the plying of small boats which hugged the sea-coast from the Red Sea, to the Persian Gulf, down to the Coromandal Coast, reveals mixtures which look odd today because in modern times these countries were compulsorily separated from their neighbours by Western Imperialism since the fifteenth century.

With all her conservatism, her adherence to a traditional way of life that has never really been in danger of destruction, Japan went out of her way towards the end of the nineteenth century to embrace an alien way of life that she believed to be necessary to her complete modernisation and survival. She accepted industrialisation that made her at one time singular among Asian nations. Cultural intercourse may have set up in Japanese minds a kind of schizophrenia, not unlike that among Indians in the nineteenth and twentieth centuries, but the modern Japanese does not appear to have suffered from the inaction that a split-personality is presumed to induce. It is apparently possible to owe a spiritual allegiance to a traditional culture even as we adjust to the times in the way we act and work and live. Indeed, such synthesis may in the long run pay the individual as it pays the nation. In the Philippines, we have a meeting and a synthesis of the cultures of people of Malaysian stock that has evidently been dominated by the Catholic religion and the culture of Spain. The Philippines later switched to a very different culture — the predominantly Protestant culture of the United States of America. Today, the Filipino's is a culture apart. He is not an American in the accepted sense of that term for he bears within him the pulsating beliefs of Spain that are as different as can be from those of America, and the blood, for what that implies, of the Asian countries.

Of course, a civilization is conditioned by geography, climate, temperament and habits of the people who inhabit the area, and many other factors. Attitude towards life or religious thinking, for instance, influences directly the works of art and architecture. The Persepolis temple, the pyramids, the caves at Ajanta or Ellora are all evidence of efforts to incorporate and perpetuate religious ideals. That philosophy and art are interrelated can be viewed in the temples of Nara in Japan or the Banaras Ghats in India where the dedicated work communicates the inner perception of the artist.

It must, however, be pointed out that India occupies a unique place in the world and has time and again shown a capacity for adjustment and comprehension. Civilization in India is at once more ancient and alive than in any other country in the world. "With its spirit of assimilation, comprehension and synthesis," says Dr. Radhakamal Mukerjee, "the Indian culture has stood at once for the infinite expansion of the human community." The well-known Indian poet, Rabindranath Tagore called the land "Bharat Tirtha" or the great concourse of humanity where everyone is welcome. Mahatma Gandhi believed that this ancient land with a continuous civilization of many thousand years would have the privilege of showing a way out to a blood-spilling world. Indian dance-forms tried to keep up the purity of *Bharatanatyam, Kathakali* and *Manipuri* but at the same time many folk-dance traditions blended; they even brought, like the Himalayan *gaddi* dancers or Tibetan and Japanese mask-dancers' elements beyond the borders of India.

India has played an important role in the interaction of cultures in Asia. It was about two thousand years ago when the first Indian merchantships sailed towards the lands of South-East Asia. They reached Kamboj, Malaysia, Siam, Vietnam and Indonesia. The Sailendra Empire held sway over Kamboj and Malaysia and through the medium of language and literature, particularly Sanskrit and Pali, Hindu culture and civilization spread to the whole of South-East Asia. The cultural influence of India, as many articles in this book would reflect, today lies scattered in the numerous monuments and folk-tales rooted in Indian mythology. Though many of the South-East Asian countries subsequently changed their religion, the core of their culture remains ancient Indian in character. In many cases, Indians can discover their ancient culture in its true form outside their own country for there it has escaped the ravages of time. Hence, the necessity to review India's cultural relations with the countries of South-East Asia. These regions were once seats of powerful Hindu kingdom and empires more than 1,500 years ago, and bore Hindu names such as Champa, Yava-dvipa, Suvarnabhumi and Suvarana-dvipa.

It should be added, however, that the culture that took shape in the widespread expanse of these lands owed its content no less to indigenous sources than to the imported product. The Angkor temples thus carry such a dual imprint and are an amazing example of creative synthesis. In the words of a commentator: "Khmer culture is essentially based on the inspiration of India, without which the Khmers at best might have produced nothing greater than the barbarous splendour of the central American Mayas; but it must be admitted that here, more than anywhere else in Greater India, this inspiration fell on fertile soil." Indonesia and Thailand hold even more of such fusion. Following the Indian merchants and warriors who reached those shores after long months on the seas came the Brahmin priests. Attaining dominant positions at the royal courts, they imparted upon the ruling houses the elaborate ritualism which they had devised in their own homeland as an instrument of their authority. Palaces were the starting point. The new culture then spread out to the people enriching their spiritual life at one level, while giving them at another level the complex formalities of the rites of divine worship. As the chapter in this book on *Ramayana* clearly bears out, the ancient Indian epics, *Ramayana* and *Mahabharata,* made the strongest impact on the Indonesian mind. Adapted into the Javanese language, as also in Balinese and Malay and Thai, they became an intrinsic part of the literature and mythology in each of these countries. They remained a source of inspiration for the people through all the centuries and continued to be so even today. An Indonesian scholar has summed up these trends thus: "Great was the influence of the Indian civilization on the spiritual life of Indonesia, yet Indonesia succeeded in developing her own tremendously vital personality."

Thus, from Malay Peninsula to the Philippines, Indians continue to be known generally as "Kalings", indications of the lingering tradition that in ancient days most of the Indians migrated from the Kalinga region.

There was a time not very long ago when the four countries of the Mekong basin — Laos, Thailand, Cambodia and Vietnam — could collectively be described as the Indo-Chinese Peninsula. A mingling of the two principal streams (Indian and Chinese) is still visible.

In this process Buddhism has played a most important role. However, Hinduism too has been for many centuries a potent force in evolving cultural affinities between India, Indonesia, Indo-China, Sri Lanka, Thailand, Korea and Japan.

Even a layman is struck by similarities of customs in the various countries of Asia, such as the taking-off of shoes before entering holy places whether it is a temple or a mosque, drinking of holy water in shrines, respect for elders, teachers, etc. There are also great similarities in names of person and places in various countries of Asia, particularly Malaysia, Thailand and Japan. While Thais directly adopted names of Rama, for example, Sanskrit or Hindi names are a familiar sight even in Malaysia, though they are written in the Roman script. Even many Japanese names owe their origin to the language spoken in the North-East of India, particularly Nagaland. For example, *Japfu* or *joe* closely resemble *Chibu*, a mountain in Japan. Again Nagoya or Nagasaki may have been derived from Naga. Some of the words prevalent among the tribes in Nagaland closely resemble Japanese words, such as *Azhi* (liquor), *Madhu* (rice and beer), *Azu* (water), *Ashi* (meat), *Amichi* (cow), etc. Like the Japanese, the Nishi tribe in Arunachal, a State of North-East India, regard the Sun as a manifestation of the Supreme-Being. Like among the Khasis, ancestor worship is also a basic tenet of the Shintos of Japan.

Even before Buddhism spread to Japan, Brahmanical deities had found their way to Japan and are widely worshipped even today including, *Indra* (*Taoshaku-ten*), *Brahma* (*Bon-ten*), Vishnu (*Naraen-ten*), and others, and *Agni* is one of the twelve guardian deities in Japan. Japanese warriors went to war in helmets bearing Sanskrit *bijas.* The colour scheme in Horyji caves came to be compared to Ajanta paintings. As the great scholar Chamberlain observed: "In a sense Japan may be said to owe everything to India for from India came Buddhism and Buddhism brought civilization."

As noted earlier, Buddhism played a pivotal role in cultural intercourse among various countries of Asia. In the field of sculpture, too, there is a great similarity in the images of Buddha produced in India and various other countries of Asia, such as Thailand, Sri Lanka, Korea, Japan, etc.

The great Indian reformer and scholar Keshab Chandra Sen spoke fervently of the past greatness of Asia and pointed out that even Christianity was really an Asian religion. "Pride in Asia's achievements in bygone ages, combined with anguish at the woeful state in which it had sunk, led to a feeling of the oneness of Asia. This feeling persisted for almost a century and eventually became one of the contributory factors in the movement against foreign rule."

It is in the context of these factors mentioned above — the emergence of a national culture-consciousness, the perception of a fundamental affinity of spirit among Asian countries, and a desire to understand this affinity in the larger context of universal humanism — that the basic tenets of Asian culture could be understood.

It is due to these ancient ties that India under Jawaharlal Nehru gave unstinted support to the struggle for national freedom waged by the peoples of Indonesia and other Asian countries. The epoch-making Bandung Conference, the evolution of the concept of *Panchsheel*, the ever-widening co-operation between Asian countries — all these testify to Nehru's dynamic and persistent efforts. And as Nehru wrote in his *Discovery of India*: "I remember when I first read... some kind of a detailed account of the history of South-East Asia, how amazed I was and how excited I became. New panoramas opened out before me, new perspectives of history, new conceptions of India's past, and I had to adjust all my thinking and previous notions to them. Champa, Cambodia and Angkor, Sri Vijaya and Majapahit, suddenly rose out of the void, took living shape, vibrant with that instinctive feeling which makes the past touch the present."

The present work is an attempt to portray Asian culture through the ages in all its aspects — political organisation, social life, economic conditions, education and literature, and art and architecture. This would help in assessing and focusing the role of cultural currents in different periods. A proper evaluation of the Asian way of life in all its aspects and in different periods, has been made. It is hoped that the present study would provide a perspective for viewing and understanding Asia's cultural heritage in full.

A study of various chapters in this book reveals close similarities among peoples of Asia in the fields of games and sports, dress and clothing, hairstyle, eating habits, houses, agrarian rituals and festivals, life of fisher-folk, position of women, love for flowers and their use for spiritual purposes, dance and drama, puppet theatre, kite-flying, use of masks, etc. The two great Indian epics *Ramayana* and *Mahabharata* made a strong impact on large parts of this region and are most popular particularly in South-East Asian countries, such as Indonesia, Malaysia, Thailand, Sri Lanka and others.

In the present work, the first of its kind, an effort has been made to portray various aspects of the culture of Asian people, their similarities and diversities which would serve as a work of reference for scholars and of abiding interest to common people. The various articles have been written by renowned specialists of Asia in their respective fields to whom we owe a debt of gratitude.

Most of these articles originally appeared in the *Journal of the Asian Pacific Culture* sponsored by UNESCO during the course of several years while some others were specially written for this book. To the journal's Chief Editor, Miyamoto Shigeo, we are deeply obliged for his help and co-operation and also for supplying us some of the older issues of this journal, and to his predecessors for initiating this dialogue.

We are obliged to our friend and publisher, Kapil Malhotra of Vision Books, for undertaking the present publication.

P. N. Chopra
Prabha Chopra

Part 1

The Way of Life

An example of ukiyo-e, *woodblock prints which flourished in Japan from mid-seventeenth to mid-nineteenth century.*

Birth Customs

Birth Rites and Folk Beliefs in Thailand

A couple without children is sad and insecure for they are afraid that no daughter will look after them when they are old and no son will become a monk to save them from going into hell when they die. The Thai believe that barrenness is caused by lack of merit, therefore, a childless wife will try every means to become pregnant either by taking folk medicines or by praying for help from the supernatural beings. Moreover in an extreme case, some women will find a chance to perform a Hindu ritual by having sexual intercourse with the holy Siva lingam which is still kept in the compound of certain Buddhist Wats today. Among the Thai, it is regarded that childbirth is a crisis because it is a period of uncertainty and is "like going to war", for a woman might die. There are many beliefs and rituals for pregnant woman to perform in order to facilitate delivery and also to protect the mother and child against evil forces.

Customs and belief during pregnancy

A pregnant woman has to observe taboo in terms of words and actions in order to save herself from danger. She wears, for instance, an amulet or sacred thread around her wrists to protect the *khwan* (the soul) in the womb from flying off in terror (it is believed that the *khwan* fly into the womb of the woman during sexual intercourse) and the baby will die in the womb if its *khwan* does not return. She must also avoid going to a funeral, visiting sick people or observing childbirth because the child will be frightened and lose his *khwan.* She is encouraged to work hard so that the child will not get too fat and be difficult to deliver. However she is urged to eat a great deal for herself and the unborn child. It is also believed that the baby is created from the blending of kinds and qualities of food. For instance, if she eats fish, meat, or fruits, the baby will be a reincarnation of an animal, if she eats sweet things, the child is from the human world. From such beliefs, women in the olden days would avoid eating meat or fruits for fear of getting a merit-lacking child. However, among the fruit taboo, coconut-milk and banana are allowed since they are likely to bring fair skin to the child and help the mother to deliver the child easily, like peeling a banana.

Also during the ninth month, she would find a chance to crawl under an elephant and drink a bowl of gold-foil dissolved in coconut-milk to facilitate the delivery.

The husband, too, shares in observing certain behaviour. He should avoid quarrelling with his wife for it would cause the child to be quarrelsome. He has to avoid laughing at or making jokes with any cripple or else the child will be born abnormal. The husband is expected to collect wood for his wife's post-parturition fire which will take many days after giving birth to a child. He is also required to cover the pile of fire wood with some thorny wood to keep away the evil spirits.

Birth rites

There is not much difference between the birth of a baby boy or girl except in the case of the first child which is of great psychological and social significance for the parents. In a village, usually, a midwife is sent for when the delivering time comes and it is also expected that the neighbours will come and help. During delivery if a woman has difficult time, she is supposed to drink magic water or water which her husband has used to wash his foot, to facilitate the delivery.

After the child is born, the mother will drink a filtrate of tamarind, salt, and water to cure the womb. The midwife will cut the umbilical cord with a bamboo knife and wash the baby with soap. She usually uses salt to remove the greasy fat from the baby's body and paints the abdomen with turmeric so that baby may not get stomachache. Then the baby is put on a winnowing tray. If the baby is a boy, a book and a pencil will be placed beside him. This will make him intelligent and knowledgable. If the baby is a girl, a needle and sewing thread are given to make her become skilful in sewing.

The mother, then, performs a ceremony of linking the child to the family by asking a woman who is the mother of healthy children to winnow the tray. The woman will raise the tray up moving it in a circular motion slowly from left to right and recite the magical old words three times, "three days, a spirit child; four days, a human child". One of neighbours will act in place of the spirit by crying out: "Mine". Then she takes the tray to the baby's mother who sits in a circle of sacred thread. At this time they tie the child's ankles and wrists with sacred thread to seize and welcome its soul. They all bless the baby well.

The next step is to clean the lower part of the mother's body with warm water or alcohol. Some folk medicines are painted to make the uterus dry. The midwife will put her foot on the mother's hip and press hard, three times on each side. This is to close the hipbone and to get the pelvis back into place again. To save her from the evil spirits, it is believed that the mother has to rest beside the holy fire, the heat of which will also cure the womb, get rid of the bad blood and waters of childbirth, restore her strength and stimulate her milk. For the first-born, she is expected to stay eleven or fifteen days by the fire with the stay shorter for each successive child but never less than five days.

During the fire period, she is forbidden to eat cool things such as bananas, ice, gourds except boiled rice and salted fish and some folk medicine. She is urged to eat a special nursing curry of banana flower and vegetables. If anyone speaks of uterus pain to her during this time, she will suffer more. If a visitor speaks of the hotness of the fire, some boils will appear on her body and she will be weak for a long time.

It is also a taboo to leave the fire on an even day for she will soon be pregnant again. Before leaving the fire, the mother is obliged to thank the fire asking the spirit of fire to bless her and her child. Lustral water is sprinkled on the fire and also given to the mother to drink. After leaving the fire, however, she is still unclean and is prohibited to sleep with her husband for three months.

The placenta must be cleaned carefully and put into an old pot mixed with salt and set aside for three days before burial. As a general practice, the placenta pot is taken to be buried under a big old tree. While being carried, the pot has to be held by both hands so that the child will be able to use both of his hands properly. On the way back, the person has, if the baby is a boy, to sing or preach along the way so that he will grow up with a good voice and become a good preacher. If it is a girl the person has to pick up wood or vegetable on the way back home so that the baby will be a good housewife.

Ceremony of a month-old child

When the baby is a month old, a rite of first hair which is a purification rite is performed. An offering tray made of banana stems containing food together with candles, joss sticks and flowers, is made to the guardian spirit of the place. Actually the head of a child is not completely shaved, for a knot of hair is left in order to protect the sensitive spot of the soul. The shaven hair is placed in a cup made of banana leaf and is floated away along a running stream so that the baby will be as cool and happy as the water. Relatives and neighbours will soothe the *khwan* of the child by tying sacred thread around the baby's ankles and wrists and pronouncing a blessing upon the child. The baby is now a member of the family.

The naming of a child is done usually when the child is placed in cradle for the first time. Before placing the child in the cradle, a tomcat, a stone roller for pulverizing native medicine, a kind of gourd smeared with white powder, small bags containing paddy, sesame seeds and peas, are placed in the cradle so that the child will have a cool temper like the gourd. He will be rich and will love the place like a cat. Besides this, if the child is a male, a book and a pencil are also placed in the cradle; and needle and sewing thread are placed instead if it is a female child.

The name of the child which is written on a small piece of paper is placed beside the child in the cradle after the cat and other things are removed. Usually the father or the monk will be the person who names the child. It is also a popular belief that the spirit has a great deal of control over the birth of a human being and it is likely to bring him back at its will. So to prevent the child from being taken away, the spirit must be deceived by naming the child as a nobody. He or she is only a buffalo, a frog or a bad smelling being. However when the child grows up the proper name will be given again.

The belief and customs of childbirth described here are one of the features in Thai culture which shares some similarity with its neighbours in the mainland of South-East Asia. These reflect a blending of the indigenous belief with Buddhist and Brahmanical elements and other religious cults derived from India and China.

This traditional way of childbirth has long been practised among the Thai people of the central plain. Today, it is still found in the rural area where modern civilization has not yet come into contact. It could be expected, however, that while this traditional way of childbirth is gradually changing into a new form of modern medical care, the belief and taboo of childbirth still have significant influence upon pregnant women. We may say that from the study of Thai birth rites today, the old form of belief co-exists with the new method of medical care, and the new is a trend of change in which the old remains recognizable.

Birth Customs and Ceremonies in Japan

In Japan, the ceremonies and traditions that surround birth begin well before the infant actually comes into the world. When it is clear that a woman has conceived, she and her husband are frequently invited by her parents and the couple's neighbours to meals to celebrate the happy event, or the prospective parents may be presented with gifts of red and white cloth or *mochi*, cakes of pounded rice. In the fifth or seventh month of pregnancy (counted by the lunar calendar, so that each month is an equal 28 days and the total period of pregnancy is said to be ten months), the mother wraps her enlarging abdomen in a long band of cloth to provide support, and this *haraobi*, bearing the well-omened colours of red and white or red and yellow, is frequently received from her parents or from a Shinto shrine. In the past, many women would wear this *haraobi* right up to the time of birth.

Today, most Japanese give birth at hospitals or maternity clinics, but in the past it was usual to give birth at home or at the home of the mother's parents, with the help of a midwife. There were also frequent cases where a village would have a small building especially for use at the time of birth. Such a *ubuya* (birth house) appears in the *Kojiki*, (or Ancient Chronicles), the earliest of Japanese histories written during the eighth century. Although they are not actually used today, these buildings still remain in a number of areas, principally in the Kinki and Kyushu regions. Often, the mother would live in the *ubuya* for twenty or thirty days after the delivery. Another difference between the past and the present is that today women lie down to give birth, while in the past Japanese women customarily gave birth in a sitting position, leaning against something. A rope might also be hung from the ceiling for the mother to hold on to during the delivery.

It was believed in the past that unless the god of the mountains and attendant gods gathered, the child would not be born. Thus, in some areas, to ensure the presence of the gods, a horse might be led into the mountains to be ridden by the gods. When the horse was led into the mountains, if it suddenly reared up or twitched its tail or ears, this was taken as a sign that the god of the mountains had mounted; the horse would then be led back to the village. This custom remained alive in the folklore of the Tohoku region until relatively recently.

Another custom to ensure a safe birth was to stand a broom by the mother's pillow at night. Since it was the belief that standing a broom upside was a charm to make guests leave quickly, there are some who believe that the practice of standing the broom by the mother's pillow was designed to bring a quick birth, but it was also a practice to borrow a broom from a shrine and then lightly sweep the stomach of the expectant mother after making offerings before the broom. The belief was rather widely held that the god of birth was also the god of the broom.

In some areas, special worship of the god of birth would begin from the day by the haraobi was first used, but in the majority of areas, such worship would begin with the onset of labour pains. In many regions it was believed that if an infant smiled spontaneously, this was because he was being entertained by the invisible god of birth.

The infant's umbilical cord would be cut with a small bamboo knife or a sharpened shell, and the separated cord would be (and still is) put into a small box and retained. In some cases, the box might be buried in the earth, and since in many places it was believed that the first person to step on the spot where the umbilical cord was buried would be the person most respected and feared by the child, the father would frequently immediately step on the box.

When the child is born, rice, the staple food of the Japanese, is immediately prepared and a rice bowl filled to overflowing is often offered to the god of birth on the family alter or placed at the infant's pillow. It is a widely held that the greater the number of people who eat this rice prepared to celebrate the birth, the greater the number of children the mother will have; so in many localities, neighbourhood house-wives and others will be gathered to partake of the rice.

Bathing the new born infant in hot water is today performed by the hospital nurses, but in the past, this was not necessarily done immediately after birth and might be ceremonially performed two or three days later. In many locations around the country are wells or springs known for having provided the water used in the first bathing of famous figures or heroes. It was the practice in many regions for the infant to receive the milk of someone other than his mother for the first few days of life, and it was not unusual for this person to be of special importance to the child throughout his life. Another practice found in some regions in the past was that clothing would not be prepared in advance for the infant; at first, the new born child would be wrapped in the mother's underslip. In contrast, however, there were many regions in which clothing would be prepared by the mother's parents, and this clothing would first be put on amidst celebrations on the infant's third day of life. The use of clothing with sleeves was a special sign of celebration. A mixture of wheat and rice. would sometimes be prepared or balls of rice covered in red bean paste (called *ohagi*) would be made and offered to the god of birth or distributed to the neighbours.

Even today, there are still many places where the child is named as part of a celebration on the seventh day after birth. The name given to the infant is written on pieces of paper and prominently displayed in the home or placed at the infant's pillow.

In such places as Okinawa and the Amami Islands, it is still a custom today to go down to the seashore on the day the name is given to catch a small crab and place it on the head of the infant. In the past, it is said, the child would customarily be taken to the seashore or a riverside for this ceremony. Part of the name-giving ceremony in many cases is the making of a formal meal for the infant, and the preparation of the fish with the head and tail intact is also a necessary part of the celebration in many areas. Frequently a small stone is placed on the traditional tray bearing the formal meal.

When a child was born into a family which in the past had difficulties with the healthy upbringing of children, or when a child was born during an unlucky year, it was sometimes the practice to abandon the child at a crossroad to be picked up by someone who had been requested to do so in advance by the parents. The infant would then be returned to the original parents as a foundling, in hopes that by making it appear that the child was not the real child of the family, the difficulties of bad luck could be avoided. It was not unusual in such cases for the person picking up the "abandoned" infant to give it its name.

Around the 30th or 50th day after birth, the infant is taken for his first visit to the traditional shrine of the particular family and presented to the gods enshrined there. Even today, such scenes can be frequently seen throughout Japan. There is a difference of one day or so in the times when males and females are taken for this first visit to the shrine, with the male infant being taken earlier in many cases. The infant, dressed in clothing of brilliant colours and patterns, is carried to the shrine by its mother or grandmother, and frequently characters or marks are drawn on the child's forehead to ward off evil spirits. In many cases, if the infant is sleeping when the group arrives at the altar, he will be awakened and made to cry by shaking him or pinching his nose. It is said that the infant that cries at such a time will grow up strong and healthy, but some scholars also say that shaking the infant before the altar was seen as a means of settling the soul in the child's body.

For this first visit to the shrine, the infant is frequently dressed in a long kimono, with brilliant colours as already mentioned and at times bearing special designs of a felicitous nature, such as a carp leaping up a waterfall as a symbol of strength. The kimono may also bear the family crest, and here again, it is frequently a present from the mother's family.

In many places it is believed that since the mother's body is made impure by the birth, she may not pass through the gates of the shrine until this ceremonial first visit by the infant. The use of the separate *ubuya* was also a sign of the supposed impurity of giving birth, and it was also common to use separate fire for the mother and the rest of the household after the birth. However, some scholars also maintain that the act of giving birth was regarded as a holy act, and that the *ubuya* was a sanctified structure where the gods could be called upon to lend their strength to the delivery.

In Japan, 3 March is the Festival of the Dolls, also called Girls' Day, and girls celebrate by setting up displays of traditional dolls. For boys, 5 May is the corresponding day of celebration, when dolls of warriors or sets of model armour are displayed and large streamers of carp, another symbol of strength, are hung from poles outside the home to wave in the wind. These festivals are known to some extent outside of Japan, but it is also the custom to place special importance of the first 5 May after birth for a boy and the first 3 March after birth for a girl. The mother's parents or other relatives will often send carp streamers or warrior dolls to boys and traditional Japanese dolls to girls on such occasions.

To celebrate an infant's first New Year, a period of particular importance in Japan, it is the practice in some areas (for example, Gumma and Kumamoto Prefectures) to send ceremonial arrows symbolizing victory over evil spirits to boys and brilliantly decorated *hagoita*, or battledores, to girls.

On the hundredth day after birth, celebrations are held in many homes. Small dishes, plates, chopsticks, and other implements are purchased for the child, a tray of foods is laid out in traditional formal style, and the family goes through the motions of feeding the meal to the child. In Tokyo department stores one can even find special sets of trays, dishes, and the like for use in this celebration.

Frequently, a small stone is placed on the formal tray for this celebration, indicating according to one explanation the prayer that the infant's head, still relatively soft, will grow strong and durable, and according to another theory, the hope that the child's teeth will be strong and hard. Since the child generally begins to crawl about this time, rulers, chopsticks, an abacus, and other items may be placed in front of the child, and the parents may try to foretell his eventual profession from the items that the hundred-day-old child picks up.

In the past, it was not especially common in Japan to celebrate a person's annual birthday, and in quite a number of regions, only the first birthday received any particular celebration. In many areas it is the custom on the first birthday to distribute cakes of pounded rice to relatives and neighbours or to make a large pounded rice cake and have the child step on it or try to carry it on his back. In Nagano Prefecture and other regions, the young child may be made to put on a straw raincoat used in farming and made to look up at the heavens as part of the day's activities. It was also the belief in some regions that it is not good for a child to begin to walk too early, so that a walking child might be pushed down by hitting him lightly on the buttocks with a large rice cake. A later festival is *Shichi-go-san*, meaning "seven-five-three".

At ages three and five for boys and three and seven for girls, many children are dressed in fancy clothing and led to a Shinto shrine on 15 November. This custom began in Edo, the old name for Tokyo, during the Edo period (1603-1867), and spread throughout most of Japan. In Kyoto, Osaka, and some areas, there is also the custom of taking youngsters to Horinji Temple in Kyoto on 13 March of the year that they become thirteen years of age. This temple houses a famous statue of Kannon, the goddess of wisdom not only on 13 March but on either 13 April or 13 May. The custom of the uncles and aunts giving a boy a *hakama* (Samurai's skirt) and a girl an underskirt at such times was once quite widespread. Today, however, because Japanese adults and children alike generally wear Western clothing most of the time, this practice has largely disappeared, but even today the age of thirteen is sometimes regarded as the dividing line between childhood and youth.

Hindu Birth Rites in Bengal, India

Ceremonial union of the couple

The first ritual is known as *garbhadhan* which is ceremonial union of the husband and the wife with the specific purpose of impregnating the wife by the husband. This is observed on an auspicious day indicated in the Hindu calendar as appropriate for this purpose. This must be performed within sixteen days after the fourth day of first appearance of menstrual blood of the wife immediately following the marriage.

The rituals are as follows .

The husband cleanly dressed makes his wife sit on his left, facing east, and offer oblations to the Sun-God. The husband then stands up and takes his position behind his wife, and touches her by his hand from her shoulder to her uterus and in the course of doing so he chants incantation invoking the goddess Sinibali to give boon for birth of a long-lived son in her womb. He also prays for his wife's trouble-free delivery. After that, some women whose husbands are alive, or any boy, make the wife drink *pancha-gavya* or five sacred objects derived from the cow like some quantity of cow dung, cow's urine, milk, curd and clarified butter.

Both of them retire to bed the same night and have sexual intercourse with the specific purpose of having a son. There are certain incantations also which are supposed to be uttered by the husband at the final stage of the sexual act.

This ritual is performed only once in one's married life. Even if the wife does not conceive on this occasion, the ritual is not repeated. Nor is it repeated, when she gives birth to a daughter.

Taboo and rituals during pregnancy

When the wife conceives she has to observe certain restrictions in her movements. Some of them can be mentioned here.

The pregnant women are forbidden to look at a dead or alive serpent. Snake-charmers are not generally invited to a house where there is a pregnant woman. It is believed in some parts of India that if the shadow of a pregnant woman falls on a snake, the baby becomes blind. In some other parts of India, especially in Bengal, it is believed that if a pregnant woman casts her look at a snake, a child of crooked nature is born. But on the other hand it is also believed that a serpent removes the curse of barrenness from women. A serpent is generally believed to bestow a male child on a pregnant woman. If any one in the family dreams of a serpent it is believed that a male issue will soon be born in the family if there is any pregnant woman there.

Some of the other restrictions are:

1. A pregnant woman must not go below a palm or a plantain tree.
2. She must not cross a river nor a channel.
3. During dusk she must not visit the landing place of the family tank or any river for washing herself.
4. She must not wash fish during midday or at night for cooking or for any other purpose.
5. She must not go outdoor during midday.
6. She must not visit a house where there is a pregnant woman. If there is one in her own house she must not touch her.
7. She must not visit a house where there has occurred any death of a child.
8. During eclipse of the sun or the moon she must keep herself indoor and must not look at the eclipsed sun or the moon.

The husband of the pregnant wife also has to observe certain restrictions which are as follows :

1. He must not attend any cremation by carrying dead bodies to the cremation ground. He must not take food in a funeral feast.
2. He must not participate in ceremonial sacrifice of animals.

Anxiety of getting a male child instead of a female of the Hindu society is expressed in the ritual known as *Punsavan* performed on an auspicious day in the third month of the pregnancy.

In the early morning of the day of performing the *Punsavan*, the husband of the pregnant woman takes his bath and ceremonially offers food and sacrifices to the ancestors.

After that he seats his pregnant wife beside him and both of them offer oblation to fire, chanting proper incantations assisted by priests. He then goes behind his wife and touches her navel with his hand from behind. He chants incantations requesting the Vedic gods, Mitra, Varuna, Agni and Vayu to offer a male child to his wife's womb. Then the husband addresses the wife saying "there exists a male child in your womb".

The next ritual to be held during pregnancy is *Simantonnayan* literally meaning 'raising the parting of the hair'. It is observed in the case of the first pregnancy in its fourth, sixth or eight month. It is a very important ritual and is still observed even in urban areas, sometimes with real pomp and grandeur involving considerable expenditure. This is the last ritual before the actual birth of the child, and after this ritual is over the husband is forbidden to live with the wife until after the delivery of her child.

In the morning of the day of performing this ritual the husband takes his bath and offers food ceremonially to his ancestors. The wife also takes her bath and after decorating her body with ornaments and new clothes sits beside her husband and offers fuel to the sacrificial fire. After that the husband sits behind his wife facing east and ceremonially ties two ripe fig fruits in a thread and garlands his wife with them, uttering certain incantations. He then takes some thorns of porcupine in his hand and by the touch of them he moves his wife's hair upwards from the place of parting.

Then the husband cooks some rice mixed with sesame and pulses, and places the cooked rice before the eyes of the wife. He then asks her, "What are you seeing here?" She replies, "I see a vessel with cooked food."

The pregnant woman then visits some nearby bathing place like a village tank or river accompanied by a few elderly women whose husbands are alive. The pregnant woman ties some fruits of different (generally five) varieties in the skirt of her cloth and as she takes a dip in the water she releases the fruit into the river and quickly picks them up again. The sex of the unborn child is 'determined' by the fruit thus caught hold of.

In the ninth month of pregnancy there is an event called *Sadh-Bhakshan* literally meaning 'eating of desired food' for the purpose of entertaining the woman at the last stage of her pregnancy. The pregnant woman is invited to a sumptuous feast by her relatives and friends and is offered new clothes on this occasion. The function is confined only to the womenfolk and no male member of any family is invited.

Natal rite and folk rituals

If a son is born the father immediately offers food to his ancestors even before the umbilical cord is separated. After that any unmarried or pregnant woman or any Brahmin rubs the tongue of the child with his or her finger coated with powdered rice and wheat. He or she then takes a piece of gold and having once immersed it in honey rubs the tongue of the child. After that the father asks the attendants to separate the umbilical cord and then takes bath a preparatory to ceremonially seeing the face of his newly born son for the first time. But if a girl is born this part of the ritual is abandoned. Besides the above natal rite for a boy baby, there are also some folk rituals which are observed by the women generally unnoticed by the menfolk of the family.

The child is born in the lying-in-room which is magically protected from any possible attack of evil spirits by some iron nails, torn pieces of worn-out shoes, skulls of cattle all hung above the door and by other means of mystic character. The navel cord is immediately separated by the sharp edge of a slip of bamboo skin. The sex of the child is then announced by the midwife from within and the women waiting outside receive the announcement with eagerness. They in turn relay the announcement over a wider area by making a peculiar sound, known as *ulu* sound, made by the tips of the tongue striking against the two lips. If a son is born the sound is made five times and if the child is a daughter the sound is made three times. This is the public announcement of the birth of a child and its sex in a village.

On the first day of the birth no other ritual is performed. Birth-rites are performed on the sixth day of the birth of the child. At about ten o'clock at night, a small wooden seat is placed at the door inside the lying-in-room which in most cases is a thatched hut. A small earthen pitcher full of water and a new napkin are placed on the seat. Two canoe-shaped pots made of bark of the plantain tree, one filled with husked rice and the other with paddy, are placed at its two sides. Ripe plantains, some sweets and other ingredients of worship are also placed inside the pot which is filled with rice.

A pair of iron-bangles, a bit of a waist-band made of coloured thread, some pieces of gold and silver, a pen and an inkpot are also placed on the wooden seat. A new piece of cloth is spread on the ground before the seat and a lamp having five wicks soaked in clarified butter is kept burning all the while. It is believed that at dead of night the god Chitragovinda enters the lying-in-room and takes his seat there. The god Chitragovinda accepts the offering for himself and in return gives a boon to the new-born child. The pieces of gold and silver are intended to remind the god to bestow on the baby the boon of wealth. Before Chitragovinda leaves the room the god writes its fate with his own hand on the forehead of the child, whose future life is determined by this writing which, however, cannot be read with mortal eyes.

The door of the lying-in-room is closed and only the mother and the midwife are allowed within. Some women of the family ask from outside, "Pray, what are you doing inside?" The answer comes either from the mother or from the midwife, "We invoke the goddess Sasthi." Seven times the same question is asked and the same reply is repeated, but each time before the reply is given the mother or the midwife places the child on the floor on a new piece of cloth and takes it back again on the lap. After that the women outside make the auspicious sound *ulu* by their tongues five times if the child is a boy and three times if it is a girl. The mother and the midwife keep vigil throughout the rest of the night and both of them deliver little sermons to the child, such as not to be afraid of his/her enemies, or wild beasts like tigers, elephants and boars or ghosts and spirits and so on.

No ash or charcoal from the fire which burns in the lying-in-room can be brought outside the room before the sixth day of the birth of the child.

On the seventh or the ninth day at dawn, the housewife unnoticed by others, takes some ash or charcoal from the fire of the lying-in-room burning there since the birth of the child and places it on a piece of leaf from the plantain tree along with a *cowri* (a small shell), some turmeric, a lamp with its wick soaked in mustard oil and leaves them beneath a plantain tree within the compound of the house. She twines a thread seven times round the tree. This piece of thread is removed later and used as the waistband of the new born child for a time.

Oblation to the moon

A ritual known as *niskraman* literally meaning coming out from confinement or lying-in-room is observed in the third or the fourth moon day after the birth. This is performed after nightfall and making the new-born look at the moon is the principal object of this ritual. Therefore, a night with the bright half of the month is necessary for this purpose so as to have the moon in the sky.

The father sits facing the moon in the courtyard of his house and the mother, with the child fully covered, sits on her husband's left and offers the child to him. After that the father offers ceremonial worship to the moon. This is practically the ritual of child's ceremonially looking at the moon for the first time. After uttering some incantations the father makes his son look at the moon in the sky. Having done this he returns the child to its mother and all of them enter their home.

Name-giving ceremony

On the tenth night after the birth the name-giving ceremony is held. It may also be held on the sixth or the eighth night. At the very beginning, offerings are made to the ancestors by the father. After that the mother approaches her husband with the child in her arms having covered it with a new piece of cloth. She then offers the child to her husband and sits on his left side. The father softly touches the face, nose, eyes, and ears of the child and utters some incantations. After that the father speaks in a low voice with his face close to the left ear of his son, "thou art given this name", and utters the name given to the child. In the right ear he says, "thou shalt be known as such and such from today".

First shaving ceremony

In the third or any uneven month after the birth of the child its head is to be shaved for the first time. The ritual observed in this connection is known as *chudakaran* literally meaning 'shaving of the head'.

The father and the mother sit together and after offering food to the ancestors, the father accepts in his hands the child from the hands of its mother and worships the god Savita (the Sun). The father then pours some quantity of water slightly warm only over the head of the child. After uttering some incantations addressing the god Pusa, the father cuts some portion of hair from above the right ear of the child. He then offers his son to the barber who completes the remaining work of shaving the head cleanly.

First rice-eating ceremony

The first rice-eating ceremony is performed in the sixth or the eighth month after the birth if it is a boy and in the fifth or the seventh month if it is a girl.

At the very outset food is offered ceremonially to the ancestors by the father of the child. Afterwards some Vedic sacrifices aimed at Aditya, the sun-god are performed. Then, the child tastefully dressed with ornaments and clothes is taken into the lap of its maternal uncle who offers the first rice mixed with clarified butter to its mouth. Some incantations are also uttered by the maternal uncle while offering the food. Afterwards some ingredients like rice, inkpot, pen, pieces of earth and coins are placed on the ground before the child and the child is made to look at them. His future character is determined by the article it places its hands on at the first instance. If it holds the coin it is believed that the child will be a rich man or woman and if it holds the inkpot or the pen it is believed that it will be a scholar in its future life.

After the first rice-eating ceremony, the next ritual in a man's life is the initiation ceremony to be held not earlier than the tenth or the twelfth year of his life.

Birth Rites of the Newars of Nepal

Birth rites are found almost all over the world in one form or another. The bringing of new life to earth is a singularly awe-inspiring and sacred occasion and, if it conforms with societal rules, i.e. if it is legitimate, it is an occasion for rejoicing. It can be said that at birth ritual exists on roughly three functional levels. First, childbirth in itself can be quite dangerous for people lacking medical help. Through ritual the supernatural has been invoked to aid in childbirth and safeguard the delivery and health of the child. Second, the status of the woman having a child changes when the child is born to that of a mother. Whether it be for the first, second or third time, in societies where childbearing (and rearing) is one of women's legitimate duties, the status of a mother is something to be proud and one of the reasons for a woman's very existence. Third, birth rites are performed in order to incorporate the father as legitimate progenitor of the child and, in patrilineal societies, to bestow lineage on the child.

In Nepal, which is characterised by rich cultural diversity, one may find a variety of birth rites among the different ethnic groups. This small Himalayan Kingdom is the meeting-ground of Buddhism and Hinduism, though the hill communities still believe in the shamanistic cult of mediums and sorcerers. Nonetheless, Nepal is popularly known as the only Hindu State in the world, ruled by a Hindu King who is also worshipped by his people as the reincarnation of Vishnu. Here, we will discuss the birth rituals of the Newars, the original inhabitants of Kathmandu Valley. They are one of the most cultured ethnic groups in the country; they are skilled in metal-work, wood-carving and have their own language and writing script. Today, they are mainly known as traders and merchants and have spread to many parts of the kingdom. Wherever they settle they set up a bazaar (a shopping centre) and an urban way of life. These Newar towns in the different parts of Nepal are characterised by the Newars' unique architectural tradition of house-building with tiled roofs and artistically carved wooden windows.

Religiously, the Newars are divided into Buddhists and Hindus. Formerly, the vast majority of Newars were Buddhists, but they have been losing ground steadily in favour of the Hindus. Now we will contrast the birth rites of the Brahmins and Chhetris of Nepal whose birth rites can be said to be the most representative of Hindu rituals so as to add interest and a cross-ethnic view. Also, in order to get an overall picture of birth rituals, we shall add other practices that take place during pregnancy and childbirth, though not strictly rituals, they give meaning to them.

Pregnancy: folk beliefs, food and work

Since childbirth and motherhood give a woman status in Newar society, Newari women seek practical and religious aids to conceive. The help of the *aji* (midwife) who prepares a mixture of herbs to help conceive is often sought. By fasting on Tuesdays in honour of the elephant-headed god Ganesh and worshipping the deities Santoshimata and Bhakal, women seek the help of the gods. Amongst the Brahmins and Chhetris, a woman is considered particularly fertile on the fourth, fifth and the seventh to fourteenth days after menstruation. It is considered a man's religious duty to sleep with his wife on the fourth day after the onset of menstruation. This belief is generally not prevalent among the Newars.

As in most Asian countries, the birth of a son is usually preferred. This is so with the Newars as it is with the Brahmins and Chhetris. There are several reasons for this. In Hinduism and Buddhism a son is required to perform the death rituals for his parents so that they may go to heaven. Besides, there is an economic reason in that daughters will eventually marry and leave the family homestead. Sons will economically contribute, in one way or another, to their family all their lives. Amongst the Newars, however, if the first baby is a boy then either sex is preferred for the following children.

There are popular ways of predicting the sex of a child amongst the Newars. If the expectant mother is agile, bright of face and charming, it is said that she will give birth to a son; if she is sluggish, worn-out and drowsy, she will give birth to a daughter; if the child lies toward the right side of the womb, it is said to be a boy, to the left side a girl; if the baby starts moving in the fifth month of pregnancy it is a girl, in the sixth month, a boy; if the mother dreams of wells and ponds and eats *sel roti* (a round bread with a hole in the middle) in her dream the baby will be a girl, if of flowing water, water pipes and bananas, a boy.

Also, there are a number of folk-beliefs about certain things a woman must not do when she is pregnant such as she should not touch her abdomen during eclipses, otherwise the child will have a dark patch on its body; she should not see or touch pictures of fierce deities such as Bhairava and Narsingha so as to avoid miscarriage; she must not step over the rope by which a horse is tethered so as not to be late in giving birth since a horse gives birth to foals after twelve months of pregnancy. (Nepalese women count pregnancy as lasting ten months.) There are many more beliefs relating to almost every aspect of childbirth and child rearing which sometimes shed light on the meaning of the rituals which are also associated with these events.

As far as food is concerned there are no set rules of avoidance, though a pregnant woman seems to prefer hot and sour foods. However, she will be fed rich food cooked in clarified butter, meat, liver, etc., in order to nourish the developing baby. After the fifth month of pregnancy, Brahmin and Chhetri women are not allowed to do *puja* (religious worship) or go to the temple; after the eighth month, they may not cook *dal bhat* (lentils and rice) for their elders or touch the water they are to drink. None of these restrictions adhere to Newar women. A pregnant woman is expected to carry on with her usual daily routine of work. In fact, instead of discouraging hard work, women are encouraged to work hard in the belief that this will result in a strong and healthy baby and in a smooth delivery. After nine months of pregnancy, members of the expectant mother's natal home come to feed her and her husband's family with *dhau* (curd) and *bajee* (flattened rice) and they bring one hundred and eight sweet rice cakes. This is called *Dhau Bajee Nake Wanegu*, (feeding the mother curd and rice). It is believed that the child will refuse to be born or it will always be gluttonous with saliva dripping from its mouth unless the mother is sufficiently fed. The relatives who come to see her on this day will not do so again until they formally hear of the child's birth. Likewise, the pregnant woman is not supposed to spend a night at her parents' house again until after the child is born.

Labour, delivery and the announcement of birth

No Newar woman is supposed to give birth to her child at her own parents' house. Even if she and her husband are living with her parents she is expected to go out of the house in order to give birth. When labour starts, the *aji* (midwife) is called to help the woman who has retired to a warm, dark room where a bed of paddy straw has been laid over which a cotton sheet is spread. The straw should not be spread untidily, otherwise, it is believed, the mother will go mad. All strings and knots should be removed from the room. Men, childless women, children and the pregnant woman's mother are not allowed into the delivery room otherwise delivery will be long and difficult. As delivery approaches, the woman is given *mishrikada* (sugar water) and mustard oil to drink whilst the midwife manipulates the baby. As soon as the baby is born, it is washed by the midwife who also presses the nose, head, etc., with the idea of shaping them. She then worships, Ajima, (goddess of smallpox) by offering five heaps of items, one each of jaggery, *imu* (corum copticum seeds), ginger, black pulse and fruit.

If labour continues longer than usual, the mother is given *saga(n)*, (boiled and fried egg and liquor) as it is believed that the baby wants to eat and drink before coming into the world. If the placenta does not come out immediately, the mother is made to drink the water that has been poured from the seventh step of the main staircase and collected in a winnowing-tray. Sometimes she is hit on the back seven times with her husband's shoe; sometimes she drinks the water in which a Prithi Narayan (the unifier of Nepal) coin has been washed and, as a last resort, her husband is supposed to shake the egg-plant tree.

The child cannot be shown to its father until a *joshi*, (astrologer) has been consulted to determine whether it has been born under an unlucky astrological sign harmful to its father. If this is so, the child is not shown to the father until the unlucky period is over. But usually the father is supposed to see the child for the first time ritually on the day of the Benkay, (purifying ceremony) which takes place on the fourth or sixth day after birth.

Amongst the Newars, and not the Brahmins and Chhetris, the news of the birth is made public by informing the maternal uncle of the baby. It is rendered symbolically; a messenger is sent with a bundle containing as unbroken betel nut, a complete slab of jaggery, a little quantity of salt, ginger and *imu*. This means that the baby is a boy. If the bundle contains only half a betel nut and half the quantity of the other items, it is the signal that a girl has been born. Thus the importance of a son is symbolically expressed.

Before the purifying ceremony, usually two or three days after birth, members of the child's maternal uncle's family pay a visit which is called, *Nacha-bu-ka-Wanegu*. They present the mother and the baby with some coins, the former receiving half the amount, the latter receives the other half which the midwife takes for herself. The guests are offered a feast by the child's father.

Shortly after the purifying ceremony, the same group of guests returns and feeds the mother with flattened rice and meat. This is called *La-Na-Ka-Wanegu*. Buffalo meat, beer, and liquor are essential items in this ritual. Brahmins and Chhetris have no equivalent rituals — liquor, beer and meat are items which will never be used ritually nor consumed.

Cutting the umbilical cord

Cutting the umbilical cord is delayed only if there is some ceremony taking place amongst the *fukee* (cognatic members of the family) since it would pollute the participants. The midwife usually performs this duty. The mother and the baby are brought to the threshold of the room where the midwife stands and where she ties the cord with a *kacho dago* (new undyed string) and cuts it over a four-cornered leaf plate containing about half a kilogram of rice, some coins and a betel nut. Amongst the Brahmins and Chhetris, it is usually the mother who cuts the cord in a similar way. The cord is placed in an earthen pot together with the placenta, boiled rice, parched rice, boiled eggs, black soya bean, buffalo meat and ginger which is buried right-side up at Chhawasa (a place in every Newari locality for traditionally throwing away unclean things to the Chhawasa Ajima — the goddess of that place). It is the duty of the midwife to dispose of it and, even though the umbilical cord is cut in the daytime, it has to be disposed of at night.

The umbilical cord will not be cut when an illegitimate baby is secretly abandoned. As long as the umbilical cord is intact, the infant is considered casteless and can assume the caste of whosoever takes it in and cuts the cord.

Birth purification ritual

Amongst the Brahmins and Chhetris naming and purification takes place during one ceremony called *Nuhuran* which takes place on the eleventh day after birth. However amongst the Newars, no elaborate naming ceremony takes place. The baby is given a name suggested by the astrologer after consulting the horoscope within two years of birth. This name should never be made public since it is believed that witches and evil spirits can attack a person if they know this name. Most people cannot remember it anyway. The child's everyday name is given by its father's sister in an informal way either on the eleventh day after birth or during *junko* (first rice eating ceremony).

On the fourth day for girls and the sixth day for boys, *Benkay* (purifying ritual) takes place. Several rituals comprise purification. Early in the morning, in some places, a woman is sent from the mother's natal home with soap with which she will wash the mother and baby, a coarse undyed cotton sari and a straw mat for the mother and one for the baby.

The house is purified smearing cow-dung on the floors and sprinkling cow-milk with a bundle of sacred grass. An outsider who is not affected by birth pollution gives *fukee* members milk to drink so that they can be purified. The midwife offers rice and a few coins to the sun before the baby is taken outside into the sunshine. The mother and baby then take a bath and, on returning to the house with the baby in her arms, the mother has to pass through the smoke of the fire of paddy straw on which she had lain during and after delivery. Sometimes they put Balayo seeds on the burning straw so that the baby will be immune to the itching effect of the Balayo tree. The rest of the family, including agnates and cognates, also purify themselves by taking a ritual bath (*Nisi-Yae-Gu*). Their nails are pared and their toes stained red by the local barber. The religious rites start with the lighting of the oil-lamp, *dhiyo*, and filling the *kolosa* (container) with pure water. Three big leaf plates containing different food items are prepared for the different goddesses one of which is taken to the place where the placenta and umbilical cord were buried. Twelve different food items, such as flattened rice, soybeans, fried dried lentils, buffalo meat, chicken, etc. are placed in leaf plates which are, in turn, placed on a winnowing tray and offered to the sun by the midwife. After this the mother and father of the child sit together on the floor with the baby in the mother's lap. The midwife then gives a *tikka* (a spot placed on the forehead) to the mother and baby and puts some oil on top of the baby's head. All the guests present do likewise and each relative's household has to provide about half a kilogram of rice, about one meter of cloth and a little oil. The maternal uncle provides a hand ornament for the baby comprising gold and silver rings and a mattress, quilt and a stitched, three-layered vest. This is the first time that the baby is allowed to wear stitched clothing. Amongst the Brahmins and Chhetris, however, the baby can only wear stitched clothing at and after the first rice-eating ceremony, i.e. five or seven months after birth. The father ritually accepts the child as his when the midwife lifts the baby from the mother's lap and puts it into his — he gives money in return. In the evening, a special eyeliner is prepared to put around the baby's eyes. Some jaggery, musk, naphthalene, clarified butter and oil are placed in some muslin cloth, placed in an earthenware dish and set alight. Another dish is placed on top as a cover and the black smoke sediment is scraped off and used for eyeliner and black *tikka*. This eyeliner is not only good for the eyes but, it is said, protects the baby from evil spirits.

On the evening of the sixth day after birth, a spot is cleared in the delivery room where several objects such as a book and a pen, etc., are placed in front of the child as it is believed that Chitragupta will come and write the baby's fate and life-span on its forehead. Religious songs are sung during this evening with a light burning throughout the night. This is called *chaithi*. The Brahmins and Chhetris have a similar practice called Chaitom on the same night.

Twenty-one days or a month after birth, the mother again takes a ritual bath and the house is again purified. From now on she will be completely and ritually pure.

The rewards of childbirth

For one month after delivery, the mother is fed three times a day with rice cooked in clarified butter, chicken, sweets and other rich food. The midwife massages the mother and child three times a day with oil and after one month her services are rewarded with a sari, a blouse, some rice and flattened rice and cash payment. After a month or so the mother and child set off for the mother's natal home for a period of one month or more. Many women view this as being one of the greatest rewards of childbirth. The mother and child spend the days covered in oil soaking up the sun.

Junko — the first rice-eating ceremony

This takes place five or seven months after birth for a girl and six to eight months after birth for a boy. The exact time is set by an astrologer. As for the purification ritual it is again the responsibility of the maternal uncle to send all the necessary items — a shirt, cap, silver anklets for the child; a sari and blouse for the mother and a shawl for the father. The paternal aunt or mother sits facing east with the baby in her lap wearing the clothes sent from the maternal uncle's house. A tray containing eighty four different items of food with cooked rice and fried fish in the middle is brought and placed in front of the child. (In actuality, however, the baby is fed a specially prepared rice pudding). Another tray is placed in front of the child containing some soil, paddy, a pen, a book, etc. and the child is encouraged to choose one of the items. It is said that the object that is chosen indicates the child's future career. For example, if he picks up the pen he will become a writer.

The child is then fed his first solid food with the beak of the *Badria* bird or sparrow so that he will be clever and start speaking quickly. There is no special order as to who should feed the baby first; usually the astrologer decides. Each guest will feed the baby and present some money or another present. A feast for all the guests follows.

Prayers to Ganesh, the elephant god, is considered essential in rounding this ceremony off. The maternal uncle carries the baby in the evening, to the nearest temple of Ganesh and offer the god rice, a betel nut and a few coins.

Conclusion

Reference may be made to the main birth rites and explore a little of their significance and meaning. As we have seen, no priests or religious specialists are involved in any aspect of pregnancy and birth. The only specialist involved is the astrologer who selects the right time for the various rituals and chooses a secret name for the child. Otherwise, an important and interesting aspect of pregnancy and birth is the interplay between the pregnant woman's family, headed by her brother (the child's maternal uncle) and that of her husband. The maternal uncle plays an important part in the rituals before and after birth. He is responsible for sending members of his family gifts of food before birth. He is the first outsider who hears of the birth and again he is responsible for sending presents and ritual items for the purifying rituals and for the first rice-eating ceremony. There may be a certain amount of anxiety before birth on behalf of the pregnant woman's natal family that something may go wrong After birth there must be relief and rejoicing, especially if the baby is a boy. The father of the child plays a very minor role in the whole affair.

Birth Rituals of Pakistan

According to a Tradition of the Holy Prophet Mohammad (Peace be upon him) "Heaven lies under the mother's feet." Woman in Pakistan, therefore, occupies a central place. She is considered at the root of all happenings whether at home or in society. Many such rituals in Pakistan are woven round the women, from birth until death.

In discussing the birth rituals in Pakistan it must be understood that the common sources of habits and customs trace themselves to Islam, the great religion. The country was established as an experiment for the vindication of great laws given by Hazrat Mohammad (Peace be upon him) and the sufis and saints who came down to preach Islam to the people did so through innovative ideas mixing dogma with the essential law. Things might have degenerated to some extent through span of centuries. But even in prejudices and such customs as some people might regard as unhealthy the slow, silent forces hark back to the ideas preached by Islam.

Marriage is an instrument to perpetuate the family. After marriage parents of the newly-wed couple start expecting some issue from them. Particularly the parents of the male member are more appreciative. If two or three years pass without any issue the daughter-in-law is blamed, the poor creature is caught in mental agony. She is accused and tortured by her in-laws and even the husband in some cases. The childless woman tries to seek some divine blessing to have a child. She goes to Pirs, religious persons who are said to possess some superior power, to invoke prayers and obtain some sort of *tawiz* (amulet which is supposed to bring some divine help). This evil practice is prevalent among women folk because in doing so, sometimes they are deprived of their chastity as mostly Pirs and Faqirs are disguised culprits. Some go to shrines and make a *mannat* (a vow). In Gujrat (Punjab) women-folk go to Shah Doula's Shrine and promise that if she would be blessed by a baby she would offer her first child to the shrine. In such cases the first baby is usually male and bears a peculiar shape, named rat. The child is brought up by the descendants and beggars of the shrine. But now this practice is ceasing gradually, the parents instead of offering their born child, present a silver shape, resembling a rat. All these practices such as worshipping of shrines are non-Islamic, and are the product of Hindu culture. Muslims believe that it is the will of God that works, but still these practices are carried on owing to lack of education and ignorance.

When a woman becomes pregnant she gets respect. She becomes the centre of attraction in her husband's home. In fact, she gets extraordinary attention. The husband cares a lot about his wife, and feels deeply attracted to her. Both husband and wife start planning about their would-be child. But they always dream of having a son (I will discuss the reasons later). The pregnant woman is prohibited to go to a house where some one has died. It is generally believed that the house might have apparitions, and this might influence the would-be child. She is not allowed to have food or drink served by childless married women, and even by women whose children die after birth.

As a general custom the first child of a newly-wed couple should be born at the home of the wife's parents, for which arrangements are made months ahead. At the close of the seventh or eighth month of pregnancy, the girl (now married) is invited by her parents. If the parents can afford they present a new dress, perfume her with *attar* (a herbal perfume) and *sandal* (wood paste), adorn her with flowers and amuse themselves with music and traditional songs peculiar to the occasion. In villages small groups of professional *mirasis* (singers) chant congratulatory songs, and gather handsome rewards.

In a section of society, an attempt is made to predict the sex of the expected infant. They pour a few drops of milk on a piece of saffron cloth and if the milk leaves a white stain it is supposed to be a girl. If the stain is yellow then it would be a boy.

All female relatives, friends and neighbours begin to assemble in the house in the ninth month and the expectant mother is advised not to wear fine clothes and jewellery.

In some families *fateha* (prayer offered on some eatable thing) is offered by a *moulvi* or a religious person or by the eldest male member. The offering is made in the name of Bibi Fatima (daughter of Hazrat Mohammad — Peace be upon him).

The eatables (generally sweets) are distributed to seven women considered auspicious and fortunate. These women fill the pregnant woman's lap with seven kinds of fruits, vegetable, and sweets. It is an omen, that woman's lap will likewise be full and might never be empty. (It means that the children would live longer and prosper). Widows and barren women are not invited; it is considered an ill-omen. This practice is borrowed from Hinduism. In Islam, of course, there is no prejudice. During the three months (seven to nine) a *dai* — a midwife by tradition and not by education — is hired by the girl's parents. She attends the pregnant lady, and rubs and smears her. This is useful for the health of the pregnant woman and her would-be child. Everyone rewards the *dai* according to his means but she is paid more on the birth of a boy.

When the baby is to be born the mother is given a warm apartment. The woman is brought to the bed with the assistance of the family midwife where she is confined for forty days. After the delivery a handkerchief is tied on the head and a belt of thick cloth round her abdomen and she is laid on bed or a sheet spread on the ground and by the side of her bed an iron knife or any other weapon is kept to ward off evil influences, ghosts and apparitions.

After birth something shining such as *fanam* (a piece of silver, or un-used knife) is given to the midwife for cutting the navel cord. The cord is then deposited in a large earthen vessel together with copper, iron and a betel leaf and buried in some corner of the house. It is believed that the person whose navel string is buried loves this place very much. If somebody does not want to move from a certain place people ask him "*Kyia yahan tumhara anwal nal gara hai?*" (Is your navel cord buried here?). The knife is not used for any other purpose but is kept near the mother until the *chilla* (fortieth day). When the child is bathed or taken out of the house the knife is carried along, in fact the knife is always near the mother and the child. The infant is washed with warm water (in every season) and bound in swaddling clothes; he is carried by the midwife to the assembly or male relatives for the *azan* (Muslim call to prayer). The *azan* is spoken loudly in the right ear of the child. The opening words of the *azan* are "*Allah-o-Akbar*" (God is Great). This is done by some religious preacher, if present, dip his finger in honey or sugar paste, or chew a little of the date-fruit and insert a small quantity of it into the infant's mouth, before the child starts breast-feeding. This is done to ensure that the wisdom and learning of the sages might be imparted to him.

The diet of the new mother for the six days consists of *uchwanee*, a boiled preparation of sugar, a little coarse wheat flour and *ajwaen* — seeds of a medicinal plant. In some families she is given *harre-ra*, a mixture of wheat and flour, sugar and ghee (butter) boiled to paste. Some people give her light food like *khoshka* (butter fried rice) with little salt and black pepper. After the sixth day the mother may resume her normal diet. She takes boiled water for forty days. A red hot horseshoe or any other piece of iron is slated and allowed to cool in the water after being boiled.

Among some people, the woman does not comb her hair for forty days after child birth. She wears a handkerchief tied on her head. She is not permitted to leave her room except for bathing. In some superstitious families, when a visitor — male or female — comes into the room, they throw some *ispund* (seeds of *lowsonia*, a plant whose leaves are used by women to colour the palms and nails) on the fire in the belief that in doing so, there will be no evil influence which may have accompanied the visitor. Great care is taken that no dog or cat enters the room; even the very name of cat is not allowed to be mentioned. The cat is considered a witch. Some people make a small black blot on the forehead of a child to prevent evil eyes or shadows falling upon him. If the child is a girl, a black bangle or black thread is round on the wrist.

The birth of a son is immediately announced with greetings and joy. All assemble and enjoy themselves. There is music and songs are sung. Some people hire dancing girls. The observance of this custom is very common among the uneducated. The professional singers and dancers pray for the child's life. The traditional wish is "*Allah bache ki umer daraz kare*" (May God bless the child birth long life). In this way they collect a lot of money from the relatives. Gifts are given to the new-born, both in cash and kind. Some relatives donate a lot of money just to show-off even if they can't afford it. The birth of a son is generally considered the biggest occasion for celebration. Money is spent like water. *Dais*, professional singers and dancers are rewarded lavishly and many families even get financially ruined in the process. The birth of the second or third child — male or female — is not as well celebrated as the first one. The naming of the child takes place either on the day of its birth, or the second day. There are many ways this is done. The offspring of a Muslim belongs to his father's tribe, consequently the father's name or the family name is given as surname. If the father of the child is a Syed, the child's name will be Syed Ajaz. If he is Moghal his name terminates with words Mirza, Aga or Beg such as Mirza Ahmad or Ibrar Beg, etc. Among Pathan women the word Khatoon or Bano is added at the end. Among Syed women the words Begum, Beebee or Be Nissa is attached; e.g. as Safdari Begum. In some families the infant obtains the names of some of the family's members, as that of the parents' father, grandfather or great-grandfather. Sometimes the new born is given Holy names, for instance, Mohammad, Ibrahim, Ali Abbas, Fatima or Zainab, etc. Some people add the word of Ghulam (Servant) with pious names — like Ghulam Mohammad (servant of Mohammad, Peace be upon him) or Ghulam Abbas (servant of Abbas — grand son of Mohammad, Peace be upon him). In educated families, learned men assemble for the purpose; they suggest names from the Holy Quran suiting the high station in life such as Ahmad (most praised) and Arshad (most upright). Parents who think that the child is the result of the blessing of some *Pir* (Saint) or some shrine name their baby as Piran Ditta (saint-given) or Pir Bukhsh (saint-gifted). Some mothers, out of love, call their children such names as Moti (pearl), Heera (diamond), Mukkhan (butter), Chan (moon). Some names are suggested according to day and time. For instance if the child is born on Sunday between six and seven the child is named in honour of *Shams* (sun); as Shamsul Islam.

Chatti (the sixth day bath) should be observed on the sixth day, but usually takes place on the seventh or ninth day. The child is washed thoroughly with hot water and a *kurta* (shirt) made of any old article of dress worn by some great personage who lived to a considerable age. After the child has been washed the mother, too, is given a ceremonial bath (*chatti*), preferably by the sisters of the child's father. The water used for bathing is boiled with medicinal herbs like *neem* (margosa leaves) and *shumbalee* (leave of a chaste tree). It is a domestic treatment. At this time, it is usual to give some money to the midwife. If the infant is male the midwife is rewarded with a new dress. This custom is observed by the rich and the poor. On this occasion a feast is given to the women-folk (men having no part in this ceremony); it is accompanied by merry-making and dancing. In some families the sisters of the husband demand from their brother a handsome gift, usually money. It is called *naig* (sister's share). In some families the parents of the girl despatch presents to their female friends and relatives on a large platter carried on the head of the midwife, and each individual's portion is parcelled out. It consists of *pun-jay-ree* (a caudle prepared of medicated seed flour, country gum arabic, poppy seeds, sugar and oil of greese) and *pan soparee* (betel leaves and areca nut). When any relation or friend receives the parcel, it is assumed that birth has taken place. The ceremony is not observed on the birth of every child.

The *uqeeqa* (sacrifice on shaving of the child's head) takes place on any convenient day after the birth; it is also called *moondun* (to shave). In the morning the child's head is shaved by a barber. Those who can afford prefer to have the head of the child shaved with a silver-mounted razor. A silver cup is also used for water. Both are given away to the barber who receives rice, wheat and cash. The shaved hair of the child is preserved in the family and their weight in silver or gold is given away to the poor. *Moondun* is followed by the slaughter of an animal in the name of God (two goats or sheep for boy and one for girl). The goats should be one year old, and perfect and without any blemish. While offering it the father of the child repeats an Arabic prayer; the significance of which is that "Almighty God, I offer the animal instead of my own offspring. In the name of God do I sacrifice this goat or sheep." The meat of the sacrificed animal is distributed and some cooked and served with rice or bread to the relatives, friends, neighbours and the poor. According to Islamic law this meat or cooked food should be distributed to the poor. The child, his parents, his paternal and maternal grandfathers and grandmothers may not eat the flesh. The bones, skin, feet and head of the sacrificed animal are buried under the earth. Some people leave a tuft of hair unshaved in the name of particular saints, and take great care that nothing unclean contaminates them. They allow the hair to grow for four or five years and go to the shrine or the saint to have the hair cut. Such hair is termed as *jumal bal*.

Chilla (bath) is observed on the fortieth day. Until then the mother is considered unclean. She cannot pray, fast, touch the *Holy Quran* or enter a mosque. All relatives and neighbours are invited on *chilla*. The midwife and close relatives wash the child and the mother and child are given new clothes. *Kheer* (rice and milk) and *polaoo* are cooked and *fateha* is offered in the name of Hazrat Mohammed (Peace be upon him). The guests bring presents on a tray covered with a shining cloth. Cash must be offered and given to the new born usually in his or her palm.

It is customary for the child's maternal grandmother and father to give away new clothes and jewels (if they can afford) to the child, his mother and father and most family members of child's father. This custom is called *chuchak*. If possible a silver or wooden cradle, sugar, some other eatable things and some cash is given. These things are taken by the mother (of the infant), while proceeding to her in-law's house. In this way the parents of a girl have to bear a lot of expenses; firstly they bear the entire expenses of birth of her first child and also to provide a lot of things to her in-laws. The poor parents of the girl have to spend a fortune to satisfy the demands of the in-laws. The custom may be, of course, regarded as bone to our society.

In some villages on the *chuttee* and *chilla* days eunuchs are engaged but usually they come on their own accord to dance, sing and play. It is customary for them to search out a home where a son is born. They dance at the house of parents and get handsome reward and do not leave the house until they get something. If a girl is born they do not get much.

In the evening after the wash on the fortieth day the mother is taken out into the open air with the infant in her arms. She is asked to count a few stars. After this they shoot a couple of arrows in the air. The mother and child are now free to go out and visit relatives and friends. This is the end of the confinement.

When the child is of about four months and can clasp his hands the action is construed as desiring *laddoos* (rounded sweets) and they are immediately ordered and distributed. After seven months close relatives are again invited to a feast; *polaoo* (rice and meat) and *kheer* (rice and milk) are cooked. A little *kheer* is applied to the child's tongue. It is repeated twice. The child is now allowed to take other food.

Dant nekulna (tooth appearance) is celebrated with distribution of *ghoongneean* (small rounds of wheat and molasses). When a girl attains the age of a year her ear-lobes are bored by degree. When the girl has been of two or three years she has 13 holes on the right ear and 12 holes on the left. But now this practice is confined only to the uneducated and ignorant.

Sal-girah (birthday) also called *burras ganth* (annual knot) is celebrated in the upper class of society, and is not common among the middle or poor people. In some families *fateha* is offered in the name of Hazrat Noah (Peace be upon him). The reason is that Noah lived to a ripe age.

Circumcision of a male child is generally performed after seven or eight years of birth. But in some sections of society, it is done during the third or fifth year. It is considered a big occasion and is observed like the marriage festival.

It is very natural for mothers to sing *lorri* (lullabies) when the child is in their lap or in the cradle. But in some parts of Pakistan professional bed-singers visit the infants. They take him in the arms and sing songs which according to our belief, Hazrat Halima (the woman who brought up the Prophet Mohammad — Peace be upon him) used to sing for Hazrat Mohammad (Peace be upon him). The singers are rewarded with wheat, sugar and rice.

Some of the rituals discussed above, are wasteful and do not serve any purpose for the development of a healthy and enlightenened society, but are in fashion owing to lack of education.

Fortunately, there is a healthy change in the outlook of the urban society. But as Pakistan is a land of villages, these rites appear to be deeply entrenched.

Birth Ceremonies in Trunyan, Bali

Introduction

The village of Trunyan lies on the east of Lake Batur in the district of Kintamani, on the island of Bali. This rather remote village can be reached from the village of Penelokan of Kintamani descending down to the lower rim of an ancient crater by motor car, to the edge of the crater lake Batur, and from there by motor boat across the water. The people of Trunyan are not primitive, but belong to an ancient and conservative tribe known to outsiders as 'Bali Aga' (Mountain Balinese), or 'Bali Mula' (Original Balinese). The people themselves do not like to be called by the first term, but prefer the second, or better still 'Bali Turunan' (the Balinese who came directly from the sky). The first term has a derogatory connotation, that of being non-Javanized Indigenous Balinese who is crude and uncivilized. To Trunyanese love to be called the Bali Turunan, because they believe that their ancestors had come directly from the sky to the centre of Bali, Trunyan, and that they are the original Balinese.

The Trunyanese culture is Balinese, but compared to the Bali Hindu (who form the majority of the population) culture, includes more elements, which are probably the remnants of a pre-Hindu Megalithic culture of Bali. The Trunyanese subsistent economy is based on horticulture, supplemented by lake fishing, trade, and raising pigs and oxen. The kinship system of the Trunyanese is based on the principle of patrilineal descent, and the residence pattern is patrilocal. The religion of the Trunyanese, at present, is a kind of Balinese Hinduism. Yet although the liturgy is already Hindu, the religion is basically animistic, in that it includes the worship of spirits, ancestor spirits, supernatural power and almost no Indian Hindu gods at all.

Marriage

One of the important stages in Trunyanese life cycle is birth ceremony, but in order to have a clear picture of it, we must have a little knowledge of their marriage ceremony first, which is quite complicated.

Marriage in Trunyan society still adheres to *dadia* endogamy, that is marriage between people who belong to the same patrilineal minimal lineage. Marriage between patrilineal cross cousin is preferred, though marriage between patrilineal parallel cousin is considered to be incest. *Dadia* endogamy will insure a Trunyanese to reincarnate in his own *dadia*, and not into another *dadia* which is not liked by them.

The marriage age in Trunyan is about twenty-five for man, and twenty-four for woman, but there is a tendency that the younger generation is marrying at an earlier age. Up to the present time, premarital sexual union has been and is still the rule between teenagers. Marriage in Trunyan is initiated in one of the three ways : by proposing, by eloping, or by kidnapping. Among the three ways, eloping is the most preferred and popular one. The reason according to the people is that it is based on mutual love.

Premarital union is permitted by the custom of Trunyan, because the purpose of marriage there is for procreation; so that expensive marriage ceremonies will be held, only after the man is sure that he will get an offspring from the girl that he has chosen to be his wife. This is the main reason why a bride in Trunyan is mostly already with a child when she stands before the "altar"

After a young man has chosen a prospective girl, they manage to make love in secret, and this is mostly done in the dark of the night, in the girl's house when her family is not at home, or in the hut built in the corn field. If later on, the couple feel that they do not belong to each other, this experiment of sexual union is discontinued. And it is considered to be all right, as long as the girl is not pregnant. If she is pregnant, both are brought to the village traditional council to be tried. If both agree, they get formally married. If not, both are fined, and the child born out of wedlock is considered to be an illegitimate child, and belongs to no one's *dadia*. But the poor child could be made legitimate to its father's *dadia*, after it grows up and goes through a purificatory ceremony.

If the union is all right, the lovers elope and hide in one of the man's relative's house. Having performed this grand *pas de deux*, the man sends his delegate to inform the girl's parents that they attend to get married. The delegate has to bring along with him ceremonial betel leaves. If the offering is eaten by the girl's father, it means that he agrees with the marriage. If refused, it means that he disagrees. However even though he keeps on refusing to eat the betel leaves, the marriage is considered to be valid if the delegate keeps on coming to offer him the betel leaves for three consecutive days.

After the six obligatory days of hiding, the couple go out to visit the girl's and the man's parents and relatives, to make amend for the wrong done. From that time on they may lead the life of a married couple, but they are not yet considered to be full-fledged members of the traditional village and may not enter the village temple before they have performed the four stages of expensive marriage ceremonies called *mebiokaon, meperagat/mekala-kalan, bakti pesaren,* and *mepekandal* respectively. The function of these ceremonies are; to purify the couple having performed sexual intercourse; to free them from the bad influence of the demons; to inform the gods that a marriage ceremony is about to take place in the front courtyard of the main temple; and to make them confirmed as full-fledged members of the traditional village.

Birth ceremonies

According to the Trunyanese belief, conception is the result of the union between the woman's *semara* (white blood) and the man's *buiken* (seed). Miscarriage could happen if the foetus is devoured by the *kala* demon. Thus birth is considered to be full of danger.

To prevent this and other misfortune, there are many taboos to be observed by the pregnant woman in Trunyan, such as they must always carry some amulets given by the native healer *(balian usada)*. During pregnancy woman is forbidden to contact physically defective persons, such as the deaf, the hare-lipped, the blind, and the crippled, or else her child will be born with the same defect.

A woman does not receive a special treatment during her pregnancy. She is expected to help her husband in the field till her last day of pregnancy. To facilitate her birth, a special ceremony called *toya penyeseg* is held for her, when she is four months with child. At that ceremony she is given holy water *(toya penyeseg)* to drink by the native healer. During her pregnancy, her husband is not allowed to cut his hair, because it would hamper the process of the birth of their child.

Childbirth in Trunyan, as in other Balinese villages, is a male affair in the sense that it is handled by men. The midwife is also male and the husband acts as the chief assistant. He is the first person to handle the baby after it is born and to care for the afterbirth.

Childbirth in Trunyan is in fact an extended family affair, because even the little children are allowed to witness the process. Childbirth to a Trunyanese child is not something secret. For them it is nothing new, and you cannot fool them with your childish stork stories.

As the front door of the house where is the parturient woman is opened widely during the labour, the neighbouring children can be seen crowding in front of it watching the scene. From the door we can see the parturient woman squatting on a long low bench, wearing a *sarong*, with her back facing the front door. On her back sitting on the same bench is the male midwife *(balian tekuk)*, who holds her waist firmly and gives her a downward during the labour. In front of the woman squats her husband, ready to receive the baby, the moment it is born. During the labour the woman is not allowed to lie down on her back, but to sit straight up leaning on the chest of the male midwife. In order to keep her in that position, a maiden is assigned to pull firmly her knotted hair upward. This is done because there is a belief that if she lies down, her amniotic fluid will flow to her head and kill her.

If there is complication during the labour, the male midwife will ask the help of the native healer who with the help of his magic formula and holy water would smooth things up. The baby's umbilical cord is cut, only after its placenta is out from the womb, and it is cut with a bamboo knife on a piece of a turmeric root. This is done so in order to prevent the umbilical cord from retraction into the womb again. The umbilical cord is cut by the baby's father. The remaining cord is first rubbed with rice flour paste mixed with candle nut and red onion, and then bound with a piece of cotton thread. The baby's body is first sprinkled with holy water mixed with vinegar, then cleansed with cream made of lime and mashed turmeric and washed with lukewarm water. After the bath the baby is given its first food of masticated candle nut made by one of the woman attendants. This food is believed to cleanse the baby's stomach. From this time till the baby is three months old, it is dressed only in rags, and no new clothes are allowed to be put on it, for fear that the new born baby's soul will misunderstand it as a sign of not being wanted in the family and leave the new body it has just reincarnated; it is the custom among the Trunyanese to dress the dead with new clothes during mortuary ceremony.

Soon after the baby is put in the basket, the father has to take care of the child's "four siblings" which consist of placenta umbilical cord, blood and the amniotic fluid; for if their bodies are not well taken care of, their souls will not guard the safety of the child who is their brother. First the placenta and the umbilical cord are mixed with kitchen ash, and put into a half coconut shell, and before they are covered with the other half of the coconut shell, they are covered by pieces of beautifully coloured cloths. These cloths will magically make the baby beautiful when it grows up. This coconut shell and the pandanus mat which has been stained by the parturient woman's blood and amniotic fluid are bound together and brought to a place called Tantanbuni to be hanged there on a bush. The person who does this task is the father of the baby. While carrying this bundle, he is not allowed to speak too much, for fear his child will grow into a chatter box. Before leaving the holy place the father has to cleanse himself by submerging himself into the lake in clothes. On his way home he picks up three little pebbles from the lake, to be used as amulets for his baby against evil spirits.

Returning from Tantanbuni, the father has to light a campfire for three days in front of his house, to announce the birth of his child, and to drive off the evil spirits who want to harm the baby.

At the night of the day the baby was born, a baby welcoming ceremony, called the *pemapag rare* is held, where offering is given to the soul of the newly reincarnated soul. This ceremony is conducted by the male midwife.

Besides the *pemapag rare*, the following ceremonies are held in association with the birth of a baby in Trunyan.

Tutug Telu : this ceremony is held at night when the baby is three days old, and is also conducted by the male midwife. This is an important, because it is the name giving ceremony. What is interesting about this ceremony is that although the name is picked by the parents, the choice is made by the baby's soul. The male midwife burns three bamboo sticks bound by cotton wool, soaked with coconut oil. Each stick represents a name given by the parents, and the last extinguished stick is believed to be the name chosen by the soul of the baby. So if the stick representing the name I Sueca is the last extinguished one, it means that the baby's soul has chosen that particular name to be used in this incarnation. In order to have the name stick forever to the boy, the scorched cotton wool is rubbed on all the limb joints of the baby.

Before the name giving ceremony, the baby is called by the temporary name of *Mantag* (penis) if it is a boy, or *Kemog* (vagina) if it is a girl: According to the Trunyanese practice the parents are addressed as *Nang Mantag* (Father of Mantag) and *Men Mantag* (Mother of Mantag) respectively. But after the name giving ceremony, the father is addressed as *Nang Sueca*, and the mother *Men Sueca*; and the father is allowed to cut his hair which has not been cut since his wife became pregnant.

After this giving name ceremony, the parents enter the state of *mabrata*, a taboo state, when they have to observe some food taboo and action taboo. The duration of the taboo state is one month and seven days. The foods that are considered taboo are for instance every food fried with oil. If the fried food is eaten by the mother, the baby's skin will be infected by ulcer. The action taboo, for instance, is that the parents are forbidden to cut a vegetation that produces sap. If this taboo is violated, the baby will bleed without any reason at all. Or the parents are not allowed to split a coconut, otherwise, there will form a cleft on the baby's skull. But all these could be avoided by eating all the taboo foods and performing all the taboo actions during the name giving ceremony.

Tutug Wolu: this ceremony is held when the child is eight days old; and the ceremony is meant for the child's guardian spirit, the *Empu Rare*.

Tutug Duadasa: this ceremony is held when the baby is twelve days old, and is the ear lobe piercing ceremony. On this day the baby is allowed to leave its dwelling and to see the sun for the first time, for at this age the baby considered to be strong enough to withstand the evil spirit power.

Tutug Bulan Pitunga Dina (or Lepas Berata) : this ceremony is held when the baby is 42 days old. Its function is to free the baby's parents from the taboo.

Tutug Telu Bulanan : this ceremony is held at night when the baby is three months old. Three months is a crucial age, for from this day on, the soul of the baby is considered to inhabit its body for good. The baby is allowed for the first time to wear new clothes and adornments. For this occasion a piglet is roasted to be offered to the baby's soul.

Tutug Enem Bulanan (Otonan or birthday ceremony): this ceremony is held when the baby is six months old. This ceremony is important not only to the Bali Trunyanese but also to other Balinese, because in Bali the birthday is celebrated once in every six months. The functions of this ceremony are: to assemble all the souls of the "four siblings" who are believed to have strayed to other places, and to placate the soul of the baby, so that it will be contented to dwell in its present body.

Tutug Dua Dasi Bulanan: this ceremony is held when the baby is 12 months old, and is the initial hair cutting ceremony. The offering becomes manifold, because besides this ceremony, the parents have also to give a birthday ceremony. The ceremony becomes more sacred if the baby's hair is matted, because it means that the soul of the child is impure. The hair is then kept in the baby's personal medicine box, and will be buried in the patrilineal minimal lineage shrine during the teeth filing ceremony which will be held when the family has amassed enough fund for the extravagant ceremony. The *Tutug Dua Dasi Bulanan* ceremony is the final ceremony in connection with childbirth, and after that, the periodical *Otonan* ceremony is held in every six months through a person's life, and held for the last time six months after his or her death.

Finally, in connection with the birth ceremony, there is one more ceremony worth mentioning, that is the ceremony held for certain child who is born in the unlucky week of the Balinese year called the *Wuku Wayang*. A person born in this unlucky week will have a sickly body, so to avoid it, he must be neutralized against the evil power of the *kala* demon, with a certain purificatory ceremony, called the *Salah Utu* ceremony or the *melukat* ceremony. This ceremony consists of three stages, from the simple to the extravagant one. It is conducted simultaneously by the native healer *(balian usada)* and the *dalang* priest who will perform the purificatory shadow puppet play on this occasion.

Marriage Customs

Marriage — Variation on the Theme in Sri Lanka

Sri Lanka is a land of great traditions. These traditions, whose early origins are rooted in the autochthonous "Yaksa" and "Raksasa" cultures (pre-historic) have thrived over the passage of several millennia with the distinctive mark of Buddhist influence from pre-Christian centuries onwards. The marriage customs of Sri Lanka too are rooted in this stream of ancient tradition.

In pre-historic times the attempt by Ravana, the lord of Lanka, to abduct Sita, proved fatal to the very existence of his kingdom, which is recorded in the epic "Ramayana" of Valmiki. However Ravana's attempt is preserved in Indian tradition as the Raksasa form of marriage which the anthropologists prefer to call marriage by capture.

With the dawn of recorded history a similar disaster befell on Sri Lanka on the occasion of a royal wedding festival. Lanka fell before the invading army of the eponymous foreigner Vida (Pali: Vijaya) who took the city Sirisavatthu unawares while a grand marriage festival of the daughter of the ruling monarch was being held there. This Homeric type tragedy at Sirisavatthu, a massacre unleashed on a revelling crowd, recorded in the chronicle "Mahavamsa" also provides the earliest reference to a marriage festival in Sri Lanka (cir. 5th century BC). Marriage customs in Sri Lanka today, especially among the major community, the Sinhalese, is a perpetuation of a series of rituals of a time-honoured ceremony which initiates the bridal pair into a state of matrimony.

The ritual conducted on the "Magul Poruva" (Bridal dais) is most colourful and is the matrix of all rituals connected with a Sinhalese marriage ceremony. The "Magul Poruva" is the hymeneal altar constructed on a raised wooden platform in the bridal hall. Seats are arranged all round for the guests to observe this customary form of Sinhalese marriage. Various theses have been advanced for the origin of the Sinhala "Magul Poruva", but none seem to have provided a conclusive answer. It may be safely said that it is yet another relic of an ancient custom preserved by the Sinhalese.

With her bridegroom, the Sinhalese bride ascending the "Magul Poruva" to go through the rituals, attired in her lily-white bridal robes, her tresses heavily braided with jewellery and flowers, provides a most colourful event and a fascinating moment for the onlooker. On either side of the "Magul Poruva" are placed "Punkalas" (brimming vases) which symbolise prosperity and fertility. The vases are decorated with coconut lamps trimmed with coconut oil and wicks. A new mat is spread on the "Magul Poruva" and a piece of white cloth is spread over the mat — a symbol of purity. Rice, betel leaves and coconuts are placed on the "Magul Poruva". In some areas baskets containing milk-rice, oil-cakes and plantains are placed on the Magul Poruva.

Little before the auspicious hour for the "Poruvesituvima" (ascending on the Magul Poruva) ceremony, the bridegroom having saluted his parents in the traditional manner steps out of his residence to go to the wedding house accompanied by his friend (the grooms' man) and relatives. A younger brother of the bride receives the bridegroom at the threshold of the wedding house by pouring water over his feet from a clay trough (koraha) placed at the entrance. The bridegroom drops a golden ring on the "Koraha" as a token of thanks for the person who bathed his feet. Nowadays a metal basin would replace the "Koraha".

At the auspicious hour the bride and the bridegroom are led to the "Magul Poruva" by the respective elders of the two families. A maternal uncle of the bride unites the right thumb fingers of the couple and ties the nuptial knot, pouring over it water from a golden pitcher, while a bevy of girls arrayed before the couple chants "Jayamangalagatha" (auspicious verses meant to bring blessings and prosperity on the couple). The maternal uncle receives a present of a suit of clothes from the bridegroom. Several traditional customs follow in succession, which may vary a little according to each province, caste or social rank. The couple exchanges presents of wedding apparel which is known as "Talipilihuvamaruva". The bridegroom presents to the bride a white silk cloth by placing it around her body and ties the "Mala" (gold necklace) round her neck. All these are a pantomime which signifies the husband's duty to provide his spouse her wherewithal; also enjoined by the Buddha in the "Singalovadasutta" and valued much by the Buddhists of Sri Lanka. The feeding ceremony follows at which the bride feeds the bridegroom with milk-rice and ripe plantains. This act of the bride denotes her obligations to attend to the comforts of her husband from that day onwards. The bride's mother is then invited to come forward to receive the "Kirikadahela", a milk-white cloth which is the traditional gift of the bridegroom to the mother-in-law. It is the custom of the mother-in-law to keep this piece of cloth carefully until the couple is blessed with their first born baby, when she presents the "Kirikadahela" back to be utilised for making baby shirts and linen required for the new born babe. Then follows the custom of the "Hurulubedima" or distributing handfuls of betel leaves by the bride to all her near relatives as a token of her farewell. Next an elderly uncle of the bridegroom invites the couple to descend from the "Magul Poruva". As they step down a coconut is broken into two halves with one blow of a large knife (Katta). This is done usually by the "Henemama" (the washerman) and is supposed to bring good luck to the couple. The wedding dinner follows, at which the bridegroom's party is served first. The newly wedded pair then leaves the wedding house for their honeymoon.

The above is a brief description of the prevailing marriage customs of the major community — the Sinhalese. The minorities, Tamils, Muslims as well as the aboriginal tribes in Sri Lanka — the Veddas, the Rodiyas too follow marriage customs peculiar to them.

The marriage customs among the Tamils who form the prominent minority community in Sri Lanka too are of early origin. In some instances they have striking similarities with Sinhalese marriage customs. It is natural for two communities living amicably together in the same land for thousands of years, to share and absorb rites and customs common to each other.

It is customary to erect a "Manavarai" (lit. a throne, which is a Pandal-like structure) in the bride's house at a Tamil marriage. When the bridegroom's party is seen approaching the bride's house, a party of married ladies go forward to receive him and as soon as he arrives at the "Pandal", the bride's mother or sister presents him with a cup containing a drink prepared out of bruised plantains and milk. They invite him to sit on a raised seat placed under the "Pandal". The bride now arrayed in her wedding apparel is carried in a palanquin to the temple with every mark of respect. At the temple she is made to undergo various rites, after which she is carried back in the palanquin to the wedding house and made to sit by the side of the bridegroom upon a mound of earth. This mound of earth has been raised earlier near the "Pandal" and on which is placed a ball of cow-dung ornamented with "Kusa" grass to represent "Pillaiyar (God Ganesha). The brahmin priest now initiates the bridal rites by tying a yellow thread round the right arm of the bridegroom and the left arm of the bride who are seated facing the east. In the square pit near the "Pandal" a sacrificial fire is kindled by the brahmin priest while chanting sacred hymns or *mantrams.* At this stage the bridegroom fastens the "Tali" (gold necklace) round the bride's neck while several married women present, put some paddy and betel leaves into a seer and whirl it thrice round the heads of the happy couple. The brahmin priest breaks the coconut into two with a single blow of a knife. Next the priest puts the little finger of the bridegroom's right hand round the little finger of the bride's right hand and places a round "Pottu" mark on their foreheads with a paste of sandalwood and sacrificial ash. Sometimes the bridegroom himself places a "Pottu" mark on the bride's forehead. The couple is then made to circumambulate the sacrificial fire thrice from left to right throwing into it handfuls of paddy mixed with flowers. Once this is over the bride's father takes his daughter's right hand and places it on that of the bridegroom's and pours over them water repeating sacred formulae. The couple resumes their seats and blessings are changed by the brahmin priest. Various other rituals are performed for seven days.

The marriage customs among the minority community, the Muslims of Sri Lanka although do not differ much from their fellow countrymen, yet have their own peculiarities. With the blessings of the priest, the bridegroom's party proceeds towards the bride's house in pomp. The bridegroom either rides in an open carriage or walks surrounded by his friends and relatives. On their arrival, a boy, generally a brother of the bride, washes the feet of the bridegroom with rose-water for which he is rewarded with a gold ring. He then proceeds with the bridegroom to the hall where the bridegroom takes his seat on his haunches before the priest. A document read before the bridegroom, by the priest is signed by the bridegroom, the bride's father, the priest and two other witnesses. After this the priest takes the bridegroom's right hand in his own, repeats a formula in Arabic, three times in succession and asks his willingness to take the bride as his spouse. The bride too is asked in the similar manner by the priest. This is followed by tying the *Talla* (gold necklace) and clothing the bride with a silk apparel by the bridegroom. Then the bridegroom and the bride sit on the bed nearby and the young man has his first look at his life partner, for up to that time she remains heavily veiled. What follows is a grand repast, for the men first and women afterwards, with plenty of food and no other drink than water, hot or cold.

Marriage customs of the Rodiyas, an outcast community of Sri Lanka, often referred to as 'handsome beggars' too are worth recording. On the auspicious day the bridegroom proceeds to the bride's house with friends and relatives. A pingo load of presents and refreshments too is taken. The essential ceremony of a Rodiya marriage too is centered round the "Magul Poruva". The couple stands on a Magul Poruva which among the rich is a tastefully decorated structure, whereas there may be no Magul Poruva at all among the poor. At the lucky hour, the bridegroom ties a "Mala" necklace, often made of silver, round the bride's neck. The marriage rite proper is duly performed by an elderly relation of the bride or her maternal uncle, who ties the thumbs of the right hands of the couple with nuptial thread and pours water over it. After the ritual and feasting the bride is conducted to the bridegroom's house.

Among the "Veddas", the aborigines of Sri Lanka, marriage is a simple affair. Their jungle habitat and primitive living may be the reason for such simplicity. The young man goes to the girl's house at the auspicious hour with such bridal gifts that he could afford to procure. These may include a few yards of cloth, a jacket, a handkerchief, a necklace of beads, two bangles and a hair-pin or two. He may or may not be accompanied by others. The bride attired in her new trousseau, is handed over to the bridegroom by her parents. The bride then ties the waist-string round the bridegroom's waist. The new couple then goes to live in a hut put up by the man as their home. Some spend their honeymoon in a jungle cave or some such sylvan resort. The waist-string plays an important part in the Vedda marriage as does the necklace or the ring in others. This is made of bow string hemp. When a woman has tied round the waist of a man a string of her own twisting he becomes her husband. Marital fidelity is observed very strictly by the Veddas among whom polygamy or polyandry is rare if not absent.

Conspectus

Among all the communities in Sri Lanka, marriage arranged by the parents or elders, is most common, where the "Kapuva" (match-maker) plays an important part, while love matches among young men and women too are not rare.

Caste is observed strictly in marriages arranged by the elders. However, the widespread of higher education has slackened the rigid caste feelings and among the educated there is a tendency to overlook caste wherever possible. This may also be a result of the impact of several social reforms in the recent past by which an equality of opportunity and status to every member of the society was made possible. The new wealthy class, a product of modern industrial and commercial ventures, has rendered possible the breaking up the hereditary caste barrier in regard to marriage.

The "Binna" marriage or the matrilocal practice whereby the husband goes to live at the home of the wife (as against the "Diga" or patrilocal method) is prevalent even today among the Hill Country Sinhalese (The Kandyans).

Infant marriage which is actually a betrothal arranged by the parents while the couple is too young to think of marriage is also occasionally heard among the strictly orthodox Hindu Tamils of Sri Lanka. This is in fact a necessity to continue family ties and preserve the purity of one's caste.

The auspicious times as fixed according to astrological calculations still set the pattern for the various rituals in the marriage ceremonies in Sri Lanka. Among the Sinhalese and the Tamils, the horoscopes of the bride and the bridegroom are examined to find whether they agree in regard to the ten different astrological points — "Dasaporondama" in Sinhalese and "Tasaporutta" in Tamil. Ironically enough prospective brides and bridegrooms have sometimes to wait many years until they pass well beyond their marriageable age, to strike at an agreeable horoscope for marriage to be finalised. Dowry (Davadda in Sinhalese) which in the past was a most desired item, often a must in a marriage, is gradually fading out. But still men rarely eschew a handsome dowry from their in-laws, while women take it a pride to be given away in marriage with a big dowry. Divorce is considered as an unorthodoxy both by the Sinhalese and the Tamils as well. Divorce by law-suit is unheard among the less urbanised communities and is almost absent among the Veddas and the Rodiyas. Polygamy is not discouraged for the Muslims, but in Sri Lanka, may be owing to the influence of Buddhist and Hindu ethics, monogamy is the rule among all the communities.

With modern trends in social patterns and standards, the old institutions that regulated marriage customs among the various communities in Sri Lanka too have mostly changed. Original symbolisms and ritualistic meanings of the various rites and ceremonies associated with the marriage have been forgotten. But still, in Sri Lanka ceremonial rites on the occasion of a bridal are preferred, if not for the sake of their colourfulness and glamour, as an attempt to preserve the age-old traditions cherished by their forebears over the past for more than two millennia.

Marriages in India

arriage or *Vivaha* is by far the most important social institution all over the world. It is the basis of procreation and perpetuation of the human race. As such this institution is as old as the human race.

Marriage customs, ceremonies and rituals differed from tribe to tribe till the advent of organised religions. Judaism, Christianity and Islam gave a religious tone and context to this institution and prescribed rules and rituals to be followed by their followers at the time of marriage.

The customs and practices of the people and areas in which these religions had their origin deeply influenced the rules and rituals laid down by the founding fathers of these religions. Christians and Muslims all over the world follow those rules and rituals. Therefore, Christians and Muslims living in India follow the same rules and rituals of marriage as Muslims and Christians elsewhere. But since most of the Indian Christians and Muslims are converts from Hinduism and are rooted in the Indian soil, they continue to follow the old Indian customs and ceremonies including folk songs that have become part of the marriage celebrations in India.

Unlike Christianity and Islam, Hinduism is not an organised and regimented religion. As explained in the "Hindu View of Life" by the scholar statesman and late President of India, Dr. S. Radhakrishanan, "Hinduism is a way of life, a cultural stream and not a religion in the conventional sense of the word. It is a commonwealth of all the sects and "panths" of Indo-Vedic origin which are tied together by common acceptance of allegiance to "Dharma" or "Dhamma", the code of moral conduct which was evolved in India but has a universal relevance. It has nothing to do with religion or any particular prophet, book or way of worship.

The Indian or Hindu way of life has room for wide local variations. But in regard to basic human institutions like marriage, it has developed some common rituals and ceremonies which are the common feature of Indian or Hindu marriage all over India.

The Indian savants and law makers knew the importance of sex instinct and the varied factors that influence the human approach in the matters of sex and heart. They have therefore prescribed eight kinds of marriages. They include:

1. Brahma Marriage : It is a marriage between a boy and girl endowed with qualities of head and heart, good character, education, etc. with mutual consent.
2. Dev Marriage : Gi`ing away the well decorated and accomplished girl to the boy after performing yajna is known as Dev *vivaha.*
3. Artha Marriage : A marriage arranged after getting some reward or monetary benefit from the groom is described as "artha" *vivaha.*
4. Prajapati Marriage : A marriage arranged to further a social or political end is known as "Prajapati" marriage.
5. Asura Marriage : It is a marriage solemnised after making a payment to the bride and groom is known as Asura.
6. Gandharva Marriage : A union brought about by mutual attraction without reference to age, place or social practices of the bride and the groom is known as "Gandharva" *vivaha.*
7. Rakshasa Marriage : A marriage with a girl taken captive in a war or taken away forcibly is called "Rakshasa" *vivaha.*
8. Paishach Marriage: Forcible sexual intercourse with an unwilling girl or a girl of an unsound mind is described as "Paishach" *vivaha.*

These eight kinds of marriages cover the entire range of unions between man and woman prevailing all over the world. It points to the wide vision, deep grasp of human frailties and realism of socio-cultural leaders and law givers of Vedic India. But they commended only "Brahma" and "Dev" marriage. They have been the rule in India for ages in the past. The other kinds of marriages are looked down upon and "Rakshasa" and "Paishacha" varieties are condemned as inhuman and anti-social. But they are not entirely ruled out. Their existence is recognised.

One important feature of Indian marriages is that due importance is paid to the genetic factor. Marriages with near relatives on the paternal or maternal side is not permitted. Marriage between parties living in different and far off villages or regions which have no close relationship is commended. It is universally accepted in India that progeny of such marriages is genetically superior and conducive to the preservation of high quality of the family.

Importance is also given to the social and caste status of the parties. Inter-caste marriages are also not ruled out. But marriages within the caste groups are preferred.

The age factor is also kept in mind. The ideal marriage is one between a boy of 25 and above after he has completed his studies and girl of 16 or above. A difference of nine years between the age of the girl and the boy is considered to be ideal.

Marriage in India is a sacrament and not a contract which can be broken at will. Therefore, monogamy is a rule. Taking a second wife is permitted to have a male child with the consent of the first wife. But in practice, the rulers, the rajas and the *samants,* some time had more than one wife. But the ideal as prescribed in the life of Shri Rama is one wife and total commitment to each other.

Arranged marriages are the common practice. Among the upper castes, particularly Kshatriyas, the right of the girl to choose her partner in a "*Swayamvar*" or open competition between suitors was accepted. But in course of time, it became an exception rather than a rule.

Marriage celebrations are long and elaborate. They are spread over the more than one day. But the key ceremony is the circumambulation of the sacrificial fire by the bride and groom and "*kanya dan*" by the father or guardian of the girl to the groom. Until and unless, the circumambulation of fire is completed, marriage does not get the soul and legal recognition. Among the Sikhs, their holy book *Granth Sahib* takes the place of the sacrificial fire. The bride and groom have to go round it four times, whereas among non-Sikhs, the circumambulation is completed in seven rounds around the holy fire.

The first step in the marriage is betrothal. Then a date for marriage is fixed when the groom goes to the bride's place accompanied by relatives and friends — the *barat.* The marriage procession terminates at the bride's place or the place fixed for the marriage feast. The *barat* is received by the father, relatives and friends of the bride's family amidst the chanting of the Vedic *mantras.* It is followed by the garlanding of the bridegroom by the bride and of bride by the bridegroom. The *barat* departs after the marriage feast, but the near relatives stay back for the marriage rituals which are performed at a time fixed in consultation with family *purohit* or priests.

After the rituals are over, the bride is bade good bye by her mother, father and other relatives with due ceremony. The bride then departs for the bridegroom's place.

Marriage is generally preceded by "Sangeet" when folk songs are sung at both bride's and groom's places on the marriage eve. That night, *mehndi* or henna is applied in decorative patterns on the hands and feet of the bride to be. The ritual is also performed at the groom's place when henna is applied on his hands and feet. The next morning, the groom is applied turmeric paste before bath. The bride also takes bath after applying "ubtan" or traditional herbal paste including turmeric. Generally red or saffron coloured clothes are worn by the bride and turbans of the same colours are worn by the heads and close relatives of both the families.

Except for the actual rituals, other ceremonies are common among Indians of all castes and religions. Muslims, not only in India, but also in Pakistan and Bangladesh, follow the same practice and ceremonies. Marriage songs of Pakistani Punjab are exactly the same as marriage songs of Indian Punjab. They are loaded with words drawn from Sanskrit.

Although marriage practices are almost common, the status of brides and wives after marriage differs in two Punjabs. The Muslim religious laws framed by Prophet Mohammed and his Arab companions gives almost license to the husband to treat the wife as a "field" for enjoyment and procreation and discard her at will by uttering "Talaq" thrice. He can have any number of wives, but not more than four at a time. As a result, Muslim women are less than equal and do not enjoy even some of the basic human rights. That explains the growing demand among Indian Muslim women for the common civil laws which may put them on equal footing with the Hindu women socially and legally.

The pomp, show and glamour of Indian marriages is unique. That is why many foreigners especially Europeans and Americans, get attracted to it and like to get married in the Indian way.

With the world getting smaller every day due to scientific inventions and elimination/distance, a common world culture is being evolved. The Indian marriages have therefore begun to influence the marriage ceremonies outside India as well.

The Cosmos, Weddings, and Honeybees

In the distant past, chaos filled all space. Out of this chaos there appeared a goddess, and in the midst of the chaos she created the earth and all the living things — plant, fish, and animal — that lived thereon. Having done so, she finally conceived a child within herself and gave birth to a male child, himself a god. The goddess dearly loved her god child, but she knew that he alone could never give rise to further children and a line of descendants, so at last the goddess married her god child and bore him a large number of offspring. The children born to the two gods were mankind. It was thus that Man was created, bearing the stain of cursed incest between mother and child.

Because the goddess made the earth and all things living on earth, she was called the Great Mother, and while she created the earth, she was the very earth itself. Mankind, however, unable to bear the dark shadow of original sin that stained the creation of the human race, tried in many ways to purge that original sin. The simplest and most ingenuous of these attempts was the interpretation that the goddess incorporated both the male and female sexes and their attributes, and that the marriage to the child god was a symbolic representation of this duality. The most representative examples of such a sexual duality, however, were demons, which would thereby mean that mankind is descended from demonic ancestors. Another alternative interpretation which was advanced held that the goddess gave birth to two children, a young god and goddess, who in turn married and gave birth to the human race. This, too, bore its own shadow of guilt, again that of incest, and with this rationalization, man's very birth made him the unwilling heir to original sin. Consequently man must invariably meet death some day, returning to the womb of his ancient mother, the earth, and once again emerging into this world in a new life, it was thought.

Such a "monistic" approach to the process of the birth of mankind had added to it an additional concept of the "cosmos" which lends a new dimension of meaning to man's attempts to explain his origins. Cosmos stood in contrast to chaos, and within the realm of the cosmos, a divine order controlled all and assigned and fixed in their divinely appointed places all the primal elements floating aimlessly in the unordered mass of chaos. Cosmos also possessed a finite boundary to its domain, a boundary at which cosmos touched chaos. What was of the ultimate importance was that along with a boundary, cosmos also possessed a hub, a centre, a heart.

The cosmos was the result of the sacred wedding of god and goddess, those two awesome giants — the female, — goddess of earth — as already mentioned, and the male, the god of the skies. Since these two gods, however, were so deeply in love with each other that they were constantly in each other's arms, they had to be forcibly separated to create a place for mankind, to which they had given birth. It was thus that the cosmos was created, with its tri-level structure of heaven, earth, and the underworld, through which there stretches a great cosmic axle tying together these three levels.

Through such a view of the world and its creation mankind was finally able to escape the black burden of original sin which surrounded mankind's birth. It was also necessary, however, for man to procure food with which to sustain himself, and this need led man to set the plow to the earth, marring the earth goddess, mankind's Great Mother, but through this mother's sacrifices gaining sustenance from the fruits of the earth. This action, while giving man life, also carried its own grievous penalty, that of eventual death for all men. There were others who believed that the sacred cosmos was the product of the mystical marriage of the two gods, who themselves were generated of their own accord in the midst of chaos. In such a theory, the two gods proceeded to provide the earth with all that was required for life thereon. But in the effort of creation, the goddess herself perished and entered the dismal world of the dead far beneath the earth. The remaining god, bereft of his loved one, tried to follow the goddess into the underworld to lead her back to the land of the living, but this act, contravening the sacred order of existence, was doomed to failure. The heartbroken god returned and ended his role in the creation of the world by creating the gods who became the ancestors of mankind. With this explanation of the creation of all things, mankind was at last freed of the burden of original sin, but man was fated by the rules of the sacred cosmos to follow the goddess, the original ancestor, into the world of death.

Thus the order which rules the cosmos, created out of the sacred marriage of these two gods, became a theory of dualism, composed of a wide range of mutually dependent principles, male-female, life-death, heaven-earth, above-below, good-evil. Attention must also be paid to the way in which the cosmos itself is set in contrast to chaos. Just as before the creation of all things, chaos surrounds the cosmos and is filled with all manner of strange writhing monsters trying to devour the shining cosmos.

The cosmos itself possesses its own strange characteristics. Its size is elastic and takes on a myriad of shapes, at times encompassing all of heaven, earth, and the underworld, at times becoming a single country and people within a fixed territory. At other times it may contract to a city enclosed in a stout wall, a castle with its high towers and dismal dungeons, a village encircled by a fence, or a single hedge-encompassed home. It may even be the microcosm of one individual human being. The individual human, however, as a microcosm is, in a manner of speaking, an "incomplete cosmos" lacking one of the basic dualistic principles of the cosmos, that of the male-female contrast. Thus, so long as there is no mutually complementary male-female relationship, the microcosm will remain incomplete.

This aim of completion of the cosmos through creation of a mutually complementary relationship has long been the basic principle behind the wedding ceremony. Here the bride and groom, in some sacred place apart from the course of daily life, are re-enacting the creation of the cosmos through the marriage of the god and goddess. The two to be married begin by dressing themselves in garments that are totally different from those worn in their ordinary daily activities, either the traditional garments of the nation or the highly formal apparel of the culturally advanced nations, expressing the distance — either in time or space — separating the ceremony from ordinary life and thus identifying the bride and groom with the ancient gods who created the cosmos. And since the couple is re-enacting the mystic creation of the cosmos itself, the wedding ceremony must be conducted with solemn seriousness. There are limitations on those who may participate in the ceremony, and in particular, the location in which the ceremony is conducted must be different from those for other ceremonies and must be a small, more limited area.

The bride and groom, having created the new cosmos, must then fulfil their duty to complete the contents of this cosmos. Among the nations of Asia, the wedding dinner is held as a very important part of the wedding ceremony, representing the completion of the new cosmos. The large hall in which the wedding dinner is held represents the new cosmos just created by the couple, and a brilliantly shining chandelier fills this new cosmos with light. In Japan, the bride and groom often remain silent throughout the wedding dinner, and the *nakodo*, the go-between, announces to all present that he has witnessed and attests to the marriage ceremony. The bride and groom, of course, are present as god and goddess, and a qualified human must announce the actions of the couple to the common mass of human being who are present. Those invited to the wedding dinner are seated in a fixed, predetermined order, and as those participants represent all things constituting the new cosmos, their fixed seating order represents the sacred order of existence come into being in this new cosmos. The food provided here represents the abundance and prosperity of the gods' new cosmos, and at the same time this food is invested with a sacred spirit of its own through the gods' act of partaking thereof. This mystic spirit is communicated to all those present and allows them to become members of the new cosmos. At such wedding dinners held in Japan, the guests are often presented with souvenirs of food which, when distributed to be eaten by those not present at the dinner, allow them too to become members of the new cosmos.

It is thought that in the distant past such wedding ceremonies were conducted only by the king, the head of mankind's basic body of government. The king was not merely a leader of government. The god of heaven and the goddess of earth, having created the cosmos, were parted and had to live in the heavens and beneath the earth. Man, thus provided with a place to live, felt that it was good to live apart from the gods, but he still needed some way to protect himself from the domination of the forces of evil living in the surrounding chaos. To do so, mankind made a personification of the gods through whom man could call upon the spirits of the god of heaven or the earth goddess and thereby forestall the inroads of chaotic evil. This personification was the king, and thus the king and queen had a responsibility to create a new cosmos and protect the people of the land from evil, as well as to provide food for the people and prosperity for them and their descendants. The political and social system of the country is no more than the cosmic order, just as the whole of the products of the nation is symbolically the same as the food provided at the wedding of the king and queen. Especially good examples of such a phenomenon are provided by Japan, Thailand, and other nations where pictures of the emperor and empress or king and queen are often placed in the living room. Such pictures transform the home into a cosmos created and watched over by the king and queen, with those living in the home thereby becoming members of that cosmos.

This explains why there are no countries without kings, as well as why, in principle, there are no single kings nor queens who do not give birth to children.

The inhabitants of the new cosmos created by the marriage of the king and queen — in other words the nation — follow the example of the king and queen by themselves holding marriage ceremonies and by thus creating their own cosmos. It is doubtful, however, whether all the people of any country can have such a marriage ceremony. In various areas of Southeast Asia, youth groups systems have developed under which boys and girls of a certain age join together and, where they are tested and instructed in approaching maturity before finding their mates and being married. Here, too, there are serious doubts as to whether all the members of such youth groups are able to marry. A good many of such young people probably have no chance to marry and remain single all their lives. People who have no opportunity to marry may remain in the youth dormitories, sometimes entering specialized occupations or forming special groups which learn and pass on specialized jobs or knowledge. Such people have made for themselves the sacred space they require to protect themselves from domination by evil, but no matter how many members of the same sex — each an incomplete microcosm — may gather, they will still be able to form only an incomplete cosmos, an imitation cosmos. This imitation cosmos is also a definite territory within set limits, an area ruled by a certain order. This order is naturally not dualistic but monistic and therefore can never be at rest, but must always be moving endlessly in a fixed direction. Should this motion ever cease, the imitation cosmos will fall in ruins.

An additional observation which may be made about such an imitation cosmos is that its members are never born within the cosmos but are invariably added to the cosmos by entering from outside. There is thus no male-female contrast, an absolute necessity in the creation of life, and the imitation cosmos leads only a genderless existence. Using a bit more modern terminology, this imitation cosmos is an "organization".

There are constant efforts made to turn such an imitation-cosmos organization into a complete, finished cosmos. One example is the call for "Japanese-style industrial management" that is so often made in Japan. Companies have made attempts at building living area that encompass both the employees and their families, renting their workers pleasant company homes and providing a wide range of welfare and recreation facilities, and in addition, company officials may serve as go-betweens in arranging marriages between workers within the company. And yet, whenever the president of such a company makes an appearance, whether in the company offices or in photographs in company publications, the president's wife is never to be seen. When a worker reaches a certain age, he must retire and is cast out of this company cosmos. This imitation cosmos thus, in the last analysis, can never become a true complete cosmos. If, however, the individuals who constitute this organization each have their own spouses, it does become possible for each of them to create his own cosmos.

A short while ago, the president of a famous Japanese company tried to challenge the limits of such a system. He and his wife formed a new religious sect and became the leaders of this new religion. The president built a shrine atop the company's head-quarters building and forced all the employees to become members of the sect. In a very short while, however, the company's performance plummeted and the president was forced to resign.

The members of such an imitation cosmos are unable to escape the neuter of the structure within which they live and work as they are compelled by a strong need to try to construct a cosmos of their own. Thus all manner of people have held wedding ceremonies and have sought places to live, leading to a wedding boom which in turn has resulted in the explosive growth in population which has produced today's society. Apparently, the concept of dualistic cosmos furthered the development of human society and culture, with the help of its counterpart, the imitation cosmos, the most effective means of conquering the chaos. Although the ancient god of heaven and the goddess of the earth created only one cosmos, there are today innumerable multitudes of microcosms. Thus, the sacred order of the cosmos having reached into every nook and cranny of the world, there has arisen a movement in opposition to this order — the Women's Liberation Movement. The point most strongly stressed is that there exists a true equality between male and female, which might also be called a strong drive toward "degenderization," with male or female fundamental aspects evinced. Such an orientation to me portends a return to chaos through the breakdown of the cosmos ruled by the sacred order based on the principle of opposition of dualistic, mutually complementary factors. This may, of course, be followed by the creation of a new cosmos with a new order of existence. "Women's Lib" is without a doubt the forerunner of such a development, but if one looks for a type of society in which almost all the members are neuter and bear divided responsibility for a variety of functions, one immediately thinks of bees and ants. Such insect societies are type of imitation cosmos in which the members are driven forward at full speed toward the single aim of preservation of the species. The queen bee (naturally enough, there is no such thing as a king bee) serves the sole purpose of reproduction. This being so, "Women's Lib" may be a gloomy omen of the future collapse of our present cosmos and the formation of a huge imitation cosmos in which humanity plunges forward single mindedly toward the goal of preservation of the species.

Tradition and Change of Marriage in Korea

The foundation of marriage customs in contemporary Korea was established in the middle of the Yi dynasty. The decline of Buddhism, which had been the national faith throughout the 500 year reign of the Koryo dynasty (918-1392), due to the corruption and demoralization of the monks brought the collapse of the Koryo. At this time neo-Confucianism was imported from China and enthusiastically accepted by a group of young state officials. These officials finally brought the fate of the Koryo dynasty to its end and created a new dynasty, Yi. Thus the Yi dynasty (1392-1910) from its inception repressed Buddhism and ruled the country according to the Confucian political ideology. The philosophy of Confucianism, especially that of neo-Confucian ideology of Chu Hsi, played a major role not only in the realm of politics but also in every sphere of daily life in Yi dynasty Kŏrea. As a result traditional customs had been drastically modified or changed. The marriage custom was not an exception. From the social structure point of view the Yi dynasty Korea may be characterized by a kinship oriented society or a family society. In this setting, the fundamental goal of the institution of marriage was not so much the pursuit of happiness for the bride and groom as to meet the obligations to the family and ancestry.

At the same time marital arrangements, at least among the aristocratic class, proceeded according to the rules set by *Wen-Kung-chia-li* by Chu Hsi (a book on family rituals).

The procedures of marriage include; 1) Eui-hon (negotiation of marriage through a go-between), 2) Nap-chae (declaration or transmission of intention of engagement to the bride's house), 3) Nap-pae (engagement ceremony) and 4) Chin-young (ceremony for bringing and receiving bride at the groom's house).

The four major procedures in the marital arrangement will be described as follows:

Eui-hon

In the Eui-hon stage it is mainly the go-between's act. The go-between is given the task of visiting the house of both the prospective bride and groom and he investigates the family background, social and economic status of the family, the person's appearance, character, talent and personality, for both parties. The go-between is selected normally from among the relatives or acquaintances of one of the prospective parties. Marriage was also occasionally arranged by professional go-betweens. In both Korea and Japan, the go-between traditionally played a major role in the marriage arrangement. There is a distinction, however, in the responsibility of go-betweens between the two countries. While the go-between's role and responsibility terminate at the time of the establishment of marriage in Korea, the Baishyaknin's responsibility in Japan is extended even after the establishment of marriage.

Nap-chae (declaration and transmission intention of engagement)

The prospective groom's family examines the information about the bride and her family supplied by the go-between. If they intend to pursue the matter further, the head of the groom's household sends in Sa-ju-dan-ja, in which the time, date, month, and year of birth of the groom are written, to the bride's house. The Sa-ju-dan-ja is customarily wrapped in a kerchief of red cloth when it is sent to the bride's home. When the Sa-ju-dan-ja reaches the bride's home, they let a fortune-teller prognosticate the future harmony of their marital life by reading the Sa-ju (four pillars if literally translated: the hour, day, month, and year of one's birth) for the çouple. This is normally known as the practice of Goong-hap. In other words the Goong-hap is a kind of fortune-telling based on the principles of Yin-yang (the cosmic dual forces in principles of Chinese philosophy) and Gan-ji (sex-agenary cycle). Although Goong-hap was no more than an act of superstition, it was widely practised and believed among nearly every strata of the population, especially among women. Even among the well educated class, the success of marriage arrangements was very often determined by the Goong-hap.

If the outcome of fortune-telling is judged to be positive, the bride's family let the groom's family know about their intention of engagement by sending the Taek-il-dan-ja in which the date for the wedding is proposed.

Nap-pae (engagement ceremony)

Nap-pae consists of procedural rules for the engagement ceremony. It involves sending congratulatory letters and gifts from the groom's family to the bride's house for the successful agreement for marriage. The letter is called Hon-seo (a letter of marriage), which is written in a standardized form or sometimes in a creative style.

The types of gift varied from region to region. In Seoul it was customary to send blue and red silver and silver threads. In other places sometimes gold and silver products, clothes, and food stuff were also sent as gifts. Historical records indicate that the practice of sending too many luxurious gifts among the rich families often became the target of criticism and sometimes the government openly discouraged such practice.

The money sending practice as the engagement gift often attracted opposition. Nevertheless the custom of sending money as an engagement gift to the bride's house was quite prevalent among the middle and lower classes and continued until recently among some segments of the Korean society. It is uncertain whether the money-sending practice was simply a form of congratulatory expression or it was done as a bride price.

Once the ceremonial process of the Nap-pae was completed and the engagement formalized, it was considered to be a permanent and unbreakable contract. It was written in the laws of the Yi dynasty that "if a woman marries another man after receiving Hon-seo, a letter of intention for marriage, the head of bride's household shall be punished by the law and ostracized".

It was often observed especially among the upper class that the bride had to live throughout her entire life as a virgin in case of a death of the groom after receiving the Hon-seo.

Chin-young

Chin-young prescribes the ceremonial rules for receiving the bride at the groom's house. This is the most important act in the institution of the marital process, especially under the patriarchal family system. However, the prescribed rules had not been fully realized in actual practice during the Yi dynasty. In the following some of the unique conditions in the traditional Korean marriage custom that prevented the full realization of the Chin-young will be discussed. Ancient customs of Korea are not well known. Fragmentary historical records and materials from the archeological excavation highlight some aspects of traditional marriage customs in Korea. One distinct feature of the Korean traditional marriage custom emerges from these historical records; that is, when marriage takes place, the groom first goes to the bride's house and lives there for a considerable period. One of the Chinese historical records described the marriage custom in Ko-gu-ryo (37 BC - AD 668, one of the dynasties in the three kingdom era Korea) as follows: "When their daughter becomes engaged to a man, they build a little cottage right behind their main house for the couple. The groom comes to the bride's home, identifies himself and begs permission to enter the bride's room. He repeats the begging three times before the bride's parents let him go in. When children are born and grown up, then the groom takes his bride with the children to his home." Another historical record describes the marriage custom of Ko-gu-ryo: "When man and woman love each other, they marry. The groom's family sends only some pork and wine. The groom's family is not expected to send other valuables. If one does so, it is regarded as shameful since, when it happens, it is considered to be a slave sale rather than a marriage."

These two records are too brief to provide a comprehensive understanding of marriage custom in Ko-gu-ryo. However, they shed light on an important aspect of the marriage customs of the ancient Korea, although we do not know for certain whether the customs described above are practised by one segment of social strata or in all levels. The procedures described above clearly point to the fact that the courtship practice was quite free among young people and marriage by the couple's own choice was the dominant form in the Ko-gu-ryo period.

This custom of marriage based on the couple's free choice in Ko-gu-ryo is quite a contrast to the strictly arranged marriage by parents in the Yi dynasty, which under the strong influence of Confucian ideology forbade free contact between men and women and strongly condemned marriage by the couple's own choice.

Traditional customs of the three kingdom era seem to have undergone little modification until the latter part of Koryo dynasty, when the neo-Confucian ideology began to flow into Korea. As this new ideology became rooted in firm ground in Korea in the middle of the Yi dynasty, the traditional customs of family life and marriage underwent a fundamental transformation. Amazingly enough, however, the tradition for the groom to move into the bride's house at the time of marriage did not change very much.

Although procedural rules prescribed in Chin-young began to be promoted in the latter part of Koryo dynasty, their implementation was strongly advocated by Chung, Do Jeon who played a crucial role in founding the Yi dynasty.

According to the Yi dynasty Chronicles, a recommendation was made by the Board of Rites to the king in the spring of the 15th year of Tai-jong (1415), the third king of the Yi dynasty, "The old tradition of marriage in the preceding (Ko-ryo) dynasty prescribes that the groom moves into the bride's home and bear, and raise the children in the bride's house thus the feeling of affection and appreciation of the grand-parents on the mother's side is enhanced. When one parent dies, in case of government officials, a 30 day leave is granted to them. This practice is still being continued in our dynasty and does not differentiate between the relative importance of the family of the father's side or of the mother's side. It is therefore recommended that the mourning period is to be limited to 9 months and a 20 day leave is to be granted in the case of the death of grandparent on the mother's side. It is also recommended that the mourning period be limited to 6 months and a 15 day leave be granted in case of the death of one of the wife's parents. This recommendation was accepted by the king. The king at the same time instructed the Board of Rites to draw up detailed procedural rules of Chin-young and received the report accordingly. However the written procedures were not actually practised." The kings in the following years tried to implement the rules of Chin-young without much success. Finally, King Joong-jong, the 11th King of the Yi dynasty, in his 12th year of reign (1517) received the queen at the marriage ceremony strictly according to the rules of Chin-young, which was followed by some aristocrats and nobles. However, the practice did not last very long. Thus a great scholar of the 18th century Korea, Yu, Hyung Won deplored in his book *Ban-kye-soo-rok*, "The aristocrats are old fashioned and often violate the rules of *li*, thus the groom goes to the bride's house upon marriage. Accordingly, when a man marries, it is commonly called Ibjang in Korean (to go to the father-in-law's house) rather than Chui-cheo (to bring the bride home). This practice for Yang to follow Yin is against the principle of nature and to violate the proper rule of conduct between men and women." Even the absolute authority and power of Yi dynasty could not alter the indigenous custom of the groom staying at the bride's home for a considerable period; therefore, a compromised form of marriage incorporated the essence of both old and new elements. The act of bowing to each other to be husband and wife and exchanging wine, the principal ceremonial act of marriage, always takes place at the bride's home. It thus became customary for the groom to stay at the bride's home for three days (in some cases, only for one day), before he introduces his wife to his own parents at the groom's house. Often, especially for rich families, the bride stayed at her home for several years after the marriage ceremony actually had taken place.

The marriage procession of the groom going to the bride's home followed the pattern described below. In front of the procession two lamp-men with a pair of candle lamps covered in red silk lead the way. The lamp-men are followed by a goose-man, in red clothes with a purple hat, carrying a wooden carved goose (sometimes a live duck is substituted). The goose-man is then followed by the groom dressed in a light pink robe, silk hat, and a pair of cloth shoes riding on horseback who is flanked by an umbrella man. The end of the procession is made up of two men representing the groom's family. Once the procession reaches the door of the bride's home, the groom gets off the horse and walks on the straw pad to the inside yard. In the yard, there is a tent which contains a festively decorated screen and a high-legged dining table. The groom takes the wooden goose from the goose-man, sets it on the table and performs two full bows and a lesser bow. The bride's mother then takes the goose, wraps it in her long skirt, and puts it in the bride's room. After this procedure, the most important ritual of the marital ceremony — the ceremony of bowing to each other and exchanging wine between the groom and bride — takes place on the Dae-chung (big wooden floor). Thus the formal wedding ceremony ends. For the Woo-rye — the ritual of the bride going to the groom's house to pay respects to the parents-in-law — it was customary for the bride's parents to send a variety of gifts, including a dried pheasant, to the groom's parents.

Jeon-an, the ritual for dedicating the goose described above, had long disappeared in China, where the tradition first originated. It is a puzzle that this ritual nevertheless continued so long in Korea. There are several interpretations as to the reasons why the goose was used in the wedding ceremony. One thing is clear, however, food as a gift takes a special importance in ancient societies and must have aroused feelings of happiness and gratitude among people. Records indicate that among the ancient customs of the Shilla dynasty, marriage gifts only included food-stuffs and the kind and quantity of food as gifts varied among the rich and poor. As mentioned previously, in the Ko-gu-ryo dynasty, also, the wedding gifts to the bride's home consisted of pork and wine only. These practices testified to the importance of food as a wedding gift.

This old tradition of exchanging food-stuffs as gifts might have been easily transformed into a form of goose and pheasant in the Yi dynasty.

Since the liberation in 1945 from the Japanese colonial rule which lasted 36 years, Korea for the first time in its history has become free to contact the outside world and is exposed to the new ideology of democracy. The Korean War of 1950-1953 not only inflicted heavy material damage, but also disturbed many traditional social structures of Korea. The economic development plan, begun after the Korean War and intensified in the 1960's, has laid the foundations for a capitalistic economic system. Under these processes of economic and social transformation in the recent past, many traditional elements of Korean family life and marriage customs have changed. These changes may profitably be compared to those that occurred to traditional marriage patterns upon the institution of the Yi dynasty and its alien ways of neo-Confucianism.

Nowadays, it is not uncommon to observe a marriage that takes place as a result of romantic love affairs that were traditionally viewed as sinful. However, it took nearly two hundred years in Yi dynasty before traditional marriage custom was transformed into a new form under the influence of neo-Confucianism. Likewise for present day Korea, undergoing as it has, such profound structural and economic transformation, it is not surprising that traditional elements still persist that entirely new modes of conduct have not emerged. Marriage in the Korea of today is not strictly arranged by the go-between, yet it is not entirely romantic love that leads into marriage. The dominant form of mate selection today takes elements from both the arranged marriage and love match. When prospective mates are introduced by parents, the final decision is left with the partners themselves. When two prospective mates wish to marry as a result of romantic love first, then it is customary to earn the consent of their parents for final approval.

In upper-class society, the traditional practice of the four principal rituals of marriage has long since disappeared. The three rituals, Nap-pae, Jeon-an and Woo-rye which had been widely practised in simplified form among the commoners in former days, also have become less frequently practised. Today church weddings are common among Christians within the Christian tradition. Non-Christians normally perform wedding ceremonies in a commercial wedding hall presided over by a civic leader or a celebrity. After the wedding, the couple immediately leaves for a honeymoon. The couple starts marital life at the groom's parents' home, the bride's parents' home, or finds an entirely new home by themselves depending upon the circumstances.

In spite of these changes, this does not mean that all traditional elements of the marriage customs have disappeared.

The custom of delivering letter of marriage and gifts to the bride's home by the groom's friends on the day before the wedding is a revised contemporary form of the Nap-pae. This custom is still practised in Korea today. The ritual for the bride to bow to the groom's parents in a separately prepared room at the church or at the wedding hall is universally practised. This is also a revised form of the traditional wedding ritual, even though it formerly took place at the groom's house.

Though a new form of marriage is being developed, blending both traditional and modern elements, one thing is clear. The poetic country scene of the wedding procession under the clear and high sky of Korea; the groom on horseback and dressed in a red and blue costume; and the bride in a colourful hand-carried ga-ma (cart) marching among the company of her friends and relatives; this scene has long disappeared.

The Japanese Way of Marriage

The go-between

Though marriage in Japan has seen many developments, some aspects of the institution go back over a thousand years. Then, as now, there was a strong emphasis on marriage between people of equal social standing. The aim of marriage among the upper classes then was the unromantic one of forging links among influential families. The main institution in Japan which for many centuries helped bring suitable partners together and smooth the path to wedlock was that of the go-between, or *nakodo*. Though go-betweens initially restricted their services to the rich and royal, after the Meiji Restoration of 1868 the custom filtered down to lower levels of society and the *nakodo* became universal in Japan. Dealing as he or she does with affairs of the heart, the go-between needs to be a person of considerable social skills. Unlike the *nakodo's* impersonal modern counterpart, computer dating, the spirit behind the go-between is purely altruistic, though the role carries with it much prestige. The go-between identifies couples that he or she thinks would make an ideal match, researches the all-important details on family background and arranges the couple's first meeting. The go-between is always present at his meeting, which usually takes place at a smart hotel or restaurant. After the first meeting, the two parties then signal whether they want to meet again and continue towards marriage. A fast decision is essential when working towards an arranged marriage, as it is considered poor form to meet more than three times without having very serious matrimonial intentions.

Love not connections

For many years after the system became widespread, arranged marriages were the commonest way for the Japanese man or woman to meet their life's mate. Since the Second World War, however, there has been a growing trend among Japanese of "love marriages." The love match is more along the lines of matrimony familiar in the West and dispenses with the time-honoured offices of the go-between. In 1965, a significant change occurred in the Japanese pattern of marriage. In that year, the number of love matches exceeded that of arranged marriages for the first time. Since then, the trend towards the love match has continued: a 1991 survey indicated that only 13% of Japanese now find their partners through go-betweens. Yasuhiko Yuzawa, professor of sociology at Tokyo's Ochanomizu University, comments, "Recent decades have marked quite a turning point in Japanese attitudes towards marriage. Since the last century, arranged marriages had been the norm, but the trend away from tradition and custom that has come with the modern age has meant that younger people have started to think differently about how they find their partners."

Pressure to marry

At one time, the Japanese, swayed by the strong Confucian ethic of fidelity to the household, felt it was an individual's obligation to get married. Indeed, in many professions, individuals were not considered fully responsible adults until they had tied the marital knot. At one time, there was a good deal more social pressure on women to get married early, as Prof. Yuzawa explains" "A survey of the late fifties showed that most women felt they had to accept an arranged marriage out of duty to their families. At that time, too, there were fewer job opportunities for women who had reached the normal marriageable age, and this made them more amenable to proposals.

Shopping around

In addition to the trend towards the love marriage in Japan, another significant development that has occurred over recent decades has been that Japanese are gradually getting married later in life. Before the Second World War, 50% of Japanese women were married by the age of 25, but a 1989 finding shows that this figure had decreased to 15%. The same picture is also seen with Japanese men. At one time, men commonly get married in their 20s, whereas today many are still unmarried by the age of 30. A national census in 1990 showed the unmarried rate among males in their late 20s to be 64.4% as against a female figure of 40.2%. One of the main reasons for the difference in the figures is the ratio of the sexes in Japan, as Prof Yuzawa observes, "Today, Japanese men between the age of about 37 and 45 have problems because of the imbalance in the population. Japanese men on average marry women three years younger than themselves, but the number of men in this age group is 20% greater than that of women who are three years younger." Another factor that makes it more of a buyer's market for Japan's would-be brides is the way in which Japanese couples tend to meet. Among white-collar workers, over half of love matches are the result of office romances, but since the female: male ratio in Japanese offices stands in the female favour, the Japanese office bachelor is up against strong competition. Muriel Jolivest, Assistant Professor of French at Tokyo's Sophia University, believes that the attitude of the Japanese male also plays a role in these figures: "There's quite a difference between Japanese and Western men in the way they regard women and marriage. For the Western man, one of life's great goals is that of finding a suitable partner. But for Japanese men this is not the case. I think that Japanese men need to find greater fulfilment in their personal lives rather than in their work."

Future trends

With regard to how the situation with marriage in Japan will develop in the future, Prof. Yuzawa echoes some of Asst. Prof. Jolivet's feelings". "One of the main barriers to happy marriages in Japan has been the Japanese work ethic. For many Japanese men, work is the most valuable aspect of their lives. This attitude is beginning to change, and there's now more of an emphasis on leisure in Japan. But for society as a whole, as well as for the individual, it is important that this trend continue." However, that situation may develop, Japan's wedding agencies and hotels are not despondent about the current state of their industry. After the postwar baby boomers, the second baby-boom generation is the most populous group in Japan, and this generation — at the age of 18 to 22 — will soon be at the main marriageable age. For Japan's wedding industry, the prospects for the next decade couldn't look more promising.

An Indian miniature, "Dhola and Maru riding a camel", late eighteenth century.

Dress and Hairstyle

Dress and Clothing of Bangladesh

Culture is an integral part of human behaviour in the society. It shows the development of the human mind and spirit by training and experience. This intellectual development of people from generation to generation is the paramount determinant of civilisation. Man is born in society. He is nursed in society, finds his degree of fulfilment, his character and his limitations is society. As a social being, the first thing he has to do is to cover his body with some sort of clothing, which differs from country to country and from time to time. Thus, the traditional culture of a particular country can best be represented through an analysis of different clothings and costumes used by its people. Generally, by clothing we mean all the garments and accessories worn by a person. Dress means to provide with clothing which adds something that improves the appearance or heightens the effectiveness of the person. Now, in the case of Bangladesh, as in the case of other countries of the world, dress and clothing depend upon some physical and social factors. The physical factor includes the physiography and climate of the country while the social factor takes into account the over-all social set-up as well as the influence of religion. Along with these, the economic condition of the general people is also an important factor.

Bangladesh is a developing country with agriculture as the main source of livelihood. The economy is agriculture-oriented and about 90 per cent of our total population live on it directly or indirectly. So their dresses are such that they are convenient for agricultural activities. The agricultural people are mostly rural.

But with the advent of science and technology, urbanisation is taking place to a great extent. Various sorts of big industries are going to be set up in different parts of the country. People are coming in their thousands from villages to industrial cities. As they change their occupation from a village farmer to an urban industrial worker, their costumes also change in accordance with their jobs.

Basically, therefore, the classification of the people of Bangladesh according to their dresses can best be shown with the help of the following chart:

(1) Rural
(2) Urban — (a) Upper, (b) Middle, (c) Lower Class
(3) Tribal.

But before analysing their chart, we shall have to take into account another very important factor, i.e, religion. The two most important religious communities of the country are Muslims and Hindus. The Muslims form about 77 per cent of the people and the Hindus form the majority of the other religious communities. The Hill-Tracts of Chittagong are mainly inhabited by Buddhists, the only indigenous Buddhist community in the sub-continent. There are also a number of native Christians in the country. The Muslims and the Hindus live side by side, — and there is hardly an exclusive Muslim or Hindu village in Bangladesh.

Now, keeping in mind the influences of economic-factors and those of religion we can analyse the above three categories of people and see what kind of clothing they do use.

First comes the rural population of Bangladesh. We have mentioned earlier that about 90 per cent of the population of Bangladesh live in villages. Cultivation, animal husbandry and fishery are their main occupations. Almost all of them use the same dress; i.e, a "Lungi" and a vest called "Genji". "Lungi" is made of a piece of cloth about 2 to 2-1/2 yards in length and 44-55 inches in width. It is used to cover the lower portion of the body. During the summer or rainy seasons, the village workers generally do not use "Genji". The upper portion of their body remains uncovered. Another important thing used by them is called "Gamcha". It is also a piece of cloth usually 2-1/2 yards in length and about 27 inches in width. The villagers use it as a towel, and during working hours in the rainy season the farmers and fishermen wear it in place of Lungi, the upper portion of the body remains uncovered.

The people from the Hindu community use "Dhoti" in place of "Lungi". "Dhoti " is a cloth of about 5 yards length and 1-1/2 yards in width wrapped with front and back tucked below the naval and around the hip.

On certain occasions, the village people use shirts or "Panjabis" (a full sleeved shirt without collar). These are mostly used during Eid or other festivals or during marriage ceremonies. The typical dress of a Muslim bridegroom in rural Bangladesh is "Pyjama" and "Panjabi" and a cap called "Topi". The well-to-do families of the villages use "Sherwani" over the "Panjabi". "Sherwani" is a long coat with closed neck. The Hindu bridegroom use "Dhoti" and "Chadur"- a long wrapper for upper portion of the body. The influential persons in the villages, whom we generally call village "Matabbars" use "Lungi" or "Pyjama", a "Panjabi", a "Topi" and sleeveless coat with an open front called "Fatua".

The main dress of the village women of Bangladesh is "Sari". It is a long piece of cloth 5 to 6 yards in length and about 1-1/2 yards in width. "Sari" is not only the dress of village-women but a common dress of all the women-folk of Bangladesh — either Muslim or Hindu. The women from common village families use "Sari" as the only clothing of their body. But ladies from well-to-do or conservative families use Blouse and Petticoat called "Saya" inside their "Saris". The brides are dressed with colourful "Saris" and ornamented with jewelleries, — either of gold or of silver. Gold is mainly used by rich families, while silver is the main ornament for common village women.

One thing about dress is remarkable in the villages of Bangladesh. That is, both rich and poor use the traditional dress. Both a well to do farmer and a landless peasant use "Lungi" as their main dress. The difference lies in the price of the item. Rich people use "Pyjamas" also but "Lungi" is the common dress to all the people of rural Bangladesh.

But this thing is not present in the urban society. In a city, a man from an upper class or a middle class family will never come out from his house wearing a "Lungi". Even a modern educated young man in a village can easily go out for marketing wearing a "Lungi" and a shirt or "Panjabi". But he will hesitate to go out for shopping in the same dress in a city. So, the class system is prominent in urban life as far as the dresses are concerned.

In urban society there are three classes, the upper class, the middle class and the lower class. The people from the lower class include those of factory workers, rickshaw-pullers, domestic servants, and many others. They are actually the sons of villagers who have come to the cities in search of a job and generally use the same traditional dresses as those of the villagers. The middle class people are those working in different government or private offices with a background of general literacy and education. They use both traditional "Pyjama" and "Panjabi" as well as modern western dresses of trousers, shirts and in special occasions suits and neckties. While the common village-people generally do not cover their feet with shoes, almost all the people from the middle class and upper class families in cities must use shoes. The women use "Saris", blouse and petticoat, but the quality of the garment and the manner of wearing it is different from those of the village-belles. The women from a middle class Hindu or Muslim family use the same dress. But men from Hindu Community use "Dhoti" and "Panjabi" along with the western dresses. During Eid or Pooja festivals, the people from different communities use their traditional dresses. The Muslim during "Eid" wear "Pyjama", "Panjabi" and "Topi", and sometimes "Sherwani". The Hindus, on the other hand use traditional "Dhoti" and "Panjabi" during their "Pooja" festival. In both the festivals, the ladies from the two communities are clad with costly and colourful "Saris".

The dress of few upper class of the urban society is more or less the same as those of the middle class. The only difference lies in the cost of the garments. Moreover, the people from so-called upper class are more acquainted with the change of modern fashion.

The younger generation in the urban society is more inclined to western dresses. Sometimes they mix the western dress with the traditional one. As for example, it is a trend among the student community of Dacca, Chittagong and other big cities of the country to wear ornamental "Panjabis" along with bell-bottom trousers. The school boys use half-pants and shirts. The girls of colleges and universities use "Saris" and blouse, "Salwar", "Kameez" and "Dopatta". "Salwar" is a special type of "Pyjama" meant for girls. "Kameez" covers the upper part of the body, and "Dopatta" is a piece of cloth usually 2 yards in length and 1 yard in width. One thing remarkable about the dresses of men and women in Bangladesh is that a man from a typical middle class family or upper class urban family wears western dress very easily, — but even a most modern lady from an affluent family will hesitate to use western dresses like skirts, gowns, or minis and maxis. "Sari" is the main dress of Bengali women, — rural or urban, educated or illiterate, modern or conservative. We can say that our ladies are more conservative about their dresses than our gentlemen. Only the school-going minor girls below the age of 12 or 13 years do wear frocks or skirts or any other type of western dresses. After reaching a particular age they switch over from frocks to "Salwar" and "Kameez" and finally to "Sari".

The usual dress of an urban bridegroom is "Pyjama", "Panjabi". "Sherwani", "Nagra" and "Pagri". "Nagra" is an ornamental shoe with a long front usually used by the "Mughal" emperors of the sub-continent. It is also called "Selimshahi" named after the Mughal Prince "Salim" (later emperor Jahangir). "Pagri" is to cover the head. It is a long and narrow piece of cloth wrapped round a cap. The Hindu bridegrooms use "Dhoti", "Panjabi" and "Chadou", — and their heads are covered with a long cap called "Topar". The dresses of brides are same in both Muslim and Hindu communities — i.e, costly "Saris", blouse, petticoat and jewelleries. The Muslim bride covers her head with a "Dopatta", while a Hindu bride wears a"Topar" on her head which is a bit different in shape from that used by the bridegroom.

Then comes the third category of people, namely the tribal race. The tribal people of Bangladesh live mainly in the districts of Chittagong Hill-Tracts in the Southern Eastern part of the country, and in some parts of Mymensingh, Rangpur, Dinajpur, and Sylhet districts. The people of Chittagong Hill Tracts are mostly Buddhists. They are called "Chakmas" and "Murangs". They use "Lungi" as their main dress. Even women of this area use "Lungi" and buy sleeved blouse. Those who come to towns and get education use western dresses and their women use "Saris". There are some primitive tribal women in the interior part who do not use blouse even. The tribal people of Mymensingh district in the northern part of the country are called "Garos". With the influence of Christian Missionaries, many of them have adopted Christianity as their religion. They use shirts, trousers and other western dresses. Their women generally wear "Saris". But those who live in the forests generally lead a rather primitive life, — cover their body only with a small piece of cloth around the hip. Even their men use ear-rings and other ornaments made of metal. The women generally use two pieces of cloth, one for the upper portion and the other for the lower part of the body. The tribal people of Rangpur and Dinajpur districts in the North-West of Bangladesh are called "Santals". They also wear primitive dresses like the "Garos". But those who have adopted Christianity use modern urban dresses.

"Khasias" are the tribal race of Sylhet district in the North-Eastern part . Their dresses are like those of "Chakmas". Most of them work in the tea-gardens. A typical "Khasia" woman generally wears a two piece "Sari" and blouse. Like the "Chakmas", the "Khasias" are also mostly Buddhists.

Excepting few tribal races, the whole of Bangladesh is a land of one nation, namely the Bangalees. Of course, the tribal people are also Bangalee to their heart, but they have got some specialities of their own. Otherwise, the whole country seems to be a single family. Since it is a land of one nation people wear almost similar dresses here. Even in our neighbouring country India, — which is a vast country with different races and religions, we find various sorts of dresses and costumes there. But this variety is not that much prominent in our country. People are mostly rural and thus very simple about their clothing. Only the urbanisation makes the dresses complex, but we have already seen earlier that about 90 per cent of our people are simple villagers, who live mainly on agriculture.

Climate and Culture — Costume in Asia

"The search for beauty" — This desire is the basic force that has led Man to adorn himself from head to toe with a variety of garments. The world around, people of every tribe, ethnic group, or nation have applied their ingenuity to this goal, seeking materials with which to drape their bodies, devising in addition to these garments a wide variety of accessories with which to decorate themselves. Applying cosmetics and other decorations directly to the body itself and even mutilation of the body were probably originally connected with religious ceremony, but later these methods also became essential means to self-satisfaction and self-display. In these ways, the origins of costume lie deeply rooted in human character, but on the other hand, seen in terms of geography, adaptation to climate and natural environment also represents another important factor. Bruno Taut, the German Japanologist, once praised the Yukata, the traditional light summer garment of the Japanese, as a skilful adaptation to the climate of Japan, but this is merely a matter of responding to the demands of marked seasonal changes in climate, such as are found in Japan, by changing modes of dress and selecting suitable colours and designs of their garments, but at the same time, there are patterns which are common throughout any given region, and these are closely related to the features of the climate of that region and the people's psychological adaptation to that climate. The history of the ways in which man has perceived the natural environment and climate of the many diversified regions in which he resides is also entwined with adaptation to climate and selection of modes of dress. In this way, the various peoples of the world, each in its own region and under the influence of its own particular history, have developed their own distinctive styles of dress. The advances made in transportation and communication in our modern world are undeniably leading the world toward homogeneity, so that new and beneficial developments quickly diffuse throughout the world, enveloping or altering the old, but many forms of dress are being preserved in the form of folk or ethnic costumes. There are many cases where such ethnic costumes continue to be one's "best clothes" or the accepted form of formal dress, as is the case with the Japanese kimono, and there are no few cases in which such folk costumes continue to be used as everyday wear.

Further, one major principle of the geographic distribution of costume is that the higher the level of development of an economy of consumption within a given society, the greater the resistance and desire to escape from the limitations imposed by the natural environment. Such a desire encourages a trend toward more unrestrained freedom in colour and design. However, in the societies of developing countries such as exist in many parts of Asia, the environmental limitations still play a major role and preserve strong conservative elements. In other cases, such as seen in India, Burma, and several other regions, historical elements or ethnic pride act as powerful forces to inhibit the outright acceptance of foreign elements of dress and costume, thus impeding the process of acculturation of such foreign elements.

When one takes such matters into consideration in reviewing the traditional "clothing culture" of Asia, one finds that it is indeed possible to divide Asia into a number of cultural areas.

East Asia

As a region, East Asia covers an immense area, and the various sub-regions have each shown their own particular development of clothing. Culturally, however, the basic form seems to have developed in China. As long ago as twenty centuries before Christ, silk weaving was to be found in China and a variety of clothing materials were available. Even from the distant past, the clothing style for both men and women was broad-sleeved loose cloth garment tied at the waist with a belt or length of material. Until about the seventeenth century, this style was the general form of dress. This was, naturally, an adaptation to the particular climate of Asia, with its high summer temperatures and frequently high humidity. It is likely that this is also related traditionally to the western Asian caftan-like garment with long skirts, which will be touched on later. In the seventeenth century, Manchurians from the north came into power in China, and under their influence a body-fitting tunic style tight cloth garment came into use. Such a garment is related to similar forms of cold-climate garments found in Northern Europe. Thus two different lines of clothing were merged in China. Even today, the Mongols' dress reflects this merger, as they wear body-fitting under garments and trousers topped by outer garments appropriate to the season. Variety in colours, too, has historically been related to the level of society. In general, blue has traditionally been the colour most frequently used in the everyday wear of China's agricultural class. As has been pointed out by philosopher H. Keyserling, this is a colour that perfectly matches the clear blue of the skies of northern China. As the Chinese today clothe themselves in "people's clothes" and wear workers' caps, they are reflecting a new acculturation to changes in the social system, changes which have again worked their influence on the attire of the Chinese.

Archeological remains indicate that the dress of the ancient Japanese was a type of simple pullover robe, but with the progress of cultural exchange with China, the Chinese culture influenced a change to a board-sleeved type of garment which resembled lounging clothes. This, in time, developed into a style with smaller sleeves and eventually produced a uniquely Japanese style of attire — the kimono.

One characteristic of Japanese costume lies in the close relationship with climate and nature over the many generations. As the seasons change, so do the flowers and grasses of the land, and these were incorporated in the cloth woven by the Japanese to produce a variety of patterns. This tradition of employing a wide range of plants and flowers in the designs of clothing has been carried forward, so that even today the mature Japanese woman's kimono makes use of the same types of design. Thus, in a manner of speaking, the patterns and colours of clothing provided the Japanese with the medium for expressing their feelings toward nature.

The attire of Korea has also seen its share of historical transition, but throughout its various styles, it is still evident that the influence of China has been far-reaching.

Southeast Asia

Whether one speaks of natural environment, ethnic association, of culture, S.E. Asia is a region of complex patterns, and attire, too, appears in a variety of types and levels. The basic form, however, for both male and female has been a type of simple loincloth worn only on the lower half of the body. This, of course, is closely related to the tropical climate of S.E. Asia. The torso is left unclothed. A more advanced form of this garment is the *sarong*, a basic style of garment that is highly suited to a region of tropical lowlands. The *sarong* is a strip of cloth some two meters by one meter, with the two ends joined and sewn together to form a hoop of cloth that is wrapped around the lower half of the body. Since there have also been areas and times (such as periods in the history of Indonesia) in which the accepted mode of dress consisted only of a lower garment, with the upper portion of the body left exposed, this gives sufficient reason to believe that such a *sarong* constituted the basic form of clothing for such regions. The *sarong* of Indonesia, the *panung* of Thailand, and the *lungi* of Burma all fall within this class and are also linked with the Indian *dhoti* and sari to be mentioned later. But even within S.E. Asia, there are mountainous regions and other cooler areas where the pullover type of attire, with a hole or opening in the materials through which the head is passed, is common. The dress of the Karen and Meo peoples living in the north of Thailand are good examples of this phenomenon. In this area, the nights are cool, or even cold, and a lower garment alone is not enough. Thus, with progress in the art of weaving, this need probably gave birth to a type of simple pullover attire. In short, these two styles, the loincloth and the pullover, were the basic forms of dress in S.E. Asia, and with the addition of cultural influence from China or India, they gave rise through history to the diverse styles of costume to be found in this region today.

Such Chinese influence can be seen plainly in the *aozai* of Vietnam, split far up the side and worn in combination with trousers, while the *slendang* worn in Indonesia and Thailand reflects Indian influence.

It has become a custom for Indonesians of all classes to wear the *sarong*. This is, of course, true for the woman, but even though in recent years a man's working clothes have often come to consist of short pants and a T-shirt, when the men return home, they still tend to change into a *sarong* for casual wear. The *sarong* is cool and convenient.

Another major reason that the sarong continues to be used is its connection with traditional Indonesian batik, an art into whose outstanding designs and colours is woven 2,000 years of Indonesian history and psychology. It is also interesting to note that there are geographic variations in the basic colours used in batik: while quiet browns and deep blue are preferred in some regions, other areas lean more toward brighter and showier primary colours.

Burma is a country of strong conservatism in dress, and the Burmese people maintain the tradition of wearing the *lungi*. Just as is true of the Indian *dhoti* and the Indonesian sarong, *lungi's* continuing popularity derives from its being best suited to the country's climate. Basic dress consists of *lungi* accompanied by an upper garment, the *engee*. In the past, the primary colours were most common. Today, prints account for a major share and bright colours have come into use, but there has still been no change in the basic form of the garments.

In Thailand, the traditional costumes for the general populace, male and female alike, has been the *panung*, worn on the lower half of the body. This is a loincloth-like garment that resembles the *dhoti* of India. To this, females added the shawl-like *pahom* as an upper garment. With this was worn a hat, the *ngop*, woven from bamboo or palm. Black was frequently used as a colour for the *panung*. In recent years, however, this traditional Thai costume has been undergoing major changes. Most of the males today wear shirts and trousers, while females have taken to wearing a blouse along with a *sarong*-like *panung*. The *pahom* remains, but in the form of a light sash worn diagonally, hanging from one shoulder over the blouse, and as such it has developed into the same type of garment as the slendang of Indonesia. When the *panung* is thus worn, the overall effect clearly indicates the trend toward Europeanization of attire. One basic condition for such acculturation is development of economic power to a level that will permit such changes, combined with flexibility in the ethnic psychology. In this respect, Thai possesses an aspect that is totally different from Indonesia, Burma and other countries in S.E. Asia. But even within the general changes which have taken place in Thailand, there is still one point in the country's panorama of costumes that remains unchanged from the past- the Buddhist priests in both town and country have retained the saffron robes traditionally worn as they wander barefooted through Thailand's roads and streets.

The Philippines would basically belong to the loincloth cultural area, but in recent decades the country has been subject to strong influences and displaying an increasingly high level of acculturation in dress. In this point, the Philippines is similar to Thailand.

India

India is often called a subcontinent, and just this term would imply, there are marked differences in dress and costume from region to region. Where one Indian wraps his head in a heavy turban atop a thickly bearded face and garbs himself in a *dhoti*, another goes turban-less and clean shaven, wearing a white "Nehru cap" and a white jacket with a stand-up collar. There are many women wearing a colourful variety of saris while other adopt a long coat and loose trousers as their form of attire. A variety of complex factors — ethnic, religious, social and many others — has led to this situation, but for the country as a whole, it is possible to pick out some common, or in other words, overwhelmingly frequent, patterns of dress. For the male, for example, the *dhoti* and turban; for the female, the sari.

The *dhoti* is a seamless loincloth worn on the lower half of the body, and depending on the region, there is a wide range of methods of wearing this simple garment. The turban, too, varies in colour and way of winding from region to region, but originally it was the universal head-wear of followers of Islam. This religion arose in western Asia, and turban can be thought to have spread in India along with the eastward advance of Islam. The distribution of the turban is thus generally heaviest in western India.

The sari has become one of the symbols of India, but it too is a single seamless piece of cloth long enough to be worn about the whole body. There are of course a number of regional differences in the manner in which the sari is worn. In contrast to the seamless sari, there is a combination of fitted garments consisting of the Kamiz, a blouse-like upper garment and loose trousers called salwar. This costume probably has a western Asian lineage. Even in areas where this fitted attire is to be found, a sari may frequently be worn on top of these clothes for formal occasions, and thus it may truly be said that in reality, the distribution of the sari covers all of India. But in any event, here again we find that these basic forms of dress are well suited to the hot climate of India.

The variety of colours generally used is one of the costumes of India. The turban, for example, may be found in white, blue, light violet, or other colours, and the colourful decoration of the women's garments is in itself one of the typical characteristics of India. Messrs. Battachariya and Hossain treat the subject of costumes of India in greater detail elsewhere in this issue.

The attire of the Indians is, of course, not limited to the *dhoti*, turban, sari and similar garments; a remarkably wide range of accessories has also become an essential part of the costumes of India. Even the poorest villagers bedeck themselves with a variety of ornaments. The creation of elaborate personal ornamentation of precious and semiprecious stones, gold and silver is one of India's traditional handicrafts, and among the designs used in such crafts are many which could well become tomorrow's fashion around the world. The followers of Hinduism also have the custom of painting their bodies with diverse signs and patterns, in some cases dying their hands or feet with henna or saffron and in such actions are included not only elements of decoration but elements of magic as well. There is a conspicuous absence in India of the type of cultural acculturation of dress which may be seen in other regions. One reason for such a phenomenon is that the Indian cultural traditions, strongly rooted in Hinduism, has been resistant to the penetration of elements from abroad. Both the turban and the sari are tied to ethnic pride, a fact which may be called major characteristic of costume in India. And just as may be said for other cultural elements, the *dhoti* and sari have had a stimulating influence on the development of *sarong*-type attire in S.E. Asia. In this sense as well, India has indeed served as a fountain of culture of S.E. Asia.

West Asia

Seen from the air, the dominant colour of West Asia is brown, and the lives of the people are swayed by the awesome natural forces that accompany the extremes of dryness and heat that reign in these desert-like lands. As a matter of course, the dress of these lands must permit the people to adapt to and withstand these conditions. The type of garments found in the humid tropics which leave much of the body exposed to the elements is not appropriate to these lands. The general dress of the Arabs is a white pullover-type of robe, and the head is completely covered. When the women go out of doors, they cover themselves with long black veils. These and other garments best display the adaptation to the climate. White is a response to the desert nature of the land, and black is used in contrast to white and as a colour which absorbs the strong rays of the sun. The loose clothing is particularly effective in the ventilation that it provides, and headgear and veil are essential to protect the wearer from sun.

In addition to the demands of climate in this area, a veritable crossroads of people, a variety of cultural elements — Arab, Persian, Turkish — have worked their influence in a complex mixture, and Islamic influence has also been strong in these lands. Each of these elements has contributed to the pattern of traditional costumes in West Asia. The custom of women hiding their faces behind veils was reinforced by the precepts of Islam.

In recent years, there have been active movements in West Asia to dispense with traditions, and this acculturation process is still in progress. The women of Turkey were the first to rid themselves of the veil. This was watched and imitated by the women of such cities as Baghdad and Teheran, but the veil continues to be part of the traditional dress in many areas. Thus, the flowing robes and traditional colours, deeply rooted in natural conditions of the land, can still be called the basic folk costume of many of the countries of West Asia.

In summary, while the basic theme of adaptation to natural conditions appears among the people of all areas of Asia, history and ethnic psychology have been at work forming the particular patterns and styles of clothing with which Asians garb themselves. And it is possible to follow the threads of mutual influences that have resulted from exchange even among widely separated regions.

Rich Variety of Clothing in India

Introduction

Indian costumes have taken their own shape and form, as elsewhere, according to the climatic, social and even political changes that mark the vast span of the Indian territory. In a certain way they also reflect the vicissitudes of the country's long history. They have changed and are still changing, according to taste and utility, yet they tied to their old and traditional moorings. They are shaped by the unavoidable contacts with the outer world but at the core conform to Indian sentiments of bashfulness and dignity. Against this perspective, Indian costumes are to be studied and described.

The basic elements: Sari-sarong-ghagra-salwar

The Sari with its endless variety in texture and in colour, in lay-out and in decoration, is the predominant female costume of India. It plays down the wearer's sex, and yet is the most feminine of all known female costumes. Nearer to this is the Sarong worn in the far eastern regions of India. Shorter than the Sari in total length and coarser in texture and simpler in design, it is wrapped around the breasts from the height of the armpits and below them, reaching only midway between the knee and the ankle. The Sarong is a short-cut, in a way, to the Sari. The counterpart to this in western and southern regions of India is the Ghagra which consists of a densely pleated skirt in plain texture, generally coloured, and mostly designed and bordered. Worn at the point of the navel, it is supplemented by an upper bodice to cover the breasts, known locally as the *Choli*, with the grown-ups wearing a scarf (*Orhna*) covering the bodice. The scarf in this case serves as the much too necessary Indian veil. Completely different in conception is the Salwar which with Kameez constitutes an entirely distinct combination. The Salwar is a pair of trousers tapering downwards, close-fitting ones, though invariably closed at the ankle. The Kameez, the upper garment to this, is a long tunic, and is a sort of loose shirt, buttoned up at the front and at the wrist and flared at the end, coming down to the mid-thigh or the knee. Essentially the outcome of closer contacts with the immediate western neighbours, e.g. the Afghans, the Salwar perhaps bears a remote element of similarity to the dress in Central Asia from the second to the ninth century and carries a definite influence from the Islamic dress of the Mughals. This answers best to the colder climate of the north-western regions and better dispels the dry heat of summer in those regions. A scarf or *Orhna*, which is short, light and invariably of a different texture, serves as the veil, being taken over the heat from the right covering the breasts and thus completing the ensemble.

Blouse-orhna

The upper garment which goes with the Sari is an Indian blouse that developed originally from an indigenous garment used as a breast support. The early form, more or less a tie-at-the-back support for the breasts, was known as *Choli*, though in its more modern evolved form it retains its older name. In fact, *Choli* and blouse in its Indian version are synonymous, though the *Choli* is, strictly speaking, the earlier brassier for the Indian women. And the earlier form, the *Choli*, is still in use in remote parts of India given to the older customs and uses. The *Choli* in the blouse style, full-sleeved, also acquired a distinctive form being combined and continued with the Ghagra at the waist in specific region of the Hill States of the seventeenth and eighteenth centuries, as is reflected in contemporary Pahari-miniature paintings. In certain cases the lower part of the dress, the combined Ghagra, shows mostly horizontal bands of variegated colours, as in regions around the valley of Chamba.

The *Orhna* is a longish scarf made usually of fine silk or cotton, plain or decorative, and is used as a veil to cover the head from the back leaving the face visible as little as possible in certain cases, e.g. a newly wed bride in her husband's place, serving to be used both for a sign of modesty and of bashfulness. It, however, starts to be worn as soon as a girl attains puberty. In a slightly variant use of the *Orhna*, it is flung over the shoulders, with the mid-portion resting on and covering the bosom. With a short Sari, it makes up for the short flowing free end of the regular Sari. In its use with the Ghagra, one end is tucked into the centre of the waist and the other end is taken by the back from the left and then drawn up to rest on the head. One corner of this end is passed under the right armpit from the back to be tucked into the Ghagra at the left.

With the above basic garments, the Indian ladies' costumes display an endless variety. They vary from region to region according to older traditions and modern taste, sometimes according to caste, sometimes to religion and also sometimes to the traditional avocations followed. Added to these, there would further be variations with the secluded tribal people as opposed to the urban sophisticated society. There are, also, festive, occasional and performing dresses in almost all sections and regions of this vast country.

Kurta-dhoti-pugree

The male Kurta is a full-sleeved, loose fitting, collar-less, front-buttoned tunic type of garment for the upper body and is of late origin. The traditional wear was the Chadar or the Wrapper, followed by an overlapping full-sleeved cotton coat fastened at the ends by strings, at the two sides — a type which is still retained with some orthodox people in parts of India.

The *Dhoti* a piece of cloth, five yards long in varied width from 42 to 48 inches, worn in different modes, and marked by a simplicity in texture and colour. Worn with pleats in the front, it is generally taken back between the things in pleats and tucked into the waist. The other way known in the Punjab and the South is to wear the cloth wrapped around the body at the waist level with a knot in front as in the former case and at the sides as in the latter.

A variety of costumes in different regions: Kashmir

Starting from Kashmir, the northern-most State of India, the dress here can be described as a blend of the Hindu and the Muslim, being influenced through successive periods of its history by the Buddhists, the Hindu and lastly by the Muslims and bearing at the same time a clear stamp of the Afghan and Central Asian contributions. Strangely enough, it is only here that the Hindus and the Muslims dress themselves the same. Caused by the climate needs of extreme cold, the *Salwar* here forms the common lower garment equally for male and female, both tight-fitting and loose, as in neighbouring Afghanistan. The only contrasting feature lies, however, in the close-fitting ends at the ankles of the females dress being highly decorative and embroidered in the traditional way of shawls. The full-sleeved, yet loose upper garment known locally as 'pherna' is loosely gathered up at the sleeves and is full gown covering an under wear. The cloth used in the garments may be of pure wool or a mixture with cotton, or Jamewar, i.e. a kind of brocaded wool. These garments are characterised by embroidery at the front opening, at the joining of the shoulder and the arm, and at the ends of the sleeves revealing motifs of the chinar leaf, apple blossoms, almond nuts and forms of various birds, much in the fashion of the shawls. A flat and close-fitted cap sometimes embroidered at the borders and used both by male and female, completes the ensemble, and is a local substitute for the veil, specially with the poorer section.

Himachal Pradesh

Bordering Kashmir, Himachal Pradesh, the hill area of the Bordering Kashmir, has a distinctive dress for its diverse and colourful groups of distinctive ethnic units. Here the dress, evolved out of necessity for the almost nomadic life led by the different ethnic groups and also for the cold hilly climate, is almost the same for the male as for the female, except that the female attire is more ornamental and decorative. The total ensemble consists mainly of a loose Chola, reaching from the neck up to the ankle and is made, in case of those specially for women, of wool, and sometimes, of cotton. This is worn over a pair of tight trousers which is seen only at the ankle and near the heels. While heavy ornaments of beads or multi-chained necklaces mark the distinction, the general pattern conforms to the Kashmiri basis. The ensemble is complete with a cap, sometimes with a conical shape as mostly used by the Gaddis, a shepherd tribe, and also sometimes retaining its tight-fitting, flat type generally preferred by the poorer section.

Above all this, however, areas like the Chamba valley, have a more common wearing style with the adoption of the very loose-flowing Ghagra with a thin quarter-sleeve of the Chola type for the upper garments, and a decorative Beladal for the forehead. This pattern seams to be Mughal pattern.

Punjab

Very few dress-types in India can be called form-fitting, and the Punjab costume perhaps comes nearest to this designation. Here the women wear a three-piece ensemble in which at least the upper garment is tailored to the measure of the body. And though the upper garment, the Kameez, plays down the sex, the lower garment, by the parting of the trousers, has a suggestion of the sex. While the male is recognisable by the turban in its peculiar folds, clearly distinctive from that of the Rajasthan male, the female dress of the Punjab is distinguished by its Kameez or the Kurta shaped along the elevations of the female body and by its very formal type of Salwar. Though there is no cap used by the female, the ensemble is complete with designed *Orhna* which is generally of cotton but may be of velvet or wool. This latter is taken from the back, over the back of the head, leaving a part of the hair and the forehead open, returning to the right shoulder and joining the part hanging on the left shoulder, thus covering the breasts. In case of the newly weds or those in the presence of elders in the father-in-law's place, the veil is drawn further down coming upto the tip of the nose. The bride's Salwar, as already noted elsewhere, is also a bit longer and almost covers the feet.

The modern version of the *Orhna* or the Dopatta, is a very fine cloth, usually four-and-a-half feet long with a deliberate transparence, that hangs over the shoulders with ends flung towards the back, and the middle portion gathered up in folds. It rests on the bosom and the Kameez or the Kurta is tailored to the shape of the bosom.

The distinction in the Salwar, between the male and the female types lies in the shorter length of the male ones, and the absence of colour or decoration.

The male dress is marked by the Pugree invariably in one colour, taken in a peculiar mode as to conceal the tuft on head. The lower garment is an Achkan with a Churidar or tight pyjama.

Rajasthan

Much of the drab colour of Rajasthan's arid landscape is brightened by the very colourful dresses of its women. With a few very minor variations, the basic Rajasthani costume of the female consists of a Ghagra, which is nothing but a densely pleated skirt, with a bias for deep colours, sometimes interspersed with printed or embroidered butis (flower-buds). Yet for a good proportion of the women, the Sari forms the usual lower garment for the ladies, especially of the more well-to-do households. Contacts with other parts of India have drawn the Rajasthani women more towards the Sari these days. The Ghagra in Rajasthan is usually worn with an undergarment in the form of the tight-fitting Salwar. The Saris or the Ghagra of Rajasthan have distinctive designs, mostly floral, either in embroidery or prints. The tie-and-dye print of Jaipur and other areas constitutes a special contribution of Rajasthan in cloth-printing. The Ghagra generally goes with a tight-fitting bodice wherein the upper valley of the breasts is given a separate patch with a distinctive colour with sometimes the midriff left bare especially with working women. Both together appear to be a practical dress for women whose daily life is quite hard. In cut and fashion, the bodice is short-sleeved and open at the back, tied by strings drawn from the corners. In one of the variants of this, specially among poorer ladies, there appears a hanging flap at the front from above the breasts down to the point of the belly. The more recent turnover to the covered back type is, however, as popular as the Sari of recent adoption. The entire conception of the Ghagra being that of a multi-petalled lotus, it is sometimes formed by joining a number of triangular pieces broader at the base, generally about twenty-five yards of cloth making one Ghagra. A Ghagra by its very nature is an all-purpose garment — it admits of high decorative elements, it is suited to serve as warm clothing and to keep away heat and dirt, and finally is thus designed to keep movement free, and gait rhythmic. Worn at the waist line but often below it, it leaves an element of appeal. The ensemble of the Rajasthani women's dress is completed, as may be expected, by the *Orhna* (Scarf), which is tucked in at the line of the Ghagra, and covering the midriff, is taken round the back to hang on the face up to the eye-line. The *Orhna* also provides a profuse decorative element and occupies a unique position in weddings, on traditional festive occasions and in general community life. The display of colours in one's *Orhna* is a matter of pride for a Rajasthani woman. It is believed that a Rajasthani bride must choose the right colour and the appropriate design in her Chunri (*Orhna*) which would best please the groom. It is taken as ominous for the success of a match.

It occupies, in a way, the centre of a woman's vanity and songs are composed in praise of the Chunri.

Each festive dress of the Rajasthani woman is meaningful and according to prescriptions. For example, while invoking the rain-god in the monsoon season, the women of Rajasthan put on orange coloured Ghagra, with *Orhna* showing wavy lines signifying flowing water.

It is the custom of upper class Rajasthani women to indicate they are married by wearing a narrow strip of cloth of distinct colour over the front of the Ghagra. More conservative women following the traditional prescriptions would wear an additional transparent veil covering the entire face to maintain modesty while going out of doors or at home before elders. The nobleman's male dress in the heat of Rajasthan is a long coat to the calf, parted at the sides, over an underwear of Churidar to the ankle, and tied at the waist, with the head-gear tilted at the left.

Gujarat

In Gujarat, west and south-west of Rajasthan, the Ghagra is in use though mostly confined to the peasant and the outdoor working class. The rest of the people wear the Sari, where in most cases the Ghagra retains its use as an undergarment in a less-pleated variety, as is proved by the fact that even as a petticoat, the underwear Ghagra is embellished, being reminiscent of the original practice of having the latter as the principal wear. For a Sari, the Gujarati style is marked by the dominating pleats at front tucked into the petticoat. In part of Gujarat, known distinctively as Saurashtra, the women's dress consists exclusively of the Ghagra and the men's dress is composed of a loose Pugree, a double-up Kurta tied by strings and a pair of breeches loose from the waist to the knee and tight-fitted from there downwards to the ankle. While the Ghagra is colourful, the entire men's dress is in spotless white, except the red Pugree.

The tribal dress current in the different regions of Gujarat represents as many varieties as are the physical types and the variations in the customs and avocations followed. The closed bodice of coarse cloth with a veil for the married people are the common elements in these.

Maharashtra

In Maharashtra one encounters a change in the way the Sari is worn. Here almost half the Sari is wrapped from one end, around the waist and then the rest taken gradually up the body with folds on the right hip from above the knee and finally over the left shoulder going as a veil and falling to the right. Thus Maharashtra is the dividing line between the north and north-east on the one hand, and the south on the other, except Kerala. The Maharashtra Sari is perhaps the longest being sometimes upto eleven yards long, as against six yards in the north, since this is needed to allow for the wrapping around and the pleated end that goes to form the tail (Kaccha) tightly taken along the sex-line to the back and tucked into the waist at the mid rib. This is, however, less exhibited, being worn loose in the case of aristocratic women, but in the case of poorer ladies, e.g. fisherwomen, the appeal of the parted buttocks is marked clearly by this tail (Kaccha). This allows a freedom of movement, though consequently, however, the style keeps a portion of the leg from the calf to the ankle bare. With poorer women, specially doing manual labour, the Sari is short enough not to be able to cover the leg much beyond the knee, and not providing a veil either for the head or for the bosom.

In Maharashtra the male dress is characterised by a Pugree, i.e. a turban, made by folds of cloth colourful in themselves. While this is invariable with peasants and labourers, the recent pedagogues would prefer to have a fixed flat type of Pugree bearing a resemblance to the folded type. The general lower garment is a Dhoti shorter in length than the one used in Bengal. The Kaccha of the Maharashtrian leaves one end untied as in many other parts of northern India. The upper garment, originally an over-lapping Kurta, is presently replaced by a plain one common in many parts of northern and north-eastern regions of this sub-continent.

Uttar Pradesh

Uttar Pradesh or Northern Province is constituted of an area in the Indo-Gangetic plain which is marked by the more elegant type of dress, especially so far as Sari wear is concerned. Yet this province reveals also the prevalence of the two types of the basic female dress; the Ghagra and the Sari, mostly one exclusive of the other but sometimes both over-lapping each other in the same area. It is here also that the Hindus and the Muslims come very near each other in dress. While, for example, originally the Sari was the Hindu tradition, the petticoat and blouse descended from Ghagra and the *Choli* from the Muslim contribution. While the Muslim Ghagra of Uttar Pradesh is a long pleated skirt reaching from the waist to the ankles, the shorter Ghagra which comes down to only the calf and is more densely pleated, is a Distinguishing Hindu version of the same. In both the cases, the *Orhna* completes the ensemble, and in Uttar Pradesh, it is more used for covering the bare parts of the body than as a mere decoration only.

The Uttar Pradesh Sari, famous for its quality in cotton, silk and brocade sets the norm for at least its own State and the adjoining State of Bihar. One end of the Sari is wrapped round the waist and tucked with pleats at front, while the other end is taken from the left hip up the back and over the head falling ultimately on the bosom from the right shoulder. This is entirely different from the way in which a Sari is worn in Bengal. The common element in this area with Bengal is the display of the cross-wise border though in the former case it is at the front, and in the latter, at the back.

Bihar

Bihar shares almost the same style of wearing the Sari except that more than elsewhere, the pleats at the front are gathered up so as to compensate for the petticoat which is only used by those in closer contact with cities and towns. The sign of modesty, the veil, used by the married women, is of fine cloth and taken over the head as a separate piece, though the modern reaction is to discard it altogether. The upper garment is a bodice with sleeves and is known locally as Kurti.

Most areas of this province are inhabited by different tribal people whose primitive dresses still prevail and which for the females in some cases, e.g., the Juangs, are confined only in a tied up loin cloth with a little tuft hanging at front, the rest of the body being left bare. On the other hand, some tribes, like the Santhal, have a preference for Saris for the ladies who wear it, however, in a different way, viz. that one end of it is closely wrapped round the loins, the remaining part moving from the right, passes over the left shoulder over the breasts leaving part of the right bosom exposed from the side. No blouses are worn, except by richer women, and no veil is used by either the married or the unmarried. The male dress of the Santhal consists of a bordered Dhoti which does not go beyond covering the knee with one end sharply taken back and tucked at the waist and the other end wrapped round the waist with a final knot at front. With the body bare, a wrapped up short cloth in a sort of Pugree is worn on the head.

The Extreme East (Assam, Meghalaya, Manipur, Mizoram, Nagaland, Arunachal)

The extreme east of India, beyond Bangladesh, is characterised by a variety of tribal groups and so also by divergent sets of dresses. The basic dress for the women consists of Mekhala, which is the lower garment and the Chadar or wrapper forming the upper garment. The Mekhala, which is nearest to the Sarong or the short Sari, is worn round the waist without pleats, in some cases from the navel line, and in others, from just below the line of the armpits. This is made of a rectangular piece of cloth and measures three yards by one yard. While the Mekhala and the Chadar constitute the ensemble with the poorer section of the people, the richer ladies have a bodice as the upper garment and an undergarment, a petticoat, below the Mekhala. Married women have an additional piece to cover the midriff, called Riha, which is wrapped around and is tasselled at ends for decoration. The above basic dress has assumed variation with different tribal groups like the Lakher, the Mikir, the Khasi and others.

Orissa and the South

Orissan dress for the female consists of the Sari, though its right end being taken to the right after a knot at the left waist leaves the right leg partly bare. Use of a stitched garment for the torso is modern and is used by the more sophisticated people. The male dress is almost similar to that in West Bengal except that the typical Chadar on the shoulder is absent. Common to Maharashtra, except for Kerala, the South Indian women's dress consists usually of the long Sari, seven to ten yards, where the pleated end is taken at the back through the legs. Sometimes an additional wrap is worn to hide the pleats which are revealed only slightly at the ankle. In any case, the taking of the pleat is ceremonial and traditional. In the Kerala area, the Sari is wrapped like a skirt around the waist in several rounds, the upper garment being only a blouse superimposed by a short scarf. Some of the tribal people, e.g. the Todas of the Nilgiris, wear a thick vertically striped Sarong-type Sari tied around the body from above the breasts and hanging down a little beyond the knee. For a Nair woman, on the other hand, the torso is left bare.

There are wide variations not only from region to region in South India, but between daily wear and occasional, as on marriage, etc. The manner of drawing the upper part of the bust is also variant in the several distinctive parts of South India, the only common element being the absence of the veil formed by the Sari. A bodice is usual upper garment. While this is so with women whose husbands are living, the widows cover their heads and trim their hair to hide their misfortune.

There are variations according to castes, and sometimes according to occasion. A Panta Kapu farmer of Andhra Pradesh for example, would have only Dhoti and a Chadar as the upper wrap with an elaborate Pugree generally of bordered silk.

West Bengal

The Bengali women's dress, mainly constituted by the Sari, has undergone changes due to political turnover during the last two centuries. Earlier, and in interior village even now, there was no separate upper garment over the torso except a wrap of the Sari. The British impact brought in the use of blouse. Another influence was marked in the introduction of the Chemise which was a combination of a sort of loose blouse and a petticoat.

On formal occasions, a blouse was put on over the Chemise. With the introduction of the bra, after more Western contacts, the Chemise was completely put out of use except by older ladies.

A special feature of the Bengali way of taking the Sari is to draw the free end from the right hip for covering the bust diagonally and over the left shoulder, returning to the front from under the right armpit leaving the right arm free. The decorative cross-wise border is displayed half in front and half on the hip.

While the mode for household wear has no pleat in the Sari, a frontal bunch of pleats is an invariable in out-door wear. The male dress, originally an overlapping and string-tied cotton garment in white for the educated, gradually gave way to the kurta (Known in Bengali as 'Punjabi'), with a Chadar which is broad-folded and put on the left or the right shoulder showing the decorated end. The Dhoti would have one end tucked at the front pleated bunch, often held at the lower end by the left hand, and the other pleated and taken to the rear through the parting of the thighs and tucked at the waist.

Modern dress: Reaction to tradition

For the younger and the modern generations, ladies' wear remains the Sari in cases where this has been the tradition, though the mode is greatly simplified and conforms broadly to the two types, viz., that current in the Uttar Pradesh and the other in Bengal. The preference for Salwar-and-Kameez is noticed only with teen-agers and very sporadically. In areas where the latter set is the norm, the modern trend has brought in more appealing cuts.

The modern reaction to men's dress of yester year in all different areas considered above has resulted in almost exclusive use of the trousers and the shirt, rather a bush-shirt, with all the ultra-modern modifications thereof — a direct result of Western contacts. However on religious or social occasions, young people still prefer traditional wear.

Dress of Mongolian People

The dress of Mongolian people displays national peculiarities being very much suited to the cattle-breeders' nomadic way of life, economic features and the country's natural climatic conditions.

Historical sources give evidence of many kinds of dress that Mongolians used to wear. For example, during the Mongolian empire period, married women wore original hats called "Bogtoga", which were very tall and slender, and made out of wood-bark. They were covered with silk, which was decorated with valuable pearls, precious stones and feathers on top. Archaeological findings revealed many kinds of hats like these. The Mongolian *del* or robe was quite different from those of today. *Del* is a general term for traditional Mongolian coats, which resemble the Japanese kimono. According to scholars, the *del* almost reached the ankles and had no collar, simply wrapping across sideways. This ancient form of collar still persists among lamas' costumes and some winter *del* made of wool and fur. The *del* was fastened together by a leather belt decorated with various kinds of metals, sometimes pure gold, as proved by archaeological evidence. The forms of belts, hats and other clothing of that period can be observed more clearly from the statues of the time.

Although some details changed throughout history, the national costume retained its original style until the beginning of the twentieth century.

Mongolian costumes differ in shape and purpose. There were everyday costumes for men and women, for summer and winter, as well as special clothes for holidays and ceremonies. In olden times the Mongols had a great variety of street-clothes, head -gear, and ornaments. The way a person was dressed showed to what ethnic or social group he belonged. The rules for wearing each style of dress were dictated by ancient traditions and customs.

The details of the married woman's costume are interesting and significant. Costumes and ornaments of married women in the western, central, and eastern parts of the country differed from each other. The wives wore an "uuji" (something like a long waistcoat without sleeves) over the traditional *del.* Women from western Mongolia had the privilege of having a large white collar on the *del* and their costumes were very free and loose. But the women of central and eastern Mongolia wore a *del* with high shoulders and the collar, hem and sleeves were decorated with intricate designs. Great attention was paid to the ornamentation of the head-dress. In the older days it was believed that the hairstyle should resemble the wings of an eagle. Women wore their hair smoothly combed back, and an artificial string was glued to the front of the *tatuur,* on both sides of which hung pendants made of strings or pearls. They pinned their hair with silver hair grips and slides. In winter, Mongolian men usually wore *del* made out of sheep or lamb's skins, as well as lynx, sable and fox pelts. In summer, men preferred *del* of different coloured cotton fabrics. The Mongolians wore many kinds of hats in all seasons of the year. Both men and women wore hats decorated with fur: sable, silver fox, red fox and others.

In summer the Mongols wore both *malgai* hat (made of plush with a velvet upturned brim and pointed crown) and top hat (*tortsog*) consisting of six gores. Mongolian boots are the same for men and women but they vary from one ethnic group to another. There are many kinds of boots, called Mongol, *tookuu, kanchin, buriat,* etc. and some of them are worn even today.

Today, especially in the city, Mongols prefer to wear European dress. The national costumes of the small ethnic groups of the past are almost forgotten now, and the clothes of Central Mongolia are most popular.

Reverence for Man's Hairstyle in the Traditional Imagination of Mongols

Mongols, like other peoples in the world; have had an age-long reverence for man's hairstyle, for it was considered that these hairstyles had magic power. So, adoration of men's hairstyle has had a decisive role in rites and traditions among all nationalities and peoples, being passed from generation to generation.

The tradition of hair veneration is vividly evidenced nowadays in the ceremony of babies' hair cutting. When a child reaches a certain age a special ceremony is held to cut the natal hair under the strict observance of ritual. This ceremony usually takes place when a boy reaches 3 or 5 years and a girl 2, 4 or 6 years. Before organising the haircutting ceremony it is obligatory to choose an auspicious day which usually falls in autumn or summer depending on the sex of the child. On the fixed day the child puts on its best clothing and adornments, relatives and best friends from the neighbourhood are invited specially and a festive table is prepared with ritual food including boiled meat, dairy products and a celebratory meat dish, while presents are distributed to children.

One respectful person touches the hair of the child, thus beginning the ritual of the hair-cutting ceremony. The person who is selected to touch the hair of the baby first should be born in a favourable year for the child according to the lunar calendar. He or she cuts a small lock of hair on the forehead of the baby, and only after this do the other guests follow suit, each cutting off a small lock of hair with scissors specially chosen for the event. If one of the child's relatives is absent during the hair-cutting ceremony for some reason, then a bundle of hair is left untouched on the nape so that later on he or she may come and cut it off.

At the end of the ritual the hair of the baby is either shaved completely or a small bunch of hair is left untouched on the forehead which is then called a "salmai"; or two small locks of hair are left at the nape in the form of horns, in which case they are called "kegul" or "ever" (horns). The mother of the child gathers the cut hairs, wraps them in a silk cloth and preserves them as a talisman or charm for the long and happy life of her baby.

The rites are usually accompanied by offerings and good wishes for the child, and obligatorily with eulogistic verses and songs of praise, which represent a specific form of the people's folklore. As a present, the child may be offered a baby goat, lamb, or even a horse.

This rite dates back to the Stone Age. Written sources evidence that the tribes populating Central Asia between the second century BC and the early part of our century had the tradition of wearing plaits braided in a certain manner, which were compulsory attributes for a man. Epic Mongol legends contain a great deal of facts concerning the adoration of and reverence for the hair as a symbol of the honour and invincibility of the hero. According to the heroic epos there was among the Mongols a tradition something like scalping. If we take the shamanist point of view widely held among the Mongols, apparently the ancient Mongols worshipped the so-called "zuld" which represents the head, lungs and hair altogether. This was considered to guard the soul of a human being. In the various heroic epos where the combat of two heroes is described, they each strive to capture the "zuld" of the other as a symbol of victory. However, following the principle of "part instead of parcel", the hero needed only a token of the "zuld" from the defeated enemy, namely his braid. For a steppe warrior there was no greater disgrace than to lose his tresses. The "Altan Tobchi", a historical chronicle compiled in the seventeenth century, says that the above tradition had been observed up to the fifteenth century.

The forms of such hairstyles are of great interest to us. Those of the ancient peoples like Hunnus, Xian-Be, and Zhuzhan, who were the predecessors of Mongols, have not been thoroughly studied yet due to the lack of information sources. Many rich materials have been preserved relating to the hairstyles of the Kidans which enable us to imagine their original form. The Mongols of the thirteenth-fourteenth centuries wore very original hairstyles, which were quite different from those of all other peoples of the world.

This is why all the travellers who visited Mongolia at that time pointed out the originality of the Mongolian hairstyles. Among these travellers were Zhao Hung, Pen Da Ya and Shu Ting from China, and Plano Carpini and Fra Ruburquis from Europe, who visited Mongolia in the thirteenth century. They left detailed and reliable descriptions of the way of life of the Mongols at that time. It is not surprising that their descriptions concur. They unanimously stated that at that time all Mongolian men, regardless of social status, shaved the hair on the top of their heads in the form of a horse-shoe, leaving a lock to be brushed onto the forehead and the greater part of the hair at the nape which was divided into two "tails" hanging behind the ears. These accounts agree to minute detail with those left by other medieval travellers in Mongolia.

There are also magnificent fine art monuments which prove the truth of the above-mentioned facts. These are, first of all, a group of portraits representing Mongolian Emperors, which are now in the Imperial Palace in Beijing. These emperors have the two "tails" falling behind their ears and the lock of hair falling onto the forehead which absolutely conforms with the descriptions of the medieval travellers. Hairstyles were depicted in the Persian miniatures of the fourteenth century, known as "Persian-Mongolian" from their style of depiction. These masterpieces were no doubt influenced by ancient Central Asian art.

Many of these miniatures, show scenes of the way of life of Mongolian emperors, as well as people of mongoloid origin in Mongolian dress with the above mentioned hairstyles.

The same styles were shown in the pictures of Chinese painters who were working at the palace of the Mongolian emperors, as well as on the Turphan frescoes. The fact that these works were made in places so far apart attest to their veracity.

Moreover, in the epic legends and historical chronicles there are some colourful descriptions of hairstyles and it is not surprising that their names correspond to those being used in contemporary Mongolian language. For instance, in the heroic epos the word "kukel" is often used, which means the forehead part of the haircut. "The Secret History of Mongols", a magnificent monument to the spiritual culture of the Mongols compiled 750 years ago, as well as the "Collection of Historical Chronicles" by Rashid'Ad'Din, given the same word in the form of "kagul", "kegul" and

"Kakul". At the present time the Mongols use the word "huhul" or "guhul" to mean a lock or bang of hair falling onto the forehead, or a forelock usually left on the head of a baby during the hair-cutting ceremony. Furthermore, this word was expressed in the Russian language as "hohol", also referring to the fringe common among the Zaporozi Kazakhs of the Ukraine. A word which we come across in the "Secret History" and which means the hair left at the nape, in our days is used in certain regions of Mongolia as "Sirbegel" or "Shiverlig" to mean a needle-case for women's hair.

Another important source for reconstruction of the hairstyles of the medieval Mongols are the stone statues, mostly found in the eastern part of the country. These monuments greatly differ in their inscription and style from the more well-known ancient sculpture commonly found in Central Asian territory. The analysis of the objects depicted on them, as well as results of excavations in burial places where these statues were erected, convincingly prove that they belong to the medieval Mongols. On these marvelously made statues, besides clothes and objects of adornment and household articles, men's hairstyles were engraved with the highest skill in a natural form which belonged to the thirteenth-fourteenth centuries. This again proves the importance of symbolism in the imagination of Mongols. These monuments or statues are of special value to us for they enable us to understand the form and construction of these hairstyles. It is also of great interest that these same styles, so natural in appearance, were discovered in a tomb excavated in Eastern Mongolia and dating back to the thirteenth-fifteenth centuries.

The strict observance of traditional forms in the hairstyles was perhaps dictated by their symbolic importance in the imagination of the ancient Mongols, and at the same time It served as one of the main features of their ethno-differences. It is a fact that the Mongols in the thirteenth-fourteenth centuries not only strictly observed the wearing of plaits themselves, but also forced the people of the countries they conquered to wear similar braids.

In the changing political circumstances which came about in Central Asia, the ancient form of the Mongol hairstyle was replaced by one long plait on the nape, with the forehead shaven completely. And the ancient hairstyle, together with its name, now survives in its original form as a ritual in the hair-cutting ceremony for children.

The Folklore of Hair of the Maori in New Zealand

Hair styles for men

The portraits of the Maori, the Polynesian aborigines of New Zealand, drawn by Sydney Parkinson, the artist who accompanied Captain Cook in his first expedition to the Pacific (1768-1771) and died on the way back to his home country are precious documents that show what the Maori were like before European contacts. What particularly impressed me were the exquisite tattoos on their faces, but the focus of this article will be on their hair styles.

The men in the old pictures had long hair tightly bound into small topknots. This hair style was called *koukou* or *ngoungou.* The men also wore several feathers in his topknot as decoration. The most treasured ones were the tail feathers of a rare bird called *huia* (Heteralocha Acutirostris), which were black with white tips. The feathers of the albatross, long-tailed cuckoo and blue heron were also highly valued.

The men wore precious combs made of whalebone. On the man's comb a small carving of a male figure could be seen. Whalebone combs were treated as family treasures to be handed down from generation to generation, and there is a story of a man being severely scolded for wearing the comb which his father had kept for his eldest brother. There were other variations of men's hairstyles. For example, hair was bound into several small topknots, sometimes as many as 8 of them. Another regional hair style called *tikitiki* was formed by combing the hair up on top of the head and passing it through a ring 4 to 5cm in diameter, thus making a topknot with the hair around the ring, which was pressed against the head.

As men's hair styles required much time and skill to arrange, it was said that they could not even sleep using wooden pillows once these beautiful hair styles had been made up. These styles, however, were for people of higher social rank, and lowly people simply grew their hair down to their shoulders. Women also wore simple hair styles. Unmarried women had short hair, whereas married women braided the hair and wound it around the head. However, according to the legend, the mother of Maui, the trickster god of the Maori, wore her hair in the *tikitiki* style. Maui was called by another name, Maui *tikitiki* a taranga, because he was carried hidden in the hair of his mother.

Tapu and the head

The reason why men of high social rank paid so much attention to hair styles seems to be that they probably considered that hair was directly connected to the head. For the Polynesians, the head is the source of *tapu.* Tapu in the

Polynesian language is the origin of the word "*taboo*" in English, and *tapu* means both "prohibited" and "sacred". According to the Polynesian way of thinking, *tapu* is a special power which is inherent in a person depending upon his/her birth. Men have more *tapu* than women, the first child has more than the second and a chief has more than his followers. *Tapu* is concentrated in the head as well as other parts of the body. And strangely enough, *tapu* flows out like electricity when it comes into contact with any object. If someone or something touches the body of a noble chief, that person or thing becomes *tapu*; and if an ordinary person becomes *tapu*, it means that he has committed a fatal transgression which may cause his death. Therefore people, be they of high or low rank, have to be cautious not to invite any disaster caused by *tapu* through their careless actions. While a chief is sleeping, his *tapu* flows out from the point of contact between his head and the bed. Therefore, if he sleeps in someone else's house, the master of the house asks him the next morning not to leave anything behind. Then the chief touches with his hand the place where his head was the last night, and touches his nose with that hand. By doing so, he absorbs with his hand all the *tapu* which flowed out of himself during the night and returns it to his body.

Thus, the head is considered to be a very important part of the body. It is said that a big war once broke out due to a question asked of a woman, that is, "Is your brother using firewood as a pillow?" It was an intolerable insult that the pillow where the sacred head was placed had been referred to as 'firewood'.

Hair cutting

To touch the head, which is *tapu* itself, and to cut the hair growing there, required a religious ceremony for the Maori. Of course, customs varied from one region to another. In one region, for example, hair cutting was to be done on a fixed day of the year. On that day 1,000 or more people from neighbouring villages got together at a designated place, and no-one was permitted to eat until all of them had finished cutting. Also they were forbidden to light fires except for burning the cut hair. This kind of mass hair cutting was, however, not so common. The places for hair cutting were mostly beside springs or rivers where rituals were usually conducted. As for the time, it was at night in some regions, and morning in others. When several rituals were conducted simultaneously, hair-cutting was done at the end to mark the finish of all the rituals.

The tools used for hair-cutting were knives made of sharp pieces of obsidian. First of all, a priest offered a prayer to the knife and the hair-cutter. Then the hair-cutter held a bundle of hair in one hand and cut it with the knife in the other. But Te Rangi Hiroa, a well-known ethnologist who has a Maori mother, once saw cut hair, pieces of obsidian and a wooden plate which were apparently discovered behind some rocks. On the wooden plate, there were several knife marks. He assumed from these marks that this wooden plate was place under the hair so as not to pull it, and it was cut on this plate.

Cut hair had to be either burnt instantly, hidden somewhere or installed in the altar, or *tuahu*. Or sometimes the guardian god was called upon to prevent someone from using the hair for evil purposes. It is said that Captain Cook saw a bundle of hair twined around the twig of a tree in a cave. To dream of hair cutting was an omen of misfortune which might fall upon one's elder brother or his son.

The relatives of a dead person cut their hair. Some people cut all the hair short, some cut only one side short and kept the other side as it was, and some left a bundle of hair long and cut the rest short. In some regions, people burnt off the hair by pressing a brand to it. All of these hair styles were signs to express deep mourning over their relative's death. Occasionally one or two hairs were pulled out of the head of the dead person, and an incantation was uttered to these hairs so that the dead person's spirit would not come back to this world and threaten the living. The asymmetrical hair styles similar to those of people in mourning could be seen, on the eastern coast, on the heads of the messengers who went to other groups for help during battles. Those messengers cut the hair on one side of the head very short and smeared the scalp of that side with red clay. Because of this outstandingly strange style, everyone could understand the purpose of their visit at a glance.

Hair as a tool of magic

The reason why people took so much care of cut hair was that they believed that hair had magical power. During battle, soldiers cut a lock of hair from each of the enemies they killed and brought them back to their village as trophies. Then priests conducted a ritual using these locks of hair, in which a prayer was offered so that the defeated enemies might fail in taking revenge even if they tried to do so. For someone who had ill feelings against you, the following method was effective. First, you pulled a hair from your head, uttered an incantation to it, and put it in the cup he used. If he touched his lips to this cup, he would die. Hair was also used as a sacrifice to be offered to a god or other supernatural being. When a person was fishing in a canoe, and suddenly, after a strange sound, big waves surged around him he thought that it was because *taniwha* (water monsters) were angry, and hastened to pull one hair out of his head and throw it into the water. While doing so, he uttered the words of an incantation in order to soften the anger of the *taniwha* and to pacify the raging waves. Thus, he tided over the crisis.

Such an act was called *whakaeo*, and there are a number of similar stories. For example, when their ancestors were travelling in several large canoes, immigrating from central Polynesia to New Zealand, one canoe called *Tainui* was surrounded by a lot of *taniwha* near the coast of New Zealand. A priest pulled out his hair and threw it into the sea, uttering incantations repeatedly. Then the *taniwha* disappeared. The hair used in those stories includes, besides that of the head, the hair of the genitals and armpits. In other cases, when the sea was stormy and a boat was facing disaster, people threw hair in the sea, to seek the help of whales or other animals.

Before going to battle, soldiers got together in front of the hill where their ancestors' bodies were buried, and performed the ceremony called *hirihiri*. During the ceremony, the chief of each troop cut a lock of his hair, uttered an incantation and then threw it toward the hill. This was the occasion to offer a prayer to the ancestors so that they would give the power and courage to bring about a brilliant victory.

There is another story that if you set fire to some of your hair and throw it into the fire, uttering incantations before travelling, you will be safe from various disasters on the way. One man was travelling up a steep mountain in the heart of the bay of Plenty. He was so thirsty, but could not find water there. Then he pulled a hair out of his leg and threw it to the ground where, strangely enough, a spring began to gush out. This spring still has abundant water even today, and they say that an eight-tailed eel lives there. Hair was connected with fertility. When a new fishing net was used for the first time, a key member of the group pulled out a hair and put it in the mouth of a fish selected from among the catch, and then uttered an incantation, to ensure an abundant catch in the future.

Hair was also effective in curing diseases. It is said that in order to exorcise an evil spirit, the priest pulled out one hair from his own head and one from the patient's head, and put them together into the mouth of the patient. Also, when important buildings were constructed, the hair of priests was buried at the site as an offering. The hair used for such ceremonial purposes was often taken from the fontanelle area of the head.

Thus, for Maori, head and hair were the parts of *tapu* which had such special powers as described above.

Particularly, as the *tapu* of high-ranking chiefs or of priests had very strong power, it was necessary to avoid any crisis caused by the transmission of their *tapu*. In extreme cases, therefore, those people had to bear such inconveniences as not being allowed to scratch their own heads nor to wash their hair.

These customs of the Maori tribe based on their traditional religious concepts gradually disappeared as Christianity prevailed in the region, and none remain at present. Under the recent movement advocating the renaissance of the traditional culture of the Maori, various activities are being actively carried out for the restoration of their language and arts and the revival of their traditional customs. Yet, there is no effort to revive the religion of the Maori. One wonders whether it is because the Maori people have been too Christianized or whether they simply do not place any value on their traditional religion any more.

Korea: Inborn Hair

orea lacks a tale about hair that is comparable to the well-known tale about the hair of powerful Samson in the Bible. This writing is a collection of stories told among ordinary people in Korea and especially, on the island of Cheju, as well as the writer's own opinions and experiences related by aged persons.

"Inborn hair" means the "hair grown while a baby was still in its mother's womb" or the "hair a baby was born with". In other words, it is the hair which a human being carries to the world upon his birth.

It is said that "inborn hair must be cut if it grows sparse." The hair grown in the womb is apt to be sparse, yellowish, and weak. For this reason a baby can have good hair only after the hair it carried with it from its mother's womb is cut off. Good hair must possess the characteristics of being black, long straight, and glossy. One who has yellowish hair is called "Yellow" and one who has curly hair is called "Curly." Girls who have such hair are usually considered as fickle-minded, obstinate, and wicked, and are not considered beauties. If a baby's hair is sparse or yellowish it is cut frequently. Whenever she trimmed my bobbed hair when I was young, my mother used to tell me, "When you were born, you were like a rat with hair that was not fully grown. You had yellowish hair. For fear that you would experience difficulties in finding a spouse, I cut your hair frequently. So your hair has grown this much." Now my hair, though not so thick, is of fine texture and black. Often I have been asked by others if I dye my hair black. People paid special attention to the date when they cut inborn hair. It is said that people on the mainland used to cut it mainly on the 100th day after birth or on the first birthday.

The custom of cutting the inborn hair on the 100th day attached importance to the meaning of the number 100; namely, it embodied the desire for longevity. In addition, people chose the 100th day because the mother could restore herself to her normal physical condition by that time, with her bones returning to their original places, and the baby had grown up enough to hold its head upright and to discern objects. Parents used to entertain guests at a special feast to celebrate the occasion. They also gave a "birthday feast" on the first anniversary of the birth of their sons or daughters. How was the inborn hair cut? It was usual at the first cutting to leave several hairs untouched on top. The reason is not clear on the mainland, but it was presumably intended to symbolize long life. It was also believed that it was better for the inborn hair of a baby to be cut secretly by its father's sister, so that its mother would be surprised later.

On the Island of Cheju, however, the cutting took place on 8 April of the lunar calendar. Although the day is Buddha's Birthday, non-Buddhists also chose that date. The islanders believed that a baby whose inborn hair was cut that day would be protected from ailments and enjoy longevity. An aged person who was blessed with happiness and renowned as virtuous was asked to cut the inborn hair. It was also customary to leave several hairs on the top untouched. They were also considered "ropes of life" or "hairs of life" in the belief that a long hair promised long life.

It was an obligation of parents who cut the inborn hair of their baby on 8 April to observe the custom for three years; that is, they had to cut the hair on the next 8 April and again on the one after that. This is presumably connected with the custom of observing a three-year mourning period after the death of a father or a mother.

In addition, it is also said that "to have the inborn hair cut on 8 April is better than to perform an exorcism three times." An exorcism is intended to ask for forgiveness for one's wrongdoings from one's deceased ancestors or gods by inviting sorceresses to perform the rite before tables filled with food. However, a person with an ordinary level of income can hardly spare the time or money required for an exorcism. It was much easier to cut the inborn hair of one's baby on 8 April according to the lunar calendar, and to invoke the same degree of efficacy by cutting on the same date for three years consecutively.

The custom of cutting on 8 April was not limited to the inborn hair. The same rule was applied also to the cutting of the grass on the graves of one's parents and ancestors. The first cutting was conducted immediately after the funeral. The second cutting took place in the year after the death (before the *Chusok*). Several blades of grass on the summit were left untouched. On the third and succeeding cuttings, all the grass was mowed. This custom is based on the notion that a man turns three years old in the other world after death just as he grows three years old in this world after birth.

Why were several hairs left untouched?

Several hairs left on the shaved head certainly looked ugly and tempted one to cut them it one had scissors nearby. This was an intentional act aimed at incurring ridicule from others for looking ugly. People were invited to ridicule a baby with several hairs left untouched on its head. It was believed that the more a baby was ridiculed, the longer it would enjoy life without illness. The infant mortality rate was very high in the old days. The mortality rate was especially high among boys and children of distinguished families who had few descendants. They often fell sick and died young.

By contrast, children born to poor and humble families grew up in good health. It was believed that evil gods were jealous toward children of noble families and did harm to them, but they were disinterested in children of humble families and did no harm to them at all. No matter how noble the family a baby was born to, it had to be treated like a child of humble birth if it wanted to enjoy a long life without disease.

On the mainland, the cut hair was committed to flames in a kitchen furnace or thrown into the toilet. On the Island of Cheju, people threw the cut hair away on a crowded street. It was necessary to choose a good direction when throwing it away. A direction open to good fortune all the year round had to be chosen. If not, knotty problems were likely to befall the baby. The concern was mainly with ailments. Because many people walked along a street open to busy traffic, a baby with several hairs left on its head was apt to be ridiculed and abused by more people. It was believed that a baby who was much scolded and criticized could grow up in better health.

The hair of grownups, too, was treated with great care. As hair is part of the body given by parents, it should not be thrown away indiscriminately. If a hair or two were mixed by mistake in food offered at an ancestral rite, it was believed that the spirits of the deceased ancestors would refuse to eat it. If they did not eat the food, the ancestors would mete out great punishment to their careless descendants. People were very careful in disposing of hair. People called hair mixed in food "baem" (ill luck), and nobody was willing to eat the spoiled food. Scattered hairs were collected with great care and wrapped in an oil-soaked piece of paper. The paper was then set on fire carefully outside the gate after dusk on the first day of lunar January. Hair was not cut on an unlucky day. It was believed that if it were, misfortune would sneak into the household. If snakes or wire-worms were hidden in a house, they could be driven out by burning hair.

In the Choson Kingdom period, people considered hair to be part of their bodies given by their parents and treated it with utmost care. When males were about to leave for a battleground or a dangerous place, they used to cut their hair, as well as their fingernails and toenails, and leave them behind. In case their bodies were not found, their hair and nails were regarded as substitutes at funeral ceremonies. Even if a man died a natural death, the custom was to prepare five small bags of clippings in advance before placing the body in the coffin. The five small bags, containing the hair, the right and left fingernails, and the right and left toenails, were set in proper positions inside the coffin. They were cut either during the lifetime or immediately after death. This meant that he carried part of his body with him to the other world.

Thrifty women used to collect fallen hairs whenever they combed their hair and used them to protect their needles from getting rusty. If the needles were placed on a roll of hair contained in a beautifully shaped bag, they wouldn't get rusty or be lost.

These folk customs have virtually dis-appeared nowadays. Although, old people over 60 must have experienced these customs in their youth, they have gradually given way to Westernized civilization.

Our parents, who regarded long life free from disease as the greatest happiness but who, because of their backwardness in medical knowledge, did not know how to save their dying sons or daughters, used their "wisdom" and wit to devise other means. Especially in the Choson society, where distinction between the noble and the humble was extreme, it was a cherished desire to attain the status of *Yangban* (nobility). Persons of the nobility flattered the evil gods who were always ready to rob them of their children, by degrading themselves as persons of ignoble birth. People very much wanted long life without disease.

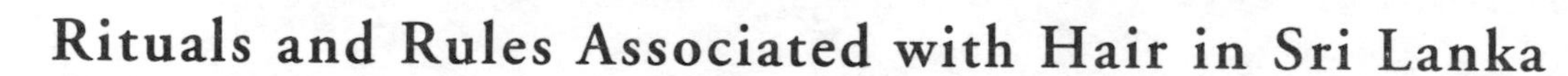

Rituals and Rules Associated with Hair in Sri Lanka

HAIR — the fibre that grows from one's head is considered to be woman's crowning glory. Hair can be cut curled, permed, scrunched, braided like Bo Derek's coiffured like Elizabeth Taylor's dyed or shaved.

Since time immemorial, hair has played a major role in myths, rules and rituals. Even in biblical times Samson's legendary strength lay in his long locks. Lady Godiva rode nude on a horse with only her hair to cover her modesty. Rapunzel let down her hair so that her lover could climb up and rescue her from a tower ... but that was all in the West.

Closer to home, in the East and Sri Lanka in particular, hair plays a vital role in all aspects of life. The 'Pancha Kalyani' or the Five Beauty Characteristics of a woman include hair, the other characteristics being skin, teeth, age and suppleness of body.

When a child is born — especially if it is a boy child, precious in the eyes of an Easterner — his hair is cut very short to ward off the evil eye, and on the more practical side to help his hair grow thick and long. The baby's hair is often preserved and sometimes worn in a locket by a mother. Hairdressers today will tell you that women's hair should be trimmed regularly or worn in a smart short style, probably coloured or streaked. Not so the Sri Lankans of yesteryear or the more conservative Sri Lankans of today, particularly in the rural areas. Hair, they believe, should be worn long — the longer the better, for long hair is a sign of femininity. It is for this reason that even today we see Sri Lankan women wearing their hair in a single plait, reaching right down to their ankles. This plait is often adorned with flowers — jasmine in particular, if the woman is attending an auspicious or festive function.

The daily trek of the lovely village damsels to and from the bathing well or river, as they chatter, water buckets in hand and towels on their shoulders, with their radiant long hair trailing behind them, is one of the most beautiful sights commonly seen in rural Sri Lanka. The longer the hair, the prouder they look. the hours these beautiful damsels spend by the water, working on each other's long tresses is a tribute to the calm, serene, slow-paced Sri Lankan village life, away from the hustle and bustle of the big city. Artistic hair styles for long hair are commonly seen in Asia. Where beautiful ornaments adorn women's hair which has been very skilfully and artistically dressed. Asian hairstylists are at their brilliant best on this type of work. At one stage, the cutting of a woman's hair was a sign of punishment, of shame. But today modern Sri Lankan women appreciate the convenience of a short and 'sassy' look.

An important ritual attached to hair is that, every time hair is brushed, the fallen strands, particularly those that have touched the ground, are either burnt, buried or disposed of in a manner whereby they will never be touched by human hands. In a country like Sri Lanka, steeped in superstitions and customs, black magic thrives in certain area, and human hair is an ingredient used in many local charms, to lure back a straying lover or break up a tottering marriage, or for other such dubious ends.

Often the person whose hair is used believes that she will be affected by the charm — hence the care taken in hair disposal.

Sri Lanka — a land of over 70% Buddhists — naturally has a large population of monks. Traditionally monks shave their heads as a symbol of their leaving the material world, and also to appear physically unattractive to others, hence leaving us to surmise that long hair is a great source of attraction, closely associated with the pleasures of the material world.

It is for this reason perhaps, that among certain clans, the close relatives of one deceased often shave their heads clean as an indication that they are in mourning. Moving back to superstition and fear of the unknown, it is a strict rule amongst Sri Lankan women not to have their hair cut after six o'clock in the evening or else they believe that they, and also their loved ones, may fall under an evil spell.

Superstition also has it that a child's hair should always be cut for the first time before he starts to speak and never during the time he is learning to talk, as there is a belief that this would cause a speech impediment.

Among the Hindu people of Sri Lanka, hair plays a very important part. At the age of one, the child goes through an elaborate ceremony when he or she receives the first haircut, and married women wear a streak of red called 'Sindhur' in their hairline to show the world their respect for their husbands. If the husband dies before the wife, she will no longer wear red 'Sindhur', and she will wear only a white Sari for the rest of her life. It is customary among some Muslim families to shave a child's head completely on the ninth day after birth and the weight of the hair in gold is given to charity in the case of a boy, and half of its weight for a girl.

Possibly the most common 'ritual' (if it may be called that among modern day women, is that of daily brushing, shampooing and conditioning. Though it may seem but a trivial detail, modern women look upon hair care almost as a sacred ritual.

Hair has always been a part of legend, of ritual, even of history, and will continue to be so.

Today's basic hair care will probably become tomorrow's legend...

Hairstyle in Filippino Tradition

ow many of us have taken the time to appreciate hairstyles and notice the various ways people fix and coiffure their hair? Once, hairstyling escaped the attention of many but more recently we have realized that each culture has placed its own significance and interpretation on hairstyle. In return, hair interpreted itself into striking cultural statements, styles and sophistications. The Philippines was not spared from this mode of the times.

For generations the headhunting people who inhabit the forest-armoured wilderness of the Cordillera mountains of Northern Luzon which has hidden them from the world, and the world from them, have prescribed a distinguished hairstyle that only headhunters who have brought home trophies are allowed to wear.

At a distance, the headtakers of Bontoc, Ifugao and Kalinga provinces seem to wear a thick helmet, but closer examination shows that this helmet is hair cut just above the ears, around the nape and forehead forming a thick curtain of bangs. A very sharp *bolo* or long knife is used. The *Minger or* headhunter adorns his hair with small bundles of black rooster feathers tipped with tiny fuchsia and yellow feathers obtained from birds of omen. The more showy bachelor-warriors add other fanciful decorations of strands of beads, boar's tusks, flowers, shells, etc. The village hero's hair is his crowning glory and to tough or stroke it, much more cut any part of it, is the greatest insult one can inflict upon him. The offender will definitely lose his head.

Today, the "helmet" hairstyle which once belonged to the elite circle of headhunters is shared by young boys and would-be headhunters who idolize and dream of duplicating their forefathers' feats. Some push themselves to the limit and pursue this abandoned unfriendly practice while the majority merely enjoy showing off a hairstyle which symbolizes prestige, bravery, honour and achievements that still fire their imagination.

In contrast to the headtakers, the slightly-built Mandayas, Manubo, Matigsalug and Tiboli maidens of the highlands of northern Mindanao, southern Philippines, spend considerable time preening themselves, giving their hair the most attention. The most potent means of winning their man is through a painstakingly arranged and coiffured hairstyle which entails a lot of combing, preening, twisting, flattening, bunning and sticking every conceivable accessory on their hair. Although separated by miles of rough terrain and thick forests, these ladies met somewhere in time, as it were, and approved a peculiar hairstyle which to this day they proudly display. Part of their hairstyle is thick, well-trimmed bangs covering their foreheads down to soot-drawn eyebrows. Hair on the sides is pulled down to frame their tiny made-up faces. An eye-assaulting array of textures and hues from beads, feathers, yarn, buttons, seeds and bells beautifully covers their pony-tailed hair, and prominently perched above all these bangles is the inevitable beaded-comb, clearly a head ornament and a vanity tool.

Other ethnic groups whose hairstyle is wedged on tradition are the Higaonons and Bukidnons who claim ancestry from the colourful Pagpagayok bird and inhabit the cleared areas of another mountain located several day's hike away from the Matigsalugs. These maidens coiffure their heads like birds, starting by parting their hair, expertly twining one part on the right and the other on the left end of a pencil-sized stick laid horizontally across the nape. To keep the twined hair in place coloured ribbons are tied. These parts are the spread wings.

This bird-hairstyle has two purposes. Firstly, it makes strong base on which to plant the ceremonial comb with fan-like ribs exquisitely decorated with vari-coloured feathers, yarn, beads, bells, coins and shells, and secondly, it has to resemble a bird in some ways to remind this maiden that she is the descendant of a mighty and colourful bird-god to whom she follows lineage and gives reverence. A magnificently embroidered kerchief is tucked over the hairdo to create a bird's tail.

What has love and marriage got to do with hair? Nothing we would say, but it has to the Bagobo tribes living on the slopes of the Philippines' highest volcano, Mount Apo in Southern Philippines. From birth, the Bagobos are warned never to cut their hair lest they court sickness, pestilence, famine and misfortune. The sacrilegious act of cutting one's hair desecrates the tribe's most honoured taboos, prompting the village elders to admonish the young to grow their hair long and healthy till their wedding day and beyond.

Weddings are occasions to fix the Bagobos' long hair in the tradition of a bride and groom. This day they reap the reward for caring for their hair. The wedding highlight consists of knocking the couple's heads together and tying their hair in a knot for unit. Woe to those are balding or have falling hair.

Beliefs and time-honoured rituals predating Spanish culture and influence to this day dominate many lowland villages. Again hair gets a fair share of attention, including thin and falling hair. Everyone, even the less vain man, wants his head full of healthy luxuriant hair, and when the problem of hair loss confronts him, there is the village medicine man who always has home-made remedies, to run to. One look at his scalp situation and the "doctor" reassuringly recommends the shaving-off of all the hair. If this does not produce a thick crop of hair, he pronounces the surest and final medication, a handful of flies squashed on the scalp. He swears in the names of all their gods that the hair will grow as thick as the forests around them.

Before the winds of change from the West blew over the heads of the Filipinos, long and silky hair was everyone's greatest pride and joy. European chronicles of the sixteenth century wrote and raved about how Filippinos kept their healthy hair shampooed with gogo (pounded bark that produced sods) and the aloe vera plant's sap, blended with newly cooked coconut oil and finally perfumed with extracts from orange leaves and blossoms. For good grooming, hair was tightly tied in a bun on top of or behind the head. Men's hair was kept short, barely reaching the collar. Those who live in the countryside continue to sport long unkempt hair, which distinguishes them from the Western-influenced urban groups.

At about the turn of the century, Western hairstyles became the vogue. The advent of electricity, moving pictures and the introduction of commercial preparations for hairstyling showered Hollywood's glittery magic on every fashion-conscious lady, prompting her to test the short and curly look. She was cute. But the advantages were only for the city. The poor *provinciana* or country maiden had nothing on hand to improve her simple village looks and, in desperation, turned to nature's wonders to find ways of equalling her city cousin's hairstyle. She turned to the lowly papaya plant. She realized that when the right amount of her short tresses were stuffed into short portions of the papaya leaf petiole and heated with a charcoal flat iron, the result was a head of uneven curls. Ordeal gives way to vanity. Thanks to Shirley Temple et al, the Filipinos have forgotten their shiny long hair once admired and envied.

It gives one a pleasurable thought that hairstyle in all its variety and function is the crowning glory of many Philippine traditions.

Hairstyle in Bangladesh

In this rapidly changing age of advanced technology, it is sometimes quite difficult to imagine life without magazines, television, films or fashion shows, which incidentally convey various latest fashions on boutiques and hairstyles to us. Consequently, since in this part of the world, womenfolk are getting more and more involved in complicated professions, they are becoming more conscious about wearing their hair in a wide range of styles. This wide range certainly varies with a number of factors like social status, professional requirements, age groups, social and cultural festivities, etc. However, no matter which socio-economic class they are confined to, women follow hairstyles which have a deeply traditional feeling, and are heavily accentuated with South Asian finesse and accessories.

Just like in any other part of the world, working women in Bangladesh tend to follow hairstyles which are rather convenience-and comfort-oriented, but somewhat attuned to western flamboyancy. These hairstyles reflect utter authority and self-confidence.

Although long hair is a moral symbol of beauty and traditionalism, working women often wear their hair in medium to short length or what is called 'bobbed' style. The front is usually well fringed to retain style and hair taken up from the sides is fastened on top to keep it tidy. Those having medium length hair leave the back loose to maintain controlled bounce and swing.

Wearing hair down to one's waist is a common feature in Bangladesh. This custom depicts oriental softness and sincerity. Elderly women, together with a fraction of working women and, of course, young maidens tend to keep such long luxuriant hair.

However, they all adopt a common hairdo called 'khopa', meaning a braid. In a 'khopa', hair is pulled back to form a coiled bun, fastened with hairpins and delicate nets to give a neat look. A centre parting is common in most cases, presumably, to complement the symmetrical effect of the 'bindi', a spot on the forehead between the brows, matching the colour of the outfit. It may be mentioned here that for religious reasons, women must conceal their 'khopas' under the long ends of the 'sari', the national dress for women in Bangladesh.

The village womenfolk, who constitute the majority of the population are very keen on wearing their hair in decorative plaits, ornamented with silver hairpins or multicoloured ribbons. They adore bright coloured accessories for their hair to match the colourful jewellery they wear. They also put homemade coconut oil in their hair regularly, to maintain quality and shine.

It is customary for young unmarried girls to wear their hair loose and falling or layered to give lift and body. Clipped at the sides of the head, it reveals the ear to show the meticulous ornamentation of gold earrings. Sometimes girls are also seen with pony tails, the hair being drawn together at the back of the head, secured and allowed to hang free over the shoulders. As a matter of fact the hairstyles favoured by young girls in Bangladesh are quite unpredictable, since they mingle influence from both east and west.

Apart from these routine hairdos there are a few special ones, highly decorative and traditional, reserved for particular social celebrations. The most alluring is the bridal 'khopa', which contributes heavily to the beauty of the bridal outfit, matching the gorgeousness of gold and silver. Back combed and puffed up in different layers, the braid is decorated with golden ribbons and hairpins along with other exquisite accessories. There are also hairstyles which are part of the costume for Bangladeshi dance which are also very decorative. Bangladesh has long been rich in culture and literature as well as tradition. The poets of Bangladesh have always been very keen to make the beauty of a maiden's hair the topic of their poems. We can conclude with a few verses from a poem of Jivananda Das...

Her hair is dark as the nights of Vidisha
Her face the architecture of Sravasti
So have I seen her in darkness,
Who asked me, "Where have you been so long?"

Sister and baby, Korea. The sister (a virgin) wears a pigtail, and the boy shows a head still retaining several of his inborn hair.

Culinary Traditions and Cuisine

India: Land of Rich Culinary Traditions

It is possible to conceive of an average Indian in almost any context. The 'Average Indian' exists for purposes of per capita income, standards of living, trends in entertainment, birth and mortality rates — but in one field of life, he remains elusive — food habits. Intensive perusal of reference books, interviews, and plain perception conclusively proves that the Average Indian simply does not exist when it comes to ascertaining his preferences in food.

Since India spans a divergent culture, climate and people, Indian food has tremendous variety. Customs, beliefs, availability of various types of food, economic trends, physical environment and climate, and religious taboos pertaining to food or the lack of them — these are a few of the influences which determine eating habits.

The availability of food is, of course, the major factor in influencing what people eat. Availability is decided by climate, environment and the physical location of a region. Generally, the kinds of food available are markedly different in three areas: the hill regions, the plains and the sea coast.

Rice is abundantly grown in the hills and valleys of India. As a result, it forms the staple diet of the hill people; rice is always eaten once a day, usually at lunch time, and flour made from wheat, maize, etc., supplements the basic diet. Strangely enough, although rice is so rich in starch, the inhabitants of these areas do not seem to put on fat. Perhaps this is due to the fact that the water in which the rice is boiled is usually thrown away, and the rice thus loses its starchy content. Also, the preparations cooked along with the rice are generally fat-free, so the overall meal is light instead of being rich and heavy.

In the plains almost everything is available, specially since a state which may not grow a particular item can always import from another state which has a surplus production. Rice and flour, therefore, jointly provide the staple diet to the people of the plains.

The people of the sea coast, again, are largely rice eaters. The scenery, whether it be Kerala or Bengal, is characteristically green with paddy fields, which provide the peasant with not only basic food but with his livelihood as well.

Religion is an important factor in determining the kind of food people eat. Meat is eaten all over India, except where religious taboos prohibit it. Since Hindus form a major portion of the Indian population, their avoidance of beef has led most people outside India to believe that Indians as a whole are not beef-eaters. Yet, where not prohibited by religious taboos, it is consumed by many communities. Meat, poultry and fish are widely eaten all over India, except by the Brahmins, who are strictly vegetarian.

A curious fact about the vegetarian food habits of certain communities is that fish and eggs are permitted. Fish, for instance, is considered a 'vegetable of the sea' and therefore it does not fall into the meat category.

Religious taboos are not the only ones which determine the eating or avoidance of certain foods. Some are based on popular beliefs which, though not generally adhered to today, nevertheless find followers in backward areas. It was commonly believed that sour limes, oranges and custard apples caused colds, a misconception since the vitamin C contained in these fruits is actually beneficial in curing colds. Pulses, which contain a great deal of protein, were avoided by people suffering from infections of any kind as it was believed that pulses caused pus. Although most of these 'old wives' tales' have not an iota of logic behind them, an observer of food habits will still come upon these pockets of belief which only years of nutrition education can dispel. While the basic food or staple diet of a region may be essentially the same as another region similarly situated — such as fish and rice in the coastal areas — minute variations in cooking mediums, in methods or spices, transform the familiar into the extraordinary and provide each dish with the distinct stamp of its region.

Indeed, the concept of certain fruits and vegetables can change in variance with the methods of preparation. In the North, for instance, the jack fruit is cooked as a savoury dish when the fruit is still raw. The moment it begins to ripen, the jack fruit season is said to be over. But in the South, the season has just begun. The jack fruit is eaten as a fruit, and it must therefore ripen before it can be consumed. It is also used in the preparation of jack fruit *halwah*, an extremely common and popular sweet in Kerala. Then again, bananas are just bananas to everyone — but in some parts of the country, you can get cooked bananas, sweetened bananas, savoury bananas and even banana chips, just like potato wafers only made of bananas and fried in coconut oil. Speaking of coconuts — grown along the sea coasts, the coconut is widely used in cooking, either as oil or in a desiccated form to add a flavour to almost any kind of food. Further inland, however, the coconut has no real influence on cooking, maintaining only the religious significance it appears to have throughout the country. The coconut generally forms part of religious offerings in Hindu prayer. The variety of India's culinary traditions is enormous — each item, whether it be meat or vegetable, is transformed by totally different approaches. The fish preparations of Bengal, Kerala and Maharashtra are vastly different from each other, although all three have easy access to fishing waters — to say nothing of the further variety presented by fish-eaters of non-coastal areas.

In the meat and poultry eating regions — generally the hills and plains, and the coastal areas only to a lesser extent — distinct influences are obvious everywhere. The rice and spicy preparations of the Punjab — buttered chicken, meat smothered in onions — contrast with the exotic art of the Kashmiri chef who cooks sans garlic and onions. Kashmiris, as also certain other communities in various parts of India, lay a great deal of emphasis on detail in preparation of food. A tradition of unusual and painstaking methods makes it possible for even a simple, tasty item to have a long history of patient preparation behind it. The meat dishes of Western India are again altogether different, and one's education is not complete unless one has sampled *dhansak* — lamb or chicken cooked with curried lentils and served with rice. Kerala is famous for its dry meat cooked with coconut. It is truly like wandering into different lands.

The different kinds of cooking mediums have a lot to do with changing the flavour of the food. In the East, the tang of mustard oil is prominent in the cooking, whereas the distinct flavour of coconut oil filters through the taste of most dishes in Southern and Western India. Clarified butter was, till fairly recently, the main cooking medium in the North, but over the years a gradual inclusion of groundnut oil has occurred. Edible oils prove cheaper for most middle-class families.

Milk products are widely consumed all over India, in many varied forms. Clarified butter is still used by families that can afford its use, and also for special preparations where it is not possible to make do with a substitute. Cottage cheese is also popular in its many forms — varieties of savoury and sweet dishes. In Indian sweets and desserts, milk is indispensable — North Indians make an infinite variety of *kheer* — rice, vermicelli, pista, almonds, etc., combined with milk, slowly simmered till it thickens to the right consistency, and finally sweetened. A similar dish is made in the South — *payasam*, a rice mixture of cashews, sugar, cereals and raisins in milk. Bengal has the richest tradition in confections, from the *rossogulla* (cream cheese balls in syrup) famous all over India, to the many kinds of *sondesh* made from cream cheese.

Indians were eating curds long before the West discovered the value of yogurt. One of the most varied and nourishing of milk products, curd (or yoghurt) is used in many ways. It is incorporated in cooking — to thicken and enrich meat preparations, for instance; it is made into buttermilk in the North and consumed in the summer months; it is whipped up and mixed with finely cut cucumber, tomatoes, onions, potatoes or mint to produce *raita*, which is inevitably found on the tables of most Indian homes with summer lunches; it is mixed with sugar and saffron for the preparation of *srikhand*, a popular Western India sweet dish originating in Maharashtra.

Pulses are perhaps the only major food common to people in all parts of India. An excellent source of protein, pulses are the 'poor man's meat.'

No meal is really complete unless it is topped off with a *paan*. The *paan*, a betel leaf containing betel nuts, a dash of lime, and a variety of spices and ingredients according to choice, is available all over India. The betel leaf also plays an important role in ritual and, like the coconut, often forms part of the prayer offering.

Indian hospitality is legendary. Even today, undaunted by rising costs of living, an Indian will very rarely refuse a meal to a comparative stranger. Coupled with this over-whelming hospitality is a wonderful graciousness of attitude. If a neighbour sends food over to one's house, the container is never returned empty; a guest who arrives for a visit at any time resembling mealtime is always asked to stay and eat with the family. A largesse or spirit is evident in the meanest of Indian homes, and the Average Indian certainly, for once, exists here — where generous hospitality is involved.

An offshoot of this largesse of spirit is the Indian's ability to find innumerable occasions for feasting. Community feasts are arranged on births and deaths, marriages and religious ceremonies, and festivals of all kinds. Festival feasts have graduated into a separate tradition of their own, with special foods associated with each festival, and fasting on certain days which permits only certain foods. Various kinds of *halwah* are the most common, made of semolina, pumpkin, carrots, or other bases which are first fried and then mixed with either milk or water, sweetened, and thickened — served with a garnish of raisins, cashew nuts or almonds.

The switch from one season to another comprises a festival as well. On Basant Panchmi, for instance which is celebrated in the North as the advent of spring, women dress in the traditional yellow colour associated with spring. A yellow dish is always served on Basant Panchmi, whether it be saffron rice or semolina *halwah* which has been given the requisite yellow colour with turmeric of saffron.

Eating habits have been greatly modified over the years, with changes in attitudes and standards of living affecting the degree of conformity to rigid rules about eating. In the good old days, entering your kitchen to cook in it (especially if you were of a high caste, which necessitated ensuring greater purity) meant you had first to bathe; thereupon you donned special clothes kept separately only for working in the kitchen, so as not to pollute the kitchen with germs from everyday clothes. You could never enter with your slippers on, and certainly not when 'impure' at the time of the menstrual period. In high caste households, only the women of the family were permitted to cook the food; for fear of contamination by those considered untouchable and of lower caste, servants were rarely employed.

Once the meal was prepared, the men sat down to eat in the kitchen. The men-folk always ate first. With the men seated on the floor, the food was served out to them on either leaf plates (which were the most hygienic since, like paper plates you simply threw them away after the meal) or on silver or metal *thalis* (plates). When eating off a leaf plate, dishes for curries, etc., were ingeniously made by moulding a section of leaf and securing it with slivers of bamboo or cane to make a hollow dish. Leaf plates are usually made from banana leaves. Containers made of unbaked clay, called *kasoras*, are used for drinking water. When *thalis* are used instead of leaf plates, individual items are served in *katories* or metal bowls.

Indian food is traditionally eaten with the hands, to mix the food to the right consistency. Spoons, knives and forks have been a latter-day import into the Indian food scene. Before starting a meal, a prayer would be followed by sprinkling water around the leaf plate or *thali* in the belief that it would purify the eating area. Since food was cooked and served at floor level, most Indians still have a passion for cleanliness in the kitchen, which has survived many of the other changes which have slowly taken place.

Indians today possess a mixture of traditional and modern attitudes, having discarded those which no longer serve a functional value. In most urban homes now, it is not necessary to take your shoes off when entering the kitchen, as the physical reason for such a custom no longer exists. Most kitchens in city areas are now modernised to the extent that cooking is no longer done at floor level, so it does not really matter whether you enter shod or unshod. Meals are eaten in dining rooms in homes where there is sufficient areas to provide separate space for this purpose. Housewives, specially working women, now tend to treat cooking as just another household chore, attaching to it none of the near-fanatical care and ritual given to it by earlier generations. The traditional culinary art is now carried on in modern and well-equipped kitchens, which prove labour and time-saving for the average Indian housewife. The actual time spent by women in the kitchen has decreased, even in cases where they do the cooking themselves. More convenient cooking methods have replaced the old-fashioned ones — instead of laboriously lighting dried dung cakes or wood or coal fires in the *chula* (earthen fireplace), the modern housewife has now graduated to matches, gas lighters and electricity for lighting kerosene stoves and gas ranges.

The *tandoor* — the traditional North Indian oven — has persisted in spite of the transition from tradition to modernity. The *tandoor* is a hole dug into the ground, with its interior walls plastered with clay. Chicken, fish, meat, unleavened bread — an array of items cooked in the *tandoor* has led to the immense popularity of tandoori food.

Orthodoxy and tradition have not, however, been entirely stamped out in India's urban areas, and certainly not in the rural areas. In fact, rituals and rules and customs continue to flourish in any area which has been left physically untouched by modernisation, where the standard of living has not changed, where the quality of life has remained the same, freezing women in their rigid confines. The rural environment is still basically the same, The necessity for adherence to basic rules for hygiene, set so long ago that they became custom, still exists for the Indian villager.

India, a land of diverse cultures, has a profusion of culinary traditions. Yet all of them — with all the variety — belong to one larger tradition. That of one country, one race, one people. The *pot pourri* of all these cultures provides a total picture of Indian food. However diverse your gastronomic experiences when embarking on a discovery of Indian food, there is one observation in common: it's a great tradition.

The Dietary Culture of Asia

Ways of eating

"What bad manners you have! Don't eat with your fingers, use your chopsticks!" For many a child in China, Korea, Japan, and Vietnam, this parents' reprimand is one of the first lessons in social manners. For each of these ethnic groups, putting food in your mouth with your fingers is viewed as an ill-mannered, rather animal-like act.

Indians, however feel that "When they eat with a fork or chopsticks, they lose the pleasure of having a meal. If they eat with their fingers, they also enjoy the heat of the food, the consistency of the curry, and the texture of what they are eating. For Indians, their fingers are like a second tongue." Thus it is better that the slanted view that eating with the fingers is unsanitary and barbaric should be discarded. The culinary arts of the world's various peoples are a cultural heritage developed over the centuries. The best way to ensure full enjoyment of each ethnic group's foods is to eat them in the same manner as they do. Even eating with the fingers has a set of manners all its own.

In Asia, the custom of eating food directly with the fingers is found in the Middle East, India, and throughout Southeast

Asia with the exception of Vietnam. In all such localities, the hands are normally washed thoroughly before and after the meal. Certainly your own hand which you have carefully washed yourself is a more reliably sanitary tool for eating than the fork or chopsticks washed — perhaps haphazardly — by someone else. Moslems, Hindus, and the members of other sects may use only their right hand for eating, with the left hand, deemed less clean and used for other purposes, never coming into contact with the food. In localities where eating with the hand is the tradition, people do not use tables or chairs, instead gathering around the food placed on a mat or similar floor covering and using their hands to partake of food from a common central bowl or plate.

In contrast, cultures which use chopsticks apportion the food among those joining in the meal, with each person eating from the individual dishes in front of him. In particular, soup and the staple food, rice, of such "chopstick regions" are served separately to each individual, and small individual bowls have developed in such regions specifically for this purpose.

The three main Western eating utensils, knife, fork, and spoon, first began to appear together on European tables in the seventeenth century. Chopsticks, on the other hand, have a much longer history and were wide-spread in China as long ago as the second century BC.Korea, Japan, and Vietnam, all of which were strongly influenced by Chinese civilization, also came to use chopsticks. Similarly, the peoples of Mongolia and Tibet, both of which border China, are familiar with chopsticks but normally do not use them in their everyday meals.

Staple foods

In the western areas of Asia, the representative food can be seen as bread, whereas in the eastern regions of the continent, rice would occupy this position. This is true to the extent that in Japanese, the term "eating rice" is synonymous with "having a meal." Let's look for a moment at these staple foods and the methods of preparing them.

First, speaking broadly, in western India and farther west, wheat is an important foodstuff, and it is all ground to flour and baked or otherwise cooked. It is used to make bread or *nan*, the large flat or bowl-shaped bread of western Asia, and in central and northwestern India, wheat flour is baked unleavened into *chapati*. In contrast, in all of Asia to the east of eastern India, the staple food becomes rice, with the whole grains usually boiled or steamed for eating without being ground to flour.

Rice and wheat are thus representative staples of East and West Asia, but the continent also includes people who find their staple foods still elsewhere. The varieties of the staple foods of these various ethnic groups are closely linked to the environments in which they live and their own histories. Here, in order to give some thought to the traditional dietary cultures of Asia, let us look at the Asian staple foods as they stood in the fifteenth century.

Mongolia to the north and Central Asia had no active agriculture, it being limited to small-scale farming in the oases, they were inhabited by pastoral nomads. For these nomadic peoples, the milk and meat of their livestock were important foods, and they ate only such grain as they could procure through trade with the farming peoples to the south.

In the deserts running from southern Iran to the Arabian Peninsula, dates were cultivated in the oases, and the dried dates were an important source of nourishment for those engaging in animal husbandry.

Wheat and barley spread northeast from the ancient seats of West Asian civilization, and a variety of barley suited to cold climates (processed into the parched barley flour called *tsampa*) also became a staple food in the highlands of Tibet. There barley held sway, while to the east in North China wheat was again the staple diet, where it was made into a kind of steamed bread called *mantou* or thick wheat noodles.

Various millets- sorghum, German millet, proso millet and the like — were introduced into East Asia from ancient India, long ago passing through the northern mountains of Southeast Asia and on eastward, eventually reaching North China and Manchuria. The ancient Chinese culture that grew up along the Yellow River of North China relied heavily on German millet and proso millet as their staples. This ancient millet-eating region, however, was later overtaken by the development of cultures whose staple foods were wheat, barley, and rice, and at present, millet remains the sole staple only in the dry Indian highlands, part of North China, Manchuria, and part of northern Korea. In India, millet is normally ground and baked as *chapati*. In North China and Manchuria, it is normally ground, formed into balls, and steamed for consumption, or else the whole grains are boiled into a gruel and eaten. In Southeast Asia, the crops of longest standing are taro, yams, bananas, and others which are not planted as seeds but which are cultivated through transplanting. These, however, were displaced to a major extent by the rice and other grains which appeared later, until today the grain-cultivating cultures have taken root in Asia to the extent that the above form the staple diet only in eastern Indonesia and on the islands that dot the Bashi Strait between Taiwan and the Philippines, though they are still important crops on the islands of Oceania where grain cultivation did not penetrate earlier dietary patterns.

One point that must be made concerning animal proteins deals with the use of the milk of domestic animals. In Mongolia in northern Asia, Central Asia, and from India westward, milk from a variety of domestic livestock is made into yoghurt, butter, cheese and other dairy foods, which serve as an important source of nourishment. However, China, Korea, Japan, and Southeast Asia traditionally have not used milk in this way. Instead, these non-milk areas developed a variety of fermented foods made from soy beans — for example, soy sauce and soy been paste — and rely heavily on these as sources of vegetable protein in their daily lives.

Religion and diet

The foods selected for consumption by various ethnic groups and their outlook on food and eating manners are closely related to religion. It is well known that Moslems do not eat pork, but other animals as well must be slaughtered by a Moslem or they cannot be eaten by followers of Islam. The ninth month of the Islamic calendar is a month of fasting, when Moslems may not eat or drink during the daylight hours. For Hindus, the cow is sacred and the eating of beef is forbidden. Many other Hindus go further and are vegetarians for religious reasons.

In China, the influence of Taoism has led to the deeply-rooted belief in food as a way to long life. Food is thus deemed to be medicinal, and all foods are classified according to their medicinal properties. For example, eggplant is medicinally effective, it is said, in cooling the blood, so that it should be eaten by those with high blood pressure. Ginger, on the other hand, heats the blood and thus is beneficial to persons with anemia. In this way, a balancing of the condition of the body is sought through food.

In Japan, through the influence of the Buddhist proscription on killing, meat was not commonly eaten up until the latter part of the nineteenth century.

Asia's three main dietary cultures

The various peoples of Asia have each developed their own ethnic cuisines through the historical interaction of environment and culture. Still, the major civilizations that have appeared in Asia have each exerted an influence on the dietary lives of the people of the continent.

Beginning from the west, the three main civilizations would be the Persian-Arabian, Indian, and Chinese.

Historically, the food structure of the Persian-Arabian civilization began with the cooking techniques innovated in ancient Persia and carried forward by the Persia of the Sassan Dynasty. With the coming of Islam, to these were added the dietary customs of the Arabs, and through the growth of the Turkish Empire, Turkish methods of cooking were also added to the culinary tradition. In the areas covered by this dietary civilization, *nan* became wide-spread, but on special occasions or among the upper classes, the rice dish called *pilau* was also frequently served. The most important meat was mutton, and a representative food in this region would be the *kebab*, deriving from Turkish cooking. Another feature is the plentiful use of hot peppers, black pepper, cloves, and other strong spices. Since this is also an Islamic region, the consumption of pork is of course forbidden and other Islamic dietary regulations rule the inhabitants' eating habits. With the spread of Arab culture to North Africa, the cooking practices of Persian-Arabian civilization also advanced into this area, and at the same time, the expansion of the Turkish Empire carried its influence as far as the Balkan Peninsula, the shores of the Black Sea, and Greece.

Cooking in the Indian civilization has as one of its characteristics the daily use of curry in meals. Here, too, through the influence of the Hindu religion, cows are used only for their milk and not for meat. A butter oil called *ghee* is frequently used in cooking. In addition to rice, *chapati* made from wheat or barley are also a staple part of the diet, and beans also play an important role in meals.

In the Chinese civilization, pork is frequently used, but traditionally the Chinese have not used the milk of their domestic animals. The Chinese also developed the fermented soy bean preparation *jiang*, primarily in the form of paste or liquid, as a ready-made seasoning. Fats and oils are frequently employed in cooking, and the use of dried and preserved foodstuffs is another characteristic of Chinese cuisine. The foods, spices, and seasonings go beyond being mere foodstuffs; they are of great importance in cooking based on their classification as medicines for long life. As mentioned earlier, the use of chopsticks and small, individual bowls is also a characteristic of the Chinese cultural sphere.

In Southeast Asia, which has been influenced historically by both Chinese and Indian civilizations, both influences are evident today — the Indian in the curried dishes and the Chinese in the use of a variety of *jiang* foods and noodles in Southeast Asian cooking.

The arid region stretching from Central Asia to the Caspian Sea has been a crossroads not only of culture but of cooking as well. In the oases from Mongolia to Sinkiang, Chinese cooking has made its mark, and Indian cuisine has penetrated to the north-west to reach Pakistan and then Afghanistan, where it has met and intermingled with the foods and methods of preparation of the Persian-Arabian culture.

The Rural Malays of Malaysia: Their Meals and Eating Habits

The Malays, otherwise known as the bumiputra, literally meaning 'sons of the soil', of Peninsular Malaysia make up over fifty-five percent of the total population of Malaysia. Of this percentage, more than three-fourths of the Malay population live in the rural areas forming the agricultural sector. The remaining quarter is dispersed in the growing industrial towns and heavily concentrated in the Federal-capital, Kuala Lumpur, and in the state capitals. They live competitively but harmoniously side by side with their Chinese, Indian and other minority counterparts. Historically, the Malays are a race of farmers and fisher-folk. In the heyday of Malay feudalism, the Malay *rakyat eked* out a living from the land and the sea and surrendered part of their harvest or daily catch to their feudal lords in subservient recognition of their sovereignty and power over life and limb. The era of British colonial adventure in Malaya marked the advent of modernisation and change to this country. After establishing her Independence in August 1957, Malaysia's road towards political, economic and social stability were firmly defined. However, the contemporary rural Malay, in spite of the incursion of modernisation and industrialisation manifest in the use of modern machinery in farming and the application of new technological skills, or in the use of power boats and machine-operated dragnets, still clings to certain aspects of his traditional beliefs and way of life. He accommodates change and yet at the same time tries hard to retain most of his cultural heritage deeply rooted in the long past.

A look into the eating habits and meals of the rural Malays of Malaysia will expose some of these traditional ways and beliefs. Food in the Malay language (now known as Bahasa Malaysia since it was gazetted as the official language of the country) is *makanan*, a derivative of the stem *makan* meaning 'to eat.' Meals are variously termed according to the time of day and hence *makan pagi* or *sarapan* is used for breakfast, *makan tengahari* for lunch and *makan malam* for dinner. The number of meals taken by a Malay villager is very often determined by his daily income and social standing. A poor Malay farmer or fisherman would be considered lucky if he and his family could afford two square meals a day, in contrast to the four square meals of a richer and more affluent landowner or fishing fleet owner. The type of food a Malay villager eats also depends upon the region or environment in which he resides. For example, a Malay specialty in the historic state of Malacca is curry called the *gulai asam peda*, whilst the *gulai masak lemak* is a favourite of the Malays of Negeri Sembilan. Nevertheless, most rural Malays of Malaysia do share certain common types of food. Rice, as in other Asian regions, is the staple food of the Malaysians. In the rural areas, a square meal would consist of rice, a spicy curry of fish or occasionally beef or mutton, a vegetable dish and a hot and pungent preparation of salt and red chilly known as *sambal*. Vegetables are usually available from the Malay villager's backyard garden or from the jungle in the vicinity of his home. These vegetables may range from *pucuk paku* or tender fern shoots and *rebung* or bamboo shoots, to *pucuk ubi* or tapioca shoots and many others. Other than these plentiful locally grown or wild vegetables, a Malay occasionally eats commercially grown cabbages, radishes or imported carrots when he makes his trip to town and when he can afford them. The Malay vegetable dish is simply prepared as it usually entails the boiling of the vegetable in water and a pinch of salt or fried in a little bit of oil. The preparation of the Malay curry or *gulabi remph* is more elaborate. The protein source, be it salted or fresh fish, beef from the nearest market or chicken from the chicken coop behind the house, is cooked in coconut milk and a preparation of finely ground spices consisting of coriander seeds, cloves, cinnamon, turmeric, aniseeds and a few others. Coconut milk is frequently used, as other dairy products are considered luxury items.

In preparing chicken, every available part of the chicken (excepting the feathers and claws) is cooked, from entrails to bones. The flesh is used for curry whilst the internal organs and entrails are cooked together with vegetables. Beef and mutton are usually bought from the nearest market or from enterprising vegetable seller-cum-fishmongers who come to the villages on push-carts or on their motorcycles. The Malay villager slaughters his cattle or goats and chicken when he holds a *khenduri* or feast especially for the wedding of his son or daughter.

Amongst the fisher-folk of the coastal region, fish, shrimp, and cuttlefish are the main diet apart from being a source of their income. If the harvest is good, part of their catch is surrendered to their boat owners or sold at fish markets and part of it kept for their daily needs. The excess fish are cut up, cleaned and dried in the sun and later used in their kitchen. Fresh water fish are also available from rivers, ponds and the irrigation canals of the rice-growing areas. Catfish, locally called *ikan kili*, are considered a delightful delicacy, and the *ikan sepat* of the *tilapia* species thrive well in the muddy *bendang* or rice-fields. At harvest time, the slush water is drained-off the *bendang* and diverted into a secondary pool where the fish are trapped. The catch is very often salted and dried and stored for future use or sold in markets to supplement the Malay man's income.

There are many ways of preparing food in the Malay kitchen. The first and simplest way is by boiling *merebus* which is usually done to vegetables and meat curries that require the softening of tough meat, or in the simple preparation of a hard boiled egg. The second method is *menggoreng*, frying as in dishes common in Malay society such as *ayamgoreng* (fried fish) or *ayam-goreng* (fried chicken). Preparation of *ayam-goreng*, for example, entails the rubbing of salt and turmeric powder onto the dressed and cut chicken and then deep frying in coconut oil. A third way of preparing of Malay dish is light frying of *menumis*, as in the preparation of a hot and spicy dish well known as the *sambal*. *Sambal*, a favourite amongst the Malays, usually consists of red hot chilly, onions, and *belacan*, a prawn paste pounded together until fine and finally lightly fried in oil. One other method of preparing food amongst the Malays is broiling or *memanggang*, as in the dishes *ikan panggang*, broiled fish, or *ayam panggang*, broiled chicken. Preparation of chicken and fish is similar to that of *ikan goreng* or *ayam goreng*, but instead of frying, they are clamped between a small, partly-split piece of bamboo and placed over a makeshift barbeque grill of burning charcoal or less expensive fuels such as coconut kernels. The broiled product is often dipped into a simple sauce prepared by slicing red chillies and onions and mixing them in a solution of tamarind juice and prawn paste (*belacan*).

The Malay kitchen can be regarded as incomplete without the following items: spices (*rempah, belacan*, and coconut), *kelapa*, and red and green chillies (*chabai merah* and *cabai api*). From the ripe coconut fruit, coconut milk is obtained by grating the coconut flesh, mixing it in water and extracting the milk from the mixture with the help of a strainer. Coconut milk is used in the preparation of several curries and other dishes and also in the making of coconut oil. The use of spices in Malay cooking dates to the early history of the Malay people. Ever since the Malacca sultanate was the spice emporium of the East, spices have been used in the Malay kitchen. They not only function as the basic ingredients in preparing food but are also used as food preservatives and in the treatment of certain ailments and illnesses by the traditional medicine man or *bomoh*. The most commonly used are cardamom seeds, aniseeds, cinnamon, cloves, coriander, pepper and many others. Apart from theses spices, the Malays also make use of herbs and grass roots like lemon grass (*serai*) or turmeric leaves (*daunk kunyit*) and its roots as colouring or flavouring agents or even to give fragrance to the food being cooked. Chillies are often used to make the food hot and pungent, so that they usually burn the tongue of a foreigner. *Belacan* is a prawn paste widely used by the many ethnic groups of Malaysis. It is never eaten for its own sake but is used more as a seasoning agent, as the *Aji-no-moto* is in Japan. *Belacan* is added to all kinds of hot *sambals*, in certain vegetable dishes and curries.

The Malays also have a penchant for preserved or fermented food. Pickles or *jeruk* are familiar to the Malay appetite. Lime, mangoes and other sour fruits are cooked in spice and vinegar and preserved for months or even years without turning bad in the least. Pickled fish (*ikan jeruk* or *pekasam*) is another delicacy to the Malays. The cleaned fish is soaked for a long period in brine and spice, or is salted and mixed with cooked rice and then bottled up for a length of time. The fermented product very often exudes an offensive smell but is nevertheless palatable to the local populace. Apart from the *belacan* mentioned earlier, there are two more local delicacies which are natives of the states of Kelantan and Malacca. The *budu* of Kelantan is actually a type of fish sauce prepared and stored for long period, whilst the *cencaluk* of Malacca is a sauce made of small shrimps. The *budu* is somewhat similar to the *bagoong* of the Philippines, famous for its odour yet appetising to the native palate.

There are many factors that determine the nature of the Malay diet. Other than the question of income of the Malay and the availability of the food in relation to his environment, there are yet potent considerations that dictate what a Malay may eat and what is taboo. These are the factors of religion and tradition. Being Malay and Moslem, religion and tradition determine food that may not be consumed. Pork is specifically mentioned in the Quran as taboo or *haram*, and thus the rearing of pigs and eating of their flesh is strictly forbidden. Amphibians like frogs, toads and certain species of crustaceans like the land crabs cannot be eaten, and the same is true of species of the reptile family. The taboo is also imposed on carnivorous animals, birds and fish, which includes animals and birds with fangs or claws. These taboos dictated by religion and tradition restrict the Malay from eating at Chinese or European restaurants, not only because of the nature of food but also because of the way the food is prepared. A Moslem cannot eat meat of animals or poultry slaughtered by a non-Moslem. A short prayer precedes the slaughtering of livestock and requires certain expertise known only to the Malay men-folk. Alcohol is never used to flavour food. Meat and fish must be thoroughly cleaned of blood and waste matter and must be thoroughly cooked. No meat may be served rare in a Malay home. Some of these conditions for preparing food reduce their vitamin potential.

In a traditional Malay home, meals are served on the floor. A woven *mengkuang* (a species of hemp) mat is laid on the floor and sometimes a piece of cloth (*seperah*) is spread on top. The dishes are arranged on the *seperah* and the plates are placed on its fringe. Where the *seperah* is not available, the dishes are laid in a large tray or *talam*. The family sits around the *seperah* or tray with the father or head of the family presiding. The men-folk sit cross-legged or *bersila*, whilst the womenfolk *bersimpuh*, sitting with both legs tucked under them and one hand supporting their body.

Eating with the hands is the fashion in most Malay homes. Spoons are usually used to spoon out food from dishes. A *kendi* or *bekas basuh tangan* or washing basin is used to wash dirty hands. In some Malay families saying the *doa*, a short thanksgiving prayer before eating, is observed. The younger members of the family must refrain from talking while eating and are to allow their elders to have first turns at spooning out food or ladling out rice. The women eat together with the rest of the family but frequently rise to replenish the contents of empty dishes or rice bowls. Burping after meals is permissible, but it is expected that a Malay say '*Alhamdullialah*' meaning 'Praised be Allah', as a gesture of gratitude after a hearty meal. Meals are often washed down with plain water or beverages like uncreamed coffee or tea. After the meal, the men-folk leave the women to clear the dishes.

The task of cooking meals is always left to the womenfolk in a Malay family. It is part of her responsibility in a rural Malay family apart from her other duties of housekeeping. In the agriculture sector, this responsibility is combined with some form of economic activity such as harvesting rice, tapping rubber or many others. In such a case, she rushes through the cooking, sometimes wrapping up her family's meals to be carried to their place of work. A simple meal of fried fish, sambal, and boiled vegetables would be a full course meal for the family members.

No matter how simple the meal is, a Malay farmer would gladly share it with his neighbours or kinfolk. A Malay house is an open house, and the basic philosophy of 'my house is your house' behind their humble generosity goes far in cultivating a spirit of benevolence and camaraderie in Malay society. Formal invitations to lunch or dinner are quite unknown. One may drop in at the oddest hour and yet be quite sure that one will have something to eat before reposing for the night or before continuing one's journey. A Malay proverb attests to this benevolent spirit — *Hati gajah sama dilapah, hati nyamuk sama dicecah*, literally meaning we will eat the elephants' and the mosquitoes' liver together, or freely translated 'partake whatever we have, be it in abundance or scarcity'.

In the villages, feasts are not uncommon and a Malay wedding feast tops them all. A cow or buffalo is often slaughtered to feed a whole village. Invitation cards are not issued as it is always expected that the whole village will be in attendance. A *hidangan* or table of food would consist of lavishly prepared curry beef, some salad made of local fruits, pickles, and a special ghee rice. Guests are served under a makeshift *bangsal* or shed by the host's kinfolk and neighbours. The Malay's *gotong royong* or *esprit de corps* is seen in preparations made for a wedding feast. From the time the makeshift sheds for guests are constructed till all the greasy pots and pans are scrubbed to a shimmering brightness, neighbours and relatives chip in to make the wedding feast a success. Pots and pans in a Malay home have changed considerably in form and material. *Metal periuk* or cooking pots, usually of aluminium or light steel, have replaced the *belanga* or clay pots. These are used for boiling rice, curries and vegetables, whilst frying is done in a deep pan called *kuali*. A *senduk* is a ladle of a half-coconut kernel with a wooden handle (now replaced by commercially produced aluminium ones), and a stove in Malay is *dapur* and is a simply constructed table with the top covered with a thick layer of sand or clay. Two steel bars are placed in parallel on top of two bricks placed on the sand or clay layer. Pots and pans are placed on top of the bars and firewood is burnt underneath them. For this makeshift type, most Malay houses have replaced wood with a kerosene stove, especially in the smaller towns as it is increasingly difficult to find wood and uneconomical to use it as fuel. Dishes and bowls are of cheap china available from the nearest town. Silver cutlery is a Luxury item and is found only in the more affluent homes. Hot water is boiled in a *cerek*, whilst water from wells or river are stored up in large earthen-ware jars called *tempayan*. Cutting knives are known as *pisau*, cleavers as *parang*, and the multi-purpose axe as a *kapak*.

The impact of modernisation upon the meals and eating habits is more profound for the urban Malay. Placed beside the many other ethnic groups of the country, he is more susceptible to changes than his brothers in the rural areas. Western cuisine, western cooking utensils, western cooking stoves and other imported paraphernalia exhibited in shop windows become part of his household belongings. Where his *kampung* brother uses a kerosene stove, he uses a gas or electric stove which at the same time can help in the baking of cakes for his tea. He more often uses good quality china for his meals, and as he sits at a table, he sometimes uses fork and spoon, a western habit he has picked up from his learning. On Sundays he invites friends to dinner or gets invited to a meal, at times complete with cocktails and barbequed steaks (imported, of course). As he hastens to fight time in a bustling city, his lunch may be reduced to only one of the instant-type foods in the form of Colonel Sander's Kentucky Fried Chicken or an A&W steak or hamburger. This pattern, however, is not typical of the Malays in cities and towns. Malays of the lower income still have much to share with the modest type of meals his *kampung kin* eat. Much of their eating habits are not lost, as a strong bond exists with the village from which they have migrated. A Malay's nocturnal visits to his place of birth, away from the city, are always there to remind him of his identity as a Malay and his cultural heritage. He still has a penchant for *belacan* and *pekasam*, though instead of eating them out of cheap china, his plates might have a foreign trade mark embossed on the base. When he burps, unconsciously he utters, 'Alhamdulliallah' as if signifying that in spite of being surrounded by change, he is still and indomitably a Malay.

Plain and Simple: Cooking and Eating in Burma

If you happen to drop in at a Burmese home at mealtime, you will certainly be invited to stay for the meal. Do not feel hesitant to accept their hospitality because they sincerely want to share their meal with you, even if the food is poor or meagre.

As you take your place at the low round table in the kitchen where you either squat down or sit on a low stook, you will find a bowl of rice fried with green peas. This is breakfast. Your host will deposit a huge portion of the meal on your plate and will urge you to help yourself.

You use either a spoon or your fingers after dipping them in a small basin of water to eat your breakfast. A cup of tea or coffee with cream sometimes goes along with the meal, but most homes prefer to have a pot of green tea instead. The Burmese take three meals a day — a light breakfast at sunup, a lunch around noon and a dinner at sundown. Lunch and dinner are almost identical. Most dishes are cooked in the morning in quantities large enough for both lunch and dinner. There can be an extra dish for dinner if the wife is able to prepare it or if she has a sudden kindly thought for her husband.

Let us suppose you happen to be again with the same family at dinner time.

You will sit with them around the same low round table in the kitchen. All the dishes for the dinner together with a bowl of rice will be set on the table and everyone is free to choose any or all. Burmese lunch and dinner are never served course by course.

Rice is the centre and substance of the meals, and it is cooked to result in clean and separate grains.

Burmese dishes consist of meat, fish, poultry and vegetables, but vegetables generally dominate. Raw vegetables such as cucumber, gourd creeper, citron leaf, mint leaf, cabbage, Bengal quince leaf and green fruits like carambola, *da-nyin* (pithecellobium begeminum), *phanga* (myrobalan), tomato and mango ginger are taken together with fish paste spiced with dried hot pepper and pounded dried prawns. This item is a must on the menu of the Burmese people both in rural and in sophisticated urban areas.

Unless the family is vegetarian, their main dish will be meat or poultry or fish, sometimes mixed with vegetables. Chicken is a favourite main dish, probably because Burma is the first country in the world where poultry were domesticated.

When fish is the main dish, fresh water fish are more preferred. Except for people in coastal areas where seafood is their daily fare, most Burmeses are not accustomed to eating sea fish and they say it does not taste as delicious as fresh water fish. They also complain that sea fish gives them muscle ache. However, with the easy availability of seafood on the market, with the persistent publicity of their nutritive values by the health department and with the fast-growing acquired taste for them, sea fish is now a regular item on the menu.

Pork is prestigious as the main dish. There is a Burmese saying: "Among fruits, mango is the king; among meats, pork is the queen." Although pork, plain and simple, may be cooked as curry, it is considered to be too rich, and dried slices of mango fruit are usually cooked with it. The sourness of the mango softens the cloyness of the meat and the resultant curry is just right for the Burmese palate. Many Burmese do not eat beef. The abstinence is not due to any religious prohibition. They only feel that it is a shame to eat the flesh of the animal which helps them produce food. They regard exen as 'comrades-at-work'.

Some of the favourite dishes of indigenous races have been adopted by the Burmese. For instance, a Karen dish called *talabaw* is very popular with the Burmese. This 'vegetable cocktail' curry is made up of many varieties of vegetables which are easily available in the jungle. Shan *pe-boke,* a soya bean preparation, when liberally sprinkled with cooking oil, is highly relished by the Burmese.

Because Burma is situated between India and China, the country has many Indian and Chinese immigrants. Many of their dishes have come to be accepted by the Burmese. As Chinese-style steamed duck is a frequent main dish, so also is the mango chutney a *la Indian,* a popular apetizer. Among side dishes, fried fish and fried vegetables are common. The vegetables used are rozelle, eggplant, corn and cabbage.

A popular side dish is *let-thoke,* which may be freely translated as 'hand-mixed affair.' It is a mixture of vegetables such as tamarind leaves, mushroom finely shredded cabbage or green papaya fruit with the balancing ingredients of oil for smooth mixing, powders of dried prawn and bean for filling, lime for sourness, fish sauce for salting, red chilly for spicing, and crisp fried garlic and onion to dress the whole. Most of the homes have a 'stand-by' side dish. It can be dried prawns pounded and fried together with fish paste, a bit of garlic, and onion, or it may be pieces of chopped dry fish fried likewise. This is kept handy in a glass container and it is used when the side dishes suddenly run short. It is also the favourite item of a picnic packet.

Soup is served at the same time as other dishes. Pure meat soups are rare. Vegetables such as lentil, cabbage, gourd, drum stick, Asiatic pennywort, *soo-boke* (acacia pennata), bean, bamboo shoot, or potato are the main ingredients, mixed with fish, prawn or pork.

The Burmese are fond of using monosodium glutanate in soup and curry despite the warnings of health authorities. Except for this, no chemically prepared condiments are used. To brighten the curries the Burmese use turmeric or red pepper powder. Most of the Burmese dishes are therefore not colourful. but the Burmese believe that the proof of the curry lies inherently in the eating.

When the dishes are rich or cloying, the housewife will prepare a slightly sour soup to offset the cloying taste. *Tamarind, kinmum* (acacia concinna) and rozello leaves are commonly used. Of these, rozelle soup is most popular because it is available almost all year round and is cheap. In the absence of a soup, a pot of green tea is usually substituted.

Desserts served at the end of lunch or dinner are tropical fruits of the season such as bananas, pineapples, jack fruit, oranges, custard apples, durian, mangos or mangosteen. As the banana can be had at any time of the year, it is a familiar dessert. In villages, jaggery serves as dessert. Instead of fruits as dessert, pickled tea-leaf accompanied by shredded ginger, nuts, sesamum, prawn powder, fried coconut bits and garlic may also be served.

Milk is not on the daily diet of the Burmese. It is not taken with meals, although on rare occasions rice boiled in milk can be a breakfast. Nor do alcoholic drinks, whether weak or strong, accompany the meals because most of the Burmese are teetotallers.

Although milk is plentiful in villages, no Burmese — not even the children — take milk as part of their daily diet.

Butter is rarely in cooking, and the same is true of coconut oil. Peanut and sesamum oil are the most used, with bran oil trailing along to be used as a substitute. Burmese cooking emphasises the right combination of flavours. The ideal combination of flavours which contribute to a delicious dish is sourness plus saltiness plus pungency. Burmese women have a special liking for sour foods. Unlike women in the West who have fondness for candy and sweet things, their Burmese counterparts relish sour things such as green mango, green tamarind fruit and Burmese salad composed of lemon, powdered dried shrimps, oil and fried garlic. Some dieticians attribute the slimness of the Burmese women to this.

There are some don'ts in cooking and eating. The Burmese will not cook a pigeon with carambola nor a rabbit with mushroom. They will not take cucumber with Asiatic pennywort nor frog with mushroom. Mangosteen is not eaten with suger, *Kaffir* bean with chocolate, and hog plum with an ice cone. Burmese books on medicine say that these combinations have toxic effects.

Native dishes prepared in villages differ very little from those cooked in towns. But there is a difference in the use of cooking utensils and methods of cooking in villages and in towns. In villages meals are cooked over a wood fire, whereas in towns they are cooked on kerosene stoves. Gas is used only in Chauk, a town in middle burma, where there are oil fields. Electricity is used for cooking almost exclusively in Rangoon and by those who are well to do.

Aluminum pots and kettles are used throughout Burma although earthernwares are still seen in village kitchens. Pressure cooker is an unknown commodity even in most towns and its use in limited to rich families in Rangoon. In olden days, a low, round lacquer table with built-in-trays was used to partake meals. Then lacquer plates, cups, saucers and spoons came into vogue. Now, enamelled plates, common chinaware and glassware have taken their place. Because Burmese dinners are simple, specific plates and bowls are not needed. Of course the exception is among people of position and those of high society who have separate dining rooms and use fine china, lovely glassware and gleaming cutlery. The Burmese use very few table implements. Simple ordinary spoons — aluminum or enamelled or china — are used to ladle curry. No special spoon is specified for soup or for dessert. Except for a big serving spoon to transfer rice and an extra-small spoon to serve fish paste mixtures, all spoons are of the same size.

As the Burmese eat with their fingers, they handle the spoon with their left hand to take curry.

On picnics banana leaves are used as plates and bamboo is cut to make cups and throw-away spoons. Bamboo tubes are also used to cook rice and to boil water on these occasions. The Burmese have about six significant religious festivals in a year. Added to these are many occasions for celebration, such as weddings, name-giving ceremonies, notitiation ceremonies and the feeding of monks, which can take place at any time of the year. On these occasions rice flavoured with coconut or butter is cooked and more main dishes and side dishes are added.

Although these ceremonies are mixed affairs, women tend to gather into groups. Invited guests sit around low, round tables and partake the food. No class distinctionn is observed and every guest eats the same food in the same way. This is especially true in villages where all members of the families are invited and are encouraged to eat their fill so that there shall be 'all quiet and no smoke on the kitchen front.'

Most of the ceremonies are undertaken bythe villages on a cooperative basis — the whole village footing the bill, that is. Neighbouring villages vie with each other as to which village can outfeed the other. The village which feeds the guests with 'pieces of pork as big as a knee cap' usually wins the day.

Private lunches and dinners do not differ much from community meals. If all the guests are men, the hostess does not join them. She will personally lead them to the dining table and once they have started their meal, she will leave them and stay at a distance from where she can keep a watchful eye on the table.

If a couple comes to dinner, then the hostess joins them to keep company. If children come with the couple, they are fed separately together with the host's own children.

It is not the custom of the Burmese to say prayers at meal times. Even at the festivals which are connected with religious activities, no prayers are said.

To belch or to make noise while enjoying the food is a breach of table manners. Spilling food on the table, leaving a large portion of food uneaten and picking one's nose or ear during meals are aslo considered as bad manners.

When the head of the family cannot immediately join the family at the table, it is customary to put a piece of choice meat or vegetable from the main dish on his plate as a token of respect. This custom is called *'co-cha-de'* in Burmese. Although general conversation at the table is permitted, superstitious people do not recount their dreams during meals. They fear that by so doing they will nullify the promise of joy.

The kitchen is regarded as the exclusive domain of the housewife and she prepares the meals for the family, sometimes with the help of her daughters, if she has any. Most Burmese husbands are not interested in cooking though there are exceptions. If both the husbands and wife are office workers she may have a maid to help her and the wife will supervise the culinary activities.

According to the traditional Burmese way of living, mother instructs her daughters how to cook and look after the home. It is therefore taken for granted that a woman knows how to cook, sew and provide creature comforts. That is the reason why very few books on cooking appeared in Burma before World War II. Those books also did not sell well because it was considered silly to learn cooking from a book. Times have changed. It is not economically possible to run a household on the income of the husband alone. Burmese women are no more home-bound and education among women has expanded. This has resulted in the employment of more women at offices and factories. Freed from the tutelage of their mothers, the modern Burmese girls neglect to learn the art of homemaking. When they marry, the duties and obligations of a housewife inevitably fall on them. Thousands of these newlyweds are now seeking information on how to run a house. This is one of the reasons why many books on cooking and home economics are coming out and are destined to be best sellers.

To recapitulate, the Burmese way of cooking and eating is a simple, convenient affair. As if to defend the plainness of Burmese cooking and homeliness of Burmese eating, the Burmese have a saying: 'It matters not if the meal is expensive or cheap; it matters most that the eater shall relish it. Then the meal is excellent.'

The Burmese eat to live rather than live to eat. This may be the reason why it is rare to find gourmets and gourmands among them. However, history has recorded an instance of a show of culinary skill and a royal gourmand.

About 400 years ago King Bayin Naung ruled Burma. One day the king entertained an envoy. Among many lavish dishes was a roasted chicken elaborately decorated. When the envoy carved it, he had the shock of his life because a sparrow flew out.

The gourmand was Narathihapate, a Burmese king who ruled the kingdom of Pagan about 900 years ago. He refused to eat his meals unless they consisted of 300 dishes. This meant a feast every day among his queens and courtiers. When the Mongols invaded Burma, he was forced to flee from the capital. During his exile his queens and servants desperately tried to fulfil their master's gastronomic desire but they could only manage to serve him 150 dishes. He wept.

Eating in Korea: Varied Dishes, Courteous Manners

Korea began its main exposure to Western culture — and began to be influenced thereby — only in the twentieth century, and particularly since 1950 the country and its culture have been undergoing rapid change. To show the somewhat liberal and modern pattern that is emerging in contrast to our older tradition, the meals and eating habits of Korea have also shown a strong movement toward Western culture in many cases, which the majority of Koreans recognize as a scientific way of living realistically. However, it is also true that our tradition of a few thousand years, with its own cultural values and reasonability, is well preserved in the people's minds, at times complementing and at times contradicting the Western way of life. The emerging patterns seem to present the Korean people with a kind of mental or cultural dissonance when they come up against such contradictions in daily life.

Actually, Korean life today shows a somewhat flexible and variable pattern according to the family, age, economic status, education, location, and other such factors. However, here an attempt has been made to treat the matter of Korean dietary ife from an extremely general and objective viewpoint.

Just as in many other lands, it is a firm tradition to have meals three times a day, normally breakfast around 8 o'clock in the morning, lunch around 1 o'clock in the afternoon, and dinner around 7 o'clock in the evening. Frequently there are also "coffee breaks" (consisting of tea, actually) between meals twice a day. There are, of course, exceptions in the case of such persons as gourmands or heavy manual labourers such as farmers, mine workers, or fishermen, who may have additional meals, perhaps consisting of a special menu. The young people of Korea, again as in many other lands, often pay close attention to Western trends in fashion, and they may diet rigorously when fashion dictates a slim figure.

Among the various traditional daily foods, boiled rice is perhaps the most representative staple food, accompanied by a variety of meats, vegetables, and eggs. *Kimchi* and other pickled or vinegared vegetables, heavily laced with hot, spicy peppers and the like, are also well known as traditional Korean foods. Among the other favourite staple foods are Korean noodles, buns with ground meat buried in their centre, and rice-cake soup. Soup-style food plays a major role in Korean dietary habits. Such soups are so necessary a part of the standard Korean meal that the formal combinations of dishes on our tables often take the form of "one soup and three other dishes," "two soups and five other dishes," "three soups and seven other dishes," or various other permutations of the same general pattern. Koreans generally season their foods or classify their tastes into four broad categories. The salty taste is provided by soy bean paste, salt, soy bean sauce, and the like. For a hot taste, we use red peppers, red pepper paste, black pepper, garlic, ginger, or green onions. Sweet foods are generally seasoned with sugar or honey, and the fourth category, encompassing other tastes, features use of a variety of flavouring agents such as sesame oil, salt, sesame powder, or bean oil.

For centuries, milk and dairy products were no more than curious foods for the common people, though they have become popular in recent years in the country's urban rather than rural areas. It is recorded, however, that milk was once one of the favourite beverages of one of the kings of Korea, so much so that he endowed milk to various of his relatives and nobles of the country.

On special occasions, or when special guests grace the home, many special foods may be served to provide some variety from the normal daily menu. The Koreans have a special, highly decorated table called the *kyo-ja-sang* for guests' use, and it bears a variety of special meat, egg, fish, or vegetable dishes. This may also be followed by other special courses, borrowing the table's name and being called "wine table," "noodle table," or "tea and fruit table".

The Koreans naturally have a wide range of tools and utensils for preparing and serving these foods, with specialized utensils for every purpose-boiling, frying, mixing and grinding, storage, and the like. Their materials also traditionally ran the gamut from stone, clay, bamboo, and wood to brass and iron. Recently, of course, we can see utensils and tools of plastic and stainless steel frequently being used in Korean kitchens, but it is still true that Koreans prize the traditional materials for their own particular advantages and esthetic values. Until recently, one of the most prized kitchen essentials was the clay jar, made from clay fired at high temperatures and used for the storage of fermented sauces or pastes.

As is well known, the use of chopsticks is one of the distinguishing characteristics of Korean meals, as are the small bowls used by the individual eaters. The chopsticks (the most popular and prized of which have traditionally been of silver) and spoons (again of silver in special cases) as well as the chinaware and metal utensils are frequently given artful decoration in the form of etched or drawn patterns or illustrations.

One note in passing on the fuel used in Korean cooking. The traditional fuels of wood, charcoal, dry leaves, and straw are being supplanted by oil, gas, coal, and electricity. The older fuels are still used, however, in many rural areas as well as in some urban regions, but in either case, the fuel system is characterized by the economical multiple use of the heat. It not only cooks the food, it is also channelled through pipes or channels beneath the floors to warm the floors and rooms as well.

The foundation has been set for preparation of the meal through descriptions of the foods, their seasonings, and the tools and utensils used. But who in fact makes the meals? Meals in Korea are principally prepared by the housewife, daughters, or daughter-in-law, but in the extended family system, more common in the past than today, other relatives may also lend a hand. Servants were also common in the past, and today as well some people hire housekeepers who can serve as cooks or assistants in the kitchen. (An interesting note in this age of "women's lib" is that some of the younger generation of Koreans complain about the tradition that the male members of the family are not qualified to cook). The location of the meal itself, as well as whether the family members eat together or not, depends greatly on the style of the house, whether traditional for modern. The traditional home does not have a separate dining room, so that the various rooms can be used for a variety of purposes. More precisely, the male family members principally have their meals together in the male quarters, with the female members gathering in the mother's room; in either case, the portable dining tables of Korean tradition are used. This pattern may be varied somewhat when special guests are present, but even then, it is an old custom that the male family members sit together only with the male guests, and the female members with the female guests.

In more modern homes, there is usually a specialized dining room where the family may gather as a whole. But even though such a place is available, the recent pace of life may still split up the family at mealtime. For example, we can see many cases where the housewife prepares a meal for those members who go out to work before she joins the remaining family members for a later breakfast. Students may take a lunch box to school and working adults usually buy lunch near their jobs. It is generally agreed, however, that it is desirable for the family to have dinner together.

Guests frequently join in meals. It is a traditional custom to invite relatives friends, or other guests to have dinner on the various ceremonial celebratory, or goodwill occasions, and such guests may also be invited to share breakfast or lunch as well. Today, there is also a growing trend toward going out with guests for a meal.

Korean manners during the meal are highly formalized. The following are some of the manners customarily observed. We have to express formal appreciation and thanks to the parents even at daily meals. As guests, we offer such thanks to the host.

Starting with the *Kimchi,* we try the rice, soup, and other dishes in turn. It is thought proper to eat rice and the other dishes alternatingly, and we must be careful not to have too many side dishes without eating rice.

Traditionally there is little or no conversation at Korean meals, and when children are present at the meal, we take care to see that they do not make too much noise. If there is some conversation, however, the speakers much avoid such topics as death or the sorrows of others, particularly at meals celebrating happy events.

The spoon is only for the rice and soup, and in the same way, the chopsticks are only to be used for the side dishes. It is also considered ill-mannered to hold the spoon and the chopsticks together.

Priority in picking up or putting down the spoon goes to the eldest male present or to the guest. In other words, other persons taking part in the meal may not begin or finish before the senior male or the guest. If necessary to wait during the meal, the spoon is placed in the rice bowl instead of being returned to the table.

It would be relevant to mention in conclusion that religion has indeed had influence on food and eating in Korea, with two different religions introducing varying factors. The two would be Buddhism and Confucianism, and while both have permeated the whole of Korean culture, the result in terms of the Korean dietary life has been a contrast between the two traditions. Buddhism, for example, produced a trend toward vegetarianism, and although pure vegetarianism is not extremely common today, the wide range of vegetables in a variety of styles of preparation found on Korean tables can be seen as a reflection of this religious influence. On the other hand, the effects of Confucianism can also be found in the eating of meat, as well as in the very ceremonial and courteous patterns in which Korean meals are conducted.

Food and Eating Habits of Mongolian People

Mongolian people like milk products in summer and autumn, while in winter and spring meat is preferred. Besides that, flour or rice is eaten quite a lot with milk and meat in all seasons of the year.

The food is mostly cooked over a fire, but sometimes steamed of fried. There are interesting methods of preparing meat by baking it over hot stones, called "khorkhog" and "Boodog". In olden times these dishes were usually prepared from the meat of wild animals, but now sheep and goat's meat are widely used. Mongols prefer beef and mutton, and horse-meat is not so popular. Within the last few years camel meat has been added to the menu. Fish and chicken are rarely eaten except by city people during the last few years. The meat is prepared by cutting up all the meat into joints, then into smaller pieces, and stewing them for a short time. There is an interesting kind of meat dish which is prepared from the internal organs of slaughtered cattle and wild animals. In addition, the hair and skin of the severed head and legs of cattle are burned, and tasty dishes are prepared from them. Beef, mutton and camel meat are dried in sun and wind and preserved for a long period, and they are called "Borts". *Tsagan-ide* (white food) is very popular in Mongolia. From milk many kinds of dishes are prepared. Fist of all, the milk is boiled and is stirred many times, and after cooling, the "*urum*" (the thick skin on boiled milk) is taken off. Further, the boiled milk is fermented and used to make yoghurt, *arts* (sour cottage cheese), and *aruul* (a dry curd sweet). A small quantity of yoghurt is poured into hot milk and fermented, and from this *byaslag* (cheese), *reezgi* (dry curds) and *eedem* (similar to cheese) are made. Mongols very much prefer *urum* and *aruul* among milk products. The people enjoy eating the above-mentioned products for lunch in summer and autumn.

During the lactation period of animals which lasts approximately 6 months, the Mongolians prepare and store dairy products for the winter. These are called "*hatuu ide*" (hard milk dishes) and can be served in a nomad's home all year round. Tea with milk is appreciated and loved by everybody, in any season of the year. If anyone visits a family, he is offered tea first. Tea is drunk at breakfast, lunch and dinner, and it is an essential part of the daily diet.

Over centuries of tea drinking in Mongolia, lots of brewing recipes have appeared, reflecting national distinctions, and influenced by the cattle-breeder's nomadic life and long standing traditions in cookery. Many Mongolians like flour tea, to which are added butter, milk and salt. This thick beverage is an nourishing as soup or porridge.

In summer and autumn seasons people love to drink *airag* fermented mare's milk. It is kept in bag made of cow's skin or in a wooden vessel. Besides drinking *airag* at home, many people are fond of drinking in the companionship of a group, chatting, playing and singing folk songs.

Pastries in China's Ancient Culture

The Chinese nation with its ancient culture of several thousand years also has rich and varied pastries.

China's pastries can be divided roughly into two categories: palace and popular pastries. The first category consists of foodstuffs for imperial palace nobles of past dynasties, though most of them were made by the ordinary people. The palace pastries were carefully made from high-quality materials, catering only to the emperor, ministers, and imperial concubines. Such pastries were required to be good in colour, flavour and taste, and to be novel in shape, and had to be constantly improved so that palace nobles could fully appreciate and enjoy them in their leisure time. Palace pastries included small steamed breads of sorghum, poria cakes, eight-treasure lotus-seed gruel, fried dough twists, "No. 1 scholar" cakes, polygonum flowers, and peach-shaped birthday cakes, just to mention a few.

Almost every kind of pastry has an accompanying folktale. Concerning the "No. 1 scholar" cake, for example, the popular legend states that, in the later years of the Ming and early years of the Qing Dynasties there was a pastry store in Kaifeng Prefecture of Henan Province, the proprietor of which, seeing many scholars coming to the city to take an examination, had sudden inspiration to make a sort of jujube paste cake bearing the words "No. 1 scholar". Instantly, he had a booming business, and "No. 1 scholar" cakes were later brought into the palace and appreciated by the emperor, thus becoming listed as delicacies of the palace.

The small steamed bread of sorghum and poria cake, too, has interesting stories about them. It is said that when the allied forces of the eight powers invaded and occupied Beijing, Empress Dowager Ci Xi fled in panic. Only half way to their destination, she became extremely hungry. Just then, she came across a peasant family which gave her a steamed bread made of sorghum chaff. Being so hungry, she felt it tasted delicious and, after returning to Beijing, she ordered the imperial kitchen staff to make such steamed bread for her. Considering that Ci Xi's taste was quite different when she was fleeing for life, the imperial kitchen cooks refined the sorghum and soya bean flour and added to these white sugar and osmanthus, making small steamed breads of sorghum which tasted delicious and looked very nice and unique as well.

It was also said that when Ci Xi fell ill, she lost all desire for food. In order to whet her appetite, the cooks carefully baked different patterns of poria cakes as thin as white paper, made from specially selected raw materials such as poria starch, pine and walnut seeds, and honey and osmanthus. The poria cakes, sweet and crisp and looking very nice, were enjoyed by Ci Xi very much. Such pastries have been handed down since then as palace foodstuffs.

There is a wide variety of popular pastries in China, their tastes unique and their names delightful. In the north alone, there are fried dough cakes, slice dough cakes, *ludagun* (snowball cakes), oil parched flour, dumpling soup, fried dough drops. Different localities and ethnic groups have their own kinds of pastries with special characteristics, too numerous, indeed, to mention.

There are also many popular pastries linked to different seasons and festivals in China. The Han people, for example, eat dumplings on the occasion of Spring Festival, *yuanxiao* (a kind of dumpling) during Lantern Festival on the 15th day of the first lunar month, *zongzi* (a pyramid-shaped dumpling made of glutinous rice wrapped in bamboo or reed leaves) during the Dragon Boat Festival on the fifth day of the fifth lunar month, moon cakes during Autumn Festival on the 15th day of the eighth lunar month, cakes on the ninth day of the ninth lunar month, *laba* porridge (rice porridge with nuts and dried fruit) on the eighth day of the twelfth lunar month. Each festival and each kind of foodstuff carries with it an interesting and moving story. A few examples are as follows.

Zongzi

For the Dragon Boat Festival on the fifth day of the fifth lunar month in China, every household on the south and north banks of the Changjiang River will take *zongzi*. *Zongzi* is made from glutinous rice and fillings mixed with sweetened bean paste, dates, sugar, ham, bacon, meat, and green broad beans. After *zongzi* is cooked, it can be eaten either hot or cold. It is delicious because the glutinous rice is permeated with the scent of reed or bamboo leaves.

Why do people of every household in China eat *zongzi* during the Dragon Boat Festival? They do so in commemoration of Qu Yuan, a great patriotic poet of China.

During the Warring States Period (475-221 BC), Qu Yuan was a minister of King Huai of Chu. Because the senior officials at the time spoke ill of him before King Huai, the King sent Qu Yuan into exile. Qu Yuan, who cherished high ambitions, despaired and drowned himself in the Miluo River because his patriotic propositions could not be realized. The day of his death fell exactly on the fifth day of the fifth lunar month. In order to commemorate this great patriotic poet, the people of Chu sailed boats, bringing with them food, and paddled the boats to midstream of the Miluo River where they threw in their food as offerings to Qu Yuan on the day.

One or two years after this ritual began, people suddenly saw in their dreams Qu Yuan wearing a high hat, a long sword by his waist, and some pearls and jade on his jacket. Everybody was elated and saluted him. Smiling, Qu Yuan came forward and said: "Folks, thank you very much for your kindness. Yours deeds show that the people of Chu are patriotic." Seeing that Qu Yuan looked emaciated, people asked him, "Minister Qu! Have you received all the rice we gave you?" "thank you for your kindness," Qu Yuan said gratefully, then heaving a deep sigh, "All the rice you gave me has been eaten by the fish, shrimps, tortoises, and clams." Everybody was indignant and said, "They shouldn't have eaten it. It's what we had specially prepared for you!"

Qu Yuan smiled wryly and said, "There are too many aquatic animals there!" Then everybody asked. "How can we prevent them from eating it?"

Qu Yuan replied, "If the rice is wrapped in bamboo leaves and made into a pyramid-shaped dumpling, the aquatic animals won't eat it, for they will think it is a water caltrop."

On the fifth day of the fifth lunar month in the ensuing year, people made the pyramid-shaped dumplings the way Qu Yuan had instructed them to and threw them into the river. However, on the second day, Qu Yuan appeared in people's dreams again, saying. "Thank you for your rice. I have had a lot; but still a great deal has been eaten by the aquatic animals!" Everybody questioned closely, "How can this be avoided?" Qu Yuan replied, "there is a way. When you deliver the rice by boat, you can make the boat look like a dragon, for all the aquatic animals are under the sway of the Dragon King (the God of Rain in Chinese mythology). When they see that the rice is sent by the Dragon King, they dare not eat it." Thus the custom of eating *zongzi* and paddling the dragon boats came into existence in the fifth day of the fifth lunar month every year. On that day, members of a family sit together to sample the delicious *zongzi*, talking about the great patriotic poet Qu Yuan.

Moon cakes in mid-autumn

The Mid-Autumn Festival falls on the 15th day of the eighth lunar month when the moon is at its fullest during the whole year. According to history, in ancient times emperors used to offer sacrifices to the sun in spring and to the moon in autumn. The eighth lunar month is middle month of autumn while the 15th day is in the middle of the eighth lunar month. Hence it has been chosen as the best day for worshipping the moon, and has become known as the Mid-Autumn Festival. It also symbolizes the hopes of the people for a good harvest after a year's hard work. Thus it has become a popular holiday of the working people.

The custom of eating moon cakes, dating back more than a thousand years, is observed throughout north and south China. It is always celebrated at night. People climb to the top of tall buildings or hills to watch the full moon. Traditionally they laid out a feast and good wine. When the full moon began to rise, they placed moon cakes, fruits and boiled green beans on a table as offerings. Then they lit sandalwood incense and candles and worshipped the moon. Because the full moon and moon cakes are both round, they symbolize wholeness or completeness, giving rise to another name for this occasion- "Family Reunion Festival." Family members love to sit together and eat moon cakes while enjoying the bright moon. There is a large variety of moon cakes. However, the methods of making them are more or less the same. The small round baked cakes of flour have different kinds of fillings. Sweet moon cakes have such fillings as jujube paste, sweetened bean paste, shredded coconut, and mixture of sugar, almonds, peanuts and candied fruit. Salty fillings are made of harm, salted pork, salted duck eggs, dried meat floss, etc. Moon cakes generally fall into two categories - northern and southern. The moon cakes made in the north have thicker and harder flour wrappings with different kinds of prints of carved patterns on them. Those made in the south do not have such intricate prints. Instead they are only marked with the names of the fillings. But they all taste good.

For centuries many tales about the Mid-Autumn Festival and the moon have added colour and poetry to the festival. One of these, the fable "Chang E Flies to the Moon," is the best known. It was said that when Hou Yi, the warrior, obtained some herbs from a celestial being which would ensure immortality, his wife Chang E stole them, and after eating them, became as light as a swallow and flew to the moon.

Today the superstition is gone but the festive activities of celebration, family reunion and enjoying the moon continue.

Laba porridge

On the eighth day of the twelfth lunar month, people will prepare gruel, or *laba* porridge, which they sometimes present to their neighbours or friends as a gift. They use either coarse or fine materials for the gruel, depending on what local products are available and what their family economic condition is like. Those who use coarse materials for the gruel might mix food grain other than wheat or rice with sundry beans. It is easy to cook and the gruel tastes delicious. Those who cook their porridge with finer materials use, besides sundry beans and, coarse food lotus seeds, water chestnuts, the seeds of job's tears, dates, chestnuts, green plums, raisins, dry longan pulps, sugared cherries, almonds, hazelnuts, pine nuts, walnuts, melon seeds, and peanuts.

Why does every family eat laba porridge on the eighth day of the twelfth lunar month? A popular legend relates that once upon a time there was an old couple who worked hard and lived frugally year-round. Their big and small grain bins were always full to the brim. However, their son grew gluttonous and lazy and married a girl as lazy as himself. Before long, they vexed the old couple to death. They became lazier than before, only eating and squandering money. After they had consumed all the food grain, they sold their land and then their house until, by the time winter came, they had consumed and sold everything at hand. On the eighth day of the twelfth lunar month, the young couple in desperation scraped together what was left in their grain bins and cooked half a pot of gruel; but before they could eat it, they had already starved to death in the corner of the house. To learn a lesson from the experience of this family, older people of every household cook the gruel called laba porridge on the eighth day of the twelfth lunar month. When serving this porridge, the elderly usually tell their children and grandchildren the above story, admonishing them to work hard, live frugally, and never be gluttonous or lazy.

People also eat laba porridge in order to commemorate the national hero Yue Fei. As the story goes, Yue Fei resisted the Jin troops and camped in the town of Zhuxian in Henan Province. The treacherous minister Qin Hui made a false charge against Yie Fei and slandered him before Emperor Gao Zong who summarily called Yie Fei back to Beijing. Feeling reluctant to lose Yie Fei, the town folks presented him and his troops with food-rice and porridge. In tears, General Yue Fei and his troops bid farewell to the folks on the eight day of the 12th lunar month. Later, when the common people heard that Yue Fei had been killed, they cooked gruel to eat on the eighth day of the 12th lunar month in memory of him, and this has become a custom throughout China.

In short, eating Laba porridge is a traditional custom among the people. Formerly in Beijing, such porridge was cooked by the people, as well as by various large temples such as the Bailin, Songzhu, and Baiyun temples, and was offered to rich alms givers. In each bowl of porridge was planted a small yellow paper banner bearing such words as "presented by Bailin Temple." Receiving the rice porridge, the alms givers would give silver in return. In the Qing Dynasty (1644-1911), The Lama Temple of Peace and Harmony, a famous lamasery in Beijing, would hold a grand ceremony on the eighth day of the 12th lunar month every year to make the occasion. The huge bronze pot - 2 metres in diameter, 1.5 metres in depth and 8 tons in weight - used to cook rice porridge at that time is still on display today in the courtyard of the Lama Temple of Peace and Harmony.

Laba porridge was also called "Five-Flavoured Rice Porridge," "Seven-Treasure Rice Porridge" and "Eight-Treasure Rice Porridge." According to Records on the Tour of Beijing, the rice porridge with the most varieties was considered the best. People who cared about food would skilfully make red dates and kernels into small animals and legendary Eight Immortals and put them in the bowl. This not only made the rice porridge more colourful, delicious, tasteful, and nice-looking but also added joy to the festival.

Because the way of making rice porridge differs from place to place, porridge cooked in the north tastes sweet and that in the south tastes salty. Northerners like to have sweet rice porridge cooked with glutinous rice, red beans, candied dates, lotus seeds, longans, walnuts, soybeans, and pine nuts, whereas southerners like to have rice porridge cooked with rice, pea-nuts, broad beans, taro, water chestnut, chestnut, gingko, green vegetables, and meat cubes. Whether it tastes sweet or salty, it is helpful to one's health if one or two bowls is eaten each day in the morning of the depth of winter. Laba porridge, cooked with various kinds of dried fruits and cereals, is nutritious, contains a lot of protein, fat, and various kinds of vitamins, and has the effect of relieving uneasiness of mind, enriching the blood, invigorating the function of the spleen, and providing vital energy.

Foreign Confectionery Transformed into Japanese Treats

Historical Development

Japanese confectionery (*kashi*, or *okashi*) has developed in the climatic and cultural environment of Japan. Although the origin of all such items can be traced to foreign countries, once imported they were transformed into something new and absorbed into the Japanese milieu. Nowadays the Japanese treat confectionery as a supplemental luxury in their diet, while their prehistoric Jomon era (until 300 BC) ancestors, being hunters and gatherers, must have made no distinction between staple foods and snacks, simply eating hunted or gathered food as they acquired it. Delicious fruits, however, may have been treated as luxury food items in that time and lifestyle.

Looking at the historical development of Japanese confectionery, we can note (1) early when fruit served as confectionery; (2) Nara (AD 710-794) and Heian (794-1192) Periods, when the rice cake (*mochi*) and Chinese pastry (*kara-Kashi*) were imported; (3) Kamakura (1192-1333) and Muromachi (1392-1573) Periods, when the Chinese sweets *tenshin* (in Japanese) came to Japan with other aspects of the So-Gen [Sung (960-1125) and Yuan (1271-1368)] culture; (4) Azuchi-Momoyama Period (1568-1598) when confectionery of Spain and Portugal reached Japan; (5) Edo

Culinary Traditions and Cuisine

Asian people enjoy sharing food with their neighbours and kinfolk at home, at ceremonial occasions and at the market places. Asian food has a rich variety in its spices, seasoning and the way of cooking from place to place.

1. *Lunch cooked 'on the spot' for farmers in Bali, Indonesia.*
2. *The small Aka tribe in Thailand dining.*
3. *The washing of the hands before eating.*
4. *Family dinner in a modern home in India.*
5. Shin-son-ro, *special Korean menu for guests in ancient times.*

Marriage Customs

Wedding processions are still popular in many Asian countries. The new couple becomes a unit of the society by sharing their joy with other people.

ঙ

1

2 3

ঙ

1. *Wedding procession in Bali, Indonesia.*
2,3. *Wedding processions in India.*

Marriage Customs

4. *A newly-wed Philippine couple.*
5. *A Japanese bride and bridegroom.*
6. *A Hindu bride and bridegroom, India.*
7. *A Korean bride and bridegroom in traditional dress.*

Hair Styles

The curtain rises
it's the beginning of new life
entering the realm of love.
The longing that filled my heart
shines in the blackness of my hair
the world is me and I'm the world.
Let us be the light of the world.

1

2

3

Elaborately coiffured hair at:
1. *A Korean wedding;*
2. *Indian marriage;*
3. *Indonesian wedding.*

Period (1600-1867), when processes for making both high-grade and less refined confectionery were perfected and both supply and demand increased; (6) Meiji Period (1868-1912), when more Western pastries and candies entered Japan with the opening of the country to foreign intercourse; and (7) the present era of mass production.

Kara-kashi (or *kara* "fruit"), made of wheat flour or rice flour fried in oil, was the first man-made confectionery in Japan, and it appeared in many delightful shapes, such as a branch of the peach or plum tree, insects, spheres, and fine strings. The Japanese, generally adept at handicrafts, take pleasure in not only the taste but also the configuration, and this tendency is still seen in present-day *kashi*. The custom of offering *buto*, a kind of *kara-kashi*, at shrines is still practised, although the process of frying in oil, apparently not suiting the Japanese taste, has been replaced by a steaming preparation.

From the end of the Kamakura Period through the Muromachi Period, the custom of having tea, buns, and other snacks (*tenshin*) entered Japan along with the Zen sect and other aspects of the So-Gen culture. Instead of the pork or jellied mutton used as filling in China for the small cakes, the Japanese version (known as *manju*) contains sweetened *azuki an* (red bean paste). Whether this bun underwent the change in content (from meat to bean) in the Zen temples of China or after reaching Japan has not been determined. This Chinese bun appears to have arrived at about the same time as what in Japan became *rakugan* (candies made of wheat flour and powdered sugar), which originated with the Uyghur at the western end of the Silk Road, reached Japan.

The arrival from Spain and Portugal of what is known in Japan as *nanban-kashi* at the end of the fifteenth century delivered a shock to Japanese confectionery, for this pastry, baked and containing sugar, differed greatly from the fried and boiled cakes known at that time. *Nanban-kashi* such as *kastera* (custard), boro, and konpeito (candies) were then transformed and refined, even during the period of national isolation (Edo Period) which followed.

The Edo period saw Japanese confectioners becoming proficient in and improving upon techniques of making the imported rice cakes and *kara-kashi*, *tenshin* snacks, and *nanban-kashi*. Japanese confectionery by the beginning of the nineteenth century had been fully developed. Up until that time Kyoto had been the centre of this activity, but in the nineteenth century Edo (now called Tokyo) confectioners displayed increased skills. Production of *senbei* (cookies made of rice flour and soy sauce), *okashi* (sweet cookies), candies and other inexpensive snacks flourished, and confectionery consumption spread throughout the general populace. The history of Kyoto confectionery, known as *Kyogashi* ("capital confectionery"), the most highly refined in Japan can be called the history of Japanese confectionery. There are both geographical and historical/cultural reasons for the unparalleled development of these foods in Kyoto. Among geographical factors were (1) the abundance of good, fresh ingredients from the farming villages surrounding the city; (2) being the capital city, all news and developments from around Japan and abroad reached Kyoto; and (3) as centre of transportation and supply routes, Kyoto accumulated products arriving from all points, Japanese and foreign. Cultural factors included (1) activities centering around palace functions and the customs of the nobility and public figures; (2) with historic Shinto shrines and main temples of the Buddhist sects located in Kyoto, numerous important ceremonies took place; (3) as centre of the tea ceremony tradition (*sado*), study and development of confectionery for service with tea was carried out; and (4) in Kyoto, a famed tourist spot with many famous historical attractions and tea shops situated in front of shrine and temple gates, much *kashi* was produced for consumption.

Forming an important part of traditional culture, Japanese snacks developed into refined products through use of indigenous materials and a wide variety of techniques. Beginning with the Chinese confectionery and continuing to develop through the influx, in turn, of a number of different cultural influences and refined processes, the variety of confectionery resulting in Japan seems to have attained an incomparable degree. Added to this are the forms and associations drawn from the structural arts, songs, and literature of Japan which became attached to these edible items.

Japanese confectionery is thought of as a synthetic art, related to all of the five senses. Each item must be pleasing to the eye as well as to the taste. The sense of touch is considered, as first the hand and then the tongue experience the texture, and the aromatic qualities of *azuki*, cinnamon, ginger, etc. are a delight to the sense of smell. Then, hearing the name of the items brings to mind their seasonal and literary associations. The *Kyogashi* tradition includes crafted, decorated confectionery. In the past, court nobles and feudal lords expressed their aesthetic consciousness by including in their banquets snacks in natural shapes such as birds, flowers, clouds, and the moon.

The confectioner himself needs to be familiar with Japanese traditions including tea ceremony, flower arrangement, songs, poetry, and classical literature to be able to devise new *kashi* and then give them attractive, fitting names.

Kashi for annual events and festivals

With four clearly defined seasons and their related events, *kashi* for the respective seasons has developed. The year begins with the new year *mochi* (rice cake) and the custom of celebrating the new year wishing longevity and health by eating decorated *mochi* and *zoni* (*mochi* boiled together with vegetables). At the Imperial palace, *mochi* of red and white colours made in thin layers are put together, served together with a lobster, an orange, ferns and dried persimmon. Most people use simple decoration, and place *mochi* in household shrines and Buddhist alters, tokonoma (special alcoves), storage areas, and even toilet rooms, and farm families present *mochi* to farm tool and field gods. In some areas, small *mochi* are affixed to tree branches and flower-shaped *mochi* signify prayers for a rich harvest.

Zoni ingredients vary from region to region, and the shape of *mochi* boiled in *zoni* dishes likewise varies, although eastern Japan generally uses square *mochi* and western Japan round *mochi*. The broth may be *miso* (fermented bean paste) flavour or clear. The tradition of *zoni* is of relatively recent origin, dating from when the use of the iron pot became wide-spread. Baking *mochi* with sweets sandwiched between layers on the first day of the year is an old custom still practised in all parts of Japan. *Mochi* containing *miso* candy of burdock has been part of the royal family's new year fare, and the *hishihanabira* (diamond-shaped flower) *mochi* , also known as *tsutsumi zoni*, is still used in the Imperial Palace on New Years' day. On the fifteenth day of the year throughout Japan, bonfires called *tondo* (or sagicho) are made to burn decorations used in the New Year festivities, and *mochi* are baked over these fires by children and adults alike.

On the third day of 9 February (Setsubun), roasted beans are spread in doorways, etc. to ward off evil spirits, and beans numbering the same as the individual's age are eaten as longevity is wished for.

The third day of the third month (3 March) is the annual Girls' Day. When *hina ningyo* (dolls) are decorated, and *hishi* (diamond-shaped) *mochi, hina arare* (crispy rice cookie), and *kusa* (mugwort) *mochi* are served. *Hishi mochi* is normally in layers of brown, white, and green, but in the Palace fifty layers each of white and green are combined and placed together with peach blossoms and willow twigs wrapped in paper and a ribbon to form a gorgeous display. The birth of Buddha is celebrated at temples on 8 April, when *amacha* (sweet green tea) is poured over Buddha figures, and puffed brown rice *mochi* and beans are eaten as nasal mucus of the Buddha.

The fifth day of the fifth month (5 May), the annual Boy's Day, is celebrated by decorating *samurai* dolls, and wrapping *mochi* in leaves of mountain bamboo and oak (*samagi and kashiwa mochi,* respectively). In the Palace, an elaborate display of one hundred bunches of wrapped iris and mugwort leaves is put together.

O-bon, the mid-summer celebration, includes making *azuki dango* (rice dough and red bean dumplings), and farm families make *azuki mochi* after their work is through. *Tsukimi* (moon-viewing) dango is made for *chushu no meigestu* (harvest moon), and pampas grass is used as decoration. *Mochi* and *ohagi* (rice dumpling covered with bean paste) are offered to ancestors' spirits at both Spring and Autumn equinox.

Kashi is included in offerings of food placed in front of shrines. In Kyoto and Nara, traditional offerings often include *buto* (a kind of *kara-kashi*), the size and shape of which varies at different shrines, indicating the respective shrine's historical antiquity. *Zoni* at shrines in Kyoto is boiled over fire taken from shrine bonfires, and large shrine and temple events have individual *kashi* piled high one atop another. Worshippers coming to shrines and temples often bring *kashi* bearing their family seals (*kamon*), and confectioners make special *kashi* for specific temple or shrine events. The respective special day may be once yearly, on the first and fifteenth days of each month, or the twenty-first day of each month (the saint Kobo Daishi's death anniversary is commemorated each month) and the day before and after (twentieth and twenty-second).

Kashi in everyday life

Japanese confectionery plays a role in the lives of the Japanese from birth of death. *Mochi* is made on the seventh day following the birth of a child, and the child on his first birth anniversary is given *mochi* to carry on his back, often tied to the back by string, in wishing for healthy growth. The holiday *Shichigosan* ("seven-five-three", for children of those ages) includes *chitose ame* ("thousand year candy"). On joyous and mournful occasions, upon entering school, graduation, entering into employment, building a new house, and other events of personal life, *kashi* expresses feelings.

Japanese confectionery is also vital as a gift item. Noting the large number of orders for gift *kashi* in records of the Imperial Palace during the Edo Period, it also appears that gifts of *kashi* for *chugen* and *seibo* (summer and winter gift-giving traditions) are responsible for high sales of confectionery these days. Taking gifts of *kashi* when visiting others is a common custom among Japanese, and buying souvenir snacks from other regions when travelling is also widely done.

The realm of *sado* (tea ceremony) is one in which congenial, refined human relations are fostered, and the formalization of the tea ceremony has brought host and guest together with the hanging scroll painting, flowers and vases, tea cups and utensils, and the tea room and garden, with *kashi* playing an important role. The *kashi* here is a combination of the host's planning and the confectioner's skill, and the confectioner may even prepare the *kashi* in the preparation area of the tea room, as in the case of the *kinton* (sweetened chestnut) *kashi*. Such interaction between host, guests, and confectioner also gives birth to new confectionery forms and techniques. Comparison of tea ceremony records of the Azuchi-Momoyama Period and the Edo Period reveals that in the former era coarser materials such as *kaya* (a kind of grass) and *kuri* (plain chestnut) were used, while during the latter period *kashi* much like those in use today were popular. The design and making of Japanese confectionery, featuring refined simplicity rather than richness, is in line with the spirit of *sado* and the dominant Japanese aesthetic concepts of *wabi* and *sabi*.

In addition to fancy high-class *kashi* there is *dagashi* (cheap confectionery) which, although finely shaped, has less refined flavour and goes well with everyday foods and coarser tea, and has therefore become endeared of the public. *Senbei* (rice cookie), candy, *karinto* (fried dough cake), bean cake, and others appear in numerous variations across Japan.

Current trends

The influx of Western confectionery in the Meiji Period gave a shock to Japanese confectioners, and there were those who studied the imported snacks and changed over completely to production of Western confectionery, while others experimented with using Japanese materials in a Western manner — the use of gelatin made from soya bean, for example. It took some time, also, for Japanese consumers to grow accustomed to the smell of butter, after which their like for Western snacks gradually increased through the Taisho (1912-1926) and Showa (present) Periods. Mass production of chocolate, caramel, and biscuits began at the end of the Meiji Period and, from the beginning of Showa, the use of automatic wrapping and packaging method progressed.

Following the end of World War II, the Westernization of Japan increased greatly. The Christmas cake is now a part of year-end customs, and in urban areas recently the popularity of Valentine's Day chocolate gifts has become apparent. Although *wagashi* (traditional Japanese confectionery) is not considered inferior in any way to *yogashi* (Western style confectionery), *yogashi* can normally be purchased more readily, without placing orders, than can *wagashi.*

Mutual influence between *wagashi* and *yogashi* is evident at present, as shapes such as flowers used in traditional Japanese confectionery are being used with imported *yogashi,* and new *wagashi* using Western baking methods are emerging.

The history of Japanese confectionery reveals many instances of imported foreign items being converted into something Japanese. In the one hundred years since the beginning of the Meiji Period, this tendency continues, as confectionery of the present undergoes further transformation.

India: Giving Back to Nature What Nature has Given

Through religions ranging from the most primitive to the most sophisticated, man has through the ages sought to communicate with the unknown Supreme powers that control his destiny. Man's dependence on man, on nature, and on the cosmos are expressed in diverse ways by the multi-lingual, multi-racial, and multi-religious population of the vast sub-continent of India.

What prompted man to turn to certain rituals expressed in various forms is a matter of great interest; in this brief survey, however, we shall focus on offerings made in the form of food. Why food offerings? Let us consider man living on this planet many centuries ago. His fear of the elements, of the power hidden from him but constantly felt, prompted him to share first with the elements whatever he was able to collect for himself - fruits, berries, or products of the hunt. Even today in many parts of the world people place food below a tree, at a road crossing, or at the family shrine. This act today is a continuation of the first man's expression, appeasing the unknown.

Along with the rural, semi-urban, and urban population there exists a large number of tribes in India with their own rituals and ceremonies. The tribal and rural population of India is culturally very rich in crafts and performing arts and, living close to nature, their joys and sorrows are expressed in the ritual connected with day-to-day life. Their offerings and rituals are very elaborate and, even though some of the tribes have been converted to Christianity or Islam, their religious ceremonies retain the flavour of their original faiths.

The Gonds, numbering more than two million, dwell mostly in the central part of India. Their festivals are connected with agriculture, though the method of celebration varies from tribe to tribe. Some of the festivals celebrated are the millet festival, *ma ahua* flower festival, and mango festival. Dancing, singing, feasting, and the drinking of *ma ahua* and rice beer is followed by the ceremony in which sacrificial offerings of pigs and fowl are made.

The Todas residing in the Nilgiris of southern India are not a large tribe numerically, but this tribe is believed to be one of the most ancient, with a long and rich cultural tradition. Their livelihood depends largely on the rearing of buffaloes. The community dairy is like a temple, and the sacrifice of buffaloes for the peace of the soul of the dead forms part of the offerings made in ancestor worship. This is done a few days after the funeral. When crops are assailed by pests, some tribes offer animal sacrifice. Generally each farming household beheads a cock and mixes its blood with margosa leaves, sprinkling this mixture in the fields. Sometimes the cock is not sacrificed, but a special ritual food consisting of boiled rice and margosa leaves is sprinkled in the fields with the belief that this special food will appease the deity and the pests will be averted.

The Baigas of Madhya Pradesh celebrate a festival known as Ras Nawa. On the festival day they go to the forest to collect honey. On their return the shamans or witch doctors prepare millet in gourds and, when it is ready, honey is poured into the vessels, after which this preparation is distributed to people attending the ceremony.

The Khasis of Meghalaya break an egg before undertaking anything of importance. This is also done to propitiate spirits, and in worship of the god of state, god of water, and the god of wealth.

Similarly, each of the numerous tribes have their own special offerings made at special ceremonies.

In ancestor worship, whole meal is cooked and offered in memory of the departed soul. In the dark fortnight of the lunar month between September and October, special foods are offered for ancestors, while according to family customs, food and clothing is given to priests. In this *Sraddha* (ancestor worship) ceremony of the deceased, sixteen items (*sodasa dana*) are offered. Betul leaf is one of the essential items offered together with food, water, *asana* (seat), gold, and silver. A variety of local beliefs are found in ancestor worship, although the offerings are generally made in memory of the departed and for the peace of the soul.

Betul leaf is offered in ceremonies welcoming gods and goddesses, religious gurus, priests, and, in some households, bride and groom. The bride is welcomed with sandalwood paste, white mustard seeds, curds, and betul leaf and nut.

In all Hindu ceremonies, the *yagna* is performed to sanctify or purify any ceremony, whether it be marriage, entry into a new house, propitiation of certain gods and goddesses for wealth or good harvest, or the beginning of student life. The holy fire is offered with *ghee* (clarified butter), vermilion, incense, rice, etc.

The principal rites which are observed in the *yagna* are performed in the great hall of the temple. Two ritual sites are established and a three-tiered platform is constructed. The offerings of leaves and flowers are placed. To the north and west of this area in the sacrificial area (*yagna sala*) a small circular pit is dug in which the sacred fire (*yagna-agni*) is kept. Into this fire the various offerings are poured — mild curd, *ghee*, honey, coconut, etc. While performing *yagna* for purifying or sanctifying, or certain ceremonies and rituals pertaining to the life cycle of man, special *mantras* are chanted for different rituals, with the offering made at specific points in the chant. All this is done in a codified manner where the priest sits facing certain directions, using certain hand gestures and position of fingers in holding the object to be offered. It is believed that the performance of these *yagnas* aids in removing evil forces and pollutants, and purifies the surroundings. Tree worship is an ancient practice in many parts of the world. In India various types of trees and plants are worshipped, some having medicinal value life *tulsi* (basil), some representing gods and goddesses (*bel* symbolising Shiva, plantain representing Lakshmi, etc.) and other mythological trees like *kalpataru* — the 'wishing tree' which fulfils the desires of the worshippers. Sun protects life, and Hindu women worship it on the 11th day following a child's birth. On this day, water is sprinkled towards the sun and sweetmeats are offered to it. A specially cooked porridge of wheat and millet is also served.

Apart from this, there is a whole series of food offerings known as *prasadam*, such as cooked food, fruits, betul leaves or nuts, or coconut. After being sanctified before a certain deity in rituals, ceremonies, and festivals or in temples or other places of worship, they are then distributed among the devotees.

Most common among the cooked foods are combinations of *ghee*, flour (of wheat, gram, etc.), sugar, milk, rice, sugarcane juice, and other ingredients.

In Rajasthan, Gujarat, and Madhya Pradesh, in the worship of the god Bheroo special sweets are cooked and offered in worship before being distributed to the devotees. One of these is *ladoo*. Gram flour is cooked in *ghee* over a slow fire and grated coconut is added while continuously stirring, after which sugar and ground cardamom is added. This mixture is allowed to cool, and round balls are made which are offered in worship and then served.

In the worship of Shitla Mata, goddess of the pox, several food items are offered. Porridge is made from jaggery and wheat, and round fried balls made of gram and wheat flour dough are also served.

The *kheer*, rice cooked in milk in which sugar, cardamom, and nuts are added is an item offered and served in all parts of the country. It is somewhat similar to the rice pudding known all over the world.

Bati, another simple dish, consists of round balls made of dough with salt and *ghee* kneaded into them. These are baked over an open fire before serving. Honey, curds, *ghee*, and *tulsi* (basil) leaf are mixed in a base of uncooked fresh milk and offered for worship, and after the prayer ceremony this liquid is distributed among the devotees. This is known as *panchamrit*, i.e. having five ingredients.

A very commonly offered *prasadam* is made of wheat flour slowly cooked in *ghee* with sugar syrup added while stirring. This semi-solid mixture known as *halwa* is also served to devotees in Sikh temples or gurudwaras, and in homes after any religious or social ceremony.

The offering is a token of what man has received from nature, and the offering blessed, returned, and shared is in remembrance of the bounty of nature.

The Vedic commentator Sayanacharya mentions that food offering left over after the completion of a sacrificial rite is praise-worthy because it is symbolic of Brahma — the source of the universe. *"Yajne, hutasishtasya, odanasya sarvajagatkaranabhuta Brahmadbedena stutih kriyate."*

Nepal: Yomari, Symbol of Social Ties

Cakes in the Newar Community

The Himalayan kingdom of Nepal has always been the meeting ground of peoples and their cultures migrating from different directions. The confluence of the Buddhist and Hindu cultures and religions has given the Nepali culture its unique character. The Newar people, believed to be the original settlers of the Kathmandu valley, possess a very rich cultural tradition, and their food culture also displays this unique feature of the Nepali culture, the co-existence of the Buddhist and Hindu elements. In the Newar communities, sweet and delicious cakes are enjoyed together with tea and home-brewed alcoholic beverages - *alia, ton,* etc. - with friends and families in formal and informal gatherings. The cakes, beautifully made, serve to cheer and relax each member of the community. Apart from providing delight in everyday life, cakes also occupy an important place in Newar rituals, festivals, and religious occasions. Cakes tend to heighten the joys of occasions such as childbirth, initiation, marriage, annual events, and other family and community festivals. Specially prepared cakes are also offered to gods and goddesses in special religious worship.

From among various types of cakes and confectionery, we have chosen one special type of cake — *yomari* — for discussion in this article, for its use reflects unique socio-cultural features of the Newar people.

Yomari

Ingredients and shape : the basic ingredients of yomari are chamalkopitho (rice flour), chaku (brown sugar), and til (sesame seed). Cooked by the process of steaming, it is actually a lump of steamed rice flour dough of neutral colour prepared with solidified sugar and sesame seeds inside. Meat, kalodal, and mugidal (paste of black and green lentil), kurauni (condensed milk), and other things are also stuffed inside for the sake of variety. A special cake known as lonchamari, oval-shaped and without stuffing, is also baked whenever yomari is prepared. (In the Newali language mari is a generic term which refers to all types of sweets and cakes.)

Yomari festivals and rituals: *Yomari* is prepared and served on the day of *yomari punhi* — the *yomari* full-moon night — which is observed in the month of Marga (around the last week of December). The festival itself is named after the *yomari* cake. On that occasion, the Newars worship Laxmi, the goddess of wealth, by making an offering of *yomari* cake, showing gratitude to the goddess for the good harvest of the year. Such worship is performed so that the family may never run out of grain-stock. As soon as the new harvest is stored, *yomari* cakes are prepared and offered, placed for four days on top of the paramedical heap of fresh paddy grains stored in granaries. This is also known as *kunpuja,* the worship of granary. Small figurines of deities such as Laxmi, Ganesh (god of good fortune), and Bhimsen (god of strength and valour and known as god of wealth among the Newars), as well as those of animals, beasts, fowls, and objects related to these deities in some way — elephants, horses, fowls of various kinds, cats, rats, pomegranate and walnuts, a rice-husking mortar and pestle — are placed alongside the *yomari.* Two female and male guards flanking the entire retinue, are also placed there. During the four-day period the granary must not be opened, and women should not see or touch the *yomari* or the granary. This last practice, however, is not strictly observed in Newar towns outside Kathmandu.

It is generally believed that by this worship the paddy grain stored in the granary will increase in quantity. This tradition originated with Newars engaged in agriculture *(jyapus),* with other Newars later adopting it. In recent times, urban Newars have begun putting *yomari* in wealth bags and cash boxes. On the morning of the fourth day, the *yomari* are taken out and, usually, only the male and female guards are cut into small pieces, distributed among all family members, and eaten with great mirth. On the evening of the same day, children go from door to door asking for *yomari.* It is also used in the mock-marriage ceremony of Newar girls known as *yihee,* marriage to *bel* (fruit of the Aegle marmelos tree), and in *burajunko,* an old folks rice-eating ceremony.

Yomari is also prepared on the birthdays of children. This custom of celebrating the birthday with *yomari* is performed on every even year up to the age of twelve. Accordingly, a garland marking the age of the child has to be prepared and put round his neck on the occasion. But in *yomari* prepared for the birthday, they do not put sesame seed and brown sugar. Instead, they include *ankhi,* grains of rice husked carefully with the fingers. The number of grains put in corresponds to the age of the child. The *yomari* taken from the garland of the child are then distributed among other people, with the belief that such distribution may prevent evil from attacking the child, possibly transferring any impending evils on to others so that the child may remain healthy and safe throughout the year.

Yomari is also related to the Annapurna festival that comes immediately after the Dasain festival in October. This festival is also directly related to the agricultural life of the Newar people of the Kathmandu valley. The temple of the deity, situated in the heart of Kathmandu bazaar (Asan), is not represented by deity images, but by a paddy-measuring pot known as *pathi.* Since this festival falls in the harvest season, it naturally has a great significance. In those places where there are no idols, grain storing is celebrated by propitiating the Ganesh deity of that locality.

Yomari is also eaten on the occasion of the Seto (white) Machendranath festival, after it is offered to the deity. Machendranath, known as Bungadev in Newari, is the god of monsoon. When the chariot of the white Machendranath — Rato Machendranath being the deity of Patan — is pulled through Asan bazaar and taken to Machendrabahal, where the idol of the deity is enshrined, and eight *yomari* are dropped from the top of chariot. People make a great rush to pick up the cakes, as they believe that one who gets a *yomari* will have good luck. Similarly, *yomari* is prepared and eaten on the occasion of Kumarijatra, the festival of the living virgin goddess.

Yomari and life rituals: Newars make a ritual visit to a daughter in the last month of her pregnancy to feed her with *dhaubaji* (flattened rice) and *dhau (curd).* They also take with them 108 yomaris as symbols of good luck. The same number of yomari is also taken by the maternal uncle of the child to celebrate the second birthday of the first child of the daughter.

Yomari and folk legend: As the legend goes, Kuber, the god of wealth, once wanted to test a merchant of Panchaladesha, believed to be situated in what is now called Panauti near Bhaktapur. Kuber went to the door of the merchant in the guise of a beggar. At that time the merchant was not at home, but his wife received Kuber with great hospitality, offering him delicious food and clothes to wear. The god was so pleased with this hospitality that he revealed his true identity to the wife and gave her a *tashi,* a common citron fruit. On his return, the merchant, learning about the god's visit through his wife and following the instruction of the god of wealth, baked the *yomari* cake with rice flour, sesame seeds, and brown sugar, and put it in the granary along with a small replica (made of flour) of the same god and the citron fruit. He worshipped at the granary for four days, during which time they ate and distributed *yomari.* Consequently, whatever they spent was only multiplied. At that time, it is said, the custom of celebrating *yomari* festival came into existence. Since then the Newars have believed that if this festival is celebrated properly, it will bring wealth and prosperity. There will never be a shortage of grains in the house, and everyone in the family will be healthy and cheerful.

Yomari is generally offered only to those gods and goddesses who are believed to take animal sacrifices, but not to vegetarian deities, who are believed to take *panchamrit,* a holy drink of cow-milk sweetened with honey, brown sugar, yogurt and *ghee.*

Conclusion

It is clear that the *yomari* is closely related to religious aspects of rituals and festivals as well as birth-rituals, and thus to the fertility cult, regeneration, and the expectation of prosperity to the family and community. Additionally, it is also supposed to make people healthy and cheerful. The worship of agricultural deities with *yomari* indicates that this festival must have begun with the coming of agriculture. *Yomari* rituals are practised equally by both Buddhist and Hindu Newars. Different cakes are prepared for each special occasion, but no festivals except *yomari punhi,* which is named after the *yomari* cake, are known by the names of the cakes prepared for those occasions.

Another unique feature of *yomari* is that, unlike other common cakes, it is not baked in the sweet vendors shop or sold in bazaars, nor is it used on other ordinary occasions. The fact that it is baked at home at certain times to mark specific festivals and rituals indicates the cultural significance attached to it. The *yomari* cake offered to neighbours and relatives on birthdays and the *yomari* festival, reflects the unique social ethos of the Newar community by its use as a symbol of social ties.

Cakes in Thai Life from Birth to Death

Recipes for traditional Thai cakes are based on three primary ingredients — rice flour, palm sugar, and coconut milk or grated flakes. Various preparation processes such as deep-frying, boiling, and vigorously stirring a dough-like mixture over a hot fire are combined with individualized shaping to give Thai cakes their distinct and unique appearance. It should be noted that *kanom,* the Thai word for cake also refers to any dessert in the form of prepared or even plain ripe fruit.

An abundance of extremely perishable exotic fruits has done much to prompt the Thais to excel in the art of fruit preservation. Surplus bananas are peeled, flattened, and left to dry in the sun or turned into banana jam. Durian, mango, and crab apple are among the well-known fruits used to produce highly flavoured jam. Acidic fruits such as unripened tamarind, wild plum and local olive are not suitable for making jam or for drying. For use as dessert, they must be neutralized by marination in brine before being sweetened.

Even wormwood vine, the bitterest of the most bitter, can be sweetened and transformed into a dessert by this process.

With a wide variety of local fruits and preparation processes, the Thais from time immemorial have concocted a large assortment of cakes and desserts, many of which have played an important role in traditional Thai rites and ceremony, or various social occasions. Ripe *hak mook* bananas are taken on a visit to a woman who has just given birth. Roasted *hak mook* banana is considered to be a proper dish for the new mother.

Kanom kai hia

Some cakes seem to have been invented in a haphazard manner. *Kanom kai hia,* a rather odd name for a cake if one understands Thai, means a cake that looks like the egg of a monitor lizard. Nothing unusual, perhaps, except to Thais, for to call someone a monitor lizard is one of the meanest and most degrading insults one could imagine. In fact, merely mentioning the name of this creature in Thai is definitely taboo!

The preparation of *kanom kai hia* begins with the stuffing of a dumpling slightly larger than a ping pong ball with cooked beans and coconut flakes. The dumpling is deep-fried, sugar-glazed, and then served. It is believed that this cake was first prepared by Lady Waen, one of the noble ladies in the service of King Rama I's Court some two hundred years ago. King Rama I, as legend goes, developed a liking for monitor lizard eggs with the sweet fruit mangosteen, a combination considered a delicacy at that time, but finding eggs of the odd creature was not easy. It was left to Lady Waen to devise the best available substitute — a cake shaped like and, if possible, tasting like a monitor lizard egg.

Cakes in wedding rites

Cakes used in the ceremony vary according to customs of different regions. Most of these cakes are in pieces that can retain their shape. In a traditional betrothal ceremony, *kanom tom,* a common kind of Thai cake, is one of the items presented to the parents of the young woman by an elder of the young man. There are two kinds of *kanom tom* shredded - the white and the red. The former is a dumpling stuffed with shredded coconut mixed in palm sugar syrup. Becoming white after boiling, this *kanom tom* is served with a sprinkling of coconut shreds. *The red kanom tom* is disc shaped and contains no stuffing. After boiling, it is rolled in red palm sugar. Both kinds of *kanom tom* are also used as offerings to deities and spirits.

The wedding ritual is also a happy occasion in which most things used are charged with a symbolic significance, and cakes that go with it have efficacious names and appearances. One of these cakes is *kanom chan,* made from sugar and flour boiled together and poured layer by layer into a flat tray. Quite often each layer is individually coloured, symbolizing the various stages of married life.

There are quite a few traditional cakes that once held prominent place in Thai traditional weddings, although Thais might not recognize any of them now.

Kanom gong is a cake shaped in an abstracted form of the wheel of a Thai buffalo cart with its spokes rendered in a simple cross. It consists of puffed rice and green or yellow beans ground together and then combined with palm sugar and sticky rice flour. The resulting dough is then used to form pieces of the desired shape. Each piece is generously anointed with a mixture of sticky rice flour and coconut milk before being deep-fried in coconut oil.

Kanom chamod is a cake prepared from dumpling stuffed with green or yellow beans. The rest of the preparation process resembles that of *kanom gong,* except that before deep-frying, three dumplings are arranged to form a triangle secured by three skewers which are then removed after the deep-frying process.

Kanom sarm gleur is a cake to *kanom chamod* in appearance, and these two cakes are usually served together, especially when used in the wedding rite. Like *kanom chamod,* it begins as a dumpling stuffed with great copra mixed in palm sugar syrup and green or yellow beans. Three dumplings are again arranged and secured by small skewers to form a triangle which is then amply glazed with a liquid mixture of sticky rice flour and coconut milk. The skewers are removed after deep frying.

The success or failure of three dumplings to remain joined together and retain the triangular configuration upon removal of the skewers after deep frying is used to predict the future of the married couple. Should all three dumplings still stick together without the benefit of the skewers, the couple will live together until a ripe old age. If one dumpling should become separated from the other two, the marriage will produce no children. If all three dumpling become detached from one another, the marriage is likely to result in a break up.

Cakes in festive and religious rites

A large proportion of the Thai population has since ancient times been Buddhist. As Buddhists, they are occupied year round in all kinds of merit-making rites, many of which are for the benefit of departed souls. According to Thai lore, foods (including cakes) offered and served to Buddhist priests will eventually be consumed by the dead to whom the merit-making is dedicated.

Cakes in midyear merit-making rites

The Thai traditional midyear is observed some time during the month of September or October, depending on the reckoning of the lunar calendar. The southern Thais are noted for their rich offerings of cakes of at least five different kinds in midyear merit-making. *Kanom dee sam* or *kanom mae sam* is shaped like a doughnut. These rings of cake are offered for the dead to use as bangles or turn into leis.

Kanom la loy mun (bird-nest cake) is deep-fried platter of pastry. These platters are to be used as pillows and mattresses by the dead.

Kanom la is a cake in the form of noodles. According to Thai ghost tales, an evil and greedy person will become a *pret* in death. The mouth of the *pret* is as small as the eye of a needle and can only ingest fine noodles.

Kanom kai pla and the *kanom gong* previously described are to be used as ornaments by the dead.

Kanam pong are deep-fried sticky rice cakes in various shapes —diamond, circle, triangle, etc. - offered for the dead to use as rafts for river crossings.

One kind of cake prepared especially for the midyear occasion is a mixed rice cake known as *kayasart,* consisting of puffed rice, peanuts, sesame seeds, and syrup. This cake is now made at all times of the year, and can be bought from many sidewalk food-stalls in Thai cities.

Pancake for merit-making.

A favourite cake of Thais young and old is brown pancake. Many Thais these days may be unaware of the practice of offering brown pancake to the priest in Buddhist merit-making. Preparation of the brown pancake begins with mixing flour, sugar, and egg to obtain a thick cream. A spoonful of the cream mixture is poured on a hot skillet and carefully spread out to form a circular shape. A coat of sugary liquid is quickly applied to the layer before a small spoonful of filling prepared from ground shrimp and coconut shreds is added. With the help of a spatula, the flat layer is folded into a half circle, removed from the skillet and served hot.

Cakes for the end of Buddhist Lent

Buddhist myth has it that Lord Buddha once spent the whole period of Buddhist Lent preaching to his mother in heaven. To commemorate the return to earth of Lord Buddha, Thai Buddhists observe two days of rites from the fifteenth day of the waxing moon of the eleventh lunar month. On this occasion, *kao tom,* steamed sticky rice stuffed with half-ripe banana and wrapped in banana leaf, is presented to priests along with usual offerings. There are too many kinds of traditional Thai cakes to describe here, many of which are still made and eaten by many Thais. Some of these may have in the past been used in ceremonies and rituals but have lost most of their symbolic significance. Further studies are needed to throw light on the role of traditional cakes in rites and rituals of Thailand.

'Toothsome Knick-Knacks' in Burma

"Cakes and ale" for the Burmese amounts to knick-Knacks and green tea which they enjoy between regular meals. Called *tha-yay-sa* in Burmese, the phrase may be literally translated as "saliva's delight."

As rice is the staple food of the Burmese, most of these toothsome items are rice-based. Jaggery — that coarse sugar made from palm sap — is the main sweetening element in the preparation of these delicacies.

The names of the refection's are mostly descriptive, corresponding to appearance and composition. For instance, "big cake like a ball" (*mon-lon-gyi*) gets this name for the simple reason that it is rather big and it is spherical in shape. The "comb-cake" (*bi-mon*) also gets this name because it resembles a comb. A doughnut-like food made of glutinous rice looks like a bangle to the Burmese and hence they call it "bangle-cake" (*mon-let-kauk*).

When the banana is the main ingredient of the "saliva's delight" it is called "banana cake" (*hnet-pyaw-mon*) and when the palmyra nut predominates over other ingredients it is named "jaggery palm cake" (*htan-thee-mon*).

A delicious solidified items made of agar-agar, sugar, and coconut juice is smooth as a slab of marble and so is called "cake smooth like marble" (*kyauk-kyaw*).

Sometimes a religious expression is used to name a cake. It is the custom of Buddhists to enshrine religious relics and precious stones in the body of a pagoda. When a cake has a luscious jelly of shredded coconut and sugar stuffed inside it, the Burmese call it "the enshrined cake" (*hatr-pa-nar-mon*).

When a banana leaf packet is used to hold the contents of a cake for steaming, such cake is called "cake wrapped (in banana leaf)" (*mon-phet-htoke*).

Some cakes have had their names changed because the original names were inauspicious. There is a cake which is baked by putting it between two shelves of burning coal. It was commonly called in Burmese "the cake baked with fire above and below" *(a-het-mee-auk-mee-mon).* The name bore ominous associations, especially at a time when insurgencies were breaking out in Burma, so people changed its name to "peace cake" *(aye-mon).*

Similarity in sound can also beget a new name for a cake. Prepared with coarse rice sprinkled with onion tops, a certain cake is usually sold in pairs, packed face to face. Its name, *mon-lin-bya* (flat pan cake) sounds somewhat like *mon-lin-ma-ya* (husband and wife cake) and, since most of the children who flock to the sellers ask for "husband-and-wife cake." the new name sticks.

The name of a cake can appear to be a misnomer. What makes a cake get the name "cake-not-free-from-tumeric" (*na-nwin-ma-kin-mon*) when there is not a pinch of tumeric in it? The only possible explanation is that it has a yellowish colour.

A cake may undergo a name change when it is associated with a popular personality. One such cake is a preparation of coarse rice, a splash of jaggery, and a sprinkle of coconut shreds. Called *bain-mon* (a lowly cake), it is a very cheap and popular tooth-some knick-knack. During World War II the celebrated Thirty Comrades of the Burmese Revolution against the British collaborated with the Japanese and marched victoriously into Burma. One of the Thirty Comrades was Bo Yan Naing, formerly a well-known student leader. He was the hero of the hour, and the popular cake took its name from this popular personality, and was re-christianed *Yan-naing-mon*. There is a festival named after a "saliva's delight." Called *hta-ma-ne-pwe*, it is held in November when early crops are harvested. In villages all the inhabitants contribute glutinous rice, groundnuts, coconuts, and sesame to prepare *hta-ma-ne* (the ladled rice). In towns, people celebrate the festival by wards. To prepare *hta-ma-ne* the above mentioned ingredients together with water and sesame oil are put into an enormous iron bowl and placed over the open flames of a wood fire. Three or four hefty young men take turns stirring the mixture until it is completely cooked. The delicacy is wrapped in banana leaves and distributed to all households.

Another preparation linked with a Burmese festival is "ball-cake-floating-on-water" (*mon-lon-ye-paw*). Pieces of jaggery and some coconut shreddings are "enshrined" in small spherical lumps of glutinous rice and these balls are put into a pot of boiling water over a wood fire. As the water festival is an annual merry-making festival, mischievous helpers sometimes insert red pepper inside some of these glutinous balls and watch for the fun when the merry-makers start eating the hot cakes.

At all pagoda festivals one can find "rice pudding cooked in bamboo tube " *(war-kyi-dauk), the* best seller in the knick-knack market. It is usually eaten with a touch of sesame oil and salt.

As Burma is an agricultural country, some rites are performed with a view to reaping more rice and better agricultural products. Burmese, Shans, Kachins, Karens and Arakanese farmers propitiate the guardian *nats* (supernatural beings) by offering steamed glutinous rice pudding and fruits. Among the fruits offered to the *nats*, coconut is must.

A Burmese cake called *mon-pya-tha-let* is linked with the military strategy of a certain king. It is a pancake with a slightly fat centre composed of coconut, groundnuts, and sesame. When a youngster greedily bit off the central portion of the cake his grandma rebuked him, saying that he was like King Sandakok who tried to take a city but failed. The puzzled grandson asked for an explanation. The grandma told him that when King Sandakok attacked a city he went straight to the heart of the city, which was, of course, well fortified. He therefore failed to take the city. He should have demolished the perimeter of the city first and then attacked the core. This remark reached the ears of King Sandakok who, changing his strategy, won his conquest.

Mon-see-kyaw, a Burmese fried cake, was related to a prophesy. When King Theebaw ascended to the Burmese throne in 1878 an ominous saying, "as there was a break in the central portion of *mon-see-kyaw,* there would emerge a person who would destroy the country, "was rife. The doomsayers interpreted that fried cake meant the palace groups such as the monarch, the princes, and ministers and that the cut signified disunity among them, and the country would "go to the dogs." Coincidence or not, Burma was annexed by the British in 1885 and King Theebaw was dethroned and exiled.

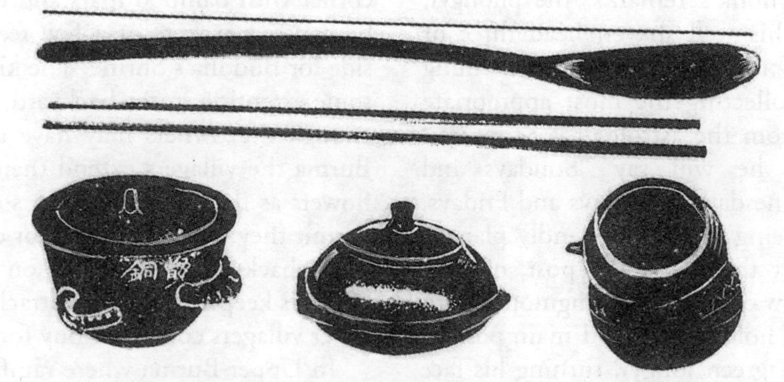

Old form of spoon and chopsticks (above) and steamer, stone pot and distiller of local spirits (below) — Korea.

Houses

Burmese House Building Ceremony

In so far as traditions, customs and superstitions are concerned there is not much difference in the construction of a house in Burma, except in the size and the amount of expenditure to be incurred. The individual preferences of the future owners of the house and the day on which the first post will be erected, according to the astrologers' calculation are very important because the astrologers' answers come out differently for the Sunday-borns and the Monday-borns.

Firstly, the husband and wife have to consult their savings box which is commonly used in villages. It will contain the of money they have so far collected by daily savings. It is still too early to start construction because until the Burmese Lent is over new constructions are not done, according to the Burmese belief. But perhaps they can invite the elders of the village to convey their intention regarding construction of a new house. The elders accordingly gather together at tea and carry out the requirements of the couple in consultation with the other villagers who have enough knowledge to calculate the required timber in tonnage, the numbers of bamboos to be used, the weight of iron nails required or if nails are not to be used the amount of jute strings to the bamboo with the thatch roofing materials. The next step assumed to be the most important is that the couple concerned must approach the Monk or "phongyi" of the village in his monastery and put forward their intention. Then the phongyi will ask both husband and wife their date of birth, the day, the year and even write down to the exact minute of the hour when the both were born. When the information is given their horoscopes can be produced. While the anxious couple is silently awaiting the revered monk's remarks, the phongyi, sitting cross-legged, will nod his well shaven head three or four times, use his right hand fore-finger to scratch something on the bamboo mat as if recollecting the most appropriate rhythm of important things from the astrological Scriptures. Then after a few minutes, he will say "Sundays and Thursdays, Mondays and Wednesdays, Tuesdays and Fridays, Saturdays and Wednesdays" being the most friendly planets, you will have to start to erect the first main post, of your house on Thursday, the tenth waxing of Tazaungmon month at ten o'clock in the morning, holding the said main post by one Thursday born, wearing a green longyi, turning his face to North East direction, at the same time reciting Buddha's First Requirement being...

Buddham saranam gacchami...
Dhammam saranam gacchami...
Sangham saranam gacchami...

Then the phongyi will have to preach at least for half an hour on Buddhism particularly the Five Precepts. The phongyi will retire.

At last one day for the erection of the first post has arrived. Village people who are conversant with carpentry have gathered. Some bamboo thuds are made ready to mark the posts of the house. And then the building and the necessary paraphernalia are complete. The husband will be busy tying one coconut and two or three bunches of bananas with some gunny ropes to the main post to be erected exactly at ten o'clock according to the instructions of the revered monk. His wife meanwhile will have been preparing hot water to make plain tea and getting ready one or two pots of rice and curry to feed the well wishing villagers who have already been standing by to help those leading the construction works.

After completion of the thuds where the posts are to be erected, the head villager will announce that everything must be ready to erect the Main Post. In the Burmese custom, the Main Post of a house is selected in the Easterly direction where Buddha's Shrine is normally placed. There may be three or four posts depending on the size of the house and the first post in the most eastern direction has to be the Main Post. If it is a small house there will be only three posts and two rooms in the house. The Burmese carpenters' terminology goes as above mentioning the post and then making rooms in between them. A bed-room has to be made by covering a corner with bamboo mats and the rest of the house need not be covered except for a few feet of extension on the frontal side for Buddha's Shrine. The kitchen may be made by having some extention in the backyard. When the plot of land is wide enough the owners may have a garden or in the villages in Burma the villagers extend their land to grow vegetables and flowers as their cash crop. In some cases where the situations permit they may keep cattle or chickens under their houses or at the backyard. Depending on their financial situation, some villagers keep a small shop attached to their original house and other villagers come and buy for their daily meals.

In Upper Burma where rainfall is negligible, the flooring is not made separately but they use the ground as their flooring by smothering it with mud. In Lower Burma, however, the rain and deltaic conditions make it necessary for every house, however big or small to have a floor about three feet above the ground to enable the dwellers to be safe from the high tides and rain water.

Timber, being plentiful in Burma, the village houses are mostly finished by timber, except for some owners who prefer brick buildings. In most of the country, the roofing is mainly thatch to protect the occupants from the hot weather. This is the main difference between the rural and urban population, the latter being better than the rural crowd, they use modern roofing materials such as asbestos or corrugated iron sheets. If a house is being built in urban area and if the area is particularly within local Municipal Limit, it is not allowed to have cattle farms or vegetation land in the same compound but only a garden.

The common belief for most Burmese is that a house should face East as far as possible or if no, South — and nowhere else. The Buddha Shrine is a must for every Burmese Buddhists. For one-storeyed house with raised flooring or in any two-storeyed houses, the number of planks used as foot-steps must be always odd numbered and never even.

In Burma, this kind of house will be occupied by about two or three generations of a family of up to six members. When the new couple become old enough to have children, and unless the house has been extended within, the children sleep together with their parents. As the children become older, the girls usually sleep in the room covered with the bamboo matting while the boys sleep in the open space of the house perhaps together with their father.

According to the Burmese civilization, after any marriage between a boy and a girl of age, the bridegroom always accompanies the bride to live together in the latter's house. So then, the house which has been built years ago will have to be altered to have a separate room for the newly weds by making a new room covered with bamboo mats or using whatever material is available depending on how much they can spend.

The rural houses or huts can never have a separate living room or guest-room whereas the houses in Urban areas have, as the civilization of Western styles has been copied. And where there are guest rooms tables and chairs are used. Again, it also depends mainly on civilization, that is to say that when the old people including parents or grand-parents sleep on the bamboo flooring, then it is regarded as very rude to let the guests or the family members sit on the chairs which are naturally higher than the place where old people sleeper or retire. In the Urban areas the people refrain from sleeping on the floor and use a bed. Therefore to sit on the chairs by either the guests or the family members could in no way be rude.

Singapore: Houses — Where East and West Meet

The houses in Singapore, with the architectural features of the traditional Malay, Chinese and European houses, are fast disappearing because of the rapid rate of urbanization and the construction of high-rise flats in housing estates. An attempt seeks to describe some of the architectural features of the traditional Malay, Chinese and European houses which were predominant until the 1950s.

The Malay house

The traditional Malay house is a single-storey house, built above ground. The floor stands on wooden or, subsequently, on brick pillars about two to three metres above the ground to keep the dampness away from the floor and to allow this open space to be used as storage space for household objects and to allow for a freer circulation of air. It has a steep, pitched roof rising to a ridge, to allow rainwater to flow easily away on a wet day and the heat of the sun to be diffused over a wider area. The roof used to be made of attap (Nipa palm leaves) which are easily replaced and have a cooling effect. Subsequently, tiles are now used in place of attap.

The floor plan of the Malay house is, in general, a simple one. A short flight of steps leads from the ground up to the main entrance of the house. Up here we find either an open verandah or else we pass through a door leading to an area which serves as a reception room for guests or a living and dining room for the occupants.

From the reception area living room, a door or a passage opening leads to the bedrooms. In between the bedrooms on either side of this area of the house is a passage which leads to the kitchen and the bathing and washing areas which are situated at the back of the house.

The materials for the walls and the floor of the house are, traditionally of wood with the walls constructed horizontally, with wooden planks in such a way as to allow for ventilation and to keep out the rain and the heat from the sun.

Recent innovations are to have walls of bricks and the floor of cement. In such a case, either the pillars supporting the floor raised from the ground are of brick or else the house is built on the ground level.

The Chinese house

The Chinese house is built on the ground level. It is a single-storey house if it stands alone, but the Chinese live mostly in terrace-houses or in "shop houses" (a name derived from the use of the ground floor as a shop and the first floor as a private residence) The houses which stand well above the road level are approached by a flight of step leading to the main entrance.

The Chinese house has also a steep, pitched roof rising to a ridge, to allow for the flow of rainwater. The roof is covered with either Chinese tiles or red house tiles common to the area.

One interesting feature is the "rooflet" which covers the front upper portion of the house, midway between the ground and the first floor of the building at the front portion of the house, to provide for additional shade and to prevent rainwater from spilling over the main entrance onto the front door. One other feature, which is a technique used for ventilation, is to have the roof falling in two stages with an overlap and a sort of clerestory of windows above aside roofs.

Each house has a front porch. When the porches of a row of houses are linked together, they form a sidewalk which may be the origin of the "five-foot way", a common feature in Singapore.

The Chinese house extends usually to some depth. Immediately after the main or front door, many of which have carvings (including also two windows, one on each side of the door) is an area used for the reception of guests as well as a living room where the family altar is installed.

Immediately behind this is a passage or corridor leading to a courtyard which sometimes takes the place of a small garden, arranged as an area with a fish pond or with potted plants. After the courtyard is an area where the kitchen and the bathroom are located.

The bedrooms are found on the first floor and are reached by a staircase situated midway between the front and the back portion of the building.

A corridor on the first floor immediately behind the staircase, leads to the bedrooms. In some cases, there is a small area on the first floor immediately behind the staircase where a few chairs or a small table may be placed.

In the case of "shophouses", the rooms in the house may be reached from a staircase situated to the side of the main door, i.e. "the shop".

The Chinese house has cement floors (except for wooden floors which some houses have on the first floor), brick and white stucco walls and ceramic tiles with floral decorations on the walls at the front portion of the house; as well as other decorations, such as classical Roman pillars and motifs derived from columns with Ionic, Doric and Corinthian capitals.

The European house

The European house is similar to the country house in England except that it is planned with white stucco walls, high ceilings and deeper verandahs. It has adopted many of the features of the Malay house, such as its pyramid-shaped roof rising to a central point and its bedrooms on the first floor (which means that they are raised above the ground floor level).

The European house is usually a two-storey house, with its framework of timber and, originally, with its roof thatched with attap, but now replaced with tiles.

Every house has a portico or porch in front on the ground floor. Living rooms can be found on either side of the wings on the ground floor, with one of these used as a dining room. The kitchen is at the back of the house.

The servant's room is found either immediately after the kitchen, or is joined by a narrow corridor leading to it from the living room, with toilets either adjacent to the servant's room or situated just to the back of the living room. On the first floor in the area above the porch is an open area which serves as a verandah or as a sort of living room enclosed with blinds. Bedrooms (with bathrooms attached) are at both wings of the house. There are usually two in number or else in pairs with a corridor and a passage before, running laterally in the front. Between the bedrooms is a staircase leading to the ground floor.

The interior of the premises may have late-Georgian plaster decorations, reminiscent of the influence of the Regency period of architecture. Other motifs are derived from those of the classical Roman period with pillars of the type decorated with Ionic, Doric and Corinthian capitals. The high ceilings and the open verandahs which, in some cases, continue the whole way round the house on the first floor, and the fretted wood work which is attached round the edge of the roof to keep bats out, are features adopted with the tropical weather in mind.

Khmer Republic (Cambodia): Houses on Both Water and Land

Introduction

Located between Thailand, Vietnam and Laos, the Khmer Republic (Cambodia) with 181,035 km² is about half the size of Japan. She has a clear geographic personality: a huge interior basin surrounded by less populated highlands. In the basin, the Khmer peasant has created an original civilization.

According to the national census of 1962, the total population was 5,728,771 inhabitants composed of 4,770,342 rurals; 546,865 urbans and 411,564 semi-urbans. The urban zones or localities having 10,000 inhabitants or more represent 9.5 percent of the total population. This source says these were in all 1,071,101 families in the whole country.

Khmer families are generally large with an average of 5 or 6 children.

Khmer rural house

The Khmer peasant and his family live in their house (Pteah) built up on piles about 2m. above the ground with light materials and surrounded by fruit trees. Poor houses have walls and roofs made of palm leaves, the richer ones have plank walls with a tile roof. Traditionally a peasant house is often located remote from the others although, sometimes surrounded by nearby houses of relatives, e.g. sons or sons-in-law. Generally the houses are grouped in hamlets of 20 to 50 units, or in villages of about one hundred roofs.

Along the river banks the lines of houses are uninterrupted. Hamlets and villages are called "Phum". In the center of rural life there is a monastery with many Buddhist monks where children learned to read and write. Every villager had a term to fulfil for a period of his life in a pagoda.

Type of houses

There are five types of houses: Pteah Roong Daul, Pteah Roong Deung, Pteah Kantaing, Pteah Pet and Pteah Khmer. Those types of houses are built up on two kinds of base: water (floating house), plains and mountains (houses on piles and houses on the ground).

Lake-dwellings are built up with wood on floating, generally bamboo foundations. The roofs are covered with corrugated iron or palm leaves. This kind of house happens to be in the great lake area (TONLE SAP) which has perhaps the most plentiful supply of fish in the world. These houses, of course, belong to the fishermen families. But houses on piles are to be found everywhere in the Khmer country, in rural as well as in urban areas. The kind of Pteah Pet and Pteah Kantaing are the most popular.

Family members and their house

Generally speaking, in a Khmer rural house there is only one generation but sometimes two. In a house there are: father, mother and unmarried children. The whole family work on their own land (rice field or chamcar). Proletariats are scarce. The rural society is aiming at social equality. In most provinces, vacant lands are abundant. Once married the sons leave the paternal house and clear a corner of the forest and build a house near his father's or his father-in-law's. Traditionally only the younger son or younger daughter live with old parents even if he or she is married.

The form of the house is often rectangular, the front of which preferably faces the East. The standard size is — length: 11m., width: 9m., height: 2.5m. For this size we arrange four rows of columns from front to back and the house is naturally divided into three compartments. The types of the houses are recognizable due to the shape of the roofs. The roofs are generally arranged in a form of one, two or three tops.

Formally the front and the left hall between two columns have no external walls but a carved palisade and their floor is at two stair steps lower than the main floor inside. At the back along the width between two columns, one third of the compartment on the left is reserved for the kitchen which is sheltered against monsoon winds which come from the south west. The other part is used as a granary for rice. The floor is made of sheets of bamboo. Today all the floors (front, hall and main floor) are arranged on the same level, and we use plank instead of bamboos. Today the granary is built up on a rising ground nearly outside the house for greaves convenience. The shower room is outside on the ground but near the house and the water-closet is behind and away from the house. In the shower there are several basins of water. To bathe we use a kind of bowl originally made of skullcap of the coco-nut to take the water from the basin and pour out the contents on the head and the body. To get up the house, there are two straight stairs, one at the front side just in the middle and another one on the left side leading straight to the kitchen.

The middle compartment is divided into two portions: a dining room and a drawing room with simple furniture: matting plaits and pillows. Formerly there were no chairs in the house. People write or eat in a sitting position. The visitors come in bare-foot and sit down on one side with their legs folded. To do honour to the visitors, the housekeeper brings betel-nut and tobacco on a tray then invites them to share these things before discussing business. The next compartment is divided into two bedrooms: the parent's bedroom and the daughters' common bedroom. When we sleep we turn our head to the south (South=Tbong=Precious stones) and our feet to the north (North=Choeng=Foot).

Formerly there were no beds in the bedrooms. People slept on the floor covered with a mat, using pillows and mosquito-nets against mosquitoes and other insects. On the corner of the compartment on the top of the parents' couch, there is an altar of a statue of Buddha or an image of Buddha for family worship.

In each compartment we find a few pitchers containing cold drinking water. To drink we use the same kind of bowl as used for our shower, but of smaller and more refined fabrication. Clothes are folded and kept inside several big boxes made of palm leaves. Today in every house we use bags and wardrobes. In the daughters' common bedroom there is a large and deep whatnot (Stack) above the head along the width of the compartment for storage purposes. The boys, when reaching adulthood, sleep outside on the veranda during the dry season. In the rainy season temporary walls are added to the structure for better shelter against the rains.

Under the house there is agricultural equipment: oxen carts, ploughs, hooks, grains mills round flat baskets used to separate rinds and bare seeds after decortication. Often mainly in central provinces (Takeo, Kandal) we find a loom to weave.

Custom and status

The house site

There is a method to choose the site for a house. Supposed a rectangular ground is chosen for building a house. The length of the ground is divided into ten parts and the width into six. One portion of the land reserved for the house is chosen between four tenths of the length from the West and five tenths of the length from the East, and three tenths from the North and two tenths from the South for the width.

Before building a house

After all necessary materials for the construction is collected, the moment and day most favourable to build a house is examined. On the day prior to the beginning of construction, the "Achar" a priest to stand on the ceremony to conjure misfortune is invited. For this, an offering composed of two trays of food and desserts, one banana tree with roots, one sugar cane, sampots (skirts) and new coats is needed. Then on the ceremony place, one principal column, two secondary columns and a girder that stands crosswise is set up. The master of the ceremony enflames waxlights and incense sticks, then he attaches the banana tree to the side column, the sugar cane to another side column and the sampots and coats to the girder. Then he spreads a mat on which he arranges the plates of offerings, then he asks "Neang Konghing Preah Thorany" or the Goddess of Earth for the ground to build. After the ceremony of conjuration, the 'Achar' makes several knots with the threads in the columns and the girder. Then he gives the order to dig the holes to plant the columns.

The day after, the Achar returns to spell magic formulars to conjure misfortune, then he recites another formular and puts a piece of money into the depth of the hole in the principal column. Then the construction starts.

In all Khmer houses two parts are very important: the gate and the top of the stairs.

The principal gate of the house must open to the East, South-west and Northeast. Its width must be half the size of its height. The tops of the stairs of the peasant house are carved in a form of some animals conforming to the wishes of the proprietor. According to an old custom the tops of the stairs are considered as the heads of the proprietors' parents and it is prohibited to put the foot on them. To respect this custom the ancients had the initiative of embellishing them as a venerated place.

Ceremony of installation

Khmer people are superstitious They forbid women and the monks to go up into a newly built house until after the ceremony of installation in accordance with ancient custom.

First the three senior persons considered as symbol of prosperity are invited, then all neighbours, all parents and all friends to participate in the ceremony.

Before entering the house, the owner walks three times around the house carrying cat with a three coloured coat, one accomplished woman and two virgins. They are followed by the other guests who come with their gifts: weaver's equipment, a stone, a coco, a knife, a bag, fowls, seeds, etc.

During the first tour, the owner stays silently playing chess inside the house. The leader makes a call: "Eh! The proprietor!" There is no answer. Then begins the second tour. When arriving at the same place, the same person calls again: "Eh! The proprietor!" Then the owner answers: "Who calls at this moment?" , then he says to himself: "Yok Tuk Kat Seh Yok Seh Ban" It means (I take the boat — Castle in western chess — against the horse and I get the horse).

The procession continues for the third tour and the leader calls again: "Eh! The proprietor!", then the latter asks "Where do you come from carrying bulky things?". Everybody answers "We were travelling from very far country, our junk was capsized, we required your hospitality and beg you to keep our property if possible!" - The owner says: "Yes! All right!". Then we beat the gongs and the drum as sign of joy.

The house is generally for the use of one generation only. After the death of the parents, the house is pulled down and old materials are brought to the pagoda as a gift to the monks. If the family is poor, old materials are to be divided among brothers and sisters or they may sell them.

Generally speaking there is not much difference between rural and urban traditional houses. The types are mostly the same, but urban houses are built up only for dwelling, they are generally elevated and the ground floor is arranged in several rooms for use according to the needs. Today, the use of modern furniture such as: wardrobes, tables, chairs, desks, beds, etc. is widespread in urban as well as in rural houses.

However, there is perhaps a little difference between the two centers concerning some aspects of the practice of custom. For instance, in town, the choice of the place to build a house and the rites have a tendency to become much more simple.

Vietnam: The Imperial Tombs of Hue

The emperors of the last dynasty having ruled over Vietnam rest in tombs scattered along the two banks of the Perfume River, westward of the ancient imperial capital, Hue.

The construction of those tombs complied to a tradition which had taken form in China over the course of time; it had elaborated and perfected itself before passing into Vietnam where it prevailed immediately, without seemingly undergoing any essential modification.

According to the tradirional theory of the creation of the universe, the terrestrial world could become homologous to the celestial world only through the royal world, which was the ladder between Heaven and Earth, the axis and pivot of the universe, the source of time and space. That was the reason why the erection of royal sepulchers, among other things, was an important matter. In particular, the selection of the site must answer the most favourable geomantic conditions, since, as stated by geomantic theories, all the future and the happiness of the dynasty would depend on that choice. On the other hand, as the cosmos could be not only figured, but actually made present in any space, conformably to geomantic laws, the construction of the tomb was never conceived independently. But in relation to the landscape with which it had to be in close connection. Ethics create esthetics: the imperial tomb forms a whole covering a vast surface, with buildings disseminated in parks planted with sundry species of trees, and where the architecture is more intimately linked to the natural context than anywhere else. The greatest emperors of the Nguyen dynasty had been also great artists by knowing how to connect their tombs with nature, with a marvelous sense of the scenery and effect.

Astrological and geomantic considerations, together with the Buddhist conception of death as a mere return to another world of eternity, had made the emperors of the Nguyen dynasty choose themselves, often in their lifetime, the site of their ultimate resting place. The most worthy of mention are:

- the tomb of Gia-Long (1802-1820) the construction of which began in 1814 and was completed after the sovereign's death.
- the tomb of Minh-Mang (1820-1840), the site of which had been chosen and the plan drawn while Minh-Mang was still alive, but the monuments of which were built only from 1841 to 1843.
- the tomb of Thieu-Tri (1841-1848), built in two years, from 1847 to 1948.
- the tomb of Tu-Duc (1848-1883), built from 1864 to 1867, at the cost of a revolt from the workers.
- the tomb of Khai-Dinh (1916-1925), which began to be built in 1920, but was finished only in 1931.

The influence of Chinese funeral architecture could be clearly discerned in the general disposition of the different elements of the tombs, which practically is the same as in Peking; especially the plan of Minh-Mang's tomb is the classic plan of the Chinese imperial tombs of the Ming, but only on a smaller scale.

The following elements can be distinguished in the sepultures of the Nguyen emperors:

- a flagged court of honour, "path of the spirit" or "way of the souls" (the Chinese *shen tao*), where are lined all along, in imposing solemnity, sculptures of caparisoned elephants and horses, and statues of civil and military mandarins.
- a Pavilion sheltering the funeral stele which relates the principal events of the defunct emperor's reign and often expresses his conception of government (especially in the case of Tu-Duc, who composed himself the text of his stele); this stele is a massive monolith, reposing on a stone table, all adorned with sculptures.
- a temple for the cult of the defunct sovereign, veritable museum of souvenirs, where are kept the emperor's mortuary tablet and his legitimate wife's.
- a terrace rising in tiers to be used for the performance of the ritual ceremonies, on festival days.
- the tomb proper, which Tu-Duc called the "deep palace", in a sacred enclosure wall closed by a bronze door.
- appended buildings erected either for the memory of the ancestors, or to house the sovereign's wives after his death and the persons in charge of the cult, or to be used as resting pavilions when the sovereign came to watch the works of his last abode, for each one of the emperors had

taken a personal interest in the construction of his sepulchre.

The disposition of these elements differs sensibly with each tomb. With Minh-Mang's (and in a lesser measure with Thieu-Tri's), the arrangement, as we have already stressed, is the one of the Ming's tombs in Peking: the different edifices are disposed on a longitudinal axis. Thus, the monuments succeed each other on a straight line: a three-arch portal; a court of honour with its stone mandarins, its stone horses and elephants which could be useful to the historian of usages and accoutrement; three-tier stairs with sculptured dragons as banisters; a platform in the middle of which stand the funeral stele and its pavilion; right and left, waterlily lakes; an esplanade with on the right and left pagoda-like constructions and at the end the temple of cult; a bronze portico; a stone bridge over a groove full of water; stairs leading to the bronze door of the funeral monument, standing against a pine wood. There are constructions on the neighbouring hills and separated from the median line by large man-dug bodies of water. On the contrary, in Gia-Long's tomb, situated in a wild but grandiose landscape, the pavilion of the stele as well as the temple of cult are no longer disposed on a longitudinal axis, but on a transversal one.

Tu-Duc gave up the disposition of Minh-Mang's tomb by setting up two groups of constructions on two different axes: on the principal axis are disposed the different monuments which compose the whole of the tomb (the court of honour which constitutes the path of the spirit, the pavilion of the stele in the middle of a large flagged court, the crescent lake which represents the moon accompanying the sun, the tomb proper); on the axis of the palace which goes with the tomb are raised the different edifices destined to the cult of the defunct sovereign. But, in every tomb, all around the principal edifices are arranged charming gardens and magnificent alleys bordered with trees. Everywhere, lakes studded with islets bearing kiosks and belvederes are spread out. In this harmonious environment, where verdure blends with water, amidst deep silence, nothing evocates the idea of death; but rather perfect serenity, inner as well as external, diffuses from these sanctuaries of indefinite repose.

The ornaments seen in all the tombs are much the same; they proceed from one another, with more or less harmony, taste, refinement, profusion, richness: banisters made of dragons carved out from Thanh-hoa granite, decorated stone screens, bronze porticoes, ballustrades in wrought iron, etc... The tombs of the Nguyen emperors are remarkable not only by their architecture; they can also be considered as museums of plastic arts. Their architectural composition allows also to assert that the influence of Chinese art may not have always prevailed entirely, and that many styles can be discernible.

However, there is a total modification of artistic concepts with the tomb of Khai-Dinh, which marks the breach with the beautiful landscape architecture of the tombs of the first four emperors of the Nguyen dynasty. Entirely built in concrete, with casings of multicoloured China potsherds, it has been an attempt of inspiration from the European taste, while giving up the best part of Vietnamese architecture, that of the association of the landscape to the monument.

In brief, one can say without risk that the imperial tombs of Hue are the most representative of Vietnamese art under the last Vietnamese dynasty. It is a pity that these artistic and historical vestiges have suffered so from military and natural disasters during the two past decades.

Houses of the Mongolian People

ne of the specific forms of nomadic dwellings is the *gher* (yurt). Historical information shows that until the end of the nineteenth century more than 100 large and small ethnic groups used to dwell in *gher*. Today, *gher* dwellers are mainly the peoples of Central Asia who speak Turkic and Mongolian languages. Many scholars relate the origin of *gher* to the history of cattle breeding. The first known example of a *gher* among the nomads of Central Asia is the ball-shaped felt dwelling of the ancient Hunnu.

Definite evidence of the Mongolian *gher* at the beginning of the thirteenth century is briefly recorded in "The Secret History of the Mongols" and in the notes of travellers in Mongolia at that time. For example, the most interesting form of Mongolian *gher* is the "*gher* with neck". The French traveller W. Roubrouc, who travelled through Mongolia in the thirteenth century has given interesting information about this, in his book, "Travels to Eastern Countries". The "*gher* with neck" was called "*Chorkhan*" by the Mongolians of that period and scholars identified it as a kind of *gher* built on a cart. In such dwellings lived kings and lords, and also military authorities.

After the Mongolian empire the *gher* developed further into the classical form in which it appears today. The Mongolians were inhabitants of Central Asia for many hundreds of years and being nomad cattle-breeders, they mainly dwelled in *gher*. But after the advent of Buddhism in Mongolia in the sixteenth century some of the population turned to a settled way of life, dwelling in houses, and this change in lifestyle greatly influenced more and more people, especially from the mid-twentieth century. Today the light, transportable felt dwellings are indispensable to the shepherds' life. Of course, *gher* are erected in the city, too. The Mongolian gher has been thoroughly thought out an dis ideally adapted to the nomadic way of life, being easily erected and taken down.

The *gher* consists of *tono* (flue), the support poles section of latticed walls, and *uni* (the bars forming the arched ceiling). The entrance must face south-east. The *gher* is protected by double coverings of felt, which are made for the outer wall of the gher, the ceiling, etc. Over the *tono* is set a square piece of felt called "*Urkh*", which is open during the day and closed at night like a window. *Tono* have several forms.

In ancient times the *uni* were constructed together with the *tono* and the *tono* would be separate from the central part; and in another form, there are holes around the *tono* in which the ends of the *uni* are fixed. The latter is more widely popular. At the entrance of the *gher* is hung the "*Und*". (door), also made of felt. There are many customs connected with life in the *gher*. One must not step on the threshold when entering it, and the felt *Und* must be lifted from the right side. But now this type of door is almost forgotten and wooden doors are constructed instead. According to the traditional custom the men-guests are usually seated on the eastern side of the *gher* and women on the other side, where the mistress is seated. However, the *gher* may be, its basic construction proportions remain unchanged. By tradition the fireplace is situated in the centre, and the kitchen is arranged on the eastern side. Beds of the master and mistress of the house are arranged on the north-east side. At the opposite side to the door, sacred possessions are displayed and on the western side of the *gher* other household possessions are arranged. A new *gher* is erected for a newly wedded couple. The *gher* is presented by the boy's family and its furniture by the girl's.

Of course, over the centuries the design of the *gher* has markedly changed. Besides their *gher* dwellings, Mongolian people also erect small *gher* for storage purposes. In some parts of the country this kind of *gher* is built square or round-shaped, and made out of willow and reed. At the beginning of the twentieth century, most of the poor people used to live in *gher* consisting only of *tono* and *uni*, which are called "Jolom" and "Khatguur". This kind of *gher* is one of the oldest forms of Mongolian dwellings.

There are other interesting dwellings called "*Asar*" (large stretched tent), "*Maihan*" (small tent) and "*Jodgor*", made of fabric. *Asar* are erected on special occasions such as religious and folk festivals. *Maihan* are usually carried by travellers and hunters even today. *Jodgor* are smaller in size and were carried on the back by lamas who visited pilgrimage centres on foot and camped in these small *jodgor* on their way. Now these are no longer used.

Today in Mongolia there are a few Turkic and Tunguus (Evenk), ethnic groups who are engaged in both cattle-breeding and deer-forming. Their dwellings differ from those of the Mongolians. The Kazakhs of western Mongolia dwell in *tureg gher*, while Turkic families in the northern part live in rawhide tents. These tents used to be covered with wood bark, but now this has been replaced by other materials.

A traditional Burmese house.

Entrances and Gateways

China: Warding off the Evil and the Wicked

Stone tablets can be seen standing at village entrances, street corners and in front of courtyards in Taian, a country in eastern China's Shandong Province. Inscribed with the name of a legendary Taishan Mountain hero by the name of Shi, the Invincible, in the form of five big Chinese characters "Tai Shan Shi Gan Dang", these tablets are said to have the power of warding off the evil and the wicked. Hence the name "House protecting stone."

The Han people in China are worshippers of the River God, the Mountain Divinity and a lot of other holy spirits in heaven and venerable souls on earth. To them, a board hung above the door or stone tablet standing in front of the house is enough to scare away the ghosts if it bears such lines as "Prime Minister Jiang is here!" The same purpose can be served if two special bricks are laid underneath the threshold. The ubiquitous Tai Shan Shi Gan Dang tablets are typical of the Hans' many traditional beliefs.

The Taian people are proud of their Tai Shan Shi Gan Dang tablets because they inspire awe and mystery in whoever sees them from a distance. These tablets embody the presence of the legendary hero, Shi the Invincible, so that ghoulish creatures will be terrified at the sheer sight of them and flee helter-skelter. The tablets are even more terrifying to evil spirits if they are even more terrifying to evil spirits if they are made of stone quarried from Taishan Mountain, one of the Five Holy Mountains in China. For thousands of years, the Taian people see these tablets as a sign for personal safety.

Such tablets are of different sizes. Those erected at village entrances are mostly *5-chi* in length (one *chi* equals approximately one-third of a metre). Those appearing in front of houses are 2-3 *chi* long. Meticulous attention is paid to choosing the materials. Granite from Taishan Mountain is seen as the most ideal material because of its hardness and glamorous hue. It is believed that tablets made of such granite are the most effective for keeping the evils at bay. Some tablets are made of brick. Inscriptions on them are usually decorated with a lion-head design of the "eight diagrams." The lion, known as the king of all beasts, and the eight diagrams can both help harness the demons. Some tablets bear a picture of Shi the Invincible. Occasionally one can see tablets bearing lines that read: "Shi the Invincible is here. He is the hero who eliminates evil spirits and saves the people from disaster."

Shandong is certainly not the only place for the "Tai Shan Shi Gan Dang" tablets. They can be found virtually all over China particularly in such provinces as Hebei, Henan, Jiangsu, Zhejiang, Gurangdong and Sichuan. They can also be seen in Southeast Asia and Japan.

Tales of Shi the Invincible of Taishan Mountain are still alive among the people in the Taian area. As to the identity of this hero, the folklore has the following sayings:

1. Shi the Invincible was a hero who performed meritorious deeds in combating ghosts. Inhabitants in the Culan Mountain in southeastern Taian claim that Shi the Invincible was one of their ancestors. He was held in high esteem because he fought tirelessly for the weak and the innocent. Whoever was insulted by the wicked come to him for help. Once, a young woman was victimized by a devil, who appeared in her room to torure her when night fell. As a result, the woman looked sallow and emaciated and was bedridden. Her parents implored Shi the Invincible to subdue the devil. Well prepared, the hero hid himself in the girl's room. When night fell and the torturer stole in, the room was suddenly ablaze with lights. Wielding a sword, Shi the Invincible fought the devil with vengeance. The fight ended with the devil running away hastily all the way south. Gratified, the girl married Shi the Invincible. The devil, unwilling to take his defeat lying down, continued to harass young women in southern China. "I'm afraid of neither heaven nor earth. Shi the Invincible in Taishan Mountain is the only guy I fear," it told its victims. It did not stay there long before it was again sent packing by Shi the Invincible who came at the invitation of the local people. The devil continued its flight south, first to Fujian and then to Guangdong. The hero chased it wherever it appeared. Then, one day, his wife said to him: "It won't do for you to go away from me for so long. Now that the devil is afraid of you, why not write your name Taj Shan Shi Gan Dang on cards or inscribe it upon stone tablets?" Shi the Invincible did as his wife told him and this method worked. Since then, stone tablets bearing the name of Shi the Invincible became the weapons in the hands of those troubled by evil spirits. Such is the background of the Taj Shan Shi Gan Dang tablets. It was said that the devil, unable to find a safe place in China, finally fled to Southeast Asia. Incidentally, two special bricks underneath the threshold for the purpose of scaring away the ghosts also symbolize the presence of Shi the Invincible. Ledend has it that once Shi the Invincible met a

family that was taking a bride home for the wedding ceremony. Four ghosts were tailing the bridal sedan chair. Seeing Shi the Invincible, the ghosts swiftly hid themselves so that they would not be discovered. They reappeared once the hero went away. But this was not lost on Shi the Invincible. Picking up two bricks and putting them underneath both ends of that family's front door threshold, he told the bridegroom: "The two bricks at the gate symbolize me, Shi the Invincible." This stuck terror in the ghosts, who dared not come and haunt the family. Since then it has become a practice among the local people that whenever a new house is built two bricks would be put underneath the threshold so as to banish the evil spirits.

2. One more saying depicts Tai Shan and Shi Gan Dang (Shi the Invincible) as the names for two intimate classmates. Tai Shan later became a successful candidate for an imperial examination at the provincial level but Shi the Invincible managed only to pass an examination at the country level. The latter was so poor that he had to stay with the former. They became bosom friends. Later generations, thinking of the rapport that had so closely bound the two together, put their names together, that is, Tai Shan Shi Gạn Dang. In order to beat foreign invaders, they believed that they could emerge victorious only when they united as one like Tai Shan and Shi the Invincible. From then on, the five Chinese characters Tai Shan Shi Gan Dang have appeared on the walls of each household.
3. According to another saying. Taishan Mountain stones had superhuman strength. One day, Hua Tuo, a celebrated doctor in the Three Kingdoms Period (220-280), was picking medicinal herbs on Taishan Mountain when one of his disciples showed him a piece of stone. The stone was inscribed with a line that read: "With Taishan Mountain here, no ghosts of any description dare start a foolish move." A witch disguised herself as a ghost in an attempt to harm Hua Tuo, only to be driven away by the stone. When the folks heard about this, they flocked to Taishan Mountain for the stones. They chiselled the characters — Tai Shan Shi Gan Dang — on them and then imbedded them in walls, hoping that this would save them from the demons.

There are so many tales about Shi the Invincible across the land that they can be compiled into a thick book. The above mentioned tales are typical ones.

Tales about Shi thc Invincible were recorded in ancient Chinese books from the Han to the Qing dynasties. For example, Shi You, author of *Impromptu Writings* in the Han Dynasty, presented Shi the Invincible as a human being. This coincided with the fact stories about the hero spread far and wide among the people and that it is widely believed that Shi the Invincible is a human being who can keep the devils at bay. On the other hand, it was said that Bixia Yuanjun, the noted Taishan Mountain Goddess, was the daughter of Tai Shan and that Qiaoguo Village at the foot of Culan Mountain was the native place of Shi the Invincible. The Shi families in the village are said to be the descendants of Shi the Invincible. The saying that Tai Shan Gan Dang denotes the stone of Taishan Mountain also rings true. From the Qing Dynasty's first emperor Qin Huang onwards, every Chinese feudal emperor made it a routine to go all the way to pay homage to the god of Taishan Mountain, the holiest of the Five Holy Mountains. The prestigious Taishan Mountain God was also regarded as the emperor who ruled all the devils in the Orient. Since Taishan Mountain is his residence, it was natural that Taishan Mountain stones had the spell to scare away all the ghosts and evil spirits.

It is not strange for the Hans to stick to the legacy left behind by their forefathers. For many years, they believed thạt once a person died, his soul would be immortal. They also believed that everything on earth has a soul. Out of their worship of immortal soul, they regarded Shi the Invincible as a human being and inscribed his name on stone tablets to ward off the evil and the wicked. Likewise, out of their notion that "everything on earth has a soul," they saw Shi the Invincible as a piece of stone from Taishan Mountain which possessed superhuman strength.

Pakistan: Gateway to Destiny

There are millions of gateways in the world but there is one in Pakistan which has no parallel elsewhere. It is known as the 'Gateway to Destiny' though it is known to laymen as the Khyber Pass.

This Gateway which makes a strong impression on its visitors is considered by many as magical, by others as mystical, and by some as mysterious, magnificent, majestic, romantic, rugged or sensitive, though none of these adjectives do justice to the great Khyber Pass.

It is, in fact, very difficult to explain exactly what the Khyber Pass is, but I think most historians were right call it the 'Gateway to Destiny.' In fact the history of the South Asian region, particularly the Indo-Pakistan subcontinent has been greatly influenced by the success or failure of the Dynasty defending it.

Through this gateway swarmed in the fair-skinned Aryans about 1500 BC and then Scythians and Persians around 522-486 BC Alexander's forces marched through this gateway in

327 BC and he was followed by Bactrians and Parthians. The area was later governed by the great Kushan Kings for a few hundred years.

The Kushan empire was snuffed out around AD 455 by the savage onslaught of the white Huns who sprang like a thunderstorm from central Asia laying waste everything that came in their way. It was a great setback for Buddhism because some of the great universities like Taxila and other institutions where Buddhism flourished were wiped out.

The Tartars invaded this region several times through the Khyber Pass and then-Mahmud of Ghaznavi used the Khyber not once but at least seventeen times in the eighth century and extended his empire up to Lahore. After the death of Mahmud Ghaznavi it was used by the Mohammad Ghori who was in fact the founder of a great muslim empire in Hindustan.

The Mongols also invaded India through the Khyber several times and then came the Moghuls in the sixteenth century who established a strong empire and ruled India for several centuries.

This gateway is now being used by the Afghan refugees to save their lives from the armies of the U.S.S.R. which are invading. Besides this historic gateway there are hundreds of others in Pakistan which are also celebrated in the annals of history. It is not possible to cover all of these gateways in one article. So only a few representative gateways are described.

Only a few hundred years ago most of the major cities of this region were surrounded by strong walls and only a few gateways, usually six or eight, were kept for going into and coming out of these cities. The walls were built in order to save the residents of the cities from enemies and invaders. All gates were closed during the night and during the war days. Such gateways played historic roles as and when the country was invaded and the cities were attacked. Some of the fiercest battles were fought around such gateways and many legends have been spun around them.

Now almost all the historic cities have spread out of their walls and in some cases it is not even possible to see the wall, but some of the gateways can still be seen as landmarks of history. These are no longer closed for the night and they remain open even when there is danger of invasion. The Harm Gate of Multan is one such landmark.

In the past it was also a tradition to build very strong walls around forts and palaces. The gateways of the forts were designed keeping in view the strength of potential enemies. There are several gateways in Pakistan though some forts are in ruins now and some have completely disappeared. Strange it is that gateways are there and now used and photographed by tourists because of their historic importance, architectural beauty and peculiar designs. Such is the gateway of the historic fort of the city of Multan which is no doubt the oldest living city in Pakistan. The fort was blown up when the British forces captured Multan in 1857. This gateway also damaged but it has been repaired after independence and restored to its original shape. Originally it was built during the fourteenth century.

There are scores of gateways of various shrines and tombs, some of which are so beautiful that it is difficult to describe them in words. Most of them are profusely decorated, some of them silver plated and some of them are opened only once a year while others are always kept open. Here is one such gate, the gate of Shah Gardez, which was built in the tenth century and is in its original shape even now. Thousands of devotees come here to pay homage to the Sufi saint who is buried here.

Iran: Through the Gateway from Chaos to the Cosmos

City gate of Shiraz

Not too long ago all the major cities of Iran were enclosed by protective walls and gateways. A number of these gates are still in use and some have been restored as national monuments. Today travellers entering the city of Shiraz from the north-east, pass the gateway of *Quran.* A copy of the Holy Book of Islam is kept on the top of the gate in a repository and, all travellers leaving the city, pass through the "Open-Gate" (darwazeh), and are thus blessed by the beneficent powers of the *Quran* and are safeguarded from the perils of the journey. That the sacredness of this particular gateway is secured by the *Quran* needs no amplification.

In Iran, anyone embarking on a journey when leaving the house passes under the *Quran,* hand-held above the head. Hands holding the *Quran* above the head, is in fact, a symbolic "gateway", not only for trips but pertaining to any important undertaking or intended action.

Before the appearance of high-rise buildings in Iran, the house-door of the common people was built lower than the height of the average person. So that, anyone entering the house perforce assumed a gesture of reverence to the dwelling place. Moreover, high above the doors tiles bearing holy names or phrases were embedded in the wall, to doubly ensure the sanctity of the home.

The gateway of the *Quran*, the symbolic gateway formed by the hands holding the *Quran*, house-doors built low with holy names above, are all significant, so far as they are the carriers of the Holy Book or divine inscription.

Now, let us examine another type of abode which gains sanctity by another scheme. The Turkoman tribes of northeastern Iran live in tents called *Yurt*. The *Yurt* is constructed, somehow, in the order or a geodesic dome. At the very centre of the *Yurt*, there is an aperture-opening through which smoke escapes. The rising smoke is a "central-pillar" directly facing the *Polar Ṣtar*. The tent, unlike the house, is a movable unit, which is exposed to the dangers of the surrounding environs. The "rising-smoke" as a "central pillar", sanctifying the space within the tent, is a notion deeply rooted in time, extending from Central Asia all the way to North America. Before taking up the "gateway of Jamshid" let us, in one broad sweep, look at the landscape of Iran, and observe what we can find in visible architectural forms. Holy shrines of Saints and their descendants dot the land, and all are active with the rites of pilgrimage. The rituals take place annually or periodically in accordance with the communal custom. In addition, there is in every village some nook, or solitary sacred spot. No communal pilgrimage is designated for such spots. These are places of repose and contemplation. Oftentimes, a lone tree at the outskirts of the central desert or in a difficult mountain passage becomes numinous. Pieces of cloth are tied to the branches of such trees for divine favour.

All sacred precincts are separated by thresholds from the surrounding environs, visible or invisible. Within the enclosure all is in the order and harmony — cosmos—, whatever is outside the limits of the sanctuary is profane—*chaos*—which means that entry from chaos into cosmos is gained only through a passage or gateway.

The vision of Paradaiza

It was in ancient Iran that the vision of paradise originated. Both the name and the concept are Iranian, meaning "enclosure". The symbolic configuration of paradise is reflected in the major gardens of Iran. To mention only one, the Garden of Golshan in Tabas, in the central desert of Iran, is a veritable paradise, with running water brought forth through subterranean channels from distances miles away.

Travellers and wayfarers traversing the desolate and barren desert, when reaching this garden-paradise, are overwhelmed with awe, knowing deeply that they have entered a blissful environ. The entry to the gate-house of the Golshan Garden, is an experience of unparalleled beauty. The shimmering foliage of the garden, framed in the archway of the portal entrance, suddenly comes into view. The intense blinding light is at once modulated and a sense of release, from the heat-radiation, is felt. Within the gate-house a cool breeze embraces one's whole being; and the echoing murmur of the hidden flowing water, underfoot, is a soothing melody to the ears. In the quadrangular reflecting pool, a fountain miraculously created ever-expanding concentric circles, in the water-surface. And, by the poolside are cypress trees swaying to and fro.

Bond between heaven and earth

The mountain ranges of Iran are the great reservoir of water sustaining life. When hot summer skies bear down upon the land and vegetation dies, the magic ritual is invoked to seek the gift of fertility and abundance.

In the absence of mountains, their replicas were created. One such early and imposing monument is the Elamite Ziggurat of Chogazambil (c.1250 BC) in southwestern Iran. The Ziggurat was "The Link between Heaven and Earth". The focal point in the Ziggurat is indicated, symbolically, by a double recessed panel — a niche — wherein the heavenly forces come in contact with the earth. Again, at the base of the Ziggurat the entrance gate leads the way to the upper and inner spot, the most sacred in the structure. Later on, that is, more than two thousand years later, the "niche" emerges as the Mihrab in the mosque, this time as the focal point for all moslems, who face the direction of the Holy City of Mecca, when praying.

The throne of Jamshid

"Persepolis" is the translation of the "City of Parsa", in western languages, but in Iran it is Takht-e-Jamshid or the Throne of Jamshid. The entire complex of Persepolis is anchored in the rocks of Mount Mercy, dominating over a vast fertile plain reigned by mountains. The first major archeological excavation Persepolis took place fifty years ago and continued intermittently until recently.

Who planned Persepolis and why was this architectural complex built? It is said that Cyrus the Great, the founder of the Achaemenid Dynasty, selected the site, and the successive monarchs brought it to near completion (518-330 BC). All the capital cities and royal residences of the Achaemenids are pasargadee, Babylon, Susa and Ecbatana, but there is no mention of Persepolis. How was it possible to conceal such a colossal structure under the veil of secrecy, for two centuries? The Throne of Jamshid was the most sacred enclosure in ancient Iran, constructed for divine purposes and more.

The true architects of the throne of Jamshid, when conceiving the structural-system, must have had an exact blueprint upon which to realize their ideas. Such a blueprint, did in fact exist, and it was in the encoded primordial forms of *Urmythos*. The throne of Jamshid came about not only as the concrete manifestation of kingly powers, but at the same time, as a copy of the mythic "City of Heaven". In Sumer, the temple and garden complex of Gudea, was one example of the sacred city.

Now we may begin to pass through the "Gateway of All Lands". The gate of Xerxes was built on the terrace which is 1,745 feet long and rises to a height of 60 feet. The terrace is scaled by a double stairway, diverging and returning on itself, leading to the "Gate of All Lands". The gateway is guarded by gigantic human-headed, winged bulls, giving the impression that they are about to walk out of the pylons.

The proclamation of Xerxes inscribed in the gate, reads in parts as follows... "By the grace of Ahuramazda, this Gateway of All Lands I made; much else that is beautiful was done throughout Parsa, which I did and which my father did, whatever work seems beautiful, and all that we did by the grace of Ahuramazda.."

Once the passage through the entrance-gate is secured, we gain entry into the most sacred shrine in ancient Iran, wherein the presiding spiritual forces are operative. As the Ziggurat, centuries earlier, was the "Bond Between Heaven and Earth", Persepolis, too was structured in every detail to function with exact coordinates, computing the celestial cycles. Time itself was deified, under the all comprehending title, *Zurvan Akarana.* This divinity regulated the revolutions of the stars, to be the absolute master of all things.

In the Iranian cosmology of Zurvanitic tradition we read that every terrestrial phenomenon, abstract or concrete, corresponds to a celestial, transcendental invisible form. Each thing, each notion presents itself under a double aspect: *Menok* and *Getik.* Our earth corresponds to a celestial earth. Every act committed here below, in the *Getik*, has a celestial counterpart, which is the true reality. From the cosmogonic point of view, the cosmic stage called *Menok* precedes the stage *Getik.*

Jamshid or Cyrus? Which one of the two is really the true architect of Persepolis? When we, once again, refer to the coded fabric of the myth for verification, the extraordinary figure of Jamshid appears. In India he is called Yama, in the old Iranian *Avesta* he is named Yima x saeta, and translated into New Persian, he is Jamshid. In Latin he is Saturnus. Saturn or Koronos had been known as the ruler of the "Golden Age". Such mythical beings do exist, but not in temporal time. Such beings, under whatever names, are resistant to falsification, and further, they do not yield to speculation of the unconscious. The most important ritual which took place in Persepolis was at the time of the New Year, that is at the exact moment of vernal equinox. The rite of passage from the old to the New Year, was pre-arranged months prior to the precise moment, when day and night were equal in duration.

Each component in the structural system of Persepolis was orchestrated and tuned to celestial harmony. Because heaven in motion provides coordinates for time and place on earth. Only the privileged and honoured persons could pass through the Gateway of All Lands. The ritual which took place within the sanctuary of the Throne of Jamshid required no witnesses. Therein the ritual was conducted under strict rules, barring contamination from outside. While each person performed the assigned act, the structural system became numinous and alive. Every symbol began to generate the mute and arrested energies, which had remained dormant till then. One must, at this time, remember that all the symbolic configurations carved in stone, were part and parcel of one unified whole. Lotus, cypress, the image of the mountain, Leo and Taurus, the serene representation of Ahuramazda, all emitted power seeking divine favour. There were five hundred and fifty columns representing the sacred grove. The inverted lotus forms at the bases of the columns made up the tempo of the procession. Indeed one can only imagine the ritual of this magnitude taking place within the vast complex of Takhat-e-Jamshid at a time receding back twenty-five centuries. As we all are the inheritors of one diversified culture deeply rooted in time, where else could we look for guidance but to the heavens? The faultless and all powerful machine, should have yielded only harmony and perfection, the reign of justice and innocence, rivers flowing with milk and honey.

India: Beginning a Spiritual Journey Toward Enlightenment

The Indian landscape is interspersed with man-made monuments in wood, brick and stone, each symbolizing man's journey to the divine, known and unknown, concrete or abstract, and to the formless and the unmanifest. Man's first awareness of the eternal waters which sustain him, the earth which supports him and the heaven and ether which protect him and the cardinal directions and space which circumscribe him led him to recreate the cosmos in words, stones, line, paint, colour, sound and movement. Each time man recreates for a particular duration of physical time — a few moments or a whole day, week, month or year, — a cosmos on earth in its never-ending rhythm of evolution, creation and devolution. The homes, cities, temples, stupas, churches and mosques man built in permanent material also articulated this self-conscious awareness of his life on earth and his journey towards the infinite, the divine and the unmanifest. In each case, first was the establishment of a centre corresponding to the seed, the *beeja*, the mythical navel-of the earth as also the human body, thereafter an immediate enclosure, a square or circle, encased the centre; a larger outer space came next and finally there was the outermost spaces, with gateways which represented the cardinal directions. The entire space was now differentiated from mundane, secular space. The enclosure was sacred space hallowed and a pathway to the divine. Vertically also there was the centre, or the seed which emerged as the tree, the pillar, the *stambha* and finally reached the pinnacle. Sacred architecture of all faiths followed these fundamentals.

This primary conception of consecrating time and space for fixed durations and recreation through either the occurrent or ephemeral or permanent arts or the construction of monumental edifices sums up the universal conceptions underlying both gateways and shrines known to all cultures at all times.

Although the remains of Mohenjodaro and Harappan culture are fragmentary, it is clear that the citadel of Mohenjodaro must have had a grand entry into this architectural edifice. The Vedas speak in many beautiful hymns of the eternal waters, earth, heaven, ether, and fire and the lords of the directions. Man calls out to the elements to protect and guard. The rituals of the Brahmans concretized these conceptions by enclosing space in the shape of an enclosure (*shala*) in which were established the three fires, domestic, terrestrial and celestial in the shapes of a semi-circle, circle and square respectively. The sacred altar was built with bricks of different sizes. Through incantation and chants, oblations and rituals, the cosmos was recreated for seven, eleven or twenty-one days and then destroyed. The multiple forms merged back to the formless; dust unto dust was the culmination. The ritual over mundane time and space returned. In terms of structures and as an outward symbol of this inner process, the outer enclosure, the three fires and circumscribing of space were essential.

In time to come, the Vedic ritual gave place to actual monuments where, through daily rituals, the same was done. The earliest archaeological remains of the historical period manifest Man's aspiration and needs to relate himself to the elements and to the vegetative, animal, human, and celestial world which surrounded him and on which his life was dependent.

Many religions were founded and each was responsible for giving a distinctive expression to these fundamental concerns. The language, form, shape, design, and architectural style were different but the underlying unity was unmistakable. One outstanding feature of all these architectural edifices, big or small, domestic or sacred, made of ephemeral or permanent materials was the one or many entrances. In domestic architecture the one entrance led to the centre of the home, the inner courtyard. In the plan of the city, the roads led out to the cardinal directions, and converged to a central place which was usually the sacred centre of the city, a shrine, stupa or temple.

In India, it is believed that Mount Sumeru rises from the midpoint of the surface of the earth as the vertical axis of the egg-shaped cosmos. The slopes of this mountain are propelled by a multitude of life, the creatures of the waters, the crocodiles, the serpents and fish, the first vegetation of the waters, the beautiful lotus, the flowering tree; the animals on the earth, the deer, the elephant and the monkey come next. The human gnomes, dwarfs and *yakshas* and the flying celestials, female *apsaras* and *gandharvas* follow. On the quadrangular summit stand the palatial abode of the eternal gods, the deathless ones (*amara*). The summit is known therefore as *Amaravati* (The Town Immortal).

This mythology of the Sumeru (mountain) and *Amaravati* (the eternal or immortal city) was adapted in the early Buddhist stupas in India to commemorate the life and preachings of the Buddha. The gateways represent the four quarters which protect the sacred world. The human figures or deities who are carved on the gateways are called the *Lokapala* (protectors of the world). They stand and guard the four entrances (gates) of the railings of the Buddhist stupas. As the doctrine of the Buddha spread, these deities of the four quarters also travelled and they are integral to the architectural designs of monuments in China, Korea, Japan and Indonesia. The most impressive amongst the early Buddhist monuments are the sites of Bharhut and Sanchi. The stupas have a simple form: the interior is a compact heap of earth, pebbles or stones which is enclosed by a layer of bricks and the bricks are in turn covered with a facade of polished stone. One or several terraces, quadrangular or circular can form the base (*medhi*) and around this base there is enough space for clockwise circumambulation. The whole structure is enclosed by a railing (*vedika*) of either wood or stone. In the case of both Bharhut and Sanchi, it is stone. Such railings are created with horizontal beams which are interlinked and vertical pillars (*stambha*). Finally there is a coping or a brown (diadem or turban). Staircases (*sopanas*) may lead up to the terraces going around the central bulwark which is called the egg (*anda*) or the womb (*garbha*) and which contains the seed (*beeja*), namely, the relic. It is crowned by a quadrangular housing or terrace (*harmika*) above which arise one or several canopies (*chhatra*). The stupa is a symbol of enlightenment and the vehicle of carrying the message of the Buddha to the four quarters. The stupa is also an instrument (a design — *yantra*) for the guidance of the devout who take the upward journey of the soul by circumambulating clockwise in a reverent attitude. Finally he ascends to the top.

The gates and railings represent the beginning of this spiritual journey. The railings and the gateways are richly carved with reliefs which illustrate the world, its vegetation, lotus trees, flowers, aquatic and terrestrial life, animals and birds, dwarfs, dryads, the yakshas and yakshis. Amongst these are the reliefs of the vase of fullness, *purna kumbha* which stands for fertility and fullness. Also there is an abundance of reliefs of the lotus, which symbolizes cosmic order and the wheel which represents the first preaching of the doctrine. There are beautiful animals, rows of elephants and deer, and winged lions. This is the mundane world (*samsara*) from which the pilgrim begins his journey: the plenty and abundance lead him to restraint and the desire to know the past lives of the Bodhisattva. So the horizontal and vertical columns of the gateways depict in profusion, the numerous lives of the Buddha in his journey towards enlightenment. The tales of the jatakas depicting the Buddha, as *Mahakapi, Mahajanaka* and *Vessantara* and *Saddantajataka* and innumerable others are seen in reliefs in the architraves in Sanchi and in the railing medallions in Bharhut. All these reliefs are in fact symbolic of the devotees' personal journey. When the pilgrim attains to the crowning terrace, he has anticipated in a figurative way his own enlightenment and the extinction of all passions which fetter him to the round of rebirth. This didactic function of the stupa is clear in all stupas ranging from Sanchi in India to Borobudur in Java. The architectural plan provides the physical opportunity for this figurative journey of the devotee pilgrim.

The North Gate of Sanchi is impressive for the two vertical pillars which support two imposing capitals (four elephants back to back) and three superimposed architraves. Each of the faces of these pillars and architraves is richly decorated with reliefs illustrating the Buddhist legend. The Southern Gateway is similar. On the outside of the upper architrave is a beautiful standing figure of Lakshmi with two elephants and surrounded by a luxurious atmosphere of water vegetation and birds. On the middle architrave is a panoramic view of Ashoka's visit to the stupa of Ramagrama and on the lowest there are six dwarfs spouting lotus stalks amongst leaves, buds and lotus flowers. On the Western Gateway are depicted some of the Buddhist symbols: there is the young elephant representing conception, the tree representing enlightenment and the wheel of the doctrine. In the middle architrave is seen the great renunciation: the riderless horse suggests the Buddha's departure from the palace. On the lowest architrave is seen Ashoka followed by a crowd of warriors and servants: he steps down from the kneeling elephant to worship the sacred Bo tee. The *yakshini*, the tree dryad is the most outstanding figure. Her arms are intertwined with the branches of the tree and her foot touches the trunk of the tree. The Western Gateway has similar scenes. Through each of these gateways the pilgrim enters the sacred stupa and gradually make a circumambulation clockwise until he reaches the pinnacle. The gateways are the beginning of this journey.

Elsewhere in India, instead of the four gateways, there are the impressive entrances and facades to rock caves. Bhaja and Karle caves in Western India have stupendous entrances which lead the pilgrim into a cave-like structure with a basilican plan nearly 60 feet long and 25 feet high. At the end of the cave is the altar in the form of a stupa around which the devotees can walk. The facade of Karle is decorated with massive figures in high relief. Outstanding amongst these are the couples who seem as if flying in air, soaring towards the heavens through the flowing curves of their bodies. These horse-shoe facades in the rock cut caves of India were the abode of monks and famous monasteries were established here. The facade and the entrance were one with only one source of light, once again suggesting metaphorically the journey of the pilgrim to the divine. These cool, half dark vaults receive dim light through the entrance above. Occasionally there is an additional vaulted upper window. Pure space without matter, without weight or any figurative sculpture inside invites the devotee to enter into the sphere and face the symbol of his outer extinction and inner enlightenment; the small replica of the stupa within denotes *nirvana.*

The tradition of the gateways and entrances also applies to the architecture of the Hindu monuments. In Ajanta and Ellora, there are both facades, single entrance and gates, if not gateways.

At the Kailashnath Temple of Ellora, also a masterpiece of rock cut architecture, the pilgrim is greeted with two figures of the water deities, namely *Ganga* and *Yamuna.* One stands on a crocodile and the other on a tortoise; both represent the gateway to the mountain Kailash or Hemavata. Ganga and Yamuna are the entries into the journey of the soul to the summit of spiritual ascension. At all sanctuaries in India from Kailashnath in Ellora to the medieval temples of the plains of U.P., Madhya Pradesh and Rajasthan to the temples in far-off Assam, the two water goddesses representing the two mighty rivers of India, are carved on the entrance gates of temples. The Ganga and Yamuna figures as guardians of the entrances continue to be popular, but in addition in the South Indian temples as elsewhere in India and especially Indonesia and Cambodia, there appear the fierce figures of the *dvarapalas* (the doorkeepers). They ward off evil, and protect the innermost shrine. Sometimes they are simple warriors seen in their Indian, Chinese or Japanese garbs. At other times, they are weird fearsome demons who guard and frighten. Metaphorically and figuratively they are the demons within the human psyche who have to be reckoned with and ultimately conquered before taking the inner journey of the soul towards enlightenment.

The devotee enters the massive gateway of Southern Indian temples, the *gopuram,* as if he were entering a fort. The door lintels are again richly carved with minor and major deities, the life of the vegetative, aquatic, terrestrial and celestial world, though the *dvarapalas* (the guardians of door) are dominant. Sometimes, they ride elephants at others lions and other mythical beings. The great *gopurams* are on the four directions of the outermost enclosure of space, (as in Sanchi) but now enlarged a hundred fold. The temple is the temporary abode of the gods on earth, the re-creation of the cosmos on earth, a fort on earth of the gods. The Central Shrine is metaphorically the Sumeru, the Kailash. The devotee enters through the gateways to take this journey, circumambulates the larger outer spaces, moves inward into smaller enclosures and finally enter the *garbhagriha* (the womb house) and ultimately the sanctum representing the seed of all creation. From outer light, he moves inward into areas of physical darkness; this is his physical state. Natural light gradually diminishes. Inwardly from the world of multitudes of forms (*samsara*) and the ignorance and darkness of his psychical state, he moves towards the shrine which will bring him inward light and luminosity. The doors of perception are opened physically and psychically through the gateways, entrances and the facades, the mythical goddesses of the waters, the guardians of the stupas & the temples. The devotee-pilgrim's journey begins here, and these concrete structures are the symbols of an inward journey temporary or enduring.

Sri Lanka: Moving Toward the Compassion of Buddha

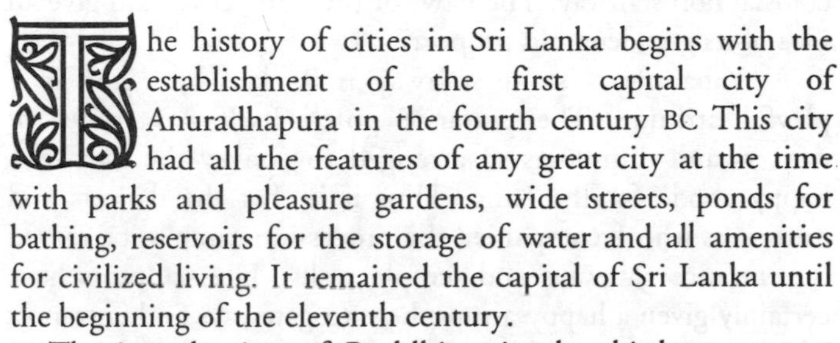

The history of cities in Sri Lanka begins with the establishment of the first capital city of Anuradhapura in the fourth century BC This city had all the features of any great city at the time with parks and pleasure gardens, wide streets, ponds for bathing, reservoirs for the storage of water and all amenities for civilized living. It remained the capital of Sri Lanka until the beginning of the eleventh century.

The introduction of Buddhism in the third century BC through the missionary activities of King Asoka of India was the beginning of a tradition of Buddhist architecture which has developed and maintained its individuality throughout the centuries. Monasteries were built of brick, stone, timber and wattle and daub. Some of the brick stupas are of colossal dimensions whilst the village shrine room are of timber and mud construction of modest size.

There developed in time an architecture adapted to different materials with symbolic ornamentation so linked with the religious beliefs of the time. Facades of buildings were decorated with heavily moulded plinths, flights of steps and entrances. Religious buildings were enclosed in walled areas providing sometimes several courtyards and procession paths linked with stairways at the cardinal points. The gateways were of simple as well as elaborate detailing.

The layout of the buildings in a monastery complex was divided into several large courtyards. The main building or *prosada* which housed the image of the Buddha was entered through a single entrance with a decorated flight of steps. A semicircular stone placed at the entrance of these buildings referred to as the moonstone, has the most intricate design and has intrigued many an art historian in its ornamentation. Paranavitana who made an extensive study of the best example seen at the shrine room of the Abhayagiri Vihara at Anuradhapura finds the detailing very expressive of the deep philosophy of Buddhism. "No one who sees any of the half-a-dozen examples of the moonstones at Anuradhapura will indeed fail to be impressed by the technical perfection and refinement of the carving in general, of the skill of the sculptor in making the intractable gneiss yield delicate details of the animal and vegetable forms, of the vigorous realism and sensitive modelling and suggestion of movement noticeable in the animal forms, of the intricacy and rhythm of the foliated scroll, of the architectonic quality of the lotus design in the centre, or of the integration of the various elements of the design to form a satisfying whole."

While admiring the form and design of these moonstones one cannot fail to realize that the designs must have a meaning in their composition at the entrance to a sacred edifice. Paranavitana says:

"The shrines at Anuradhapura, in which the object of worship is an image of the Buddha, and at the entrance to which moonstones are placed, are built on moulded platforms, the level on which the image is set up being about three feet above the ground. The edge of the moonstone is flush, with the ground. If, as we have surmised, the shrine itself is meant to represent the Palace of Tooth from which the Buddha looks down with compassion upon beings undergoing suffering in the *Samsara*, (the mundane world), the moonstone must be taken as the plane on which those who are still enmeshed in the world flux have their being, that is to say, the *Bhava-Cakra*, circle of existence and becoming."

In course of time the various motifs used at the entrance, moonstones, balustrades and guardstones began to be used independently in various decorative forms. The gateway was ornamented with forms more for their decorative character than for any symbolism in their use.

The earliest guardstones which had only a pot motif on them later changed to a pot in the hand of a guardian who held a sprouting creeper in the other hand. This same pot motif in later times has been used as an interesting design, the shape being composed of sensuous forms of five women. An ivory carving over the entrance doorway to the Red Vihara is a fine example of this form.

The *makara*, an imaginary motif of a decorative mythical animal form has figured in almost all entrance gateways of medieval times.

Stout dwarfs have been sculptured on the steps as if carrying the weight of the steps on their shoulders. Entrances and plinths are decorated with dwarfs in various dance forms. Apart from the above, the entrances to the stupa at the cardinal points contain a *wahalkada* so called because it faces the entrance.

The *dagabas* of Sri Lanka are of colossal dimensions and comprise the domical stupa, a square, raised platform paved with stone slabs, a procession pathway and roadways leading to the four cardinal points.

Facing the entrance as one climbs the steps to the sacred terrace are these decorative entrances with sculptured motifs of animal, floral and human forms. In these *wahalkadas* the animal forms of elephants, horses, lions and bulls appear in separate rows. The elephant in keeping with its stature is made to bear the load of the structure above. The lion, horse and bull are depicted running a never-ending race. It is most humorous to find amidst all this a row of dwarf musicians and dancers. Some of them are shown in acrobatic postures with their head down standing on their hands. In a simple frieze at Mihintale on a *wahalkada* is shown a procession of dwarfs bringing food and drink to Ganesha, the elephant-headed God of Wisdom.

The pot-bellied figure has also been used at entrances. A characteristics form is Padmaniphi and Sankanidhi seen at the entrance to the palace of Vijayabahu at Anuradhapura. These also appear at the entrance to stupas.

These guardian figures have in course of time been regarded as having magical powers. A person by the application of *chunam* on the face or body of the figure takes a vow for the attainment of some objective. These dwarf deities, however, do not accept requests of an evil nature. While in some instances they guard treasure they are supposed to bring ill-effects on those who attempt to redeem the treasure in their custody.

In the middle ages when buildings were of wattle and daub and of timber construction the entrances began to take the form of guard houses one sees in a fortress. The temple square in Kandy was enclosed with a wall entered through a gateway with a tiled roof. The walls of these gateways and the entrance contained the characteristic figures of a *makara* and guardian. Entrances to palaces were designed to suit their location. The Palace of Kassapa (AD sixth century) located on the rock 600 feet above the plain is entered at the midway terrace through a colossal lion stairway. The paws of the lion yet remain give an idea of its grandeur and proportion.

At Yapahuwa a stone stairway is flanked by a lion in a playful attitude. The entrance porch itself has friezes of dancers and drummers so arranged to convey the idea of a happy abode for the King. Thus it is that the dancers and musicians who accompanied the procession came to be carved on entrance gateways and temple walls. The sculptors have certainly given a happy atmosphere to gateways and entrances which otherwise would have been blocks or stone and wooden posts and beams serving only as entry to a sacred or royal enclosure.

Thailand: Protecting the Delicate Channel to Fortune or Misfortune

Beliefs concerning Animism and superstition in ancient Thai society were similar to those of other societies. These beliefs concerned invisible supernatural powers which could cause good or bad luck, fortune or misfortune to all human beings. Accordingly, there were a series of rules and taboos that had to be strictly followed for a good life.

The entrance or gateway was viewed as the very delicate channel which the enemy or the malevolent spirit could enter to cause misfortune and disaster. Therefore, the entrance or gateway had to be very carefully protected with a sacred object. This sacred object was usually the symbol of the religious belief of the people.

This belief concerning the entrance or gateway had a strong influence on traditional Thai society. In house construction, the entrance or gateway was built in the east since the east was considered as the symbol of birth and good fortune.

The house door was built very narrow. Ancient texts concerning house construction stated the house door should be about 2 feet wide. A wider doorway would bring about illness and disaster. One advantage of the narrow doorway was that it would be difficult for the enemy to get in and out. This implied the intention of self-protection.

However, this rule is no longer followed at present since a narrow doorway is also inconvenient for the owner of the house. But it has to be noted that certain taboos concerning the doorway are still practised. For example, people, especially pregnant women are prohibited from sitting blocking the doorway. It is believed that to sit blocking the doorway will cause difficulty in the delivery of the baby. Moreover, the entrance or gateway in Thai architecture is usually accompanied with a number of thresholds. There is also a taboo which prohibits stepping on the threshold. In the royal palace, this taboo is very strictly followed since there is a belief that the gates of the royal palace are guarded by a group of deities who dwell inside the threshold. Thus, anyone who steps on these threshold, even by accident or unintentionally, has to immediately pay respect to the deities and ask for forgiveness. The gateways of the royal palace were ceremonially purified yearly.

In constructing the gate of a large or important town and the royal palace, the appropriate date has to be selected by an astrologer. Some magical or sacred objects are buried at the construction site in order to protect the entrance from all enemies. The kind of wood used for construction is selected from trees with auspicious names. The gate poles are erected at certain points. The time to open and close the town gate is fixed. The corpse of the dead could not pass through the town gate. It had to be taken out of the town for burial or cremation through a special gate called "Pratu Phi" (Ghost Gate). The Pratu Phi is opened only during the daytime. There was also a Pratu Phi in the early Bangkok Period but it was demolished recently.

The Royal Palace has a total of 30 gates. Among these gates, there are two main gateways for entrance and exit. They are large brick gates constructed in the form of a "Sum Mondop Yod Prang" (A pyramidal superstructure topped with a tower), according to the Thai art style. These gates called Prahtu Pimantheved (Bimanadevavesa) and Prahtu Visethjaisi (Visesajaysri) are doubled and painted dark red and are situated in the northern wall line. There is a group of soldiers in charge of guarding these gates. The inner part of the Royal Grand Palace was used as the private residence of the Kings of the Chakri dynasty. The guards of the inner gates were female soldiers called "Klon" who were responsible for protecting the Palace against intruders into the inner part of the palace and against people stepping on the thresholds of the gates.

Since folk belief in Thailand is an amalgamation of Animism, Buddhism and Brahmanism, beliefs concerning entrances or gateways are closely related to the symbols and concepts of those religions. The entrances or gateways of important or sacred places are usually accompanied by guardian symbols in various forms, depending upon their popularity during each period in history.

Mostly, however, these symbols are made in the images of Buddhist or Hindu deities or in the forms of the animals in the Himavanta forest which are mentioned in the religious texts. The guardian deities of gateways or entrances are generally called Tikapala or Lokapala. The personal names of each deity are as follows:

Indra — guardian of the East
Agni — guardian of the Southeast
Isana — guardian of the Northeast
Varuna — guardian of the West
Vayu — guardian of the Northwest
Nirrti — guardian of the Southwest
Yama — guardian of the South
Kubera — guardian of the North.

The images of these guardian deities are usually found in religious building of Mahayana Buddhism or Hinduism (Sivaism or Vishnuism), for example, at Preasat Hin Pimai in Nakornrajasima Province or at Prah Prang Samyod in Lopburi Province. The reason for using these deities as guardians of the gateways or entrances of the religious sanctuaries is that the religious sanctuaries are places for the gods or Bodhisattva from heaven to reside. Thus the religious sanctuary has to be modelled on the Mountain of Meru which was the residence of the gods according to the religious texts.

In addition, the guardian deities are sometimes known collectively as Catura Maharaja and individually as —

Vessuvana (Kubera) — guardian of the North
Virupaksa — guardian of the West
Viruhaka — guardian of the South
Dhataratha — guardian of the East

The beliefs in guardian deities in Thai society which might have originally been imported from ancient Khmer culture have been held to the present time. In Prah Tamnak Chitlada the present Royal Residence of the King of Thailand, there are no symbols or images of the guardian deities but the names of all four entrances or gateways still reflect this belief. The names of these gates are as follows:

Prah in yochom (Brah Indra ayû jam) situated in the East
Prah Yom Yu gum (Brah Yama ayû gum) situated in the South
Prah Varun yu ven (Brah Varuna ayû ven) situated in the West
Prah Kuevn yu fau (Brah Kubera ayû phaû) situated in the North.

The use of symbols or names of the guardian deities in naming the gates of the Royal Residence is based on the concept of "Deva Raja" or "God King". According to this concept the king is considered to be the reincarnation of god from heaven. Other symbols are also commonly used as guardians of the entrances of religious buildings, namely, the images of Yaksa (Giant), Siewkang (Sieyv Kan) or Khiewkang (Khieyv Kan), Singha (Simha) and Naga.

Yaksa is believed to have supernatural power over all malevolent spirits. Therefore, images of Yaksa are commonly found in front of the gates of important religious sanctuaries all over the country. The best known images of Yaksa are in front of the gates of the Temple of the Emerald Buddha. They are generally accepted to be the most beautiful images of Yaksa in Thailand.

Siewkang of Khiewkang is constructed in the form of a human being but with a stern face and usually standing on the back of a lion in the style of Chinese art. Most Thai scholars believe the Siewkang was an imitation of the guardian spirits in Chinese culture dressed in Thai costume. The images of Siewkang are usually found engraved on the gates of religious buildings of the early Bangkok period. Some people believe

The oldest evidence of using the images of Singha as a guardian of an entrance or gateway was found at Chedi Chula Pathon in Nakorn Pathom Province which is a Buddhist sanctuary of the Dvaravati Period. According to a Buddhist text, Singha is one of the four animals (Singha, elephant, horse and bullock) which were the guardians of the universe. It was the guardian of one of the four Watergates of Anavatapta (a lake in the Himavanta Forest) which contain the sacred water that flowed down to feed all human beings. In Hinduist belief, Singha was the mount of Vishnu and Kubera. The use of the image of Singha as the guardian of the entrance of a sanctuary was very popular in the ancient Khmer Period. Later on the Thai adopted this concept from Khmer culture but instead of placing the image of Singha in front of the entrance or gateway of the sanctuary, the Thai placed it in front of the doorway of the main temple. In the present day the image of Singha has become a part of the decorative objects.

Naga (King of serpents) is also considered to be a guardian of sacred places. The Mahabharata states that Naga is half deity and half animal. It usually existed in the form of a very poisonous serpent although sometimes it would appear in the form of a human being on the upper half of the body with the lower half as serpent. Most of the countries in Indo-China have some folktales and literature which describe Naga, especially the ancient Cambodian Empire. One Cambodian folktale states that Naga was the ancestor of their kings and the guardian deity of their country. The image of Naga in the form of the great serpent is generally found in religious constructions in Cambodia. It is also commonly found in religious monuments in Thailand that were influenced by ancient Khmer culture, for example, at Prasat Hin Phanom Rung in Burirum Province. Today, several Wats in Thailand still construct the facial image of Naga at the entrance or gateway and construct its body as the rail of the stairway which leads up to the temple. The Northern Thai People believe that Naga is the God of Earth who can ordain fertility or disaster to human beings. There are many folktales describing ancient towns created or destroyed by Naga.

Recently, however, beliefs concerning entrances or gateways in Thai society are gradually disappearing. Most of the painting and sculpture found at the entrances or gateways of sanctuaries, nowadays, are constructed mainly for decorative purposes rather than to symbolise religious beliefs. Consequently, the concepts behind these symbols are becoming more and more unfamiliar to the young generation.

The North Torana *(gate) of Stupa No. 1 at Sanchi, India, richly decorated with reliefs illustrating the Buddhist legend.*

Agrarian Rituals and Festivals

Rites Devoted to Nature in Indian Peasant Tradition

Indian society is a predominantly agrarian society. About three-fourths of the people engage in agriculture for their livelihood. They are bred in ancient peasant traditions and observe an almost primitive devotion to nature that is manifested in innumerable festivals and rituals. The common features of most of these Indian festivals are the worship of the sun, the giver of sustenance and life; the worship of plants, animals, and the elements; the lighting of fires at special places that serve as centres of social life; dance; and music.

India's geographical situation has contributed to certain customs and traditions that are peculiar to India. The land, which is bounded by the Himalayan range in the north, extends southward and the Tropic of Cancer tapers off into the Indian Ocean between the Bay of Bengal on the east and the Arabian Sea on the west. This distinct geographical unity, which is maintained by mountains and the sea, marks India off from the rest of Asia. Its innumerable rivers flow across fertile lands and favourable weather conditions provide ample scope for the peasants to grow *rice, jowar, bajra, maize,* cotton, sugarcane, sesame, groundnut, wheat, barley, gram, linseed, rapeseed, and mustard. The growing of food and the rearing of domestic animals leads to a sense of security with regard to the basic necessities — particularly food. Farming and the rearing of animals have assumed an important place in Indian life that is highly valued at all levels of the society. Ritualistic activities involving nature and domestic animals have an invocatory role in society, for they express a fundamental hope for successful harvests and improvement of the herds.

In the Indian context it is also true that the various crops that are raised have given shape to many distinctive cultural patterns. With its diverse cultures, races, and religions, India has innumerable festivals that follow the agricultural cycle from sowing to harvesting. When the peasant worships nature, he expresses his hope, and sometimes, his thanks, for favourable weather conditions and a good harvest. The number of agricultural festivals in India is too large to permit adequate treatment here. However, an overview can be given with reference to some of the most popular festivals associated with the agricultural cycle, particularly to the cultivation of wheat and rice.

Sowing rituals

The agricultural year in the northern regions of India begins from the third day of the Bright Fortnight of the Hindu month Baishakh (April-May). In most places the Akhateej ("undecaying third") ceremony is performed. Rituals and customs for starting sowing in the field vary from place to place. In certain districts, the peasant goes to the field at daybreak to propitiate the earth, the mother goddesses, and the Sesha Naga, the Great Snake, which according to Hindu mythology supports the earth. It is believed that when he yawns, he causes an earthquake. The peasant carries a brass vessel and a branch of a mango tree, the tools for warding off and frightening spirits. The priest draws an imaginary line along which the peasant first digs a shallow trench and then sprinkles water over it five times with the branch of the mango tree. It is believed that the purpose behind this ritual is to ensure the protection of the crop from evil spirits.

In the Rajasthan villages, after the rains, the first day of the ploughing is observed by a ritual in which the villagers carry new earthenware pots coloured with turmeric, that they fill with *bajra* and serve as an offering to Mother Earth. A selected farmer ploughs five furrows. The ploughman's hands and the bullock's hoofs are rubbed with henna.

Is some other places, particularly in Maharashtra, commencement of the sowing season begins with breaking a coconut and throwing the pieces either side of the plough. By so doing it is believed that the soil spirit will leave and make way for Lakshmi, the Goddess of Prosperity, who is represented by the plough. The peasant watches all the omens carefully and if he notices anything inauspicious, he discontinues the ceremony and starts later in the day. When he returns home after performing this ritual, a married woman of the family gives him curd and silver for good luck. For the rest of the day, he will now engage in any transaction of money, grain, or fire.

In hilly areas of the northern region a different ritual is followed, known as Kudkhyo and Halkhyo. The Kudkhyo takes place in the morning or evening with the lighting of a lamp before the image of the deity. Rice, flowers, lemon juice, and balls made of turmeric are offered. Conches are blown and the peasant takes a handful of seed grain from a pot and carries it to the field. The peasant then digs a small area with a spade and plants some of the seed. In the Halkhyo ceremony, the turmeric balls are placed on the cattle-plough while four or five furrows are sown by the ploughmen and the servants are fed.

In the southern part of India, the ceremony is held to honour ancestors and other spirits who, if neglected, would prevent the seeds from germinating. Cocks and goats are sacrificed at some villages, while at others every villager plants a *bel* tree to ward off evil spirits.

Harvest festivals

Throughout India, festivals are celebrated to mark the end of the harvest period. Although they are celebrated at different times and places, they have many common features; for instance, the use of fire.

In northern India, the corn fields ripen and the crop is gathered during the spring. There is joy in the air and peace in the peasants' hearts. Pleasure fills the atmosphere and the young and the old dance and sing. A common sight is bonfires. In every village and city, heaps of wooden logs are collected and, after a proper ceremony, lighted.

In the north of the country, and notably in the Punjab, the festival to mark the end of the harvest season is known as Baisakhi. The first day of Baisakh is the time of biggest celebration. The festival is a mixture of abundant gaiety and subdued solemnity. Eating, drinking, and dancing fill the atmosphere with an air of joy and satisfaction. On the other hand, there is also an atmosphere of solemnity where people observe a fast for the contemplation of the deity. The festival is an expression of prosperity. Singing and dancing are its most enchanting features. Dances such as *bhangra* are generally performed to the accompaniment of a drum and rhythmic clapping and are very popular. From ancient times, these dances have been associated with the reaping of the harvest and with strength, masculinity, and joy.

This is also an occasion when, for the first time, the new corn is baked in the fire. In addition to the peasants' thanking the deity for a good harvest, the day is also for forgetting old quarrels. In central India, this ceremony coincides with Holi, the festival of colours.

In the southern parts of India, the harvest festival is known as Pongal. Tamilians celebrate Pongal in the month of January-February, on the first day of the Tamil month Thai, when the sun enters Capricorn. This is the time when the period for harvesting comes to an end in the region. Pongal is the festival marking the end of the harvest. The celebration lasts for four days: Bhogi Pongal, Mettu Pongal, and Kanu Pongal. Pongal, the name of this festival, is also the name of a dish consisting of rice, *moong dal,* sugar, and milk boiled together. The name thus signifies "plenty." The sun is worshipped on this day by offering a dish of *pongal* followed by a thanksgiving ceremony to the cows and the bullocks.

The sun, for all its bounties and mercies, is regarded as the chief deity of the festival. For the people who grew up with farming as their chief occupation, the worship of nature is an old tradition that has been in their blood from time immemorial. The ceremonial part lies in setting a brick stove on an elaborate *kolam* in the middle of the open courtyard of the decorated house. *Kolams* are floor decorations made for different occasions. A pot beautifully decorated by tying turmeric plants all around it is considered auspicious *Pongal* is cooked on this day. Huge stalks of sugarcane, just harvested, are tied around the pot and placed in the courtyard. As the pot is kept in the open courtyard, it is meant to be an offering to the sun-god. When the *Pongal* boils over, people gather around it and shout: *"Pongalo-Pongal!"* The cooked dish is then fed to all those who live in the house. When the *pongal* boils over, it symbolizes plenty and prosperity.

Apart from being an offering of thanks to nature for a good harvest, the festival is an offering to the sun. The second day of Pongal is known as Mattu Pongal, and it is celebrated by cow worship. Cows and bulls are decorated gaily, tassels of fibre are tied around their necks, and they are taken from house to house. Housewives perform *aarti* before them and they are fed *pongal* cooked from rice, sugar, and milk.

Farmers' festivals in Assam

In the northeastern region of the country, the people of Assam celebrate popular festivals known as the Bihus at different stages of cultivation. There are three Bihus; Bohag, Magh, and Kati. These are celebrated when the field is prepared, when paddy seedlings are transplanted, and when the harvest is ready. Bohag Bihu lasts for many days - from one week to one month, depending on the people celebrating it. The cattle are led to rivers to the accompaniment of songs. The cows are fed salted rice cakes. The festivity includes music and dance. Magh Bihu is celebrated in the middle of winter, after the harvest is collected. It reflects the powerful influences of the hills that surrounds the Brahmaputra valley, and the community fire serves as a centre of social life, dance, and music. Human civilization developed around the fireside, in addition to providing protection from the winter cold, fire was necessary for protection from the animals that roamed the earth in the olden days. These uses of fire have lingered on to later times. Magh Bihu, with fire as a conspicuous feature, is a living relic of this custom.

After the harvest is collected the earth is barren. The fires add colour to the landscape. They also announce fulfilment in the life of the peasant, who has collected his harvest and now finishes his work in the fields. During Kati Bihu, offerings are made to the *tulsi* plant by lighting clay lamps. Prayers are then offered for a good harvest. The Bihu festivals are enactments of that primitive urge in man that seeks expression through rituals, songs, and dances.

These festivals are predominantly festivals of joy. The drum-beats produce a hypnotic music that draw people into the world of dreams and aspirations. The Bihu dances are enactment of agriculture and aspirations. the Bihu dances are enactment of agriculture and pastoral experiences of the people. The peasant since ancient times has been interpreting in rituals and in art forms the process involved in cultivation. Bihu dances are mostly symbolic in nature and purpose.

All the festivals mentioned above are as much a part of lives of the peoples as farming is. They provide the people with an opportunity to express as well as to promote the community feeling that they share.

Sacred Agrarian Activities in Sri Lanka

An oral tradition regarding a shipwrecked prince, Vijaya (the Victorious), entranced by a demon-enchantress, Kuvanna (the Dark-complexioned), who, in almost Circe-like manner, entrapped the prince together with his following and later connived with him to establish a kingdom over her kith and kin, was recorded by monastic chroniclers of the Buddhist fraternity as evidence of the first migration of a race of men into the until-then ogre-infested isle of Sri Lanka. Whether this tale of demon habitation was a concoction of scheming merchants trying to maintain a monopoly over the gem and spice trade by scaring away their potential rivals, or whether it is a variation on a myth shared and spread by break-away groups from a common Indo-European ancestral stock, modern historians have not only seen in this story a kernel of historical truth regarding the first colonization of Sri Lanka by Aryans, but also have inferred from that premise the beginnings of agrarian life in this island of tropical sun and monsoonal rains; for a primitive subculture still persists to tell the tale that the pre-Aryan population was composed mainly of hunters feeding on the flesh of wild beasts, while the Aryan settlers were wielders of the plough and the scythe who consumed rice as the staple of their daily diet. There is hardly any reason to doubt the veracity of this interpretation and, to this day, the bulk of Sri Lanka's traditional population is agrarian, consisting of a rural peasantry mainly cultivating the paddy seed which, through the varied processes of sowing, reaping, threshing, and pounding, they transform three times a day into meals of boiled rice or porridge. Villager or urbanite, ancient or modern, they have sustained their lives on this mud-loving cereal regardless of all social change.

It is little wonder then that the life of Sri Lankans, at both the individual and the national levels has evolved around the cultivation of the paddy field. For both levels, the growing of rice is intricately interwoven with the culture and religion of the people and has acquired a sanctity and importance beyond other pursuits, superstitions, and rituals. Customs and ceremonies concerning the sowing and reaping of rice have come to be institutionalized as "the inheritance of the ages." From the first germinating of the paddy seed to the final harvesting, the individual peasant treats his task as sacred and marks each stage with a rite, rituals, or festival. Before the paddy seed is first soaked in water in a copper or earthenware vessel to initiate germination, the peasant seeks blessings from the gods through an act of salutation with palms pressed together before the selected grains and the assembled utensils.

The ploughing

While the seed is germinating, the ground is prepared for the sowing. This preparation begins with the flooding of the field to loosen the hard earth. But despite the acceptance of the Buddhist creed of cause and result, the peasant also places his faith in the planets and their grace. He consults an astrologer with customary offerings of betel leaves and a fee for advice on the most auspicious conjunctions of the starts before he begins his ploughing. Buffaloes are brought in to pull the plough at this first ploughing, when the ground is broken into clods. A lucky person is chosen to start off before the team joins in. Monarchs apparently added prestige to the agriculturist's profession by participating in this activity, a custom that is traced to the royal father of the Buddha, who, according to Buddhist tradition, with great pomp and pageantry stepped into the field at the annual festival called the Vap Magul, a custom that was revived recently in Sri Lanka when the president and his ministers themselves put their hands to the plough.

Astrology also determines the times for sowing, and at the prescribed moment the peasant takes a handful of the sprouting seed he has prepared and strews it over a corner of the field. He declares it "a sacred area" by planting a coconut flower, which for the Sinhalese is a symbol of prosperity. Some consider this marking out a way of reserving part of the yield for the gods when the time for reaping comes.

Vigilance through charms

From this day of the first sowing of the seed, the peasant has to keep watch and ward over his field, not only because of birds, beasts, and insects but also flood, drought, and disease that may be sent by man, devil, or angered god. To the mind of the Sinhalese peasant, it seems, jealousy is a malevolent power that can cause blight, pestilence, or accident to damage the growing crop. It finds its outlet through the eyes, the mouths, and the thoughts of malicious men. If a rival or foe should cast his envious eye or express his thoughts concerning the peasant's flourishing field, that would be enough to bring about un-anticipated evil or unnatural disaster. The wise farmer must therefore take precautions, and this he does by the aid of charms. Charmed sand or ashes are strewn over the field, and often, a charm ritual called a *kema* is performed with each stage of the crop's growth.

This charm is performed by a specialist, an exorcist (*kattadivala*) who takes up a potful of sand and mumbles over it the words of a Pali stanza, which in translation goes:

Abstain from evil
Do only good deeds
Purify the mind
This is the teaching of the Buddha.

This is apparently a scholastic Buddhist substitution for a magical spell dating from pre-Buddhistic times.

This done, at dusk, the exorcist walks along the boundaries of the field, with his waistcloth wrapped round his head, scattering sand on the ridges and bunds. Then, without another word, he retires to fast until he falls asleep in a deserted house to ensure that the spell will work. Four coconut-oil lamps that he has placed at the four corner of the field burn throughout the night, and no passing man or demon will dare enter the field, for it is charmed.

The reaping

The Sri Lankan peasant has two harvests, one called the *maha*, which depends for its success on the southwest monsoon, and the other the *yala*, which is the fruit of the northeast monsoon. Both harvests are periods of ritual and festival mixed with labour and merriment, awe and frivolity.

When the paddy is ripe, the farmer prepares for the reaping by purifying himself and his team, each act of theirs being decided by a lucky hour prescribed by the constellations. Thus they all bathe and put on clean clothes and, eating an auspicious meal of rice cooked in milk, enter the field at a fixed time. At the set moment, the leader cuts three handfuls of the ripe grain, which are kept on a specially erected post set apart for the god Kataragama, or sometimes for the guardian deity of the particular region, who may be either a Hindu divinity or a local god. This is kept in token of the portion to be used at the close of the harvest in the offering of gratitude to the gods, an alms-giving called the *deyyanne dane*.

After this handful of grain is set aside, the team begins its reaping, now for the first time with the women participating in the work in the field. Harvest songs are sung jointly to simple rhythms, while sweating hands move swiftly in the tropical sun, a glitter flashing, from the scythes as the gold-coloured paddy reeds fall into sheaves. But the songs, at least as they are known today, have little ritual significance and perhaps only serve to beguile and relieve the tedium of the work.

Threshing rites

The preparation of the threshing floor also involves a sanctifying ritual, though this varies in detail in different districts. In some, a magical diagram of three concentric circles is drawn with ash on the semi-circular floor or on outspread mats, and in the centre one are drawn various symbols to represent the implements used by the peasant or the articles that are buried in a central hole. In the floor, the only striking exception being a symbol of the foot print of the Buddha with its special marks. In the central circle is placed a conch-shell and a bundle of "sacred" oddments wrapped in a white cloth. At an auspicious time, a reputed "fortunate," placing a sheaf of corn on his head, solemnly walks three times round the bundle and thrice salutes it with palms joined together. The women carrying the sheafs do likewise before they relieve themselves of their burdens. The direction in which they must keep looking while they perform this rite is astrologically decided. In some districts, the chief cultivator, while walking around, recites a sacred stanza enumerating the virtues of the Buddha, which perhaps once again is a substitution spell that was used by the Aryans before the arrival of Buddhism.

On the thus-sanctified threshing floor, buffaloes are driven around, treading on the heaped paddy. When the grain is freed from the chaff, the winnowing is undertaken with equal reverence, the participants kneeling and bowing six times before the heaps.

Throughout these operations, common language is abandoned and a special vocabulary is used to refer to the items and activities involved. This is believed to mislead the demons who may be prowling around with harmful intent.

Customs prevail even regarding the distribution of the harvest among all the collaborators; the gods take precedence, while even the blacksmith who made the implements, the astrologer, and the washerman are not forgotten.

In short, the whole business from sowing to reaping is a community affair, with each person helping the other in turn, this arrangement having the name "*attam.*"

It is therefore not strange that these rituals are also performed at community or national levels. Not only are large-scale dance ceremonies called *kohombakankari* or *gam madu* performed as fertility rites, but the celebrations for the fulfilment of vows for thanksgiving and rainmaking are also observed at the national level.

Thus it is that the offering of the first fruits to the deities has become an annual festival — the Alut Sahal Mangalya, the Ceremony of the New Rice. A nineteenth-century foreigner's record tells us how it was then performed in the Kandyan highlands. It was held in January with the moon waxing and at lucky hours fixed by astrologers. The assignees were dispatched to the monasteries, the temples of the gods, the royal palace, and the treasury, in processions whose size and nature marked the reverence due to each. For instance, those sent to the temples of the gods were carried under canopies by men on foot while those to the Temple of the Sacred Tooth of Buddha were sent on the back of an elephant. All attendants were dressed in clean white clothes and set off to the firing of a cannon and to the accompaniment of music and drum.

The ceremony of the feast

Where the rice was received the ceremony of eating was held. The rice was cooked according to a special recipe and was usually prepared along with a curry of seven vegetables. This food was partaken of while facing the prescribed direction and the leftovers were offered to the gods, since it was considered too holy for consumption, except of course by the god's own attendants, the temple priests.

For rain in due season

But this was not the main agrarian festival, which actually centered on the Temple of the Tooth, for the sacred relic was and is still believed to have powers of bringing down rain, and therefore its possessor had the right to rule the country, since rainmaking was the monarch's primary duty toward his agrarian subjects. Modern archaeologists and anthropologists have claimed that, before the advent of Buddhism, the Rain-God of the Aryans, Parjanya, dominated the agricultural scene. But since the bringing of the Bodhi-tree from Asokan India, its watering has become the rain-making ritual. Still later, with the arrival of the Sacred Tooth, rain-making powers became linked with the holy relic, the worship of which quickly spread throughout the country. Around this relic and its associated beliefs evolved the now world-renowned "Asala Perahera," or pageant of August. The procession of caparisoned elephants carrying the Buddha relic and the insignia of the guardian gods (Natha, Vishnu, Skanda, and Pattini) of this one-time capital continues to draw thousands of devotees and sightseers each year. From start to finish, it is rigidly ritualistic, with prescribed performances and times for each movement. Its grand finale consists of the ceremony known as "water-cutting". In a decorated boat, the ritual-priests go forth into the river and draw a circle in the water with a golden sword and collect the holy liquid into vessels that they carry again in procession to the Temple of the Sacred Tooth. A vast social organization directed toward the maintenance of this annual ritual was instituted by the ancient kings and remains today, sustained by custom and piety.

Shortly after this annual ceremony the monsoon rains begin, and the peasantry of Sri Lanka repeat the cycle of their activities, sowing and reaping the golden grain around which a whole civilization of vast tanks and irrigation networks, architecture, and religion have grown, so much so that a visiting stranger once remarked that to be waist-deep in mud is the Sinhalese's glory. Among the Sri Lankans, in fact, the proverb has grown that the peasant washed of his mud is fit to rule the country.

In Veneration of Rice Spirits — Agrarian Life and Rituals in Southeast Asia

There have been many theories as to where rice was first cultivated. Recent evidence supports the theory that rice was first cultivated in the Yunnan province of China. Apparently, when Mr. Shuntaro Morinaga inspected over 25 whole rice grains in Southeast Asia, only one of those was white rice while the others were of a red colour. It is an established theory that the rice in Japan, before its quality was improved, was also red rice. Therefore, it is said that the rice which was originally brought to Japan was red rice and furthermore that this rice was glutinous, rather than non glutinous, rice. It is believed that the use of glutinous rice for many ritual meals and festive occasions stems from the days when our ancestors first came to these islands bringing glutinous rice with them.

In Japan there is a custom of cooking rice with red beans, to make *osekihan* (red-coloured boiled rice) on festive occasions. This custom is believed to be a vestige of the old days when red rice was mainly grown.

Several reasons can be given for the switch from red rice to white rice. Although red rice, which is more closely related to wild rice, is very sturdy, when the seeds ripen they fall off very easily. Red rice is very tasty when eaten just after it has been cooked but when it gets cold it is dry and rather tough. Besides such disadvantages, the amount of red rice that can be harvested is much less than that of white rice that can be harvested from the same amount of land. This is perhaps the major factor behind the switch from red rice to white rice. Already by the Heian Period (AD eighth century) red rice appears to have been replaced almost completely by white rice. Japanese shrine activities still retain many elements from the past. Even today, at the Takuzu Shrine in Tsushima and at the Homan Shrine in Tanegashima, the Japanese variety of red rice (Japonica) is still being cultivated in the fields owned by those shrines. The ritual connected to red rice of Tsushima, in particular, is of great interest. In a village called Tsutsu in Tsushima, 15 old families organize themselves as leaders (to) of the ritual and take turns to cultivate the red rice, which is the object of worship and wherein the god dwells. For the ritual a *tanemomidawara* (a type of rice bale made from woven rice ears) for the seed rice is at first made from the red rice that is harvested. This is hung from the ceiling of the house of that year's leader of the ritual, the *hareto*. This event is called *otsurimashi* and is held on the 17th day of the 10th month of the old (lunar) calendar. On the 10th day of the 1st month of the old calendar, the *tanemomidawara* is sent from the house of the leader of the previous year, the *hareto*, to that of the new leader, the *uketo*. In the middle of the night of the 10th day, actually at about 3 a.m. on the 11th day, the object of worship which has been hanging from the ceiling of the *hareto's kamizashiki* (a room in Japanese houses meant for those of the highest status) is taken down carefully and respectfully. The person who acts as protector of the object of worship carries it on his back and wears a ceremonial dress over it. Along the way to the *uketo's* house, the *utaguchi*, who is a good singer, sings joyous songs, and people with food and *sake* (rice wine) follow. The bearer of the object of worship cannot rearrange it on his back even if it is heavy or falling off. He must be extremely careful to humour the rice spirit or otherwise it would run away.

The group walks slowly beneath the icy moon on the 10th day of the first month. The villagers stay up and wait for the *utaguchi*. When they hear the singing of the *utaguchi*, they call out to each other that "the *utaguchi* has come" and gather outside. Kneeling by the road, they clap their hands in prayer to worship the sacred object. When the group finally arrives at the house of the *uketo*, the new leader, the sacred rice bale is hung in the middle of the *kamizashiki*, and the transfer of this sacred object is made from the old to new house. The belief that god dwells in red rice is perhaps one that existed before red rice was brought to Japan. The Yao tribe living in the northern part of Guangtong province in China consider red rice to be sacred. The Yaos cultivate red rice in mountainous areas by the slash and burn method.

They believe that red rice is superior to white rice in all ways. There is a story of the Yaos which explains the origin of red rice as follows: In ancient times rice plants yielded flowers but no rice grains. Then a noble lady sprinkled her virgin milk over the rice and splendid ears of rice grew. However, as she squeezed her breasts forcibly, they bled and this is how red rice was made.

In the continental areas of Southeast Asia the type of rice grown in dry fields was dominant for a very long time until it was gradually replaced in the years after Christ, by the type of rice grown in paddies. Furthermore, a large part of this was glutinous rice. This rice was grown in an extremely large area covering northern Thailand, Laos, the Shan and Kachin provinces of Burma, eastern Assam, Yunnan province, Guangix and the autonomous region of the Chuang tribe. Even today, glutinous rice is cultivated extensively among the hill tribes by the slash and burn method. At the time when the Japanese variety of rice, originating in Yunnan, became the fixed rice of the inland areas, the other type of rice, the Indian variety (Indica) appears to have been spreading along the coastal plains of Southeast Asia. I was once treated to a meal of rice which is a specialty of Mo Jian Prefecture at the official guest house in Simo of Yunnan province. One type of rice was called purple rice. True to its name it was of a purple colour, sticky, and had the flavour of glutinous rice. It was explained to me that this rice was for guests and that it was very nutritious. It is a special food for days of celebration. It is probably of the same variety as the Japanese type of rice — Japonica. Another type of rice was called crimson rice and was of a very deep red colour.

It was dry and had no flavour. This seemed to be non glutinous rice. The grains were rather long and I believe this rice was of the Indian (Indica) variety. It is said that there is no cultivated plant that is as productive as rice. If the yield of rice before modern technology was introduced is compared to that of wheat, it is said that in Japan the amount of rice harvested was 30 to 40 times the number of seeds planted, while in Europe the amount of wheat harvested was 5 to 6 times the amount of seeds planted. Furthermore, in the case of paddy rice cultivation, this is possible continuously for even 1,000 years. Rice is a food with multiple advantages. It is very tasty and therefore there is little need to have other foods to eat with it. While rice includes, even if a small amount, vegetable protein. *Sake*, rice wine, can also be made from rice. It can also be said that the power of rice to sustain a population, helps build an independent society with a strong sense of group solidarity.

There are probably very few Japanese people who believe that the rice spirit dwells in rice. However, there are a surprising number of people who, having been scolded by their mother if they spilt rice, or having been told to leave some rice in their bowl if they want another filling, still keep up this custom. In the past it was believed that if the spirit that is the source of the growth of all things is taken away completely, then the next growth cannot be attained.

In some parts of Japan the first ear of rice that is harvested is kept with the rice seeds. Again, among the Shan tribe of Thailand, which is also a rice-cultivating area, the first ear of rice is carefully put into a bamboo basket. Charms made of bamboo are tied many times to the basket to protect it from evil spirits, and the basket is placed on top of the rice granary. This unhulled rice, that is, the unhulled rice of the rice spirit, is used by being mixed with the following year's seed rice. Originally, the rice bale was a type of magical equipment in which the rice spirit was captured so that it would not escape. Also in Japan, the harvested ears of rice are piled up in a circular cone called *nio* in which the rice spirit is said to dwell. Among the Munda tribe of India, the branch of a plant called *soso* is stuck into the pile of rice ears and it is believed that the magical powers of the *soso* prevents the rice spirit from escaping. According to Mr. Taryo Obayashi there is a concept among many tribes in Indonesia called the "Rice Year". The year in the natural (agricultural) calendar is divided into two periods: the six months of the "rice growing year" and the six months of wait or resting period. This is also compared to the life cycle of man. Man's life in the real world from birth to death corresponds to the rice growing year which is the active period of the rice. The period as a fetus in the mother's womb and that after death, corresponds to the waiting or resting period before and after the active period of the rice. Man's life from conception to after death and the structure of the yearly cycle are thought to contain a similar basic structure. Furthermore, natives of Indonesia consider sunset to be the end of one day. The new day begins right after sunset. The days are counted from the beginning of the night.

It is said that in Japan, as well, before the established calendar of China was adopted, the natural (agricultural) calendar was no doubt used as in Indonesia. The character for year (*toshi*) and that for ripening (*toshi*) have the same origin. In the Manyoshu (a classic Japanese collection of poetry) the character for year and that for rice were both read "*toshi*". And the period from the sprouting to the harvesting of the grain spirit — this always meant the spirit of rice rather than any other grain — was apparently called one *toshi* (year). It is thought that a new year began twice — in April and November. In fact, in Christianity there is a cycle of two holidays. The first is Christmas which was originally the winter solstice. The second is Easter which is celebrated on the Sunday after the first full moon after the Vernal Equinox. The division of one year into two periods is a concept common to all agricultural peoples regardless of whether they cultivate rice or not. In many parts of west of the Kanto area of Japan, northern Korea, Southwest China and in the Hai Nan Islands, there is a festival which is held during the important time when the seasons change before the rice cultivating season begins in spring. Centering around March third of the old calendar (the Chinese agricultural calendar, that is, the Japanese lunar calendar) people climb mountains, enjoy themselves at rivers and at the beach and take special meals meant for days of celebration. At this time there are always songs and dances of young men and women and it is a time for young people to meet their mate. To give one example, in the villages of the Miao tribe along the Qingshui river, in the Guizhu Province of China, there is a "Sisters Festival" on March third. At that time glutinous rice is dyed red or yellow, cooked in a basket steamer, and made into riceballs. The young girls eat these riceballs sitting along the grassy banks of the Qingshui or on the sandy fields. The riceballs are not made simply to be eaten but are given as gifts to the young men. In return for the riceballs the young men give gifts of embroidery needles or silk thread to the young girls. At night, lively impromptu love songs are exchanged.

In this way courting is done right before rice cultivation in spring to stimulate the ripening of the cultivated crops through sympathetic magic. Furthermore the special meal for days of celebration is taken together in order to bring life back to the spirit which has been weakened from the withering of plants in winter, by sharing the power of the rice spirit with men and with the gods. On this day dummies which have been made to bear all impurities would be thrown into the river, plants that are charms against evil spirits would be hung on the entrance to homes and in such ways the people prayed for health and prepared for the coming days of work in the fields.

Entertaining the Gods — Korean Village Festivals

he ceremonial forms of today's village festivals in Korea are somewhat different in different areas and what they are called varies. However, most village festivals are intended as petitions of good harvests, good catches of fish, freedom from disease, having many sons and many domestic animals, and harmony in the villages. There are several different gods-mountain gods (e.g. Sansin), guardian deities (e.g., Sonang), or even deceased tragic heroes — who are believed to protect villages. Consequently, village gods vary from village to village. Festivals in Korea usually take place in sacred groves or at shrines on hilltops. The shrines are comprised or altars made of piles of stones, sacred trees, or tiled or grass-roofed shrine buildings. Shrines are variously called *sonang-dang, sansin-dang, dangsan,* and so on with *dang* meaning shrine. Most Korean village festivals are observed between the lunar New Year's Day (for the regeneration of time) and the fifteenth of January, the lunar Festival Day. But some festivals are performed in the autumn to thank the gods for harvest. The expenses for festivals usually come from communal rice paddies or village farms. If there is no communal farmland, villagers contribute equal amounts of money or rice to cover expenses.

Korean village festivals today may be grouped into three types. The first is mostly called *san-je* or *sanin-je, dong-je,* or *sonang-je*. Here, *san, sanin, dong,* and *sonang* mean mountain, mountain god village, and guardian deity, respectively. *Je*

means religious ceremony. A noteworthy festival of the second type is the *dang-kut*, a shamanistic communal rite offered to the guardian deity. Festivals of the third type may be grouped under the name *pyolsin-kut*. The main factors that differentiate the types of Korean festivals are the ceremonial forms and the participants. The festivals of the first type are strictly Confucian ceremonial services and are carried out quietly, without music and dance, by male celebrants. In contrast, the second and third types of festivals are followed by shamanistic music, dance, and feasts, and are conducted by professional shamans hired by the villagers. Also all villagers, both males and females, participate in the second and third types of the festivals while only males participate in the first type. Even though the second and third types are in the same ceremonial framework, the second type is popular only in the central areas while the third is found in the eastern coastal areas of Korea. Also, the third type is conducted on a larger scale than the second.

Let's take a look at examples of each type of festival. The *sansin-je* in Ommir-ri, Kyonggi Province, is an example of the first type of Korean village festival. Early in the morning of *sansin-je* in Ommi-ri, Kyonggi province, is an example of the other year, male villagers meet together at the open gathering place of the village and under the leadership of the elders, divide the work of making and raising the *changsung* (a pair of wooden devil posts) and the *sottae* (wooden altar post with wooden waterbirds on the top). First they select a suitable pine or black alder tree for these sacred poles. Then they carve, paint, and complete the *changung* and *sottae* and erect them before noon, placing them beside the old ones at the entrances of the village. After that, they conduct a service to the new sacred post with offerings of rice cake, rice wine, dried fish, and fruit, and party to the sacred post for peace and good harvests. After the service, the villagers feast on the offerings. At midnight of the service, the villagers feast on the offerings. At midnight of the same day, the villagers perform the main religious ceremony for the guardian deity, *Sansin*, on the top of the sacred mountain. Before the ceremony, a small shrine called the *sansin-dang* is built beside an old pine tree and a pair of wooden tablets for the male and female mountain gods (or sometimes only the female) are placed in it. The main ceremony is conducted very quietly according to set rules by the head celebrant and his assistants. The head celebrant of the ceremony and his assistant are elected by the villagers three days before the rite. The celebrants should be "clean", i.e., men who are not in mourning, who have not killed any animal recently, and who are virtuous and fortunate. The elected celebrants bathe, wear clean clothes, and put a left-woven straw rope across their doors and red earth in front of them to keep out evil spirits and show visitors that are set apart and cannot do any business until the rite is over. They also refrain from tobacco, liquor, and conjugal relations with their wives. No mourner or person who has been defiled by contact with a dead body or childbirth is allowed to go near them.

The offerings of the ceremony include rice wine, large pot of rice cake, meat patties, dried fish, five kinds of fruits (*jujube*, chestnut, persimmon, pear, and apple), three kinds of soup (meat, fish, and vegetable), salad, and so on. In the old days, they originally sacrificed a carefully raised bull. But nowadays villagers offer only the head, four feet, and samples of meat from different parts of a bull, all bought at a butcher shop because of the difficulty of raising enough money for a whole animal. After arranging the offering tables, the head celebrant and his assistants light candles, burn incense, offer wine, read a prayer, and then bow three times. Next they burn prices of white paper to petition for their village's peace and for a good harvest and for each family's good fortune. After the ceremony, the food is divided among all the village families that they might share good fortune.

Following the religious ceremony, the villagers get together and discuss the village's affairs. There is no feast or festival. It is said, however, that until fifty years ago a festival called the *kochang-kut* was held the day after this more austere ceremony. In the *kochang-kut*, a shaman was invited to perform a shamanistic rite accompanied by music and dance. After the shamanistic rite, all villagers, regardless of sex or age, participated in a festival that consisted of mask-dance dramas, puppet shows, acrobatics, and all kinds of entertainment. The festival used to last for two or three days. In actuality therefore, the original form of the *sansin-je* in Ommi-ri consisted of two parts: a strict religious ceremony and the *Kochang-kut*, a shamanistic festival. Festivals similar to the kind of *kochang-kut* that were held fifty years ago but that still exist today may be grouped and considered as the second type of Korean village festival. This type of festival is usually called *dang-kut*, with *dang* or *dodang* meaning village shrine and *kut* meaning shamanistic ceremony. This type of festival is conducted by professional female shamans with music and dance. All villagers participate in the second type of festival. As an example of the second type of festival, let us take a look at the *dodang-kut* in *Daechi-dong*, Kyonggi province. Daechi dong's *dodang-kut* is held every two years on a favourable day in February.

The festival is led by a shaman and her assistants and consists of twelve seances. These are: (1) *hyangch's-mullim* (expelling the evil spirits); (2) *puchong-kori* (cleaning up the shrine); (3) *Songiu-kori* (praying for peace); (4) *teakam-kori* (praying for prosperity); (5) *chesok-kori* (praying for long life for the villagers); (6) *hogu-pyolsang-kori* (cajoling the spirits of smallpox and measles); (7) *sansin-kori* (praying for the protection of the village); (8) *ch'angbu-kori* (praying for protection from misfortunes); (9) *t'ochu-kori* (praying for protection from disasters); (10) *kollip-kori* (praying for wealth); (11) *chisin-kori* (praying for a good harvest); and (12) *tuitchon-kori* (dispatching the spirits). The twelve seances may be grouped into three stages: (i) invocation of the spirits; (ii) entertaining the spirits; and (iii) the return of the spirits. The *songju-kori*, the *taekam-Kori*, and the *chesoks-kori* comprise the main parts of the shamanistic rite. Between the seances, there are intermissions. During these intermissions, villagers, both males and females, put on shaman's robes and dance to shamanistic music. They believe that this will bring them good fortune. In addition, they have feasts and perform ritual dramas.

Festivals of the third type are mostly found in Kyongsang province and the eastern coastal fishing and agricultural villages of Kangwon province. This type of festival may be divided further into three subtypes: a regular festival such as *tano-kut* (May Festival) in Kangnung; a grand village festival held occasionally as a special event, such as Hahoe's *pyolsin-kut*; and lastly, a fair-type festival. The forms of the regular festival such as the *tano-kut* are similar to those of the *dodang-kut*. But this kind of festival always includes a seance aimed at petitioning for good catch of fish and a good harvest. The *tano-kut* consists of three stages. On the night of April fifteenth, the head celebrant and the shamans go to the god's shrine on the top of Daekwan mountain and transport the god in his abode to Kangnung City, twelve miles away from the shrine. They let the god stay in the city at the goddess's shrine. On the twenty seventh of April, the villagers have a shamanistic rite for the god and the goddess. After that, from May first until May sixth, the villagers have a festival to entertain the gods. During this festival period, the villagers hold shamanistic rites and maskdance drama. They also engage in many kinds of sports and have swinging, wrestling, and archery contests. The festival ends with the return of the gods and the burning of the temporary abode of the god and things used in the festival, such as tablets, flowers, flags, masks, and so on.

A noteworthy example of the grand village festival is the *pyolsin-kut* in Hohoe, Kyongsang province. This festival is held once every ten years, or when there is a divine message from Sonang, the guardian deity. On the second day of the lunar New Year, the celebrants and shamans take the guardian deity down to the village from the mountain shrine. The deity is carried in a holy bell on the sacred pole. Then the villagers perform a mask-dance drama to entertain the deity until the fifteenth of January. The drama consists of nine acts and employs fourteen masks. The drama satirizes depraved monks, reproves corrupt *yangban* (nobles), and portrays the lives of the common people. This is an early sort of mask-dance drama for rites in rural villages. The last kind of *Pyolosin-kut* is really a fair rather than a religious rite. These usually take place at marketplaces but, are rarely found these days.

Even though Korean village festivals persist in the same general framework, they very according to the simple ethnic religious systems of the individual villages. However, general pattern of Korean village festivals are as follows: (1) election of celebrants; (2) purification for the rite; (3) invocation of guardian deities; (4) procession of the gods; (5) ritual service to the gods; (6) entertaining the gods by sacred music and dance, ritual drama, and contests; and (7) the return of the gods. This general pattern suggests that Korean village festivals were originally shamanistic, but have been influenced by Confucianism and to some extent by Buddhism and Taoism, which brought about a number of variations. Therefore, we can find a syncretic amalgam of indigenous shamanism, Buddhism, Taoism, and Confucianism in Korean village festivals.

As seen from the examples given, Korean village festivals have dual characteristics: a sincere, Confucian-type of ceremony followed by an ecstatic shamanistic rite and music, dance, drama, contests, and feasts. The characteristics of collective shamanism, such as trance, possession, and seasonal ritual drama, are all present. Thus villagers were temporarily freed from *yangban* repression to freely drink, eat, sing, dance, and even indulge in sex. Most Korean village festivals take place in January, suggesting the regeneration of time and the wish to destroy profane past time and to establish a new time. Korean village festivals generally aim at purification and the driving off of devils, petitioning for a good harvest, and so on. Village festivals also still have a social function in integrating the villagers.

Since the beginning of the twentieth century, however, Korean village festivals have been changing a lot and in various ways. In the original forms of the festivals, the religious aspects were more emphasized, even though these were inseparably tied to the entertainment aspects that contributed an orgiastic pattern to the festivals. Korean village festivals are now less religious and are more a form of entertainment and the performing arts. Among other reasons for such changes, the modernization of Korean rural society and the influence of Western culture seem to be most significant. The influence of education has made the younger generation believe that village festivals are superstitious, and they are therefore not too eager to participate. As a result, most festivals today are held very quietly by elders, without music or dance, and are strictly religious. The music, dance, drama, and games that were once an important part of village festivals have been separated from the religious aspects and have come to be identified as performing arts and public games.

New Year's Celebrations of Some National Minorities in China

Like all other peoples the world over, the fifty-six nationalities (including the Han) that inhabit China's vast territory of 9,600,000 square kilometers have their own traditional festivals. The festival rituals and customs are so varied that their celebration can be compared to the blooming of a hundred species of flowers. They are really a colourful feast for the eyes. The most solemn festival is the lunar New Year's Day, called the Spring Festival after the Gregorian calendar was introduced into China in 1912.

New Year's Day is regarded as the beginning of a period of gay time in the lives of the people who celebrate it, because no matter whether the people live in the northern or the southern part of the country, or whether they are engaged in agriculture, animal husbandry, or hunting, they all arrange their lives and work in accordance with the order of the seasons. New Year is enjoyed by the people of various nationalities because it is a time of rest and leisure after the grain has been harvested and stored along with other produce and because at this time people can indulge themselves by setting off firecrackers and fireworks, admiring revolving lanterns, performing a dragon or a lion dance, or going to drinking parties. But what is most important is that New Year's Day is an occasion that has stood for the beginning of a new period of happiness from time immemorial. Through their celebration activities, the people of many nationalities offer sacrifices to the spirits of their forbears, thank the deities, and pray for a new year of favourable weather, a bumper harvest, prosperity in livestock farming, and their own well-being and security.

On New Year's Day in many areas, especially in the south of China, the people glorify their national history, eulogize the merits of their ancestors, and offer sacrifices to the deities. Moreover, because young people of both sexes are eager to get together and entreat for love on this occasion, they participate by singing and dancing. For this reason in some places New Year's Day is known by such names as the Festival of Songs or the Festival of Lusheng (a reed-pipe wind instrument used by the Miao, Yao, and Dong nationalities). Not a few nationalities' activities on New Year's Day are even more interesting and rich in lyrical and mythical characteristics. In the valley of the river Qingshui, on the plateau of Yunnan and Guizhu, people of the Miao nationality celebrate their Spring Festival with dancing accompanied by brass drums, *lusheng*-playing competitions, drinking songs, bullfighting, and horse racing. In addition, they place drops of wine on the noses of their oxen as a token of appreciation for the animal's year-round arduous work in the fields.

In some mountain village in this area the Miao people hold "jumping slop" tournaments, the most attractive of which is the one involving pole climbing. Before dawn on that day, in the village where the "jumping slope" is organized, people hang a bottle of wine and a piece of bacon on the top of a ten metre pole that is peeled off bark and painted with chicken oil. It is erected on the slope of a hill and people come from all the neighbouring villages when the sun rises behind the mountain. After nine rounds of gunfire and nine rounds of cannon shots, the youngsters in gala attire begin their exquisite performances. The young man who can retrieve the objects on the top of the pole using only his arms and without touching the pole with his feet or body is treated as a hero by all those who join in the tournament. Pretty girls are likely to shower him with admiration.

When the pole-climbing tournament is over, the Miao young men and women choose their favourite partners and begin to dance, sometimes forward, sometimes backward, to the lyrical tones of the *lusheng*. If a couple is in love, the girl will tie a well-woven coloured ribbon to the pipe of her young man's *lusheng*. When night comes, they leave the site in pairs, some singing graceful love songs, and others playing melodious tunes on the *lusheng* on the way to the nearby villages to seek lodgings for the night. Those villagers who accommodate such guests are deemed fortunate, and those who fail to attract guests are eager to seize one or two couples from their neighbours. Spending the Spring Festival in the Dong villages by the riverside and in the foothills in the vast border region of Human, Guizhou, and Guangxi provinces, one can witness not only varied traditions and characteristics but also celebration activities on an extensive scale. On the day of the festival, members of all clans of the Dong nationality, without distinction as to age or sex, dress in their holiday best and congregate near the drum tower (a square-based, polyhedron-topped, exquisitely built pagoda-shaped building) to offer sacrifices to the shrine of "grandmother". They are led by elders of high virtue who pray for good weather and security in the village when the new year comes. As soon as the sacrifice offering is over, they fire cannon shots and play the *lusheng* in unison. As a rule, the merry young men and women are divided into two concentric circles, with the women forming the inside ring. Led by a singing master, they sing solemn song and dance to express thanks to their forbears and wishes for the spirits to share in their happiness.

From the second day to the fifteenth day after New Year's, the married women of the Dong nationality have a custom of visiting other villages. This is done in a humorous and friendly way: they disguise themselves as "beggars" or other kinds of queer persons, with their faces painted and hands smeared with mud, wearing caps made of palm leaves. They proceed to other villages in files, one after another, to convey congratulations.

Generally, when they reach village they are intercepted on the main road by those who are going to entertain them there. After they sing in antiphonal style, they are given a sumptuous feast. The antiphonal singing by both sides covers such subjects as asking the visitors' addresses, the reason they came, and about their harvest, the hosts thereby testing the wit and talent of the visitors' answers. These songs have been passed down from generation to generation from time immemorial. The people call them "songs of intercepting visitors on the road." This custom implies that through the visits of the "poor" and the hospitality shown to them by their hosts, egalitarian thinking can be propagated.

Some nationalities pass their New Year's Day in accordance with their own calendars. The actual date on which a nationality has its New Year's Day varies, and so are the names they give to this day.

The New Year's Day of the Dai people living in the Dehorn and Xishuangbana areas of Yunnan province, reputed to be the native land peacocks, fall on the twenty-fourth day of the six month of their own calendar, i.e., the seventh to the tenth day after the Qingming Festival of the lunar calendar (or 5 April on the Gregorian calendar). This is the heartening Water-Sprinkling Festival, which occurs once a year.

In the past, the Dai people believed in Hinayana Buddhism and their gala activities are mainly connected with that form of Buddhism. The day before the Water-Sprinkling Festival, they have the interesting practice of sand-piling and Buddha-washing. So doing, they wash away the diseases and calamities of the year that has just passed and pray for happiness and well-being in the year to come. When sprinkling water, aside from their pouring clean water with a ladle onto the necks of respected old people, there is no limit as to how the ordinary people sprinkle water on one another. When their gaiety reaches a climax, they may pour a whole basin or pail of water on anybody, till that person will be the happiest person in the future. Young men and women often express their love during such occasions.

For the Water-Sprinkling Festival the Dai people also hold a magnificent Dragon Boat Race on the river Lancang. People dance and sing throughout the night to the light of fireworks and torches. They perform the Peacock Dance in which they imitate the peacock drinking water, spreading its tail, climbing a tree-branch, and flying. Besides the Peacock Dance, which symbolizes beauty, goodwill, happiness, and luck, they may perform another traditional Dai dance, which is called the Elephant-Foot Dance. The Water-Sprinkling Festival of the Dai is a day of very great joy.

Despite the fact that the ways of celebrating New Year's Day varies with the different nationalities, and that many celebrations have been influenced by the changes of time and some rituals and customs are tined with superstition, one can nevertheless see in them honesty, simplicity, enthusiasm, and hospitality and the virtues of loving peace, labour, life, and integrity, which are characteristic of the Chinese people as a whole. The Chinese nation, which is composed of fifty-six nationalities, is a great nation with rich imagination and creativity. One can easily understand that these old and traditional festivals not only contribute to the social life of the Chinese people, but also add splendour and unique features to the national culture.

Festivals of India

ndia is famous the world over for its colourful, joyous and magnificent festivals. Marked with gaiety and enthusiasm, they celebrate life in its various shades and hues, forms and manifestations.

Indian festivals can be broadly divided into three categories. They are : national, regional and religious.

The national festivals are celebrated throughout the country by all people irrespective of caste and religious considerations. They are generally associated with changes in seasons, moral values and other natural phenomenon having uniform impact on all people. They include Vasant Panchami, Rakshabandhan and Deepawali. The regional festivals are confined to particular regions like Baisakhi or Onam. Religious festivals are connected with birth anniversaries of prophets and different gods and goddesses of different religious sects. They include Vijayadashmi, Ramnavami, Christmas and Id.

Vasant Panchami

As the name suggests, it is a festival which heralds *vasant* or spring. It falls on the fifth lunar day in bright fortnight or *Magh* (January-February) and is dedicated by the students to Saraswati, the goddess of learning and arts.

Holi

Known as the festival of colours, Holi is one of the most popular day of rejoicing, music and feast.

Deepawali

Diwali or *Deepawali,* meaning of row of lamps, it is the most well-known and well-celebrated festival of India.

Observed on the 15th day of the first half of the month of Kartika (October-November), it marks the return of Rama, India's national hero and worshipped by many as the incarnation of Vishnu, to Ayodhya after a long gap of 14 years in exile.

It is preceded by annual whitewashing of the house. At night Lakshmi, the goddess of wealth and prosperity is worshipped after which illumination takes place. Friends and relatives exchange sweets and gifts and children burst crackers.

Rakshabandhan

This is a unique festival with great moral appeal. On this day, sisters tie a silken thread called rakshabandhan on the wrists of their brothers. The brother who receives the thread also called *rakhi* is bound to protect the life and honour of his sister.

When a lady sends a *rakhi* to someone, however different in caste and religion from her, he becomes her brother with a moral obligation to stand by her in times of need.

Akbar made it a national festival and had a *rakhi* tied on his writs.

Today also, women and children tie rakhis on the wrists of the President and Prime Minister of the country.

Baisakhi

Observed on 13 April, it is a famous harvest festival of Punjab. It is celebrated throughout the state with great jubilation. Bouts of wrestling and kabaddi and bhangra dance are the two special features of the fairs held on this occasion.

On this day, people, irrespective of their caste and religious affiliations, take a bath in a river or canal and partake of food cooked of new crop.

This is celebrated as Bihu in Assam when people sing and dance together.

Lohri & Sankranti

Sankranti or the Indian new year falls in the month of January. It marks the solar transition from the southern planetary (Dakshinayan) to northern planetary (Uttaryan). It is celebrated as Pongal in the South.

Onam

Onam is celebrated throughout Kerala with gusto. According to a legend, this day, which is celebrated in September every year, King Mahabali visits his lost kingdom for a day. To welcome their ruler, the Keralites observe Onam.

On this day, special prayers are held for King Mahabali. They are followed by feasting and dancing. Womenfolk decorate their houses with flowers and alpana, i.e. colourful patterns on floor.

Vijaya Dashami

Popularly known as Dashera, it is commemorated by the Hindus to hail the victory of good over evil. It is observed on the 10th lunar day of *Asoj* (September-October) and is considered an auspicious day for undertaking a military expedition. It is customary worship weapons on this day.

A great attraction of this festival lies in the burning of the gigantic effigies of Ravana, Meghnath and Kumbhakarana by Ram and Lakshman at the conclusion of the nine days of theatrical shows on the epic Ramayana.

These nine-days are also called *Navratris* or nine holy nights. They fall twice a year, once in summer around March-April and in September October. Astrologically these are extremely auspicious for spiritual and material benefits.

During October *Navratris,* Mother Goddess Durga is worshipped with great devotion. Devouts fast on these days and perform special spiritual rites. In Bengal, *Durga Puja* is a festive occasion which is accompanied with great fanfare. Large idols of Goddess Durga are set up in huge gaily decorated *puja pandals* for worship. On the tenth day, i.e. on Vijaya Dashami, they are immersed in river Ganga with a prayer to the Goddess Mahishasuramardini to return again next year to bless the laity.

Shivaratri

Shivaratri, or the festival of Lord Shiva, falls on the 14th day of the waning moon at the end of *Magh* (January-February) or the beginning of *Phalguna* (February-March). It is observed for the atonement of one's sins and fulfilment of one's desires "during life and union with Shiva or final emancipation after death". Fasting, holding a vigil, or worshipping the Linga during the night are special requisites on this occasion.

Ramnavami

This is observed as the birth anniversary of Lord Rama. It falls on the ninth lunar day in the bright fortnight of the month of *Chaitra* (March-April).

Lord Rama is worshipped on this day. Devouts fast and distribute food and clothes to the needy.

Janmashtami

Celebrated as the birth anniversary of Lord Krishna. Janamashtami falls on the eighth of the dark fortnight of the month of Bhaduan (August-September).

Devotees throng to Krishna's birthplace in Mathura and Vrindavan to participate in the large-scale celebrations.

Reference may be made also to the celebrations at Puri when Lord Jagannatha is brought out in his car. Huge crowds from all parts of the country attend the festival.

Ids

The Muslim community in India celebrates Id-i-Milad, Id-ul-Fitr and Id-ul-Zuha with great enthusiasm.

Id-I-Milad or the feast of the Prophet's nativity is celebrated on 11th of Rabi-ul-Awwal with great solemnity. Special lectures on the life of Prophet are arranged on the occasion.

Id-ul-Fitr : Also known as the festival of breaking the fast *or Id-ul-Saghir*, or the minor feast, begins on the first day of *Shawal* and continues for two days. This day of rejoicing comes after the long-drawn-out fast of *Ramzan* and is, therefore, particularly welcome.

Buddha Purnima

Both the Buddhists and non-Buddhists celebrate Buddha Purnima, the birthday of Lord Gautama Buddha, with great devotion. On this day, observed on the full moon day of the month of Jyestha in mid-summer around May, devotees take a dip in the river, fast and visit Buddhist temples to offer prayers and light lamps. Ceremonial readings from the Buddhists texts are held in all monasteries all over India, particularly in Sarnath, where Buddha attained enlightenment.

Mahavir Jayanti

Followers of Vardhman Mahavir observe Mahavir Jayanti on the full moon day in the month of April-May. On this day also, the devotees offer their prayers to Bhagwan Mahavir and reiterate their pledge to follow his teachings.

Christmas

Indian Christians, like their fellow brethren elsewhere in the world, celebrate Christmas with gaiety and enthusiasm. Churches and homes are decorated, gifts are exchanged, feasts are held, carols are sung to welcome Jesus Christ on his birthday on 25 December.

Easter & Good Friday

Easter is observed with great solemnity. Devout Christians fast on this day and remember the goodness of Christ. Colourfully painted Easter eggs are also distributed to children. Good Friday is celebrated on the third day after Easter when the crucified Christ resurrects himself, as per the legend to prove his divinity. It is a joyous occasion for the Christians who celebrate it with singing and dancing and feasting after special Good Friday service in churches and cathedrals.

Bhutan: Celestial Praise of Guru Rimpoche —Tshechu Festivals

f the numerous religious festivals celebrated in Bhutan, the Tshechu, which literally means the "Tenth Day" (of the month), is regarded as the most popular and colourful. The times and duration of the Tshechu vary from one region to another, but as its name suggests, the festival always takes place on or around the tenth day of the month in the Bhutanese calendar. During the festival, which is celebrated either in the *dzong* (fortress-monastery) or in the monastery, different religious dances (*cham*), with or without masks, are performed by the monks and lay people, and in some places folk dances are also performed by the villagers.

The Tshechu is a festival in honour of Padmasambhava "One who was born from a lotus flower", popularly known under the name of Guru Rimpoche "Precious Teacher". This Indian saint contributed enormously to the diffusion of Tantric Buddhism in the Himalayan regions including Tibet, Nepal, Bhutan, etc. around AD 800, and he is the founder of the Nyingmapa "Old" School of Lamaism which still has numerous followers.

In the same way as the life of Buddha Shakyamuni, the historical founder of Buddhism, is depicted by his Twelve Deeds (*dzepa chunyi*) such as Birth, Enlightenment, Nirvana, etc., the biography of Guru Rimpoche is highlighted by the twelve episodes, all of which occurred on the tenth day (*tshechu*) of the month at different moments of his life. What follows is a summarized account of the twelve episodes: (In the following account, the twelve episodes are arranged in the order of the month of the year, on the tenth day of which they respectively took place. In order to follow their chronological sequence in the life of Guru Rimpoche, one starts with the sixth month which is the month of birth, then one proceeds to the twelfth month. Thereafter one follows the order of the month from the first month up to the eleventh month in which the last of the twelve episodes took place.)

Ist month

Pema Gyelpo (lay name of Guru Rimpoche before he entered into religion) understood that there was no meaning in the exercise of political power. Therefore he abandoned the government, leaving behind the retinue of Queens, such as Oechangma, and went to the Eight Great Cemeteries like Shitavana (Siwetshel), in order to do penance.

IInd month

Guru Rimpoche was ordained by Acarya Prabhahasti in order to convert fortunate beings to the Holy Doctrine by a higher teaching than that of the Hinayana discipline.

IIIrd month

Tsuglagdzin, King of Zahor, had a daughter called the Divine Lady Mandarava. Declining proposals of marriage, she entered religion and began staying with Guru Rimpoche, listening to his teachings. When the King came to know this, he took back Mandarava to confine her in the palace. As for Guru Rimpoche, the King issued an order to burn him alive. At this time, by the supernatural powers of Guru Rimpoche, the fire turned into water to create a lake and in the centre of the lake, Guru Rimpoche appeared seated on a lotus flower. This is the blessed lake Tsho Pema (Rewalsr, Mandi district, H.P., India) which is still today a place of pilgrimage. After this miraculous phenomenon, the King acquired faith in Guru Rimpoche and the Kingdom of Zahor was converted to Buddhism.

IVth month

When Guru Rimpoche in company with the Divine Lady Mandarava came to Ugyen (Uddiyana), Oechangma, the Queen whom Pema Gyelpo had previously abandoned, became jealous and issued an order to burn them alive. On this occasion, Guru Rimpoche showed his supernatural power which transformed the fire into a lake. Guru Rimpoche and the Divine Lady Mandarava then appeared together on a lotus flower in the centre of the lake. This miraculous phenomenon won the conversion to Buddhism of the Kingdom of Ugyen, beginning with the King Indrabhuti.

Vth month

In the country called Tharkye in the south of India, there were five hundred heretic teachers who were hostile to the Holy Doctrine. Guru Rimpoche appeared there in the form of Senge Dradrok. He made the thunder-bolt strike the five hundred teachers and exterminated them. The heretic kingdom was thus destroyed.

VIth month

The Buddha Shakya Thubpa (Shakyamuni) made the following prophecy: "After my nirvana, I will be reborn in the country of Ugyen (Uddiyana) as Pema Jungney (Padmasambhava) who will teach the Tantric Doctrine."

In accordance with this prophecy, on the tenth day of the sixth (Monkey) month of the Wood-Monkey year, Guru Rimpoche was miraculously born on a lotus flower in the lake of Dhanakosha which is situated in the north-west of Ugyen. At his birth, he looked already like a boy of eight years old.

VIIth month

The heretic King of a barbarian country named Zangling put Guru Rimpoche in a huge copper vessel, sealed it with iron nails and had it thrown in a big river. However, with aid of his supernatural power, Guru Rimpoche escaped from the vessel and flew back into the sky. The big river, instead of flowing down, started flowing upstream and the palace of the King was carried away by the water. This frightened the King, who then made an apology and took refuge with Guru Rimpoche. The barbarian kingdom was thus converted to Buddhism.

VIIIth month

In order to kill Guru Rimpoche, the heretics gave him different kinds of poisons: poisonous food through mouth, sight-poison through the eyes, poison through the eyes, poison of contagion through the body, and poisonous smell through the nose. No matter what they gave him no harm came to Guru Rimpoche. On the contrary, the splendour of his body increased in the same way as the peacock becomes more and more splendid by taking poisons. Faced with this spectacle, the heretics took faith in Guru Rimpoche and were converted to Buddhism.

IXth month

When Guru Rimpoche was making propitiation in the rock cave of Yangleshoe in Nepal, all the demons of Nepal and Tibet together tried to disturb him. At this moment, Guru Rimpoche, having propitiated the deities of the cycle of Phurpa, bound the demons of Nepal by a solemn oath and made them guardians of the Holy Teaching.

Xth month

In one of his previous lives, Guru Rimpoche was born as one of three sons of a poultry herdswoman. The three sons constructed together the stupa of Byarung khash or (Bodhnath) in Nepal and made a solemn prayer to be reborn in another life as religious King, Abbot and Teacher in order to spread the Holy Doctrine. As a result of this prayer, they respectively obtained rebirth as Khrisong Detsen, Shantarakshita and Padmasambhava.

Khrisong Detsen, King of Tibet, invited Guru Rimpoche to Tibet. In his journey to Tibet, the demons such as the Twelve Tenma, made a vain attempt to harm him. Guru Rimpoche thereby subdued them, took control of their lives, and bound them by a solemn oath. On arrival at the peak of Hepori near Samye, Guru Rimpoche bound by a solemn oath the mischievous demons of Tibet.

XIth month

Guru Rimpoche decided to go to Ngayabling, situated to the south-west in order to subdue the demons. Before his departure, he held discussions with King Khrisong Detsen at Chimphu, near Samye. For the benefit of the Holy Doctrine and sentient beings of the future, Guru Rimpoche prepared to conceal in different places in Tibet innumerous treasures of profound meaning (*terma*). He then subdued the principal local deities of each region and made them guardians of treasures in order to assure their transmission into the future. He also made prophecies which clearly announced the future apparition of discoverers of treasures (*terton*) such as Five King Tertons and Eleven Authentic Lingpas.

XIIth month

After his birth on the tenth day of the sixth month, Guru Rimpoche stayed in the heart of a lotus flower in the lake Danakosha. As Indrabhuti, King of Ugyen (Uddiyana) in the West, had no son, he adopted Guru Rimpoche and took him to the royal palace. The King named him Pema Gyelpo and entrusted with him the government of the Kingdom.

In fact, we have to add one more act which is the departure of Guru Rimpoche from Jambudvipa Continent where we live, to Ngayabling Island where he is still supposed to be active for the general benefit of the sentient beings. This act which is not included in the twelve episodes but which ends Guru Rimpoche's activities in Jambudvipa took place on the tenth day of the sixth month the same date as his birth, which was his first act in Jambudvipa.

The Tshechu festival of each month is therefore celebrated to commemorate the episode which took place in that particular month (the sixth month is the double commemoration of Guru Rimpoche's birth in and his departure from Jambudvipa). The Tshechu festival is celebrated throughout Bhutan and its date, duration and programme of dances vary from one place to another. Moreover the programme of the Tshechu is not something which is fixed forever: with the change of times, some dances are added and some struck off the programme. For example, the dance of Tamshing in Bumthang (*Bumthang tercham*) has recently been added to the programme of the Thimphu Tshechu, and for several years the dance of the Good Man and Good Lady (*Phole mole)* has not been performed in the Talo Tshechu (near Punakha). Certain dances are particular to single Tshechus. Thus, the Talo Tshechu programme has a dance of *kyung* (mythical bird *garuda*) which is performed nowhere else and the Wangdiphodrang Tshechu has the dance of Dole Raksha which depicts the story of the construction of the bridge just below the Wangdiphodrang Dzong.

Paro Tshechu

Among the numerous Tshechu festivals of Bhutan, that of Paro, a fertile valley in western Bhutan, is probably the most popular and lavish. Indeed the Paro Tshechu attracts each year hundreds of villagers from the Paro valley and surrounding areas, as well as foreign tourists from all over the world.

The Paro Tshechu lasts for five days from 11th to 15th of the second month in the Bhutanese calendar which fall approximately in March-April in the European calendar. During the five-day festival, more than forty religious and folk dances are performed by the monks, the Royal Dance Troupe and village folk. Below is given a brief account of the Paro Tshechu festival, as well as some of the most representative and popular dances, which are also performed in most of the other Tshechus.

Prior to the Tshechu festival exclusively, on the fifth day of the second month in the courtyard of Paro Dzong there is a ceremony called *chamju* which means literally "examination in dance". On this occasion, monks rehearse the dances in their ordinary habit without donning the festival costumes or masks.

The first day of the Paro Tshechu is held in the courtyard of the Dzong which is closely packed with village folks dressed in their best. The Neten (Abbot) of the Paro Regional State Monastery together with his retinue watch the festival from the balcony situated on the first floor of the surrounding building. On the first day there are five dances, all of them performed by monks, such as those of the Lord of Death and his consort (*Shinje yabyum*), the Lord of the Cremation Grounds (*Durdag*) and the Black Hats (*Shanag*). As each dance lasts for close to an hour (some almost two hours) the programme, which starts around nine o'clock in the morning, ends at three or four o'clock in the afternoon. In the intervals, and even during these solemn and dramatic dances performed with magnificent and colourful costumes and masks, clowns called *atsaras*, play the fool in order to make the spectators laugh and increase the festive mood.

From the second day, the Tshechu continues on the Deyangkha ground just above the Dzong. Each morning, monks, musicians and dancers who participate in the festival walk in a long procession from the Dzong to the Deyangkha ground and then back to the Dzong in the afternoon when the programme is finished.

Some dances are a dramatic execution of the liturgy dedicated to a particular deity. The movements of dancers are therefore minutely detailed in the dance manuals (*chamyig*) as is the case with other religious rituals performed in the temple. Through the elaborate process of the dance, one aims at evoking and "generating in front" the deity together with his retinue. Most often although the deity's inner nature is compassionate, its external aspect is wrathful in order to subdue the evil force which cannot be tamed by peaceful means. The climax of such dances is the ritual murder of the evil represented by an effigy. The evil force is thus destroyed, while its conscious principle is "liberated". The dances of the Black Hats (*Shanag*) and the Terrifying Deities (*Tungam*) which belong to this category are performed annually in order to protect the Paro valley and the whole of Bhutan from the evil force. Zangdo Pelri "Glorious Mountain of Copper-colour", the heavenly paradise of Guru Rimpoche which is situated in the Ngayabling Island, is one of the favourite themes of religious dances. For example, the dance of Ging and Tsholing (*Ging tang tsholing*) is said to have been initiated by Guru Rimpoche on the occasion of the consecration of the Samye Monastery in Tibet in order to show the people of Tibet the splendour of the Zangdo Pelri. The dance of the Three Kinds of Ging (*Gingsum*) is another example of this type. This dance is the visual representation of the Zangdo Pelri as visited and seen in meditation by the famous Bhutanese terton "treasure discoverer", Pema Lingpa (1450-1521).

The purpose of other dances is more concerned with the edification of the folk audience. Most didactic in purpose is perhaps the dance of the Judgement of the Dead (*Raksha mangcham*) which is based on the *Bardo Thoedrol* (Book of the Dead), a text "rediscovered" by Karma Lingpa (fifteenth century). This dance depicts the court over which the Lord of Death presides. Two men are brought to this court one after the other: The first man, who committed different kinds of bad deeds during life, is sentenced to Hell, while the second who accumulated good acts is sent to heaven.

The famous story of how the poet-saint Milarepa (1040-1123) saved a deer from a hunter named Gompo Dorji, whom he subsequently converted to Buddhism, is the theme of the dance of the Stag and the Hounds (*Shawa-shachi*).

In a more mundane way, the dance of the Good Man and Good Lady (*Phole-mole*), taken from the biography of the King Norzang, is more of a comical and rather crude play than a dance, and demonstrates the virtues marital fidelity. The *leitmotif* of the Tshechu is dramatically represented on the fifth and last day. Before dawn a gigantic appliqué scroll made of colourful brocades and silks is unrolled and hung on the wall of the building which faces the Deyangkha ground. This scroll called Thongdrol, "One whose sight alone gives the deliverance (from *samsara*, or future rebirth)", depicts Guru Rimpoche in the centre surrounded by the Eight Manifestations (*Guru tshengye*) which he is said to have assumed in order to benefit sentient beings. People come to prostrate themselves before the Thongdrol and touch its border with their heads. It is believed that, owing to the benediction of Guru Rimpoche, the prayers formulated before the Thondrol are bound to be fulfilled.

In sharp contrast to the silent and two-dimensional world of the Thongdrol in the morning, is the dance of the Eight Manifestations of Guru Rimpoche (*Guru tshengye*). This dance dynamically and vividly performed in the daytime gives the impression that Guru Rimpoche with all his retinue is back before the viewers from his palace of Zangdo Pelri.

Thus ends the Tshechu festival which is an annual occasion for Bhutanese common folk to remember Guru Rimpoche's past activities in our world and to refresh and strengthen their faith in him.

A masked dancer, Sri Lanka.

Symbolism of Colours

Colours through Thai Eyes

The nomenclature of colours in Thailand of old is based in no small measure on the colours of familiar natural objects which Thai folks are likely to encounter in their daily life. Thus light green is known as 'si tong on' (the colour of young banana levels), pink as 'si tabtim' (the colour of pomegranate seeds), scarlet as 'si luad nok' (the colour of birds 'blood), light blue as 'si fash' (the colour of a cloudless sky), light purple as 'si med maprang' (the colour of wild plum seeds), and so on. Many of the old-fashioned Thai dyes are obtained from parts of some plants, such as yellow dye from turmeric, and yellowish brown from the core of the trunk of the jack-fruit tree. It should be of little surprise that colours of all shades and hues could be accurately described by the Thai of the byegone era.

In the olden days, colours were not to be used in an indiscriminate manner. For instance, red was reserved for royal personages and objects. Only the royal palaces and audience halls could use red as a base colour. It was prohibited for commoners to wear red to go into the royal compound. This prohibition is evident from a provision in an old legal code which says "...whoever adorns him on herself with red flowers, wears red to pinkish-red attire and ventures to enter the gate of the royal residence or to cross the bridge leading to the royal residence, or to present him or herself in the vicinity of the royal presence be it on land or water, let him or her be stripped and his or her attire be torn..." The tradition of wearing red among members of the Royal Family, when attending the Buddhist service on Buddhist Sabbatical day, began in the reign of King Rama IV, and was undoubtedly initiated by the King himself.

Colours on the flags

The plain red flag officially named in 1897 the 'Maharaj Flag' first appeared in the reign on King Rama IV. In 1901, the King's Flag became a square featuring a red *garuda* against a yellow background. This flag is flown by the vehicle carrying the King and at a royal residence or palace where the King is staying. The practice of adopting yellow as another royal colour was reinforced by King Rama V. The Most Illustrious Order of the Royal House of Chakri created by King Rama V for exceptionally distinguished members of the Royal Family is the highest of all royal decorations. The sash part of this decoration is yellow, obviously chosen as it is the colour of the House of Chakri, King Rama VI added a new dimension to the symbolism of colours when he introduced the 'trirangha' or tri-coloured flag, to be known as the National Flag. In sports five horizontal strips in red, white, and blue, symbolizing nation, religion and King respectively.

Colours of the gods for the days of the week

According to a Thai legend which owes its origin to Hinduism there are seven gods who take turns to lord over each day of the week. The name of the god becomes the name of the day over which he supposedly presides. All these gods are the creation of Phra Shiva, the Lord of the Universe. Goddesses, holy men and animals are the raw material for the creation. They are pulverized and ground to dust before being wrapped up in a coloured material. Sprinkling the bundle with nectar for immortality and reciting a mantra, Phra Shiva transforms the dust into a god whose body colour assumes the colour of the material shrouding the dust. These gods, the material from which they are created, and the colours are :

Phra Athitaya for Sunday, from 6 lions, rose red
Phra Chandra for Monday, from 15 goddesses, light yellow
Phra Angara for Tuesday, from 8 buffaloes, dark red or pink.
Phra Buddh for Wednesday, from 17 elephants, jade green
Phra Brhaspati for Thursday, from 19 hermits, bright reddish orange.
Phra Sukra for Friday, from 21 oxen, light indigo blue.
Phra Saur for Saturday, from 19 tigers, black.

On all auspicious occasions such as the celebration of important events, the Thais in former times would make sure that the decorations and objects which were connected with the event were the colour of the day on which the celebration was organized. For instance, if the celebration took place on Sunday, the trimmings had to be in red, on Monday in yellow, on Tuesday in pink and so on. Some people in modern times may go as far as acquiring objects of certain colours on certain days, such as a black car on Saturday, a red bed cover on Sunday, or a yellow robe on Monday.

Auspicious colours to wear

Traditional Thais pay a lot of attention to which colour to wear on which day of the week. It is thought that the god will give extra favour to those who wear his colour on his day of the week. Tradition, however, allows one or two more colours in addition to the colour assigned to each day. In the past, Thai ladies could wear a skirt of one colour and a shoulder cloth of another, both being accepted as auspicious colours to wear, e.g.:

On Sunday — red or yellow skirt, pale yellow or light green shoulder cloth.

On Monday — yellow skirt, light blue shoulder cloth.

On Wednesday — green skirt, pink or yellow shoulder cloth.

Thursday — reddish orange skirt, light green, shoulder cloth.

On Friday — blue skirt, yellow shoulder cloth.

On Saturday — dark or purple skirt, light green shoulder cloth.

Poets and the Court to have had their own ideas about which colours to wear on certain days of the week. Sunthorm Phu, the well-known Thai poet of the eighteenth century, wrote 'Swasdiarksa', a didactic poem which covers a wide range of Thai etiquette. Regarding colours, Sunthorn Phu told his readers to wear purple or indigo on Tuesday, orange on Wednesday and greenish yellow on Thursday.

Wednesday represents the most unusual case as far as the Court's custom on dresses is concerned. It was related that King Rama VI once consulted his astrologer on what to wear for a party on Wednesday evening. The answer he received was 'dark purple' instead of the usual green. From this we may infer that for Wednesday, the auspicious colour is green during the day and purple in the evening. Even within the Court, two officials- the astrologer and the tailor - appeared to be at variance with each other as to which colours to wear on certain days. For Thursday, the astrologer prescribed yellow as the auspicious colour to wear, while for the tailor, it was blue.

The Court tailor also recommended blue or light blue as the auspicious colour for Friday.

Lucky and unlucky birthday colours

Along with the belief in auspicious colours for the days of the week comes the belief in lucky birthday colours. The system as a straightforward one; the colour of the day on which you were born becomes your lucky birthday colour. Thus precious objects or personal items should be the same colour as that of one's birthday. Tradition again allows not only one lucky birthday colour, but two more for grace and dignity respectively. There are, however, colours of which tradition forbids the use on certain days of the week.

Thus if one's birthday is on :

Sunday — use red for luck, green for grace, pink for dignity; light and dark blue are forbidden.

Monday — use yellow for luck, black for grace, green for dignity; orange is forbidden.

Tuesday — use pink for luck, yellow for grace, black for dignity; white and blue are forbidden.

Wednesday — use green for luck, purple for grace, yellow for dignity; pink and reddish purple are forbidden.

Thursday — use reddish orange for luck, orange for grace, blue for dignity: black, dark purple and dark blue are forbidden.

Friday — use light blue or indigo for luck, pink for grace, white for dignity: reddish purple is forbidden.

Saturday — use black for luck, blue for grace, purple for dignity; all shades of green are forbidden.

Colours, gems and attire of the gods of the planets

Superstitions about colours and associated gems are common among peoples in many parts of the world. For the Thais, objects of beauty decorated with nine different coloured gems are as believed to have the effect of a charm. The so called "Ween Noparat', i.e. a ring of nine coloured gems, is thought to bring blessings to the lady who wears it. The coronation sword of the King of Thailand, decorated with nine gems in nine different colours, constitutes a hallmark of victory. Since the reign of King Rama V, there have been royal decorations in the form of badges, starts and sahses embellished with nine coloured gems. In general the power of the nine colours should protect the wearer against harm from weapons or poisons, and from animals and fire, at the same time enhancing success in commerce and agriculture. The legend relates the nine colours of the gems to those worn by the gods of the nine planets as known to Thai astrologers. The associations are as follows :

Red (ruby); worn by Phra Athitaya, the sun God.

White (Zircon); worn by Phra Chandra, the Moon God.

Deep Pink (garnet); worn by Phra Angara, the God of Mars.

Green (emerald); worn by Phra Budh, the God of Mercury.

Black (black spinel); worn by Phra Saur, the God of Saturn.

Yellow (yellow topaz); worn by Phra Brhaspati, the God of Jupiter.

Bluish Purple (dark blue sapphire); worn by Phra Rahu (no equivalent in Western folklore or astrology).

Pale Blue (light blue sapphire); worn by Phra Sukra, the God of Venus (male in Thai folklore).

Golden Yellow (cat's eye); worn by Phra Ketu, the God of Neptune.

There is a belief concerning the colour of the gem and the attire a man in power should wear after a lunar or solar eclipse. The god of the planet which is dominant in the horoscope of the important person at the time of the eclipse is determined by the astrologer. The gem of the colour favoured by the god of that planet should be worn on the body for the following six months in order to have the full benefit of protection against all bad luck, while attire of the same colour as the gem may be worn at any and all appropriate occasions during the same period of time after the eclipse.

Colours for mourning

Colours have been used to represent or express deep feelings in a variety of ways. In Thailand colours of clothing have been a conventional way of expressing mourning. In the past, mourning colours included black, white dark purple and dark blue. The choice of colour was determined by the relationship between the wearer and the departed soul. In the old tradition, the older relatives wore white while the younger relatives wore black. Mourners who were not relatives of the deceased wore dark blue or dark purple. Exceptions have been known: King Rama I and King Rama III were recorded as having worn white at the funeral ceremonies for their respective son and daughter, both of whom died prematurely. The wearing of white may thus be considered to be an expression of forlorn love as well as of mourning.

In modern times, it is the custom for Thais of all social ranks and status to wear black to mourn the passing away of their beloved relatives, friends, and public figures.

A Rainbow of Colours: Notes on the Symbolism of Colours in Bhutan

The kingdom of Bhutan is small country of 47,000 km[2] nestled in the Eastern Himalayas between Tibet (China) and India. Except for Tibet, which greatly influenced this country's culture and gave it its religion, Bhutan had hardly any contact with the outside world until the late 1950s. This isolation helped Bhutan to retain most of its traditions, and it is country where colours still have meaning and cannot be used in a haphazard manner, be it in the religious field or in everyday life.

By a visit to the Colour Museum of Bradford in England, one can understand the significance of colours and their effect through modern science. Some of the mixing of colours and their results which are explained there are, in fact, very familiar to many Tibetan Buddhist scholars. They know the elaborated theories of colour combinations which are observed when making a religious painting, a "thangka". In the monasteries, besides its symbolic use in different rituals and mediation, colour is also very important subject which is discussed in the course of academic students.

In monastic debate, students are first taught a subject called "khadog karma" or "white and red colours", which deals with the relationship between four root primary colours and eight element/secondary ones. The subject may appear to be simple but it is the manner of phrasing the question in the debate which actually trains the mind. Before going on to practise debate in high philosophical spheres, students are required to debate on colours for months.

In rituals and mediation, colour plays an important role as each colour represents a direction, an element and a Buddha of Wisdom. Letters in white, red and blue represent the Body, Speech and Mind of the Buddha, while white, yellow, red and blue represent the four kinds of deeds. In the majority of the mandals, blue, white, yellow, red and green represent respectively the centre, the east, the south, the west and the north, but they also symbolise the Five Elements; either, water, earth, fire and air/wind as well as the Five Buddhas of Wisdom (Jina/Dhyani-Buddhas). During medita-tion, the colours are also used to represent not only different deities and the kind of mediation associated with them, but also the different "carks" (wheels) which are in one's body and on which one meditates in order to gain different spiritual powers or benefits. In the fourteenth century *Book of the Dead*, visions of colours in the immediate state ("bardo") are explained to the departed soul as the paths to different categories of existence in which to be reborn.

The prayer flags of different colours which are put up on the roof of buildings or on hilltops, represent the different elements and are erected in accordance with the astrological element of the person who offers them. For example, a person born in a Five element year would be recommended to erect a red coloured flag and never a white one, as the latter represents the Water element and that water puts out the fire. However, the numerous white prayer flags bearing inscriptions which are raised on hill sides, are in memory of departed souls. In Bhutan, these flags are usually erected the 3rd week after the death of a person and in this case, the element of the dead person is not taken into consideration. The white colour represents here the colour of Chenrezig. [Avalokiteshvara], the bodhisattva of Compassion, whose complexion is white. As for the inscriptions, they reproduce Chenrezig's prayer. "Om mani padme hum" which liberates from the six realms of incarnation.

When it comes to painting, there are many theories about colours and their usage. Boding Penchen Chogley Namgvel (1375-1451) of Bodongpa, a sub sect of the Sakyapa, writes that there are five basic colours: white, red, blue, yellow, and black — while later scholars like Sumpa Khenpo (1704-1788), Ronghta Lobsang Damchoe Gyamtsho (1863-1917) and Mibham Gyamtsho (1846-1912) agree on seven Father colours: deep blue, green, vermilion, orange, maroon, yellow and indigo and one Mother colour: white. Mixing one of the seven Father colours with the white Mother colour produce other light colours which are referred to as "sons" and there are up to fourteen such "sons". There are also rules concerning the mixing of one colour with another to produce a third colour, as well as on the use of the colours according to the quality the painter wants to reflect. It said "White and red are the flower colours. If beauty is desired, it can be derived from them. Likewise, red and yellow are the heroic colours. If majesty is desired, it can be derived from them", etc. On the other hand, rules are very strict as to the colour's a painter should never juxtapose; for example yellow and white next to each other are "blind colours'.

Thangkas which have a black background are reserved for wrathful deities which are themselves black or dark blue in this case, there is no bad moral judgment associated to this colour, cf. below), while white is very often attributed to peaceful deities. As for the gold colour, it is associated with majesty and is above all the colours. That explains why a deity whose colour is normally blue, or green, can instead be painted gold.

In everyday life, the symbolism of colours is also very much alive but it often derives from the symbolism found in the religion. When a house is constructed, a ritual is performed and "after thc digging ceremony, the site is immediately decorated with banners and flags made of cloth in four colours and facing the four directions: White to the east, blue to the south, red to the west, and yellow to the north. These are the colours of the guardian deities of the four directions". White is associated with the good qualities of virtue, peace, and with nobility while black is associated with evil/sin or inferior status. The scarf called "kata" which is offered to the lamas, or in any ceremonial occasion, is always white. The most highly priced ladies traditional dress, the "kishutara", worn on festive days has a white background. The ceremonial scarf wore by ordinary men to go to monasteries or to the administrative headquarters is white. Whitish foodstuff such as curd, butter and pork fat are signs of wealth but their colour undoubtedly adds to their prestige. To be fair-skinned is considered a sign of beauty but may also be the sign of nobility, as a noble person does not need to work in the sun in the fields or in the soot and smoke of the kitchen, and therefore does not get dark. This is perfectly evident from the dance drama called "Pholey Moley" where the princes and princesses wear white masks while the servants have black masks.

However, the white/black opposition is particularly strong when it comes to symbolize the moral values of vague *versus* evil. In the religious dance of the Judgment of the Dead, the sinner is dressed in black and wears a black mask, the Demon who records every being's bad deeds is also dressed totally in black, black pebbles symbolize the bad actions committed by the sinner, and a black cloth represents the path leading to the different hells. In contrast, the virtuous man is in white and wears a white mask as does the God who notes every being's good deeds; white pebbles symbolise virtuous deeds; and a white cloth shows the way to the paradises.

The red — or maroon — colour has a very particular status because it is mostly associated with religion. The robes of monks and nuns are maroon, as are some parts of the clothing of elderly lay people who have devoted their life to religious practices. The ceremonial scarves worn by lay priests called "gomchens" are also maroon. A wide band of red paint at the upper level of the walls of a building indicates that it is not a house but a temple. However, red is also associated with heroic virtues; the guardian deities which are clad in armour and ride on horses are often red in colour as is the whole central tower of the monastery of Deschenphug which is dedicated to the guardian deities of the Drukpa Kagyupa, the official religious school. The sacrificial cakes which are offered to these particular deities during rituals are also red. As for the high officials who are given the title of "Dasho" by the King, they carry swords and wear red ceremonial scarves instead of the white of the common folk.

Bright yellow, as in most parts of Asia, symbolizes authority and majesty, and as such is reserved for the King and for the Head Abbot of Bhutan. The King wears a large yellow ceremonial scarf and the Head-Abbort is entitled to a yellow shawl instead of the usual maroon one. Bright yellow, it is understood, is a colour which is not used in daily life and, for example, there are no yellow cars. The part of the Bhutanese flag which is yellow is the symbol of the secular authority - the monarchy. The ministers who in the hierarchy are between the "Dashos' and the King wears an orange scarf which is the intermediate colour between red and yellow. And as colours play an important role in denoting the rank of laymen in the administration, they also indicate the status of the monks in the monasteries which can be read by the colour of their upper garments.

In Bhutan, the symbolism of colours is far from being forgotten. It not only rules great part of the religious activities but also permeates daily life in the modern context. And where to find better examples than the red and yellow official signboards and vehicle registration plates which symbolize the Bhutanese nation and even more so, stress the importance of the religion and of the secular power.

Hair Styles

Close your eyes and block your ears
mountains and rivers are
whispering a song
grasshoppers are on the field
bamboo brushes the wind
life is growing bright as hair flows
from the head where spirit dwells
incarnation of the supernatural
embodied as a talisman.

1

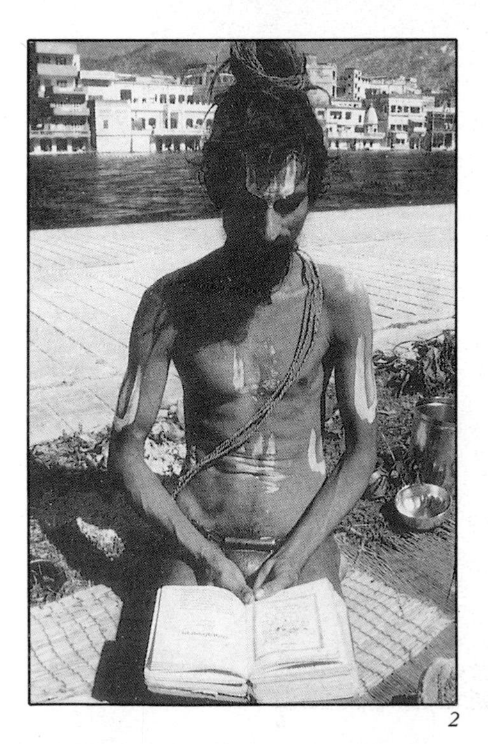

2

3

1. *Miao woman on a festive day, China.*
2. *An Indian* Sadhu.
3. Bukidnon, *member of an ethnic group, Mindanao, Philippines.*

Houses

Water, plains or mountains . . .
Asians live everywhere.

1

4

2

3

5

6

1. *Houses of some Indonesian tribes.*
2. *House of Igorots of Luzon, Philippines.*
3. *Entrance of a house in Kathmandu, Nepal.*
4. *A house of Khmer, Cambodia.*
5. *A house in Korea.*
6. *Water dwellings in Sabah, Malaysia.*

Forest and Folk Tradition

Breathing of the spirits slowly begins
insects underground start to creep
heartbeat of mother earth tells us
we human beings are also creations.
In the darkness
the creature is born,
the god manifests,
the evil spirits are everywhere
the folk tale is heard
life and death, life and death
continuing cycles
millenia upon millenia
everything so perfect, so beautiful
altogether in harmony.

Some paintings depicting Asian forest and folk traditions:

1. *'Life of the Buddha', Enlightened monks congregating in the Khan-thamat valley in Himaphan Forest, Thailand;*
2. *Shaikh Taju, 'Maharao Umed Singh, Hunting in the Jungle', India;*
3. *Ida Bagus Made Nadra, 'The Village in Bali', Indonesia;*
4. *Kim Un Ho, 'Cranes in the Forest', Republic of Korea.*

Flowers

Sweet fragrance of flowers for gods and people.

1

2

3

4

5

1. *Tree of life in full bloom, mural painting, Kalani Vihala, Kelaniya near Colombo, Sri Lanka.*
2. *Floral decorations at the Indra-jatra Festival which takes place in September; Kathmandu, Nepal.*
3. *(Left) Lingam worshipped by Indian community, Singapore. (Right) Prayer with flowers, Bali, Indonesia.*
4. *Ceremony of entrance to Buddhist priesthood, Thailand.*
5. *Jain follower offering flowers, milk, curd and fruit at the feet of huge statue of Lord Gomteshwara or Bahubali, India.*

China's Five Colours

A dialogue

When I was a child, I lived within the walls of Beijing. The place I was most fond of going, was the summit of Jing Shan (III). I would climb it and stand in the great pavilion at the centre, with sweat still on my forehead, looking out over the great panorama of the whole city. It was the centre of Beijing and also its highest point. Look! Inside a grand square of grey roofs, there was a smaller square of golden roofs, surrounded by a circle of green water. That was the Forbidden City of ancient Chinese palaces, symbol of feudal imperial power. Every time I went to school, passing under its high purple-red walls and looking up at its golden roofs, it always inspired in me a great awe. One day, my grandpa took my hand and led me into a grand door to the right of the high purple-red wall. When we stepped onto a eastern platform in a great courtyard, he stopped, and pointing to the earth under our feet asked me "My child, do you see anything peculiar about the earth here? I replied, "Grandpa, I have discovered: the earth on this platform has five colours. This side is red, that side is blue, here is white; there is black, white in the middle is yellow." "That's right. This platform is called Platform of She Ji. It has five different colours of earth to represent out mother country. These five colours — red, yellow, blue, white, and black — symbolize the five directions, namely east, west, south, north and the centre, and they symbolize too our five nationalities, namely: Han, Man, Mend, Hui and Cang" said my grandpa.

"Why are there only five colours, yet before my eyes, I see many varied kinds of colours?" I asked doubtfully "To classify the elementary colours as five, was the tradition of our ancient culture. The other varied colours were all derived from them. And I should tell you that these five elementary colours not only symbolize five directions and five nationalities, but also five elements and five emotions," said grandpa.

"Then, what were these five elements and five emotions?" I asked again.

"Metal, wood, water, fire and earth were the five elements, while happiness, anger, sorrow, pleasure, and resentment were the five emotions. Nowadays, we have science, and the five elements have become beautiful legends, but the five emotions are still a nice explanation of the relationship between the colours and our own life."

Thus having said, grandpa took me to a bench nearby, sat down and continued:

"Come! Come! Let me recite a poem to you, so you will understand the idea:

Life was a worthless paper blank,
Until green gave me development,
Red made me passionate,
Yellow taught me faith,
Blue required me to be noble,
Pink bestowed me with hope,
And grey sent me sorrow;
To complete this picture of colours,
Black will add my death,
Thereafter,
I devoted myself to my life,
Because I love all its colours."

"Grandpa", said I "It's beautiful poem, Now I know, that because colours can inspire our emotions, and different colours inspire different emotions, therefore they bear close relation to our life Isn't that so?"

"You are still a child", replied grandpa. "One day when you yourself step into life, you will gain deeper, more intimate experiences with the years".

Some reflections

Later, with this beautiful poem always in mind, I embarked upon my life. And life has really confirmed to me the close relations between the five colours and the five emotions.

I found many new experiences.

I saw that people wore white clothes and white shoes to bury their dead in the tomb; I saw that people put white flowers on their bosoms to pay respect to the memory of their past friends. Then I understood that the divine white of snow and virginity was the colour to express our sorrow and pain.

I saw a young bride with a garland of red flowers on her head, dressed all in red to be wedded to a young bridegroom who was also clothed in red. Then I knew that the firelike red was the colour to represent happiness, pleasure and festivity.

I saw a great flag reddened by the blood of revolutionary martyrs leading us to drive away a dark blue age, taking the victory of revolution, opening up splendid future before us and also resurrecting the yellow dignity of ancient culture for us. Yes, the cradle of ancient Chinese culture was the Yellow River. For thousands of years, she nourished the Chinese people; yet for thousands of years she also, with her yellow currents, changed the fertile middle land into yellow deserts.

For this reason, the ancient Chinese Emperors adopted the colour yellow as the symbol of their power. It represented dignity, authority and supremacy. The yellow tiles on the roofs of Royal Palaces in the Forbidden city even now still have the power to keep people in awe.

But, yellow, as the colour of barrenness, as the colour of deserts, was also the symbol of isolation, lifelessness, conservativeness, and impotence.

Prospective future

We are awakening from the dream under the thousands of years of this heavy yellow burden. We are looking for new colours on the vast horizon.

We introduce green waters to the yellow plateau, plant green trees, sowing green seeds to restore the original green features of nature.

The colour green should be always the symbol of progress, reform, and new life.

We open our heart to the boundless blue skies, to the limitless blue oceans, to widen our field of visions, to run abreast with whole world.

The colour blue should be always the symbol of vastness, openness, and forwardness.

Then, the five colours symbolizing the five emotions are imbued with entirely new meanings. We can follow that great poet to sing with pride:

Hereafter,
We still all devote ourselves to our life,
Because we love its beautiful colours.

A Glance at Colour Symbolism in Iran

Man has long been aware of the effect of colour on his psyche. He knew that some colours had a pleasant effect on him, while others made him sad or melancholy, and that particular colours stimulated his feelings. The symbolic role played by a colour in the culture of various peoples and nations is determined by the effect that colour produces on their psyche. For instance, in Iran, black is supposed to be the colour of mourning, sorrow and misfortune, while white represents purity, good luck, love and hope. With regard to this to some verses popular in Iranian folklore may be referred:

I am a white pigeon stuck to a branch.
The black hand to misfortune broke my wings.
O Heaven, thou should not aim thine arrows at me and break my wings further.
Helplessness has already set in on my being.

In this folklore of Byrjand, white is the symbol of good luck or bright future, and black is the symbol of misfortune and dark days ahead.

Blue, being the colour of water and sky, is the symbol of new life and the emergence of multiple beings. Water symbolizes honour, dignity, prosperity and progress. It also indicates gneiss. When we refer to the flow of water in stream, it implies one's wealth, good luck and success. The water of life' is mythical spring located in "darkness" (Zulmat). If one drinks its water, one attains eternal life. This is the same water of immortality that Elijah is said to have drunk. Blue also symbolizes the sea which is beautiful at rest and fascinating in motion.

Iranians consider blue sacred. Turquoise is a kind of blue with multiple uses. Many Iranians wear rings inlaid with turquoise. Iran herself exports turquoise of the best quality. In the view of Iranians, turquoise has the properties of talisman. For instance, an inferior quality of turquoise called "Kharmohreh" (glass beads) is hung around the necks of some pet animals or children to dispel the effect of the evil eye. Examples of this may be found in old Iranian tombs dating from the first millennium till the Sassanidd period. Similar instances are visible in engravings excavated at places of sacrifice belonging to the Hechaemenian and Parthian periods. Turquoise blue, according to the theories dealing with colour, symbolizes spirituality and is known as a spiritual colour. Its features are tranquility, riches and purity.

Thus it is predominant in all the Islamic masterpieces of architecture. This colour is like the golden mean between warm and cold colours — mostly, inclined towards blue, and having special brilliance. Turquoise in most cases is used for decorating tombs or domes.

Taking into consideration the fact that the sky is blue. One may understand why this colour is predominant in Islamic architecture, particularly in domes and minarets.

Feradun Mushiri, one of the contemporary poets of Iran, speaking of blue and its effect on the human soul, says:

"What is this whisper of water?
What is the playfulness of white clouds.
Upon the surface of a high and tranquil blue sky?
These all take you to the heights of imagination."

Furthermore, in some theories about colour, blue is synonymous with the music of flute and the form or sound of the Da'ira a circular tambourine prevalent in Iran. The tenderness and consoling quality of the sweet notes of the flute and the curved shape of the Da'ira are supposed to be imbued with blue colour.

Saffron colour, ranging from light yellow to blood red with all its properties and peculiarities has always been used in Persian poetry since antiquity, to create beautiful similes and metaphors.

During the last twelve centuries the area of the influence of Persian language has been vaster than it is today being current in many countries of the Indian sub-continent, Central and Western Asia.

Many a Persian poet has emerged from these lands. Poets of these regions have composed a number of verses about the yellow colour of saffron. They have also used numerous similes to represent different qualities of saffron.

Daqiqi Tusi (from Tus a town in Kushrasar AD 978), used the simile of saffron or saffron colour for gold. He believes that "Conquest of a country needs but two things: one is silken bright' and the other is of saffron colour. One is gold minted in the name of the king, the other is a sharp sword made of Yemeni steel".

In Persian poetry light saffron is indicative of the face of a frustrated lover who has failed to win his beloved. There are hundreds of verses in this regard, a few of which are quoted here. Nizami Ganjwi (from Ganjeh, a city in Russian Azerbayejan that is today called Kierofabad, AD 1207) says "Gold is to be offered to the beloved who loves yellow. If thou art happy with yellow it should not matter whether it be gold or saffron". The poet tells his beloved that if he has no gold to offer her, he at least possesses a saffron. coloured face.

Zahir Faryab (Faryab a town in old Khurasan presently in north-western part of Afghanistan, AD 1291) says: "If you smile when you see me, I am not to be thanked: It is my saffron coloured face that cause you to smile". Some poets in similes and allegories have also alluded to the uses of saffron and saffron colour in artistic and industrial products. Persian poets have particularly referred to saffron in the context of the paper industry, since it was used in manufacturing high-quality paper to give it the desired colour and brightness.

Sultan Ali Mashhadi (from Mashhad, the present capital Khurasan in Iran), a poet and a master calligrapher of Iran in the fifteenth century, referring to the paper industry prevalent in those days in Samarkand and Khurasan, which were famous for beautifully coloured papers, says that one has to make use of Hana (a herb whose leaves are used to produce a yellowish orange colour) and saffron to prepare good quality ink. Describing the technique of production good quality paper, he has composed the following lines:

"No colour is better than that of Hana
I tell you how this colour is prepared;
Saffron and Hana are to be mixed with a few drops of ink,
No more than this is required.
Writing with such a compound is as good as writing with gold.
This suffices to produce ornate calligraphy.
On a dark surface, colourful writing is more attractive."

The poet, in the above verse, has described the technique of ornamentation and illumination of writing, pointing out that paper should not be plain white but a little bit dark with a tingle of yellow. Saffron solution was used for writing the titles of imperial decrees and also for the headings of books and treaties.

In conclusion let us look at some of the verses in which different colours have been symbolically used by Iran's most revered and excellent poet Khajeh Hafiz Shiraz (as rendered into English by Wilber Force Clarke):

A bulbul had a rose-leaf, pleasant of hue in his beak;
And, on that leaf and pleasant food, bitter lamentation held.
Evil (of any) we utter not; inclination to the injustice (of any) — we make not;
Black, the face of anyone; and blue, our own religious garment — we make not.

. . .

In this dark night, (the world), lost to me became the path of my purpose (knowledge of the true Beloved).
O Star of guidance (the Murshid, perfect and excellent)! come forth from the corner (and help).

. . .

On account of this blue circle (the sky), bloody of liver I am; give me wine;
So that, in the enamel cup, this difficulty I may solve.

. . .

With the blood of tulips, on the rose-leaf, they have written, Saying : "(Red) wine, like the ruddy Arghavan that one, who became mature, took."

. . .

(O Zahid!) For recorded (open) blackness (of sin), reproach not me intoxicated;
Who knoweth what Fate (in Eternity without beginning) hath written on his (fore-) head?

Red and White are not Just Indonesian State Colours

From time immemorial, the colours red and white have had a special spiritual significance in the minds of the majority of Indonesians. Some prominent Indonesian scholars even believed that this deep psychological association as long as 6000 years ago during the first major migrations of ancient Indonesians from the mainland of South-East Asia to the archipelago, when the *aditya-candra* or red-sun and white-moon' cult started. Consequently it is not very surprising that towards the end of World War II when the fathers of the present state of the Republic of Indonesia, in their search for the national flag, decided to adopt red and white as the state colour, it was unanimously and enthusiastically accepted by the entire population. Since the political independence of the country was achieved through a revolution, the simple flag - which was a familiar sight to the people because from time to time it had been used as a banner by various leaders or petty kings throughout the long history of the Indonesians - very soon became a rallying point and a fighting symbol of the newly emerging country. Numerous heroic songs, poems and the like were written about it during those turbulent periods so that from then on it has been popularly and deeply implanted in everybody's mind that the red and white colours in the Indonesian national flag symbolize valiant and virtuous spirits respectively.

Because of this long cultural history, it is understandable that the usage of red and white is also deeply entrenched in the traditional daily life of Indonesians. The aditya-candra cult alluded to earlier was manifested among other things in the acceptance of red and white lotuses as sacred plants, no doubt fostered by the influence of Buddhism which flourished also in the early history of the country. It is common knowledge that the late President Soekarno cultivated these plants in the ponds of his palaces in Jakarta, Bogor and Yogyakarta, and even the bases of the flag poles in these palaces are also ornamented with carvings of these plant species. As is well-known, in India especially, the fully opened lotus flower is an emblem of the sun. Brahma, the dispeller of darkness, is believed to have emanated from this flower, whereas Gautama Buddha is often represented seated on a full blown lotus blossom.

Still within the context of this red-sun and white-moon cult, Kuda Wanengapati, or Raden Inu Kertapati, or Roung Eynao the male hero of the *Romances of Panji Cycles,* a popular and widely spread folk saga in South East Asia, but especially in Indonesia - is considered to be one of the descendants of the Sun God (Kala Surya). What is more fitting than to have princess Candra Kirana (the moonlight princess) as his idol paramour? In many other local folk tales, red and white also feature prominently, for example in the *Bawang Merah* (red onion) and *Bawang Putih* (white onion) story which is the Indonesian counterpart of the western Cinderella fairy tale. Similarly *Menak Jingga* (the ruddy duke) and *Macan Putih* (the white tiger), or *Dara jingga* (the orange princess) and *Dara Petak* (the white princess) are names of protagonists with the significant combination of colour play which appeared in the popular historical romances which took place in fourteenth century Java.

In employing red and white in their traditional daily customs, more often than not the Indonesian community put a heavier emphasis on the cultural significance rather than on the appearance of the actual colour itself. For that reason in the *meminang* creamy (the engagement ceremony when the representative family of a man officially asks for the hand of maiden in marriage) *sirih* (betel leaf) and *pinang* (areca nut) are offered and used in the ritual because Indonesians "see' red and white colour in this gesture. In betel nut chewing, besides the leaf and the nut indicated above people also use an astringent and reddish brown substance extracted from the gambier plant, as well as pinch of dirty white quick time. The red and white are supposed to signify the male's earthly lust and the strength of his responsibility to be sublimely united with the chastity and the loyal love of the female. That is why in a number of family rituals one often comes across offerings consisting of red and white puddings or cakes to signify the bond of harmony between husband and wife is leading a happy married life. Since the red pudding normally appears brown from the colour of the palm sugar used and the white pudding is creamy coloured, it is obvious that in this case too the metaphorical significance is more important than the colour itself. As can be expected, the combination of gold and silver colour used in many carvings or precious metal ornaments is a further extension of this liberal representation because it is also meant to simulate the sacred red and white colour.

There are a number of tribes in Indonesia, such as the Batak and the Minangkabau in Sumatra, the Badui and the Madurese in Java and the Torajas in Celebes, who believe that besides red and white, black should also be considered a sacred colour. This is evident from the fact that in a number of their traditional ceremonies there is ritual performed by casting a handful of three-coloured rice. In many fairs and public festivals as well as other occasions in Madura, many people (especially the males) dress up in raven-black trousers with unbuttoned loose-fitting dress combined with red and white spangled T-shirts which are considered to be the traditional costume of this tribe. The Balinese consider black so holy and dignified that they drape their deities with chequered cloths of black and white. To these people the black colour signifies the vitality of self-reliance, integrity and the will to lead a vigorous life. Therefore it has nothing to do with the symbol of mourning or the expression of grief as practised in the western world.

The Javanese mystically believe that there are magical powers in colour to overcome evil temptations and physical problems caused by human frailty and foibles. Red is considered capable of nullifying the influence of the devil as well as driving away fear and anxiety, whereas white has the ability to conquer lascivious and mischievous feelings. Black is supposed to prevail against hunger and other physical weakness of the human body. It is of interest to note that, besides believing in their magic power, the Javanese also use colour as a measure of one's understanding of good conduct. This is especially true with regard to batik colouring. For the reason it is understandable that during official ceremonies people who are familiar with Javanese courtly customs and tradition will only turn up in hand-painted batik dress of neutral and subdued brown obtained through the use of natural dye. As in the case of red and white, from this and many other instances it will be obvious that to the majority of Indonesians colours are used for their symbolic significance rather than their physical aspect.

Bhutan: Auspicious Symbols and Luminous Colours — Art and Architecture

hutan is still today a very little-known kingdom secluded in the Eastern Himalayas between India and Tibet (China). It was a country ignored for centuries whose strict policy of isolation ended only in the 1970s.

Bhutan with a land area of 47,000 km^2, has a population of Mongoloid stock. The majority of the population practice Tantric Buddhism which was introduced as early as AD eighth century by Guru Rimpoche. For centuries, monks and refugees from neighbouring Tibet have settled in the hospitable and fertile valleys of Bhutan, and have ensured close cultural links between the two countries. Because of different ecological and socio-economic conditions, Bhutan quickly developed a culture of its own. The art and architecture of Bhutan are beautiful examples of this cultural association with Tibet which has evolved into original patterns and forms, showing the true Bhutanese genius.

Bhutanese art

Bhutanese art (painting and sculpture, as discussed in this article) has two main characteristics: it is religious and anonymous. When the Bhutanese commission paintings and statues, they consider this gesture as a pious act, gaining them merit. The name of the donor is sometimes written on the work so that his pious act may be remembered. The artist is often a religious man who also gains merit doing this work; however, the artist's name is almost never mentioned.

Since the iconographic rules in Bhutanese art are very strictly fixed, the first responsibility of the Bhutanese artist is to observe them scrupulously; thus he can only express his own personality in minor details or scenes.

The subjects of Bhutanese art are: the Wheel of Life; the Four Guardians; the Bodhisattva Avalokiteshvara (Chenrezig) in his multiple forms; and 16 Arhats (Neten Chudrug); the 84 Mahasiddhas (Drubthob Gyechushi); the 1000 Buddhas; Guru Rimpoche and his Eight Manifestations; Amitayus (Tsepamey); the highest deities of Tantric Cycles like Hevajra (Kyedorje), Cakrasamvara (Demchog) etc.; the protective deities such as the different forms of Mahakala (Gompo), Palden Lhamo, Gyelpo Pehar; and various diagrams (mandalas, kyilkhor). Some of the most beautiful and astonishing paintings are the cosmic mandalas which show the conception of the World according to the *Adhidharmakosha* (an encyclopaedic treaty on Buddhist cosmology and philosophy composed by an Indian scholar Vasubandhu in the fifth century) and the *Kalacakra-tantra* (Kalacakra literally means the "Wheel of Time". This text of the tenth century exposes the basic conception of cosmology and astrology of Tantric Buddhism). We find them in Paro Dzong, Punakha Dzong, Simtokha Dzong and Gantey Gompa. As Bhutan has been the stronghold of the Nyingmapa and Drukpa Kagyupa sects, many paintings depict the spiritual lineage of these two sects, as well as the different religious and temporal Drukpa rulers of Bhutan (Shabdrungs, Desis and Je Khempos).

Paints are traditionally made from earth, minerals and vegetables, though in recent times chemical colours have been used. The material is first reduced into powder and then mixed with water, glue and chalk. The brushes are made from twigs and animals' hair. The colours are applied in a particular order associated with a symbolic meaning.

Paintings and sculptures are executed by monks or laymen who work in special workshops. The disciples of a master do all the preliminary work while the fine work is executed by the master himself.

(1) Paintings

Bhutanese paintings can be classified into three categories: those applied on statues, the wall-paintings and the scroll-paintings called *thanka.* The clay statues are entirely painted while the statues called "bronzes" are only painted on the face to underline details like a moustache and the eyes. The technique of the fresco is unknown and the surface of the inside walls of all the monasteries and temples is covered with plaster of earth, smoothed and let to dry before being painted. There is another technique which may be specific to Bhutan and which is widely employed there: a very thin piece of cloth is applied on the plaster with much care so that it is almost impossible to detect the cloth unless it peels off the wall; a special paste made of wheat flour and pepper powder is used to prevent worms from eating the cloth.

Scroll-paintings, known as *thanka,* are extremely numerous in Bhutan but they are not placed on permanent display in the temples and monasteries. They are kept rolled in huge boxes in the storeroom of the temples and are taken out only for special religious occasions. The technique of the *thanka* consists of fixing a damp piece of cotton to wooden frame. A mixture of lime/chalk and gum is then rubbed on the surface of the cloth and smoothed. A net of geometrical lines is drawn to help the artist layout the composition. Sometimes, he simply presses the cloth against a xylographic block on which the design is already engraved. He could also use the system of the pounce, or spray pattern, which consists of a printed figure on paper with holes pricked at intervals through which charcoal is pressed to produce a dotted pattern. This preliminary sketch disappears when the colours are applied. While numerous colours are generally used, some *thankas* can have a totally golden background on which the design is executed in fine black or red lines. Other *thankas* executed for special rituals are black with white and red designs. When the *thankas* is finished, it is surrounded with a silk and brocade border of many colours which also have symbolic meaning, and two staves are stitched to the upper and lower borders for suspension and stretching.

Two other techniques not involving painting are used to make *thankas:* embroidery and appliqué. Appliqué is specially done in the case of the huge *thankas* which are hung on festival days on the outside walls of the temples.

The style of the paintings has changed much along the centuries, but it is very difficult to make a precise history of Bhutanese paintings because paintings of temples which are undoubtedly old, have been repainted many times along the centuries. In the earliest temples which have kept their original paintings like Tamshing in Bumthang (AD fifteenth century), the central figure, soberly drawn, occupies most of the painting while the edges are divided into small compartments for the minor figures. The imposing proportion of the main figure, the clothes of the attendants showing the legs, and the pattern of the jewels indicate an Indian influence of the Pala-Sena Bengali dynasties (AD eighth-twelfth century). This style has highly influenced, possibly through Nepal, early Tibetan and Central Asian art. Although in the fifteenth century Chinese art had already exerted a certain influence on Tibetan paintings, it does not appear to have reached Bhutan. However many early paintings had been repainted much later as a meritorious act and some examples of this influence may have disappeared. Bhutanese painting always favoured, even after the fifteenth century, a central composition with adjacent figures like in Taktshang (seventeenth century), Tango (seventeenth century) and Phajoding (eighteenth century) monasteries. Other artists used the entire space of the walls of the cloth and produced asymmetric compositions. In this case, many figures or scenes occupy the whole space and the interest is not focused on one main figure. The artist can also freely, around a central figure, illustrate scenes of a famous person's life; an example is the illustration of Milarepa's life in Paro Dzong. Throughout the centuries Bhutanese style has become more and more ornate, the use of gold paint more lavish and landscape paintings treated after the Chinese manner. Chinese art influences, mixed with earlier impact into a harmonious Bhutanese blend, can be seen from the seventeenth century onwards. Many of the paintings are inscribed with the names of the figures represented which help to date the paintings.

(2) Sculptures

To our knowledge, in Bhutan there are no sculptures made of stone and almost no stone carvings, except some low reliefs on the *mani*-walls and on a few rocks. As Bhutan is very rich in slate, a number of large pieces of slate are intricately engraved with deities, monks and saints of Tantric Buddhism. The most beautiful are found around the central tower of the Simtokha Dzong and, as they are all inscribed, are a priceless treasure for the iconography of Bhutanese art.

Clay images are very common and are entirely painted. Their size can vary greatly from the very small images which are placed in the portable chapels called Tashigomang, to the huge statues of two or three meters high, as in Kuje and Phajoding Monasteries. Fine and even clay is either moulded on a core of wood wrapped in cloth or moulded directly without any support, the status then remaining hollow. Some small additions may then be moulded before being added to the main body. Miniature *chortens* made of clay and sometimes mixed with the ashes of the dead are called *tsha-tsha* and are very common in holy places; they are moulded before being painted or whitewashed.

Metal images are called by the conventional term of "bronzes" but are usually made from other copper alloys.

Silver and gold statues, although rare, do exist. The lost wax casting, or *cire perdue* technique which was introduced in Tibet and Bhutan by the Newari craftsmen, is widely used for the medium-size images. The tall images and the large commemorative stupas, however, are first hammered from sheets of various sizes then embossed and engraved, the separate parts being jointed by riveting. Most of the metal images and *chortens* are gilded, and some of them are even ornamented with corals and turquoises. The face and the jewels of the statues are frequently inlaid with silver and copper, and paints applied to the faces and the head-dresses. From the eighteenth century, altars and *chortens* were frequently ornamented with sheets of beautifully embossed and chiseled gilded copper, primarily in western Bhutan (Phajoding, Gantey and Thadra Gompa). Some images are made of lacquered wood and have a striking expression such as the Milarepa's statue in Dungtse Lhakhang.

Religious book covers are also made of wood, and when the books are quite precious, the upper covers are finely carved with deities and often painted or covered with sheets of the embossed copper.

It is very difficult to speak about different styles of Bhutanese sculpture because no study has yet been made of them. A Newari influence is evident in large hammered statues and in the copper halo which is located at the back of many important statues, like in Simtokha Dzong, and which is composed of *garudas, nagas, makaras* after the typical Newari *torana* (gate).

Other statues which may date back to the sixteenth century have very simple but striking features. Their bases are not carved and no real influence can be discerned from them, the statue of 4th Sha-mar Chhoekyi Gragpa (1453-1524) at Thangbi Lhakhang in Bumthang is a good example. From the eighteenth century onwards, statues were much more ornate, very often inlaid with semi-precious stones and their base carved in a double rank of petals of the lotus flower.

Paintings and statues are consecrated and a religious ceremony destined to give life to the painting or the statue is performed: a holy lama may even apply his hand prints at the back of the scroll, while inside the statue will be placed a piece of wood and papers inscribed with sacred formulas.

Bhutanese architecture

The architectural forms in Bhutan are very diverse: *chortens* (stupas); *mani*-walls, temples; monasteries; fortresses; palaces; and village houses compose a landscape which is unique to Bhutan.

Chortens are erected in memory of an eminent lama or to protect against evil spirits at dangerous place, like cross-roads and passes. They are of three styles: 1) Huge stone, often whitewashed *chortens* built after the stupa of Bodhnath in Nepal: good examples are the Chendebji Chorten and Chorten Kora. 2) Small stone *chortens* which show an affinity with the Tibetan style, common throughout central and eastern Bhutan, and are often protected by a wooden superstructure. 3) *Chortens* which show a purely Bhutanese tradition and are widespread mostly in western Bhutan: The outer structure is a square stone tower with a red stripe at the upper level and shingle roof; sometimes inside a memorial *chorten* after the Tibetan style is erected. This kind of *chorten* may be an elaborate form derived from the *chorten* with wooden superstructure.

Some of the *chortens* are linked together by *mani* (prayer)-walls. These are stone walls which support a multitude of stones carved with the sacred formulas, either of the three protective Bodhisattvas: Chenrezig; Jampelyang; Chana Dorje; or simply with the Chenrezig's formula *"Om mani padme hum"*, from which the name of *mani*-walls is derived. However *mani*-walls may also stand by themselves, without *chortens.* Bhutanese architecture is a remarkable adaptation of Tibetan architecture to different climatic and ecological conditions. For instance, in Tibet the walls are sloped and often white-washed, the windows get larger with increasing storeys, but in Bhutan the abundance of rain and of timber has given Bhutanese architecture its specific feature. Wood is used plentifully, and the doors and the windows show a supreme craftsmanship. The windows have distinctive trefoil-shaped tops and elaborate lintels which are painted with geometrical and floral motifs The pitched roof, covered with shingles weighed down with rows of stones is a very striking and original structure. Its origin was probably the Tibetan flat roof on top of which Bhutanese have put slotted trusses. The use of nails was in olden times unknown but has now become more common. Temples, monasteries, fortresses and houses have been, and are still very frequently destroyed by fire but they are generally rebuilt after the same model.

Temples (*lhakhang*) are usually one or two storeys, simple buildings with wide red stripe at the upper level of the walls and a gilded roof ornament. They may have a small courtyard. Inside the temple the walls are covered with paintings and the space is generally divided by pillars into an antichamber and a shrine. These buildings seem to be one of the earliest forms of religious architecture and have crossed the centuries, remaining intact to this day.

We can cite Kichu Lhakhang in Paro, Jampa and Sugney Lhakhang in Bumthang, all said to have been built around the seventh century, Chime Lhakhang from the sixteenth century in Punakha valley and Gom Kora in eastern Bhutan. Temples are kept by a caretaker who belongs to the owner's family or who is delegated by the State, because temples and monasteries are the properties of the state or of a family.

Bhutanese monasteries (*gompa*) are of two architectural types: the "cluster" type and the *"dzong"* type. The "cluster" type is probably the most ancient type; it consists of a core of one or two temples, around which small houses of habitation and meditation are built for the monks. Some examples of the "cluster" type are Dzongdrakha in Paro valley, Phajoding and Tashingang in Thimphu valley, Kunzangdra and Tharpaling in Bumthang valley. The *"dzong"* type is a monastery built like a fortress with a main tower housing many temples and a surrounding outer wall which serves as accommodation quarters for the monks. The most impressive examples of the architecture are Gantey Gompa near Pele-la Pass, Tango in upper Thimphu and Talo near Punakha, all dated late seventeenth century. Cheri Gompa, built in 1620 by the Shabdrung Ngawang Namgyal in the upper Thimphu valley, presents the characteristics of the two styles with a *dzong*-like main building and a cluster of small houses around it.

The Bhutanese fortress built for strategic purposes since the beginning of the seventeenth century is called a *dzong*. It can be defined as a state-monastery and a district administration housed together in a dramatically located fortress. The solidity of the sloping white walls combines with the elegance, the richness of the woodwork and the aerial feature of the pitched roof and make the *dzong* one of the most impressive forms of architecture in Asia. The basic pattern of a *dzong* is a main tower (*utse*) and a courtyard surrounded by walls which houses monks' quarters, kitchens and administrative offices: Gasa Dzong and Simtokha Dzong can be given as examples. However, very few *dzongs* strictly follow this pattern and most of them have two courtyards delineated by the central tower: one courtyard delineates the monastery and one the administrative section, like in Punakha, Wangdiphodrang and Thimphu Dzongs. The courtyard and the buildings may also be located on different levels and follow the slope of the hill: Paro, Jakar and Tongsa Dzongs follow this pattern. Tongsa is the most complex *dzong* with an intricate pattern of buildings, towers and courtyards.

Many architectural features of the temples, monasteries and *dzongs* are also to be found in the purely civil architecture but with interpretations due to different functions.

The appearance of palaces seem to have coincided with the advent of the monarchy at the beginning of the twentieth century, and are mainly found in Bumthang-Tongsa area. Their basic pattern is very similar to the *dzong*: a main building where the masters reside surrounded by outer walls in which the servants' quarters are established. However, because they serve a different purpose, these palaces have a much less severe architecture than the *dzongs*. They are profusely decorated with woodwork and even the outer walls are pierced by numerous beautifully carved and gaily painted windows. One upper room of the main building is always devoted to religion. This room, called *chhoesham* is a real temple with wall-paintings, altar, statues and books for the rituals. Amongst other palaces, Lame Gompa, Wangduchhoeling and Ugyenchhoeling in Bumthang, Kunga Rabten south of Tongsa Dzong and Gantey Palace in Paro vallery are good examples.

Village houses are not built with the same material all over Bhutan: in western Bhutan the walls are made of rammed earth while in central and eastern Bhutan, mainly stone is used. In eastern Bhutan, bamboo mats are also used to build and to cover small houses which rest on poles. However, all over the country Bhutanese houses display distinctive features: they have a rectangular shape, two or three storeys high; the upper floors are almost totally made of a framework of wood and plastered bamboo lattices; the windows are closed from inside by wooden shutters but now glass is common in the bigger villages. Although, in olden times, the framework was rarely painted, it is today more and more ornamented by coloured motifs. The roof, as is discussed above, is pitched on trusses and the open space between the flat top of the upper floor and the wooden shingles is used for stacking firewood and fodder. Traditionally in the farm-houses, which were seldom whitewashed, the ground-floor was reserved for the cattle. The other floors were reached by a ladder cut out from a tree trunk, and the walls of these floors were almost windowless. The intermediate floor, if there was one, was used to store grains, seeds and other foodstuff. The upper floor, the living quarters, was divided into small rooms which had no real definite function except for the bathroom, if existing, the kitchen full of smoke and soot due to the absence of a chimney, and the prayer-room which also served as the guest-room. The furniture is sparse: low tables; sleeping-mats which are rolled in a corner during the day; shelves for the crockery; carpets; trunks for valuable possessions; an altar; and one or two looms. A courtyard, often covered, is found on one side of the house. Nowadays this type of farm-house is still found throughout the country with slight regional differences. However, they are now almost all whitewashed and in the towns, because the house is no more a farm, windows are located at the first floor as well. The ground-floor has become servant's quarters, storeroom and kitchen, and there is a tendency to build the kitchen and the bathroom in a separate little building detached from the back of the house. The ground-floor can also be used for a shop.

Bhutan: Spiritual Living; Enthusiastic Enjoyment — Daily Life and Entertainment

Birth

The first born child of Bhutanese parents is kept away from public view the first three days, after which lamas are invited to perform a purification ceremony known as *ihasang*. When the contaminations resulting from the birth have been removed in this way, visitors drop in to offer gifts and greetings, and are in turn served food and drinks. The parents of the new-born child consult an astrologer, and the child is named according to its horoscope. If obstacles are foreseen, the astrologer will prescribe necessary remedies. Sometimes, in the event of difficulties and problems early in life, the child is renamed after deliberations with the lama-astrologer.

Immediately after the birth of a child, the mother is given a special kind of homemade wine prepared with butter, eggs and sugar, called *menchang*. The quality of the wine's taste is believed to reflect the quality of life that the new-born child will experience.

Marriage

In the traditional Bhutanese system, parents decided well in advance who their children were to marry when they reached maturity. Generally, as is to be expected, the choice fell upon the son or daughter of a friend. If the sentiment was reciprocal, the two parties reached an understanding that was both morally and socially binding, the marriage then took place in due course. This method of selecting the spouse-to-be of one's son or daughter was known as *chungnyen tag* "engagement of marriage at childhood". Occasionally, however, owing to developments that were contrary to the understanding, the proposed marriage failed to materialize. In such an event, the party backing out would compensate the other in kind.

The marriage ceremony itself was prolonged and colourful. The bridegroom, escorted by a group of friends, called *bangro*, went in procession to the bride's house. From there he brought her home at a specified time prescribed by the astrologer - in the company of her own friends, family members and neighbours, including local folk dancers. The bride's party is known collectively as *bumrog*. As the procession approached the bridegroom's house, members of the household stood outside the doorway with two bowls - one full of milk, and another full of water, symbolizing the fullness hoped for in the new life of the couple about to be married. This was followed by an auspicious ceremony called *marchang*, wherein offerings were made to the local deities. The two parties would then cross the threshold and settle in, with the bride and bridegroom seated side by side before a lama, who chanted the wedding ceremony. When this was done, the couple would sip wine and exchange their cups before being declared husband and wife. At the same time, the lama handed them eight auspicious sacred articles (*dzegye*) so as to preserve, protect and promote the sanctity of their covenant. Gifts were given to each of the couple by the guests, with either three, five or seven different varieties of cloth together with a white scarf each to the bride and bridegroom depending on the economic capacity of the giver. If the giver of the presents were elders, the white scarf would be placed around the neck of the couples.

The scene was then set for merry-making. Sumptuous food, including saffron rice, was served, liberal quantities of local wine called *chhang* were imbibed by one and all, the guests joked and gossiped, and there was much dancing. The celebrations ended only with the late hour of the night. This sort of traditional marriage is known as *lagpa marchang-gi genpi nyen* "marriage blessed by the *marchang* ceremony."

If a married couple proved incompatible, and a partner resorted to another person, he or she lost all right to property in that particular household. If the misdemeanour was committed by the wife, then the man who took her in had to bear the estranged husband's entire expenditure on her during the course of their marital life.

The *chungnyen tag* system of marriage, however, has largely died out, and the new generations of young Bhutanese men and women are increasingly taking recourse to civil marriages with someone of their own choice. In Bhutan, as elsewhere, the traditional way of life in the country is giving way to modernization, and a party, thrown by the newlyweds themselves, has replaced the elaborate ceremonials of tradition.

Sickness

Traditionally, sickness among the Bhutanese has been associated with Karmic effects, and astrologers are consulted for advice on the remedies and the *pujas* to be performed. Neighbours and relatives of the sick help out with the arrangements, as well as volunteering various other kinds of assistance. The practical application of this spirit of fellowship and good-neighbourliness is known as *kilen duglen* "sharing happiness, sharing misery," and involves offering one's good offices, both in times of happiness and misery. Of late, with the spread of modern education, more and more Bhutanese are relying on the numerous hospitals and dispensaries that have been or are being set up all over the country.

Construction of a house

When a residential house is constructed, it is customary for neighbours to assist in the physical labour. The house, in fact, is built by the local community with a mason and carpenter lending their expertise. The latter are each presented a *gho* in which to undertake their work. While the men-folk engage in the more strenuous activities, the women pound mud or help carry it to the allotted places. As in almost every other public occasion, these tasks are accompanied by much singing. There is no system of wages for the hours of labour worked. Instead, the owner of the house serves food and wine to one and all during the period of construction - from morning till evening.

Once the house is completed, lamas perform exorcism rites before the consecration ceremony, or *rabney*, is held. At this time, the house-owner expresses his gratitude to the mason and the carpenter in a typical gesture known as *dartak* by giving each of them a complete set of traditional dress, including a scarf. He also presents them with other gifts in keeping with his ability, but there are no hard and fast rules as to what these should be. All the other guests, without exception, also make presentations to the mason and carpenter. This is not only recognition of their indispensable craftsmanship, but there is also a superstitious belief that if they are not given due honour, their retaliatory prayers can bring about the collapse of the house. According to tradition, the mason and carpenter are to be treated with the same respect as one's parents, teachers, and personal god.

The consecration ceremony also includes *pujas* for the prosperity of the inhabitants of the new house. The rituals are followed by drinking, dances designed expressly to confer good wishes, and other festivities.

Death

When death occurs in a Bhutanese household, the corpse is cremated. The day of the cremation is not fixed, but is decided upon in consultation with astrologers. Thus, if the time is auspicious, the body may be cremated soon after the death occurs. On the other hand, a full month or more may elapse before the right date for cremation arrives.

Following a death, a member of the concerned family, along with another member of the community, calls on a lama astrologer with a present of four meters of cloth (i.e. the size of a *gho*), and other gifts. The astrologer places his astrological charts and papers on this piece of cloth, ascertains specified details regarding the time of death, the age of the deceased, his name, and the age of the family-head, etc; he then deduces the astrological meaning of the death. If the death is likely to cause hindrances to the community in question, then the community representatives are asked to inform the community to perform certain remedial *pujas*. Alternatively, if the bereaved family is likely to have inconveniences, then the responsibility of performing the *pujas* falls on the family. In either case, the *pujas* must be completed by the 21st day after the death.

The ritual ceremonies in the house of the deceased being on the fourth morning after the death. The major rites, conducted by a team of lamas, are held on the 4th, 7th, 14th, 21st and 49th days. In between the respective days, until the 21st day, one lama remains to chant prayers and feed the soul of the departed. From the 21st until the 49th day, all worship is forbidden in the house, but is performed instead in a monastery. After 49 days, it is customary to hold a *puja* within the household so as to both purify the spiritual atmosphere, and to bring prosperity and happiness to the family members. Neighbours play a prominent role in this event, for they not only bring consolatory offerings of food and wine for the bereaved, but also help carry firewood, water and other necessities to the house.

If possible, the well-to-do invite the Je Khempo to sanctify the cremation ceremony. Otherwise, another influential lama is called for the occasion, and service takes place in the Central Cremation Ground. The less well-off have to rest content with lamas lower down in the monastic hierarchy, and an alternate site suitable for the event. Neighbours come with traditional butter, tea, food and gifts, and place money near the body in a symbolic gesture of goodwill for the departed soul. Relatives or persons close to the deceased sometimes perform a *ngowa* - a special *puja* on behalf of an individual for the release of the loved one's soul.

Ceremonials relating to promotions

Coloured scarves (*kamne*) are awarded to meritorious officials who have made significant contributions to their country in one capacity or another. The convention is somewhat similar to the conference of knighthood in the United Kingdom. The chart below shows the different colours of scarves prevalent, along with the rank entitled to people wearing them.

Yellow: the King and Je Khempo
Orange: Ministers and Deputy Ministers
Red: Senior officials
Blue: People's representatives in the Royal Advisory Council and in the High Court
Red with white stripes in the middle: Deputy Administrator in the District (*dzongkhag*)
White with red stripes: Assistant Administrator
White: General public.

Orange and red scarves are presented personally by His Majesty the King, while those lower than the red scarf are awarded by the Home Minister. The event is one which calls for celebrations, and the recipient of the honour is carried home in procession by friends, admirers, and well-wishers. Once home, in traditional Bhutanese style, he sits cross-legged on an elevated seat, with a variety of fruits, sweets, and

Bhutanese tea tastefully set before him. Silver bowls and containers filled with this food rest on an intricately patterned table that itself is a superb testimony to fine Bhutanese craftsmanship. *Thankas* hang behind and around him on the walls, while groups of lamas and associates range themselves on the floor in front. A religious ceremony called *zhugdre*, which is performed on all auspicious occasions, is then carried out, thus solemnizing the promotion.

Later, when it is convenient, the promoted officials throw a magnificent party, where the practice of *dartak* referred to above (cf. Construction of a House), again meticulously adhered to, with the guests offering presents of either three, five or seven different colours of cloth. In the event that it is not economically feasible for a person to make the presentation in full, symbolic strips of cloth and/or cash are given instead, thereby preserving the time-honoured custom.

Other Bhutanese customs

While it is not possible, with the brief confines of this article, to touch upon each and every custom prevalent in Bhutan or, for that matter, to deal with any one in full, a passing mention may be made of some interesting and ancient customs which have been suitably modified with the changing times.

In olden days a person approaching a *dzong* — a fort which also served as the ecclesiastical and administrative centre of a particular area — had to get off from his horse at the *chorten* in the neighbourhood of the *dzong*, take off his hat if he wore one, put on his *kamne* or scarf, and proceed on foot for the rest of the way. If he donned a sword while entering or passing by the premises of the *dzong*, he would have to keep it hanging by his side rather than have it hang behind him for the convenience of walking, as he was otherwise wont to do. Even today, it is obligatory for all Bhutanese to wear a scarf while entering a *dzong*, and Red Scarf and other senior officials must also carry a sword in the prescribed fashion. Neither officials nor visitors may cover one's head in the immediate vicinity of a *dzong*, and even open umbrellas, which are a symbol of royal or religious authority, are strictly forbidden.

During the yearly festival held to mark the winter solstice in every Bhutanese village, most of the adult males go off to shoot archery. The children — and occasionally the adults too — skip along from house to house in the evenings in lively, playful groups shouting benediction on behalf of each family therein: "May the fields be filled with grains! May the stables be filled with horses! May the butter-container be filled with butter!" etc. It is customary for the family concerned to invite the party in and serve them tea or drinks. Gifts of rice or other foodstuff are also presented to the visitors.

Nine evils day

It is believed that on the nine Evils Day, the nine demons get together to hold their annual meeting, and with them away, people interested in buying a plot of land quickly avail of the opportunity to do so. Otherwise, the general rule for the day, which is observed as a holiday, is: Do no work. Do no good things. Eat, drink, and be merry!

The Nine Evils Day, which falls on the 7th day of the eleventh month of the Bhutanese calendar, is followed by the Uepa-Lagtong Day on the 9th. Literally, *uepa* means 'poor' while *lagtong* means 'empty-handed', and this particular day, as its name signifies, is considered inauspicious - inauspicious, that is, for the giving of gifts or money or, for that matter, any article whatsoever. The belief is that the giver will end up losing all his fortunes and possessions and inevitably sink into poverty. However, the recipient is believed to enter into a period of good fortune.

Sports

Archery is the national sport of Bhutan. It is played with enthusiasm throughout the year, and the young and the middle-aged alike can be seen trooping off after lunch to indulge in their favourite pastime. In fact, archery contests are an essential part of most festive occasions in the country. The archery ground has two decoratively painted wooden targets, each measuring four feet by one foot, and placed at a distance of about a hundred and fifty yards from each other. Both teams move concurrently from one target to the other in the course of a contest.

An archery competition between one village and another, or one *dzongkhag* (district) and another is an important event. *Pujas* are offered to the local deities before a match, for the contest is considered as much a trial of strength between the deities as between the participants themselves. Additionally, an astrologer is engaged by each side, who even prescribes the direction of entry into the archery ground. The visiting side is traditionally given the right of choosing the target it wants to aim at first and may also choose the food it wishes to take during its stay.

A *marchang* ceremony is performed at the venue, and the supporters of each team, accompanied by seven, nine, or eleven women dancers, take positions along the ground. The dancers act as cheer-leaders, as it were, and apart from encouraging their own side, they also try to dishearten their opponents with cries and gestures. Whenever a player scores a point, his colleagues jump and shout and leap into the air. A game comprises thirty-three points, which are computed according to a complicated system. Once the contest is over, the member of the victorious side who has hit the target the most number of times or who has scored the winning point, is carried off the field in procession on the shoulders of his team-mates amongst much jubilation and dancing. Drinking and festivity follow, and the losers offer prayers so as to avenge the defeat in the next encounter.

Another popular sport, originally played by lamas, is the *degor*, in which a round, flat stone weighing about a kilogramme is thrown from the palm of the hand at a target twenty-five feet away.

In winter, when the harvest has been collected, and the annual *pujas* are being performed at home, the Bhutanese invite their relatives and close friends for drinks and food. It is not uncommon for two such *pujas* to be performed simultaneously in adjacent houses. During breaks between the periods of worship, a member of a house might enter at unawares into another and at some suitable opportunity secretly leave behind a spinning-wheel with rice tar smeared on it. If he is caught in the act, the occupants of the house subject him to some very hearty ragging, and have a great deal of fun at his expense. If, on the other hand, he successfully makes his getaway, once outside he draws the attention of the house-members to his prank, who then give him chase, though usually in vain.

The conditions for a test of skills in a *degor* engagement have now been met. The spinning wheel and rice tar constitute a challenge, as it were, with the unpleasant implication that if the lamas of the house are not manly enough to take it up, they may as well resign themselves to feminine pursuits like spinning and cooking!

Of course, laymen too have increasingly taken to the game of *degor*, and groups of youngsters may often be seen indulging in homemade variations of the game in fields, parks, and side-streets.

Other traditional sports include the *soksom*, in which a wooden spear, held at either end, is hurled at a target; *khuru*, similar to the game of darts, in which the projectile has a sharp nail at one end and feathers at the other; *bjib*, in which a three-pointed device similar to a boomerang is spun through the air at the target; *keshey* (wrestling); *pungo-do* (shotput); and *sherey parey*, in which one contestant grasps the wrist of his opponent who then must free himself to win.

Fisher-Folk of Asia

Fishing and the Fisher-Folk of Asia

For the Asians, fish stands alongside rice as a staple of their diet, and it is a major source of animal protein, but in the past fishing has lagged somewhat behind industrial development and agricultural development. With the exception of Thailand, which has been working since before World War II to foster marine industry, scientists and technicians working to promote the development of the marine fishing industry, these nations tend to be heavily weighted towards rubber, tin, tea, and other industries left over colonial days. In addition, the income of the people of these nations have been low, so that fishing has not been able to gain an industrial footing.

Recently, however, these lands have turned to development of marine resources as part of their overall economic development programs, and also as a way to absorb the under-employment population in the fishing villages and raise their standard of living. There is, however, no single "Asian fishing industry," and fishing takes on a variety of aspects depending on geographic and economic conditions, so that this short consideration cannot hope to be comprehensive or detailed. Instead, we will look only at the general features of the fishing industry in Asia.

Asia is different from other continents in the large proportion of paddy agriculture, but its fishing industry does not differ greatly from that in other regions, the main differences consisting of the ocean environment, the types of fish fauna caught, and the stage of development, which of course depends largely on the social and economic conditions of the country concerned.

The countries of Southeast Asia and Southern Asia are divided into the South China Sea, the Andaman Sea, the Indonesian Sea, and the Northern Indian Ocean, thus encompassing the tropical seas twenty degrees north and south of the equator. One feature of the marine industries in these tropical waters is that the water temperature remains high the year around and that there are over 200 species of fish that can be taken here. The northern part of the Atlantic Ocean the northern Pacific, and other regions in the higher latitudes have only limited varieties of fish, such as cod and herring, but a single haul may yield up to several tons of primarily one species of fish. In contrast, while the tropical waters feature a wide variety of species, the volume of catches falls short of this level. This difference is due largely to the difference in the prevailing ocean structures, with the tropical zones lacking in the ocean currents, upwelling, and other conditions that go into the formation of fishing grounds.

In general, the relatively flat ocean bottom from the coastline to a depth of 200 meters is called the continental shelf, and the sunlight and nutritious salt content of the water leads to photosynthesis which supports the abundant growth of plankton and fish in what could even be called an ocean oasis.

The South China Sea, including the Andaman Sea, has the world's second broadest shelf, 2.57 millions square kilometers in area. The area of the Indian Ocean's continental shelf, however, is very small if the 610,000 square kilometers of the Bay of Bengal and the 400,000 square kilometers of the Gulf of Arabia are excluded.

Nevertheless, the Asian continent is blessed with a variety of large and small rivers which arise in Himalayas — the Mekong, Menan, Irrawaddy, Ganges, and Indus to name just a few. These rivers have formed broad, flat deltas in their lower reaches, forming both rice-producing areas and a treasure-house fish at the same time. During the rainy season, the large Tonle Sap Lake in central Khmer (Cambodia) receives backflow from the Mekong, greatly expanding the lake, and the Tonle Sap is well known as one of the most abundant lakes in the world. During the Monsoon season, the central plain of Thailand is flooded by the waters of the Menan, Moekhlong and other rivers, sending the fish into paddies and forest to spawn. The fish thus grow in the paddies along with the rice. With the arrival of the dry season, catfish, snake-head, and other varieties of freshwater fish flow downstream with the draining water, where they may be caught with bamboo pots, wing set nets, lift nets, and other simple fishing equipments providing a supplemental source of income to the rural people. Another means of catching fish is the trapping pond, a small pond dug along the banks; seeking deeper waters, fish gather here during the dry season, where they may be captured. In the delta regions of many rivers, natural salt-making is conducted. Shrimp fingerlings also flow into these salt forms along with the sea water. They then grow to about ten centimeters in around two months, when they are shipped to market. In recent years, many such salt ponds are being converted solely to shrimp breeding and raising.

Fish are most abundant around the mouths of the rivers, where shrimp, crabs, and shellfish (green mussel, askshell fish) may be caught, and traps, pots, and the like continue to be used, operating on the principle of the ebb and flow of the tides. Until the 1950's, a small set net called *poe* in Thai and a *kelong* in Malay was the most typical feature of the fishing industry in Southeast Asia, but later, with the quick development made in trawling and purse seine fishing operations, the *kelong* has progressively disappeared. Viet-Nam and Thailand are famous for the fish sauce and shrimp paste by fermenting varieties of small fishes.

Nylon nets from Japan began to enter Southeast Asia during the 1950's replacing the cotton nets in use, and the new gill nets and cast nets led more catches of India — Pacific mackerel, chub mackerel, Spanish mackerel, skipjack, and yellowfin. Whether at sea or on inland waters, the gill nets and cast nets have become favourites of the artisanal fishermen of this region. There was rapid growth in small trawlers from West Germany being around 1965. Until that time, Mexico had been the leading producer of prawns in the world, but its catches began to fall. From about this time, Japanese and American demand for shrimp grew sharply, making this a period of a shrimps boom." The small-scale trawlers began to appear throughout Southeast Asia, from Thailand, Malaysia, and Singapore to Savah, Sarawak, Indonesia, and India. With the coming of the 1970's, Southeast Asia became the World's prime producer of shrimp.

Almost every variety of shrimp is produced here, brown and black tigers, pink, white and yellow shrimp and many others. During the fingerling stage, these shrimp are raised in the region around river mouths, after which they are moved to deeper areas around 25 meters in depth so that they may spawn. The volumes of shrimp and the amount of rain are said to be closely related. In Sri Lanka, the young shrimp are raised in lagoons near river mouths before they go out to sea to lay their eggs. In the shallow lagoons they may be caught by hand or with cast nets, and at sea they are caught using gill nets. In the case of Sabah, Sarawak, Indonesia, and other locations shrimps activities are operated as joint ventures with foreign enterprises, often suing double-rigger trawlers specifically designed for shrimp fishing.

Production by the Southeast Asian fishing industry over the last 15 years has grown from a mere two million tons in 1960 to 8.6 million tons in 1974. The average annual rate of growth is 7% a very high level compared to the worldwide average of 4%. The most dramatic growth has been shown by Thailand, which more than tripled its marine production from 500,000 tons in 1965 to 1.69 million tons in 1973. As a result, however, of the increase in the number of trawlers, there has been a considerable drop in fish resources, and fishing restrictions have become for necessary to protect such resources.

Shrimps account for about 10% of the trawlers' catch, and after thread-fin bream, lizard fish, crab, squid, and other valuable types of fish are removed, the remaining 60% of the catch is made up of assorted small fish called "trash fish". Part of such trash fish may be used as feed for ducks and catfish or may be turned into fish meal, but many countries' trawlers simply discard the trash fish in the sea. Since about 30% of the trash fish are young of commercially valuable fish, the efficient handling to trash fish is also an important matter in terms of protection of resources and utilization of these valuable species. Sri Lanka rises out of the Indian Ocean, and since except for its, northern parts, the island has few shallow areas, and the fishing industry consists mostly of cast net fishing in the many lagoons. Various mesh size of gill net are found in the cost and deep-sea fishing for Spanish mackerel, Indo-Pacific mackerel, skipjack and other pelagic species. The fishing season is also limited by the monsoon, which are in general a major problem in furthering the development of the fishing industry in the Indian Ocean. Much of the coast is blocked by coral reefs, and there are few level beaches for beach seine fishing, so that 20 or 30 different groups of net fishermen may use the same beach in rotation, a method necessitated by the great surplus population of the fishing villages. In order to bring about the development of the fishing industry in Asia, elevation of fishing technology must be combined with improvements in the processing of catches and transport facilities, and an important step to this end will be the construction of port and harbour facilities and cold storage facilities. The ancient system of caste still remains strong in such countries as India and Sri Lanka, and the fishing industry is often despised as being below the status of many of the caste. Many of the people engaged in fishing also take what chances they find to leave fishing itself for marine commerce or other jobs on land. Removing such social constraint is also a vital factor in the development of the fishing industry in these lands.

Finally, let us take a brief look at the lives of the fisher folk. Fishing was originally conducted as a supplementary activity of the farming population, but as populations grew and cash economies took hold, fishing came to be an industry in its own right. In Asia, inland fishing and freshwater fish breeding are still generally considered seasonal sidelines for the rural population, but full-time fishermen spread from southern China and southern island until at present, there are many locations where they have formed waterborne communities at river mouths and islands from which they carry on their fishing full time. In Thailand, Malaysia, Singapore, Sabah, Sarawak, and similar areas, almost all of the persons carrying on trawling, purse seine fishing, and other commercial fishing operations are ethnic Chinese fishermen with funds enterprising spirit. Malaysian fishermen seem to suffer from a constant shortage of funds, and many are artisanal fishermen who live from day to day using their cast nets, gill nets, and the like from the shore. In addition to these, the sea dayaks, ancient inhabitants of the region, and others, nomadic folk of the sea, lead a wandering existence seeking pearls and lobsters. Since many of the fishermen of this region have neither lands nor assets of their own, they often receive their rice and other daily goods from the fish wholesalers, to be paid for later with their catches. It is very difficult for such fishermen to escape the vicious cycle of control by the fish wholesalers, who have both the necessary funds and set the price for the fish.

But life is even more difficult for the fisher folk of Indonesia and Sri Lanka. Many of them own no boats or equipment of their own and must borrow them from the fish wholesalers or rich men of the village, becoming in effect "tenant fishermen". Life in the Malay fishing villages follows the same pattern each day: as the fishing boats return to the beaches early in the morning, the wives come down to the beaches to remove the fish from the nets, sorting them, carrying them to the morning markets, and exchanging their small income for rice and other necessities.

In order to improve the poor economic state of the coastal fishermen, the various countries are providing financing for the fishermen to purchase boats and equipment, promoting the formation of fishing cooperatives, and supporting cooperative sales through the fishermen's own efforts. In Sri Lanka, the government rented 3.5 ton powered boats to fishing cooperatives and offers loans with long-term repayment conditions, but even under such favourable conditions, repayments are not being made on schedule. The low level of fishing cooperative activities indicates not only the strength of the fish wholesalers but the low educational level of the fishing population as well. Dealing with such problems will require elevation of the fishermen's education, strengthening of the systems for financing the cooperatives, improvement of marketing, and a variety of other steps.

A Glimpse of Philippine Fisheries

Introduction

Although fish is one of the most important food items in the Filipino diet, its production is still not sufficient to meet the needs of a fast-growing population. Philippine fisheries statistics, as compiled by the Bureau of Fisheries and Aquatic Resource (BFAR), show that in 1975, only a total of 1,336,000 metric tons of fish was available for 43 million Filipinos, which means that the per capita supply of fish is only 31 kilograms per year.

The fishery resources of the Philippines consist of around 2,000 species of finfishes, a few species of shellfishes, and other edible aquatic and fauna. All these are distributed over the marine areas, the different bodies of freshwater, and the brackish water swamplands.

Unfortunately, only the coastal, inshore waters and small portions of the deep sea are exploited. The territorial open sea and adjacent international water are exploited only by a very few Filipino fishermen.

Fisheries production

The country's major sources of production are the commercial fisheries, inland fisheries, and municipal or sustenance fisheries. Commercial fishing covers powered fishing vessels with three gross tons or larger, municipal fishing covers less than three gross tons and some non-powered vessels which are primarily utilized for sustenance; and inland fisheries covers fishponds which are converted bodies of freshwater such as lakes, dams reservoirs, marshes, etc., and brackish water swamplands, mainly used to culture milkfish; and the estuarine areas converted into oyster beds.

In 1975, fish production through commercial fishing was approximately 500,000 metric tons. Since there are various species of finfishes in the Philippines, various fishing gears are used depending on the characteristics of their habitat and aquatic populations. The most common gears used in commercial fisheries are bagnet, beach seine, gill net, hand-line, *muro-ami*, purse seine, push net, otter trawl, long-line, and round haul seine.

FAO-UNDP, through a Special Fund Deep Sea Fishing Development Project, estimated the potential annual Yield of Philippine territorial waters at around 1.65 million metric tons. Moreover, experts also concluded that the exploitation of the remaining potentials for commercial fishing will involve moving into deeper and more distant waters; and that the municipal fishery resources is approaching its potential. The Philippine Government through BFAR is making steps to conserve municipal fishing resources and improve municipal fishing, which is the major contributor to the country's total fish production.

Another major step undertaken by BFAR is to accelerate development of the inland fisheries. Present fishpond production, composed of 95% milkfish, is estimated at 106,500 metric tons utilizing 176,000 hectares and contributing only 8% of the country's total fish production. The projects of BFAR are targeted towards increased fishpond areas and improved yields.

Milkfish industry

The cultivation of milkfish, locally called *bangos*, is a very lucrative industry. It assures an estimated annual investment of US $50 million. Milkfish is generally cultivated in fishponds employing directly about 170,000 people. Fishpens are also used for the same purpose, this being practised in Laguna de Bay, the largest freshwater lake in the country. However, the industry is faced with a major constraint — the lack of stocking fry to sustain its expansive and intensive development. Current annual production of fry from natural grounds is placed at about 500 million. The total annual fry requirement from the development fishponds is 930 million, while another 360 million is required for the fishpens in Laguna de Bay.

The Aquaculture Department of the South Asian Fisheries Development Center (SEAFDEC), based in the Philippines is trying to overcome this constraint through its research projects on the spawning of the milkfish. At the same time, the Aquaculture Department also conducted a socio-economic survey of the aquaculture industry in the Philippines, with the cooperation of the Philippine Council for Agriculture and Resources Research (PCARR).

One such study gathered and assessed date on the cultural practices employed by fry gatherers and concessionaires. Fry gathering which is seasonal is usually practised from February to December, although the peak season occurs only from April to June. The prices of the fry vary with the season, region and the type of buyer. Usually, the price is dictated by the concessionaires. Fry gathering requires a relatively small amount of capital investment. Assets are simple and consists mainly of catching gears; basins, pails and cups; earthen jars; small items such as pandan bags, lamps, dyeing materials, etc. Only very few own bancas or rafts, and these constitute the second largest items.

In many cases, the relationship between the fry gatherer and the concessionaire appears to bear a resemblance to the landlord-tenant relationship of the agrarian system prevailing in the Philippines. Most of the fry gatherers were under the concessionaires. Only very few reported having received amenities in the form of basic needs, medical needs, educational needs or gifts on special occasions. Other gatherers had some kind of financial arrangements with the concessionaires, in the form of cash advances which are usually paid during the same fry season that they were incurred. The cash advance was usually used to purchase gear and other materials for the gathering.

Only 58% of the fry gatherers owned their residential lot, the others either rented or were provided with lots by either relatives, landlords or fishpond owners. A radio was owned by almost three out of four fry gatherers, however, one gatherer owned a TV set. The major problems faced by the gatherers and concessionaires is the low and fluctuating price of the fry. This is followed by the inaccessibility of buyers and insufficient storage facilities.

Fishpond industry

The average annual fish production through fishponds is estimated at 600 kilograms per hectare. Techniques have been developed to increase the output from 600 to about 2,000 kilograms of fish per hectare per year.

Fishpond areas in the Philippines are either owned or leased from the government. Pond owners and caretakers devote seven months of the year in the industry, four months in other occupations mainly fishing, and are idle for only one month. General repair, cleaning, drying and levelling of pond bottom are among the various aspects of pond preparation, which takes about four weeks. During the process, pests and predators are also eradicated using pesticides and tobacco dust.

Fertilization, using organic and inorganic fertilizer, follows. Stocking the ponds is done when enough growth of lab-lab is noticed. When this natural food is insufficient, supplementary feeding is practised utilizing rice bran and bread crumbs. Harvesting of the stock is determined by the size of the fish. Various methods of harvesting are employed, among these are pond draining, gill-netting and using fish traps.

The very common problems encountered by the operators are lack of credit assistance, fluctuating prices of input and output, lack of technical support from field technicians, and lack of government programs for increased production.

Fishpen aquaculture

This innovative concept to harness the productive potential of lakes and other bodies of freshwater was introduced in the Philippines in 1965. This was tried to seek new sources of food and animal protein in response to the country's fast-growing population. The term "fishpen", according to the Bureau of Fisheries and Aquatic Resources (BFAR) means fish enclosures made up of closely-woven bamboo screens, nylon screens or other materials attached to poles staked to the water bottom enclosing a given inland water area for the purpose of culturing fish. This is now a common sight along the lake towns of Rizal and Laguna, covering an area of about 7,000 hectares. The advantages of fishpens are: 1) very high production in a very short period of culture — one hectare of fishpen Yields no less than 10,000 kilograms a year compared to only 3,500 kilograms in a freshwater fishpond or a very low 500 kgs. per hectare of natural production in lakes; 2) they serve as refuge and breeding grounds of the fish to sustain natural fish production in the lake; 3) they also augment the income of the local fishermen, thus helping the improvement of the way of life of the lake shore inhabitants. The disadvantages are : 1) big risk involving adverse weather conditions such as typhoons and floods; 2) risk in the selection of site, construction and management of fishpens; 3) risk in acquiring production, inputs such as netting materials, cost, availability, quantity, kind, species, transporting and stocking of fish fingerlings; 4) risk in the so-called "fish kill", a natural phenomenon in the lake. The Bureau of Fisheries and Aquatic Resource (BFAR) requires a license to operate a fishpen from those people who are interested in utilizing inland waters for fish culture. This license is valid for five years subject to renewal. Only Filipino citizens are entitled to get permits. Priority is given to bonafide residents of the locality where the inland waters are located.

Limbon-Limbon: A fishing village in Laguna de Bay

Limbon-Limbon, one of the many fishing villages along the coast of Laguna de Bay, is located in the western part of Morong Peninsula, whose southernmost tip is Tapao point. This village is being governed by a Baranggay (Council) headed by a Captain and six members. Community life is characterized by rich Filipino cultural values as evidenced by elaborate *binyagan* (baptism) and *Kasalan* (marriage rites). Existing infrastructures in the village include barangay roads, water and electrical system, public transport, elementary school buildings and a basketball court. The only available means of land transport for the villagers are tricycles with regular trips up to another village. Alternate public vehicles are motorboats that take passengers up to a nearby village. Motorboats do not pass by Limbon-Limbon because of a small port. There are only four publicly owned artesian wells in the village, and eleven are privately owned. Electricity is provided by a private firm called Talim Electric Company. The village, has prefabricated-type school buildings which provide schooling up to Grade 3 only. There is also a semi-permanent chapel where spiritual worship is held every Sunday.

The total population of the village is 560, with 44% employed in sustenance fishing which consists primarily of capture fishing methods using traditional fishing gears such as *panalap* or scoop net, *pante* or purse seine and *baklad* or fish traps made of bamboo sticks.

For the womenfolk of Limbon-Limbon, embroidery is their main preoccupation. Aside from sustenance fishing, Limbon-Limbon residents are also working in fishpens, which was earlier discussed. Eighty per cent of the households own inexpensive goods such as radios, plastics plates, etc. Ownership of home appliances such as stereo, T.V., refrigerator, electric stove, etc, is very limited.

Water and fishermen's festivals

The Philippines, the only Christian country in the Far East, is known for its many fluvial festivals held throughout the year in commemoration of the feast days of patron saints of various towns and municipalities. This has been a part of Filipino tradition and culture. In most cases, water festivities are held to thank Gods and saints for a good harvest or in case of fishing, for having a good catch; sometimes, they are held to request for a better harvest or better catch. The most popular of such festivals is during the Feast of Penanfrancia. It is held every 19 September in Naga City, Camarines Sur in the Bicol Region, southeast of Manila. The celebration begins with the transfer of the Lady of Penanfrancia image from the Penanfrancia church to the Naga Metropolitan Cathedral, followed by novenas and vigils. The feast culminates with the fluvial procession carrying the Virgin on a *casco,* a decorated large boat, along the Bicol River back to the shrine in Penafrancia. Other festivals are :

- The statue of the town's patron saint, San Sebastian, is submerged in water and later borne in a procession down the Lumbang River.
- Fluvial festival (Apalit, Pampanga) — 28-30 June
- On the feast of St.Peter, fishermen place the saint's image on a barge and row out in a water procession. Bocaue River festival (Bulacan)
- The Holy Cross of Wawa is taken on an elaborately decorated barge escorted by groups of boats as it sails through the river.
- Pateros River festival (Pateros, Rizal) — 29 July
- A celebration held in honour of the town's patron saint, St. Martha.
- Feast of the Immaculate Concepcion (Malabon, Rizal) — 18 December

The patroness of the Philippines is honoured in Malabon in an evening fluvial procession.

Life in Fishing Villages in Burma

The monsoon breaks, the sky virtually falls, as the Burmese expression goes. The south-westerly is "wild and dank with foam." The Irrawaddy rages. Thunder and lightning strike. All elements conspire to overturn the frail craft, rolling from side to side, in its efforts to resist the waves that push it out into the Bay.

But, undaunted, the fisherman in the boat rises up from his seat, holds high in both hands a platter containing offerings and shouts at the top of his voice: "My Lord Abo! I invoke thee! Help me. Eat this rice and curry. Drink this rice-wine. And have pity on me!

Is it coincidence? For, suddenly, all is calmness — no stir in the air and no stir in the sea. Yet the old man of the boat continues shouting louder and louder

Abo, or Bobo, or Bobogyi, as he is affectionately called, is the guardian *nat* (spirit) of the Burmese fishermen. He is hard of hearing, and unless you yell till the veins in your neck get taut, he won't hear you. But once you are heard, rest assured you will be having a good catch.

This propitiation, executed in the simplest manner possible, is all that is required of the fishermen working in the Irrawaddy Delta. Reward, which is often more than the effort, comes in the form of herrings, mainly *ngathalauk* (hilsa, cat fish of the variety of *ngadan* (*gagata gagata*), the Indian salmon called *Kakuvan* in both Lower and Upper Burma, but *ngaletkwa* in Arakan, mackerels, pomfrets, anchovies, featherbacks, prawns, shrimps and what you will.

Fishermen catering to the needs of the general public employ a variety of implements such as drag nets, drift nets, bag nets, scoop nets and fixed nets. A simple type of drag net is the *swepaik* used in shallow waters of the *chaungs* (rivulets) and sand banks. It is a rectangular net sized according to the nature and purpose of the task to be performed. The *paikwunbu* (distended-stomach) has a large bag of small meshed net about 1,500 feet in length and twelve feet in depth. A representative type of drift net is the *hmawpaik*, usually smaller, but sometimes attaining the proportions of a *paikwunbu*. It has head ropes buoyed up with floats made of empty shells of dried bottle-guard as well as ground ropes weighted with lead, or brick-bats or pieces of burnt clay. The net hangs up like screen below the surface of the water. It is extensively used for catching hilsa prized by gourmets.

A bag net is about 40 feet long, usually fixed; but when operated from moving boats it is suspended between the two crafts which are lashed together and paddled upstream. A scoop net is conical, about 30 feet long, attached at its edges to bamboo poles suspended as above between two moving crafts. The *hmyinpaik* (shrimp-net) is a scoop with bamboo handles for operation by two men when the boat is not used. The common fixed net is the *paikdamin*, usually 15 feet long, for catching small shrimps and prawns and other fry if cutlass or ribbon fish and gar fish, which all go in good combination into *ngapi* or fishpaste, made by pounding with pestle-and-mortar, not manipulated, but pedalled. This bag-like contrivance is submerged under water being attached to posts planted in the river-bed. Its mouth is stretched open facing the direction of the current. The free end of the net has a string tied to floats made of bamboos or hollow coconuts, which trail in the current and keep the entire length of the bag stretched out. When a similar but larger bag net is attached, nearly submerged, to a rectangular wooden framework built on a mudflat at the mouth of a river, it is called *sanda*. This type is used in Eya, at the mouth of the Irrawaddy, and in Zibyuthaung, at the mouth of the Ye River in Tanessarim.

When folks do a large-scale operation with such elaborate implements out in the treacherous waters, they are constrained to invoke the help of the senior guardian angel, Ushingyi Nat, for safe travel and general welfare. His origin being the sea, he is called "the Lord of the Sea-water", whose domain extends to a point below Prome which was, according to legend, a sea-port in days gone by. He is the Orpheus of the Burmese pantheon. Mythology has it that while he, as a mortal, was travelling in the high seas with his companions, he played the harp whose music had the water-nymphs so enthralled, that they refused to let go the Ship. Lots were cast to find out who had brought bad luck. The harpist drew the unlucky number, and was thrown overboard. The unlucky Maung Shin — for, that was the name he went by as a mortal — is now immortalized as Ushingyi, compassionate towards both farmers and fishermen alike, although actually he has nothing to do with fishing. He is propitiated with the offerings of sticky rice, bananas, split coconuts, jaggery (palm-sugar) and pop-corns. But no rice-wine for him, please! He is, unlike Abo, a teetotaller.

In main channels and estuaries fishermen work throughout the year. During the monsoons they establish along the banks of the *chaungs* temporary hamlets that prove a haven for them. From there they go out fishing and send the catch, stuffed with crushed ice in deal-wood boxes to the nearest village called by the Inland Waterways motor launches. This is how fish go to the Rangoon markets. When the monsoon is over, all fishermen return to their native place where fish-paste, fish-sauce, dried fishy, salted fish and dried prawns are processed.

Even from afar one can easily recognize a fishing village by the presence, at its waterfront, of rectangular bamboo platforms, 40 by 30 feet or thereabouts, built on stilts. In September/October when a clear sky heralds the advent of the cool season, the fishermen bring their catch directly from their fishing zone to the fishermen's village in big boats, each with an average carrying capacity of 200 baskets of the paddy (about 8 tons). It consists mainly of *hmyins* (small shrimps) and damins (small fry, usually of gar fish), ribbon fish and the "Bombay Duck". They are then spread out on bamboo matting occupying the entire platform, sprinkled with salt, and allowed to ferment by the action of the sun for several fortnights. When nearly dried, they removed to the *nagapi*- godown, pounded, seasoned and stored in Pegu jars or other receptacles made of bamboo and *dhani* (nipa palm). The liquid oozing out from the mass of *ngapi* is reverentially drown by pipes and stored as fish-sauce. All these are done by the female of the species represented by the mistress of the house, her daughters and her "workwomen".

These platforms for the drying of fish and prawns are connected with the houses by means of "bridges" of long bamboo poles tied flat together and supported on posts of round logs. As the village is inundated almost throughout the year, there are no proper roads. Their place is taken by long and winding walking-platforms, about four feet wide, substantially built with iron-wood posts and planks.

When a fisherman's house bustles with activity, it creaks! Imagine a "four-posted, three-roomed" structure, with *dhani* roofing, bamboo-mat-walling and split-bamboo-flooring, with an outhouse attached, where the thud-thud of fish-pounding is going on. It not only creaks, but sways like a person possessed by a *nat*!

Of course the village also has a good many number of timber buildings belonging to prosperous fishermen having good connections with fishery cooperatives and the State-owned Pearl and Fisheries Corporation. Their success in business is proclaimed by the blare of the ubiquitous "National" transistor-radio, complete with amplifier. On festive occasions (which are many) before the beginning and after the end of the Buddhist Lent, from July to October, an unholy blend of "pop" and classical music screeches and howls for Abo to plug his divine ears with whatever material is available in the abode of *nats.* But in this mundane world it is sheer entertainment for villagers, young and old. The Burmese love *pwes* (theatrical performances) which, however, are not readily available for those who lead an almost submarine life.

The lot of the fishermen in the *inns* (inland fisheries) appears to be much better than that of their counterparts in the estuaries, for the *innthugyis* or managers who lease them from the government can build substantial house with timber and corrugated iron sheets, which are a status symbol for the well-to-do. The *inns* can be seen everywhere in the low-lying areas of Burma, but the Henzada Island, between the Ngawun river to the west and the Irrawaddy to the east, and the Maletto swamps, some 30 miles to the west of Rangoon, are the best known.

The work-sites in the *inns* are stationary and permanent; and the nature of work demands that all folks lead a communal life in order that all can work together collectively for mass-production.

Fish spawn between April and mid-August. So the fishing season is from mid-August to March 31. During the closed season, fishermen collect round logs, bamboos, rattans and creepers or vines (to serve the purpose of ropes) and make fishing implements out of them. In the estuaries a net is a prerequisite for fishermen; but here in the *inns* the basic requirement is a screen of split bamboo called *yin.* It is strung together with rattans or creepers in the same manner as a "chick" blind is made.

These *yins* are usually fixed to the *ses,* or obstructions thrown across as stretch of water to prevent the escape of fish downstream. But they are also used as movable *gyanse* which is kept upright in the water with lumps of clay fixed to the bottom. It is dragged across a piece of water to a fixed fence where fish are caught.

The commonest and the most useful kind of *se* is the *myinwunse* (horsebelly) which is a *yin* cut down in the middle for some part of its length to below the water-edge, and fixed to the bed of the *chaung.* On the opening thus formed is fixed a tray, sloping a little upward, to which fish are driven by force of current. A cage-like trap is called a *sokkat* which is a wide-mouthed, hollow cylinder tapering toward the end. *Ngayant* (snake-head), *ngagyi* (torpedo fish), *ngakhu* (scorpion fish), *ngagyin* (marigata) and *ngabat* (fresh-water shark) are the most prized products of the *inns.* Snake-heads are dried and sold as *ngayantchuk,* a rival to the *kakuyanchaul* (dried Indian salmon) of the estuaries. The salted *nagakhu* and *ngagyi* are the delight of the Burmese housewives.

Under such a work load described earlier, the fisherman's weather-beaten back would almost break. But with festivities galore, his lift is one of cheer, come rain or shine. With the initiation, a decade or so ago, of cooperative movement in Zibyuthaung and also is in Moemakha, 25 miles west of Rangoon, cooperatives have sprung up in major fishery areas together with their ancillaries of cooperative markets, cooperative stores and cooperative dispensaries and clinic. Even an *ahlu* (offering to Buddhist monks) or a *shinbyu* (novitiation ceremony) or a *kinmuntat* (naming ceremony) is being conducted on cooperative basis to the joyous din of drums and cymbals, supplied in a cooperative way by village theatrical troupes contributing their talents to gain merit. And where such talents are absent — which is very rare — cassettes with their "loudspeakers" come to the aid of the whole village in festive mood with their instant music.!

Fishermen in Malaysia: Plain Living with Poor Returns

The Malaysian boy aspires to be an artist. He lifts his brush with a flourish and begins painting ...

Chances are he will finish with a little cameo of wooden shacks (called *pondok* in Malay) by the sea, interspersed with coconut trees and there are fishing nets draped gracefully to dry in the sun — a boat on the horizon. The fishing village may be a sources of aesthetic inspiration. But is the fisherman's life true to that pretty picture? I should say it is much less than beautiful. Plain sailing, it is certainly not.

There are over 80,000 fishermen in Malaysia. The majority are in Trengganu, a state in the East Coast. Here they total about 14,000, parts of the small populace providing the other 12 million or so in the country, with that valuable source of proteins. Scattered all along the cost, one will find their essentially rural life-style fascinating.

The making of the fisherman begins as early as when he is fourteen. And throughout his life he works hard but there are many reasons for his poor returns.

The consumer — indignant about the upward rise in the price of fish (besides everything else) — will probably wonder at the paradox: the *ikan kembong* variety for instance (mackerel), in 1968 was $0.20 per kati. Today it is $1.20. *Udang galah* (lobsters) fetch $7.00 per kati. Pomfret is sheer luxury. Where does the money go?

In the first place, very few own their own boat. Most are hired. Sometimes they are in constant debt with the wholesalers who help them over bad patches, like during the monsoon or *tengkujuh*, when the East Coast is exposed to the full force of the North-East Monsoons between November and March. The fishermen's hardship is most felt during the season when sheets of heavy downpour come down non-stop for months. The waves of South China Sea swell up. Small boats will surely be swallowed by the powerful currents, especially at the river mouths. Even big boats will have difficulty in trying to haul in their catch. During these times their livelihood depends a lot of the fish which the fisherman's wife dried during good times. In the evening when the tide is low, he will collect cockle and other shellfish. These popular seafoods may also be shelled and dried.

The East Coast fisherman's wife is also engaged in the cottage business of making *keropok*, a kind of crackers made from flour and fish (or prawn). In all sizes of distorted ovals, they are inevitable souvenirs (to be relished, fried) for the tourist and visitors to the East Coast. The fisherman also helps to make *keropok* when he is unable to go to sea.

The Fishing Industry in Malaysia is predominantly small scale, using a variety of traditional gear and small boats that can only afford to exploit the sea area a few miles from the coast. A fisherman sweats for his living. He leaves home for the sea before the sun has melted the chilly dawn. He comes home when the streaks of solar cruelty sears his hair. And he might not return depending on his catch. He might have to head home the next day, or the next. It is always uncertain. The sea is his home, fishing his livelihood. Death and hardship is very breathing and islets his shelter when the sea rages. An average monthly income for a *awak-awak* (normal crew) is $70.00 Ringgit (30 US Dollars). A *taikong* (skipper) earns an average of $150.00 Ringgit (60 US Dollars). There are bountiful seasons when they get as much as $200.00 Ringgit (80 US Dollars). This sounds adequate enough for subsistent living. But the average fisherman usually has to support a family of 6 children or more. Only lately have they been actively encouraged to plan their family.

That income too has to be stretched over period of poor catch. This is when the wild ferns and shoots they pick in the *belukar* (secondary jungles) serve not only to supplement their family diet but also the family's finance. The tourist will find the fisherman's daily toil, his hustle and bustle from the sea to the shore to the village, a fascinating panorama.

Their way of living is colourful, even their attire. The heat at sea perhaps explains why he is clad only in batik sarong. Elsewhere in Malaysia the batik sarong is normally worn by women. His head will be wound with a length of broad cloth (about a yard broad). To go to sea they wear pants under the sarong, that of the cheapest worn materials.

As far as fishermen utilising small boats are concerned their buyers are *peraih* (retailers for the local market) who will be waiting on shore beneath the coconut trees. Soon as the boats are beached the *taikong* will announce the floor price for a particular box of fish.

Presently the government is encouraging the open auctioning of the catches. Existing ones are in Kuala Terangganu in the East Coast and Lumut on the West Coast. More such complexes will be built under the third Malaysia Plan. The Government also gets aid from the United Nations for more modern methods.

But overruling these efforts is the fact that the fisherman himself is depleting marine resources by concentrating a few miles from the shoreline.

The local experts believe that the answer lies in deep water fishing. At this stage the government has secured Korean collaboration to exploit the deep waters of South China Sea. The government also tries to help in other ways, providing text-books for their children, housing facilities and supervising the fisherman's associations and cooperatives. Most important the government tries to diversify their activities and where they are more flexible, expose the alternatives like pioneering new land schemes.

Their children are educated and not encouraged to follow the father's footsteps to the sea. The population of 80,000 is a bit too heavy on the exhausting supply. The Malaysian fisherman will not be affluent for a long times yet. Even his richer brother on the West Coast is facing difficulties.

A fisherman from Tanjong Keling (Malacca) has complained that dirty tar and oil have stained his nets. The damage costs him $600 and more debts which he is thus indisposed to suffer. Pollution is fast catching up with him at a time when the fisherman needs to upgrade his standard of living. Yet he is a contented Yokel. His main port of relaxation is the *kedai kopi* (coffee shop).

Whenever these fishermen come back from the sea they never fail to stop by and talk at the shop for at least half a day before he goes home to be greeted by his wife and children, who regards this habit as a matter of course.

The coffee shop will receive these fishermen again after they have done with the necessary homely routine and put out the nets to dry in the sun. Besides these idle hours at the coffee shop they also hold open shows of traditional dances (Makyong and Menora) and Wayang Kulit. Or else they play giant tops, or if the wind permits they will fly kites. Thus he takes his hard life in his stride.

Hardship to him is as natural as a smile, a puff of *rokok daun* (cigarette of rolled leaf and tobacco) and brown children laughing into the camera.

Behind all these scenes, the Government continues busy implementing various projects and drawing up more to upgrade the socio-economic status of the fishermen. Where the government has not intervened with their scheme of uniform timber housing, the fisherman's home is a wooden shack on stilts with a tapa roofing.

Fisheries in Malaysia come under the Ministry of Agriculture and the direct responsibility of Fisheries Division. There is also a State Directorate of Fisheries responsible for fisheries matters in their respective states.

In addition to the Fisheries Division, there is also a Fisheries Industry Development Authority (MAJUIKAN). The primary objective of the Authority is to accelerate the expansion of the fishing industry particularly that of the East Coast. The Authority is concentrating especially on activities that will facilitate the transfer of low-productivity inshore fishermen to the modern sector of the industry.

The Fisheries Division on the other hand will continue to give special attention towards the improvement of physical infrastructure, particularly harbours and to the continued expansion of training and research facilities and of extension services.

Established within the Authority also is the marketing Board which is involved with the marketing of fish in order to provide competition in the market, to increase returns to the fishermen. It is also aimed at improving market facilities, upgrading the quality of fish, stabilising prices and expanding market outlets for fishery products.

As a fast developing country, the Malaysian fishing industry has its shares in getting international attention and aids. To date the industry has received assistance from the Government of Canada (under the Colombo Plan), France, the Federal Republic of Germany, Japan and Belgium. A development plan for the East Coast has been formulated by the Asian Development Bank (ADB) and its implementation is already under way.

However, future requirements by the Malaysian fishing industry for specialized and international aid will center around the socio-economic and technical aspects of small-scale fisheries development. In this regard, direct assistance is being rendered by the UNDP/CIDA Funded FAO Project, the regional South China Sea Fisheries Development and Coordinating Programme. One the whole, the Malaysian fisheries have developed rapidly over the last decade, with the catch reaching a record of 525,600 tons in 1974. In spite of the tremendous Government efforts to update the living standards of the fishermen, life in the fishing villages goes on as usual. The fishermen go about their daily work, some unaware of what is being done to help them.

The wives pray for their husband's safe return, worried of the many hidden and unforeseen dangers of the sea. But the fishermen seem not to worry... he goes to sea hoping for a better catch. I once met a 50-year-old fisherman who had just escaped the wrath of a storm. For fifty days he starved, bobbing in the waves till finally found by a foreign merchant ship and taken to a Burmese port. After a month, the paperwork was finalised and he was sent back home. He was offered another job in a factory and the government offered help. His response was a proud declaration that fishing is his profession.

The above is not an isolated case. The daily papers often report news of missing fishermen.

But into his late sixties, the sea is his life, friend or foe. His soul steeped with the sea-salt.

He will return to the sea....

Japan: Fishermen under Female Protection

There has long been a saying among the fisher folk of Japan "Just one hull between you and hell." The life at sea has always been a dangerous one, not only for the Japanese but for men who work the seas in any region. The rigours of the fisherman's occupation have birth to beliefs and practices designed to offer prayers for boats' safety.

One of the representative beliefs in Japan is the honouring of the "funadama" or "spirit of the boat". The intercession and protection of the deity referred to as the funadama is sought not only for the small traditional boats but for large, modern fishing boats and huge tankers as well. The object venerated as the embodiment of the funadama — the "sacred object" in Shinto terminology — may be a pair of small wooden male and female dolls, an assortment of five varieties of grains, 12 old coins, two dice, strands of a woman's hair, or a variety of other objects, at times even including a women's lip rouge. In the case of a woman's hair, it may be from the wife of the ship owner, captain, ship's carpenter, or someone else connected with the boat. The sacred object is generally enshrined at the launching ceremony or is privately enshrined by the ship's carpenter the night before the launching. In small traditional boats, the mast is often raised and the sacred object placed underneath, but in the case of large, engine-powered vessels, it is enshrined on the bridge. It is said that when a storm approaches, the funadama cries out a warning as a sign of impending danger. After a major accident, a shipwreck, or a long period of poor catches, the sacred object may be replaced.

The most important characteristic of the funadama, however, is that the spirit is believed to be female. It is for this reason that Japanese sailors and fishermen dislike having one single woman come aboard — which would displease the female funadama. When it is absolutely necessary to take a woman aboard, she is given a mirror or a woman's photograph to take with her. The mirror reflects her image, so that there appear to be two women, and the same end is served by the photograph. The fishermen also try to avoid having a women on board while she is menstruating, or a woman (or her husband) soon after she has given birth, representing a blood taboo.

Though there are few such examples, an excellent indication of the feminine nature of the funadama is the occasional adoption of a living human — a young virgin girl — as the sacred object. When the boat comes in from its fishing, the catch may at times be presented to this living funadama as an offering.

There are also certain words that the fishermen must avoid while at sea because of their unlucky connotations. Only while the ship is away from its port, these unlucky words are replaced by "offshore words" with more desirable associations. For example, the Japanese word for monkey is *saru,* but in different contexts, the same pronunciation may represent the verb "depart", so that a monkey is referred to by the phrase "man of the mountains." A Japanese pear is called a *nashi,* but this is also a cognate of the word for "none." To avoid any unfortunate influence on their catch, the fishermen substitute the word *ari,* meaning "having." While the funadama is primarily a guardian deity, such practices make it seem that she is also assigned a role in ensuring an abundant catch. Belief in a deity called the funadama could also be found in the southernmost part of Japan, Okinawa. This was not applied to the traditional-style fishing boats but involved practices for the large cargo ships called "yanbaru-sen." The yanbaru-sen were large, junk ships, and just like the Chinese junks, they bore two round wooden eyes on the prow. These eyes kept watch over the sea ahead, warding off evil spirits and protecting the ship from dangerous shoals. The most representative of the Okinawan beliefs regarding protective deities was the veneration of the "Onari goddess." Okinawa has for centuries been strongly influenced by the culture of the Japanese mainland, but the reason that the funadama practices were not applied to the small traditional fishing boats is that there were stronger belief already present in Okinawa, the worship of this Onari goddess. In Okinawa, "onari" is a term of address used by brothers toward their sisters, and there is a marked belief that the males of Okinawa are safeguarded by their sisters. As representatives of the protective Onari goddess, the sisters are treated with importance in daily life. This is clearly a reflection of the spiritual dominance of the sisters over the brothers. As the men went out to fish the seas, the women constantly prayed for their safety, and before setting out for distant waters, the brothers would visit the Shinto shrines accompanied by their sisters. When they set out, the sisters would give a small towel to their brothers and the women to their loved ones. It was believed that having such a gift from the women would guarantee one's safety. The funadama and onari goddess are different in form, but they share the basic characteristic of being female.

One representative belief in a protective deity for ships found widely in China and particularly throughout the southern regions of the country is the veneration of "Ma Tsuou". The legend of Ma Tsuou relates that she was born on one of the islands of Hokken province (Southern China), and the main temple of Ma Tsuou is located here. Ma Tsuou was the youngest daughter in a family of seven children, one son and six daughters. Since the son, the oldest child, was a weak, undependable fellow, the parents constantly wished for another son. As they were believers in "Kannon", they offered up prayers to this Goddess of Mercy. The Goddess appeared in a dream to give the mother a pill. Later, at sunset on 23 March 960, a brilliant red light illuminated the parents' room at just the instant that Ma Tsuou was born. For the first month of her life, she made no sounds at all, so she was given the name "Silence". At age 13 she was enlightened by a Taoist priest, and at 16, she began to act as a channel for the power of spirits, showing a divine nature by seeking out and purging evil and otherwise helping the beings around her. She would frequently appear mounted on a cloud, sailing across the sky. At noon on 9 September, 987, according to the legend she ascended into heaven. One example of her miracles occurred when her father and brother were shipwrecked. While she was at her home weaving, she appeared to them in a dream and rescued them.

There are a number of famous temples dedicated to Ma Tsuou, including the well known Ma Tsuou Temple of Macau but such temples can be found throughout Hokken province and everywhere in Southeast Asia that Chinese have settled.

In the Philippines, Malaysia, Indonesia, Singapore, and other countries, where there are Chinese and Chinese temples, Ma Tsuou is honoured — not only by fishermen and sailors but by the others as well, reflecting characteristics which go beyond protection of the seas.

In Taiwan, the belief in Ma Tsuou covers the entire island, and it is said that 383 temples take Ma Tsuou as the principle deity. Since one feature of Chinese temples is that almost all honour a wide variety of beneficent gods together, the number of temples where Ma Tsuou is worshipped, though not as the principle deity, is also extremely large.

The worship of Ma Tsuou as a protective deity of boats and fishermen came to Taiwan from the mainland, brought by the growth in sea traffic between Taiwan and Hokken in particular across the Taiwan Straits. Large numbers of Taiwanese craft took to the seas, and accidents were frequent, bringing the spread of Ma Tsuou's veneration, so that Taiwan eventually surpassed the mainland in the popularity of Ma Tsuou. There are other gods whose protection is sought by fishermen and sailors, but Ma Tsuou remains the central and most important. While the junks were still in frequent use, prayers for peace and safety were offered to Ma Tsuou before the sailing date was set. While under sail, incense would be burned, primarily by the captain, before the shipboard image of Ma Tsuou, and on safe arrival at the destination, gold paper would be burned as an offering. If the boat seemed in danger of being shipwrecked, all on board would make fervent prayers to Ma Tsuou for her intervention. When a new boat was built, a lucky day would be selected, the keel would be installed, gold paper burned and firecrackers set off, and the leader of the carpenters would offer up prayers to the goddess along with red bean-paste buns. When the construction was completed, a propitious day would again be chosen for the attachment of the round wooden eyes at the prow, and with the attachment of these eyes, it was thought that the boat's spirit first entered into the boat. The launching, too, would be held on a lucky day, and the owner would invite the carpenters and his friends to a banquet to celebrate the new boat. Following the launching, another propitious day would be selected for the installation of an image of Ma Tsuou in the ship's stern. The wooden statue of Ma Tsuou would be about 15 cm in height, made by an artisan specializing in such statues. A Taoist priest would be called on to preside over the enshrining and worship. After long periods of poor catches or after an accident, a priest would also be called to purify the boat by driving out the evil spirits.

There have also been some instances of the worship of Ma Tsuou in Japan in such areas as Okinawa, Kagoshima, and Nagasaki. The most important characteristic of Ma Tsuou for the present purposes, however, is that she is female. The Philippines, Malaysia, and Indonesia have a variety of methods of fishing, both traditional and modern, but today very little of the fishing population of such countries lives in a simple trading economy, living lives centered around urban or rural markets and trading their catch with inland farmers. In addition, most of the fishermen of these lands are either Muslims of Christians, faithful followers of the teaching of the Koran or the Bible. Particularly from the southern part of the Philippines to Malaysia, Singapore, and Indonesia, when the fisher folk are faced by danger, they pray to Allah. This does not mean, however, that folk beliefs of centuries past have completely disappeared. Just as Chinese fishermen pray at their temples and also consult a professional shaman called a "tanki", the Malaysians and Indonesians, too, have similar customs. For example, the Malaysian fishermen may call on a type of shaman called "bomo" when they are beset by trouble or illness. The imams — the priests of Islam — are the formally acknowledged religious leaders, but the bomo are still the leaders of the shadow world of religion and folk practice.

The bomo frequently go into trances, bringing forth the voices of gods believed in by the local population, and they also diagnose and treat illness. Various events and happenings as well as sicknesses are thought to be caused by spirits. In lands such as Japan and China which have a long history and yet are still open to the outside world, folk beliefs often remain extant deep below the surface of new culture. In the developing nations, undergoing rapid change, such folk beliefs appear to be declining rapidly with the introduction of new culture and development — and this trend is all the more marked in fervently Muslim areas. In Oceania, there is a marked belief that women — either women in general or wives or sisters, depending on the case — are spiritually superior to men and that they use their spiritual powers to protect the men as they go out to fish; the strength of this belief makes one wonder whether Southeast Asia was not the same before the coming of Islam and Christianity. One could even say, perhaps, that the precise rise and then fall of the tides, the waxing and waning of the moon, the cycles of menstruation, pregnancy, and fertility, have formed a view of the relationship between the women and the sea not only in Southeast Asia but around the world.

Catching fish with a basket-type net, Pakistan.

Women in Asian Villages

Thailand: Stability in Transition

A nation of farmers

Thailand, earlier known to outsiders as Siam, is a tropical and agricultural country in Southeast Asia. The people call themselves Thai and have always proudly referred to their country as "Muang Thai" or "Prades Thai." The reason is simple, for the meaning of Thailand, "the Lord of the Free", is largely one of linguistic and political definition. The Thai government in 1937 announced officially the change of the name from Siam to Thailand to symbolize the nationalistic significance of the ethnic name, Thai. The earlier name was resumed in 1945, but later in 1948, the name Thailand again became its official designation. Thailand has a population of 36,218,000 according to the Population Census of 1970. Its population growth rate of 3.1 per cent is one of the highest in the world. More than 80 per cent of the whole population live in rural areas, and approximately nearly 80 per cent of Thailand's population live and work on farms. Farmer's lives indicate the Thai way of life not only because they form the majority, but the standard of their living is considerably lower than enjoyed in the cities and towns. They live simply in their small houses built from bamboo or teak. The village in which they were born and live is the most important unit of the Thai social system. The people's habits and customs are based mainly on agriculture and religion. The great majority of the Thai population is village dwelling people who profess Hinayana Buddhism (96 per cent).

In the Thai social system, the village is the smallest administrative unit. There are about 50,000 villages in Thailand. They vary in type, size, and in the agricultural produce grown, depending upon location, regional variation in soil fertility, availability of water supply, general population density, and other factors. Generally, each village has its own headman elected by the people of the village. The headman's principal function is to look after the welfare of his people. Thus, he is looked up to by the villagers as their elder who will be ready to assist them with any problem.

Thai village life

The majority of Thai villages nowadays can be reached and visited by outsiders from the highways, along village roads, canals and rivers. Ways of communication between remote villages and the outside world are more difficult: along rough roads, cart tracks, and even jungle trails. For the latter, it is very hard for villagers to contact neighbouring villages and the district centres. It may take from several hours to a few days to get to town especially during the rainy season. Fortunately, the former type or the accessible villages are more numerous than the remote and isolated ones.

Nearly every village has a primary school, either a permanent or non-permanent structured type. In some places, three or four small villages may have a school which is centrally located. Primary school vacations vary from region to region, and even in different parts of the same region. Usually, in farming regions, the schools close during the planting season which comes in the rainy season, in order to let children help their parents in the field. In all the villages, except the newly set-up ones, there is a Buddhist monastery called *wat* which provides facilities for religious, social and cultural activities of the rural people.

Economically, the villagers are self-sufficient. They live close to the soil, growing their own food which consists mainly of rice. Some build their own houses and make their own implements. Apart from rice, which is their staple food, they raise cattle, pigs, and chickens for sale rather than for family consumption. The use of money is prevalent except in the isolated areas where some sort of barter system still exists. Glutinous rice and fermented fish are the universal foods among villagers in the North and the Northeast regions of Thailand.

Thai villages in general are poor in comparison with city standards of living, for instance : lack of household furnishings, lack of cleanliness and sanitation, lack of dietary and nutritional knowledge, lack of adequate transportation and mass media communication, and other proper facilities. In the rainy season, food is plentiful, but it is scarce during the dry season. Regularly the ordinary meal is rice or glutinous rice in some parts of the country with cooked or uncooked fermented fish, chilli peppers, and some vegetables. Those who are more well-to-do may have more dishes with fish, meat and vegetables. Fish are caught from shallow streams, canals or rivers near the village. Other kinds of meat such as chicken, beef and pork are prepared for special occasions, festivals and ceremonies. However, the problem of malnutrition still exists among villagers especially children who show symptoms of food deficiency. The majority of the rural population is also in need of a public water supply. Natural water sources in villages are mostly from wells, canals and rivers which villagers use without purifying tablets. Most rural people do not have toilets and they use the rivers, canals, or woods for the purpose. Inadequate health and sanitation facilities such as those mentioned have helped to diffuse communicable disease, especially during the dry season.

Receptivity or resistance to change of any Thai village would depend upon several factors. They are probably: location and natural resources of the village itself, the personality type and local culture of the people, the lack of village leadership, limited opportunities and the educational level of villagers, inadequacy of transportation and communication, motivation of the people, the roles and performances of local administrative officials and so on. In fact, villagers in general are innocent, sincere, hospitable, and courageous. They consider themselves inferior and are eager to learn the ways of city people. They have strong beliefs and firmly follow traditional values and practices resulting from their Buddhist religion. The educational level of villagers is rather low and limited.

Thai villages in transition

It is interesting to note that in the past decade, Thai villages have changed and continue to undergo change. These changes are a result of fundamental and technological forces. Various programmes on community development have been undertaken at several stages for the well-being of the rural people and the progress of the country, by both governmental and non-governmental agencies in accordance with the National Development Plan. Up till now Thai villages have developed in many ways. Village roads were laid out; artisan wells constructed whereas houses and fences were repaid or remodelled. As to women, permanent waves and hair beauty were introduced. As to women, permanent waves and hair beauty were introduced. Wedding and party invitation cards were introduced and are now popularly used. Girls in villages learned folk dances and modern dancing. Formal adult and youth organizations in the modern sense were introduced, for instance, the farmer organizations, the farmer cooperatives, the 4-H clubs, and the teenager's clubs. The Farmers Federation of Thailand and the folk volunteer groups have recently been introduced. In fact, farm activities organized by informal groups during translating and harvesting have long been known in Thailand but with no continuity nor permanence in the process. They were organized temporarily according to the actual village needs and problems.

The most significant change which should be mentioned here is farming methods. Since the importance of rice in the life of Thai farmers depends on climatic, geographic, traditional, and other factors, Thai farmers are likely to be conscious of the role which rice plays in their well-being and survival. On many farms, rice is produced primarily for family use. On others it is an important product for sale as well as for home consumption. Even though traditional agriculture is still thoroughly characterized by mono-cropping system with rice being the predominant crop, many of the Thai farmers now produce rice in some combination with other cash crops such as maize, corn, and cassava. This surplus production varies according to soil, water supply, farm sizes, labour, capital and management. On farms where rice is produced in very small amount, other crops predominate with production of meat and poultry. These other crops, plus cottage industry, livestock, and even labouring outside the village, all make relatively equal contributions to the family income. However, the subsistence farmers do not buy fertilizers, insecticides nor selected seeds, and they still farm and use methods and practices in the way their fathers and forefathers did in the past. It may be said that changes in the crop patterns regarding farm organization and management are occurring. However, change is slow growing out of the experience of the rural people although open to some innovations.

Modern farm equipment, such as the substitution of draft-animals for tractors and the use of fertilizers, is now widely being used. It is not an uncommon sight in Thailand to see women and girls riding tractors on the farms. There are a considerable number of them who have been influenced to change. Both men and women know about fertilizers, irrigation pumps and other kinds of modern equipment which are readily available in the local market. Changes in farming techniques have taken place rapidly in larger rural communities, but they do not exist in the very remote and isolated areas. These changes have brought about some other changes. Traditional values are also changing. As evidence it should be mentioned here that the free collective labour, of neighbours helping each other in transplanting and harvesting, is disappearing. It has been replaced by hired labour. The materialistic hospitality, as termed by the writers, is now taking the place of the spiritual hospitality. Money, it seems, is becoming an universal value almost everywhere in the world.

The villagers' pastimes have also had some change. New forms of modern recreation such as radio-listening and movie-going are beginning to affect the rural people due to better transportation and communication facilities. Nowadays transistor radios are widespread among villagers. Each family tries to have at least one set. However, their recreation and social activities remain and revolve around the family household, the neighbourhood, and the *wat* as well. Visiting and neighbouring are still the pattern of their daily life. Much of the family leisure time is spent in casual talks and informal activities within the family and in the neighbourhood. Small stores in the village usually serve as coffee houses and men's meeting places. The village headman's house is also a meeting place of the male villagers. Daily newspapers do not reach most villages except those in large greatly populated areas.

Family life

The life of Thai women in villages is interesting and undergoing changes. Before going a step further, let us talk about the rural family a little bit so that the readers may get more insight and better understanding of them. In most villages the basic social and economic unit is the clear family which consists of husband and wife and their unmarried offspring. In addition, a few relatives may live with them either as dependents or unpaid extra labourers depending upon their ages and family ties. The average size of a Thai rural household is relatively large, consisting of about 6 persons. The household primarily forms the social, residential, and economic unit. Generally, the father is the head of the family and the family name comes through him. Both sons and daughters inherit property equally. Children address their father with the term *paw*, and the mother with the term *ma*. The descent is bilateral, kin groups being reckoned through both father's and mother's sides. Even though marriage in modern Thai society is legally monogamous, polygamy is not uncommon in the rural areas. Marriage in Thailand, particularly in rural areas, takes place at an early age. Most rural girls frequently marry between the ages of seventeen and twenty three thereabouts, and boys between the ages of twenty and twenty-four or so. Legally, no marriage can take place until the boy is seventeen and the girl is fifteen. In urban areas, sometimes girls and boys are married at later ages, because nowadays they tend to think of their professional security before marriage. Bachelors, especially in rural areas are rare, because marriage and birth of children is the ultimate goal for all village women. With a son, a woman is given hope that she will obtain religious merit through his ordination into the monkhood (customary at the age of twenty), and with a daughter, she is assured that she will have someone to care for her in her old age. Young people in Thai society, rural as well as urban, do their own courting and make their own choice of mates. However, they rarely choose their partners without parental approval. Most Thai parents like their children to marry into families of the same economic and social status. Marriage payments as a sort of "brideprice" are involved in the majority of Thai marriages both in urban and rural areas. The payment is meaningful in the sense that it is the recognition of the girl's place in society.

According to rural customs, after marriage, a newly wed couple usually live for a time in the house of the parents of one spouse or the other. By and large, residence with the wife's family is preferred among the rural people. Then as soon as the couple can afford it, they may set up a separate household which may be adjacent to parents' or kins' house within the same village or in some other village. As such, social patterns of cooperative work and frequent visiting, keep neighbouring households, (whether kin or not), in close contact with each other's activities, needs and problems.

Women in the family

Rural women play a very important role in agriculture. It is indicated by their virtual equality with men. They participate fully in daily farm work and other activities as well as in their own domestic responsibilities. Women in villages work side by side with men in the field, for instance, ploughing with the buffalo, planting and transplanting, weeding, harvesting, repairing the dikes or local dams, hauling, and working even on village roads and dam construction. Only heavy tasks and operations such as wood cutting, land clearing, and house building are exclusively men's work. However, they even help men in thatching roofs and other minor construction work. They also concentrate on cottage industries such as cotton and silk and mat weaving, depending upon the geographical region. Besides their work in the rice-fields, rural Thai women dig and clean canals and ditches, mound land, and fish in the ponds, canals and rivers. They carry water from the village wells, which are sometimes a long way off, cut and fetch firewood. They tend livestock, pound rice in motors, cultivate fruit and kitchen gardens, and also do household chores — cleaning, cooking and washing. In the remote rural areas, women during pregnancy, work hard up to the day of delivery, and only a few days after giving birth, they resume their normal work.

In the household, a village women or a wife's role is very important. She does not only perform routine tasks such as preparing food and serving the meals, keeping the house orderly, and looking after her children, but also she controls the family finances and makes all the important decisions regarding household expenditure. Decisions-making concerning farming equipment and children's future education are made by the husband with the wife's consent. However, the wife may not interfere with whatever her husband does outside the home because it is not considered to be her concern.

In infancy up to adolescence the village child spends most of its time with the mother, gradually learning through contact with play groups or through indirect contact with adults. In village farm families, children are still an asset, because their help, skills and earnings enrich the family. They are loved and cared for by the elders. They are the centres of interest and unity of all family members. Girls as well as boys are equally desired. They are reared in the affectionate care of parents, and in many cases, parents treat and care for their daughters more than sons. Proof of this can be seen in the marriage of the daughter, as it is customary for the son-in-law to go and live close or even in the same compound with the wife's family. Both sons and daughters will provide cherished care for the parents in their old age, but this is expected particularly of daughters.

In villages, the man plays a minor part in looking after and training the children. Being the head of the family, he has a heavy burden in taking up family duties. He is the leader of hard tasks in the field, and it is his responsibility to provide income and equipment. Thus, the village woman or the wife plays a vital and major responsibility in rearing children. To girls, the mother is the girls first teacher. The girls, from the earlier age are taught how to prepare daily food, to take of younger siblings, and other household duties.

The mother instructs them with a view to preparing them to be good housewives and mothers in the future. Carrying water and pounding rice are commonly the duties of the daughters and granddaughters. They are taught to cook rice, spin cotton and weave. A mother with small children and no one to help, is very busy and hardly has any free time. Both boys and girls are taught to show equal filial respect and deference to the mother and father, but very often boys are naughty to their mothers. In fact the relationship between the mother and the son is very close but indulgent. In Buddhist teaching, the mother is regarded by her son as more important than his wife. Even though a son makes his own choice of a wife, he seldom chooses a mate without parental approval, especially the mother's. The mother is the central figure around whom the family gathers and she acts as a peace maker in family disputes. If a son disagrees with his father, it is the mother who reconciles them. If brothers and sisters quarrel, the mother brings them together. Rural girls are also expected to obey their fathers and wait upon him with respect. They, in general, are more permissive than girls in urban areas. Due to rural environment, living close to the soil, with primarily folk-community-type relationships, they are rather care-free. Both boys and girls, from an early age, are brought up alike. Childhood is very happy and care-free. It is not uncommon in Thailand, particularly in rural areas, to see a younger sibling under one year old being carried around on the hip of the little older sister while the mother is working in the field or marketing. Small babies and girls like to play underneath the house. They may enjoy the home-made swings with their older siblings, but frequently they play with clay dolls and do native games.

From the age of seven until about twelve years, both rural boys and girls spend most of the day at the village school.[1] By this time, a girl helps her mother increasingly with the household chores and begins to assume more responsibilities in domestic life: caring for water buffaloes, looking after younger siblings and helping in the rice transplanting. During this period, girls in the cloth weaving areas are taught the rudiments of the cloth-making process while boys are taught how to fish and hunt.

All members of the farm family live and work as a unit-eating their meals and working in the fields together. Women and children help the male members in carrying for the water buffalo, and in transplanting, harvesting, and threshing rice crops. During the planting season, the men plough, the women sow, and both sexes including children, work when the rice is to be transplanted. Children look after the cattle and scare the birds away when the rice is growing. The interval period between planting and harvesting, and the period after harvesting are spent in comparative ease and leisure with many feasts and religious festivals during October and November.

To supplement the family income, rural women and rural girls may spend the morning at the village market, selling eggs and vegetables which are collected and sold rather than eaten at home. In the household, the wife and the girls prepare the family meals. A farm girl at about 12 years old knows how to cook rice and help in meal preparations. They always get up early in the morning to prepare rice, sometimes with dishes to be offered to the monks who come in the village from the monastery at about 6 or 7 o'clock with their bowls in hand. In some areas, the women with their husbands bring food to the monks at the monastery. Even though women cannot enter the monkhood which is expected of the sons, due to the tenets of Buddhism, they may confirm to other patterns of filial obedience. Ideally a woman should have an obligation to assist her parents until they later die. Usually the youngest daughter and her husband (but not always) must look after her parents in their old age until they pass away. On festive occasions, ceremonial feasts, or religious merit-making[2], rural women also play a large part in preparing the feasts for this as part of their duty. Old village women may participate in minor activities around the household and help in looking after young children. Generally, they retire from work and spend more time in religious activities. In Thai rural and urban society, more importance is attached to age differences than to sex differences. Great respect is theoretically given by children and other family members to grandparents. Long life is prayed for and old age is idealized.

Woman in ceremonies and festivals

It is interesting to note that in Thai villages, all periodic family affairs and ceremonies such as weddings, originators, and cremation have a significant religious character. Merit is most usually made through giving meals and things to the monks, and often these presentations take place in collective ceremonies. Women are responsible for providing the meals which are given to the monks and to the guests at the close of any religious ritual.

There are many religious festivals and holidays around the year in which members of the rural Thai family participate. The Buddhist monasteries in Thailand are the meeting places of the people for ritualistic purposes and public rejoicing. The family joins because of spiritual as well as temporal values. Such occasions not only urge people to cooperate in merit-making, but they also lead to social interaction. The Buddhist New Year or Songkran Festival, which is fixed on the first full moon of April, is the most important of the religious and social activities of the year. The festival lasts three to five days. Numerous social activities take place including feasts and games. Girls and women in particular attend in their best holiday clothes to the *wat*, offering special food to the monks. They enjoy the festival because it is a time of merit-making and social gathering among young women and men. With the changes in nearly all aspects of human life brought by modernization. Thai women especially rural women are more conservative in preserving old customs and manners. Most Thai rural women nowadays are reluctant to imitate Western culture such as new styles of modern dance, the practice of free love and trial marriages. As mothers and housewives, they take it as one of their most important duties to bring up children according to their traditional culture and customs.

The changing situation of women

Village women have more children than those in the cities. This is not necessarily because they want more children but may be because they are less effective in controlling their fertility due to their limited education in family planning and some traditional values involved in their perception and understanding.

Family planning which was introduced a few years ago is now gradually accepted by village women, but it still has no effect on their birth rate. On the average, Thai women continue to have about 6.9 children by the time they complete their reproductive years of fifteen to about forty-four years old. Although today there are slight regional differences in costumes especially among women, the majority of them tend to dress alike. Women, particularly in cities and towns, always go about in blouses and skirts, or one-piece dresses. The most fashionable style is blouse and pants. Village women generally wear blouses and the skirt-like *pasin,* a piece of cloth about one and a half yards sewn in a tube and folded at the waist and tightened by a belt. On going outside the house or to any public gathering, the older women may wear blouses and skirts while the young ones wear the styles similar to those worn by city women. Young country girls sometimes enjoy wearing blouses and pants. In the fields, men wear black shirts and black loose trousers, while women wear navy blue or black long sleeved blouses and black *pasin* skirts, because the colours are fast and durable. Farmer's hats are used by both sexes. Most young women and girls have permanent waves, long or short as they like, depending on recent fashions.

Thai women in villages are not very active in politics. They have less interest in internal issues as well as international politics than city women. The indifference or lack of interest of village women towards either national elections or other government activities and current political trends is probably due to their limited opportunities, their low standard of education, inadequate transportation and communication facilities, and the lack of information media such as newspapers, radios and televisions. They are self-contained and happy as long as the family gets enough rice and fish to eat, suitable shelter and appropriate clothes, have occasional festivals at the Buddhist monasteries, and the children are properly educated. They are expected to be polite, modest, generous, throughout and devoted. They are neither race nor language conscious at all. Several female adults in some isolated areas who were interviewed by the writers a few years ago, came up with a very impressive conclusion. "All that I care about is that I belong to the human race and speak the language understood by my people. I know that my country is Thailand, ruled by a handsome king and a beautiful queen. That's all". It is interesting to note further that the government of Thailand is now moving to upgrade the rights of Thai women in every way to equal men by submitting a draft bill to Parliament which, if approved, will allow married women or widows to use their maiden names. This will include village and city women alike.

References

1. According to the Primary Education Act promulgated by King Rama VI in 1921, and which became wide-spread in the rural areas after the revolution of 1932, four years of primary schooling is compulsory for boys and girls of seven years of age until they are fourteen.
2. During good deeds as merit for future life.

Indonesia: Superstition — Why?

Society in general

Life in the villages in Indonesia is far different from that in the cities. The people are very simple in their way of thinking, simple in carrying out their daily activities, and have a great sense of helping each other and their aim in life is to live in peace and to have enough food and clothing. Society in the village is far from being lively, not as we usually think of it in the city, where activities are multicomplex. For instance, in the mountainous regions most of the people are working on a single project which is agriculture. So when we visit a mountain village, we will find only rice fields and here and there areas where vegetables are grown. As Indonesia is a rural country, no wonder that the village population finds its living in agriculture. While in the villages along the shore where most of the population are fishermen, we often find fishnets and fishing boats lying idle during the day.

Life depends on nature and therefore they are compelled to work hard. If sometimes the weather is bad, raining all day long, day after day, which causes floods, or again sometimes protracted drought, their efforts may be in vain, bringing great hardship. Based on these experiences they must work hard on days when the weather is favourable.

They haven't begun to think about how to make better use of the soil to improve their yields, so as to lighten life's burden in lean periods caused by adverse weather. It is also still far from their thinking to give their descendants education for better living in the future.

In the course of development, situations like these must improve, only step by step.

As a first step, there is need to improve the communication media in order to get information to the people on agricultural matters, and thereby introduce new methods of cultivation concerning improved rice seeds, kinds and types of fertilizer, care of the plants, which includes combating plant diseases and methods of irrigation.

Information activities are usually directed by a village-chieftain as the most influential and responsible man in the village. To an approach of his kind the villagers are susceptible enough.

Otherwise if the information is done by someone they don't know, even if the man is an expert, they will flatly lend a deaf ear to him. To the villagers, something new means something uncertain. They need clear proof to be convinced. Basically the aim of this expert's information is to enhance yields so that the standard of living will be improved.

In carrying out their daily activities the farmers help each other very much, implanting paddy seeding, weeding as well as harvesting. They are never short of helping hands. If the farmer needs extra hands, they just ask aid from another farmer and promptly get it voluntarily without minding compensation. This is not only the case in husbandry, but in all kinds of jobs, such as in building or restoration of a house, etc. We call this kind of helping each other *gotong royong,* meaning a sense of duty towards each other where help is needed.

This is not the case in towns and cities. Here *gotong royong* is uprooted by services valued in money and the sense of helping someone else is lacking.

Hard work becomes a characteristic of the farmer applying more efficient methods, they begin to gain better yields. Nowadays communication in other farther regions is not so hard, thanks to the improvement of communication media and this makes it easier for them to sell their superfluous crops and in exchange to buy non-agricultural goods which they need for their family. They sell their superfluous goods by themselves or by way of a go-between. We call this go-between *tengkulak.* If they sell the goods themselves they gain a little profit, although not very much, but if they use a *tengkulak* they usually get no profit. However, this is the usual method and so the *tengkulaks* become richer and richer while, they, the farmers, have a continuously bad bargain if they have to sell fruits and vegetables because they are not like the *tengkulaks* who always try to keep prices as low as possible in buying and sell as high as possible. These goods are highly perishable and won't hold very long, they have to sell them at the first opportunity even if they suffer some loss. This is better than having spoiled things in the basket. Some farmers choose to sell the goods themselves. In that case they sometimes use a bicycle as transportation, two or three bales loaded on and riding into town or market in a line, one after the other. If there are too many goods to be transported in this manner, then they might hire a truck.

The Government is well aware of this situation and persuaded farmers to save their money by setting up farmers-banks. Saving money is something new to farmers but gradually they will come to know the benefits and to some extent answer the Government's expectation in setting up farmers-banks. But there's something else that causes this money savings to not achieve the aim as expected. Nowadays, going to town is so easy, that they go as frequently as they like, and so begin to know the towns better and better. They find there so many things they had never yet eyes on before in their villages, such as motorcars, radios, television, etc.; that it is no wonder that farmers, who have a little savings at their fingers begin itching to lay hands on all these things at long last and succumb to the temptation. They sometimes come home with all these luxurious things that are not really urgent to the production process. They get the feeling that having all these things, they become loftier in the eyes of fellow farmers measured by village standards. They don't stop to think about buying better tools that can save time and effort in cultivating the soil, or in weeding, or in combatting insects that can harm the plants. It also never comes into their minds to provide better schooling for their children so that they will become useful in the production process as well as society in the future. Based on all this we can say that it still is a long way ahead in the future before the farmer achieves a living on better and higher standards.

Women's role in the daily life

Farmers spend a great deal of their time toiling in the fields. They leave at dawn and come home at dusk. Only in time of sowing seeds, weeding and harvesting, do the women come to their aid. They are so occupied in the field that there is no time left for them to do any work at home. This is left to the care of the women. On the other hand, their women also have to work hard. They get up very early to prepare breakfast for their husbands who also must leave very early, as well as for the children. Breakfast usually comprises a cup of coffee or tea with some edibles but no rice. Later that day at noon they have to prepare lunch for their husbands which must be delivered to the field since their husbands never come home for lunch. If the family has a boy to do this, then it usually is his job. Otherwise the housewife must do this herself. In so doing she sometimes takes all the children along and then the whole family have lunch together in the field. The house is then empty, but they don't have to worry about this, since larceny never occurs.

And later towards the end of the day, the housewife once again has to prepare supper. So that is the task of a farmer's wife, day in day out. And if there is a baby in the family it is not seldom that the house-wife carries out her activities with the baby cradled in her arms.

In the village, farmers usually live in groups. Each group comprises four or five houses. They have a common space where the children play together. Parents don't have to worry that the smaller children will go astray. These children also have a sense of togetherness and the bigger children will look after the smaller ones.

If cooking for lunch is finished and before she takes it to her husband in the fields, the wife does some washing and rinsing. Usually she does it together with other house-wives at a brooklet or stream nearby. They talk and laugh with each other as they do this job joyfully and this makes their burden lighter in the village life.

Coming home from the field, she may again stamp paddy for planting rice while keeping eyes on the playing children until she has something else to do, like preparing meal for supper. In all this family duty she gets help from the bigger children like gathering wood for the fire, etc. Then comes the time for rest, late in the afternoon near dusk before going to sleep. It is the most enchanting period of the day. They sit together in front of the house, talking about things to be done the following day, laughing and singing. There is more joy when it is moonlight.

Villagers don't go to the market every day. Market is one of the less frequent characteristics in the village, usually only twice a week. Then they buy the most essential goods like sugar, coffee, salt and salt fish. Only once in a while do they buy other things like clothes, etc. They don't buy vegetables as they plant these themselves, if not in the field, then as an after crop plant, or they may plant vegetables in the premises around the house. There is no need for meat as they generally have popularly at home and sometimes sheep or goat.

A farmer's family is often large as planned parenthood is strange to them. This is also another reason that life's burden for a farmer's wife is so great although there is added help from the older children in the kitchen as well as outside, such as gathering wood for the fire. But nowadays, sponsored by the Government, they have commenced to give information about planned parenthood throughout the village. Villagers begin to realize that having many children means a heavier life's burden, especially if they are in a bad shape financially. They now also realize that children don't need only feeding, but that there must be education, clothing, space in house, etc. They now come to think that every additional child brings along additional trouble.

When the children grow older and bigger and are able to help mother in the household, then she can breather easier and have some spare time. Recently they are using this spare time to take part in courses in home economics, which is very useful for the family, like sewing, cooking and child education. They are introduced to sewing children's clothes so that if they can do it themselves, it will be cheaper than buying ready made clothes. In cooking they learn to serve better nutritional meals that will result in having healthier children. In child education they learn to know that better educated children are more useful to the community. To think that sending children to school is but a waste of money is a wrong view point.

It is a general opinion in the village that having a boy is much luckier than a girl child, because a boy is expected to help father in the field for better results. It is evident that parent's assessment of a child lay in the fact of how fat this child could help the parents in the production process as a grown-up later on. As to a girl, their opinion is that she will be tied to the household especially the kitchen regardless of her education. Therefore the chances for boys is always better than girls in obtaining better education. Girls are supposed to be very strict in religion and it is merely enough if they can cook as a precondition for their future. It is not a rare case that girls grow old at home waiting for some man to ask for their hand and have few happy experiences. Therefore illiteracy among girls in the village is very high. They have not the opportunity to learn more about a proper household, unlike their sisters in the towns and cities who are better situated and know as much about the household as their mothers are supposed to know.

Fortunately nowadays, there are courses given in the villages that open parents eyes to give their girls opportunities in education for use in their future life.

Formerly, before farmers realized the meaning of school education, their children grew up with nature. They didn't know writing and reading. They knew only playing the grazing and herding of cattle. When they were grown-up they became also farmers like their fathers. But it is different now, often farmers know the meaning of education. They may go to school to get education as best they can.

Farmers no longer expect their children to follow parents in their career. Especially for boys is this true if his parents are somewhat well to do, then they may choose education as high as possible.

Girls on the other hand get only a chance to finish elementary education. Sometimes they get an opportunity to take part in home economic courses but not in higher education. So there is still a difference between girls and boys. A boy can have the choice — what kind of education he prefers — while for a girl, there is only the future household.

No wonder that the woman's role in the household is very, very extensive.

Women's role in cultural matters

Community in the village in by and large small community that is based on brotherhood. In all aspects the people are tied strongly to customs and habits they inherited from their ancestors that has become a tradition. Human relations is based on brotherhood, and norms and values as well as function for the individual is, pre-stipulated from the very beginning, from the time he is born. Aside from the ties with tradition there is something else that is very detrimental and this is supersession. Creative efforts is society can run head on against this tradition and superstition.

Superstition as part of tradition lives on persistently as older people hand it down to children, and their children in turn to grand children. The manner of doing this is by way of stories told by older people, whenever they happen to be together. Elders always say "you must not do it" it is not allowed by custom or habit, etc." But they never say why it is not allowed. They always tell us the story that we are saved from calamities or maladies, because we perform these customs and habits well. Thus in all this the rational is lacking.

As people in the village are mostly strictly religious and obedient to elder people, the youngest never ask "why" and merely accept what the elders tell them and they in turn hand down to their children exactly in the same manner. Usually the elders who tell about these customs are the mothers. While the baby is still in the mother's body, usually in the seventh month of pregnancy, the baby is burdened with all these customs and ceremonies in order to be delivered well. Again when the baby is 40 days old, all kinds of ceremonies are performed to ward off sickness. In the course of the child's growth, many kinds of edibles are prohibited to be given to the child so as not to harm his soul. Even when the child is grown-up he is not free yet from this "so and so" without knowing why. If boys are confronted with so many prohibitions, girls are even more so.

These traditions are applied not only to youngsters but even to older people in performing their daily activities and they never dare to violate them.

In time of planting and harvesting, ceremony must be performed, also when building a house.

The women's value of prime help to her husband has an important role in performing these ceremonies. They have to prepare everything and in handing down these traditions to youngsters they also have their say, no less than the husband. In time of misfortune in the household or in the field (crops) as well, they never seek ways outside of tradition. The question is always whether the ceremonies were performed well. So great is the influence of tradition on the village which is governed by the past. If we would lead the village society into a better standard of living, the best way will be to persuade villagers to leave traditions that are harmful to mankind and show them there is something else we call "science" that is much more rational and useful than tradition.

And the key is to approach to women folk.

Nepal: Women's Ethnic Groups

Introduction

Nepal, though a cradle of ancient civilization, was little known to outside world till quite recent years. It was partially due to the policy of the then ruling family, which remained in power for one hundred and four years and partly due to its geographical position. It is a landlocked country. It lies between Tibetan Region under the People's Republic of China in the north and the Republic of India in the south. It is an independent sovereign kingdom.

There are three regions in Nepal Himalayan, Midland and Terai. The very topography of Nepal — provides it with the wide ranges of climatic conditions varying from the freezing cold of the Himalayan region to the sweltering heat of Terai. Midlands' hills and valleys generally have a salubrious climate.

The people of Nepal can be divided into two distinct ethnic groups — the Indo-Aryans and the Mongoloids. People of Mongoloid groups are the Rais, Limbus, Newaris, Magars, Gurungs, Tamangs, Thakalis and Sherpas. Brahmins, Thakuris and Chetries are the people of Indo-Aryan group.

Nepal is predominantly agricultural country with over ninety percent of population drawing direct substance from agriculture and allied occupation. Two major religions of Nepal are Hinduism and Buddhism. There are more than fifteen different dialects spoken in the country, however, Nepali is spoken as a national language. Because of the climatic and geographical conditions of the country one can note the varied characteristic features of the people of Nepal.

Life of village women

Being a mountainous country communications are difficult, and therefore village women know very little about other villages or communities. The life of a village woman is very different than the life of a woman of the city. The daily routine of village women is routine like a clock. Life is really monotonous by schedule from morning till evening. Of course she has to devote most of her time to the family members as a devoted wife and daughter-in-law. The Nepalese woman is a wonderful mother because she breast feeds all her babies until they are three or four years of age. She is also a great partner in running the household. She gets up very early in the morning about three or four a. m. depending on the work. Her day begins with grinding corn, beating and winnowing, and after the grain is ready she prepares food for the family. She then brings water from the nearest stream or waterfall on the hill, but in the Terai area, she fetches water from a well or river. She must also see if there is enough fuel in the hilly areas. In the Terai area wood as well as dried cowdung and hay are used for fuel. She must also look after the domestic animals as well.

Brahmin women

The Brahmins are scattered all over the country, mostly in Terai low lands, and also in midlands. The Brahmin woman belongs to a higher cast and her men folk are usually priests. They perform marriage ceremonies, religious ceremonies and are usually found working in the temples. While here men folk are busy performing priestly duties, she usually has to clean the floor of the house with a mixture of water and cowdung. Traditionally, women are skilled in making *duna* and *tapara* — small bowls and plates made of out fresh leaves. After finishing her household work she also has to work in the field, cultivating, planting and harvesting crops. Women of Nepal are very fond of bright coloured saris which is called *fariya*. Married women must wear red bangles, also rein vermilion powder called tika on her forehead and a bright green fine glass bead necklace called *potey*. Their long hair is usually done in a plait which hangs down their back with a red tassel. She must cover her head with a shawl in the presence of elders, specially in laws. The girls are married at an early age and the new bride finds difficult to adjust in a new home in which the mother-in-law usually helps the bride to take over the responsibility of the house. The mother-in-law gives training in all fields of the household and gradually hands over the responsibility of the house. The mother-in-law gives training in all fields of the household and gradually hands over the responsibility to her daughter-in-law. Her first job in the morning is to prepare bath water and clothes for her husband who has to do Pooja-rituals-every morning.

Socially the Brahmin woman is very much liked by her friends and neighbours of other castes. She helps in all the religious performances of the village folks. She is usually gay and has a full sense of honour and is always helpful. If she becomes a widow, she must restrict herself from the usual social customs. She will not wear any gay colours, nor any jewellery and will not eat meat. As a rule she cannot remarry again. Most of her life besides her household work will be spent on religious activities. If she comes from a poor family, her burden is greater and she will have less time for the religious deeds, because she may have to go and work in the field, and bring the firewood and cut grass for the cattle.

Newari and Sherpa women

The life of a Newari woman in the village is quite different from that of a Brahmin woman. Although Newari people of Nepal are inhabitants of Kathmandu valley they are also scattered in the hills and Terai area. The farmer class of Newaris of the valley of Kathmandu are called *jyapu*. They are a highly complex group divided between Hindus and Buddhists. The Newari women have olive skins with gentle smiles and are soft spoken. Traditionally Newari girls are married to a fruit called *bel*, before they are actually married to the men. The bel-fruit marriage takes place before puberty. This marriage is considered to be a real one according to the belief of the Newari people, and her marriage to a man is considered only as secondary.

The Newari women work equally hard with their men in the fields. They are wonderful weavers, and weave their own clothes. They take part in community singing and dancing. Their life is simple and their role in society is only as home maker, whereas the women of Sherpa community, who live in the high mountainous region are completely different. The Sherpas are of Tibetan descendent. The houses are loosely scattered on the slopes of Mt. Everest. As most of their men folk are guides and porters for the mountain climbers and go away from home for many days, the whole burden of the house falls up on their shoulders. Their daily routine would be about the same as any village woman, since she also looks after the cattle and makes cheese out of yak's milk. As a rule they do not drink milk but make lots of butter for domestic cooking and for ritual butter-lamps. They never sit idle, and are constantly on the move, working either in the field or gathering wood for the winter or weaving carpets. Living in the remote and inaccessible mountain regions they are distinctive in their character. The Sherpa women are gentle and hospitable even to strangers. Unlike the Brahmin women of Nepal they have more freedom in the house as well as in the society. Some Sherpa women join the monastic institutions and become nuns. Until now there has been very little social change among the Sherpa women as they live in remote areas of the mountains — Himalayas, where transport and communication are yet to be developed. They only come across the trekkers and mountain climbers. In recent years a hospital, a primary school and few health posts have been established. A few Sherpa girls are trained in Kathmandu for health post, and get training as health worker, health assistants, assistant nurse-midwifes and registered nurses. These girls who come for training in the city go back to their own villages as they are used to their own climate and environment. Farming methods are old and primitive but the people now have radio programmes on new methods of farming. They have no electricity so that the transistor radio has become a great medium of communication which brings them in contact with the outside world. They have very good personal relationships among the villagers, helping each other's need and enjoying together the group festivals. Although primary school is now established, there are still very few girls who know how to read and write. The government, as well as the Women's Organization of Nepal, are helping them to drive out illiteracy by opening morning and evening classes in adult education. In each village Sherpa women are now members of the women's organization, and every year they are invited to the city to participate in various activities.

Women of other groups

There are other ethnic groups such as Rais, Limbus, Gurungs, Tamangs, Thakalis, Tharus and Dhimals who belong to Indo-Mongoloid group. Rai women are famous for their beauty, they are shy yet gay and lively people. Gurung and Tamang women are fond of colourful dresses and ornaments and they are both Hindus and Buddhists. They love community singing and dancing. Tharus and Dhimals women are other ethnic groups who live in the southern part of Nepal in the Terai area. There are not social changes among the Dhimal women, but they are skilled in handloom and weave beautiful patterns and designs. The traditions are still handed down from generation to generation. They highly respect their elder women folk and respect them by bowing before the feet of their elders. Tharu women have more freedom than other ethnic groups. They have a wonderful ability for artistic creation. They keep their houses very neat by keeping the floor always clean with fresh red mud, while the walls of the houses are painted with white clay and red mud. Both sides of their door from the outside are beautifully decorated with low relief designs with primitive motifs. They have a wonderful sense of design and these artistic works are carried out by Tharu women. They decorate their arms and legs are heavily tattooed and they wear heavy ornaments. Frequently they join the religious festivals with singing and dancing.

The village women of Nepal are gradually changing their village life. They are getting education and therefore changing their pattern of life. After finishing primary and secondary education, they may come to town for college and university education. Some outstanding girl students get scholarships for further studies abroad. The village women are becoming more aware of family planning.

Education, family planning and women's organization help them to change their old traditional attitudes. Changes are coming to the villages slowly but definitely.

Pakistan: A Hard but Rich Life

Rural families

Pakistan is essentially an agricultural country in character and the large majority of women reside in the rural areas. Female population comprises about 47 per cent of the total; of these about 80 per cent are dependent on agriculture and their lives are conditioned by the nature, type of land and farming practices in vogue over the generations.

A typical rural family is a joint family with centuries of tradition behind them which has become entrenched through the generations. In the family social structure the male is the head, major decision-maker, financier and farm entrepreneur. This should not, however, lead one to conclude that the role of a woman in the farming community, at home or on the farm is essentially passive or limited to rearing children or attending to minor odd jobs. It is difficult to comprehend a male farm operator without the active participation of female members of the household. The latter attend to them from a young age and thus acquire expertise. The peasant women are working women; not only do they work in their homes and bring up children but work in the fields picking cotton, winnowing, threshing, husking, cleaning grain, making cow-dung cakes for fuel, feeding livestock, churning milk and a host of other chores. Primarily the farm size in Pakistan is small; about 50 per cent of the farmers either do not own land or if they do the size is so small as not even to provide subsistence living; only 25 per cent have what may be considered as economic holdings. The small farmer is faced with a host of problems in which the womenfolk join hands to help. Had labour been hired for all jobs the cash returns of the farmer would be further reduced. Female family labour force is thus a blessing, although it means a large family to support.

A rural woman's busiest period is at harvest. Since family's repayment capacity is low and the family lives a hand to mouth existence, the product is sold soon after harvest and the womenfolk get busy to bring it into marketable form to be carried to the *mandi* (wholesale market at town level). The produce is carried usually on bullock carts driven by men but women and children also accompany the farmer many times and utilize this opportunity to make household purchases not available at village shops. In the business of selling the produce and striking a bargain with the purchaser, the women is not a participant.

Duties of women

A woman is associated both with the farm and the house. Her daily activities begin by rising early in the morning before the sun, feeding the livestock (cow, buffalo, goat and poultry), milking the cow and churning the milk so as to have tea, milk or lassi (drink prepared from whey) ready for the family breakfast along with *roti tandoori* or ordinary roti (flat unleavened flour bread) baked on an iron plate known as *tawa* or mudoven. The better-off-farm woman cooks *parathas* (bread with admixture of butter or ghee). She provides this for the family so that the men folk may go to work in the fields and male children to school, which in some cases may be even some two or three miles away. Besides attending to cooking she collects dried twigs and small branches of trees to help in burning the fire. She normally uses cowdung cakes for fuel or wood from a tree felled from the farm by male family members. An important duty is also to draw water from the village well, pour it into pitches and carry it home. A village woman can be seen carrying two or three pitchers at one time by carefully balancing two on the head and placing one on the side and upholding with one arm. This is a heavy duty job which takes a lot of a village woman's time. Government has plans to provide piped water, particularly for drinking, which would be hygienic as well as a time-saver. Sometimes a lift pump is installed on a village well for pumping water. On the contrary piped water is available in the urban areas and an urban woman is freed from the drudgery which a village woman is subjected to.

The mid-day meal consisting of *roti*, cooked vegetables or sliced onions is prepared by the housewife. She places it on a platter tied in a coloured cloth and carries it to the farmer working in the field, which he enjoys under the shade of a tree or near a water channel or well. The village housewife does not eat with the men folk but at this hour two or three such women who have carried the mid-way meal get together for a chat. Just as cooking is purely a female job, so also is cleaning the house, sweeping the floor with a broom and washing clothes. Ironing clothes is uncommon in the village although the urban woman has become accustomed to using an electric iron.

A woman in the rural areas has but few household possessions, mostly consisting of a few utensils, *charpois* (beds) knitted with straw rope and wooden legs, bowls to wash clothes, pitchers, glasses, spoons and quilts. Generally a family cannot afford separate charpois for all children and which are shared with brothers and sisters. These *charpois* are used not only for sleeping at night but also during the day to sit on instead of western style chairs. The latter though used by some villagers are not very popular yet.

When these *charpois* are also used for guests, they are covered with beautifully and carefully embroidered sheets and pillows with embroidered cases.

The family's living quarters generally consists of one or two rooms with thatched roofs or brick roof; seldom is there a place for livestock away from the family house. The livestock is housed nearby or under a tree.

Differences between provinces

Pakistan has four major provinces other than the northern and tribal areas. The national language, Urdu, is largely understood by the womenfolk and even spoken by some but it is usual to communicate in the distinctive local dialect. Sindhi is spoken in Sind, Punjabi in the Punjab, Baluchi in Baluchistan and Pushto in the North-West Frontier Province. Each of these has dialects peculiar to the people of a region.

Handicrafts of each region are a speciality in themselves in which women excel. The women embroider a distinctive design for the long frock used by the Sindhi women. *Ralli* (patchwork) is very popular and coverlets are made in multi-colours. Besides, all articles of daily use in the village have some embellishment. Baskets of palm leaves and wicker work are also important part-times and a means of adding to income. In the province of Punjab there is a distinctive craft in every small district. Women are, however, very fond of embroidery, crochet and spend much time in making bedsheets, pillowcases, tablecloths and embroidering clothes in very fine stitches that they wear. The speciality of Baluchi women is mirror work bags, shirt collars, chair cushions, etc., and colourful silk embroidery of the womenfolk in the North-West Frontier Province.

The main dress of the village woman is *shalwar* (trousers), *kurta* (shirt) and *dupatta* (2 ½ yds. long and 1 yd. wide cloth worn over the head and shoulders). *Shalwar* and *Kurta* patterns differ somewhat in the different provinces as also the style of wearing the *dupatta*. In certain parts of Punjab province women wear *lungi* or *lacka* instead of *shalwar*. The Sindhi *shalwar* is called *sutthan*, the *kurta* known as *cholo* and the *dupatta* as *poti* or *chunni*. A Sindhi rural woman's costume also is *kanjri-lahnga*.

A bride dresses in red with silver and gold jewellery depending on the family status. Glass bangles are worn both by girls and married women and their absence is a mark of widowhood. Lavish sums of money are spent at wedding ceremonies and families enter into debt following the traditional customs of dowry and serving meals to the participants. Serving meals to mourners who come to attend a funeral is also an old custom. A woman on this occasion usually dresses in white as a sign of mourning; it is almost compulsory for women to attend marriages and funerals of persons in the *biradari* (larger kin-group) derived from the Persian word *birader* (brother) and hence brotherhood. Women participate in singing and dancing, they sing and the instruments they play are distinctive in each province. The *dhol* (drum) and *'luddî* dance performed in a ring by young girls dressed in different colours is very popular. In the Punjab besides Sammi which is performed typically by women in the rural areas. In the province of Sind the Jhoomer and Jamalo folk dances are loved by both the men and women folk as is also the Atan dance in Baluchistan Province. On festive occasions such as "Eid", women dress in gay coloured clothes and visit their near and dear ones. It is also customary for women of the *biraderi* to call on a widow on the first "Eid" after her husband's death. Women cook vermicelli which are served to the visitors on "Eid" day. Women in the villages do not normally observe *purdah* (segregation; wear burqa when going out of the house) as do women in urban areas. If they did it would seriously interfere with their work in the fields. A girl, however, is taught to be modest, docile, obedient to her elders, unassertive and to defer to male members of the family. A psychological feeling of dependance on the male members is inculcated and self-reliant traits discouraged. In urban areas the situation is not the same. In the large cities of Karachi and Lahore the pattern of behaviour is different; young girls go to school and college unsecured and are taking up independent careers in larger numbers. Marriage in villages are arranged by the elders usually within the clan; these take place at a rather young age due to the economic condition of the parents.

The present situation and future development

In the field of education the rural woman has had no initiation. There are almost negligible schooling facilities and, therefore, the peasant woman is illiterate since only some schools exist for boys in the rural areas. Government attention is directed towards establishing schools in the rural areas which besides making men and women literate will also help towards breaking up some traditional chains. These schools will emphasize on providing training to women to help them in their work on the farms, e.g., poultry and livestock breeding, vegetable farming, home-economics, hygiene and nursing. It may be mentioned that medical facilities in the village are almost non-existent, except a primitive Dai, and the mother usually treats her child or husband by giving herbs, etc., the knowledge of which has come down to her from her elders. In case of serious illness the patient is taken to the nearest town doctor. There are no kindergarten or creches for children of working mothers In fact the latter do not exist even in the urban areas not to speak of rural areas.

Government has launched several programmes for rural development in which women are expected to play an important part. Technological progress is being introduced which farmers are gradually accepting. Government through the Agricultural Development Bank is extending credit facilities for purchase of tractors and other machines and besides farmers are being encouraged to use improved seeds and fertilizers which are both imported and domestically produced and supplied to the farmers; improved implements and methods of cultivation are being introduced to bring about a transformation in the traditional agronomic structure and provide better returns to the cultivators. An increase in income of the vast majority of the rural population will exercise an important influence on the lives of womenfolk in the rural areas as they will have access to better facilities and amenities of life. Education and training and provision of better medical facilities will equip them to play a more active role in the development of their country. Besides, price increases are changing old customs and traditions, particularly those associated with wedding ceremonies and funerals and a change is beginning to manifest itself, due to government effort as well as voluntary social effort. Changes in economic conditions are changing the life-patterns of both men and women

Iran: Carpet and Fruit

Introduction

Woman — an intriguing figure through the ages — has appeared in a vast range of images in human history, from exalted goddess to domestic drugs. At one time the object of adoration, the ideal of poet's dreams, the supreme principle of life giving, she might also exert the supernatural influence of a high priestess or wield the political power of a despot. Yet, at other times, she is feared as a temptness or reduced to the role of a slave — with subservience to the masculine oriented society.

In the varied environment of Iran from the Tarid plain of Khuzestan to the high plateau of Fars and from the Mystical peals of Azarbaiyan to the lush Caspian shores — the role of woman has undergone a succession of changes. In ancient times women enjoyed considerable prestige and authority. She took part in the creation of the Persian Empire (mid-sixth century BC). However, few of Iran's neighbours chose to emulate this positive creative concept. Instead they elected to treat woman with disdain and to look on her as an inferior human being, unworthy of being considered as a contributing citizen. This negative view of the woman swept into Iran in the mid-seventh century witnessed a definite increase in the number and types of activities in which women participated. But despite this increase and growth and despite the safeguards provided women by the constitution, the Iranian woman in effect remained limited in her channels of social and political activities. Her ultimate liberation awaited the reforms of Reza Shah, the Great, and the Banning of the veil, 1934, and the law of 1936, giving rights to women to enrol in the universities and right to work with men in various professions. But again active progress awaited the commencement of the "white revolution" led by his Imperial Majesty the Shahanshah Ariyamehr.

Iran, a vast land, some, 1,648,000 square kilometers in size with a population of only 33 millions, has more than 15 million female inhabitants of which 9,856 are women in agricultural work while the remainder take care of the family, helping their husbands with the live stock in the making of daily products. Most of the women of the villages weave rugs, carpets and make other sorts of handicrafts according to the climate and the environment of their local region.

As the country has many varying features in its landscapes, climate and altitudes, as well as in agricultural products, local arts, dresses and costumes of varied ethnic groups, so the way of life is varied region by region. There are many dialects and languages in Iran, though the official language, spoken by the majority of the people is Farsi.

Women in the villages

The women in the villages must often work harder than men. Early in the morning the woman prepares tea in a samovar and serves her own home made bread. She cleans the house, prepares the meals, feeds her children as well as her husband's workers. Each family usually has besides the farming land and a piece of garden, cattle and poultry, which the woman also takes care of. According to an ancient custom, milk from the herds of three or four families of the neighbourhood is collected at one house for a certain number of days so that each woman has a chance to make additional daily products which will sell either in the city nearby, or at the village shop. Most of the families have garden of local fruits — vineyards in the high lands, oranges on the Caspian Sea, and dates in the south on the Persian Gulf. The abundance and variety of fruits, e.g., different sorts of grapes, mellons, almonds, nuts, plums, and pomegranates keeps the woman busy all through the year. She helps her husband in the garden and in the picking and drying of the fruits from which she makes different delicacies, sherbets and jams, usually served over the *korsi* during the long winter nights. *Korsi* is a certain ancient heating system. It is a small table covered by a beautiful cover and around it's four sides, different hand made cushions are provided, so that the members of the family may sit and lean on the table. For the heating, a big iron plate from the blazing fire or a special electric heater is used, which gives a warm and intimate atmosphere for the evening gathering in the villages. Dry fruits makes a portion of Iran's exports to other countries. On the Caspian Sea, the woman helps her husband and so one can see women in their colourful local dresses, working in the rice and tea fields, which makes a beautiful sight. The women also raise bees as well as silk worms, from which they make and wear as beautiful silk clothes. In the highlands and in the central provinces around Loot Desert, the agricultural products are mainly wheat, barley and cotton and various sorts of Mediterranean fruits. The women of these areas make beautiful carpets, rugs and sheep-skin coats and tapestries. Sometimes the woman makes more money than her husband in carpets and rugs, and the best Persian carpets are from the villages of Meshed, Tabriz, Torkeman Sahra, Esphaham and Kashan, which can be easily distinguished by their design and their colours. As the winter is very severe in these areas, the women take care of the household which the husbands usually work in the big cities.

Social development of women

The "white revolution" was launched in 1963, principally to bring reform to the rural areas of Iran. Apart from land reforms, equal legal rights for both sexes opened new career possibilities for women. A literacy corps was established shortly afterwards. The corps is dedicated to the improvement of education in the villages. This corps filled a gap in the lack of teachers in the rural areas. Its principle objective was to eradicate ignorance and illiteracy and prepare the villagers for a better life. To reach this objective, it dealt with the villagers social, economic and health problems as well as their formal education, by which it succeeded in the formation of a health development corps. These corps are composed of girls and boys who help their sisters and brothers in the villages, which also doing social service work in these various corps. An increasingly greater number of village women are enrolled in literacy classes, despite the attitudes of the village men.

Teaching activities of the literacy corps are as follows :

a) to hold evening classes for adults who are taught the three R's at a functional level,
b) to run theatre groups for young people as a way of providing health entertainment,
c) to establish libraries and encourage people to use them, and
d) to establish scout groups, in order to prepare children for the responsibilities of life.

By June 1975, about 1,000 Cultural Houses had been organized nation-wide and 181,799 families made use of these facilities. In these Houses the women have a chance to learn different vocations, as well as being able to watch T.V. and movie films.

In 1968, the National Association of Cultural House with the Crown Prince Rega as Honorary President was created. These Cultural Houses are intended to become centres in which rural people will learn about Iran's cultural heritage, and discuss basic problems of this age and learn the principles of social disciplines and cooperation. They will also provide facilities for cultural pursuit by the "new owner-farmers"

The Iranian women's organization under the presidency and guidance of her Imperial Highness, Princess Ashraf Pahlavi, at present directs its attention to the campaign against illiteracy, the guidance of women in family planning, and the formation of educational art classes in the villages and rural areas. The activities of this campaign are as follows :

1. The establishment of a family guidance training centre aims to train 200 people in the field of family guidance during the Fourth Development Plan; to offer the necessary guidance in the fields of family problems, feeding, health, and child care. (To date thirty-nine persons have been graduated.)
2. Establishment of the village social workers' institute, which aims to train the personnel required to familiarize rural women with their duties in a modern village and improve the situation of village families.
3. Establishment of short-term classes throughout the country for instructors in the fields of nutrition, health, family planning and mental health.

Formation of vocational schools across the nation.

Right now there are quite a few women of the villages who are members of village councils or provincial councils. Quite a few women are among the members of the board of cooperatives. Though the women of Iranian villages have a long way to go, we hope that in the very near future, that the rural women like their sisters in the cities will be able to play an increasingly significant role in the continued development of our country.

A Cambodian village woman carrying water.

Forest and Folk Tradition

Thai Culture and Forest Preservation

Thailand has long been one of the rice-producing basins of Asia, especially in the past when natural resources were still abundant. Due to the climatic conditions, which vary little as seasons change, life is simple, humble and carefree. Even the four basics of food, clothing, housing and medicine among the Thais are simple and related to nature. One striking example is the Pha Khaw Ma, or loin-cloth, which can be adapted for all purposes, namely as clothing, towel, head turban, belt and baby hammock. It is unbelievable that we derogate such simplicity which relates to nature as 'backwardness'. The abundance of forests in the past was not due to chance, but to the wisdom of our forefathers who appreciated their value. Wood was only used for building shelters to live. Temples and big monuments were constructed with bricks and mortar. From looking at the Thai way of life, one can learn a few interesting ways to preserve our forests.

According to various teachings of Buddha, forests are to be preserved as a source of peacefulness and serenity. Nature marks the rhythm of a Buddhist's life. The main events in Lord Buddha's life, namely Birth, Enlightenment and Nirvana, all occurred under the shade of a tree. The First Teaching, with the first monk, took place in the forest. Even the period of Lent is marked for meditation inside the temple so as not to do harm to living creatures in the rainy season, the time when all plants and animals are born and grow. One of the 227 precepts is not to destroy green young plants. Lord Buddha himself once said: "All monks, as long as you love life within the forest, you will never deteriorate", and on another occasion: "All those who make gardens, grow trees, build bridges, dig ponds, and give shelter, these deeds will always grant merit to them". Abundance has left its mark even during the last 50 years. Tales were recounted to show our ancestors' wisdom in saving our forests. These tales might not be scientific, but served well to present life as part of nature and *vice versa.* Over the last forty or fifty years, near most villages there existed dense forests, sometimes regarded as wastelands. In these forests stood all types of trees. These shady forests, inhabited by wild animals and birds of all species, were regarded as sacred. Under the shade of a big tree, a piece of ground was cleared and spirit houses built. Each house was empty inside, but in front of its stood various animal statues, with pots of incense, candlesticks and vases of flowers. Sometimes coloured cloth was tied around the pillars of the spirit houses. The number of spirit houses varied according to the beliefs of each village. There were the "Spirit Houses of the Ancestors". Anyone who walked past showed respect to the houses, thus respecting the forefathers of the village. Local festivities were celebrated with gifts and offerings to the spirit houses. Merry-making took place on the ground in front, marking the unity of all villagers through their forefathers and invoking their blessing. Such were the beliefs and tales that accounted for the peace of the village.

The forests around the spirit houses became sacred ground, to be passed through with respect for the forefathers, as well as for the wild belonging to them. From the spirit houses in the forests came the blessings for peace, love, hope and encouragement for all the villages. All the trees around the spirit houses were therefore left to grow on their own. Those who cut trees were tormented by their conscience for having stolen from their own forefathers. Exceptions were made, however, for those in trouble, who could ask for permission to look for wood, mushrooms, and ants' eggs for their survival, without having to endure the forefathers' curses. Psychologically, beliefs in their ancestors greatly affected the villagers' way of life, so much that forests remained green as the breathing spaces for all villagers, unity marked their efforts, and the wicked ones were deterred from sin. We can even say that the ancestors' spirit houses served to unite men for the purpose of doing good deeds as well as preserving the forests for common use.

In some areas, Buddha statues are enshrined outdoors or in a pavilion. For instance, in the province of Maha Sarakham in Northeast Thailand, not far from the community, a medium-sized Buddha statue was enthroned for people's worship in a hall on the bank of a river, not far away from which is situated a virgin forest with trees over a hundred years old. In this forest live over 500 monkeys, which freely enter passing vehicles, take away food as they like, and roar back if obstructed. We have to realize that this forest is their territory and we are only invited at our own risk. With the Buddha statue, the ruling monkeys and the forest, this should be called a "model communal forest". With its site on the riverbank, and various festive activities under shady, peaceful trees, the pavilion has retained its traditional values which link man with forests and nature. Despite the distance between the forest and man, the most destructive enemy of trees, cultural beliefs have well managed to maintain existing forests.

While travelling, one can see coloured cloth of bright red, yellow green or pink, tied around huge trees' trunks as a symbol of worship. Trees over 100 years old have witnessed many events and protected travellers. Whether trees should be worshipped because of the residing gods or goddesses depends on one's belief. Nonetheless, trees are beneficial to all for their peacefulness, for air and water, for unity as demonstrated in communal work like rice planting, harvesting, threshing, housing and road construction, and pond digging. Festivals deriving from the way of life of the majority of Thai people, who are farmers, are marked by the seasons. Most depend on when or how much it rains. Rural customs are celebrated according to the rice-growing process such as the traditional Rocket Firing to predict the amount of rainfall, or the Cat Procession to invoke rainfall in time of drought. Some customs of laymen to mark Buddhist ceremonies, which may not be so appropriate within the temples, can also be held in this pavilion. The pull and push of different traditional influences continuously affect the rural way of life in one way or another to varying degrees. They retain their predominant role until influences from outside begin to alter the existing pattern.

In places far away from the community, a belief in the sacred gods of mountains and forests serves to inhibit men from destroying natural resources. Forest products are indeed sources of food, medicine, and wood for fuel and shelter.

Since the reign of King Mongkut in the early nineteenth century, the impact of westernization has forced itself on countries like Thailand. Western civilization has meant materialism, a new culture forced upon a traditional self-supporting society, fairly balanced between the material and spirit worlds, based on four basic human needs, wrapped in simplicity, and co-existing with nature without exploitation. It is unfortunate that improved communications rapidly and gravely affect all parts of society. Economic changes affect man's beliefs and way of life, even in a community or a family. Competition breeds selfishness in all levels of business which gradually seeps through to all sectors of the community. Materialistic urges destroy the goodness in an individual or society which once served as the defence of the Ancestor Pavilion, together with its forests and ceremonies. Some remnants are revived, but only superficially, without essence. Rightly or wrongly, it is extremely difficult to obstruct the wave of materialism, to decrease the 'desires' which make man exploit others. Selfishness has come to hasten the pace of environmental destruction. Pollution reflects man's advance towards suicide. Before it is too late, wisdom has to be sought. However hard it may be, man may have reached the turning-point where he must look back to recover the environment, to return the earth, water, air, forests and mountains to nature for his own survival. The existence of the forests which our forefathers have saved and passed on to us is not sufficiently appreciated. We still cannot feel the direct link between forests and life. Unheeding, we do not realize all the consequences of our actions, until we are faced with crises resulting from the destruction of the forest, namely flood, drought, change in seasonal climate, and pollution. These crises should awaken one's conscience to seek a means to protect the forests which are being destroyed. The effects of deforestation are now felt by all, even those who were responsible for the destruction. Movements to prevent deforestation, to mobilize men to plant young trees and make serious efforts to preserve all kinds of existing forests, have become necessary.

Nonetheless, the fact remains that one cannot hasten the growth of new forests. Money and technology can destroy the whole forest in an instant, but cause great pain to humanity. Wildlife ceases to exist due to lack of forests which give shelter for protection. Time cannot be restored, especially the time that trees take to grow large enough to give shade. Money, no matter how many times more than the profit that was gained from deforestation, can never bring back the forests. Injustice is done to our children by depriving them of the chances to see our forests, and to nature by human negligence of its priceless values.

What counts most in forest plantation is continuous sincere effort on the part of all. Patience and perseverance are needed to constantly re-awaken everybody's consciousness to the values of the forest.

Ways are being sought to solve the present crisis and, maybe we can learn from our ancestors' traditions. Though they could not have imagined the problems of environmental pollution and deforestation we are now facing, they managed to conserve trees in their own time. Are we to destroy everything before having a chance to appreciate it?

Deforestation is a common problem in all countries to varying degrees. The environment has to be protected worldwide, simply for everyone's survival.

Philippines: In the Shade of the Forest

The old Datu was sitting at the edge of a deserted logging road beyond Opis high in the mountains of Bukidnon, Mindanao. A young flimsy Makaranga tree with its big red water-lily like leaves gave him some shade from the growing heat of the day. The valley and the mountain range opposite were once the forest lands of his people, the Manobo. He was looking out over the valley, but he could not see; he was nearly blind.

He explained the demise of his people: "We had our own way of seeing the life of the forest. But some time ago others came and they only saw logs, not life. They were more powerful than the spirits of the forest, so we were forced to see what they saw. When the logs had gone, the forest had gone, and life too. Everyone left us, even the spirits. We are blind."

The primary forest only stretches for a few kilometers in this mountainous corner of Mindanao where thousands of square kilometers have been logged. According to government figures hardly 2% of the Philippines is now covered with primary tropical rainforest. Commercial logging opened up these once awesome forests. Marginalized lowlanders in their shifting existence followed, searching for a little nutrient-rich soil to grow corn. As a result, the tribal communities shrank back up the mountains unable to protect the diminishing forest from the blind demands of society.

Though government officials did come, it was never to manage the forest. Politicians got involved as logging was good politics, but they never knew the forests from where their funds came. The Asian timber trade has fed well on such local injustice and blighted many countries, turning them from green to brown.

Many of the Asian tropical forests, like those of the Amazon and West Africa, have already been destroyed. The obvious difference between the Asian and Amazonian forests is the continuous vast mass of the Amazon as compared with the tropical continental edge and archipelago of Southeast Asia.

However, a crucial difference is the number of people living in these forests. About a hundred million indigenous people live in Asian forests from India across to Papua New Guinea, while only a few hundred thousand live in the Amazon. Therefore, such countries have added socio-cultural responsibilities. The destruction, of the forests has meant the destruction of both the life-giving resources of these people and their cultural expression of life. With the widespread forest destruction. Filipinos from all levels of society are now asking: "What have we done?" Economic planners have forgotten that the agricultural base of Philippine society has been tied-in with the forests. Neither is foresight a strong point of Filipino farmers; ironically this is explained by the attitude that, in times of need, there are always the forests for potential food cultivation. These people also now recognize the importance of the forests in times of climatic extremes and are striving to protect areas that stabilize and sustain community life.

Many blame the economic or political systems, national and international. Others blame Christianity's fixation with heaven. Christianity, in its association with urban wealth, lowland farming, or migrant subsistence never knew anything was really amiss. The country's dominant religion remained oblivious to the forests — to the splendour and fear of a verdant mystery central to other beliefs — and so to their destruction. Hope for the Philippine forests and for the different cultures is greatly dependent in the Philippines upon an increasing articulation of Christian attitudes to the surrounding world.

Out of this estranged relationship of the Christian Filipino and the forest arises a hope that all is not lost: that the mountains will once again be green and rivers be clean. This is often expressed in very contemporary ways of reforestation and watershed management. But there is an upwelling of a deeper sentiment: that these islands once clothed in forest are a gift of friendship – a gift from God. The relationship with the creator has suffered, so has the gift, and now the effort must be made to correct the injustice to the land and its people.

To see how this is coming about we must look at the religious practices and how they have been inspired by the changing environment. Anyone who has visited the Philippines during Biernes Santo (Good Friday) and seen the personal and communal enactment of the passion of Jesus will recognize the centrality of suffering for the Filipino in establishing anew the relation with God. Such cultic expression was a major source of hope for renewal in society during the times of martial law and the loss of human rights in the 1970's. Similar enactments of Jesus' passion now express the people's suffering and loss of a stable and productive land. Environmental activities in rural areas use images of the suffering Jesus. Today, he is seen as suffering with those living in degraded forest lands and struggling with them through peace and justice to establish again the forests.

The roar of a chain-saw announcing the death of another tree, bulldozers ploughing across the back of a forested hillside, or logs being dragged from a dwindling forest are seen as occasions for reflection and are used in the symbolic dramatization of the Stations of the Cross. Images of forest destruction have become a focus of community prayer.

In protest at the destruction of the local environment, a coffin containing the limb of a tree or just a mirror is used to symbolize the death of Kalikasan (Nature). The mask of Jesus crowned with thorns is also used in demonstrations against legal logging. With the inauguration of a reforestation programme, a cross may lead the way in the procession up to the barren hills. The suffering of the whole of creation that Jesus came to redeem is recognized and given faithful expression in these actions.

Liturgies of the Earth are heard as people grow in wonder of the forest and fear its demise. Prayers for reconciliation of the people with the land, and for the return of the forests, along with offerings of seedlings during the celebration of the Eucharist, are some of today's cultural expressions of the community's changing relation with the forests and experience of God. The planting and caring for a tree is a prayer full of hope. In relating to the forest the faith of all the people is being revitalized as God is again being found everywhere.

Usually when we speak of the divine present in our surroundings we think of the old cultural ways where there are spirits for everything. Belief in spirits of the forest like that of the Manobo datu have persisted among Christian Filipinos, but less as a fearful and placating relationship. Christianity did not substitute the cult of the saints for the spirits of old. The importance of fiestas and the close connection of patron saints with harvest festivals are seen in part as protecting the people from the feared spirits. Unfortunately Christianity appointed no patron saint of the forests.

Christians normally do not view the forest as the place of God nor see in a particular tree any divine nature. Even the medieval monastic tradition sought to tame the forests of Europe in cultivating a contemplative garden. However, in the Philippines, where economic development has touched everything and seen it turn to dust, there is a growing fear of disaster. People sense a loss of awe and are saddened by their destruction of the forests. People know God's sufferance amongst them as they, together with the land, become poorer. Here begins the acknowledgment of the divine as being present in our relation to the forests.

From this experience there stems the willingness to develop a deeper sense of sanctuary. Some tribal groups like the Bontoc keep sacred groves, parts of the forest are preserved for religious rituals performed at critical periods in the life cycle of the community (birth, death, harvest, sickness). This sense of right-relation and its expression is sought in the context of Christian retreat houses and the need for areas of natural beauty where people can rest and know God's presence, particularly during the Easter season. Christian reflection increasingly acknowledges the association of the forests with the life, wealth and well-being of the community.

The Philippine legend "Si Malakas at si Maganda" (the first man and woman), who came from a split bamboo, underlies the Filipinos' earliest relation with the forest and a life which even today is sustained by the constant need for bamboo. Filipinos have always recognized that all life is of divine origin and is sustained by divine presence. Though the forests are being destroyed the gift of creation and the giver are still to be found; there is hope.

As Filipinos seek such relation with the environment there is another tree that keeps the spirit of the forest alive, instilling fear and wonder even among city children far from the forest. Nobody cuts a ballete tree. Ballete trees are still found along the old streets of Manila. Their tortuous trunks turning and binding each other until they reach the sky are full of nooks, crevices and crannies containing all sorts of insects, lizards, bats and spirits. It is a forest itself, crammed with life, and people wonder at its endurance. The boldness of the tree, its strength and shade is respected rather than feared; it calls people to be still. In this growing scientific era a ballete is not to be thought of as merely cleaning the air, but is to be sought out as a sign of life, a reminder of the divine. To pray under a ballete is a natural thing to do.

Those who seek out life under a tree recognize the blindness of our society and the extent of our exhausted forest life. Today we contemplate a new image of the forest as that of something sustaining our lives, through its richness and beauty. Not only those of us who live in the forest, but those nearby and far away, need to express thanks for such a gift. All the more, Christians will now have to work to protect the environment knowing that God is manifest in the thick, green forests - present in the shade of creation.

Japan: Okinawa's Utaki

In ancient Japan people believed that gods dwelt everywhere in nature, and especially in wooded places. This belief lives on in modern-day Okinawa. After the twelfth century, especially in Okinawa, people began to call woods where the gods dwelled "taki", or, "utaki". The word "utaki" is made up of the prefix "u" and the stem "taki", "u" meaning to honour or respect and "taki" meaning mountains or woods. Thus the original definition of *utaki* is, sacred mountains or sacred woods.

The custom of creating *utaki* spread from the south northeastward through the more than sixty islands making up the Ryukyu chain which extends a thousand kilometers between Taiwan and the Japanese island of Kyushu. In ancient times in the Ryukyus, when people built a village, they were certain to make *utaki* at its centre. Today, therefore, wherever there is a village, there too is an *utaki*. In an *utaki* is found with no surrounding village, this means that blood relatives from two villages joined together in one village, abandoned the other, with only the *utaki* surviving to mark its site. The form and distribution of *utaki* thus provide clues to the history of village life in Okinawa.

The structure and form of Utaki

There is nothing man-made in the *utaki* except perhaps a small altar where incense is burned. The place abounds with huge thick trees, symbols of the gods. Making skilful use of topography, as a god would, the villagers sited their *utaki*. The basic structure is "mu" which means "there is nothing". As gods will push aside artificial works, *utaki* must be kept as pure land. Therefore *utaki* have various shapes depending on topographical features.

The distribution of Utaki

According to Ryukyu Yuraiki there are great numbers of *utaki* — 29 in Shuri; 8 in Hana; 143 in Kunigami; 210 in Nakagami; and 297 in Shimajiri. In the lheya islands there are 22. 37 are found in the Kerama islands, 29 in Miyako, and 76 in Yaeyama.

The priests of Utaki: Noro

A *noro* is a member of a paid priesthood of women who owns a piece of land. Her duty in olden times was to pray regularly at the *utaki* for the king's long life, for the prosperity of the king's family, for good harvests, for peace and the people's safety, for safe voyages, and so on. Beginning in the fifteenth century, the highest ranking *noro*, called "ogimi", was appointed from among female members of the king's family. The first *ogimi* was the younger sister of Sho Dynasty King Shin. Under the *ogimi* was "kimi" and under *kimi* were "oyanoro". *Noro* formed the bottom rank of this hierarchy. There was one *oyanoro* in each "majiri" (a district including cities, towns, and villages) who supervised the *noro* found in every village.

Notable Utaki and their functions

1. The King's Utaki (Seifa Utaki)

Seifa is known as the most holy place in Okinawa and is called "sayaharake". There is a legend that *Seifa Utaki* was created by "Amami Kiyo" herself, she being the goddess who created Okinawa. In the enclosure of *Seifa* is a primeval forest of banyan trees. Deigo trees, bamboos, palm and hemp palm trees rise toward the sky so thick and tall that they dim the light. Two towering rocks are positioned leaning against one another. There are eight "ibi" (holy spots) within the *utaki*. At one, there is an altar for the worship of Kudaka Island. The altar is situated so that there is a direct sight line to Kudaka through the arch formed by the two rocks.

The coronation of the Ryukyu Kingdom's highest ranking priest (Kikoe Ogimi) was held in this most holy *utaki*. On an auspicious day in September (by the lunar calendar), at six in the morning, the *ogimi* left her castle to greet the king. They exchanged a parting cup at the king's castle, Shuri Castle. The *ogimi* departed from the "Akata Gate" dressed in white and riding upon a white horse.

Two ceremonial ladies from Chinen Village led her towards Yonabaru in a procession of over two hundred attendants. The procession stopped at a hut near the *utaki* in Yonabaru. There the members prayed to a sea god, "Nirai Kanai". Leaving Yonabaru they headed for Chinen through Baten and Sashiki. At every village along the way, *noro* and village officials welcomed them. They proceeded along surrounded by warm welcomes and the sound of "mich Kuena" (special procession music).

Before they entered the *Seifa Utaki* they rested at a hut nearby. At midnight they made their pilgrimage to *Seifa*. *Kikoe Ogimi* offered rice and wine at six places within the *utaki*. Seventy *noro* from Chinen and Kudaka sang "umui" and "Kuena" to the accompaniment of the drum. Their singing voices echoed through the wood. At a sign given by the Kudaka Island *noro, Kikoe Ogimi's* honourable name was born. The group then all stood and blessed *ogimi's* birth. "Yarashi" and "Kuena" choruses all at once rose.

At four in the morning, they returned to the hut to rest. At five, in the *Seifa* courtyard, fifteen *noro* with their hands pressed together to *ogimi* and to the sky danced a holy dance and the ceremony ended. On their way back home they passed through Tamagusuku village and Ozato, arriving at *Kikoe Ogimi's* castle about five o'clock in the evening. On the ruin of *Kikoe ogimi's* castle now stands Shuri Junior High School looking down upon the four seas.

2. Binnu Utaki

Binnu Utaki is located on the east side of Shuri Castle on a small hill about 150 meters above sea level. The whole area toward the south is topographically gentle. *Binnu Utaki* is quite a noticeable wood, truly a sacred place. "Bin" means "houo" in China and refers to an imaginary bird. So *Binnu Utaki* is a sacred wood where "houo" lives. The site also looks out toward Kudaka Island and is a worship place for that island. *Binnu Utaki* is celebrated by a Shuri Senior High School song:

Look up to *Binnu Utaki*
Thick greed of 1000 years
With a splendid view of the sea of Naha
Whose waves have lapped for ten thousand years.

3. Chinen Mori

Chinen Mori is a ruined castle on a round hill in the south of Okinawa. Omorososhi (an epic book of 22 volumes completed in 1623) describes it thus:

Chinen Mori: Chinen Wood Castle
When the goddess Amami Kiyo descended
To create Okinawa.
Chinen Wood, the birthplace of Okinawa.
Chuzan Seikan (written in 1650: a historical book of six volumes) describes the creation myth.

4. Kudaka Kuba Mori

Kudaka Island is a small island east of Okinawa. There is a sacred wood on the island called "kuba mori", or also, "kubo no utaki". *Kuba mori* is situated away from the village. Within there is no intrusion of human life; stillness prevails broken only by the sounds of nature. Men are prohibited from entering the *mori.* It is also closed to women except when a religious service is held there. No one has broken this rule for hundreds of years.

A religious observance called "*Izaiho*" is held in the wood once every twelve years. *Izaiho* is a ceremony for women who will soon be in the service of a god. On the appointed day all the women return from other islands to join the ceremony. A twelfth year fell in 1990 but unfortunately the service had to be cancelled because the island has lost so many inhabitants that there was no one available to conduct it.

5. "Takmori", Naze City, Amami Oshima

Amami Oshima is located north of Okinawa and is in Kagoshima Prefecture. Naze is the island's main city. The people of Amai use different terms for *utaki*: "Agami yama" (worship mountain), or "Kami Yama", (god's mountain).

In Naze City, the city assembly debated whether or not they should keep their *utaki* as a sacred place. They finally decided to keep the place but use it for a different purpose. It is now named "Agami Yama-koen" and used as a place of rest and recreation.

6. Utaki in the Miyako Islands

The Miyako Islands include Miyako, Iraby, Tarama, Ikeba, Ogami, Kurijima, and Minna.

Irabu has a population of seven thousand. There are seven villages but eight *utaki*, showing that there were formerly eight blood-related villages. Every blood-related village had one *utaki*. Later the present social structure formed. In spite of the consolidation into seven villages, the *utaki* are kept as before. In Miyako, where social change proceeds at a moderate pace, the social structure changes only slowly. In Miyako, the priest is called "tsukasa" rather than "noro" as in the other islands. "Nakasone tumiya" is a hero who unified the Miyako islands for the first time in their history. He came from a powerful clan which contributed to the line of rulers of the Ryukyu Kingdom. When the "oyake akahaci no ran" revolt broke out, Nakasone suppressed it. His distinguished service was recognized by the king. His wife was appointed "O-amushi", or, the wife of a ruler, and given the highest priestly position.

Under O-amushi ranked "kami tsukasa" followed by "sani amu". O-amushi owned land, and had two male and four female followers. On New Year's day, the day of the winter solstice, she made a pilgrimage with her attendants. When her followers' terms were up, she requested new terms from the king and then appointed new followers. In Miyako, sixteen *utaki* are known so there are sixteen *noro*.

In Irabu, a particular sequence of religious observances was established by "Iando no Omu" in the year 1522. As recorded in the "Utaki Yuraiki", an ancient record of *Utaki* origins, the details of the *tsukasa's* duties were as follows:

1. In February, the first prayers for a good grain harvest were to be offered.
2. During April, prayers for the rice and millet harvest were to be offered. In order to perform the rice and millet harvest festival, *tsukasa* had to collect one pinch of rice grain and millet to offer to the gods.
3. In May and June, the "setsu matsuri" or changing weather festival was held.
4. In September, a social service was held.
5. In October, a fire god festival was held.

7. Yaeyama: Mori and Wan

A feature of Yaeyama Utaki is that their names, god's names, and site names are quite clear, since many of them were created in recent years.

The following legend is told about Puriwan, Kuroshima: In the old days. "Yamatun chu", or, people from the Japanese mainland, found their way at last to the island of Kuroshima after a long journey. As they were about to land, they discovered a snake coiled around the mast of their ship. Believing that a god had disguised himself as a snake and had protected them during the long voyage, they released the snake on the island. Since then snakes have lived in Kuroshima. Now there is a god to provide safe voyages enshrined there.

A sacred site named "Fuzumari" can also be seen in Kuroshima. "Fuzumari" in the Kuroshima dialect means "takamori" or a high wood. Fuzumari was the site of 'fire duty' during Edo times. The fire was made on top of a hill to signal an emergency. From the southern tip of Japan, at Hateruma island, to the very western tip at Yonaguni island, to Kuroshima, Iriomote, and on the Miyako islands (Tarama, Kurima, Miyako island itself), people made signal fires to communicate urgent messages to the Shuri Kingdom office. In every island today, the fuzumari is still maintained carefully.

Akamata, Kuromata, and Umutu

In the Yaeyama Islands, the southernmost islands of Japan, the *Akamata, Kuromata* festival is held. These are masked men-gods completely covered with leaves who appear at "puri", or corn harvest. The first day of the festival is devoted to giving thanks for the year's rice harvest, the second to praying for and endeavouring to predict a good harvest for the next year.

The ceremony is held at "on" (In Yaeyama, *utaki* is called on). Komi in Iriomote island is the mecca of this festival and there it is a little different from that in Yaeyama. Three main gods, *Akamata, Kuromata,* and *Shiromata* appear from "umutu", or, "the original place", and bless the villagers. Another view holds that Akamata and Kuromata are gods, who visit from far away in the sea to give a good harvest.

The harvest festival was held during June on the lunar calendar. It was not only devoted to the harvest; it was also a time for joining the *Akamata,* Kuromata group.

In Komi village in Iriomote, young men reaching the age of seventeen, born in Komi and of good morals, were accepted to join. So the youths of the village took care to behave well. When a boy is about thirteen, he is registered as a candidate for entering the *Akamata, Kuromata* group. From then until he reaches seventeen, the boy's behaviour will be carefully supervised by grownups.

Upon becoming members of the group, young men also become part of the village council. A leader will be chosen, and the whole village will be kept in good order. Iriomote island had contributed to "Yamato Chofei", or imperial family, since the seventh century, and the island was the centre of the Yaeyma islands. In the Middle Ages, the islands owned ship-yards and contributed to the Ryukyu Kingdom's trade with other countries.

Akamata, Kuromata spread not only in the Yaeyama islands but also to Kohama island, to Arakaki island, and to Miyara in Ishigaki. Today the festival is still actively held throughout the islands. At the festivals of Kohama and Miyama only two gods appear, *Akamata* and *Kuromata.* The festival of Arakaki island is a little different. There, in addition to *Akamata* and *Kuromata,* a parent and child couple appear, four gods in all.

At Komi village in Iriomote, the *Akamata, Kuromata* festival is closed to the media. No one is allowed to take pictures or videos or make recordings. It is such a solemn event and the villagers' devotion to it is so deep that there is no prospect for opening it to the public in the future. This island has many wild creatures, including "Iriomote Yamaneko" or, the Iriomote wild cat. The people's love of nature, and their belief in and feelings toward the gods make the life of the island abundant.

Laos: Forests and Tribes

Laos in the past was a land of forests with plenty of elephants. It was called "Lan Xang" which means "a million elephants" because "there were so many elephants that it was named that way". One should think of how large the forest was, to be the home for so many elephants. That was in the past. At the present time, there are few forests because most of them are being destroyed. This is a big problem now in our country as well as many countries in Asia.

There is an expression which says, "A big tree must be haunted by spirits just as a beautiful girl must be loved by her boyfriend". This is the general belief of people in our country. The forest is the most important of natural resources, especially for those who depend on it for their living. Many of them are the tribal people that are sometimes called "mountain people" because they prefer to live in the forest on the mountain. They cut trees down and then when the land is dry, they burn the wood to fertilize the soil for planting rice, which is their principal food. Usually, in Laos the forest grows on the mountain. It is more difficult to divide the forests up, so we call them "Phou Pha Pa Dong" which means 'mountain forest' or 'forest on the mountain'.

As the forest is a natural resource in which people live and earn their living, they consider it to belong to ghosts, spirits and gods because these sacred and mysterious things create and preserve it. The people's duty is to be grateful and respectful to them. If they do not sacrifice correctly, it may bring harm and if the spirits are angry with them, they may cause disasters.

Therefore, the forest is a symbol, a sacred and mysterious realm for them. They do not understand nature, so they are afraid of it. It is necessary for them to satisfy the spirits. From this concept, many rituals have arisen.

To clearly understand the beliefs of Lao people, we should consider their religious and cultural background. Their original beliefs came from animism. First, they worshipped their ancestors and some spirits. Later, Indian culture came to Laos in the form of Brahmanism the people accepted it because it was similar to their own beliefs. Brahmans worshipped gods that are higher than spirits, but embody the same meaning. Then Buddhism came to Laos. The people welcomed it with pleasure as their national religion, but they did not give up their old beliefs. They mixed them and practised them side by side.

This is their religious background, so it is very difficult to classify which elements stem from animism, Brahmanism and Buddhism in their beliefs and behaviour even now. Through this background, we can see that people's beliefs related to the forest have their roots in these religions. That is to say, they believe in spirits, gods and man; the spirits come from animism, the gods from Brahmanism and the belief in man from Buddhism, that is, from the Lord Buddha. Spirits prefer to live in the forest and so do the gods. Even the Buddhist monks like to live in the forest to practise meditation.

But the tribal or mountain people believe in animism. They worship their ancestors and sacrifice to the spirits of the forest. For example, when they establish their farms and the New Year comes along, they will celebrate and sacrifice to the spirits. The important thing to do first is to ask permission and protection from the master of the forest before cutting trees in preparation for rice cultivation. When the harvest is successful, they bring friends to worship the gods and offer sacrifice to the spirits of the forest to express their gratitude and thanks.

Besides this, some tribes follow very strict traditions. For example, a woman who has an illegitimate child has to be fined one water buffalo which is killed as a sacrifice to the master of the forest. This shows that the forest has a great influence on people's behaviour.

There are many legends and myths connected with the forest in Laos. According to one of the legends, long, long ago there was a man, a good hunter, who lived with his mother. One day he took his bow and arrow and went into the forest to hunt. Unfortunately, that day he caught nothing. As he wandered through the forest, he came across a huge tiger. He was frightened and ran, and climbed up a tree. But the tiger did not go away, and was waiting for him down below. He cried and thought of his mother. Finally, he prayed to the master of the forest and asked the spirits to look after him. The spirits of the forest took pity on him. They took the tiger away and brought the man down. Some of them gave him food and some gave him shelter. Early next morning, they took him to the king's park and told him, "If someone asks you a question, do not say anything except the word 'Ama'. It means 'yes'. And then you will be lucky." And then the spirits disappeared.

At that time the king of that realm died. His people were seeking a new king. They sent off a king's cart to select a king by luck and fortune. The cart went to the park where the man was and stopped near him. They saw him and questioned him. "Who are you?" "Why are you here?" "Yes," he answered. "What is your name?" they asked. "Yes," he responded. "Were you sent here by the gods?" they asked again. He answered, "Yes," as usual. The people decided to make him their king because his answers and behaviour suited their purpose. When he became king, he helped the spirits in the forest, particularly the master of the forest. The king was very grateful and respectful to the spirits. He decided to build a village near the forest as a shrine where sacrifices would be made to the spirits and the master of the forest.

This legend shows the beliefs of the people concerning the master of the forest and spirits. They are able to bring a man good luck and happiness, so it is best to show gratitude to them by not destroying the forests.

In most of the villages, especially in the countryside, one will see the spirit houses, which are shrines or sacred places to the villagers. Near by the "Ho Poo Ta" which means "house of the grandfather, forefather or ancestor". There will be a lot of big trees and plenty of wild animals because no one can cut the trees or hunt the animals there. The Poo Ta spirits will be angry if someone destroys the trees and animals. They may bring danger or make the villagers sick, or cause some disaster. This is a good way to ensure that the people preserve the forests.

Before cultivating the rice at the beginning of the rainy season, they will celebrate rituals to Poo Ta and offer sacrifice for good luck in their harvest. This ceremony comes from the cultural background of ancestor worship in the form of sacrifices to the spirits, expressing the gratitude of the people to the ancestors for the preservation of nature and the environment.

Besides the preservation of the forest through these traditions and beliefs, the government and local authorities create some rules of taboos forbidding people to cut trees and make fires in the forest without good reason.

The tribes or mountain people who make their living on the mountain by cutting trees to clear land for rice cultivation are now being persuaded to come down to the lowlands to grow rice there.

India: Forests in Folk Tradition

Forests have been a part of the cultural heritage of India since time immemorial. The natural beauty of forests has been described beautifully by the great poet Kalidasa in his play "Shakuntala", which is considered his masterpiece. Describing the abode of the heroine (Shakuntala) who lived in a forest, he wrote that the cottage was surrounded by "waterbodies", full of lotuses, the trees vied with each other to bend towards the cottage to soften the effect of the sun's rays, the soft breeze made the multicoloured flowers swing with its song, and drops of rainwater fell from the leaves to wash the roots of the trees. The sylvan surroundings enabled deer and peacocks to move about freely without any fear whatsoever.

The natural setting of the forests was in perfect harmony with the life-style adopted by our saints and preachers. The soft cool breeze bringing aromas from all directions, the purity of nature in the form of the forest and clear waters of the lakes, streams, waterfalls and rivers and lush green flowering trees afforded a place where the saints could lead a life of calm and quiet away from the palaces and worldly riches. They lived in caves and thatch huts; ate roots, fruits, shoots and flowers; wore clothes made of animal skin and prayed under the shade of tree canopies. Living in forests enabled our ancestors to develop and identify with nature. They developed friendship with trees, birds and animals, learnt to live off the land, and discovered many useful herbs and medicinal plants which have been handed down to us for generations. In the great epic Ramayana, Lord Rama, during his wanderings in the forests, ate roots and fruits and slept on grass. He made friends with monkeys and bears who helped him in his fight against the demon King 'Ravana' who had ten heads. The mythological bird 'Jatayu' fought with Ravana to protect Rama's wife Sita whom Ravana was abducting. In his devotion to Rama, Jatayu laid down his life. The attachment to nature of the forest dwellers is beautifully described by Kalidasa at the touching farewell given to Shakuntala by her native 'friends'. The deer stopped eating the grass, the peacock halted in the midst of his dance, the creepers shed tears in the form of yellow and worn-out leaves.

Forests have been an inalienable part of the evolution of Hindu religion. The great epics *Ramayana* and *Mahabharata* have been written against the backdrop of the wanderings of the protagonists in the forests. Lord Buddha and Lord Mahavira retired to the forests from their palaces and sought enlightenment in the peaceful surrounding. The saints performed 'Yajnas' or religious sacrifices in the forests and practised penances of the most severe kind to enable them to have communion with God. Nature worship of deities like Agni (fire) and Vayu (wind), clouds and rain, originated with man's desire to please the Gods of nature. Trees, stones, and animals were worshipped and offerings made to them.

Education was dispensed by saints in the forests both to pupils from royal families and to commoners. Learning was imparted in the open and the pupils had great reverence for the teacher. At the end of the training period, the pupils acknowledged the teacher's efforts by giving him a 'Guru Dakshina' or teachers' award. Teaching dealt with the art of archery and other forms of warfare, use of forest materials for making bows, arrows etc., community life and living in harmony with nature. Students were also taught worldly wisdom by citing examples from nature. The animal world came in very handy for such teachings. The stories of 'Panchatantra' abound in the wisdom gained through the actions of animals. Three 'dull' sons of King Amrashakti were taught the 'ways of the world' by their teacher Vishnusharma simply by relating stories of birds and animals. Each story ended with a moral which was well-absorbed by the pupils. Among the more famous of these stories are 'The Hare and the Tortoise' (moral — slow and steady wins the race), 'The Rabbit and the Lion' (moral — 'brains beats brawn') and 'The Hunter and the Pigeons' (moral — unity is strength.)

Arts and crafts flourished in the forests in the pre-historic days. The favourite places for such activities were caves where people lived and utilised their spare time profitably. The paintings of the Ajanta caves and sculptures of Ajanta, Ellora and Elephanta caves have captured the imagination of people from far and wide. Natural pigments and stones were used for the arts. The subjects related to gods, goddesses, animals, trees, plants and the like. Similarly, religious instructions of edicts were engraved on stones to enable the common man to read and follow the teachings. The beauty of forests, however, is overshadowed by the myths prevalent about the dangers of forest life. Traditionally forests have been considered the abode of wild animals and evil spirits. The problems associated with forest life have been summed up beautifully in the epic Ramayana. Lord Rama was exiled to the forests for fourteen years by his father as a consequence of the wish of his stepmother Kaikeyi, who wanted the Kingdom of Ayodhya for her own son Bharat. Rama's wife Sita insisted on accompanying her husband. Rama tried to dissuade her by narrating the hardships associated with life in the forests. According to him, tracks in the forests were full of stones, and thorns, and there were steep mountains. The deep gorges, fast flowing rivers and streams were difficult to negotiate. The dark caves were inhabited by unknown spirits. Wild animals making bloodchilling sounds caused fear even among the brave. One had to guard against huge and fearsome vultures and snakes. To cap it all, groups of demons capable of taking on deceptive forms roamed about freely, stealing or eating men and women. The deceptive forms adopted by the demons were used to lure kings, hunters and other human beings into a pre-conceived plan whereby the forces of evil could prevail. In the Ramayana, the demon Marich took on the form of a deer to tempt Sita with its golden skin while the demon Ravana took on the form of a saint to carry her forcibly from her cottage when she was alone. At times, the demons demanded food and offerings from the populace, threatening them with dire consequences if they refused.

Forests were considered the ideal place for exiling 'unwanted' persons. The theory was that the exiled persons would not be able to return from forests and would be 'out of the way' of those parties who were interested in their exile. The protagonists Rama and the Pandava brothers in the epics *Ramayana* and *Mahabharata*, respectively, spent a large part of their youth wandering in forests. In traditional folklore, defeated kings, cursed men and women and disobedient children were sent to forests as a punishment. An uncouth character is referred to as 'Junglee' — meaning 'of the forests' — alluding to the unwanted and outcast persons living there.

The difficulties of forest life gave rise to a number of superstitions, especially relating to animals. The braying of a donkey or the howling of a jackal are ill omens. A cat crossing one's path would bring ill luck. On the other hand, sighting a fox or a herd of deer is an auspicious sign. If a snake covers a sleeping person with its hood, he will have a long life. In addition to natural omens, men and women had to face the curses of saints if they were annoyed at the disturbance of their prayers.

Forests have long been the backdrop of our civilisation. Traditionally, the Indian life span is supposed to be a hundred years divided into four parts or 'Ashrams' of twenty-five years each. Life starts in the forests when young boys go there to learn in the first 'Ashram'. The cycle is completed when man returns to forest in the last 'Ashram' to seek communion with God and to give up worldly pleasures in his twilight years.

Advancement of scientific knowledge and spread of communication have destroyed many myths about forests but their awesome mystery still remains a part of our life.

Mongolian Folk Tradition

Fine Art

Mongolian fine art has a rich history and reflects the people's life and labour. Fine art is one of the origins of any nation's culture. It is an aesthetic reflection of human emotions, imagination and handicraft.

Embroidery

Mongolian nomads not only decorated their dwellings, but also made pictures on silk. They embroidered various small articles such as bags for containing bowls, tobacco pouches, etc. Hats, clothes and boots were also embroidered for the nobles.

Besides this, religious books were ornamented and embroidered. The Golden Fund of museums preserves some examples of this art: "White Tara", "Mongol Boots", "Ochirvanni".

Painting

Mongolian painting began to develop more than two thousand years ago from simple rock drawings. Uigur paintings of the eighth century prove that this art was flourishing in Mongolia and Asia long ago. buddhism was the main theme of the painting, and it developed into a fine art form.

B. Sharav is the painter who linked the old with the new in his art. The Mongolian way of life was depicted in his famous work "One Day in Mongolia" and various portraits.

The traditional painting was influenced by European art. The Mongolian painters L. Gavaa, O. Tsevegjav and Ts. Doripalam are famous not only at home, but also abroad. They made a great contribution to the creation of new art based in tradition and trained several generations of painters.

At present, new and different artistic trends are emerging, and creative young artists are developing the national art.

Sculpture

Deer carvings in rock constitute the historical monuments of ancient times. Thousands of these rocks are evidence of the development and wealth of sculpture in ancient Mongolia. Under Gageen Zanabazar, a prominent religious figure and famous sculptor of the seventeenth century, created 21 *tara* (consorts of Buddha), which show the beauty of Mongolian woman. Zanabar laid the foundation for the depiction and praise of the human form in Mongolian sculpture.

Now there are many famous sculptors such as S. Choimbol, A. Davaatseren, N. Jambal and L. Dashdeleg.

The monument to D. Sukhbaatar by S. Choimbol is a symbol of Mongolia and it gives an idea of our country to foreign visitors. It is a unique example of a Mongolian horse-rider represented through the medium of sculpture.

It is hoped that creative young artists will further contribute to sculpture in Mongolia.

Mongolian folklore traditions

Among oriental nations Mongolia is famous for its rich folklore tradition. Heterogeneous genres of folklore such as ancient myths, proverbs, sayings, good wishes, blessings, tales, epics which depict the happiness, yearning and wisdom of the people, have been inherited by our people and passed down orally, from generation to generation, since time immemorial. Even in the primitive stage of development during the struggle with nature and the domestication of wild animals, labour songs, and verses and melodies on livestock breeding emerged and came down to our day, evolving in accordance with our cultural development.

It is a history of thousands of years of herdsmen's long, drawn-fencing sheep and other national peculiarities, melodious and eloquent verses, proverbs, tales and epics integrated into present day life.

While Mongolian folklore was passed down by word of mouth in pre-literate times, the parallel development of oral and written traditions of folklore has entered a new stage in this period of national script, as is evident from contemporary stories, epics, proverbs, and benedictions.

Mongolian heroic epics

Epics are a classic genre of Mongolian folklore. They are rooted in epic songs which depict the valour of courageous heroes of the tenth century, and in the twelfth and thirteenth centuries they flourished and large epic songs and long verse epics were created. In this, Mongolia was distinguished among Asian countries, and the epics "Geseriada" and "Jangar" ranking with supreme world poetry such as the "Iliad" and "Odyssey" of Greece, and the "Mahabharata" and "Ramayana" of India, were created.

In the development of epics the ideology of the emperor Genghis Khan's state had great impact and played an important part in revealing the powerful and heroic events and aspirations of the steppe nobles.

The inheritance of the Mongolian people's epic has become more and more enriched, and epics such as "Bum Erdene", "Khan Kharankhui", "Daini Khurel" and "Dsul Aldarkhan" which depict the prosperity of the people, were created and handed down to the people of present-day Mongolia by contemporary reciters of epic songs like Jilkher and Parchin. Their successor, epic-teller B. Avirmed, has recited epic literature in our day and for this merit he was awarded the 1991 State Prize of the MPR.

Mongolian folk songs

The Mongolian folk song is one of the most ancient forms of musical and poetic art of the Mongols. History books recorded their wolf-like melodical singing in the time of the Hsiung-nu, Mongolian folk songs could be classified according to function as songs of everyday life, ceremony and dancing. As for their genre they are divided into lyric melodies, narrative songs for performing art, response songs, tragic melodies, humorous and festive songs.

There are two basic forms: short songs and long songs. Short songs are more popular and have short tunes, sharp rhythm, originality and vivacity, and are connected with daily life and activities, and combined with beautiful decorations. But the Mongolian long song is of the classic genre, in philosophical style, evocative of vast, wide spaces. It also demands great skill and talent from the singers in their breathing abilities and guttural singing techniques.

There are in Mongolia a number of already-established schools of Mongolian long song in certain local regions. According to its scale and composition, Mongolian long song could be classified into 'lesser long songs', 'long songs' and 'majestic long songs'.

Mongol khoomi

Mongol *Khoomi* is a musical art to be delivered with the help of a guttural voice and specific way of breathing. It can be regarded as musical art - not exactly singing but using one's throat as an instrument. Professional *khoomi* performers are only found in certain areas with a certain tradition and geographical location. The Chandmani district of Kobdo *aimag* (province) is the home of *khoomi*. A number of well-known *khoomi* performers of Mongolia were born there. One tone comes out as a whistle-like sound, the result of locked breath in the chest being forced out through the throat in a specific way, while a lower tone sounds as a base.

The style of *khoomi* can be distinguished, according to the direction of the air breathed out, from deep in the lungs. For example:

- *Harhireaa khoomi*: under strong pressure of the throat, the air is breathed out while a lower tone is kept as the main sound.
- *Bagalzuuryn* (laryngeal) *khoomi*: locked breath is exhaled while being pressed close to the larynx.
- *Tagnainy* (palatine) *khoomi*: the locked breath is exhaled while being pressed close to the palate.
- *Hooloin* (guttural) *khoomi*: the locked breath is exhaled past the end of the tongue.
- *Hamryn* (nasal) *khoomi*: the locked breath is let out through the nose.

In fact, *khoomi* is an art of not only single but double throat singing, in which both upper whistle and lower tone are included. Rendering of a song vocally, combined with lower sounds and whistle, produces polyphonic singing.

Khoomi is the specific and classic genre of Mongolian traditional music.

Mongolian folk instruments

Since their origin, Mongolian folk instruments have long been developed, evaluated, improved and enriched through historical links with musical instruments of other nations in Asia. Mongolian folk instruments can be divided into eight groups according to the material of which they are made such as metal, bamboo, stone, clay, etc.

They also could be classified as wind instruments-*bishguur, limbe, buree* and so on; stringed instruments - *khuur, khuuchir, biwa* and *tobshuur*, python - skin instruments, and drums of different sizes and shapes.

Five of the folk instruments - *morin khuur, shudraga, limbe, khuuchir* and *yoching* are usually considered to comprise the classic quintet. The *morin khuur*, a two-stringed lute with a wooden sound box and scroll carved in the form of a horse's head, is the instrument that comes closest to expressing the deep feelings of the Mongolian heart. The *shudraga* is a three-stringed lute with a circular wooden sound-box covered with skin. *Khuuchir* is a two-stringed spike fiddle with a skin-covered body, and *yoching* is a board zither.

Design on ritual costume, Sumatra, Indonesia.

Flowers

Lotus — The Sacred Flower of India

Known in Sanskrit as *Kamala* or *Padma,* the lotus is perhaps the most perfectly representative flower of India. It is rooted deep in Indian myth and its presence dates back to the beginnings of pre-Aryan history in India... The striking beauty of its semi-ellipse with radiating petals, tightly wrapped bud and large disc-like leaves has enthused the imagination of philosopher, artist and poet, and the lotus has permeated all aspects of Indian life and thought, earning for itself a prominent place in the Indian tradition. Used even today as a common votive offering, it is a vibrant link in a 5,000 year-old living culture.

Lotus goddess

This flawless lotus draws its nourishment from the depths of water. Through it, nature reflects the concept of the primordial life-giving forces from which the universe arises. It is this idea that leads to the religious connotation of the lotus, which is by far its most important function. The lotus Goddess is the early form of the goddess Sri Lakshmi, an important divinity of the Hindu pantheon. Brahma the creator, Vishnu the preserver and Shiva the destroyer form the all-encompassing trinity of Hindu mythology, under whose sway the whole universe is said to exist. Sri Lakshmi, portrayed standing on the lotus, is the consort of Vishnu. She is the focal point of female energy, the force corresponding to the concentration of male energy existing in Vishnu, the preserver. She is empowered to protect the fertility of the soil and the riches embedded in the heart of the earth. It is for this reason that Lakshmi is associated with the lotus which is the symbol of fertility and creation.

The Hindu gods were said to dwell not only in the realm of heaven but also in the plant and animal kingdoms. Shiva is symbolized in the *bilva* tree, Vishnu in the *myrobalam* and Sri Lakshmi in the lotus. In every Hindu home Lakshmi — the Lotus Goddess — stands with Shiva, Vishnu, Krishna (an incarnation of Vishnu), Saraswati (the goddess of knowledge) and Ganesha, the elephant god (the remover of obstacles). The pious Hindu offers prayers to her, for she is said to endow the devotee with success, fame, health and long life.

Yantra — power diagram

In another dimension of Hindu thought, tantric *yantra* have incorporated the sacred lotus. A *yantra* is a sacred, geometrical diagrammatic representation, designed to aid meditation. *Yantra* of varied structures help the disciple to attain each set goal. Later by progressive practice, the *sadhaka* or aspirant, can seek timeless truths beyond the concrete world of matter and energy. It is his goal to gain the inspiration that takes man beyond Self to merge with the Absolute, from which all energy emanates and into which it recedes. These 'power-diagrams' (*yantra*) have been evolved to channel the mind of the aspirant to unravel the mysteries of a higher consciousness. In lotus-*yantra,* the progressive radiation outward of the lotus petals depicts the soul in the process of spiritual fulfilment.

Rice flower art of Rangoli

From religion and philosophy, we now turn to the significance of the lotus motif in everyday art, popularly known as *rangoli.* Otherwise known as *alpona* in Bengal, *aripana* in Bihar, *mandana* in Rajasthan, *osa* in Orissa and *kolam* in Tamil Nadu, this traditional flower design or decoration is made out of rice powder or paste and coloured powders. In traditional Indian homes, *rangoli* is used at the doorstep, on the threshold and in the *puja* room (prayer chamber). *Rangoli* patterns have a symbolic meaning and incorporate some of the fundamentals of the sacred *yantra* mentioned earlier. The idea behind the art of *rangoli* is to cleanse and prepare the doorstep to bring in well-being and prosperity, by warding off evil spirits and welcoming the gods into the home. They employ a rich variety of designs comprised of dots, lines and floral motifs, with specific *rangoli* for special occasions. Dynamic *rangoli* lotus designs are very popular all over India. The number of petals varies; there are 5, 8, 9, 16, 32 and 1000-petalled lotus designs. Looking into the meaning of one such *rangoli,* that of the eight-petalled lotus, reveals the representational significance of this folk art form. Each petal has a particular meaning. Three of them denote the ego, intellect and mind (three facets of man), while the remaining five denote the five elements — ether, air, fire, water and earth. They reflect the internal and external world, the physical and the metaphysical, and thus depict the interaction of man with the elemental energies. Thus, even at the level of everyday life, the auspicious lotus is continuously relevant.

Lotus blooming from a god's navel

In Indian sculpture the lotus emerges as a predominant symbol. On the *torana* gates of the Sanchi *stupa,* built in the more elaborate Mahayana style, the goddess Lakshmi is seated on a fully open lotus flower, with lotus buds and blooms surrounding her. She holds a lotus, and there is a vessel filled with these flowers. It is significant to note that the lotus Goddess and the Hindu lotus-symbol of fertility are abundantly used in Buddhist sculpture, drawing on the earlier motifs of the sculptural tradition of the sub-continent. Later, in Gupta sculpture, *Vishnu Ananthasayina*, the reclining god Vishnu resting on the serpent Anantha, has a perfect lotus bloom growing out of his navel. The underlying symbolism seems to represent the fact that the lotus, symbol of fertility and creation, has blossomed forth from the Divine essence within Vishnu. Another interesting example of the lotus used in sculpture is the lotus-seat of Brahma, the creator — the very creator is supported by a lotus, seemingly that of Sri Lakshmi. However, in later sculpture, this lotus pedestal came to be used as a base for all gods and goddesses. The sculptor finds a close affinity to the lotus and uses it as a support for Shiva and Parvathi, Ganesha and many other deities.

Indo-Islamic architecture

During the Indo-Islamic period, new and alien influences were brought into India. Indigenous artisans have left marks of the earlier Indian tradition even as they erected Islamic structures adorned with calligraphy. In several monuments, carved lotus medallions are repeatedly found flanking arches. In the Taj Mahal at Agra and the tomb of Safdarjang and several other Islamic buildings with domes, one sees an inverted lotus-like flower marking the pinnacle of the dome. Inner domes of tombs and mosques are also crowned with patterns of the spreading lotus. At the Rang Mahal in Delhi's Red Fort, an elaborate lotus in smooth marble forms the base of a fountain. In the mosques at Mandu and Ahmedabad and the buildings of the erstwhile capital Fatehpur Sikri, the lotus continues to exist in the delicate 'stone-traceries'.

Lotus-eyed, lotus-faced...

Indian literature is known for its richness of metaphor and its exquisite poetic imagery. Descriptions of the lotus and descriptive epithets incorporating this flower enrich the texts. The great Indian epics Ramayana and Mahabharata, the Vishnupuranas and the works of Kalidasa and Bhasa are noted for their nature imagery. A few simple examples showing the nuances of descriptive words based on the lotus are: *padmini* — one possessed of the lotus; *padmavarna* — lotus-coloured; *padmatakshi* — lotus-eyed; *padmadalayatakshi* — eyes as long as the petals of the lotus; and *padmanana* — lotus-faced.

The lotus image also lives on in popular Indian names. Kamala, Kamalika, Kamalini, Kamalakshi, Padma, Padmalochani, and Padmavati are a few of the many names derived from the lotus.

Paintings

The classic frescoes of Ajanta contain an outstanding portrayal of the Bodhisattva Avalokiteshvara Padmapani. They depict a bodhisattva wearing a bejewelled crown, in his hands he holds a resplendent lotus bud symbolizing creation. He stands out screne among spectators who crowd around him and the muted colours of the natural dyes enhance the beauty of this rare painting. In the miniature paintings of the Kangra, Basoali, Rajput and Mewar schools, delicate paintings of Krishna, Radha and the *gopi* (shepherdesses) are depicted. In many such paintings, the artist with his single-haired brush carefully represents abundant lotus blooms in their natural settings. Such scenes abound in a variety of natural habitats in India and can be seen and experienced even today.

In quivering fingers of dancers

India has a rich variety of classical and folk dance traditions. Rhythm, graceful movements and sensitive expressions together with *hasta-mudra* (had gestures) play an important role in the interpretive aspect of dance. Hands become 'vehicles of speech', and an intricately formulated visual language, both expressive and artistic, has been evolved. The dancer's hands form elaborate symbols representing words and ideas. The sun, moon, peacocks, fish, deer, tridents, altars, kings, gods and goddesses are all deftly represented. The lotus has its own *mudra* (hand gestures). The *padmakosa* is a *mudra* that depicts the lotus bud and the *ala padma*, the full-blown lotus. With gently quivering fingers the dancer celebrates the blooming of the lotus. In Indian music too, the lotus is a common epithet used in song. In one of the initial *geeta* (elementary songs), a child learning Karnataka music sings "*Sarasijasana Janani*" (the Mother Goddess seated on the lotus). Later, the mature singer invokes the goddess — '*Kamalambam bajare*' (may the Goddess Lotus be worshipped). Innumerable expressions of melody evolve around the lotus.

Lotus posture in Yoga tradition

In the ancient tradition of *yoga* the body is prepared to achieve spiritual awakening. In this process the energies of the body are harnessed and directed. The *sadhaka* (disciple) sits in the *Padmasana* (the lotus posture) with legs crossed, the soles of the feet facing upwards, hands placed on the lap with palms facing upwards, eyes concentrated on the tip of the nose, body erect and breath controlled.

He prepares himself thus for the moment of self-realization when he will transcend the physical.

The lotus, symbol of fertility, encompasses the beginning and culmination of all creation and spiritual evolution. At every level of Indian thought and life, it merges with the reality of contemporary living. The lotus — sacred flower of India — remains eternally relevant.

Flowers and Islamic Architecture

Two sources of floral arabesque

Flowers and floral geometric designs are a major motif in Islamic architecture. They are used to overcome the *horror vaccui*, and are executed in every decorative architectural medium known to the Muslims, from stucco to gemstone mosaic. The impetus for the development of intricate non-figurative floral patterns or arabesque, which were to become the hallmark of Islamic civilization, came from two sources. One supposedly was the heavily iconoclastic semitic roots of Islam, which manifests itself in an Islamic injunction forbidding the creation or display or images of living beings. Another source, one condoning gardens, is in the *Quran* itself.

Give thou good tidings to those who
believe and do deeds of righteousness,
that for them await gardens underneath
which rivers flow.
(*Quran.*, Sura 11:25)

Earthy manifestation of paradise

To the Muslims of the seventh century, these verses showed the path Islamic artistic expression should take. The birth-place of Islam, i.e., Arabia, and the surrounding areas of the Middle East, were dry harsh lands, where people devoted their lives to harnessing recalcitrant waters and outguessing nature in order to live. In such utilitarian circumstances a garden was unimaginable, and a flower was a thing of great beauty and luxury. Only in God's paradise could one enjoy the flowing water, shady trees, sweet-smelling bushes and flowers of nature, for only there was subsistence not an issue. On Earth, men who were rich and powerful enough to control nature in a garden were worthy of being kings. To the Muslim patricians, gardens and flowers were symbols of sovereignty and power. To the less fortunate they were symbols of God's beneficence and bounty in the life hereafter, and the multiplicity of His creation. Thus flowers were given religious and secular approval, and applied to intricate geometrical patterns that Muslim architects and artists had developed using Greek mathematics coupled with mystical philosophy.

Common idioms, individual sensibilities

Architecture throughout the Muslim world has drawn from a common set of artistic and decorative idioms. Cultures from diverse geographic areas have also manifested their own individual sensibilities in their buildings. In floral architectural decoration, the shared motifs come from the lands the Muslims conquered; the vine scrolls and acanthus leaves from the eastern Mediterranean region, the rosette and palm tree from the ancient Near East, and the lotus from Egypt and India. Of course, all these were transformed to a certain extent by their alliance with the Islamic aesthetics of geometric continuity.

In Turkey, although the classical or shared idiom provided the basis of architectural decoration, other flowers were also represented. In the portals of a thirteenth century stone building in Anatolia (Ulu Cami) exist ornately carved floral cornucopias in deep relief, with the acanthus leaves split, filled with filigree, stretched and curved, and placed next to palmettos and overworked lotus to create a fantastic tree. Historically similar subjects had been created by the Byzantines, but in mosaics, and none so organic and burgeoning with life. By the sixteenth century, architectural decoration had toned down and was more two-dimensional. Iznik tiles on the walls of the palace of the Ottoman sultans, Top Kapu Saray, are painted with hyacinths, carnations, and tulips, interwoven with spiralling vegetal scrolls and lotuses. Large areas are often covered with flowers faithfully copied from nature, but painted in such vivid or unnatural colours that they defy identification. Similarly in Iran and Southern Asia, flowers were rendered in every known architectural decorative medium: stucco, tile, fresco, and faience, gemstone and mirror mosaics. The arabesque reached its zenith on the domes and cupolas of the seventeenth century mosques of Isfahan. Split acanthus leaf and vine scrolls vied with extravagant lotus nodes and palmettes, while the odd peony-like flower and leaf were used to fill space and balance the design. Soon the acanthus leaf was to lose what little naturalism it possessed in the arabesque and be rendered like a handkerchief fluttering in space. Though the Mughal emperors of southern Asia borrowed floral ornamentation from Iran, they altered it: stucco arabesques became more plastic and organic, while marble inlay became more subdued. European influence in the seventeenth century and the native naturalism of the Indian artist is manifest in the marble and stucco portraits of the rose and lily found on the interior palace walls. Another idiosyncrasy was the predominance of twelve and sixteen-petalled rosettes used to mark the empty wall space of spandrel or arch.

If an inventory were made of the flowers in Islamic architectural design, the list would be brief and boring. What distinguishes Islamic floral patterns are the variations of a single motif. The vine scroll, palmette, or rosette rendered in stucco in southern Asia is quite different from one in Spain; the arabesque on a cupola in Cairo is not the same as one in Isfahan. The difference lies in the rendering of the subject. In Spain the arabesque is like filigree, in Cairo it is bold and angular, in Isfahan, colourful and fluid, and in India, bold and serpentine. The design is the same, but the spirit and eye are different, and this manifests itself in differences in the components of the design. For example, the variations on the lotus or acanthus leaf in the Islamic world must be innumerable.

Illusory world in architecture

Flowers have also appeared in other ways in Islamic architecture. Often, large gardens were laid out with a conscious intent to create a *Quranic* paradise on earth. The patron, often a king or prince, would enjoy his garden from a well-placed open *kiosk*, which, in turn, was richly ornamented with floral patterns, and covered with carpets woven in the *chahar bagh*, or four-part garden, design. In warmer countries like Iran and India, these garden *kiosk*, supplemented by tents embroidered with floral patterns, became the summer palaces of the kings. During the harsh winters of Iran, the architectural ornamentation of the winter palaces was augmented with colourful paper flowers and free-standing gilt trees bearing jewelled flowers and birds. The fourteenth century palace in Granada, Spain, Al Hamra, was built around courtyards filled with flowers, sweet-smelling bushes, and running water, so that from every exquisitely ornamented room, a door or window would ensure access to a charming exterior garden. Each exterior scene was reflected in the floral stucco tracery of the interior walls. This rich vegetation, both man-made and natural, created in Islamic architecture an illusory world with nebulous boundaries, symbolising the labyrinth at whose centre lies power and hidden knowledge-gnosis.

Prevailing even now...

Today, flowers are seldom used in architectural ornamentation, for the decorative techniques of old are too expensive for individuals to afford, and the modern state favours more utilitarian architectural forms. However, flowers and floral motifs continue to hold an important place in the Islamic world. Throughout the Middle East and southern Asia, interior decoration relies on the floral motif in carpets, textiles, pottery and metalwork. Added to this the flower has retained and added to its symbolic significance; besides evoking Paradise, it is a symbol for passion, purity, earthly beauty and spiritual love, to name but a few. Flowers adorn saints' tombs, are stuck on to the hats of the Chitrali tribesmen and are worn by beautiful women from Indonesia to northern Africa.

Ikebana and Cherry Blossom Viewing — A Japanese Attitude toward Flowers

The natural landscape of Japan is full of variety and shows changes with every season. In the mountains and fields many flowers bloom from spring to summer and from summer to autumn and in the autumn the fruit on the trees ripen and the leaves of deciduous trees change colour.

The cherry blossom, the Japanese national flower, is found all over the country and there is a large number of garden varieties as well. The flowers bloom every year around 20 March in the south. As the days grow warmer the cherry blossom blooms in different parts of the country and in about two months, by mid-May, they blossom in the north. "The cherry blossom front line moves north."

The colouring of the leaves in the fall, together with the cherry blossoms in the spring, are the two highlights of Japan's natural beauty. The spectacular colouring of deciduous trees is represented by the maple and the leaves begin to turn red around 20 October in the north. "The front line of the trees changing colour moves south" and by the end of November the leaves of the trees in the south begin to change colour. Although the spring cherry blossoms are quite a sight, the subtle hues of the tinted autumn leaves are also of outstanding beauty and are often described as brocade-like.

The Japanese have treasured such scenes woven by nature and this has given rise to special feelings towards plants including, of course, flowers.

Flowers in ancient literary works

The variety of plants and their uses which appear in the *Kojiki*, the oldest historical record in Japan that was compiled in the eighth century, and the *Manyoshu*, Japan's oldest collection of poems, also gives us an idea of the great interest in plants held by people in ancient Japan.

In the *Manyoshu*, in particular, of a total of 4,500 poems, about a third are poems about a variety of 160 types of plants, many of which use flowers metaphorically to express some inner emotion. The plants themselves are primarily for practical use and it is not recorded that they were at this time picked to be put in a vase and admired. However, with 138 poems on the bush clover, 87 on the pine, 112 on the plum and 42 on the cherry blossom, showing considerable interest in beautiful flowers and trees, so perhaps, it may be said, they did pick flowers and put them in vases to admire. Thereafter, in the *Kokinwakashu* and the *Makuranososhi*, written from the latter part of the tenth to the eleventh century, there are records of flowers being placed in a vase, giving evidence that flowers were being enjoyed in that way by this time.

Sacred medium where gods visit

On the other hand, before the Japanese began enjoying flowers in this way they believed, from ancient times, in trees and flowers as sacred media. People believed that sacred spirits lived within trees and flowers or that the gods visited these plants, so that trees and flowers were placed in special places which were then considered sacred sites or they were planted in everyday places which people hoped the gods would visit. This idea of the gods visiting plants served as the basis of prayers for an abundant harvest or for purification in pre-celebration of the harvest and gave rise to various customs within the agrarian society. Even today vestiges of those customs can be found in different parts of the country. Many of the sacred media were indeciduous trees. That these trees kept their leaves green all winter gave them a semblance of immortality which made such trees symbols of everlasting life.

Although the most representative flower used in Buddhist offering is the lotus, in time beautiful flowers of all seasons and branches of indeciduous trees also came to be used as offerings.

Such customs as worshipping plants as sacred media, offering flowers and generally admiring the beauty of flowers eventually led to the birth of *ikebana*, or flower arrangement.

Manifold significances of 'flower'

The meaning that the word 'flower' has to the Japanese mind is quite broad and the word is used to indicate not only individual flowers and flowers in general, but also, grasses and tree branches in certain contexts. Especially in *ikebana* any plant that is used is simply called 'flower'.

Furthermore, in Japan 'flower' would mean specifically the cherry blossom. Found all over the country the cherry blossom is most familiar to the people and considered a natural calendar which, by the flowering of its blossoms, was thought to predict that year's harvest. The cherry blossom which bloomed in full glory was a pre-celebration for an abundant rice harvest and the people rejoiced at its flowering as if they had been promised the joys of a rich crop in the fall. First among all flowers was the cherry blossom.

In Japan the quality of flowers is projected onto things that are beautiful or flashy regardless of whether or not they are plants and, for example, someone is said to "have the quality of a flower". That is to say that that person has something 'flowery' about him/her. There are also many words that include the character for flower. The Japanese idea of flower is very broad and the word 'flower' has many shades of meaning.

Ikebana — an everyday art unique to Japan

Ikebana, flower arrangement, was born around the fourteenth century from the idea of plants as sacred media and practice of flower offerings and admiring flowers placed in a vase, as mentioned earlier. The practice of placing flowers in a vase to enjoy their beauty is universal but *ikebana* differs from other such practices in that the flowers in one vase are given a definite style or arrangement.

At first the flowers were arranged as offerings so that their arrangement took the form of flowers placed vertically in a vase, or the 'standing flower' style. Thereafter, between the fourteenth and twentieth centuries six major styles of *ikebana* evolved under the influence of different historical periods and architectural styles and these are still in existence today.

What *ikebana* expresses within one vase is the natural environment of Japan — the fields, mountains and waterfronts — and the arrangement of the flowers reflects the artists' feelings towards them. In particular, the emphasis that is placed on the origin of each flower, including its environmental surroundings, is a reflection of the Japanese view of nature.

Originally *ikebana* was practised among the court nobility and *samurai* (warrior class) families but in the eighteenth century it spread to the wealthy townsmen and by the nineteenth century it was widely practised among the common people. In present times, especially since the second World War, there has been a great *ikebana* boom, and if those who have taken *ikebana* lessons even once are counted the *ikebana* population amounts to thirty million and the number of different *ikebana* 'schools' is said to be 300 or 400.

In *ikebana* there are certain rules as to what type of flower is to be used in each season or on certain holidays and many of these rules are still held today. This again reflects a certain view of nature and special feelings for the flowers. Today, however, many arrangements are based not only on the traditionally-used flowers but also on the beauty of the colours and shapes of the different flowers themselves.

People gather around cherry blossoms

Along with *ikebana*, a custom that is unique to Japan is flower viewing. Although *ikebana* is a way of depicting nature, it may be said that it is also a way of appreciating nature by bringing it closer to man. Flower viewing on the other hand involves going to the blossoming flowers themselves to appreciate them as they are. It is a view of nature as a macrocosmos. As the word 'flower' itself meant the cherry blossom, flower viewing too generally means cherry blossom viewing. To a Japanese, a spring without cherry blossoms is no doubt unthinkable.

People also go plum blossom viewing, but unlike the plum whose individual flowers each bloom as if unfolding gradually, the cherry blossom blooms and is gone in seven days. As the saying, "a cherry tree unseen for three days" (that is, a cherry tree unseen for three days may already be in full bloom or it may have lost its flowers completely) indicates, an entire cherry tree blossoms very quickly. It is perhaps the way the cherry blossoms bloom that has captured the Japanese heart. The cherry blossom also loses its petals very quickly. A certain gallantry is seen in the way the cherry blooms suddenly and is gone in a whiff, and this gallantry is considered of the highest virtue, which makes people relate to the flower even more. The custom of flower viewing seems, from literature and picture scrolls, to have been practised among the Heian nobility by around the tenth century and, just as many customs were passed on from aristocratic and *samurai* families to the common people, flower viewing also spread to the Edo populace by the seventeenth century.

The picnic beneath the cherry blossoms gave the people a chance not only to view the beautiful flowers but also to come out into the warm spring air after a long, cold winter, and for the oppressed common people, to throw their cares to the wind. With the mild spring climate people became light-hearted. With food and drink and merrymaking among friends and neighbours the spirits rise. All formality is laid aside.

Falling and fallen petals have their own beauty

The blooming of the cherry blossom is beautiful indeed but the way its petals fall off is also a sight worth seeing. The petals scattered by the wind are described as a 'flower blizzard' or 'flower storm' and their sight is also greatly enjoyed. There is a custom of viewing cherry blossoms at night as well when people get even more high-spirited than during the day. The beauty of the cherry blossoms highlighted against the dark of the night will be described by any Japanese as of "unsurpassed beauty".

The way flowers lose their petals, and flowers seen at night suggest the world after death — they seem to belong to another world. We are offered a chance to participate in the joys of a world of dreams that is beyond reality. Life after death — a land of happiness — is reflected in flowers or leaves such as petals of cherry blossoms, the camellia flowers or deciduous leaves that have changed their colour falling in the garden. Some gardens are even landscaped for such an effect. This effect has also been adopted as a motif in flower arrangement.

Seeking natural beauty

People also go out to view other blossoms. Enjoying the sight of beautiful flowers is, after all, a release from mundane reality. People go to see peonies and wisteria in May, irises in June, the lotus in July, bush clover in September, the chrysanthemum and colouring leaves in October, all in the same spirit as a continuation of flower viewing.

In Japan there is a word that means 'snow-moon-flower'. This points to the beauty of each season which is enjoyed through snow-scene viewing or moon viewing just like flower viewing. The beauty of the moon or of a snow-covered scene is appreciated with similar feelings to those evoked by various flowers.

Annual events and flowers

Besides *ikebana* and cherry blossom viewing, there are various aspects of Japanese life closely associated with flowers. Among such annual events, I will mention two, Doll's Festival in March and Tango Festival in May.

March third is the girls' seasonal festival which is also called the Peach Festival. A set of *hina* dolls is put on display with peach blossoms to celebrate this day. The *hina* dolls are remnants of images used for purification ceremonies. Paper is cut into human form and the body is stroked and floated on water in the belief that this would purify the person represented. This custom is still observed at shrines. These images of man later became dolls.

The peach came to Japan from China where in ancient belief it was thought to purge noxious vapours. This belief was adopted in Japan where the custom of drinking peach wine with a floating peach blossom was observed at the Imperial Court. As the Doll's Festival came to be celebrated among the people the practice of decorating dolls with peach blossoms also spread. The peach is used as a decoration to purge noxious vapours and in the hope that young girls may grow as pretty as peach blossom. Yellow blossoms go well with the peach so that rape-blossoms are always added to the peach decorations. In the past a yellow Japanese rose was used. The Doll's Festival is also held in many areas a month later on April third. May fifth is the Tango Festival (Boy's festival) which is also known as the Iris Festival. This custom also came from China. On this day there is a custom of displaying warrior dolls and carp streamers, placing branches of mugwort and irises (sweet flag) on the roof and taking an iris bath using iris leaves. It was a day to purify the body and purge it of evil spirits with the medical properties and smell of the iris or mugwort and pray for the healthy growth of boys.

Rice cakes wrapped in oak leaves and rice dumplings wrapped in bamboo leaves are also eaten on this day.

Thai Sensitivity and Wisdom Reflected in Flowers

Country full of flowers

Abundant is Thailand in flora species ranging from ferns, flower plants and fruit trees to large trees that supply timber for building and industry. An almost endless number of flower plants are to be found all over the country. Many of these plants bear flowers which give off a perfume-like fragrance. Like people, flowers are blessed with different 'personalities'. Their beauty can be fabulous, exotic, subdued or mysterious. Irrespective of their peculiarities, flowers of all descriptions add to the delights of Thai life. Indeed, for the Thais who live under the tropical climate, flowers and plants have always been an inseparable part of their livelihood. In early times, flowers featured as a matter of course in cooking, cosmetics, decoration, medicine, and worship. With the advent of modern technological development, the traditional role of Thai flowers has somewhat diminished. On the positive side, knowledge of bio-engineering has enabled Thai horticulturists to develop hybrids and render rare flower species available to a greater mass of the public.

It is mindboggling to give a fair estimate of the number of floral species now existing in Thailand. The task becomes somewhat simpler when one limits the effort to a specific genus. Take orchids for instance. There are probably well over one thousand species of wild orchids now flourishing in the Thai forests. Most of them bear flowers all year round. During the hot season, the spectacle of Dendobrium aggregatum hanging from overarching branches of a large tree is a sight to behold. Their purple and bluish colours tend to exert a cooling effect on trekkers who brave that hot and humid weather. In winter, Paphilpedlum exul rhynchostylis adorning the canopy of a large towering tree greets the eyes of those who choose to enjoy the Thai jungle in the cold part of the year.

There is a motley array of indigenous plants which flower during some particular season of the year. It is a great pity that most Thais rarely associate flowers with seasons. This may be partly due to the abundance of floral plants in Thailand plus the fact that green thumbs can induce any flower plants to bloom at any chosen time of the year. Of all flowers grown in Thailand, about two thirds are scented. The scents of Thai flowers can be delicately light, extremely evanescent or even intoxicating. As in many aspects of life, nature has its own way of compensating. Unscented flowers are usually more colourful and more attractive than the scented kind.

Flowers sung by travelling poets

Thai flowers have always had special meanings for poets of antiquity. It is a common practice among Thai romantic poets to associate women with flowers. Peculiar to the Thai language and culture, many first names of persons do not indicate whether individuals are male or female. There are a few exceptions. One of these is when names of flowers are used as first names. In such cases it is most likely that persons with such names are female. A fair approximation to a treatise on Thai flowers and names of Thai women of the past can be found in so-called 'travelling poems'. In this type of verse, poets, most of whom are men, describe the beauty of local flowers and their reminiscence of women in their lives.

Flowers to cure the disease

Man's dependence upon plants for the essentials of his existence is common to all cultures. Leaves, stems, trunks and roots have been used as food, drink and drugs in numerous ways.

The uses of flowers for such purposes are not, however, as well known. For example very few modern Thais know that *dok kajorn dok kae* (Sesbania grandiflora) and *dok snoh* (Strychnonos nuxvomica) can be consumed as cooked vegetables. *Dok sarapee* (Mammea siamensis), *dok mali* (Jasmin smabac), *dok bunnag* (Mesua ferrea) and *dok pikul* (Mimusup lengi) in alcohol or hot water are considered mild medicines good for heart complaints. *Dok kamfoy* or safflower (Carthamus) and *dok kalong* (Bauhinia) employed in the same way are supposed to bring down high fever as well as to lower blood pressure. *Dok rak* (Calotropis gigantea) is an antidote for various forms of skin diseases and *dok lien* is a chief ingredient in a medicine used for deworming and strengthening a weak bladder.

Dok mali (Jasmine sambac), *dok kradanga* or *ylang* (Cananga odorata), and other flowers which have a sweet scent are used to give fragrance to cakes, drinking water and dresses.

To beautify, to mourn

Traditional Thai women employ a variety of flowers to beautify themselves. A 'champa' flower (Michelia) suspended from the hair over one cheek adds glamour to a tanned skin and dark brown eyes. A hibiscus flower may be tucked above an ear. Many kinds of flowers can be made into garlands which are worn around chignons or the neck and the wrist.

In the annual traditional homage-paying to teachers, Thai school *children* or even university students present three kinds of flowers to their teachers. They are flowers of the egg-plant tree, the ixora shrub and grass. These flowers are thought to symbolize humility and the fertile stage of wisdom and learning.

Flowers are used by the Thais to mourn death. *Dok songlin* (tuberose) is the only kind of flower used for this purpose and perhaps nothing else. The reason is obvious: its over-powering scent to the point of sickening is a morbid reminder of the grim occasion.

Pretty but unfavoured flowers

Some floral plants such as *dok champa* (Michelia), *dok lantom* (Frangipani), although they bear rather pretty flowers, are not grown in the gardens of most Thais. They are likely to be found in the compounds of a Buddhist temple or even cemetery. The names of these flowers in vernacular only convey either sadness or an ineffectual situation. Thai scholars have suggested explanations for this strange practice and taboo. According to one explanation, these plants, in spite of their sturdy and healthy appearance, in fact have weak and brittle branches and thus present a real risk to the life and limbs of the children who might be tempted to climb them and sit on their branches. Names of ill import are given to these trees to discourage the Thais from growing them near their homes as a measure to protect young children from possible dangers.

Flowers with fascinating names such as *dok rak* (Calatropis) meaning the flower of love, and *dok baan mai roo roay* (Gomphrena) meaning the flower which knows nothing of fading, are made into garlands and bouquets and presented to a bride and bridegroom on their wedding day.

Lotus, net, and chandelier

Thai floral decoration, an art long in practice since the early times of history, makes use not only of flowers but also leaves, branches, pins, thread containers and other accessories to hold the composition in place.

One of the most basic forms of Thai floral arrangement is *poom.* This is made up of flowers arranged into a lotus shape on a stem glass bowl. The lotus form is made possible by sculpted moist sand. *Dok baan mai roo roay* or bachelor's buttons on pins are stuck one by one into the sand until the whole surface is covered. The pattern is achieved by the use of flowers of different colours.

Another type of Thai floral arrangement is in the form of a net cover over a saffron robe folded into a rectangular shape. Flowers used are crown flowers (*dok rak*), bachelor's buttons (*dok baan mai roo roay*), and jasmines (*dok mali*).

Similar to the net-type floral arrangement is the flower curtain prepared from the same types of flowers.

The Thai floral arrangement that proves most popular among the Thais and visitors to Thailand is the chandelier type. For this type of floral decoration, banana leaves and stems are also used. Although hung from the ceiling the chandelier-type floral decoration is never used as a chandelier but simply as a floral decoration.

Symbolic patterns

Flowers in their natural state and otherwise have captured the human imagination in an almost magical way. Artists and philosophers are known to be inspired by the beauty of flowers. Objects and events which carry special significance to man have been symbolized by flowers of various descriptions. In Thailand, three lotus buds represent the Buddhist Triple Gems, i.e. Lord Buddha, Dharma and the Buddhist Sangha. In modern times, many institutions have adopted some flowers to represent their organizations, for example: *chamchuri* (Samanea saman) by Chulalonghorn University; *dok pradoo* by the Royal Thai Navy; and *dok mali* (Jasmine sambac) as the symbol of Mother's Day.

Gold shower flower — the national flower of Thailand

One question that flower lovers outside Thailand would like to ask their Thai counterparts concerns the flower which represents Thailand. Unknown to many Thais is the fact that there is such a thing as the Thai national flower. About three decades ago, an astute gathering of horticulturists convened by an authority no other than the Ministry of Agriculture deemed it appropriate to declare *dok rajpreuk,* flower of the royal plant (Cassia fistula) known under the English name of 'gold shower flower', as the national flower of Thailand. This is one of the trees that blossom during the hot season. The golden shower tree with its luxuriant racemes of bright yellow flowers drooping gently in the sun augurs well for Thailand and her people.

Thailand, for all its rich treasures of flower plants, has no national flower garden. In some ways the Thais do not really need it. At Chatuchak Public Park in the northern suburb of Bangkok, there are a multitude of nurseries which sell what appears to be an endless variety of pot flower plants. These include those that are indigenous to Thailand and those that have been recently introduced to their new home. During weekends, Bangkokians and visitors flock to the areas to admire and buy flowers and plants which they may have seen for the first time in their lives.

Flower Appreciation — A Chinese Tradition

Long history of flower appreciation in China

In the early years of the Zhou dynasty over 2,000 years ago, books were written classifying various kinds of flowers and their names, and poems were compiled extolling the beauty of flowers. Details of flower appreciation were described in such works as the *Records of Chrysanthemums* by Liu Meng in the Song dynasty (960-1279), the *Chronicle of Flowers* compiled by Chen Yong in the Southern Song dynasty (1127-1279); The *Book of Flowers* by Wang Xiangyu of the Ming dynasty (1368-1644), and the ancient book the *Peony*. Numerous poems and rhymes have been written ever since ancient times expressing people's emotion and sentiments on flowers.

Plum — advanced guard of spring

Noted for its ability to withstand frost and cold, the plum is the "advanced guard" of the 24 major flowers which greet the coming of spring. The Chinese people cherish a deep attachment to plum blossom. Pine, bamboo and plum are extolled as the three famous plants of the winter season. Plum, orchid, bamboo and chrysanthemum are regarded as the four best flowers and plants, with plum taking the lead. It has inspired countless poems, paintings and anecdotes.

With its unique quality of blossoming in the winter, the plum is highly symbolic of man's character. From ancient times to this day, it has had a far-reaching spiritual influence on the Chinese people. Throughout China's history, revolutionaries and patriots have adopted the image of the plum to symbolize their own aspirations and will.

Plum trees and politics

The famous Qing philosopher and literary figure Gong Zizhen(1779-1841) composed the masterpiece "On Sick Plum Trees" as a metaphor for the political situation. It said that cultivation of the plum was very popular in Zhejiang and Jiangsu provinces. However, in the eyes of the feudal ruling class, plum trees with twisted trunks were charming while those with straight trunks were misshapen. Branches had to be thin because thick branches were thought to be unsightly. As a result, plum plants were grafted, and the branches were over-pruned. The tender branches were cut and the straight trunks were bent, and their growth was thus checked. These plum trees were "sick". In his fury, the author bought 300 potted plum plants and set up a clinic for sick plums. He was determined to devote the rest of his life to curing the ill-shaped plum trees. Of course this is a satire on how the feudal ruling class repressed talented people. Through this masterpiece, the author showed his noble aspiration of devoting himself to the promotion of talent.

'Professor Plum'

Chen Junyu, a contemporary botanist specializing in the cultivation of plum trees, is known for his character, which is similar to that of the plum. A professor at the Beijing Institute of Forestry, he devoted more than four decades of his life to the cultivation of plum trees at the Beijing Botanical Garden. Unfortunately, during the ultra-Leftist time of the 1960s, the 2,000 plum trees he and his colleagues had cultivated with painstaking care were rooted out with a bulldozer. This almost killed him. Utterly disillusioned, he was forced to move from Beijing to Nanjing. After he came back to Beijing upon his rehabilitation, the first thing he did was to visit the plum orchard at Fragrant Hills where he had worked. To his surprise he found three surviving trees. The next day he took his luggage to the botanical garden and set about cultivating the plum trees.

The plum garden has now been restored. People in Beijing who love the plum need not travel to the south of China to see it. This plum botanist says, "The character of the plum is similar to the character of the Chinese people — reserved, and keeping its feeling under control. Plum is not only charming, but has the novel quality of withstanding bad natural conditions." He is one of those who suggest that the plum blossom should be made the national flower.

Peony — the king of flowers

Others, however, feel just as strongly that the peony should be the national flower. In the last years of the Qing dynasty, it was so named.

It is regarded as the king of flowers for its large, fragrant blossoms and gorgeous colours. There are more than 300 varieties. Through the centuries many books on peonies have been written, and some ancient poems portrayed it as the national flower: "Like rosy clouds, the peony blossoms; their brilliant and fascinating colour spreads out in the vast field. The blossoms of other flowers greet this national flower." Some peonies are named after the places where they originated, some for their rare colour, such as *zi yan duo zhu* (startling purple overshadowing the shining pearls) and *yin shui jin lin* (silvery ripple and golden scale), and some after beautiful women in history. There are such names as *yutian xiun* (jade celestials), *xue furen* (snowy lady), *feiyanhongzhuang* (flying swallow clad in red), *fen xiang nu* (delicate maidens in pink costume) an *sui yang fei* (tipsy Concubine Yang).

Tipsy concubine Yang

Zui yang fei is named after Tang Emperor Li Longji's favourite concubine Yang Gui Fei. One day in the late spring of 743, Emperor Li Longji and Yang went to the Chenxiangting Pavilion to admire peony blossoms. The noted singer Li Guixian from the imperial song and dance troupe performed for them. Unsatisfied with his old songs, Emperor Li Longji said, "Now that we are here to admire these precious flowers, how can you entertain my concubine with such old songs?" He ordered Li to bring a piece of paper and asked the poet Li Bai to improvise some new verses instantly. The sight of the garden full of charming peony blossoms in front of the Chenxiangting Pavilion filled the poet with inspiration. He picked up his brush and wrote three poems.

While Li Guixian sang the songs with new verses, the emperor played a jade flute to accompany him. Leaning against the balustrade, Concubine Yang sipped a glass of grape wine. The Chenxiangting Pavilion still exists, and the peony plants *Wei zi* and *Yao huang* are still grown in Xi'an. However, instead of emperors, concubines, generals and royalty, the admirers are ordinary people.

Unyielding to power

The peony was loved not just in the imperial palaces in ancient Chang'an (today's Xi'an), it was grown widely in ordinary people's homes. It was only years later that Lyoyang surpassed Chang'an in the cultivation of peonies. Legend has it that on a snowy day Empress Wu Zetian (624-705) declared that she planned to tour the imperial garden the next morning. She ordered that "spring must come instantly, and the flowers must blossom before dawn."

Early next morning all the flowers blossomed ahead of season, yielding to the empress's power, except the peony. Empress Wu was furious and ordered 4,000 peony plants to be removed from Chang'an to Luoyang. But contrary to her expectations, the peony flourished in Luoyang. On learning this, Empress Wu ordered all the peony plants to be burned. But after the fire, the peony blossom took on a more striking red colour, a great attraction to people. And it became the new *jiao* (burnt) *gu* (bone) peony.

Luoyan people and peony

In the Song dynasty (420-479) the peony became the biggest attraction of all the flowers in Luoyang according to the *Chronicle of Customs* by Ouyang Xiu. When peonies were in full blossom, a Luoyang tradition for both rich and poor officials and commoners, was to decorate homes with peony flowers. People toured peony gardens and music could be heard everywhere. Rich and noble families would hold banquets, inviting guests especially to admire the peony blossoms they had grown. Literary figures wrote lyrics, essays and poems to extol the fascinating peonies.

Legend has it that one high official held a banquet in the peony blossoming season. When the guests arrived, they were surprised to find no peony flowers in the banquet hall. After a while the official asked a servant, "Is the fragrance coming?" His man answered, "Yes", and the host ordered a curtain rolled up. A fragrant smell instantly came from the inner chamber. Ten beautiful young ladies singing and carrying cups of wine and stringed instruments walked gracefully into the hall. The charming women, clad in white and decorated with peony flowers on their collars, danced and sang. When the performance was over, the curtain was lowered. After a while, up went the curtain again and a fragrant smell filled the air. Another ten ladies appeared, clad in peony-patterned costumes. A total of ten performances were presented at the banquet while ten rounds of wine were drunk. All the songs performed at the banquet were related to peonies. This was a rare, grand instance of peony appreciation! Today, peony flowers are grown throughout China, in the south and north. They symbolize the prosperity and bright future of the Chinese people, and also happiness. As an ancient poem says: "The flower blossoms to the will of the people".

From the depths of their hearts

Flower appreciation requires sophisticated taste. "Appreciating" flowers is not the same as "looking at" flowers. As a special art, flower appreciation requires a strong aesthetic feeling and can produce a rich and comprehensive response. In other words, a fascination for flowers can inspire in people a noble response from the depths of their hearts. The accomplishments Chinese people have made in flower appreciation are unique and special.

Part 2

Folk Dances in Asian Villages

Design of dancing figures modelled on that found in the Piman Patthaya Palace in the Royal Palace of Thailand.

Folk Dances

Folk and Tribal Dances of the Indian Sub-Continent

For untold centuries India, with its vast variety of ethnic groups, races and cultural groups has been a veritable treasure-house of dance and music.

The contemporary Indian classical dance forms which are governed by elaborate technique and stylized systems of both pure movement and 'mime' have had their origins in the dances of the common people. This many-hued garden of dances has not only survived as a vestige of the past, but continues to have the inner vigour and vitality to influence and shape more sophisticated and self-conscious art forms. Thus, the folk and classical forms in India are not mutually exclusive: they are in continual dialogue. The classical forms occasionally provide the thematic content and gravity to folk forms; the folk forms provide the freshness, strength and buoyancy to modern forms.

There is not a region, a valley or mountain, a sea-coast or a plain, which does not have its characteristic folk dances and songs. From Kashmir in the North to Kanya Kumari in the South, from Saurashtra and Maharashtra in the West to Manipur and Assam in the East, each region district and community has its particular folk music and dance. Roughly speaking depending on the level of social and cultural development, these dances can be grouped under the three categories of tribal, village folk community and traditional ritual dances.

The themes of the dances are simple but not naive; sometimes they revolve around the daily tasks on the field of sowing and reaping the harvest, of pounding rice, of weaving textiles, of catching birds and insects: at others they celebrate victory in war or the success in a hunt: and yet at others, it is the abstract movement of an actual ritual performed to propitiate the gods, or dances which may have a magical import. Finally there are the community dances for all seasons and festivals when men and women dance for sheer joy to celebrate Spring, the Rains, Autumn and Winter. Men and women and children all dance; there is no cleavage between performers and audience: everyone is a participator, a creator. There is no entertainer and entertained.

Nature has silently and unobtrusively fashioned the movements of the dance, as it has the lives of the people who continue to live in continual communion with it. The Himalayan mountainous ranges extend over a large area in India; all the dances of the mountains have something in common, whether they come from Kashmir, Himachal Pradesh or Uttar Pradesh or Darjeeling. The bend of the knees, the long swaying movements, the intertwined arms recreate the undulating ranges of the Himalayas. The agitated movements and abrupt changes of posture in the otherwise flowing lyrical movements of the Eastern region particularly Assam and Manipur, speak of sudden storm and uprooting of trees. The tense and watchful and carefully choreographed attitudes in the dancing of the Nagas of NEFA (North East Frontier Agency), Meghalaya, Manipur and Assam denote the unknown perils of the jungle. The dances of the fishermen of Saurashtra suggest the roaring waves of the sea while the folk dances of the plains present a different picture of colour and rhythm by contrast.

Folk dances of particular regions of India have both a regional autonomy and features which are common to other regions of India. While the ecology, environment and agricultural functions give a distinctiveness, legend, myth literature unite them to other parts. The dances have survived through many centuries of Indian history and have provided a continuity to the Indian tradition which is not stagnant, as it is constantly adapting itself to new conditions and assimilating influences. Pliability and flexibility is of essence: scope for self-expression, improvisation, is the secret of its survival.

As has been mentioned above, all these dances in their staggering multiplicity can be divided into the dances of the tribal and rural communities of India. A tribal belt runs through all parts of India be it the Himalayas from the North to the East; or the plains and the marshlands or the sea-coasts. All these varied groups comprising many racial and ethnic strands ranging from the Austric to the Mongoloid, from the Aryans to the Dravidians, are people who represent the pre-agricultural state of civilization. While most of them have taken to agriculture and tool cultivation today, their dances and music continue to recall the functions of hunting, fishing, food gathering and animal husbandry. A whole group amongst these several hundred tribes is known by the generic term Nagas. They constitute the Zeliangs, the Maos, the Tankhuls, the Ao's, the Mizos, the Deolas, the Garos and many others. Their dances revolve around the 'hunt' and many ceremonies and rituals connected with them. Some of these are closely related to similar dances in Thailand, Burma, Philippines and other parts of Asia. One amongst these is of special relevance as a Pan-Asian dance. In India, it is performed largely by the Mizos and is called the Bamboo dance.

Perhaps, originally the dance was performed as part of the death ceremonies, today it is purely secular. Here four long bamboo poles are placed across one another. The square thus formed is opened and closed with the beat of the drums by men who sit near the ends of the poles. The dancer hops on one foot outside the cross when it is closed and inside when it is open. The dance becomes more intricate when two or more persons dance together to the bamboo pole clapping and the fast tempo of the accompanying drum. This requires practice. Today the dance is very popular in the whole region and is being practised in schools and colleges.

In deep contrast to these dances of men and women dancing in straight erect postures with nothing but drumming or vocal music as accompaniment are the dances of the tribes of the plains and the marshlands. The richest amongst these are the dances of the Ho's and Oraons of Bihar, the Marias of Bastar in Madhya Pradesh and the Santhals of Bengal. Kaksar is a typical festival dance performed by the Abhujmarias before reaping a harvest. First the deity is worshipped and then the dance is performed.

The men appear fairly attired with a belt of bells around their waists: so do the women, in short brief saris, but richly bejewelled. The dance provides the occasion for choosing life partners: the marriage or marriages which so emerge are enthusiastically celebrated. The rhythms are complex, the choreographical patterns varied. The bells belts of the men dancers and the jewels of the women add to the variety of rhythmical patterns of the dance. The instruments used are *dhol* (cylindrical drum), *timiki* (bowl-shaped percussion instruments) and *bansuri* (a kind of flute).

Bihar

Close to lush marshlands of Madhya Pradesh and yet very different are the tribes of Bihar. Amongst these the Ho's and Oraons are rightly famous for their vigour and vivacity.

Dance and rhythm runs through the veins of the Oraons of Bihar. Men and women vie with each other in creating choreographical patterns of extreme complexity and intricacy. Jadur and Karma dancers of Oraons denote a series of festivals, which start in March, April and end in June. All these dances are essentially harvest dances meant as a prayer for the betterment of the crop. These dances are also an abstraction of the everyday agricultural operations of the people. The dancers are unusually graceful and the dances have a very well defined structure. To a just few notes of close intervals, the melody is sung and danced in slow tempo. Men and women form separate rows, interlocking patterns of the arms and the legs are intricate, gradually the tempo builds until frenzy.

The musical instruments consist of *nagara* (bowl-shaped drum), *Kartal* (clappers) and *khetchka* (wooden clappers). The leader holds a staff of peacock feathers and the drummers (medal players) join the dance at various points.

Andhra Pradesh

Mathuris: Migrations from one part of India to another were common in India. One such migration seems to have taken place hundred of years ago of group of people from North India to Andhra Pradesh in the South. The Mathuris claim their descent to the line of the Northern Raja Pritivisingh Chauhan of the North. Today they are settled mostly in the Adilabad district of the Deccan. They celebrate festivals through dances, chiefly the Holi (Spring festival) and festivals revolving around the life of God Krishna. The Mathuris dance two favourite numbers, the *Lengi Ka Natch* and *Lingi*. The musical instruments mainly consist of drums and *jhanj* (the brass plates) which create a clanging sound.

Uttar Pradesh

From the Northern Himalayas regions come many dances which belong to the village communities. Himachal and Northern Uttar Pradesh is the home of many interesting colourful dances. Two popular favourites come from Jaunsar Bavar in Uttar Pradesh. The festival of lights called Diwali is celebrated throughout India at the end of autumn. On a dark night lights are lit and presents are exchanged. This is also the time for the home-coming of married women. The dance begins with semicircular formations: it breaks into single files of men and women: the song which accompanies is usually set as questions and answers. With gliding movements, graceful knee dips, the dance progress, until one or two amongst the women proceed to the centre to rotate discs on their fingers or sometimes pitchers full of water turned upside down over their heads. So perfect is the balance that not a drop of water trickles out of the pitchers.

The musical instruments resemble those used by the dancers of Himachal Pradesh comprising a *narsingha* (a large trumpet), brass bells, barrel-shaped percussion instruments and bowl-shaped drums.

Punjab

In the Punjab, a virile agricultural dance called the Bhangra is popular originally and is closely linked with the ritual importance which is given to wheat. After the wheat crop is sown, the young men gather together in some open field under the light of the full moon in answer to the beat of the drum. The dancers begin to move in a circle, so that as many newcomers who wish to join can do so without breaking its continuity. The circle goes on widening until a large open circle is formed with the drummer as the leader. The leader, with a large drum hung in front stands in the centre and plays the *dholak* (the drum) with sticks. The dancers naturally first begin with a slow rhythm, with an abrupt jerky movement of the shoulders and a hop-step: this is followed by many vigorous movements of the whole body and the raising of both hands to the shoulder or above the head level. After the circle has been well established and the tempo of the dance has accelerated, the two main dancers dance within the ring in a kind of duet. This is followed by pairs emerging from different sections of the circle, dancing in the central arc and returning to their respective places in the circle. The pair of dancers can execute many variations, ranging from graceful to virile movements, circles, pirouettes, jump and extensions of legs, jumps, and leaps. A skilled Bhangra dancer may even perform some highly complex acrobatic movement of the torso touching the floor, through a spinal back-bend or letting another dancer stand on his shoulders, while he dances on his knees. Since there are no rigorous rules of the Bhangra it leaves an overwhelming impression of fresh spontaneous vigour and vitality, its movements are nevertheless characteristic of the masculinity of the Punjabi and cannot be mistaken for anything else. In choreographical patterns, besides the circle and the semi-circles, sometimes two-tier or three tier circles of one group of dancers balancing themselves on the shoulder or arms of another group of dancers standing in a circle can also be seen. The whole formation moves in a fast rhythm. A dwarf is included in the party and he has an important role to play.

Kashmir

And further North in Kashmir the occasions of the dance are many. Men, women lie in the lap of snow-clad mountains throughout winter, spring brings new life and a reawakening. Rouf is a typical dance of the women at spring time with across interlocked separate rows made and each sings a different line of the song, almost as a question and answer. The steps are light moving backwards, and forwards with slight swings and sways. The composition is charming for its simplicity and spontaneity.

This is but a sampling of the vast store-house of tribal and folk-dances of the Indian sub-continent. From these have emerged the varied classical traditions of Indian music and dance.

A Glance at Nepalese Folk Dances

Imagine a world map showing all the countries in a size in proportion to the richness of their folk dance tradition. Small though it is in actual size, Nepal would certainly appear as one of the largest countries on such a map. The themes of Nepali folk dances know virtually no limitations. The folk dances presented here offer a fine example of how, through these dances, the Nepali masses not only celebrate and worship but also protest against poverty, exploitation, and war.

Like every other country of southern Asia, the kingdom of Nepal has several dialects. Its folk dances can also be divided into fourteen zones and 75 districts, and almost all of the kingdom's numerous folk dances have their own distinctive characters. In Nepal, the Crown was the source of ancient Nepalese culture, and the folk songs and folk dances spread throughout the kingdom are an integral element of ancient Nepalese culture.

According to the old texts, Lord Shiva was the chief teacher for dance, drama, and folk song. Here in our country are a variety of old stone inscriptions, such as the Balaram pedestal stone inscription near Gorkhanath Cave in the Gandaki zone in Gorkha, giving mention of musical instruments and a players arrangement committee. Nepalese history also tells us of ancient evidences of literature, song and musical instruments.

According to Nepalese legend, musical instruments gradually appeared in the hands of the ancient Nepalis as they were developed and produced by the more skilled of their fellows. In Nepal most probably the sites of the earliest music must have been the indigenous shrines, temples, stupas, or monasteries, where daily hymns were sung in the Hindu or Buddhist worship services. Even today, we may see primitive instruments such as the conch shell, *damaru, ghayali,* and *sahanai* as they are used in the different temples of Nepal. The people first learned religious hymns based on the names of the gods and goddesses. Then the ancient folk began to sing folk songs, and the folk dances likewise may have had their origin in the distinctive Nepalese celebrations held during the fairs and grand festivals of the different villages. Whenever and wherever there is any fair or the celebration of any grand festival, folk songs are sung and folk dances displayed and brought to life through the infectuous cheerful mood of the local peasants. Each and every example of folk dance has its own significance, the folk tales, songs, and dances drawing their essence from the deep well of primitive civilization.

Nepal has a wide variety of folk dances, and new folk dances have been created by the local people in their gay, festive mood after the completion of their harvest work. Every community thus exhibits folk dances that carry some sort of particular local significance and characteristic. The local peasants have developed their own folk dances of the rice-planting and harvest seasons, expressed through the medium of the folk songs in their local language. These folk dances express the character of the Nepalese culture, religion, and social way of life.

Some Folk Dances of Pakistan

Recovery of the dancing doll from Moenjodaro, the principal city of the Indus Valley Civilization reveals that dance tradition in Pakistan is as old as Moenjodaro itself, i.e. 5000 years old.

The folk dances in Pakistan are generally associated with festival occasions or seasons of sowing, harvesting and others.

The pattern of folk dances, however, changes from region to region. Being so the folk dances of Frontier and Baluchistan are different from those of the rest of the country though there are some common dances as well. The folk dances of Frontier are very manly and some of them are even associated with the display of swordsmanship or sticks in place of swords.

Luddi dance

It is a very popular dance in the villages all over Pakistan. This dance is related to triumph or success. It is also performed at the time when the fields have been prepared for sowing or at any other successful occasion. It is not necessary that this dance should be accompanied by songs but when it is, the songs are down to earth ballads which reflect their own emotions. This dance is performed by males as well as females but separately.

Sammi dance

It is a special dance portraying the pathos of love. This dance could be performed in any season. It is a very popular dance of the Pothwar area of Pakistan.

Jhoomar dance

Jhoomar (or Ghoomar) literally means spinning or going round. It is danced by the women of Multan, Muzaffargarh and Bhawalpur. It is a dance of sheer romance, beginning with a circle, breaking and forming into patterns as it progresses.

Dhamal dance

This dance is popular all over Pakistan. It is a dance of the fakirs of the saint Shahbaz of Sehwan Sharif. It has however, grown in popularity during the recent years and it is now performed all over the country. The dance is performed by the Malangs during moments of ecstacy.

Hai-Jamalo

This is also a very popular dance. It is performed by males as well as females but separately. It is performed on occasions of happiness and festivity.

Khattak dance

It is performed by sturdy Pathans of Frontier. It is performed by men with long handkerchiefs and sometimes with swords. Wearing embroidered, colourful waist coats and baggy trousers, they dance to the tune of *shenai* (a king of flute) and drums. There are many versions of Khattak dance according to various tribes. This dance is not related to any season and it could be performed on any occasion of success and festivity.

Kalash dance

This dance is only performed in the Kalash Valley of the Chitral District of Pakistan.

South-East Asia: Dance-Communication between Gods and Men

Sitting on the bank of the Rajang River, the large river that flows through Sarawak in eastern Malaysia, or going into the woods to rest and refresh one can deeply sense the true vitality of nature. The songs of the many varieties of birds, the chirps of the insects, the cries of the beasts — all mixed with the wind in the trees to create an unending chorus. Nature was alive and speaking to man. Not in the choice of man, of course, but the sounds seemed to come from another realm of nature, hidden beyond the nature that man usually observes, calling in a ceaseless assertion of its existence.

Man sits quietly and alone, steeping himself in nature. Suddenly the birds stir, the eyes of the beasts flash, and the insects set up an almost silent rustle. The eye of man meets the eye of the rest of nature. At such instants, man becomes strikingly aware of the world he shares with other living things. Nature becomes more than an order of things that Man observes as if from atop a pyramid — instead, he recognises a world which he shares with all the birds and beasts and growing things. Our fathers before us no doubt had such experiences frequently. Our ancestors imitated the birds. They imitated the dances of the animals. There even survive dances that represent the behaviour of smaller beings, fish and insects.

The source and history of such dances are all different, but in Japanese festivals one could find reproductions of the dances of birds, and the dance of the deer was also performed. In the distant past, according to records, there were also crab dances. The dancers would don a headpiece of a bird and a robe bearing feathers, personifying the spirits of ancestors as they came into and left this world, or they would drape themselves in the skin of a deer or imitate the form of a crab in their dances. By doing so, they promised human participation in the universal order of existence. And even though it has largely disappeared, the frog dance does remain in certain localities. This type of dance is also referred to as the spider dance, but whether frog or spider, the dance deals with beings related to water, and as such these dances have been deemed rain dances.

Such phenomena can of course be seen both in Japan and in other lands as well. Throughout Southeast Asia, masked or costumed dances passed down over generations are quite common, and not a few of these represent birds and animals. For example, the Akhas of northern Laos have bird dances, and the Yaos dance a one-legged dance where the performer fixes a live chick atop his head. The women of the Kenyahs of Borneo fix rhinoceros bird feathers to their fingers and perform an elaborate dance that imitates the motions of such birds as they walk along the edge of the water. There are, of course, a great variety of dances wherein the dancers wear strange masks or costumes and transform themselves into spirits and ancestral gods. On Bali in Indonesia there is a very well-known dance that depicts the song and dance of the monkey army of Hanuman.

Setting aside the historical background of these dances, the world imitated and expressed therein is not merely a world of man alone but one shared by man and beast and spirits. The leading and most far-reaching scholar of the indigenous Japanese *Weltanshauung* in literature is Norinaga Motoori (1730-1801), and he has presented a precise perception of the roots of song and dance. According to his theory, the emotion, the surprise, of the instant of meeting between man and nature generated the spontaneous cry of "ah", and this cry of emotion eventually took on the full-fledged form of song and dance. The origin of all song and dance, he says, is in this cry, this shout of "ah!" To the ancients, "god" was the name applied to the source and fountainhead of such emotion. "The gods are as described in ancient literature, but the term denoted a being of supernatural authority, a being to be held in awe. Not just man alone but the birds, the beasts, the grasses and trees, and even the seas and mountains themselves are 'god'."

This ancient concept of "god" was not in any way generated by delusion or misinterpretation. Instead, it was born out of the meeting of hidden Nature and one's true, essential self, and out of the emotion and impact of that confrontation.

Such motions as "jump, turn, and sit" are the basic forms of dance. The dancer stamps the earth and jumps into the air, or moves around some central object — a pillar, a stone monument, or perhaps a person — or, again, may sit facing some certain point or object. In ancient Japan, there was a *toka* or "stamping song" performed at the start of the new year, and the dancers would stamp on the ground to quiet the evil spirits. There were other dances where a wooden tub would be laid on the ground and stamped upon to summon the gods. Further, by stamping on the ground, the body in reaction rises into the air, symbolising the link between heaven and earth. Such dances still can be found in some localities.

Dances which are centred on moving about a focal object are too numerous to mention in detail here. (In passing, it is thought by some that one of the Japanese words for dance, *mai*, came from *mawaru*, meaning to go around). The *Bonodori*, danced throughout Japan at the summer Festival of Lights, the *Ramvong* of Thailand, and many other harvest festival dances of agricultural societies incorporate this element. The people dance in a circle, and thereby, the person at the centre becomes imbued with the essence of the gods. Such a belief can be widely found. Even today, the shaman as he seeks to heal and many games of children include repeated circling about the focus of attention, bearing hints of the attempt to call down the gods to the central person or otherwise influence his spirit. Beginning from this basic action of moving in a circle, the dances took on greater refinement and more colourful form.

The seated position is used to welcome persons of rank or importance and is the posture used toward the gods. Though this, too, encompasses a large number of points worthy of consideration, let us make only that brief observation. Whatever the case, dancing with or without song was more than a mere collective community recreation, more than simple entertainment. Dance was a method for each tribe or community to communicate with its gods as well as an expression of the emotion of being in communion with those gods. Moreover, those gods were to be found everywhere in nature around us.

Popular Dances in Burma

Popular dances

Dancing is an expression of joy and the Burmese have ample occasions to express their rejoicings. Each month of the year has a festival of its own at which dance and music prevail. Together with some 50 ethnic groups who have their own gala occasions, Burma seems to have dancing all year round. The most popular dance among the Burmese is *do-but* (short drum) dance. Historians say that it originated round about 1857 from a village dance practised near Mandalay, the old capital of Burma during the days of the last Burmese king. The musical instruments usually used are two short drums, *hne* (trumpet or clarinet with a broad bell-shaped mouth), a pair of cymbals and two bamboo clappers (castanet). This dance is performed at every and any occasion and it could therefore be called "the dance of the common man." The dancer, usually attired in a ludicrous imitation of princely costume, wear bangles and flowers, and paints both his cheeks with *thanaka* (murraya paniculata), fragrant cosmetic. His dance steps are sprightly, his hand movements are deliberately jerky and with pouted mouth he mimicks the professional *mintha* (dancer-singer-actor). There is an element of mischief and humour in the dance. One of the most popular characters which the *do-but* dancers assume is that of U Shwe Yoe (Mister Simpleton), a legendary elderly man with a bushy moustache, who wear a *gaungbaung* (turban) and wields a tiny paper umbrella. He hops, he struts and he twirls the small umbrella while he waves his other free arm energetically. At the same time he goggles at the audience and makes faces at the crowd. The accompanying music is loud, brisk and merry.

At times the leader of the music group shouts impromptu wisecracks which are incorporated into a song. The others clap and join in the chorus.

The other popular dance is *ozi* (pot drum) dance which originated during ancient times. Finding the picture of the dance in a white *parabeik* (folded board made of bamboo) owned by King Mindon, the second to last Burmese king, historians deduce that the dance must have begun as early as 1750. The dancer may be of either sex, dressed in princely attire and prettied up. With a pot drum suspended on his left side, he beats the drum with the ball of his right palm. At times he uses his left elbow to hit the drum in tune with the dance. Sometimes he raises the pot drum above his head while he dances with a fling and a flounce. *Ozi* dance is accompanied by a pot drum, *hne*, a pair of cymbals and at least two bamboo clappers.

When this dance is shared by two-dancers, the additional dancer, usually a girl, clashes the cymbals to the beat of music.

Although *ozi* is basically a Burmese dance, other ethnic groups like Shans and Kahins adopt the dance as their own. Originally a dignified dance which is courtly, elaborate serious, it has also been parodied to amuse the audience. There are also *ozi-yein* in which four or five pairs of pot drum dancer and cymbal player participate. They dance harmoniously and elegantly to the tune of the music.

Nat-propitiation dances

Burma is a Buddhist country but there still lingers a belief in *nats* (spirits) who guard the houses, farms, trees, mountains, springs, rivers, seas and what not. These superstitious persons propitiate the *nats* with a ceremony followed by dance and music when they start planting paddy, when they start building a house, when they start on a fishing or hunting trip, and when an epidemic overruns their place. To appease the guardian nat of farms and to persuade it to bring good crops, farmer observed a ceremony at which a slow, dignified dance called *bon-gyi* (big drum) is performed. It takes place near the farm where the seedlings are to be inserted in the ground which has been ploughed. Two musicians with big drums, slung around on their sides, beat the drum in consonant with the tune while a male dancer crashes a pair of cymbals and a female dancer goes through classical dance movements.

The dance begins at about 7 o'clock in the morning when the planters start their work. Cheered by the dance and music, they continue until noon when they break for lunch. After about an hour, the planters resume their work and so do the dancers and musicians. Both groups work until sundown.

Dances of wizard, ogre and animals

Of numerous dances connected with supernatural beings, the most famous is the *zaw* (wizard) dance. This numinous character who owns a magic wand can fly in the air and can concoct a medicine for long life. In his dance he leaps in the air to show his prowess in flying, jumps to show his ability to move from a tree top to another and thumps his wand furiously on the floor to depict him as grinding medicinal herbs. The dance is said to have originated in the early nineteenth century.

The dance of *biloo* (ogre) probably derived from the famous *Ramayana* which originated in India. The dancer stamps his feet savagely on the floor, flourishes his ever-present sword and glares around to search for his enemies. He wears a mask of an ogre and he is dressed in a costume of deep red, green and black to denote his ferocity.

Some dances are associated with animals such as lion, elephant, water-buffalo, dragon, peacock and monkey but there is no such thing as a dog dance. There are also dances related to mythical creatures such as *tonaya* (half-snake and half-dragon), *manuthiha* (half-lion, half-man with two bodies and one head), *galone* (a fabulous bird of immense size), *keinnari* (a legendary animal with a body of a bird and a human face).

Dances of ethnic groups

Among the ethnic groups, the Kachin dance called *manao* is the most famous. According to a Kachin legend the gods of the Sun created the *manao* dance in the beginning of the world. The gods invited the birds which were flying around in the air to the dance. On their way back home, the birds found a banyan tree loaded with ripe golden fruits. They had a feast and they danced around the tree in the same way as they were taught by the gods. A human couple living in a country situated in the middle of the world saw the dance, adopted it and it eventually spread far and wide. Invitations to the *manao* celebrations are sent out one month ahead. A string with small knots represent a formal invitation. The invitee cuts one knot each day and the last knot corresponds with the first day of the ceremony. The invitees bring gifts such as rice, salt, liquor, buffalo, hen, pig and apparel for the host.

At the place where the ceremony is to be held, *manao* posts, like totem poles, are erected. These posts are made from trees which are entirely free of imperfections. Before these are felled, appropriate *nats* are appeased by observing a ceremony in their honour.

The *manao* festival mostly lasts eight days — four days for *nat*-propitiation ceremonies and the remaining four days for dances and music.

As a custom, buffaloes are chosen as a sacrificial animal but hens and pigs can also be substituted. After the ceremony the meat of the animals together with strong Kachin rice wine is served to the celebrants and the guests.

The celebrators then dance around the eleven *manao* posts while the musicians play two long drums and three gongs. Both sexes participate but they dance without touching each other bodily.

The Karens have *htolitone* dance which is their national dance. It is rhythmic, vigorous and exuberant. It is a mixed group dance, consisting at least six dancers and at most 12. The dancers bend their bodies forward, then arch backward, at first slowly and then, after gathering tempo, the dance movement becomes snappy and tripping.

Among *Taunghus* in Shan States their popular folk dance is called *maung-sine* (gong) dance. Twenty to sixty villagers participate in the dance which is more or less a fairly slow march. The music is supplied by two big gongs, six small gongs, a pair of big cymbals and another pair of small cymbals.

Most of the marital Nagas believe in spirits and they have four spiritual festivals related to agriculture. The host villagers invite other Nagas from neighbouring villages and hold a feast for seven days. Wearing feathers on their head and scantily dressed, they beat their feet on the floor and make vigorous movements.

The sea-faring Salones, indigenous natives living in the southern tip of Burma, are also spirit worshippers and they believe that there are sea-nats, and island-nats. They are afraid that the nats may prove destructive and hostile at any time and so they appease them by giving sacrificial feasts and dances. Both men and women take part in the dances which are held at about six months' intervals. They do not have any special costumes for the dance which is spontaneous, bold and energetic.

As mentioned earlier, the Burmese dance for joy. That is why there are no dances at funerals. However there is one exception. The Burmese do dance at the funerals of the *phongyis* (monks) because they believe that the *phongyis* "return" to the celestial abode when they leave this mundane world and this indeed is a time for rejoicing.

Folk Dances in the Rural Areas of Indonesia

Viewed from the development of the Indonesian traditional existence, art is an integral part of the social life of the Indonesian people. It is woven into the social structure of daily life, performed habitually by the people and appraised as the most valuable social property. Both visual and performing arts are marked by magical, religious and sacred functions, which are designed to bring peace, security and welfare to the people. There is thus a great number of art forms in all parts of Indonesia, but we will focus our attention on dance as it exists and grows in rural areas.

In the process of its development in Indonesia, dance has undergone development in harmony with the growth of the structural life of society. The various forms of folk dance have experienced changes in their functions, shifting from their role as a part of traditional ceremonies and rites or religious functions to become a show or entertainment for the community. In the process, many of the forms of folk dance also saw improvement in their artistic value, resulting in a firm, fixed pattern of form as well as of movement which gradually came to be known as classical dance. Despite their adaptation to other forms, folk dances still remain alive in the rural areas. Here, they have also undergone a development process, so that three channels of form of folk dance can be found in such areas.

The first channel found from time to time is folk dance which still retains its function as a part of traditional ceremonies.

The second channel is folk dance which has undergone changes in function and developed into social dance, especially among the youth of Indonesia.

The third channel is folk dance which has developed into other forms of dance, particularly those regarded as entertainment for the local public.

Though folk dance belonging to the first channel retains its function, we can also find various forms of dance which have obviously undergone some changes in their presentation. Various folk dances which had the original function of accompaniment for worship have developed into dances to welcome guests. Examples of such dances would include, for instance, the Pendet dance, the Reog dance, as well as the Kuda-Lumping dance.

The rapid development of science and technology in today's world has had a direct influence on the existence of folk dance in the rural areas. Better communications have brought about improvement in the inter-relationship and cultural exchange among the various regions. Folk dances have developed to the extent that they have grown out of their natal environments, escaping direct identification with the original societies that gave them birth. The folk dance thus hastened to change its function and develop into a show-performance or light entertainment.

A careful study of the forms of folk dance, particularly in the rural areas, shows that it is rather difficult to differentiate between dance and the theatre. This is due to the tradition of performance of folk dance by a group of people and not by a single dancer, with the dance presentation always accompanied by traditional music. Direct communication takes place between the dancers and the audience through dialogue as well as through the movement of the dance. One example is the Tayub dance, also called "Ronggeng" in West Java, one of the forms of folk dance which has grown up particularly in the rural areas. This Tayub dance normally consists of a group of female dancers and players of traditional music. The Tayub dancers peddle their dance or take part in ceremonies in return for some fee for their performance. During the performance, the Tayub dancers may stop to invite the audience or guests to dance together with them. If a member of the audience or one of the guests is asked to dance, he may then choose his favourite melody to accompany the dance. Those who invite the Tayub group to perform should themselves know how to dance and sing. In its process of development, the Tayub dance underwent changes and improvement in form and value so that it gradually became an entertainment for the upper classes of the community, including the elite and the nobility. In this way, the Tayub dance in fact became a performance of dance and traditional music in which the dancers competed in displaying their knowledge in the field of traditional music. In the course of its development, the Tayub dance also experienced changes in character. The original character as a performance of dance changed into a display of wealth and strength, often resulting in riots and disorders. Because of this, the Tayub dance has virtually disappeared for many years.

In fact, forms of dance such as this Tayub dance are found not only in Central Java and West Java but in other areas as well, where they are known by such local names as Ronggeng, Gandrung, or Joged. We can, however, see some indications that today's world might bring about the disappearance of the forms of folk dance in rural areas of Indonesia. These indications seem to be the result of several situations such as the following:

1. As a result of increasing cultural exchange among the regions of the country and even with other nations, the arts of the various areas are influencing each other. Forms of folk dance which have shown less potential have been neglected or even eliminated, or at least have undergone changes and have been inclined to drop their identity as folk dances of the rural regions.
2. As a result of modern ways of thinking, there is a tendency for folk dances to absorb elements of dance from outside the community environment without heed to factors which might eliminate the identity of the indigenous arts.
3. The migration to big cities by the rural folk has presented some obstacles to the continuity and even the existence of folk dance in the villages.

To overcome such problems, the Government of the Republic of Indonesia has taken measures to discover, guard, preserve, guide, improve, and research forms of traditional arts all over Indonesia. The continuity of the forms of traditional arts will be selectively overseen and their quality improved and developed further in line with community development and the social structure of the Indonesian people. In this way the local community will be made aware of its function as guide, leader, and supporter for the development of arts in its respective region. For this purpose the Government has organised a variety of festivals, performances, and seminars. Just one example is represented by the First National Festival on Folk Dance, held in Jakarta from 28 to 30 November, 1977. This festival was organised by the Directorate for the Dissemination of Arts, Department of Education and Culture, and here, twenty provinces presented various forms of folk dance indicating the specific characteristics of their respective regions. Several of these dances deserve mention here to indicate that they are still alive and developing in rural areas.

Saman dance of Aceh

This dance is performed by men. They kneel down in several rows, and the performance is carried out by a large number of people; the ideal number of participants is an odd number, and the dancers usually come from the mountain area of this region. The dance movements are symbolic aspects having various names, such as *tepok, kirep, lingang, lengek, guncang,* and *surang-saring.* The movements are expressed in variation, sometimes slowly, sometimes very quickly. Movement (the form) is considered the source of the dance movement characteristics of Aceh, which develops in harmony with the situation and the condition of the environment. The poem (the vocal element) is recited by the Syeh (performer), who usually sits in the centre of the group. The other artists dance together and while doing so also sing in he specific rhythm of the region.

The contents of the poem recited can be adjusted to meet the need or the particular condition: it can be religious instruction, information, tradition, development, or various other topics. The dance with its poem is thus communicative, instructive, and magisterial in order to promote spiritual strength and heroism. The characteristic costume for the dancers of the region consists of head covers (*bulang teleng*), trousers and short-sleeved shirts, a sarong worn by the dancers around their waists, and other clothing, all of which are adorned with the specific designs of the region concerned. The Saman dance was created by Syeh Saman, a well known teacher of Islam who came to Aceh many years ago.

Joged Pingitan dance of Bali

This is a form of social dance in Bali, a very lively and demonstrative dance accompanied by a set of traditional musical instruments called "tingklik gegrantangan". Unlike the Joged Bumbang dance, the Joged Pingitan dance is based on history taken from the repertoire "Palegongan" as found in "Prabu Lasem" and also in "Calon Arang". The dance is called Joged Pingitan because there is something *forbidden* (*pingitan*) during the performance. Unlike the Joged Bumbungan dance, where the dancers (*pengibing*) may touch and hold their counterparts, the dancers in the Joged Pingitan dance may not have any contact during the performance. This dance was formerly preserved and developed in royal courts and was considered entertainment for the kings. It is said that the female dancers consisted of the king's concubines living outside the palace. It is understandable, therefore, that ordinary men would not be permitted to touch and hold them.

Kembang Topeng dance of Jakarta

The Kembang Topeng dance is one of the folk dances of Betawi and has developed for more than a century in Jakarta and its surroundings. As a common folk dance, the Kembang Topeng dance is improvised with spontaneous dance movements. Seen at a glance, one may have the impression that this dance emphasises the erotic aspect. But seen more humorously, the Betawi community finds life beautiful and interesting and sees this dance entirely as an enjoyable entertainment and pastime. The Kembang Topeng dance can be performed by one, three, or five couples of dancers, and each couple symbolises a sacred union. In this presentation we find five couples (as a symbol of the balance of the cosmos: west, east, north, south, and centre), indicating the different kinds of character encompassed in this dance.

Ketuk Tilu Karawangan dance of West Java

The movements of this dance are generally improvised and consist of a king of self-defence movement *(pencak)* and reflections of physical movement in a particular condition. The dynamics and tempo of the movement are influenced by the song accompanying the dance.

Sirang dance of West Kalimantan

This dance describes a method of curing a patient. According to local belief, a man becomes sick because the "spirit" is taken away by a demon from the other world. To cure the patient, a priest's help is needed in order to bring the spirit back to the patient. "Bensirang" means to ask for a priest's assistance. This dance illustrates how the priest (*mamang*) unites his soul with the patient to fight the king of demons (Pantau Ajan) and his followers in the other world so that the priest can retrieve the spirit and bring it back to the patient. Then the priest sticks a man's wooden figure to the patient so that from that time on he will not be bothered by the demons.

Tandak Gero dance of Nusa Tenggara Barat

The Tandak Gero dance is one of the traditional arts of Lombok. It can be found in the village of Lenek in the district of Lombok Timur. The performance of the Tandak Gero dance is held usually at the end of harvest, and it is considered an entertainment after a hard day's work.

Baduwi folk art of Yogyakarta

The Baduwi folk art exists among the common people in the district of Sleman and the surrounding countryside. This art was borrowed from the Arabs by ancestors who visited Arab lands. This art has been passed down from generation to generation and has been adapted to the conditions of the Indonesian people. As the Baduwi folk art has been greatly enjoyed by the common people, it has been adopted as a representative folk art of this area. The theme of the dance illustrates a group of young men or soldiers doing their exercises in preparation for battle. The performance is given at night to celebrate Islamic holidays, weddings, and other festivals. The dancers are men and the number may be large or small as the occasion demands. The accompanying musical instruments consist of three small drums (*terbang genjring*), one *jedor,* and one drum. The vocalists are all men, numbering three, four, five, or even more. The poems sung are taken from the holy *Al Qur'an.* These poems are sung by the singers alternating with the dancers.

Local Japanese Folk Dances

From the ancient past, folk dances in Japan have been the people's representation of a wide range of faiths and beliefs in spirits and presences — the spirit of the sun, of water, of fire, and of prosperity among many others. A basic structural characteristic which these folk dances share with other folk dances throughout Asia is the link that so many have with agriculture.

Drum dances

Drums can be found everywhere around the world, and drums are an essential element of folk dances throughout Asia as well. Japan has a plentiful variety of such dances, where the performers step, jump, or leap as they beat their drums. The drums are used not only for their rhythmical properties but also to appeal to the dancers' spirit and call up a special energy that induces a type of trance state. The rhythm of the drums and the intoxicating energy of the dance form a channel to the gods and the spirits. This type of dance is often used to pray for rain.

Kanko Odori (Sahachi, Ise City, Mie Pref.)

"Kanko" derives from the drum, called a "kakko," worn at the waist of the dancer. The face and head are covered with a veil of hairs from the tail of a white horse. The dancers wear a colourful fitted garment in a stripped pattern. A skirt of straw is worn about the waist, and the whole appearance is designed to represent a being from the other world.

Taiko Odori (Ohyagyu, Nara Pref.)

Many Japanese folk dances began as symbols of welcome to the gods and spirits, and for this purpose, a wide variety of symbolic representations of the gods have been created. In this *taiko odori* (drum dance), the dancers carry *bonten*, a symbolic wooden rod with paper-strips to invite deities, on their back, and they leap around the area, pacifying the spirits of the earth.

Gojinjo Daiko (Wajima, Ishikawa Pref.)

Here, the dancers wear weird masks as part of their costumes. The ferocious expressions of the masks derive from the day when, during battle, soldiers would don such masks and beat their drums to inspire fear in the hearts of the enemy. The performers set up strange cries as they dance, and their frightful appearances are the very personification of demons come to this earth from another world.

Circle dances

In Japan, there has long been a belief that the circle is the symbol of the sun. As such, to form a circle was in a way to consecrate the site concerned. The circle also represented a type of completion or attainment of perfection, and even today, when something is brought to a finish, where a Westerner might use a phrase such as "shipshape," a Japanese might say "done up like a circle." One typical example of such a dance occurs at the Bon Festival, held at the middle of July. Men and women, young and old, gather in temple grounds or plazas to dance in a large circle. The original purpose of this dance was to console and send off the spirits of the departed who return to earth each year at this time, but it soon became a collective entertainment of the villages as well as a prayer for a fruitful harvest the coming autumn. This dance, in Buddhist terms, also represents a release from the constant cycle of reincarnation. And at times of abundant harvest or good catches from the sea, the circle dance is also a wish for the continued joy of fulfilled prayers.

Kujira Odori (Miwazaki, Wakayama Pref.)

The *Kujira Odari* (literally "whale dance") has continued to be performed at the time of the capture of a great fish, the dancers forming a circle to offer their joyful thanks to the gods.

Stick dances

The stick dance is found throughout Asia and can also be seen in almost every part of Japan. The dancers' striking of the sticks does not represent battle; instead, hitting the sticks together in a cross symbolizes the chasing away of evil spirits

Boh Odori ("Stick Dance") (Hitoyoshi, Kumamoto Pref.)

Tachi Odori ("Longsword Dance") (Ohama Nishizu, Fukui Pref.)

Paddy fertility dances

In many Japanese farming villages, one can find anticipatory ceremonies held at the start of spring under the lunar calendar, imitating rice planting to pray for fruitful harvests of the traditional "five grains" (rice, wheat, millet, beans and darnel). The dances that form a part of such ceremonies are whirling and turning dances which include no jumping or stamping which might disturb the spirits of the rice seedlings.

Otaue ("Rice Planting") (Kasuga Shrine, Nara Pref.)

This ceremony is held in paddies owned by the shrine to pray for the growth and development of the seedlings. The actions of the ceremony and the depiction of the form of a bull seek to cause a sympathetic response through the mock rice planting.

Izouno Otaue Sai ("Rice Planting Festival") (Shima-Isobe, Mie Pref.)

To seek the fertility of the paddies, the participants call gods and spirits down to a symbolic large fan (called "ohuchiwa") erected in the paddy. So that the humans as well may partake of the blessings of the gods, participants may splash the consecrated paddy's mud on each other or rub it on their own faces.

Animal dances

There has long been a belief among many peoples that through a process of mimicry, a person may avail himself of the characteristics or attributes of an animal or object by imitating its appearance. This belief is found in the many Japanese folk dances featuring animal costumes.

Harukoma (Sado Island, Nigata Pref.)

The dancer dons the head of a horse and prances around to the accompaniment of local folk songs to celebrate the arrival of spring. The name of the dance implies 'the energetic horse of spring,' and the horse is seen as the messenger of the gods.

Shirasagi no Mai (Senso-ji Kannon Temple, Tokyo)

As a prayer for good harvests, this dance depicts the *sagi*, or snowy heron, which eats injurious insects in the rice paddies. It is said that this dance was originally performed as a ritual designed to expel epidemic disease.

The legendary phoenix (ho-o) not only links heaven and earth as it flies back and forth, it also brings portents of good or evil. Here, the dance prays for abundant harvests of the five grains and at the same time to pray for rain. It is said that rain will fall the day after the performance.

Dances of the gods of fire and the mountains

Since fire devours things in its flames, it is also thought to be able to devour evil spirits. Fire is thus used as a means of cleansing and purification. The spirit of the mountains, too, can be of help to mankind since it will descend to chase away spirits of evil inhabiting the earth.

Sacred Lamp Festival (Shingu City, Wakayama Pref.)

The sacred fire presented as an offering to the gods is brought down from the mountain to drive out evil spirits.

Onibashiri (Gojo City, Nara Pref.)

Three dancers representing parents and son, wear huge demon masks and accompany a burning torch.

"Celestial Child" dances

The "celestial child" refers to a child in a Shintoist procession, and in Japan, such a "chigo" is venerated as a symbol of the gods and deities along with another figure, the *dojo* or virgin maiden. There are many folk dances centered around the *chigo* or *dojo*, and these children, as a link between the worlds of heaven and earth, have been regarded as channels for the sacred words of the gods.

Okina Mai (Naratsuhiko Shrine, Nara Pref.)

The *Okina* (old man) represents a god. The *chigo* as *senzai*, forgoer to clear *okina's* way, dances to celebrate the coming of *okina* and expresses the god's message in his dance.

Ayakomai (Kashiwazaki City, Niigata Pref.)

This dance is performed gracefully by maidens 14 or 15 years of age or younger.

Macchanu, the son of Hanuman, in a Thai mask play.

Masks in Folk Theatre

Masks of Sri Lanka

Sri Lanka's age-old ritualistic and rural theatrical pageants are still conducted with much solemnity today. The traditional masks or *ves muhunu* associated with these ceremonies are therefore not just show-pieces or curios to decorate affluent apartments. They have a meaningful existence in ritual and other such performances. The rituals have sprung from esoteric practices based mainly on the belief in the power of the Unseen to direct Man's destiny. Although the Buddha is stated to have rid the Island of the evil machinations of the devils, they still appear to affect the destiny of some of the Sri Lankans. For instance, Annie Besant describes, in the London *Daily Chronicle* (1893), an evening she spent with the devils of Sri Lanka. What she was actually doing was participating in a devil dance.

These devils would naturally have become more restive and vehemently ferocious when reporters and photographers attend their festivals at night. But today, they don't seem deterred by these intruders, perhaps realizing that those who may have been capable of exorcising them, the witch-doctors, are not that powerful, having taken to other lucrative professions. The *kattandiyas*, for that is the name for the witch-doctors, have their reasons: their previous clientele now prefers to go to the newly opened rural health centres. With little fear of being exorcised the devils are left in peace and cohabit happily with progress! Yet the fact remains, as pointed out by Faubian Bowers, that "Almost every Sinhalese is a devout Buddhist, but in the back of his mind ineradicably exist his pre-Buddhist atavistic fears and superstitions." (*Theatre in the East.*) Perhaps the unsophisticated villagers may be living witnesses to that utterance in Shakespeare's Hamlet:

"There are more things in Heaven and Earth, Horatio,
Than are dreamt of in your Philosophy."

The villagers still believe in the occult control of the spirits who are supposed to act like an invisible ether.

Before the devils are exorcised they have to be introduced to the patient. This is done mainly through impersonation — the focus of attention being the masks the dancers wear. The ritual masks could be divided into two categories to facilitate study — (1) The *tovil* masks, and (2) a specialized group of *tovil* masks known as *sanni* masks. *Tovil* ceremonies are curative ritual performances which are varied, elaborate and complicated. Detailed analysis of each variety and each individual dance-area is beyond the purview of this article. *Sanni* in Sinhala denotes a malady. Those prone to superstition still believe that diseases arising out of the morbid state of the three humours — aerial humour, bile and phlegm — are the results of demonic activity. There are 18 such ailments which are commonly known as the *daha ata sanniya.* Each malady-causing demon is symbolized by a separate mask. The ritual connected with this type of masked dancing has a cathartic and psychosomatic effect.

Tovil masks

Almost all the masks of this variety belong to the demon mask category. Since a dancer has to impersonate the demon who is made to appear before the patient, his make-up, dress, and above all the masks, have to be faithfully worked out to bring the demon into proper focus. If there is a specific mythological narrative on the origin of the demon, the carver's task becomes easier. We can cite the case of the demon Maha Sohona — "The Great Devil of the Grave Yards" in this respect. He is supposed to haunt cemeteries in the guise of a great hairy bear. How he came to possess a bear's form is very interesting. The story goes that king Dutthagamani of Sri Lanka had ten warriors. One of them, Godimbara, had a pretty wife. When the couple were attending a festival, a demon called Jayasena, who had developed a liking for the wife, cast a spell over her. Godimbara sensed this and challenged Jayasena to combat. The very next moment one sweep from Godimbara's left foot (was it a karate kick I wonder?) saw Jayasena's head reeling in the air. God Saturn pitying him, hastily grafted a bear's head on to the remaining trunk of the body. The devil thenceforth started preying on corpses strewn in grave-yards, whereupon he came to acquire the name Maha Sohona. The mask worn by the performer therefore assumes the face and head of a bear of the were-wolf type. Some masks carvers make the face look more dreadful by introducing two fangs at the two corners of the mouth. The ferocious demon is seated on a pig and sports a young elephant in his hand to have an occasional sip of its blood! The dancer executes several rounds of strenuous dance steps in front of the arena known as the vidiya (a shed constructed with strong sticks driven into the ground and onto which are tied several rows of other sticks, the structure being divided into passages decorated with banana stems and young coconut fronds). The dancer, who is a lithe-limbed young man, is sometimes perched on the structure. He swings, gambols, jumps and falls on the ground with a thud while the drumming reaches a crescendo. The exorcist converses with the demon. The dialogue, like in the Elusian mysteries of Europe, abounds in scurrilous and bawdy language at the end of which the demon is constrained and brought into submission.

Many of the masks worn in these ceremonies are only half-cut masks and do not cover the entire face and head, unlike the masks in the rural theatre. In a *tovil* ceremony, the dancer has to converse freely with the exorcist. The mask has to be light and easy to talk through. The teeth are therefore separately fitted so that the lips can be moved easily.

Sanni masks

Except for one or two masks of this variety others do not cover the entire face. In this manner Sanni masks become easily viable, thus facilitating long, drawn-out conversation between the masked-dancer and the exorcist or the drummer. These masks portray the symptoms of the disease on the one hand and the devilish features of the character on the other. The eighteen diseases are as follows: *boota* — delirium: *amukku-shivering: gulma* — abdominal pain: *vedi* — fits: *kanu* — blindness: *kora* — lameness: *golu* — dumbness: *bihiri* — deafness and Insomnia: *vaata* — paralysis: *pita* — billiousness: *naaga* — disease of the glands: *kola* -swollen throat: *seetala* — cold shivers: *demala* — disease of the stomach: *murtu* — fainting: *ginijal* — high fever: *aboota*; and *deva* — hypnotic ailments.

Since the mask is named after the disease it symbolizes, the carver's task appears to be easy. However, it requires much skill to register such symptoms as dumbness or abdominal pain on the mask. The mask of dumbness has a gaping mouth and the look on the mask, needless to say, is jocular. The two sets of teeth are carved separately and fitted later onto the mask. The dancer moves the teeth in quick motion so that the clattering of the teeth creates the effect of a man trying to talk but without success. This mask is sometimes caricatured as having a cobra capelle rising from a nostril. There is a tradition that cobras do not have ears! The mask of the demon causing death, the Maru Sanniya has two protruding eyes, a pointed nose and gaping nostrils, while the head is capped by one or two, or even three tiers indicating flames. The characteristics of the mask become more evident when the dance sequence is analysed. For instance, the demon causing high fever is depicted with red eyes and flushed mouth. The dancer shivers from the burning sensation and even invites the exorcist to bake pancakes on his back — the burning sensation has produced enough heat for the purpose! The demon causing cold shivers dances into the audience in a hilarious manner and invites the audience to provide him with a match-stick as the cold is unbearable. A colourful mask used in the *sanni* ceremony is that of the *Maha Kola Sanni Yaka*, the leader of the *sanni* demons. This mask displays all the *sanni* demons at once. The main mask comprises two cobra capelles on the sides, five cobra hoods in the middle, and two huge cobras coiling upwards at the two ends, while the demon is made to devour a child lying prostrate in his mouth. It is probable that this mask was not used in the actual performance but more as a mask-structure to hang the eighteen *sanni* masks.

Ritual theatrical masks or dance-drama masks

The artistic skill of the indigenous mask carver is clearly noticed in the masks worn in the rural opera known as *kolam*, which is at best a visually heightened art of caricature. It is confined to the southern coastal belt of the island. The characters in a *kolam* performance enact a variety of episodes seemingly disjointed yet having an underlying unity, through mime, dance and song interspersed with impromptu dialogue. All the dances are executed to the rhythm of the low-country drum or *yak beraya*. One cannot absorb the meaning of the mask dance without comprehending the background to the performance which has an expository story content. In its early stages, *kolam* seems to have been connected with fertility rites. The story goes that the queen of King Mahaasammata, the first legendary ruler, was subject to a peculiar *"dola-duka"*, or pregnancy desire, to see a masked dance! Many performers vie with each other in the attempt to satisfy the queen. They do not succeed. The king in his anger and disappointment goes to sleep and refuses to eat. His fast becomes an unintended act of merit. A goddess carries the news to Sakra, the God of gods, and asks him to help the king. Sakra details Visvakarma, his Divine Artisan, to do the needful. On the following day the gardener of the royal park discovers the masks and a book detailing the performance. The king, realizing what has happened, hastens to the park and makes arrangements for the ceremony by which the queen's peculiar desire is appeased. Whatever the origins of the myth, it provides the skeletal structure on which the whole performance is based. In fact all the existing *kolam* scripts retain this story, thus suggesting that *kolam* was originally a pregnancy ritual. Even the composition of some of the masks support this assumption. *Kolam* dances are held nowadays for amusement and fun on ceremonial occasions. One of the characteristics of *kolam* is that it displays a kind of theatre-in-the-round, where the performing area — *Karaliya* — is circular and the audience is seated close-by occupying all but the small "green-room" area at the rear. There is a partition between the spectators and the "green-room". It is known as the *Ves Atta* which is constructed with sticks sufficiently strong and to the height of an average man. The actor wearing the mask remains behind this until his turn comes to enter the arena. An authentic *kolam* performance can be divided into three stages to facilitate study. The preliminary rituals like the lighting of the coconut oil lamps and the invocations to gods followed by the dances of stock characters comprise stage one. The royal party enters the Assembly and demon and animal dances are enacted before them. This is stage two. Stage three is the enactment of a story by masked dancers. The story may be taken from legend oı from Buddhist birth stories.

All the stock characters wear masks. Since a *kolam* performance has become a field of humorous parody and burlesque, it provides enough scope for satirising. The stock characters in *kolam* are broad types. In a fairly representative performance today the following stock characters appear: the drummer, his wife and sons; the soldiers, the village headman and his assistant; the Mudaliyar and his scribe; the laundryman and his wife; the moorman; the money lender; the old couple; the Tamil couple; the European couple; the foreign beggar, etc. The artists have utilized these masked-dance sequences with a significant artistic point. Moreover the satiric expressiveness and range of the mask, the teasing form of the dance, and witty backchats and the farcicality of the action of most of these characters all underscore the bold attempt of the folk artist of caricaturing each and every individual whose traits and manners he thought were questionable!

The drummer — Anaberakaru — is a drunken misfit. He is old and feeble. The mask carver portrays all these qualities with a few wrinkles on the face, a few protruding teeth, sagging cheeks and a pointed chin. A long, flowing beard is separately fitted or cut on the mask itself. The lines on the forehead, wrinkles on the sides, and the beak-like pointed nose coupled with sharp Shylock eyes complete the cunning mind of the money lender — Hettiya. An interesting feature noticed in the carvers of Sri Lanka is the innovation of new faces caricaturing different officers in authority. The face of the police inspector in a troupe from Amabalangoda, near Galle, is presumably an attempt at caricaturing the face of the Kaizer Germany. The artist Gunadasa had seen his photograph in a calendar. The mask of the Mudaliyar, an official during the colonial regime, symbolizes his haughtiness and what the artist considered as his foolhardiness. The pointed nose, thick eyelashes, side whiskers extending from the ear lobes far down the side of the face — all complete the satirical image of the official. The wife of the drummer — Nonchi — is an old woman, but she still wishes to be in the company of youngsters. The mode of representing the "wench in spite of herself" is very appealing. A lonely tooth, white in colour in a surrounding black face catches the humour of this coquettish character. Very often the dancer wears two maniac stems to suggest her drooping breasts!

Mask-making

A mask is generally worked out of *vel kaduru*, striychnox nux-vomica, grown near paddy fields. The wood is light and durable. Carving of the mask involves a ceremonial process. After the virgin trunk is cut into sizable blocks, the correct size and level by using chisels and gauges. Then the wood is hollowed from inside and is kept on the kitchen shelf to dry. The wood has to be completely dry (since it contains latex) before dressing and hollowing. If a mask is kept on the kitchen shelf for six months, it will last nearly 150 years. Regarding large masks of the demon variety and those belonging to the royal party, the width of the block of wood is not sufficient to make the masks from one block. The ear lobes, crowns and head-dresses are therefore carved separately and fitted on to the main mask. There are thus as many as three separate tiers in the case of royal masks. In the past, traditional paint — *alliyaadu* — was used, but today ordinary lacquer is utilized.

The Khon: The Thai Mask Play

Mask play in Thailand, a tradition of high aesthetic value, is known to all Thais and to worldwide admirers as the *khon*. It is not fully determined when and where it originated. So far as one can trace through the help of historical records, the *khon* might have been introduced to Thailand during the Ayudhya Period over 300 years ago. Since its introduction it has gone through various stages of evolution and adaptations. The records show it was played for such occasions as the Court coronation, in which the *khon* play would accompany other items, e.g. shadow plays, war dances, etc. It is logical to believe that the *khon* represents the influence of the Hindu culture in India which pushed its way over the border through the Bengal state to Thailand. The European traders who visited Thailand during the reign of King Narai the Great in the Ayudhya Period also made special mention of the *khon* in their trading documents.

The *khon* is a kind of Thai classical play which implies "the wearing of masks by performers". These masks indicate the personalities of their wearers and have a variety of designs. Since the performers wear masks and are therefore unable to utter any kind of sound, there then has to be a sort of "reciter". However, the clowns who wear no masks still carry on their dialogue in the ordinary way. Later on it became the preferred habit for those taking human roles as well as roles of celestial beings not to wear masks. These performers still keep to the former tradition of non-utterance. All performers of the *khon*, therefore, have to conform their steps and poses to the recitations and songs of the choruses.

The recitations of the *khon* are of two types; the *kampak* (recitation) and the *jenraja* (dialogue). The *kon pak*, or reciter, has to be conversant with his subject and should know the rhythm of the dancer's movements so that he may be able to regulate his recitations and pauses in consonance with the requirements of the technique of the dance, for it is mostly his utterances that guide the dancer's movements. The *jenraja*, on the other hand, admits interpolations on the part of the reciter. The *khon*, therefore, has to rely for its perfection upon the coordination of dancer, reciter and orchestra.

The story that has been used for the staging of the *khon* is the story of Rama, the Indian hero who is immortalized in the Hindu epic *"Ramayana of Valmiki"*. The Thai version is called *"The Ramakien"*.

The *Thai Ramakien*, which was composed for the classical dance, exists in many versions. The only one which is found to be complete is the version of King Rama I, while the one most suitable for presentation on the stage is that of King Rama II. In the adaptative forms introduced by the Fine Arts Department, the versions of King Rama I and Rama II form the main basis, namely the sung portions. Recitatives and dialogues have, however, often had to be composed for each of the episodes performed.

There are still *khon* texts which are not based on the versions of these two Kings. The best known was the version written by King Rama VI which appears to more resemble the classical *Ramayana of Valmiki* through its English translation.

The greater part of the Ramakien is concerned with the wars of the two kings, Rama, the King of Ayodhya, and Tosakanth, the King of the island of Longka. Rama and his brother Lakshman, together with Rama's beloved consort Sida, had gone to take up a hermit's life in the depth of the forest when the demon king, Tosakanth abducts Sida and takes her to his palace near the city of Longka with the hope of marrying her.

The brothers start in pursuit. Hanuman volunteers service and through him they win two allies in the persons of Sukrip, King of Khitkhin, and Thao Mahajombhu, the Great King of Jombhu. They then march with their allied armies to the seaboard to the south of the Indian subcontinent, opposite the island of Longka. They then acquire as another ally Piphek, a brother of Tosakanth who had been banished by the demon king. He is a highly skilled astrologer.

Rama's army was ordered to build a causeway made up of stones to enable his troops to storm Longka. Having crossed the newly built causeway, the allied simian armies lay siege to the city of Longka. After a long series of battles with the demons of Longka and their allies, the armies of Rama are eventually successful. Tosakanth, having exhausted the sources of all help from relatives and allies, resolves upon going out himself to give battle with the enemy. He is finally killed in battle. Rama then consecrates his ally, Piphek, as King of Longka and returns with Sida to Ayodhya where he resumes his reign. The epic goes on to record a good deal more fighting, but save for the single episode of the adventure Rama's sons, these subsequent campaigns hardly find their way to the stage.

While conducting the siege of the Longka City, pavilions were built by the simian army for their use. The fighting forces of the two rival kings are therefore sometimes known as the "Pavilion Army" (Rama's) and the "Longka Army" (Thosakanth's).

The mask is perhaps the most important characteristic of the *khon*, for through it more than any other thing else, one distinguishes the variety of roles. Conformity to certain characteristics, however, is well apparent. The dress and the mask designs of a demon are made to create a sense of ferocity and strength; whilst those of a human hero are majestic and graceful, female parts beautiful and gentle, and the simian role restless.

Generally speaking, divine and human roles no longer wear masks and are represented in natural colours. Rama is green of complexion, whilst the brothers — Bhrot, Lakshman, and Satrud are painted red, yellow and purple, respectively, as in former times.

Other unmasked players are women, upsorn (celestial maiden), wives and daughters of demons, e.g. Queen Montho and Suvanamatcha. But the *khon* of later or recent periods prefer to have actors play the parts of gods without masks. The same holds for the female demon (Yakshini). While male demons still retain their masks, the female demons on the other hand have demon features painted on to their natural faces.

Those that are still required to wear masks in the *khon* play are monkeys, demons and animals. *Khon* masks for demons and monkeys are divided by teachers of drama into two types: the Peaked Mask and the Bald Mask. Thus four categories are recognized: Demon Peaked Mask, Demon Bald Mask, Monkey Peaked Mask, and Monkey Bald Mask.

Furthermore, each mask possesses individual characteristics of shape, decoration, colour and facial expression. The following are sample descriptions of the mask and appearance of major characters in the play.

Tosakanth, the King of Longka, generally has a green complexion with a 'crown of victory' which is, however, differentiated by two tiers of faces within the crown, one of demons representing his ten faces, and a top one of a celestial face.

Indrachit, his son and heir, also has a green complexion with a peaked crown. His role is attributed with a Few human characteristics not usually associated with demons, e.g., the human ear flaps and his dance movements.

Kumbhakarn, next brother to the King of Longka, being attributed with an aesthetic disposition, wears no crown but a coronet. His complexion is also green.

Piphek, another brother, also green in complexion, wears a gourd crown.

It is not clearly evident by what principles the various roles are assigned their individual masks. Most of the principal demon crowns which are easily traceable to their parentage. The leading ones wear a 'crown of victory'.

There are also additional features for distinguishing the demon characters, such as the eyes which are of two types: bulging or crocodile. The mouths are also of certain types: clamping or snarling. Tosakanth, for instance, has in his facial characteristics rows of visages to signify his ten faces; the mouth is of the snarling type and the eyes bulge.

Maiyarab, another major actor in the demon camp, has on the other hand a clamping mouth and crocodile eyes.

The mounts they adopt in battle are usually a chariot but some invariably ride a horse or an elephant. The weapon used, though often varying, consists of a club, while leading demons use bows instead.

Another noticeable feature is that demons wear coats of mail on top of their vests which are in contrast to the colour of the coats. This is in contrast also to the simian dress of Rama's camp. All monkeys irrespective of ranks wear coats of an identical colour with the masks. On these coats are designs of hair indicating their bare bodies.

On the whole, the simian masks are simpler than those of the demons. The simian kings, Pali (green) and Sukrip (red) as well as the King or Jombhu (blue) wear the *'yodbat'* crowns with an insertion at the top. A similar crown is also worn by the demon Indrachit. This may indicate a high royal rank. Ongkot, though being heir to the throne of Khidkhin as Indrachit is to the one of Longka, wears a gourd crown. Three monkey chieftains, though of great imminence, do not wear crowns but are given coronets. They are Hanuman (white), Nilanon (red, being an incarnation of Agni, the Fire God), and Nilapat (black, being an incarnation of the God of Death).

There are other monkey chiefs who wear coronets and distinguish themselves by the colours of their complexion. One or two have similar colours and become distinguishable by their mouths which are either close or open.

There are 30 different masks designed for the "Bald Monkey" category. All of them are of similar shape so it was found necessary to rely on colour (in relation to the colour of costume) and on other facial characteristics for identification. For example, a mask of yellowish red belongs to Nilanon, of bronze colour to Nilapasan, of copper colour to Nila-ek, of faded lotus colour to Komut, and of purple colour to Keyun. But masks of the same colour are further differentiated by facial expressions, and also by the weapon carried by the characters. For example, the white monkey with gaping mouth and trident is Hanuman, while another white monkey with closed mouth and dagger is Sattaplee. Two black monkeys, one lacquer-black and the other dull black, look almost identical. They are Pimon Parnorm having a mask with a mouth close and Nilapat with gaping open mouth.

The differentiation by colours is applied also in the case of peaked masks. The Yodbat crown of bright green belongs to Pali; if dark blue, it designates Thao Maha Jombhu, and if of Chinese red, to Sukrip. At present, monkeys of the Tiew Pet and Chang Kiang are rarely represented on the stage, so that a description of their masks is not necessary.

There are more than one hundred different demon masks used in the *khon*. In the making of these masks, there are rules to follow to avoid confusion. Fourteen different groups of demon masks can be recognized: crowns with Kranok top worn by Phya Thut and Maiyarab; with fluted top worn by Phya Khorn and Satthasun; with cock's tail top worn by Virun Chambang and Banlaichak; with gourd-shaped top worn by Piphek; Chiewha; with round gourd top worn by Kuvennuraj, Paovanasun; with fluted gourd top worn by Banlaikan, Wanyuwik; with bamboo-sheath top worn by Thosakhirivan, Thosakhirithorn and Ramasoon; with three cornered peak worn by Thappanasoon, Swahu, and Marrij; with Hang-lai (pattered tail) top worn by Trimegh; with Naga (powerful snake) top worn by Mangkornkanth; with multiple heads worn by Tosakanth with 10 heads; Trisian with three faces; with uncrowned or bald masks worn by Kumbhakarn and Moola-phalum; bald masks as worn by junior officers in general; and masks of demon privates and clowns. Eyes and mouths are also brought in for differentiation. They are: snarling mouth with bulging eyes (e.g., Thosakanth, Kumbhakarn); clamping mouth with crocodile's eyes (e.g., Maiyarab, Trimegh, Mangkornkanth); clamping mouth with bulging eyes (e.g., Indrachit, Ramasoon, Suriyabhob); and snarling mouth with crocodile's eyes (e.g., Piphek and Phirap). However, the above combinations and shapes were not adequate for positive identification, so colour was also used to help identify one hundred and more demons of the *khon*. For example, many demons who wear Granok-top crown masks can be identified by the colour of their faces. Kurepan is lilac, Phya Thut purple, Vaitan light blur and Saeng Athit chinese red. The fluted-top crown mask with a green face belongs to Phya Khorn. The same crown with a vermillion face belongs to Satthasoon. Yellowish red identifies Sataloong, cinnabar red Kumbhannuraj and clay-red Pathutan.

Therefore a slight error in colouring may easily lead to confusion. If such case happens then other attributes have to be taken into consideration. For instance, both Phya Thut and Kuhn Prahat have purple faces but the former carries a lance and the latter a club. After weapons, costumes and war mounts are the next differentiating factor.

Presentation of *khon* or mask plays in Thailand is divided into five major forms:

a. *Khon Klang Plaeng*. This is the open-air mask play, in which such items as military reviews and battles are staged. The accompanying music takes the form of marching tunes, while the text consists of recitatives (*kham phak*) and dialogues without singing.

b. *Khon Rong Nork*. Also called Khon Nang Rao, this is a variety in which the play is performed on the stage with a pole, the latter serving as seating. The pole is placed towards the back of the stage, flanked by a simple curtain on which is painted a scene of mountain or forest. Like the above variety there is no accompanying tune, and only recitations and dialogues are required. There are, as a rule, two *piphat* bands (bamboo xylophones), one at each end of the stage. A development of this variety, called the *Khon Norn Rong,* is often adopted, in which a preliminary performance takes place on the first day and the main presentation on the second. The troupe stays the intervening night on or near the stage. The preliminary performance consists of inaugurative music (the *Homrong*), a sort of overture which is repeated in every set and episode of a performance. Then performers do the pole dance, which is in turn followed by the short episode of Pirab, the demon who, being in the habit of catching food or any living creature staying into his park, tries to devour Rama and his brother who are wandering in search of Sida. Pirab is eventually killed.

c. *Khon Nah Jor* or the "mask play in front of the screen", is a variety in which the presentation resembles a shadow-play. White cloth is spread as the background of the stage.
d. *Khon Rong Nai,* meaning the Court Mask Play. This variety has the greatest affinity to the dance dramas of the Court, consisting of singing as well as recitations and dialogues. The stagecraft is as well more elaborate than in other forms of the *khon.* Presentation is not divided into acts or scenes.
e. *Khon Chak* (stage play type of *khon*). This is a modern, adapted version of the *Khon* that can be presented on modern stage.

The *Khon* reflects to large extent the exactness and intricacy of Thai choreographic technique with full observance of formalities within the profession. No one, for instance, may cross the stage during a performance, except those dressed for their parts. It is for this reason that stage hands who carry properties onto the stage are required to adopt some kind of theatrical dress while performing their duties. Neglect of this formality is regarded as discourtesy to the traditional Master of the Dance and Music.

Another belief is that no performance may end in a tragedy. If Rama or his brother is wounded in battle, the performance must continue till he is cured or restored to life. Similarly the final defeat and death of Tosakanth is considered by professionals as a taboo and is never performed.

To all Thais, the *Khon* or masked play has been regarded as an integral part of the nation's cultural heritage. It is made up of various branches of the fine arts encompassing dramatic and choreographic manifestations which make it one of the world's classic traditions.

For Thailand, the *khon* does not seem confined to the stage alone. It is well known that its influence has deeply permeated our everyday life for centuries and everlasting. It is also true that the masks which are used for the *khon* play, once made for dramatic arts, have become or rather have been transformed by the creator, the performers and the public into sacred objects which are to be worshipped by all.

To some, the *khon,* masks have been both regarded and treated as *objets d'art* which could be at the same time the subject of sentiment, adoration and respect. Such a leading Thai personality as M.R. Kukrit 'Pramoj, the former Thai Prime Minister, also has his altar a mask of *Phra Phirap,* the Master of the *khon.* The realm of the *khon* mask's adorers has expanded into the field of collection and hobbyists.

The creation of the *khon* masks requires special artisans and skilled workmanship. It has its own right to claim a unique status of art. Specialists in this field have gradually become extinct. In the old days, Prince Chalerm Lakanawangse Kromamuen Vorawatsupakorn, a son of King Pin Kloa (the second king in the Rama IV reign), was recognized as a very famous mask maker. His works are now kept in the National Museum collection. At present, only two persons in Thailand are recognized as *khon* mask makers of acceptable standards. They are Mr. Chit Kaewduangyai and Mr. Charoonsawat Sukhsàwasdi, and both are retired officers and learned their skills from preceding masters of *khon* arts.

Eight different steps can be described in the process of the *khon* mask making. It begins with the structuring of the model with clay. The clay model, which is called *hoon long nai* (inner model), is then converted into a plaster model or lel or baked in the oven to convert the model into baked earthenware. From the hardened model the maker now has to revert to the process used in making *papier mache,* which involves pasting the model with *khol* paper tissue (made from paper pulp plant called *khoi*) by using rice flour paste as the adhesive. Pasting-up is done until it reaches an appropriate thickness. Then the pasted model will be left to dry in the sun. While it is still half wet, the model will be pressed by bamboo instruments to ensure that all the curvatures and the entire surface of the model are contacted and no air bubbles are left. Once the model is dry, then comes the removal of the well-set pasted paper which took the form of the hardened model beneath. This is done by cutting in half and sewing the two separated portions together.

The blank paper mask is then touched up by the lacquering process (known in Thai as *kah naeh*) to ensure proper details on the face of the mask will be made separately on cowhide. The patterns are then transferred to the mask. The next process is that of inlaying gold-leaf on the Thai black lacquered surface. In applying the colours to the mask, the mask maker uses powder colour pigments (in Thai, *sih foon*). No enamel paints can be used, as this would produce a shining surface on the mask which would make it unsuitable for stage plays. In adding beauty to the mask some prefer to decorate the forehead frame with glass flakes or ruby flakes. The more luxurious masks even use mother-of-pearl as the material for artistic patterns on the mask.

The most important part of *khon* mask making is the enlivening of the mask with lively eyes. This process, which is considered a vital step, moves the *khon* mask far beyond the status of *objet d'art* and instead makes it a sacred entity in the realm of arts. Religious ceremony is called for at the time of adding the eyes to the mask, and due to the blessing, one expects the magic eyes of mask to cast a magic spell on the world. Therefore, any time that the *khon* mask is to be used by the performer, he has to recite a prayer both to God and to the master of Profession. In so doing, he taps their mental power to ensure a good performance.

The Masks and Masked Plays of Southeast Asia

The origins and functions of masks

Few of us truly realize the wealth of artistic culture possessed by the peoples of Southeast Asia and the degree to which it has been refined and elevated. There exists a massive volume of cultural materials as recorded on monuments and in ancient document and literature, as shown more concretely in the expressions of sculpture, relief, and paintings, and as demonstrated in everyday life through customs and traditions, ceremonies, dance, dramatic performance, and the like. Today, cultural science in each of its fields is conducting research which will throw a new light on Southeast Asian Culture.

Among the most valuable of such cultural materials are masks and masked plays. The origins of masks as objects of veneration for use in ceremonies lie far in the distant past, and it is reported that the ancient tribes of Java — followers of animism — and various peoples of the surrounding areas of Borneo, Bali, and Sumatra possessed such masks. Masks used in dance and plays can also be found in a wide range of areas other than Bali and Java — for example, Malaysia, Thailand, Cambodia, Laos, and Vietnam — and ethnic traditions and myths involving masks still remain alive in such areas today, but it is not clear whether the cultural element of masks existed in such areas from the distant past or whether they are comparatively recent imports.

Masks have generally served a variety of functions with the aim of transforming personal appearance, though it has frequently been the case in Southern Asia that masks served as a means for the wearer's metaphysical transmutation into a god, ancestor, spirit, or mythic hero taking the form of a supernatural being. Through the act of donning the mask, the wearer both protects and conceals the part of the anatomy deemed most important, thus submerging his own personality to bring forth the ancestor, spirit, or mythic hero represented by the mask itself.

The functions performed by the masks vary somewhat from region to region, but in general, they can be thought to be of the following two major types in Southeast Asia:

1) Masks of supernatural beings, used for worship.
2) Masks of a uniform character used for amusement and entertainment.

The following discussion will center on these two types of masks.

Masks as objects of veneration

In such places as Bali, Borneo, and Sumatra, ceremonial masks are indeed used in ceremonies, but in addition to this function, the very act of wearing a mask for dancing or performances is in itself an object of religious belief, for through faith in the magical properties of such observances, the dance itself can become a prayer or even, at times, an effective means of driving away evil spirits.

Masks which represent only a temporary possession by spirits of one's ancestors, guardian spirits, mythic heroes, and the like also belong to this genre, and even when this type of mask is not in actual use, it may also be viewed as sacred and be carefully stored in some place of special religious meaning or importance.

The *Topeng* masked play passed down on Bali is in general known only as a play, but the masks used in the performance are not kept, as is often true, in the homes of the performers. In the case of the *Topeng* seen in the village of Sanur, the masks are kept in a small shrine in the forest, and when the masks are viewed, one must wrap around his waist the same sash — called a *saput* — that is customarily worn when entering a temple. And only after receiving the permission of the caretaker priest of the shrine can the masks, each wrapped in a white cloth which signifies veneration and stored in a bamboo basket, be viewed. The villagers each day bring offerings of flowers or holy water and worship the masks. In the village of Kuta, a mask known as "Barong" — a guardian spirit of mankind and a representative of the brilliantly shining sun and goodness personified — is carried around the village at dusk, when evil and mischievous spirits wander the earth, to the accompaniment of simple music and the ringing of gongs and cymbals to drive the spirits away. (It may only be coincidence, but the lion dance or *shishimai* of Japan in origin carries the same significance). This Barong mask, along with the Rangda mask that represents the opposing forces of evil, is wrapped in white cloth and housed in a special building. The Barong and Rangda masks, as expressions of the eternal opposition of these cosmic powers, are essential elements in the ceremonies at Pura Dalem, the temple of the dead, and such ceremonies are accompanied by large amounts

Folk Dances in Asian Villages

In the single motion and dynamic movements of folk and tribal dances in Asian villages, whether they are harvest dances, rain dances, masked dances, or animal dances, we can trace an important method for a community to communicate with its gods, ancestors and nature, expressing desires, prayers and emotions.

1

2

3

4

1. *Sword dance; a typical solo dance of northern Thailand.*
2. *Warrior dance of the Kalinga, Philippines.*
3. Kargam *dancers carrying a brass pot filled with water, South India.*
4. *Dancing on the temple grounds; Bali.*

Asian Music Scene

Music, a living form of feelings and emotions, has various faces in Asian life. In many countries of the region, traditional and folk music is a part of the enjoyment of daily life, while in some countries — where the Western influence is strong — pop music has begun to crowd out traditional forms.

1

2

3

4

5

1. *A street-musician of Nepal.*
2. *Performance in Folk Art Village in Su Wung, Korea.*
3. *Music at the Water Festival in Thailand.*
4. *Chinese in Singapore, celebrating the New Year.*
5. *Drums at Harvest Festival in South India.*

Animals and Folk Culture

Since the dawn of human civilization animals have played an important role in man's world. The special attributes of animals have inspired his religious mind, imagination and aesthetic creativity. Here are some examples of animals in various art forms that have enriched the cultural and spiritual world of Asian people.

1

2

3

4

5

1. *Bull-shaped coffins made of wood and cloth at a funeral procession in Bali, Indonesia.*
2. *Nine Dragon Wall, Beijing, China.*
3. *A statue of Hanuman, monkey god at Wat Phra Keo in Bangkok, Thailand.*
4. *Painting of Ganesha, elephant god, Nepal.*
5. *19th century painting of Hanuman in fierce mood* (Raudrarupa) — *Paithan, Maharashtra, India.*

Puppet Theatre

Various forms of puppetry have enriched folk life in Asia as popular entertainment, often connected with religious ceremonies. Puppets, or the shadows of puppets, animated by the great skill of puppeteers act out traditional myths and legends and invite the audience to the world of romance and mysticism.

1

2

3

4

5

1. *Traditional Korean puppet theatre.*
2. Yakshagana *puppet in Karnataka, India.*
3. *Burmese puppet show.*
4. *Glove puppet play* Wu-song Defeats the Tiger *in Fujian province, China.*
5. Wayang purwa, *the art of leather puppetry in Jogjakarta, Indonesia.*

of offerings before the masks. The Barong mask is implored to protect the dead from evil spirits, and it is said that presenting the masks with sufficient offerings will satisfy them (the evil spirits) and direct their attention away from the spirits of the dead. Both of these practices are evidence of the faith placed in the magical powers lurking behind the masks.

The poem "Kidung Sunda'," which relates the battle of King Sunda and King Hayam Wuruk in ancient eastern Java, describes the death of King Sunda. The elaborate funeral for the king, the poem states, included priests who donned masks to transmute themselves into the king's ancestors. The masks used in this case were made to resemble the face of the king. Today, as well, the *Wayang Purwa* shadow performances were once preceded by a ceremony wherein the dalang, the chief puppeteer or performer, who revealed the stories or teachings of the gods through his art, put on a mask resembling one of his ancestors in order to call the ancestors' presence at the performance, though such observance is not widely seen today. As can be seen from such examples, masks have had the property of temporarily housing the spirits of gods or ancestors, and for that purpose they carried the symbolic function of representing some supernatural existence. The fact that such masks were revered and worshipped and also kept in sacred confines reflects the belief in sacred confines reflects the belief in the magical power attributed to the masks which underlay such practices.

Masks as amusement and entertainment

Masks also serve another function beyond religion, that of amusement and entertainment — these are the "dramatic" or "play" masks. Such masks express the typical characters appearing in plays and join with the beat of drums and the unfolding of the drama to add greatly to the performance's atmosphere. Such a genre would include the *Topeng* of Bali and Java, the *khon* of Thailand, and the story-telling plays of Malaysia, called the *Penlipur Lara*.

Judging from the functions of the type of mask, they are regularly used only as accessories to the drama, but in some cases they do retain the mystical properties that can still be seen by crossing the Indian Ocean to Sri Lanka, Nepal, and Tibet. For example, traditional masked plays of Bali called Caron Arang and Barong Landung use masks that inspire fear in the hearts of local viewers; such masks include the demoness Caron Arang who spreads fatal disease among the villagers and the giant beast Jero Gede Metjaling who comes from the island of demons to cause magical death throughout the village. The factors directly generating the fear in this are the masks themselves, and the persons playing these roles are themselves transformed into Caron Arang, Jero Gede Metjaling, and other characters. The dramatic structure is added thereto to develop in the hearts of the spectators an actual fear of the world of the spirits, felt as both real and imaginary at the same time. In the forms of the actors wearing these masks are seen in the forms of the various demons and monsters, and although the spectators know that the performers are villagers like themselves, the sight seen is that generated by the masks. Although the masked plays of both Java and Bali bear the same name of *"Topeng"*, they differ somewhat in dramatic structure. In Java, the performances consist largely of stories of the Javanese prince Panji, and an extremely strong symbolic approach is applied: rather than the flow of the story, which is viewed as secondary, the nature of the masks which symbolize the play's characters is taken as the telling factor in the Javanese *topeng*. The play unfolds as the viewers link together the images of the various masks which appear, images which have taken on set forms for specific types of masks, a feature that is also shared with the shadow plays.

On the other hand, the *topeng* of Bali draws its stories from the historical tales of ancient Java, centering on the tale Babad as the main source for its themes. Its performances are primarily portrayals in dance, and the motions and gesture of the dancers must express the character symbolized by the masks. In addition, the story, including the most important portions, is acted out by clowns. In the case of the Javanese masked plays, the lead actors are not permitted to speak, but the clowns may speak at will, constantly parodying the lead roles. In Bali, however, the clowns take over the leading roles, themselves unfolding the drama.

The masks of the clowns are half masks (demi-masks), which signifies that they are permitted to speak. Since the masks used in Japanese folk plays for old men, the only ones allowed to convey the words of the gods to the people, had detached jaws that were moved by hemp strings, and the masks used in Italy's *Commedia dell'arte* were half masks, it is interesting to note that the masks used by clowns take a common form, in the past as today, in the East as in the West.

The reason for the use of the demi-mask in the Malaysian *Penlipur Lara* is also to allow the wearer to speak so as to carry forth the story of the play, and a large variety of masks are used to portray the characters in the plays.

In watching such masked plays, the people learn their group's myths, legends, and historical tales, at the same time learning about life through the knowledge, philosophy, and moral systems presented therein. In addition, through the ancestors, gods, spirits, and heroes symbolized by the masks, the masked plays also bring alive again through the medium of the stage the fading memories of the ancient past.

Korean Mask Dance-Drama

Masks have long been used in Korean drama and ritual. Some masks have had a purely religious function: shaman masks and the *Pangsangssi* funeral masks inspired by Chinese models. Other masks were made for more overtly theatrical purposes: The *Ch'oyong* masks used in a carefully-paced palace dance, lion dance masks, masks worn in village festivals, and the masks of the ten major folk mask dance-dramas.

The first historical record of Korean mask dance appears in a Japanese historical work, the *Nihon shoki,* which mentions that Mimashi (Kor.: *Mimaji*), a native of the old Korean Kingdom of Paekche (18 BC — AD 660) learned *Gigaku* (Kor.: *Ki-ak)* at the court of the Kingdom of Wu in Southern China, then went to Japan and taught *Gigaku* to the Japanese court in 612.

Gigaku were mask dances on Buddhist themes presented with musical accompaniment. Of Central Asian origin, these dramas were introduced into China as a means of proselytizing Buddhism. From China, the dramas spread to Korea and Japan. The Japanese have preserved hundreds of *Gigaku* masks but none of these ancient masks have survived in Korea. The next historical record of mask dance in Korea is found in the *Ogi*, or "five plays", written in the ninth century by the renowned scholar Ch'oe Ch'i-won of the Silla Dynasty. Three of the five plays in this manuscript were performed as mask dances. It is believed that numerous other mask dances were performed in the three kingdoms of Silla (57 BC — AD 935), Koguryo (37 BC — AD 668) and Paekche. Old Japanese music books list the names of ten mask dances brought from Korea at an early date, thus suggesting the popularity of these entertainments on the Korean peninsula.

Mask dances were performed throughout the Koryo Dynasty (950-1391) and until the end of the Yi Dynasty (1392-1910). In the early part of the Yi Dynasty, one cycle of mask plays, *the Sandae-dogam-nori,* enjoyed government sponsorship. In the seventeenth century, frugal officials called for the termination of royal patronage, and performances of mask dance-drama were discontinued at court. Tradition holds that thereafter, the now-unemployed actor-dancers roamed through the countryside and performed before commoners. Thus, the old court drama was transformed into what we know today as the *sangdae-dogam,* folk dramas.

Korean mask dance-dramas performed in recent times fall into three broad categories: First, there are those dramas which developed as purely local traditions and were performed at village rituals. Representative are the Pyolsin ritual drama of Hahoe, North Kyongsang Province, and the Kwano masked dance-drama performed as part of the Tano festival held in late spring at Kangnung on the East Coast. The second category is a cycle of folk dramas found throughout Korea which folklorists call the *sandae-dogam* tradition. Surviving dramas in this tradition — the Yangju Pyol Sandae Nori found near Seoul, Pongsan mask dance-drama and Kangyong mask dance-drama from the Northwest, the Ogwangdae (Five Actors Play) and Yaryu (Field Play) dramas from the far South, and the Kkokttu-gaksi puppet play performed by roving players — all encompass roughly the same sequence of dramatic action.

Finally, there is a lion dance, probably of Central Asian origin. The Lion Dance of Pukch'ong, from Northeast Korea, was performed as part of the New Year festivities.

Let us consider two regional variations of Korean masked dance-drama in the *sandae-dogam* tradition.

Yangju Pyol Sandae Nori

The Yangju Pyol Sandae Nori developed as a local variation of the *sandae* drama cycle performed throughout the Seoul region. The old town of Yangju was located at a busy intersection from which roads fanned out to several towns. Yangju was also an important stopping point on the way to Seoul. Here were to be found numerous wine houses catering to travellers and here, until recent times, was the office of the Country Magistrate. The old town is rich in historic remains: a Confucian shrine, memorials to officials, a Buddhist temple, and various stone ruins. In this setting, the drama was developed and handed down by minor officials associated with the office of the Country Magistrate. The play is performed today by their descendants.

Traditionally, the Yangju play was performed on the eve of the lunar new year, on the eighth day of the fourth lunar month (Buddha's birthday), on the Tano festival (the fifth day of the fifth lunar month), and on Ch'usok (the autumn harvest festival on the fifteenth day of the eighth lunar month). Performances were also held on special occasions such as the country magistrate's birthday.

On lunar new year's eve, the Yangju Pyol Sandae players put on masks and went all through the office of the magistrate and the government office, driving out evil spirits from each and every corner. Then, they went around the town inviting the village folk to come to a performance. It was at this time that the people donated money and rice to the players to cover performance expenses. Total expenses for a performance were born by wealthy men of the town, merchants, and others, but the performers received no individual payment for their services.

In traditional times, the play would be performed at the *Sajik-kol*, a shrine dedicated to the god of earth and the god of grain. A performance would go on all night by the light of a bonfire. Today, the play is almost always held in the daytime in the front courtyard of the old Confucian shrine.

In the past, offerings would be made in a small-scale ritual before the start of the play. Food offerings would include ceremonial wine, cakes made from glutinous rice flour, fruit of three different colours, the head of a cow, and pig's trotters. After the completion of the ritual, the players would partake of the food and wine, and with the added inspiration of the wine, the play would begin.

The Yangju Pyol Sandae play, like other masked dramas of Korea, is composed largely of dance with accompanying music to which song is added. Further, it includes scenes where speech is entirely absent, employing only pantomime and gesture, and other scenes where both monologue and dialogue appear, largely for the purpose of jesting as well as for acting out the part of the drama which calls for speaking roles. The dramatic action of the Yangju Pyol Sandae Nori, as in other dramas of the *sandae-dogam* tradition, reveals satire, lust, comedy, and lamentation as portrayed in the antics of the apostate monk, bankrupt gentry, shamans, dancing girls, servants, and commoners of all ages. Thus, the drama contains all the characteristics of traditional Korean folk literature. The themes of the play may be broadly outlined as follows:

1. Ceremonial dances for the exorcism of evil spirits and shaman rituals.
2. Satire of the ideological hypocrisy of apostate monks.
3. Criticism of the privileged status of the gentry.
4. Conflict between male and female as a critique of the tyranny of the male.
5. The misery of the everyday life of the common people.

The plot of the Yangju play, though similar in outline to other Korean mask dance-dramas, does have its own unique characteristics. The other plays depict a triangular relationship between husband, wife, and concubine, while in the Yangju play, a commoner (a police inspector) wins away the concubine of a man of letters. The triangular relationship here is not so much an expression of the conflict between male and female, but rather an expression of the rivalry between commoner and gentry. The privileged class is the object of severe contempt. The masks used in the Yangju Pyol Sandae Nori and in other Korean mask dance-drama cover the whole face and are attached to a cloth hood which covers the performer's head. These masks are thus similar to the masks worn in Greek drama and to the *Gigaku* masks preserved in Japan. The colours used for masks symbolize the "five directions" (north, south, east, west, and centre) and thereby have special connotations in the symbolic scheme of folk religion. As with the masks of China and Japan, white symbolizes the good and noble, while black connotes evil.

Though formerly carved of wood, Yangju masks are today made of gourd. Bits of pine bark, string, cloth, and fur are used to fashion features. Compared with masks in the Pongsan style, considered below, the Yangju masks are relatively realistic. The masks for each character are made according to a basic form. However, different craftsmen have added their own touches. Masks produced today have all the charm and beauty of old Yi Dynasty craftsmanship. There are 22 masks in the Yangju play with some masks used twice to accommodate the 32 characters in the play.

Masks include: two Sangjwa (young Buddhist monks), the first of these masks also being used for the character named Toryongnim, a boy or unmarried young man of the Yangban class; Omjung (the boil-faced monk); four Mokchung (Buddhist monks), Yonip (Lotus Leaf), and Nunkkumjjogi (the winker); Wanbo (a monk); Sinjubu (the acupuncturist); Waejangnyo (the procuress and mother of the young dancing girl), which is also used for the Haesan-omom (the midwife) and Tokkinui (the oldman's daughter); Nojang (the old monk); two Somu (little shamanesses), used also for the Aesadang (the dancing girl) and Tangnyo (dancing girl) roles; Malttugi (servant), also used for Sinjangsu (the shoe-seller) and Tokki (the old man's son); Wongsungi (the monkey); Ch'wibari (the prodigal), also used for the role of Soettugi (another servant); Saenim (a scholar of the Yangban class); P'odo-pujang (the police inspector); Sin-harabi (the white-bearded old man); Miyal-halmi (the old woman); and Ch'wibari-ai (Ch'wibari's baby) represented by a doll with a small-scale Ch'wibari mask. Tradition holds that *sandae* masks were burned or destroyed after a performance, but the players relate that around sixty years ago, masks were no longer destroyed. Players kept the masks in a special shrine near the performance site and repaired them once a year. After the destruction of the shrine, masks were kept in the players' houses.

The Yangju Pyol Sandae play has been designated Important Intangible Cultural Property No. 2 by the Korean government, and nine players are recognized as performers qualified to preserve and perpetuate this art.

Pongsan mask dance-drama

Although the plot of the Pongsan Mask Dance-Drama is clearly of the *sandae-dogam* tradition, the music, dance, and dialogue of the drama carry the distinct flavour of Northwest Korean folk art.

Pongsan, in the northwestern province of Hwanghae, was a thriving market town during the eighteenth and nineteenth centuries. Here, produce and grain were bartered and local handicraft industries flourished. As a market town, Pongsan had the additional advantage of being on the route taken by Chinese diplomatic missions bound for the capital. Prosperous townspeople fostered a local tradition of mask dance-drama, and players were called upon to perform at welcoming ceremonies for visiting Chinese envoys.

Adopted from the *sandae-dogam* drama performed throughout Korea by roving players, the local theatre began to appear in the early eighteenth century under the tutelage of a low-ranking government official. From that point on, a distinctly regional flavour came to be reflected in the Pongsan drama. Originally, the play's primary function was religious; performances were held to commemorate the birthday of Buddha on the eighth day of the fourth lunar month. In the nineteenth century, the mask dance-drama was incorporated into a magnificent folk festival held to celebrate Tano, the fifth day of the fifth lunar month. The Tano festival was held at a relatively slack point in the busy agricultural calendar, just before the arduous work of summer rice planting begins. As part of the festival, a performance of mask dance-drama would be held to expel evil and invoke blessings for a good harvest in the coming year.

Like similar forms of Korean mask dance-drama such as the Yangju Pyol Sandae Nori of the Seoul region and the *Ogwangdae* Nori (or "Five Actors Play") of the South, the Pongsan Mask Dance-Drama combines dialogue, dance, and music. The Pongsan Mask Dance-Drama is unique, however, in the use of quotations from classical poetry. Interspersed with prose dialogue, the poetry is chanted to drum rhythms.

Before the start of the play, performers stage a formal parade in full costume on the way to the performance site. After the parade, it was customary to perform a ritual for the guardian deities of the performance. The play would usually be performed at night in an open space by the light of a bonfire. First, farmer's music would be played and folk dances performed to the accompanying rhythm. When a large audience had assembled, the masked figures of the young monks would appear and the play would begin.

The first episode is a ceremonial dance scene in which four young monks appear and greet the deities of the four directions by bowing reverently to the east, west, south, and north of the performance area.

Then, eight Buddhist monks enter, one by one, and each monk introduces himself by speaking and dancing. When all eight monks gather together they resolve to dance and sing instead of going back to their callings as monks.

A dancing girl, the Sadang, appears followed by seven Kosa, entertainers. The seven Kosa sing and dance with the Sadang, with the Sadang initiating the song and with the seven Kosa then taking over.

In the next episode, an old priest falls in love with a young shamaness and is seduced. The flirtation between the old priest and the shamaness employs only dance, body movement, and gesture, but the result is superb comedy. This sequence is considered the very best in the Pongsan Drama. Next, a shoe-seller and monkey enter. As he sells the priest a pair of lady's shoes, the shoe seller comments on the degenerate life of the old priest. Then Ch'wibari, the prodigal, appears and challenges the old priest for the favours of the young shamaness. He is successful, and the old priest is forced to leave. The young shamaness bears the prodigal's son, but abandons it. The prodigal, however, is proud of his son.

The fifth episode is the Lion Dance. A lion comes to punish the degenerate old monk and the eight other monks. One of the monks pleads with the lion for forgiveness, swearing that the monks will never do such worldly things again. They are forgiven, and the monk and lion dance together.

The next episode depicts three aristocratic brothers and their servant Malttugi. Malttugi continuously makes fun of the three noblemen through audacious remarks and clever double entendre. He arranges a pigsty as the lodging place for his masters who are so ignorant that they don't even know what a pigsty looks like.

The final episode concerns as old man and his wife, Miyal. Miyal enters looking for her long-lost husband. She sees a musician and describes the ugly appearance of her husband to him. When she exits, her husband enters, looking for his wife. He seeks the same musician and describes the ugly appearance of his wife. Knowing that the old man's wife has just passed by, the musician tells the old man to call her. Miyal calls back and the old man and his wife are reunited. But Miyal finds a pretty concubine standing beside her husband. The three quarrel, and Miyal is killed. A shaman ritual for the dead wife concludes the play.

As with the Yangju play, three themes are evident in the dramatic action of the Pongsan play: satire involving degenerate monks, mockery of aristocrats, and the portrayal of the everyday life of the common people.

The masks used in the Pongsan Mask Dance-Drama are made of *papier-mache.* Though the characters in the play are 34 in number, only 26 masks are used, as some of the characters borrow their masks from other characters. Compared with the masks of other Korean mask dance-dramas, those of Pongsan are by far the most grotesque in form, especially the demon masks of the eight Buddhist monks. There are sharply contrasting colours, with an emphasis on red, white, and black. Pongsan masks include: four Sangjwa (young Buddhist monks); eight monks whose masks are also used by the six Kosa; the Sadang whose mask is also used by the Somu, or little shamaness who seduces the old monk; the old monk, the shoe-seller, the monkey, and Ch'wibari, the prodigal; Saenim (the first Yangban aristocrat), Sobangnim (the second Yangban); Toryongnim (the young Yangban); Malttugi, the servant; the old man; the old woman Miyal, the old man from Namgang, and a shamaness who uses the Somu mask; the lion; and Ch'wibari's baby here again represented by a masked doll.

The Pongsan Mask Dance-Drama has been designated Important Intangible Cultural Property No. 17 by the Korean government. Eight dancers have been recognized as qualified to preserve and perpetuate this mask dance-drama.

Masks in Japanese Folk Entertainment

Devil masks

At *Setsubun,* the start of spring, the Japanese scatter beans about their houses to drive out evil spirits. This particular mask — that of the devil that is driven out of the home by the scattering of beans — is perhaps in general the best known mask in Japan.

The image of "devil" appears not only at *setsubun* but in a great variety of folk entertainments. Among the many examples that could be cited is the variety of "flower festivals" celebrated throughout Aichi Prefecture, where the "Yamami", "Sakaki" and a variety of other devil dances are included in the celebrations. These devils affect huge masks much larger than the normal human face, wear red garments, and carry huge broad axes as they dance about in a foot-stamping step designed to wake up the sleeping spirits of the earth and ensure fortune for the coming year.

Among the folk activities of the Oka Peninsula of Akita Prefecture is the *Namahage* devil dance. On the last day of the year, the devils go from door to door seeking crying or lazy children in order to bring good luck to the home during the coming year. In addition to such New Year ceremonies, there are also summer Festival of Lights ceremonies throughout Iwate Prefecture, at Kosai Temple in Chiba Prefecture, and at other locations around the country which include a variety of devil dances.

Lion dances

Among the most widely distributed of folk entertainments involving devils is the lion dance, or *shishimai,* which is said to account for fully half of such folk presentations. Even though the term "lion dance" is used, the masks employed in the dance may also represent boars, deer, dragons, tigers, or other animals. The dances generally take one of two forms. One is the single dancer, where one person dons the mask of a deer, dragon, or the like and dances with other persons similarly garbed while beating a drum which he carries. This form is a characteristically Japanese form of lion dance and is found primarily in eastern Japan. The other type is the "team" dance, where two or more persons together form a single lion or other animal in a type of lion dance brought from abroad. The lion, as a mystic beast that drives away evil spirits, often leads festive processions and is also included in *bugaku, dengaku,* and *kagura,* forms of dance and dramatic performance. In the *daikagura* and *gongenmai* dances, the lion is even given the important role of a god.

Dengaku masks

When one thinks of Japanese masks, the first thing to come to mind is no doubt the *Noh* mask, and little attention is given to the masks of *dengaku, kagura, sarugaku* and other similar performances handed down from earlier ages which are closely tied to the folk beliefs of their respective periods. Japan has long been a basically agricultural society centered on the raising of rice, and there is a large number of *dengaku* dances. The *dengaku,* which were developed during the Heian Period, derived from rice-planting activities and ceremonies, marking the importance of such activities in the lives of the ancient Japanese. Today, particularly in the mountain areas of Nagano, Shizuoka, and Aichi Prefectures, there are still performances of a large number of *dengaku* dances using such *sarugaku* masks as old men, lions, demons, and the black-faced *sanbaso.* For instance, the *dengaku* of the Nishiure community of Misakubo, Shizuoka Prefecture, is a representative example. Here, the *Yoshuku* ceremony held at the New Year to ensure a year of abundant harvests is composed of *dengaku* performances in the fields using masks from the *sarugaku.* The setting is appropriate, as the term "*dengaku*" itself means "performance in the paddies."

Kagura masks

The *kagura* are performances of sacred music and dance celebrating the gods of Shinto. With the exception of the *Mikagura* of the Imperial Court, folk *kagura* are divided into three categories: *torimono-kagura,* which involves using the sacred Shinto tree *sakaki* in the dance; *yudate-kagura* in which water is heated in a large kettle and splashed on the dancers circling around it; and *shishi-kagura* which uses lion masks. One form of the *torimono-kagura* is the *Izumoryu,* which includes one section popularly called "*masked kagura*"; the masked dances recorded in such ancient Japanese histories as the Kojiki and the Nihonshoki were generally of this type. The roots of the *Izumoryu kagura* lie in the *Sada-shinnoh* passed down at Sada Temple, and this form of masked *kagura* may be found throughout the country under such names as *Iwato-shinnoh* and *Jindaishinnoh.* Most of the masks used in the *Iwato-shinnoh* are relatively recent creations based on the *Noh* mask. In the same way, the *satokagura* of Tokyo during the Edo period, a form of *torimono-kagura,* featured a large number of animal masks including foxes, monkeys, dragons and the like.

Flower festivals and the Snow Festival, Winter Festival, and Saruyama Festival of Shimoina Gun, Nagano Prefecture, belong to the *yudate-kagura* category. These festivals feature dancing through the night using a large number of masks such as demons, long-nosed Tengu, old men, and sorceresses to represent the gods in this masked dance.

The *yamabushi-shinnoh*, among the best known of the Tohoku region's folk entertainments, is called by a variety of names such as *nohmai, bangaku,* and *gongenmai.* As part of the performance of the *jinjimai* lion dance, these dances are performed on woven *tatami* mats and use masks to represent the gods or lovely women and warriors from the legends peculiar to this region.

Other folk masks

The *ennen* masked dance of Moetsu Temple and Chuson Temple in Hiraizumi, Iwate Prefecture, is performed by the Buddhist priests after certain services. The *rangeemai* dance of Kokubun Temple in Shimane Prefecture is a *chigobugaku* (a dance performed by children) and incorporates dances similar to the *ennen,* using masks of bodhisattvas and old men. In addition, in the "Ceremony of Welcoming the 25 Bodhisattvas" held at Taema Temple in Nara and Joshin Temple in Tokyo, a great number of bodhisattva masks are used as the priests walk in procession while chanting a sutra. Another quite distinctive performance is *Dainenbutsu-kyogen* comedy in which the masked dancers act out a pantomime.

Summary

The people of Japan have for thousands of years harboured a belief in gods living in another world, and at festivals, these anthropomorphic gods make their appearance through the use of a great variety of masks. The majority of the masks used in the various folk entertainments included in these festival celebrations have been carefully preserved (in form at least) and handed down over the generations as representations of the many gods, both feared and respected, to be found in the villagers' environment.

Noh: The Masked Drama of Japan

Leading up to Noh

The oldest form of dramatic presentation in Japan is the *gigaku.* At the ceremonies and services of large temples, the ceremonies would be accompanied by entertainment in the form of a series of short farces presented outside the temple. The farces would be full of laughter-provoking coarse jokes and allusions, presented through mimes, musical performances, dance performances, or masked plays. The *gigaku* mask was a large, deep mask that covered not only the face but the entire head. In general, the eyes were large and round, and the nose and mouth were also large holes, creating a humorous effect amidst the bold violence of the image. It is said that over 200 ancient masks are preserved at such temples as Horyuji and Todaiji and at the Shosoin in Nara, but these all-important *gigaku* masks seem to have completely disappeared during the Kamakura period (1185-1333).

It is possible to follow the history of the use of masks from *gigaku* through *bugaku* dance and *gyodo* masked sutra-reading processions, but the latter two forms involved entertainments adopted from abroad, dancing to accompany musical performances, or folk or religious ceremonies, and it is thus difficult to call them masked plays. The oldest type of presentation encompassing truly dramatic contents and form and still existing today is thus the Noh play. The Noh mask has been influenced by the earlier *gigaku* mask and the *bugaku* mask, and through the addition of highly-polished carving techniques, the Noh mask has become a unique dramatic means of portraying a wide range of characters.

Use of the Noh mask

"It is not the man who sees. It is the mask." This remark in the writings of Kongo Iwao, a past master of Noh, is highly suggestive of the relationship between the Noh actor and the Noh mask.

The Noh actor, having finished putting on his costume before the play, goes to the *kagaminoma,* or "mirror room." There, seating himself before a large mirror and receiving his Noh mask, he carefully dons it and then observes himself in the mirror. All of his will and concentration he pours into the mask, transforming himself from his normal, very day personality to the character represented by the mask. Through this transformation, the actor appearing on stage has become one with his mask in mind and body. The mask is the basic element in the creation of the part, and at the same time the mask itself creates its own role.

Noh is called a masked play, but not all persons appearing in the performance wear masks. The lead actor, called the *shite,* and a supporting actor called the *tsure* do indeed wear masks in a great majority of cases to portray specific roles. On the other hand, a third member of the drama, called the *waki,* never wears a mask regardless of the play being performed. The reason is that the *waki* is invariably a male role, and the *waki* always portrays a contemporary of the period when the Noh plays were created. The *shite* and *tsure*, too, with few exceptions, do not wear masks when they are portraying living male roles. In Noh, however, performing unmasked is called *"hitamen"*, *"men"* meaning mask, and the existence of such a technical term itself indicates that the use of masks in Noh is considered almost a universal practice.

What roles, then, call for masks? In general, the masked roles are elderly characters, all the female roles (for Noh has traditionally been performed only be males), ghosts, gods, demons, animals, and spirits.

A myriad of masks

The masks of old men have the characteristic feature of hair on the chin and sides of the face, and generally have wavy wrinkles and gentle eyes. When gods or spirits of warriors take the form of humans, they often use the masks of old men.

Female masks are the pride of Noh. They take a wide variety of forms depending on the age and character of the role — the innocent little girl; the maiden who combines a prim appearance with a touch of coquetry; the voluptuously charming beauty; the middle-aged woman who gives a sense of the trials and worries of life; the high-born lady; the woman burning with jealousy, the divine angel; and many, many others. While all of the female masks share such common features as hair parted in the middle, long, slightly down-turned eyes, and round, slightly smiling mouths, it is still simple to see the features that set each type of mask apart from the others. The Japanese sometimes use the phrase. "as expressionless as a Noh Mask." This phrase is unfortunate and, of course, mistaken. By only a delicate change in angle of the various features of the mask, the expression represented can change from great joy to despair. Far from being expressionless, the Noh mask can present an almost infinite range of expressions. The masks of ghosts, gods, demons, animals, and spirits are also found in great abundance. Natural human features are used for such roles as the spirit of a warrior who, having been defeated in battle, has taken his own life but is denied rest by a delusion of love that could not be fulfilled in this world. Other types include the demon who has tried to harm humans but who is driven away by the power of a sutra; gods who come to bring blessings to man, appearing from heaven or from the depths of the sea; and the spirits of spiders, foxes, or lions. The masks for such supernatural roles may carry horns on the forehead, have large, glittering metal eyes, and show a red tongue projecting from the open mouth, thus freezing a momentary expression of violent emotion. At present, some one to two hundred varieties of such masks are in use in Noh plays.

The *Kyogen* — comedies presented between performances of song and dance presentation of Noh, the *Kyogen* uses a realistic dialogue type of presentation, so that the function fulfilled by the mask is not so great as it is in Noh.

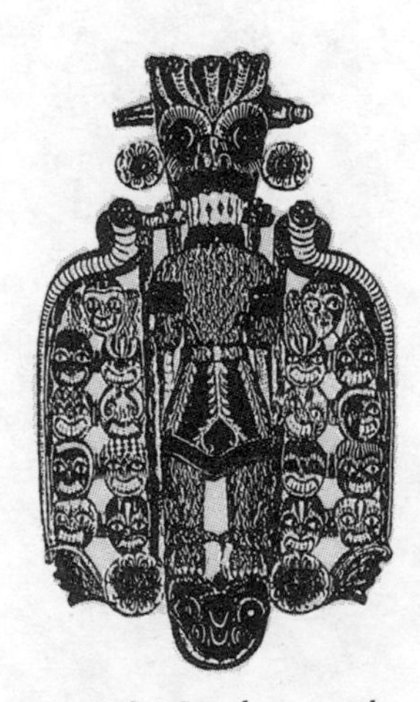

A Sri Lankan mask.

Part 3

Asian Music Scene

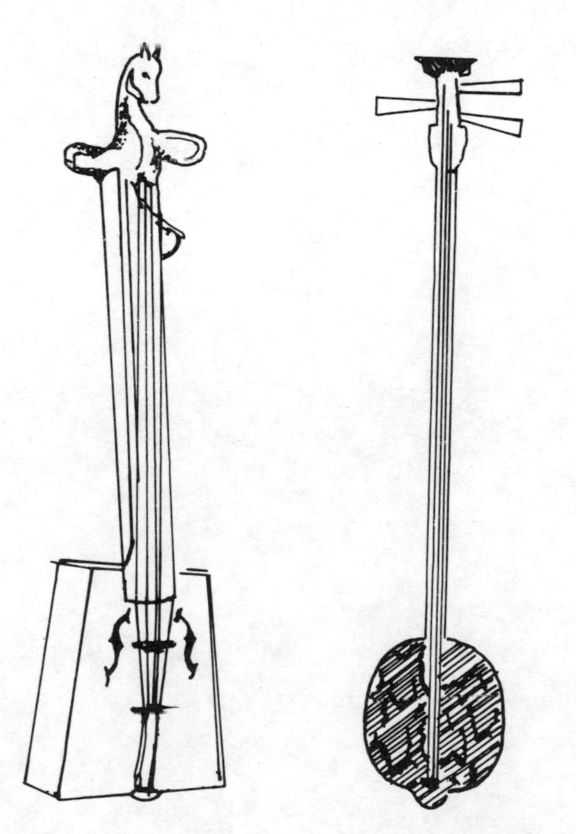

Mongolian musical instruments; Morin Knoor (left) and Shudraga (right).

Asian Music Scene

Music Horizons in India

From ancient times, the cultivation, enjoyment and appreciation of music has occupied a position of vital importance in Indian culture at all levels and in all spheres of life. So much so that music has been proclaimed the one means of attaining the accepted goal of human life in terms of socio-economic, affective-aesthetic and spiritual values. This all-embracing pervasiveness of music in the traditional cultural value of India can be envisaged in three broadly demarcated areas with interactions and mutual exchanges through the ages. These areas are:

(i) Folk, tribal, and similar varieties pertaining to the different regions and subregions.
(ii) Temple traditions connected with religions and cults.
(iii) Traditions in classical or art music.

(i) Folk and tribal varieties

These have all along been an integral part of the socio-religious life of rural and tribal communities all over India. Throughout the present century, however, and especially in the last few decades, the impact of industrialization and technological advancement has brought about changes in living patterns. As a result of these changes — the mechanization of agricultural processes for example — some of the lively varieties of functional music have gradually lost their relevance. Nevertheless, ceremonial, festive and ritualistic songs and dances, many of which are group activities, still continue to occupy a place of vital importance in the basic fabric of Indian life.

One important and noteworthy point is the marked similarity in respect of melodic arrangement as well as rhythmic movement to be found in the songs of the different regions of the country — a fact that suggests the underlying unity of basic human emotions and their manifestation through sound and rhythm as part of a common cultural heritage.

India's traditional concept of 'integrated, total theatre' with an abundance of music, dialogue and histrionics is very much alive today in several regional art forms. For instance, Tamasha of Maharashtra, Bhavai of Gujarat, Khyal of Rajasthan, Rasleela, Nautanki of Uttar Pradesh, Kuddiattam, Kathakalli of Kerala, Yakshagana of Karnatak are all important cultural activities in their respective regions. Allied to this abundance of musical experience is the rich and fascinating variety of musical instruments — both melodic and percussion — to be found in the folk and tribal musical lore of India. A point of interest is that many of these instruments resemble in their essential characteristics the descriptions found in ancient learned treatises in Sanskrit on Indian Music.

After India became independent in 1947, this folk and tribal art-lore was accorded a special place as part of India's national culture. As an important activity encouraging cultural integration, it inspired government at both central and state levels to make particular efforts to preserve and propagate its various expressions. With a view to acquainting the whole country with this rich heritage, music and dance festivals were organized from time to time. The mass media — radio and gradually television, too — are also playing a role in this endeavour. Where there is any danger of significant folk and regional art forms being forgotten or neglected, centres for their cultivation, providing specialized training, have been set up by the Sangeet Natak Akademi and the government, and others are projected.

(ii) Temple traditions

In some prominent shrines like those of the Vaishnava cults and Sikh Gurudwaras, there are long-established traditions of music as part of the daily routine of worship. There are, at these shrines, resident musicians trained in particular styles, techniques and compositions. These varieties of music often attract large audiences, and in many congregations music forms an essential part of the prayer service and devotional-spiritual discourses.

(iii) Classical traditions

Indian classical music comprises two broadly distinguished musical systems — Hindustani music, prevalent in the northern, western and eastern regions, and Karnatak music prevalent in the southern parts of the country. In spite of major and minor difference in the delineation as well as in the styles and techniques, there is a marked and fundamental unity between the two. Both are melodic systems and the Raga concept is the quintessence of the musical matrix for both. 'Tala' or time measure is the rhythmic, shape imparting component for both. Closed compositions set to Raga and Tala with ample scope for further elaboration are common to both. Both systems have roots in the ancient system of Hindu music originating and nurtured in India's philosophical traditions.

From the point of view of India's classical, learned, or art music, the twentieth century stands out as the most historic and prolifically expanding period of all. Indeed, it has been a period of resurgence, of social and cultural change, an age of a total musical explosion.

From the stage when art music was an exclusive privilege of the noble and wealthy, when the learning of music was confined to a few professional families, when musical activity was considered taboo in the intellectual sections of society, this century has moved on with tremendous strides. Changed social attitudes and perspectives, creating new opportunities for the pursuit and enjoyment of music among all sections of society, have been a vital factor in the horizontal progress and expansion of music in India. However technological advances in the recording and broadcasting of sound have endowed music with a truly revolutionizing dimension — almost as if the muse of 'sound', descending from her heavenly abode, had graciously agreed to dwell in metals and plastics. The art of a creative musician who in the context of Indian music creates a new, elaborate musical structure every time he performs, can now have an existence independent of himself. Though the radio, the gramophone and tape recordings, the general public is coming into contact with classical music, and growing awareness and interest is evident everywhere. Music conferences, societies, academies and Centres for the Performing Arts form a 'live' factor in the increasing availability of music to large numbers in a vigorous, direct form. Attendance at some of these programmes, particularly in big cities like Bombay, Calcutta, Madras, and Delhi, may run into hundreds and even thousands. This is an indication of the growing interest among the general uninitiated public in classical music. Both the vocal and the instrumental styles of the Hindustani and the Karnatak systems are being made available to listeners all over the country.

New avenues

After the advent of the 'talkie' film, during the last four decades or so, formidable amount of film music has come into existence. By and large, though, in recent decades, Indian film music has tended towards a more unconventional miscellany of sounds. Its easy dubious charm is all-enveloping, and records and radio have been instrumental in its widespread dissemination among the masses.

Alongside this development, great deal of non-film popular music has arisen in response to a demand for new modes of expression with an 'of the moment', contemporary relevance. The themes are varied — devotional, patriotic, romantic, and lyrics with a ready appeal. Musically, there is a conglomeration of regional, folk, classical and also non-Indian elements. Community and group singing is gaining a lot of ground too, with a number of professional and youth choirs being formed.

Moreover, with opportunities for high national honours and awards, academic and professional positions and engagements, subsidies and organized promotion on his behalf, the musician is now entitled to high social status.

Thus India is ringing to the sound of music. A streamlined sense of direction is perhaps yet to emerge. The total picture, however, is one of an affirmative assurance and suggests a favourable future.

Singapore: "Instant Asia" — Varieties of Music

"INSTANT ASIA" is a catch-phrase adopted by the Singapore Tourist Promotion Board to lure foreigners to Singapore. Daily at a seaside hotel in Pasir Panjang on the West Cost an "Instant Asia" show is presented featuring the song and dances of Singapore's main ethnic groups: Chinese, Malay & Indian.

While such a cultural diversity does provide a varied fare for the tourist, this dissimilarity imprints itself on life-style patterns and also on musical tastes. Thus in any discussion regarding the music of Singapore, no common canvas can be painted, instead, a diversified picture embracing the peculiar diatonic progression of Chinese melodies, the languor and subtly exciting rhythms of Malay music, the complex rhythmic structures of the table of the English educated people would have to be presented. This complexity is further aggravated by a host of dialect groups within the Chinese majority.

This multi-racial characteristic is clearly illustrated in the programmes of Radio and Television Singapore, which is run by the Ministry of Culture. The time distribution of programmes per week for Radio is as follows:-

Malay 126 hrs
Chinese 147 hrs
Tamil 105 hrs
English 126 hrs

And for Television

Malay 11-1/4 hrs
Chinese 26 hrs
Tamil 9-1/3 hrs
English 57 hrs

The only other radio station is Rediffusion, a commercial enterprise which leases out a total of 85,000 sets and relays its programmes through a wired broadcast system. Because of commercial considerations, programmes are mainly in Chinese and English.

An examination of the above reveals heavy emphasis on English and Chinese, with Malay and Indian playing a secondary role and all this closely tied to the nature of the population distribution, with the larger part of the people being English speaking.

Western music

The English speaking peoples of Singapore naturally tend to the West in their musical preferences, and with modern rapidity in dissemination, pop stars of the West are automatically the idols of the Singapore teenager, and the latest fads and idiosyncrasies of Western pop music be it rock, soul or country and Western, immediately catch on with the young English speaking Singaporean. Charts which give the top tunes currently in favour in English and America are hardly any different from those in Singapore.

To combat the pop craze, the Ministry of Culture has embarked on a series of concerts to attract both young and old to the more serious forms of Western and local ethnic music. These concerts are heavily subsidized with nominal charges for admission to the "Music for Everyone" series and free admission to the "concerts for the Young" and "Meaningful Music" series. Attendances at the "Music for Everyone" series has increased appreciably during the past few years. The aim of these series is to give opportunities to local talented musicians to perform in a formal concert and also to scout for new talent. Foreign professionals are also featured and the services of such musicians are usually obtained through the courtesy of foreign embassies in Singapore. "Concerts for the Young" are held in the Lecture Hall of the National Library and as its name implies, features talented young musicians from around 8-15. A new series has recently been started, "Meaningful Music", which are music appreciation lecture concerts for young people to develop an interest in serious music.

The National Theatre also regularly presents programmes for the serious music lover; foreign orchestras and large cultural groups are often presented in the 3,500 capacity theatre. Because of the semi-open nature of the theatre, acoustics can sometimes be a problem. Previously, the National Theatre maintained a symphony orchestra, which gave concerts under the baton of such would famous conductors as Ron Riklis and Norman del Mar but, because of heavy maintenance expenses, this orchestra had to be disbanded. In the private sector, impresario Donald Moore helps to keep the serious music flame alive with the importation of the big names in music.

There are a number of music societies catering for the amateur music maker and music lover. These include the oldest music society in Singapore, the Singapore Musical Society, which is now pursuing a very successful series of household concerts, the Chamber Ensemble, Which annually presents two to three concerts and the Metro Philharmonic which has a fine orchestra and choir.

Music as a profession

A music teacher in Singapore earns on an average of about $1,000/= to $2,000/= per month*, which is quite high by local living standards. Professional musicians however are not so lucky in that there are no professional orchestras in Singapore. Because of this, it is exceedingly difficult to find sufficient competent musicians to form ensembles and orchestras. Those with exceptional performing talent normally go abroad to find employment and those that remain behind resort to teaching as their chief means of subsistence, performing as and when required for nominal sums.

Employment in hotels, restaurants and nightclubs however is more remunerative. Here, there are two categories of musicians, those which have taken up the traditional instruments of the dance orchestra, e.g. trumpet, trombone, saxophone, etc. and who can competently read music notation and those who form beat groups using electric guitars and synthesizers. The latter rely on head arrangements of the latest hit records, mainly using chord symbols to effect cohesion. Hotels and restaurants which feature floor shows, usually engage two or three bands including a dance orchestra to play the orchestrations required for floor shows and cabaret acts. These bands circulate around the various entertainment establishments of the hotel, performing for about an hour in each place. Working hours are normally form 9.00 p.m. to midnight or 1.00 a.m. with extensions on Saturdays and holidays. Employment is on a contract basis for 3-6 months with musicians earning $1,000/= to $3,000/= per month. Because of the necessity to change entertainment frequently, employers have resorted to importing musicians from abroad, mainly from the Philippines and Hongkong. Immigration laws however are very strict and require the employer to engage on local musician for every foreigner employed.

Radio & TV

Way back in the 50's when Singapore was a British colony, Radio Singapore maintained a chamber orchestra comprising mainly of expatriate musicians. While this tradition has been maintained, the composition of the orchestra has completely changed and now consists of trumpet, trombone, saxophones and a rhythm section under the leadership of Mr. Ahmad Jaafar with Mr. Rufino Soliano as Dy. Leader. Augmentees are used to supplement the orchestra on a part time basis. All members are very competent musicians preferring to play western music but because of the dictates of policy and the dearth of good Malay and Chinese recordings, the orchestra is mainly used to back such singers in local Malay and Chinese radio and television productions. Members of the orchestra

* In the year 1976-77 — Singapore dollars

are paid a monthly salary of between $1,000/= and $2,000/= per month. Singers and musicians who are engaged to appear on local radio and television productions are paid on a graded basis. Musicians are paid approximately $15/= per hour for their services, whereas singers are paid per appearance in a programme averaging $60/= to $80/= per programme. Most radio and television music programmes like "Bintang Irama", "Rangkaian Melati" and "Chinese Variety Show", are pure variety shows with a few comedy acts thrown in. One perennially favourite programme has been the "Talentime" series which is an annual competition for singers and musicians. "Talentime" which first started as a radio programme some 15 years ago, is now a heavily sponsored television programme with sponsors providing fantastic prizes for eventual winners. This series has also acted as a stepping stone for some of Singapore's more successful recording artistes.

Chinese music

Previously there was a marked division between the English educated Chinese and those who received their education in Chinese schools. However this has become a thing of the past with the introduction of compulsory bi-lingualism. In schools children are required to learn two languages and the ultimate choice is English, either as a first or second language. Although Mandarin is the language taught in schools, some of the dialects spoken at home are Hokien, Teochew or Cantonese.

Traditional Chinese music when performed, is closely related to religious festivals. During the month of August, the Chinese opera or wayang is performed in various districts in Singapore. A temporary shed is erected, electricity connected and under the glare of neon lights, actors and actresses reenact the history of ancient China. The accompanying orchestra consists of melodic instruments on side, usually a yang chin (zither) and one or two er hus (violins) and drums, gongs and cymbals on the other side. The melodic instruments usually accompany the singers whereas the percussion instruments are used mainly to dramatize the development of the plot.

The traditional Chinese funeral is an elaborate affair, the length of the funeral procession dependent on the economic status of the deceased. Music is a prominent feature in such processions and beside the incongruous western brass band traditional Chinese music accompanying the processions consists purely of about 25 to 30 cymbal like gongs and huge drum all beating out a steady rhythm. The Chinese orchestra is a recent development but is quickly gaining popularity. The Chinese orchestra is built on the same principles of the symphony orchestra with its four main sections of strings, woodwinds, brass and percussion, but with one main difference. Because of the lack of brass instruments in the range of Chinese instruments, the string section is divided into plucked and bowed strings.

At present, the People Association runs a very fine orchestra. The full time instructors of the orchestra are paid salaries ranging from $400/= to $800/= per month with other musicians being paid part time allowances. One orchestra which has won honours abroad is the Singapore Youth Chinese Orchestra run by the Ministry of Education sponsored Young Musicians' Society. Members of the orchestra have won awards at Teeside and the Llangollen Eistedfodd in Wales. At Llangollen in 1974 the Singapore Youth Choir caused a major upset in the Youth Section when it won 1st Prize beating some of the finest Youth Choirs in the world.

Popular Chinese music

Whereas serious Chinese music has a limited following, Chinese pop music has made a big impact. Walk into any small coffee-shop, barbershop, small eating house or big restaurant and you will find Chinese pop music pouring out of hidden speakers. Walk along the beaches or along the many public parks and you will find one in every group carrying a cassette recorder playing the latest Chinese hit tunes.

To define a Chinese hit tune is just as difficult as to define a Western pop hit. Is it the melody, the lyrics or the singer? Fortunately or unfortunately, Singapore is not wholly caught up in the lucrative pop song production business. Most of the songs which become popular emanate from Taiwan, which is undoubtedly the nerve centre for pop songs for the Chinese peoples which populate East Asia. A close second is Hongkong, where songs specially composed for films catch on with the local Chinese who see the films. Pop music from Taiwan and Hongkong flood the Singapore market mainly through Lp's and cassettes with the Ep gradually losing favour. Although the music backing for most of the songs are heavily western influenced using the latest rhythms, the melodic outline retains a Chinese flavour which together with the Mandarin lyrics distinguishes it from its western counterpart. However, the prevalent western pop feature of composer/singer being the same person, e.g. Elton John, Carol King and Gilbert O' Sullivan is not evident, moreover no pop groups on the scale of Led Zeppelin, Deep Purple, Brotherhood of Man or ABBA have risen to prominence in Chinese pop music. What generally happens in Singapore is that local record producers study the popularity of imported songs, collect a dozen to sixteen of the most popular, and engage a local singer with a local beat group to record the songs. Chinese people in Singapore prefer the simplicity of the guitar group to the lush strings, brass and reeds employed to back Taiwan singers on the original recording. In the uncertain world of pop music, singers come and go and Singapore is no exception. During the 50's, singers like Poon Siow Keng and Foo Soo Yin held sway. Poon Siow Keng had an unusually low voice, which was high suited for sentimental ballads. EMI used to send her to Hongkong for recording sessions. In the 60's a new breed of singers came into the picture. Singers like Rita Chao and Sakura added new dimensions to Chinese pop music which came under the influence of the twist, rock and cha cha. Although there are a number of recording artistes in Singapore today, one name however need to be mentioned — Chang Siao Ying, who has retained her popularity for the past 10 years. Her first taste of success came when she won First Prize in a Talentime contest organized by Rediffusion. For two years she hedged off recording offers, finally succumbing to releasing her first record "Three Dreams" which was an instant success. "Three Dreams" was originally a Japanese folk tune with Chinese lyrics added. Since then she has cut nearly a hundred records and her fame has spread throughout South East Asia. Some of her records have been sold in U.K., Holland and America. Her musical activities however have been confined purely to the recording studio, having never taken up a nightclub engagement and only making personal appearances for charity shows. At one Red Cross Charity show in Bangkok, she was presented with a bouquet of flowers from Queen Sirikit of Thailand and she has always cherished this honour. Chang Siao Ying is a very happily married woman, spending most of the time with her family, playing table tennis, or going swimming.

Malay popular music

Whereas in traditional Chinese music there are no definite rhythms and as seen in the wayang (chinese opera), the percussion section is used mainly to emphasize the melody or dramatic development, several exciting rhythm patterns have developed in traditional Malay music, like the kronchong, joget, masri, etc. The kronchong is romantic in character with a slow lyrical melody, but the accompanying rhythmic pattern gives a double tempo feel which together with floried ornamentation by the guitar and pizzicato accentuation of the rhythm by the cello has made it a perennial favourite with the Malay community. The joget is a lively 2/4 or 6/8 dance of Portuguese origin, passed on to the Malays when they occupied Malacca during the seventeenth century. Other influences include Arabic, because of the Muslim religion and India.

In order to preserve the Malay identity, the joget and Kronchong are often used by modern pop composers as vehicles for their compositions. Modifications however are made, such as heavier accentuation of the beat in keeping with present day tendencies in pop music. Whereas the Chinese have developed their own instruments, the Malays use western instruments, e.g. violin, accordion and guitar to form the traditional ensemble.

Today, melodies and character of accompaniment faithfully follow pop styles currently in vogue in the West. Melodic phrases, harmonies and rhythms are carbon copies and if not for the language the difference would not be recognizable. The centre for creativity and production is Jakarta, Indonesia, where talented composers and singers abound and whose records are constantly exported to Malaysia and Singapore. Singapore does have its Malay singers and during the 50's and 60's the EMI studios in Orchard Road were kept busy producing records for the large market in Malaysia. With the split between Singapore and Malaysia, Malaysian singers who previously used to come to Singapore for recording sessions, now record in Kuala Lumpur where new recording studios have been set up.

Names like P. Ramlee, Saloma, Asiah and Momoh have long been household words among Malays in Malaysia and Singapore. P. Ramlee, apart from his singing abilities, was also film director, script writer, composer and actor. His untimely death a few years ago was indeed a great loss. His wife Saloma was for a long time the queen of song and together with Asiah and Momoh were the stars of the EMI studios. With the passing of time new names have cropped up like Kartinah Dahari and Julie Sudiro. Today Milah Hussein, Rahimah Rahim and Anita Sarawak are the top names in Malay pop music in Singapore.

When they take up nightclub work, most Malay singers usually sing in English as the demand is for English or Chinese songs. There are no Malay nightclubs as such and Malay songs become popular through records or radio and television.

Take Milah Hussein as an example. At night Milah sings at the Peking Restaurant in Orchard Road, where there are three other Chinese singers. As this establishment is more famous for its food, entertainment is on a modest scale as compared to those provided in theatre restaurants and nightclubs. At the Peking, Milah sings mainly in English as hardly any Malays patronize this place. Because of the large number of Japanese patrons, she has included Japanese songs in her repertoire and also a few Chinese songs.

Mainly self taught, Milah started singing in public at the early age of 12 in a radio programme with an amateur group "Four Plus One". Today she draws more than a thousand dollars a month singing at the Peking. Milah has an unusually husky voice which thins out when she reaches out for the higher notes of the scale. Coupled with a very pleasing and appealing personality, she was selected to represent Singapore in the combined Asean Radio and TV stars tour of 1975. For her television and radio appearances, Milah usually sings Malay or English songs depending on the requirements of the programme, but for her records it is purely Malay songs.

This bi-lingualism is not an unusual phenomenon as the government, in order to effect better communication between the multiracial people has made bi-lingualism an educational policy. Musicians themselves have to be versatile to interpret the unconventional diatonic leaps of Chinese melodies, the ever-changing western pop hit or the intricate rhythmic patterns of Malay music.

This then is the contemporary music scene in Singapore, as complex as the peoples who populate this little island, a complexity which has led to the coining of "Instant Asia" a phrase to all intents and purposes eminently applicable to multi-racial Singapore.

[Note : all currency used in the article refers to Singapore Dollars.]

Folk Songs of Mongolia

In the Mongolian steppes, people are proud of their treasure of folk music dating back some 1000 years. There are many beautiful songs that add to the cultural heritage. They are a crystal mirror which reflects the ancient history of the country, the essence of the national spirit and the echo of the ancient times.

The traditional folk songs are classified into nine categories according to the text: 1. Lyrical songs, 2. Songs of life, 3. work songs, 4. comical songs, 5. military songs, 6. historical songs, 7. religious songs, 8. revolutionary songs, and 9. songs taken from literature. According to their musical structure, they may be divided into types, *bogino duu* (short song) and *urtyn duu* (long song).

Bogino duu is the original form of Mongolian folk song. The characteristics of this types are small range of tone, fixed rhythm, and asymmetrical and fairly flexible structure. Generally speaking, the folk songs of Mongolia are based upon a pentatonic scale without semitones. From the beginning of this century, the repertoire of short songs has broadened to include new themes, such as urban and revolutionary songs. *Urtyn duu*, the long song, has a long and continuous melody on a free rhythm, in a broad range full of *tremolo* and ornamental notes. It reflects vividly the boundless plain, the wild range of mountains and nomadic life of the people. Long songs can more precisely divided into three types:

1. *Besreg urtyn duu* (simple long song), 2. *Urtyn duu* (long song), 3. *Aizam urtyn duu* (solemn and exalted long song).

Besreg urtyn duu is the shortest form of the long song, in other words, the lengthy short song. It is affectionate and lyrical in nature and its range is not so broad as the other types. It has a simple form without falsetto or *shuranhai*, which is also typical of the other long songs.

Urtyn duu, the most popular form of long song, depicts love for the motherland, the beauty of nature, and deeds of heroes. It has a broad range of tones, a melody in a slow tempo with rich ornaments, and falsetto.

Aizam urtyn duu has a solemn and exalted character with a deep psychological expression, using double falsetto and delicate ornamental notes.

The characteristics of the long songs may be summed up as follows: In the first place, there are no restriction in meter. Therefore, it allows the full play of imagination, improvised and free singing. In the second place, the range of voice is broad enough to suit the character of the song. Most of the short songs have the compass of one octave, having the third interval, while the compass of long is two octaves, having sixth and seventh intervals. In the third place, the notes take a great leap in long songs. Notes abruptly jump from higher note to lower note, or the other way around. In the fourth place, the solemn long songs require the singer to have the prefect technique of singing, great artistic expressions and the broad mind and maturity to allow improvisation. The singers of Mongolia know that singing technique means the technique of breathing. Therefore, they train themselves to acquire the skill of controlling breath and technique of breathing extremely. At the same time, they are skilled in vocal and phonetic requirements, such as pronunciation, vocalization and sound effect. In the fifth place, the solemn long songs are rich in melisma. The composition is so complicated that it is difficult to reflect all the delicate ornaments in it.

Anybody who listens to a superb long song of Mongolia cannot help feeling admiration and marvel at the song. Now, let me introduce one popular song each of the short song and the long song.

Ehiin Ach (My Dear parents)

This folk song is of the *bogin duu* (short song) type, which is simple in rhythm and structure. It is an expression of gratitude to parents.

■ *My Dear Parents*

1. My Dear father,
   Made a cradle for me from Urel.
   My dear mother,
   Woke and fed me at her breast,
   At night in cold winter.
2. My dear father,
   Made toys for me from Nars.
   My dear mother,
   Fed me at her breast,
   At night in chilly autumn.
3. Getting a tall bay horse ready
   At night in winter,
   I will go to see my father
   Who is old and gray-haired
   Early tomorrow morning.
4. Getting a slender fine house ready
   At night in autumn,
   I will go to see my mother
   Who is old and gray-haired
   Tomorrow at sun rise.
5. Mountains are covered with snow.
   Thinking of my old father and mother,
   I cannot stop singing songs.

■ *Zambu Tiviin Nar* (The Sun of the Rose-Apple Land).*

This folk song is of the *urtyn duu* type. In the slow and free melody, it depicts the glorious haven that provides the light and sorrow of human life. The singer freely improvises her own verses from the first verse of the written text.

The Sun of the Rose-Apple Land

1. Yes, the sun of the rose-apple land
Eternally glittering and ever bright
On all of this earth's beings
Fairly sheds its golden light, alas, doesn't it?
2. Yes, like the beaming of the sun
The benevolence of my people
Will equally bless everyone
Who is honest and gentle, alas, won't it?
3. Yes, as sunshine through the rent
Short is one's life indeed
But believing it will ever last
Many are deluded so badly, alas, aren't they?
4. Yes, it is toilsome indeed
once aged and grey headed
to learn what you missed
When young and bright-minded, alas, isn't it?

*According to the traditional Mongolian cosmography, this is the southernmost of the seven major continents which surround the mythical mountain Meru.

Japanese Popular Music: "Radio Culture" and "New Pop"

ne of the characteristic features of Japanese culture is the way in which the cultural elements of a variety of lands exist side by side in harmony, exerting a constant influence on the existing culture and generating a new resultant culture. Music is certainly no exception.

The music listened to by the Japanese as a part of their daily lives is extremely diverse, and in addition to the particularly Japanese popular music of the Japanese masses, the young people of this country are also avid fans of rock, popular music, and jazz from the United States and Britain, the chansons and canzone of France and Italy, and even, recently, the folk music of the Andes Mountains of South America. A piece of foreign popular music makes its debut on Japanese radio and at almost the same time it becomes a hit in its native country, and a wide range of foreign performers are constantly — and very successfully — appearing in concert in Japan.

But although there are a great number of Japanese fans of foreign music, there are limits to each type's popularity; American popular music and rock are for the young, and chansons are the special province of their own "aficionados". The music that receives the broadest support from the public in general is Japan's own original popular music.

At present, this wholly Japanese popular music is divided into two main categories. One of these is conventional popular music, wherein the efforts of separate singers, composers, and lyricists are brought together by the music industry to create a song which is then presented to the public. The other category is something new to Japan, developing just during the last ten or so years, and is represented by a singer who writes the lyrics or music or both of a song he performs, thus using the existing music industry but operating outside of its conventional channels. Let us look first at the features of the first category. The majority of the popular music today aimed at the Japanese masses is composed of vocals, with almost no pure instrumentals, and this feature has been present throughout the history of Japanese music. During the latter half of the nineteenth century, however, Japan was opened to the West after over 200 year's existence as a "closed country," and the active modernization of the country was begun. This same point marked the beginning of a major qualitative change in the music of the Japanese masses. Japan's modernization has constantly followed the path of observation and duplication of contemporary Western society, and the same sort of process has been at the core of Japanese musical development as well.

One major factor in determining the musical tastes of the Japanese people has been musical education. In the musical education provided in Japan during its modernization in the nineteenth century, modern Western music was held up as the ideal, with Japan's traditional music being ignored either as "pre-modern" or as beneath notice. The scale used in school music was a blending of Western and Japanese scales, but because of a lack of basic understanding of the structure of Japanese music, this scale had some features in common with Japanese traditional music but was basically different. As shown by the brilliant results of Zoltan Kodaly of Hungary, musical education based on the independent musical sensibilities of an ethnic group can give rise to a rich musical art, but in spite of this, Japan followed the opposite course for a century. Though the aim was the Westernization of the Japanese people's sense of music, it is unreasonable to expect the rhythms, scales, method of vocalization, and other basic elements of foreign music to be grafted onto Japanese musical tastes overnight, and the Japanese masses have unconsciously come to give their allegiance to a form of popular music that has various elements in common with traditional Japanese music. As a result, today's mass popular music is a strange blending of Western music and Japanese music as it had developed up to the introduction of Western musical influences. This popular music, with its particular characteristics, developed around the beginning of the twentieth century, but up to and after World War II, it was strongly influenced "by" American popular music, so that while it still retained traditional elements, a mass music very close in form to that of the West steadily gained ground. The result is that today there are two main lines of mass music in Japan, one still strongly tinted by traditional elements of Japanese music and the other, as described above, strongly Western in nature.

The popular music of the Japanese masses, unlike Japanese folk music with its strong ties to particular localities, become popular throughout the country through the influence of the record industry. With the spread of radio and television, the music industry developed as a distinct entity following the war and become able to create fashions in music. Popular music, just as the term implies, takes as its audience huge numbers of people throughout the land, and as such it relies heavily on the mass media. Let us look at the relationship in Japan between the music industry and popular mass music.

Music is experienced only indirectly through the mass media of radio and television. Either or both of these media are present in virtually every Japanese home, whereas the whole family joins in watching the same thing on television, the radio is a more personal possession, and there may be several within the same household. In the urban areas there are both privately-operated television broadcasting stations and a semi-government system, for a total of about eight channels. Every day at least one or more of these stations, with the exception of one educational channel, broadcast popular music programs, most of these having an audience in a studio or hall shown watching the singers on stage, with the audience participants drawn from persons who have requested tickets. Television has a largely visual cast (the faces and movements of the performers, etc.) in its presentation of popular music.

Radio, on the other hand, offers a total of around eight private and semi-government stations (including one educational station) on the medium wave band and one private and one semi-government station on short-wave. Radio is the most effective medium for popular music, and musical programs are incomparably more common on radio than on TV.

In particular, broadcasts on some private radio stations go on 24 hours a day except on Sunday, with almost the entire day being devoted to programs dealing with popular music, including that from abroad. Since the make-up of the listeners varies depending on the time period, the daytime features older popular selections aimed at the housewives, while the evening hours are largely given over to English and American rock and popular music for the young, along with Japanese popular music strong in the same elements as such foreign music. The late-night broadcasts from one to five a.m. are in particular put together with the young in mind, forming what could even be called a type of "late-night radio culture." The reason that young people are listening to radio late at night in such numbers is the "entrance exam war," the excessive preparation required for the entrance examinations for senior high school and university. In today's Japan, the university from which one graduates has a major bearing on the rest of one's life, and teenagers must spend many long hours in study and preparation for the university entrance examination. While pouring over their books, they listen to the late-night radio broadcasts in part to stay awake but also in large part because the music presented accurately reflects the tastes of the young.

Further, the disc jockeys on these programs are quite often popular musicians themselves, practitioners of the new popular music mentioned earlier. In the case of radio, the programs often accept request postcards from the listeners of have telephone facilities in the studio for a direct give-and-take with the at-home audience, thus soliciting the participation of the listening masses.

In addition to these two mass media, the music industry also includes cable broadcasts. Such cable broadcasts offer a selection of channels, mood music, Japanese popular music, American popular selection and the like, for use by coffee shops, restaurants, bars and other eating and drinking establishments, department stores, supermarkets, boutiques and other shops, Japanese "pachinko" pinball halls and similar game centers, and variety of other establishments contracting the background music service. People are thus exposed, at times without conscious awareness of the fact, to such cable music broadcasts as they meet and talk with others, shop, eat, drink, or play.

In this way, people come into contact with currently popular songs or new selections through the mass media and cable broadcasts, and also through newspapers, magazines, and other printed matter, and they go out and buy recordings of those that catch their fancy. Almost all homes in Japan now have record players, stereo sets, or tape recorders (particularly cassette tape recorders), and listening to records and tapes has become an everyday activity. Stimulating the public's purchase of such records and tapes is the ultimate goal of the music industry, and the industry is exerting a wide range of efforts to this end.

Thus, popular music becomes a product for sale in so far as the music industry is concerned, and lyrics, melody, the attractiveness of the performer, and his or her background, and various other individual elements are packaged and presented as a whole for the public's consumption. In short, a singer finds himself singing a song set before him by the composer and the lyricist, and such a song is often far removed from the performer's own experiences, feelings, and personality. It was just such a wide-spread situation that generated a new trend in popular music as mentioned above. Several years ago, around 1964, the English rock group, the Beatles and American folk singers such as Peter, Paul, and Mary, the Brothers Four, and Joan Baez exerted a great influence on the youth of that day, gradually fostering ideas of harmony and deep concern for the nuances of rhythm that had not originally been a part of the Japanese approach to music. New introductions were not limited merely to musical techniques: the youth of Japan were also exposed to the method of expressing one's own assertions in the form of a song, a phenomenon which can be seen in protest folk music.

One particularly marked development was that the young people from 15 to 25 — regardless of the level of their proficiency and regardless of whether or not they aimed at becoming professionals — took up guitars and first started to play music of foreign composers, little by little beginning to compose their tunes and lyrics. At the same time, many amateur groups were formed, centering on the electric guitars the members had learned to use after the example of foreign rock groups. Various rock and folk bands began to hold concerts in all parts of Japan, winning many followers but also refining their own music and eventually becoming able to attract a wide range of supporters in addition to the limited number of ardent rock and folk fans. This can be clearly seen in the greater and greater number of their own original musical numbers placed on the popular music hit charts by such groups beginning around 1972. This was of course in part the result of the "ready-made" music industry's interest in this new trend and its use of such music on records and in the mass media, but seen from the musician's point of view, these new-wave musicians have used the music industry as a means of placing their own compositions before a broader range of the public. Such new music went beyond the conventional popular music, which gave the public only prepackaged, ready-made music, by promoting among the Japanese people an active, enthusiastic attitude toward music.

There are even some people who have begun to think about their own cultural roots as they relate to music, taking another look at the traditional music of Japan. This makes it seem increasingly possible that Western music and American popular style will no longer be the only ideals, but that a new form of Japanese popular music may arise. Another possibility is also appearing — that Japanese popular music will escape its present state of mere passive listening to become a leading medium for active self expression.

The Philippine Pop Music Scene

After 400 years under the Spanish regime and another half century of American rule, the Philippine has become so westernized that its pop music scene is dominated by the usual names leading the top hit charts in the United States and England.

As in many countries where rock and soul have made rather deep inroads, Filipino youngsters are very familiar with pop artists like Elton John, Eric Clapton, Diana Ross, Roberta Flack, Dionne Warwicke, Stevie Wonder, John Lennon, Paul Mc Cartney, Helen Reddy, Paul Simon, Art Garfunkel, the Jackson Five, the Stylistics and many more whose names will fill up a long list.

Switch on any radio in the Philippines and nine times out of ten, you will get a good dose of rock, soul, the hustle, the salsa and just about any other form of pop music. Turning from station to station will get you the same results. It has been estimated that about 80 to 90 per cent of the programming of Philippine radio stations is made up of pop music in its varied forms. In Metro Manila, with a population of same five million, there is only one radio station exclusively broadcasting classical music. The rest are pop-oriented from sign on to sign off, which is an average 18 hours a day. The lopsided emphasis on pop is not without reason. Recording companies with foreign tie-ups have sufficient resources to make disc jockeys play only the records they want promoted.

Toward the Filipinization of the music industry, the newly organized Philippine National Entertainers Association (PHILNEA) led by Victor Wood and Julius Obregon, has however undertaken positive steps to remedy this situation, with the Kapisanan ng mga Brodkaster sa Pilipinas (KBP) a private organization sanctioned by law to police the radio and TV profession, into cleaning the broadcast industry ranks. The Broadcast Media Council, the policy-making body headed by Teodro Valencia, also took steps to help stop the current "payola" system by prohibiting disc jockeys from selecting what records are to be played in radio programs. As a result, Philippine radio stations are now obliged to play at least one Filipino recording for every broadcast hour. This may not be much but still, it means that something concrete has been done to give Philippine music a better airing by the Philippine broadcast industry.

The executive vice president of the Manila Entertainment Corporation, Oskar Salazar, who was at one time connected with several top recording firms in the Philippines, has observed that about 90 per cent of radio time is allotted to the playing of foreign records and only 10 per cent for Philippine songs.

"As a result," he said, "this has undermined the incomes of singers, composers, musicians and others in the Philippine music industry. Recording companies prefer to promote foreign records because of the big financial reward in selling them. But if this continues, this would defeat the program of the government to encourage Filipinos to patronize Philippine products and the moulding of a new Filipino character." The Philippine Musicians Guild headed by Alfredo Robles joined ranks with the PHILNEA in pressing for the improvement or working condition for Filipino musical artists in the entertainment and broadcast industry.

The Department of Trade Secretary Troadio Quiazon gave the assurance that after the inter-agency committee which he created had submitted its probe study, the Department of Trade will propose measures to President Marcos to improve the Philippine music industry. Among the proposals is the establishment of a government regulatory body to be known as the National Music Commission, which would be empowered to regulate and supervise the music industry. It would be self-subsidizing and would have quasi-judicial powers to handle cases like copyright infringement, royalties and the like.

Early in September this year, the broadcast and music industries agreed to adopt guidelines embodied in a resolution signed jointly by the Philippine Association of Recording Industries (PARI) and the Filipino Society of Composers, Arrangers, and Publishers (FILSCAP), and in a memorandum of agreement by the PARI and the Kapisanan ng mga Broadkasters sa Philipinas (KBP).

The resolution allows other recording companies to record Filipino compositions upon payment of just compensation. This is intended to provide maximum exposure and additional benefits to Filipino Composers, record companies which have existing as well as future exclusive rights to Filipino compositions.

To ensure regularity of payment and accurate reporting of royalties earned by composers, payments will be made within 45 days from the end of a semester. The payment of royalties shall be accompanied by a certificate under oath of the company treasurer stating in detail the amount of royalties earned by the composer concerned during the preceding semester.

There have been earlier attempts to produce pop music with a Filipino identity. One of these was Pinoy Rock, which reached its heights in 1974. Among the groups most active in promoting it were the Juan de la Cruz Band, Anak Bayan, Birth of the Cool. Basically, Pinoy Rock is hard rock improvised by Filipino rock bands and were it not for the country of origin, sounds very much like the imported kind. But for all the sincere efforts of its exponents to come up with a Filipino version of rock, Pinoy Rock did not quite catch on and by 1976, hardly a small group of followers remained to sustain it.

Jingle, the leading Philippine pop music magazine, wrote: "It seems Pinoy Rock would remain a dream once more; after a brief beautiful scene two years ago. It seems the few good heads who could sustain it have problems of their own that they can not seem to make up their minds. To lead and help are two different things. The movement of Pinoy Rock music badly needs leadership and the people who are qualified would not come out, in total force. For fear of burning out? Martyr complex? No organization. And no funds. No unity. Are we really that cynical about Pinoy music? Meantime, Pinoy Rock, swept even more way by the Manila Sound, the Hustle and the Salsa, remains a baby. An ugly one now." The magazine contends that Pinoy Rock's drug connotations, prejudice and suspicion, added up to hasten its fadeout. It also pointed out that "as long as the ego-tripping psychedelic rock displays are gross and blatant, society won't accept Pinoy Rock. They should either compromise; e.g. make less complex and less confusing music, make good public relations, or rot with their 5 to 10,000 adherents."

Pinoy Rock was followed by the so-called Manila Sound, which had a stormy beginning. The pioneers of Manila Sound are two rock groups, the Hotdogs and Cinderella. Hotdogs made a big hit in 1974 with its "Ikaw ang Miss Universe ng Buhay Ko" (You are the Miss Universe of My Life) timed for the Miss Universe contest held in Manila that year. The group's follow up song "Pers Lab" (Pilipinized spelling of "First Love") was a greater success and bigger earner. The Cinderella's recording of "T.L.Ako Sa 'Yo" (My Love for you is True) and other local compositions in the same genre attracted the attention of the KBP. According to the broadcasters, many of the Manila Sound songs had double-meaning, distasteful lyrics. They also fund the use of corrupted Philipino-English lyrics, an insult to the national language. Perhaps, it was more of the controversy rather than anything else which propelled Manila Sound to national prominence and when the KBP finally relented, more songs in this idiom were to eventually flood the market.

The Manila Sound is considered a breakthrough of sorts because it represents a new trend in the Philippine recording industry: Instead of recording songs imported from the US and other foreign sources, or merely Pilipinizing their lyrics, local artists are singing and recording songs written by Filipinos. What is more important is that such recordings are being brought, some in volumes that have pushed western imports down from the top hit charts which they had always dominated in the past.

The Hotdogs, today rated on the best money-making rock groups in the Philippines, was organized by Denis and Rene Garcia. The group is busy making recordings, going on live performances, doing TV commercials and coming up with more Manila Sound songs.

The Cinderella, a group of nine, is made up of two girls and seven boys who hit the mark when they recorded "T.L. Ako Sa 'Yo." The group started out as a joke among Bobby Guzman, Sonny Ilacad, Snaffu Rigor, Celso Llarina, Willi

Cruz, Yolly Samson and Lourdes de Leon. Recording under the Sunshine label, the Cinderella has a number of best-selling LPs to its credit.

While the Manila Sound is still making waves and recordings continue to sell, there is at the same time a renewed interest in the Tagalog (or Pilipino) pop song. In Pinoy Rock and Manila Sound, it was not unusual to mix Pilipino and English words or phrases, considering that most Filipinos are bi-lingual. And it is seemed to be a sure-fire formula for crashing into the pop market.

Lately, however, pop songs are being written using straight Tagalog(or Pilipino) lyrics. One recent hit, "Sa Aking Pagiisa" (In My Loneliness) was written by a young songwriter, Fernand Feramil, a student at the University of Santo Tomas. Realizing the growing demand for pop songs with Pilipino lyrics, Vicor Music Corporation signed up Rico K. Puno, one of the biggest name in Philippine entertainment today. Previously, Puno had been singing on the nightclub circuit and marking a hit with his unique vocal styling, somewhat reminiscent of Johnny Ray, and doing American songs with Pilipino lyrics.

Puno believes that songs in Pilipino can very well be accepted by the elite and the mass market. He has also done recordings of older Filipino hits like "Buhat" by Mike Velarde and "Kapantay ay Langit" of George Canseco in soul style. Another of his hits was "Namamasyal sa Luneta" (Strolling in Luneta) which is considered a trend setter.

The new emphasis on songs with Pilipino lyrics has made Filipinos more aware of the songs written by an earlier generation of composers like Mike Velarde, who wrote "Dahil Sa lyo", "Silayan", "Minamahal Kita" and many other hits; Ariston Avelino, Tito Arevalo, Levi Celerio, Tony Maiquez ("Sapagka't Kami'y Tao Lamang"), Santiago Suarez ("Bakya mo Neneg"), Contancio de Guzman ("Bayan Ko"), Restie Unali, Leopoldo ("Dahil Sa lsang Bulaklak") and Josefino Cenizal ("Hindi Kita Malimot"). Among the younger composers writing in this genre are Willi Cruz ("Araw at Gabi"), Orlando llacad and Emy Musngi.

Another interesting development is that Filipino songwriters now tend less and less to copy the styles of Tin Pan Alley and are turning out songs that have distinct Filipino sentiments. Happily for them, this is what is selling most in the market today.

Today, more albums of songs with Pilipino lyrics are being released. The roster of artists featuring all-Fillipino repertoire or adaptations of American hits with Pilipino lyrics is likewise growing.

A newcomer who is already a big name in the Philippines is Celeste Legaspi, who like the reigning queen of songs, Pilita Corrales, is blessed with both good looks, a beautiful voice and talent. A talented actress as well, she frequently appears on stage with Teatro Pilipino at the Cultural Center of the Philippines.

Her latest album entitled "Celeste" offers 10 American songs with lyrics in Pilipino by the well-known director-dramatist Rolando S. Tinio. This new concept in entertainment is explained by Tinio thus:

"Translating foreign pop songs into Pilipino is not intended as an exercise in fadmongering or yellow music-making. Rather, it is an attempt to fill up the Pilipino ear with insights into common experience, nuances of thought and feeling, and discoveries through the lyric consciousness of the human world (especially the world of love), not ordinarily found in original song writing. The purpose of translation is not to stifle or replace original creation, but to open doors and windows for native genius by showing new possibilities and approaches for the Pilipino creator. Miss Legaspie's repertoire derives from the objective of the two pop song concerts sponsored by the Department of Public Information in cooperation with the Cultural Center of the Philippines through Teatro Pilipino."

Of course, the enduring Pilita Corrales is still the top Filipina singer both on stage and on records. Born in Cebu of Filipino Spanish blood, she started in show business not as singer but as disc jockey. She eventually made it to the Manila stage in 1958 and has made singing tours in Australia, Singapore, Hong Kong, Kuala Lumpur, Las Vegas, Honolulu, San Francisco, Los Angeles, Toronto, Washington D.C., in addition to TV, nightclub, and concert performances whenever she is in the Philippines.

Among her most cherished awards is that of Best Singer in the Second Tokyo Music Festival in 1973. Although the Philippines' entry, a song written by Jose Mari Chan did not make it, Pilita's singing was enough to attract the judges' ears into voting her Best Singer of the event. Pilita has recorded 22 long-play albums and 260 singles in the Philippines, Australia, the United States and Japan. Her versatility includes not only Filipino songs done in Pilipino and Cebuano, but English, Spanish and Japanese compositions as well. Also in the list of Philippine pop singers is Nora Aunor, whose phenomenal movie career has earned her the title "Superstar", actually started out as a singer. Despite her busy TV and movie schedules, she still finds time to do recordings. Among her latest albums are "Lady Guy", "Si Nora Nuon at Ngayon", and "In Love", all under the Vicor label. Didith Reyes, Jacqui Magno, Louie Reyers, Tillie Moreno, Norma Ramirez are also among the names often mentioned among the country's leading pop singers. Among the males, there are Basil Valdez, Florante de Leon, Pepe Smith, Rustie Fabunan, Pabs Dadivas, Boy Camara, Paul Galv, Victor Wood, Bobby Gonzalez and Ric Marique, Jr.

These singers represent a wide range of styles ... from rock and soul to ballad, folk and all Filipino. Each has merited public acclaim doing his own thing and indications are that each will continue to be ranked among the leaders and trend setters of pop music in the Philippines for a good many more years.

The pop scene is also dominated by singing groups. Besides the Hotdogs and Cinderella mentioned earlier, there are others like the Ambivalent Crowd, the new Minstrels, and the Circus Band.

Also worth mentioning is the Filipinos Singers which concentrates on all Filipino repertoire. The group is led by Ernie de la Pena, singer-composer-lyricist-record producer. Others in the Group are Nora Hermosa, Raye Lucero, Robert Denis, Roy Notario and Merle Maglonzo. The group is known for its authentic interpretation of native songs and their albums are bought not only by foreigners but their own countrymen as well.

But while record producers and singing stars are making good money, the same cannot be said for Filipino song writers. Their counterparts in the United States, Japan and Europe share equal billing with performers and make very good money, too. But in the Philippines, songwriters have to take on other jobs if they want to keep from starving. The situation has not yet reached that point where a Filipino song writer can make a comfortable living from his songs and from the royalties that should be given to him by recording companies.

Although there is a group called the Filipino Society of Composers, Authors and Publishers (FILSCAP) headed by Felipe P. de Leon, little has been done so far to raise the income levels of songwriters. The FILSCAP is actually an organization whose main purpose is to license original songs and collect royalties due songwriters for performance uses of their works from radio stations, nightclubs, hotels, theatres, movie companies, jukebox operators, and all users of recorded music for commercial purposes.

Recent government moves have been taken to improve the lot of the Philippines' artistic minds. However, the implementation still has to be pushed hard for these moves to be truly effective. For instance, presidential Decree No. 49 protects intellectual property and sets the guidelines for the corresponding reward due creative people.

In 1974 the government also sponsored a national song-writing contest "Paligsahan sa Musika." Its main objective was to discover singers as well as song composers-lyricists and music arrangers. However, the winning songs, for some reason or other, never became national hits. There have been other song writing contests but as has been pointed out, not one of the winners achieved success on a national level.

Meanwhile, the KBP and BMC are doing their part to Filipinize the pop music scene by implementing such objectives as:

1. To give life and meaning to the provision of the New Philippine Constitution Article XV, Section 9, Subsection 2 that Filipino Culture shall be preserved and developed for national identity.
2. To improve music programme content of stations relevant to Filipino culture and traditional Filipino compositions.
3. To provide opportunity for growth and development of Filipino music with international appeal.
4. To encourage and improve quality of Filipino compositions, performing talents and musicians.
5. To create incentives and assure local producers of promotional airplay and exposure of their products competitive to foreign recordings.

Under this atmosphere and a growing nationalistic feeling among the Filipinos, it is no longer an idle dream that one of these days, foreign influences can be minimized and future generations of Filipinos can grow up, listening to and singing songs expressive of the national hopes and aspirations. Meanwhile, there is a lot of hard work ahead. Values have to be changed; tastes must be remoulded; and efforts redirected towards improving the quality of the songs, with better music, lyrics, arrangements and equally better performances. Far more effective than nationalistic exhortations in shaping the public mind is the quality of the products offered to them. And from the kind of recordings being produced lately, there is every reason to be hopeful that the Philippines pop music scene will become an important factor in uniting the masses and sharing the human experience and aspirations that can only be expressed best through music.

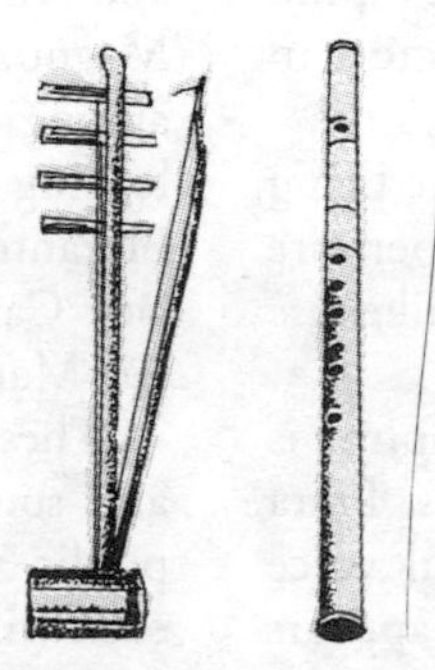

Khuuchir (left) and Limbe (right); Mongolian musical instruments.

Part 4

Animals and Folk Culture

Animal motif on tiles of the Han dynasty (China).

Animals and Folk Culture

The Serpent Lore of Bengal, India

The serpent is an object of worship in different forms among the Hindus throughout India. In Northern India especially from Kashmir to Bihar and over the whole of Madhya Pradesh or Central India, the serpent is offered worship as an anthropomorphic male god known as Vasuki, the Naga Raja, or the king of the serpents. It is represented in a life-size image carved in stone in the position of standing the eight principal serpents of the Indian Epic, the *Mahabharata*, forming a canopy covering its head with their spread-out hoods. As serpents live under the earth in holes, the chief serpent is considered to be the king of the nether worlds.

The serpent worshipped in the eastern regions of India, from West Bengal including Bangladesh up to Assam, is represented by an anthropomorphic female goddess made of earth or clay though in more ancient times it would also be made of carved stone. She is considered the queen mother of the serpent race and known by the name of Manasa, a word of unorthodox origin. In almost all of southern India the serpent is worshipped in its zoomorphic form either through images representing serpents with their raised hoods or actually as live serpents residing in holes within the shrines or outdoor anthills, where they are supposed to live. Images of serpents in their zoomorphic forms are made from clay or earth, iron or some metal, especially brass, unlike the Naga Raja Vasuki which is always carved out of stone by regular sculptors.

The serpent-cult in Bengal

Of all the places in Bengal the area covered by the western part of the State, which is comparatively barren and hilly, has undoubtedly the largest number of votaries of the serpent-deity Manasa. Even to this day notwithstanding urban and industrial development over this area the serpent-worship there, is a very well-developed cult. Almost in every village a visitor will come across one or more serpents' shrines which are simply low mud-walled huts with roofs covered by straw situated within the house-quadrangles of some lower class Hindus or Hinduized aboriginals. Daily worship is offered in the most humble way in most of these "shrines", but during the four months of rain from July to September daily worship with special care is offered to the deity. People of the various groups of the rural community among the Hindus ungrudgingly join the worship through the orthodox section generally disassociates itself with it. In the Northern part of Bengal the serpent-cult is also very widely prevalent. Both anthropomorphic and zoomorphic images of the serpent-goddess carved in stone in classical sculpture have been recovered from this area. They belong to the period up to the twelfth century. Over this area there is no permanent shrine of the serpent-deity nowadays. The worship is held once in the whole year with great pomp. The orthodox Hindu serpent-festival known as Nagapanchami held by the upper cast Hindus practically throughout India is almost unknown here. It is a folk festival which is performed here by all sections of the people.

The worship is held either at the public places of such worships or in the houses of the individual worshippers on the last day of the Bengali month of Sravana (July-August). This is practically the middle of the rainy season when cases of snake-bite reach a peak. No image of the deity is generally made, but on this occasion zoomorphic forms made of earth of eight principal serpents of the traditional serpent legend of the Indian Epic, the *Mahabharata*, are offered worship. Sometimes also only one serpent representing Astika of the same legend is also worshipped in the same way. In most cases instead of any image a piece of branch of a milky hedge plant, as stated above, is worshipped as the seat of the serpent-goddess. Special offerings, consisting of milk and fried rice and sometimes milk with banana are offered to the deity on big-sized arum leaves. The mud floor of rooms, outer courtyard, and veranda of the houses are beautifully decorated with special designs of rice-paste drawings resembling the winding gait of the serpent. The womenfolk abstain from taking food on that occasion in some places, because it is believed that on this particular day the serpents generally enter the ovens of the rural householders in order to warm up their bodies which had been drenched constantly by rain water for the last months. Therefore, to kindle fire in the household ovens is to disturb their taking rest for the day and is dangerous. In most Hindu families no meal is, therefore, cooked on that day. Barring a few minor exceptions, on the whole, there is a unity in the rituals of serpent-worship over the area along the Ganges in South Bengal. Over this area there are public places of worship of the serpent-deity in almost every village on the prescribed date, invariably before a milky hedge plant which grows in size as the years roll by. People assembles there irrespective of caste and creed and offer their worship without, however, any animal sacrifices.

Sometimes the higher caste Hindu women, instead of going over to such places of public worship perform the rituals at their respective houses with the assistance of the Brahmin priests.

Serpent-worship is almost like a national festival in the eastern part of Bengal though it is held only once a year during the rains. Animal sacrifice is an indispensable adjunct to the rituals in this part of Bengal.

Owing to the wide prevalence of the cult among all classes of people in eastern Bengal, a very elaborate and complicated ritual has developed over this area with regard to its observance. Though the mode of worship is fundamentally the same, they differ in detail to a considerable extent.

The annual celebration of the serpent-worship here is held on the last day of the Bengali month of Sravana when the whole of eastern Bengal is practically covered by the vast sheet of water deposited by the overflow from the neighbouring States of Assam and Meghalaya. People irrespective of caste and creed build images of the snake-deity Manasa and worship her in their own houses individually in each family with sacrifices of goats, pigeons and ducks. There was a time when buffaloes also used to be sacrificed on such occasions.

The image of Manasa generally has arms, with two clay snakes spreading their hoods on either side of her shoulders. After the worship is over, the image is ceremonially immersed in the river. Over some places, a boat race festival is also held on the occasion of the ceremonial immersion of the deity. The special feature of the serpent festival over this part of Bengal is the rice-paste drawings *(alpana)* made by the womenfolk on this occasion. The entire venue of worship is decorated with drawings representing serpents in various designs. Around these drawings other paintings illustrating the chief incidents of the principal Bengal snake-story are also drawn. Coloured powders are used in such drawings. From the first day of the Bengali month of Sravana until the end of the month when the worship is held, the principal snake-story is musically recited in parts every day after nightfall before the assembly of the members of the family, male and female, and this is listened to with the greatest attention and with a feeling of spiritual devotion. The legend as recited is as follows:

The serpent legend

Once upon a time there was a merchant named Chand. He was a great devotee of Siva and on no account would agree to worship Manasa, the serpent-goddess. Once Manasa appeared before him and asked him to worship her. Chand insulted her instead and drove her away. Manasa determined to take revenge on him. Chand had six sons all in the teens. Manasa sent her most venomous serpents to mix poison into their food. They were thus all killed. Chand was still undaunted. When his last son Lakhindar was to be born within a month or so Chand started for a long mercantile voyage. In the middle of the open sea Manasa appeared and asked Chand to offer worship to her before he proceeded further. Chand still refused to do so. All the fourteen vessels of Chand full of cargo were sunk in the sea by the machinations of Manasa. Chand somehow reached the shore of a foreign and unknown country and after twelve years of sufferings reached his home.

His youngest son Lakhindar was only twelve years of age. Chand due to the pressure of his wife Sanaka agreed to give him in marriage even at that early age. A bride was soon found. Her name was Behula. She was a good dancer and the daughter of a rich merchant. The date of the marriage was settled.

The serpent-goddess appeared in a dream before Sanaka and warned her that unless her husband worshipped her before the marriage of her son, she would kill her son with a bite in the nuptial chamber. Sanaka was alarmed and she informed Chand all about the dream. Chand gave her his assurance that he would baffle the evil design of Manasa. Sanaka was assured. After the marriage rituals were over the couple was made to enter an iron chamber built by Chand to baffle the design of Manasa. There was no passage even for air and light in the chamber. Nothing could enter into it after iron doors were closed. Strong guards were also posted all around the place so that nothing could come near it. By midnight Lakhindar fell asleep within the chamber. Behula was keeping herself awake on that happened there. But all of a sudden Lakhindar cried out that he had been bitten by a snake. Behula saw in a twinkle of an eye the *kalnagini* (a small species of deadly snake) disappearing through a small hole made somehow in the wall. Lakhindar died almost immediately. According to the prevalent custom the body of Lakhindar was floated down the river on a raft. Behula accompanied the body. It is believed that Behula reached heaven with all that remained of the body of her husband and revived the life of her husband having pleased the gods and goddesses there including the serpent-goddess Manasa by her dance performances.

The snake-story in folk entertainment

The narrative of Chand and Behula, the principal snake-story of Bengal, has contributed to folk-entertainment of a secular nature also from a very ancient time. There are four principal forms in which the narrative has been adopted for this purpose. They are *Bhasan Yatra,* or a popular form of folk-drama, *Rayani,* a form of musical entertainment, *Jagaran* or musical narration and *Putul Nach* or puppet dance.

Bhasan Yatra is a form of Bengali rural theatre performed in a most crude form in which continuity of the theme is often interrupted due to indiscriminate interpolation of out of the place dance and music. The people are more interested in fun than in the story which is traditional and, therefore, known to every body.

Rayani is a musical performance through which the snake-story is narrated sometimes in great detail. Besides the musical performance an exhibition of doll representing the main characters and incidents of the principal serpent-story is also held. Some times the dolls are made bigger then life size. The hero of the legend Chand is made to ride huge elephant made of earth and most realistically painted in various colours. *Rayani* can be performed any time of the year. It is generally performed before a marriage ceremony is held in the family, invoking the blessing of Manasa for the couple.

Jagaran is the simplest of all the performances of this nature. It is not expensive and only a few participants are necessary to perform it. It is in a sense musical recitation of the narrative by the principal traditional musician supported by his two or there repeaters. This seems to be the oldest form of public performance of the serpent-legend in this country. Only a very few musical instruments purely of traditional character are utilized on this occasion. With the development of other forms of entertainment this most simple form has now almost gone out of use. Only in remote villages where traditional life still exists, this form of musical recitation of the serpent-story still can be heard during the rainy season.

Putul Nach, or puppet dance of the serpent story, is a very popular performance especially in the southern part of Bengal. The life-size rod puppets are used on this occasion. Songs, prose dialogues and dances are performed according to the demands of the situation with great artistic ability. The scenes in which the body of Lakhindar is floated down the river and of the dance of Behula before the gods in heaven are beautifully performed by the artistes.

Serpent-motif in folk art

The delightful colour and peculiar features of the serpent have been a source of inspiration for artists since primitive times. Though animals in general formed the chief model of primitive art, the serpent, due to elastic body and graceful movement, offered the most convenient object for artistic adoption. An angry serpent with its raised head and spread-out hood, however dreadful, is undoubtedly one of the loveliest sights of the natural world. It is, for these reasons that the serpents have occupied a prominent position in art and sculpture all over world. In Hindu and Buddhist sculptures also serpents play a very important part. It is, however, undeniable that classical art stands in very close relation with folk art. It is on the basis of the folk art that the classical art develops, most of its constituent factors being derived from popular elements. Again during the period of its decadence it takes refuge among the people at large who appropriate the different elements of its lofty ideals than in their own way. Therefore, still to this day numerous serpent designs are displayed through different works of folk art in different parts of India. Bengal has the most prominent share of contribution to it.

In Bengal folk art manifested itself at its best in the rice-paste drawings or *alipana* as drawn by the womenfolk on ceremonial occasions. In the course of serpent festivals certain serpent drawings are made in which artistic ability of a very high order is sometimes displayed. There are numerous designs drawn in different regions.

Over certain areas of Bengal a small house made of a species of Indian aquatic weed known as *shola* or Indian cork is offered worship along with the earthen image of the serpent deity Manasa. On all sides of the slanting outer side of the roof and roof walls of the tiny house, not more than two feet in height, beautiful coloured drawings are made of the serpents, the serpent-deity and the hero and the heroine of the serpent legend. This is known as *karandi*. On the day of the immersion of the deity it is also floated down the river after the worship is over.

There are scroll-paintings in which the serpent-legend is painted from the beginning to the end. Features of serpents have a prominent place in them. The jar which is worshipped in lieu of the image over certain areas is also beautifully painted with the figure of the serpent-deity. Sometimes hoods of serpents are also carved out of such clay jars which are backed or dried in the sun.

Snake-charmers and their festival

The Bengali snake-charmers constitute a social group by themselves popularly known as the *badiya* or the *bede*. They have been carrying on their profession of catching snakes, extracting their poison and selling it to medical men and also of playing with live serpents in the public as a means of their livelihood. This is a very ancient practice and profession in Bengal for a particular group of people. Members of this community of snake-charmers of Bengal hold annually a festival which is known as *Jhampan*. It literally means an open-air stage built to exhibit tricks with live snakes. It is held on the last day of the Bengali month of Sravana or the day on which the annual worship of the serpent-deity is held almost throughout Bengal. The festival is still held with great enthusiasm in the western part of Bengal.

Mythological Animals in Nepal

Animals have been a part of man's world since the beginning of civilization. Primitive man identified himself with animals and mimed their prowess and strength in various activities. The special attributes of animals have, in fact, inspired man's worship of them out of admiration or fear. It is especially in Asian cultures that animals are found to be still worshipped as guardians, holy messengers or vehicles of the gods. Animals are intricately woven into the fabric of culture, religion and beliefs of the people, thereby occupying not only a physical but also a spiritual significance in their lives.

In this article, we would like to highlight the close relationship that exists between man and animals in Nepalese folk life and culture especially with regard to religion, philosophy, arts and literature. Because the people of Nepal belong to diverse ethnic groups living in varied geophysical terrains, a colourful variety of beliefs, practices and depictions of animals may be encountered. Specific animals, both real and mythical, play important roles as guardians, and *vahanas* or vehicles of particular deities, during festivals and rituals and in art and literature. Traditional medicinal value is attached to charms and amulets made from their body parts, and folk beliefs and taboos are associated with them.

Role of animals in religion

In Nepal, two main religions, Hinduism and Buddhism, as well as form of Animism and Tantricism are seen to influence and govern the imagination, beliefs and cultural practices of the people. The philosophy of rebirth and transmigration of souls that emanates from these religions is thus intimately linked with the manner of treatment that animals receive. They are worshipped as vehicles of the gods or as gods incarnate, or for their own specific qualities.

Animals as incarnations

Both Hinduism and Buddhism offer a rich pantheon of gods and goddesses who may be freely inter-adopted. Hindu gods and goddesses spring from the one Trinity formed by Brahma, Vishnu and Maheshwar who are personifications of the three fundamental processes of life — creation, preservation and destruction. Together with their divine female consorts, they assume many divine forms as well as incarnate themselves as human beings and sometimes, even as certain animals. Incarnations are believed to occur whenever evil outbalances good in the world and because the gods wish to help their devotees. In Hindu mythology, Vishnu is believed to have become incarnate as a fish, a tortoise, a boar, and man-lion. Some of the demi-gods of Hinduism are animal and divine personages such as Hanuman (Monkey-god) who was the faithful servant of Rama, and Ganesh (Elephant god) who is the remover of obstacles.

Similarly, Buddhist literature also narrates that the Buddha in his previous lives had taken birth as a lion, a hare, a deer, a white elephant, a monkey, a crow, a dog, a peacock, an eagle and a jackal.

In Tantricism too, animals have been regarded as incarnate beings.

Animals as guardians and *vahanas* (vehicles)

Animals serving as guardian deities and vehicles are considered as animals of fortune. They include real as well as mythical animals. The fact that even gods and goddesses use their services for travelling emphasizes the great importance these animals are imbued with in the folk culture and imagination.

Among the animals that feature most prominently as guardian deities of temples are the lion, who is the vehicle of the goddess Durga, the terror form of goddess Shakti; the elephant who is the vehicle of Indra and goddess Laxmi, who symbolizes wealth; the horse who is linked with the sun and the chariots of the gods Indra, Agni and Mitra, manifestations of the holy Trinity. The horse which guards the four corners of temples takes the form of the flying horse 'Kusala' as is found in the Krishna temple in Patan, Kathmandu. The dog who is guardian of Yama, the god of death's gate and vehicle of Bhairab identified with Yama, is also common. More rarely, the rhinoceros and camel are found guarding the entrance of temples.

Among the mythical animals, the *garuda* who is half eagle and half man symbolizes speed and is a favourite guardian deity. It is also the only one of its kind found in the whole of Hindu art. The *garuda* bears Lord Vishnu on its shoulders. Sometimes it is depicted as riding on a lion while carrying the god on its back. Lord Vishnu and his consort Laxmi are often portrayed as riding the *garuda* together. Laxmi also uses the owl as her vehicle. *Nandi* the bull, is considered to be the vehicle of Lord Shiva, who also has snake coiled around his symbolic of his power over death. The bull presides as a guardian deity before every Shiva temple in the docile, kneeling position. A famous myth relates that Lord Shiva accepted the overlordship of the animal as his vehicle after the two had fought a duel. The bull also serves as the secondary vehicle of the goddess Durga. The buffalo is considered as the vehicle of Yama, god of death. The deer serves as the vehicle of Vayu, the god of direction. The antelope is depicted as a vehicle of Chandrama, god of the moon. Not the least among vehicular animals is the rat or mouse who carries Ganesha.

Among birds, the peacock, also known as sun-bird, is the vehicle of Kartikeya or Kumar, the celestial god of war and love. Goddess Saraswati, embodiment of wisdom and consort of Brahma, who often rides on the swan and tortoise, also uses this bird as her vehicle. The gate of paradise, it is said is guarded by the peacock.

The vulture is regarded as the vehicle of Saturn represented as one of the most malefic of planets. In the Ramayana, the story of Lord Rama, it functions as the opponent of the demon King Ravana who kidnapped Sita.

Snakes figure as staunch guardians of deities and kings forming a celestial canopy over them in single or mixed formation. Often, they are imagined as multi-headed, and are depicted with the *garuda.*

After the *garuda*, the *makara* is another mythical vehicular animal. It is a remarkable hybrid creature imagined as crocodile, elephant, fish and other creatures in variation. The composite creature is the symbol of Varuna, god of ocean. Separately, the crocodile is the vehicle of Ganga, the sacred river, while the elephant and fish are symbolic as one-time incarnations of divinity and are associated with fertility and longevity of life. The *chimaera*, another fabulous mythical creature with a lion's head, a serpent's tail and a goat's body, is considered as the guardian of tombs, temples and monasteries.

Likewise, the mythical dragon with a scaly supermuscular body, and wings and fire in its breath, functions as the militant guardian of temples and monasteries.

Animal worship in rituals and festivals

In the myriad festivals that form a part and parcel of Nepalese folk life and culture animals occupy distinct positions of respect and adoration. In fact, there are three major festivals of national significance that go by the names of certain animals. Among these animals are (a) the cow which is the national animal of Nepal worshipped during the Gaijatra or cow festival, (b) the horse which is worshipped during the Ghodajatra or horse festival, and (c) the snakes which are worshipped on the Nagpanchami or Snakes'Day and also during the Bisket on New Year festival among the Newars.

a) The Gaijatra which falls in August or September, is a time when the cow, sacred to Hindus, is venerated. She symbolizes wealth and abundance and is regarded as the saviour of souls so that a gift of a cow is revered as the greatest of all gifts. On this day, the *janai* or protective thread tied on the wrist three months earlier, is tied to the tail of the sacred cow in the belief that after death, the cow will help the person's soul to cross the Vaitareni, the most ill-omened and terrifying of all streams that has to be passed before reaching yama's gate for judgement where thousands upon thousands of soul are waiting. The cow is believed to push open the gates with her horns to let the souls enter heaven.

This is why on this day the family must honour the soul of their dead members. This is done by sending a cow or a young boy gorgeously costumed to represent one accompanied by the family priest, musicians and a *yogi* (hermit), to participate in a mock procession around the city. Festival dances of other animals such as the lion, the bear and monkey also take place during this festival.

The significance of the cow as a mediator of souls is again manifest in the role ascribed to her during the *shraddha* or annual death ceremony performed for the dead family member. Gifts of money or kind given to the priest at this time are identified with the gift of a cow. The gift of a cow is also used for annulling defects of an unlucky horoscope.

During the Tihar of five-day Festival of Lights falling in late October or November, the cow is worshipped along with the crow and dog who are considered Yama's messenger and door keeper respectively. It is on the third day of this festival that the cow is worshipped as the earthly form of goddess Laximi. The cow was also among Lord Krishna's companions when he took birth among the cowherds.

The killing of the crow is, therefore, expressly forbidden by Hindu culture and tradition. It is not unusual for people to swear by the cow as by the holy books when they want to express themselves.

b) The Ghodajatra or festival of horses falls in late March or in the first week of April. It is believed that the ancient tradition of kings drawing a cavalcade of horses around the temple of Bhadrakali in Kathmandu, and of a herd of horses stampeding over a threatening demon Tundi, has led to the observance of this festive occasion which has come to be synonymous as the national equestrian and athletics day. Successful horse-racing on this day is believed to auger well for the victory of Nepal in overcoming her enemies.

The horse is regarded as the symbol of the vehicle of life with the rider as the spirit. A white horse is considered auspicious because of its association with the celestial white horse of Indra, god of heaven. It is even said that the tenth incarnation or Kalkiavatar of Lord Vishnu will assume the body of a white horse.

c) On the occasion of Nagpanchami, which falls during the monsoon in late July or early August, snakes are worshipped by the farmers and in homes since they are considered auspicious for bringing rain and wealth.

Legend says that the whole of Kathmandu valley was once a lake known as Nagahird wherein resided Karkot Naga, the king of snakes with his companions, and it was the Buddhist saint Manjushree from China who struck the Chobar hills which split, letting the water drain away. Karkot Naga was given a permanent home in the Tundah Pond beyond the Chobar gorge and it is believed that he still resides there.

Another version of the story recounts the occurrence of a severe drought in the valley and how all the snakes who had caused it, were subjugated. They are believed to have presented portraits of themselves in their own blood to the reigning king promising that droughts hereafter would be dispelled when one of these images was worshipped.

Their request is fulfilled to this day. In every home, on this fifth day or Panchami, the lintel beam over the entrance is cleansed with water and cowdung and a picture of snakes is pasted on it. Food and incense are offered in the name of the snakes while imploring their protection and blessings.

During the Machendranath Jatra of festival which is observed in June before the rice-planting season, a *bhoto* or sacred vest studded with jewels is shown to the public. This vest is supposed to have been given to a farmer by a snake who is the guardian of precious stones and jewels.

During the Bisket festival which marks the Newari New Year the heroism of a legendary prince who slew two serpent demons is celebrated.

The snake appears as an ambiguous creature because it is both life-giving and also death-dealing. Snake worship is therefore inspired by fear of its wrath.

Animal sacrifice

Though animals are worshipped they are also used for sacrificial purposes. The apparent contradiction in animal sacrifice and animal worship is explained by the belief that transformation of life into another form is the very nature of the universe. Animals are sacrificed in order to provide the gods with power to fertilize the earth for a rich harvest. It is also performed as a measure of propitiation or expiation

Among sacrificial animals, the fowl is regarded as the symbol of a demon and is therefore killed to please the gods. During the Dasain festival which is analogous to Christmas for Hindus, mass slaughter of buffaloes is ceremoniously carried out on the eighth and ninth days to appease goddess Durga who slew Mahisasur the demon disguised in the form of a buffalo. The sacrifice takes the form of 'Panchabali', literally meaning 'sacrifice of five different animals and birds.' These are the cock, duck, goat, sheep and buffalo.

Folk beliefs and taboos regarding animals

Certain animals and birds are considered messengers of good or evil fortune. Among them are the crow, parrot, eagle, peacock, cuckoo and goose. It is said that misfortune will prevail on hearing, seeing, or meeting certain animals. The owl hooting on the roof-top, the dog, cat or jackal crying at night, are considered ill omens. The crow crying may mean good or had news. The dreaming of a lion by pregnant women means that she will give birth to a strong. If she sees a swan, she should beget an intelligent child. Seeing an elephant in dreams has been interpreted as the omen of some portentous event because Mayadevi, the mother of Lord Buddha had seen a white elephant in her dream before Buddha was born. Similarly, seeing a snake in dreams is a sign that the woman will conceive. A cat or a snake crossing one's path is never to be taken lightly as it is a symbol of bad luck. However, if one meets a cow feeding her calf or if a mongoose or crow crosses one's path on the right side, it is good.

The sight of a boar or hog is considered to give rise to wounds attacks and hostilities from enemies. Some people, however, consider it a positive sign which will mean sons, riches and happiness.

It is believed that if a dumb child is fed with peacock meat he/she will get back his speech. The 'learned' parrot is believed to know the four Vedas. So, if a child is slow to talk, a grain of rice dropped by it should be given.

Some believe that magic words may charm the snake to resuck its venom from the wound it has inflicted.

Animals in decor, paintings and handicrafts

The depiction of various animals in wood carvings, stone carvings and paintings may sometimes serve as purely aesthetic motifs, but most often, they are symbolic. The most commonly found animals in art and decor are the peacock, frog, elephant, dragon, fish, snake and crocodile.

The peacock is a popular motif on windows and doors. Its eye feathers make beautiful fans.

Adorning stone water taps and wood carvings are the animals connected with water such as the elephant, crocodile, fish, snake, tortoise, and frog.

Ritual utensils are beautifully supported by and engraved with various auspicious animals such as the lion, elephant, snake and mythical and supernatural animals like the *garuda*, the flying horse, flying lion, dragons, crocodiles with feathery tails, multiheaded snakes as well as Tantricism-inspired guardian deities that have a human body but the face of a crow, parrot or owl. The *toran* or ornamental panel above temple doorways usually have a *garuda* or clan deities posed in sombre meditation, with whips of clouds on either side. The *garuda* is always shown as trying to swallow the clouds. This is interpreted as the garuda swallowing its arch-enemy, the snake. A deeper level of interpretation is that the artist, through this symbolism, is attempting to link heaven and earth.

On the *tunal*, or struts of temples, can be found animal-faced human guardian deities. The *makara* and elephant are popularly carved on the supporting beams of tables. Animal motifs are very common as decorations in front of huts in the Terai parts of Nepal.

The most popular animals in traditional paintings have been the bull, deer, dragon and fish. The latter and some parts of animals, such as the yak's tail, eyes of the deer, are auspicious motifs in paintings. Vultures and jackals are depicted on paintings of the Shiva-linga and Chaityas. The ritual umbrella used in weddings and religious festivals are adorned with images of deities with their animal vehicles or guardians.

Greetings cards, writing pads and lines are also printed with lucky animal designs.

Carpets, terracotta and metalwork employ the dragon, Yak and peacock as famous themes. Terracotta figurines of the elephant, lion, peacock, fish, horse, rhinoceros and tortoise are sold as flower pots while snakes ornament the pots and candlestands made from terracotta. The same animals as well as fowls, dragon, *makara* and *garuda* are carved in metalwork.

The roles played by animals in Nepalese folk culture thus emphasize the sympathetic view towards them. This, in essence, is an extension of the philosophy that man has to pass through eighty-four non-human lives before taking birth as a man and that man must live in harmony with nature in order to preserve himself.

Naga: The Most Significant Animal in the Thai Culture

Living in a basically agrarian society, as do the majority of people in Southeast Asia, the Thai believe in numerous fertility-protective spirits and guardian deities. Today Thai farmers still practice the ritual worship of the rice goddess and the Lokapala or the tutelary deities of four cardinal directions. Myths and legends which are associated with some animals and the fertility of the earth, water and the rain are also common in rural Thailand. Among all animals, both real and symbolic, the most significant animal always plays an active role in Thai culture is the *naga*, the symbol of water.

Throughout Thailand the *naga* or the Hindu mythical serpent appears in various forms. The myths of this animal have deeply influenced people's thoughts and beliefs as represented in the motif of Thai art and the practice of the fertility rites, as depicted in the folk tales, and as appears in folk belief and ritual.

Naga vs. Garuda

Though the origin of the *naga* is from Hindu mythology, Buddhist and Hindu representations of this popular divinity do not differ much from each other. In Thai the term *naga* means "a great serpent" or "the king of snakes" possessing supernatural power. It represents the life-bestowing, fertilizing element of the terrestrial waters. The only opponent of the *naga*, the *garuda*, is generally represented with wings, human arms, vulture legs and a curved, beak-like nose. *Garuda* is the vehicle of the god Vishnu, and as the protector of his people, a king was traditionally compared to Vishnu. The *garuda* naturally became the emblem of royalty, and to this day still graces the royal standard.

According to myth both the *naga* and the *garuda* were sons of the Sun god. Once the *garuda* accepted to bet from the *naga* to predict the colour of the horse that their father would drive the next day. Without knowing the dirty trick of the *naga*, the *garuda* lost the bet and a lot of *garudas* were killed by the *nagas*. Therefore the garudas took revenge by catching and eating all the *nagas* they found. This became one of the motifs of Thai art represented by the *garuda* in a triumphant position above the *naga*.

Naga as Buddhist guardian

An important function of the *nagas* is that of "*door guardian*" and as such they frequently appear at the head of the stairs of Buddhist temples. In this role their attitude is one of pious and fervent devotion to the Buddha. Another unique type of sculpture that typifies the art style of Thailand is represented by the Buddha seated in meditation sheltered by the *naga's* hood.

The legend that explains this art form is based on an event that is supposed to have occurred shortly after the Buddha's attainment of enlightenment. While the Buddha sat in meditation under the tree, Muchalinda, a prodigious cobra which dwelt in hole, perceived that a great storm would begin for seven days. He issued quietly from his dwelling and with the coil of his body enveloped the body of the Buddha seven times; with the expanse of his giant snake-hood as an umbrella he sheltered the blessed head until the rain stopped.

Another version of this story adds that the *naga* requested the Buddha to call the person to be ordained *naga* in memory of his fervent devotion. This is why the Thai call the ordinand *naga* in the Buddhist ordination ceremony.

Naga as the symbol of fertility

There are many stories concerning the *naga's* role as creator and destroyer of the topography and human settlement. The *naga* is always mentioned in Thai legend as the hero who claimed descent from the union of a human hero. In the Northeast of Thailand, *naga* is believed to be the creator of many important rivers, mountains, and ancient cities. However the most popular story which was widely circulated in the region is the romance of Pha Daeng and Nang Ai.

"The son of nagaraja fell in love with Nang Ai but the girl had already the own lower, Pha Daeng who was a young prince. Her father decided to sponsor a sky rocket competition. Whoever won the competition would receive his daughter Nang Ai as his wife. Unfortunately the *naga's* rocket was defeated. To fulfil his desire, he transformed himself into a white squirrel to seduce the girl. But the *naga* was shot to death by Pha Daeng and his flesh was eaten by the townsmen. After that at night there was a storm that flooded the city, turning it into a big lake and all the people who ate the meat of the squirrel were drowned. Pha Daeng tried to save Nang Ai by taking her away on a horseback but failed. She fell from the horse and was taken away by the ghost of the *naga*."

Naga and rain-making ceremony or fertility rites

The folk tale of Pha Daeng and Nang Ai is believed to be the origin of the lighting the sky rocket ritual or *bun bang fai*. This ritual is very important to the villagers who believe that it will help to bring regular rains for a good crop and happiness to the commune. It is customary that during the dry season which falls in May of the lunar calendar, the rain-ceremony of lighting the *bang fai* is held.

The *bang fai* is a kind of firework, composed of a bamboo shaft with an iron tube about one metre long and containing gun powder attached to its head. It is traditionally decorated splendidly with a figure of the *nagaraja*, made of cardboard and coloured paper. The presence of the figure of the *naga* reflects the belief in *naga* as the god of water. As soon as the *bang fai* is completed, preparations for its procession and exhibition begin. The procession of the *bang fai* is composed of cars, trucks and a group of men and women who sing and dance along with the troupe. When the *bang fai* is to be lit, the villagers build a stand of bamboo poles in an open space on which to lean the rocket, and someone is requested to climb up the tower to light it. A well-made *bang fai* will shoot into the sky for a distance of nearly a mile.

Apart from this ritual, the significance of the *naga* as the contributor of water is represented also on Songkran or the Thai traditional New Year feast. During Songkran days, people will celebrate by throwing water on each other. On this day, there will be a prediction of a fertile or barren year, according to the number of the *nagas*. If there is only one *naga* in the calendar, a good rainfall can be expected but if there are more than four or five, there will be a low rainfall, and there will be a drought if there are seven *nagas* in the calendar. For it is believed that if there are too many *nagas*, each of them will be lazy and disagree as to who will contribute the water.

However, if the weather is still dry and there is no rainfall, another form of rain making ritual will be performed. For people can not begin to plough their land in time. The Thai also believe that the female cat is a symbol of fertility. Therefore they catch a female cat and put it in a fish basket made of bamboo. The cat is carried in a procession through the village accompanied by a number of villagers. They sing with one voice as loud as they can the well-known words in connection with such a procession. This is usually accompanied by a drum or a gong. Where the procession stops people will come out and drench the cat with water and this may be considered an inducement of rainfall. Some of the words of the songs are as follows:

"Hail Nang meo (female cat)
Give us rain, give us consecrated water to pour on the Nang Meo's head.
Give us rice, and give us a wage for carrying the cat.
The rain falls in four copious showers
A thunder bolt strikes a nun.
Strip off her clothes and see the pudendum.
The rain pour down heavily, pour down heavily"
(From Phya Anuman Rajadhon: 1968)

Also after the rice in the field is tall enough to be harvested, the first threshing ritual will be performed before the actual threshing takes place. And again the importance of the *naga* as the controller of fertility is observed in the ritual which is generally performed in Northern Thailand.

"The orientation of the threshing board must correspond to be position of the serpentine Naga King, a subterranean deity which controls fertility. The naga King's body lies along one of the cardinal axes, and his exact position varies according to the month of the year. During the "first threshing" the board must be positioned so that when the sheaves of rice strike the board, the rice passes over the Naga King's scale back and beats against its stomach. Otherwise the rice grains will become lodged in the creature's scales and the crop yield will be low." (Richard Davis; 1974)

In conclusion, the study of myths, folktales and rituals, which are concerned with the *naga* in Thai culture as described, indicates to some extent that before the coming of Hinduism and Buddhism the indigenous belief system might have had some connection with the cult of *naga* worship (or snake worship) as a symbol of fertility (Srisakara Valliphodama: 1976). And after that this animistic belief was gradually mixed with Hinduism and Buddhism until it became one element of a new religion.

Myths and Folklore of Animals in Asia and Oceania

In ancient times, various peoples who lived in Asia and Oceania had developed unique culture in their individual courses of history. On the other hand, there had been various migrations of people and cultural exchanges among the peoples since prehistoric times. Therefore, there is a multiplicity of myths and folklore of the animals or ideas and beliefs while there are also conspicuous similarities and consistency.

The life style of the hunting tribes who made their living by hunting wild animals was closely connected with the animals. The majority of the peoples in Siberia have long been practising stock raising and yet there was the deep rooted old view of the world of the hunting tribes in their minds. Therefore, the animals they hunted played important roles in their myths. For instance, there is such a myth as described below among the Dolgan.

Once upon a time, there were the bones of an elk on the bulge of rock wall at the remotest beach. A young boy came to this place to make certain whether the sun set into the west diving into the bottom of the sea or just gliding away on the surface of the sea. The boy gave life to the elk bones as he was taught by his mother and went into the sea riding on the elk. He found that the sun set into the bottom of the sea. After that, one day when the young boy sitting on the beach was watching the sun rise, he realized that the sun rose from the two places at the same time. One sun rose up to the sky as usual and the other one approached the boy, gliding on the surface of the sea, and was found, upon investigation, to be that elk.

In other words, as pointed out by Okladnikov, that elk was not only the guardian of the young boy but also the sun itself. It is also interesting to note that the young boy brought the elk to life again from the bones. This idea of resurrection from bones can be found in many parts of the world, especially every so often in Northern Eurasia. This is one of the outstanding features of the view of the world of the hunting peoples.

Among the wild beasts, there are some useful animals like the elk from which edible meat can be obtained. On the other hand, some animals like the wolf do harm to human beings and also to domesticated animals. However, the wolf was worshipped as the ancestor of the tribe by Turkic pastoralists in inner Asia. For example, according to the myth of the Kao-ch'ang who established the kingdom to the west of Mongolia and Altais at the end of the fifth century, Shan-Yu, the king of Hsiung-nu, had two beautiful young daughters. He did not like to let his daughters marry human beings but wished to give them to heaven and placed them on a high stand built in the uninhabited land in the north. Then, a wolf came and barked day and night. The younger daughter alighted from the stand saying that the wolf came there by the order of Heaven, and ignoring her sister's pleas became the wife of the wolf and their children became the ancestors of the Kao-ch'ang.

Speaking about the wolf, a dog is a domesticated animal closely related to the wolf. It is interesting that myths and folktales similar to that of the wolf just mentioned above have also been related about the dog. A particularly famous myth is the one described below, which is found in the *Hou-Han-Shu.*

In ancient times, the Ch'uan-jung had come to invade China. The Emperor Kao-hsin proclaimed that he would give his daughter to the one who would cut off the head of the enemy general. He had been keeping a dog named Pan-hu, and in a little while the said dog came back with the head of the enemy general in his mouth. The emperor had no choice but to give his daughter to the dog. Pan-hu ran away to the Southern Mountains with the princess on his back and lived in a cave there. The princess gave birth to six boys and six girls, who became the ancestors of the Wuling-Man.

The said myth recorded in the fifth century has been transmitted to date in almost the same form as the myth of the origin of the Yao tribes from southern China to northern Indochina.

It is a commoner idea to regard a dog as man's cooperator rather than his mate. For instance, there is the following tradition in Iwata-city of Shizuoka prefecture in Japan. A long time ago, about the beginning of August every year, a white arrow would come from nowhere and stick to the house where a young beautiful girl lived. This meant that the beautiful girl would have to be put into a white coffin alive and offered before the deity of the Tenjin Shrine, at midnight on the 10th day of August in the lunar calendar. At about the beginning of the fourteenth century, a travelling Buddhist monk who had heard about this cruel custom came to the shrine one night. Then he secretly hid himself under it, and heard an evil deity tell someone "Don't tell Hayataro of the country of Shinano about this". This Hayataro was in fact a dog kept by the Kozenji (The Buddhist Temple of Kozen) in the country of Shinano (present Nagano Prefecture). The monk then borrowed the said dog and put it into the coffin and offered it before the deity of the shrine. At midnight when the evil deity appeared and broke the coffin open, the dog came out to fight and killed him. It is said that since then this bad custom came to an end. It is also said that this evil deity was either a big raccoon or baboon. This legend clearly expresses the idea that the huge wild animals are evil beings for men while a dog is a friend.

As for the origin of the dog, there are various kinds of myths and legends. According to the myth of the Maori in New Zealand, one day the culture-hero Maui went out fishing and began to quarrel with his brother-in-law, Irawaru, because he did not divide the catch but intended to monopolize it. It was said that in order to punish him for his egoism, Maui transformed him into a dog. Although the dog has had a close relationship with man, it has not always been highly valued.

The ancient Iranians thought that the animal first created by the good god Ahra Mazda was a bull. Although this bull was attacked and killed by the malevolent deity, Ahriman, the seed of this primeval bull was carried to the moon and thereby purified. It was said that after a while, a cow and a bull were born from the seed and following them, 282 couples of various kinds of animals appeared.

What we must pay attention to in this myth is the close relationship between the moon and the bull. It was said that this primeval bull of Iran was "a white bull shining like the moon". India is famous for sanctifying the cow and this idea was already clearly expressed in the *Mahabharata.*

The connection between the sun and horse forms a contrast with the connection between the moon and bull. The idea of connecting the sun and horse can be found from Europe in the west to China in the east. One typical example is the idea of the chariot carrying the sun. In contrast to this, in ancient India, it was believed that Surya, the sun god chases after his lover, Ushas the Dawn Goddess, driving a seven-horse carriage. Also the idea of the horse was quite often linked with the worship of heaven and the kingship. Among the traditions of ancient Korea, according to the Samguk Yusa, one day when the ancestors of the six clans gathered at the upper part of a river in Chinhan to elect the ruler, they found a white horse kneeling down at the side of the Najong well at the foot of Mt. Yangsan. When they approached the white horse, they found a purple egg nearby the horse and the horse went up neighing to the sky upon seeing the men. A son came out of this egg and he later became the founder of the Silla Kingdom, the king Hyokkose.

Among the myths and traditions about birds, the "Swan-Maiden" ones are most commonly found almost all over the world. It is especially widespread in Asia and also the parts of Melanesia and Micronesia in Oceania. Its Javanese version in Indonesia describes as follows: Long, long ago, a widow picked up a baby boy in the woods. The boy became an expert of the bow when he had grown up. One day while he was walking in the woods chasing after the birds, he happened to come to the side of a beautiful pond. There he found several heavenly maidens bathing in the water. He stole one of the feather robes hanging on the tree by the pond. All the heavenly maidens returned to heaven except the one whose feather robe was stolen. She had no choice but to remain on earth and she became the wife of the hunter and children were born between the couple. As the husband wondered why the stock of rice never diminished, one day, he secretly took off the cap of the kettle and looked inside and found only one ear of rice. However, as he had opened the cap of the kettle, the supernatural power of his wife was lost and they had to obtain more rice somehow to meet the demands of their daily life. Thus, the stock of rice in the granary had been diminished and finally the feather robe concealed underneath the rice came out. Although the heavenly maiden returned to heaven by wearing this feather robe, from time to time she came back to earth to suckle her child. This child grew up and became a beautiful young girl like her mother.

In this tale, the idea that the heavenly maiden has the power to control fertility is well expressed. The myths and legends of the birds bringing the seeds of grain to mankind have been widely distributed in East an Southeast Asia.

Fish have been an important source of food and familiar to the inhabitants of the Oceanian Islands and yet they often became fearful animals. There is, for example, the following tradition from the Torres Strait between New Guinea and Australia. Once upon a time, when a man called Mutuk was fishing at a lagoon, the fishing line got entangled. Therefore he dove into the water to disentangle the line. Then a huge shark happened to pass and swallowed him unhurt and it swam to the north passing the Mangrove Island. Mutuk noticed that the shark was now swimming in warm water and felt cold when the shark sank into the deep water. Finally the shark swam in the direction of the Boigu but was stranded because the tide was on the ebb. When the sun shone on the fish, Mutuk felt the warmth and became aware that the fish was now on the shore. Then, Mutuk took a piece of sharp shell stuck behind his ear and cut open the belly of the shark and went out of the fish. Mutuk noticed that he lost the hair of his body completely while he was inside the belly of the shark. This legend in which a huge fish swallows a man, similar to which is the tale of Jonah in the old Testament, can be found often in Oceania and Indonesia. Folklore of this type makes us recall the mystery symbolically played frequently at the initiation ceremonies in New Guinea in which a young boy is swallowed by a crocodile-like monster and comes out of it later.

In myths and folklore, not only animals that actually exist but also imaginary ones play important roles. In China, the phoenix, chi-lin (unicorn), turtle and dragon were important as sacred animals and they were called the Four Spiritual Animals although they are only imaginary except the turtle.

A dragon in China is an animal symbolizing kingship. When the legendary emperor Huang-ti was looking at the tripod made of the copper of Shou-shan, a dragon descended from heaven. The Emperor rode on the dragon and went up to heaven saying that God summons him. The retainers intended to follow him and more than 70 men rode on the dragon. However, when the dragon ascended to heaven all the men were thrown off and the mustache of the dragon held by the men came off and dropped down to earth together with a bow of Huang-ti. The men left on earth cried, holding the mustache and bow. The idea of the Chinese people linking the dragon with kingship deeply affected various other countries in East Asia.

China: All Creatures Great and Small

It is almost impossible to determine exactly when human beings began to develop close bonds of affection with the other creatures, but we do know dogs, sheep, pigs and cows have figured hugely in man's history ever since there was history to record. Man and the other animals on earth have lived together in close association since the dawn of human civilization.

In prehistoric China, our ancestors had close relations with the other animals. Many of the ornaments of the Upper Cave Man in China 18,000 years ago were from animals such as feathers, fish bones, teeth, shells, etc. Fish, bird, deer, frog and other animal motifs are found on the earthenware vessels of the Painted-pottery Culture of the Neolithic Age.

Animals were intimately woven into legends of the prehistoric period. The two legendary sages, Yu and Shun were supposed to have emerged from an animal state. And Fu Xi, who lived earlier than Yu and Shun was said to have a long, bushy tail. Myth has it that Qi, the first ruler in the Shang dynasty (circa 16-11 century BC) was born after his mother had swallowed the egg of a fairy bird.

Of course, all these are fables, but they are illustrative of the fact that in the history of China, the birds and beasts and our ancestors were inseparable from each other.

But one must not speak only of what is pleasant to hear, that man and animal lived together in close communion for survival. When slave society arose, through ignorance and superstition, huge numbers of animals together with tens of thousands of slaves were buried alive to accompany the dead slave-owners. These funerary sacrifices included young elephants, deer, girls and boys.

All living things have competed in various ways to survive with man emerging as the winner. The mountains, rivers, flowers, beasts and birds and insects and fish have all become the booty of the victor in the war for survival — man. They became his to use and existed only for him.

A few lines in a page cannot cover the story of all the animal forms which came into use in writing. It can be seen how closely the Chinese pictograms resemble the image of animals: shell, tiger, sheep, fish, tortoise, elephant, horse, deer, turtle-dove and bird. Apart from these stylized pictograms, bird, fish and tadpole script found on ancient bronze, jade and stone artefacts have been found. From the first to the last stroke each stroke in each character of these scripts contribute to the shape of the animal it takes after. Even today, village artists write couplets on scrolls with characters in the shapes of followers and birds with bamboo pens in various bright colours. They are characters from afar but, close up, they are colourful paintings.

Animals appear constantly as subjects of metaphors, from the old classic *The Book of Songs* to contemporary folk ballads and folk sayings. Animals are referred to in many places in *The Book of Songs.* For example, "Bustards flapping their wings flock to tall, ancient trees. The crying deer graze in the wilds." Folk songs and sayings mentioning animals are too numerous to count. Many are very succinct, pithy one-line or two line rhymed saying carrying a profound meaning. For instance:

Hypocrisy is a cat which says it doesn't like fish
A bird does not depart until the branch withers.
Don't expect the tortoise to walk quickly.
The louse on the tail of the cow always has its share in the end.
Examples of two-line rhymed sayings are as follows:
The pattern on its back doesn't make a bee a tiger;
Nor a horn on a snail, a cow, either.
The crane flying in the sky is lean;
The frog squatting on the ground is fat.

In philology, lengthy tomes have animals discoursing learnedly. In Greece, an owl is symbolic of wisdom and learning. In China, it has always been associated with evil, and animal portending terror and catastrophe. Only the natural scientists speak well of them, claiming that owls are not harmful to man at all. Zhuangzi, the Daoist philosopher of the Warring Sates period (475-221 BC) mentioned them twice in his "Autumn River Essay" on philosophy. "There is a kind of phoenix in the south. This noble bird perches only on the paulownia tree; eats only fruits; drinks only from pure springs. Owls, however, relish dead mice they find occasionally. When the phoenix flies by, they try to frighten the phoenix away. The phoenix *disdains* dead mice. This shows that a different nature has different demands." Du Mu of the Tang dynasty wrote in his poem: "Withered lianas, old trees and drowsy crows." The withered lianas and old trees are enough to evoke forlorn desolation. "Drowsy crows" and "ancient trails, biting wind and lean horses" which follow heighten the bleak desolation. Han Wo, a contemporary of Du Mu, wrote in one of his poems: The stream murmurs to itself and the sun sets itself. Neither dogs nor chicken are seen, only cawing crows. Desolate and vacant, not a shadow can be found round the villages but flowers." Here, crows are used to underline the desolation and wretchedness. Li He, another member of the literati of the Tang dynasty has another altogether different description of a "lean horse": This is no ordinary horse. It was sired by the Celestial Horse. The bones of the lean horse ring as of metal. It may be lean but it has the strength of steel. Since ancient times, the animal motif has been variously depicted. Sometimes animals are lofty and great, other times they are ugly and mean, but that is all created by people to answer different needs.

Are not venomous snakes, sly foxes, ugly toads and sneaky weasels animals people abhor, all familiar animals in Chinese classical literature? In the folk opera, "Liu Hai as the Golden Toad" a three-legged toad is one of the main characters. This story has been widely enjoyed by people for thousands of years. However, toads in general are not well received, in spite of the newspapers and magazines constantly telling people that the toad preys on insects harmful to man. The toad is the object of disgust to people. This loathing for the toad is implicit in many sayings, such as the following:

A toad lusts after a swan's flesh — aspiring after something one is not worthy of.

Toads under the bed posts — unsuitable material for the purpose.

A toad leaps onto the foot — It doesn't bite, but is enough to make one's flesh creep.

The four-legged toads in life can never hope to become as lovable as the three-legged on in the story of Liu Hai.

In the popular legend, "The Cowherd and the Girl Weaver", magpies build a shiny silvery bridge, the milky way, once a year for the two lovers to meet. People, old and young, in China and abroad, all remember the masterful Monkey King and the lovable Bajie, the Pig in the "Trip to the Western Regions". In this story the two animal characters become real living beings people can relate to.

Pu Songling of the Qing dynasty (1644-1911) has so successfully created lovely and good-natured images of fox fairies and weasel spirits, like "Jiao Na", "Xiao Cui" and "Qing Feng", that any man would love to have a wife like the last, although she is only a weasel spirit in the world of mortal men.

Animals have played a big part in man's life. They are with him in his food, home, travels, and in illness and in health and on occasions like funerals, weddings and births. The bird and animal motifs are second only to flowers in designs for clothing. But in the overall composition, prominence is given to birds and animals.

In bird and animal motifs, the bird, the butterfly, the dragon and the phoenix are the most popular. There is a great diversity in the designs of these motifs which vary with the locality, conditions and tastes. All these motifs are considered auspicious signs. Homophones are popularly employed. For example, "Ji" meaning chicken is the homophone of another ideogram meaning good luck, and similarly "bian fu" the bat the "fu" for fortune, "lu" deer to "lu" for his position and good pay, "yu" fish to "yu" for abundance and "xi que" magpie to "xi" for joy. Children wear hats and shoes with the likeness of a tiger and clothing embroidered with the tiger, scorpion, centipede, poisonous snake and toad motifs, as venom is supposed to be the best antitoxin. Girls love the mandarin duck motif as it is the symbol for ever-lasting love, while the old people usually prefer cranes and peaches, symbols of longevity. The dragon motif is masculine, while the phoenix motif is feminine. There is a very clear distinction.

Whole books could be written about the dragon and the phoenix in Chinese art. It is not clear as to when they first appeared, but they were already in existence at least over three thousand years ago, judging by the inscriptions on the oracle bones and tortoise shells found in Yin dynasty ruins. They were not, however, as well developed as they eventually became.

Anyone who has been to Beihai Part in Beijing knows there is a magnificent porcelain wall called the Nine-Dragon Wall there. Dragons and phoenixes are creations of the imagination, but one never feels repelled by them. On the contrary, as one stands before this wall with its nine writhing dragons, one cannot but be attracted and filled with a profound sense of respect and admiration for the consummate artistry of the ancient artists of China and their contributions to the world.

There are many other motifs of mythical animals similar to the dragon and the phoenix. There is the unicorn, *kui* and the strange bird with the body of a beast and even the flying figure of a bird with twin human heads.

During the long Chinese New Year holiday when the Yuan Xiao Festival falling on the fifteenth of the first month is celebrated, people devote their skills and talents to making lanterns of many shapes and kinds. There are fish, prawn, dragon and lion lanterns of marvellous ingenuity. When the Qing Ming Festival comes round in March, people turn to making kites of fantastic cunning. Kites in the shape of swallows, eagles, goldfish, centipedes and the mythical Monkey King soar into the sky. The smallest fry will plead tearfully for one, even if it is only a simple tadpole of paper and slivers of bamboo.

Animals again appear to join the rejoicing of men of the fifth of May, during the Duan Wu Festival. Girls embroider animal motifs diligently and deep into the night. On the seventh of July, the meeting of Levers, when the legendary Cowherd and the Girl Weaver meet again, gaudy lanterns of diverse designs light up along the rivers. On the Moon Festival in mid-august, Every family is busy making cute little rabbits of dough. Our animal friends, as can be seen, are always present to share our joys and add colour to our festivals.

In conclusion, some examples of the intimate bonds that exist between animals and the cultural life of the Chinese people may be reiterated.

When a baby is born, relatives and neighbours are given eggs that are dyed red. At weddings, a boy clasping a large rooster is put inside the bride's sedan. When old people pass away, they are said to leave this world on flying cranes!

But when people slaughter chicken and fish for banquets, we think they do not always remember that *ji xiang and you yu* are homophones for "good luck" and "abundance", as well as for "appetizing chicken" and "have fish!" It's all a joke!

Animals in Malaysian Folklore

Living in or at the edge of the wonderfully luxuriant rain-forests that have supported myriad vegetable and animal life, the indigenous people of Malaysia have come to know their environment very intimately. On their hunts and gathering expeditions they have come not only to recognize the different family groupings of plants and animals but have also been able to make out their distinguishing characteristics. They have in fact, over the generations, gained a knowledge of the habits and personalities of these members of a community that they share together. The humans have entered into the life of the fauna as it has become a real part of their living.

For generations the proto Malays and the Malays have in effect depended on both the plants and animals of the forest for their food and even livelihood. The animals are present in the life of the Senoi, Temiar, Kadazan, Murut and Malays in many intricate ways. Besides being hunted for food, as in the case of the jungle fowl, wild boar, deer, monkeys and innumerable species of birds, some of them have been tamed, reared, and even made to work for men. Jungle fowls have caught and reared and even crossbred with the village strains; so it is with the wild boars. In the states of Kedah, Trengganu and Kelantan, monkeys are trained to pluck coconuts from tall palms.

This is the practical level of relationship between man and animal. But animals do also pay a great part in the ritual lives of the different peoples, and without doubt the rituals of the various people in this country are amazingly varied and rich. Among animals, the fowl, both the hen and the cock are the most often used. White hens are often presented to the *bomoh* or folkhealers whenever a patient has been cured. The black cock, with black feathers and flesh, *ayam selasih* is a rare breed and is also given to the folkhealer as a present for successful treatment of disease. It is sometimes offered by the *bomoh*, to the spirits to help locate lost gold or precious articles. The black fowl is in itself a medicine for serious illnesses like leprosy. Among the Kadazans or Dusuns of Sabah fowls are prescribed as payment for transgressions of the lesser *adat* or customary laws. For more serious communal offences buffaloes are prescribed. Animals are among the most important sources of medicine and even poisons for Malaysians. One sometimes still crowds encircling a medicineman who has only a metal container with the horns and bones of the *kambing gurun*, the serow, a rare mountain goat, in a solution of oil. In fact, all parts of the serow are valued by Malays as medicine, especially the saliva, bristles, meat and bones. For fractures, wounds and rheumatism, a solution from its horns is used for curing yaws. The buffalo too contributes to Malay medicine. Scrapings from its horns are used for wounds in the eye or other chronic wounds.

The honey bee is fairly universal in its medicinal importance. Mixed with other herbs or extracts it is often used for sore throats, coughs, numbness of the feet, rheumatism, feeble mindedness and even as an aphrodisiac.

The list of medicine and cures from animals is bound to be a very long one, and it is hoped that this very brief sampling does illustrate how very important the animal is in the longevity of man himself. Man is not only dependent on these animals for his food but also in his struggle to be healthy.

Due to new surroundings and the introduction of easy access to modern medicine, traditional medicine unfortunately is losing ground too fast. Pills, capsules and the hospital replace the traditional cures and *bomohs*. However, in the field of general folklore and literature the animals are still ever present in stories that find their existence not only through the spoken word, as they were told in days of old, but also in the more permanent printed works. Used in school reading texts or general reading these stories have found a new and vigorous life after the 1950's. An attempt may be made to sketch some of the roles of the main animals in Malaysian folklore, through a very special collection of fables that has been classified in Malay as the *cerita-cerita mergastua* or animal tales, that bring forth a deep knowledge of the animal kingdom.

Several of the more popular fables are trickster stories that are collected in the *Hikayat Sang Kancil* (the stories of the Mousedeer), that focussed on the cunning and guile of this small yet elusive creature. However, one also sees a process of maturing in the tales, on the part of the protagonist. In the second series he has turned into the Pacifier of the Forests, bringing warning groups of animals together. In the last series, *Hikayat Pelanduk Jenaka* (Stories of the Comic Mousedeer) he has been elected as the King of the Forest.

The *kancil, pelanduk* or mousedeer is both hero and clown, and is wily and full of tricks. Belonging to the deer family and known to be a fast runner in the tracks of the jungles, it is elusive to hunters, and as quick in the mind too. In fact it has become the symbol of cunning and later of wisdom for other creatures of the stories. George Maxwell describes the *Kancil* admirably well in his *In Malay Forests*:

> "It is the smallest of all the deer tribe, the daintiest, and the most exquisitely formed little creature that can be imagined. A full grown animal is barely eight inches high; and so small is the scale upon which it is built that its feet, with their delicately cloven hooves, have not the thickness of the slimmest penholders."

Such a delicate animal, fast and pretty, no doubt appeals not only to Malays but also Orang Asli, First Malaysian children, as possible pets, especially with its big 'pleading eyes and all the grace and elegance of a gazelle'.

In the jungle it is always a victim of both man and the bigger animals. It thus must survive through its swift movement, guile and cunning. For example, in a famous story *kancil* spotted ripe berries on the opposite side of the river. Unable to cross the water on his own he summoned the crocodiles to surface, and be counted, as commanded by King Solomon. When the reptiles surfaced and arranged themselves in a row he jumped onto their bodies and playfully knocked on their heads, in the process of carrying out the command of the King. As soon as he reached the other bank he jeered at their stupidity, always arousing mixed feelings in the listener of admiration for his cunning but also a dislike for his unkindness, and deriving pleasure by hurting or troubling other animals. Thus in another story, in revenge, a crocodile bites his hind leg. But sharp of mind, the *kancil* quickly picks up a stick of bamboo and dangles it before the reptile saying that it was not his leg that was bitten, but a mere stick. On hearing this the latter releases the real leg and catches the stick, thus freeing the *Kancil.* Naughty and often unfair (in a perhaps unfair world), he uses bigger and stronger animals, both his predators and friends, for his own survival. Once, caught in a deep hole-trap and unable to climb to the surface, he was asked what he was doing in the hole alone, by passing animals. Incidentally too at that time the skies were brewing a storm and the clouds were dark and scuttling across the heavens. Quickly he responded that the skies were falling and he was taking cover. When they heard this the elephant, tiger and the other animals jumped in to join him. As soon as they were in the trap the *Kancil* taunted them by twisting their private parts, to the anger of these animals. Unable to stand it any longer the elephant wound his trunk around the small body of the mousedeer and threw him to the surface, thus again freeing him from his initial predicament.

A trickster, quite egocentric and always ready to outdo others he has often behaved as a practical joker. Even though not hunted by the tiger, for example, he has played unkind tricks on him. Passing by a sleeping coil of python, he once told the tiger that he was guarding king Solomon's belt. The tiger, aroused by curiosity, pleaded with the *Kancil,* to let him try it on Eventually the latter agreed, on the pretext that permission had been obtained from the King himself. From a safe distance *kancil* watched the tiger winding the snake around his body and being strangled by it.

Popular among children the stories of *kancil* also include incidents when this cunning animal was deceived by creatures smaller than him, as in his race with the river shells. The shells have arranged it so that every time the mousedeer calls out, there always is a member of their tribe to respond, thus making out that the shells were always before him. At last *kancil* concedes defeat without knowing that he himself has been tricked. *Kancil's* crowning act was how he defeated the ogre who terrified and robbed animals of the fishes that they have collected from a lake. Several animals were put on guard, but all of them ran away, frightened out of their wits. At last these animals pleased with the *kancil,* now their King of the Forest, who came to their help riding a white *seladang.* He arranged to have all the animals collect rattan and fashion them into nozzle and nooses. After they left, the *kancil* made a fire. Seeing this the ogre approached him, but with a limp, from his rheumatic pains. *Kancil* offered to help him, before giving him the fishes. The ogre, a ready patient, fastened the nozzles, nooses and loops onto his body, with the help of the mousedeer himself. The latter then asked the giant to shake his body hard, which in fact tightened the rattan over his body.

The mousedeer stories are also found among the various groups of the First Malaysians. The story of the *kancil's* trick is fairly similar in the Orang Asli version. So is the story of how it tricked the tiger into beating the wasp's nest saying that it was the gong of King Solomon. Many of the Orang Asli stories are attempts at explaining (to children) the state of things in the forests, especially those concerning animals. Thus we see how in the story of the tapir, a conceited animal meets his fate. This tapir was once 'proclaimed by all the animals in the jungle as the most handsome because of his imposing size and fine physique and his beautiful cost of glossy black hide. He spotted a brutal horn on the top of his head like a rhinoceros and he was endowed with enormous strength.' However his physical beauty and strength made him a vain and arrogant animal. Once, coming to a community of poor rats who have been belittled by him, he was given herbs to intoxicate him. While he was drunk they sawed off his horn, painted his back white and filed off his carnivorous teeth. For shame the tapir now lives alone, and is herbivorous.

Indeed, animals appear not only in the medicine cures, comic and moral stories, but in Malaysia, as in other countries, they turn up in various art forms, in imitation or in the abstract. In the various sates of Malaysia, we see designs, patterns, and shapes which were inspired from the artists' knowledge of the animal world. Pandanus weavings have designs called *siku keluang,* elbow of the fruit bat, *sisik ikan,* fish scales and *tapak harimau,* tiger's footprint.

In textiles too animals are chosen. In the *songket* cloth in which silver and golden threads are used for the designs and pictures birds are favoured, especially the peacock. The *songket* is a Trengganu specialty. Also from Trengganu are found bows of fishing boats decorated in bright-coloured, stylized carvings of the *bangau* or egret. This decoration is functional, rising from the old belief that egrets are good fishers and will guide the boats to rich fishing grounds.

Birds are traditionally related to Malay woodcarving, especially with the craft of the *kris* or dagger. The *kris,* a traditional weapon often endowed with magical powers, a revered heirloom in most families, is also a thing of beauty. The hilt or handle of this dagger is carved from good and strong wood or various species, from tasks of elephants, and sometimes even from silver and gold, studded with precious stones. Many of these hilts copy the heads of different birds like the *rajawali,* eagle, or even the chick. The latter is known as *anak ayam patah tengkok,* the chick with the broken neck.

Animals, live or in symbolic art forms have a very rich and meaningful presence in the lives of Malaysians, past and present. Besides fables and carvings, poems and songs are heavily populated by them, because Malaysians look upon them as creatures of God that share the same earth and enrich their lives, provide comparisons and models for life and art. Animals and nature complement man and neither can exist without the other in the grand design of things.

Animals in Melanesian Folk Stories

The Institute of Papua New Guinea Studies has a Folklore Archive of nearly 4000 items. These are somewhat unevenly collected so that in the following data it should be borne in mind that researchers have collected more heavily from the East Sepik Province than, for example, the Northern Province. Nevertheless, from the stories collected so far we can begin to see a pattern emerging in accordance with geographical location. That is, since Melanesian communities have many more similarities than difference we are not as conscious of the narrow differences in the stories (although these exist) as of the broad difference based on coastal, highland, inland and island locations.

In the stories, animals are friendly or unfriendly with each other, kill, aid or have sexual intercourse with humans, have their physical attributes and behaviour explained, become or have been humans. The stories, when analysed, explain history, law and order, religion and biology. For example, a number of stories explain sexual reproduction by relating how early man and woman discovered by accident how male and female genitalia fit together. Many stories explain the universe, creation, supernatural interference in daily life, supernatural presence in animate and inanimate things, life after death, codes of behaviour dictated by the dead, in other words, Animism, which undoubtedly remains the strongest and largest single religion in Melanesia today.

Law and order, that is social control, is very much the basic theme of the many functional stories collected. If it is undesirable to be greedy, for example, the person who eats too much is punished by fate. In a story from Central a greedy husband is deliberately overfed by his wife and has to spend all his time in the toilet until he becomes a phalanger, an animal which is always defecating. The phalanger is thought of as a stupid animal in the area. The message is clear: food is scarce and must be shared.

The stories also serve as a political device, as in the Hebrew texts, in which Moses is victorious and his political enemies defeated. The legend makes Moses God's man and the executed become Satan's men. Likewise, in Melanesian legends, "we" won, and therefore "they" have sins ascribed to them. Several stories collected are fairly obviously derived from European teaching and some stories have introduced biblical themes. These include stories about foxes (which do not exist here), the Seven Princesses and so on. More particularly, the Christian Bible is one of the four books which semi-literates get to read or which illiterates have heard read. The stories are gripping especially in view of the fact that for a century at least the Bible's religious sponsors, the Europeans, so dominated the animistic sponsors in power and economics.

Not surprisingly the distribution of the stories reflects the geographical location. Mermaid stories belong to East New Britain, which is an island province. East Sepik, a coastal province, leads the field in pig stories and in the snake stories but, interestingly enough, not in crocodile stories, which one thinks of as belonging to the coastal provinces of Gulf of Sepik. Bird stories, particularly cassowary storied, also come predominantly from the Sepik. The ritual of the cassowary is prominent in the West Sepik and a film by Chris Owen (The Red Bowmen) has been made about this. Dog stories come mainly from East Sepik, North Solomons, Western and Eastern New Britain provinces and it would be interesting at some later date to discover the historical reason for this. In the West Sepik, it has been noted, the dog population is large and the dogs are of a noticeably different breed, with whiskers almost like a cat's. They were perhaps a dog/cat hybrid!

One story not yet catalogued has appeared in the journal *Oral History* and presents a problem. In this Western Province story, the eyes of a platypus have been pricked out with thorns for ritual reasons. But no living specimens or bones of this Australian animal have ever been found outside Australia. The area from which the story comes however, was connected by a land-bridge with Australia before the end of the last ice-age. Did the platypus once reach Melanesia or was the story imported by Western Province people after visits to the Torres Strait islands or are some Western Province people descended from Australian Aborigines? A very long time ago an early wave of Aborigines passed through Melanesia.

Although animal legends reveal acute observation of behaviour, statements do not always accord with scientific knowledge. In the coastal province of Central, a shell of one species which rides around on a shell of another species is wrongly thought to be the male of the second species. In West Sepik the gravel sac on the neck of a female cassowary is wrongly thought to be a nipple with which she feeds the baby bird. Bats are sometimes thought of as birds and porpoises as fish. However, sometimes we cannot be sure of our own assumptions. Baimuru people of the Gulf claim surprisingly and obstinately that the crocodile which we always think of as carrying its victim in its jaws, always seizes and carries it in its claws, at least in their very muddy waters. No explanation is given in the legend but when questioned, the answer comes that crocodiles cannot hold their breath under water with the mouth open. The stories collected go on to explain that the drowned victim is dragged out of the water and devoured on a mud flat. In many crocodile stories the monster is brought to the surface by magic and singing where it is speared. There are many natural explanations for this, not least of which is that puncturing a crocodile's hide reduces its ability to stay under water. In some legends, the crocodile marries a human, and today one can hear villagers cover their grief after a tragedy by saying that the victim was married by the crocodile (or python). It will be interesting to see if shark stories contain the same element.

A bee story from the Sepik explains the funding of a clan. The story revolves around a female who is pursued by black bee and herself becomes a bee. The oral history behind the legend suggests that the bees are darker migrants who conquer, marry and overwhelm linguistically weaker, earlier, fewer in habitants. However, we cannot be sure of this since sometimes the earlier group speaking a less widespread language wins in the long run even when the incoming group assimilates the existing group. Further collection of folklore in that and contiguous areas may help to make the story clearer.

Large birds figure prominently in Motu legends. The bird is, of course, a convenient device for moving the hero/villain around quickly in the story of different sites. From Central comes the story of the tragic god-like figure of Uro who, on his flight as a bird around the Motu Villagers, is brought down by stones. Significantly, "Uro" is the word for pot, an important item in the traditional Motu economy. The village men throw stones at him because he is an handsome man/bird admired by the women. Because only women make pots, the insult to Uro is also a dig at the women, or so one might speculate. Uro is not a prime-moving god. Rather he is a minor god with human frailties but more than a culture here since his behaviour helps to explain division among the Motu tribe. Many of the stories will be found to be widespread. A well-known example has gained the name of the Ogre-Killing Child. The son, or twin-sons, of a slain man kills a marauding monster which can be giant, an eagle or a boar, etc. In some versions the avenger dresses as a bird to lure the eagle. In the twin-son versions the twins might be two clans living symbiotically or a major clan split into left and right branches. The story seems to be telling us that they cooperated to defeat the enemy. The monster is barely human even when a giant, but it betrays intelligence, speech and guile. The geographic suitability of the type of monster is becoming apparent. In one part of Central the giant is called a "not-man" which is also the name of an extinct clan whose ancestral cave has been located. One can see how earlier inhabitants who dwelt in a cave and had to be fought against could be thought of collectively as a monstrous animal. The story often ends with the saved tribe gathering to celebrate.

Animal motif on tiles of the Han dynasty (China).

Part 5

Bamboo Culture

A Japanese drawing of bamboo.

Bamboo Culture

Buluh: Long Association with Malaysian People

Even in a tropical rain forest in Malaysia where vegetation is luxuriant, bamboo (buluh in Malay language) is an exceptional plant. It is not only the fastest growing, pushing its shoots up at the rate of 10 to 12 inches in a day, but bamboo has also established itself as one of the oldest plants which have been culturally associated with man in this region. In fact, it is hard to imagine the existence of such rich varieties of ethnic food, musical instruments, household objects, farm implements, *objet d'art*, custom and rites and even some very apt linguistic expressions that we find in the culture of the people in this country without bamboo.

In most parts of lowland Malaysia where the climate is constantly hot and humid, bamboo grows throughout the year. As a result, monopodial bamboo which silently creeps underground in winter and bursts into life in Spring at regular intervals is unknown. So is the romantic image of poets and painters walking among bamboo groves experiencing spiritual bliss and drawing their inspiration from winter moonlight flickering through a thousand leaves. Because, due of their incessant growth, all varieties of bamboo grow in cultures. A single cluster of bamboo which can occupy a space of 30 feet in diameter is a thickets of twisting roots and crisscrossing stems crowned by a soft umbrella of green foliage. This feature of growth makes bamboo among the most efficient plants for conserving soil on barren hill-slopes or river-banks. Since the thickets are seldom penetrate by men, or even sunlight, it is common beliefs that large bamboo clusters are natural abodes for all kinds of spirits, goblin and fairies not to mention snakes and other lowly creatures. The characteristics of bamboo combine many attributes unknown in many other natural lives. These features give rise to the many diversified functions which men have derived from it. Bamboo is soft and conforming when young but rigid and stubborn when old. It is hollow and yet its outer skin can be fashioned into very efficient cutting edges comparable to any razor. It is strong enough to be used as pillars for supporting considerable weight and yet split bamboo can be woven into intricate designs. The tender bamboo shoots are constant delicacies but the fine hair on their protective sheaths is an itching menace and a common ingredient among the Malays for making lethal poisons. In traditional Malay life-style, the use of bamboo often transcends social and class barriers. A festive rice cake which is made from glutinous rice and coconut milk baked in bamboo over open fire is not only served in humble homes but is also relished among the nobilities. It is to be common practice to scatter bamboo thorns beneath the house during later stage of women's pregnancy to ward off any evil spirit lurking nearby. Before disposable hypodermic syringe and surgical tools became a part of modern medical practice, Malay midwives had used bamboo splinters for cutting umbilical cords of newly-born babies casting them away each time after us. The act of circumcision in the same manner is still being practised in remote villages and post-surgical infection in these cases is notably rare. Until the firing of crackers and other loud explosive devises during the nights of annual festivities were banned for their public nuisances and the hazards they caused to life and properties, loud booming sounds of bamboo canons were a common feature. For this purpose, a 6 to 8 feet of the largest possible wild bamboo is hollowed out except for its lowest joint and a tiny hole is bored a few inches away from the jointed end. The detonation is achieved by igniting a piece of wet carbide which is positioned inside the bamboo beneath the hole.

The Malays attachment to bamboo for their musical expression is one which is more fundamental than just being a convenient source for their musical instruments. The epitome of the most pleasant musical sound that can be produced by human vocal chord is always likened to the sound of bamboo. In the legend of the Princess of Gunung Ledang in which her enchanted garden bursts into life orchestra accompanying what in today's term must be a very large symphonic choir, bamboo provides all the wood-wind and percussive backing.

A bamboo musical instrument is indeed a common heritage over a very extensive area in Asia and as such it must be the most important natural source for producing all varieties of sound. Among the aboriginal people in Malaysia where the use of metal is rare in music, bamboo is nearly the sole source for rhythmic as well as melodic expressions. The large variety of flutes, zithers, clappers, harps are well-known instruments which are made of bamboo. Bamboo is also combined with other natural objects such as gourd or coconut as resonators to make it into mouth-organs or idiophones. But, perhaps the most unique of all the musical instruments associated with bamboo, if one can call it so, is a 'lantai lompotan' or a jumping floor common to Muruts in Sabah. For a 'lantai lompotan' a sunken floor of about 9 feet square is constructed with layers of bamboo cross-beams supporting it.

Several dancer-singers stand in concentric circles on the floor and through shifting their body weights and hopping movements cause the floor to bounce up and down. On the downward bounce the floor hits the cross-beams underneath creating percussive rhythms to accompany their songs. Throw a piece of bamboo in the deepest water and it floats. In this situation the structure of a length of bamboo with its series of almost water-tight compartments is very much like that of a modern ship except that in the case of bamboo, even if all its holds are flooded, it still retains its buoyancy. With this unique characteristic, it is not hard to imagine that bamboo has been used as floats either in fishing devices or as means of water transportation for as long as we care to remember. In Malaysia, where large rivers often begin from treacherous terrains cascading their ways toward calmer valleys, a bamboo raft is about the only means of transportation which is safe and economical although somewhat slow. It is still a common practice for indigenous dwellers of highland areas to load their bamboo rafts with jungle produce, shoot the rapids and drift along until they reach a settlement or township. After disposing off all their merchandise and the rafts which are dismantled and sold as bamboo pieces, they track home overland only to begin all over again when a new raft is constructed and enough jungle produce has been gathered. In some river towns on the east coast of Malaysia the rafts which were once used as transports are turned into dwellings gradually developing into a community of raft houses with their own characteristic life-styles. Photographs of multi-storied buildings under construction with girds of bamboo scaffolding were once a popular cliché to denote development in Asia. Whilst in reality the pictures offer a tribute to the plant for having found a new purpose for men, there is also doubt for the many social overtones that they carry. But if you think that the sight of tiny dots of spidermen deftly manoeuvring themselves to fix a window twenty floors above the ground is enough to send cold shudders down your spine, you should take a close look at some of the men whose occupations are to gather edible birds' nest, wild honey or guano in lime-stone caves. For, a lime-stone cave is often a steamy dark void soaring vertically hundreds of feet from the ground. Its wall is dotted with cracks and crevices and its stalagmited floor is slimy with remnants of century-old bat's droppings. To get to the roof where the richest deposits are found, pieces of bamboo, each no more than 2 to 3 inches in diameter, are secured to the cracks zig-zagging their way upward. In scaling the cave to the top, the worker does not have to depend on the damar-resin torch with which he has to find his direction in the dark but also to contend with swarms of bats which are disturbed by his presence.

Man's long association with bamboo has taught him to draw certain conclusions from its characteristic and relate them to his own experience. In the case of the Malays, some aspects of their world-view are reflected in their similes, proverbs, metaphors and other linguistic expressions which draw inferences from bamboo and its characteristics. In the Malay language there are innumerable references to bamboo which illustrate wisdom, morality and teachings applicable in many situations in life. In order to express the fact that education should begin during the formative stage of a person's life, the Malays state that the shape of bamboo can only be controlled when it is still in the form of shoot. The expression 'like bamboo clumps and a river bank' simply expresses a spirit of interdependence between two closed allies. A good model for a career diplomat is perhaps to behave 'like bamboo in the wind' which is apparently genial and amicable but firm. But, a bamboo gun or rifle is not particularly complimentary when used to describe a person for its very obvious reasons. The legend that once there was a princess who was born of a bamboo clump called 'Putri Buluh Betong' is not only widespread among the aboriginal tribes in Malaysia but occurs in many of the early Malay literature as well. All rulers in Hikayat Raja-Raja Pasai, Hikayat Merong Mahawangsa and Cerita Kelantan claim their genealogy from this totemic personage instituting a sacral belief that a bamboo clump is not just an ordinary bush to be taken for granted.

Kawayan: Versatile Uses in the Philippines

Distinctly an indigenous plant claimed as the world's tallest grass, the bamboo luxuriantly grows throughout the Philippine archipelago. It has thrived and proved its cultural, historical and economic worth since per-literary historic times. It gives prominent aesthetic accent to the rustic landscape as if to symbolize strength, toughness, resiliency, and suppliant character of the populace,

Nature and propagation

The Philippine bamboo, or native *kawayan*, is classified by botanists as *Bambusa spinosa* belonging to the huge family or natural order *Gramineae*. This is one of the largest groups of fast-growing grasses characterized by hollow, cylindrical, woody, jointed stems with solid nodes at intervals. This plant has creeping, jointed underground stems or rhizomes which reproduce by sprouting light pith stems called culms. The young shoots grow several inches or sometimes more than a foot overnight. The culms grow to a height of 60 ft. (18 meters) or more. The bamboo's hard outer layer which is impregnated with silica turns dark green or yellow when it matures after 2 to 5 years.

A bamboo is an easiest vegetation to propagate. Cuttings good for propagation can be taken from matured stem having lateral buds whose nodes have dense roots. A seedling can also be grown from a cutting of a matured culm with three nodes intact. A small opening is made at the upper portion of each of the two hollow chambers of the internodes wherein fresh water is poured. This bamboo pole is planted vertically such that the portion with holes measuring 50 centimeters is exposed and the lower portion measuring 70 centimeters is buried in the ground.

Varied economic uses

Man's progress could be recounted to the attributed to the marked extent to which he controls or manages, understands, and utilizes constructively the resources available in his environ. Archeologically, the bamboo has been a universal provider long before the colonizers came to the Philippines. Its mundane uses have been explored it being a principal source of raw materials for utilitarian and decorative purposes. The natives have fashioned their dwellings, tools and devices for livelihood, domestic implements, articles, tools and devices for livelihood, domestic implements, articles, ornaments, musical instruments, and many other products out of this cellulosic material.

Over the centuries, specialized skills to optimize the use of this plant have been employed. What dominated the scene during the early times was the architecture purely of Malayan taste.

The usefulness of this multipurpose plant which has been providing considerable material and aesthetic benefits, has been accepted as a part of the Philippine experience. Its tested values in the past are still being felt as those relate to the needs, standards and technological developments of modern life-style.

The uses of this versatile bamboo are innumerable. Bamboos are used as sturdy construction materials. A great majority of the framework of rural houses in the country is constructed from seasoned bamboos. The posts, walls, floor, roof and ladder of the nipa hut are made of bamboos. The natural beauty of interior decorations is captured through decorative panelings. The adornments of dwellings made of variegated, attractive and artistically crafted articles such as flower vases, wall decors, book shelves, lamp shades, hangings, fans, and other domestic ornaments are among the products of bamboo culms.

On account of durability, accessibility, and workability, a bamboo is a potential source for livelihood. In major occupations like farming and fishing, implements, devices and articles are made of closely woven or open interlaced bamboo strips or matured stems. Harrow and sledge are some of the farm implements made of matured bamboo poles. In fishing, fish traps, crab traps, push nets, rafts, mast and outrigger for bancas, and corrals made of portable bamboo fences set along inland and open waters are common useful devices and implements made of bamboos.

Domestic and agricultural activities make good use of bamboos. Of great value are the jointed stems of varying sizes used for tube and water containers, measuring device, cylindrical contrivances, bucket, mouse trap, savings box, baskets, hats and other household utensils.

The young bamboo shoots and rhizomes are edible foods. They can be cooked or pickled, and even canned for commercial purposes. Bamboo leaves are good fodders for livestock.

Social and cultural values

The bamboo finds its way in the foundation of a Filipino culture. Whenever there are social and religious affairs, and other special occasions, the bamboo is the most accessible material used for decorative and structural purposes.

During fiestas, national holidays or occasions when special guests and dignitaries visit the place, a festive atmosphere and a gesture of hospitality are created by putting up huge, artistically designed bamboo arches. Games, floral parade, agro-industrial fair, or cultural presentation during fiestas use to great advantage the bamboo in constructing Maypoles, *pabitin, palo sebo*, fences, floats, and exhibition booths. It is the traditional way to bid good-bye to the old year and greet the forthcoming year with bamboo cannon fires during New Year's eve. Artistically decorated lanterns made of bamboo splits form part of the customs and traditions pervading the Christmas season.

Bamboo musical instruments have established the Philippine identity in the musical world. Some such instruments which are by no means limited to cultural communities are the flutes and similar wind instruments, the stringed instruments like the bamboo guitar and violin, and those belonging to the linguaphone and percussion categories.

The bamboo tubes cut in varying sizes and shapes of one or more internodes with a small hole drilled at the other end, produce resonant, standard tones chromatically scaled in two octaves. The bamboo hand or orchestra is an ensemble of these wind instruments complemented by other bamboo instruments which could produce Philippine folk and classical melodies.

The famous bamboo orchestra known as *Pangkat Kawayan* or "Singing Bamboos" of Quezon City, Philippines, composed of 50 grade and high school students, plays a hundred instruments made of bamboos. This group has been the ambassadors of good will to advanced and developing countries. The tradition of *musikong bumbong* has been preserved through this bamboo band or orchestra.

But the most unique instrument which has achieved the heights of grandeur and fame with its wide range of varying tonal qualities and fascinating sounds is the priceless century old Philippinese' Bamboo Organ. Considered the oldest musical instrument of its kind in the country and the only one of its kind in the world, this instrument was built by Fr. Diego Cera, a Recollect friar from Graus, Spain, Who was assigned to Las Pinas, Rizal, in 1818 and finished after four years. This 160 years old bamboo organ is 6.7 meters high, 4.17 meters wide and 1.45 meters deep, with a total of 1,031 pipes, 122 of which are horizontal metal trumpets, 7 are small special pipes and the rest numbering 902 are bamboo flute pipes.

In order to restore the bamboo organ to its original state, this stately instrument was sent for repair to Germany by the House of Klais in Bonn in July 1973 and returned to the St. Joseph's Roman Catholic Church in Las Pinas after 20 months, with a triumphant welcome.

This world famous bamboo organ is a national heritage which has drawn remarkable impression and praises from visitors here and abroad.

Economic prospects

Bamboo craft is becoming a promising field in developing local cottage industries. The demands for handicraft products like furniture and other useful household articles are limitless considering that local consumption keeps on increasing. More over, there is a growing acceptance and good market potential abroad for various bamboo products.

With the recent development in bamboo technology, creatively made bamboo products are produced in commercial scale. What can, however, be further explored in order to produce best quality items and consequently command high prices in the competitive market are new processes and designs of new bamboo products.

Since a bamboo can be used practically every purpose as wood, there is no limit to its usefulness except perhaps man's ingenuity.

Ta-Ke: Practical, Aesthetic and Religious Values in Japan

The bamboo of Japan

Japan is home to a wide variety of bamboo, including native varieties *Phyllostachys bambusoides* (in Japanese, *madake*) and *Phyllostachys nigra form. Henonis* (hachiku), and *Phyllostachys pubescens* (*mosochiku*) introduced from China and spreading throughout both countries, as well as such species of *Sasa* (bamboo grass) as *Pleioblastus sect. Nezasa* and *Sasa Veitchii*, and the volume of production of these is as great as their variety.

The Japanese archipelago was born of volcanoes and is covered in soil that includes crystals from the weathering of igneous rock, and the bamboo growing out of this soil generally has a dense, hard structure characteristics of Japanese varieties. Particularly in Kyoto and the vicinity, the granules of quartz are quite small, lending an added measure of hardness to the bamboo grown there.

Edison, in his early experiments with the electric light bulb, succeeded in producing incandescent light using a filament *madake* bamboo from Kyoto. Cotton eventually replaced bamboo as filament material, but for eleven years beginning in 1887, Japanese bamboo was the major material for such applications, and was exported around the world.

The fact that the stalk of bamboo is hard accounts for its bright luster; the luster presented by Japanese bambooware and the precise alignment of grain uncovered by the craftsman's implements are indeed beautiful, in a great many cases creating items that are both practical at the same time deserving of appreciation as works of artistic handicraft. Further, the musical instruments made from Japanese bamboo — the *shakuhachi*, the *koto*, and a variety of flutes give forth a rich range of sounds and are an essential element in the traditional music of the Japanese people.

The revered bamboo

From the ancient past, among all the growing things found in Japan, the Japanese have given special position and special reverence to bamboo and *sasa*. The shoots of *mosochiku* may grow up to 120 centimeters a day, a rate almost unimaginably great compared to other flora and equalling or surpassing a year's growth for a variety of trees. One adjective that may be applied to such a rate growth is *takedakeshii* — ferocious — and it is from this word that bamboo, or *"ta-ke"* in Japanese, is said to take its name. The dynamism contained within bamboo and bamboo shoots was viewed as a holy manifestation, and they frequently serve as the "god-body" worshipped in Shinto shrines as the embodiment of the spirit of a god. The leaves of the bamboo plant also contain vitamin K and other elements and were doubly revered for their disinfectant properties. The ancient Japanese would also place fruit in bamboo cylinders and allow natural fermentation to create fruit wines, but at this time the fermentation would not proceed well unless green bamboo was used along with a stopper of *sasa* leaves, and these strange powers of bamboo and *sasa* attracted the belief of many Japanese, a belief that can still be found today around the country.

In the ancient past, when Amaterasu Omikami (the sun goddess who was the highest of the deities in the myths of

Japan's creation) became angered and hid herself in a cave, throwing the world into darkness, Amenouzumeno-mikoto danced before the cave with *sasa* leaves brought down from heaven and succeeded in tempting Amaterasu Omikami from the cave, being light back to the world. This was the origin of *kagura* — sacred music and dance — and the performance of *kagura* by shrine maidens holding *sasa*, believed to have the magical power to convey to man the words of the gods, was the forerunner of later Noh music and dance.

Whenever a ground-breaking ceremony is held in Japan, the site is sure to be encompassed at the four corners by green madake bamboo linked by a cord to keep the evil spirits away from the site.

Japan, as an agricultural country, is the home of many agricultural ceremonies, and since it is believed that rice, the staple crop, cannot be grown in ground that is even slightly impure, a great many of these festivals are for the purification of the land or as prayers for abundant harvests. Bamboo and *sasa* appear without fail in these ceremonies. As the Tanabata Festival, held in July, short inscriptions bearing the writer's wishes are attached to great bamboo plants as prayers, and at the New Year, bamboo is placed at the entrance of the home along with pine as a welcome to the coming year and as a prayer for the safety of the family members during the year.

Sasabune-bamboo grass boats

In the early summer, *sasabune*, boats made from the new-green leaves of *sasa*, have long been revered as sacred boat of the gods. When children make such boats, they exercise special care, and even when they fail to make the boat properly and have to discard it, they are careful never to stop on one of the *sasabune.*

It is believed that each October 1, all the gods of Japan gather at Izumo-taisha shrine in Shimane Prefecture, and here, too, the vehicles of the gods are taken to be the *sasabune.* In making these *sasabune*, the local people rise early in the morning and carefully purify themselves before going into the mountains to find clean, perfect *sasa* leaves to create the boats of the gods.

During the reign of Emperor Godaigo (1318-1339), *sasabune* would be made and launched at sea during times of stormy waters to appease the goddess of the sea. It was customary, it is said, for eight such boats to be made so that all the gods would gather around and calm the upset spirit of the goddess. The fresh green of the *sasabune* represents youth, and at the same time it is a sign of purity and holiness, and for these properties as well as its ability to preserve food, "*Sasabune Sushi*" has become a feature at festive times in the Niigata area. A *sasabune* is made from *chimakizasa* (Sasa senanensis), and in the boat are placed balls of vinegared rice with slices of squid or shrimp on top. These *sushi* are eaten without using chopsticks; the *sasabune* is customarily held in the hand and the *sushi* are eaten directly, an approach that seems to add to the enjoyment of the *sushi.* There is even the belief that to eat these sushi using chopsticks or other utensils will soil them and lead to an upset stomach. It is known today that the vitamin K in *sasa* leaves prevents the deterioration of *sushi* served in the leaves, but this effect has been recognized for centuries in Japan, an example of the perhaps unscientific but highly practical knowledge arising in everyday life. In making a *sasabune*, a leaf is pulled from a *sasa* branch (which must be relatively long), leaving about 10 centimeters of stem. About 6-7 centimeters of the stem is folded back on itself, the bottom part of the leaf is bent in two places, and the folded point is pressed through the leaf to give it the boat shape. Sometimes, the boat may be made by bending up both ends of the leaf, and the stem is placed so that it stands up and appears to be the mast of the boat.

Takenoko

In the minds of the Japanese, *takenoko*, bamboo shoots, are one of the typical foods of spring. The main feature of new spring *takenoko* is its crispness, a texture that cannot be found in canned goods, vegetables, fish, or meat.

In April or May, if one visits the regions where *takenoko* is produced, one can partake of *takenoko* cookery at its best, cooking which makes use of *takenoko* just dug up. The trick in cooking delicious *takenoko* lies in removing the vegetable harshness of the bamboo shoots. This process most often requires long years of experience, and the boiling of the *takenoko* is thus usually the job of the older women in the household.

First, the *takenoko* is dug up in the early morning, the tip is sliced off diagonally, the upper portion is lightly pierced with a knife, and the *takenoko* is placed with the skin intact in water left over from washing rice. To the water is also added ten percent rice bran of wood ash, and red pepper is also added for flavour. The *takenoko* is boiled over a high flame for about two hours, until it can be pierced with chopsticks, after which the heat is stopped and the *takenoko* cooled. When it is thoroughly cooled, the skin of the takenoko is removed and it is placed in water for about two hours to remove the rice bran or ash and the harshness. The *takenoko* is then flavoured with sugar, soy sauce, *sake* (rice wine) and the like and is served together with seaweed or added to raw rice and boiled.

Bamboo and the Japanese residence

The Katsura Detached Place in Kyoto is one of the treasures of Japanese architecture, and a full half of materials used in the buildings of the this 350 year old place is bamboo. Attics, windows, porches, panelling, and other portions are all of bamboo, and the combination of the straight and curved grains of the bamboo gives an overall feeling of simplistic beauty and luxuriance. As one passes through the main entrance to the place, one sees the bamboo fences stretching left and right, unfolding a vision of simple yet strong design in the vertical lines of the huge bamboo and the horizontal binding of slender *mosochiku.* Along the bank of the Katsura River is a bamboo hedge formed of living bamboo bent and intertwined in a cleanly lined a powerful impressive mass of life. Within the palace, one can see the simplicity of decoration carried out in the delicate bamboo inlays of the ceilings and the strength projected by the bamboo of the rafters, in thicknesses as required by their locations. Moving further into the premises, one can find other buildings where bamboo has been employed to superb advantage as halls, windows, bamboo nails holding other bamboo elements in place, gutters, and in many other applications, each elements adding to the overall beauty of the structure. This variety of applications of bamboo and its many revelations of loveliness are integral to the beauty of traditional Japanese architecture.

The ebullience and diversity of application of bamboo is one of the features of traditional Japanese architecture of that period, but today bamboo is steadily disappearing from Japanese building, taking away much of the distinctive flavour. Nevertheless, particularly in remote regions, one can still find many dwellings that have bamboo as the ceiling, pillars and posts, and panelling.

Today, however, once in while, lovers of Japanese tradition will occasionally build homes centered around bamboo pillars and other bamboo parts, but such structures have become much more expensive than wooden construction, the standard method of building today, and such homes appear to be mainly for show.

Bamboo gardens

Bamboo has long been revered as one of the abodes of the gods, and the stalks and leaves of the bamboo hardly change colour the year around. With such traditional value and esteem, it is not at all unusual that bamboo should be planted in gardens for esthetic appreciation.

In recent years, Japan has moved progressively toward the nuclear family, and great number of residences have been built within Japanese narrow confines, but this rapid expansion in the number of homes has made it impossible to create new gardens from replanted old bamboo, and further, after building their new homes, many people do not have enough money left over for an elegant garden. Particularly in the case of public housing complexes, hundreds of the same trees are necessary to form their gardens, and expense thus becomes a major factor in creating such gardens. In this sense, few plants or trees surpass bamboo and *sasa* in price and versatility. In recent years, more and more Japanese are planting their new gardens in bamboo, which displays its lovely leaves the year around and offers a greater and more entrancing variation over the range of greens than conventional flowers and trees. The leaves on the slender branches, the graceful green fall of the leaves' tips, these speak to the hearts of men and give them peace.

Bamboo requires only a relatively low level of light to carry out its photosynthesis and can be planted between tall buildings or along streets where the air is polluted. With just a little fertilizer, a little water, and a little care, bamboo can create a quiet, peaceful environment. In our cities, where tall buildings are springing up like forests, nothing could be better to protect privacy and create a composed environment than the 10 meter growth of ***mosochiku*** and its concealing green. Bamboo is indeed a fascinating and wonderful gift nature.

Bans: Valuable Material in Nepalese Life

Nepal is a land of ancient culture, the home of many rituals and festivals and of a way of life handed down over the generation. In religion, in social activities, and in daily life alike, an important — even essential — element of Nepalese culture has been bamboo and items made therefrom.

Perhaps the best way to illustrate the range and scope of the relationship between bamboo and the people of Nepal would be to give few brief examples that come to mind from history and from life today. According to a Chinese traveller who visited Nepal in the seventh century, people wore in their ears ornaments of decorated bamboo (which is called "bans" in Nepali, related to the Sanskrit word "bansha" of the same meaning). In the Terai region today, boys, girls, and women still pierce their ears with fine sticks of bamboo as adornment. In a more practical sense, bamboo pens were used in writing texts long ago by both Hindus and Buddhists.

The Nepalese people have used bamboo objects for centuries in traditional worship, especially religious ceremonies, fasting, rituals, and local festivals.

There is a Buddhist custom that children below thirteen years of age observe holy fasting known as "bamboo stick fasting." It is held once every at the full moon of Ashad (June/July) in Patan Hiranya Verna Maha Bihar and Kathmandu Paravath Maha Bihar Itumbahal.

Both Hindus and Buddhists have festivals consisting of lighting hanging lamps at their homes. On the occasion of this holy festival, a young bamboo pole with the leaves left attached is set up in the courtyard or top of the house, and the people worship by offering a light daily in the evening during the month of Kartik (October/ November).

Bamboo shoots are used for local grand festivals such as Chudakarma and Upanayan and in wedding receptions as well, themselves festive occasions.

In the Ayurvedic culture, the best quality bamboo plants and even roots are used to make traditional homemade medicines. Bamboo shoots also provide a source of sustenance, since both the moist white fresh shoots and dried shoots are edible. According to the law of His Majesty's Government, it is strictly prohibited to cut young green bamboo plants without permission of the concerned forestry division, although bamboo is available in every part of the kingdom. The young green bamboo plant is protected for the value it holds as a very useful material for the Nepalese, and this measure also helps ensure a sufficient supply of bamboo. There are more than 3,000 villages in Nepal and the rural societies need bamboo and its products in their daily life.

The relationship of the rural people and bamboo has always been very close from birth to death. Long bamboo pipes are used in the hilly region as containers for carrying water, and in the Rai society, when someone dies, the people must use bamboo pipes for drinking beer after the funeral. In the Terai region and hilly areas, bamboo arrows have been used for hunting in the forests. An arrow made of a bamboo stick with strong twisted thread fixed in it is used to kill birds and animals in the forests by expert hunters.

Bamboo is also a major material in the weaving equipment used in many villages, and has been for centuries.

There are various shapes of baskets made of bamboo such as the *kharpan, doko, dalla,* and *thunches.* These baskets are very useful for the peasants, labourers, and middle-class population in transporting luggage, grains, and daily commodities. All the village dwellers know how to weave such baskets, as well as *chaki* (baskets for religious function) and *chalni* (for sifting wheat, rice barley, and other grains).

Various villages are famous for producing special kinds of bamboo objects. In the Lalitpur district, there are several villages which specialise in making the *doko,* and the Tamang family of Kathmandu are experts in producing traditional simple bamboo combs with handles. Likewise, the Pyang villagers are noted for producing different varieties of *pyang.* The type of *pyang* (bamboo case) with a tight lid has been very useful to Nepalese traditional Ayurvedic physicians for storing the scented medicinal powders of their art since the late medieval period in the Kathmandu Valley. Medium-sized and large *pyangs* are used mostly by the Jyapu, who belong to the farmer class.

Bamboo has also served in the musical life of the Nepalese. The bamboo flute is identified with Krishna and has been used for centuries by Nepalese musicians as one of the most popular and most economical musical instruments in all of Nepal's various ethnic societies. In a slightly different form, bamboo pipe was combined with buffalo horn to create an ancient traditional musical instrument for towndwellers. This kind of traditional musical instrument is used once a year in the three main districts, Kathmandu, Lalitpur, and Bhaktapur, in the month of Bhadra (August/September).

Brief as these comments have been, they have been able to show only a small sampling of the many ways in which bamboo has been used by the Nepalese and has served its users. Even with the introduction of new, modern methods and culture from outside, the importance of bamboo has remained central to traditional life and culture here, and it is no exaggeration to say that it will continue to maintain its position of importance.

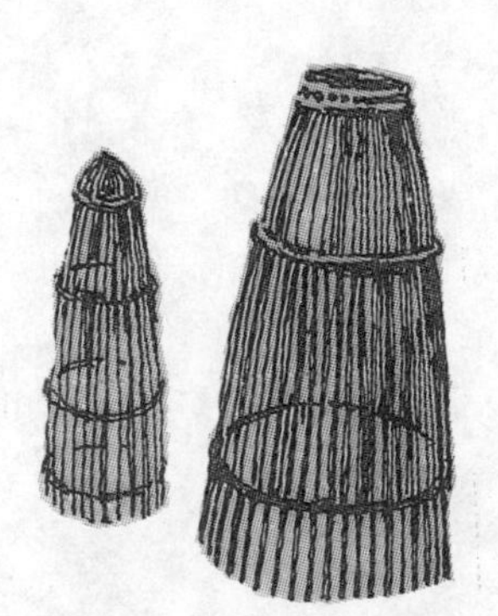

Traditional fishing baskets, Indonesia.

Part 6

Performing Arts

Representation of a village folk dance of the state of Orissa, India.

Performing Arts

Korea: Inheritance and Preservation of Traditional Dance

Korea's traditional dances are composed of the court dances, having their origin in the literati culture, and the folk dances which sprouted out of the common culture.

The court dances can be classified into the *Tang'ak* (Chinese dances) and the *Hyang'ak* (native Korean dances) which are performed in ceremonies, and sacrificial rituals dances. The folk dances can be classified broadly into shamanist dances, Buddhist dances and popular dances. Among them, the first two are performed by persons holding religious posts, exorcists or priests.

The popular dances are classified into people's dances and artistic dances performed by accomplished dancers. The people's dances include group dances such as *Noraech'um* (dance with songs), mask dances, and miscellaneous dances. The artistic dances include farmers' dances, mask dances and woman-entertainer dances.

The people's dances and the artistic dances share many similarities and at a glance, they do not have distinct characteristics. However, the peoples' dances are more concerned with daily life, festivals and are non-professional and playful, whereas the artistic dances are occupational, commercial and professional.

The farmers' dances are not uniform in style, but have five regional characteristics from the Kyonggi, Ch'ungch'ong, Yongdong, Yongnam and Honam regions.

The artistic dances include both professional farmers' dances and mask dances in the northwestern, central and southern regions on the Korean peninsula. Included in the woman-entertainer dances are *Sungmu* (monk's dance), *Kommu* (sword dance) and *Salp'uri ch'um* (exorcist's dance).

What causes the extinction?

Some of them, however, are no longer extant, while others have been preserved by the government by being designated as important intangible cultural properties. Dances that have become extinct or are on the road to extinction include *T'aptori* (dancing round the pagoda) among the Buddhist ritual dances and *Noraech'um* among the peoples' dances, and burial dances, designated as miscellaneous dances. The *T'aptori*, originally a group dance in the form of a procession, was performed at temples by common dancers who went round the pagoda praising the Buddha for his profound virtues or praying for their individual happiness or the well-being of the state as a whole. As temples did not sponsor these dances regularly, they naturally fell into disuse and moved toward extinction. Dances like the *Noraech'um* were group dances in which commoners expressed their joy and sorrow. These too have become extinct, in this case as a result of the erosion in the traditional faith of farmers and fishermen, and changes in their environment. The burial dances have disappeared, as biers are rarely used, having been largely replaced by the motorized hearse.

Under protection of the government

Dances preserved and inherited in a relatively good condition are mainly those that have been designated by the government as important intangible cultural properties. Two examples of this are the court dances and the ceremonial dances, preserved by the National Music Institute. The court dances are performed on stage two or three times a year, while the ceremonial dances are presented in ceremonies at the Royal Mausoleum and the Confucian Shrine each spring and autumn. As the two are taught at the National Music High School as part of the regular curriculum, the scope of their inheritance is being widened, and Korea now has a rich repository of graceful court dances. The court dances were rich in ceremonial elements, as they were performed before the sovereign, and were held in supplication for his long life, prosperity of the dynasty, national peace and glory and a fruitful year.

The ritual dances, on the other hand, were designed to glorify the memory of the kings, royal subjects and sages, while civil dances were intended to praise literary talents, and military dances extolled martial virtue. These ritual dances were religious ceremonial dances aimed at propagating Confucian truth, upholding the ideals of benevolence, cultivating human virtues and promoting order and national peace. Shamanism was a religion that spread mainly among Korean women. Many women in the lower stratum still embrace shamanist faith. Sounds of shamanist music attract them to the place of an exorcism, where they interact with the sorceress in a dance intended to communicate with gods. Through exhilarating dances, they try to temporarily forget their woes. Enjoying the mental state of being in a paradise, they are reborn into the scene of their real life.

The shamanist dances are performed by sorceresses who are believed to be capable of invoking gods. Their dances are designed to receive descending gods, and in rapture, they unleash various divine dances while bestowing happiness on spectators. The hereditary sorceresses, after presenting various divine dances, unfold god-pleasing dances, god-mimicking dances and sending-off dances. One thing shared commonly by these shamanist dances is that they are designed to ward off disasters and bestow happiness on people by drawing strength from spiritual beings through communication with the soul. There are regional differences in shamanistic dances and they have been designated by the state as important intangible cultural properties for better preservation. In can be said that the shamanist art helped Korea's performing arts greatly in creating new forms.

Tojangdori (going round the exercise hall), one of the Buddhist ritual dances, is performed at present at Haein-sa Temple, providing an opportunity to train the body and the mind and fortify the resolve to national defence.

One of the service dances, *Chakpobmu*, is intended to lead the deceased to paradise after cleansing their souls, as well as to pray for health and long life for living souls. These dances are preserved at several temples, including Pongwon-sa, for presentation at services.

The farmers' dances are representative of Korea's folk dances. They constitute the most deeply rooted art of life in Korea, and they have been held since ancient times in farming and fishing villages throughout the country. On the fifteenth day of the first moon by the lunar calendar, the farmers' dance troupe visits all households with the intention of expelling evil and greeting happiness. In cities, the dances are taught at schools, and cities compete in the dances.

The *Sungmu* and the *Kommu* falling under the category of the woman-entertainer dances, are designated by the government as important cultural properties and transmitted from persons skilled their art. The *Salp'uri ch'um*, containing the basic movements of the women's dances, is taught in the department of dance at colleges and at girls' high schools, and is growing in popularity as a folk dance.

These dances, the most artistic among Korea's traditional dances, were created toward the close of the Choson period . The *Sungmu* was influenced by the drum dance of Buddhist ritual. This, however, does not mean that the *Sungmu* is a Buddhist dance. This is a dance created by artists from the woman-entertainer chamber who were influenced by Buddhism.

The Sword Dance in which the dancer holds two swords, dates back to the Silla period. This was originally a court dance and its present version was first performed at schools of music in the southern region. It also has been designated by the government as an important intangible cultural property. We have viewed the contents of Korea's traditional dances as well as examples showing how they have been preserved and inherited. At present they are being further refined by the National Dance Company.

Performing Arts in India: A Continuing Tradition

In the Indian tradition the "performance aspect" is only the manifestation of a greater and more deeply rooted cultural ethos-whether it is the philosophical concepts that are finding expressions in the performance, or the religious beliefs, or, the celebrations of a social, agricultural, religious festival, of a particular community or tribe. Then, again the performance has many aspects/levels to it — whether it is the sophisticated art form performed on the concert platform for viewing by an elitist audience, or the songs or dances performed in religious institutions like temples, churches, *gurudwaras*, etc. for devotional or ritualistic purposes or, the traditional theatre or puppetry forms performed in various parts of India utilising elements of stylised gesture, movement patterns, music, make-up, costumes. All these derive their content from mythical legendary characters and the technique and grammar of performance from texts like the Natya Shastra (second century BC to AD second century).

Then, there are the multitude of performing forms in all art forms — theatre, dance, music, puppetry, narrative and story-telling which are performed by the people where the audience and performer both participate.

Similar categories are available in dance. However, one must note that these are not watertight compartments. For example, a dance or a narrative story-telling performance will have elements of music, movement and mime, gesture language and the word content.

Another factor that must be noted is the close inter-relationship or inter-dependence between the literary, visual and performing traditions in our country. Stories from the epics or myths and legends whether they are now in written form or whether they were, or are passed down by word of mouth (oral traditions). These were the source of inspiration to numerous visual forms. Scenes were sculpted on monuments or painted on walls of caves or monuments, as also illustrations for manuscripts on palm leaf and later in the medieval period on paper. Scenes painted on cloth, paper scrolls or simple paintings like the *padha* of Rajasthan or *patachitra* or *chitrakathi* of the Eastern and Western regions of India are popular even today. In these forms the combinations of the visuals accompanied by the text narrated in song, in addition, to movement and mime are used for communication. Communication or participation has its most multi-faceted or multi-pronged approach in the narrative forms in India where literary text, painting, elements of dance, *abhinaya* (mime and drama) and music, both vocal and instrumental, combine to give both performer and viewer/listener the most aesthetically satisfying experience.

With reference to the aspect of preservation of the performing arts, let us see how or why they have survived for so many centuries. These may indicate how to ensure their survival in the future. Through the ages, the cultural and artistic forms of manifestation have survived in this sub-continent, due to the main reason that these arts were relevant to the sub-culture or social group performing these activities — a particular song or folk tale or floor design continued to be because it was part of the daily life of the people.

The mountains, rivers, sun, moon, the seasons, to the Indian all these are sources of inspiration for creative expression, be it through word, line, colour, form, sound or movement and mime. There are numerous verses describing nature or the environment, the flora and fauna. Stories told in these verses are painted or sculpted on the walls of monuments, they are sung — the gesture language in dance depicts these stories through mime and movement — episodes are also dramatised. It is thus seen that in India there was not much danger of extinction of the art forms till recently, as these forms were relevant and formed part of the daily life of man. Artistic manifestations related to the agricultural cycle, the life cycle, the seasons — all these were not likely to need special programmes for preservation as they were very much connected with life's rituals, ceremonies (both religious and social).

In fact performing arts were the direct manifestation of these. Episodes from the myths and legends were sung and danced. A third character of the performing arts is its close relationship with the environment and nature, should the environment change, the performing arts would be rendered out of context, baseless and hence, meaningless.

In ceremonies conveying agricultural activities and the rituals connected with the first breaking of the earth/soil for sowing had accompanying song, dance, playing of certain instruments. The birth of a child and the various stages of development of his life were also accompanied by songs. The verbal or literary content of these songs ranged from the highly philosophical, to the sheer ecstasy of aesthetic joy, to the mere mundane and naughty or sometimes even verging on the so to say vulgar. So also the musical expression varied from the use of the highly sophisticated Raga Sangeet to the not so stylised melodic patterns of the rural areas to the utterly simple tunes or repetitive note combinations of the songs sung by the vast tribal community — living in various parts of India. The thing to note is that sometimes the most philosophical and highly evolved thought or concept could be expressed in a simple tribal dialect and sung in a totally unsophisticated melody by members of a community on a specific occasion.

Another reason for the survival of the arts was its flexible creative and ever-changing nature. Also the traditional forms were not static in performance or expression. The content that was to be communicated as well as the method or creative manifestation flowed like a river which was mobile — at times placid, turbulent, in spate of flood, nearly dried out, changed course occasionally, mingled with streams, but the inherent quality, i.e., water did not undergo change. The secret of the continuity of tradition in India as also the ability to absorb aspects of other cultures and its concept of 'Unity and diversity' has made our traditions to be fluid and mobile which cater to the aesthetic and social needs of the times. A fourth aspect of performing arts in India is the ways or methodologies used for training in the arts, that have led to their survival and contained creativity. The classical forms with a grammar and complex codes were passed from one generation to the other, by the teacher through the oral tradition. Learning the art meant living with the teacher, to acquire not only skills of the art, but the subtleties of philosophical meaning and interpretation. It was a question of building the mind and body, cultivation of ideas and skills, of developing the aesthetic sensibility through contemplation and self reflection.

The point that the need for preservation did not arise till very recently in India was due to the relationship of the performing arts with daily life. The impact of modernisation or development of industry has created this need. A song that was sung for a particular occasion — e.g. sowing, harvesting will no longer be relevant when tractors and other machines take over the work done by human beings. At best that song will be preserved — recorded, documented and later *taught* to people who are not connected with agriculture, thus making it a purely entertainment oriented song.

Then there is another level of the artistic form which sensitises one to the beauty, cleanliness, aesthetic communication, which are essential features for the development of the personality of man. The Indian arts at all levels bring out this ability to communicate with oneself. The outer manifestation or activity performed by the artist is basically an inward coming together of all faculties and sensibilities to energise the inner core of the thought process which then flowers/blooms to expression in a variety of forms according to the temperament training, cultural ethos of the artist. Such forms like sophisticated or stylised forms of music of dances performances connected with certain rituals are also to some extent slowly dying out due to again the change in pace of life and need to achieve or see results as quickly as possible — so the time that was required to be spent in first learning the grammar and technique for the correct expressions of a particular art form is now no longer available — this time span of learning, being with the masters also developed the ability to concentrate, sharpen the intellect, sensitise one to the development of aesthetic communication — it developed the spirit of endurance, it generated love and respect for the master, the guru, the perpetrators of the art form. It created a rapport between the performer and the audience, in fact the two became the one — both participating in the *rasa* that emerged out of the aesthetic joy or *ananda*. It is said that the *ananda* or joy emerging from the experience of artistic expression was, or is equivalent to the eternal or spiritual bliss that one experiences by communication with the Supreme Being. What is required for agencies, especially government agencies, is to identify the various teachers, *gurus*, available in the field, in all the manifold forms of dance, music, theatre, puppetry and narrative, story-telling forms and to provide assistance to these teachers to train students in their art, in the manner in which they learnt it. It would also be necessary to document, through the use of all possible media to draw the whole process of teaching and the complete repertoire of the art forms. An in-depth documentation of the social geographic, occupational, religious and philosophic aspects of the art, must also be undertaken to understand the essence of the form, its vibrancy and creativity. In this area in India, the government has schemes for honouring artists for training students with scholarships, and financial aid. Documentation of the arts is also being undertaken, however, so much more has to be done. Attempts are being made to build a firm foundation in early school education to give students an opportunity to study the arts, to discover and develop their talents, to ensure the participation of the young generation in the continuity and development of the arts.

Papua New Guinea: Cultural Change and the Performing Arts

Papua New Guinea comprises 400 islands which are populated by about 3.5 million people. Geographically, these 3.5 million people live in a variety of environments, ranging from coral atolls and islands, high-altitude mountain ridges and valleys, to mission stations and cities.

Apart from the diversity introduced by the modern-day arrival of people from other parts of the world such as Europe and Asia, in physical appearance ethnic Papua New Guineans are one of the most diverse people in the world. This diversity ranges from the very light skinned wiry-haired peoples of the Papuan coastal regions to the very dark woolly-haired people of the North Solomons, while in between there are varying degrees of light and dark skin colour. In stature the diversity also ranges between that of the tall seaboard dwellers and the short stocky highland dwellers.

Linguistically, there are three official languages, English, Tok-Pidgin and Motu. English was introduced by Europeans. Tok-Pidgin is a lingua-franca which developed during the early years of Papua New Guinea's colonial history and has its roots in a number of languages, such as English, German, Malay and many Melanesian languages. Of these three, Tok-Pidgin could be regarded as the National Language because it is understood and spoken by almost eighty percent of the population. But ethnic Papua New Guinea's speak an estimated total of at least 700 different languages. Most of these languages are quite distinct from one another.

Culturally, Papua New Guinea is said to belong to the Melanesian area. But to say that Papua New Guinea is part of the Melanesian culture area by no means implies that the 3.5 million people all share the same culture. On the contrary, the cultures of PNG are as diverse as the physical appearances of the peoples themselves, the geographical environment in which they live and the languages they speak. We get a glimpse of this diversity when we look at some aspects of their cultures such as their social organizations, social and political structures, religions and economic activities. Despite this internal diversity, Papua New Guinea is considered to belong to Melanesia culturally because the cultures that are found here have certain components akin to those found in the rest of Melanesia.

Culture change and adaptation

Prehistorians believe that the ancestors of people who lived in Papua New Guinea when the first Europeans found them, came from the West. It is believed that they came from the direction of Asia through the islands of Southeast Asia, then to the islands of Papua New Guinea. Prehistorians also seem to believe that there may have been a number of waves of migration from the general direction of Asia, to Papua New Guinea and thence to the other islands of the Pacific. This being so, as archaeological evidence suggests, cultural change as a result of contact with other people is not a new phenomenon in the region. Whatever changes that may have occurred during the early years of settlement of the region can be discerned through the work of archaeologists and prehistorians, a lot of which is speculative.

The cultural changes that we can talk about with some degree of certainty are those that have occurred in the last one hundred and twelve years i.e., since the arrival of Europeans. This is because of the availability of records.

Anthropologists agree that cultures are not static but are ever changing in response to new situations, ideas, innovations and changing circumstances. Circumstances may be climatic or environmental, and ideas and innovations may appear from within or without. It is recognized that one of the main reasons for cultural change is intercultural contact.

In pre-contact PNG, although the people lived in what appeared to be small isolated communities, there is evidence to suggest that they had ways and means of communication and interaction with other people, particularly their close neighbours. In a number of regions of the country there were a number of trade networks in which people of different cultural and language groups participated. This was one of the ways through which ideas and innovations were transmitted from society to society and in turn caused cultural change in the recipient societies.

At the south-eastern end of the mainland of New Guinea there was and still is a trade network known as the *kula* ring. In the Bismark Archipelago trade links existed along the shores of the island of New Britain between number of tribal groups and between the Duke of York Islands and New Ireland in the east. On the main island of New Guinea there were trade links between the northern shores of Madang, the Sepiks, the Highlands Cordilleras and the southern coast in the Gulf Province.

The *kula* ring is located in the group of islands off the south-eastern tip of New Guinea known as the Trobriand Islands. Two of the main features of this ring are that it involved the exchange of two kinds of valuables known as *muwali* and *soulava*. Secondly, these two valuables flowed in opposite directions in the ring, one going clockwise and the other anti-clockwise.

The exchange of these valuables involved large parties of men travelling for months away from their homelands in flotillas of canoes. While the two valuables were the focus of these exchanges, other things were also exchanged, such as less valuable items, food, utilitarian objects, magic and other non-material items. Clearly this was an important vehicle for the interchange of culture in these islands. In the Bismark Archipelago, the trade link between New Britain and New Ireland centred mainly around two different kinds of shells, the cowrie shell and the *pele*. The cowrie shell came from the West New Britain area. This shell, in its modified form, is known as *tabu* and used by the peoples of East New Britain and the Duke of York Islands as a form of valuable. The men from East New Britain sailed on long canoe voyages to the west to trade for the shells. In exchange for the *nasa* shells they brought back with them a variety of items including food and the *pele* shell which was produced on New Ireland. On these voyages it is understood that along with the trade there was also a lot of interaction between the voyagers and their host communities. From the above kinds of situations we can say that cultural changes as a result of cultural contact was not a new phenomenon to Papua New Guinea when the Europeans arrived at the end of the last century. But one thing we can say about this contact between Europeans and PNG societies was that the magnitude of the impact was far greater than anything that had happened before. This impact was felt in all areas of life of the indigenous people of PNG.

The impact of western contact on the performing arts

One aspect of the lives of the indigenous people of the country which was effected by Western contact was the performing arts. Common to many PNG societies were ceremonial and ritual performances. The degree to which these aspects of life were affected varied from one culture area to another.

This depended on a number of factors, three of which were the intensity of Western influence, the ability of such performances to withstand outside forces and, thirdly, the adaptability of such performances to changing situations. Two such aspects of the performing arts will be discussed here to present some insight into this. These are two kinds of ceremonial performances, one of which suffered badly through contact and became extinct, while the other was able to adapt and continues to flourish due to changing conditions after contact.

Hevehe

Hevehe was a general term given to a series of ceremonial performances found in the Elema language area of the Gulf Province. This series of ceremonies centred around the initiation of males. These initiations were performed at certain intervals which extended over periods between the ages of eighteen and twenty-two years. Altogether there were seven stages of initiations through which all males had to go through before becoming full adults, all of which were marked by ceremonies.

The end of the last of these initiations was marked by a prolonged ceremony in which hundreds dancers wearing masks known as *hevehe* appeared and performed. The centre of ceremonial activity for this last initiation was the *eravo*, a long house.

The initiations and accompanying ceremonies were elaborate affairs which required long periods of preparation and availability of manpower. In addition the *eravo* were huge structures which were built over long periods and also required a lot of community effort. In a way the whole life cycles of communities revolved around these initiations and the building of *eravo*.

With the arrival of Europeans, many able-bodied people left the Elema area lured by the prospect of employment with Europeans, or by the towns. This effected the manpower strength in the communities and, consequently, preparations for initiations and ceremonials. The effect of outward migrations in these communities was felt very quickly indeed.

Apart from the outward migration, there was another important factor contributing to the decline in the ceremonial life of the Elema people. This was the Christian missions which established themselves in the area. In the early years, as part of their teachings, these missions spoke out against traditional cultural practices, branding them as being heathen and urging the people to abandon them. At a later stage, some Elema people who had some idea of the Christian teachings began to interpret some of them for themselves and their people. As a result of these interpretations some came up with the idea that if all the black people abandoned and destroyed their traditional cultural practices they would be like the white men. Thus they advocated the destruction and abandonment of all cultural artifacts and ceremonies. This destruction and abandonment of cultural artifacts and practices was known as the 'Vailala madness' which swept the whole Papuan Gulf Coast and was recorded by early anthropologists.

As a result of these two main factors, the last *hevehe* to be performed in the Elema area was in 1912.

The *Tubuan* ceremonies

The *tubuan* is a conical mask figure which is found among the Tolai of New Britain. This figure represents the male cult which is often referred to as the Tubuan Society. Like the *hevehe* of the Elema, the *tubuan* was also involved in the initiation of young men, although this was not seen as its main function. It appeared mainly in association with certain ceremonies, in which it was the principal performer.

One main factor which is central to traditional Tolai cultural activities and without which *tubuan* appearances are not possible, is *tabu* (shell money). It has been said that *tabu* permeates Tolai culture and that without it such culture would not exist. *Tabu* is little *nasa* shells about two thirds the size of a pea, with their backs knocked out and strung onto rattan. It is used both as a currency and also for ritual ceremonial purposes. As a currency it is graduated into a number of units but the basic unit is the fathom which has about 400 shells. Today as a currency it can buy anything from a bundle of peanuts to a packet of sugar to a bottle of whisky. As a ritual object it is ceremonially given or received in funeral, marriage, land transfer and other kinds of ceremonies. It is also ritually given and received in *tubuan* ceremonies.

Before the arrival of Europeans, *tabu* was the pivot of Tolai economic, social, political and cultural life. Ever since the first Europeans arrived among the Tolai, in the form of German colonialists, many attempts were made to stamp out the use of *tabu*. For instance the German Colonial Government ordered the manufacture of glass beads to replace it. The missions also did their part in trying to stamp it out. As a result, during the eras of successive colonial administrations, Tolai cultural activity was at a low. This declined even further during and after the Japanese occupation in WWII, due to the destruction of large stocks of *tabu* during the war either in bombing raids or by Japanese soldiers. It was only after the war and many years later when *tabu* stocks had been replenished that Tolai cultural activities were on the increase again.

There are two main reasons for the survival of *tabu* today. Firstly, there is its importance in commercial exchange. Secondly, it is the important in ceremonial exchange which has implications for the social and cultural life of Tolai people. Because it is important in commercial exchange, people use it, and because it is important in social and cultural life, people want to own it.

As stated above, *tubuan* ceremonials are part and parcel of Tolai cultural life. Any waning of the importance of *tabu* will spell a decline in the Tolai social and cultural life including the *tubuan* ceremonials.

Japan: Diversity as a Source of Cultural Vitality

Japan, being an island country, has had fewer cultural exchanges historically, than those countries on the Eurasian Continent. Furthermore, from the second to third centuries BC, a social structure based on land cultivation had become dominant. This social structure, unlike that of the nomadic people in northern Eurasia, which was based on a highly migratory lifestyle, tended to encourage a relatively settled life in villages which developed into self-sufficient communities and in which the villagers remained from one generation to another.

Due to the nature of this predominant social structure, the performing arts such as music, dance and theatre, which developed in a particular area, were generally developed by the people who had settled there and passed on to the next generation.

Consequently, Japan's performing arts have developed in relatively closed environments and mainly by word of mouth from one generation to the next.

At the same time, the Japanese people in the past have enthusiastically accepted outside influences as a stimulating force in developing their own culture.

It may be said that in Japan, the new and the old in the performing arts of different periods, have existed side by side, at times contradicting or clashing with each other, and have been passed on together. And it is precisely for this reason that Japan can be called a treasure house of traditional performing arts.

However, looking back of history, there have been times when, just as the power to absorb new influences was very strong, a great part of the old forms were lost all at once.

The period in which this tendency was most extremely manifest was that transitional era from the feudal to the modern age, the Meiji Restoration (1867).

The Meiji restoration and its after effects

The Meiji Restoration set out to abolish a feudal system under which various isolated and self-governing local communities containing large populations and ruled over by powerful lords were in their turn controlled by a central political or dominant rule, and to establish a system under which all people were equal and national administration would be carried out through the free expression of the people. The model for this new system was the socio-political structure of Europe. As Japan worked to accomplish this transformation into a modern nation, the model that Europe offered as an ideal extended to the realm of culture as well. The government encouraged the introduction of European performing arts such as music, dance and theatre, educational systems and religions, which began to inundate the country. The distinctive feature of Japan's performing arts is that they are closely connected to local festivals. The Japanese believed that human life was protected by each element in the natural environment, the sun, water, earth trees and grass, and that god resided in each of these elements. At the same time they worshipped the gods of life — that is, their ancestors. The seasonal festivals served as occasions on which to call upon the god and to sing, dance and perform in an act of intermingling with the gods. Therefore, the popular performing arts were based to a large extent on a significant religious element.

However, with the sudden influx of European culture, the festival which had developed in local areas based on local beliefs were frowned upon as superstition and obsolete custom, and the related performing arts were rejected by the Japanese people themselves. Compared with the performing arts of Europe their own forms seemed restricted to very limited local conditions, and soiled by the smell of earth and salt and life. In this way the traditional performing arts of Japan entered a period of rapid decline.

This tendency was further accelerated by the educational system of the time. Under the newly enforced compulsory education system it was European folk music that became the standard material for musical studies while almost all Japanese music was rejected. Japanese musical instruments were excluded from the educational scene and the piano and organ became the primary teaching instruments.

Rediscovery and regeneration

However, after the initial tumult of the Meiji Restoration, as society began to regain its composure, people began to re-evaluate the role of the popular performing arts and to see the songs, the dances and the theatre once again as an embodiment of the spirit and sentiment of the people, as their very history and as the best vehicle for promoting a popular culture. This led to the development between the 1920s and 1930s of a movement to preserve traditional culture as such as well as a movement to create performing arts for a new era, merging the highly 'artistic' methods of European art with the traditional methods found in Japan. The movements to develop old folk music into a new and modern folk music, the experiments among Tokyo's artists and scholars in staging rediscovered music and dance of various localities and the passion with which musicians and dancers worked to revive traditional music to give it a role in modern society, were all apart of the rediscovery and recreation of the traditional performing arts.

Hakushu Kitahara's "New Folk Song Movement", the beginning of the "Local Folk Song and Dance Club" for local youth which was started on the occasion of the completion of the Nihon Seinen-Kan (Japan Youth centre) for youth organizations and the establishment of the "Folk Performing Arts Association" the forerunner of the Folk Performing Arts Academic Society, are all examples of the cultural climate of the time.

Developments after the Second World War

Thus it looked as though the traditional performing arts would be revived. However, Japan's defeat in the Second World War called for fundamental reconsideration of traditional culture itself.

For one thing, material cultural properties were affected in that many buildings had been devastated by the war, while the lives of many who had been the transmitters of Japan's non-material cultural property had been lost. At the same time, a reaction developed against the ultra-nationalism of pre-war times. The local shrines in pre-war days had been the symbol of Japan as the "land of the gods." The belief in the will and power of the gods boosted the morale of both those who fought war and those who stayed home to protect their village. With defeat, the shrines were this time taken as the symbol of a militaristic Japan. In an attempt to erase the horrible memory of war, there was a growing tendency to reject the shrines and all their related activities which were closely associated with the war. As a consequence traditional performing arts also faced a rapid decline. Furthermore, Japan once again began to follow in the cultural footsteps of the West, particularly of the U.S.A. That is, Japan's youth preferred jazz to the ritual lion's dance.

Continuation and preservation today

Now that over forty years have passed since the end of the war, how are the traditional performing arts being preserved today?

On a national level, the Cultural Properties Protection Act exists to ensure that both material and non-material cultural properties are preserved, recorded or given increased performance opportunities. In response to the national movement, local self-governing bodies have been working to preserve cultural properties, including the traditional performing arts, by establishing their own Cultural Properties Act. Their enthusiasm has been such that a Cultural Properties Act now exists on most levels of self-governing bodies, from the prefecture and city to the town and village. It may be said that in legislative terms there is an established system foot the preservation of cultural properties.

However, financial support for such preservation is still insufficient. As a result, the administrative bodies serve to support members of local communities who, on their own initiative and based on their own financial capacity, form committees which, in actuality, are the main vehicle of preservation.

Of the traditional performing arts, those considered to have high artistic merits, such as *Kabuki*, *noh* and *bunraku*, are performed in theatres that have been established for that purpose, that is, the National Theatre, the National Noh Theatre and the National Bunraku Theatre. The National Theatre has also been making efforts to preserve and to introduce other traditional performing arts to a wider audience, by staging performances of *gagaku*, *shomyo* (a performing art related to the temple), traditional local performing arts, classical Japanese dance and classical Japanese music. Meanwhile, Western performing arts such as ballet, opera, and classical music, which have been adopted since the Meiji Period have enjoyed a wide following. There are over ten orchestras in Tokyo alone and many performers in these fields have enjoyed international acclaim. A Second National Theatre is now being planned for these arts, in recognition of their history and role in the cultural life of the people as well as the need to publicly support them.

In this way efforts are being made on a national level to support the preservation and continuation of traditional performing arts as well as to encourage the development of new arts in as many ways as possible. The insight shown in these efforts merits much praise.

However, support for the individual performing arts has not been sufficient. The only institution which is capable of educating successive performers of the traditional arts is the Japanese Music Course in the Faculty of Music of the Tokyo National University of Fine Arts and Music. There is no special institution for the training of such students. There is no national dance company or theatre company. The great number of traditional performing art forms makes it impossible to include all of them in a national company or to choose representative ones from among them. We believe Japan can learn much on this point from other countries. There have been long-standing discussions on how to incorporate traditional performing arts into the school curriculum in order to foster a wider knowledge and deeper understanding of these arts and on how to thereby contribute to their future development. As a result, traditional performances have been included in the school curriculum's music education, in order to familiarize students with these arts. However, this is not sufficient as students are offered only an incomplete appreciation of folk songs, *noh*, *kyogen* and so on, through records and other audio-visual material. The schools' extra-curricular club activities serve to supplement this. Actual training in local performing arts such as festival music, the lion's dance, and *bon* dance is actively carried out. It can be said that these extra-curricular club activities are making a contribution to the training of future performers.

One factor behind this situation is the change that has occurred in Japan's traditionally agricultural society. The agricultural population, which once comprised 80% of the overall population, has now dropped to less then 20%. With more and more young people moving to work in the cities, the local communities are inevitably left with only the elderly and children to support their traditional performing arts. However, the situation is seeing some change. People are beginning to think twice about the merits of an economically and cultural centralized society and to recognize the importance of local communities. Young people are beginning to return from the cities to local regions in what is known as the "u-turn" phenomenon. At the same time, the idea that the promotion and refinement of local culture and local performing arts leads directly to the re-creation and re-construction of a new local society is beginning to win wider acceptance. In this context, the traditional performing arts are also being given new life.

Local power

When the local culture is thriving, it is a reflection of the cultural vitality of the country as a whole. This can be witnessed in Japan's cultural history. *Noh*, an art form which was popular in the courts of the middle ages, had its origins in a local festival performance called *Sarugaku*. *Kabuki*, which flourished in the central cities of the Tokugawa period, grew out of the local *Kabuki* dance and *Furyu* dance, while the puppet theatre which was highly popular at the same time in the cities similarly had its roots in the very simple religious puppet theatre found in coastal villages. In this way the local performing arts were brought to the cities where they were refined. While the local culture was thriving it was possible to create a culture of national significance. In light of this, it may be said that the promotion of traditional performing arts depends on the development of those local arts which are born of the passions of a people deeply attached to their land and its lifestyle.

Reconsidering the tendency toward uniformity

The rapid adoption of Western culture after the Meiji Restoration did, in fact, enrich Japanese culture on the whole. However, at the same time, Japanese culture itself became exceedingly uniform, resulting in a period which lacked the vitality to create anything new. Even at present, it seems that the ability to create great works of art has declined when compared with the distant past. The tendency to passively accept the trends imported from Paris and New York to Tokyo and from there to local areas, saps the life out of artistic creation.

The *bel canto* method of singing which originated in Europe, has been used in the musical education at schools since it was adopted in the Meiji Era, and its use has been fervently supported. For the past several decades even the singing method employed in Japan has become Westernized and the Japanese method of singing has become simplistic. However, with the recently increased exposure to the varied vocal expressions of Asia's diverse folk music, there is a growing realization that beautiful as the *bel canto* method may be, it is simply one method and not necessarily a definitive one. Various vocal techniques, such as groaning, shouting, singing from the stomach and singing with the throat contracted, are being applied in many musical forms to create unique musical effects.

A message to Asia

Culture is developed in the regions and refined in the central areas. In order for the world's culture to develop and flourish it is necessary for the various ethnic groups to cultivate their own culture to mutually stimulate each other and thereby create new art forms. We believe that the ideal conditions for cultural development depend on this contribution to the artistic creation of the next generation. Under the influence of the West, there was a tendency to belittle the distinct qualities of the national culture in Japan, which, we believe, existed in other Asian countries as well. It is necessary to make a reassessment now and to take another look at our own traditional culture.

Furthermore, we must not forget that there is more than one traditional culture. There is no high or low in the local culture of each area, since each artistic form that has developed there is based on the life of the people.

Today, the countries of Asia, including Japan, should recognize and respect the diversity which is the distinct characteristic of Asia, unmatched even by the West. Asia is a richly stocked treasure house of folk culture. The question that must be asked by individuals as well as by administrations, is the vital question of how to protect and develop this vast treasure.

Museums in Asia

"Modernization of museum activities in Asia" is an excellent theme to explore at this time. The countries represented at the Asian Cultural Centre's Roundtable Conference on this subject — Australia, India, Iran, Japan, Korea, the Philippines and Thailand — may all be considered leaders contributing significantly to the general movement of modernization of museums in this region, in varied but appropriate ways. All have great museums; all are striving for a more active role for their long established museums, are planning new museums and, in general, are creating programmes to meet the present and future needs of their societies.

"Modernization" in the present context may perhaps be defined museums widely useful, in relation to contemporary social developments and needs.

To anyone following the growth of museums in Asia, particularly during the past decade, a definite trend towards change, improvement and modernization is obvious. In some few countries, modernization may still be in the stage of debate, but generally it provides illustration of concrete accomplishment. It takes the form of construction of new buildings and/or renovation of old buildings, the general renewal from every point of view of long established institutions, and the creation of types of museums new to the region. Parallel is the general improvement of exhibition presentation in museums of every kind. Likewise, techniques of interpretation of museum collections, and of supplementing them appropriately, that is, providing programmes of an educational and cultural kind, are now being studied and improved forms are being introduced according to national conditions and requirements. Load and other temporary exhibitions, sometimes from abroad as major items of official cultural exchange programmes, are additional signs of an increasingly active role for museums. Even more important, though not in public view, are improvements in museological/museographical techniques of every kind, growth of professional and technical training for museum personnel, and, most important, concern and increasing provision for scientific conservation of museum objects.

Generally speaking, budgets in support of the development of museums and of the diversification and broadened application of their services, though certainly improving, lag somewhat. Also the status of museum personnel, as compared with other government and university employees, is not always satisfactory according to international standards. However, progress can be seen here as well. Possibly it may be attributed in part to the demonstrably increased contribution that museums now make to formal and popular education. Perhaps, too, the dawning appreciation of museums' potential role in tourism, especially Unesco's "cultural tourism", with its promise of earnings including foreign exchange, gives the museums an added economic value for practical administrators and political leaders, in addition to the scholarly and scientific prestige formerly admired. In any case, it seems indeed that a new perspective, has opened for museums in Asia.

Because of the large number of great civilizations in Asia and their antiquity it is not surprising to discover that the museum of archaeology is, in general, the oldest and most predominant type of museum in the Asian world. Almost always national museums in Asia consists of archaeological collections of the country. Site museums are an important and fairly recently developed addition to this category. Evidence of a nation's past is greatly valued in defining its identity and provides a sound foundation for present and future cultural growth. Frequently the arts — including decorative arts, folk and tribal arts — and historic material, have been added to national or regional archaeological collections. Asian countries are rich in ethnographic material and their contemporary arts are varied and important. Evidence of history also accumulates and this material must also be preserved. Eventually each field justifies a separate museum and most Asian countries are providing them.

Museums of natural history were often founded in Asia at the same time as the archaeology museums, sometimes, indeed, were originally intended to form a part of these museums in the effort to create "general" museums. However, with only rare exceptions the museums of natural history failed to develop at the same rate as the archaeological museums. A few countries in Asia even now have no scientifically based natural history museum open to the general public. But such museums are being planned, for their importance is recognized in relation to the development of natural resources and for better understanding of the environment and its protection. History and personalia museums tend to be fairly recent creations in most Asian countries and, in some cases, are associated with the attainment of independence, serving as memorials as well as a basis of public instruction.

Museums of applied sciences, of industry and technology, are still more recent types, but already they are widely recognized as of particular value for developing countries. In Asia they are still relatively few in number, but where they already function they represent a conscious effort to apply museum techniques and resources to the problems of developing nations which are passing from agricultural, village societies to technologically oriented, urban, industrialized economies. As they represent a new form of the museum, one obviously of direct usefulness to development, they merit special attention here. They undertake instruction in applied sciences and technology for all ages and segments of the population, but they are particularly valuable in attracting young people to careers in these fields, for which trained personnel are so greatly needed. Japan has notable museums serving this field, but the most spectacular example of such a museum in Asia at present is the Singapore Science Centre now under construction. It will include both technology and the life sciences and will concentrate on exhibition activities and teaching. Possibly the science programme most realistically directed to reaching the village and rural populations — of outstanding importance in Asia — is found in India.

Mobile exhibitions and varied extension services to rural areas are provided by the Council of Scientific and Industrial Research's Museums, respectively at Calcutta and Bangalore. Here perhaps it is pertinent to point out that in a very real sense museums are today part of the worldwide search for knowledge and understanding, as well as of the dissemination of varied information as instruments of education. This international aspect of the museum movement is emphasized and served by Unesco and by ICOM. Since the war the exchange of information has been encouraged by *MUSEUM*, Unesco's quarterly on museum techniques, and by ICOM News, but especially by museum leaders' travels abroad to see museums elsewhere and by participation in international meetings (for example, Unesco's and ICOM's various seminars, ICOM triennial General Conferences).

Notable in recent years is the effort to develop regionalties, cooperation and activity for museums in Asia. The ICOM Regional Agency in Asia is one step in this direction. Various meetings on museums, or including them, such as the Roundtable Conference of the Asian Centre and the Japanese National Committee for ICOM; ICOM National Committee meetings, like those held in Malacca, December 1972; the current series of surveys and seminars of the SEAMEO's ARCAFA Project Development Office; and various museum meetings now being planned, represent this trend. Unesco's Intergovernmental Conference on Cultural Policy in Asia, in Yogyakarta, December 10-19, 1973, including museums as cultural agents, puts an official stamp of approval, at the highest intellectual level, on this regional emphasis.

Another indication of the trend to modernize Asian museums, is the growth of non-official professional associations of museum workers, concerned with the improvement of museum techniques and practices. They do not as yet exist everywhere as formal societies. In some countries informal gatherings of dedicated professionals, for discussions of museological subjects and the improvement of techniques and related matters serve this purpose. In others, the National Committee for ICOM undertakes this role of professional leadership. The emphasis on the contribution of museums to education is an international development of great importance since the war. In Asia the guided tour of museum galleries has long been firmly established almost everywhere. Relatively new in Asian museums, and a recognition of their broadened use for the community at large, is the growth of specific activities and programmes related to exhibitions, but supplementary to the lecture tour and on a higher level of professional instruction. Thus all kinds of museum programmes appropriate to their respective subject fields, designed to supplement formal education in schools, colleges and universities, but also to fill profitably leisure time, are found now in the process of development in Asian museums. Continuing education in cooperation with museums, directed to all ages and economic levels of the population, is undoubtedly one of the most important example of the modernization and broadening services that museums are now called on to contribute to their communities. It promises to be particularly valuable to Asian countries. Another sign of an increasingly modern attitude in Asian museums is the tendency to develop the scope of archaeological and arts collections in order to present the local material in a national context, then to include examples from other countries or regions, thus providing general background and the possibility of comparative study. The museums of Japan, especially those of Tokyo, exemplify brilliantly this latter museum development. No country in Asia can as yet provide such a comprehensive report on the archaeology and arts of the world as can Japan.

More obvious indications of modernization are, of course, the tremendous improvements in the presentation of collections in public exhibitions, the skills developed in providing supplementary information in labelling, with graphic devices such as maps, charts, diagrams, drawings, photographs and audio supplements of various types. Everywhere in Asia this trend reflects the concern of museum leaders in the respective countries to improve their services to the general public.

These visible aspects of museum progress are based on a general modernization behind the scenes, the result of growth of professional leadership and skills. In some countries university level training in museology has been introduced. The preservation of museum collections is almost everywhere of great concern, prompting establishment of scientific conservation laboratories with appropriate staff and scientific equipment. Research on the scholarly level increases, but it also emphasizes more than in the past all types of popular publications, ranging from *Guides* to the galleries to picture postcards, and thus extends the influence of museums far beyond their own walls. These few examples of museum modernization are cited here as a sort of index to what this international professional organization for museums (ICOM) observes as a general and significant trend in the region towards improvement, increasing influence and greater recognition, not only in scholarly and scientific directions, but also in broad popular appeal and services to society. It is obvious that the influence of museums is growing everywhere in Asia and that their value now is widely recognized.

Representation of a celestial figure, nineteenth century, Republic of Korea.

Part 7

Puppet Theatre

A Thai shadow theatre figure.

Puppet Theatre

Wayang Purwa — Transmitter of Indonesian Culture

What is Wayang Purwa?

Wayang Purwa, the most popular of the Indonesian performing arts, is here defined as "the form of performing art in which flat leather puppets are used, in the presentation of a repertoire which initially came from the Hindu epics: the Ramayana and Mahabharata". This definition consists of two parts, separated by a comma. The first part of the definition distinguishes *wayang purwa* from other kinds of performing arts which present the same repertoire but do not make use of flat leather puppets as their "actors and actresses", such as the Sundanese *wayang golek* of West Java, and the *wayang wong* or *wayang orang.* The former uses three dimensional wooden puppets, the latter is performed by the human *wayangs.* The term *wayang* itself literally means "shadow" in the Indonesian languages, but in the course of time has also come to mean "performance" and "actors and actresses", mostly the former.

The second part of the definition distinguishes *wayang purwa* from other types of *wayang,* which, although making use of flat leather puppets, do not have as their repertoire stories derived from the two Hindu epics. *Wayang gedog,* for instance, uses the East Javanese Panji legends as its repertoire, *wayang suluh* uses stories from the Indonesian struggle for independence, formerly used by the Information Agencies, and *Wayang wahyu* uses Biblical stories, introduced by the Catholic Church in Central Java. If we use the term *wayang* to refer to any kind of performance in which the director plays an active part on stage, we find that there are over seventy different types and styles of *wayang* in Indonesia.

Compared with the other forms of *wayang, wayang purwa* is definitely the most popular, many of the other being regarded as rather "dying" forms of art.

Personnel, equipment and audio-visual elements of Wayang Purwa

The following table gives the names of the personnel, equipment and audio-visual elements of the *wayang purwa.*

A. Personnel & Equipment	*B. Audio-Visual Elements*
Personnel:	Visual Element:
1. *Dalang* (main artist)	1. *Subetan* (puppet movement)
2. *Niyaga* (musicians)	Auditive Elements:
3. *Pesiden* (lady singer[s])	2. *Janturan* (declaimed narration)
Equipment:	
4. Wayang puppets	3. Chariyos (narration)
5. *Kelir* (cloth screen)	4. *Ginem* (dialogue)
6. *Balenchong* (oil lamp)	5. *Suluk* (mood-song)
7. *Dhebog* (banana long)	6. *Tembang* (song)
8. *Kothak* (wooden chest)	7. *Dodogan* (knocking sound)
9. *Chempala* (wooden sound)	8. *Kepyakan* (rappingknocker)
	9. *Gending* (melody)
10. *Kepyak* (metal rappers)	10. *Gerong* (male instruments)
11. *Gamelan* (musical chorus)	11. *Sindenan*(song [s] by *pesinden* [s])

Please note that the total number or the different types of personnel and equipment is eleven equal to the number of the different kinds of audio-visual elements of *wayang purwa.* This 11-11 method of approaching and analyzing *wayang purwa* is considered a simple way to study this interesting yet complicated form of traditional art.

The *dalang* or main artist, besides being the sole puppeteer who manipulates the puppets throughout the night, is also the director of the performance and directs the musicians and singers who sit behind him. A *dalang* is usually a man. The number of *wayang purwa dalangs* in Indonesia is estimated at 20,000, of which less than fifty are women. Throughout the all-night performance — the performance generally begins at 9 p.m. and lasts until dawn — the *dalang* sits on the stage facing the cloth screen, giving coded orders to his crew on what melodies to play, what songs to sing, when to start, to soften, to slow down, to stop and so on. The skills of a *dalang* ran in families and were handed down orally, but they can be learned by anyone wishing to become a *dalang.* Since 1923, starting in the court-city of Surakarta in Central Java, *dalang* schools have been set up for those who are interested. Besides being an expert in performing, a *dalang* must also be versed in classical literature, and must master the various forms of speech and an extensive vocabulary of the Javanese stratified language, its philosophical and even mystical contents. This makes him not only an entertainer or performer but also a wise teacher and transmitter of cultural values.

To accompany a *wayang purwa* performance there are usually 13 musicians called *niyaga* or *wiyaga.* They are mostly men who play at least 15 different kinds of musical instruments. (Two *niyagas each* play two different kinds of instruments). The most important one for the *dalang* is the drummer, because he is the one who usually receives the *dalang's* coded orders and transmits them to the other musicians. The sound of his drum also accentuates or illustrates the puppet movements and serves to enliven the performance as a whole.

The *pesindens*, or lady singers are the most recently introduced performers in a *wayang* performance. Although they did not commonly appear at the beginning of this century, the *pesindens* are now considered necessary. There is at least one *pesinden*, usually two, but occasionally 25 *pesindens* or more in one performance. A large number of *pesindens* gives a spectacular impression.

The flat leather *wayang* puppets are usually made of buffalo hide, the best ones being made of scurvy young buffalo hide, which does not contain fat and can best retain the glued-on colours. Although *wayang purwa* is meant to be a shadow play, the puppets have long been coloured, besides being carved and attached to sticks, since more people view the performance from the *dalang's* side. The traditional colours are produced by using mixtures of colouring agents and glue which are painted onto the leather. The sticks are made of buffalo horn. These *wayang* puppets do not depict human figures in their natural form, but are highly stylized, each portraying what to the Javanese symbolizes a certain meaning, a feature of the character of the depicted figure, whether hero or villain, god or man, male or female.

A professional *wayang purwa* set usually consists of around 200 puppets, although the well-to-do *wayang* lovers may have 400 or more.

There is a term referring to the various forms and expressionistic characters of the various figures as portrayed in the puppets. This term is *wandha*, which for the puppet figures means their character or mood expression. As character expression, the *wandha* of a certain puppet is different from the *wandhas* of other puppets depicting different characters. But there are also various *wandhas* of certain figures; the more important the character is, the more are his or her *wandhas*, so that Arjuna (the famous *Mahabharata* hero) can be portrayed by different *wayang purwa* puppets, each showing him in a certain mood.

In one performance, the *dalang* usually uses not more than 60 puppets. The rest are mounted on both sides of the stage, kept in the wooden chest, or laid on the right hand side of the *dalang*, all according to set rule, so that the *dalang* and his helpers know exactly where to find the needed puppets. What is considered the "stage" is the part of the screen left open for the performance, which is approximately five feet wide at the centre of the up-stretched screen; the rest of the screen, on the right and left sides of the *dalang*, are covered by the decorating puppets. Generally the bad characters are mounted on the left hand side of the *dalang*, the good ones on his right hand side. The *kelir* or cloth screen is usually made of white cotton cloth and measures approximately 5 metres long and 1.5 metres wide, with the borders (usually red) about 8 to 10 cm. at the bottom and somewhat wider on the other sides. The *Kelir* is stretched upwards and side-wise in front of the *dalang*. The red border at the bottom indicates ground level. The shadows of the puppets are cast on the *kelir*, with an oil lamp (blenchong) hanging over the head of the *dalang*.

The *blenchong* is a coconut-oil lamp made of bronze in the form of flying eagle. Its cotton wick extends from its beak, and its spreading wings and tail serve as a reflector. During the all-night performance, the *blenchong* has to be refilled several times and its wick regularly extended. The flickering light produced by the *blenchong* makes the *wayang* shadows look alive. Nowadays, people make frequent use of electric lights or gas lamp. But those who prefer the more mythical and mysterious atmosphere produced by the not-so-bright flickering light of a *blenchong* decry this "secular" change, although they also realize that the modern lamp is more practical and easier to handle, producing a brighter light which enables many people to clearly see the puppets and their shadows.

Two banana logs called *dhebog* are positioned under the up-stretched screen; one is placed on the other, the upper one attached to the screen while the lower one is close to the *dalang*. The upper *dhebog* is used for mounting the puppets who in a scene have a higher status, the lower one for those of lower status, status being determined by age, rank, relative position in the family tree or a combination of these factors. Those lower in status mounted in the lower banana log will appear as if they were sitting on the floor, while those higher in status will appear as if standing, their feet touching the lower red border of the screen.

A wooden chest called *Kothak* normally serves as a storage box for the *wayang* puppets and other equipments such as the *kelir*, *chempala* and *kepyak*. During the performance, the *kothak* is placed on the left hand side of the *dalang*. When the *dalang* knocks the *chempala* against the *kothak*, this wooden chest functions as a sound-box.

The *chempalas* or wooden knockers are usually made of teak wood. There are two kinds, one about half the size of the other. The larger one is approximately 20 cm. long with a diameter of about 5 cm. This is usually held in the *dalang's* left hand, and is used to knock the *kothak* to produce the sound effects and coded orders he requires. When his two hands are busy manipulating the puppets, he uses the small *chempala* which holds between the toes of his right foot, for he sits cross-legged, his right-foot crossing his left thigh.

The *kepyak* or metal rappers is usually made of three pieces of bronze plate measuring about 15 cm. long and 10 cm. wide suspended on small cords or chains to the outer side of the *kothak*. The *dalang* hits it with the toes of his right foot or with the small *chempala* held between the toes of his right foot. The *gamelan* or musical instruments nowadays consist of at least 15 different types, mostly made of bronze and generally of the percussion type. A small bamboo flute (*suling*), one or two horizontal drums on wooden stands (*kendang)*, a two-stringed violin-like instrument (*rebab)* and a wooden xylophone *(gambang)* are the non-percussion instruments.

The eleven kinds of personnel and equipment explained above produce the eleventh different kinds of audio-visual elements of a *wayang purwa* performance. Now, the eleven audio-visual elements will be explained.

The term *sabetan* meaning puppet movements can actually be understood in several ways. It means "how the dalang manipulates the puppets", or "how he manipulates the puppets in battle scenes", or " the puppet movements." The first and second meaning are sensed by the audience sitting behind the *dalang*, the second meaning being more commonly used while the last meaning of the term is usually sensed by those watching from the shadow's side. Traditional rules and conventions govern the postures and movements of each character to convey the emotional state of each figure, all of which are popularly known and have to be mastered by the *dalang*.

The *janturan* is the declaimed narration. The contents of the various *janturans* are traditionally set in beautiful prose, declaimed by the *dalang*, at which time music is played softly. The function of the *janturan* is to set the stage for particular scenes, relate to the audience the country or place where the scenes takes place, what personalities appear on stage, and what will be the topic of their conversation A *janturan* can also serve to describe notable things appearing on stage, such as the beautiful and magnificent gate leading to the inner quarters of the palace or the royal magic carriage. The *dalang* has more freedom in reciting the *chariyos/kands* or narration, having only to observe literary rules governing the classic Javanese language and to demonstrate familiarity with the proper use of this stratified language. The function of the *chariyos* (usually not accompanied with music) is to relate to the audience what happens on stage, what has just happened in a certain scene, or what will soon happen. The *dalang's* mastery of classic as well as modern-day Javanese, or his lack or mastery thereof, will clearly show in his chariyos, since its content is not fixed by tradition.

In reciting the *ginem/pochapan* or dialogue, the *dalang* has to be able to speak in the different voice of the various characters. Each voice expresses the character of a *wayang* figure. An excellent *dalang* is able to speak in over forty different voices; he should at least be able to speak in thirty different voices to pass as a qualified *dalang*.

Very characteristic of a *wayang* performance is the use of *suluks* or mood-songs. In a *wayang purwa* performance, the verses are taken from classic poems, many dating back to the eleventh and twelfth centuries, such as the Old Javanese *Kakawin Arjuna Wiwaha* (mid-eleventh century) or the *Kakawin Bharata Yudha* (mid-twelfth century). Verses from more recent classic works are also used, such as the classic poems of Yasadipura (end of eighteenth century) and Mangku Negara IV (mid-nineteenth century), or even later ones. Sung by the *dalang*, the *suluks* function to set the mood in the scene, whether it is dignified serenity, romantic love, anger, deep sorrow, or any other mood being felt by the figure(s) on stage. There are over 40 different kinds of *suluk*, for each of which verses can be used from the various classical sources.

While the *suluk* is sung by the *dalang* to set the mood for certain scenes, the *tembang or sekar* is, although actually sung by the *dalang* also, sung by the character on stage in his or her "own" voice. The verses used can be modern or classic, and the singers are usually the clown figures.

The *dodogan* or knocking sound is the sound of the *chempala* knocked against the *kothak*. The *dodogan* not only produces the needed sound effects but also serves as coded signals or orders to the musicians and singers.

The *kepyakan*, a raping sound produced by the *kepyak*, produces sound effects to enliven the performance or accentuate the puppet's movements and actions. The Javanese classic repertory contains over 1,000 *gendings* or melodies many of which are used in *wayang purwa* performances. Over 150 melodies are used in the various performances, although during one performance not more than thirty different melodies are played. Traditional rules govern the considerable number of melodies and allow only the playing of suitable melodies for certain figures in certain places or moods. In *wayang purwa*, the Javanese hold strictly to rules governing harmony between sound (melody and voice), form and posture (*wandha*) and movements (*sabetan*), all of which are felt to portray the character of a particular person.

Occasionally, the *gerong*, a male chorus of some of the musicians *(niyagas)* enlivens the performance. The verses are usually taken from recent classics, mainly from nineteenth century poems. Like the *gerongs*, the *sindenans*, the song of lady singers, make use of recent classical poems and recently composed verses.

Structure and contents of the plays

Wayang purwa is one of the very few structured plays in the world. The all-night play is invariably divided into three parts. This three-part division is traditionally set, each part consisting of acts and scenes. The first part presents the problem of the story, the second part shows the complications of the problem, and in the final part the problem is finally solved with the good side overcoming its difficulties. The contents of the play, as shown in the various acts and scenes, consist of various topics from daily jokes to sophisticated discourses on philosophy and mystical doctrines. The classical figures speak in dignified and lofty languages, while the clowns provide the jokes, conversations and songs which relate the performance to contemporary conditions and issues. It is through the clown scenes that the *wayang purwa* can always keep up with contemporary topics and problems.

The repertoire of Wayang Purwa

As mentioned at the beginning, the *wayang purwa* presents "a repertoire which initially came from the Hindu epics: the *Ramayana* and *Mahabharata*". The word "initially" is important, because there are so many differences as to justify the opinion that the Javanese (and other Indonesian ethnic groups as well) have their own version of *Ramayana* and *Mahabharata.*

The whole repertoire is divided into four cycles: on gods and demons (7 plays), on Lokapala, a prelude to the *Ramayana* (5 plays), on the *Ramayana* (18 plays) and on the *Mahabharata* (147 plays) — a total of 177 plays. This means that to perform the entire repertoire it would take 177 nights, each nightly performance lasting approximately nine hours.

In what respects do the Javanese *Ramayana* and *Mahabharata* differ from their Indian versions? The differences are numerous, but a few marked ones will be mentioned here. The traditional clowns who always appear in any *wayang purwa* performance, Semar, Gareng, Petruk and Bagong, serve the good side and invariably assist it to victory and are pictured in the *wayang* repertoire as deities incarnate. Semar, the wise, old, ugly and fat man, the father of the other three, is in fact a powerful deity, who voluntarily descends to earth to guarantee the victory of good over evil. He is the elder brother of Shiva, also called Bathara Guru in the *wayang*, and whenever the latter acts unjustly against Demar's earthly masters, Semar stands up to defeat Guru. If this sounds strange to our Hindu friends, they will be even more surprised to know that in the *wayang purwa* world, both Shiva and Semar, along with other gods in the Hindu pantheon, are presented as descendants of the Biblical (or Qoranic) Adam!

The spread of Wayang Purwa repertoire

Although the *wayang purwa* is mainly a Javanese form of art, its repertoire with slight differences from region to region is shared by other forms of performing arts familiar to other ethnic groups in Indonesia. The Sundanese of West Java know the stories, which are performed in their *wayang golek*; the Balinese have their own style of *wayang purwa*; the repertoire is also used in *wayang wong or wayang orang*, and the stories are also known in Kalimantan and performed as shadow plays. Altogether, the *wayang* repertoire is known to the Javanese, the Sundanese, the Madurese, the Balinese and the Banjarese of South and East Kalimantan. The other ethnic groups in Indonesia are not totally unfamiliar with the stories, for they are also contained in school textbooks, newspapers, periodicals and so on, written also in the National language.

Can Wayang Purwa be a medium for change?

The question has often been asked whether a traditional form of art, like the *wayang purwa*, can be made medium for change. Modern day cosmopolitans tend to look at tradition and its many manifestations in a negative way, regarding them as hindering the course of progress, shackling the behaviour of man who is forever trying to move ahead, to acquire the new and to live a better life. In the eyes of modern man, especially those living in the big cities of the developing world, tradition is associated with backwardness and out-of-date cultural values which must be laid aside if they wish their countries to develop sufficiently and compete effectively in the modern world. This attitude is shared by many living in the Indonesian cities. Yet the question can be asked whether a nation or people can really rid themselves of the past and live entirely with newly acquired values and systems.

Relying only on the modern and new would serve merely to produce failure and disillusionment, and create a communication gap between the relatively few modernized and educated city dwellers and the mass of the people. The latter still hold to their old cultural values and cannot be made to change their way of life, largely because they do not understand the messages conveyed to them by modern leaders unwilling to accept or use their cultural frame of reference.

It seems that the above communication gap exists in Indonesia, for the reasons given below, and that *wayang purwa* can function to bridge this gap between the urban and the rural population between the sophisticated city dwellers and the uneducated villagers, the greater part of the population. Although according to the 1971 census 81% of the total population live in the rural areas, the modern mass media are largely confined to the cities. Moreover, what is termed the mass media proves not to be powerful a means of change as would be imagined, simply because they are not as widely spread as expected. For a population of 141 million, the total newspaper circulation is estimated at a ratio of 10 to every 1,000 people. Add to this the fact that they are mostly found in the few big cities, especially in Jakarta, where up to 60% of the total circulation of national newspapers is thought to be centered. The other mass media do not present a better picture. The total number of television sets is estimated at 1.3 million*, of which up to 70% are found in Jakarta.

Probably the radio functions as the most potentially powerful medium for change, for it is estimated that around 10 million are found in the country, and thanks to the invention of the transistors, even those living in remote rural areas can listen to radio broadcasts. However, in a country where the per capita income is estimated at US$175 (using the 1973 price-index), with an estimated 60% living under the poverty-line of US$75 per annum, it is rather difficult to believe that the mass of people living in the rural areas can afford to buy a radio set, the cost of which represents at least a two-month income for most people.

On the other hand, the *wayang purwa* with its widely known repertoire, along with the other forms of traditional media such as the Sundanese *wayang golek*, the Balinese and Banjarese shadow plays are deeply anchored in the hearts of the people and are for them a familiar cultural frame of reference. *Wayang purwa* is especially very popular, both in the rural and urban areas, being performed from the Presidential palace down to the remotest villages in Java and elsewhere. Compared with the relatively few movie theatres — there are only 1,100 throughout the country, found mainly in the cities — the 20,000 *wayang purwa dalangs* can reach the people more effectively, because *wayang purwa* relays messages contained in and relevant to a familiar cultural

* 1971 Census

framework. Such is also the case when compared with the other forms of mass media.

Ever since the early fifties, the government-owned radio stations have regularly broadcast and are still broadcasting *wayang purwa* performances through at least four radio stations. Those in Semarang, Yogyakarta, Surakarta and Jakarta take turns broadcasting the weekly all-night performance.

The question may be raised whether *wayang purwa* traditional art form, can possibly convey new ideas and concepts. Put another way, can *wayang purwa* serve as a medium for change and modernization?

The answer to the question is YES, for *wayang purwa* itself, in the course of time, has experienced change and has shown itself able to adapt to new ideas and concepts. It has incorporated changes in language and religion, and has modified its repertoire, which now contains the universal elements of Hinduism, Buddhism, Islam, etc. Moreover, in the clown scenes, *dalangs* can always insert modern ideas into their jokes, conversation and songs, as these scenes are not bound by rigid rules governing the classic parts of the performance. Nowadays, people can attend a *wayang* performance with a famous *dalang*, broadcasts by radio throughout the country, in which the traditional clowns discuss family planning, the introduction of quick-yielding varieties of rice, and any other modern topic. At the same time, the ethical values which have universal application, and of which there are many expressions in the *wayang* stories, can still be retained, providing a link between the past and present, between the classic and the modern. The *wayang purwa* performance techniques as described above are native to Indonesia, for although Indonesians have absorbed so much from Hindu culture and its Sanskrit literature, the terms referring to the elements of the plays are non-Sanskrit and not otherwise foreign in origin. This fact gives the Javanese and other Indonesians a sense of pride, a pride needed by a people who have to struggle hard to adjust themselves to the modern world, a pride which can help them overcome their difficulties to develop their country in order to live a better life and realize the dreams for which they have fought to achieve independence. And if the modern mass media have failed to integrate the rural and urban people and have thus created a communication gap, dividing minds rather than consolidating people, *wayang purwa* and other forms of popular traditional arts can provide this link between the largely different views of the urban and rural population. It can help to eliminate this communication gap, preventing schisms in a society which desperately needs a united effort to succeed and move ahead.

The Ancient and Popular Tradition of Indian Puppetry

As in other spheres of cultural manifestation, there is a staggering multiplicity of forms, styles and genres of the puppet theatre of India. From the West to the East (Rajasthan to Bengal & Assam), from the North to the South (Uttar Pradesh to Kerala), there are string puppets, rod puppets, leather puppets, shadow puppets in different parts of India. They constitute simple folk drama in some parts, family entertainment in others and highly ritualistic drama in yet others. In all parts they are complimentary to the live theatre of the region: there are many common features in the format and styles of the live and the puppet theatres of each region. The contents are the pervasive myths & legends of India, often centering round the Ramayana and the Mahabharata in their regional variations or the tales of legendary heroes and heroines particular to the area.

The antiquity of Indian puppet theatre, has been much debated and no consensus has been arrived at on the crucial problem of whether the puppet theatre preceded or followed the highly developed theatrical tradition of the Indians. Scholars, foreign and Indian, have disagreed vehemently on this point. Be as it may, it is quite clear that the epics Ramayana and Mahabharata (twelfth to tenth century BC) knew of puppetry as an art. In the latter, there is a very definite reference to the puppet Chitrangada (the name of a heroine of Manipur with whom Arjuna falls in love). Equally important is the term *sutradhara* (master of strings) used by the grammarian Panini in the fourth century BC. The word is a generic term which is used for any master artist or craftsman and thus equally applicable to the architect of a temple, a sculptor, carpenter (i.e. maker of images), and a director of drama. Indeed, AD second century text on the Indian theatre arts, the Natyashastra, consistently uses the term *sutradhara* for the director.

Indian literature also provides evidence of the use of another term, *chhaya nataka* (literally shadow theatre) from AD second century onwards. Medieval literature and poetry both of Sanskrit and the regional languages is replete with references to puppet and shadow theatre.

Despite this antiquity and the status given to puppet and shadow theatre, in contemporary Indian puppetry has been widely popular at the rural level rather than either the tribal or urban levels of Indian society. This is accounted for by the lack of patronage to this particular art in the medieval and post medieval periods, by the courts and feudal noblemen. In this respect the history of Indian puppetry is substantially different from the developments in Java, China and Japan, where it acquired a high sophistication in a court and urban milieu. Except in Kerala, Andhra and Karnataka in the South, where puppet theatre is closely identified with a village and a permanent site, puppeteers in India, especially from Rajasthan, Madhya Pradesh, Bengal and Orissa are itinerant performers comprising a family of two or three who present puppet theatre as and when the occasion demands. The puppet stage can be an improvised stage from the legs of a bed stand or a sheet tied to wooden poles. The lighting is invariably from a lamp or torch with an oil flame. The puppet play presented by the family folds its dramatic personae — the puppets — in a box or a bundle and moves on. But this modest equipment creates stupendous high drama which holds audiences of children and adults in a trance for hours.

String puppets or marionettes

The string puppets are ancient and popular. Although known to other regions, the string puppet traditions of Rajasthan and of Karnataka are the most developed.

In Rajasthan, the theatre and the puppet is known as *kathaputli* (wooden doll) and the performer *kathaputli nata*. The puppets are normally two feet high, their faces are carved of mango wood by the puppeteer with knives, chisels and mallets. The features are stylised with large eyes and pointed noses. In effects, the colours of the Rajasthani puppets are strongly reminiscent of the late Rajasthani painting. A character can be clearly identified by the crown or turban, nature of moustache and particular shade of paint of his face. The puppet characters recall medieval Rajasthani history; little wonder that the origin of Rajasthani puppetry is attributed to Amarsingh Rathor, a famous nobleman of medieval Rajasthan around whom many legends have been woven.

The upper limbs of the Rajasthani puppet are made of stuffed rags so as to provide flexibility of movement. The carved arms can be manipulated in innumerable ways. They spring to life, are thrown around swiftly and dexterous manipulation of the pliable arms creates the impression of agility.

The puppets do not have any lower limbs nor are these necessary. All characters wear full richly gathered skirts which makes it possible for the puppeteer to suggest all manner of movements such as walking, running, dancing and slumping to the ground in a dramatic movements.

A variety of animals especially camels and horses associated with Rajasthani chivalry appear on the puppet stage along with humans. These are not carved: instead they are made of cloth cut and sewn to shape and then stuffed. Normally there are no separate moving parts and this makes it a little difficult to suggest movements of only the legs, neck or torso: however in actual performances these puppets have an extraordinary pliability.

The puppets are manipulated by two continuous strings — one from the head to the waist and the other from one hand to the other. The strings are just wrapped around the fingers of the puppeteer who whirls the characters with amazing skills, sometimes making them strut like arrogant nobles, at other times making them run and dance and at yet other times raising the figure, filling the skirt with air like a balloon and suddenly dropping the puppet so that the skirt spreads all around. The warriors enter combat, women dance and weep, and acrobats perform impressive movements by turning backwards or walking on ropes. A whole world of chivalric romance, fun and frolic is recreated.

The musical accompaniment is minimal, comprising the recited and sung passages by the puppeteer and his wife, a drum and nowadays sometimes a flute or harmonium. The stage is the simplest: the puppets are hung on a bamboo pole against the background of a cot, (a bed stead), the proscenium is provided with a *sari* or other cloth which hides the bamboo pole and provides the sky line and the wings on either side, from which the puppets appear and into which they disappear.

Through these modest means and simple techniques, the Rajasthani puppeteer achieves a very distinct type of theatre with a vast range of movements, gestures and expressions. Today, the technique has been refined to include more strings, a wooden string control mechanism and some new directors have even experimented with providing the puppets with legs. The Rajasthani marionette is being used in schools for educational purposes and in community programmes. The themes are not restricted to Amar Singh Rathor and the medieval tales of chivalry but include modern themes. Puppet groups have travelled widely in both India and abroad. Recently, one such troupe achieved great success in the U.S.A. String puppets also flourish in other parts of India, particularly Karnataka, Orissa and Tamilnadu. The richest amongst these is the form known as *gombeyetta* in Karnataka. It is the closest counterpart to the human theatre form of the region called *yakshaqana*; it shares all the characteristics of this dance drama form in stylisation, make-up and costuming.

The puppets are about eighteen inches high. They are also carved from wood like the Rajasthani puppets, but the makers are professional wood carvers or stone carvers who sculpt images for temple and for ritual chariots. Sometimes these puppets can be as high as 35 inches. The faces are painted in the same manner as the stylized make-up of the live theatre. While the good characters have a basic pink or flesh coloured make-up, the evil characters are painted red and black. The style of moustaches, forehead lines, etc. distinguish one character from the other. The make-up techniques of these puppets are akin to those followed by Chinese opera, Japanese *kabuki*, Indian *kathakali* and *yakshaqana*.

Unlike the Rajasthani puppet the arms, hands, thighs, calves and feet are all lightly carved. All these parts, however, are appropriately padded with cloth. The wooden skeleton has joints at the neck, shoulders, elbows, hips and knees. This enables the puppeteer to use any of these joints singly or in combination for the articulation or movement. All the joints are loose and allow for great flexibility of movement and variety of manipulation. All portions of the puppet are suitably attired with rich jewellery, breast plates, shoulder, wrist, and ankle ornaments as in *yakshaqana.* The headgears are elaborate and variegated. Some characters wear turbans, others crowns and other elaborate crescent crowns as in the live theatre. Normally six strings are used to manipulate each puppet, and if the puppet holds a musical instrument or a weapon, an additional string is used. One end of two of these strings is fixed to the ears and the other to a single bamboo or wooden short stick. This enables the puppeteer to create symmetrical movements. This pair of strings controls the movements of the head and the neck. The next two strings are attached to each of the elbows at one end and to another stick at the other. This horizontal stick is placed at right angles to the first controlling stick of the ears. A third pair of strings is similarly tied to the knees and controlled by another cross bamboo stick. Thus the puppeteer holds three bamboo sticks counterpoised in a definite arrangement and controls the movement of each part of the body through the six strings. This string and stick method is the precursor to the more refined control mechanisms which are employed in modern marionette theatre. Through this system the puppeteer can manipulate the puppets in many skillful ways and is able to co-ordinate the movement of the different limbs. When appropriate, he utilises the seventh string for the instruments or weapons.

Many scenes in *yakshaqana* shows require the collaboration of two puppeteers. In sequences where a warrior rides a horse one puppeteer manipulates the horse, while the other manipulates the rider. The swift union and co-ordination of the two puppeteers is incredibly quick and effective. Indeed the backstage of the *yakshaqana* puppet *gombeyitta* is as interesting as the front because the puppeteer walk, dances and jumps in a manner that is identical to the movement executed by his puppets. The puppeteer sings the songs, recites the dialogues in the appropriate melody and rhythm (*tala*). He provides the music through vocal accompaniment and the double ended drum (*maddala).* In the war scenes there is sounding of the vertical drum called *chende.*

The dialogues are spoken by one or two accompanists and there is a lively interspersion of song passages, prose dialogues and drumming.

The stage comprises a raised platform roughly 12 feet by 8 feet in size and about six feet high. An upright wooden frame with an opening of 1 or 2 inches by 32 inches is placed on the stage. There is a front and backdrop on this frame. The backdrop is normally black, so that the puppeteers cannot be seen. As in human theatre the overall director of this theatre is the Bhagavatar who directs the play and synchronises the roles. The lighting is provided by an oil-wick lamp: this is appropriately subdued and the dramatic climaxes are highlighted by characters holding torches.

The themes of these plays are drawn from the two Indian epics, the *Ramayana* and the *Mahabarata.* Through the puppets epic theatre is recreated effectively. The puppet master conceives and executes this drama with great devotion and artistry; the result is a most satisfying aesthetic spectacle, comparable in range of emotion and expression to any live theatre.

The string puppets of Tamilnadu are close second to those of Karnataka although they are not quite as elaborate and ornate. The Orissan puppets resemble the carvings on the Orissan temples particularly that of Jaganath temple in Puri. The puppets are about 24 inches high with wooden arms and legs. The arms are joined at the shoulders and the legs at the hips. Compared to Karnataka they have limited manipulation possibilities.

The Tamilnadu marionettes have their own distinctive charm. The faces are beautifully carved and their contours are like those of the sculpture of Tamilnadu. The arms are joined to the shoulder and have subsidiary articulation points at the elbow and the wrist. Known as *bommalattam* these puppets are manipulated through both strings and rods. The head and neck of the puppets are manipulated through strings tied to a cane control worn on the head of the puppeteer. The ring on the turban of the puppeteer determines the movement of the head and shoulder of the puppets; with the stretching, drooping or turning of his neck, analogous movements are recreated by the puppet. Iron rods are attached to the hands of the figures and these are manipulated from above by the puppeteer. The plays presented are the same as those of live human theatre of Tamilnadu called *bhagavatamela.* These are based on episodes drawn from the Ramayana and the Mahabharata. Depending upon the skill and artistry of the manipulator, he can present the full repertoire of the classical dance form called *bharata-natyam.* Often the audience watches with spell-bound thrill the puppets execute intricate movements of the dance style. A full musical accompaniment is provided by an ensemble comprising a drum (*mridangam*), cymbals, flute and clarinet and of course vocal music of a very high standard.

Shadow theatre

While other examples of the marionette theatre from India could be cited, mention must be made of a few outstanding traditions to show puppet theatre in India. Although not as highly sophisticated and variegated as the *wayang kulit* tradition of Indonesia (both Java and Bali), Indian shadow theatre has a long tradition and variety. Shadow theatre (*chhaya nataka*) is mentioned in early Sanskrit works of AD second century Many Sanskrit words are indicative of the wide prevalence of the traditions in different parts of India. Today they are chiefly concentrated in the shadow puppet theatre of the state of South India particularly Karnataka, Andhra and Kerala and a magnificent form in Orissa in

Eastern India. Another rare and interesting form is known to Goa.

In Andhra, the shadow puppet theatre is known as *thol bommalattam* (shadow doll play). The shadow puppets are large-size figures ranging from 72 inches to 60 inches. Three areas are particularly associated with puppet making in Andhra — namely Kakinada, Madanapalli and Nellore. Each has a distinct style. In earlier days both in Karnataka and in Andhra, particular characters were designed from different animal hides. For example, the antelope skin was used for holy characters, wild sheep or buffalo hide for evil characters and demons and domestic goat or sheep skin for humans.

By a variety of assemblage and articulated techniques a fantastic range of movements can be recreated. Fifty or more puppets could crowd a large Andhra shadow theatre screen. Today while the number of characters is not vast the epic dimensions of the characters are unambiguous. High drama is created through manipulation and the verbal and musical support of the manipulator. Like the *wayang kulit* dalang the Andhra puppet master is polyvalent master who can sing, recite, manipulate and handle instruments at the same time. Castor oil lamps provide the light and enhance the depth of the puppets. The stage is an improvised structure comprising a screen often made by a *sari.* The presentation of the play is preceded by an elaborate ritual comparable to those performed in Java in Indonesia, and Karnataka and Kerala in India. The Kerala shadow theatre is called the *thole pavakoothu*. Similar to the *thole bomallattam* of Andhra and Karnataka it is in some senses more simple and austere. They are not manipulated through joints, nor is a dynamic movement aimed at. Neither are they as colourful as the Andhra and Karnataka puppets. Their distinctiveness lies in their presenting a ritualistic performance through many nights based on a particular version of the *Ramayana* from Tamilnadu written by a great writer, Ramban. An elaborate ritual precedes the performance and night after night different episodes from the *Ramayana* are presented serially. This shadow theatre does not include other plays in its repertoire.

Goa in western India and Orissa in eastern India are the home of two other very distinctive types of shadow theatre. In Goa, it is called *chitarakathi* and in Orissa *ravanachhaya* (the Shadow of Ravana). The *ravanachhaya* is a shadow theatre from full of unique vitality and dynamism. Unlike the Andhra and Karnataka shadow puppets, these are smaller in size and the leather is not coloured. They are not designed ornately or with intricate patterns but instead their charm lies in the high degree of abstraction, symbolism and the varying sizes of shadows they can cast on the screen. The hide is carefully prepared (formerly restricted to deer skin) and then the character is perforated appropriately. The sizes vary from six inches to 18 inches. As many as 500 shadow puppets may be required to present a full length performance. Sometimes more than one puppet is made for the same character as in the case of Hanuman for whom there is a small diminutive and a large Hanuman. The screen of the *ravanachhaya* is simple, comprising a four of five yard cloth like a *sari* which is tied to two poles and flaked by a number of mats. The light is provided by an earthen lamp with three wicks. The puppeteers sit on the ground in-between the lamp and the screen and recreate this exciting thrilling drama which is as simple as it is sophisticated.

These are but a few examples of the vast variety of puppet forms known in India. Rod and glove are also popular in other parts of India. Chief amongst these is the *putul natch* of Bengal and the glove theatre of Uttar Predesh. One could add many more examples but this sampling may provide an insight into this ancient and vital form of theatre which links the traditions of India with those of Egypt & Turkey and Iran on the one hand and those of Burma, China, Japan, Indonesia, Cambodia and Thailand on the other.

The Rich Variety of Asian and Oceanian Puppet Theatre

Puppet theatres, which were created by various races in many areas of the world, and had developed while creating their own traditions, had gradually lost the significance and popularity that they once enjoyed. However, the situation changed rapidly after World War II, and puppet theatres have received attention as "a revived art".

Especially in the Asian areas, puppet theatres have a long tradition, and, have revived and used as education for children and as daily cultural activity. Several nations in Asia were released from a long colonial occupation after the War, and they have reconstructed their own cultures and arts. In the Oceanian areas, modern puppet theatres also became active after the war.

The birth and the development of puppet theatre

The origin of the puppet theatre has long been the subject of controversy. Richard Pischel (1849-1908), places the origin of puppet theatre in India in his book, "The Home of the Puppet", Charles Magnin (1793-1862) says it is in Egypt; William Ridgeway (1853-1926) disagrees with Pischel. In any case, the relationship between the birthplace and development of puppet theatre and Asia is deep, and Asia has great weight in the world history of the development of puppet theatre. Original styles of puppet theatres seem to come from many sources. In animism man can rhythmically move tools, vessels, copies of things, and object which are shaped like holy spirits among others, in order to approach the spirits which are believed to exist inside the objects and communicate with them.

Two examples of very simple objects used as puppets are "Oshira-sama" which remain in the Tohoku region of Japan, though the puppets there are used mainly for prayer or incantation by maidens possessed by spirits, and tins called "marotte" which were held by clowns who served at the courts in Europe. Each is a stick puppet, of which the top is a head. A man handles the other part of the stick. Both festivals and towns must have played a big role in the process of its development in which the use of the puppet for incantation becomes public entertainment. The result that was gradually formed in this process, was mingled with old puppet dances of each region, and then, that process created distinctive styles and regional traditions.

In Europe stick puppets as simple structures have changed into marionettes which are hung from sticks and handled from above, and into puppets manipulated by both sticks and threads. This latter kind still remains today in Sicily, and in some theatres in India and Czechoslovakia. Now they are mainly marionettes in Europe.

In the meantime, in the Asian areas rod puppets handled by sticks from the bottom developed. Rod puppets have been popular in India, China and Thailand since early times, and *wayang golek* and *wayang klitik* in Indonesia are especially famous.

Rod puppets in Asia had a great influence on modern puppet theatres in Europe. It is said that Richard Tescher, an Austrian who is one of the most famous artists in modern puppet theatres after World War I, was inspired by the puppet theatres of Java which had been displayed at a Dutch museum during his trip. He recreated brilliant rod puppets through his study. Today the rod puppets in Czechoslovakia, where they are flourishing most, are named "Javjka" or "Vajanga". So it is obvious that this form of puppet theatre in Czechoslovakia originally comes from *wayang* in Java.

Shadow puppet theatres developed significantly in Asian and Near East countries such as China, India, and Turkey, and are the same as rod puppets in terms of both handling and functions. In China, the puppets of the shadow play are supported mainly by sticks attached to a part of the throat and handled by the sticks at an angle against the screen. In India, Indonesia and other South-east Asian countries, the epics, Mahabharata and Ramayana are performed very often. The shadow play puppets are supported by sticks attached vertically from the heads to the toes of the puppets. The shadow play puppets are handled by sticks attached at right angles to them. We should not forget that the shadow play of China influenced that of France, and French shadow plays called *ombres chinoise* flourished in the nineteenth century.

In Japan manipulation of sticks has developed in various and complex ways. Usually glove puppets are handled by inserting the fingers of one hand into both the head and the hands of the puppets. However, in Japan, with a few exceptions, traditional glove puppets are moved by handling short sticks attached below the heads of puppets. Their operation is unique. The Bunraku puppet is manipulated by three assistants. One handles both the head and the right hand of the puppet; the second, the left hand; the third, the legs. The Bunraku puppet combines simple rod puppet functions with complexity of movement. The Bunraku has an obvious Asian character on the basis of the functions of rod puppets and their handling.

International relationships and today's growth of puppet theatres

In 1929, UNIMA (Union International de la Marionnete) was founded in Prague, Czechoslovakia. Its activities were stopped during World War II. However, UNIMA was reestablished after the War and its activities have rapidly spread throughout the world from Europe which was its center before the war. Because of that, the puppet theatres of Asia and the rest of the World were firmly joined, and the new wave of modern puppet theatres has been spreading throughout Asia and Oceania. Puppet theatre troupes from Russia and Eastern Europe visited Mongolia, China, Vietnam, and North Korea. They have built up their state puppet theatres in their own countries. The activities of modern puppet theatres in Australia and New Zealand are progressing. Particularly in Australia there are puppet theatres that are aided by state government, and located in Sydney, Tasmania, and Melbourne, and a lot of groups are active.

The international relationship of performing puppet theatres reached a high point at the First International Puppet Theatre Festival held in Bucharest, and the movement has become very active through the international festivals that are now held in each country one after another.

On the other hand, however, a lot of Asian traditional puppet theatres are introduced to the world by documents and photos, even today, and it is worried that this valuable inheritance may be lost without enough research.

The following are precious theatres, and thus far not introduced worldwide as live theatre; the water puppet theatres of Vietnam that are floated and handled from far away; the string puppets of Burma and Lanka, shadow plays of Malaysia, Cambodia, and Thailand; the Rajasthani marionette and the Tamilnadu puppet manipulated through both strings and rods in India.

The International Puppet Festival of the Asian-Pacific Area 1979 was held in Tokyo, in August, under sponsorship of UNIMA of Japan, and it was attended by troupes from many countries in the Asian and Oceanian areas such as India, Korea, Thailand, Japan, Australia, and New Zealand; puppet theatre personnel of Thailand, the Philippines, and Indonesia, and there were documented reports form Sri Lanka. Kkoktu-

Gaksi, a traditional Korean puppet theatre, was performed by Namsadam of Korea, and appeared first time before international audiences.

Puppet theatres in Japan have been developing differently, even in comparison with other Asian countries, Japan seems to have the most puppet theatres in the world, in terms of variety of styles and one of the highest levels of art in the field of traditional puppets — the *Bunraku* puppet. Modern puppet theatres in Japan, that were born as one of the new theatrical movements near the end of the 1920s, have developed along with traditional puppet theatres as professional puppet theatres. The activity of the professional puppet theatres has given rise to amateur puppet theatres. Traditional puppet theatres have cooperated with modern ones and both have developed actively. About 10 years ago, the Puk Puppet Theatre was established in Tokyo, and it serves as the centre of the nationwide puppet theatrical activity

At the Festival mentioned before, the Asian Oceanian Puppet Theatre Conference was also held, and they discussed today's problems of puppet theatres in these areas. It was pointed out that today's puppet theatres are also used to educate in the schools and to educate the public about social issues such as birth control, but that there are many countries that face financial problems, difficulties in training technicians, and difficulties of growth because of the lack of social recognition. All of these factors point to the many problems which Asian and Oceanian puppet theatres and their rich traditions face in modern society.

The Last of Sri Lankan Puppets

The puppet theatre of Sri Lankan has somehow survived the ravages of time more successfully than most other theatrical arts of the country. It is indeed surprising that, presented in a rural setting, it can still draw a crowd with its unsophisticated charm. It is perhaps the child in us — the spectators to which the puppet shows appeal when it projects through its stock characters a picture of life, both realistic and naive, spiced with a fine sense of humour.

If puppetry, both shadow and marionette types, originated in Asia and spread to the West, where it developed and evolved into modern theatrical forms, its relative lack of development and gradual decline in several parts of Asia is to be lamented. The only form of puppetry now existing in Sri Lanka, the marionette, is facing the same situation. A few puppeteers still maintain their ancestral vocation while any plans of development or rehabilitation of the art comes up against a series of problems such as competitive theatrical forms, heavy financial disbursements and above all inadequate patronage.

Sri Lanka most probably inherited the art from India and preserves in certain parts of the country, particularly in the south, the same type of string puppetry as is preserved in Rajasthan, the original home of Indian puppetry, and in South India. The method of manipulating human and animal figures was known even in the days of her ancient king, for references are made to dolls and motivated images in the ancient literature of Sri Lanka. In Sinhalese the puppet is *rukada* (derived from Sanskrit *rupa* and *khanda*) meaning a 'miniature figure ' or 'replica' or 'doll'. It probably signifies any figure made of wood or any such material, originally, but is now used solely to denote a 'puppet'. The carving of animal figures or puppets was, and still is, a skilled art confined to particular groups of craftsmen. At some stage in the development of the art, some of the craftsmen, who had realised the entertainment value of the figures, formed themselves into a group, and began to put up shows at street corners, junctions and under the trees in towns and villages. Like their counterparts in the west, these itinerant puppeteers in the village were not slow in availing themselves of the opportunity of providing easily enjoyable amusement through puppet shows at fairs and religious festivals. They charged no gate and depended entirely on the small collections they made from the appreciative audience. They either introduced popular religious characters from the Buddhist Jatakas or dramatised some well-known episode from history. These themes were intended to evoke religious fervour among the masses or to appeal to the national sentiments and patriotic feelings of the spectators.

Puppetry as a dramatic art is comparatively recent in its origin in Sri Lanka, and the stimulus to use puppets for the purpose of drama came from a variety of folk-drama locally known as *nadagama*, a kind of operetta, which was very popular at the turn of the century and has influenced the traditional puppet play in its form and style of presentation. Owing to this influence the puppeteers use *nadagam* texts, borrow the music and use the instruments (harmonium and drums) of the folk play and even reproduce the recitative and dialogue portions so slavishly that there seems to be hardly any originality in the presentations as a puppet play. From its very inception the traditional puppet play has been closely connected with the folk play on account of its popularity and perhaps sustained it. Not only was the borrowing confined to the text and music but the *nadagam* actors, themselves, played the roles of puppet actors and manipulators during a performance. Such artistes who were accomplished in both forms of acting were able to take to puppetry when the *nadagama* gradually declined and even today, the outstanding puppeteers of the South have been proficient as *nadagam* players or artistes natured in the folk-play tradition. The puppet play in its present form has somehow survived because it has been able to adapt itself, unlike the *nadagama*, to the changing circumstances and living conditions of the villages.

The puppeteers of Sri Lanka form a closely knit community, now confined to part of southern Sri Lanka, where the art grew and flourished along with the other folk arts such as *kolam* (mask dances) and *sanni* (ritual dances) performed regularly then because the rites and rituals connected with them played an important role in the life of the people and also provided the necessary entertainment to the entire community. Today there are about three to four separate troupes of traditional puppet players practising the art. They are so closely related to each other that they seem to have inherited the common traditions and skills of the art from the same source, an ancestral teacher. It had been the practice for puppeteers to own jointly a collection of puppets, which later passed into the hands of another and from him to his pupils. While the puppets changed hands in this fashion jealousies and rivalries among the pupils introduced a competitive spirit. Consequently the more talented pupils began to make their own puppets, closely following the models of their former masters thus kept the tradition alive. Except for one or two of the older generation still with us, the puppeteers practising the art today are young and have taken to it partly from a sense of duty and also find a vocation by practising the art.

Though small in number, a puppet troupe requires a combination of the skills to make it a workable and successful group. About five of the troupe form the nucleus of regular members who should be trained in the difficult art of manipulating the strings of puppets. The rest are singers, instrumentalists and stage hands in charge of the screens and stage arrangements. The two artistes who provide the accompanying music on the drums and harmonium, often sing, simultaneously, when the story demands. Some of the puppet manipulators themselves, recite the verse portions and speak the dialogue in shifts as the play proceeds. The singers and instrumentalists work on a contract basis, making themselves available to any of the troupes which demand their services. They are in fair demand because their knowledge of the entire repertoire of *nadagam* songs and music enables them to play for any troupe at short notice.

The puppet stage is an improvised structure made by the troupe which normally brings along with them a few screens, curtains and decorative panels. The base of the puppet stage is set at a height of about two feet from the stage floor. The puppeteers manipulate the puppets by standing on a bridge fixed above the stage floor and masked by black screens forming the background for puppets.

The average height of the puppets appearing on the stage is four feet, but some of the principal heroes of a religious or historical play are made in life-size proportions. The latter type depicting royalty or nobility like King Sir Wickrama Rajasinghe and his Courtiers are often presented in seated postures with hardly any movement coming from the puppets as they are too heavy for manipulation. All the troupes use a common repertoire of plays based on *nadagam* texts and the collection of puppets in the possession of a troupe may be as large as 200. The stock characters presented with every play are the *konangi* or *bahubhutaya* (clown), *vidane* (a type of village official who acts as a presenter), *sellapillai* (a Tamil word meaning 'boy player') and the dancing girl. All the four figures except the *vidane* are dancing puppets. The *konangi* appear first in a pair, performing an introductory dance swaying to the rhythm of the drums. After their introductory dance a narrator appears and introduces the main play. When several scenes have been presented, it is time for an interlude, the players and the audience simultaneously feeling the need for a change. Comes the *vidane*, an excellent caricature of rural officialdom, mimicking and gesticulating, his comments directed towards something topical or a contemporary event of some significance. Other interludes which follow at regular intervals, present stock items. These subsidiary scenes enliven the puppet show and add the necessary spice to it. Among them stands out the *Carter's Episode, a sine qua non* in the traditional puppeteer's presentation anywhere. The scene depicts a carter, a drunkard and a policeman engaged in a hot exchange of words. As the curtain opens on the scene a brightly painted cart is seen jogging along, driven by a carter in a merry mood. He is the worse for liquor and as the car moves it keeps to the right side of the road (an offence against traffic regulations) and knocks down a pedestrian at the same time. A policeman then appears on the scene and proves too smart for the latter with his witty and sarcastic rejoinders. The humour is at times coarse and could be a little obscene, but the audience always reacts to it with uproarious laughter as the carter is made to mount and dismount from his seat, times without number at the behest of the policeman. This repeated mounting and dismounting from the seat, a device deliberately overdone to the immense delight of the spectators, is something the puppet show can present in its inimitable fashion. After feeling a little more sober and thinking of taking revenge for the treatment meted to him by the policeman, the carter turns towards the man, injured by the accident and crumpled up on the seat. He abuses him and belabours him with his stick, the blows being punctuated with deafening roars of laughter. The above items remind us of one of the most important features of the puppet show, namely improvisation, which allows the players as well as the audience to derive maximum entertainment. Even the practice of not having a fixed text proves a great asset to the layers in improvising and adapting the dialogue to suit the occasion.

The last of the stock scenes, thrown in at a significant stage of the performance, is a display of dancing given by the dancing doll called the *Bombay Dance.* The item seems to be an import from India, a cheap imitation of a Bombay dancing girl, perhaps a craze at the time it was introduced. Gaudy and garish in appearance, the female figure is able to produce delicate neck and facial movements and supple wave — like hand movements — all done with grace and finesse to demonstrate the master puppeteer's expertise. This sort of dance item has indeed became a very common feature of the traditional marionette shows of many countries of Asia introduced for the purpose of giving variety to the programme and for revealingly manipulating skill of the puppeteer.

The stories have heroic, patriotic or religious themes. One of the most popular in the list is the tragic story dealing with the ill-fated Kandyan King, Sri Wickrama Rajasinghe. It is based on a theatrical text and contains all the ingredients of a drama, full of intrigue, misdeeds and horror, that can sustain the interest of the audience and evoke their sympathy. The Buddhist Birth stories or Jatakas also have an unfailing appeal to rural audiences. The *Wise Vidura and King Vessantara* have been highly appreciated for the Buddhist ideals they reflect and the values they inculcate. Suffering, born of dedication of truth and renunciation of worldly life, two virtues of an aspirant Buddha, are conveyed in a highly emotional tone by song, dialogue and puppet action. The puppeteers who feel the pulse of the audience are able to work out particular scenes to suit the mood of the people on such occasions.

In the light of the above situation and factors connected with its growth, the traditional puppet show has always remained popular among the rural folk. A puppet show is generally arranged in connection with a religious festival, a national celebration and the locale invariably is the precincts of a temple or school as befits the theme of the performance. It would not be inappropriate to mention the developments that have taken place both with regard to the efforts made for maintaining and improving the state of the traditional marionettery and in connection with recent attempts at introducing new techniques and styles of puppetry. The puppetry has not been able to gain permanent footing on account of its obvious limitations and, therefore, it has been practised by the poor artistes and patronised to great extent by the poorer classes of society. If artistic traditions of the past have fostered that art these very same factors have also hindered its growth. The puppeteers for the most part have no general education in artistic matters and been carrying on a tradition merely for the sake of preserving it. They have remained so orthodox and even fanatical in their ideas regarding training and transmitting their skill and know-how to the younger generation that they are reluctant to teach the art to anybody outside their family circle. It is only in a few instances that suitable pupils within the inner circle have successfully pursued the ancestral vocation. By and large, the younger generation of these families have turned away from this vocation owing to the deplorable conditions prevailing.

The government has been aware of the above circumstances and in recognition of the value of puppetry made several attempts to foster it. The Art Council of Ceylon and the Department of Cultural Affairs have for the last two decades given grants to puppet troupes for training the young in their workshops and also organised festivals and exhibitions of puppets in addition to inviting foreign experts for conducting courses and renowned puppet troupes for performances. All these endeavours have been beneficial in keeping the art alive and appreciated for its entertainment and theatrical values, but have had limited effect on developing the art in a substantial manner.

The puppetry activities which certain collection trainees and especially university students (under the auspices of the University Puppetry Society) indulged in deserve special mention. For nearly five years (1960-65) students with an aptitude for puppetry pursued their interests in making and manipulating both hand and rod puppets — an experiment done of the first time here — and staged playlets based on popular stories. These performances were always popular in university circles and in schools mainly because the new styles of puppets and their methods of presentation created great enthusiasm among both children and adults who wished to something different from the traditional show for a change. It is a pity that these activities could not be continued for lack of adequate facilities and the difficulties of organising the work at a purely voluntary level. A local puppeteer, playing with marionettes made and manipulated entirely in the Western style, has made the headlines recently with his shows given at hotels on special occasions. With his troupe consisting of family members, he has shown the potentialities of modern puppetry as a medium of whole-some entertainment. He was also commissioned to present a playlet based on a national religious theme during the Non-Aligned Conference held in Colombo a few years before. In conclusion it must be said that the potentialities of puppetry in its dramatic and educational aspects have still not been exploited in this country. It is our hope that a greater degree of understanding of puppetry and its value among the young in particular will contribute to a greater appreciation of the art and promote its development.

Multi-National Character of Australian Puppetry

In the living-room of her home in the Blue Mountains outside Sydney, surrounded by reminders of years gone by, one of the pioneers of puppetry in Australia reminisces on the early days. Edith Murray speaks of such individuals as Alan and Key Lewis who carved many small wooden marionettes and performed in the schoolrooms of the "nineteen-thirties" and she remembers Bill Nicols whose work in tertiary education institutions provided many with their first contact with puppetry. Edith Murray herself started a small puppet theatre in a hut donated by a local council in a Sydney suburb in 1949 and it was here that Richard Bradshaw, today perhaps the country's foremost puppeteer, received so much of his early experience.

Edith's recollections continue — the names and the memories seem endless. The small figure of Mrs. Murray has been a familiar sight for many Australian puppeteers for many years — she has seen the puppet theatre in Australia develop from infancy to its present state. Today the variety of puppetry in Australia is enormous. Puppets in Australia are alive.

For many years in Australia the work "puppet" immediately summoned the image of a "Tintookie". Peter Scriven established the possibility of successful large scale puppet productions in Australia with his 1956 production of "The Tintookies". The name itself is Australian Aboriginal and means "little people of the sandhills". The origin of Scriven's marionette theatre, however, lie far from Australia.

Scriven, who had earlier studied with Bill Nicols, had the good fortune to meet with Igor Hychka while overseas. Hychka had worked and travelled with one of the great European marionette theatres of this century, the Teatro dei Piccoli of Vittorio Podrecca, an Italian puppeteer who travelled the world with his gently satirical puppet productions.

Hychka and Scriven together adapted the techniques developed by Podrecca, maintaining many of his theatrical devices and yet creating a theatre form with a strong Australian content. Scriven's puppets were like Podrecca's long-stringed marionettes worked from overhead in a scaled down version of the traditional European picture-frame proscenium stage. Obviously such an arrangement involved large amounts of equipment and large casts of puppeteers and this, combined with a puppet cast of, in some productions, up to a hundred marionettes, presented considerable problems on the company's tours of Australia and Asia. Scriven's final production in this form was in 1975, but the style was carried on by Phillip Edmiston's "theatre-strings" company for several years. Phillip, puppeteer trained under Scriven, continued the direct influence of Podrecca and the grand theatricality of the Italian puppet master, will no doubt continue to hold a strong attraction for puppeteers for many years to come.

It is often said that in Australia we have no tradition of puppetry, although of course there have been the occasional Punch and Judy shows since the early days of the colony. In a sense that is true; it is impossible to point to one tradition and to say that here we see the origin of the puppet theatre in this country.

Yet to go on from this and to say that no traditions are represented here and that the Australian puppeteer must create his art in a cultural vacuum or else merely mimic overseas trends and traditions would be a misrepresentation. Australian society is one of the most cosmopolitan in the world, a society of immigrants, and the present Australian population represents a complex mixture of cultures. Several of these cultures possess long-standing traditions of puppetry and some of these traditions are already being revived and developed here today.

To ignore the presence and influence of the diverse cultures found within Australia today not only impoverishes our perception of the Australian heritage, but denies the very nature of Australian society.

The largest immigrant groups in Australia that have come from non-English speaking cultures are the Greek and the Italian populations. Both Greece and Italy have for many centuries enjoyed the puppet theatre in various forms and this heritage must now be seen as part of the Australian identity.

In Greece the shadow play performed with flat leather figures held against a thin muslin screen and illuminated from behind has long been a popular entertainment. In Sydney, Kostas Zouganelis is heir to this tradition. Kostas makes his own puppets in the traditional manner, cutting his figures, usually seen in profile, from thin leather and then staining them with coloured oils. The use of the oil has the effect of making the jointed figures translucent so that the shadow produced by them assume rich, muted tones when held against the large, white shadow screen.

In Greece the shadow play centres around the vain and impetuous character of Karagosis, a bawdy and not entirely well mannered gentleman whose provocatively satirical comments on the life of the country have scandalized and delighted generations of children and adults alike. In Australia, Kostas and others adapt the Greek tradition to the new country, telling new stories, creating new characters and interpreting a new society through the eyes of the old rascal, Karagosis. At an exhibition of puppets from around the world, held in the Sydney Opera House in 1979, Kostas performed with his shadow puppets, delighting many school children and gently increasing a new generation's awareness of their country's heritage.

On the Mediterranean island of Sicily a flamboyant form of the puppet theatre has existed since the sixteenth century. The bloodstained tales of Ariosto's "Orlando Furioso" have been enacted by large and colourful puppets, some being almost life size and weighing up to forty kilograms. These Sicilian "marionetti" are operated from above by means of a heavy metal rod attached to the head of the figure with another lighter rod leading to the puppet's right hand which often wields an iron sword. Although the method of control is so simple the carriage of Orlando and the knights, princes and villains of the medieval legends is magnificent. Clad in polished brass armour, plumed and brilliant, they stride and strut across the wooden stage floor, stiff-legged and fiercely proud. Today in the inner Sydney suburb of Marrickville it is possible to watch these heroic figures being created anew. The medieval armour is still being beaten by hand in the traditional manner, the battles are still being fought, the legends continue to enthrall.

Giovanni Bronzini began making his marionetti while still living in Sicily. After migrating to Australia yearned to continue with his art and to teach others what he had learnt. Working in a disused army hut, Giovanni carves and paints the wooden heads, he beats the armour and costumes his figures. Through conducting workshops he passes on these skills and at last count Giovanni and his pupils had completed the construction of thirty figures of the Orlando cycle as well as many others for different stories. Each puppet involves four weeks of work, working for ten hours a day, and performances have been given in both Italian and English .

While the work of such individuals as Kostas and Giovanni represent only a small part of the entire range of work being done in the puppet theatre in Australia, perhaps it is not too idealistic to see their contribution as the beginning of a long overdue recognition of Australian's unseen heritage. With the establishment of the Independent and Multicultural Broadcasting Corporation in the near future their work, and the work of others, will surely gain greater recognition. The IMBC or "fifth channel" is soon to begin broadcasting a television service for the ethnic communities and already moves have been made to incorporate traditional puppetry into the channel's programmes.

Australia's many cultures are represented in the puppet theatre in other ways, not only through the direct continuation of traditions such as we have seen above. One of the more socially adventurous puppet troupes in Australia is Polyglot, a Melbourne-based group working in the schools. Polyglot has based its performances on a recognition of the country's multicultural nature and developed a show which attempts to relate to the many language groups found in Australian cities. Picture an audience of young children, many of whom speak English as a second language, their original tongue being perhaps Greek or Spanish or Turkish or any one of a number of languages. A puppet show is about to begin. The children in the past have come to expect that any performance they see will be in English — after all this is Australia, isn't it, and in Australia we all speak English, don't we?

The show begins, but this isn't English. What language are the puppets speaking? Some of the children are confused; but who is that smiling over there? He obviously understands what is going on. Yes, he understands because he speaks Turkish and this is a story performed in Turkish. Polyglot performs in six languages, stories from different countries being told in the appropriate language. How does an audience react when confronted with such a show? Ideally the children in the audience who, for example, speak Turkish will feel encouraged to explain the Turkish story to their classmates and in return will be told about the other stories. Polyglot aims to encourage children to explore the many cultures from which they and their classmates come. It is through such attempts as this that Australian puppetry can begin to reflect the true nature of Australian society.

And what of tomorrow? What can we expect of the future in puppetry? Puppetry in 1980 is in the midst of a "boom period". Public interest in the art form has never been so high in this country before. Of course this is encouraging; it is exciting and yet there is a danger. Unless the very highest of standards can be maintained in this flurry of activity audiences will soon lose interest, and the "boom" will have been nothing but a flash in the pan. Let us assume for the moment that this does not happen, that audiences do continue to grow and to find enjoyment in the puppet theatre, and the puppetry continues to flourish.

A suggestion of one possible future development can see in the Sydney Dance Company's production, "Poppy". In this exciting modern dance piece puppets, made by Joe Gladwin, occupied the stage alongside the dancers, providing a dramatic visual element that could hardly have been achieved by other means. A huge rod-puppet figure, representing a teacher towered above the dancers and in another scene a number of life-size figures danced together with the human performers with startling effectiveness. Co-operative efforts between puppetry and other forms of theatre could offer exciting possibilities for the future.

The greatest potential strength of Australian culture lies in a rich eclecticism, drawing upon the many cultures and many artistic forms now represented in this country, allowing the wealth of tradition to which we are all heir to develop and to grow in a new environment.

Japan: From Sacred Puppets to Bunraku Puppet Theatre

Essence of puppet theatre

The essence of puppet theatre lies in the expression of emotion by means of puppets, which is quite different from human theatre, which represents feelings by the direct physical movement of actors. Moreover, in terms of structure, the human theatre is composed of the elements of actor, drama and audience while the puppet theatre consists of puppet, puppet-manipulator, drama and audience. Thus the role of the actor in the human theatre corresponds to that of the puppet and the puppet-manipulator in the puppet theatre. This is why the human theatre and the puppet theatre have developed their own peculiar expressions separately.

Puppet theatre may seem incapable of expressing feelings of a psychological or realistic nature. However, *bunraku*, the most well-known Japanese puppet theatre, is capable of expressing the most complex of feelings. Furthermore, the puppets are able to manifest scenes of unreality and the fantastic which cannot be depicted by human actors, freely performing arts such as flying in the air and diving in the sea.

For immobile puppet to mobile puppet

As for the origin of puppetry, many scholars who study the puppet theatre say that it traces back to the ritual ceremony or to the production of magic effects in ancient times. As regards source of the Japanese puppets, first of all, it might be conjectured that the puppet developed from a rough-cut branch or stick said to be possessed by deities. This early form is called *katashiro* (or figure representing the gods) and then the next stage of development is the personification of this *katashiro* into *hitogata* (or human figure). The *hitogata*, being possessed by deities, is supposed to operate in both the material and spiritual worlds. There are clear examples of this.

When you go into an agricultural society, you will find scare-crows in the paddies. These scarecrows have the dual purposes of protecting crops from animals or birds and driving away bad spirits. The straw effigy, or *wara-ningyo* in Japanese, is also known to exterminate crop-destroying insects with spiritual powers. Thus the primitive puppet was immobile, but our perception of it, even nowadays, is based on a belief in its spiritual powers. From the influence of folkloristic religion, this immobile image became a mobile puppet. Since this process is very important in understanding the puppet theatre as a whole at the present, we will examine the puppets as it was at this primitive stage, which survives even now.

The materials transformed into puppets which were occupied by gods or deities were mainly mulberry or peach trees. A man was used as the medium between a deity and the puppet, and it was believed that not he, but the mysterious powers of the deity, moved the doll. We will find that this primitive form is still found in *oshira-sama asobi* (or, performance of the god named Oshira) in the Tohoku district of the north-eastern part of Japan and in *ebisu-mawashi* (or, barbarian dance) in the Chugoku and Shikoku districts. The former, *oshir-sama*, is made of a piece of wood and manipulated by a maiden who is called *itako*, a psychic medium. She has puppets on both hands, to which the deities descend and tell the *takusen* through her mouth. *Takusen* means an oracle declaring the god's will. This act is regarded as having ritualistic significance. As another example, *ebisu-mawashi* represents the action of fishing for sea bream, while chanting propitious words. The sea bream is said to be a lucky fish in Japan. This puppet dance can be thought of as sympathetic magic to assure a good catch and the chanting of propitious words as being done by a servant of gods or deities.

The two examples mentioned above lead us to the following conclusions: first, puppet performances symbolize sacred acting and second, puppet manipulators utter the words of a deity through their mouths. Third, they are able to communicate with deities either through inherent instincts or through acquired training by aescetic exercises. Fourth, the puppet manipulators are considered to be sacred persons, as are *itako* and Shinto and Buddhist priests who all played an important role in the history of Japanese performing arts. It can surely be said that the puppet manipulators carry on the tradition of the *itako* and priests to the present day.

On the contrary, we have other information which has been found in eighth century documents of the Nara period, which say that the puppet manipulators come from Seiiki, the present Central Asia. On the whole, wandering performers in both Seiiki and in Japan were the original persons who communicated with deities and spirits. At this stage, this puppet entertainment seems not yet to have been developed into true drama. In Japan the actual puppet theatre flourished after combining with a new form of storytelling, called *joruri* which rose in popularity in the middle of the Muromachi Period (fourteenth-fifteenth century). Afterwards the *Samisen*, a three-stringed instrument, was introduced from Okinawa, during the Keicho era, in the early Edo period (sixteenth century) and this was the true beginning of the *bunraku* puppet theatre.

Local puppet theatre

There are many puppet theatre troupes in various parts of Japan, but most of them do not have a permanent theatre.

Puppet theatre is performed on the occasion of religious festivities. When the puppet manipulators are not engaged in performances, they are engaged in work such as farming, fishing, office work, and so on, traditionally succeeding to their fathers' work. Provincial puppet theatre was brought by groups of professional performers, who taught the technique of manipulation and performing to the local people. During the height of popularity of *Kabuki*, that is to say the Horeki era (1751-63) to the Edo period, some puppet manipulators who could not find enough work in the large cities moved to local areas, settling there for life. At this time puppetry descended into the milieu of popular entertainment.

The development of present-day society has produced various forms of plebeian entertainment; in particular, television, after the Second World War has reduced traditional performing arts to a position of lesser importance, making them relics of the past. But now, when we ask questions about traditional culture and its value, these puppet theatre troupes throughout the country gain our serious attention. Nevertheless, the lack of successors and lack of concern for antique matters continues to this day. As stated above, if the puppet theatre is to flourish in the future, the puppet manipulators must express through the dolls what human actors cannot perform. The more the puppet theatre displays this inherent advantage over human theatre, the more we can appreciate the value of the existence of puppets.

Bunraku reached its peak in the art of puppet making and puppet manipulation during the Edo period, so people presently engaged in puppet theatre work should pay close attention to the superior expressive possibilities that *bunraku* developed at this time.

After studying the puppet theatre in Asian countries it is no exaggeration to say that there is no country which has so many types of puppet theatres as Japan. Puppet theatre shows us the distant world standing aloof from space and time which we have forgotten. Actors who perform on the stage may satisfy our emotions, but the puppets, manipulated by the puppeteers, act out myths and the cosmos on the microcosm of the stage, upon which deities and spirits dance for joy. The movements of the puppet are the god's emotions, and the puppet theatre provides us with a place where there can be communication with deities and spirits, and also harmony between human beings and heaven and earth.

A Brief Introduction to Puppet Shows in China

uppet and shadow shows in China are twin sisters. Both are characterized by their long history, rich variety, wide popularity and solid foundation.

The puppet show has history of more than 2,000 years, while that of the shadow show, though a little shorter, is also no less than 800 years.

The wooden puppet unearthed from a Han Dynasty tomb in Shandong province in 1979 is 137cm high, almost as tall as a man. The whole piece is made up of 13 wooden parts (excluding the small rotten ones). With the joints nicely carved, it can sit, stand and kneel just like a man. String-puppets of the later period might have developed out of puppets of this kind. It shows that an embryonic form of the puppet show already existed in the Han Dynasty (206-8 BC).

"Reminiscences of Dongjing" (By Men Yuanlao) is a book describing the life and customs of the people in the capital of the Song Dynasty (AD 960-1276). Some parts of this book are devoted to a description of the grand occasions of puppet and shadow show performances, and contain a record of names of some popular performers of the time. The is also a description of vivid scene in which puppets rowed a boat and took hold of a living fish in a performance given in the Waterside Hall of the Royal Palace.

Two earthen pillows of the Northern Song Dynasty were unearthed in Henan Province in 1979. On them, there are clear pictures in red, green and yellow of children fiddling with stick-puppets and string-puppets. This is additional evidence that, in artistic level and degree of popularity, puppet and shadow shows of the Song Dynasty had already reached the stage of full bloom. It also shows that children were very fond of this form of amusement.

There are a great variety of puppet and shadow show in China: The big stick-puppet of Yilung Country in Sichuan Province is of the size of an ordinary man, while the "single puppet" of Guangdong Province is only a few inches high.

The beautifully shaped string-puppets of Fujian Province in South China remind one of fair figures in the frescoes of temples in the Tang Dynasty or of the images of gods or goddesses, while the string-puppets of Shansi Province in North China are rather simple and rough in modelling as well as in costumes and make-up, with a folk style of their own. The pouch-puppets (or glove-puppets) show that puppets which belong to different schools are quite different in style even in the same part of the province of Fujian, such as Southern Fujian. Some are at singing and acting while others excel in acrobatic skills.

There are three different kinds of puppet shows that are performed by only one performer: the "bed sheet show" of Sichuan, which is lively and vivid, the "shoulder-pole show" of North China, which is dexterous and skillful and the "one-man-team" of Guangdong, which captures the audience with its consistency and integrity of plot.

There is also a "human-puppet show" in Lingao Country of Hainan Island. Its distinguishing feature lies in the audience's seeing both the puppet and the performer at the same time. It has a history of more than three hundred years and is very much loved by the people of that area. Silhouettes of characters cut out of paper are known as "shadow entities". They are placed against the screen-like "shadow window", which is also made of paper. In ancient times, when the lights of lamps or candles were thrown on the perforated and transparent "shadow entities", images of flowers, birds, insects or fish, different movement of flying, diving, running and jumping as well as different moods of happiness, anger, sadness and merriment were displayed clearly on the "shadow window". Now, cattle and donkey hides have taken the place of paper in making "shadow entities", "paper windows" have been replaced by "cloth windows" (now called "screens"), and candle lights by the electric lights. Modern performances, as a result, really look somewhat like the movies. No wonder some people call it "the predecessor", "the most ancient form" or, with some exaggeration, "the ancestor" of the movies.

There is still another kind of puppet show that we should not fail to mention here: the iron-stick show. Though its operation is quite similar to that of the shadow show, its performance is basically the same as that of the puppet show. It is rare variety of puppet show now, and can be found only in the southern part of Fujian Province. It is said to have evolved from the puppet show and is called "paper show" in the Chaozhou-Shantou area of Guangdong Province. Since the iron-stick show does not need any light or screen, it can be performed in the daytime. It is a favourite of the people of the area.

The puppet show of China has behind it hundreds of years of artistic practice and is an embodiment of the wisdom and labour of innumerable artists. All these factors have contributed to the consummate skill, exquisite modelling and clever costumes and make-up of the different varieties and schools, each having its own characteristics, blazing with colour and rich in artistic styles. For example, the stick-puppet of Guangdong Province has a pair of expressive eyes. It can cast glances quite naturally and freely and can express exactly the thoughts and feelings of the character by a wink or turn of its big eyes.

The stick-puppet of Shanghai, with its fine postures and ingenious make-up, can convey its feelings very well by a flutter of its dress and a sweep of its sleeves. There is also the stick-puppet of Hunan Province, which is famed for its quick, accurate and energetic "leg actions". It stamps and kicks as if it had a pair of sensitive legs of flesh and blood.

The string-puppet of Fujian Province can perform extremely difficult actions in the twinkling of an eye, such as, the consecutive actions of thrusting the sword back into the sheath again as soon as it is pulled out.

The stick-puppet of the Chinese Puppet Art Troupe of Beijing creates a puppet art with a novel and unique style of its own, by combining the characteristics of the puppet art of different parts of the country and absorbing both ancient and modern, indigenous and foreign techniques of expression in modelling, costumes and make-up, lighting, scenery, and music.

As for the shadow show, Tangshan is noted for its musical accompaniment. With voices rising, falling, pausing and resuming in its own unique style, it is known both in our country and abroad as the "shadow tune". The western school shadow show of Beijing is also famous at home and abroad for its traditional simplicity in modelling, elegance in colour, delicacy in lining and exquisiteness in the art of leather silhouette cutting.

The shadow show of Heilungjiang Province incorporates skilful light projecting. It attains the desired artistic effect by duly changing focuses to bring skilled technique into full play and thereby creating a desired atmosphere. The puppet show of Hunan Province is based on children's stories of tables. It is noted for endowing every figure in the show with its own character and feelings by imitating the ways animals fly, run or climb, thus giving scope to the special skills of the shadow show and making every show ardently loved by the old and the young alike, and even more so by the children. Puppet and shadow shows have popular among the people in about 90 per cent of the provinces and cities in our country as well as in number of countries and regions abroad. Naturally, they have all become forms of art that the people love to see and hear.

China has a great number of professional puppet and shadow artists. Take the province of Hunan for instance. In that province alone, there are as many as 5,000 workers of shadow art and over 1,000 troupes. For some counties in Zhanjiang district of Guangdong province, there are as many as 200-300 workers of puppet art and more than 100-200 troupes in each county.

The puppet and shadow shows in China traversed an extremely arduous path before liberation. It is only after liberation that they gained a new life and have been developing vigorously ever since under the policy of "letting a hundred flowers bloom; weeding through the old to bring forth the new". Quite a number of plays based on children's favourite fables, fairy tales and children's stories, such as "The Riot in Heaven", "The Flood of Jin Shan", "The Borrowing of a Palm Fan" etc., have been collected, produced and put on the stage. Shadow as well as puppet shows either with sticks, pouches or strings of many provinces and cities, such as Beijing, Shanghai, Hunan, Fujian, Guangdong, etc., have been to various countries to give performances and take part in international contests, playing an active role in cultural exchanges and the promotion of friendship between peoples. After the smashing of the "gang-of-four", it has become possible again for the puppet and shadow artists to work untiringly for the "four modernizations" of our socialist construction. The specific forms of presentation of puppet and shadow shows fit in very well with all the age groups of children. Take pouch-puppets for example, which appeal to all the three characteristics of children before school age, i.e. love of toy, story and amusement. The carrying on of puppet show activities in the kindergarten will have marked effects on children in their development of language, thinking and action.

In recent years, organs of women's federations, education, public health and culture working together with workers of literary and art circles and workers of puppet art have made explorations on different occasions in "children's puppet show activities" in a number of kindergartens in more than ten provinces and cities in China. Experience shows these "children's puppet show activities" have a marked effect on the physical development of children (especially the growth of their limbs and fingers) and on the consolidation of what they learn in their studies.

Today, this old popular art of China has not only become a good means for enlivening the cultural life of both children and young people, raising their moral standards and disseminating scientific knowledge, but also a good means of education for children before school age. This is why some people call it "living teaching aid".

Under the leadership of the Institute of Theatrical Workers of China, the puppet and shadow artists are now making preparations for the setting up of an "Institute of puppet and shadow art of China" for the purpose of uniting the workers of the trade as well as persons concerned, and of studying the problems of "how to make puppet and shadow shows serve hundreds of millions of children", "how to raise the quality of puppet and shadow art", "how to carry on artistic and technical exchanges in this field," etc.

Thai nang talung *shadow play.*

Part 8

Cinema in Asia

Cinema in Asia

Masterpieces of Asian Cinema

The best-known films from Asia, those of Japan excepted, are Bruce Lee's kung-fu films from Hong Kong and the many works by India's Satyajit Ray, most notably his trilogy *Pather Panchali* (1955), *Aparajita* (1956) and *Apur Sansar* (1959). Although India ranks third behind the United States and Japan in the number of films produced yearly, the great majority of these are simply vehicles for popular Indian music and dance and are not known abroad. Satyajit Ray was the first Indian filmmaker to be recognized internationally as an artist of the first rank. His reputation was established with his first film, *Pather Panchali*, a work which describes the everyday life of a typical family in the remote Indian countryside and explores the deep, sensitive relationships that exist there between parent and child, sister and brother, man and nature, and family and village.

The film opens with an attractive and young brother and sister who charm the audience with their disarming demeanor. Their mother argues with an elderly woman relative who has been sponging off of them, finally driving her out of their home and into their neighbor's. Ray succeeds in this scene in conveying the sadness of this old woman with a good measure of humour. Later in the film, the old woman senses her death is near and returns to the original household, only to be treated evermore hard-heartedly. The old woman pours water from a jug into her hands, splashes it on her bald, sun-baked head and smiles sweetly, creating a face with the power to move hearts never before seen in the cinema.

The children wander off to watch the trains go by, but are caught in the rain on their way home. Just as the rain begins to fall, the camera zooms in on a beetle scampering across the surface of a swamp. After a young girl, drenched in the rain, catches pneumonia and dies, her younger brother throws a necklace previously stolen from a rich child into this swamp in her memory. The swamp grasses that obscure the surface of the water suddenly open up to receive the necklace, and then quietly close in a ring around it. Nature in this film is not simply beautiful nor analogous to character, but indeed an actor capable of subtle expression.

Aparajito is the sequel. The final scene in *Pather Panchali* depicts an impoverished Brahmin family living in the Bengal country-side circa 1910 who have lost their daughter and decide to leave the village and the sequel resumes the story after they have resettled in the city of Benares along the Ganges. *Aparajito* portrays the poor of India and the emotions we share with them through such scenes as the banks of the Ganges at dawn, an old man practising yoga, a performer telling stories, the tragic death of a father, a flock of doves taking off into the sky together, and the pathos and beauty of life seen through the eyes of children.

The mother and her son eventually return to the countryside where the child, named Apur, is made to attend school. Audiences inevitably smile as Apur, a bright boy, pleases his teachers by reciting a poem before the school inspector. Apur, now grown and desperately eager to attend university in Calcutta, fights with his mother who does not want him to go. Finally, she capitulates and sees her son off, saying farewell with a lonely smile that moves us with her beauty, a beauty now made lean by the suffering she has endured.

Apur Sansar completes the trilogy. Apur has graduated but, discouraged by unemployment, impulsively marries a friend's sister. Their happiness is cut short, however, when his bride dies in childbirth. Years later Apur suddenly reappears to claim his son, a son he had abandoned and left with his wife's relatives.

These three films, simple and restrained in their making, eschew artifice and in its stead communicate an intimacy through the actor's facial expressions. Satyajit Ray has continued directing masterpieces, such as *Mahanagar* (Metropolis, 1963), *Charulata* (1964) and *Ashani Sanket* (Distant Thunder, 1973).

China is the largest nation in Asia, but the only Chinese films that have achieved any international fame have been kung-fu films made in the colony of Hong Kong, in which the Chinese actor Bruce Lee uses every kung-fu technique ever invented to vanquish the villains, both Western and Japanese.

Chinese films of course have long been made in both China proper and Taiwan. Films from the People's Republic, with a population estimated at one billion, reveal much of what has been happening there.

Between 1966 and 1976, most of the Chinese working in the film industry did not, in fact, make films but rather were ordered to rural areas to assist in agriculture. Reportedly, during the Cultural Revolution only eight films, so-called "model films" dictated by Jiang Qing and her followers, were made. It now appears, however, that the industry has revived rapidly" fifty-two feature films were made in 1978, and sixty-five in 1979. If revivals and foreign films are included, a total of 139 full-length films were distributed in China in 1979.

The author who visited the studios in Beijing and Shanghai, learnt that Chinese filmmakers, due to the Cultural Revolution, feel they have fallen far behind recent advances in motion pictures. Though there were so many excellent films from the 1930s and 1940s the post-Cultural Revolution works were not impressive. Many films are made simply to attack the Cultural Revolution, the best of which are said to be the recent *Tear Stain* and *Troubled Laughter*. Both portray the so-called agents of the Gang of Four as nothing more than despicable hooligans. This stance may somewhat mollify those who suffered under the Cultural Revolution but hardly speaks for those who supported it. A film in China today must attack the Cultural Revolution, or it is never made in the first place. I was reminded of how in Japan during the war films were inevitably militaristic and patriotic, yet after the defeat tables were turned and all films had to criticize what they had recently praised.

One recent film *From Slave to General* did, nonetheless, strike me as a masterpiece. An ambitious and dense historical film, it is the story of a serf from one of China's minority races who died on the front lines with the People's Liberation Army after fighting for over twenty years, from the 1920s until the 1940s. It may be hard to imagine a soldier who could have survived twenty years of continuous war, but like Japanese samurai of the Sengoku period (Warring States period), there were indeed many incredible warriors among the Chinese. This film may have been intended to educate the Japanese and perhaps people everywhere in the history of the Chinese people's revolution, but as a work of art this film captures, with understatement, the valour of a national hero.

The Chinese magazine "Popular Film", with a circulation said to be over two million, awards its Hundred Flower Prizes each year on the basis of a poll of its readership. In 1979 the prizes went to *General Ji Hongchang*, about a general who fought the Japanese during the Second World War; *Tear Stain*, the story of a party official dispatched from the Central Committee to research and restore the name and reputation of an artist who had died of persecution by a local party organization during the Cultural Revolution; and *Little Flowers*, the saga of two sisters once separated but reunited during the War of Liberation.

The 1980 Hundred Flower Prizes went to *The Tenth Bullet Hole* and *Dan Xin Pu*, two films that declaim against the Gang of Four, and Romance on Lushan Mountain, the story of a daughter of a former general in the Chinese army living in the United States who returns to China and falls in love with the son of a party cadre. Of these, *Romance on Lushan Mountain* was especially popular with the audiences.

Today in China there are many films that were once targets of fierce attack from partisans of the Cultural Revolution but have now been popularly revived. Among them are not a few masterpieces. One example would be the 1937 *At the Crossroads* starring the famous actor Zhao Dan, a film depicting young people who, highly educated yet unable to find work, refuse to be disheartened by their poverty and instead struggle to help each other. The film is executed with lightness and comedy, and though it candidly reflects the lives of the Chinese proletariat under pre-Liberation conditions, it is filled with a combination of humour with pathos highly reminiscent of Chaplin.

Crows and *Sparrows* (1949) began production in Shanghai before Liberation but was completed afterwards, and as a result vividly records the turmoil just before the victory of the communists between the Shanghai citizenry and the Guomindang government. It is surprising that a work ruthlessly exposing the corruption of the Guomindang could be made in a city still under its control, and in fact its style, both severe and rich, fairly parallels that of the contemporaneous Italian neo-realist cinema.

The Lin Family Store (1959) is a chronicle of 1931, the year of the Shanghai Incident. Lin runs a general store in the country that, because it continues to handle Japanese goods, has its business hurt by the mass anti-Japanese boycott of that time. Lin, now desperate, bribes the police and sells his stock at cut-rate prices to refugees from Shanghai, but the Guomindang, the police and other stores, fearing how dangerous the situation is becoming, conspire to put Lin out of business while still enjoying his bribes. Finally, the defeated store owner flees in the middle of the night absconding with the meager sums that poor people had deposited with him. This film is an excellent example of the best use of realist techniques in the Chinese cinema. The process of the destruction of this one store is pursued with such acute and accurate description that one feels one can really understand how it must have been for a certain class of Chinese in a certain period of history; and yet, for the very reason, this film was roundly criticized during the Cultural Revolution as capitalist for sympathizing with petty-bourgeois elements.

The 1964 *Sisters of the Stage* is the story of two actress sisters in a rural travelling company. Both had once been stars on the Shanghai stage, but they parted ways when one joined the proletarian theatre and the other married a money-hungry theatre-owner. Yet after the Revolution, they find themselves reunited in their hometown and their lives come together once more. The latter half of the film, a story of the Revolution told simplistically, is tedious but the first half, with its beautiful scenes of the troupe travelling in the countryside, communicates a touching sorrow. This film, too, was attacked in the Cultural Revolution for its "disgraceful" obliteration of class lines in the sisters' reconciliation. It was exactly this sort of criticism that put so many Chinese filmmakers behind bars, or in extreme cases, forced their suicides.

The recent sad news from the Chinese cinema has been the death of Zhao Dan. The films he starred in from the 1930s and 40s, such as *At the Crossroads* and *Crows* and *Sparrows*, are considered to be masterpieces on a par to those found anywhere in the world, but after passing the duration of the

Cultural Revolution in prison his health faltered and, unable to star in Noboru Nakamura's joint Sino-Japanese production of *An Unresolved Issue,* died without making a comeback. Zhao was so respected that Vice Premier Deng Xiao Ping and other officials paid him a bed-side visit, yet just before his death he published an essay, much like a last testament, in which he accused excessive government control of killing the arts in China. It shall be interesting to see how China's leadership will respond to Zhao Dan's words.

The Republic of Korea, too, has produced a number of noteworthy films. There is, to cite one, the 1972 *Ahn Chung Keun, Martyr.* Ahn was the assassin of Hirobumi Ito, the first Governor-General of Korea under the Japanese colonization, and for it he is considered a national hero. The film recreates Korean history as it describes the Japanese suppression of monarchy, the patriotic movements that arose throughout the length of the peninsula as a result, and the subsequent harassment by the Japanese army. It was in these times that Ahn and his fellow conspirators swore a blood pact to fight and defeat Japanese imperialism.

The climatic scene in which Ahn assassinates Ito in Harbin station is quite spectacular. Within the station building are crowded a great many Chinese, Russians and police to welcome Ito, yet Ahn manages to get within striking distance and shoot him. Full of suspense, it is a scene that masterfully portrays the passion of radicalism.

Ahn is incarcerated, tried by the Japanese authorities and executed. Even in this final sequence of the film, it does not labour to characterize the Japanese with contempt or hate, but rather as a strong enemy that Ahn and his fellow patriots stood up to and fought bravely.

Thailand has given us an important film entitled *The Scar* (1978), a romantic tragedy somewhat like "Romeo and Juliet". Set in the swampy rice paddies of southern Thailand in 1930, the love between the two children of feuding families unfolds. One scene, beautifully done, shows the consummation of their love in a rice paddy. The female lead was played by a champion swimmer, but the film communicates true passion in such scenes as the one in which her lover waits for her hidden in the tall grasses, or in which the two of them first bathe and then race a water buffalo, or where they swim together to a holy shrine located in the middle of a river, embrace in the water among the reeds and pledge their love before the shrine. The girl's father, adamant in his refusal to allow her to marry her lover, packs her off to the city leaving the young man alone in the village. She is subsequently adopted into a rich family and one day returns to her old village with her upper-class fiance in tow and refuses to even speak to her former lover who has, ever since she left, swum night after night out to the shrine where they had pledged their love and played his sad flute, hoping its music might reach her ears wherever she be. When he learns upon her return that her feelings for him had faded, he swims once more out to the shrine, battling the monsoon rains, and beseeches it to tell him why she has broken her vow of love.

It would not be appropriate to call this rather spoiled young man a romantic hero. He falls upon his rival in love and murders him. He laments his lover's fickleness with tears so exaggerated as to suggest the monsoons. European romances — like "Romeo and Juliet" — have their share of reckless, impulsive youths but certainly the spoilt child nowhere resembles the image of the European hero. He is somewhat like the baby who refuses his mother's breast only to make her fret. In the last scene, having resolved to confront his lover's obdurate family, he dies in the middle of the swamps. Yet his lover, possibly due to the intercession of the shrine, suddenly finds her love for him reviving and jumps into the swamp after him, embraces his dead body, stabs herself and dies in the reddening water. The scene is an impressive one, but not without the embarrassing sentimentality of an endlessly demanding hero surrounded by the blood of an endlessly understanding heroine. There is another good Thai film, *The Country Teacher,* also made in 1978. Here a college graduate leaves Bangkok to become a teacher in a rural elementary school in the northeast. He is successful in several ways; he improves his pupils' performance by using the popular puppet theatre as a teaching tool; and he fights malnutrition by converting the school courtyard into a productive garden. *The Country Teacher* is a serious film yet it still pokes fun at the arrogant school principal. It is a pastoral, enjoyable and entertaining motion picture, while it also indicts the pretentiousness of officials and the corruption of merchants.

In the latter half of the film, the young teacher uncovers a secret lumbering project in the jungle and exposes it in the local newspaper. Should enough trees be felled, serious flooding would result. The young teacher is consequently targetted by an assassin hired by the lumberers and murdered. Unfortunately, this gangster film-like latter half regrettably clashes with the leisurely lyricism and humour of the first half.

The level of film in the Philippines is also high. There is one masterpiece, called *The Queen of Burlesque,* which deals with the lives of the dancers and performers in a strip-tease show, and in the process defines with an awesome and raw sense of reality the poverty of Manila. There is one particularly powerful scene in which a dancer falls in love with a young man, but loses him when his mother literally drags him home by the collar. The dancer, abandoned, drowns in her sad tears. Mothers in the Filipino family are said to be quite powerful.

The Filipino cinema is considered the most technically accomplished in Asia, perhaps because so many Filipino filmmakers have studied in the United States. What contributes to the uniqueness of Filipino film is the conspicuous influence of Spanish and American culture and, especially interesting, the native culture engendered by the collision of Western civilization with that of the indigenous Tagalogs. Compared with other cinemas around the world, one finds in Filipino film certain parallels with the Brazilian,

Cuban and Mexican traditions. In Filipino films to-date, only mixed-blood actors have risen to stardom, but there is a widespread feeling that within the next few years a full-blooded Tagalog will achieve fame. In Indonesia, a series of comedies entitled *Inam, the Sexy Maid* has been very popular. The status of a maid in Indonesia is rather humble, but in these slapstick films the maids usually seem to get the upper-hand over their upper-class employers. These films are both funny and substantial.

Film production in Asia continues to remain high, largely because television is not yet universal and movies are still the king of entertainment. Furthermore, national consciousness, still important in Asia, is articulated through its various cinemas and thus meets with enthusiasm from audiences. All these countries are beset with difficult, complex political problems, and in many of them open debate is difficult. It is within this context that Asian filmmakers exploit their abilities to continue to build vital and relevant cinemas.

Vigorous Revival of the Chinese Film Industry

To Chinese, the second spring of the '80s is the fifth spring after the terrible decade of chaos and cruel destruction. The so-called "cultural revolution" was a cultural blight, a dark decade in China's long and splendid cultural history. During those years, the world's biggest cinema audience was starved. The Chinese screen was a blank, a desolate desert. When the long winter was finally over, the great cultural desert began to bloom with life again. Among the bright flowers which the return of spring revived is the film industry.

The fifteen years between 1966 and 1980 can be divided into three stages: the bleak period during the ten years of turmoil; the period of restoration after the downfall of the Gang of Four in 1976 to 1978 when the third plenary session of the 11th Congress of the Communist Party of China was held; and the period of rapid development since.

The two years of restoration after the Gang of Four was ousted saw the Chinese cultural circles busily repairing the massive damage, the criminal activities the Lin-Jiang cliques had caused, repudiating their ultra-leftist line and rehabilitating the people those two cliques had defamed. As the deleterious influence of the Gang of Four could not be eliminated overnight, artistic creation was still severely handicapped by the remnant ultra-leftist line. Although the situation did show a degree of improvement, people were still more or less just recovering from the stultifying effects of ten years of ideological repression. The same phenomenon was observed in the film industry. There were few films which reflected important and acute contemporary issues, films which showed how the "cultural revolution" engendered widespread misery and social evils, films which described and criticized the Gang of Four. These were the sort of films which were wanted. Moreover, what films there were, were not of a very high standard technically and artistically. A few films taking their themes from recent revolutionary history, such as *We Are Eighth Armymen* and *Two Eighth Route Youngsters* drew large audiences by their portrayal of fine revolutionary traditions, particularly the close ties between the Party and the masses during those years of war. Some spy thrillers such as *Hunter 99* attracted a lot of attention, particularly from the young people who were probably seeing such films for the first time.

Then in the winter of 1978, the film industry began to develop again. This took place after the ideological and political line was established at the third plenary session of the 11th Congress of the Communist Party of China. In 1977 there were 14 feature and stage drama films produced. The number rose to 46 in 1978, 65 in 1979 and 82 in 1980. As mental shackles were discarded and the policy of "letting a hundred flowers blossom and a hundred schools contend" was implemented, realism came into its own again. Cramping, debilitating taboos were smashed one after another. Heartening changes took place. the range of subject matter was widened considerably and burning issues of contemporary life appeared on the screen. The films improved technically and artistically. Here are some salient points:

One. Veteran proletarian revolutionaries such as Chairman Mao, Premier Zhou Enlai, Marshals He Long and Chen Yi and others are portrayed for the first time and presented on the Chinese screen. This can be considered a landmark in the history of the Chinese cinema. *The films Dawn's Light, The Newspaper Boy* and *Death of the General* proved extremely successful. Their success lies in part in that veteran revolutionaries were not made out to be "immortal beings", but were depicted as flesh and blood men who, by their moral character attained a stature greater than most men.

Two. New approaches were made in describing war. The films *Xiao Hua (Little Flowers), Anxious to Return, Cradel of Love* and *Stars So Bright Tonight* all have one characteristic in common. Instead of building a story centred on the war or a particular battle, these used war or a battle as the backdrop against which the fate of the individual linked to the fate of a class and the nation is played out, expressed through the joys and the sorrows, the aspirations and the feelings of the characters caught up in the throes of war. The revolution unfolds on the screen sensitively and naturally through the depiction of compelling human emotions and through superb characterization. The films have powerful appeal and vivid artistic vitality. In these, people no longer and incidental to the story. They take centre stage and the story revolves around them. *In General Ji Hongchang* and *From Slave to General* it is through these men's lives, their actions and their thoughts and feelings that the audiences come to know of the battle and situation. Moreover, these two films successfully recreated on the screen two high-ranking generals, each with his own distinct personality and Chinese to the core. The films mentioned were very popular. They won citations at the Third "Hundred Flowers Competition" sponsored by the Chinese Film Workers" Association and awards from the Ministry of Culture for outstanding films and best works by young producers. (Awards were only for films produced in 1979. *Stars So Bright Tonight*, produced in 1980, did not enter the competition.)

Three. The films boldly unfold the social conflicts and struggles, exposing and denouncing the bad and the evil, and enthusiastically extol truth and virtue. Film-making was put directly to the service of social comment. This has become the dominant theme in Chinese film-making today One third of all films produced in 1979 and 1980 dwelt on the crimes and the victims of the Gang of Four, with the Cultural Revolution as the background. Representatives of this style of films were *Tear Stain, Troubled Laughter, Reverberations of Life, The Holy Mission, Where Silence Reigns, Loyal Overseas Chinese Family* and *So Near Yet So Far.* They were stark revelations of the horrors inflicted on society by the Gang of Four and conversely, were works which showed the heroic fight the people put up and which give voice to their feelings. A departure from this were *Night Rain in Bashan Mountain* and *Romance of Tianyun Mountain,* both produced in 1980. The first is a piercingly accurate depiction, in a rather light lyrical vein, of the national pride and revolutionary indignation smouldering deep in the breasts of the Chinese people during that long agonizing decade. The other, *Romance of Tian Yun Mountain* adroitly shows with fine artistry, the fate, the mind and the character of one man through the eyes of three women. The complex, interlocking relations among the characters are cleverly used to explore the causes of that deadly decade of chaos and intrigues which began in 1966.

The film makers, committed to the cause of the revolution and the people have turned their attention to simple human situations and tried to discover for the audience the elements contained within them. They have found everyday living exciting material for their art, the work, study, life and love of the younger generation in the new historical stage for example. In many of the new films, the focus is on the young people. They extol socialist ideals and praise the young people working for the realization of the Four Modernizations. At the same time they have not turned away from exposing, denouncing and satirizing the decadent and the ugly things in life. This can be found in the films *What a Family, Sweet Affair, The Youngsters, Twins Come in Pairs, The Second Handshake, Swallows Return, Not For Love, Romance on Lushan Mountain and Love* and *Inheritance.* Many of them have been commended for their wit and artistic presentation and their closeness to life.

People's democracy, laws and legality have also become subjects for the creative abilities of the scriptwriters. *The Tenth Bullet Hole* and *Inside* and *Outside the Court* are vivid illustrations of the principle that all men are equal before the law. The unrelenting, uncompromising pursuit of justice is the theme, one which found in audiences an immediate response.

Four. Veteran stars have found themselves sparkling now in a galaxy of younger stars. A look at the films produced in the last two years shows older actors and actresses, directors and scriptwriters doing a fine job. One can sense in them the drive to make up for those lost years. But they have keen competition from a rising younger generation. There are many new names on the 1980 awards list among the more familiar names. The above is only a brief personal view of the Chinese screen today. The Chinese film industry is making progress but everyone in the industry is well aware that the number and quality of the films so far produced are still far short of demand. But behind the films one can sense the driving urge to do much better, to create works to match the new era and to satisfy a social need.

Indian Cinema: A Huge Juggernaut on the Move

he Indian cinema is a vast juggernaut that was put together in a colonial setting but one that had already, in the 1920s, outproduced Great Britain and threatens, as we look towards the close of the twentieth century, to obliterate even more national boundaries that it has done so far in vast sections of the Middle East and the Far East.

This juggernaut moves on a unique inner momentum and fuel powered by a production ratio of almost two full length, feature films every day, produced in over a dozen different languages and seen by, at the very least, some eighty million people within the country every week. This polyglot home market is the linchpin of the entire edifice. Side by side, and radiating like spokes from this inner hub, are as many as 650 regular film magazines of all shapes and description and the world's largest short film producing organization, the Films Division. To go back, briefly, to its beginning, Indian audiences were introduced to a projected motion picture in the same year as British, Russian and American audiences were — in 1896, barely a few months after the historic unveiling of the *cinematographe* in the basement of the Grand Cafe in Paris by the brothers Lumiere. The flurry that this aroused in rival entrepreneurial circles spurred the brothers to send their agents to far corners of the world to both win friends as well as revenue and to influence peoplc in favour of their radical invention. The Bombay showing, initially scheduled for three days only, continued in spite of the monsoon for many more days and *The Times of India* of 27 July 1896 records "At the desire of a large number of Bombay residents who have flocked recently in spite of bad weather to see the Kinematograph, the patentee has obtained fresh lease of the Novelty Theatre for a few more nights". By the end of July, the shows, already advertised regularly in *The Times of India*, had acquired tow distinctive Indian characteristics. "Reserved Boxes for Purdah Ladies and their families" were announced, indicating the thrust towards capturing women and indeed the whole family as potential audiences. Also, for the first time, a broad scale of admission rates was introduced. From the initial one rupee blanket rate, prices now ranged as low as four cents and as high as two rupees. This wide price range was to remain a salient feature of film exhibition in India, important to its future growth and ability to attract ever new sections of the society.

Alone among the great film industries of the world to have been born and developed in a totally colonial setting, the Indian film industry never looked back after the production of the first Indian film, "Rajah Harishchandra", to have been completed in late 1912 by one Dadasaheb Phalke. A Brahmin with an unquenchable thirst for knowledge, Phalke was obsessed with painting, play acting and magic from his childhood, spent in the idyllic surroundings of Nasik, near Bombay. His introduction to cinema in the form of a Christmas show of *Life of Christ* around 1910 changed the course of his life — and subsequently of Indian cinema. After the showing, he came home, determined to make something similar on the life of Lord Krishna. He persuaded his wife to accompany him to the next showing. According to family tradition, the Phalkes had no cash in the house and money had to be borrowed from neighbours and relatives for transportation and cinema tickets. Meanwhile Phalke's determination grew and along with it the growingly desperate measures with which every iota of money was scraped together to obtain a passage to England, get both equipment and guidance and upon return, to make his film. A major problem that he faced — that of casting the heroine — reveals the decadent state of the arts in that period. Successive assaults by foreign invasions on the classical Indian performing arts had left Indian drama, dance and music so feeble that it had almost come to mean that there was no room in these erstwhile sacred precincts for any but the lowliest of the low, the prostitutes and the perverts, the sexually depraved and the social outcastes. Try as he might, Phalke could not persuade even a prostitute to act in his film. It was then that he turned to a cook with a slender form and hands that could pass muster for the legendary queen, Taramati. Both Phalke and A. Salunke, the cook turned actor-actress, became successful to such a wild extent with that first Indian film *Rajah Harishchandra* that Phalke went on to make more than a hundred other films in the following years and Salunke became the forerunner of today's mass-appeal, popular film start, both male and female rolled into one!

Phalke's experience was to be symbolic of the future growth of Indian cinema as a whole. The upper-crust social elite, well-versed in European etiquette and Western social mores, took little or no note of Phalke as they continued attending Western films at big metropolitan cinema palaces. Nor did the English language newspapers notice the new phenomenon on the social and cultural scene. As for Phalke, he neither advertised in them nor bothered about this long-to-continue indifference. He was reaching out to a different public, a faceless, nameless mass audience to whom his screen heroes and heroines were palpable, flesh and blood creatures and whose impact on them was electrifying. When "*Rama*" appeared on the screen in *Lanka Dahan* or when *Lord Krishna* finally made an appearance in *Krishna Janama*, men and women in the audience threw themselves before the screen in hysterical prostrations of devotion and frenzy.

Travelling by bullock cart, with projector, screen and film, Phalke set the tone for other producers who also became the exhibitors of their own wares. And to far and near, the fame of the new medium, the moving picture, spread. The people came out in hundreds, thousands and ultimately millions. They seldom paid more than four or even one and two cents for admission, sat on the ground and readily lapped up this new variation of their favourite operatic forms of dance and music. To date, the Indian film is unique in its extensive use of song and dance, a carry-over into another art form of a theatrical tradition that goes back to the hoary age of Sanskrit drama. It was not until 1953, more than twenty years after the introduction of sound on the Indian scene that the first film without singing and dancing was produced. Since then, while a parallel art cinema movement has grown and blossomed into quite a viable bloom, the mass cinema has shown a literally endless and unquenchable thirst for the musical genre that is peculiar to Indian cinema. Nor has the audience shown any sign of outgrowing its standard and well-worn love of a few rigidly formulaic themes. Beginning with the classic obsession of Indian artistic tradition with the fight of good against evil, and the ultimate victory, of course, of the former, a few variations are worked in. A perennial favourite is the archetypal villain, a smuggler or dacoit, a completely macho image, surrounded by sleek objects like a panther or a pretty girl against a gaudily decorated, highly ornate set, framed by henchmen with bald head and menacing looks, made up to look like American G.Is.

Simple, near-mimetic imagery, use of a language that is easily understood in far-flung parts of the country; excellent, very lavish and sophisticated camera work; special effects and stereophonic gimmicks go a long way to cover the banality of the themes and the near vacuity of intellectual content in the formula film. Though the modern hero is a far cry from the older, simpler village yokel style of a good man, the anti-hero has yet to emerge on the Indian screen. A few warts on his character apart, the script must always justify his deviations from the law however serious they may appear. And in any case they must be transitory and either death or the law must take its course in the end. Whenever the hero is an out-and-out criminal, as in the recent blockbusters, *Kalicharan* and *Don*, his double, the Mr. Nice Guy, is always around to surface at the correct cue. The expedient of the double role not only means gold at the box-office but it also gets around, in a very simple manner, the problem of showing the public's favourite hero with a multiplicity of action-oriented, yet good-to-the-core facets. Of late, a new genre, the dacoit drama, has become phenomenally popular. The trend was triggered off by the runaway success of *Sholay* (over 140 weeks at the biggest cinema in Bombay) in which a special team of British stuntsmen worked to create the fast-paced, thrilling spectacle of train-top chases and blood-curdling fights between the bad guys and the good guys. Part Robin Hood, part Rama, the ideal of all Hindus, the hero of a typical Indian film is the champion of the weak and the defenceless, preserver of family loyalty and honour, especially of his parents, and going further up the scale, of his mother, and always a true patriot, motivated by the most self-sacrificing, if obviously shallow, patriotism. Women are further straitjacketed. It is only in the last four or five years that a heroine has been shown as a real flesh and blood creature who may love a man other than her wedded husband or who has been raped and not forthwith rejected from the home. But cliches abound all too often and it is only in the parallel cinema, the cinema of regions and production centres other than Bombay and Madras, that socially relevant films are being made. Both the central government at New Delhi and the government of states like Karnataka and Kerala, West Bengal and Maharashtra, indeed even hitherto somnolent areas like Assam and Orissa, are aiding the art film movement with special subsidies and grants. This aid comes not a minute too soon nor can it ever suffice to break the stranglehold of the economic compulsions that characterise the mass film. With an overall capital investment of Rs. 721.5 crore and a total employment figure of over 2 million, Indian cinema represents the country's most indisciplined capital intensive industry. It does not receive finance from any respectable financing institution and with break-even ratio of only 25%, it is India's most conspicuous laissez-faire, tenacious and successfully operating blackmarket set-up. The era of super-hits has already given way to super-super-hits and a handful of actors have reached the commanding heights of drawing six and seven figure payments. The vicious financial circle is further complicated by the fact that Indian cinema has the highest tax levy in the world. Some 40 to 50% of all income earned at the box-office goes to the federal government and a tax levy can some-times be as high as 120%.

Some, though by no means as high an amount as ought to be ploughed back, is put into the financing of institutions and bodies which have aided the growth of quality cinema. One of these is the Film and Television Institute of India, set up in 1961, and recognized as one of the best equipped film schools in the world. Another is the Film Finance Corporation which has this year been amalgamated into the newly established National Film Development Corporation and which pioneered the financing of off-beat, experimental films from new and yet untried directors like Saeed Mirza's *Arvind Desai Ki Ajeeb Dastaan* or Muzaffar Ali and his *Gaman*. In the last two years alone, over 50 films thus aided by government, figured in the honours list at various top international festivals such as in Berlin, Cannes, Montreal, Chicago, Karlovy Vary, Mannheim and Moscow. This has been the logical culmination of the trend of world interest in Indian cinema beginning in the fifties with the interest aroused by Satyajit Ray's world famous trilogy, *Pather Panchali, Aparjito* and *The World of Apu*. Since then many serious, highly talented and successful film makers like Mrinal Sen, Shyam Benegal and Girish Karnad have carried forward the work of mirroring social reality truthfully and artistically. From the South have come deeply committed and sensitive film makers like G. Aravindan, Girish Kasaravalli, T.S. Ranga and T.S. Nagabharana. From Bengal we have a whole new crop of young film makers like Goutam Ghose and Buddhaded Dasgupta. The absence of women film directors is sorely noticed among these talented ranks and it is very much hoped that the debut of someone like Sai Paranjpe (whose first film *Sparsh* won a number of awards last year) will be the forerunner of many more women entrants to the ranks of the "other" cinema. There is little doubt that their problems will be a multiplication of those already existing for the male film makers of the new school. They function under extremely difficult conditions. Lack of adequate finances, of course, is the basic problem. The realistic, low-budget film, whether in Hindi or in any of the regional languages, shows both a devotion to technique and film craft as well as a steadfastness in ideas and convictions. In comparison, the commercial cinema, with the at times embarrassing abundance of its resources, has extreme poverty of ideas. It continues to sell dreams, refusing even side-long contact, let alone head-on collision, with social problems and urgent individual predicaments. When the problems are raised, their solution is offered through the medium of fantasy. But to be fair to the impact of commercial cinema, it has constituted independent India's most wide-ranging integrating factor. However formulaic its brand of songs and dances, they have an unquestioned hold over millions of multilingual spectators and this is reflected even in radio and television. The radio's main lifeline, the commercial channel, subsists only on film songs. As for television, its most steady and eager audience is for the two week-end commercial films telecast throughout the country.

What is the scenario for the future? For the eighth consecutive year, more films were made in India than anywhere else in the world. More than half of the 700 films made in 1979 were produced in South India where Government subsidies, tax exemptions and a compounding scale of entertainment tax, encourage production.

Britain and Dubai continue to be the largest export markets for Indian films, followed by Singapore. Last year's export earnings in these areas were the highest ever. Hongkong and Thailand are seen to be slowly declining while the exports are picking up in Indonesia and Malaysia.

The most pertinent cinematic forecast made by futurologists is that, come the year 2000, the possibility of an Indian superstar heading the national government is not a surrealistic nightmare! The victory of Ronald Reagan in the United States and the ascendancy of the superstar of Tamil films, M.G. Ramachandran, to the post of Chief Minister of the large and populous state of Tamil Nadu are signs of how the medium and the message are becoming one.

The Exciting and Excited State of Philippine Movies

Our title needs an explanation — especially to people who are conversant with the current crop of Filipino movies. "What excitement?" the typical Filipino moviegoer with fairly educated tastes would ask. The question is rhetorical — The man knows that there's almost everything to deplore concerning the general quality of Philippine movies today. The word that easily comes to everybody's tongue is trash, and it doesn't take much cinema savvy for one to be able to say it. Local film critics, backed up more by a literary sensibility than by a truly filmic one, do not tire castigating Filipino movies for being artistically inferior. These film critics may not seriously qualify for their role, but they certainly arouse the enmity of no one when they express their dissatisfaction, except of course the movie-makers themselves.

With, of course, some exceptions Filipino movies are too blatantly crude in their approach to the art of film-making. One has only to ask a very basic demand "Is the movie entertaining?" to hit the nail right on the head. For if there is one failure that should be disturbing to the Filipino producer's peace of mind it is that he cannot seem to come up with a movie that is really memorable as a piece of entertainment, that stays long in the minds of the movie-goers who are always out not for art but for entertainment such as say a Bruce Lee film does. Why so? The answer is simple, so simple that a sensitive observer senses something painfully ironic in it all: the reason why Philippine movies are not so hot even when it comes to sheer entertainment which presumably is the commercial movie-maker's only aim is that there is little art, or to use a term less highbrow, little craft, behind them. It is ironic how Filipino movie-makers — particularly the producers — take the artistic motive to mean bad results in the box-office, and therefore take the idea of art and the idea of entertainment as necessarily clashing opposites. This is an argument that has evidently convinced even the more artistically ambitious among Filipino film-makers so that compromise has become their tacit modus and policy. The Filipino film craftsman will make films that are commercial in intent and in the process cater to the supposedly inferior tastes of the mass consumers, sacrificing his artistic conscience because, presumably, it cannot be helped. The commercial nature of the work justifies what he is doing. As for his more serious artistic ambitions, he, after a string of such commercial compromises, can perhaps be allowed the luxury of making an artistic movie, a "pang-Cannes" movie, meaning a film not bothered by the box-office bugbear but freely aimed at the heart of his Muse, at international recognition, at the Cannes. The rift between these two interests — the artistic consciousness and the film producer's business consideration — may not have been there in the beginning. "Since its beginnings in the 1920's" says a U.P. professor in a paper prepared for the Third World Studies Program, "it has been the obsession, especially among film artists, to produce movies that are not only artistic and significant but more importantly, commercially successful." The professor quickly observes that as it turned out in the history of Philippine film-making the two goals wouldn't mix. This history bears witness to the sad parting of ways between film art and film entertainment. The paper continues, "In the late forties and early fifties, the so-called art films like *Biyaya ng Lupa* (Blessings of the Earth), *Badjao, Anak Dalita* (Child of Woe) and other classics were isolated individual achievements that could not even create a trend." The study does not tell us what specific films in those days were commercial hits. But it does when it comes to the films of the sixties, recalling a decade when a new Filipino film genre was born — the bold or *bomba* film in which nudity and actual sex was cinematographed for the benefit of a public that was discovered to be amazingly prurient and responsive. It can safely be said that with the possible exception of the years when Filipinos were seeing movies for the very first time there was never a time when they flocked to the theatre with such hungry and eager expectation. Filipino producers pounced on this porno phenomenon with unabashed opportunism. Possibly, they too shared the excitement, apart from the excitement of sure money. Never was the word trash so right. The proliferation of *bomba* films killed the artistic conscience in such a total fashion. But the bomba phenomenon could have had happier circumstances besides the exploitative vigour of Filipino film-makers. Read more perceptively it need not be an argument for the belief that trash makes money and art doesn't. In fact the Japanese erotic masterpiece *Empire of the Senses* is an overpowering proof that films with a heavily explicit sexual content need not be trash, that *bomba* and art are not necessarily enemies. By implications, to regard artistic effort and popular entertainment as irreconcilables is perhaps erroneous. For there is one thing that makes the cinema an enviable art form, which today makes the Filipino literary artist and the musician and the painter jealous, it is its capacity to fulfil both artistic expression and popular entertainment. That *The Godfather* is both commercially and artistically a triumph surely must inspire, if not haunt, the Filipino film-maker. What must hit him between the eyes is the fact that *The Godfather* is successful commercially largely because it is a well crafted work. When we search for a local counterpart to *The Godfather*, that is, a Filipino film that was successful on both levels, is Lino Brocka's *Tinimbang Ka Ngunit Kulang* (You Were Weighed But Found Wanting) back in 1975. The film represented a breakthrough by a new wave of Filipino film-makers that had its seeds in the late sixties. In the late sixties PETA, a theatre group, was organized. It produced worthy theatre efforts which were noteworthy for their use of both local literary material and foreign masterpieces translated into the Filipino language. PETA proved, among other things, that Filipino directors *can* direct and Filipino actors *can* act. The PETA people however were soon to realize that the cinema offered possibilities of artistic fulfilment not accessible to the theater. For instance, a wider audience, Moviedom was very short of talent; PETA felt it could provide it. It was a question of migration. Brocka was the PETA talent who was able to leap the hurdle. "No other movie has been appreciated and favourably received by academe, critics, professionals, the industry, and the public at large. *Tinimbang* appealed to all sectors of society and indicates that there is a local audience for "quality films."

Brocka however couldn't quite duplicate the same amount of success in his latter works, a curve which tends to enforce the opinion that art and the box-office in the country rarely meet. His beauteous works like *Insiang* (1976) tend to bring back the tradition of Filipino film classics like *Badjao, Biyaya Ng Lupa*, etc., loved by refined art circles but not ravenously received by the moviegoers. Those who loved *Tinimbang...* and who continue to expect a lot from Brocka look on helplessly as they watch the box-office still dominated by artistically inferior movies.

To recoil in disgust from the latter is understandable. The disgust has become capitulation in Gerry de Leon, a master Filipino film-maker of an earlier generation. De Leon is best remembered for his filming of Jose Rizal's novels — *Noli Me Tangere* and *El Filibusterismo*. Inactive for about two decades now, the master, in a recent interview, expresses a radical despair with the present system in the Filipino film industry, — pointing out that it is at the mercy of production costs and thereby defeated from the beginning. Regretting that he and his colleagues have yet to come up with a film like *Rashomon* which spearheaded Japan's entry into the international movie market, De Leon says "We may not be able to do so unless the government steps in". He therefore speaks out for total government subsidy of the movie industry.

De Leon's stand ties up very well with the inside story of Lino Brocka's *Jaguar*, the Philippine entry to the last film festival at Cannes. Hailed as his most exciting film since *Tinimbang...*, *Jaguar* was, without exaggeration, a heartbreaking labour of love. The movie and no producer. Brocka whipped up whatever amount of money he could and counted on the support of fellow artists who were willing to work with him for lesser fees than they usually got. The star himself, Philip Salvador, did it for free. The film was a gamble — it took chances on the makers getting a percentage of the profits. How the movie fared in the market is a story that again speaks sadly of the seeming distance between the Filipino film artist and the Filipino movie audiences: *Jaguar* couldn't break even in the local market, but it made profits abroad.

There are not too many local film directors with Brocka's courage, although there are others equally talented — Celso Ad. Castillo, Ishmael Bernal, and most recently Marilou Diaz-Abaya among them. All are young, and — with the exception of Diaz-Abaya who is the latest to emerge — now sufficiently familiar with the harsh pains of local movie-making. They constitute the consciousness that the country is not short of creative talent in all aspects of film-making. They may yet bring about a wave of cultural renaissance. But aren't they rather the exception? One asks. Well, yes and no. These people may not be to rule but *they are the trend.* They are to future. One must make up to it: the Filipino cinema is getting to be exciting. Brocka and his colleagues are an inspired lot. But they have to face up to the two main problems that beset the Filipino film artist today: financial support and a stubbornly unresponsive audience. We have said that it is Brocka's courage that singles him out as the leading Filipino film-maker of today, apart from sheer talent. But perhaps there is a better word: ambition. Brocka is without doubt the most ferociously ambitious film-maker in the Philippines today. It is a paradox that he is doing not quite to expectation with the local audience. His films are marred by a very pronounced preoccupation with the downtrodden, with victims of social injustice. This film artist's heart seems to belong to the slums — to some weirdly spawned village at the foot of a mountain of garbage — to quote from *Jaguar.* His success with foreign audiences adds to the paradox.

The shape of things to come with regards to how the exciting new generation of Filipino film-makers will be able to entrench themselves in the box-office is a matter of conjecture. In the meantime, the producers have their own nasty experience of the box-office problem. The most recent one is that of competition from imported films, mostly Hollywood and Hong Kong martial arts movies. These imported films have become such a threat in the local market that Filipino producers in 1977 pushed for a legislation to control the importation of films. To date, nothing has come out of it, although occasionally the press calls the attention of the public to the problem. Another difficulty shared by producer and film creator alike is the government-backed censorship that has ruled the industry since the seventies — perhaps a reaction to the porno films of the late sixties. The grounds for censorship are sex, violence, and political controversy. As so often happens, creative expression can feel itself trammeled. The well-meant idea of censorship, of protecting public morals, can be a barrier between artist and audience — can be, as a matter of fact, destructive. A case in point, is Ishmael Bernal's *Manila By Night.* The film's realistic dialogue, which happens to be one of its powerful qualities, prompted the censors to take up arms full-scale. The result is a severely bowdlerized version, *City after Dark*, which nonetheless is impressive enough to elicit enthusiastic responses from the critics. Bernal is a very sensitive film director — more purely aesthetic in his approach than Brocka in that we do not perceive in his works the same tone of social protest that characterizes the letter's films.

Because the Filipino film producer has narrowed down his box-office strategy to invariably opting for what is proven to sell, he has held on tenaciously to the starsystem. The big stars are Fernando Poe Jr., Dolphy, and Ramon Revilla. These stars are so big that they produce their own films.

Fernando Poe Jr. and Ramon Revilla are action stars. Both portray a heroic image on screen which the movie-goers have come to love. Poe's hero is one who wins in the end because his heart is noble and his fists and gun are faster. Revilla on the other hand is less realistic in his approach and more folklorish — his heroes are supernaturally powerful, aided by their amulets — something which the native psyche does not find difficult to accommodate. Both the Poe hero and the Revilla hero are really carrying on a tradition which dates back to the years immediately following the Second World War. The classic movie in this regard in *Misteryoso* (Mysterious) which was a serialized comic strip made into a movie. The story tells of a guerrilla fighter who defeats the Japanese army in every encounter because he possesses mysterious powers such as invisibility at will and a warning star that shines on his forehead whenever danger approaches. The Filipinos fresh from the experience of being a captive people naturally responded to this tale with irrational sympathy. The star of this film, Armando Goyena, was not strictly an action star for he played other types. The role of action star went to Efren Reyes Jr. who gained a faithful following by local cinema-goers for over two decades. Film criticism that would criticize a Fernando Poe or Ramon Revilla movie for lack of realism, for fantasy, for escapism, for being untrue to life is perhaps wide of the mark because it fails to take into account the sociology behind their popularity, to take stock of the national psyche. As we pointed out earlier film criticism in the country has, itself, much to learn. So much the better. It is all part of the general excitement of film-making in the country today — an excitement that see-saws between the virginal mentality of Filipino movie-goers and the sophistication of foreign film masterpieces shown, usually free, by the cultural arms of foreign embassies whose countries are generously sharing their hoard of film classics and masterpieces, the Thomas Jefferson Cultural Centre, the British Council, the Goethe Institute, and the Alliance Francaise.

Japanese Film Today

The Japanese film industry entered the decade of the seventies with the bankruptcy of the Daiei studios. Daiei had been one of the major film companies in Japan, the company that gave us such films as Akira Kurosawa's *Rashomon* and *Kenji Mizoguchi's Ugetsu Monogatari.* Known throughout the world, Daiei was the most successful of all the Japanese studios in the 1950s. Thus its sudden demise was greeted by the Japanese film world not with any glee over the failure of a competitor, but rather with shock that if Daiei could go under today, anyone might be next tomorrow. The history of the Japanese film industry in the seventies commenced with the "Daiei fiasco" and continued to beat one retreat after another.

The major motion picture companies have from the very first maintained their own monopolistic control of production, distribution and exhibition. The effect of this "block booking system" was to continually distort competitive market forces, and in the nineteen-sixties, with the growth of television and the diversification of leisure-time industries in Japan a basic structural defect was revealed in the film industry, a defect which finally impoverished Daiei. Studios were far too slow to expand beyond production proper into direct marketing of their films to the audiences, and then when confronted in the 1960s with a dramatically diminishing film-going population, all the majors — not only Daiei, but Shochiku, Toho and Toei, too — were compelled to slash the scale of their operations by firing personnel and abandoning their plans for both diversification and production. The past ten years of Japanese film is fairly typified by the failure of the industry to rise to the challenge of a film audience a mere one-tenth of what it once had been. The oldest film company in the country, Nikkatsu, now has the former head of a communist labour union for its president and just barely manages to make money producing and distributing pornography.

Although it is true that Japanese film has forsaken large-scale productions for ever — fewer and cheaper ones, it is not true that this has helped the industry. The floodgates in Japan have been opened wide to foreign films, principally American. The major American studios have all opened offices in Japan that handle distribution, and the Japanese themselves compete all over the world to buy the rights to prominent films. Japanese movies are doomed to vie with foreign ones as well as each other: in the nineteen-seventies, American blockbusters such as *Jaws, Star Wars* and *Close Encounters of the Third Kind* swelled the number of theatres exhibiting American films, and their box-office receipts outdistanced any Japanese product. Shochiku and Toho were the companies that provided their theatres for these, and other, American films, and it was only through their cut of the profits that they have remained financially solvent. Yet, the short-term gain foretells a long-term loss: the Japanese film industry continues to lose its creative vigour.

The aforementioned monopoly of production, distribution and exhibition by the established Japanese studios has meant that independent productions have not, as they have abroad, met with great success. Consequently any move on the part of the majors to decrease either personnel or production has resulted not in increased activity by independents but instead an absolute reduction in the size of the industry. The paralysis of the studios has conspicuously stagnated the vitality of existing personnel and stymied the development of future actors, writers, directors and technicians. At the same time, management has grown more conservative and wary of financing any film that might involve a risk. For example Toho, with the strongest exhibition network in the two largest cities of Tokyo and Osaka, has stopped all production and now only exhibits other studios' films, and yet thereby managed in 1980 to gross over fifty million dollars, the healthiest balance sheet in the industry. No doubt Shochiku and Toei will soon follow suit.

The seventies were, for Japanese film, a time for a basic re-orientation of the industry towards entertainment and away from serious cinema. To that end, there has been a degree of experimentation. Capital from a number of sources flowed in which both helped, and altered, the industry. All sorts of enterprises, such as publishing houses, television networks, advertising agencies, department stores, foreign film distributors and even quite small businesses, either wholly financed or co-produced films in the 1970s. Initially, some degree of success was assured by novelty and by the considerable sums these firms spent on publicity. Most famous of these newcomers is Kadokawa Films, a spin-off Kadokawa Books, which has profited by making movies out of what they publish and effectively tying together the advertising campaigns of both products. Such Kadokawa films as *Inugamike no Ichizoku (The Inugamis)* and *Ningen no Shomei (Proof of the Man)* have substantially increased their revenues. However, in 1980 Kadokawa made a film entitled *Virus* with the intent to market it widely abroad, and so used a good many American stars and staff and filmed on locations as far away as the Arctic Circle. The scale of the production was spectacular, but so was its failure. Should any film made by an independent concern be successful in the small Japanese market, its profit will still be slight, and should it fail, the losses are immense. Filmmaking in Japan today is a dangerous gamble. Basic flaws in the industry that have resulted in far less production served to demoralize and humiliate Japanese film in the seventies. Yet there is also danger inherent in the increased reliance of the industry on simple exhibition, because it is clear that audiences will not pay money to see just anything. Even supposing theatres were to show nothing but European and American films, there is a limit to them, and Japanese wish to see only what is most current. Moreover, film today is no longer the property of solely theatres. Television makes available daily both domestic and foreign films, and eight-and sixteen-milimeter as well as videotape versions of films for home consumption continue to proliferate. Japan in the 1980s will no doubt see the advent of pay television. The consumer, treated to an ever-increasing variety of products to choose from, will necessarily grow more discriminating. One can already see that films in the theatres have begun to respond to more selective tastes. The Japanese economy may be presently in a slump, but compared to other Asian nations and even to the industrialized nations of the West, Japan is by any standard affluent and film can certainly survive, but we are faced by two choices. Either the industry can make block-busters of such scale television will be unable to broadcast them, or it can make individualistic films that cater to specialized interests. Kurosawa's 1980 film *Kagemusha (The Shadow Warrior)* is an example of the first alternative. *Kagemusha* is certainly not Kurosawa's best work, and its popularity rests in no small part on his past reputation, but it nonetheless possesses demonstrative value as a "theatre movie", a movie whose sweeping story and cinematic beauty — reminiscent of a Japanese picture-scroll — would be compromised on a small television screen. The box-office hit of 1979 was *Ginga Testudo 999* (*Galaly Train 999*), an animation film that delighted young audiences with its fantastic world of science fiction. The success of this film in both Japan and Southeast Asia points to the popularity this sort of film can command.

Films made to satisfy individual tastes have only appeared intermittently, but with growing frequency. For example, Mitsuo Yanagimachi's 1979 *Jukyusai no Chizu (The Nineteen-Year-old's Plan)* and Yoichi Higashi's 1979 *Mo Hozue wa tsukanai (No More Easygoing)* are two films made by directors who were not trained in the major studios. Both take up the topic of young people trying to survive being young, a feat the heroes accomplish by falling in love with their heroines. *Jukyusai no Chizue* was well-received by audiences abroad, as well. There are a great many young people in Japan today making their own eight-and sixteen-milimeter films. The proliferation of this equipment in Japan is probably the most rapid in the world. These aspiring filmmakers, following in the footsteps of Americans like Stephen Spielberg and George Lucas, must be given a welcome. In the university first-year film students are given eight-milimeter cameras and told to work together on joint projects; second-and third-year students work individually on their own films; and finally, for thesis films the students are required to write and then film (or videotape) their projects on their own, though assisted by professionals such as scenario writer Yoshitaka Yoda, cameraman Kazuo Miyagawa and others. It is now in the university film programmes, and not in the major studios, where new talent is being nurtured.

Among the films that appeared in 1980, Kazuki Omori's *Hipokuratesutach (The Hippocrates Gang)* and Sogo Ishii's *Kuruizaki Sanda Rodo (Crazy Thunder Road)* are works by directors still in their twenties who shunned toys to play with cameras in high school and then college. *Hipokuratesutachi* is a film in the tradition of American *Graffitti* that portrays with wit the lives of medical students in Japan, but also explores the darker, hidden sides to their characters. The film is quite appealing in its madcap look at a medical school.

Kuruizaki Sanda Rodo is the story of some youths who are travelling on their motorcycles across the scorched earth of some unidentified country. The plot concerns a self-destructive protagonist who commits himself against a gang of violent and right-wing young men. Both films were very low-budget, but they have breathed fresh life into Japanese cinema. The outlook for Japanese film in the 1980s cannot be called rosy; but neither can it be called moribund.

Part 9

The Ramayana in Asia

The final and fierce battle between Ravana and Rama (Paithan painting in the Raja Kalkar Museum, India).

The Ramayana in Asia

The Epic of Epics

There are moments in history when to a single individual a universal' light is revealed. The experience of the individual transcends his subjectivity and becomes perennial, illuminating and immortal. Valmiki, the author of the epic Ramayana, was one such individual to whom this revelation of experience came at a moment of violence done to a pair of birds at the most sacred moment of mating. The story of the *kronch vadha* inspired compassion (*karuna*) in the being of the poet, and from it emerged the grand narrative of a life of God on earth. Created out of the experience of compassion, it developed into a mighty spectacle of life in its dimensions of private love and public duty, action and renunciation, the joy and the glory of power and the fortitude of banishment.

This epic, more than any other single literary creation, has permeated every nook and corner of the land of its creation and travelled into other lands far and near, for the kernel of the story is capable of retaining a universality and yet adapting and modifying itself to local traditions, circumstances and genius. Little wonder that for over 2000 years the Rama theme has fascinated, and inspired poets, writers, sculptors, painters, musicians, dancers, puppeteers, and ballad singers over a vast geographical area extending from Mongolia, Central Asia, and Turkey to China, Japan, Indonesia, Malaysia, Sri Lanka, and of course, Nepal, Thailand, Burma, Laos, and Cambodia. Countless versions of the Ramayana are known in nearly 40 languages of the world dating from the second to the nineteenth century. Contemporary versions of the theme continue to find a place in modern literatures and dramatic performance. Although it is impossible to guess the number of versions which are known, ranging from the *Buddhist Rama Jataka* to *Janaki haran*, a rough reckoning tells us that there must be over 500 versions of this epic in India and elsewhere in Asian and other countries.

The influence of this epic on the plastic and performing arts is equally extensive. From the earliest panels of Deogarh in India dateable to AD fourth or fifth century, there is a sustained interest in this theme over the centuries. Today large panels of beautiful wood carving continue to be created in Bali and Java. Scrolls are painted in Thailand, and innumerable murals are executed in different parts of India. Great panels of the Ramayana story are seen in the Indonesian temple complexes of *Prambanan* and *Penataran*. The Hazar Rama temple in Hampi (Karnataka state, India) presents a panoramic view through reliefs, and the great bronzes of the Chola period present Rama, Laxmana, and Sita.

Through the performing arts the Ramayana has left a deep impact on the people of India, Nepal, Thailand, Burma, Cambodia, Indonesia, and Malaysia. The theatre revolving around the Ramayana has a plurality and a multi-dimensional character which is bewilderingly diverse, complex, and fascinating. Performances range from the humblest village show where the Ramayana is chanted by a single ballad singer to the most sophisticated stylized theatre as seen in the traditions of Thailand, Cambodia and Indonesia. There is then also a whole range of puppet theatre built around the Rayamana: string puppet Ramayana shows in Burma, the glove puppets of Malaysia, the Wayang Kulit and Wayang Golek of Indonesia, the shadow puppet called Ravana Chhaya in Orissa, Thola-pavakoothu of Kerala in India and more. Mask theatre forms are equally popular.

This brief account only points at the phenomenal spread and impact of an inspiring story which repeatedly has displayed its contemporary significance.

Professor Matsunami Yoshihiro outlines the significance and appeal of the Ramayana in a very concise manner. His brief outline points at the fundamental significance of the story and its varied interpretations of meaning. He draws attention to the fact that the Ramayana theme can be related to the theme of fertility of earth and natural phenomena. There is great meaning in this. No matter where the story travels and what becomes of other characters, the role of Sita and the birth of Sita never undergo any change. Sita is Mother Earth the principle of fertility and creation and this is a universal concern at all times. Pertinently, Prof. Matsunami also draws our attention to the juxta-position of order and disorder, and back to order. The peaceful life of Rama's father Dasharatha is disrupted through the emergence of selfish desire, disorder is the immediate consequence until the battle with Ravana is fought and Rama returns; there is a clash, as the forces of chaos, of desire, power, greed and those of harmony, renunciation, and order interact.

Alongside is the theme of duty, duty in action despite personal suffering and turmoil. Altogether the Rama theme holds significance in the contemporary world because it brings to the fore the constant play of the forces of life and death, of order and disorder, of fertility and abundance, of union and separation, and of the constant need to suffer privation in order to be chastened and purified.

Sita appears again and again, at all times as primaeval energy which must be put through the test of fire. So does Ravana, for he represents power without wisdom and in each time and age new meaning and validity is given to this character, a symbol of human ambition. Rama is duty incarnate.

Professor Mattani Mojdara Rutnin presents a very beautiful picture of the living cult and tradition of the Ramakien in Thailand. She tells us how Rama was the ideal for all kingship in Thailand and the long tradition of all kings assuming the title "Rama" in Thailand. The relationship of temporal power and spiritual power is brought out beautifully. It also shows that a myth becomes a reality in the life of both royalty and the people as the conduct of the citizenry is also governed by the inspiration of the myth.

The great panels of the Rama theme in Wat Phra Kheo (Emerald Buddha Temple) and in modern Thai painting is outlined. All this is living proof of the efficacy of the Ramayana story.

Bali is a home of Ramayana, as is also Java. Although the Kawi Ramayana is closest to the Bhatti Kavya, many versions of the Ramayana are known in Java and Bali. Each area of Indonesia has its own version, and these versions have studied at some length by scholars.

Dr. Bandem gives an account of these versions and the scholars who have worked on the role of the Ramayana in Indonesia. They signify the vital role of the Ramayana in domestic ceremonies of Bali, including wedding, cremation, and right of passage ceremonies. One has only to experience the performance in Bali to be convinced on the deep impact of the story on the life and people of Bali and their most beautiful, sophisticated and sensitive arts. Innumerable forms of presenting the Ramayana are known. Dr. Bandem's narration gives a brief account of these as also the diverse versions. Most important is the role of Hanuman in the Southeast Asian versions. Unlike the character of Sita, this character undergoes many, many changes when it travels outside India. The Balinese Hanuman is dynamic and dutiful, and yet unlike his Thai counterpart, he continues to be a celibate. Faithfulness is known to Hanuman in all versions. Shri Tulasi Diwasa Joshi and Abhi Subedi describes the role of the Ramayana in Nepal. Nepal has been a great repository of the traditions of the Ramayana and other epics. Localization of themes of place has taken place in a manner which makes it impossible to dissociate Rama and ancient Nepali history. They once again prove the great popularity of the Ramayana in the written and oral traditions.

Finally, Professor Shankara Pillai provides a window to the plurality of traditions involving the Ramayana in India. He tells us of the situation in Kerala (southern India) where the Ramayana is painted as murals and dances are performed in many styles. Elsewhere in India, there likewise large numbers of variations in form.

Where does the secret of the continuity of Rama theme lie? It would appear that even when the theme seemed to run into dry sand, it never died, for the oral tradition sustained it. Also, the role traditions supported, supplemented, and complemented the traditions of the written word and of brick mortar, clay stone, colour and paint. It was also responsible for facilitating processes of assimilation without 'electric shock' experiences and providing the basis of integrated amalgamation. The world view, the affirmation of the life/death continuum, and the adherence to a concept of cyclic time through a method of transmission has led to artistic creations on the Ramayana in every century including the twentieth which have many dimensions. A single spectacle has elements in it which can be traced back not to one moment of historical time, but to several; it has other elements which echo cultures of distant lands; and yet the creation is new and contemporary with a distinct identity and personality. It is not an artificial resurrection of a dead language, a piece of antiquity, but a living reality of the present.

And yet more vistas and avenues of exploration await the interest of creative minds and artists. Kamban the Tamil poet begins his Ramayana by the words: "As a cat standing on the shores of the ocean of milk thinks it can lick up the whole ocean, I hope to retell the Ramayana story already told by Valmiki". From Kamban to Gandhi in India, from the Rulers of Campa to Maha Eisey in Khmer and from the rulers of Srivijaya to Dhani Nivat, creative minds in Asia have been drawn to this epic of all epics.

Significance and Appeal of the Ramayana

The Sanskrit language has from ancient times been in use in India. This language is much like classical Greek and Latin and, furthermore, is closely related to modern European languages. There are in use even today two epics written in Sanskrit — the Mahabharata and the Ramayana. The former is thought to be a historical account of the internal discord and resulting war within the tribe of Bharata, while the Ramayana is the tale of Prince

Rama's adventures in pursuit of the demon king Ravana to retrieve his abducted wife Sita. Whereas the Mahabharata is not attributed to a specific writer, the more fantastic and imaginative Ramayana, displaying a more technically polished literary style and known as the origin of later elegant court poetry and prose, is credited to the author Valmiki. Both of these two epics have influenced the cultures of India and southeast Asian countries, but the Ramayana has been particularly influential outside of India, not only in southeast Asia but also beyond into central Asia, China, and Japan. This topic of influence will be taken up again later.

The Ramayana is made up of seven chapters. The work as read today was not written all at the same in history, as it contains progressively added portions; however, the main and oldest portion of the epic is believed to have been written sometime between 500 BC and 300 BC

The story of the Ramayana cannot be related in detail here, but the main points of the epic stated very simply would seem to be as follows:

In Ayodhya, the capital city of the country of Kosala, there was a king named Dasharatha whose three queens bore him four princes, of whom Rama was the eldest. Rama, following a contest, received as his wife Sita, daughter of Janaka, king of the country of Mithila. (the above from *Bala-kanda*, or "Childhood chapter").

King Dasharatha had decided upon Rama to succeed him, but Kaikeyi, one of his queens, persuaded him that her son Bharata should inherit the throne and Rama should be banished to the forest for fourteen years, so Rama took Sita and, accompanied by his younger brother Lakshmana, they entered the forest and lived as wanderers. Soon after, King Dasharatha died, whereupon Bharata sought out Rama and implored him to return to Ayodhya to reign. Bharata managed only, however, to return alone with Rama's sandals to place by the throne as he reigned in Rama's place. (from *Ayodhya-kanda*)

In the forest, Rama met hermits and came upon numerous demons with whom he battled. Then Shoorpanakha, sister of the demon king Ravana, appeared in the form of beautiful maiden to entice Rama, only to be rebuffed by him and then disfigured by Lakshmana's sword as she attacked Sita. Next, Ravana, desiring Sita for himself persuaded his wily uncle Maricha to assume the form of a golden deer to attract Sita. Ravana himself then appeared, abducted Sita, and killed Jatayu, king of the eagles, who tried to protect Sita. Shortly thereafter, Rama met the demon Kabandha, who prophesies that Rama will meet Sugriva, king of the monkeys. Rama then heard a voice from heaven in the forest, instructing him as to how to retrieve Sita. (from *Aranya-Kanda*, or "forest chapter")

Ravana carried Sita across to the island of Lanka, his domain, while Rama and Lakshmana travelled south in search of Sita, coming to the land of the monkeys and meeting their king, Sugriva, who had lost his kingdom and wife to his elder brother Vali. After Rama helped Sugriva vanquish Vali and regain wife and throne, Sugriva ordered Hanuman, his general, to help in search for Sita. As Hanuman and his monkey soldiers proceeded to search, Sampati, brother of the slain eagle king Jatayu, appeared and informed them that Ravaṇa had taken Sita to Lanka. The host of monkey travelled south to the crossing point for Lanka, where Hanuman prepared to leap across the wide channel from the mountain of Mahendra. (from *Kiskindha-kanda*)

Leaping from Mahendra and flying for four days through the air to the island of Lanka, Hanuman searched discreetly for Sita. Entering Ravana's palace, he discovered a distressed, pale Sita seated under an Ashoka tree in Ravana's pleasure garden. After revealing himself as Rama's messenger and assuring Sita that Rama would soon come to rescue her, Hanuman jumped back across the channel to his waiting army, and reported to Rama. (from *Sunder-kanda*, or "beautiful chapter")

Rama, receiving Hanuman's report, set out together with his brother Lakshmana and the monkey troops. Hearing of this, Ravana set about preparing for the decisive battle with Rama. Vibhishana, youngest brother of Ravana, proposed that Sita be returned to Rama, thereby sparing Lanka destructive fighting; whereupon Ravana, furious at such a suggestion, banished his brother who then, disgusted with Ravana's evil regime, joined Rama's ranks. As Rama prepared for the crossing to Lanka, Hanuman's troops produced rocks and trees to build a bridge across the channel. Crossing, Rama's army surrounded Ravana's castle, and the battle began. Ravana's son Indrajit came out with his forces and fought Rama, Lakshmana, and the monkey army fiercely with his sorcerer's weapons. Lakshmana managed to shoot Indrajit but fatally wounded. Hanuman, however, flew to the Himalayas for life-giving herbs for Lakshmana and his own fallen troops. Flying back to Lanka with the entire mountain Kailasa, he then returned it to its place in the Himalayas after the herbs had revived Lakshmana and the monkey troops. The Lakshmana killed Inderjit with his last arrow. Hanuman flying with Mt. Kailasa in his hand is featured often as a theme in paintings and illustrations.

At last, the battle between Rama and Ravana. After a long and violent fight, Rama killed his diabolical rival and proclaimed Vibhishana King of Lanka. Rama, delivering Sita, momentarily doubted her chastity, whereupon Sita called for a funeral pyre of firewood to be built, and then lay upon it to prove her purity. The god of fire Agni appeared and handed Sita to Rama, assuring him of his wife's purity. (from *Yuddha-kanda*)

Rama, Sita, and Lakshmana then returned to Ayodhya, accompanied by Sugriva, Hanuman, and the monkey army, where they were warmly welcomed by Bharata and people. Rama was proclaimed King of Koshala, and thereafter they lived a life of happiness. (from *Uttara-kanda*, or "concluding chapter")

The above is a very brief outline of the Ramayana. Concerning the content of the narrative, numerous scholars have given their interpretations, among which the opinion that the Ramayana reflects some historical fact(s) in ancient history is evident. It is thought that the journey south to the island of Lanka (believed to be present-day Sri Lanka) by Rama's entourage relates to the southward migration on the Indian subcontinent by the Indo-Aryan people.

There are scholars who interpret the story of the Ramayana on the basis of its correlations with natural phenomena. Among such views is the connection of the Ramayana with farming, with Rama's rescue of Sita from Ravana corresponding to the arrival of the monsoon, and the monkey army to the clouds accompanying the monsoon. Sita, certainly, is a personification of the cultivated field. Generally, however, it is agreed that analysis of mythical tales on the basis of historical events or natural phenomena should be undertaken with careful consideration. Such tales are not necessarily related to either historical or natural phenomena Myths, then, should be interpreted primarily as myths.

Then, what meaning does the story of the Ramayana bring to us?

Closely examining the story reveals a curious thing. In the first chapter (*Bala-Kanda*), Rama's birth and marriage, conceding of the throne to his brother Bharata, and retirement to the forest are described. The primary setting is Ayodhya, capital of Kosala, and the story, centering around Rama and dealing primarily with relationship among human beings, is realistic. In contrast, from the second chapter on, the tale moves out-side the realm of realism. The beings Rama comes across are numerous demons, a phantom bird, the surrealistic and mythical monkeys, as well as gods and saintly hermits. This portion, overall, is quite imaginative and fantastic, and the central theme is the conflict between Rama and Ravana. Then, in the conclusion, Rama and Sita are reunited and return to Ayodhya for Rama's instalment as king. The Ramayana story, then develops in a progression from peaceful conditions, through Rama's banishment to the forest and various battles, and back again to peaceful conditions. The situations in which Rama is placed are first static, then kinetic, and then again static, as moves from Ayodhya to the forest and the island of Lanka, and returns to Ayodhya.

In another sense, Rama's travels from capital city to forest and then back represents a progression from civilization to primitivity and back to civilization. In other words, the progression is from a realm of order to one of disorder and back again to order, or from cosmos to chaos and back again to cosmos.

In the Sanskrit epics, the forest is portrayed as a decidedly fearful place. Even in the *Rigveda*, India's most ancient sacred scripture, we can note that Aranyani, goddess of the forest, does not make contact with the dwellings of humans. As seen in the literature of India, the forest contains dangerous wild animals, and spirits prowl while some places are hunted by demons. It is, then, natural that Rama should in the forest come upon the powerful demon Viradha, with Shoorpanakha, Ravana, and other demons such as Maricha.

The forest is certainly a place to be feared. In spite of this however, in the *Rigveda* the forest is also represented as a place where the forest goddess grants food from abundant nature, making it a source of benefit for humanity. In it the gods appear, saintly hermits reside, and fragrant flowers and sweet fruits are in abundance. To the hero Rama, as well, the forest has its beneficial side, for this is where he meets numerous helpful hermits, is armed by the gods, and assisted by the phantom eagle Jatayu; furthermore, then road to Lanka, treated as an extension of the forest, features the aid of Sugriva, Hanuman, and the other monkeys.

The fact that in the Ramayana the first two chapters are set in realism while from the third chapter (*Aranya-kanda*) on the content suddenly becomes fantastic is not implausible. As stated previously, the forest is both the abode of gods and saints and a place where assorted diabolical beings prevail, so the story in that setting would necessarily appear fantastic and surrealistic.

We see, then that the forest is both hazardous and benevolent; in other words, it reveals itself as being ambivalent. This corresponds to Rama's kinetic condition in this part of the story.

Rama's kinetic condition is itself manifested in two phases. The first of these is his "separation" from his wife Sita, and the other is his "conflict" with Ravana and the other diabolical figures. While the theme of loving couples being separated in the forest is not uncommon, in the Ramayana the parting of Rama and Sita marks the take-off point in the drama and also becomes the cause of the ensuing conflict.

Now, what is the factor that moves Rama from a state of stasis as heir apparent of the throne in Ayodhya to the unstable, kinetic conditions of succeeding chapters? It seems obvious that this factor is his abandonment of his claim to royal succession, and then what returns him to stasis and stability are his reunion with Sita and re-establishment of his right to rule. The Ramayana, then, is made up of the following five motifs: (1) a static Rama, (2) by abandoning his right to rule, (3) enters into a kinetic state in the ambivalent forest, then (4) through the retrieval of Sita and assumption of the throne, again (5) is returned to a state of stasis. Among these, (1) and (5) appear to be contrastingly opposed to (3), while (2) and (4) are likewise antithetical.

It is worth noting, however, that the static Rama at the beginning of the tale clearly differs from the static Rama at the conclusion. The former had yet to establish his ruling authority, while the latter, after passing through his ordeal in the ambivalent forest, was installed as king. This process, the initiation of the person Rama, forms the core of the narrative. More than a simple initiation, it is that of a king, and can be viewed as a mythological coronation.

In the process of initiation, a person is lifted by the initiating agent from the realm of everyday events and placed on a higher level, and then returned to functioning as a normal human being and, furthermore, by passing through the process is established as a new person. This rebirth', as such, requires the 'death' of the individual to allow the emergence of the 'new being'. It follows, then, that the initiating person or agent serves to transport individual to the realm of 'death'. In a mythology like the Ramayana, the role of initiator is most often played by a wicked figure. The demonic beings encountered by Rama prior to his climactic meeting with the demon king Ravana served to carry forward the progression to its resolution.

In ancient India, the celebration corresponding to coronation was known as *rajasuya*. Being a process of more than one year in duration, it was a synthesis of numerous relatively small-scale ceremonies with many priests required and was, therefore, a very costly event. Also, it seems that such ceremonial pomp as is found in a normal coronation today would have occurred a number of times in the lifetime of a king in ancient India.

In the process of this ceremony, the prospective king would be transported to a symbolic state of death by rites administrated by officiating priests. This state, lasting about one year, involved the observance of a variety of strict austerities. The new king would then be 'born' out of this state of 'death by the *adhiseka* (unction) ceremony, the climax of the long observances. On this occasion, the new king would stand on the skin of a tiger with both arms raised as four priests, one each to the east, west, north, and south of the initiate, poured water on his head from special cups. The water itself, a special mixture of sixteen or seventeen type of water collected from special places, was known as the water of *rajasuya*, or "water which gives birth to a king".

The ceremony of *rajasuya*, then resembles structurally the Ramayana story. The not yet established king Rama through his trials and experiences in the unfamiliar forest finally emerges to be installed as a 'reborn' king.

The king in ancient times, believed to embody cosmic meaning, was the personification of fertility and abundance, and should he lose his fertility powers he would need to be again 'reborn' through the *rajasuya* ceremony. The reason behind the assassination of kings, incidentally, is thought to be related to this concept.

In another incident in the Ramayana bearing on the right to rule, Rama gives his sandals to his brother Bharat, who places them at the throne. Likewise indicating the connection between sandals and the royal prerogative following the *adhiseka* of the *rajasuya*, the initiated king was traditionally driven in a chariot and, upon leaving the chariot, fitted with a pair of sandals made from wild boar hide.

Summarizing the points of significance in analysis of the Ramayana can be done as follows. The focal point of and reason for both the epic and the *rejasuya* rites was, generally, initiation and, specifically, the initiation of a king. However, neither was the Ramayana based upon the *rajasuya* ceremony nor was *rajasuya* evolved from the Ramayana; in other words, cause-and-effect cannot be considered between the two. It is likely that the basic concept of the initiation of kings emerged both as a tale composed of words (the Ramayana) and a ritual comprised of actions (*rajasuya* ceremony).

Also, whenever read or heard by people, the tale itself has served to draw them from the everyday world into a state of fascination and wonder, then returning them refreshed to the reality of living. This could explain why the Ramayana as both a tale and esoteric teaching has been passed on and achieved such popularity, not only in India but throughout Asia. The reading and telling of the story has come to have a ritualistic function in itself. Readings of the Ramayana and representations of Rama in dramatic arts can be interpreted as such, and the popularity among Indians today of such beautiful Ramayana-based poetry as "Ramcarit manas" by Tulsi Das (1532-1623) is evident. The appeal of the Ramayana continues to reach the hearts of people. The Ramayana has had its effect in Japan as well. Its story appears in *Hobutsushu*, written by Taira no Yasuyori near the end of the Heian period (792-1199), and indications are that the ancient *bugaku* (court dance music) piece "Doragaku", coming from the country known as Dora (believed to be either Bali or a part of Thailand), is closely related to be Ramayana. In more recent times, studies closely tying the Japanese legend of Momotaro to the epic of Rama have been published. Furthermore, international literary societies and other research activities dealing with the Ramayana are flourishing, and we can anticipate further significant research results to emerge in the future.

The Rich Tradition of the Ramayana in Kerala, Southern India

It is just before dawn. In the twilight gray we are passing over rough ground full of shrubs. The guide is a farmer, full of enthusiasm in showing us a great monument of his native place. He points. "There is the Seetha Kshetram — the temple devoted to Sita, the Indian image of chastity."

In Vayanad in the tribal belt of Kerala, one comes across many instances like this. There is a place believed to be abode, or *asram*, of Valmiki, the saint who sang of Rama. There is lamp made of granite at another place believed to be the spot where Sita gave birth to her sons. Again, in the high ranges, on your way to the famous pilgrim centre of Sabarimala, are found two footprints known by devotees as Sriramapadam (the footprints of Sri Rama). The local belief is that Kerala, together with certain other places in the south, is the region when Rama, followed by his brother Lakshmana, roamed about in search of his beloved. Sabarimala itself got its name from the devoted tribal woman Sabari who in her enthusiasm tasted each fruit before offering it to her beloved Rama — an act by which all the fruits became the *echil* (refuse) of Sabari. Rama, the story goes on to relate, took them with relish and blessed the simple-minded devotee. Names of places and persons denote the impact which this *ithihasa* has on the people of this region, and Kerala is not alone in this respect. This has happened in almost all region throughout India. Rama, Sita, Bharata, and Lakshmana have all become household names, and a blessed martial pair is always compared to Rama and Sita.

All these factors indicate that the two *ithihasa* of India *Ramayana* and *Mahabaratha* — are not merely epics, in the most conventional meaning of the term, and that their relevance is on a larger scale in the context of Indian society. It may be true that the two *ithihasa* were the outcome of the Aryan culture and form part of the composite base on which the entire Vedic knowledge is structured. Indian philosophy, as well as its aesthetics, is pyramid-like in structure, the strong base being the *ithihasa* and their narrative-dramatic structure. In the process of this structuring the Aryan mind was always alert to recognize the pulsations of the qualitatively rich native culture and thought, so that these are very ingeniously incorporated in their concepts. Thus, the *ithihasa* rank among the motivative forces that helped integrate the Aryan and non-Aryan cultures. Legends relating to episodes from the *Mahabaratha* and *Ramayana* are many, and are prevalent all over India. These show quite a number of interesting points of departure from the original tales. It might be argued that all the legends and ballads connected with these *ithihasa* resulted from the spread of *Ramayana* and *Mahabaratha* in correspondence with the spread of Hinduism; but, the basic concepts of certain legends and their ecological back-grounds, which are inseparably integrated, show that the case may be just the opposite. Perhaps the names of characters and certain external patterns in the development of the story might, upon close examination, be found to belong to a later period (and, of course, be influenced by Vedic culture), but they show a structural basis more ancient than the characterization, the mixture of Sanskrit and native languages, etc., which are elements of the external structure

'*Mavaratham Pattu*', a well-known ballad in Malayalam based on Mahabaratha, is one example of this, Bhima is the hero of this episode in which the settings, the important events that happen — Bhima succumbing to the bite of a snake, which was arranged by the Kawravas; his dead body being transported down a river to the sea, where the nymph-like Kanyaka of the Naga clan rescues him; their love at first sight; etc — are described in detail. It is clear that the hero's name and certain references are the only factors relating the theme to *Mahabaratha*, and that they are external additions to the total structure of the ballad.

These instances show that, beyond being two epics of extra-ordinary dimensions, the *ithihasa* have certain points of entry and integration into the totality called Indian culture, even at the grass roots level. They have gone beyond the urban level of communication and sensibility, touching the core of our cultural milieu — the rural and the tribal.

Malayalam literature had its influx of Sanskrit from quite an early period. It is believed that Aryan immigration occurred earlier in this narrow strip of coastal land than in other parts of South India, and that the nature of the impact was different. The considerable amount of Sanskrit in our language has made its contributions both positive and negative. Vocabulary was enriched and, on the other hand, quite naturally, some Malayalam words were relegated to the background, some even to total extinction. However, regular Sanskrit studies and a new genre of forms based on Sanskrit prototypes developed. From the tenth century through the sixteenth, a series of writers were trying to evolve a new literary language, the syntax of which was comprised of Tamil, Malayalam, and Sanskrit words. For this experiment all the major poets except one took *Ramayana* as the basis. Their efforts culminated in the composition of *Adhyatma Ramayanam*, a translation from the Sanskrit text with appropriate attempts at deviation and epitomization. Thunjathu Ramanujan Ezhuthachan is considered to be the father of modern Malayalam, succeeding in his endeavours in the sixteenth century.

Ramayana in traditional theatre forms of Kerala

Examining the traditional theatre forms of Kerala at all three levels — tribal, rural, and urban, the impact of *Ramayana* is still alive and active in the life of the ordinary Indian citizen. In rural and tribal theatre we can find that *Ramayana* has made an impact in terms of subject matter. Even in forms highly ritualistic in nature the impact is apparent.

Theyyam

Theyyam is one such form. This ritualistic happening, which could have originated in ancestral worship of the rural people, and may have extended beyond the family's inner circles to become a total social experience of a rural area, is quite an uncommon, exquisite form the appreciation of which demands sophisticated artistic responses. Rich in colour and movement patterns, this form grows out of a myth rooted either in ancestral worship or hero worship, through an elaborated code of pre-Aryan religious rituals culminating in a theatrical spectacle which astonishingly coordinates bodily rhythm with music, light with colour, and songs with chantings. This live spectacle is even now predominant in the northern district of Cannanore in Kerala. Many theatre artists, painters, and archeologists are attracted by this form, and there are visitors to all the interior *kavoo* (where these events happen) in every 'season'. Of these various *theyyam* (there are said to be more than 150 varieties), some deal with characters and situations found in *Ramayana.*

Bali theyyam usually performed by the Kammalar Caste (Aikkudi Kammalars — "pot makers of the five houses") is one such example. The main theme is the fight between Bali and Sugreeva, and the ballad-like song *thottam* is sung along with the stylized movements of the fight. Similarly, at Andaloor Kavu near Tellichery in the Cannanore district, many *theyyam* based on the Ramayana are performed every year. Sri Rama (locally known as Daivathar), Lakshmana, Seeta, Hanuman (here called Bappan), Lava, and Kusa, are all *theyyakkolam* of Tallichery. Hanuman, the ideal *sishya* (disciple) of the ideal *guru,* is portrayed in more than one form. There are interesting makes made of wood, the lower portions of the arecanut leaf, and other indigenous materials.

Kummatti

A form called *Kummatti,* a social entertainment somewhat resembling the commedy prevalent in Trichur and nearby places, is mobile, visiting houses of a particular area and enacting the playlets with stock characters and situations. All characters use wooden masks, and the body of the actor is fully covered with long, green grass found in abundance immediately after the monsoons. This entertainment, hence, is associated with harvest seasons and festivals like *Onam,* the Malayalam new year harvest festival.

Seethakkali

Another interesting tribal dramatic form is *seethakkali.* We might think that it is based on *Ramayana,* having Seeta as the heroine, but a casual look at the performance reveals that *seethakkali* has merely adopted the heroine's name. *Seethakkali,* an interesting narrative dramatic piece (as many tribal forms are), takes another course of action. When an unknown performer wants to tell the story of a young wife who is having many varied, enduring experiences, she is called Seetha — not by a sophisticated author, but by a tribal dancer.

Tholpava koothu

Puppetry is also one of the most ancient forms, and the leather puppets made in Kerala are peculiar in many ways. Their size, the manipulation done by the *pulavar* (chief artist), lighting system used, and music accompanying the act are all peculiar to Kerala. This form, still very much alive in the district of Kerala called Palghat bordering on Tamil Nadu, properly uses *Kambaramayana* as its text. The Rama vs Ravana fight and dramatic incidents before and after from the subject matter. As *Koodiyattom* has its own physical theatre (koothambalam), *Tholpava koothu* (leather puppet drama), has its physical theatre, generally called *koothu madam* — a small structure quite appropriate for the artists to hang their curtain and arrange broken coconuts on a long panel to give an even lighting system for the shadows to be created. Like the sophisticated *Koodiyattom* which has an elaborate and scientific performance text, *Tholpava koothu* also has a detailed performance text which is specifically structured for the purpose. These are called *atal pattukal,* i.e. songs prepared for performances. The basic text for the same is a Ramayana written by the great Tamil poet Kamban. It has been transformed to become the *atal pattu,* performed for twenty-one days.

Tholpava koothu is generally performed in front of Kali temples. Why so? What is the relevance of Rama's story before the village goddess Kali, the daughter of Siva, who took birth to destroy the demon king Darika. The myth has quite an interesting explanation for the same. It was while Bhadrakali was engaged in the battle with Darika that Rama at another battlefield faced Ravana and killed him; thus Kali missed the real spectacle and was unhappy over that. Hence, Rama's story is being enacted through the medium of leather puppets before Kali for her enjoyment and satisfaction.

Kathakali

Among the more sophisticated theatrical traditions, *Kathakali* is the most famous. It is believed that *Kathakali* emerged out of *Ramanattom,* a form codified by the king of Kottarakkara. The legend is that when Kottarakkara Thampuran, a 'southerner' inquired of Zamorin of Calicut who had *Krishnanattom* (a highly sophisticated form) at his command, whether it would be possible for him to send the troupe for some royal celebrations, Zamorin refused and ridiculed him, saying that no 'southerner' could enjoy such a sophisticated art form. This not only infuriated the king, but also offended the sensibilities of his royal advisors, and as a result a new form was structured. It was based mainly on *Natya Sastra,* the monumental book on dramatic aesthetics, and was called *Ramanattom* to contain the story of Rama. *Ramanattom,* in fact, was greatly influenced by rural traditional arts prevalent around *Kottarakkara. Padayani,* another form quite spectacular in its appearance and ingenious for its use of space and local materials to create a universe of its own, has also influenced *Ramanattom.*

Similarly, *Velakkali,* with its footwork adopted from *Kalaripayattu* (the martial arts), might also have contributed its share. These were the origins of *Kathakali,* the natural outcome of *Ramanattom.* Kottarakkara Thampuran, not only the exponent but also a poet wrote literature for performances for which *Ramayana* was made the common base. There are eight texts subscribed to him: *Puthra Kamestti, Seeta Swayamvaram, Vichinnabhishekam, Khara Vadham, Bali Vadham, Toranayuddham, Setha Bandhanam,* and *Yuddham.*

Philip Zerrali, currently assistant professor of the Theatre and Drama Dept, at the University of Wisconsin, has described his first impressions as a member of village audience for a rural performance of *Kathakali* (cf: The *Kathakali Complex: Actor, Performance, Structure,* pp. 12-13). Of these eight stories, some stories, like *Bali Vadham* and *Thoranayuddham,* were quite popular for their performance value among *Kathakali* enthusiasts. There had been attempts to codify all these *attakatha* and present a complete performance titled *Sampoorna Ramayana.*

Ramayana in modern theatre

The instances described above from the three levels of traditional aesthetics — the urban, rural, and tribal — indicate how *Ramayana* has been a source of inspiration for various traditional forms on the thematic level. Modern theatre also has made a few meaningful attempts to relate the story of Rama, emphasizing the conflict he faced in his duel capacities of ideal emperor and ideal husband. The couple portrayed in that magnificent epic, going together through the joys perils, sorrows, sacrifices, and incomparable togetherness in marital bliss, is a source of rich material for any work of art, anytime in human history. The gripping situations through which the story unfolds will continue to inspire many a genius. In modern Malayalam drama, the late C.N. Sreekantan Nair has attempted to present a trilogy of plays based on *Ramayana, Lanka Lakshmi,* and *Kanchana Seeta.* The first depicts the family drama resulting in the exile of young Rama to the forest. The second play is Ravana and his fight with the godly hero. In *Lanka Lakshmi* the playwright has tried to give his own interpretation of the Ramayana story. His hero is Ravana, and he is not a single individual but the proud product of tribal ancestry holding on to its illustrious glories. He sacrifices himself for his *vamsa* and thus becomes the hero of the tribe. The last play tries to show the conflict between the duality in Rama (the emperor and the husband) and his relationship with Seeta in these two capacities. These three plays are written basically in a realistic style and are being performed in many places.

Thus *Ramayana* continues and will continue to inspire the minds of not only the elite and the urban, but the rural and tribal as well, for in its pages there is no end to sensitive, subtle, and close human relationships.

Ramakien — A Living Cult and Tradition in Present-Day Thailand

The cult of Rama and the Thai monarchy

The cult of Rama has been associated with Thai life, culture, tradition, religious beliefs, and social and political institutions since the beginning of Thai history. Prior to the founding of the first kingdom of Sukhothai in the fourteenth century Thai tribes migrated to this fertile river basin and settled down, first as subjects to the Khmer rulers, later as their equals, and finally as their rulers. Although the cult of Siva god of destruction, was predominant in the royal, religious, social and cultural structures of the Khmers, the Thais chose Vishnu, the god of preservation of their patron god and based their kingship, as opposed to the imperial and aggressive rule of the Khmer emperors, on the cult of Rama, Vishnu Incarnate. They also incorporated Buddhist into Vaishnava Hinduism to make their monarchy and political and social structures more peace-oriented. Rama also came to be thought of as one life of the bodhisattva (future Buddha). Thus the cult of Rama merged conveniently with the Buddhism which become the national religion and the foundation of Thai society and culture.

Many Thai kings from the Sukhothai period in the fourteenth century to the present time have affixed the name "Rama" to their proper names; for example, King *Ram*kamhaeng (Ram, the Brave), King *Ram*esuan (Ram and Siva, or I-suan). The formal title of "*Ram*athibodi" (Rama, the Protector Lord) was used with the names of various kings since the first king of Ayudhaya U-thong who reigned from 1351-1369. The later kings in the Ayudhaya period used this title whenever they or their councils considered it to be appropriate. Kings of the present Chakri dynasty of the Ratanakosin (Bangkok) period are all called "Rama" and are numbered from Rama I (1782-1809) to the Present Rama IX (1946-) This tradition was strongly supported by King Vajiravudh, Rama VI (1910-1925), who wished to revive and reinforce the sanctity of the monarchy with the cult of Rama and divine kingship by mythologizing the dynasty and the position of the king as the god-king, Vishnu Incarnate. During his reign, the myth and cult of Rama was manifested both in literary and dramatic forms, as well as in many court ceremonies, which he revived from original Hindu origins. The king composed many episodes of the *Ramakien* for his amateur *Khon* (mask dance-drama) troupe consisting of young courtiers, sons of noble families and his close associates. Throughout these literary scripts, the king tactfully inserted important political and social messages. One of his major policies was to encourage among his men a strong sense of loyalty to the throne and patriotism, both of which were very much needed during that time of political threats, internally as military powers attempted to overthrow the absolute monarchy, and externally with the influence of socialism, Marxism, and communism. The mythical aura of Rama as the divine and righteous king served to support King Vajiravudh's insecure position among the military who had attempted an unsuccessful revolt in 1912 against the king himself.

King Vajiravudh made an explicit effort to adopt the *Ramakien* as the national epic and to carry out research on the origin and development of this cult of Rama in association with the Thai monarchy. He was among the first group of scholars who discussed and proposed many theories concerning the significance and symbolism of this cult for the Thai nation. *Ramakien*, in the past a major literary and dramatic work, has gained a socio-political dimension in the twentieth century through the philosophical, literary, and dramatic achievements of this king. Rama is no longer a mere mythological character, but the personification of the Thai king, the Enlightened Ruler, the Renaissance Universal Man, the divine king as well as the humanist. He is a god living among mortals, becoming one of them while possessing all divine qualities. These conflicting elements and characteristics divine and human, were evident also in the behaviour and daily conduct of King Vajiravudh himself. At times he would be very liberal and human, yet at other times he enjoyed playing the role of divine being amid pomp, royal regalia, spectacular court ceremonies, and dramatic performances. Royal attire imitated as closely as possible that of Vishnu and Rama as depicted by artists in traditional paintings, and was, in turn, copied by dancers in the performance of these classical plays to the point that King Mongkut, Rama IV, established a law prohibiting dance troupes to use costumes which resembled too closely those of the royal family. All these traditions show the strong associations and relationship existing between the religious concept and monarchy and between political and cultural institutions.

The name of the present dynasty, "Chakri" itself is closely related to the Vishnu-Rama cult. It means the 'Holder of Chakra (discus) and Tri (trident); lethal weapons of Vishnu which came to form the royal emblem of the present dynasty. The name "Chakri" was also used as title of the Commander-in-Chief or Minister of Defence in the Ayudhaya and Early Ratanakosin (Bangkok) periods. King Rama I, the founder of the Chakri Dynasty, was formerly Chao Phraya Chakri, Minister of Defence and Commander-in-Chief in the region of King Taksin of Thonburi. It was probably to relate to his former military position as well as to sanctify his kingship that the name "Chakri" was given to his dynasty and family with the approval of the council of ministers. It directly associates the family and kingship with Vishnu and Rama the ideal King, the righteous monarch as opposed to Thosakan (Ravana), the unrighteous despot.

There has been quite a lot of development in the promotion and glorification of this Vishnu-Rama cult in the present monarchy. For example, the royal emblem of Garuda is used on the royal flags, stationery, and offices of the royal government or institutions under royal patronage, even after the Revolution of 1932 when the absolute monarchy was replaced by a constitutional one. The mythological animals and birds decorating the royal throne, temples, palaces, furniture, utensils, and personal effect of the king and his royal family are all related to the Hindu myths of Vishnu and Rama blending harmoniously with *Jataka* stories about the previous lives of the Buddha and bodhisattvas. According to traditional Thai beliefs, Rama and bodhisattva are synonymous and, thus, Thai kings personify both divine beings.

Soon after his ascension to the throne and the unification of the country, King Rama I commissioned in 1783 the construction of a new Royal place and the Royal Temple of the Emerald Buddha on the opposite bank of the Chao Phraya River across from Thonburi city, the capital of King Taksin, his predecessor. The new capital was to become the second Ayudhaya and even to surpass it in beauty, wealth, and prosperity to glorify as well as to justify his succession to the throne after the tragic death of King Taksin, who was executed for alleged insanity. Rising from a common background and the ambiguous military position of Commander-in-Chief of all the armies, besides having been the closest comrade-in-arms of King Taksin and a loyal subject during that short and turbulent reign, King Rama I saw the necessity of legitimatizing his kingship and creating this splendour after the fall of Ayudhaya, the long series of civil wars, and the internal conflicts among the peers. These cultural and artistic achievements were tributes to his reign, evidence of the stability and richness of this southeast Asian kingdom in the eyes of its neighbours. The new "city of angels," Krung Thep, or formally called Ratanakosin ('god Indra's city of jewels") was to be the centre of this region under the able leadership of a new line of great kings.

King Rama I also commissioned the court poets to compose, compile, and edit the missing episodes of the *Ramakien* to make a complete collection of the drama and to establish it as the national epic. It was to serve a two-fold purpose — culturally, it was a combined effort of poets who had scattered all over the country after the fall of Ayudhaya kingdom and later came together under the new Chakri dynasty, while politically, it was a means for the king to expound his policies of a centralized government under the absolute monarchy. The epic directly and strongly promotes loyalty and dedication of a military and civil officials to the god-king. This was essential to the unity and stability of the new kingdom following the political factionalism caused by the war with the Burmese and internal conflicts among military chiefs. The sacred myth of Rama, the legendary heroic and righteous king, the personification of all kingly virtues, was then an important attribute of the new monarch. Thus the *Ramakien* and cult of Rama as Vishnu Incarnate were associated with the Chakri Kings more than any other monarch in the history of Siam, especially in times of political need, instability, and crises. The glorification of the king as a god-king has never been so explicit, grandiose in scale, and spectacular as in the Chakri Dynasty. The long span of peace and prosperity and fertile international relations, both commercial and diplomatic, have further enhanced the legitimacy of the Chakri kings in the eyes of the world as the divinely anointed rulers and leaders of this part of the globe.

King Mongkut, Rama IV (1851-1868) soon after his succession to the throne revived all the sacred Hinduistic and Brahmanistic customs and court ceremonies which helped to strengthen this image of god-king and Enlightened Ruler for international viewers and Western powers who coveted this small kingdom as a future colony. Royal and public dramatic presentations of the *Ramakien* were very much encouraged by this king foresight. After a long absence of dramatic activities during the region of his pious brother, King Rama III (1824-1851), King Mongkut issued a royal announcement that the new monarch wished to see more festive *khon* and *lakhon* (dance-drame) by private troupes to show that Siam was a country of long cultural heritage and wealth and not a land of barbarians to be colonized by foreign powers. The king himself composed an episode of the *Ramakien* depicting the return of King Rama to rule Ayodhya after his long exile. The episode symbolically and metaphorically represents the king's personal experience in entering monkhood during his brother's reign to avoid political controversies over the succession to the throne. His ascension to make a new era of opening up to the west and establishing foreign relations in order to survive as free nation amid threats of colonization.

The major effort of King Rama IV was continued and further expanded by his son, King Chulalongkorn (1868-1910), Rama V. "Father of the Modern Age of Thailand", as he is known, King Chulalongkorn with his wise policies and long, stable rule, succeeded in steering this small nation through the storm and stress of the Western colonial struggle to conquer the East. His achievements in modernizing the government, social systems, and way of living enabled the Thai nation to survive as a free country and to bargain with dignity with the Western powers. During his prosperous reign, considered a golden age in modern Thai history, there were many royal court ceremonies and dramatic presentations of *khon* and *lakhon* as well as other types of traditional and modernized forms of entertainment, including the Westernized speech drama and operetta. *Ramakien* became more relevant to the new generation through these experimental modernizations in stage presentation and theatrical technique, e.g. set design, sound and lighting systems, innovative costume design and construction and Western concepts of theatre construction. The king, an enthusiast of Western ways and a notable host-King to numerous royal visitors from Western countries, encouraged modern adaptations of this ancient epic to suit the new rhythm and life style of his generations and to cater to Western tastes in order to present to these prestigious dignitaries the rich art and culture of Siam. It seems that the urgency in modernizing his state and the social and cultural structures of this nation stemmed from political and economic pressures, both external and internal. Many court artists and dramatists, notably Prince Narissaranuwadhiwong and Prince Narathip Prahanphong, the king's brothers, and Crown Prince Vajiravudh contributed to this new movement in their modernized *khon* and *lakhon.* Branching out from the traditional roots, new forms of dance-drama such as *lakhon phan thang, lakhon dukdamban,* and *lakhon rong* (dance-drama-operetta) gained more popularity than the old style of presentations. *Ramakien* still remained a favourite subject even in this new age.

Ramakien and modern Thai painting

The turning-point in Thai art was the nineteenth century, when the realism and naturalistic perspective of Western-style painting penetrated the traditional Thai two-dimensional, linear, and symbolically abstract forms in intricate, stylized designs. Prince Narisaranuwadhiwong was among the first to introduce this new trend in his drawing, painting, and stage design in the late nineteenth century and early twentieth century. He was also a talented composer and dramatist whose works are now regarded as masterpiece of the era. In his art work as well as his music and drama he succeeded in merging the two trends, idealism and realism, in an aesthetic balance, which is symbolic of this age of "East Meets West". These two contrasting trends still exist today in contemporary Thai art. Two of the most significant artists of the present generation are Chakraphan Posayakrit and Thawan Datchanee, the former representing the continuation of traditional romanticism and idealism, the latter the Westernized expressionistic realism.

Chakraphan, the more popular and better understood artist of the two, has the advantage of working close to the heart and spirit of the Thai people, and expresses his ideals and concepts through a variety of artistic forms. His paintings are in oil, pastel, acrylic, and watercolour. He also works through numerous commissions, both royal and private, on mural paintings, stamps, puppets, decorative fans, and dance costumes. His counterpart Thawan, on the other hand, appeals more to Western admirers and Westernized intellectuals who are familiar with expressionistic style and surrealistic forms and who demand new artistic expression of their contemporaries as a sign of cultural progress. While Chakraphan's Rama, Sita, and Laksmana grace through beautiful and idyllic landscapes, Thawan's grotesque ogres, gigantic gorillas, and baboons display inhuman, supernatural, and cannibal forces and frightening power in violent *Ramakien* battle scenes. Though both artists are devout Buddhists, Chakraphan's romantic idealism contrasts sharply with Thawan's vigorous expressionism. They each have individually a deep understanding of the religion, and practise Buddhist meditation in their private lives as well as expressing their religious beliefs and philosophical concepts in their works.

Chakraphan had worked on the restoration of the eighteenth century *Ramakien* mural painting in the Emerald Buddha Temple, which greatly explains his personal attachment to the traditional style and interpretation. However, being a contemporary artist in the twentieth century, he develops his new techniques and approach to communicate with his generation. On the other hand,

Thawan grasped the essence of the *Ramakien* and its major characters, then liberated himself from traditional ways to create and interpret the epic according to his own understanding using new forms, composition, perspectives, and colours. His *Ramakien* characters, such as Honuman, Phali, Ongkhot, and Thosakan, all possess supernatural strength and power while those of Chakraphan embody grace and beauty. These two artists are sometimes compared with Raphael and Michaelangelo in their contrasting artistic styles.

Thai classical dance-drama: modern methods of training in relation to the Ramakien and stage performance in modern times

Thai classical dance-drama relating to the Ramakien is performed in many theatrical forms. The most notable and ancient is the *Khon* a mask dance-drama dating from as far back as the fourteenth and fifteenth centuries. Some historians believe that it developed along with the *nang*, dance-drama using large leather puppets in the Sukhothai period around the fifteenth century. Others contend that it was first recorded later in the Ayudhaya period in association with martial arts and military pageantry in the Vishnu-Rama cult and later as a court ritual and form of entertainment. As with all traditional dramatic and dance forms, *khon* and *lakhon* developed from religious rituals relating to the worship of gods of the Hindu pantheon, most specifically Siva and Vishnu, both of whom are gods of classical dance, each of different occasions in Hindu mythology. While Siva danced in creating the universe and destroying evil, Vishnu (or Narai to the Thais) in the Ramakien "Episode of Narai Prap Nonthuk" (god Narai defeating Nonthuk, an ogre) danced at the command of Siva to punish Nonthuk (Nantaka), an impudent ogre. In this fatal dance, god Narai, in the disguise of a beautiful goddess, tricks Nothuk into imitating her dance movements. The god finally succeeds in leading the ogre to point his index finger, endowed with Siva's fatal power, at his ankle, thus disabling him. The mythological dance movements of Siva and Vishnu became the basic classical dance movements studied and performed by Thai court ladies and dancers, male and female and these movements were later transmitted to public troupes outside the royal court.

The teaching and training of Thai classical dancers has continued from generation to generation from its beginning to the present without interruption despite wars, political and economic crises, and even the changes following the Revolution of 1932, when the absolute monarchy was replaced by a constitutional monarchy under a democratic government. The art of *khon* and *lakhon* lives on through many changes in the administrative and educational systems to adapt this ancient art to new society and public functions.

Individual coaching and strict supervision by court dancers over their proteges, whom they regarded as members of one big family, inevitably changed after the Revolution to a more modern method of teaching classes and groups of pupils from a lower social background, and who were registered in the National Academy of Dance under the Department of Fine Arts, Ministry of Education, which replaced the Department of Royal Khon and Lakhon of the old regime. The training of dancers became public and was no longer a prerogative of the privileged few within the royal court as it was in the past. Under the so-called democratic system, i.e. absence of social classes and separation between courtiers and public, these young dancers from a tender age of nine to young adulthood dance daily after their classes in formal education. They are classified by physical appearance and inclination into four major groups: *Phra* — heroic and refined male role, Nang — refined lady and heroine role, *Yak* — vigorous ogre role, and *Ling* — lively and acrobatic monkey role. A formal division of classes and curriculum geared towards teachers training and production of professional performers for the public has replaced the traditional aristocratic life-long training without specific professional aims or career-oriented purposes. Thus the tradition can survive through economic hard times in this new approach to the fine arts.

Production of the *Ramakien* at the National Theatre at present cater, therefore, to school pupils and middle-class audiences, instead of to the non-playing aristocrats and public of the past when all royal and private entertainment was open and free to all under the sponsorship of royalty or wealthy noble families. However, on some social occasions, the old way of patronization of dance and dramatic performances for the public as a form of charity or merit-making is still found. Mom Ratchawong Kukrit Pramoj, former Prime Minister, was the first to revive the traditional role of *Khon* training for the elite, future leaders of society and government, starting the training of *khon* at Thammasat University in 1973 for students in their later teens and early twenties who had no previous training in the *khon* or *lakhon*. M.R. Kukrit's intent was to preserve this cultural heritage in the personal experience of these future leaders of the Thai nation, and to train them in the traditional art so that they would absorb naturally through this rigorous training the essence of Thai social and political philosophy and structures and the "Thai Identity". It is a revival of the traditional practice of aristocrats and military officers in the Ayudhaya and Early Ratanakosin periods to receive training in martial arts and *khon*, which is closely related to martial arts, to learn discipline necessary for administrators, warriors, and political leaders. The ethical and social values expounded by the idealized characters in the *Ramakien* and their relationships to work, war and domestic affairs have long been regarded as models in moral conduct and social behaviour for the elite. It was with this aim that M.R. Kukrit initiated this *khon* training on the university campus for the class of leaders who no longer come from the aristocracy but from the middle-class. There have been many performances by them, both in Thailand and abroad, all of which have been very successful. The new and modern interpretations written and directed by M.R. Kukrit give new insights into the centuries-old literary and dramatic master piece. The new generation of *khon* audiences who come to see the Thammasat productions look for witticism and relevance to their own age, which M.R. Kukrit had wisely and tactfully added to the traditional text and style of presentation.

It is only through living in one's own personal experience and being absorbed in body, mind, and spirit that a national cultural heritage can survive significantly and creatively in this modern age of technology and materialism. The search for the right medium, method, and system for the modern generation is in itself an art. Thus *Ramakien* live on as an essential part of the Thai people, who are now sharing this rich national treasure with the rest of the world.

An Inexhaustible Source of Delight and Ethical Precepts in Balinese Society

Ramayana is the monumental poem which represents the fight between Rama, the king of Ayodya, Rawana, the king of Alengka. As an incarnation of the God Wisnu, Rama is a personification of good, while the ten-headed giant Rawana is a symbol of evil.

The Balinese version of the Ramayana story is written in the Kawi language in an elaborate poetic style. To students of Indonesian literature, this Rama and Sita legend is known as the *Kakawin Ramayana* or the *Old Javanese Ramayana* (*OJR*). The *OJR* is divided into 26th *sargah* (episodes); each *sargah* ranges in length from 62 to 214 verses. The total length of the epic is 2651 verses.

The *OJR* is still very popular in Bali, and almost everyone is very familiar with the essential sequence of the story. Episodes from the epic are not only depicted by means of many forms of performing and visual arts; the *OJR* has also become a standard source of material on moral and right conduct in Balinese society. The story is written down on *lontars* (palm-leaf books) and copies of it are owned by most Balinese priests noblemen, artists and scholars. The Hanuman character is one of the most popular among the youngsters of the island. When a hidden Hanumam dancer makes "*ngote*" (a special "squawking" vocal sound) behind the gate, the children cheer and clap their hands for they know that their favourite character is about to appear. So popular is Hanuman that when a puppeteer creates a scene in which Hanuman is temporarily dead, the children might cry aloud.

The *Old Javanese Ramayana* is a masterpiece of Indonesian literature, and it has been studied in detail by Poerbatjaraka, Hooyakas, Zoetmulder, and others. The origin of the epic is still very obscure; it is popularly attributed to the mythical author Yogiswara. Scholars say the *OJR* was not based on the famous *Ramayana* of Valmiki, but was written as an adaptation of the more recent Indian version of the Rama and Sita legend known as *Ravana Vadha*, composed by Battikavya in the seventh century. The Valmiki version was only made known to the Balinese through its English translation, which arrived on the island after World War II.

The *Rawana Vadha* was probably translated and adopted into the Old Javanese language of Central Java around the ninth century. In this period the story of Rama was beautifully carved in the stone relief of Prambanan temple located exactly on the border between Yogyakarta and Surakarta. The Ramayana series is carved on the inner side of the balustrade wall of the Ciwa temple, beginning with a scene of the God Wisnu enthroned upon the world-serpent Ananta; it continues up to when the monkey army led by Hanuman crosses the sea to Alengka. The story is continued on the Brahma temple (south of the Ciwa temple in the Prambanan temple compound).

Contemporary with the Prambanan temple, the *OJR* is the oldest extant piece of Kawi literature and is the only literary work which has been reliably dated in the Central Javanese period, prior to AD 930.

The central Javanese period ended with King Mpu Sendok shifting the royal government from Central to East Java. Mpu Sendok was succeeded by his son, King Dharmawangsa. The later was replaced in time by his son-in-law, King Erlangga, whose mother was an East Javanese princess married to King Udayana Warmadewa of Bali. King Erlangga was the ruler of East Java from 1019-1042; under his administration the temple of Penataran was erected. At Candi Panataran, near Blitar in East Java, we find scenes of the Ramayana carved on the temple base. They begin with Anoman's mission to Alengka as an ambassador and end with the death of Kumbhakarna, Rawana's younger brother. It is very important to note that the Penataran reliefs were carved in an almost two-dimensional manner; their stylized shapes are prototypes of the present-day leather puppets of Bali. Under the rule of King Erlangga, the relationship between Java and Bali became very close. This caused many forms of performing arts, music, dance and literature to be exported to Bali.

The *Ramayana*

1

The *Ramayana*, a magnificent epic created in India more than 2,000 years ago, has also travelled into other Asian countries, leaving a deep impact on the life and culture of the people.

2

3

4

1. *Latticework showing Rama, Lakshmana, and Hanuman, Laos.*
2. *(Above) Hanuman wooing Supanmatcha, golden mermaid; Khon (mask dance drama) of Ramakien, Thailand.*
   (Below) Cambodian dance drama of Ramayana.
3. *Hanuman meeting Sita and her attendant in Lanka; Cake Dance of Bali, Indonesia.*
4. *Gigantic statue of Ravana waiting to be burned; Dussehra Festival, India.*

Textiles

Such gorgeous hand-woven textiles take so much time and patience to make, that they must be something more than mere wrapping for bodies or decoration. Not just for practical use, they are a way of touching the gods, or expressing love for families and children. Motifs and colours on textiles from all over Asia are often strikingly similar.

1

2

3

1. *Patola, with elephant and plant motifs, India.*
2. *Bold geometrical design of two-headed nagas with hook and lozenge motifs. Silk on cotton, probably from Xieng Khouang, North Laos.*
3. *Mantle of Maa tribe, inhabiting an area from Vietnam to Cambodia, with* Phi *(spirit figurès), with human and bird motifs.*

Batik

4

5

4. *A pattern of clouds, rocks and animals against a rich ivory-coloured background in the northwest coastal town of West Java.*
5. *A fauna and flora design; Yogyakarta, Indonesia*

Embroidery

In many Asian villages, the art of embroidery has been handed down from mother to daughter. Through dextrous and laborious needlework, women display their aesthetic creativity and express their love for the family. Colourful designs and motifs are taken from nature, folklore and myths for a rich variety of decorations and dresses, wedding gowns and religious ornaments.

1. *Central section of a wall hanging showing a cypress tree surmounted by the stylized form of a woman's face depicting the sun; Isfahan, Iran.*
2. *Rectangular piece of Malay gold-thread embroidery.*
3. *(Left) Balinese dancer.*
   (Centre) Balinese couple wearing traditional clothes of gold-thread embroidery worn on very special occasions such as a wedding or tooth-filling.
   (Right) Embroidered dress of Sri Lanka.
4. *Wall hanging showing Ganesha in an abstracted form; cotton and silver gilt threads on coloured cotton ground; Saurashtra, Gujarat, India.*
5. *Embroidery of Kathiawar, Gujarat, India.*

Kites

So many different kites speckle the Asian sky, linking heaven and earth with one slender string. Some of them may carry prayers for an abundant harvest, or healthy growth of children; others proudly demonstrate their beauty, speed or elegance.

1

3

2

4

5

1. Wau Jala Budi — *a kite closely connected with the life of fishermen, Malaysia.*
2. *A peacock kite, Thailand.*
3. *A bird kite; Sri Lanka.*
4. *A double gold-fish kite, China.*
5. *An Indonesian kite.*
6. *Brightly coloured kites of India.*
7. *A rectangular* Mishiki-e-kite, *made in Tokyo, the most common traditional Japanese kite.*

6

7

Today a number of versions of the Rama and Sita legend are found in Bali. They are: *Uttara Kanda*, a prose story about the birth of Rawana; *Satrughna*, a prose work which describes the coronation of Rama, the banishment of his wife Sita, and the birth of their two sons, Kusa and Lawa; *Kapiparwa*, a prose account of the fight of two famous Monkey Kings Bali and Sugriwa; *Kuntir*, a poem on the same subject; *Agastya parwa* which tells of the great bird, Jatayu, whose soul reached the heavenly world after his body was cremated by King Rama; *Sumanasantaka*, devoted to the ancestors of Rama; and perhaps others. None of these more-or-less minor works has been of importance to the makers of Wayang Wong, who have relied primarily on the *OJR* as the major source.

The survival of the Ramayana stories in Bali continues to be supported by the very active *seka mabasan* (reading clubs) which exist in most villages of the island. The clubs are made up exclusively of male members, except in a few villages where female members may take part. They are devoted to the learning of the song texts, recitation, analysis and discussion of the language of the stories. The club meetings are usually held twice a week for about three hours or so in the evening at the *bale banjar*, or village community hall. Once every six months the group performs for the temple festival (*odalan*) in its own village. In *Pura Maceti* of Gianyar Province, recitation aloud from the Ramayana goes on for three days in succession. The best-known experts from all over the island are invited to participate in this special event. Selections from the Ramayana and other traditional literature such as the *Adiparwa, Arjuna Wiwaha, Sutasoma,* and *Ludhaka* are read aloud. The *OJR* is considered to be the most *wayah*, or venerable, of these classics.

Prior to the Dutch colonial period, which began in South Bali in 1906-1908, public education was only offered at schools known as *masisya*, which were conducted in the house compounds of the Brahmana Priests, who always kept the *OJR* among the books in the family collection. The Ramayana was esteemed for its didactic passages as well as for its great venerability. Pupils from all castes attended the *masisya* schools. For each category certain passages were felt to be appropriate sources of moral instruction. Thus, the episodes in the *OJR* in which the proper conduct of government is discussed were felt to be good instruction for members of the caste of rulers, the *ksatrya*. The *jaba*, or low caste people, were edified by precepts drawn from such passages as building the bridge to Alengka, in which the loyal and energetic tribe of monkeys proves its devotion to Lord Rama by working very hard to build the bridge. The Ramayana is one of the principal Balinese source for ethical precepts.

Today in modern Bali, the recitation of the Ramayana epic is often found as part of the wedding, cremation, and rite-of-passage ceremonies. *Magedong-gedongan*, the baby shower ceremony is usually accompanied by a whole night *mabasan*, and *gender wayang* music is used to accompany it. It is traditional for the Balinese *dalang* who perform the shadow puppet theatre to own collections of palm-left manuscripts containing, among other works, the texts of the old Javanese classics, or for them to have access to collections owned by Balinese noblemen. In the Balinese tradition, the *dalang* is ever a teacher of the populace, expected to edify as well as to delight the ruling *cokarda*. For this purpose, the Ramayana has provided an inexhaustible source.

In Bali, such archaeological remains as Candi Prambanan and Candi Penataran have not yet come to light. The Balinese portray their favourite characters in the form of single statues, rather than in elaborate pictorial compositions. A collection of statues which represent an episode of the Ramayana story can be found in *Kehen* temple of Bangli Province. A single, large figure of Hanuman (the White Monkey) can be found in Tegal Tamu village, Gianyar Province; the statue is believed to be a sacred figure, and is used to protect the population and their ward. In Bali the Hanuman is always associated with Bima, the second hero of the Pandawa family, as they are both considered to be sons of Bayu, the God of Wind. It is possible that the function of these two characters in Balinese life is connected to the ancient Javanese Bima cult.

In the old days, the Ramayana episodes were among the most popular themes of *parba*, oil painting on shrine walls. From this, the classical painting style on canvas has developed, and this art is still practised in Kamasan village, Klungkung Province, where the oldest masks of Wayang Wong are preserved. Today, episodes from the Ramayana continue to provide an inspiring theme for all types of paintings in the village. Wayang Wong, a total theatre of Bali, takes its stories exclusively from the Ramayana. Due to the structure and characteristics of the play, the Ramayana is not normally used in its entirety as the story for a single Wayang Wong performance. It is used only in parts, and each part is presented in a standardized play structure. Unlike the Javanese Wayang Wong plot, in which the story might be written down in a form of *pakem* (play script), in Bali the script is never written down, but rather is transferred orally from one village to another; each time the structure of the story is re-adapted into the stereotypical structure of the *Wayang Wong*. The *OJR* provides a fertile text, rich in possibilities for the choreographer to use in creating his plots for the play. No two performance of *Wayang Wong* are quite the same, even though the same episode might be presented. The plots are created according to the condition of the troupe.

The entire story of the Ramayana has been put together as a plot for the Balinese *Sendratari Ramayana*, a modern Balinese dance-drama genre performed without dialogue. The story is narrated by a dalang who comments on the action from his seat near the orchestra. *Senderatari Ramayana* is intended for the modern audience, which may not understand the rarefied and complicated Kawi language used in *Wayang Wong*. The performance lasts for only two hours or so. In it the pantomime rather than the spoken dialogue is emphasized. Reflecting the influence to *Wayang Wong* from Pujungan village, Gianyar Province, the *Wayang Wong* makers from Pujungan village choreographed a version of the whole story of the *Kakawin* for performance during their tour in Europe in 1974. The idea was perfectly accepted by the Western connoisseur, but, lacking Kawi dialogue in the presentation, it created an odd emotion in Balinese audiences and was not a success in Bali.

The *OJR* has also been divided into short episodes when used to make *Wayang Wong* plays. A lengthy *Wayang Wong* performance might employ only one or two *sargahs* for its source as can be seen in the story of "*Kumbhakarna Lina*", the "Death of Kumbhakarna". This event is depicted in 85 lines in *sargahs* XXII and XXIII of the OJR. This is sufficient material for a complete performance. The idea behind presenting a story based on limited sections of the epic is based on the intention of the choreographer to present a complete philosophical point for each *sargah*, since each *sargah* might have a single idea behind it. Additionally, by performing a plot with a simple outline, more elaborate choreography can be included in the play.

Presently, more than twenty versions of stories for *Wayang Wong* are known. To name a few: *Kumbhakarna Lina*, the death of Kumbhakarna (based on *sargah* XXII, XXIII); Matinya *Prahasta*, the death of the Prime Minister Prahasta (XXI); *Kautus* Hanuman, Hanuman as a scout (VII, VII, IX, X, XI); *Anggada Duta*, Anggada as an ambassador (XVIII); Kaejuk *Cukasarana*, the capture of Minister Cukasarana (XVIII); *Kapandung Dewi Sita*, Rawana kidnaps Dewi Sita (VI); Kuntir, the fight between Bali and Sugriwa (VI); *Ngawangun Situbanda*, the construction of the bridge to Alengka (XVI); *Katundung Wibhisana*, the banishment of Wibhisana (XIII, XIV, XV); *Nagapasah*, the punishment of Rama and Laksmana by a world serpent by Indrajit, the son of Rawana, through his magic arrow (XXI); and *Uwug Lengka*, the destruction of Alengka kingdom and the death of King Rawana (XXIV).

Cak dance

One Balinese dance that may have been inherited from the pre-Hindu period is called the Cak dan ce. The Cak dance is actually a part of the Sang Hyang dance, a Balinese trance dance. Accompanying the Sang Hyang dance are two singing groups, a male and a female choir. The male choir of about 150 member chants rhythmically the words "ecak-ecak-ecak-ecak" over and over again; thus the male choir is called "Cak". Today it is often separated from its earlier function and performed independently, while this dance still is popular in Bali as the Cak dance. Today, the Cak uses the Ramayana story as its theme.

The creators of Cak introduced a dramatic episode into the performance, performed by a small number of skilled dancers in simple costumes. Again, the Ramayana was the source, and the first story to be given was the abduction of Sita. This was a very simple presentation, to which a battle sequence pitting Sugriwa against Rawana's son, Meganada, was later added. This and subsequent innovations were devised first in one village and then quickly copied by the others, as more and more Cak groups came into being. Today, to foreigners the Cak dance is known as Kecak or "Monkey Dance".

In the next section of this presentation a summary is given of the Ramayana story based on the OJR. The OJR was edited and published by H. Kern in modern Javanese characters in 1900. He and H.H. Jaynboll issued a Dutch language prose translation at intervals between 1917 and 1936, while I Gusti Bagus Sugriwa has published a translation of the OJR in Balinese. The story is as follows:

The abduction

Rama, an incarnation of the God Wisnu and the personification of good, is the crown prince of Ayodya. Because of the ambition of his step-mother, he is in voluntary exile with his beautiful wife Sita and his faithful brother Laksmana. Sadly they are wandering in the forest, trying to console one another.

Across the sea, Rawana, ruler of the kingdom of giants known as Alengka, is the personification of evil. He has seen Sita and fallen in love with her while flying through the forest. Planning to capture her, he asks the giant Marica to lure Rama away from her. With his magic power Rawana changes Marica into a golden deer.

Playfully the deer approaches Rama, Sita and Laksmana, then moves temptingly away. A strong desire to keep the exquisite creature as a pet creeps into Sita's heart. She begs Rama to capture the deer for her. After instructing Laksmana not to leave Sita in any case, Rama goes in pursuit of the deer.

Sita and Laksmana wait anxiously for Rama. Suddenly, a cry for help pierces the forest — it is Marica mimicking Rama's voice. Sita, believing it to be Rama calling for help, urges Laksmana to run at once to his rescue; but Laksmana will not disobey his brother's request to watch over Sita. Sita's fear grows to a frenzy and she accuses Laksmana of being disloyal. Unable to refuse her entreaties any longer, Laksmana makes a magic circle with his dagger around Sita to protect her from danger and then departs.

Rawana, who has been waiting, approaches Sita and tries to seize her. At first he cannot because of the magic circle, but the frightened princess steps out of the circle and he carries her away by force.

Rama has trouble in capturing the golden deer so he shoots it with his arrow. Once again it becomes the giant Marica. Very angry, Rama kills the giant.

At this point the great eagle Jatayu, a friend of Rama's father, is flying through the air when suddenly he hears a woman's cry and recognizes Sita. He attacks Rawana viciously. Rawana strikes Jatayu with his magic sword and the great bird, fatally wounded, falls to the ground. Rawana takes Sita up again and flees to Alengka.

Rama and Laksmana arrive as the dying bird lies helpless on the ground. Jatayu tells Rama that Sita was abducted by

Rawana, and then dies, as the incarnation of Wisnu, sends Jatayu's soul to heaven.

Hanuman, the messenger

Rama has made an alliance with the monkey army. He singled out Hanuman to be sent to Alengka as a messenger to see to Sita's well-being and to demand that Rawana return Sita or his country will face destruction. Rama hands Hanuman his ring as a token to Sita that Hanuman is his messenger, Hanuman tells Rama to consider it done. Rama and Laksmana are consoled. Hanuman departs for Alengka where Rawana rules.

The search

In the garden of Tamansoka, in the state of Alengka, Sita is being entertained by Rawana's wives and Trijaya, Rawana's niece. In spite of their effort, nothing short of reunion with Rama can make her happy. Rawana comes and tells his wives and Trijaya to leave him alone with Sita. Rawana attempts to woo Sita but is refused. His temper flares and he tries to kill Sita but Trijaya, alert to the situation, stops him. Rawana leaves the scene. In the meantime, Hanuman has been watching the whole thing anxiously. He does not want his presence to be known by Rawana, lest he will not be able to communicate with Sita. After Rawana leaves, Hanuman comes down. Sita sees him and, thinking this another or Rawana's tricks, rages at him. Trijaya sees things a little more clearly. Inquiry is made, and Hanuman presents the token from Rama to Sita. Seeing the ring, Sita's grief is intensified. Hanuman is very sad to see Sita's state, and is extremely furious with Rawana, who has caused the tragedy. He tells Sita and Trijaya to step aside; he will demolish Tamansoka. Tamansoka is ruined. Two giant guards hear the noise and come to the scene, and a fight between the guards and Hanuman ensues. Hanuman is captured and placed on a pile of wood which is immediately set afire. He breaks loose and leaps from building to building, setting the whole city on fire.

The battle and victory

Hanuman has returned to Rama's camp, and the monkey army has crossed to Alengka. Duels occur between Laksmana and Kumbhakarna, a giant prince who feels that his brother, Rawana, is wrong.

He goes to war just to seek death. Rama's fight with Rawana ends with the capitulation of the latter.

Rama, Laksmana, Sita, and Hanuman reunite and return to Ayodhya, where Rama is to be crowned king.

We close the story here, for to go on would lead to an unhappy ending.

Forming the Matrix of Nepali Culture

Introduction

The impact of the Ramayana in Nepali life and culture is very broad. The tradition of the Ramayana in Nepal is very ancient and significant. The oldest copy of the Sanskrit Ramayana of Valmiki, as well as a number of other old copies of the epic prepared in medieval times when Nepal was a great meeting ground of scholars, have been preserved in Nepal. It is necessary, therefore, to present in brief the history of the Ramayana tradition in Nepal; the main object of the article, however, is to demonstrate how deep the impact the Ramayana is in Nepali life, culture, sculpture and literature. A brief survey of both the written and the oral tradition of the Ramayana in Nepali society is presented here to illuminate this impact.

The ancient tradition

According to the Hindu belief, Lord Siva was the original narrator of the Ramayana story. The Vedas and the Puranas indicate that the kingdom of Nepal lying to the south of the great Himalayas was the abode and the playing ground of Lord Siva, who first narrated the story of the Rayamana to his consort Parvati.

It is also said that the first ever Sanskrit epic poem of the Ramayana was created by Valmiki in the land of Nepal. *Nepal Mahatmya*, the fourteenth century description of the temples and holy places of Nepal, mentions that Valmiki had spent some time in the Kathmandu valley, creating the Ramayana at the confluence of rivers at the southeastern base of Dolagiri hill, the seat of the oldest temple of Changunarayana. After completing the epic, the poet installed the *mahalinga* of Lord Siva in this place, which, after the name of the poet, is called Valmikeswormahalinga. The *Mahatmya* mentions that Valmiki returned with his disciples to his hermitage on the bank of river Tamasa near a place called Bhainsalotain in Navalparasi district lying in the southern *tarai* (plains) region of Nepal. It is also believed that a great sage Viswamitra also known as Kaushika, lived on the bank of the famous Koshi river of eastern Nepal. Ramayana mentions that this sage had taught archery to Rama and Laxmana, and had also taken the two brothers to Janakpur for *swoyambara* and subsequent marriage to Sita the daughter of Janaka, the king of Janakpur.

Janakpur, which lies in Nepal, was the capital of the ancient kingdom of Mithila. King Janaka had announced that he would offer his daughter Sita in marriage to one who could bend the great bow of Siva. Rama not only bent, but also broke the bow and got Sita's hand in marriage. The place where Rama broke the bow (*dhanusha*) is in Janakpur and is itself still known as Dhanusha. People believe that the pieces of the broken bow of Siva still lie hidden in Dhanusha.

There are other places and names in Nepal associated with the story of the Ramayana. It is believed that as Hanumana, the great soldier of Rama, was returning after carrying a chunk of the Himalaya, he got very thirsty and broke his journey on the bank of the river Virbhadra, the same spot where Valmiki was to create the Ramayana, and installed a *linga* there which is called Hanumandisworlinga. This place later became famous as Hanumattirtha, or the pilgrimage of Hanumana. Similarly, there is a place called Ramdhuni, or the bonfire built by Rama, in Sunsari district in the eastern *tarai* region of Nepal. It is believed that Rama used to build big fires there during the period of his banishment. The fire is continually kept burning even to this day. The two sons of Rama were born in the hermitage of sage Valmiki, in the Navalparasi district of Nepal where Sita had taken refuge after her banishment. It is very difficult to distinguish the legends from history, but it cannot be denied that some of these beliefs have a certain degree of historical relevance.

Rama in temples, carvings, and murals

The images of Rama and Laxmana have been carved on the struts of almost all the ancient famous temples of Nepal. Additionally, Rama finds place in the temples of other deities like Siva and goddess Bhawani, by virtue of being one of the ten incarnations of Lord Vishnu. This, in turn, demonstrates the religious harmony and characteristically important coexistence of faiths. What is more, Lord Siva has narrated the story of Rama, and in his narrations, Siva speaks of Rama with great veneration.

In Janakpur there is an old temple of Rama and Janaki (another name of Sita). The beautiful murals in the temples present the visual story of the Ramayana. The most spectacular of all the carvings consecrated to Rama in Nepal can be found in the Krishna temple of Patan built by Sidhinarashingha in 1637. The entire visual story of the Ramayana has been carved onto the outer walls of this temple built in the golden age of the Malay period. King Pratap Malla of Kathmandu constructed the *Hanumandhoka* and installed the statue of Hanumana near the gate to the Basantapur palace, a centre of attraction for visitors today.

Rama and ancient Nepali history

We have already seen that images of Rama were installed in the old temples of Nepal as early as the first century AD because the Vaishnav sect of the Hindu religion had already been accepted in Nepal. During the long reign of the Lichchavis (AD fifth to late ninth century) the Vaishnava sect had become the dominant religion in Nepal. The Lichchavi kings used to call themselves the king of the sun race, or *suryavamsi*, and the great descendants of the great dynasty of Rama. Thus Rama was their ideal god-king. The influence of Rama can be seen in inscriptions as well. For instance, the inscriptions feature such names as Ramshil, Ramaswami, Armada, etc. In the Pashupati area there is a Lichchavi period figure or Rama dating back to the eighth century. Besides, the linguistic genealogy believed to have been written in the fourteenth century mentions a Ramayana play in four acts — *Chaturanka Ramayana* — performed in the Lichchavi period, c. fifth century.

Written tradition

The written tradition of the Ramayana in Nepal is quite old, too. From the evidence available, the written tradition of the Ramayana can be traced back to the early medieval period. A Sanskrit scholar of Tirhut Pradesh of Nepal had presented a beautiful copy of the Ramayana written on palm leaf to a Nepali official named Ananda in the year 1019. That is the earliest known copy of the Valmiki Ramayana.

In medieval Nepal the stories of the Ramayana were written in the then prevalent languages of Nepal such as Maithili, Newari, Sanskrit, and Prakrit. The Valmiki Ramayana was popular during this period. There is good collection of Ramayana manuscripts written in Old Devnagari, Devnagari, Newari, and Maithili scripts on palm leaves, Nepali paper, and ordinary sheets at the national archives of Nepal. These manuscripts, products of various times, show how deeply the Ramayana has influenced Nepali life and culture. During this period many plays based on the Ramayana were written and performed on various occasions; such, in fact, had become the order of the day.

A play entitled *Mahiravana Vadhopakhyana*, based on the story of Ramayana was written by a poet called Jayat in 1337, when Jayari Malladeva was the king of Kathmandu valley. By virtue of his popularity, Jayat received the title *Kavi Kamalabhaskara*. Another Malla king, Sumati Jaya Jitamitra Malla (1663-93), was a scholar of Sanskrit, Maithili, and Newari who wrote the long Ramayana play *Ramayananataka* in 15 acts. The works of another famous poet of this period, Dharma Gupta, include a series of Ramayana plays in Sanskrit, among them *Ramayananataka* and *Ramabhitseknataka*. The first play makes due acknowledgment to King Jaya Singh Mall for the encouragement that the poet received from him to write the play. Similarly King Ranajit Malla of Bhaktapur was a scholar of the Sanskrit, Newari, and Maithili languages. With the assistance of Ganesh Sharma, he wrote a long *Ramayananataka* in 40 acts, inspired by a copy of Valmiki Ramayana written by poet Kashi Nath that he had received in 1727. Poet Kashi Nath himself wrote a Ramayana play, *Balmikiramayananataka*, in 1765. The Ramayana plays were performed in festivals, birth and initiation ceremonies of princes and princesses, and in marriage ceremonies.

The popularity of the Ramayana was not confined to the Kathmandu valley. It was equally popular in the Himalayan kingdom of the Khas Mallas in the Karnali region of Nepal, as well as in the southern kingdom then called Simraungar lying in the *tarai* region of Nepal which had become a great centre of learning. Many scholars from this kingdom came to Kathmandu during medieval times. Their impact is discernible in some of the Ramayana plays written in Kathmandu during that time.

From the second half of the eighteenth century, when modern Nepal came into existence, the written tradition of the Ramayana assumed a new dimension. As the Nepali language spread far and wide in the kingdom, people began writing the Ramayana in that language as well. The Ramayana written in the years 1841-53 by a poet named Bhanubhakta Acharya, often regarded as the premier poet of the Nepali language, occupies the most prominent position among them. However, the metaphorical use of Rama in Nepali speech and prayers was evident even before Bhanubhakta popularized the Ramayana among the common people.

The predecessors of Bhanubhakta had also written the Ramayana in various forms. The *Adhyatmaramayana* (a comprehensive story of the Ramayana in Prose), story of the last section of the Ramayana by an anonymous poet. Lanka chapter of the Ramayana by Padma Sharma, the *Adhyatmaramayan Balun* of Patanjali Gajurel written in the folk medium named *balun* (a form of dance-drama), and the *Sundarakandaramayana* of Raghunath Pokhryal were quite popular. Bhanubhakta assimilated all the assorted trends of the Ramayana prevalent before him, mainly writings of the regular poets and Rama prayers prepared by the Gurus and followers of the *santa* cults, principal among them the Josmani cult.

The impact of Bhanubhakta's Ramayana on Nepali letters and Nepali culture was felt very deeply after him. The tradition of Ramayana writings has continued even up to the present. Poet Moti Ram Bhatta, wrote devotional songs based on the Ramayana of Bhanubhakta. In modern times, the late poets Lekhnath Poudyal, Balakrishna Sama, Somnath Sigdyal, Laxmi Prasad Devkota, Bhimnidhi Tiwari, and several other poets have made use of the Ramayana in various forms.

The Adhyatma Nepali Ramayana of Bhanubhakta was the first true Nepali epic story of the Ramayana. This Ramayana became popular through its use of the language of the common people and its achievement of literary excellence. Additionally, the values represented by the Ramayana of the poet were in harmony with the values held by Nepalis society — his Rama was a Nepali Rama, his Sita was a Nepali Sita, his Hanumana was Nepali Hanumana; the story flows in a manner familiar to the Nepali people; and Nepali folk-life, social ethics and practices, cultural values, and the Hindu religion and philosophy find reflection in the Ramayana of Bhanubhakta. Mention should also be made of another factor which is no less responsible for making the story of the Ramayana popular among the populace — namely, the appeal of the *Adhyatmaramayana* which elevates Rama to the position of God. To understand why the *adhyatmaramayana* was extolled by the Nepali poets, and why it was so well received, we must go back to the history of Nepal.

Nepal fought a war with the British government in India in 1814-16, and at its conclusion signed a treaty which ended the history of land victory by the kingdom of the Nepal. On top of that, the charismatic Prime Minister Bhimsen Thapa was imprisoned and subjected to a humiliating death. The effect of the downfall of Bhimsen Thapa must have deeply shaken the sensitive poets, who wrote poems in praise of him. The court intrigues, coups and counter-coups, cold-blooded murders, courtiers fight for power and royal favour, and the subsequent Kot massacre in 1846 had plunged the nation into despair and insecurity. Now circumstances forced the people to become introverted and, as a result more devotional and religious-minded. This sudden and jolting swing from the external world to the internal world of religion was responsible for the production of religious poems by poets of this period. The people and poets alike read the stories of the *Adhyatmaramayana*, and the Ramayana of Bhanubhakta fulfilled the deep-seated need of the Nepali people. The Ramayana of Bhanubhakta was sung by farmers, cowherds, soldiers, bards, scholars, carpenters, hawkers, fighters, and lovers; valleys, dunes, plains, mountains, gorges, and hills began to echo with the singing of the Ramayana. Ramayana became the song of the Nepali people. In this sense, its role in the task of national and cultural unification is very great indeed. Nepali emigrants to India became one under the Ramayana, forgetting their differences of castes and creeds. They still celebrate the birthday of the poet in the form of a festival, and the Ramayana is the symbol of their unity. The influence of Bhanubhakta's Ramayana is very great in the folk-culture in Nepal. In weddings, for instance, people representing to the two parties of the bride and bridegroom exchange verses from Bhanubhakta's Ramayana in a mood of competition. Such duets are very popular among the great majority of people in Nepal and, the Ramayana is recited on several other occasions, too. Rama and Sita as presented in Bhanubhakta's Ramayana are regarded as the paragons of virtue, and the victory of Rama over Ravana has symbolic victory of justice over injustice, truth over falsehood, and light over darkness. This symbolic excellence of the Ramayana has long been accepted in Nepali culture, and Bhanubhakta's Ramayana has presented the symbolic excellence of the Ramayana in simple and effective poetic style, winning the hearts of the millions.

Ramayana in oral tradition

Many religious stories are prevalent in oral traditions of Nepal. The Ramayana is one of them. The Ramayana features in various songs and dances as well as in folk-ballads and singing such as *balun*, *Khaijadibhajan*, *dharmari*, *hori*, and *chaits*. Similarly, in prayers, alliterative verbal repartees, and in the songs of the bards — the *gainnes* — the ideal characters are extolled profusely.

The *balun* is a very ancient form of folk singing in Nepal. The subject matter of the *balun* derives primarily from the story of the Ramayana. Poets have also utilized this medium to the Ramayana. *Sitajikochait, Ramjikochait* and *Hanimantakochaits* are popular ballads in western Nepal. These *chaits* are believed to have been in the oral tradition long before the coming of Bhanubhakta's Ramayana. Their versions of the Ramayana differ considerably from the original version of the Valmiki Ramayana. Besides *chaits,* other forms of ballads and singing are also popular in western Nepal.

Many oral traditions of the Ramayana are prevalent in other parts of the Kingdom. For instance, *Sitalachomanasambad* is one in which the dialogues between the two characters at the hour of crisis when Rama goes after the golden deer is presented. In prayers sung to the accompaniment of the tambourine called *khainjari,* we can hear the moving story of the Ramayana. In all these ballads the character of Rama as a hero is presented in an entirely original manner. Rama and his folks all have Nepali associations and Nepali sentiments. So much so that the Cheapang and Kusunda tribes and the Nepali bards — the *gaines* — claim to be the descendants of Rama. Dances of the Ramayana are performed on various occasions. In the famous *Indrajatra* festival of Kathmandu, dances based on the ten incarnations of Vishnu are performed. The Hanuman dance, popular in the Baglung valley in western Nepal, depicts its own version of the Ramayana story, featuring, for instance, the dance showing Hanuman fetching Sita from Lanka.

The name of Rama is used in popular expression and sayings. Men and, sometimes, women are named after Rama. The most common and most popular prayer among the Hindus is *hererama hererama ramarama harehare,* and *ramram*! is a very popular expression of greeting and a word used to demonstrate one's compassion. Rama hymns are chanted in the funeral procession. In day-to-day life, *rama* is used as a counting term. Usually *rama* means one.

Many festivals are associated with the Ramayana in Nepal. *Ramnawami, Janakinawami, Bibahapan-chami,* and *Badadasain* are the most important. *Ramanawami* falls on the ninth day of the white moon in the month of March. This day, celebrated as the birthday of Rama and national holiday in Nepal, spent saying prayers and decorating the temples of Rama and Krishna. People fast on this day, and processions of tableaus or pantomimes of the Ramayana are taken around. Talks are given on the theme of Rama and his impact on the society and culture, and fairs are organized. The greatest fair is held in the Rama-Janaki temple in Janakpur. Thousands of people from all over Nepal and India come to attend this fair.

Janakinawami is the birthday of Sita, which falls on the ninth day of the white moon in the month of April. There is an interesting story about the birth of Janaki — daughter of king Janaka — or Sita. Once a great famine occurred in the kingdom of Janaka. The king, to lift this state of depression, performed a great *yagya.* At the end of the *yagya* the king himself went to till the barren land with a gold plough, and from the furrow emerged a beautiful girl who was later named Sita, or "furrow-child". This day is celebrated with great enthusiasm in Janakpur and other places of Nepal

Bibahapanchami is celebrated especially in Janakpur itself. The marriage of Sita and Rama is commemorated on this day, when tableaus based on the story of the Rama-Sita marriage are taken out from the Ram-Janaki temple to the open ground. Thousands of people come to see this festival. *Dasain* is the greatest festival of the Hindus. It has become a national festival in the same sense as the Christmas and the Easter festivals are in the Christian world. On the tenth day of the white moon in the month of October, Rama is said to have prayed to Goddess Durga and acquired strength, then killed the demon-king of Lanka and rescued Sita. This day is celebrated as the victory of truth over falsehood and light over darkness.

Conclusion

In conclusion, we can say that the impact of the Ramayana on Nepali life and culture is very deep-rooted. This becomes evident from the Nepali belief that the first Sanskrit epic story of the Ramayana was created by Valmiki in Nepal. The Ramayana has found expression in Nepali inscriptions, sculptures, carvings, murals, and manuscripts that almost fill the pagodas, temples, walls, archives, and libraries in Nepal. The influence of the Valmiki Ramayana was quite wide-spread in the ancient and medieval period, but in the modern kingdom of Nepal its place was taken by the *Adhyatmaramayana.* The close study of folk legends prevalent in different parts of the kingdom, and the analysis of manuscripts written at various times tend to suggest the all-pervasiveness of the influence of the Ramayana in this country. Nepalis feel at home with the Ramayana, for Sita was the daughter of a Nepali king Janaka, and Rama came to Nepal to marry her; and above all, a Nepali poet wrote the epic story in Nepali. The Nepali state has declared the three figures, king Janaka, Sita and poet Bhanubhakta, as national heroes. Indeed, the Ramayana has deep into the lives of the people, forming the very matrix of Nepali culture.

Part 10

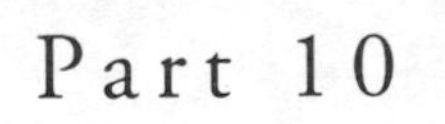

Games and Pastimes

Painting of Japanese children playing with bamboo horses (eighteenth century).

Traditional Sports and Games

A Rich Variety of Chinese Traditional Sports

China is a multifarious country, its splendid culture created by the peoples of various nationalities, each with its own time-honoured culture. From ancient times, these people have devised varied and colourful sports and handed them down from generation to generation. Being part of the age-old civilization of the Chinese nation, traditional folk sports are loved by the people. Some traditional folk sports not only benefit the people's health, but are also imbued with patriotic significance in encouraging people, to struggle courageously against evil forces. Physical, moral and intellectual education have thus been combined in a remarkable way.

Dragon-boat racing

Dragon-boat racing fully exemplifies the form and content of traditional Chinese folk sports.

Historical records show that some 2,000 years ago during the Warring States Period (475-221 BC), Qu Yuan, a brilliant statesman, thinker and great patriotic poet, was framed by sycophants and sent into exile by a fatuous and self-indulgent ruler. To protest against the dark rule and show his ardent love for his country, Qu Yuan drowned himself in the Milu River on the fifth day of the fifth lunar month in 278 BC According to legend, when the local people heard that Qu Yuan had jumped into the river, they tried to rescue him in boats. To cherish the memory and mourn the death of this great patriotic poet, the fifth day of the fifth lunar month was set aside for the "Dragon-boat Festival." People in the southern part of the country held commemorative activities every year on that day, rowing boats on the lakes and rivers so as to grieve over Qu Yuan's death. Later, these activities developed into boat racing, with the people decorating the bows of their boats with dragons on that day to show the unity of the Chinese nation. This is the origin of dragon-boat racing.

Dragon-boat racing during the Dragon-boat Festival is very popular in the southern part of china. It is both ceremonious and exciting, with huge crowds of people gathering on both banks of the river, their cheers mingling with the din of gongs and drums. The individual ethnic groups hold their dragon-boat regatta at different times. That of the Han people falls on the fifth day of the fifth lunar month, for the Miao people it is from 24 to 27 May, while dragon-boat racing for the Dai people is held during the grand Water-Sprinkling Festival (about ten days after the Pure Brightness Festival of the fifth solar term).

Dragon boats are made of sturdy and lightweight wood, and can be divided into two structural types, one with an inverted "V" shape and a large body with thirty to thirty-two oarsmen, while the other has a square stem and a small body with twenty-six to twenty-eight oarsmen. The dragon boat is generally twenty to thirty metres in length and one metre in breadth. But there are some large dragon boats in Guandong Province with eighty oarsmen. Dragon boats are categorized as gold, silver, red, black, blue or multicoloured according to the varied colours of the decorated dragon heads, and the costumes of a boat's oarsmen should be in conformity with the colour of that boat's dragon head. For example, oarsmen of the gold dragon boat should be in yellow, and those in the coloured dragon boat be wrapped with yellow turbans and wear coloured shirts with colourful silk belts. When these dragon boats speed ahead on vast rivers or lakes that empty into the sky, people looking at them from afar seem to see real dragons flying into the clouds. It is really a magnificent sight.

Young people always regard their participation in dragon-boat racing as a glory. In order to select the best oarsmen, tryouts are held in every village. Formerly, those who could carry fifty kilograms of rice around the village and step into the door of the ancestral hall of the village would qualify as oarsmen. Nowadays, with the village as a unit, elimination series are held first, with finalists taking part in festival dragon-boat racing. The number of dragon boats taking part varies from place to place; there are a dozen or so boats in some places, and fifty to sixty boats in other localities.

Long ago, victory in dragon-boat racing was not determined by first reaching the finishing line. Spectators on both banks of the river would hang out strings of silver coins on bamboo poles, and the oarsmen who seized these were the victors.

Later when the victor came to be decided by who reached the finishing line first, the distance for dragon-boat racing was not fixed. Depending on the specific conditions of the surface of the water, it ranges from several hundred to several thousand metres. A straight stretch of water is, however, always chosen as the arena for the competition. Big bamboo poles standing in the water serve as starting and finishing lines. As soon as the starting order is issued, there is a deafening sound of drums over the water, and the dragon boats make a dash for the finishing line. The cheers of viewers flanking the river resound like thunder, and the whole scene is imbued with a passionate and joyous atmosphere.

Shuttlecock

Shuttlecock, another-traditional folk sport with a long history in China, was developed from ancient "rubber ball" (a kind of football). Records about shuttlecock kicking date from the Tang Dynasty (618-907). *A Biography of Eminent Monks — Stories About Indian Monks and Buddhas of Shaolin Temple at Weisongyue* of the Tang Dynasty recorded that Shamen Huiguang, 12, kicked reversely a shuttlecock five hundred times at a stretch on a railing. The Origin of Things of the Song Dynasty (960-1279) states, "Nowadays, children take to kicking something called shuttlecock, which has a lead bottom tied up with a sheaf of chicken feathers, in threes or fives. They have many ways of kicking, such as kicking it up-wards, reversely, onto the knees, bellies and foreheads. It was developed from rubber ball". During the Qing Dynasty (1616-1912), shuttlecock was listed by emperors as a military training item. The above records show that shuttlecock is not only an ancient sport loved by people, but also a game of skill — a combination of sport, dance, acrobatics and game. At the 1912 shuttlecock exhibition match held in Beijing, players displayed more than one hundred ways of kicking. In 1984, shuttlecock was officially listed as a state sports event. Shuttlecocks have a bottom made from a coin or a piece of lead, tied up with a sheaf of long or short chicken feathers, of pieces of paper, or strips of cloth or wool. When kicked, they roll upwards like colourful, dancing butterflies and fall like flowers against a sheet of grass.

There are four basic ways kicking shuttlecocks — kicking with the inner side of a foot, the outer side of a foot, the knee and the instep — but the four can branch out into a diversity of skills, such as kicking with both feet, kicking with a jump and kicking reversely. In some cases, people kick shuttlecocks high up into the air or onto the head, shoulder, elbow, back, chest or belly, and then kick with the foot again.

In recent years, shuttlecock kicking has developed from a collective game into a sports event. The playground is halved by a net, with players of the two teams deployed on either side in a contest with features of football, badminton and volleyball. In March 1984, Beijing played host to the first shuttlecock invitational tournament.

Shuttlecock is a group contest that requires individual skill, and is of great entertainment value to the audience.

Men and women, old and young, can play shuttlecock anywhere and anytime and in either a complex or simple way. It is entertaining, interesting and enjoyable, and contribute to good health.

Horse racing

Horse racing, popular in areas peopled by minority nationalities such as Xinjiang, Tibet, Inner Mongolia, Yunnan and Guizhou, is held mostly on happy occasions. This activity dates far back into the Spring and Autumn Period (770-475 BC) when, according to the *Records of Historian — A biography of Sun Zi and Wu Qi,* Sun Bin a noted ancient strategist, with his wisdom helped Tian Ji, a general of the State of Qi, to win at horse racing against nobles. The record has it that Sun observed carefully the racehorses and found that the three horses of Tian Ti ("best", "better" and "good", rated as to how fast they could gallop) were no better than his rival's corresponding horses. Before the race began, he advised Tian to sue his "good" horse to meet his rival's "best" horse and take the loss. In the second race, he advised him to use his "best" one against the other's "better" one, and won. In the final match, Tian's "better" horse beat the other's "good" one. Thus, Tian Ji had two victories against one loss.

The *Xiyang Miscellaneous Group* records that, a Tang general named Xia was able to strike from a galloping horse a dozen coins set on the ground over twenty metres away one by one with something like a polo club. He was also able to throw boiled beans onto thorns fixed on walls, and did writing on the back of galloping horse. Ancient horsemanship was really incredible.

During the Yuan Dynasty (1271-1368), horse racing events were often held, as the ruling Mongolians were good at shooting from galloping horses, and horse racing became increasingly popular in subsequent dynasties. People of different nationalities have varied customs and diverse ways of racing horses. Generally speaking, there are two ways, "walking" and "running". The first type of competition determines, which horse "walks" faster, more stable and graceful, while the latter tests the speed and endurance of the horses. The distance is fixed, and the first horse to reach the destination is the winner.

Horse racing has found its way into the annual Nadam Fair of Father Snake: "From which well do you drink?"

Inner Mongolia, the "April 8" and "September Lusheng (reed-pipe wind instrument) Meeting" of the Miao nationality, and the "Dragon Boat Festival" of the Shui nationality. "Girls pursuit" is a very interesting kind of horse racing traditional to the Kazak and Uygur nationalities. Held on grassland around the fifteenth day of the seventh month each year, it is most loved by the young people. On that day, couples of boys and girls riding horses proceed slowly towards a designated place. Within the given distance, boys can express their love for the girls riding by their side as they please, and the girls are not supposed to show any sign of irritation or objection. On their way back, the girls run after the boys and may whip them if they can catch up with them. At this stage the boys may not hit back. This often greatly amuses the large audience, and the grassland resounds with laughter. As soon as the game begins, the boys are seen to bend over to the ears of the girls, whispering their love for the girls, who then flush to the roots of their hair; they look just like sweethearts to the audience. On their way back, however, there will be a different picture, with the boys running away helter-skelter or dodging the girls' whips. The audience will then be filled with anxiety or convulsed with laughter, Of course, careful observation will show that the girls are not whipping the boys hard and that their whips often fall onto the horses hindquarters, spurring the animals to run faster, but whoever has offended his girl will be rewarded with a whipping, naturally.

"Running off with a sheep" is also a popular sport of the Kazak, Uygur, Kirgiz and Tajik nationalities. It is held mostly on happy occasions. The two types are; (1) Collective game, carried out by two teams. A beheaded sheep whose intestines have been removed is laid in a designated spot. At the report of a gun, members of both teams spur their horses forward toward the sheep. The person who grabs the sheep then has to rush to the destination with the help of his fellow team members. Members of the other team, of course, do their utmost to seize the sheep from their rivals. Whoever delivers the sheep to the goal gains victory for his team. (2) Individual game, conducted by two people representing their own respective units. Whoever brings the dead sheep to the goal is the winner. In accordance with local custom, the winning side will have the sheep roasted on the spot and enjoy the mutton together with all the horsemen, adding lustre to the festival.

There are only a few of the rich and colourful traditional folk sports loved by the various peoples of China.

Revival of Ssirum — Korean Folk Wrestling

Ssirum, perhaps the ultimate one-on-one contest, is a traditional folk sport for individual men in Korea who like to pit their courage, strength and skill against those of a worthy opponent.

Today, three national *ssirum* championships are held annually in Korea during such folk festivals as *Taeborum* falling on the fifteenth day of the first lunar month, *Tano* on the fifth of the fifth lunar month and *Ch'usok* on the fifteenth of the eight lunar month. The winner of each of these contests receives the title *Chonha Changsa*, or Grand Champion.

In addition, there are seven weight-class championships, and the winner in each class is called *Changsa* (Champion). The Grand Championships can be participated in by any *ssirum* enthusiast, regardless of his weight and his club, and the Grand Champion is thus considered the strongest *ssirum* wrestler in the country.

Ssirum contestants are classified into four weight divisions, and a particular class championship can be participated in by only those *ssirum* wrestlers whose weight falls within a that category.

There are also numerous amateur *ssirum* contests held throughout the year in the country, averaging about two *ssirum* contests a month.

Ssirum contests are held in a sand ring nine meters in diameter. Before the fight, the two contestants tie a sash called *satpa* around the waist and the crotch, one blue and the other red, and the fight starts with the two contestants grasping the sash of the other. The one who takes the other down on the sand emerges the winner. Because *ssirum* does not require any equipment besides *satpa*, and because *ssirum* can be fought by any man and is easy to understand for any spectator, it has been traditionally popular among the Korean people.

In *ssirum* not only strength but also skill is needed to take the opponent down, and there are many specific skills -- 54 offensive and 54 defensive skills, each of these with variations. *Ssirum* is a body-to-body fight in which one takes the other down, and its origin is difficult to establish with certainty. At the beginning of human history, men must have needed some sports to develop strength in order to hunt and protect themselves. Development of strength and quick movement by means of some physical exercise must have enabled the early inhabitants of the Korean peninsula to gather food relatively easily for their survival as a race, and such physical exercise must have developed eventually into *ssirum* as it is enjoyed as a sport today.

In 1905, a mural painting in a Koguryo (first century BC to seventh century AD) tomb was discovered in the Tungkou Plains of Manchuria. The tomb, believed to have been built in the fourth century AD, is called *Kakcho-ch'ong*, meaning *ssirum* tomb, because the painting shows a *ssirum* match scene. Based on this *ssirum* painting, this sport is believed to have been popular among the Koguryo people, since the early years of Korean history.

In the middle of the fourteenth century, King Ch'unghye, the twenty-eighth monarch of the Koryo Dynasty, was an enthusiastic *ssirum* fan to the extent that he not only enjoyed the sport as a spectator but also as a contestant. He held *ssirum* matches in the palace, and he himself fought a palace eunuch, according to historical records.

Popular as it was in ancient times, *ssirum* had been a declining sport until recently. With the influx of Western sports and their rapid spread among the people, *ssirum* had lost much of its popular appeal. As a result, the traditional sport had slipped outside the public interest.

But *ssirum* has never disappeared from Korea. It just lingered in the background. With the forming of the Korean Folk Ssirum Association in 1983, *ssirum* gained momentum for a rapid revival into an explosive popularity. For instance, the Fourth Grand Championship, held in June 1984, marked a 65 per cent view rating when it was televised across the country, and the gymnasium was full each day during the match, with many would be spectators having to return home to view it on television.

As *ssirum* gains popularity, so does the Grand Champion. He is a kind of idol to adults as well as children, becoming one of the two most popular persons in the country, the other being the top pop music singer.

What are the reasons for *ssirum* gaining such popularity in such a short period? Many reasons can be cited, but the foremost reason is that the sport is easy for everybody to understand and enjoy. Of the two fighters, the one who takes the other down on the sand emerges the victor. There is no need for spectators to know a complex set of rules.

Another reason is that because the fighters wear only short pants and a sash and compete in a contest of strength, it can be said that *ssirum* is a rather primitive and instinctive sport that has a strong appeal to modern people overcome by a mechanized civilization. In *ssirum* fighters modern people find their lost muscle, and this causes them to be enthusiastic about this sport of body-to-body confrontation.

Recently in Korea there has been a movement among intellectuals to rediscover traditional Korean culture. The movement, together with the revival of *ssirum*, has helped remind people of their common heritage and inspire a kind of nostalgia for the lost pieces of traditional culture.

Every Korean adult male must have experienced competing in *ssirum* when he was young, and his enthusiasm for *ssirum* is therefore great.

When a *ssirum* fight is staged, a festival mood is in evidence around the ring, with gongs and drums playing farmer's music and singers and dancers in traditional Korean dress singing and dancing.

Ssirum contenders usually represent the balanced beauty of the human body and the baroque-style beauty of massive forms, and artists like to draw them. When one *ssirum* wrestler dumps his opponent down on his back, the falling body presents the beauty of rotating curves in the air. When the fighter swiftly moves his body to employ various techniques or puts forth his all strength against the opponent, one may be reminded of Michelangelo's works.

In the *ssirum* fight, we find movements of tension, flexibility, panting, bursting confrontation, the display of a skill against the rushing force, and finally the falling body scattering sand. *Ssirum* is, however, a peaceful symbol of strength, grace and drama.

Popular throughout the Ages — Sumo, the National Sport of Japan

History of Sumo, Japanese traditional wrestling

Sumo, first became known as Japan's national sport in year 42 of the Meiji Period (1909 AD) with the opening of the Ryogoku Kokugikan (national *sumo* stadium), but has a long history in Japan, dating from the third century BC (early Yayoi Period), as a widely practised ceremony, known as *shinji sumo*, petitioning the gods for abundant harvest of crops. Although contests of strength such as *sumo* are found throughout the world, the distinguishing feature of *sumo* in Japan in that, more than simply a sport, it is inseparably associated with agriculture as a ritual addressed to the gods. In Japan, not only *sumo* but other contests like traditional horse racing, archery, and tug-of-war are events that involve calling upon the gods for their favour.

According to Yamato Period records from around the sixth century AD, adjacent villages would select contestants for a *sumo* match, the outcome of which would supposedly indicate which village would enjoy the more successful harvest. This *sumo* developed among the common people came to be favourably regarded by the nobility, and was then adopted as a palace function in the form of *sechie sumo* (sechie is an archaic word meaning a festive meal in honour of the deities). This *sechie sumo* first appeared about 1200 years ago, during the reign of the emperor Shomu in the late Nara Period, as a ceremony in the Tanabata Festival held on the seventh day of the seventh month. Then, in the Heian Period (794-1191) it seems to have been instituted as an annual event, taking place in the eighth month, to predict the fortunes of the people in the coming year. The fact that *sumo*, *jarai* (archery contests of New Year festivities), and *umayumi* (equestrian archery contests of the fifth month), known collectively as *sandosechi*, existed as important palace ceremonies cannot escape notice in a survey of Japanese cultural history.

Sachie sumo became an annual tournament of splendour in the Heian Period, accompanied by *bugaku* (court music and dance) and merry-making in the palace garden, for the emperor and his favoured subjects. For this occasion, strong and skilful contestants were gathered from the provinces, and the event grew in scale up until the end of the tenth century.

The *sumo* ring of today was not yet in use; instead a space of the palace grounds, was designated, and the match was decided by throwing one's opponent to the ground or causing him to touch the ground with hand or knee.

As *sechie sumo*, carried out for some three hundred years, lapsed along with the transfer of power and influence from the court to the military families, *buke sumo*, or *sumo* as a martial art, emerged. With the beginning of the Kamakura Period in 1192, what was once a gay court ceremony became a military discipline, an everyday training exercise for soldiers. *Sumo* wrestlers became soldiers and took their combat skills to the battlefield, and *sumo* became something to enjoy as part of drinking parties on days when no battles needed to be fought. In periods of peace, these soldier wrestlers returned to their homes and functioned as teachers of *sumo*, and the sport gained popularity throughout the country.

In what is known as the age of civil wars (1477-1572), *sumo* was promoted as an indispensable martial art for the *samurai* (warrior). It recorded that the famous Oda Nobunaga, head of *samurai* class, organized a *sumo* tournament for the entertainment of important persons, recruiting men of strength from all the provinces, with he himself presenting a prize of a bow and arrows to the winner.

Finally, when the wars were ended and the entire country unified under the shogunate of Tokugawa Ieyasu at the beginning of the Edo Period (1603-1868), jobless *samurai* were grouped into professional *sumo* associations, and *sumo* again became an entertainment spectacle. In Osaka and Kyoto, benefit *sumo* (*kanjin sumo*) events were used to raise funds for construction and maintenance of Shinto shrines and Buddhist temples as well as roads and bridges, and even after this *sumo* ceased to be used in fund-raising it was allowed to retain the name *kanjin*, for all *sumo* matches had to occur with the permission of a governmental office in charge of the temples and shrines. The *kanjin sumo* instituted primarily in Osaka and Kyoto was subsequently brought to Edo (the present Tokyo) with the Tokugawa shogunate and became increasingly popular, with famous grapplers. In this Edo *kanjin sumo*, to form and features for present-day *ozumo* ("grand sumo") developed.

It was in the Edo Period, then, that *sumo* came to be an important means of entertainment for the common people while, at the same time, provincial feudal lords (*daimyo*) recruited and supported their own teams of *sumo* wrestlers, who would wear their *daimyo's* crest or emblem on their decorative aprons when entering the ring in contests against wrestlers of other *daimyo* teams.

Directly following the three hundred years of isolationism in the Edo Period, the Meiji Reformation of 1868 did away with the privileged military class, and *sumo* wrestlers formerly under the patronage of *daimyo* were suddenly unemployed. Then, in the fourth year of Meiji, an edict against the long hair and sword-carrying custom of the *samurai* still allowed the characteristic *mage* (top-knot hairstyle) for *sumo* wrestlers, and from the year Meiji 17 (1884), when *sumo* was held at the Shibahama resort palace for the emperor, the sport began once more to gain in popularity.

Before long came the golden age of *sumo* with rivalry between the two *yokozuna* (champions) Hitachiyama and Umegatani, and in 1909, as mentioined at the beginning, a *sumo* tournament hall was completed in the Ryogoku district of Tokyo and named Kokugikan (National *sumo* stadium).

Sumo tournaments, fomerly held outdoors in temporary structures or tents and scheduled as ten-day events to allow for delays due to rain or snow, from the Meiji Period on have been carried out regardless of weather conditions.

Sumo has, then, come down to us from the ancient days when it was rooted in the lives of the people as an agrarian ritual, through *sechie sumo, buke sumo*, to the today's *ozumo*.

Sumo and the ring

While there are numerous kinds of wrestling found in the world, the *dohyo*, the ring in which *sumo* contests take place, distinguishes Japan's brand of wrestling from all others. It is within this circular ring, and due greatly to the space limitation it places on the wrestler, that the numerous techniques used in competition and the depth and beauty of *somo* exist.

This *dohyo* is 4.5 metres in diameter and the ring bordering it, made of rice straw, is five centimentres above ground level. Long ago, when there was no *dohyo* used, spectators and wrestlers sat to make a circle in which the bouts took place. Later it became a circular or square place enclosed by poles with a rope tied to them encircling the ring. Then straw rice-bags came to be used as the ring border. Finally the present form of *dohyo*, specially made straw rice-bags buried halfway into the ground, was systemized, probably in the middle of the Edo Period.

Victory goes to the contender who first either forces his opponent out of the ring or forces him to make contact with the ground with any part of his body except, of course, the soles of the feet. It should be noted, however, that even should the foot or feet of a wrestler extend out over then *dohyo*, as long as the outside of the ring is not touched the bout continues. In such instances the five-centimetre-high *dohyo* plays an important part in deciding the outcome of the match.

There are seventy different winning techniques recognized in *sumo*, all of these based on one or more of three principles: *tsuki* (slapping or thrusting), *oshi* (pushing), and *yori* (grapping or clinching). Particularly enjoyed by spectators is the technique *utchari*, in which the apparent loser, balanced on his heels on the ring border, arches his back and lifts his opponent off the ground and, turning his own body to one side, throws him out of the ring.

The contest takes place in the limited area within the *dohyo* but, at the same time, skilful movement and strategy in that circular space allows employment of many techniques, making the ring, in a sense, a place of no limits. For example, in the championship bout of the autumn 1984 tournament, the victor Tagaryu turned the rush of his 215 kg. opponent Konishiki (nicknamed "The Hawaiian Mosnster") to his own advantage by grasping his arm and spinning him around the ring, thereby turning him from his target and causing him to lose his balance and go down on one hand. *Sumo* has, it appears, evolved its depth and appeal from the rules and limitations it abides by.

Unlike other grappling sports such as wrestling, boxing, and even judo, in which competitors are divided into weight classes, in *sumo* the smaller wrestlers find themselves up against larger opponents, as there is not classification by weight. Herein lies another attraction of *sumo*, that of a small contestant winning through skilful use of technique.

The ring and the formal beauty surrounding it

Suspended by ropes above the *sumo* ring is the *tsuriyane*, a roof-life structure patterned after the roof of a Shinto shrine. From the four corners of the *tsuriyane* are hung tassels that indicated the four seasons of the year — green for spring, red for summer, white for autumn, and black for winter.

In addition to the coordinated styling of the ring itself, there is the heavy silk kimono, such as those worn about six hundred years ago by Ashikaga Period *samurai*, and black imperial court hat fashioned after traditional Shinto priest hats, both of these worn by the *gyoji* (referee), and, as for the wrestlers themselves, the *mage* (top-knot hairstyle) and apparel — the *keshomawashi* (decorated apron) worn in *dohyoiri* (ring-entering ceremony) and *shimekomi* (loincloth), also known as *torimawashi* — that combine to produce a traditional Japanese stylistic beauty.

How a sumo match progresses

The *rikishi* (wrestler) first enters the dressing room, goes through warm-up exercises, and waits to be called for his match. With two matches yet to precede his own, he goes out and sits at either the east or the west side of the ring, depending on the affiliation of his *heya* (training "stable").

When his name is called, the *rikishi* climbs into the ring and goes through pre-bout procedure, including stamping heavily on the ground (*shiko*), rinsing the mouth with water, tossing salt into the ring (a purifying ritual), and clapping the hands together twice, followed by opening both hands to signify that he is without weapon and intends to grapple honestly and fairly (this is called *chiri o kiru*). The referee (*gyoji*) is fully engrossed in leading, observing, and judging the competition from the time both *rikishi* step into the ring until they leave it.

Before the two *rikishi* grapple, they do what is called *shikiri* — slowly lowering their fists to the ground and crouching down to stare into each other's eyes while checking their own balance and posture. If their feeling and state of readiness are not mutual, they return to their respective sides (east or west) and toss more salt into the ring, then repeat the *shikiri* ritual again or a number of times until they both simultaneously lunge at each other. During this ritual their psychological states are brought together, and the will to fight and overcome, as well as level of tension, becomes increasingly stronger. If *shikiri* continues up to the four-minute time limit, the referee orders them to begin the bout. Both *rikishi* lower their hands and hips a final time, then leap forward to wrestle. Bursting into action at the instant when the breath is held is considered to the best way to begin a bout.

Shikiri, well understood by Japanese *sumo* fans, impressed former Mexican president Portillo, who commented at the exhibition tournament in Mexico: "*Sumo*, more than simply a sport, seems to be the way of the *samurai*. Through the *shikiri*, where both contestants combine their mutual respect, trust, and intentions, the intensity of the bout becomes as a ball of fire. *Shikiri* and *tachiai* (the sudden meeting of the contestants that follows) display well the concentration and resolve of the wrestlers. Anyone who desires to know about the Japanese should observe *shikiri* and *tachiai* of *sumo*."

What the Japanese people like about sumo

Mankind has from ancient times enjoyed giving expression to the fighting spirit by pairing off and attempting to topple each other, and *sumo* represents the orderly exploitation of this natural competitive urge.

Sumo fans in Japan appreciate the fearlessness and daring involved in two contenders meeting each other's challenge, bare-handed and clothed in only *mawashi* (loincloth). The match features an all-out effort in a short time period, and rules are simple, and the outcome of the match is readily understood. The one-on-one competitive situation in *sumo*, furthermore, quickly involves the spectators emotionally and, at times, makes one feels as if he or she were actually there in the ring grappling.

To the Japanese people, *sumo* is sport that has long been familiar and well-loved in their environment. Practically every middle-aged and older Japanese man has in his youth experienced *sumo* first-hand. *Sumo* has occurred on the grounds of temples and shrines, on public grounds in towns and cities, and in schoolyards, with a simple circle drawn on a patch of sand serving as the ring. It is something that can be done nearly anywhere in any attire, with a sport or utility belt as *mawashi*.

Japanese people have, however, had increasingly less experience with *sumo* since the end of World War II. One reason for this is the entry of a number of sports from the West. It seems, nonetheless, that Japanese youths, although larger in size with each generation, have less body strength than before, and the Chamber of Commerce and Industry for Youth, with an eye to the value of *sumo* as a discipline as well as a sport, is currently promoting a nationwide programme of *sumo* for children, known as *midget sumo*. The resurgence of sumo is also evident in clubs and competition in elementary, middle, and high schools, as well as universities and social clubs, with university *sumo* grand champions frequently going on they become professional *sumo* wrestlers.

Popularity of sumo in Japan and abroad

Honbasho (major *sumo* tournaments) are held six times during the year, (three in Tokyo, one each in Osaka, Nagoya, and Fukuoka), and between tounaments the wrestlers take *sumo* to fans in other parts of Japan by holding matches in cities and areas where there are no *honbasho*.

The length of *honbasho* has increased from ten days to twelve, and finally to the present fifteen days.

These *honbasho* are televised live and have a consistent viewing rate unsurpassed by other sports broadcasts, indicating the considerable popularity of *sumo* as a spectator sport. The public broadcasting network NHK presents each tournament in its entirety, and commercial television stations offer condensed *sumo* programmes.

In 1964, young Jesse Kuhaulua (known in the *sumo* world as Takamiyama) came from Hawaii to Japan to complete in professional *sumo*, and in 1972 became the first non-Japanese wrestler to win the grand championship, causing a sudden rise in the popularity of *sumo* among foreigners, and video-taped *sumo* came to be shown on television in Hawaii.

Fans, including young people, women and foreigners, look forward to seeing their favourite wrestlers enter the ring, and the appeal of *sumo* is spreading to other parts of the world. This is shown by the reception given to recent goodwill exhibition matches in USSR, Mexico and China.

"Tail Eating Snake" Game of Thailand

There are no people in the world who are without some forms of games and sports. Ancient records of many countries tell of man indulging in all kinds of games and sports, some of which are still played today. Such early games and sports activities probably began with children imitating the actions of their elders. Boys may play with toy weapons concocted from sticks of discarded appliances and girls may dress themselves up as princesses or queens. Given the richness of the child's imagination, there could be an infinite number of children's games all over the world.

Over a long time, these activities may have developed into proper sports and games. It is noteworthy to distinguish child-play from game and sport. Child-play is more or less a spontaneous activity, for when a child is playing, he is directing himself according to his inclination at that time. But players in a game of sport are expected to follow a set of understood rules or agreements. Such rules may be sketchy or ambiguous; nevertheless they are rules which all participants should observe in order to make the game or sport proceed with interesting effects.

Some traditional games and sports played by Thai adults are quite competitive, and the incentive to win is very strong. Included in this category are Thai martial games and sports. There are also other Thai adult's traditional games and sports which do not result in winning or losing for either side. The purpose of this type of game or sport is simply to ensure a good time for all.

Thai children's games and sports are no less interesting than those of adults. A toss or drawing at the beginning of some children's games decides the role of each team or players. This preliminary is often accompanied by gibberish or rhyme-chanting. Once the game starts, children are drawn together in pursuit of the same objective, with each one trying to follow the rules of fair play to the best of one's ability. Participation in games and other enjoyment is truly sacred to the child. Children's games and sports are not to be looked upon as merely a means for children to release energy, but also as activities to generate physical and mental strength for the task at hand.

Some anthropologists compare games and sports for children with rite and rituals for adults. Rites are perceived by anthropologists as the rules of conduct which tell how humans should conduct themselves in the presence of sacred objects. Rites and all that they symbolize serve to draw people together, to renew feelings of solidarity. Children's games and sports can provide all of this for children.

In Thailand there is one childrens' game which fits the foregoing description. The name of the game in the vernacular is *ngu kin harng*, literally translated as 'tail-eating snake.' This game in more or less the same form is played by children in many parts of Thailand. From all available evidence, the game, or at least its prototype, may have been in existence since the beginning of Thai history.

Snakes are known to fascinate peoples all over the world. Large serpents, dragons and *naga* feature in folktales, legends, myths and decorative art of many cultures. The fascination of the Thai people with these creatures does not limit itself to material and literary arts, but finds its way into the world of sports and games.

The 'tail-eating snake' game is generally considered to be a game for small children, although young adults sometimes play this game during the time of the traditional new years festival. The stage version for a public audience is performed by Thai dancers to the accompaniment of traditional music.

As a game proper, the number of participants is not restricted, but is normally kept to between seven and ten players. The game is a contest between one player and the rest. The one player, who comprises one team, is called "Father Snake". The other team is headed by a player to be known as 'Mother Snake', while each of the remaining players in this team is to act out role of 'Baby Snake.'

To start the game, all Baby Snakes are lined up one behind the other to form a standing row, with Mother Snake standing at the head of the line. Except for Mother Snake, each one in the row uses both hands to hold the one in front by the waist. When this is completed, Father Snake takes up his position facing Mother Snake.

Mother Snake and Father Snake now proceed with a dialogue which is a crucial part of the game. The verbal exchange goes something like;

Father Snake: "Dear Mother Snake."

Mother Snake: "Yes, Father Snake?"

Father Snake: "From which well do you drink?"

Mother Snake: "We drink from the well in the sandy ground."

Mother Snake and Baby Snakes in a chorus: "Round and round we go."

The row of Mother Snake and Baby Snakes then moves from side to side to simulate the sidewinding action of a snake. Then comes the second round of the dialogue.

Father Snake: "Dear Mother Snake."

Mother Snake: "Yes, Father Snake?"

Father Snake: "We drink from the well in stone."

Mother Snake and Baby Snakes in a chorus: "Hone and hone we do."

Once again the row of Mother Snake and Baby Snakes moves from side to side to simulate the sidewinding action of a snake. This is followed by the third round of the dialogue.

Mother Snake: "We drink from the well in grief."

Mother Snake and Baby Snakes in a chorus: 'Lief and lief we do."

Again the row of Mother Snake and Baby Snakes moves as it has done before. After three rounds of a similar dialogue comes the fourth, which somewhat departs from the previous three.

Father Snake: Which is edible, head or tail?"

Mother Snake: "The middle part and all that avails!"

With this answer the climax of the game begins. Father Snake immediately rushes at the line of Baby Snakes to catch the last Baby Snake in the line as his first victim while Mother Snake will do her very best to fend off the attack and protect all her Baby Snakes in the line. Father Snake, unhampered by the connected long row of Baby Snakes, always succeeds in detaching and capturing the last Baby Snake in the line. The captive is subjected to a cross-examination which goes as following;

Father Snake: "With whom do you want to stay, Mom or Dad?"

Baby Snake: "I stay with Dad."

Father Snake: "Down in the hot chilli sauce with your ripped of head, Young Cad!"

Alternative lines for the caught Baby Snake and Father Snake after the question, "With whom do you want to stay, Mom or Dad?" are as follows;

Baby Snake: "I stay with Mom."

Father Snake: "Down the river to the jungle in the cast-off raft, Old Chum!"

The game may terminate with the dialogue between Father Snake and its victim or begin again by immobilizing the Baby Snake caught and cross-examined, and going through the same procedure

The 'tail-eating snake' game may seem trivial and pointless to the modern mind, yet every aspect of the game is full of symbolic significance. The symbolic representation serves to remind us of many things that we many have long forgotten. The dialogue of the game hints that women in the distant past were the providers of water. It also presents the traditional images of the father and the mother. The father, of course, represents authority and one to be feared, appeased and propitiated, while the mother is associated with solace, gratification and protection.

Some see in the game a description of married life, which is bound to have a few ups and downs. Whenever the family is broken, children are destined to their own fate.

Any symbolic representation by nature is open to several interpretations. No matter how many ways it can be interpreted, some elements of mystery always persist. In the case of the 'tail-eating snake' game, the puzzle lies in the name of the game. Why a snake and why should it eat its own tail?

Sports and Games in India

India has always had a very dynamic and exciting tradition of indigenous sports and games. The credit for this goes to the unique Indian way of life that recommended complete personality development through various exercises and activities. Some of them like chess and yogic exercises have travelled wide across the globe and gained international recognition.

Of the outdoor diversions, kabaddi, wrestling, kite flying, hockey and cricket are enjoyed by all and sundry.

While games like carrom board and Chinese Chequers are well assimilated into the Indian system, outdoor sports like squash, badminton, lawn tennis and table tennis are still the privilege of the few.

Yoga

Although a spiritual term meaning addition or union with God, the word Yoga has come to denote various bodily posture as practised by spiritual seekers to keep their body healthy and mind sharp. Its capacity to enhance mental concentration and instill confidence has made it a hot favourite of all those embarked on the path of personality transformation all over the world.

Chess

Like Yoga, Chess, too was originated in India. It travelled far and wide first through the Arabs and then the Roman Empire.

In ancient times, India was a great exporter of chess boards and chessmen made of ivory and studded with diamonds and other precious stones.

It remained the favourite past-time of kings and nobles all through the Indian history.

Even today, Indian players are making their name in this game. Most prominent among them is that of Grand Master Vishwanathan Anand.

Chaupar

Like Chess, Chaupar or game of dice, has a classical antiquity. As one of the oldest indoor diversion of the Indian people, it finds its most celebrated reference in the great epic *Mahabharata* where Kauravas use it to defeat their wronged cousins, Pandavas.

It was also a favourite court game next only to chess. It was more popular among ladies as it requires less concentration than chess.

It is usually played between two or four players on the lines drawn on the floor itself.

Pachisi

As another game of dice of gutis, it has been quite popular with both rural and urban populace. *Do guti, tre guti, nau guti* and *bara guti* are the names given to its different types. Two pieces are used in *do guti,* three in *tre,* nine in *nau guti.* The game of guti played in Madhya Pradesh resemble closely to that of *bara guti* played in Punjab.

Chaugan

Popularly known as polo today, chaugan was patronised by kings and nobles alike. It was, as is now, played on sprawling grounds also called chaugans after the game. All princely states in pre-independent India boasted of at least one chaugan, the more famous of them being the chaugan of Chamba and Jaipur.

The game has always been played on horseback with each of the ten players holding in his hand a chaugan stick with a crooked end. The ball was taken hold of it by that end and was either slowly taken to the circle by the players or was forcibly hit, the horseman galloping after it to pass it between the posts which are equivalent to goals.

Hockey

India's national game, hockey, not long ago, was a symbol of the country's sportsmanship. Much of the credit for this goes to players like legendary Dhyan Chand or Babu. Hockey found early reference in Indian literature, especially the Bengali literature, where there is a reference to the playing of *dhophari* which was in fact a hockey game played with a crooked stick and a ball in the rural areas.

But it came to the national centrestage only after becoming tremendously popular in Punjab. It soon became the most popular national game with India donning the proud mantle of world champion in the 60s.

Wrestling

Better known as *Kushti* in the entire Indian sub-continent, wrestling is still one of the most entertaining outdoor diversion among the youth.

One reason for its unabated popularity is its benefit of a sound health and strong physique to its regular practitioners.

This is perhaps the only outdoor game which is equally popular in both rural and urban areas.

In villages, matches or dangals are held on every festive occasion.

Boxing

A favourite pastime of the urban youth, boxing is getting increasingly popular as it provides excellent opportunity for body building.

Boxing sans its modern trappings, i.e. masks and gloves have long been popular in India.

Mallkhamb

Very popular in Maharashtra, mallkhamb is an ancient Indian game designed for young boys to ensure their strong and supple physique.

As the name indicates, *khamb* or a pillar, well-oiled in advance, is left to be climbed by players. Their skill lies in scaling the tall slippery pillar swiftly without falling within a stipulated time.

Lazium

It's another favourite of school children. In medieval period, a game similar to the modern form, was made compulsory by the great Maratha ruler Shivaji as part of the daily exercises of his huge standing army.

Martial sports

Martial sports have always found favour with people fond of risk and adventure. India has had a glorious tradition of archery and swordsmanship. Our great epics *Ramayana* and

Mahabharata celebrate them as essential accomplishments of an intrepid warrior. Classical personages like Rama and Arjuna were excellent archers. Indian archers have always drawn inspiration from them, including Eklavya, the self-taught contemporary of Arjuna.

Interestingly, India's national champion in archery Limba Ram is a tribal youth who learnt this sports from his elders in the family.

Swordsmanship has also found favour with soldiers all through the history. Today also, it has avid practitioners in the country.

Horse riding and racing

Both these sports evoke great interest among Indians, young and old alike. Both have been a source of outdoor diversion as well as livelihood ever since man learnt to tame the horse.

In ancient and medieval periods, horses were used in chariot races. Horse riding was very popular and skilled riders were highly praised. But things have changed now. It is no longer a popular outdoor diversion. Today, it is confined to a privileged few due to heavy expenses involved.

However, horse racing continues to be popular as it provides the people an opportunity to speculate and gamble. The thrill of victory makes gamblers throng to the race course all over the country.

Bull and cow race

Villagers all over India still derive great pleasure from the races of bulls and cows regularly in villages. These races are marked with great fanfare and festivity.

They are very often held on festive occasions and are accompanied by great fanfare.

Fishing

Much in vogue in India, like anywhere else, fishing is dear to those found of relishing fish and other marine products.

Fishing on a large scale for commercial purposes has also become very lucrative business. However, man's lust for lucre has resulted in poaching in the case of some rare species like the susu dolphin found in the waters of Bay of Bengal.

Boating

In a land of many rivers, boating comes naturally as a good community entertainment.

Boat races are held in almost all parts of the country, especially in Kerala during Onam celebrations every year. Along with boating, yatching is also becoming increasingly popular.

Swimming

But there can be no fun like swimming. India may not have won laurels in international swimming competitions, but almost every Indian born near a stream, river or sea, knows swimming.

It is as ancient as chess or chaupar or yoga.

Cricket

A vestige of India's colonial past, cricket has virtually become a national obsession in the country. The pride of place which once belonged to hockey, is now occupied by cricket.

This has had an adverse effect on other games especially hockey and football which are more suited to Indian clime and ensure greater community participation besides including feelings of sportsmanship and brotherhood among players. However, with its galaxy of cricket players like Kapil Dev, Sachin Tendulkar and Sunil Gavaskar, India has made a mark in this game.

Football

Like hockey in Punjab, football is more popular in West Bengal. It is much like by fun-loving Calcuttans. Football genuinely needs to be promoted, much like many other games, to the national sports scene to enable India make its mark in this game too. Interestingly, this game also has an interesting classical reference. Krishna, the epic hero of *Mahabharata*, was fond of playing the game of ball with his friends and fellow cowherds.

Adventure sports

Trekking, mountaineering, skiing, scuba diving and car rallies are being keenly promoted by Indian authorities as part of their tourism development plan. While mountaineering and trekking are not new, scuba diving and skiing are getting increased attention.

Mountaineering, trekking expeditions and car rallies evoke great interest in both men and women alike. Bacchendri Pal, the first woman to ever scale the Everest is an Indian.

In addition to these well-known sports and games, every state and region of the country can boast of distinct and popular diversions. For instance, the *Gedi* game of the tribals of Madhya Pradesh or the bamboo dance of Nagaland are a beautiful combination of skill and aesthetics.

"Arnis de Mano" — Philippine Martial Art

Its origins

In the book *The Way of the Warrior,* written by Howard Reid and Michael Croucher (Century Publishing, London), the authors theorise that the original roots of what are known as martial arts in Asia go back to the highly feudalized societies of China and India prior to 500 BC The People's Republic of China as we know it today was then a hodgepodge of small independent states constantly at war with each other. The conflicting parties of the time on occasion "would even hold single combat (a style of warfare that was essentially a martial art) before their opposing armies, to decide the issues at stake". The same feudalistic societies encouraged the development of individual fighting skills in relation to travelling merchants, who must have employed bodyguards to protect themselves and their goods from brigands The potential for small-scale, close-quarter combat was rife in such circumstances; therefore the need for skilled martial arts practitioners.

The routes of commerce would eventually extend to Indonesia and Malaysia, and then to the Philippines.

It would thus appear that, far from being truly indigenous, *arnis* is just a variation of fighting skills tracing back to the world's oldest civilization.

Records of the Shri-Vishaya Empire, dating back to AD eighth century refer to *kali* (Malay for blended weapon) as the martial art of the early island inhabitants of what is now the Philippines. The migration of Malays with the subsequent intermarriages resulted in a lending of techniques, but the original term *kali* remained.

It is said that ten *datu* (chieftains) from Borneo, remnants of the erstwhile Malay Empire, contributed to the growth of the art by requiring their warriors to learn and master it for the tribe's protection. In time, *kali* became part of the youth's learning processes in much the same way as reading and writing.

The Spanish influence

On 7 April 1521, a Portuguese's explorer named Ferdinand Magellan arrived on the island of Cebu as the head of a Spanish expedition. Cebu's Rajah Humabon readily embraced the new religion (Christianity) proffered by the newcomers but the neighbouring chieftain on Mactan Island would not, nor would he pay tribute. Incensed by the defiance, Magellan launched a punitive sortie but was instead repulsed in the famous Battle of Mactan, in which Magellan lost his life. There is every reason to believe that the Mactan warriors, led by their chief Datu Lapulapu, were skilled *kali* practitioners. Magellan's chronicler, Pigafetta, who survived the debacle, wrote of "sticks hardened by fire" as some of the weapons used by the native against them.

Lapulapu's successful repulse of Spain's first inroad into the islands did not, however, prevent the latter from eventually colonizing the archipelago about five decades later.

Roots of the term

Arnis, the term used to describe the fighting art today, comes from the Spanish *arma de mano* (harness of the hands). Other terms used are *eskrima, estocada, pang-olisi and pagkali — kali.*

Suppression of the art

Under Spanish domination, *arnis* was banned ostensively for being "too brutal." It is easy to understand why many think the real reason is something else.

The ban forced the practice underground, but it surfaced during fiestas and other celebrations in the guise of *moro moro* and similar folks plays.

Evolution into a sport

When the Americans replaced the Spaniards after four and a half centuries of rule, the Philippine fighting craft resurfaced countrywide. *Arnis* clubs came into being, propagating the skill from one generation to the next, primarily as a form of self defence. The Americans would call it "stick fighting" because *arnis* protagonists use wooden poles.

Official recognition of *arnis* as a sport came only in 1975, when the National Arnis Association of the Philippines (*NARAPHIL)* was formed. Four years later, on 24 March 1979, a national tournament was held in Cebu City. A second tournament followed in Manila, the Philippine capital, in August of the same year.

The country's leading exponents

Perhaps because it was the first and largest trading centre of the Philippine archipelago even before the arrival of Magellan, the province of Cebu is the acknowledged centre of the most skilled *arnis* practitioners in the country. In the two and only national tournaments held to date, the champion in the Masters Division came from the Canete family of Cebu City. Long before the official recognition of *arnis* as a sport in 1975, the Canete clan were already in the forefront of *arnis* development in spite of the traditional secrecy such fighting arts were known for. In 1932, the *Doce Pares* (twelve pairs) club was formed by the *Canete — Saavedra* families of Cebu. Similar smaller clubs would follow countrywide and, in time, competitions would be held.

The early *arnis* encounters were bloody, even occasionally fatal affairs. There being no formal rules, the winner in a match emerges when his opponent either simply is unable to carry on or surrenders. Protective devices of any kind have traditionally not been used.

The country's most colourful *arnis* fighter is the youngest of the Canete clan, Ciriaco "Cacoy" Canete. His exploits include a fairly recent duel held in Cebu where a challenger from another club was beaten to submission in a matter of less than a minute. Of him, Reid and Croucher Write:

"There were 12 children in the family, eight boys and four girls. They were all taught the traditional form of *eskrima (arnis)* by their father and uncles. The youngest boy was taught mainly by his older brothers.

"He turned out to be the sort of man who can rethink the accepted patterns of thought and action. Cacoy Canete has greatly advanced the level of skill and techniques used in *eskrima.* He was concentrated on using a light, hardwood stick approximately 75 centimetres (2-1/2 ft.). long. He fought more than 100 challenge matches and was never beaten. These challenges were real fights in which neither armour nor protection were permitted, and which end in the collapse of submission of the loser".

Arnis fights are not limited to the sue of sticks. In *eskrima,* unlike most other systems, the weapon skills are just the starting point. Should the stick be lost as in a disarming stroke, variations using bare bands are allowed (or resorted to in actual combat).

Eskrido

In the 1950s Cacoy Canete studied judo and karate. From that training, he experimented with the *eskrima* and judo, blending their techniques. Thus were incorporated into the traditional *arnis* strokes the Oriental sweeps, throwing and ground work techniques. When he considered the enriched style sufficiently different from classical *eskrima,* he coined the term "eskrido". It obviously derives from *eskri(ma)* and *(ju)do.*

Without intending to, this blending and the coining of a different name may well give us a clue to the many forms of martial arts the world over. It is a safe bet that many ancient cultures developed truly indigenous fighting techniques, but as people from other lands came by with other forms, inevitable blending occurred. The *eskrido* episode is a fine example.

Tribute to arnis

Likely as an offshoot of the book *The Way of the Warrior* and BBC film documentary on Asian martial arts that preceded it, a movie is now in the works featuring *arnis* Grand-master Cacoy Canete and Mike Williams. Directed by Wilfrendo Milan and produced by Dr. Frank Scalercio, Jr., it is titled "Eye of the Sun".

Arnis has finally come of age.

Games of Mongolian People

"Tsam" — religious mask dance

Tsam is mystery play based on Buddhist mythology. In ancient times Tsam were per formed in big monasteries. This art of dance is almost forgotten now. Tsam originated in ancient India, and was brought to Tibet a thousand years ago by the divine Padmasambhava, renowned for his victories over demons and spirits. In the sixteenth century it spread to Mongolia. In Mongolia Tsam was enriched with elements of witchcraft and the pagan traditions of the nomads. The mystery play formed part of the local Buddhists' cult rites. The Mongolian Tsam costumes and masks, as well as stage sets, differ considerably from those used in other Buddhist countries. They contrast sharply in colour in accordance with local tastes, Monglian masks were in bold primary colours — red, black, yellow, white and blue — and therefore looked more expressive. The masks were big and bright so that the audience could see them clearly. They were much larger than life-size, but however big, all the masks were invariably made in strict conformity with the canons of religious decorative and applied arts. Masks were masterfully done and lavishly decorated designed to inspire awe and veneration for the deities. They were made from papier-mache and richly inlaid with coral, gold, silver and precious stones, and painted with gouache and mineral dyes. The ancient masters had a great talent for harmony and use the most effective combination of colours.

The *Tsam* masks depicted the main Buddhist deities which numbered several dozens. During the nineteenth century, numerous monasteries were built in the country and magnificent *Tsam* performances were staged there. One performance a year was given at each of the 700 major monasteries. The last one was performed in the late thirties in the square in front of the Choijin-lama's monastery in Ulaanbaatar.

There were three types of *Tsam*: the first presents episodes from the life of Milaraiba, a famous Indian hermit poet of the eleventh century, the second is about Khan Gassar, the folk here and the third, Erlik, Tsam, is about the struggle between good and evil.

The performers of the mask dance enacted ancient ritual dances and scenes from the lives of heaven-dwellers and heroes. By their movements and gestures the actors conveyed the idea of the eternal triumph of good over evil and life over death. Wearing various coloured masks and performing a dynamic dance with jumps, they led an old man with a long white beard out of the temple. He was the Lord of the Life Supporter, accompanied by six boys. When all actors were assembled, the bull-like Yamaraja, the lord of Hades came onto the stage. he wore rich clothes adorned with gold and silver and precious stones and a terrifying mask topped with a crown made from skull. And with his participation, the dance were performed.

For *Tsam* performances long preparations were necessary. Rehearsal one or two months prior to the event under the guidance of an experienced high-ranking Lama. Some of the *Tsam* scenarios have survived. One of them, about Gessar-Khan, contains 94 acts. Apart from the scenario proper, it includes a detailed description of the costumes and masks, and an explanation of the symbolism.

Naadam

In Mongolia, the national sports festival is called *Naadam*-the most famous celebration of the traditional way. Wrestling, archery and horse-racing are the Three Main Games of Men which are rotted in the mists of antiquity and continue to be very popular among the Mongols today.

In twelfth-thirteenth century, military festivals were widespread, at which men tried their strength and their steeds' agility. From the seventeenth century onwards, *Naadam* contests were held regularly during religious holidays. Since 1922, they have been held on the anniversary of the people's revolution. Wrestling is the most national and popular of all Mongol sports. It is the highlight of the Three Games of Men. Historians claim that Mongol-style wresting originated some seven thousand years ago. The technique and ritual of Mongolian wrestling is distinctly national. There are no weight categories or age limits in Mongolian national wrestling. The wrestlers were heavy boots, a very small tight-fitting loincloth, a pair of sleeves which meet across the back of the shoulders, resembling a tiny vestige of a jacket, and pointed cap of velvet. The contestants come out on the field leaping and dancing, flapping their arms in imitation of an eagle. Each wrestler has his attendant herald. The aim of the sport is to knock your opponent off balance and throw him down, making him touch the ground with his elbow and knee. The loser walks under the raised arms of the winner in a sign of respect, and unties his vest, after which the victor, again leaping and dancing, takes a turn round the flag in the centre of the field. The victor is awarded symbolic prizes — biscuits and *aruul,* or dried curds; once he has tasted these, he offers them to his seconds and to spectators.

Traditionally, either one thousand and twenty-four or five hundred and twelve wrestlers participate in the contest. Today the latter number usually take part. At the Republican Naadam nine rounds are held. Those who lose in one round are eliminated from further rounds.

A wrestler who beats five opponents in a row is awarded the title of "Republican Falcon"; one who wins seven rounds is given the title of "Elephant". A wrestler becomes a champion by winning nine rounds and is given the title of "Lion", and if he wins two years running he is called "Giant". If a wrestler becomes a third-time champion at the Naadam the attribute "Nation-wide" is added to his title, and the fourth time, he is styled "Invincible".

The winners of the tournament receive honorary titles and are also awarded various souvenirs. But for them, the main award is the truly nation-wide popularity and fame that they gain.

Horse-racing is a normal part of the Naadam. This sport is also centuries old, dating back to the Bronze Age.

The horses for the Naadam races are selected a month before the big day. They are then taken to a adequate pasture separate from the heard and trained. Racehorses are divided into several age groups: two, four and five years old; over five years; and stallions. The riders are aged from 1.2 Mongolian children of these ages are good riders, as both boys and girls have been riding since infancy. As the popular saying goes, "The nomad is born in the saddle"

Small saddles are made specially for children, but they usually prefer to ride without them. They are not only superb riders, but also skilful tacticians. They know how to hold the horse back so it has enough strength to last the entire distance of the race. Competitions are not held on special race tracks, but right across the steppe, where riders are confronted with various obstacles such as rivers, ravines and hills. The distance varies according to the age of the horse, between 15 and 35 km. The riders are dressed in bright, colourful and comfortable clothes. On their backs are various symbolic pictures. Symbolic ornaments and designs also embellish the horse-cloth.

The most exciting moments are the start and the finish. Before the beginning of the contest the young horsemen ride round the starting point three times yelling the ancient call, "Giingo!", a kind of war-cry. When all the horses step behind the boundary lines, the starting command is given and the riders surge forward, setting in motion the long-awaited race. The winning riders do a full circuit of the stadium, each accompanied by a herald. The winning horse receives the honorary title "Forehead of Ten Thousand Race Horses" and the five runners-up are awarded medals. They are popularly called the "Koumiss Five". In accordance with tradition, the riders on the winning horses do three laps of honour, then ride up to the grandstand, and each child is offered a large bowl of *airag* — fermented mare's milk — from which he drinks and then pours some on the rump of his horse. The herald in turn, chants in poem-form the virtues of the house, its rider and owner. But there is also a interesting tradition is connection with the losers. Honour and praise of the winners of the race is to be expected; but the losers are also rewarded and honoured. After the awards ceremony for the victors, the racer who came in last is led up to the main stand with his young rider. The loser's face shows vexation and shame. But the spectators do not make fun of him. Instead they shout encouragement and try to give him confidence in himself. The national story-teller recites a special ode to the loser. The ode encourages him with words expressing faith in his future success.

Archery

Ample information about archery can be found in literary and historical documents of the thirteenth century and even before. It is an ancient sport of the Mongols which can be traced back to as early as 300-200 BC According to historians, archery contests began in the eleventh century.

The Mongols use a compound bow built up of layers of born, sinew, bark and wood. When unstrung it is not straight, but curved. Archery is more archaic and ritualistic than other sports. All archers adopt the same stance and posture. The target consists of a row several meters across, of small woven leather rings, some painted red, which are laid out laterally on the ground. The openings face upwards, providing a challenging exercise in trajectory for the archers. In olden times, women did not participate in the contest, but in the last few decades they have started to do so. The distance is about 75m for men and 60 m for women. Men shoot about 40 arrows and must score not less then 15 points and women shoot 20 arrows and must score at least 13 points using the same bows as the men.

When the arrow hits the target, a group of people standing near the target, acting as judges, raise cry "Puukhai!" and make sings with their hands to indicate the result. The one who scores the most points is the winner and the title of *Mergen* (or Supermarksman) is bestowed on him or her.

Japanese children playing "war"
(Painting of about thirteenth century).

Children's Games in Asia

Picture-Drawing Songs of Japanese Children

The children of Japan make use of a large number of songs to accompany the play-time activities that play such a large role in their lives. Among the most interesting of these are, in particular, the picture-drawing songs. Children of every country, in some form or other, begin at an early age to depict the things in their environment that attract and please them, or else very familiar scenes or people, using still rough and unformed lines and curves. It is also common for children to mumble quietly to themselves as they draw — telling themselves the story of the drawing or, perhaps, imitating the sounds of the objects, cars and the like, which appear in their picture. While such an accompaniment to the act drawing is extremely common, when the quiet mumblings take on the characteristics of a "song" — displaying to some extent a definite melody and rhythm--they become something altogether different. At this point, a song, combined with the simple action of drawing, leads to a whole different phase of development. The most important element is no longer whether the picture is well or poorly drawn. Instead, the emphasis is on the enjoyment of the intertwining of the picture and the song--the text and melody and rhythm--that is sung as the picture moves toward completion. Let us explain in the following order the characteristics of these picture-drawing songs: 1) their characteristics as a form of play; 2) the types of drawings and texts; and 3) their musical characteristics.

Characteristics as a form of play

The first characteristic we will examine is that as a rule, picture-drawing songs are a form of play for one child only. Among the play songs of Japanese children there are many which require at least two playmates. For children, of course, any type of game or play activity is more enjoyable when it can be shared with other children, and many interesting activities contain elements inculcating rules, wisdom, and attitudes regarding social interaction and group relations. Picture-drawing songs, on the other hand, can be enjoyed together by several children, but only one child will actually draw the picture. In this, these songs differ from forms of play in which children must coordinate their voices and actions. This characteristic is directly reflected in the music of the picture-drawing songs and is an important factor in determining the nature of those songs.

The fact that there need be no coordinated action leaves a great deal of margin for individual, rather than group, creativity in the picture-drawing songs and provides the possibility of improvisation. As a result, even though the product of the process on different occasions may be the same picture, each child may, during the process, select the text or melody that suits his particular image or mood at the moment, and thus there is a wide range of variants for the same song. A second feature is that even in a restricted area with as little as a piece of chalk, a child can enjoy a picture-drawing song. Requiring far less space than a playground and far less than for hide-and-seek and similar action games, picture-drawing songs are possible in narrow back streets, in a corner of a classroom, in the narrow canyon between city buildings, or almost anywhere. If paper is unavailable, there are always the dirt on walls (if the child doesn't mind being scolded for scribbling on walls); if there is no chalk, a child can use a stone or a stick to draw in the dirt. In short, picture-drawing songs require only the very simplest of tools or accessories, and a child can easily enjoy this activity any time he wishes with an absolute minimum of restrictions.

Such a total ease of enjoyment, when combined with children's abundant creativeness, means that countless new picture-drawing songs and variants are constantly being born, soon to pass out of existence. Among this mass of short-lived picture-drawing songs, however, there will be some that the children come to like in particular, and these will become fixed in a more-or-less concrete form and will be passed on. Among these, again there will probably be some "masterpieces" which are particularly apt combinations of picture, text, and melody. Next, let us examine some such "masterpieces."

Types of drawing and texts

Children use the shapes of letters, characters, and objects related to the song's text in completing their drawings. Or perhaps it would be better to say that the words of the text are selected so that the characters or objects, in symbolic form, may be used in the picture. The methods of creating a drawing may be broadly divided in the following way: a) use primarily of characters of the Japanese language (*hiragana* or *Katakana* — Japanese phonetic characters — or numbers); b) use primarily of representations of objects (for example, drawing three circles to represent three eggs); and c) use of characters and objects in a combination of types a) and b). Each syllable "he no he no mo he ji," is represented by a single *hiragana* phonetic character in the drawings, and these are written in a particular order to produce a human face. This is one extremely popular example known to every Japanese. The *kana* phónetic characters are derived from Chinese ideographic characters which, after being imported to Japan, were highly abbreviated and simplified and came to be used solely for their phonetic values. Learning the *Kana* syllabary is one of the very first steps in the education of Japanese children, and combining selected *kana* characters results in a very comical face and expression.

In type B — representations of objects — the child while singing "mimizu, tamago, ame arare" (some worms and three eggs, some rain and some hail"), draws the objects named and while drawing the circle of the head, finally sings " al to iu ma ni tako nyudo" ("and oh! all of a sudden, an octopus appears"). In terms of text, the order of elements and the line of thought is really of little importance. Actually, words have been chosen to fit the shapes and forms of the drawing, and such nonsensical contents linking these symbols and words plainly hold more interest and fun for the children. The final set phrase "all to iu ma ni..." (the short, sudden "a" being an expression of surprise) ties together and completes the drawing, and the more unexpected the result, the greater its effect — a device used in a variety of songs. With the final stroke, there is a thrill which releases all the anticipation built up while waiting to see what kind of picture will be produced. In addition, for the children of Japan, an island country encompassed by the sea, feelings about the octopus are quite different than those in the West; rather than being very unpleasant and unattractive, the octopus is viewed almost fondly as a very familiar and humorous animal. This is an integral part of this drawing's status as a "masterpiece," for no matter how many times it is repeated, it is always interesting and full of a sense of familiarity.

By juxtaposing two 3's, 4, a baby *tanuki* or raccoon dog is drawn, but there are two different texts, A and B, for this one drawing. Text A gains its effect through use of a final wrapping-up phrase to complete the picture. Text B, on the other hand, features a phrase often used when drawing animals — "draw a pointed beak and we've got...." The *tanuki* of this drawing is well known and loved by the children of Japan as a humorous leading figure in Japanese folk tales and folk songs.

An elaborate picture-drawings song for girls, incorporate thickly-drawn letters of the alphabet, *kana* characters and numbers in the drawing. It also displays a customary pattern of picture-drawing songs in the words used for drawing faces and hands — "Rokugatsu muika wa Sankanbi" ('The sixth of June is the P.T.A.") — and those often used in other picture for drawing feet — "Tate tate, yoko yoko, maru kaite, chon" ("Draw a line, one more line, cross it, cross it, cross it, circle point"). In either case, along with a pleasant play of sounds, this example also shows the efforts that children put into making inconsistencies in the text fit together as they draw a unified systematic picture. The above examples are, of course, representative of only a limited sampling of Japanese children's picture-drawing songs. And as mentioned earlier, children are constantly trying out new creations, making the total number of such picture-drawing songs extremely large. One important point is that these creations are the result of borrowing existing elements out of the past and employing customarily used phrases, and if the creation is uninteresting, it is mercilessly discarded. A further interesting point is that in these pictures, a high proportion of the things depicted are faces, human figures, or related objects; when animals appear, they are usually comparatively small (*tanuki*, ducks, fish, octopus, etc.), with landscapes and scenery seldom making an appearance. Granted, concrete objects such as fans, paper lanterns and the like to sometimes appear, but even these are limited to objects which are both directly and commonly experienced by the children and provide interesting material and subjects for their drawings.

Musical characteristics

Examining the structure of the melodies of picture-drawing songs, we see that in general melodic structure falls into one of two classifications: a) melodies in which the accents of the words are reflected unchanged in the melody; and b) those which make use in part of the melodies of songs learned at school or from other songs.

Speaking broadly, the Japanese language has a three-level system of accent, high, medium, and low, which is unrelated to rhythm but which is tied closely and directly to melody. A shift from high to low accent may be the only difference between two totally unlike words with the same absolute phonetic values. The song sung quietly by a child as he draws will naturally reflect the most common accents of the words of the text, and the great majority of the melodies of picture-drawing songs belong to this type a).

Scores 1 and 2 present a simple 2-note melody, and in the examples in Scores 3-5, one intermediate note (fa) is included to create a re-sol tetrachord. This is the normal basic structure both of the songs of Japanese children and of the folk songs of adults, and it is the simplest form taken by melodies when Japanese casually put their words to music. In the picture-drawing songs, the "ambitus" is likewise very restricted.

Type b), as shown in Score 6, has a comparatively wide ambit, with pentatonic scales being very common. Such melodies are composed, rather than naturally developed, melodies, and children use them where they prove convenient, sometimes adapting them slightly and sometimes combining them with various new texts.

The basic rhythm of the picture-drawing songs is a two-beat rhythm, as is also the case in traditional Japanese music. Attention must be paid to the tempo of the song, however, because when many things must be drawn to the accompaniment of a song which has a comparatively small number of beats, there are frequently changes in tempo, with the song at times being drawn out slowly to allow time for work on the picture, at times even being interrupted and being made to wait on the picture. Such variations in tempo no doubt derive from the emphasis being placed on the drawing rather than on the song, also reflecting the fact that picture-drawing songs are play activity for one single child. An additional more-or-less characteristic feature is that even in the case of as simple a drawing as a single line and a single circle, no one really cares whether the actions are necessarily coordinated with the song. This phenomenon is also found in Japanese working songs, where it is not felt absolutely necessary that be an exact correspondence between the motions of the job and the beat or rhythm of the song, seemingly one characteristic of the Japanese.

The cities and towns of modern Japan are plagued by problems of a deteriorating environment as population concentration becomes increasingly dense. For children, this means that space for playing is decreasing, and ever growing academic competition for grades and the resultant advancement to better schools is also gnawing away at the proportion of children's lives devoted to play activities. These circumstances are bringing about changes hour by hour in the forms of play and the play songs that Japanese children have enjoyed in the past.

The picture-drawing song is a very characteristic type of Japanese play song, found outside Japan, it is said, only in Korea and perhaps one or two other countries. At present, these picture-drawing songs are increasing in proportion to other play songs, and just what is the meaning of such a phenomenon? In terms of the picture-drawing song's nature as a form of play that can be casually enjoyed alone in a restricted area, unbothered by cars, is it a phenomenon to be welcomed? Or conversely, will children remain unchanged in any age, constantly putting to use their abundant creative powers in ways dictated by the changes in their environment? Since television today has an undeniably important influence on the lives of the children of Japan, in closing let us introduce a picture-drawing song, "Kawaii Kokku-san" ('The Cute Cook"), that was borrowed from children by a certain composer, who adapted it slightly but kept the melody basically unchanged, added accompaniment, and broadcast it via television. While this song has many variants reflecting the accents and idioms of various regional dialects, it is one picture-drawing song that is found in every corner of Japan.

Children's Games and Songs in the Philippines

hildren from the Philippines, like children all over the world, love to play games and sing songs. Playing is serious business for Filipino youngsters and are an important occupation. There are a variety of games that Filipino children play, such as: small and large group games, indoor and outdoor games, quiet games and games that make use of physical movement, relay games, conversation games, guessing games, musical games and games using special objects or equipment. These various games may belong to any one of 3 categories: a) traditional Philippine games, b) foreign games, c) Philippine adaptation of foreign games.

Transition of children's games

To draw a clear demarcation line distinguishing Philippine traditional games from Philippine adaptation of foreign games, and to trace the real origin of many of the traditional games is difficult. It could be said however that some of them have Spanish, Indian, Indonesian, Malay or Chinese elements since these peoples played an important part in the history of the country and influenced many aspects of Philippine life and culture.

The Filipinos had their own native games before the Spaniards came into the country. In the third century of Spanish rule, it is said that the Spaniards did not encourage the playing of games or sports of any kind among the Filipinos except for the latter part of their occupation, when a form of physical education was added as a subject in the school curriculum, of which playing games was only a part.

It was only during the early part of the American regime that modern games and organized play first introduced. This was done by American teachers in the Philippines via the public schools. Upon the formulation of the course of instruction in the public schools in 1903, the playing of games, together with calisthenics, was required of all children in the schools all over the country as part of the physical education requirement. After the second world war, games and sports have become an important part in everyone's life.

The more popular Philippine traditional games Filipino children play are "Harangang-Taga", "Sipa", "Siklot", "Sungka", and "Luksong-Tinik".

Singing games

Songs in singing games are usually short and easy to sing and the text usually relates to what the games is all about. Sometimes the words are a form of advice directed to the "it" telling him what to do in order to catch another "It". Some songs are in the form of dialogues sung alternately by the "it" and all the players.

Philippine singing game songs are sung in the dialect of the particular region from which the singing game originated. There are however some native songs with English text making the place of origin difficult to determine.

An old native singing game is the "Aswang-Aswang". "Aswangs" are blood-drinking vampires believed to exist in the Visayas. Mention of an "Aswang" is a very effective way to scare children.

The game is played by 10 or more children. A circle is drawn on the ground. A child is chosen as the "Aswang". The "Aswang" stays outside the circle, while the rest of the children remain inside. They sing the "Aswang-Aswang" song. The "Aswang" ("It") goes around the circle and tries to touch another child. (The children shout "Uy" at every attempt to touch them.) The children move about as fast as they can to escape the "it". Whoever is touched becomes the "Aswang" in turn.

Aswang-Aswang

Translation:

(Children) Beware of the Aswang it might catch us all.

(Aswang) I'll have plenty to eat if I catch you all.

A singing game of the llocanos in the North is "San Pedro" also called "Halaphalap" and Taptapay".

The players choose a leader then arrange themselves in a circle. The leader blindfolds a player ("it") and make him stand within the circle. The rest join hands and go around singing this song.

San Pedro

Translation:

Come, come right away!

Catch anybody and be changed at once!

At the end of the song, the blindfolded child touches one of the other players and tries to guess his name. If he makes the right guess, they exchange places. If the guess is not correct (he is limited to only one guess) he goes back to the centre while the children sing and start going around again.

A Philippine singing game that shows definite traces of Spanish influence is "Bordon de los Bordones". It might even be an adaptation of an original Spanish game. The words are Visayan interspersed with the Spanish "Bordon de los Bordones". This singing game makes us of a ring or a piece of stone. The children select a king and a catcher, then join hands and sit down on the ground forming a circle. They sing the song while secretly passing the ring from one hand to another until it reaches the king. The catcher watches this passing of the ring carefully, and approaches the player he thinks is holding the ring. The player caught is given a punishment by the king. He may be asked to sing a song, recite a poem or do something else which the king deems be a fit punishment. If the catcher fails to catch anybody, he himself is punished by the king.

Bordon de los Bordones

Translation: Bordon de los Bordones,

The ring of the king is dearer than someone's ring

Keep walking until you reach the place of the mighty king.

Philippine traditional games are more popular nowadays among children in the rural areas than among boys and girls in the cities. In these metropolitan areas, children play more of foreign outdoor games like pingpong, badminton, touching ball and rope skipping. Indoors, among the favourites are jackstone, pick up sticks and Chinese checkers.

In the last 30 years, foreign singing games have also become very popular among Filipino children. These are more often played than the old Philippine singing games.

The most well-known foreign singing games are "London Bridge", "Have you Ever Seen A Lassie" and "Dollar, Dollar". They have been sung and played by Filipino children since about the 1930s. "Little Sally Water", "Shoo Fly" and "Bean Porridge Hot", however, are some of the more recently introduced foreign singing games played by city children. Thought most of the native singing games do not seem to be sung and played as often as before, a few have retained their popularity. "Pen Pen de Sara Pen" is one. In its original form this singing game was short. The current version includes recent additions which has made it a 3 short-section song. The text consists of nonsense rhymes strung together.

Pen Pen de Sara Pen

Children's Games in Pakistan*

Imitation is one of the most powerful instinctive urges pronouncedly operative among the children whose games are by and large an imitation of the occupations and attitudes of the various social groups. It is through them that children not only entertain themselves but also unconsciously train themselves for various rules that they have to play in a particular society. Although there is a slight variation in children's games in the various

* Almost similar children's games are in India, especially in North India

provinces of Pakistan yet on the whole the pattern is similar everywhere. One may even venture to say that the pattern may be uniform the world over if allowance is granted to the degree of sociological development that has taken place in various parts of the World. A few of the children's games in Pakistan are described below:

Guryan (dolls)

Dollmaking and doll-playing is probably one of the most commonly pursued games of children everywhere. Groups of children get together to recreate the entire ritual of life through dolls. Grandmas who are retired and have much leisure make dolls for the children, out of otherwise unusable pieces of cloth. As they grow, children themselves make dolls which are usually modelled on a variety of Physical human contours with which they are familiar. The most fascinating aspect of doll-playing is the marriage ceremony arranged by children independently between he-doll and she-doll. The details of the ceremony run parallel to the details of actual marriages. Engagement, marriage songs, banquets etc. are arranged. Marriage parties are taken out and received. In fact the entire atmosphere of marriage is recreated by children.

Churian (bangles)

Girls play with broken pieces of bangles. By placing a piece on another a push is made.. If the underlying piece leaps up it is considered to be won by the girl who strikes.

Chhatapoo

A diagram is drawn with a piece of coal indicating rectangular spaces, usually 10 in number, with a narrow space in the middle which is a sort of obstacle in the games. With one leg suspended in the air a piece of stone is pushed with the foot on the ground in a manner that the dividing line of each rectangular space is not touched nor the piece of stone allowed to stick up on the line. If it so happens, it is regarded as a foul, and the player is out. The one who pushes the piece of stone through the spaces and brings it to the starting point successfully is considered to be winner of the games. This is a popular game and is usually played after the rainy season when children merrily get out of their houses after the weather has become pleasant.

Lukkan meti (hide and seek)

On moon-lit nights groups of children escape from their parent's vigil and run away to play hide and seek. One child is blindfolded and the rest scatter hiding themselves in nooks and corners. The blindfolded child has to seek out and catch one of his play mates. When he succeeds in doing so his turn is over and it passes on to the one who is caught.

Kokla chhapaki

Girls and boys sit in a circle in the open ground or in a spacious compound and form a circle. One of them holds a sort of whip made of twisted cloth. With this whip in hand the child proudly goes around the circle, sings a song and looks for any child who may chance to look backward. The moment such a child is caught the whip holder has a go at him. The one who is caught looking backward swiftly takes the whip in hand and repeats the whole performances. So the game goes on.

Gulli danda

It is very popular game, played with a "gulli" which is a piece of wood, about six inches long and has pointed ends. It is played throughout Pakistan mostly by children by occasionally but grown-ups too. They divide themselves into two teams who toss a coin to decide which team will be "in" first. A small hole is dug and the "gulli" is placed on it horizontally. A member of the team, that won the toss, throws the "gulli" up in the air and the other team does the fielding as players do in Hockey. If the thrown-up "gulli" is caught in the air, the player goes out. If it touches the ground, the player, comes on to bound it off by pressing it down at one of the pointed ends and by giving it a push with a stick when it rises up. The standing team tries to catch the "gulli" before it touches the ground. The same performance is repeated till the player is out. Each team plays in turn and stands to lose or win on the score of its players.

Kabaddi

Kabaddi is a game mainly for grown-ups yet children also play it with zest and pleasure. A line is drawn between two poles fixed in the ground. The two teams stand on either side of this dividing line. A player belonging to opposite side goes over to the other side pronouncing "Kodi Kodi", a meaningless word indicating the continuity of the player's breath. While on the other side the player has to wrestle his way through the opposing team and take care not to be caught or lose his breath. If there is a break in his pronouncement of "Kodi Kodi" or if he is caught by one of his opponents, he is regarded as a loser. But if he successfully runs across the lines and rejoins his own team, he is a winner. Obviously, the victory of the team depends on the performance of its members.

Jang planga

It is a very ancient game still played by children in villages in the vicinity of Rawalpindi. 5 to 20 boys participate in it. One of the boys takes a stick and passing it under his leg throws it away. One of the players runs off to catch the stick while the rest climb up the trees around. The boy with the stick follows them and if he succeeds in catching anyone, his turn is over and it passes on to the boy who has been caught. Catching the runaway boys is not easy, as they usually climb down the trees by catching twigs and run off to climb another tree. One poor boy may some times have to run for an hour to catch hold of his reliever.

Bander killa

In this game a large number of boys form a circle and fix a stump in the centre of the circle. With the stump is tied a string which is held generally a boy standing in the row. Around this boy are got together the shoes of the rest of them. The boy with a string in his hand flies around his legs alternately while everyone of the other boys try to pick up a shoe. If the boy happens to strike another boy with his leg, his turn is over. But if somebody succeeds in picking up the shoe and avoids being touched by the leg of the boy with the string he beats the fellow with that shoe.

Akhrot (nuts)

Nuts are used to play this game. A hole is dug in the ground. All the participants pool one nut each and the boy who wins toss gets the first turn. He rolls all the nuts on the ground towards the hole. The nuts that pour into the hole are won up by him and if he happens to strike one of the nuts outside the hole with a striker he wins the entire pool. But if he fails to do that, the turn passes on to the other party, and so the performance is repeated.

Latoo (top)

A circular shaped wooden toy with a leg and a nail stuck to the leg is called a latoo, or a top. A string of fine thread is rolled on the top starting with the leg going to the upper edge. Then if thrown down with a downward swing. The string is held back and the top moves round and round very quickly on the ground. Large number of boys get together and draw a circle fixing a top in the centre. Then the players swing their tops at the one that is fixed in the centre.

Clay houses

In the rainy season when the rain is over and the ground is wet, young children move out of their homes and try to make houses with the wet clay. The clay is rolled on to one of the naked feet and is patted by hand till it secures the shape of roof. Then the foot is drawn out leaving behind the clay structure which is later embellished by fixing small doors to it, usually made of straw.

Chaur sipahi (thief and the constable)

In the villages incidence of theft brings the villagers into contact with the police whose crude and harsh methods of investigation are often talked about. Children observe and hear all this. So they are tempted to enact the whole story in their games. Boys get together, some act the role of the police, others that of thieves. It is really delightful to see how innocent children wear frowning looks as constables and imitate the cunning ways of thieves. Laughter and fun are the feature of this dramatic performance.

Fashion — New and Old — in Traditional Children's Songs in Asia

"Old songs" and "New songs"

Fifteen years ago, teachers were under the impression that children's songs that had been traditionally transmitted to children in various form of children's games, and sung with such activities as hand-clapping, ball-bouncing, and rope-jumping had largely disappeared, although they themselves used to sing them when they were children. Their view was that in the age of radio and television, those old songs had largely disappeared and that even the existing few, if any would have little to do with rhythms of the hustling and bustling society of today.

However, the children in Japan know numerous old traditionally transmitted children's songs. And yet, most of those songs had gone through various changes so that there were few outward similarities with the traditional songs. In short, traditional children's songs are not simply handed down to later generations, but they all go through the stages of transformation as they are sung by each generation of children. In fact so much so that within the period of a little more than ten years, they are hardly thought to be the same songs. Consequently, the concept of "old songs" does not exist in reality. Popular, well loved songs have been constantly transformed in the process of transmission, and eventually many new words and melodies are added to them. Nor is the concept of "new songs" really meaningful. For in many cases songs that sound completely new and strange to us are new versions of the "old songs" we used to sing when we were children. For example, the recently popular song called "Let's Fly a Man-made Satellite" and the game goes with it seem quite new at first glance. But, in reality, the song is based on the traditionally transmitted children's game, "Irohani Kompeito", and can be regarded as another version of it with appropriate changes to fit the space age. Such examples as this are too numerous to cite. Consequently, with regard to traditionally transmitted children's songs, we should no longer use the distinction between the old and the new, but instead think that songs are popular because of the constant creative changes of their traditional elements by children of a new era.

Cities and villages

There is another point we should not overlook. It has to do with the misconception that traditionally transmitted children's songs are inherently old-fashioned. Many people tend to think that more old-fashioned children's songs exist in villages and secluded places in the mountains than in cities. To be sure, in cities there are few traditional arts left. There is an immense popularity of such international musical phenomena as rock music, contemporary popular songs and classical music. But these phenomena are largely limited to the adult world, and particularly to the commercial music industry. As for the world of children, television creates a wide influence, and this fact is equally true in cities and rural areas. It may even be said that, in some ways, rural areas are more open to the influence of television than cities.

But that as it may, cities enjoy a higher distribution rate of traditionally transmitted children's songs than rural areas and that the surrounding areas of large cities and small to medium sized local cities enjoy the highest distribution rate. Over against this, the distribution rate of songs in rural areas is generally low and their variation is small. This tendency is even more pronounced in isolated islands and mountain villages.

Our further research on these factors has led us to the conclusion that there exist close relationship between the variation in the songs and the scope of human interaction. In short, mountain villages and isolated islands enjoy little influx of people from outside. This accounts for the small development of new songs and new games in those areas. All the villagers do, in most case, is simply to repeat what has been handed down to them; therefore they enjoy no increase in their repertoire, unless there emerge creative geniuses of songs and games.

On the other hand, cities have a very high mobility rate. City children often experience saying good-bye to their "best friend" who is moving to another city or receiving total strangers into their peer group. And these new members with a strange accent and colloquial expressions introduce them to songs and games hitherto unheard of. Thanks to these "nice presents," a new comer who would otherwise be timed and shy suddenly finds himself as a popular star among his new peers. This kind of constant stimulation and human interchange enriches the variety of traditionally transmitted children's songs and accelerates their transformation. And yet, we find exceptions among children of closed families in cities. Those children who are prohibited by their parents from playing with their peers are in the identical situations as those of children in mountain villages and isolated islands. Certain activities that parents consider as more educational (viz. learning to play the piano and the violin) than songs and games that involve actual playing with peers often block children's creativity and spontaneity when forced on them.

Children's songs in Asia

The difference between cities and village with regard to traditionally transmitted children's songs in one country is, to a certain extent, applicable to other countries. In reference to the areas, the Eskimos in the North Pole who have such games enjoyed even by adults as "cat's cradle" have relatively few songs. The Vedda tribe of Sri Lanka has almost none. The social structures of the Eskimos and the Vedda tribe are too simple to allow enough human interchange for the development of new children's songs. Compared to the Eskimos and Vedda tribe, such east and south east Asian countries as Japan, Korea, and Indonesia and the southern European countries such as Spain and Portugal, and South America have, in general, numerous traditionally transmitted children's songs. The point to be noted is that highly industrialized countries as the U.S.A. and Japan have many children's songs.

However, the industrialized countries in western Europe have comparatively few songs.

Generally speaking, in Asia there is more variety in children's songs than anywhere else in the world. Asia, due to its cultural and human interchange as well as a fair spread of education, may be compared to small medium sized cities and to the surrounding areas of large cities in any country. And yet, there is a difference between children in the arid lands in the west of Asia and those who live in the monsoon areas in south east Asia as far as the environment for games is concerned. And this difference is also reflected in the area of children's songs. Then, too, the social structures and the educational systems certainly create impact upon their development.

Unfortunately, we have not sufficient information to make a responsible judgment on the intriguing question of the impact created by the natural environment, political, economic and social structures of the various countries in Asia, upon the traditionally transmitted children's songs, as it relates to the product of the children's spontaneous and creative culture.

Some points of interest

Let us list some interesting phenomena of traditionally transmitted children's songs in Asia in the hope that they may provide us with some clues to the foregoing intriguing questions.

(1) Both Japan and Korea are rich with a variety of "picture-drawing songs" (*ekaki uta*). In drawing a picture, a child makes a stroke or line in rhythm with the songs he is singing climaxing with the sudden completion of an unexpected picture. This thrilling game, however, is game for one person, not played in a group of peers. This particular game emphasize the visual imagination and the movement of the hands is more important than body movement. This phenomenon is shared in common by the adult world of Japan.

There were not many *ekaki uta* some forty years ago. But today when children are deprived of playing in groups due to the shortage of play grounds and various other social circumstances, these individual and visual games have developing to greater extent. In fact, in Tokyo there are as many as one hundred picture-drawing songs. Interestingly enough, however, there are few picture-drawing songs in other areas in Asia. It has been reported that Tibet, Iran and Egypt have one or two, but the number is almost nil compared to Japan and Korea. Consequently, picture-drawing songs are a phenomenon not shared by all the Asian countries. Nor does urbanization seem to have any direct relationship with their development. This is an area that will require further research.

(2) In such west Asian countries as Turkey, rope-jumping without songs is popular. Although in Japan it is almost impossible to play the game without singing jump-rope songs, children in Turkey seem to enjoy the activity of jumping-rope itself. We may conclude from this fact that the Turkish children are interested in the rhythms of the activities of the activities themselves. This is seem in Europe as well.

The preceding observations are applicable to ball-bouncing songs (*maritsuki uta*). What captures the Japanese children's interest and attention is not the action of bouncing the ball itself, but rather how ways (methods and rules) of ball-bouncing are in agreement with the words and rhythm of the song he is singing. This is the reason why Japanese children almost never play the game without singing the ball-bouncing songs. But in west Asia there are ball-bouncing games without songs. Also there are many games the purpose of which is solely to count how many times a child can bounce the ball without failure. Thus it is clear that although both west Asia children and east Asian children seem to enjoy rope-jumping and ball-bouncing, the contents of the games, in many cases, are quite different.

(3) Children in India enjoy singing religious songs at night to the accompaniment of drums. And girls in Egypt like to sing wedding songs in chorus while still in elementary school. As these examples show, certain children's songs do not necessarily accompany games. In Japan such songs as "petition songs" (Negai Goto), "slander songs" (*warukuchi uta*), and "parodies" (*kae uta*) belong to this category. Our classification of traditionally transmitted children's songs is as follows:

1: Play songs without gesture
2: Picture drawing songs
3: Play songs using marbles and rocks
4: Play songs for Bean Bags
5: Ball-bouncing songs
6: Rope-jumping songs
7: Rock-scissors-paper matching songs
8: Hand clapping songs
9: Game songs with body movement
10: Game songs for large group to decide "IT" (Ogre)

"Play Songs without gesture" are regarded as important in Japan, and we find a few such songs in Taiwan, Korea, and south east Asia, although they are not as important as in India and west Asia. Children in India repeat with the patience almost unthinkable to children in Japan the name of Sita-Rama, a bisexual God of love, and enjoy the subtle rhythmic changes of drums that accompany the name calling. And Egyptian children's group singing of wedding songs cannot be simply explained away by saying that they are product of their wishful expectations of their future. Perhaps their impulse which could be termed as "purely musical interest" captivates the children's minds. As the imagination of east Asia children is stimulated by visual games, so is the imagination of the children in India and the Arab countries stimulated by purely musical imagination.

Be that as it may, if the seeds of rich creativity are still productively growing today in various and diverse circumstances, it is the obligation of the adult to observe them carefully so as not to tramp on them, even if they cannot actively help them grow. The systems of music education in Asia should be reformulated in accordance with the social and cultural environment in which those systems are rooted.

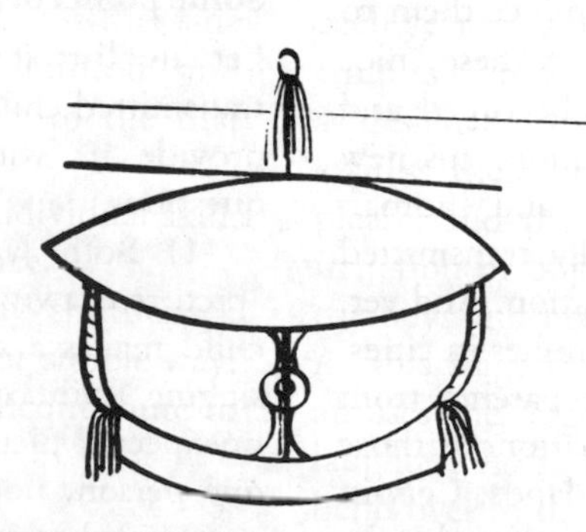

Traditional Malaysian "moon" kite.

Kite Flying

Kites Flourishing in Ahmedabad, India

Entranced by the pristine perfection of kite of exceptional beauty, a proud Maharaja once doffed his turban, placing it in homage at the feet of the kite maker!

Kite flying casts a spell that is universal and no barriers of class, age or sex mar this festival of joy. For a few brief hours, the trials and tribulations of everyday life are cast aside. Kites pursue one another in the sky and many a kite string is cut in fierce battles fought with skill and ardour.

The loser merely shrugs and starts afresh; there is no rancour, no hurt, no long lasting rivalry. All is enchantment. A legend has it that kite-flying came to India with the soldiers of Alexander the Great when he invaded the country in 327 BC, but there is of course no proof of this. It is undoubtedly a very ancient and popular sport because the great poet Tulsidas in his famous "Ramcharitmanas", writes of Rama's having flown a kite on a particular day! Namdev and Eknath, two famous medieval saints, mention kites in their devotional poetry.

It is certain that by the seventeenth century, kites were very well known throughout North India, and kite-flying was a sport in which princes, kings and nawabs took part. It was a sport that they indulged in for months and the *firkees* or reels they used often had elaborate inlay work on them.

Kite flying day in Ahmedabad

Kite flying day is a festival of joy. With the close of winter, the sun moves northwards into Makara (Capricorn). This heralds the festival of Makara Sankranti of Uttarayan meaning the northward journey, which falls on the 14th of January every year. There is a burst of activity the day before, as the entire city, taking advantage of the national holiday, makes frantic preparations for it. Shops in the alleys, streets and byways of the city are flooded with seemingly inexhaustible supply of kites of every colour, size and design — an iridescent kaleidoscope of colour. Their rainbow hues are matched by those of the numerous types of threads, *dori*, specially dyed and treated with ground grass and glue. Bundles of thread are piled up in every nook and corner of the kite shops, for the buyers of all ages who throng the shops throughout the day. There are kites to suit every taste and every pocket. They range from the small kite in one bright colour for the beginner, worth perhaps five paise to the elaborate, multicoloured, connoisseur, worth as much as five rupees a piece. Preparations for the great day usually begin two months ahead and kite makers from other northern and eastern cities flock to Ahmedabad, where perhaps, more kites are sold than anywhere else.

In 1967, in Ahmedabad, two million kites were flown on one day alone — the 14th of January. Kites worth Rs. 1,100,000 were sold and the thread sold was worth Rs. 700,000. Ahmedabad is the Mecca of all kite-makers. And the city on that day, once seen, is never forgotten. Excitement mounts as the day approaches, reaching a climax before dawn on the actual day of Makara Sankranti. Men, women and children are up at 4 o'clock in the morning, while it is still dark, and with the first rays of the dawn they are at their vantage points on the roofs of the city. Every area of the city reflects the same enthusiasm — where it is the rich man's mansion, the poor man's single room, or the street urchin's pavement home. Some equip themselves elaborately, wearing dark glasses against the sun to protect their eyes, and finger guards to prevent cuts from the sharp kite threads, and even visored caps if they feel like it. It is a family festival — one in which women and children join with abandon and eyes are trained skyward that day.

On the streets, there is a burst of drum beats and the excitement mounts. Soon the azure, cloudless sky is splashed with innumerable specks of colour as kites sway, bob and swop over the rooftops. Battles are won and lost. One kite may cut as many as fifty and a kite battle may entangle half a dozen lines, at a time. The lines are manipulated expertly by their owners holding whirring reels in their hands, and occasionally tugging on the treads so hard that they cut their fingers.

The season is highly auspicious and a good one in which to begin any new venture. Grandmothers tell their grandchildren that it is a "golden day". People are especially generous at this time: beggars are given alms; gifts are changed among friends; women put on new bangles and children are given toys; cows are fed wheat and gahu; and new fruits are sold in large quantities throughout the city.

It is certainly a sport which has captured the imagination of everyone. People lose themselves in it and forget their cares during Uttarayan. When they have cut a rival kite, they shout gleefully "katte". Lively discussion on kite-flying go on all the while, and stories of famous kites or well-known incidents are told and re-told. Kite-flying experts speak about it in epic style as if they were discussing something as important as the shastras. Throughout the morning, and until it is dark, the sport continues. Even food is eaten on the rooftops, to the sound of radio and tape recorders.

On the street below, those with meagre resources lift trapped kites delicately from wires or trees, using long poles or lengths of branches. Sometimes in a crowded area, entire trees are festooned with kites that have got entangled in their branches. Telephones go out of order. Kite threads get entwined on the horns of cows, and around cars, rickshaws and passing scooters. Children enjoy themselves thoroughly, collecting the scattered threads of different colours and sometimes piecing them together to fly their kites or to play other games with them. They tie stones to one end of a string, using them as slings to capture the threads of kites which are flying somewhat low. This sling is called a *langariya.* They also play a cutting game, called *gacharke*, to test the quality of each other's threads and see whose threads gets cut first.

By nightfall, the box kites with lamps inside, called *tukkal* are sent floating skywards, sometimes as many as seven on one long string, their lights flickering like moving stars in the night sky. The sport continues into the next day which is called Vashi Utran, but at a somewhat reduced tempo. Children go around with the pieces of thread they have collected. Women sometimes wash the thread to remove its coating of glue and ground glass and use it for stitching.

Mohamed Ustad and his workshop

Mohamed Ustad, who lives in Jaipur, is a man who has made kite-making his life's work. He started making kites at the beginning of the first World War and has never stopped. He said, "I Have only three things to do — to age, to respond to the Azan, and to create kites!"

He is a short man but slim and wiry. He has keen, bright eyes and, although he appears quite alert, he is rather reserved by nature and does not talk very much. He sports a small moustache and a white beard, and is clad in a coloured *lungi* worn under a fine *kurta* or loose shirt. His shoes are fine and well polished. He wears a cap only when he goes out, but he keeps it beside him as long as he is seated within the shop, near the doorway. No one can enter or leave without his knowing. When he speaks, it is usually to give someone instructions.

He spends four months of the year in Ahmedabad, making kites, because, he says, he makes more money in those four months than he does the rest of the year in Jaipur, although he is equally famous there.

He specializes in making simple kites and not the ornate variety. He considers it most important that each kite should fly well. He said, "The thing which flies is a kite and like to make one that flies really well". In his shop, the only kites one will find are the *sada patang,* simples kites. When he started his career, he used to make 50 kites a day alone and sell them himself. Now he employs a number of kite-makers for the work, whose ages range from 6 to 60. Although he is called Ustad or master, he does a number of odd jobs which a master craftsman or artist would perhaps not do.

He is also not averse to taking suggestions from any one. However, he does keep an eye on everything and notices everything that is going on.

When he visits Ahmedabad, he rents a house and all the workers he employs stay there with him, living and working together. The room is about 15 feet square but is sufficient room for everyone to work.

Each worker has small bench, a wooden plank placed on two bricks for support. They keep the *lahi* or glue to the right of their seat. This glue is made out of arrowroot, *morthuthu*, a mild poison which keeps insects at bay, and sugar, which is added when the *lahi* is ready. It keeps the *lahi* of a consistency that prevents the kite paper from wrinkling. There are piles of kites in small heaps, in three corners of the shop. The room has two shelves about four feet off the ground, where finished kites are kept once the day's work is over.

The shop serves several purposes. It is of course primarily a workshop. But at meal times it becomes a dining room, and at night, it is their bedroom.

Ustad has worked out a very careful programme for each of his workers so that they may make the best possible use of their time and that the work man get done quickly. He helps to mend kites which have been damaged in the process of making. He also negotiates with buyers. The kite-making target for a worker is normally 800 a day. The kites made in addition to his quota is his own.

Lalbbai is the most senior worker and the most important person after Ustad. He is about forty years of age and sits at the rear of the shop in a corner. He has worked with Ustad for about forty years. His job is to cut the paper according to the size of the kite to be made and to fix *Dhhadhha*, placing horizontal bamboo sticks to the fine paper, after it has been cut. The paper comes from Germany and there are as many as twenty colours. His two assistants arrange the sheets of paper one on top of the other, so that he can cut for twelve kites, at one time. After that, he gathers all the fine sticks of bamboo into a bunch, holds them vertically and taps the end of the bundle on the ground. He pulls out the ones he needs from the top and places the rest aside. His next step is to take on oil lamp which has seven to eight wicks all around. He lights the wicks and places the lamp flat on the floor, passing the bundle back and forth, after which he reverses the bundle and does the same. The strips of bamboo now have pattern on them, and are properly seasoned for use. He deftly attaches a strip of the right size vertically on the cut sheet with *lahi.* This is called *dhhadhha.* He then fixes a bent strip of bamboo, called *khamp*, horizontally across the *dhhadhha*, reaching the two corners above the tail. Here he folds the ends of the cut paper at each corner slightly over the bamboo.

Fallu, a boy of twenty is learner. After the *dhhadhha* is fixed, he takes up a small triangular piece of paper for the tail and places two sticks, *tilli*, on the two sloping sides, attaching them on with *lahi* and folding the edges of the paper over the *tilli*. He sticks another triangular piece over this again so that the *dhhadhha* is firmly fixed.

Hafiz is the most active boy in the group of workers. He holds the kite firmly upward and draws the *dori* or thread along all the four edges to measure it, turning the kite as he works. He then places it flat on his bench, applies lahi to the kite and folds each of the four edges over the thread he has measured. When this is done he sticks two small pieces of paper called cheppi near each end of the arched *kaman*, to secure the bamboo firmly. Two other pieces are struck on the *dhhadhha* as well, one at the tip of the kite and another not far from the tail. He does this without measuring the kite, working rapidly all the while. Two other workers are Kallu, a boy of twelve, and Bhop, an eight-year-old boy. Who do the same type of work silently and quickly in addition to household work.

Ustad proudly said that kings used to patronize the master kite-makers but that they cannot do so now because times had changed. He said that at Karoli, near Jaipur, he had a kite-making friend, who made a kite of such a beautiful design from various different pieces of coloured paper, which he had joined together geometrically that it was a real work of art. He said his friend would not part with the kite even for five hundred rupees, because it had the kind of inlay work in paper, which the Taj Mahal had in stone. Mohamed Ustadji has deep desire to make a memorable kite. He said, "I will create a kite, the like of which no one has yet produced."

Tales of Malaysian Kites

The bully and the giant kite

The famous seventeenth century Malay annals, *Sejarah Melayu*, relate the story of a celebrated royal bully, Raja (Prince) Ahmad, whose mammoth sail-like kite, strung with what today could only be called two-hundred pound line fit for shark or marlin, struck terror in the hearts of hundreds of innocent fliers whose only desire was to be left alone to fly their kites or battle among their own peers. Whether for fear of facing ignominious defeat from such an overwhelming adversary or lest their plebian handiwork amidst such a real display incur royal displeasure, a completely empty sky would ensue at every appearance of Raja Ahmad's menacing monster. But, just as in legends and tales, all bullies meet their match eventually. In the case of Raja Ahmad, his match came in the form of one nimble Hang Isa Pantas (Pantas meaning speedy) — the Speedy Gonzales of the Malacca Kingdom — whose natural wisdom and wiliness, combined with a sense for aerial warfare, taught him that an outsized and unwieldy kite would eventually succumb to speed and maneuverability despite its heavy fortification.

The story goes that Hung Isa Pantas fashioned himself a most agile kite — a bedevilled genius that could soar into the clouds, nose-dive, loop and treble-loop all within the flicker of an eye — and glazed its string with the finest ground glass and with this masterpiece gained overnight the reputation as a giant-killer, thus redeeming much of the humiliation suffered earlier by his friends and relatives.

A symbol of beauty and grace

Further back in history, almost embedded in the traces of the land's primeval culture, is the belief that a kite, the product of loving care bestowed on it by its maker, is a symbol of Beauty and Grace. A certain rice farmer who once found a lost child wandering among his desolate rice paddies discovered to his boundless joy that the child not only grew up to be a women of utmost physical beauty but also, through her presence, graced the farmer with endlessly abundant crops which brought great prosperity to him as well as his neighbours.

Ignorant of these fact that the mysterious maiden was in fact the Spirit of Rice, the farmer's wife, in a fit of jealousy at her husband's overzealous attachment to the maiden, drove her away from the village one day. She, and her husband, and the entire village then discovered that her disappearance had brought a turnabout in their newly-gained fortune, and they were gradually reduced to poverty. An oracle was then consulted, who revealed that to make amends for the wrong, the farmer had to design an object of great beauty which could fly and the same time simulate the wailing sound of a lamenting women. Thus the kite was born, along with the tradition of associating its physical attributes with those of heavenly bodies and celestial beings and of enhancing the kite with a vibrating strip of palm-leaf that continuously drones lamentable tunes in the wind. Having discovered that the object he had constructed and flown had restored his fortune the farmer instructed all his neighbours to fly kites constantly in the belief that the kite would ensure their crops' success and harvests' abundance.

The story of the magic kite

The story of Dewa Muda, an episode from the repertoire of Makyong dance-drama, deals in large part with kites. This story reflects and attempt to rationalize the practice of kite flying, to draw from kiting a more sophisticated meaning that would raise it from the level of mere childish amusement. As is typical of this genre, the story tells of an earthly prince who was enchanted by a celestial princess.

To win the hand of the princess, he had to travel to her land on his mother's magic kite, which was richly adorned with jewels and precious stones. Legend has it that on reaching the princess's country, the prince was faced with the problem of anchoring his aerial mount due to gusty wind. The prince's first attempt to anchor it to the truck of a huge tree resulted in the tree's being uprooted by the wind. His next attempt to secure it to a large rock also ended in failure.

Having failed to secure the kite at every attempt, the prince in desperation turned for advice to his companion and counsellor. The characteristic remark attributed to this counsellor was, "Your Highness, I have witnessed with great trepidation the numerous failures that Your Highness has encountered in trying to secure your venerable mother's kite. Since no object on this planet could withstand the tremendous force unleashed by this wind, I would advise Your Highness to anchor your kite to your heart. I can assure you that in this universe , no stronger basis for doing anything is known than the heart," The prince immediately took heed of his companion's advice and the kite was securely fastened.

A deep-rooted attachment to kites

The multifarious nature of Malaysian attachment to kites and kite-flying can be observed through the traditions that reflect the Malaysians' world-view and the interest which has continued to develop over the centuries and remains strong even today.

Malaysians make a clear distinction between a kite as a piece of square of rectangular paper with a tail, which can be purchased from any local grocery-store, and one which demands stricter discipline and rituals that can only be executed and understood by an informed adult. They even have different words — *wau* and *layang-layang* — to describe these two levels of involvement. While a *layang-layang* can be made from any available garden bamboo, a wau not only demands a special type of wild bamboo but also stresses stems which grow toward the sunrise. It is customary to season bamboo strips for making *wau* by soaking them in mud for as long as a month. Malaysians have not only adopted a kite as the emblem for their national airline but also welcome important guests by displaying arrays of exquisitely designed kites carried by local beauties. In Malaysia today, a kite-flying festival is one of the most colourful events in the country's annual calendar, drawing thousands of kiting enthusiasts from all of Malaysia's thirteen states and from overseas as well.

Japanese Kites — Rich in Variety, Rich in Beauty

The kites of Japan have their main fascination in the pictures and designs they carry, and because Japan did not establish relations with other lands until the latter part of the nineteenth century, the particularly Japanese culture and social development that rose up in Japan's various regions gave birth to an almost infinite variety of kites. The materials that went into these kites are Japan's durable bamboo, with all its lightness and flexible strength, and *washi* or Japanese paper that also offers durability and high receptivity to colours. Perhaps it was precisely because of these materials, and the skilled and sensitive fingers of the Japanese, that such fabulous kites were born into the world.

A representative type of kite is a rectangular one bearing a drawing of a samurai, called the *nishiki-e* or "colour print" kite. This type of decoration derived from the *ukiyo-e* ("floating world" paintings) and *nishiki-e* that appeared in the 1770's to become one of Japan's best known classic arts. These paintings were carried by merchants from Edo, the old name for Tokyo and the centre of Japan's domestic trade, to every part of the land, so that many kites created in the various localities were based on the *nishiki-e.* and *ukiyo-e.* To the north, the kites of Tsugaru. Aomori Prefecture, have a touch of elegance in the style of the famoûs artist Hokusai. The hexagonal kites of the Japan Sea region feature innovative brushwork in the style of Toyokuni, and the characteristic Suruga kites of the Pacific coast areas hint at the style of Kuniyoshi. Hokusai, Toyokuni, Kuniyoshi — all were leading artists of the Edo period (1603-1867). In this way, the Japanese *nishiki-e* kites that took paintings as their main feature spread from eastern Japan to western Japan, giving rise to new types along the way. But the whole of Japan was not completely cut off from the outside world. Kyushu, the southernmost of the four main islands in the Japanese archipelago, had been visited by foreigners since the 1400's well before Japan closed its doors on contacts with other lands. The people of Kyushu had been introduced to types of kites from China, Southeast Asia, India, and even Portugal and Spain, had absorbed their various elements of style, and had incorporated them into the native Japanese kites of the region. The *hata kites* of Nagasaki appear to have been strongly influenced by Indian styles, as were the *dojin* kites of Kitakyushu by the Chinese and the *baramon* kites of the Goto Islands by the Southeast Asians. The adopted elements, however, were ingeniously blended in Japanese fashion.

The central part of Honshu, the largest of the Japanese islands, was the point of convergence between the purely Japanese rectangular *nishiki-e* kites and the foreign-influenced Japanese kites from Kyushu. The resulting "mixed-blood" kites showed a mixture of structural and decorative styles from both, with such varieties as the butterfly kite, tomoe kite, bekkakko kite, and crest-design-kite, *tomoe* kite, *bekkakko* kite, and crest-design kite are typical creations native to this area.

This phenomenon, this mixing and melding, created a traditional Japanese art form that has been passed down to us today, and the skies of Japan have thus become a veritable treasure-house of a myriad of kites.

This history and customs of Japanese kites

The oldest definite reference to kites in Japan is found in the *Wamyoruijusho* of the year 930. This encyclopaedia dictionary lists kites under the names *shiroshi* or *shien* — in either case, *shi* means "paper" while the rest of the terms are other readings of Chinese characters for the bird called "kite" in English. Despite the assignment of Japanese name for kites, the terms used to describe the kites are all from the Chinese language, so it may be interpreted that originally there were no kites in Japan and that they were brought in from China.

At a later period, around the fourteenth century, kites were called *ikanobori* or simply *ika*, "climbing squid" or "squid". This age in Japan is called the era of Warring Kingdoms, and kites found use in battles as a substitute for rallying flags or as a means to inform allies of one's location. A besieged castle might also attach communications to kites and let them loose, in hope that the wind would carry the documents over the heads of the encircling enemy and eventually into the right hands.

With the establishment of the Tokugawa shogunate in 1603 after the civil strife of a century of warring had been quelled, kites became the playthings of the children of the warrior class, and as decades of peace and civil order continued, kites also became toys of the commoner's children as well. Kite flying was a favourite pastime of the people of Edo, children and adults alike.

Such was fervor the Edoites put into their kite flying, however, that just as disturbances may break out at sporting events today, there were frequent quarrels and fights among the kite fliers. Despite government efforts to control kite flying, it became progressively more popular, due in large part to the role that kites had come to play in the people's festivals and in religious activities and magic spells as well. The Japanese saw kites as linking heaven and earth with one slender string, and it became a deep-rooted custom to send up kites to pray to the gods for an abundant harvest, for the safety of one's family, and to tell a person's fortune. The *yakko* kite of Oji, Tokyo, is itself viewed as a talisman for safety from fires and may be hung in the kitchen or elsewhere where fire is used so as to ward off disaster. The fishing village of Chonan in Chiba Prefecture features a *sode* kite that is prayer for good catches, while the *tongari* kite of Osuga Village, Shizuoka Prefecture, is flown on the birth of a son as a prayer for his safe growth and development. In addition to these, it is also interesting to note that in the Tohoku and Japan Sea regions, which may spend a considerable part of the year under heavy snows, there are many devil kites designed to drive away evil spirits, while in the warmer, brighter areas facing the Pacific Ocean, there are many intended to brighter good luck, such as those depicting Kintaro, a figure from Japanese legend who has become a symbol of a child's safe upbringing, or Tenjinsama, the god of learning who serves as a hope for wisdom.

Kites today — giants take to the air

Kites were at their most popular during the latter part of the shogunate and into the Meiji era, that is, from the seventeenth century through the end of the 1800's. In the Meiji era, however, Japan was opened to the world, and Japanese energies were directed at catching up with the nations of the West. During this period, the kite steadily declined in popularity, in part because of the fascinations of such innovations as trains and electricity, and in part because these very innovations, particularly in urban areas, reduced the open spaces needed for kite flying.

With the death of Emperor Meiji, Japan entered the Taisho era in 1912, and then again the Showa era in 1926. As urbanization progressed, highways appeared carrying floods of automobiles, high-rise buildings sprouted around the landscape, and ever greater numbers of people flocked to the cities. As a result, it became no longer practical — in fact, almost impossible — to fly kites in the urban areas. More recently, however, there has been something of a resurgence of kiting, as many inhabitants of the cities, seeking even a little respite from the crowding and pollution, go to the suburbs and use whatever open space is available for their leisure activities, including the flying of kites. In fact, there have recently been examples of kites getting caught on electric lines and at times even stopping the Shinkansen "bullet train", super-express pride of the Japanese National Railways.

Perhaps much of the fascination that kites hold for modern Japanese is that — unlike the cars and airplanes and other conveniences with which we are today so familiar — the kite moves without electricity, gasoline, or any other artificial power. If this view is true, the situation is ironically precisely opposite that when such inventions earlier distracted the Japanese from their kites.

It is often thought in Japan that the New Year season is the customary time for kite flying. That, however, has been the tradition of the Kanto region around Tokyo, and in the Tohoku region, an area of heavy snows, kite flying must wait for mid-March and the melting of the snows. For Nagasaki in Kyushu to the south, April is the favourite season, while in the Tokai region along the Pacific coast of Honshu, strong seasonal winds lift the kites aloft in May. The seasonal winds in Niigata on the Japan Sea are best and strongest in June, making that the kiting season there. At some times in certain areas, an entire town or village may turn out to launch huge kites in kite festivals that can attract considerable numbers of sightseers. Let's look at some representative examples of these kiting spectacles.

Neighborhood Kiting Competition, Hamamatsu, Shizuoka Prefecture: In early May of each Year, the young men of some 66 neighborhoods gather to compete in flying kites eight to ten meters in length, all to the pounding of drums and the blare of trumpets. The air is filled not only with kites but with the spirited cries of participants and spectators alike in an impressive masculine festival.

Kite Festival to Celebrate Infants, Ikazaki, Ehime Prefecture: During early May of each year, large kites are flown to celebrate the birthdays of male infants who reach one year of age during that Year. The names of such children are painted on individual kites that are flown by the fathers.

Giant Kite Competition of Showa, Saitama Prefecture. On the fifth day of the fifth month of each year, the residents of the northern and southern parts of Showa gather to fly red kites for the north and white kites for the south. The kites bear felicitous inscriptions in large characters, and they serve as prayers for the year's abundant harvest. The two sides compete to see which can fly their kites the highest, and the higher they go, it is said, the greater will be the harvest.

Tug-of-war Kite Festival of Shirone, Niigata Prefecture. Various towns and villages lie on either side of the river that flows through the Shirone area, and in early June of each year the inhabitants come together to fly large kites, some up to fifteen meters in length, from their respective sides. When kites from the two sides become entangled and fall into the river, the people rush to pull on the ropes the kites bear, and the side which pulls the kites to its own banks is the winner.

Festival of "Crying" Giant Kites, Naruto, Tokushima Prefecture: This gathering features the largest kites in Japan and in the world — up to twenty meters in diameter and 2,500 kilograms in weight, with 3,000 sheets of Japanese *washi* paper covering the frame. The giant kites are sent aloft along the seashore in Naruto on a windy day in June or July. A hundred or more people hold on to the heavy ropes of the kites, ropes that are attached to five or six boat anchors firmly buried in the ground. As the huge round kites float in the air, they set up a crying sound that accounts for the name of the festival.

Kites today and the men who make them

The age of machines is gradually yielding to the age of computers. But the creation of kites remains a task for the human hand. The sheets of paper must be set in place by hand one after another, and the colouring must also be done by hand, today just as in the past. The need for manual labour has kept the kite from being a subject for modern enterprises' mass production, and for economic reasons among others, the 3,000 kite artisans working in Japan before the Pacific War have dwindled to a hundred or less. In so many cases, the remaining artisans, some of them direct inheritors of generations of kite-making techniques, are working in retirement, as it were, and when they die there will be no children or apprentice to carry on their traditional techniques. Perhaps this loss of traditional heritage in the process of urbanization could be called another form of urban pollution.

Today, a number of boards of education around Japan are promoting a movement to have the skills of these traditional kite artisans declared national cultural properties and to protect them as such. The Japan Kite Association is also working to show Japan's youngsters the joys of kite flying and to promote kiting festivals, and full members of the association have grown to 1,000 across the nation. Recently, kiting fans from other countries have begun to visit Japan's kiting festivals, and under Foreign Ministry sponsorship colourful exhibitions of Japanese kites have been held overseas to enthusiastic receptions. For the traditions they represent and the rich variety of style and shape and decoration they offer, Japanese kites fully deserve to be preserved for future generations.

Kiting: An Afghan National Sport

History

Only scanty information is available, but it appears that kiting was first introduced to Afghanistan during the region of King Abdul Rahman, who ruled about 100 years ago. Afsar Ali, an Indian printer hired by the Afghan Government, is the first person known to have brought a kite from India into Afghanistan. His kite, however, did not resemble those used in Afghanistan today. Afsar Ali's kite was made of reeds and paper, joined together by glue in a shape like a fish with a long tail, and unlike today's kite, it made a buzzing sound when in the air. Kiting gradually attracted many citizens of Kabul and consequently the sites for kiting had to be moved from the city to the outskirts of the capital. The most famous makers and fliers of kites at that time were Khalifa ("Master Craftsman") Satar, Ata Mohammed, Sediq, Mohabet, Noor Mohammed, Mir Ahmad, and Khalifa Rajab Ali. These pioneers changed the shape, style, and manner of flying, and glassing the string — a process by which the string (hand line) is rubbed with a special paste and sharpened for kite fighting — was one of their innovations.

Kiting in Afghanistan did not start and is not used as a folk-craft or a means of conveying prayers, nor as a means of fortune telling or as charms against misfortune. Rather, kiting has been an amusement and hobby, but it has also gained the status of a national sport. Today kiting is seen all over the country; even the villagers take part, and the Afghan Olympic Commission has included kiting in its list of national sports.

Today, kiting in Afghanistan falls into three categories, namely pleasure, competition, and championship. Those who fly kites for pleasure get satisfaction merely from sending the kite aloft and controlling it by a hand line. Those who fall under the competition category, both amateurs and professionals, either get pleasure from fighting their kites with others or want to gain recognition for the final championships. The third group consists of those striving to participate in the Afghan National Olympics' special play-offs for the kite championship.

Materials used for kite making

Glue: The main source of glue is the root of a plant which grows in the mountains of Afghanistan. The main root of the plant is dried and ground into a powder called "sherishi-kaye." The powder and water are mixed together until a thick mixture, something like machine oil, is produced. Commercial glue is available in Afghanistan, but kite fliers hesitate to use it, partly because they are not sure whether it will fully serve the purpose and partly because foreign-made glue is more expensive.

Paper: A strong, durable tissue paper is used for making kites. Among the various kinds of colourful paper in the markets, those from China, India, and Japan serve the kite makers best. Kite makers tell a paper's quality by feeling it or by holding it up to the light. It is believed that a paper's even ruggedness allows constant air pressure to hold the kite in the air and give good balance. Paper through which light can be seen evenly will give resistance to the wind when the kite is in the air.

Wood: Bamboo forms the kite frame and bow. Bamboo poles may be imported from India, and the bamboo used as the packaging for freight may also be used. The poles are bought second hand, split into small pieces, cut to length, and carefully trimmed with a knife to give constant flex and perfect bending.

String (hand line): The functions of the string are, first, to supplement the kite's frame, helping to hold it together and keep its shape. Second, it provides a bridle at the kite's front for balance and attachment. Any kind of string can be used in the frame and bridle but that for the hand line must be cotton, since the hand line for competition kites is coated with ground glass mixed with adhesive, and materials other than cotton string are useless. For competition kites, a glassed hand line of the same thickness is used for all kites in the competition.

How to make kites

Paper available in Afghanistan comes in rectangular sheets of 75 by 50 centimeters. The size of the kite is measured by *parcha*; one *parcha* equals one quarter of a sheet and the most common kite is made of three parchas glued together so that the pieces do not overlap more than half a centimeter. At this stage, glue is applied to one side of the "arrow", the vertical member which has been previously prepared and cut. The paper is then divided diagonally, and when the glue of the arrow is dry, the bow is next glued so that the end of the bow matches the symmetrical corners of the paper. Usually at this stage, the two ends of the bow are connected with a piece of string that is loosened or tightened to obtain the desired curve of the bow. Later, when the glue has dried, the string is removed.

To keep the paper edges from tearing, a thin string a little longer than the perimeter of the kite is used. The string is first divided into two equal parts and the middle of the string is tied to the upper part of the arrow. Half of the string is then glued to one side (two edges) and the other half to the other side of the perimeter. Both halves of the string rejoin in a knot at the bottom of the arrow. Six knots are used when reinforcing the edges with this string: one each at the top and bottom of the arrow, two at the points where the bow joins the line of the paper, and two at the two corners where the ends of the arrow are glued to the paper. When the edges and the string are glued together, the overlap should not exceed half a centimeter.

To further strengthen the kite, special patches are used. The biggest patch also carries the tail of the kite and is made of the same quality paper as the kite but with a different colour. This patch is in the shape of a beard and is fixed at the bottom of the kite. The other two patches are small; one is fixed at the top and the other at the intersection of the arrow and bow. The tail although not long, balances the kite and also produces a pleasant sound. Some extra patches of different colours and designs may be used for decorative purposes, according to the taste of the kite makers or fliers.

Tying the bridle is the last step in kite making. Though it seems simple, this is a job that requires expertise and experience, for the final performance is greatly affected by how well the bridle is tied to the kite. Before the bridle is tied, two places are marked for making holes. One is at the intersection of the bow and arrow and the other is one inch (or about 2.5 centimeters) below the mid-point between this intersection and the bottom of the kite. At each location two holes are made by a needle, and the string is passed through each hole to hold the bow and arrow at the top and the arrow at the bottom. To tie the hand line with the bridle, an extra loop is tied to the bridle designating the exact place where the hand line should be connected. It must be mentioned that tying this loop needs an expert's hand.

Strategy and principles of kite fighting

A good fighter is one who knows his opponent well and can recognize the best quality kite, distinguish types of strings, and follow the wind direction while flying the kite. Some believe that one of the most important secrets of a kite fighter's success is the strong confidence and hope that he or she will win. Kite flying does not require too much academic knowledge. Practical experience and skill are all that one needs to become a good kite flier and fighter, but some general principles are as follows.

Before fighting

- A pre-check of the kite at the fighting site, especially of the balance and the size in relation to the wind, is considered a good habit for the experienced kite fighter.
- Since the kite fighter has to move and even run with the kite when fighting, it is essential for him to locate his position in advance so that while moving he will not be blocked by trees, ditches, or parked cars.
- Kite fighting, being a sport, requires proper clothing such as light garments and canvas shoes for free movement of the arms and legs.
- As the glassed string is very sharp and can easily cut the fingers, special leather finger covers should be worn. Some people use medical plasters on the forefingers. Gloves, however, should not be used, for they do not allow enough flexibility of the hands.
- Kite fighters must be able to distinguish the different qualities of string with regard to glassing and thickness to obtain the best performance.
- To ensure better performance of the string, the spool should be kept in a plastic cover when not in use. Contamination by greasy materials will ruin the string and consequently bring loss of the game.
-

While fighting

- A good kite fighter must have good control over the fighting situation and must be able to follow the wind direction and divert the opponent's kite from the wind.
- The best kite fighter, regardless of the type of wind, tries always to keep his hand line straight and avoid curving.
- A good fighter does not try to be economical; the more and faster the string is released during fighting, the better the chances become to cut the opponent's string.
- Spool holding is an important part of successful kite fighting. Most professional and even some amateur kite fighters use a well-trained spool holder (a young boy). If the spool is held too tightly, especially during the fight, the forward motion of the string may be retarded, bringing a loss. Holding the spool too loosely, on the other hand, is also dangerous, since this may allow the string to fall on the ground, damaging the string or wrapping it around someone's feet.

Kites of Long History in China

There is, perhaps, nowhere in the world where you cannot find an excited little boy, clutching one end of a string in his hand, racing a kite overhead. The kite is probably one of the most widely liked toys of all time.

In 1955, a little Chinese boy let go of his string, and his huge kite, loaded with Chinese good-will, soared up, and away all the way to France into the hands of a group of children in Paris — in the feature "The Kite," jointly produced by Chinese and French film-makers.

The kite has also had its place in natural science. In the early eighteenth century, it was through his famous kite experiment that Benjamin Franklin was able to draw lighting down to the ground, thus proving that it was a form of electricity. This led to his invention of the lightning rod, a contribution to modern civilization.

The earliest mention of a kite in recorded history can be found in China. An ancient Chinese chronicle has it that in the second century BC, the Hang dynasty general Hang Xing (?-196 BC) used the kite to give his command signals in a campaign. During the five dynasties (AD 907-960), the nobles of Later Tang were known to have flown kites in their palaces. The "Record of Inquiries among the Masses" says that: Li Ye made a paper kite in the form of a hawk to which he attached a string and flew over his palace. Later, he tied a section of bamboo to the hawk's head, so that the wind, whistling through the bamboo, made a pleasing sound as that of the flute."

This showed that simple musical instruments were already being affixed to the kites of this period and played in the air by the winds from heaven. Poems of the time also described the "music of the Kites," testifying to their long history in China.

Even today, early spring days often find the sky over Tiananmen Square speckled with colour, as kites of all description soar aloft. Kite-flyers include not only children but also adults and even elderly people — an indication of the wide participation in this recreation.

In Asia, the Kites made in China and Japan bear the closest resemblance both in structure and in shape. Chinese hawks and butterflies have improved much in recent centuries with the addition of Japanese features. And in both countries, kites are not only toys but a form of decorative art. Some of the best are displayed in sitting-rooms as *object d'art.* Beijing kites are typical of Chinese kites in general. In the early 1970s, a treatise "The Craftsmanship of Kite-making in the North and South" came to light. Experts believe it to have been the work of Cao Xueqin, famous author of the eighteenth century classical novel, *The Dream of the Red Chamber.* In this paper, Cao Xueqin described the various types of kites found in the northern and southern parts of China and the processes by which they were made. This treatise was given by him to a friend with the surname of Jin, who handed it down to his family, which became the renowned Jin family kite-makers of Beijing. Another well-known kite-making family with the surname of Ha also lived in Beijing.

Beijing kites can roughly be divided into four types. The first is the "hard-wing" type, where bamboo slivers are tied together to form the framework, with a long rectangle in the middle, wings to the sides slightly tipping to the back, and a tail at the end. It is then pasted over with white paper and painted with swallow or goldfish designs or figures, most of which are heroes and beauties of stage and folklore. Two favourite characters of the latter type are Monkey Sun Wukong from the mythological novel, Pilgrimage to West and the Immortal Liu Hai in the folk tale " Liu Hai Fishes for the Three-footed Toad."

The second is the "soft-wing" type, where the wings are removable. These come mostly in the shape of hawks, butterflies, dragonflies and phoenixes, with their convex bodies giving a realistic impression when flying through the air. The wings can be taken down and put away in a box when not in use. Instead of paper, sheer silk fabrics are pasted over the frame and painted with great artistry.

The third is the "chain" type, where many sections, each around 30 cms across, are linked together at distances of 30-40 cms. As many as 24 sections can be linked to form a dragon-kite, with a dragon head at the very front. Once up in the air, it swishes and swirls in the best tradition of that awe-inspiring creature. Strong cords are needed for such a kite, as the pull of the wind is necessarily much stronger than for a single kite.

The fourth type can only be termed "miscellaneous" — mostly in cylindrical forms, such as palace lanterns and water pails. Clever craftsmen sometimes put a propeller, wings and a tail to the pail and form an airplane-kite. Crabs, bats and catfish, offshoots of the "hard wing," also belong to this category. The last would be a monstrous fish head with a long silk tassel. When up in the air, it gives a fine imitation of a fish swimming through the waves.

A kite is made in three major steps: First, soft bamboo slivers are tied into frameworks of the required shape, light, sturdy and symmetrical. Chinese *xuan* paper or thin silk is then stretched taut over the framework. The last step is to paint the designs. This is a special art, and the designs are often exaggerated and decorative. A swallow, for instance, would be painted black on a white background, with flowers and a meadow under its wings. Particular pains are taken with details. Sometimes, tiny windmills are put in as eyes for the butterflies, fish, and dragons and coloured streamers as tails. Kite-flying is an art in itself, requiring expert knowledge of the wind direction and velocity, so that the exact moment can be chosen to make a kite rise into the air and stay there. The flyer has to keep in the right position, using his arms to control the delicate balance. Kite races are contests of both skill in handling and in craftsmanship. On the fine days when these are held, viewers are treated to rare sights. A kite of a "beautiful lady" would have a little flower-basket climbing the kite-string until it meets an obstacle, then it would tip over and shower confetti from the skies. This is called "The Goddess Scattering Flower Petals," Then two swift swallows would cut through the air, close on each other's tail. These are actually linked by elastic bamboo slivers. Music from the spheres, from instruments on the kites, is as much enjoyed today as it was a thousand years ago. Such competitions not only raise the craft to higher artistic levels but also lead to lasting friendships. As to "kite fights" which had as their aim the destruction of each other's kites, these are now no longer held.

In China, the end of winter and the coming of spring are the ideal times of kites, when there are more clear skies and fewer squalls. With the departure of winter, people love to go out into the sunshine and limber up and strengthen their eyesight with this sport. The ancient book, *Miscellany* says that kite-flying helps children to drain excess inner heat. Actually, it means that kite-flying is a health building sport. And this is true not only for children, but also for adults.

Cartoons and Comics

Picture Story Books of China

Picture story books made their appearance in China as early as 1925. This first picture book was put out by a publishing house in Shanghai. The picture and story were based on a Chinese classic novel, *Journey to the West.*

Graphic art in China began with separate pieces of drawings. In the Wei Dynasty in the sixth century, serial story pictures inscribed on stone slabs could be found. The magnificent Dunhuang frescoes included serial story pictures drawn in the Sui Dynasty (518-618). Most of the pictures were either interpretations on Buddhist scriptures or biographical sketches of Sakyamuni. Generally speaking, the pictures dealt with šimple subject matters. Graphic writings or landscape drawings were used to separate one picture from another with unique esthetic effects.

With the flourishing of dramas and novels in the Yuan Dynasty (1206-1368) and Ming Dynasty (1368-1640), the graphic arts made great headway when artists were called upon to do elaborate illustrations for books. Some well-known novels were richly illustrated, the upper half of every page being pictures, or an illustrated page following every page of text. As many as several hundred illustrations could be found in a single book. Then there were the "Pictures of the Sage," based on the life of Confucius, containing over hundred pictures. Different versions of this series of pictures have been found in different parts of China. Some are stone inscriptions, some are coloured paintings, others just sketches. Easy reading, which is in itself a merit, is the most prominent feature of a picture story book. The fact that the Chinese language is a difficult one and such books with illustrations cater to the popular needs had long been understood by Lu Xun, founder of the new Chinese literature, when he said that picture story books could be weapons for enlightenment. Lu Xun in a number of articles, called upon artists and writers to pay due attention to and exert themselves in the production of picture story books. Lu Xun added that in the creation of picture story books, artists on a par with the great Renaissance painters Michelangelo and Da Vinci would emerge.

Nearly half a century has elapsed since Lu Xun made his appeal. Meanwhile, the production of picture story books has made great progress. It is to be noted with satisfaction that artists of picture story books are very serious in their work, which they regard as an art. Characters are created with exquisite precision and vividness. Various artistic techniques are employed so that picture story books could be appreciated by the general public with some primary school background. It is natural that children are the most avid readers of picture story books. These books, which they read outside class, help much in increasing their knowledge and broadening their horizons. Picture story books depicting lives of children are their great favourites. For many years there was a picture story series, "San Mao Goes Wandering," which appeared regularly in the newspapers. Sam Mao (meaning "three hairs" the name given to the little character in the picture series) was always finding himself in all kinds of predicaments. In this way, the artist and caricaturist, Zhang Lo-ping of Shanghai, exposed the evils of the old society before liberation. In the hearts of readers, San Mao was a lovable little boy who seemed to have really existed and was a character with whom to sympathize.

Today the Chinese people are making great effort to modernize industry, agriculture, science and technology, and national defence. Zhang Lo-ping has created a new life for San Mao. The little boy is no longer a little "vagabond," leading a life of misery, but is now a bright student who studies hard and shows keen interest in scientific experiments. Zhang Lo-ping has given a new title to his picture series "San Mao Loves Science."

Picture story books available for children include those which are based on, for example, children's stories, fairy tales, or stories of animals. They are drawn and written for children of different age levels, having different interests. Some picture story books are adaptations from foreign novels or ancient legends. Take, for example, the picture story "Master Dong Guo," the pictures of which are drawn by Liu Ji-you. The story is based on an old legend about a kind-hearted man who rescues a wolf only to be eaten up by the wolf. In the mid-Ming Dynasty, there was a series of eight pictures about this story. Now after recreation, the story of Master Dong Guo is told in a picture story book containing 80 pictures with more complicated plots. Through stories such as this one, our artists aim to teach young children that they should love the good and despise the wicked.

But the popularity of picture story books extends beyond children. In some cases, the most enthusiastic readers are found among the adults. Picture story books adapted from well-known Chinese and foreign classics, which have always had a strong influence in China, are sold in tremendous numbers. Actually, through the medium of picture story books, the original works are popularized among the people. Now picture story books adapted from works of such famous writers as Lu Xun, Guo Mo-ruo, Dun, Ba Jin, Lao She are available and find great popularity. There are picture story books versions of the most influential classical novels in China, including *A Dream of Red Mansions, Outlaws of the Marsh, Journey to the West,* and *Romance of the Three Kingdoms.* There are also picture story books based on single episodes from a classical work, as for example "Wu Song Hunts the Tiger" (an episode from *Outlaws of the Marsh*), which glorifies the hero of the story for ridding people of a scourge. Another picture story book "Havoc in Heaven" (a story taken from *Journey to the West*) sings praise to the spirit of a rebel.

These stories are old time favourites.

Different schools of art manifest in drawings for the picture story books. This might be compared to a hundred flowers in bloom, all vying for beauty. Still, most artists favour traditional line drawings, which are also popular among the general public. There are many artists famed for their skill in exquisite line drawings. A drawing from *The Western Chambers* by a female artist, Wang Shu-hui, has won a first prize.

Picture story books are painted and circulated in great numbers in China. Generally, the first impression of a book runs to 1,000,000 copies. Some picture story books are reprinted time and again totalling nearly 10,000,000 copies. The picture story books are greatly appreciated and welcomed by the general public and a bright future may be predicated for this form of art.

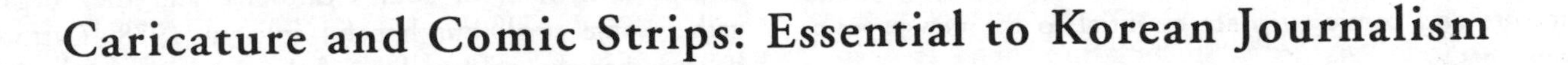

Caricature and Comic Strips: Essential to Korean Journalism

It is believed by most Korean cartoonists that the originator of the cartoon in Korea was Kim Hong-do (1760-?), a famous Korean artist who played an active part in the field of folk painting in the late eighteenth century. He was the first artist who introduced cartoon — like humour to the traditional folk drawing world. His works, in idea and plot, had some feeling of the cartoon about it. But we cannot call him a cartoonist.

It was in the early 1920s that the first group of professional cartoonists made their debut in Korea. And today, after sixty years, hundreds of people are engaged in cartoon drawing. The drawing titled "Sirum" (Korean form of wrestling) is one of the famous drawings by the Kim Hong-do. As the drawing shows, he surely had a talent for cartooning. He described the scene of *sirum* match in a light and humorous manner. Two wrestlers' desperate looks straining to win, the looks full of excitement of the spectators around them, and its comic composition give us a hearty smile.

It was not until "Bong-i" and "Kim-byol-jang-i" were carried in the monthly magazine Yadam (the hidden stories) in the mid 1920s that completely plotted cartoons were introduced in Korea.

As for the newspaper comic strips, "Mongtongkuri" (the fool) of No Shim-sun was run for the first time in the daily paper Chosun llbo, and it was followed by the works of Woongcho which were introduced in the form of caricature in the monthly Shindonga and the Jokwang.

There is a drawing by Woongcho, in which are shown the regrets of the Korean people at the partition of the country, and the pent-up feeling of the people who were praying for the unification of the country.

It is not, however, going too far to say that Kim Young-whan who is famous for his cartoon character "Kojubu" (Mr. Nosey) took the lead in drawing completely composed cartoons. With his works at the head, "Old Man Gobaoo" of Kim Song-whan, "Notol Jusa" (Mr. Guffaw) of Shin Dong-hun, "Dookobi" (Mr.Toad) of Ahn Eui-sup, "Aunt Walsoon" of Chung Woon-Kyong, "Galbissi" (Mr. Skinny) of Lee Sang-ho, "Jadong-i" (Clever boy) of Kil Chang-dok, and the caricature of Park Ki-jong who was the pioneer of the genre were presented successively.

During that time the Korean War broke out and the world of the cartoon underwent the war. But in the maelstrom of the war they continuously produced various works for adults and children. It may be safely said that they played the part of the engine, placing the world of Korean cartoons on a stable foundation.

"Old Man Gabaoo" is an example of the most popular cartoons of Kim Song-whan which has lived longest among the newspaper comic strips.

Korea has made remarkable economic growth during the past ten years, which was eventually accompanied by serious inflation. To check inflation and currency expansion, the government employed a tight money policy at last. Ahn Eui Sup drew a satirical cartoon on the policy. The pollution problem is today's hottest issue in the world. To solve the serious pollution problems, the Korean government established the anti-pollution law some years ago. But increasing factories, vehicles, wastes, and so forth, have made the environment worse and worse. Now we have another similar law, the nature protection law, and the whole nation is trying to save nature from dying of environmental pollution.

Chung Woon-Kyong took up this issue in his "Aunt Walsoon."

The Korean people's moral sense which has been based on Confucian ideas is often reflected in cartoons. A comic strip drawn by Lee Sang-ho is one example. The Koreans have learned to observe loyalty, filial piety, and courtesy both at school and at home.

The Koreans love peace and kindness, and especially, they put the highest value on respecting their elders and helping others.

The comic strips drawn by Kil Chang-dok are very popular among children, and have been run daily in a children's newspaper since 1970.

Park Ki-jong Keeps the first place in caricature drawing in Korea. When the first caricature by Mr. Park appeared in a newspaper, it summoned a great and favourable reaction from readers. And today, every paper and magazine carries caricature of the notables of home and abroad. Editors believe that the caricatures can make a stronger impression on readers than photograph can. Now, no one denies that the caricature and comic strip are essential to the newspaper as refrigerants.

Covering the most important events of the day, comic strips also give laughter and relaxation to the readers. A survey disclosed recently that the comic strip fans have been increasing for the past ten years, and more than half of the newspaper readers read the comic strip first, before the other articles and coloums.

Ko Woo-young's serial cartoon "The story of Yim Kok-jong" (A Korean Robinhood) appeared as the first newspaper's serial cartoon, and has enjoyed an explosive popularity among readers.

Mr. Ko is now drawing "The romance of Three States" a famous Chinese classical novel, for *The Daily Sports* and it also records a hit. About 800 magazines are used by cartoonists for a larger arena of their activity than the papers, because there is no magazine that has no cartoons in it. And the noticeable increase of the titles of magazines since 1970 in Korea, especially such publications as weeklies, popular magazines, and children's and ladies' magazines, has given a great opportunity not only to the existing cartoonists but also to the newcomers.

It was not until recently that the comic books for adults flourished. Children's comic books have a long and glorious history, but those for adults could not find their market until 1977. Some people cartoonists have made continual efforts to create the market for adult's cartoons, and they began to gather some small but hopeful fruit in 1978. Cartoonists believe that the golden days of the cartoon are coming in Korea, and that they can make the country and the society they live in brighter and more cheerful through their cartoons. That is the reason why they are trying to make better cartoons, even at this very moment.

Cartoons and Comics in Japan: Putting Laughter into Everyday Life

The relationship between cartoons and laughter

It was once thought that laughter-producing elements were essential to cartoons, and no doubt many people still have that feeling today. But are cartoons and laughter really inseparable? In our opinion, no. We think it unnecessary to always seek a link between the two and in fact, there are many cartoons which completely eliminate the element of laughter. It even seems appropriate to say that the boom which Japanese cartoons (*manga*) have experienced during the last ten or more years derives specifically from the way in which so many of them do not even attempt to be funny.

Around the end of the 1950s, a certain school of young Japanese cartoonists came to the conclusion that there should also be cartoons that were not tied to the comic element, and they began to produce cartoons for young people that featured realistic drawing and stories, giving this new type of work the name "drama cartoons" (*gekiga*). This was perhaps the first example of Japanese cartoons being consciously freed from the constraints of the comic element. Since then, the combination of the new approach of the "drama cartoons" with the traditional techniques of earlier story-telling cartoons has permitted a wider, richer range of cartoonic expression, and this in turn has contributed to the present boom in Japanese cartoons.

This is not to say, of course, that the element of laughter is today totally absent from Japanese cartoons. Laughter remains one of the strongest and most effective techniques of the cartoonist's art, and many comic cartoons aptly and effectively reflect the lives and feelings of the modern-day Japanese. While keeping in mind that comic cartoons represent only a part of the whole field of cartoons in Japan, it is interesting to note the way laughter is introduced into and presented in Japanese cartoons and at some of the recent cartoons that have won particular popularity.

Imagination and life

Today, the most popular comic cartoon is the "Doraemon" series by Fujio Fujiko. This has been turned into an animated television cartoon series that has attracted a wide range of young fans, and in paperback edition alone, "Doraemon" has been able to draw such an audience and such a faithful following?

The "hero" of the series is a robot from the future, named Doraemon and shaped as a cat with snowman-like proportions. One day he appears in the room of a Japanese primary school pupil named Nobita and thus takes his place in the world of today. Each episode, consisting of ten or more pages, revolves around the adventure that Doraemon and Nobita have or the disturbances they create.

These adventures and experiences or disturbances tend to follow a single pattern. Nobita, who is perhaps a bit lacking in spirit, strength, and intelligence, finds himself confronted by a situation with which he cannot cope. Doraemon thereupon applies his superior powers as a robot from the future to help or rescue Nobita using a convenient item from his collection of tools and other possession. (It is perhaps worth noting that while "Nobita" takes the form of a common Japanese male given name, it is also a cognate for a word meaning "to be tired out" or even "to be at one's wit's end.") This pattern clearly appeals to the children who are the readers or viewers of the cartoon, giving it a strong fascination by acting out in a way the dreams and fantasies of the children. The things that Doraemon pulls out never fail to solve the problem, no matter how difficult; for him, and by extension for the children reading or viewing Doraemon, nothing is impossible. Since Doraemon is a robot from the future with supernatural powers, it might be thought that this cartoon could qualify as science fiction, but actually this is not true. The stories and the images that they project are firmly rooted in everyday life, and even Doraemon himself gives no particular feeling of science fiction. He takes the stylized form of a cat, an animal familiar to the children, and he even gives the impression of a huge toy cat come to life. He did not arrive via time machine or spaceship but merely appeared from inside one of the drawers of Nobita's desk. Even when he pulls something out of his pouch to solve seemingly impossible problems, then item used is a toy or some other object from everyday life, and despite their supernatural powers, these things give little if any supernatural or futuristic feeling.

It is in fact the very mundane nature of Doraemon's miraculous possessions that seems important. Granted they have supernatural powers, they are all familiar items from everyday life. Perhaps it would be better to say that in the world of this cartoon, everyday objects take on supernatural powers. For example, a toy helicopter becomes able really to fly, and Doraemon's television can show the future. Biscuits can turn anyone eating them into an animal, or supernatural flute can suddenly change the attitudes and actions of the person who hears it. One's shadow becomes separated from oneself and takes on a life of its own, while lipstick makes anyone using it suddenly talk flatteringly to everyone, and a seemingly ordinary pencil gives all the right answers to a test at school. In short, the fascination of "Doraemon" lies in the way in which everyday life is transformed into a world of magic, of the future, while still remaining familiar and highly identifiable to the children. Putting this another way, imagination is given the chance to fly while still retaining its contact with the children's everyday lives. The same cartoonist, Fujio Fujiko, also had an earlier cartoon series called "Q-taro the Ghost" which was also popular for a similar type of fascination, and the same elements can be found in another, slightly earlier cartoon by Shigeru Mizuki about a ghost named Kitaro.

Microcosmic societies in Cartoons

The way in which today's most popular cartoon, "Doraemon", has based itself firmly in everyday life is something of great interest to me. The settings it presents are far from rare or unusual. Quite the contrary, the adventures and experiences in "Doraemon" are the very things that are constantly occurring in ordinary homes and neighbourhoods, and with the appearance of Doraemon and Nobita as well as Nobita's parents, his friends, and their neighbours, there is plenty of opportunity for the humour of everyday life to come to light in this cartoon. In just the same way, the "comic" cartoons of today are all firmly based on everyday life. Here, let us look at a few examples of such cartoons.

Until recently, "Boy Policeman" by Tatsuhiki Yamagami was extremely popular with children and youths. It featured a primary school pupil who, surprisingly, wore a police uniform, and this boy, named Komawari, always managed to stir up a variety of comic confusion. Here, too, except for the fact that the boy is wearing a policeman's uniform, the cartoon presents only scenes of everyday life in attaining its comic effect. The other characters in the cartoon are Komawari's classmates at primary school, his teachers, and his parents, and the situations that arise because of his often extravagant words and actions are all played out at school, at home, in the neighbourhood — in other words, in the surroundings of everyday life. The comic confusion of "Boy Detective" is carried even further, even to almost farcical proportions, in Tsubame Kamogawa's "Macaroni Apartments." But here too, all of the characters, all of the situations are developed in a thoroughly feet-on-the-ground approach.

Recently, the works of Hisaichi Ishii have become extremely popular among Japanese Youth, and these works can be characterized in just the same way. "Hang On, Tabuchi!" features a clumsy but determined professional baseball player named Tabuchi, and he and all of the other characters are drawn from the real world of professional baseball. The situations all involved the joys, troubles, and experiences of Tabuchi's everyday life, during games and away from the ballpark, as he tries — not always too successfully — to prove himself as a ball player. In "The Part-timer", the main figure is a poor university student who, as the name of the series implies, spends most of his time doing side jobs to eke out his living. This series presents the lives, experiences, and attitudes of the young with a comic touch.

This observation — that a large proportion of the cartoons popular with Japanese youth base their humour in everyday situations — can be made about a wide range of other cartoons as well, such as "Tensai Bakabon" ("The Idiot Genius") by Fujio Akatsuka which takes place in the home and neighbourhood of the main character; Mitsutoshi Furutani's "Dame Oyaji", also unfolding in the home and neighbourhood; and "Herenchi Gakuen" by the Goh Nagi, which is a comic series taking place in a school. Other examples would include "the Cheer-leaders," a series about a university by Do-o-kuman and "Parkside Police Station" by Osamu Akimoto, which deals with life in the old Shitamachi area of Tokyo. While the precise methods of provoking laughter may differ, all these cartoons and more have the common characteristic of the everyday situation they present.

Similar observations can be made about the comic cartoons directed more at adults. For instance, Sadao Shoji draws a series entitled "Shoji" and the central character of the same name is a low-ranking employee of a company. His desires and ambitions and the difficulties he invariably gets into trying to fulfil them are humorously depicted, calling to mind the actual joys and disappointments, successes and failures in the everyday lives of average workers. "The Section Manager" by Shunji Sonoyama also takes place in a company, featuring a section manager trying his hardest to be liked by all his superiors and subordinates and seeking to be respected at home. The same type of characteristics also appear in the comic cartoons by such popular cartoonists as Sampei Sato, Yoshiji Suzuki, Hosuke Fukuchi, Shuhei Nishizawa, and Taira Hara.

While the comic cartoons for the most part are based on everyday life, the "drama cartoons" referred to above make no particular effort to incorporate such mundane elements. Their plots in many cases are on the contrary far removed from everyday life, dealing with young men who have devoted their lives to baseball or motorcycles, for example, heroes whose one goal in life is the mastery of the martial arts, friendship or love that wins out after many trials and tribulations, the burning sense of justice on the part of a young police detective, or else historical dramas or space fantasies that depict the adventures of young Japanese. In these ways, the drama cartoons exploit the virtually unlimited potential for cartoons of the fantastic, the impossible, the unreachable. Still, the comic cartoons rely completely on situations from everyday life to produce their laughs. Their stories are founded not on fantasies or impossibilities but on the sights and sounds and persons that can be found around the cartoon's readers and in doing so they depict a microcosm of society. Perhaps one essential element of comic cartoons is timeliness in their use of subject matter drawn from the trends in politics, the economy, or society at large. In Japan today, however, there is a marked lack of such satirical cartoons and parodies. The trends in society in general are of course reflected in, for example, "Doraemon" and the works of Hisaichi lshii,. and political and social trends have a small degree of influence on the cartoons of Sampei Sato, Yoshiji Suzuki and others. However, in each of these cases the "macrocosm" of society at large and developments therein are not reflected directly in these artists' cartoons, and the presentation of a social microcosm remains the central focus of their approach to cartooning. For example, even when political and economic affairs are taken up in the cartoons, they appear only to the extent that they affect the everyday lives of the cartoons' characters. Thus, such cartoons lack a feeling of satire or parody and seek to amuse the reader with their intrinsic humour.

Just what is the source of such a personal, microcosmic approach to such cartoons? One point that can be made for certain is that in post-war Japan, a *perit bourgeois* democracy has for better or worse taken firm root. On top of this, the great majority of the Japanese view themselves as being middle-class, and this middle-class consciousness has been supported by the nation's capitalistic prosperity. No doubt much of the highly personal orientation of Japanese cartoons stems from such a situation.

In fact, the method of graphic depiction used in Japanese comic cartoons could itself even be called bourgeous or neutral. The styles of drawing are not complex or abstruse, but simple and lacking in deviousness, soft in feeling, and simple without a great deal of shading. In short, they are uncomplicated and even naive, with no overwhelming feeling of either masculinity and femininity. These characteristics are in sharp contrast to the features of non-comic cartoons, and no doubt this is in large part responsible for the almost total lack of single-frame satirical cartoons. In other words, through these simple, "natural" forms of depiction based on a personal, microcosmic approach to the world at large, it is difficult to compress the elements of satire or parody into a single frame; it is by far simple and more effective to apply this approach to softer, gentler humour stretching over several frames.

This has been only a brief consideration of the comic cartoons as they stand in Japan today, but one problem comes to light. At first glance, one might feel moved to claim that the highly varied comic cartoons are just variations on a single cartoon series, "Sazae-san" which has been drawn by Machiko Hasegawa and loved by a wide range of the Japanese people for over thirty years. It is obvious to anyone familiar with Japanese cartoons that this is perhaps the most representative example of a comic cartoon that thoroughly applies a personal philosophy and way of looking at the world that is presented in a microcosmic society. But are the many other comic cartoons mere variations on this theme? Or more importantly, how does the microcosmic world of comic cartoons relate to the essential power and appeal of cartoons in general? To reply to such questions, it is necessary to look a bit more closely at the forms that laughter takes in today's cartoons.

Desire as the source of laughter

First, let us look again at "Doraemon" and its humour. The story development in this work follows roughly the same pattern for each episode, as described below.

- Nobita is presented with a difficulty or problem in his everyday life.
- Doraemon uses his supernatural powers to give Nobita a useful object.
- Nobita uses the object to solve his problem and is overjoyed at having been able to reach a solution that make him appear omnipotent.
- Carried away by the powers that the object gives him, Nobita decides to use it for another purpose, or to play a joke. This results in confusion that Nobita cannot resolve by himself, or the object gets out of hand.
- Nobita switches from rapture to despair, and Doraemon retrieves the object and restores sanity to chaos.

This story development can be further simplified as: problem in everyday life, realization of one's dream, further difficulties caused by joking, and restoration of the state of everyday life. In other words, the humour comes from the overuse or misuse of the miraculous object, and the blessing of having one's hopes and dreams realized turns into a curse.

Why then is the object misused or overused? Needless to say, this is because of the compelling strength of Nobita's desires or dreams, and the very strength of the central character's wants gives rise to laughter.

This type of comic element in Doraemon can be found in highly similar form in other comic cartoons. For example, in "Boy Policeman," the laughter arises out of the gross confusion that is caused by the lead figure's extravagant desires, so that here too, it is the unbridled (and uncultured) desires expressed in the cartoon that generate that laughter. In the case of "The Part-time," the following four-frame cartoon strip is typical. The hero is writhing on the ground clutching his stomach. At his side is a friend who is holding up a paper bag and explaining to a policeman that the hero is in pain because he ate the chocolate bars that were in this bag, which he had found in shopping centre. The policeman immediately exclaims that this is another case of poisoned foods left around by a indiscriminate murderer (referring to various incidents that had in fact occurred about that time). But the friend explains further, saying that there had been 50 chocolate bars in the bag when the hero found it. The policeman notices that the bag is now empty, and he disbelievingly asks whether the young man writhing on the ground had eaten them all. From the circumstances, however, it appears evident that that is just the case. The homour here is the sudden shift from seeming emphasis on an indiscriminate crime against society to the greedy hunger of the hero as the cause of his troubles.

Almost precisely the same approach can be found in "Shoji." Here the core of the comic strip is desires or dreams; for instance, the hero Shoji does his best to make himself attractive to women but always fails, or else he runs out of money and tries to talk the restaurant owner into feeding him for free. In other cases, Shoji may talk about what he might do if he won one of the national lotteries, but whatever the situation, the story revolves around Shoji's wants and dreams. No more than an average white-collar worker, Shoji still has wants that far exceed his ability to achieve them. The humour of "Shoji" lies in the striking contrast between what the hero wants and what he can get, and in the impotence of his efforts at success. The common feature of the desire depicted in these cartoons is probably the triviality of the desires involved. The problems of Nobita in "Doraemon" grow out of minor, even insignificant happenings in everyday life, and in "Roy Policeman" the hero's extravagant and at times vulgar desires are of equally small importance to everyone but the hero. The type of wants and desires seen in "The part-timer" and "Shoji" can also he called extravagant on the one hand or ridiculous on the other, but in neither case of any great importance to society at large.

The very triviality of the desires presented in all these comic cartoons is the humour they offer, but they also reflect the realities of the microcosm of society that the cartoons depict. Putting this in another way, laughter is always rooted in the physical or material, it would seem. The source of laughter is in its presentation of desire, and so long as this desire — be it material desire, hunger, sexual desire or the like — is depicted in concrete, trifling form, the laughter itself seemingly cannot be metaphysical or conceptual. In fact, there is a large number of comic cartoons, but there is practically none that takes metaphysical problems such as the anxiety of life or its lack of logic and rationality as the material from which it weaves its laughter. This fact alone should serve to indicate that the humour of comic cartoons is by no means black humour.

The appeal of the comic cartoon

In light of the personal, microcosmic worlds created by comic cartoons as described above, it seems only natural that the laughter in the cartoons should be highly physical or material. So long as such cartoons are based on a highly personal outlook and philosophy of life and so long as they depict the trifling desires of everyday life, laughter will be inseparably tied to the common character of daily life. What does this fact mean in terms of the essential appeal of cartoons? First of all, there is significance in the lack of cartoons' departure from reality. It seems that no matter how cartoons seek to base themselves in everyday life, their use of laughter as springboard to carry the reader beyond mundane concerns is the essence of the comic cartoon. As we have already seen, all of the comic cartoons give birth to laughter from the confusion and disorder caused by desire. This confusion, however, never reaches such ridiculous or impossible proportions that everyday life is torn loose from its moorings and thrown into chaos. This point is common to

"Doraemon" and "Boy Policeman", "The Part-timer" and "Shoji" alike. Even in "Macaroni Apartments", the confusion of scenes and words may approach farcical proportions and vary from instant to instant, the microcosmic society presented in this cartoon is never turned completely topsy-turvey, cut loose from all restraints and order. The laughter that appears in these comic cartoons is safe, secure laughter, not the laughter of danger or anxiety. One could even say that while the humour of these cartoons invites a smile, it does not stimulate a belly-laugh. This characteristic of Japanese comic cartoons would probably also explain the lack of black humour in Japan. There are of course some exceptions. Something akin to black humour can perhaps be sensed in the works of Funio Akatsuka, Yasuji Tanioka, Hiroshi Kurohane, and Shigehisa Sunakawa, for instance, but even in such instances, the black-humour elements appear only momentarily, and there is no sense of the usual order of things having been disrupted completely. In short, virtually all the Japanese comic cartoons that can be found at present positively recognize the existing order of society, doing so in their adoption of a realistic microcosm of society as their basic approach. The readers of such cartoons are amused by the way in which they can recognize the trifling nature of the cartoon characters' problems and thoughts and their relation to the readers' own existences. From this there can be no denying that the cartoons of today thus lack the critical facility essential by nature to cartoons.

Nevertheless, more should be said than just this. There is one other element in the comic cartoons of today that should not be overlooked. That is the way in which these cartoons, no matter what trifling microcosm they may deal with, do not try to escape the boundaries of this microcosm but instead emphasize the positive aspects of the mundane. More specifically, one can look at the various heroes of these comic cartoons. No matter how many times he fails, Nobita of "Doraemon" always jumps at the next miraculous object provided by Doraemon, and after becoming once again elated, he once again fails. Komawari, the star of "Boy Policeman", feels no shame in his own uncouthness and extravagance which bring on his troubles and without hesitation continues his tricks and plots and confusion. The hero of "The Part-time", far from being at all shamed of the trifling, insignificant nature of his own actions and his own desires, pushes forward positively with his wants and dreams, acting regardless of the almost certain hapless outcomes. The lead character of "Shoji" is not in the least fazed by his momentary failures and embarrassments, nor does he recognize his own impotence in the face of the world around him; undaunted, he continues to be motivated and directed by his trifling desires, ever hopeful that sometime, he will succeed.

What is most impressive about these various heroes is most likely their invincibility of spirit, of motivation. This blatant spirit of invincibility in the face of failure gives the cartoons their own special impressiveness, and this in turn is precisely the fascination of these cartoons, a fascination and power that awakens a response in the hearts of the cartoon's many fans. Once again we can ask: Just where does this fascination and appeal lie? Again the answer is this: In the thorough-going way in which each desire, even the most trifling, is pursued within the microcosm of the cartoon world.

What impresses one most is the way in which these cartoons become almost a hymn of praise to these trifling, everyday desires and aspirations. The fact that the character's aspirations are not ambitious but humble does not seem to me to be a negative factor. In fact, the more humble or trifling the desires, the more they seem to suit the everyday life of the cartoon's readers and the world presented in the cartoons, and within the reality that they depict, the cartoons accurately and continuously depict the microcosm that they have faithfully created.

From the very outset, cartoons have been essentially a simple mundane depiction of things and scenes from everyday life, and the current popularity of cartoons in Japan faithfully maintains this long tradition. The very commonplace nature of the Japanese comic cartoon is a reflection of the everyday dreams and desires of the everyday people who turn to cartoons for their reading pleasure.

Komiks: The Filipino National Literature

Provender of fantasy, facts, opinion and entertainment, the "komiks", or the illustrated weekly magazines of the Philippines, are notoriously the great escapist fare of millions of semi-literate Filipinos. It is the one medium of communication that can boast of reaching every population group in a country with pronounced language differences. Would-be social historians love to point out that the "komiks" magazines are the literature of the lower classes, much of the rather elitist Filipino literature being inaccessible to the masses of uneducated, barely literate Filipinos. One can also note the striking creative swing between political satire and narrative form. But what is perhaps most interesting is the way "Komiks" literature reflects, over half a century, the changing position, tastes, aspirations, and world view of the Filipino masses. The comic magazine did not stand out as a clear and independent branch of the mass media until well into the '40s. Before that and as far back as the nineteenth century, there was caricature, the cartoon and the comic strip. Above all, there was Jose Rizal, the Filipino national hero, who was also the country's first cartoonist.

The climate of Rizal's time was suited to a literature of dissension. The last decades of the nineteenth century were marked by stirrings of revolution and the violent toppling of 350 years of Spanish rule. That Rizal, the master propagandist, should have been drawn to caricature in order to denounce Spanish injustices was inevitable. Unfortunately, none of his illustrated attacks on the corrupt colonial system of his time survive. We get an idea of his work in his whimsical and witty rendering to the Filipino folk table, "The Monkey and the Tortoise," which appeared in a study of Filipino and Japanese folk tales published by Truebner's Record in London in 1889. Paradoxically enough the Philippine revolution also paved the way for a new colonial power to entrench itself in the Philippines. The American occupation of the Philippines was a sharply sensed disjunction in the Filipino psyche that spawned a number of satirical magazines like *El Tio Verdades* published in 1899 and Biro-Biro in 1901. Both magazines were written in Spanish and profusely illustrated with two-toned colour cartoons and caricatures. In 1907, following the birth of Filipino political parties patterned after American prototypes, a vernacular weekly took over the format of *Ei Tio Verdades* and *Biro-Biro. Lipang Kalabaw* as the new magazine was called, took a militantly nationalist stand, satirizing American do-goodism and Filipino parrotism. Its two creative spirits, Fernando Amorsolo and Ireneo Miranda, went on to become two of the country's foremost painters. Amorsolo was posthumously awarded the National Artist Award in 1974.

The man who was to start the Philippine comics on its glorious way was Tony Velasquez, creator of the immortal Kenkoy. In 1928, Kenkoy appeared on the pages of *Liwayway,* a weekly literary magazine in Pilipino and overnight, a national hero was born. Kenkoy, with his ukelele, Valentino hair, bell bottoms was a ludicrous portrait of the Filipino of the time pathetically trying but barely succeeding in keeping up with his American mentors. The strip started a national tradition of satirizing the fads and vanities of a rapidly westernizing country. It also stood as some kind of symbol of the passage of Filipino caricature from the heavily political to a lighter airier world.

The advent of the Second World War put a temporary stop to the development of the new medium. The Japanese invaders stamped out all vestiges of Americans in the country, beginning with the English language and sweeping away with it the ubiquitous "funnies." But came war's end, and the comics were back with vengeance.

This time the Americans bought something that would figure importantly in the eventual development of the mass media in the Philippines. The comic book was nothing more than a collection of comic strips, only this time the strips were no longer three-frame gaga but running stories. Comic books were the means by which millions of G.I.'s in far-flung theaters were able to stay in touch with their homeland. Thus was grafted unto the imagination of every Filipino child born after the war the adventures and feats of Tarzan, Captain Marvel, Superman and a host of comic-book heroes. Thus was also born the germ of a new medium of communication in the country.

Halakhak (Laughter) was the first Filipino comic book published after the war. it was edited by Isaac Tolentino, published by Jaime Lucas and carried the work of the illustrators, cartoonists and novelists who were to make the "komiks" what it is today: Mars Ravelo, Francisco Coaching, Francisco Reyes, Larry Alcala, Hugo Yonzon, Viscount Mananzala, Jessie Santos, Ross Chanco and Tony Velasquez.

Following its stateside progenitor, *Halakhak* was a collection of illustrated serials, editorial opinion, political satire, social comments, some of which were overtly intended as an incentive to social change, advocating for agrarian reform and protesting against the presence of the Americans. *Halakhak* was to reach a 20,000 circulation and came out with 10 issues, but it failed to build a mass readership. Again it was Tony Valasquez, who saved the comic strip from extinction. Valasquez correctly read the taste of the reading public for illustrated and serialized novels. With Ramon Roces as publisher, he came out with *Pilipino Komiks* in 1947. Unlike *Halakhak* which was a blend of satire and illustrated stories, *Pilipino Komiks* devoted most of its pages to the serialized novels. Cartoons, whenever they were used were relegated to the role of curtain raisers of "dividers" between the big stories. The new magazine was an instant success, proving the soundness of Velasquez's editorial and business sense. Today, *Pilipino Komiks* leads a pack of 44 other titles in the komiks magazine market with a circulation of 175,000, out of a combined circulation of two million copies a week.

The new "Komiks" magazine was seldom comic in either form or content. Gone was the satirical element; much of it was in no sense particularly humorous. "Comics" rapidly become a misnomer, as a local writer, the late Cloduald del Mundo pointed out. (The KPPKP or the Association of Publishers and Editors of Philippine Comics magazines prefers the term, "illustrated magazine.") They were not merely for children, they were widely read by adults. (A recent survey states that 60% of those who read comic books are adults of 20 years and above.) They often tended towards the commercial and the sensational. A random sampling of "Komiks" titles reads like a carnival of freaks: Alonica and Bubonica, the Rat-Faced Ladies; Dyesebel and Kleng Kleng, Mermaids; Dabiana, the Superfat Lady; Bakekang, the Ape-faced Lady; Petrang Kabayo, Half-horse and half-woman.

The "Komiks" magazine today is a cloudy area comprising fantasy, freely appropriated myth, and indeed any fiction not rooted in the here and now. The same themes of love, adventure, detective, war, figure over and over again and, given the Filipino predilection for adapting without thought from foreign models, almost always occur in some never-never land of knight errants, helpless ladies, straight-shooting cowboys, Roman and Greek temples or outer space, giving ample demonstration of the multi-coloured strands from which Filipino culture has been woven.

As the popularity of the comics spread, along with cartoons, the two began to divide. The most common distinction is that cartoons and strips are generally found in daily newspapers while the illustrated serials lord it over the "komiks" magazines. But the divisions are enough. While the writers and illustrators for "komiks" magazines were developing their story-telling skills, cartoonists and comic-strip creators were sharpening their humorists' eye. Their field was the daily newspaper cartoon, the editorial cartoon and the comic strip. Where the "komiks" writers wove melodrama and fantasy, the lampoon artists hurled social comment and satire. The latter's gaze ranged over a world that included politics, contemporary mores, religion. It was a world that was dismayingly urbanized and westernized. Following the steps of Kenkoy, Francisco Reyes' *Kalafu* and J. Zabala Santos' *Lucas Malakas,* the local counterparts of Tarzan and Popeye, respectively, attested to the fact that, after 30 years of American tutoring, the Filipino was properly westernized creature. Larry Alcala, one of the few cartoonists to have successfully straddled the two worlds of the comic strip and the komiks magazine, cast a baleful look on this incipient Westernization, ridiculing his countrymen's clumsy handling of their new-found language with clever world-play in *Kalabog en Bosyo,* a strip loosely adapted from Batman and robin. Malang's *Kosme the Cop* and Ben Alcantara's *Gore and His Jeepney,* made gentle fun of the foibles of common folk. Much later in the turbulent sixties, Nonoy Marcelo's *Tisoy* caught the public fancy much as Kenkoy did some 20 years before. *Tisoy* was about the dilemma of the urbanized Filipino youth, caught between generations, not wishing to go back to the insular provincialism of its elders and yet unsure of where to go. In a business dominated by the foreign syndicated strips, Tisoy succeeded in outpolling in 1968 all the foreign and local strips put together. It was a victory of stores for local cartoonists who labour in a field that does not pay well (in contrast to their colleagues in the "Komiks" magazines) and whose works are unfavourably compared to the imported product. But that too seems to be changing as more and more local cartoonists and illustrators are coming into their own. Corky Trinidad, cartoonists of the defunct *Philippine Herald,* now a resident of Honolulu, is the only *Filipino* cartoonist enjoying U.S. syndication. Illustrators like Tony Zuniga, Ernie Chan, Alfredo Alcala, Nestor Redondo, Madz Castrillo, Alex Nino, Nestor Leonidez, and others are regular illustrators for the big American comic magazines.

Whatever the fare of individual cartoonists, it seems that the fateful dichotomy is here to stay. Social comment and the cartoonists who are its exponents have the daily newspapers while the "komiks" has come into its own as an original publication and has grown into a major industry. Today, the Komiks is unquestionably the most influential mass medium in the Philippines with an estimated readership of 16 million. Filipinos young and old, educated or not, manage to read at least one or more "komiks" a week. Not even the movies can boast of reaching a third of the population as can the "komiks." Not surprisingly the movies and the "komiks" have found one another. Komiks writers and illustrators tailor their creations for the movies market and motion picture producers and directors mine the komiks for material. The relationship is so strong that not a few comic books devote a third of their output to the gossips, intrigues, and publicity stunts of sundry movie personalities. Given the unreal character of most "komiks" fare, the kinship between the two was inevitable.

Cartoon Techniques Widely Applied in Thailand

Thailand can probably consider itself a veteran of the cartoon world. The beginning and development of the cartoon in Thailand date back as much as a century or so when the country first opened up to the influence of the western world. One might give credit to H.M. King Rama VI for introducing the cartoon form to the Thai people and ensuring its popularity. In his palace magazine, "Dusit Samit," His Majesty displayed his wit and considerable artistic talent in his caricature of a member of his Council of Ministers! He was much acclaimed for the humorous characterization which emphasized a bulging head and greatly protruding waistline. Thus, the cartoon may have had a firm beginning in Thailand by fulfilling the needs, at first, for both satirical expression and recreation.

The caricature form of the cartoon is commonly used by local and international cartoonists since it can give a message in a more effective fashion than verbal statements could tactfully describe. Caricatures offer a distorted clue to the person or subject being portrayed, but in such a humorous way that the emotional impact of the message is toned down to a socially acceptable degree.

A long-time cartoonist who had an extensive following among Thai readers and scholars was Thanya Utthakanon. His works were published in Weekly magazines. His cartoon style was recognized as being both aggressive and almost unbearably penetrating in character. Choa Phraya Yommaraj, the Minister of the Interior at the time, for instance, was wildly imagined in Thanya's mind as appearing distortingly and provocatively bald. The Minister's head was drawn to look like a hawk's head, which the Thais consider to be so ridiculous looking that it was a prime insult.

Sawas Jutharop was another pioneer in the Thai cartoon world. He introduced to the Thai readers serialized stories presented entirely in cartoon form. Most often, the cartoon technique was implemented to illustrate and simplify some difficult literary work in order for it to appeal to larger audience. Chan Suwanakul, in particular, drew cartoons for the purpose of simplification. He based all of his cartoon serials on the book *Loke Niti Kam Klong* ("World Proverbial Tales in Verse Form"). Since it was an extremely difficult literary work, rewriting it in cartoon form made it easier for the general public to read and comprehend.

Chalerm Vutthi-kosit drew cartoons under the pen name of "Chalermvuth." He was assisted by Changchan Chankana, better known as "Pranboon," who wrote the narratives. Their cartoons appeared every week in *The Monday Daily Mail*, one of the most widely read and popular magazines. Readers were often so addicted to Chalermvuth's cartoons that every week they eagerly looked forward to seeing what he would come up with next.

Wit Suthisathien's cartoons used still another creative approach. He presented the heroic deeds of the Bang Rajan Stockade, which had fought for freedom against Burmese invaders during the downfall of Ayuddhya, Thailand's former capital. Wit's work appeared in the *Polenchit Weekly* about 30 years ago. By then many artists were using their own independent approaches which revealed diverse usages and applications of cartoons as another form of art.

Two famous folk tales, "Raden Randai" and "Praya Noi Chom Talad," for instance, were creatively told by Wit in cartoon serials for the first time in the *Sri Krung Weekly* and the *Thai Ras Weekly*. This led to a new avenue of wonder and excitement in the world of cartoons in Thailand. The same was true when Sawas Jutharope, another figure in the cartoon world, created "Sangthong" and "Kraithong" in cartoon serials.

Sawas created a comic character named "Khun Muen," Which actually resembles the world-famous "Popeye." The impact of Sawas' Khun Muen, or the pseudo-Oriental Popeye, was so great among the young readers of the country that a cartoon portrait of Khun Muen became a popular logo embroidered on the garments of young admirers of Sawas' work. Despite the heavy work demand, Sawas could reach his maximum productive capacity of one cartoon piece per day.

The most prominent cartoonist in Thailand today, devoted to the profession, is Prayoon chanyawongse, the only Thai Magsaysay awardee in cartoon arts, Prayoon draws cartoons not only as a means of livelihood, but also for fun and goodwill. In a very few years, he rose from a beginning schoolboy cartoonist to world renown. During the prewar years his work appeared sporadically in the *Suphabboorut Weekly* and the *Prachamit Weekly*. His best known work was a serialized cartoon presentation of a lively folk tale, "Chantha Korope." While he does not earn a fortune, Prayoon makes up for his earnings as a cartoonist by living a happy and contented life.

In 1960, or ten years prior to his winning the Magsaysay Award, Prayoon's work also won the first prize at the "Cartoons for Peace" contest in New York in which more then 300 entries were received from 30 different countries. Three entries were submitted by Prayoon, one of which, "The Last Atomic Bomb Test," was announced as the winner. Surprisingly, Prayoon had no formal training in drawing nor does he believe in the naturally gifted talent. He believes that the way to success for cartoonists is through hard work and practice as well as through one's sincerity and belief in the profession. It brought him great satisfaction when H.M. King Bhumibhol introduced him to Walt Disney, the cartoon giant of the western world, with whom he eventually at the Disney Production Centre in Burbank, California.

Unlike his predecessors, who merely specialized in a single application or a one-sided usage of cartoons in their expression of mankind, Prayoon found himself inking his cartoons for diverse applications. The application of cartoons in everyday modern life varies to a large extent according to the cultural and environmental pattern of each society. In Thailand, since cartoons have existed for a long time and the Thais are an artistic people by nature, the cartoons seem to reach a good cross-section of the population and to be increasingly diverse in situations and applications. Therefore, it can be said that the Thais have a deep appreciation of cartoon art.

In fact, one can see that the modern cartoons are in a new phase of their developmental process. Perhaps it might be said that the basic and primary role of cartoons is to be an "art appetizer." While serving such a role, cartoon application in artistic expression also serves as a provocative inducement of interest, i.e., as an "art stimulant,"

In Thailand, satirical cartoons are still very popular. Daily and weekly satirical cartoons are produced by political cartoonists; some of the more well-known ones include "Arun" in the English papers, the *Nation's Review* and the *Bangkok Post*; Prayoon chanyawongse, better known as "Sook Lek," in the *Thai Rath Daily* and *Siam Rath Daily* and *Weekly*; "Virachon" in the *Daily Time;* "Chai Ratchawat" in the daily column under the title "Pooyai Mah kap Thung Mah Moen" or "The Chieftain Mah and the Mah Moen Prairie", a political humorist in the *Thai Rath Daily*, Aed Daily News" in the cartoon column, "Palad Kliang Khon Keng" or "Goody, Goody Kliang, the District Administrator" in the Daily News;

"Ad" in the *Siang Puangchon Daily*, and "A-Ngoon" in the *Matichon Daily*.

During the period of newspaper censorship under the martial laws of Thanom's regime, for instance, the curb of press freedom was humorously reflected in Prayoon's own self-caricature with his mouth sewn shut. The sewn mouth picture appeared continuously until the censor was abolished. Prayoon focuses on criticism of unfair practices and injustice in society. At one time he spoke out against the misuse of official cars and vehicles by government officials. Because of his bold cartoons, the government finally took steps toward devising measures to clamp down on the abusive practice.

Two other cartoon approaches have been introduced by the Thais as well as by international cartoonists. The first is the injection of humour into serious subjects. Again, Prayoon is an expert. His theme, "Sapadon Wan La Nid Chit Chaomsai," was one of the best known serials in the *Thai Rath Daily* each week. The theme could be literally translated as "A Little Touch of Joke Every Day Makes Life Wonderful." True to Prayoon's reputation, the fascination of his work is derived both from the witty narrations as well as from the humorous elements of the drawings themselves.

As was mentioned earlier, the major role of cartoons is their educational objectives. The cartoon technique is used to illustrate a text, making it easier to read, as in difficult literary works. Lately, cartoonists such as Prayoon use cartoons to explain such topics as gardening, plants, housekeeping, cooking and nutrition, and earning a living in general. Prayoon himself has published collective volumes of his cartoon works in pocket book form. There are more such books forthcoming. The latest development in cartoon art in Thailand has been its increasing use in advertising, in both reading materials and television advertising.

As in other countries, the cartoon reading audience probably consists mostly of young people. Best known among the young readers in Thailand are cartoon magazines as *Tuay Toon*, *Chaiyapruek Cartoon*, and *Tookata* (Doll). Surprisingly, however, even though these magazines have a greater reader audience than do adult cartoons, they suffer from a tremendous fluctuation in market demand. They very quickly go out of business only to reenter under a new name.

In sum, Thailand is indeed moving ahead in the fun world of cartoons in every possible sense. Their popularity among an ever-increasing audience has presented a challenge for both more and better cartoons and cartoonists. The cartoon may one day take its rightful elevated place in the world of esthetics.

Pakistan: Many Young Cartoonists

Pakistan is the cradle of one of the ancient civilizations of the world which flourished in the Indus Valley between 2500 and 1500 BC While examples of cartoon drawings have been discovered in Egypt, Iraq, and many countries of Europe strangely none has been found in any of the relics unearthed in Pakistan. Either this delightful art form was unknown to the ancient people who lived here or they were temperamentally too serious to indulge in such a flippant pastime. Thus, cartooning is one of the few art forms which has become a regular feature of journalism here only in the recent past. What is intriguing is that even after coming under the influence of successive waves of different races from Greece, Central Asia, Arabia, Turkey, and Iran and the rise and fall of their respective civilizations, which witnessed extensive cultural diffusion, this art form still did not emerge here. If cartooning, like other forms of art, reflects not only the milieu in which a nation flourishes but also the temperament of the people, then it is equally strange to observe that the people who lived in what is now known as Pakistan were never divorced from the blessings of wit and humour. Even during the pre-independence period, there were many famous Pakistani humorists and satirists whose work was streaked with the waspish sting of satire and delightful raillery. Also, there had been many journals, such as the *Oudh Punch*, printed in Rude and influenced by the renowned British magazine *Punch,* which offered enjoyable humorous reading material. Even such magazines did not print cartoon strips, except for a few caricatures of some adversaries through rather grotesque drawings.

Thus, it is evident that the growth of the art of cartooning in Pakistan has mainly been in our own times, beginning with the dawn of independence. In other words, the real history of this fascinating art in Pakistan is only about 32 years old. Besides the lack of tradition, one reason for this could be that when the sub-continent was ruled by an alien power, English was the official language of India. As such, most important newspapers were published in English which could simply reproduce cartoons drawn by well-known British cartoonists. There is no doubt that many other newspapers were then being published in Urdu which later became the national language of Pakistan. But none of them printed cartoons. Occasionally, if they did, then it was in a style which now looks crude and immature.

That state of affairs has completely changed now. Although some popular foreign comic strips, such as Schultz's "Peanuts" and Appeleby's "Gambols", continue to appear in Pakistani newspapers, a large number of Pakistani cartoonists have also emerged during the past three decades. Most of them are young but they possess deep insight into the social, economic, cultural, and political problems of the people. Much of their work reflects various aspects of contemporary life, often high lighting some incongruous situation or human weakness. So far, except for Nigar Nazar, a female cartoonist who has lived abroad and hence has successfully assimilated the work of many European and American masters, very few have tried their hands at drawing cartoon strips. Similarly, except for Anwar, none has successfully projected the antics of only one character. There is yet another cartoonist, Sadaquat, who takes his readers almost daily to a typically Pakistani family whom he calls the "Fussy family." Through them he comments with skill on what he feels about life around him.

These cartoons appear mostly in daily Urdu and English newspapers, and only a few appear in magazines. Their pungent appraisal of contemporary happenings usually relies on minimum detail and even fewer written characters. With less stress on words and more on drawings, they try to communicate the underlying message effectively. Frequently, their targets come from the realm of public affairs, exposing the shortcomings in social customs and the missteps found in the life of the common man.

A quick survey of Pakistani cartoons shows that gag cartoons are more popular than political cartoons. In most cases they reflect, thematically, the prevalent social and economic conditions.

Some of the common themes are inflation and soaring prices of consumer goods, especially before festival times. The amusing comments of children very subtly poke fun at human faults and at the quality of life. Nigar Nazar, whose comic strip is titled "Gogi Giggles," appears in Islamabad's newspaper, the *Muslim*. Her amusing observations about the International Year of the Child and on the acute shortage of potable water in Islamabad, Pakistan's ultra-,modern capital city are delightful commentaries on an important aspect of life.

Due to rapid urbanization, most large cities of Pakistan have been facing shortage of potable water. This theme has been exploited by almost all Pakistani cartoonists. For instance, Aziz, the well-known political cartoonist of the *Morning News* in Karachi, projects it grimly under the title "Keeping the Traditions Alive". Mirza, a young cartoonist whose work appears in the Urdu newspaper *Jung*, also in Karachi, uses a news items to expose this depressing state of affairs. Sadaquat, Whose "Fussy Family" cartoons appear daily in the *Muslim*, ridicules the water supply arrangements of CDA, Capital Development Authority. Then on the subject of the ever-increasing cost of living, Sadaquat has another enjoyable cartoon. His lampooning of the working of government departments such as the Post Office is also very subtle.

Public transport is yet another problem which has plagued most city dwellers for almost three decades, and the sad situation is a target of many cartoonists. For instance, Jamshed Ansari, who was killed in an accident at the prime of his career, depicted hilariously how people usually travel in public buses in large cities. His cartoons appeared in a biweekly journal, *Ahang*. Zaidi, a prolific cartoonist who now draws for *Jung* in the mode of Osbert Lancaster's "Pocket Cartoon", ridicules another aspect of the public transport system, the uncaring attitude of bus conductors. Many interesting cartoons have been published regarding railway and air services, one of the best being Tanvir Khizr's which exaggerates the frequency of the late arrivals of trains. Like Aziz, Anwar is a senior cartoonist, drawing almost daily for *Lahore's Pakistan Times* for some time. His stock character is Nanna, a lovable young boy, reminiscent of Hank Ketcham's Dennis, who pokes fun at everything which intrigues him. For instance, in a cartoon, he observes how white sugar is available only in the black market. In another, Nanna expresses his opinion about the dwindling educational standards. Anwar occupies an important place among the gag cartoonists of Pakistan for his subtle humour and the incisiveness of his message.

During recent months, the sufferings of the common man have been the favourite theme of many cartoonists. Aziz's "Save Me" is an attempt to summarize the general predicament and true state of affairs. Frequent power breakdowns due to the inefficiency of the agencies concerned is another subject which seems to require the cartoonists' attention. They have satirized the agencies and attacked the social and moral abuses which have been responsible for this deterioration in services. Vai Ell (Yusuf Lodhi), who draws simply, somewhat in the style of James Thurber, attacks WAPDA (Water and Power Development Authority) which supplies the electricity to a vast area. Although he uses more narrative than the other cartoonists, his remarks, such as the advertisement of a radio set *inter-alia* condemning the poor quality of television programmes, are still subtle. The Muslims make up a major portion of his audience.

Javed Iqbal's forte is his attacks on corruption and inefficiency. His approach is direct and his satire biting. In one of his recent cartoons published in the Urdu daily, *Nawa-e-Waqt*, he criticizes venomously those whose job is to take care of highways.

The art of cartooning which may have originated in Italy in the sixteenth century and which spread far and wide, reached Pakistan relatively late. Presently, the interest in this delightful form of pictorial journalism is great and has resulted in the emergence of many new talented cartoonists. The future of the art of cartooning in Pakistan looks bright.

Cartoons: Mirror of Bangladesh Society

artoons are a mirror of contemporary culture, in both its lighter and more serious sides, and the nine short years of Bangladesh's journey into being are perhaps more memorably captured in cartoons than in any other medium. Although cartoons did appear during the British and the Pakistan period, to fill up a gap on a page, to illustrate some funny sketches, to accompany a juicy narrative, cartoons were never accepted as a "serious" form of expression or as a regular feature in any magazine. The situation has substantially improved since the foundation of Bangladesh. Particular credit goes to a weekly review called *Bicitra* and to a talented young artist named Rafiqun Nabi, who signs himself as "Ranabi". Even so, it is possible to excavate in literary archives various precursors of the Bangladesh cartoon. Although journals have been published in this part of the former British Empire since the early nineteenth century; it was not until World War I that pictures, including a few cartoons, found their way to journals and periodicals to any extent. For the most part the drawings that are found in these publications are all too serious; sombre portrayals of the gifts of nature and landscapes were their forte, a somewhat melodramatic illustration of the newly acquired tragic sense of life. Then, three literary publications suddenly appeared as a counterfoil to such sobriety, i.e., Rajshekhar Basu's *Goddalika*, Abul Mansur Ahmad's *Ayna* (The Mirror), and the *Food Conference*, which are amply illustrated with comic pictures, opening for the first time this dimension to the connoisseur. The illustrations in the first two publications are based on foibles of human nature and the disjunctures of society, but they so well pinpoint certain emotional aspects of Bengali society that they are still popular, along with the masterpieces of humorous writing they accompany. The third book, the *Food Conference*, dealing with the politics which caused the great famine of 1943, enjoyed widespread success, and its illustrator, Qazi Abul Qasem, started contributing cartoons to daily and weekly journals. This was a heyday for politics. The future of the British in India was being determined and a *intellectual elite* was beginning to take shape among the Bengali Moslems. The creation of Pakistan and of Bangladesh were just a matter of time. Qazi, using the penname "Dopeyaza", became very popular. One of his earlier drawings, "Hungry Bengal and Famine Commission", Published in the Daily *Azad's* Eid special number of 1944, shows a donkey symbolizing hungry Bengal pursuing carrots on a stick that will never reach its teeth. The carrots stand for the Commission constituted by the Government to solve the food problem, which to be sure it never solved. The same issue, which was published in the form of a magazine, printed many other cartoons and comic drawings, mainly by Qumrul Hasan, then a young artist who has now become a celebrated master. Qamrul used the penname of "Bhimrul" (meaning the bee) and his cartoons often do carry a sting. Also during World War II, Zainul Abedin, who was to become later the doyen of fine arts in Bangladesh, first gained fame for his stirring sketches of the Bengal Famine of 1943. Later on, he drew some caricatures of the political events of the day. Following Abedin's example, Qumrul Hassan, Rashid Chowdhury, Murtaza Bashir, Debdas Chakravarty, Mizanur Rahim, and others drew cartoons and caricatures which often found use as posters to incite patriotic fervour during the liberation struggle. A few pioneer cartoonists deserve special mention — Mostafa Aziz (Aziz), Qayyum Chowdhury (Qa-Chow), Mahmud Zamir, Subhas Dutt, Kalam Mahumd (Birbal), Hashem Khan (Chabi Khan), Nazrul Islam (Nazrul), Rafuqun Nabi (Ranabi), Titu, Serajul Jug (sarda) and Banizul Huq (Baniz). They have all produced memorable cartoons during the decade.

The publishing of cartoons as a feature began earlier. The daily *Morning News* of Dacca in the 1950's introduced cartoons and comic strips. Two good cartoonists named Aziz were attached to the paper at that time. One was a Bengali. They became very popular for their political cartoons. Charles Schulz's American strip "Peanuts" was also reprinted regularly during this period and inspired several similar series in Bengali. One series, called "Pratidvandvi" (The Rivals), was published for some time in the daily *Bangla*. Another, called "Tokai", featuring conversations between a middle-class boy and a shrewdly perceptive street-urchin, appears regularly in the weekly *Bicitra*. Two famous western strips, "Barbarella" and "James Bond", have recently been published in the two weeklies *Bicitra* and *Sacitra Sandhani*, respectively, which perhaps demonstrates the participation of Bangladeshis in a collective international fantasy life. "Barbarella" has been re-illustrated by a local artist, Syed Lutful Huq, but "James bond", the symbol of international intrigue, has been left with his original round-eyes pallor and bootcamp beefiness.

Social criticism in the form of small "pocket cartoons" has become very popular. These, framed in a small, column-wide box on the front page of newspapers, comment on problems of day-to day life and contemporary events. Cartoons by Arup appeared regularly for some time in the daily *Bangla*. Pocket cartoons by other artists appear in a few other dailies and weeklies. One such artist, Nazrul, has done a caricature of himself overwhelmed by the ready supply of subject matter in Bangladesh, bearing the caption, "After drawing so many gags, I am still gagging." One sees the hapless face of the artist blotting the upper-class interviewer whom he has started to draw with bamboo-sized brush. Cartoons hanging on the wall bear such title as "Unemployment Problem", "Population Problem", "Food Problem", Flood Problem", "Nepotism Problem", Nutrition Problem", "Canvas Problem", "Colour and Brush Problem", etc. He is standing on a sheet entitled 'Society...', and another with the title "Mountain of Problems". Nazrul's cartoon appeared in *Bicitra* on 14 September 1974.

Bicitra, a magazine offshoot of the daily *Bangla*, has played a major role in popularizing cartoons in Bangladesh. Its awareness of the role it plays in mixing a few objective chuckles with the solemn business of nation-building is shown by an advertisement it used to carry: "Don't read *Bicitra* if you are not free prejudices." The means for exposing such prejudices is frequently a cartoon. *Bicitra* has published more than a dozen issues with full-page cartoons on the cover and quarter-page cartoons elsewhere. These illustrate national problems in the field of education, electricity supply, administration, airlines, food policy, price hikes, smuggling, hoarding, research activities, and so on. Politics has been more marginally, though not superficially, touched on by the cartoonists. The affairs of general and presidential elections, the voters' dilemma, and the conflict between bureaucrats and politicians have received attention from several cartoonists, most significantly from Nazrul and Ranabi during the years following liberation (1971). Their criticism, however, is cautious and muted, perhaps showing more what publishers will risk publishing than what cartoonists would like to draw. Many of these cartoons seem to project a kind of frustration instead of instantly touching our funny bone. They only succeed in producing a muttered response of "All too true."

Four artists, all Fine Arts graduates, have been associated with *Bicitra*. They are Kalam Mahmud (who sometimes uses the penname "Birbal"), Syed Lutful Huq (Lutful), Nazrul Islam (Nazrul), and Rafiqun Nabi (Ranabi). At present, it is Ranabi who is featured most often. His "Tokai", mentioned above, is published weekly on the editorial page. The pronouncements of his street-wise urchin are often witty and insightful in depicting Bangladesh society. Rafiqun Nabi, now forty-one years old, has been drawing cartoons since 1964 when he was associated with the daily Newspaper, *Purbadesh*. Because of his prolific production and regular appearances on television, he is now the most popular cartoonist in Bangladesh. He is a skilled water colourist and has also received training in making wood-cuts in Athens. He now teaches at the Bangladesh College of Arts and Crafts. *Bicitra* has published an album of his cartoons, and this year one of his cartoons (along with one from Nazrul) found a place in the exhibition of the International Pavillion of Humour at Montreal. Following the success of *Bicitra*, the weekly *Sacitra Sandhani* also started publishing cartoons as a regular feature. One of its artists, Titu promises to become a leading cartoonist in the future. The cartoon in Bangladesh is still in its infancy, but it is developing very quickly. Not only readers, but even TV watchers, are now regularly exposed to cartoons, showing the importance given to them. Recently, a Bengali equivalent of *Mad* magazine called *Unmad* ("Mad" in Bengali), has appeared. Its first four issues attained considerable success. The group of seven young artists who are drawing the cartoons to illustrate the grotesque and bizzare stories of *Ummad* seem well on their way to a big success. Clearly, Bangladesh has not lost her sense of humour despite her problems and poverty.

Bangladesh was once a land of opulence. Her people were playful and knew the niceties of life even as they were serious seekers of knowledge. It is to be hoped that the developing wit of her cartoonists can be seen as a harbinger of good things to come for the country as a whole, and that her leaders will show tolerance to these public jesters and permit them free sailing. It has always been the character of great political leaders to be able to laugh at themselves. it is said of Charles de Gaulle that every Wednesday morning during his tenure as French Head of State, he used to wait eagerly to read *Le Canard Enchaine*, the famous satirical weekly. The serious general is supposed to have especially enjoyed the journals cartoons and cirticism, which primarily caricatured his personality. It does not seem surprising that the man who brought France the greatest political maturity and international respect it had enjoyed in more than a century should have also had such a great sense of humour. We are encouraged to hold similar hopes for the future of Bangladesh.

The Inimitable Indian Cartoonists

The Indian cartoonists, like their counterparts the world over, freely and fearlessly draw cartoons as satiric and biting comments on the contemporary issue and leaders. In the process, they display consummate skill and artistry in lampooning, criticising and ridiculing people, parties and the ever-changing political scenario.

The strength of a political cartoon lies in its ability to convey an idea boldly, trenchantly and humorously using minimum of space, sketches and words. Sharp visual appeal, immediate perception and a spontaneous reaction distinguish cartoons and caricatures from printed matters of all kinds. "If a picture is worth a thousand words", as the saying goes, then the cartoon — not the comic cartoon but the cartoon of commentary — is worth a thousand words. Although a cartoon requires a much smaller space than the editorial, its appeal is often much greater. It is for this reason that a cartoon is regarded as a symbol of a society's level of political consciousness and maturity.

Its inherent appeal, wit and satire not only reflect the mind of the cartoonist but also hold a mirror to the ground realities obtaining in a particular social and political milieu.

History and politics seen and understood through the eyes of master cartoonists tend to become an exciting and thrilling experience.

Being an ancient country, India has had its share of this art since the dawn of history. As the earliest form of communication, next only to the spoken word, the story of cartooning dates back to the earliest man and the pre-historic cave paintings. In India, certain schools of paintings particularly the Madhubani cones closer to caricature with its crude but impressive sketches.

Later, the same spirit of humour and satire which immoralised the character of "Vidushak" or court jester in Indian drama began running through the mighty pens of great Indian cartoonists. This accounts for the immense popularity enjoyed by famous cartoonists like Shankar, Rajinder Puri, R.K. Laxman and many others for their unique perception of life and reality.

As a pioneer in the field of political cartooning, Shankar, starting in the pre-independence era, became well-known for his drawings distinguished by that "supreme ease of characterisation" that marked his work from those of his peers like Low or Strube. His cartoons rarely had the common man. His "Shankar's Weekly" like the British "Punch" or the American "Puck", became a household name as a first and foremost instrument of amusement, laughter and political satire in India.

The Illustrated Weekly of India, June 1972, beautifully summed up Shankar's contribution: "With him, dreaming up things is a hobby, collecting dolls an obsession, writing and illustrating books for children a passion, and exposing human follies and making gentle mockery of them through cartoons a way of life. Shankar does not just dream and stop at that, he chases his dreams till they surrender".

He began his career as the staff cartoonist of the Hindustan Times. He rose to become the internationally renowned cartoonist through hard work and dedication to his craft.

Shankar was a trendsetter. He left an indelible mark in the field of political cartooning. He paved the way for others to experiment and innovate.

The appearance of the "common man" in the cartoons of R.K. Laxman provided the extraordinary insight into the actual mood of the people. The balding, bespectacled, perpetually awe-struck common man of his continuing pocket cartoon series "You Said it" is a source of fun for millions day after day.

According to Laxman, "his (common man's) is the omnipresent eye; he appears everywhere, in political chambers and in slums, with ministers and pan-wallahs, but never speaks a word. He is ever the eaves-dropper on the remarks of others, including his slightly foolish wife who does all the talking for him".

As a sensitive artist, Laxman owes debt to the early Anglo-Saxon cartoonists of 1940s and 50s notably of the Punch school.

If Laxman chose to speak for the silent majority through his little man, Rajinder Puri favoured a direct confrontationist approach through his bold cartoons characterised by brilliant insight and sharp visual appeal.

Rajinder Puri is both versatile and controversial. Cartoonist, editorial writer, political columnist, satirist and political activist, he shot into limelight with his *coup de grace* entitled "Retreat from Moscow", published in the *Hindustan Times* in 1962, the critical year of Chinese invasion. This one cartoon provoked twenty-five MPs to write to the editor asking his dismissal. But he escaped unscathed.

A laughing indignation at the disintegrating quality of life and politics the world over is the underlying theme of Puri's cartoons that remain outstanding for their sympathetic attitude towards his fellow countrymen. His cartoons startle with their pungent wit and scathing humour.

Reckoned as one of India's powerful and influential cartoonist, Puri started his career as a newspaper cartoonist branching out to writing political commentary, and later, writing satire. He worked for *Manchester Guardian* and *Glasgow Herald* in Britain, and for the *Hindustan Times* and the *The Statesman* in India. Since 1970, he has been freelancing and syndicating his own work. His cartoons appear regularly in *The Statesman.* He has also authored four books on Indian politics.

Like the American Thomas Nast, Puri has added force to his cartoons through a new feeling for culture and has given accuracy to the art of cartooning in India.

Taking a cue from Puri and Laxman, cartoonists like Sudhir Dar, Ravishankar, Vijayan, Ajit Ninan, Unny and Sudhir Tailang have added variety to this craft. However, broad stylistic variations are easily discernible in their cartoons.

Sudhir Dar's forte lies in poking fun at the very apparent aspects of daily life. His political cartoons are mild in nature with light-hearted banter evident all through.

Ajit Ninan, on the other hand, uses cartoons as impact device to score a point with wit and dexterity. His cartoons have a broad sweep and are generalised in nature.

Ravishankar's cartoons entitled "Off Tangent" attempt to highlight the reality behind the appearances with subtle humour.

Known for tackling politics at the level of ideas, both Ravishankar and Vijaya have made a mark for using their cartoons as weapons of ideological warfare. However, with Vijayan drawing cartoons is more often an extension of his intricate thought process. With his stark lines and sweeping black brush strokes, he has developed a distinct style of his own.

A somewhat similar style is discernible in the cartoons of Unny. His cartoons are distinct for being full of literary allusion and are at times obscure in comprehension. However, his pocket cartoon, "Business as Usual" comes through as a very lively and succinct comment on the day-to-day life of the nation.

The cartoons of Sudhir Tailang, in contrast, have a soft and languorous appeal. They too are mild in nature and score a point more on the strength of the inherent idea than drawing.

Cartoonist Ranga has inimitable style. He is one of the few cartoonists who understands the tricky and intricate rules of the political game. He too excels in touching the vulnerable spots with utmost felicity.

Abu Abraham stands apart for his sharp but never to be missed sense of humour. An inveterate caricaturist, he keeps line to the minimum. In his personality and travel sketches, he uses the enormous range of subjects for a "Psychological warfare" which results in his best cartoons distinguished by scathing indictment of political sham and hypocrisy.

The growing popularity of political cartoons in India is a measure of our times. As a visual projection of ideas, its appeal continues to be most direct and intimate. A cartoonist, therefore, is neither an apologist nor an analyst. He is an intellectual, a realist and a pragmatist armed with a sharp sense of humour and an eye for the bizarre.

According to Annibale Carracci, a cartoonist stands at par with the classical artist as both see the lasting truth behind the surface. "Both try to help nature accomplish its plan. The one may strive to visualise the perfect form and to realise it in his work, the other to grasp the perfect deformity, and thus reveal the very essence of (man's) personality." No wonder, a good cartoon, like the work of art, is more true to life than reality itself.

Keeping pace with the changing times, the Indian cartoonists too are using their talent to inform and educate the masses with honesty and diligence. As enlightened torch-bearers of society, they are the watch-dogs of public morality.

A cartoon by Zhang Lo Ping (China).

Part 11

Embroidery, Textiles and Batik

An applique of Ganesha (elephant headed Indian god) on a wall hanging, Gujarat, India.

Embroidery

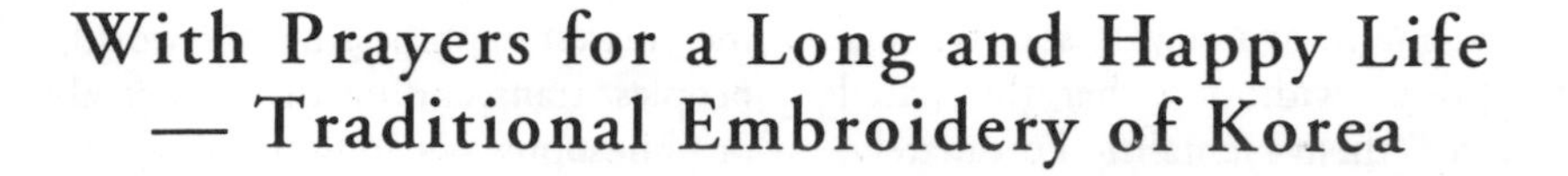

With Prayers for a Long and Happy Life — Traditional Embroidery of Korea

In prehistoric times, when early peoples were beginning to weave cloth with fibres and make clothing, they introduced embroidered decorations upon the surface of the cloth. It seems that the embroidery of that remote age was used as to symbolize either high social status or primitive faith; hence, the embroidered designs were simple.

Unearthed Korean relics dating from the Neolithic and Bronze Ages include a large number of various bone and stone needles, and stone and earthen spools used for winding thread. From these spinning and weaving tools it is certain that the early Koreans produced cloth for wearing, and applied embroidered decorations to their clothes. Embroidered articles have not yet been found among ancient relics, however, so it is impossible for us to evaluate the actual items. Most of the embroidered relics extant date back only to the eighteenth century; there may have been many causes for this, but we must first cite the attributes of the fibres themselves.

Whereas gilt, bronze, or stone handicraft items and even pottery can be preserved for long periods, embroidered articles are subject to rapid deterioration. As another cause, we may refer to cases in which embroidered works, however carefully they may have been preserved, were burned or plundered during frequent foreign invasions. This being the situation, we must rely on fragmentary old records of textiles and embroidery. Based primarily on such references, the historical development of Korean embroidery, may be attempted.

In *Nihon Shoki (Chronicles of Japan)*, a Japanese book of history and legend compiled in AD 720, it is recorded that a Paekche woman by the name of Chinmojin, who was skilled at needlework and embroidery, crossed the Sea of Japan at about AD 340 and taught Japanese women the arts of embroidery and other needlework. Next, the fact that one of the three artists who drew the ground sketches for *Ch'onsuguk Mandara Sujang* (a Buddhist drapery designated a Japanese national treasure and preserved at the temple *Chuguji* in Nara) was a Koguryo man named Kasoil is confirmed in the inscription on the back of the drapery. There are further instances of Korean embroiderers, painters, and other artists crossing to Japan and offering technical guidance to the Japanese in early times. The foregoing examples indicate that Korean culture had by then attained a considerably advanced state.

In *Samguk Sagi* (Historical Records of the Three Kingdoms), the oldest extant Korean book of history, it is recorded that Queen Chindok of Silla personally embroidered *T'aep'yongga* (Song of Peace) in 20 lines on a silk cloth, each line consisting of five characters, and made a gift of it to the T'ang emperor in AD 650; hence, we may infer that embroidery was treated as a valuable handicraft, fit to be presented as a diplomatic gift between nations.

At the Sokkuram cave temple, Pulkuka-sa Temple, Tabo-t'ap (Pagoda of Many Treasures), and Sokka-t'ap (Pagoda of the Buddha) shown in Kyongiu, Buddhism reached the zenith of its prosperity in Silla. It seems certain that various kinds of Buddhist embroidery flourished there.

According to *Kogum Ch'anggi* (a book recording the history of Pulkuk-sa Temple from the time of its foundation), it is recorded that a hall of worship was constructed within the precinct of Pulkuk-sa Temple in AD 886 as a memorial to the deceased king. In memory of the deceased king, the queen became a nun and embroidered his portrait in collaboration with Wonhae, a nun who was renowned as the best embroiderers. The embroidered royal portrait was enshrined on the wall of the hall of worship, with an entreaty that the king be admitted to paradise. In the following year, Wonhae embroidered a portrait of the Buddha and enshrined it on the wall of the same hall. A poem speaking highly of the skill of Wonhae remains today.

The art of embroidery was brought to full bloom in the ages that followed. Its development owned much not only to the affluence of the upper class in conjunction with economic development, but also to the traditional education of women-folk; that is to say, weaving and needlework were regarded as basic skills of household management — skills which all women were required to master from childhood, whether they were of high or low social standing. As a result, embroidery as a women's tradition was passed on without interruption until the early part of the twentieth century.

Embroidery purely for the sake of appreciation emerged in Koryo in the early part of the twelfth century, adding to the tradition of embroidering decorations on the surface of dresses and on cloth. This was called *sudo* (embroidered painting).

On a silk cloth framed with a green line, flowers with animals playing among them, bamboo, birds, and fruits were embroidered. It is said that a *sudo* was superior in terms of technique and shape to the *sumak* (embroidered curtain) hung in the yard at the time of a palace banquet.

In addition to the above decorations embroidered on various ceremonial tools, flags, dresses, pillows, and horse-equipment came into great vogue in aristocratic society. It is regrettable that only descriptions without either the actual articles or pictures depicting them remain. Fortunately, however, a single item, *Sagye P'un-gyongdo* (Potted Scenes in the Four Seasons), remains today, enabling us to get just one glimpse of this aspect of Koryo embroidery.

At any rate, embroidery increased in importance, forming a part of women's life irrespective of differences in their political and economic status. It may be assumed that the scope of embroidery expanded during the Koryo period, as attested to in old records such as *Koryo Togyong*. The tradition was inherited by the Yi dynasty, and from that period we still have many examples of a variety of Korean embroidery to compare. In particular, embroidered works made by commoners, as in the case of ordinary handicraft items, present harmony in simplicity, utilizing humour and delicate handiwork to express natural beauty, thereby finding an important place in Korea's traditional embroidery. Besides the embroidered articles made by commoners, those required by royalty and men of the upper class were produced by professionals employed in government offices whose works, in compliance with the taste of the palace, became standardized to display refined skills and dignity.

In comparison with the work of professionals, embroidered articles made by commoners are generally less refined and orderly in their materials, composition, colours, and technique, but many of them reflect the unaffected pure feelings of life and the sincerity of the common folk as they are. The kinds of embroidery practised by the commoners were multifarious, being applied as embroidered decorations to all things made of cloth ranging from screens to trivial daily necessities. Although it may be that there is no nation which does not possess embroidery, it can be said that Korea is exceptional in terms of the propagation of embroidery among the lower strata of society.

With what patterns did ancient women try to express Korean characteristics in their embroidery? We find that they repeatedly embroidered designs that in brief terms symbolized "happiness in this world". The most frequent motif is a pair of birds resting on a branch of a flowering tree. Emerging frequently in this motif are the phoenix (imaginary auspicious birds) as well as peacocks, pheasants, and duck (all auspicious birds), and plum, chrysanthemum, peony, and paulownia flowers. These flowers and birds symbolize harmonious and blessed conjugal love. Since most of the screens extant today show pictures of flowers and birds, it is apparent that people regarded a happy married life as the most blessed life in the world.

After flowers and birds, ten other creatures and natural objects regarded as symbols of eternal youth and longevity appear as subjects for embroidery. These are the sun, clouds, mountains, water, cranes, deer, tortoises, pine trees, bamboo trees, and the herb of eternal youth (an imaginary plant). Some or all of them may emerge in a given work. The Korean people longed for many children and life without worries as the greatest happiness in this world, a longing common to all peoples, transcending the higher abstraction level of religion or philosophy. Various embroidered patterns symbolizing this attachment to happiness were applied to dresses, screens, *norigae* (decorative knots), handbags, chopstick pouches, brush pouches, and a great number of other items. We find that embroidered decorations were applied even to shoes which were easily worn out. Ho Nansolhyon, Korea's representative poetess of the sixteenth century (1562-1590), left a poem, written in Chinese characters, entitled "Swinging." Mentioned therein is a pair of shoes made of leather and wrapped in an embroidered silk cloth.

After swinging
She alights with her neat embroidered pair of shoes
And stands in the yard without words.
Her thin blouse is wet with sweat;
She, feeling chilly,
Forgetting to ask someone to pick up her fallen hairpin.

As to the materials used in Korea's old embroidery, thick silk or patterned silk was used most often as the base material. In a few exceptions, woollen fabrics were used. Taut coiled threads were used for the embroidery work, and the technique of embroidering closely was employed.

Compared with the technique of using thinly coiled threads or that of weaving rush-mats with thick and loose threads, the art of embroidery requires much more manual work, and therefore more time. As a result, embroidered articles are more delicate on the surface, and more durable.

Natural dye-stuffs, such as those extracted from mineral and vegetable stuffs obtainable in Korea, were used. Their ingredients were of a high quality, resulting in the attainment of considerable beauty in colour.

We might as a final consideration compare Korean embroidery with that of China and Japan. Chinese embroidery is delicate and shows precision in technique. Its expressions are magnificent but very formal and orderly, while Japanese embroidery, as a result of a strong emphasis on colour, is brilliant and light but extremely stylized in handicraftsmanship.

Compared with the embroidery of these two countries, that of Korea, though less precise and orderly, achieves reasonable unity as various elements are harmoniously combined. The art of embroidery, of course, as all other arts, well reflects the climatic and cultural characteristics of its progenitors. The nation's embroidery relics are at present preserved in the

National Museum of Korea in Seoul, in university museums, and by individual collectors. In terms of quantity and quality, the Museum of Korean Embroidery is the most significant repository. For the first time in Korea, a special exhibition of traditional Korean embroidery was held at the National Museum of Korea in Seoul in 1978, and the catalogue of that exhibition was later published, with an introduction, as a book. It is presently being published in Japanese.

What is the present situation of education in embroidery? They teach embroidery at Ewha Women's University, and its graduates have formed the Noksu-hoe society, which, meeting once every year, is the only organization of its kind.

Evoking Virtue, Gaiety and Warmth — Embroidery in the Philippines

Popularky known as an ornamental needlework applied to fabrics, embroidery has been a woman's art for centuries. As a folk art, embroidery, done by hand, is a creative, relaxing pastime, usually engaged in by rural folk. This needlecraft entails skill and patience, and displays the utility of beauty. It evokes associations of feminine touch and virtue, keeps in step with styles and fashion, conveys personal gaiety and warmth, and supplements family income.

Historical and cultural background

In existence for innumerable ages, embroidery in its various manifestations represents the collective efforts of many generations. The art of embroidery with the needle, mentioned in the Vedas of India and in the Book of Exodus in the Bible, existed in the days of Abraham, and has evolved with cultures the world over.

Historical accounts of the Philippines dated as early as the tenth century (AD 982) are found in Chinese annals, although records covering the Philippines' pre-Spanish period are few and sketchy. The early Chinese influence in the Philippines was apparently more economic than cultural or social. Since intricate gold- and silver-thread embroidery is known to have been produced and increasingly stylized in China for centuries, it is probable that these embroidery products had been casually traded in the Philippines and the craft as such was imitated by the people.

Detailed accounts of Philippine history date from the sixteenth century, during the period of Spanish rule. Christianity was the greatest contribution of Spain to the islands, and churches, monasteries and convents were adorned with finely and beautifully embroidered altarpieces and vestments. Interest in embroidery for both religious and non-ecclesiastical use was stimulated, as embroidery ateliers (studios) were founded and gained popularity. Costumes of nobles and other elite personages were elaborately stitched with floral patterns, and this elegant apparel clearly distinguished them from the rest of society. Thereafter flourished the art of needlework.

The American domination in the early twentieth century introduced to the Philippines the democratic way of life. Home economics education including embroidery came to form part of the school curriculum. The introduction of the electric sewing machine for use in embroidery work has rendered somewhat obsolete the old-fashioned skills of needlecraft, yet school children and adults still learn hand needlework as well as machine needlework. Hand-embroidered products are, however, far less varied and decorative than those produced by finely-engineered sewing machines, and machine-created "readymades" are increasingly available nowadays.

Embroidery materials and tools

Like other artists, embroiderers consider several factors pertaining to personal satisfaction, and convenience when working with embroidery. These include: good fabric and needles, appropriate and sufficient thread of various colour groups, well-fit thimbles, sharp and suitable scissors, a well-arranged embroidery kit or box, and sturdy frames or rings to hold the fabric.

Selection of fabric depends upon the use for which the embroidered product is intended, the embroidery technique to be applied, and the kind of thread to be used. Fabrics made from natural fibres of plants like pineapple, or *pina*, and *abaca* (manilla hemp) were commonly used before the introduction of synthetic textiles on the market. *Pina* cloth is till preferred for the more delicate and substantial stitching of costumes and dresses for special occasions.

Cotton fabrics, sturdy enough to withstand frequent use and washing, as well as being comparatively inexpensive, are preferred for embroidered linens, curtains, and furnishings for casual use. Silk fabrics have the distinct features of being soft, glossy, and of fine texture, which make them ideal for dresses, and blouses, and for draperies and furnishings in luxuriously furnished rooms. Thanks to rapid developments in the manufacture of fabrics, a wonderful variety of synthetic textiles are being manufactured these days, providing a wide array of fabrics for embroiderers and end product users to choose from. These modern fabrics are readily available and reasonably priced; hence, they are used extensively for embroidery.

A lavish decorative scheme distinguishes embroidered products from other types of handicrafts. Embroidery designs themselves are usually dainty and imaginative, making optimum use of simple, natural shapes to enhance intricate patterns of stitchery. Designs of flowers (e.g. roses), vines, *nipa* huts, fighting cocks, and a folk dance using bamboo called *tinikling* are popular motifs in embroidery. These designs drawn from nature are modified, producing unique geometric shapes. Conventional designs influenced by modern art are also evident in the arrangement of flowers, leaves, stems and vines in a variety of shapes and patterns. The combination of various designs, where elaborate stitching schemes are coordinated in all-over decorative patterns, is characteristic in the embroidery of costumes and dresses designed for special occasions. To make them richly decorative, substances such as gold and silver thread, precious stones, beads, sequins, pearls, feathers, and roses fashioned from satin are sometimes used.

Embroidery stitches and designs

A great variety of embroidery stitches are sued to produce the desired effect, and embroiderers can even choose from among several techniques using the same stitch, depending upon the type of embroidery being done. When laying stitches side-by-side, thereby forming intricate borders, the embroiderer must consider colour harmony, proportionate effect, and thread weight in order to convey to the recipient the intended impression of the embroidery.

Different kinds of stitches are employed in satin embroidery, and *calado* exemplifies this type of Philippine embroidery. In *calado* additional threads are drawn over the stitched portions of the design, after which the warp and woof threads are drawn alternately to complete the *calado.*

"Philippine ladder" is another of the characteristics of Philippine embroidery. Hem-stitching is employed: however, no threads are drawn. Elaborate cut-out motifs which utilize needle point are also judiciously employed in our embroidery. The distinctly Filipino *barong Tagalog*, an elegant, richly embroidered shirt for men, is of a very rare workmanship. Be it authentically patterned, or redesigned to conform to contemporary taste, this lavishly embroidered dress shirt draws its appeal from implementation of the rich heritage of embroidery techniques in use during the Spanish era.

Embroidery products

Changes in education and other elements of culture have stimulated both originality and the revival of yesterday's fashions. This is evinced by the designing, redesigning, and duplication of embroidery products to give fresh appeal suitable to contemporary tastes.

Embroidery producers have sought continuously to produce and improve a wide variety of products, and originality in design and use of techniques reveals the indigenousness of the varicoloured embroidery products of the Philippines. Whereas the stitching of decorative designs formerly done exclusively on textiles, now leather and other native materials like bamboo, *buri* (coconut bough midrib), and rattan are often utilized. Locally available materials like *abaca* fibre and straw are used as threads.

Varied are the embroidery articles produced in the Philippines, among which the following are popular:

1. dress articles for men like Filipino barong Tagalog, dresses and skirts for ladies, and baby and doll dresses;
2. household items like bedsheets, pillowcases, table covers, curtains, living room set covers, cushions, place mats, doilies, wall decor, lamp shades, letter holders, waste baskets, and rugs;
3. personal effects like lingerie, handkerchiefs, shawls, slippers, step-ins for ladies, bags (handbags, evening bags, travelling bags, clutch bags, school bags), fans, and beach hats.

Embroidery — An economic activity

Embroidery exists in the Philippines as a small scale economic activity carried on mainly in the home. It is engaged in by many women throughout the Philippines, but the best quality of embroidered dress articles and linens come from Southern Luzon — notably the provinces of Batangas, Laguna, Rizal, Bulacan and Quezon — and from the Visayan Islands area, particularly in the provinces of Antique and Iloilo on the Island of Panay.

Children nowadays learn basic skills of sewing and embroidery in the intermediate grades, stitchery of different kinds being part of the Home Economics curriculum in the elementary and high schools. Most Philippine embroiderers, then, first learn this craft at school.

Occupational prospects in the embroidery industry

Embroidery products are attractive and useful, and the market is expanding, both here and abroad. Embroidery articles made in the Philippines and exported to other countries command a high price, and demand for these items is stimulated by national and international trade fairs displaying various Philippine crafts. Producers and exporters in the embroidery industry, however, like their counterparts in other cottage handicraft industries, are facing challenging problems. Some major problems are: difficulties in access to financing, increasing costs of labour and production, rising operational expenses (especially in shipping), lack of research development (particularly concerning design requirements of buying countries), conflicting market strategies, and the inroads resorted to by competitors.

Transforming embroidery, a simple art of the home, into an industry that will boost family income and contribute to the national economy is no simple task. Hence, embroidery is one of the cottage industries presently being encouraged and supported by the national government in the Philippines.

"Wind the Warp with Gold Thread": Malay Gold-Thread Embroidery

Guessing a hidden object concealed in out-stretched clenched fists is a game played throughout the world. For the children of Kuala Kangsar, however, there is an added dimension to this simple game that gives a fifty-fifty chance to players guessing whether a coin is hidden in the right or left hand. Here, the players accompany the game by chanting a rhyme made up entirely of words and jargon that allude to the intricacies and splendour of one of the most well-known forms of handicrafts in Malaysia — gold-thread embroidery.

The players sing in unison:

Form a circle with thumbs and forefingers;
Follow the diagonals, and return to straights;
A king hither;
A king thither;
Amorphous form;
Wind the warp with gold thread;
Wind the warp with gold thread;
Wind the warp with gold thread;

Nestled amidst an undulating landscape and lush rice-fields irrigated by one of the most legendary rivers in the country is the royal town of Kuala Kangsar. This historic town is not only famous for its grand palace and mosque, but is also known as the only remaining sizeable home of Malay gold-thread embroidery.

Like a number of the traditional arts in Malaysia, it is often said that embroidery, particularly in regard to its design and functions, is a derivative of the Indian and Chinese traditions, with strong adherence to Islamic and indigenous principles and beliefs by its later practitioners. The workers, who spend long hours crouching over wooden-frame stretchers, dexterously inter-twining golden threads over stencilled designs, are women, particularly young maidens, whose fame as skilled embroiderers was once justifiably considered as an asset to their marriageability. Gold-thread embroidery required very little equipment. Basic to all requirements is a silk or velvet ground, preferably dark royal blue or crimson in colour, and gold-braided thread. The tools consist of needles, wooden-frame stretchers, sharp penknives or razor blades, and paste made from tapioca starch. Three cards of ordinary Manila paper are pasted together into one sheet, which is then dried under a hazy sun and pressed, usually under a mattress. From this dried and flattened threeplied card, design motifs called pitch, or *hempelor* in Malay, are cut out. The complete cut-outs, resembling intricate paper doilies, are then placed on stretched grounds and, by using needles, gold-threads are stitched around the pith, resulting in embossed gold designs on rich velvet or silk grounds. The finished products are eventually detached from their stretchers, and are either sold as pieces to be used by the buyer for ornaments, or made into various objects which are sought after for weddings or other important social functions.

Of all the social functions in Malay society, the wedding is undoubtedly the one in which gold-thread embroidery plays the most important role. A bridal chamber, often silky and diaphanous, is considered incomplete without the end-panels of pillows and bolsters, drapes, curtain hooks, hand fans, and bridal mats embroidered in gold on crimson grounds. It is not uncommon for the more well-to-do families to commission bedroom slippers, pillowcases, and bedcovers to be similarly embroidered. In such a case, due to expense and sheer discomfort, the bride would discreetly be advised by an elder to remove the ornamental coverings before bedtime. At a betrothal or engagement ceremony, groups of five or seven gifts (it is customary that gifts be in odd-numbered sets) are presented on silver or brass trays, covered with embroidered square silk or velvet cloth. When taking the marriage vow, the bridegroom, conventionally dressed in white, sits on three, five or seven layers of embroidered mats, while the bride sits on a similar configuration in the privacy of her own room, nervously awaiting the ceremonial handshake with her future husband and his offer of the wedding ring, which culminates the vow.

Like many traditional handicrafts with limited ceremonial use, the Malay gold-thread embroidery at one time faced a bleak future. Since most embroidered materials last for a long time and are invariably kept by their owners as heirlooms to be lent to relatives and friends, markets became scarce. Over the years however, new users for this ancient embroidery have emerged. Some institutions, including palaces, universities, and colleges, have adopted gold-thread embroidery for robes and braids for ceremonial dress.

With the introduction of new materials and technology, and the trend of rising costs and other constraints which universally threaten the future of such traditions as gold-thread embroidery, it is difficult to ascertain just how long the children of Kuala Kangsar will continue to chant their rhymes while their mothers and sisters crouch over their embroidery work. Perhaps the shrinking of a traditional hand fan to less than half its original size, which used to easily cover the face of a bride or bridegroom during a wedding ceremony, is ominous, although in this case the reason for the reduction is not entirely economic. Since prospective spouses nowadays are already well-known to each other's parents and relatives before marriage, it is no longer necessary to reveal them publicly for the first time during their wedding ceremony. In such a case a token fan, more ceremonial than functional, suffices. On the part of the wedding couple, wearing heavily-tinted glasses (!) would perhaps lessen the ordeal, concealing nervousness or discomfort during the long and often tedious ceremony, a role once also assigned to such fans.

Stone and Mirrors: Embroidery in Pakistan

Embroidery, one of the ancient traditional handicrafts, is extremely popular in Pakistan. Throughout the country a great diversity of embroidery styles and motifs can be seen on various items of daily use, from headgear right down to footwear (most notably on shirts and *saris*), from pillow covers to sofa cushions, and from bedcovers to curtains.

Embroidery work in Pakistan is not restricted to any particular area. The tradition is so pervasive that every region strives to produce better quality work than the others, although some regions are famous for a particular type of embroidery work. Before explaining various regional styles of embroidery, let me mention two unique sites in Pakistan — the Chowkundi tombs and the Makli necropolis — which are known throughout the world for their "embroidery in stone".

At Chowkundi, one of the most beautiful historical sites in Pakistan, there are about forty sites of tombs built of angular stone slabs placed one upon another spread over an area of several hundred square miles. There are myriad floral patterns and geometrical designs to be found on the huge slabs of stone, carved with such supreme craftsmanship and with as much precision as if embroidered on silk. Fine examples of coordinated line and form, these tombs display an intricate network of various patterns incorporating triangles, rectangles, squares, and circles to form well-balanced and charming symmetrical designs. Patterns resembling lotuses and sunflowers profusely adorn these Chowkundi tombs, and some also have verses from the Holy Quran inscribed on them.

Makli Hills, the largest necropolis on earth, is the site of thousands of graves, many of which are enclosed in magnificent tombs, their domes supported on rows of stone pillars. Abundant intricately engraved designs and "embroidered" floral patterns grace these pillars, and a few of them are further embellished with glistening azure-glazed tiles.

Two provinces of Pakistan — Baluchistan and Sind — are famous for a wide range of distinctly decorative style of embroidery. The Thano Bula Khan area in Western Sind is renowned for lavishly embroidered wedding shirts, fully covered with intricate thick silk embroidery and mirrorwork. In addition to these wedding shirts, this area is also famous for shawls (*chadara*). Many extraordinary pieces of embroidery come from Thano Bula Khan, including children's dresses which are ornately embroidered on bright satins, some with their traditional circular motifs, which also frequently decorate the *abocchnais* (women's *chadars*). Lasbela, a nearby region of Baluchistan, has its own decorative embroidery style closely resembling that of Thano Bula Khan, although the colours are more muted.

The greatest variety of Sindhi decorative styles and techniques are employed in embroidering the *abocchnais* (shawls) usually worn for public occasions. Such shawls are also presented to the bride as part of her trousseau. These and other Sindhi embroideries are traditionally stitched on ground cloth of either white or red.

Scarves and shirt-front pieces are also popular embroidery products of this area. The difference between the decorative styles of Baluchistan and Sind can be recognized by making a comparative study. Although embroidered shirt-fronts are traditions in both regions, the Baluchi *Pushk kurta* is distinguished by matching embroidered cuffs, and by a pouch called *pudo* centred on the lower half of its front. The most intricately embroidered *pushks* are produced in Makran and other coastal areas of Baluchistan.

The embroidered shirt-fronts from the bordering areas of both provinces contain similar large geometric patterns of blue, yellow, white and red which cover the entire ground cloth. However, the stitches used are different, and the Sindhi examples from Dadu and Jacobabad are thereby distinguished from the Baluchi embroideries of Marri.

The embroidery on shawls and shirts-fronts of other areas is different from that of the two areas described above. Embroidery work on curtains, bedcovers, pillow covers and cushions is now rather hybridized, so it is difficult to discern to which area a particular design belongs.

Many embroidery stitches, although common to both provinces, have been uniquely adapted to their respective decorative schemes. *Hurmutch* work, most notably produced in the Makran and Hyderabad districts, has four overlapping layers of stitchery. Into the first two layers, similar to the interlaced herringbone stitch, are interwoven two layers of darning stitchery. Today most *hurmutches* are embroidered with cotton and synthetic threads, although silk was traditionally used. China-stitch embroidery, known as *Kutch,* is frequently made with a needle resembling a crochet hook. It was a common technique in the

Subcontinent. Armenia and near the Caspian Sea in Iran. This suggests that the Baluchis may have introduced it to Sind and Baluchistan.

Kutch, produced almost exclusively in the two provinces of Sind and Baluchistan, is among the many forms of stitchery incorporating mirrors into designs. Originally, small, round pieces of mica were sewed onto the cloth with button-hole stitches. Contemporary embroiderers have substituted for the mica mirrors which also range in size from 1/4 to 1/2 inches, but Sindhis sometimes use larger sizes as well.

There are numerous local styles of mirrorwork. For example, mirrorwork embroiderers from the Khairpur, Shikarpur and Mirpur Khas areas in Sind use thick layers of button-hole stitchery to accentuate the stalks and leaves of floral patterns. Umarkot, Sanghar, Hyderabad and Kashmir are some of the noted mirrorwork production centres in Sind.

Countering the Anonymity of Daily Routine — Embroidery in Iran

Embroidery is one of the oldest applied arts in Iran, and its intimate and personal quality has a wide appeal. It is especially valued as a traditional skill handed down from generation to generation, from mother to daughter. It is also a means of self expression; a love for individuality countering the anonymity that comes from daily routine. Essentially, it fulfils a spiritual need for beauty and adornment in the East; for prestige is acquired through personal adornment that functions also as a status symbol and as a source of pleasure for the eye.

Embroidery is regarded as one of the oldest techniques for embellishing garments known to man. As textile is fragile, few specimens of material evidence survive; however, the costumes of the nobles and guards on the stone bas-reliefs of the ruins of Persepolis in southern Iran suggest embroidery, and Alexander the Great is reported to have been 'amazed at the splendour of the embroideries he found there. To show his countrymen... he sent home the embroidered tent of Darius". Some samples from the Achaemenian period (550-330 BC) have been recovered from the frozen barrows of Pazyryk in Siberia. A saddle cloth from barrow No. 5 has a delicate floral spray, with flowers and birds on coarsely-woven tussah silk clearly worked in chain stitch with coloured silk threads.

The Roman historian Florus has recorded how in 53 BC, in the final episode of the battle of Carrhae, the exhausted troops of the Roman general Licinus Crassus gave up when the troops of the Parthian king Orodes "unfurled their brilliantly-coloured, gold-embroidered banners in the afternoon sun".

Chinese dynastic histories record that the first Chinese embassy was sent to An-shi, Arascid Parthia, in 105 BC, at which time silks and embroideries must have been included in the exchange of gifts. Excavations in 1965 at Tunhuang in the Kansu province of China unearthed a panel of silk embroidery, datable AD 487, similar to wall paintings uncovered by Stein, le Coq, and other archaeologists in the depiction of five figures in garments "quite un-Chinese... [showing] Sassanian influence."

In the centuries that followed, neighbouring "Byzantine embroideries copied the ornate designs of Persia in rich colours, often enhanced with gold and silver threads and pearls... (and) for many centuries they were considered superior."

The first sample of actual embroidery that has come down to us belongs to the Seljuq period (AD 1037-1157), and a strong Chinese influence can be detected in its design, as well as in technique employed. With the Mongol invasion of Iran (thirteenth century) and the establishment of the Timurid dynasty (fourteenth century), the Chinese influence became even stronger. The miniatures of that period give a good picture of contemporary embroideries. Marco Polo visited Kerman in the thirteenth century and wrote of the excellence of the gold embroideries produced by the women there. During the twelfth century, the so-called "Persian-style embroidery" spread to Sicily together with silk brocade weaving.

Chardin, in his thorough work on Safavid Iran (sixteenth and seventeenth centuries), admires the fineness of the Persian embroidery which "exceeds" Europe's as well as that of the Turks that "we so much admire."

Utilitarian purposes

Embroideries were primarily produced to satisfy the demands of the large households in the cities and in rural and tribal areas, and we can divide this handicraft into two categories: 1) embroideries done to fulfil the demands of the court, the nobles and the richer merchants; and 2) embroideries done to satisfy the needs of rural and tribal peoples.

Sometimes embroideries were produced to be used as presents, whether on a personal or state level, such as presentations to or by various visiting dignitaries.

The embroidery embellished clothing and headdress (in particular, the skull caps for men) especially made for festive occasions and weddings. The young girls sat at their mother's knee preparing their bridal dowry that was to serve them for a lifetime; the more elaborate pieces worn for special events such as the birth of sons and the ensuing circumcision ceremonies and other celebrations.

Needlework, furthermore, also graced a multitude of household goods, such as quilted bedcovers, door hangings, tablecloths, prayer rugs, cushions, cradles, etc., in addition to tents and rich trappings for horse and camels. A myriad of small objects were also decorated with needlework: covers for pen boxes, scissors, combs, *kohl* containers, purses, and so forth.

Influence from floor coverings

The development of embroidery in Iran has been directly influenced and inspired by floor coverings, the most primeval of household goods for a people that initially led a highly mobile life-style and dwelt in tents. Their first concern was a habitable shelter and some sort of floor covering to sleep on. Embroidery, like most other forms of art in Iran, is highly decorative. It is closely allied to the weaving of carpets or *gelims*, the forte of Persian art. Floor coverings were made by the women and girls of the household, primarily for use in the home. The families were large, and the handicrafts were done in a congenial atmosphere, the womenfolk seated on the floor. The composition, designs, and colours of the carpet or *gelim* were thus very familiar to the craftswoman, and were adapted to suit the motifs of textile weaving as well as embroidery. Even today this relationship exists.

The carpet is a miniature of nature at its best in an otherwise parched, arid, and sun-drenched landscape, with vast expanses of open space punctuated by rugged, lofty mountains, in which man is overpowered by nature. The Persian garden, *pardis* (from which the English word "paradise" is derived), is a most important symbol used in the Iranian arts. The garden on the rim of desert, such as the Bagh-e Golshan in Tabas (in the northeastern province of Khorassan) is indeed akin to paradise!

Motifs and designs

The designs used abound in elements from real life. Motifs of the embroideries are inspired predominantly by an infinite variety of flowers, *trees* (especially the cypress), plant forms (in particular the *boteh*), birds, animals (wild sheep horns in tribal areas), and fish. Frequently these designs are stylized and transformed into abstract patterns. Compartmentalized geometric forms also abound and, it is sometimes difficult to identify the original inspiration. Many of these designs are steeped in folklore and derive from ancient historical sources. In rural and tribal areas, in particular, needlework motifs are derived from mythical ideas of ancient cosmogony and are used symbolically. With the passage of time, however, they have gradually come to fulfil mainly a decorative purpose.

An important feature in the composition of these embroideries is the perfect harmony and sense of balance and symmetry that should emanate from them. There is a flow of motion, but it is bounded by an organized pattern. The repetitive quality of the motifs results in visual rhythms that give the embroidered articles a highly decorative character. The craftswoman has to work within the strict confines of tradition, and cannot give free rein to her creative imagination; she can only innovate. Patterns of embroidery on the whole usually consist of a central medallion with a special design on the four corners. The embroidery is always framed with bands of design, and the background is spattered with floral elements, the aforementioned *boteh* being a very popular motif.

Calligraphy is also used as a decorative element, mainly consisting of Koranic verses; or in some cases, a few lines of poetry.

Urban embroideries

Needlework for the court, nobles, and richer merchants, was done mainly in the cities, and supply and demand depended heavily on the so-called patrons of art who encouraged the use of sumptuous textiles and embroideries for their garments, household goods, and the articles destined for presentation and trade.

In the southern provinces, Isfahan is a very important centre of urban crafts, as is also Shiraz. These cities are both well-known for their opulent covers, hangings, cushions, etc., and needle-work used to adorn garments.

To cite a few examples, a variety of gilt embroideries were produced up until the early part of the twentieth century, such as *dahyek-douzi*, embroidered on velvet with gold or silver thread, and laid and couched with small couching stitches forming various designs. This needlework was executed on richly ornamented gift covers and on hammock-style cradles. Usually these pieces were backed with a coarse cotton fabric waxed to produce stiffness. Another variety, *naqdeh-douzi*, was embroidered with flat metallic strip gilt thread in floral designs on velvet, taffeta, and net to embellish the short-pleated skirts worn by women over their trousers in coordination with the *chadores* (long head-veils).

Other varieties of embroidery done until quite recently include the popular *golab-douzi*, or chain stitch done with a hook. It is embroidered in bright colours on a variety of fabrics (cotton, muslin, linen, and silk) with freely executed designs on a host of objects. *Sokmeh-douzi*, or drawn work, involves drawing out certain waft and/or warp threads within a given area. Designs follow a defined pattern, and the open spaces are filled in with embroidery stitches, thus creating a lacy effect. This is then combined with fine chain stitching. *Khameh-douzi*, another example, is a whitework embroidery consisting of a satin stitch in geometric patterns covering the entire ground. There is, less frequently found, a continuation of the traditional *poulak-douzi* done with gilt sequins on a variety of hangings, effectively setting off arabesques and designs of a central motif, such as a cypress tree sometimes surmounted by the stylized form of a woman's face depicting the sun (*Khorshid Khanom*) and a host of birds, fish, animals, flowers; or the paraphernalia necessary for a successful wedding, framing the bride and groom. Yazd and Kerman, in the central and southern provinces, respectively, were reputed for their very fine handloom textiles (silks, *chine* silk taffetas or *ikat*, cotton, velvets, wool shawls, etc.) on which embroidery was done with silk and gilt metal thread. Yazd is also renowned for the excellent needlework done by the Zoroastrian women on their traditional bridal costumes — a continuation of the Zoroastrian Sassanian tradition. Panels of needlework are linked by finely couched cord, and motifs include stylized trees (the cypress), animals, birds (especially the cock), flowers, and geometric designs in stem stitch, overcast stitch, and the cross and interlacing stitches, so fine that a magnifying glass is required to see them.

Kerman is especially celebrated for its brocaded woollen shawls called *termeh*, and its embroideries done on handwoven woollen fabrics with wool threads. This type of embroidery is known as *selselen-douzi* or *pateh-douzi*.

In the southern coastal province, Bandar Abbas, bordering on the Persian Gulf, has its own distinctive type of embroidery.

Gilt metal needlework, *golab-douzi* is a combination of a delicate tracery of chain stitch interspersed with embroideries done in silk, with fine handwoven edgings and spattering of sequins. The garments of the local women are characteristically embellished in this fashion.

Rasht, the capital of the province of Gilan on the lush and verdant shores of the Caspian Sea in the north, is famous for its superb and very colourful wall hangings embroidered with the chain stitch *golab-douzi* and worked with a hook. The use of applique (in particular) and patchwork are a distinctive feature of this type of embroidery. It is, moreover, characterized by its use of flannel wool (*mahout*) as the foundation material, woven so as to appear like a fine grade of felt. Rasht supplied this type of embroidery to the Safavid court in Ardebil in the sixteenth and seventeenth centuries, and this tradition continued well into the twentieth century; it was, moreover, executed by men. In the northwestern province of Azarbaijan, a type of beadwork, *monjouq-douzi*, was very popular, probably derived from Achaemenian and Sassanian periods when pearls and gems ornamented carpets, tents, and garments. A variety of small objects were covered with beads (sometimes a few real gold beads) worked into very fine and colourful designs.

Tribal and rural embroideries

There was needlework done for the rural and tribal regions to satisfy the personal needs of the large families there. It is in this second category that a more traditional cottage industry was preserved, and the work, while being just as fine as that in the urban handicrafts, has an additional touch of creativity and evinces a sense of liberation from strict conventions in its treatment of form, colour, and design.

In the western province of Kurdestan, the Kurds are a partially settled, partially nomadic people of Iranian stock whose population spills over into Iraq and Turkey. Their distinctive type of embroidery, done on wall hangings, as well as on covers, horse blankets, and various articles of clothing such as skull caps and puttees (leggings), emulates miniature carpet designs. Sangsar is a village nestled in the lush green hills north of Semnan, in north central Iran. The Sangsaris are a pastoral people travelling widely to seek pastures for their flocks. They produce fine *gelims* and woollen covers, and the embroidered headscarf of their women, made until quite recently, is of particular interest. The embroidery is done on a plum-coloured hand-woven raw silk. The motifs, with stylized flowers and leaves in panels interrupted by bands of geometric designs, reflect the influence of *gelims*.

The embroidery done by the Turkoman tribes in the north and northeastern provinces of Mazandaran and Khorassan is particularly striking and fine. The Turkomans straddle the frontiers of Iran, Soviet Turkmenistan, and Afghanistan, and history tells us that they came in waves from Central Asia. Their handicrafts consist mainly of rugs, saddle bags, *gelims*, felts, and tent bands. The Turkomans, feeding the silkworm on the mulberry trees, are well-known for silk textiles and embroideries used primarily to ornament their magnificent tribal costumes and the fine covers for their camels, made exclusively for their personal use and to add to the bridal dowry.

The embroidery is extremely rich and intricate, and adorns trouser cuffs and neck openings, side slits, hems, and the cuffs of robe sleeves. The women of the Tekke tribe, in particular, are famous for their needlework, since their costume, using an additional robe with false sleeves, and worn with the left armhole draped over the headdress, is still the most elaborate found among the Turkoman tribes. Repeated geometric patterns and motifs suggesting flowers and leaves, as well as the horns of the wild sheep, a familiar sight in the Turkoman environment, are among the traditionally abstract embroidery motifs used that seem to be attempts at pictorial treatment. The embroideries are done in red, plum, black, yellow and/or white on a red or plum-coloured raw silk handwoven fabric. Embroidery in the southeastern provinces of Seistan and Baluchistan is very rich and copious, especially that found in the latter province. It is used mainly to adorn the trouser cuffs, sleeve cuffs, and bodices of the local women's and girls' clothing, and covers the entire background of the base fabric. The colours used are lustrous; predominantly orange, red, and plum, with touches of other colours. Some mirrorwork is also incorporated, held down by a buttonhole stitch.

In Seistan the embroidery looks quite different. It is mostly done with white mercerized cotton thread on white cotton fabric, the edges of the embroidery finished off in black. The entire background is filled with a variety of geometric patterns, each one having a specific name.

This bird's-eye view of the embroidery of Iran illustrates that all neighbouring countries, this case those of the Middle East as well as Central Asia, display affinities to each other while retaining unique characteristics. This is largely accountable to such historical events as invasions sweeping established frontiers aside and pushing peoples into new geographical areas, the establishment of commercial ties, and other currents in the ebb and flow of influences from neighbouring countries, causing a cross-fertilization that enriches any culture.

Stitching Colour and Variety into Life — Embroidery in Indian Villages

In India, each region and community is distinguished by its unique textiles and traditional costumes. The many regional contributions emerging throughout the long history of this industry have given rise to endless varieties of weaving, printing and embroidery styles. A characteristic of most art forms in India is the simultaneous development of arts and crafts by the rural, tribal and urban communities.

Embroidery is an ancient art, one that finds a home in most parts of India, where embroidery itself varies from the rural patchwork designs using pieces of old cloth to the embellishments of royal robes with gold thread and pearls. Such social variations of this art form have co-existed and, in turn, inspired the development of one another in different areas.

Forms drawn from the natural environment (e.g. trees, flowers and animals) abound on the surfaces of Indian fabrics. Each region has its own motifs and style of representation, and motifs found in embroidery are also found in the prints and weaves of that region.

Textiles in India are found in countless varieties of cotton, silk and wool. Embroidery can be found in different regions on all these base or ground materials, and on other materials such as leather and wickerwork. The basic categories of embroidery techniques found are: a) threadwork or stitching techniques using cotton, silk and wool; b) applique or patchwork in which small pieces of cloth are stitched onto the ground material to form designs (gold and silver thread, sequins and/or mirrors are also often attached to the cloth); and c) quilting techniques incorporating use of stitches and applique. Often these embroidery techniques are combined together, as in the case of applique coordinated with threadwork.

Threadwork embroidery

In India, as in many parts of the world, threadwork embroidery is widely practised. The beauty of this form of embroidery seems to lie in the textural quality created by the tiny stitches superimposed on the flat surface of the ground cloth. The colours and combinations of them in relation to the ground cloth further add to the charm of this form of textile decoration.

Stitches found worldwide, such as cross, chain, herringbone, satin, and blanket stitch, are used in India, though in different regions they are given different names, and are used to form a variety of traditional designs and symbols. The stitching technique used dictates, as it were, the form of the design. In the case of the cross stitch, the motifs tend to be as delicate as the crystalline formation of a snowflake, whereas the satin stitch forms full, smooth intense areas of colour that completely hide the background cloth.

In the northernmost state of Kashmir, embroidery is found on clothes and shawls. The woollen carpet called *namdas* features crewel embroidery using the chain stitch, as floral designs and creepers are formed by parallel rows of chain stitch. The designs are embroidered on pale-coloured backgrounds in rich blues, greens and other colours.

The desert area of western India is the home of numerous communities that use embroidery to enrich the design of their clothes. Garments for adults and children, for male and female, are decorated with brightly coloured threadwork embroidery. Household items such as the cloth hammock serving as the baby's bed, pouches, and coverings are richly embroidered with a variety of stitching techniques. Cows, camels, and horses belonging to the communities of desert and rural areas of Rajasthan are draped with tapestries embroidered with bold designs of coloured thread and mirrors. Embroidery on leather shoes and saddles is also done with threadwork.

The stitches used in Rajasthan range from chain, herringbone, satin to blanket stitch and are used to create motifs and borders of flowers, animals (often peacocks), and scenes of everyday life.

Adjacent to the south, and on the western border of India, is the state of Gujarat, where the communities of the Saurashtra and Kutch have developed a unique form of embellished textiles. Here, the interiors of the houses are decorated with embroidered items.

The entrance to the house is adorned with *toran*, a cloth strip (often coloured) embroidered with coloured threads. The *toran*, hung across the upper frame of the door, is a "welcome" sign to both guests and householders, and for festivals and occasions more elaborate *torans* consist of border designs and motifs of flowers and animals in a variety of colours using different stitches. Inside the house, large square embroidered pieces called *chaklas* are hung on the walls. These coloured cloths are similarly embroidered with coloured threads and mirror work.

The Kathis are a nomadic community of Gujarat whose embroidery tradition is famous throughout India. Embroidered cloth serves as everyday clothing for women and children, and ritual and ceremonial items are also specially prepared. The Rabari community, engaged in animal husbandry, has a distinctive embroidery tradition. Every girl begins to embroider from an early age. The outline of the design is sometimes made first, drawn free hand using a 'paint' prepared out of red mud and water and applied with a sharpened twig. Dark backgrounds of black, red, and green are worked with vibrantly coloured threadwork designs and mirrors. The women of this community can still be seen wearing long flouncy shirts and blouses, their heads covered by an *oudini*, a veil made up of strips of cloth sparkling with colourful motifs and mirrors. Pouches, for precious belongings of the brides, and money belts are all embroidered similarly.

In the southern state of Karnataka there is yet another form of embroidery, *kasuti*. On the dark backgrounds of hand-woven cotton *saris* and blouses, the women embroider stylized motifs of animals and plants, using delicate cross and running stitches. The area of the *pallu*, or end of the *sari*, is more fully covered with small cross stitch motifs.

In Punjab, northern India, an important item of a woman's trousseau is the *phulkari* made by the bride herself. (*Phulkari* means "flowerwork" or "flowering"). On a coarse rust-brown cotton cloth, silk threads of yellow, white and green are used, and the darning stitch is employed in vertical, horizontal and diagonal movements to create elaborate geometric designs until little of the base cloth remains visible.

This darning stitch is often used to cover the entire ground cloth with geometric shapes of solid colours which suggest an abstracted garden; hence, such designs are called '*bagh*', meaning garden. These may be *panchranga bagh* (five-coloured garden designs) or *satranga bagh* (seven-coloured garden designs). There are also different types of garden designs, depending on the layout and geometric forms that are used. In some *phulkari* designs geometric forms of flowers and birds are also found, and more of the ground cloth is left exposed. The beauty of the *phulkari* lies in its smooth silken texture, where the embroidery becomes a part of the fabric, and the rust-brown ground cloth is seen only as borders separating the shapes of yellows and white.

Another threadwork technique, evolved for use on finer cottons and muslin, and sometimes on silk, a 'shadow-work' called *chikan* is associated with the city of Lucknow in Uttar Pradesh, northern India. In *chikan* work, coloured threads are not often used; rather, silhouette designs are created with satin and herringbone stitches done in cotton thread. On the reverse side of the ground cloth, the satin and herringbone stitches fill in a pattern of flowers and leaves, while from the front side all that is seen through the fine cloth are the opaque forms of the design and the outline made of tiny stitches. Drawn threadwork and knotted stitches also enhance the appeal of this form of embroidery. *Kurta*, a traditional long collar shirt for men, use such *chikan* work to highlight the neck line, the shoulder seam and the edges of the shirt tail. A similar form of embroidery is to be found in the eastern state of Bengal, where it is referred to as Dacca embroidery.

In Himachal Pradesh, a northern state of India, a unique style of embroidery is used to enhance the *rumals* (kerchiefs) that are presented to friends and relatives at weddings and festivals. These tokens of friendship are made out of an off-white square piece of silk. The embroidery is unique in that it is done in such a manner as to render the embroidery identical on both sides. Running stitches with return stitching to fill in the gaps creates the outline of the design on both sides. Being square in shape the *rumal* usually has a central design with a border or motifs on the edges and corners. The social and religious significance of these *rumals* is reflected in the themes used in the embroidery, often depicting stories of the god Krishna. Threadwork embroidery is also found in other areas of the country, such as Manipur in the northeast and Bihar in the east, as well as in the south of India.

Applique work

The application of cut pieces of coloured, printed or textured cloth on the ground cloth has an aesthetic quality quite different from threadwork embroidery. In applique work, the designs, formed with solid patches of colours, are bold. Appropriate threadwork and colour of the thread used to attach the patches can add to the harmonization of the patches and the ground cloth. The most well-known styles of applique work are found in the states of Bihar, Orissa, Gujarat and Tamil Nadu, though this type of embroidery is also found in other regions. In the state of Bihar, applique work is called *khatwa*, and is used to decorate canopies set up for festive occasions. White applique motifs of trees and flowers are sewn onto plain backgrounds of red and green cotton. Often the applique motif is cut out in a single piece, however elaborate the design might be.

Applique work in the eastern state of Orissa is centred in a town called Pipli. Temple umbrellas, canopies and fans are traditionally decorated with colourful patchwork designs. Geometric shapes of coloured cloth are cut out and stitched in to build up the border design and form stylized flowers and animals. Since applique work is often used in the adornment of such large areas of cloth, colour harmony between the patchwork and the ground cloth is essential. In Orissa, both the background cloth and patchwork cloth are in plain colours, mainly black, white, red, and green. The general effect is that of abstract geometric blocks of intense colour, with little textural variation in the cloth.

In Gujarat, the applique technique is used mainly as a means of re-using old yet beautiful remnants of cloth. The patchwork pieces, therefore, are coloured and sometimes printed. Household items such as bedcovers and baby hammocks are decorated with applique work in which a variety of coloured cloth, textures, and prints are carefully balanced in forming motifs. Sometimes the central portion of a large patchwork carried scenes of everyday life and the whole piece is framed by a patchwork border design.

In Gujarat and Rajasthan there are communities that affix tiny circular or triangular piece of mirror or mica onto their embroidered clothes. These mirrors are encased in a frame of blanket stitches, and positioning of the mirrors is related to the general scheme of the embroidery. Mirrorwork can be found here on both household items and clothing. On garments it is especially beautiful, as the mirrors catch the light swaying with the movements of the wearer.

Applique work is also found as a type of temple decoration in Tanjore, in the southern state of Tamil Nadu. On backgrounds of white, black, or red, geometric border designs and flower motifs are created by the application of plain coloured cloth pieces.

Zari embroidery, found in different parts of India, is used by different communities and religious groups, such as the Muslims, Hindus and Christians. The application of gold and silver thread and a variety of gold or silver sequins as borders and on the edges of silk, satin and velvet materials is an age-old art form. Royal robes, ceremonial garments, and ritual objects were often decorated using this method.

Quilting

This technique of stitching together piled layers of cloth have given rise to a simpler but no less charming form of embroidery, in which designs are created by the running stitch that holds the pile together. Bedcovers and jackets are decorated with such quilting designs. Additional thread work and applique are added to further highlight the quilted design.

In Bengal, *Kantha* embroidery has been developed from the ingenious recycling of old drapes and *saris* to make household items such as bedspreads, covers, and pouches. Designs with the running stitch are created with different coloured threads. Scenes of animals, including fish and birds, and all kinds of life abound on the surface of the *kantha*. Similar quilting techniques have been developed in the states of Bihar, Gujarat and Rajasthan.

Today, much of India's hand-made embroidery is being replaced by machine embroidery that fashions new designs for new requirements; however, most of the examples mentioned above are still being made by women in villages and towns in all parts of the nation. The care and patience with which embroidery has to be done, as well as the countless varieties and motifs that have been designed, reveals the importance of this art form in the daily life of the people, and displays the creativity of those belonging to all levels of society.

Museums such as the National Museum, New Delhi, and Calico Museum, Ahmedabad, house some of the finest collections of embroidered materials of the past. It is, however, in the villages of India where one can see how much colour and gaiety embroidery adds to life.

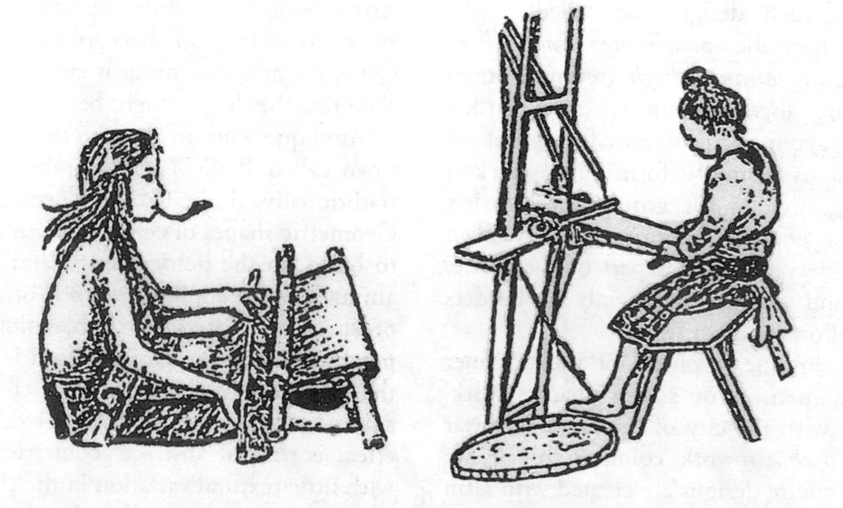

Hand weaving of textiles in South-East Asia.

Textiles

The Iranian Textile

Weaving as a combination of art and industry has a long history in Iran, going back to the millennium before Christ. Traces of sheepswool textile have been found dating from 6500 BC

During the excavations at Susa, in the layers corresponding to 3500-3000 BC, two bronze knife blades were found, which were covered with pieces of fossilized cloth; and in excavations at Marlik, small pieces of cloth dating from the latter part of the second millennium and the beginning of the first were also found.

Generally, objects dating from different periods of our civilization testify that weaving in this region has continued unceasingly up to the present time; and as with other industrial and artistic phenomena, the ups and downs of history have played a decisive role in its development. So it is one of the most important sources for gauging the particular economic, political, cultural and climatic factors prevalent in every society.

Certain pieces of cloth and weaving instruments testify to the presence of this craft in the Achaemenid period.

The Parthians also produced fine wool and linen fabrics, and subsequently learned how to weave silk cloth. The abundant production of all kinds of silk cloth continued from Ashkanian times through the Sassanian period.

Decorative motifs of Sassanian cloths include geometrical designs of circles or ellipses, either separate of tangential, which form frames, usually containing human or animal figures, different kinds of birds, and occasionally mythical creatures such as the "Simorth" (a fabulous bird).

Sometimes these figures are placed symmetrically within the frames, in which case the principles of juxtaposition and symmetry which are the essentials of the art are fully observed. Occasionally, between two symmetrical designs, there is a "tree of life". This is a motif which occurs in many different cultures, and is usually shown in the shape of the sun. In Islam, this tree is presented as a tree of light and God's grace, in the form of the olive tree which provides both sustenance and oil for lighting lamps weaving in the Islamic period.

With the advent of Islam, great development took place in various sectors. During the first and second centuries of Hejira (the early Islamic centuries) we see the continuance of the Sassanian artistic traditions as before, but from the late second century and early third century of hejira, writing begins to appear on textiles, the Kufic characters with which the Koran was written. In using this method of writing to express the holy verses of the Koran and traditional themes, the artist, by mingling figures and characters and creating harmony between them, has shown his ardent virtuosity and good taste.

During the early Islamic period, various kinds of cloth were woven in the different regions of Iran. In the third century of Hejira, in the towns and cities of Khorassan, Gorgan Azerbaijan, Deylam, Kurdistan and Fars, which were the most privileged provinces of the Islamic Empire, there flourished a fine silk weaving industry, and it was considered their most important source of revenue. *Dopoodi* was one of the most outstanding of these fabrics. In towns of Fars, polychrome embroidery and gold brocade were woven. In Isfahan silk and cotton cloth was produced, and from Tabarestan came various expensive silk and wool clothes and dresses.

The land of Khorassan encompassed the cities of Marv, Neishabur and Herat, which were famous for their fine cotton and silk cloth and a certain kind of silk brocade.

Samarkand was renowned for a kind of cloth known as *Simgown* which was woven with silver thread.

Khusistan, in the fourth century of Hejira, had the largest silk factory in Iran.

The textiles of Khuzistan included *diba*, Khaz (wool and silk cloth) and light cotton and silk cloth. There was no *Khaz* like that of Shush.

Shiraz had its matchless *Monir*, and in Easa fine, delicate garments, *Monir* and chequered silk curtains were produced. In the seventh century of Hejira, one specialty of the period was a kind of striped silk cloth with variant designs.

Kirman and Tabriz were considered the important centres for silk cloth and brocade.

In the ninth century of the Hejira, with the Timorid Dynasty ruling in Iran, patterns and cloth weaving became extremely elegant and elaborate. The cities of Khorassan, Tabaristan, Gorgan and Deylam were celebrated for a kind of silk cloth whose warp and woof were composed of gold and silver threads.

During this time, in Tabriz, silk and cotton articles, taffeta and raw silk could be found. From Gilan, silk was carried to Sultanyah and from there it was exported to Damascus in Syria, to Turkey and to Kafa in the Crimea.

In Shirvan a great deal of cloth was produced and thence carried to Sultanyeh. From Khorassan, woven and raw cotton and coloured tissue were brought to Soltanyeh.

In the course of the tenth and eleventh centuries of the Hejira, weaving attained its peak of perfection as regards beauty and variety of texture.

During the thirteenth and fourteenth centuries of Hejira the art of figure painting became prevalent, and all the arts, including weaving, tended towards portraiture and naturalism. The ingenious calico makers were perhaps the first group of artisans who joined this movement.

During the reign of Shah Tahmasp, Tabriz, as the capital of the country, was the artistic centre of Iran. There developed a special school of weaving in which medallion flower and plant designs, scenes of hunting, animal and bird motifs were predominant. On the whole, the Safavid period, from the point of view of weaving could be called a 'golden age'.

During this time all sorts of silk cloth were woven, i.e. plain silk fabric, silk with gold thread, and silk velvet.

Safavid brocade is unrivalled for its expertness of design and harmony of colours. It was usually offered by Shah Abbas as gifts and presents to the courts of European rulers.

There are distinctive techniques for weaving brocade, one of which is *zari daraee dar*.

One of the finest and most elegant art forms of this period is embroidery of various kinds, with special names. One is *Khameh doozi* (embroidery with raw silk) which is special to Rasht. It is often done on velvet and broad cloth. Pieces of cloth are cut into floral designs and stuck on the cloth and then embroidered over with silk. Another kind is known as *Khatami*; in this, small coloured pieces of cloth are set side by side and sewn on to a ground and then embroidery is done over the stitches.

Another kind of cloth which was produced in the Safavid period was a kind of velvet with varieties of raised flowers in seven colours.

Images

The images and designs used to decorate the cloth fall into the following categories:

1. Plant designs
2. Human figures displayed in banquet and battle scenes
3. The different images of animals and birds which, like flowers and plants, have essentially symbolic roles in Iranian weaving. In principle, animals have a special place in the culture of Iran. Some of these animals are symbols of good omen and joy while others are signs of inauspiciousness and misfortune.
   The lion in Iran represented Mithra, the Sun God. Moreover, he was the symbol of the constellation Leo in the zodiac. Among the Shi-ites of Iran, the lion is the symbol of Emam Ali. Since Safavid times, the lion has acquired a particular importance, and this tradition grew to the extent that statues of this animal were put on the tombs of heroes in the shrines. This tradition was current until recently in the villages of Fars, Bakhtyari and Azerbaijan.
4. Images of imaginary creatures like *Simorgh* and dragon
5. Design in the form of an altar.
6. The use of different scripts (Kufic, Naskhi, Tholth and Nasta'ligh) in which Koranic verses and traditional literature were written.

A Glance at Lao Textiles

Background

Many anthropologists and historians today believe that the Lao race have moved back and forth several times through the region of the Indochina peninsula and the south of China (between the Houang Ho and Yang Si Kiang rivers), due to regional conflicts and instability. In 5000 BC the Lao (or Lawa) and Javanese race were the prehistoric inhabitants of this land. Then, after 4000 BC, the Lawa and Mon-khom (origin of Khmer people) races simultaneously dominated the region, inter-exchanged art and culture, and accepted the influences of the ruler. According to archaeological findings and linguistics studies, the Lao population today consists of four main ethnic groups: Lao-Tai, Hmong-Yao, Tibeto-Burman and Mon-Khmer.

The Lao textiles discussed are those of the Lao-Tai group, whose weaving techniques developed and attained a high enough level to produce intricate textiles for the royal court of the Kingdom of Lan Xang many centuries ago. Thus Lao-Tai textiles have a long and distinguished background, as noted in Chinese historical documents which recount that the Lao-Tai people established the strongest Kingdom in the south of China around 1000 BC and practised sericulture with great skill.

Characteristics of the textiles

By doing comparative studies on the designs and colour composition of some textiles 100-200 years old, and the elaborate descriptions of costumes and silk garments in the Thao Hung Epic[1] and Maha Vetsantra Jataka[2], we have been able to identify the origins of designs and motifs. The main sources which inspired the imagination of the Lao-Tai weavers were probably the mythical creatures of the legends and folk tales, and the natural environment of trees, flowers, leaves, fruits, mountains and clouds. One of predominant motifs in Lao-Tai textiles is the Naga or river snake. In Lao-Tai language, there were various names for these creatures: Nak, Eua, Luang, or Munkorn[3].

Their importance could be related to the legendary ancestry of the Lao-Tai race; it was said that the father of a tribal chief "Ai-Lhao" was a dragon living in the Mekong River. 22 out of 200 folk tales collected by Vannasin Magazine for a contest in 1987 revealed the relationship between the giant snakes living in the Mekong river and its tributaries, and the Lao-Tai people who usually build their houses near the water. There is further evidence in tattoo designs; for Lao-Tai people, the favourite body tattoo is still the dragon or *maen korn*.

The other dominant motifs are also mythical creatures transfigured from wild animals and birds, such as the long-nosed lion (*kosa-sing)*, the long-nosed deer (*to mom*) and the giant swallow (*to hong*). Many geometrical motifs such as lozenges, triangles, spirals, hooks and keys also appear in Lao-Tai textiles. These figures of mythical creatures and geometrical motifs could be reproduced by different weaving techniques such as, *mat-mi (ikat), lai kid* (continuous supplementary weft), *dta mok* (discontinuous supplementary weft), *luang* or *kor*[4], and *mak mai*[5]. In former times, Lao-Tai weavers (along the basin of the Mekong and Nam Ngum rivers) were well-known for their *pha mat-mi* or *ikat* textiles, for which they used the finest silk yarn from the inside of the cocoons. They spent days, months or maybe even several years weaving a beloved piece. For example, it was written in the Thao Hung Epic that the hero's mother took seven years to weave a shawl for her son.

As mentioned above, the Lao-Tai people have been practising sericulture for many centuries. Besides producing silk and cotton yarn, the Lao-Tai people are expert in organic dyeing, using roots, leaves, grains, tree bark and flowers. The design composed of multicoloured motifs is one of the features that distinguishes the antique Lao-Tai textiles from those of other ethnic groups. Lao-Tai women have inherited their dexterity and the secrets of weaving and plant dyes from generation to generation through family links especially mother to daughter. Not only do they have to deal with the lengthy and arduous process of dyeing but also they have to observe some taboos. For example, even now, it is forbidden for a woman in menstruation to stay around the place where the process of dyeing with *Nam Kang* is taking place. If she does, the colour will not fix in the material.

The traditional loom of the Lao-Tai people is typical of Southeast Asia. The main components are strings, heddles, treadles, beater and seat. Weavers in the Vientiane region began to import the wide steel-clad beater from Thailand 10-15 years ago, but the other equipment for weaving and the loom is still made by local craftsmen (reeler, spinner, spindle roll, etc.). The size of the beater may vary from 15 cm to 110 cm. While the other ethnic groups use rough cotton yarn to weave on a backstrap tension loom, the Hmong-Yao tribes use plant fibres to weave the cloth textile, or buy it from neighbouring tribes.

How can we identify textiles from various regions? In spite of the common origin of the Lao-Tai ethnic group, migration throughout the country and displacement during war-time have affected, to a greater or lesser degree, the characteristics of the textiles. Topo-geographical factors appear as local symbols. For example: the cool weather in the northeastern area of Laos (where the Lao-Tai people build their houses on the plateaux and in the mountain valleys) engenders rough texture and contrasting bright dark colours. One can easily recognise a classical *Sin Mi* (or tube-skirt in *Ikat*) from this area by this richness of the weaving techniques (usually 3-4 types), high-contrast colour and intricacy of designs. Red, black, indigo, white or yellow, green, and orange alternate. The dominant and favourite designs are Nak (giant river snake), and birds in abstract form. The Lao-Tai weavers along the Mekong and Nam Nagum basins are also reputed for their fine, soft silk *Sin Mi*, which are also multi-coloured but muted in tone. The main designs are geometrical and taken from nature (animals, trees, flowers ....). In contrast with the intricately patterned hempieces or *Tin Sin* of the Lao-Tai from North-east Laos, the classical *Tin Sin* of the Lao-Tai along the Mekong and Nam Ngum basin are narrower, single-coloured and often woven by simple technique called "*Tam Lae*" or "*Lai Kid*".

Social and cultural significance of the textile

Up to the present time, women have been the weavers of all kinds of traditional textiles. They are responsible for the production of the family clothing from its beginning in the planting of a cotton crop (or mulberry to feed the silk worm), through its completion in the weaving of cloth and the sewing of the final garments. Thus, women's role is closely linked with the social value of the woven textile. A woman could gain distinction for being a good weaver and have the opportunity to earn the respect of her husband and his relatives. If the weaver belonged to the aristocracy, the textile, product of her creation, would be even more appreciated. The wedding tradition of Tai-Deng ('Red Tai', an ethnic subgroup of Lao-Tai) offered large dowry to the bride if she could furnish the household with textiles woven on her loom, in the form of pillowseats (Art Sana), mattresses, blankets, shawls, curtains, mosquito-nets, etc.

It is interesting to note here that the textile still plays an important role in rural Lao society. The typical Lao-Tai house consists of a large communal sleeping room (for all members of the family), a kitchen and a hall. Therefore, thick dark curtains are used to separate the rooms. A black mosquito net is one of the main household items for the newly weds.

Which Lao-Tai textiles are still in vogue? Since the very first decades of the twentieth century (during the period of French colonisation) until now, the production of woven textiles of Lao-Tai people along the basin of the Mekong and Nam Ngum rivers has gradually been decreasing, due to the importation of industrial textiles, synthetic yarn and "readymade" clothes. These goods had been imported in limited quotas as commercial exchange for many decades.

But in the last 10 years, textiles from many socialist countries have been imported as aid in unlimited quantity. This has practically stopped lao production of textiles in rural areas as well as in town. Only the traditional and ceremonial costumes for women are still woven in quantity. For the Lao-Tai people, both living in Lao P.D.R, and abroad, traditional clothes such as those for weddings and religious ceremonies are still very popular. Vientiane Municipality has become a production centre for silk textiles used as shoulder cloths and wedding costumes of high quality for export and domestic consumption. There exist four private companies and one state enterprise for cotton and silk textile.

Around the capital, ten villages are reputed for their traditional textile production (Phonekaeng, Ban Hom, Bo-Oh, Suan Mon, Chom-Phet, Nong Boua Thong, Koun Ta, Wattay, Phan Manh). The tourist demand for antique textiles has led to a great increase in the number of antique-textile shops in Vientiane during the last few years (over 100 shops — a tremendous number for a town of about only 300,000 inhabitants).

While foreign visitors appreciate the antique Lao textiles, Lao women themselves remain attached to their beloved "Sin". Although, there is no strong law forbidding female employees and students in high school and University to wear modern-style skirts, jeans, trousers, and dresses, it appears that Lao-Tai women are very keen to retain their traditional "Sin". They have been wearing this style of straight skirt called "*Sin sam ret*" for over thirty years to match blouses of any modern style.

Because of its social value, the Lao-Tai textile will continue to play an important role in the Lao cultural identity as well as the national economy. As for the weavers themselves, their skills will contribute a great deal to the family income. It could also help to preserve the solidarity of the family unit as young weavers work at home.

1. "Thao Hung Epic" is a historical literary work which provides vivid information about the ancient society of Lao people around the 13-14th century.
2. "Maha Vetsantra Jataka" is a masterpiece of Lao literature of the 16th century.
3. Local terms for the river snake in Lao language differ from one region to another.
4. "Luang" or "Kor" is a weaving technique of Tai Lue.
5. "Mak Mai" or "Mab Mai", is a technique of weaving by traditional loom.

Varied and Colourful Chinese Handwoven Textiles

China was one of the first countries to develop silkworm rearing, silk reeling and weaving, dyeing and printing as well as embroidery, several thousand years ago. As early as the beginning of the New Stone Age, China invented the original spinning tool — the spinning weight (spindle) and the original weaving device — the waist loom; and then in the latter half of the New Stone Age, in addition to cotton, bast fibre, kohemp and wool fabric manufacture, the silk weaving technique was created, a special contribution to the world's ancient history. According to historical records and unearthed articles, the techniques of hand "jacquarding" silk fabric and handwoven goods — such as cut silk brocade, very popular before the Tang Dynasty (618 AD), were also invented in China between tenth and eleventh century BC.

In the Tang Dynasty, a new process of brocade weaving emerged by changing from warp weave to weft weave, so that the disadvantage of the smaller pattern unit on the warp faced brocade could be overcome. In the history of textiles, the modern three-elementary weave, plain weave, twill weave and satin weave, had all emerged in China by the Song Dynasty (960 AD). The gold thread weaving, raising and swivel technique invented before the Tang Dynasty, were combined with satin weave in this period, producing a number of new varieties and colours, which are still used to make outstanding handwoven fabrics.

The traditional weaving device for handwoven fabric is the foot loom which can still be found in the minority national regions today. Zhuang brocade, for example, manufactured at Guangxi Binyang Mill, is really woven on a traditional loom known as a "bamboo cage loom". This loom is of bamboo construction with a shedding jacquard-type mechanism bamboo cage. It is an improvement on the older type of machine, the multi-healed and multi-pedal loom, because the bamboo cage loom has an ingenious mechanism using fewer pedals to control a multi-healed. In weaving, the bamboo cage loom employs three shuttles to achieve a weft effect on the face of the brocade, in which one shuttle weaves the weft-faced figuring, another shuttle the ground colour effect and the third shuttle the plain back.

Rich and colourful Chinese handwoven fabric has enjoyed a high reputation since ancient times. A piece of brocade with paired-sheep, paired-bird and leaf designs, unearthed from an ancient grave, shows an excellent silk fabric of high quality handicraft art from ancient times. The fabric construction belongs to a kind of warp backed weave, employing thirteen figuring healed frames and two extra plain healed frames in weaving. As a four-colour warp brocade, the silk fabric contains two groups of dyed warps in forest green, white and deep red and in forest green, white and orange respectively, but forest green is used as the ground shade. In the pattern, the pair of sheep signifies good luck and happiness, two pairs of speckled birds between the trees constitute a unique design and the tree motif looks like a "lamp-tree" with numerous white flowers round it. This lamp-tree, with its leaves popping up one by one, symbolizes the flower of life which will shine forever.

Since ancient times, most minority nationalities in China have been able to weave different kinds of beautiful coloured brocade. A few samples of the national handwoven fabric are listed as follows.

1. Zhuang brocade

Zhuang brocade was produced as early as 618 AD (Tang Dynasty), and had become widely known by 1368 AD (Ming Dynasty). A superior quality brocade decorated with dragons and phoenixes, it was used as an article of tribute in the past. In this brocade, cotton yarn is used for the warp, and silk thread for the weft; the cotton yarn is usually plain, and multicoloured silk threads are used for weft. Zhuang brocade is exquisitely woven and the pattern is very bright and colourful. In the pattern, a geometrically constructed lozenge motive constitutes the body, a circular, swastika-shaped (*wan-character-shaped)* or wave motif the ground, some peculiarly shaped dragons, phoenixes or animals the main design, regularly spaced across the fabric.

Zhuang brocade is mostly used for the Zhuang women's national costume, the piping of collar and border, waist band, headscarf and wrapped skirt, as well as tablecloths, cushions, handbags, quilt covers, wall hangings and screens, etc. Some beautiful silk handkerchiefs made with special care, showing ingenuity and great originality, are commonly used as authenticating objects for young people to express their love.

2. Tong brocade

The Tong Nationality has long history of textile manufacturing. Tong brocade is one of their famous handicrafts. Certain colours such as violet, pale purple, blue, and white, being dominant in the patterns of Tong brocade, give it a distinctive character. Almost every Tong family has its own weaving machine known as a "Dou loom". Patterns in their fabric designs are mostly straight lines, such as herring-bone, cross-over □-shaped (*kou* character-shaped) and swastika-shaped designs, etc. Motifs in the design are usually those common to the mountain area including animals, plants or household utensils, etc. In some large Tong brocades, patterns usually draw their material from ancient myths or legends. Sometimes a young Tong girl with a heart full of tenderness weaves her lover's name into the brocade to show her faithful, firm and constant love.

3. Dai brocade

The clever and deft Dai people are expert at weaving brocade, and their products show fine workmanship and exquisite characteristics. Even in ancient times, the Dai girls were able to weave beautiful brocade, as later Han Dynasty historical records described it was richness and the vast quantities of silk used. A lozenge motif is generally used for the main pattern in Dai brocade, but other colourful weft designs may emerge as the lozenge motif direction. In weaving, fine ramie thread is employed as the ground and coarse bast fibre yarn the coloured weft, so that the colour effect will fully emerge on the fabric face. Dai brocade weaving employs a waist loom.

4. Coloured webbing and coloured goods of Miao nationality

Making the best use of different coloured-silk yarns as the main raw materials for weaving, the coloured webbing is generally about five feet in length and one to three inches in breadth, with figures and characters on the fabric face and fringes of various colours at both ends. Coloured webbing is commonly used by Miao men and women for waist band and suspender as well as salon apron. Both coloured webbing and coloured goods are usually seamed on the moveable portions of the clothes such as cuff, shoulder, back flap and skirt sweep, etc., so that the beautiful inweave may appear now and then when the portion is moving, showing a distinctive flavour.

The Miao have created a splendid national culture and art in their lives over a long period of time. They possess superb skills of textile manufacturing and show exquisite workmanship in dress tailoring. Generally speaking, a lady's splendid costume ensemble incorporates both knitting and cross-stich work. It is said that a "silver-like dress" takes several years to make.

China's national brocade, as used for clothing, is briefly described above; however, other articles including embroidery, Batik prints and brightly coloured printed and dyed goods are also extensively used for clothing. Since China is a great family of fifty-six nationalities, different brocades and fabrics manufactured by different nationalities living in Northeast, Northwest, Southeast and Southwest China are noted also for their different workmanship and characteristics which are closely associated with geographical environment, weather conditions and national disposition.

Textiles of India

The handwoven textiles of India have an ancient and glorious history. Cotton has been grown, spun and woven here for the last five thousand years, while the weaving of silk, wool, hemp and flax also dates back several centuries.

Indian fabrics were renowned throughout the world for their beauty. They were exported not only to neighbouring countries, but also to the West and Far East, where they inspired many local styles and patterns.

Indian textiles were also influenced by other cultures. The Mughal influence was perhaps the greatest, and provided many new techniques and designs which the Indian craftsman assimilated, to produce fabrics of even greater beauty. the ancient Indian craftsman traced his lineage back to Vishwakarama, the Architect of the Heavens, Lord of the Arts and Crafts.

His creations formed an integral part of the social, cultural and religious life of the people. Rituals and ceremonies, as well as festivals and fairs, for instance, played an important role in determining the nature of different textiles and garments. The finest creations of the craftsman were offered to the gods. Beautiful textiles clothed and adorned the deities. They also served as coverings or containers for objects used during worship.

The structure of India's ancient caste-system and that of the traditional joint family, bound people to specific occupations and thus ensured the continuity of different crafts. Within the tremendously rich and varied textile traditions of India, every technique has been practised for centuries, with an instinctive sense of proportion, colour and harmony. There are over ten million weavers — predominantly male — in India today, weaving almost four thousand million metres of cloth a year. India has 3.8 million hand-operated looms, the largest number of handlooms is a single country.

The great diversity in Indian textiles reflects the diversity in India's climate and vegetation, as well as the cultural and religious diversity of our people. Practically every social group has its own preferences and norms in colour, design and fabric, though there is much more intermingling in these today.

Colour has always had a special place in India's weaves. A deep knowledge of colour chemistry and indigenous dyes was largely responsible for the superlative quality of Indian fabrics. Colours are much more than mere means of decoration. They are suffused with emotional meaning and rich associations. Red is the colour of love, of good omen, worn by brides to signify marital bliss. Yellow is the colour of fertility. A new mother wears yellow, symbolizing prosperity and fruition. Saffron is the colour of spring. It is also the colour of renunciation, worn by yogis or holy men, who are one with the earth but free of all attachment to it.

White is not merely a single shade. The Indian craftsman could distinguish between the white of ivory, the white of the jasmine flower, the white of the August moon, the white of clouds after rain and the white of the conch-shell.

The wide variety of motifs that embellish his weaves also reflects the sensitivity of the Indian weaver to his environment. The beautiful red and gold leaves of the chinar tree of Kashmir, cherries and apples, butterflies and kingfishers — all adorn the fabrics of this northern state. Among the traditional motifs in the fabrics of the coastal state of Orissa, are fish and flowing streams. The Indian weaver also drew inspiration from his religion, incorporating religious motifs, such as temple spires, into his weaves.

The weavers of Bengal, who wove the famous Baluchar saris, wove scenes of contemporary relevance into the fabric, such as those of temple, a durbar, of court and even a picture of a steam engine when it was first introduced into India. The art of weaving these "historical" saris had almost disappeared, but has now been revived, with the addition of new designs. All Indian textiles were traditionally handspun and handwoven. The popular name for such textiles today is "khadi". Cloth that is hand-woven, using mill-spun yarn, is referred to as handloom cloth.

The three major raw materials for hand-woven textiles in India have always been cotton, silk and wool. Cotton is grown in the fertile plains of western and southern India. Silk worms are reared on a large scale, particularly in the forests of the east and north-east, while sheep-rearing on the northern mountains, as well as on hills elsewhere in the country, yields an abundance of wool.

Cotton

Cotton is naturally the king of fibres in a tropical country like India. Ninety percent of our hand looms weave cotton cloth. India's fine cottons have been known and celebrated the world over, for centuries. Names such as *bafta hava* (woven air), *ab-i-rawan* (running water) and *shabnam* (evening dew) indicate the beauty, the delicacy and the translucent quality of these ancient weaves.

Silk

Silk, indigenous to India, is obtained from the wild tasar, muga and eri worms. But these attractive silks form only a small part of India's silk manufacture today. Fine silk from the mulberry-eating silkworm, which was probably brought to India from China, now accounts for most of India's output. Soft and lustrous, silk was traditionally considered the most suitable fabric for ceremonial occasions. It was worn for births and marriages and the finest silks were offered to temple deities. This tradition may explain the growth of silk weaving centres around ancient temple towns like Varanasi in the north and Kanchipuram in the south of India.

Wool

The most exquisite of woollen fabrics — the shawls of Kashmir — bear eloquent testimony to the weaver's art. The magnificent Shahtush shawl, for example, is so soft and delicate that it can pass through a ring, yet so warm that it can hatch the egg of a pigeon!

Handwoven textiles can be broadly divided into two categories — plain and patterned. Patterned textiles can be further divided into those patterned while on the loom and those patterned after weaving.

India was famous for both plain and patterned textiles. The finest of her plain textiles were the gossamer-thin muslins of Dacca (now the capital of Bangladesh). It is said that the Mughal Emperor Aurangzeb once rebuked his daughter for appearing unclothed, when she was, in reality, clothed in seven layers of muslin!

Among several techniques of patterning cloth while it is being woven, the two most outstanding are the ikat and the brocade techniques.

Ikat

The word "ikat" is a Malayan word and comes from "Mangikat" which means to bind, knot or wind around.

The ikat technique is the tie and dye of yarn before weaving, in such a way that the required colours and patterns appear in the woven fabric. In the single ikat technique, only the warp or the weft are tie-dyed. In the double ikat process, both warp and weft are tie-dyed separately, producing woven designs of incredible richness and beauty.

The three Indian states of Gujarat, Orissa and Andhra, specialize in ikat weaving, each state having developed its own variations on the basic technique. Gorgeous ikat fabrics, with their jewel-like colours and their eye-catching plant, animal and geometric motifs, grace many an auspicious occasion. The double ikats of Gujarat are counted as valuable heirlooms, carefully preserved and handed down from mother to daughter.

Brocade

Brocaded fabrics are those in which patterns are created on the loom by thrusting the pattern threads between the warp, to create the required design. The introduction of these separate weft threads into the fabric, led to the brocade technique being known as "loom embroidery." Depending upon the nature of the pattern thread, brocades can be classified as cotton brocade, silk brocade and zari brocade (using threads of gold and silver).

Many exquisite brocades have come from the looms of Indian weavers, to grace weddings and other festivities. The most dazzling of these is probably the *kinkhab* proper, or cloth-of-gold brocade of Varanasi. Here threads of gold and silver were woven so densely that the base of silk thread was hardly visible. Such heavy brocade was used more for royal furnishings, than for clothing.

The traditional garments of both men and women in India were unstitched lengths of fabrics draped around the body. Men, for the most part, wore a turban wound round the head, a *dhoti* or *lungi* tied round the waist, and a shawl or scarf over the shoulder.

Women wore a lower garment with another, thinner, piece of cloth covering the upper part of the body and sometimes the head. These two cloths later developed into the one-piece sari as we know it now, with regional and socio-cultural variations in length, design and draping style.

While many men, especially in the urban areas, gradually adopted the Western shirt and trousers, Indian women, by and large, have continued to wear the sari.

Innately graceful and versatile, easily manageable for work in fields, factories and offices, as well as in the home, the sari is the life and soul of the handloom industry. Its infinite variety for every occasion, could only be created by the skilled and sensitive hands of the weaver.

For generations, the finest Indian saris were woven on throw-shuttle pit looms, which are easy to operate and occupy little space. In many areas, these have been replaced by fly shuttle pit looms, which have most of their advantages and three to four times their productivity. For weaving longer yardage (as for sheets and furnishings), the more expensive frame looms are most appropriate.

Simple bamboo loin looms are used by the tribal women of the northeast, to weave their colourful fabrics. These looms are easily portable and allow plenty of scope for free designing. The time-honoured crafts of India suffered a decline during the British occupation of the country. Fortunately Mahatma Gandhi's crusade to revive the spinning wheel as a symbol of national pride and self-reliance, ushered in a renaissance of India's traditional skills. Through the efforts of the Government along with dedicated researchers, designers, economists and sociologists all over the country, India's rich textile traditions are, for the most part, being preserved and revitalized.

The production of handwoven cloth is almost 8 times what it was in the 1950s, while the worldwide demand for textiles crafted in India has increased fortyfold in the last two decades. Much has been done. Much remains to be done. The struggle to adapt ancient crafts to a changing environment goes on.

The wealth of a nation is measured not only by its financial resources. It is measured also by the creative outpourings of its people; and by the arts and the crafts through which these outpourings find expression. Measured by this standard, India is indeed a wealthy country.

The Traditional Weaving of Indonesia

Indonesian traditional textiles are diverse in material, technique and colour. Approximately 350 ethnic groups living in the Indonesian Archipelago produce loom-woven textiles ranging from simple plain cotton or other fibres to complicated cotton and silk ceremonial clothes with gold and silver thread. Each region has its own distinctive traditional dress for daily use and elaborate ceremonial and ritual occasions such as rites of passage, birth, circumcision, tooth-filling, wedding and funeral. Ceremonial dresses are also worn for agricultural festivals especially at harvest time.

In certain areas they produce non-loom products such as bark cloth (Central Sulawesi, Kalimantan, Maluku), bead and seed embroidery (Kalimantan, South Sulawesi, Lampung, Nusa Tenggara Timur), twisted or knotted bast, as well as leaf.

The varied tropical environment of the islands of Indonesia, provides many sources of plant fibres; cotton banana fibre, pineapple, several palms, orchid leaves (special orchid fibre, *serat doyo*, East Kalimantan); all have been widely used in Indonesia, and later on silk thread was used. Bark cloth and plaitwork in fact exist in mainland and South-east Asia as well. A prehistoric find in Indonesia, a stone pounder with stripes on it, was probably used to pound fibre to make cloth. This bark cloth technology disappeared, probably with the development of the loom and the arrival of imported cloth; however, the Bada and Kulawi people of Central Sulawesi, who live in the highlands, and mountains, still make this bark cloth, which is called *fuya* and is worn on special occasions.

Another prehistoric find was pottery fragments and tea pots from Sentolo Yogyakarta. They were decorated with geometric patterns exactly the same as the geometric motifs on woven cloth and batik. These geometric decorations are also found on prehistoric bronze kettle drums.

This prehistoric evidence shows that weaving, as known in South-east Asia, came from Yunan, Southwestern China, about two or three thousand years ago. Which fibre was used first for weaving, has not yet been determined.

The Indonesian islands are located at a trade crossroads, where they have for centuries been open to commercial contact with India (Hindu and Islam world), China and Europe as well. This contact influenced the indigenous skills and materials, and the cultural influences have been absorbed and accommodated alongside older indigenous elements. The traditional textiles of Indonesia also demonstrate the variety of ways in which foreign ideas, material and even techniques have been incorporated into Indonesian fabric.

Uses of traditional textiles

In Indonesia, a piece of cloth may serve many functions in ceremonies and rituals which are all intimately related to the people's life and world view.

Woven textiles articles are used daily, such as *sarong*, *selendang* (shawl), *gendongan* (baby carrier), headcloth, belt, and even bags. The use of textiles in celebrating rites of passage is most significant. The outstanding *pelepai*, or 'ship cloth' from Lampung is displayed as a wall-hanging at important rituals such as wedding or circumcision. *Pua*, a long cloth from Kalimantan, hangs on the wall inside the longhouse during ritual ceremonies. Certain batik patterns, like the *sidomukti*, are reserved for use at weddings.

Certain textiles have religious and magical significance and their presence is important. The *kain geringsing* is used throughout Bali at weddings and tooth filling ceremonies which initiate a member of society into adulthood.

The Sumbanese ruling families formerly saved the finest textiles for funerals. The corpse is dressed in valuable cloth, draped over to form a huge mound. Relatives and members of the community bring beautiful textiles as funeral gifts.

In the Payakumbuh area of West Sumatra, the *kain bakucuang* is usually taken to a house where a person has died. It consists of a *kain songket benang makao* (gold thread *songket*) made into a roll to wrap the corpse. This is compulsory for all the female members on both sides of the family. After the deceased has been carried out of the house, the rolls are taken back by the owners. Formerly tose *kains* were wrapped around the deceased and taken into the grave, but nowadays they are only symbolic gifts.

In many regions textiles reflect the basic dualism of traditional Indonesian society, the dualism of the complementary male and female elements of the cosmos. Textiles are classified as female, because they are mainly produced by women. Exchanging dowry in marriage ceremonies, the female members of the bride's family give valuable items such as weapons, metal articles, money, buffalo, horses or pigs. In many parts of Nusa Tenggara Timur, the bride's family supply, besides textiles, other items such as beads and ivory, and the groom's family offer gold, horses, and buffalo.

Clothes are important in affirming family and clan relationships. In Lampung the *kain tampan*, a small square cloth, formerly played an important role in symbolic exchange between partners in a lineage-related marriage. These *tampans* were used to wrap ceremonial food at marriage negotiations. They were returned after the food was received, their role being to strengthen the lineage relationship. Exchange of ceremonial food in marriage is also part of the Minangkabau wedding ceremony. The food is wrapped in a square cloth decorated with gold thread floral motifs. These are brought by female members of the groom's family to the bride's family.

The *ulos*, cloths of the Toba Batak people in North Sumatra, are predominantly important in the relationships among *dolihan natolu*, the bride's family (hula-hula), the groom's family (*boru*), and the members of the same family or lineage, semarga. At a Batak ceremony, an *ulos* must be given by the family of the bride to the parents of the groom, and another to the groom himself. The dowry and the gifts given by the bride's family work as a system of distribution and sharing of goods among the three groups of *dalihan natolu*. A special gift, *ulos ragi idup*, is given by the parents to their pregnant daughter as a symbol of transferring their strength to her.

It is called '*ulos ni fondi'* which means '*ulos* of her soul'.

Textiles in many regions are definers of social relationships and, especially, a means of signifying status, position and wealth. Certain motifs are associated with or restricted to certain aristocratic families.

In Sumba, *sarong* with supplementary warp decoration, called *lau* were worn, only by royalty and noble-women. Only the king and the men in his service could wear red or rust-coloured black and white animal-patterned cloth known as *hinggi kombu*, while common people could only wear the same kind of cloth in blue and white, called *hinggi kaworu*. Nowadays, *hinggi kombu* are widely worn by men of all classes.

Textiles play an important role in the lives of the people who make or use them all over the Indonesian archipelago.

Women and textiles

Weaving in Indonesia, as elsewhere in South-east Asia, is traditionally a woman's occupation. Men spend most of their time hunting and farming. Women also spend their time helping men in the fields to seed and harvest. The rest of the time they stay around the house, take care of the children and make their own clothing. In early times the Sumbanese women planted and harvested the cotton by themselves and they followed all the steps of the weaving process: spinning, dyeing and weaving cloth. The Dayak men in Kalimantan, as well as in other areas of Indonesia, assist in making the loom, as most woodcarvers are men.

Since thread is now purchased from traders, and due to other social and economic changes, not all women weave to supply their own needs. Some dye and weave for income, and supply the members of their community with their own women's traditional textiles.

Great patience and skill are required in the work of ikatting, dyeing and weaving the threads. The whole process may take several months or years. In Sumba it takes a year and a half to finish a cloth, and in Tengganan, Bali, it may take eight years or more to finish a *geringsing* (double ikat) weave. Women as weavers have a large role in preserving traditional methods and designs, and thereby their regional identities in the form of costumes. Formerly in some areas, a woman had to know how to weave; it was an essential skill. The Balinese believe that if a woman does not know how to weave, someday in the hereafter her *sarong* will be torn by dogs to shame her. In some areas the weavers have to fast; and the Dayak weavers in Kalimantan get their inspirations through dreams.

A Pande Sikek weaver of West Sumatra is of the view that when she has a problem in arranging the *songket* motifs, she just takes a break and goes to pray, especially early in the morning, and soon afterwards she has ample energy to create a beautiful motif on the cloth. Certain traditional motifs have a symbolic meaning in the Minangkabau *adat*. These *adat* rules are preserved by women in weaving, while men orally preserve their *adat* in *petatah-petitih*, or proverbs, which are usually employed in traditional speech.

Linking Intricate Workmanship with Dynamic Feelings — Handicrafts of Bhutan

While the spirit of a new age is gradually making its presence felt in almost every facet of contemporary Bhutanese life, the Royal Government is leaving no stone unturned in its determined efforts to balance its rapid socio-economic progress with a proportionate emphasis on the maintenance and furtherance of its distinctive cultural and religious heritage. Thus the revolutionary modernization that the country is at present witnessing has not, unlike in many other countries, left behind a trail of economic dislocation or psychological alienation.

The handicrafts of Bhutan, rich in range, unique in character, and renowned in their intricate and superb craftsmanship, reflect a vigorous and thriving tradition that has come down untouched through the ages. While in good measure this owes itself to charitable royal patronage, the Government has of late given priority to the organized production of these skills. Five handicrafts centres have been set up in Thimphu, Paro, Dhokar, Tashigang, and Tongsa. At the same time, the Department of Industries and Mines has undertaken a programme of expansion of production in a wide range of crafts and cottage industries, aimed at meeting domestic and export requirements through such measures as the utilization of improved tools and techniques, the provision of training skills, financial assistance and marketing facilities, and the introduction of rigorous quality control.

Applique, embroidery, and sculpture

In all Bhutanese art forms, religious themes predominate. Highly decorative and ornamental, Bhutanese art shows influences of Tibetan, Indian, and Chinese traditional styles, but these are ingeniously adapted to the Bhutanese setting and temperament. Because of their essentially non-secular nature, it is the monastic centres in the country that are the chief repositories of Bhutanese art.

At the same time, most Bhutanese art is anonymous. Whether carving a statue or painting a scroll, the Bhutanese artist is, so to speak, enacting a spiritual exercise, and the thought of name or fame is indeed far from his mind.

The painted or embroidered *thankas*, or religious scrolls, display a particularly high degree of craftsmanship, and include some of the most significant art pieces in the country. Many are large in size, and the giant *thanka* at Paro Dzong in silk brocade applique is 91 ft by 100 ft. Endowed with a brilliant colour scheme, it depicts the sacred figure of Guru Padmasambhava and his various manifestations. Other notable *thankas* are housed in the Phajoding Monastery in Thimphu and the National Museum in Paro.

Applique and embroidery are also applied to banners and dancing costumes. Of late, even neckties and ladies' scarves are made from fine silk and brocades.

Though the country can boast of some magnificent statues in rhino horn, bronze, coral, mother-of-pearl and a variety of other materials, here an attempt is made to confine only to clay figures and slate carving. Exquisitely modelled and painted statues of clay represent an age-old craft owing its origin to religious tradition. A few skilled craftsmen operate in the vicinity of *dzongs* and temples, while others are found at the commercial centre in Thimphu. Clay workmanship is seen in temples and dzongs, and in the recently-constructed Memorial Chorten in Thimphu. Carving on black slate is another traditional craft of Bhutan. Figures of guardian deities and Buddhist teachers are carved and preserved for worship, and may also be seen in the stone panelling of *chortens.*

Wood carving and masks

Wood carving is done extensively on pine, walnut, betula, erithria and sisoo woods. The delicate workmanship can be seen in buildings and furniture, including the traditional tables called *chhodoms.* Altars for worship in general have intricate carving and painting work. Beautifully carved and lacquered wooden panels are sold as souvenirs.

The regions of Bumthang, Mongar, Tashigang, Wangdiphodrang, Khen, Paro and Thimphu are known for their skilled carvers. Famous mask carvers come from Bumthang and Wangdiphodrang. Figures depicting deities, goddesses, and animal and human faces are used in mask dances during annual festivals.

In recent times, wooden masks have found a considerable market as room decorations. Lighter types of masks are made from a mixture of sawdust, animal glue, canvas cloth and hand-made paper.

Metal work

Round and rectangular shaped boxes with intricate workmanship are made of silver. Ritual vessels and bowls are made of copper in combination with two more metals. Embossed brass is fixed on bamboo pieces to make decorative containers called *palang* for liquor and other liquids. Traditionally designed chain brooches (*koma*), pendants and earrings are made of gold, silver, or a combination of these two metals. The production, however, is limited. The same high skill is seen in the metal handle of ceremonial swords. Castings of statues and bells from copper and brass are also very famous. Metal craft is widely spread throughout the country, with an organized centre located at Dechenchholing.

Wood turning

Yangtse in Tashigang district is one of the most famous places for Bhutanese lacquered wooden cups and bowls, with skilled craftsmen also found around Paro, Mongar, Wangdiphodrang, and Tongsa. Turned on foot-operated paddles, the wooden articles are given a fine finish by polishing with *sae*, a milky extract obtained from a species of the *rhus* plant. It is similar to the Japanese lacquer, *urushi*, the world famous wood-polishing agent. Wooden cups with and without silver plating are widely used for serving food, while lacquered dinner sets are becoming increasingly popular in the country.

Bamboo and cane crafts

Though a variety of bamboo and cane basket-work is manufactured almost all over the country, the famous *palang* (wine-container) and *bangchung* (food-container) come from Dagor in Shemgang and some areas of Mongar district. To this day in Bhutan, woven cane and bamboo containers are used as house-hold utensils in the remote villages, but in the towns they serve more as decoration pieces and souvenirs. These items are popular among tourists and have great export potential. Bamboo hats, lamp-shades, butter containers, tea strainers, and curd containers are manufactured mostly around Wangdiphodrang for commercial purposes. Getana, under Chimakothi sub-division, is well-known for its basket and winnowers.

Textile products

Handloom weaving is the most important and widely-spread craft in Bhutan. Fabrics of narrow width with highly organized and compact patterns are woven on loin looms, mostly for traditional garments, such as the *gho* worn by men and the *kira* worn by women. The colours are often derived from vegetable dyes. While Bumthang and Thimphu specialize in woollen products, silk products are woven around Tashingang and Mongar. Cotton-based products are woven in Kurtey and other districts. Vast possibilities exist for the design of high-class fashion garments. Furnishings and linen, based on Bhutan's unique textiles, have good export potential.

Shoulder bags are made out of cloth specially woven for that purpose. Woollen blankets are woven and used as wrappers as well as for floor coverings.

A few typical hand-woven fabrics of Bhutan are:

1. *Yatha* (thick multi-coloured woollen fabric) to be used for making jackets and over-coats;
2. *Matha* (woven from finely-twisted woollen and cotton yarns in check patterns, maroon being the predominant colour) to be used for *gho* and *kira*;
3. *Setha* (patterned in checks, but with orange as the predominant colour) to be used for *gho* and *kira*;
4. *Phyanab* (woven from natural black wool, thick in structure and considered good for health) to be used for *gho* and *kira* by the older people.

A fabric called *khezi* is made from yak hair and used exclusively for making bags because of its unbelievable resistance. It is woven in stripes of natural white and black and can be used for making carpets and travel bags.

Strong rope is made from the hair collected from the yak's tail.

Handmade paper

The traditional craft of making paper by hand developed during the time of Shabdrung Ngawang Namgyal, a period which saw the development of scripture in Bhutan. Subsequently, the craft spread throughout the country, and the home-made paper was used for copying mantras and religious teachings. This paper, which is available in three varieties, is still used today in remote areas for the preservation of important documents and the printing of religious figures for worship. It is also used for making strong envelopes, and for wrapping gifts. Tongsa, Paro, Tashigang, Kurtey, and Bumthang are among the places in the country where the craft of making paper is still practised.

Batik

Homage to Indonesian Batik

Batik has become a household word in today's world. Many forms of surface textile design have been labelled with the name batik. Although upon closer scrutiny only a few of them are produced through the true wax process which from olden times was known as batik.

The word batik itself comes from the root *tik* meaning drop or droplet in the Malayo-Polynesian language family. Droplets or drops of wax are applied to textiles, mostly natural fibres such as cotton and silks. The essence of batik making is the use of wax or other dy-resistant material to cover parts of the cloth not to be given particular colour.

Various instruments are used to scoop up the wax. In Indonesia the most popular instrument used for handdrawn batik is the *canting*, a copper spout placed on a small bamboo stem. The liquid wax then flows out on the material.

To many Indonesian who really appreciate the beauty of true batik, handdrawn batik is the only type of batik that merits the label "batik", in spite of the fact that subsequently in order to meet the demand for more mass produced batik the *cap*, copper block was invented.

The origins of batik

The debate about the origins of batik still goes on. Various theories have been launched, some of them mentioning Ancient Egypt and China as the lands of birth, next to theories that defend the Indian subcontinent as the source.

Whatever the origin of batik may be, it is on the small island of Java in the Indonesian Archipelago that the art of batik reached its highest peak of development and refinement.

To the people of Java batik does not just mean a piece of cloth or an article of dress, it is the embodiment of Javanese life and philosophy.

The batik artisans of Java drew their inspiration from various parts of life, creating patterns and motifs that were closely connected with other sections of Javanese culture.

In Indonesia batik was and is essentially a people's art, traditionally done by women — although some exceptions exist — either privately in the home or collectively in small workshops.

The princely families of Java on the other hand played a vital role in encouraging and sustaining the art of batik, acting as "tastemakers" constantly refining and correcting patterns.

They were true "patrons" of the art of batik, this then explains why the variety of batik patterns is staggering. Court ceremonies, religious occasions and even magic was attributed or connected with certain patterns of batik.

Interrelationship of the art of batik with other aspects of Javanese cultural life

Among the important preservers of batik patterns were the puppeteers or puppet makers, who through the shadow play or *wayang* brought drama and religion to life. The *dalangs* or puppetmakers designed patterns on pieces of leather, perforating them with sharp knives and subsequently selling them to batikers in the market. Charcoal powder was then blown through the leather into the cloth creating patterns for the batik-maker to follow.

Protocol at the Court of Java played an important role in the development of batik patterns. Certain motifs such as the Majestic "Parang Rusak Barong" were traditionally regarded as sacred, used only for the Ruler's magnificent ceremonial robes or as part of offerings to the spirits of royal ancestors.

It is also still a popular belief that the wearing of a certain design can ward off illness; another could bring luck and good fortune to the wearer, particularly a bridal couple on their wedding day.

Certain other designs were reserved for the Palaces and the rank and origin of the wearer determined the design he wore, more or less like the Tartans of the Clans of Scotland.

Cultural influences on batik patterns

Each batik centre in Java has its own favourite patterns and colour combinations and it is especially the colours that differentiate one region style from the other.

The Royal capitals of Yogyakarta and Surakarta in Central Java mostly use colours that are dark brown, blue and white or cream, while the batiks of Cirebon, a north west coastal town of West Java with a style of its own favours patterns like clouds, rocks, gardens and animals against a rich ivory-coloured background.

The small coastal towns of the North Javanese shore were closely associated with Chinese immigrants and their batiks show the highly decorative bird and flower patterns in colours like pinks, yellows and blues showing clear Chinese influence. At the beginning of this Century a group of Dutch women set up their own batik enterprises in various parts of Java. The batiks they produced were meant to be worn by women of European descent and thus reflected the taste and colour sense of Europeans. The batiks they produced incorporated "new" motifs taken from the flora and fauna of Europe.

Even figures from European fairy tales came to be drawn on sarongs for these Dutch ladies. It was therefore not unusual to encounter Little Riding Hood or the Sleeping Beauty on batik cloth. The use of chemical dyes imported from Europe enabled them to make a vastly wider range of colours.

Categories of batik design

There are two main categories of batik design; those based on geometric motifs and the free form designs based on stylization of natural forms and symbols.

Among the geometric designs the most popular are the kawung, an ancient design consisting of touching or intersecting circles; the ceplok, a general name for a whole of series of geometric designs based on squares, rhombus, circles, stars, etc. Although fundamentally geometric, ceploks can also be abstractions and stylizations of flowers, buds, seeds and sometimes even animals; the lereng patterns which consist of slanting parallels diagonal bands there are many variations of this basic striped patterns.

The free form designs known generally as semen, range over a bewildering variety of patterns. Here the batiker has greater freedom, and provided certain basic rules are observed, a considerable degree of improvisation is allowed. The common element is the use of leaf-like tendrils for the background.

Sometimes the design consists of only leaves or buds. Others depict animals or insects on a background of leaves and buds. Today's batik patterns have evolved from the more free form semen concept. It has already been mentioned how patterns from Europe, mostly flower and bird motifs have entered the field of traditional batik design. Another new influence was the use of patterns based on motifs from weavings from areas outside Java such as Sumatra, Borneo, Celebes and East Indonesia. In the constant search for new patterns linked with the diversification of the use of batik material, even the use of human figures as batik design was introduced.

In the past the advent of Islam affected the development of batik design in the sense that it prohibited the depiction of all kinds of forms of human life. As a result the batik designers were forced to try and find a way around this prohibition. The obvious solution was extreme stylization and abstractions. This now is not the case any more. Since the late fifties increasingly realistic patterns have come into fashion. Today one even sees Balinese dancers as well as heroes from the Ramayana and Mahabharata epic batiked in three dimensional form.

Current and future trends in batik designs in Indonesia

The invention of the *canting cap* — a copper stamp used to apply wax — put batik production on a semi-industrial basis. This development has further been followed by the use of screens in the process of screen printing batik patterns, eliminating entirely the use of wax in the production process.

The decline of the finely hand-drawn batik is the inevitable result of this competition. Many batik makers are compelled to speed up their work and coarsen the colours, even the imperfections of the craft have now become desired effects.

On the other hand, the new diversification of the uses of batik material has given the batik industry a shot in the arm.

While the traditional materials were cotton and silk, now batik manufacturers and batik designers are experimenting with different kinds of materials, including wools, voiles and manmade fibres. Batik is now used as wall decorations, household items and linens, a departure from the limited use of the cloth for just clothing apparel.

The use of chemical dyestuffs has opened the horizons for new colours and shades, making the steeping process far quicker and simpler. A disadvantage is of course the rapid decrease in the use of vegetable dyes.

As far as patterns are concerned, next to the creation of entirely new patterns based on non-Javanese motifs, there is a clear tendency to preserve ancient designs, be it in another proportion. The batiks of today in Indonesia use larger proportioned patterns. This is of course a result of the fact that the finer and smaller patterns are more laborious to make but also a clear indication that the personality of Indonesians — in particular Indonesian women — has changed. Indonesian batiks nowadays are meant to be noticed and reflect the more assertive personality to the wearer.

With the introduction of batik for Western style apparel, new arrangements of patterns and design are incorporated. The adjustment of batik patterns to requirements of dress cutting is now a common thing. The usual length of traditional batik of $2\frac{1}{2}$ metres has now been abandoned. Materials presently come up to about 30 metres.

With all these new developments nevertheless, one cannot deny that today, fine quality hand-drawn batiks, whether in the original forms or new variety of uses, are very expensive and their production limited. It is hoped therefore that in a world dominated by machine, there still will be an interest in crafts, and batiks. This interest will encourage Indonesians and foreign audiences to preserve and revive this ancient handicraft, which incorporated a whole way of life, to which Indonesians should be a most cherished treasure.

Batik in Singapore

Batik, the art of printing on fabrics with the dye-resist method using wax, is popularly believed to have come to Singapore from Indonesia via Malaysia.

Up to date leading manufacturers in Singapore have looked to Kelantan and Trengganu, the states on the East Coast of Malaysia, for their skilled workers and acknowledge that the traditional Singapore patterns are inspired by the block prints of Malaysia rather than the hand-painted delicate, intricate designs of Indonesia.

Yet, history has it that the art or rather, craft of batik came to Singapore first from Java in 1920s or by 1930 at latest, according to Constance Sheares, formerly of the National Museum, who wrote a book on Batiks in Singapore.

The Singapore batik industry had manufactured block-printed batik till the advent of Japanese force in 1942 when all the textile factories were made to produce loin cloths for the entire Japanese force in Singapore and the Malayan Peninsular.

The industry then transferred itself to Kota Bahru in Kelantan and later to Trengganu, both of which are now the centres for batik manufacturing in Malaysia. After the War, textile factories in Singapore concentrated on the weaving of fabrics from imported silk and cotton yarn. A revival of batik occurred in 1971 when factories, hit by the rising cost of raw materials, began reverting to the production of batik. Some enterprising young Singaporeans, inspired by the vogue the craft enjoyed in Europe and Australia began experimenting with the craft unhampered by traditional notions of set styles or methods.

Today the batik industry in Singapore, though not a major one, is outstanding for its emphasis on innovation and creativity rather than on carrying on an ancient time-honoured craft. A few major factories concentrate on the export market while there are a few back-yard type family establishments in villages which churn out ready-to-wear batik clothes for the local market at very reasonable prices.

Ready-to-wear batiks mark the major difference in Singapore-made batiks. They are seldom, if ever, made in the set Yardages for the sole purpose of use as *sarongs*, the wrap around traditional skirts of Indonesia and Malaysia which are worn with a blouse. Besides manufacturing batik in fabric form, to be made up into garments, Singapore-made batiks are associated with made-up garments with the batik designs fitted specifically to the design of the garments. In such cases, the designs are printed on after the garment has been sewn up and this style of garment has gained popularity because of its made-to-order look.

S.A. Shahab and Co. Pte. Ltd., perhaps Singapore's largest batik manufacturer, echoes the progress of batik in Singapore. Started in 1930 as a weaving factory, it began experimenting with batiks in 1968 with the aid of two women who introduced their ideas of design to the management.

Converting to batik in 1971, the factory catered mainly to the local market till 1977 when it became entirely export oriented. Today, 95 percent of its products are sent to markets in Europe, America and now, Africa, while only five percent finds its way to the local market. The factory produces both fabrics and ready-to wear garments in equal proportions. While "traditional" Malay motifs and bright colours are still used sometimes, the designs are characterized by an untraditional freedom of movement and are unconstrained by set ideas of what should be. Geometric designs are popular as are distinctive flower motifs.

According to Mr. Sarkasi Said, one of Singapore's leading batik artists, who now hand paints fabric lengths for garments on an exclusive basis, this lack of constraint is the strength of Singapore-made batiks. He said: "I trained in Indonesia under the famous artist Affendi. Though my methods are meticulously traditional, as are those employed by our batik manufacturers, my designs are abstract and influenced more by the *avant garde* in the international world of art, than by traditional Indonesian or Malaysian designs. "You could say that my batiks are more creative efforts rather than examples of craftsmanship. And my creativity reflects the excitement of life in Singapore. "Being at the crossroads of several cultures, our works also reflect the influences of many cultures."

Sarkasi is perhaps the man who produces the highest quality batiks in Singapore since he insists on personally designing and hand-painting each piece of fabric. His works are of course more expensive than those produced at the factory level and are marketed through My Souvenir Shop and the Singapore Handicraft Centre. Encouraged by general interest in his fabrics, he says: "I am thinking of going into export but of course not in large quantities. I would like to appeal to the exclusive market and am considering training a few craftsmen to execute my designs, all of which are signed with the name Yangtze, my own label name."

Another batik artist who has gone into manufacturing is Seah Kim Jool. He is concentrating on larger-scale industry and produced block-printed batik for garments, household linen, and even souvenir items like hats, key chains and wallets. All the blocks are designed by Mr. Seah himself and the factory called Singapore Batik Manufacturers, employs designers for the garments.

Unlike the batik produced in surrounding countries, there is no distinctive design or colour used in Singapore batiks.

Each manufacturer lets his imagination run freely and ideas come from all over the world. Shahab Weaving Factory for example, employs an European designer based in Germany as a consultant. She travels to Singapore twice a year and in the meantime, she studies the trends of fashion in Europe and sends over her designs for the garments and fabrics.

"I don't think any other country is ahead of us when it comes to keeping in step with fashion," says Mrs. Gek See, a housewife-turned manufacturer who markets under the label of Crazy Tracy. She concentrates exclusively in producing ready-to-wear garments, printing on the designs after the garments have been made up. She says: "I depend a lot on the high quality of the garment industry in Singapore. We comply with international standards and there is no problem finding people who will make up the garments in special designs."

Mr. Kareem S. Khadaied, the Marketing Executive of Shahab Weaving Factory said: "The batik industry in Singapore has the backing of a well-developed garment industry and our port and banking facilities are unequalled." He added that the lack of restrictions on the import of fabrics means that batik manufacturers in Singapore can choose the best fabrics to produce fashion goods acceptable in even the most discriminating of department stores. The fabrics used for batiks are mainly cottons and voiles.

"We offer commercialised batik which is within international standards in terms of sewing, dye-resist and colour fastness and yet it comes within the definition of hand printing." said Mr. Kareem. The marketing strategy is modernised as are the designs, fabrics used and sewing methods, but the method of producing batiks in Singapore remains faithfully traditional.

"We do not mind changing and modernising as long as it does not compromise the quality," said Mr. Kareem.

Our manufacturers still use the traditional method of dye-resist by wax and the chops themselves are made by master craftsmen from Kelantan or Trengganu. The actual chopping of the wax is still done on a bed of pliable banana stalk, the printed cloth is then immersed into a prepared dye bath and the process may be repeated several times, depending on how many colours are to be used. While production is streamlined as far as possible, the process of batik manufacturing is still very personalised with workers enjoying freedom of movement as they do not work in production lines.

Batik in Singapore looks towards the future to meeting the fashion needs of tomorrow's world.

Batik Art in Sri Lanka

Five hundred and forty-three years before the birth of Christ, Prince Vijeya from the Indian subcontinent met Kuvana, a Queen of ancient Sri Lanka, "seated under a tree, spinning as a hermit-woman might". Throughout the twenty-five intervening centuries of this country's kaleidoscopic past, there has been no dearth of evidence of the colourful attire with which her inhabitants bedecked themselves and ornamented their places of residence. The early methods and techniques of designing and dyeing and preparation of materials have been lost in the mist of history, but the perfected art form remains enshrined in the genius of her people and in the traditional image which permeates the mind of her artists and craftsmen in every bustling town and remote, drowsy village.

At what period of ancient history the systems of batik manufacture came into use is not known. Certainly batik did exist in a primitive form in very early times when resist-methods and techniques were undoubtedly the *mode d'emploi* in the preparation of ensembles to adorn royalty and the unnumbered thousands of exponents of ancient indigenous dance forms which found expression all over this picturesque island.

There is room to consider Chinese and Egyptian influence when one remembers that Sri Lanka in pre-Christian times was a trading outpost on the ancient Silk Route stretching from China to West Asia, and we know for certain that the Phoenicians, Greeks and Romans reached this emporium of trade with their merchandise. Old batiks have been found in Egypt, and there is even the conjecture that waxing techniques are likely to have originated in China. The paintings of garments depicted by the fresco figures of India's Ajanta have decorative motifs known to have been batik influenced, and the related sixth century frescoes of Sri Lanka at Sigiriya can also make a somewhat tenuous claim for common characteristics. Fifteenth-century Chinese references to the people of Sri Lanka indicate that Indonesian textiles were used even to add colour to the coiffures of both men and women.

As in every other country, religion formed the vehicle for the expression of art in Sri Lanka, and the great Buddhistic tradition of the faithful gave craftsmen wide scope for their variegated artistic endeavours. The numerous Buddhist temples which punctuate every village in this island of 25,000 square miles are repositories for art in its many forms — and textured and designed fabrics are no exception. The artist seeks every vestige of inspiration to re-vitalize our contemporary life, and in doing so he grapples with the fluidity of art embodied in his religious thinking.

Today, in a mechanised, commercially competitive world, the Sri Lanka batik artist searches for the residual aesthetic traditions in his people's intuitive longings and translates them into expressions where they find a place of eminence in the world of art. However, he is very much alive to the fact that craftsmanship in batik has to meet contemporary demands.

Decorative techniques have to be used that allow batik manufacture to satisfy and serve both ornamental and utilitarian work-a-day purposes. In the modern batiks of Sri Lanka, to some extent traditional colour preferences have been systematically maintained. The influence of temple, cave and fresco paintings pervade most items which have received acclaim and won encomiums at exhibitions of batik art held in many of the world's capitals. A common characteristic of the Sri Lanka batik is the well-defined central motif amidst a tastefully-blended surround of conventional Sinhala decor. This is essentially an indigenous factor and is easily identified when placed alongside the crowded composite productions of other Asian countries..

Of late there has been a dramatic change from the ultra-traditional to the most modern in design appeal. It has been a privilege and a joy to introduce into the world of batik a variety of both stylized and natural figurations of the fauna and flora of Sri Lanka. Ours is a small country, and when one realises that the export potential of batik art is greater and broader in compass than the narrow confines of our shores, the need to satisfy the connoisseurs of the affluent countries has to be taken into consideration. This does not for a moment mean that we are bargaining our traditions for a mess of pottage or that we are forsaking the traditional norms of our indigenous art, but that we are using non-traditional patterns and motifs as vectors to carry our basic artistic talent into the appreciative lap of the batik-loving world.

Unlike other Batik-producing countries, Sri Lanka has had the courage and is sufficiently bold to adapt and change colours and themes while retaining the purity of her techniques. A decade ago, we were mainly concerned with wall-hangings and simple items of decorative outfits. Today we are applying the art and craft of batik to the most fashionable trends in haute couture. And we are striking new ground. Batiks from Sri Lanka are now creeping into the homes and villas and salons of the Western world in the form of furnishings and household apparel, and they are being designed in such a way as to blend subtly and tastefully with their settings. Furthermore, there is another direction to be considered. Today the trend towards modern art has to be complemented by furnishings which have a surrealistic emphasis. Pattern-pieces have to be worked out both for their flowing line arrangements and their coercive abruptness of decorative design. As the outcome of a nascent trend in Sri Lanka batiks, it is possible proudly to offer three-dimensional productions that are eminently suitable for various aspects of household ornamentation. This has been made possible by evolving techniques in the application of colour and by the use of newly-devised instruments. Yet it must be borne in mind that Sri Lanka batik manufacture uses 100% wax-resist systems and does not in any way indulge in cheap labour-saving methods of direct colour application or in unreliable transfers of waxed colours. Sometimes the work is so elaborate and intricate that the finesse of the end product results in its being easily mistaken for a print and challenges close scrutiny. This is the outcome of craftsmanship of a high order which invests the Sri Lanka batik with a superiority of design-quality that excels the mass of mediocre pieces that flood the markets of Europe and the America. Sri Lanka's appealing polychrome batiks with their dominant colours set against a muted back-drop of neutral shades have spread their influence even as far as the leather trade, and today even footwear and ladies' handbags and jerkins have been caught up in this trend.

Batik-designed caparisons have been made for the ceremonial dress of elephants and for the tusker bearing the sacred receptacle of the hallowed Tooth Relic of the Buddha in the annual Perahera or religious procession held in Kandy. Costumes for stage plays are employing batik art. Religious banners and altar-cloths for Christian churches are making use of batik. Replicas of ancient flags and banners and standards of the various districts and korales are being used in batik for decorative purposes, while schools and other institutions are using batik for their banners and the ceremonial dress of their school bands. Massive pandals for the Buddhist festival of Vesak use batik emblems and patterns.

The tones and quality and intricacy of Sri Lanka batiks are thus ideally suited for inspirational themes, and these help to draw the confidence of connoisseurs who seek designed fabrics for multifarious purposes. Legendary scenes from the centuries-old epic of the Ramayana have been translated into illustrated batik friezes. The Danta-Hemamali historical episode where the Princes Hemamali brings the sacred Tooth Relic of the Buddha into Sri Lanka hidden in the dark tresses of her hair is beautifully depicted on the batik canvas. The twenty-century-old love story of the Sinhala prince Saliya who renounces and forsakes his right to the throne of Sri Lanka because of his morganatic marriage to a maiden of lowly rank, is subject matter for recent batik art. And the field has no limitations except the self-imposed restrictions and discipline in the techniques of our strict waxing systems. There is little doubt that Sri Lanka can claim a place of honour on the artistic dais which she has mounted through the sheer perseverance, inspiration and hard work of her dedicated batik artists.

Indian Batik

ost Indians believe, perhaps naturally, that the art of batik originated in their land. Like most popular beliefs, however, this is an erroneous one, for batik, as it is known to us today, has been practised in India only from a relatively recent date, 1923 to be precise.

In that year Rabindranath Tagore, on his tour of South East Asia, was impressed by the craft as practised by the Indonesians. Returning home, he sent his son Rathindranath and his daughter-in-law Protima to Indonesia to learn the craft. Even before setting foot on Indonesian soil, Protima had picked up the rudiments of batik from a Frenchman, Mieux, an artist of some merit. On their return, batik was introduced as a craft subject at Santiniketan, and Rathindranath and Protima were joined there by the renowned artist Andra Carpes and Gauridevi Bhanja. Together, they produced some very delicate batik designs on cotton and silk.

The artists at Santiniketan had no difficulty in introducing Indian motifs in the craft of wax-resist textile dipping.

All they did was to revert to the original Indian motifs and designs in place of the ones used by the Indonesians.

These were Indian in origin, and had been taken to South East Asia by Hindu merchant and Buddhist monks centuries earlier.

To quote Jeanine Auboyer, Chief Curator of the Musee Guimet in Paris, regarding the Indian influence on Indonesian cultural life "Indian culture penetrated the countries of South East Asia entirely by peaceful means. This was the result of a series of enterprises by traders, adventurers, scholars and monks.

Operating from Indian settlements that had been founded in about the first century, these men brought the highly refined culture of India to people whose way of life was perfectly suited to Brahmanic and Buddhist teachings ....

"When works of art in durable materials appear in these countries, they are already heavily influenced by Indian characteristics.... Nevertheless, it is impossible to know whether the Indian influence caused a radical change or whether it was superimposed on a pre-existent basis. It seems likely, however, that an extraordinary impetus was given to the arts by the presence of the Indians....

"Indian influence was soon assimilated and formed a basis upon which local work was undertaken... Each of the South East Asian cultures adopted the Indian forms according to its own particular character, for their art was not a slavish imitation, but genuinely creative."

This would be welcome evidence for those firm in their claim of an Indian origin for the art of batik. Their belief would be further strengthened on perusal of the comments of another authority:

"It is doubtful if any surviving batiks can be dated earlier than the second half of the eighteenth century and it is perhaps significant that most of the early pieces which do exist, for instance in the National Museum, Jakarta appear on the one hand to have been made with Indian handloom cotton, and, on the other, show conspicuous Indian influence in their floral motifs."

However, none of this is conclusive proof of the Indian origin of batik, and, there are other claimants as well. Some of the costumes discovered in the Beni Hassan tomb in Egypt (2100 BC) have on them printed designs executed apparently by the resist method used for batik. This could conceivably argue an Egyptian origin for the craft.

But whatever its origin, the present Indian tradition of batik does not go further back than 1923, and 55 years is too short a period for any art form, especially one which has only recently come to be regarded as a fine art, to evolve a national tradition.

Batik is practised only in a few isolated centres in India. In east India, the centres are Santiniketan and Calcutta; in Rajasthan, such centres may be found at Jaipur. Barmer, Jaisalmer and other districts bordering Pakistan; in west India, Bombay and the Saurashtra region of Gujarat. Kanu Nayak and J. Roy run batik schools in Bombay. Vijaya Heremuth, Savitri Sattar and Savitri Sonia are other well-reputed artists of the city, who have exhibited both at home and abroad. Among the prominent practitioners of the craft in north and east India are Gauridevi Bhanja at Santiniketan, Devayani Krishna in New Delhi and the present writer in Lucknow. The prominent artists of south India are Vasudev and P. Paramsivam, who work at Cholamandalam.

The technique used by batik makers all over India is the same — the wax-resist method borrowed from the Javanese practitioners of the craft. It is only in the Barmer and Jaisalmer region of Rajasthan that a special local clay is used. This is obtained from small pools which dry up in the summer to leave on their beds a spongy layer of mud and dead insects.

The spongy clay is mixed with lime, soap and gum to make a thick paste, which is used as a "resist" and transferred to the textile's surface by wooden blocks. In earlier days, vegetable dyes were used for Rajasthan batiks, but since they now fetch good prices and are produced on a large scale, chemical dyes are used.

Batik has become a craze in India and Indian batik has found markets abroad.

Some of the leading Indian batik artists, most of whom are women are, Geeti Bhattacharya, Ina Mitra, Vasudeva, Prabha Panwar, Arnawoz and S. Paramesivam. While they have chosen many different subjects for their art, they have shown special favour to the Indian gods and goddesses and to folk heroes. Batik designs at Santiniketan were in the main inspired by folk motifs and decorations used in the Ajanta murals and the great Indian temples.

Close-up of a Batik cap, Indonesia.

Part 12

Myths, Superstitions and Heavenly Bodies

An early Chinese stone-rubbing showing one of the ten suns crossing the heavens from the east to the west.

Myths, Superstitions and Heavenly Bodies

Iranian Homage to the Sun and Moon

In modern Persian folk-literature there is a story entitled 'Prince Leo the Renowned' (*Amir Arsalan e Namdar*). It relates the adventures of a prince who falls in love with the portrait of a princess in Byzantium (or *Rum*, as the Eastern Roman Empire was known to Moslems). The story follows the pattern of the *Thousand and One Nights* in that the Chief Story-teller of the Court used to make up and narrate the tales every night to put Nasereddin Shah to sleep. The story is full of anachronisms. Many of the scenes and characters in disguise are contemporaries of the author who lived in nineteenth century Iran, but descriptions in the story betray the little knowledge he had of the European surroundings of that century with touches of medieval life.

During his adventures in quest of the princess, the hero of the story gets involved with two ministers of the king. They are called the Vizier Sun and the Vizier Moon. The former is a man of good character, true and faithful, and tries to help the prince in his quest. The Vizier Moon, however, is an evil, treacherous villain.

The story as we have it is a century old, but on some levels it draws on older material, among them possibly the characters Sun and Moon. But in classical Persian literature we do not find any evil attributes of the moon, although the sun, as giver of light and life, is considered more beneficent to mankind than the moon. Perhaps the darkness of the night that surrounds the moon suggests dark elements that may affect its nature — hence the evil character of the Vizier Moon who contrives to carry out his treacherous plans mainly in the dark of the night.

Otherwise, both the sun and the moon represent beauty and goodness in Persian language and literature. Dozens of compounds, such as moon-face, describe the beauty of the beloved both in prose and poetry. The most common and the highest expression of beauty is 'the moon of the fourteenth night' — the full moon. And the crescent moon is likened to the beloved's eyebrow. The handsomeness of the male is usually described by the sun, though the sun more often represents high rank, generosity and prowess. Thus the sun is more related to male, and the moon to feminine, aspects of beauty.

Only once in a winter folk-song we find the sun addressed as a woman:

O, Lady Sun, pour forth your light!
Spread out a handful of rice!
We are the children of wolves,
We are dying of cold!

Numerous names, male and female, are formed in compounds with sun or moon. However, in representations of the sun in folk-art, the disc is shown with eyes, eyebrows, nose and mouth and no moustache, which may represent a female face or perhaps a young boy. In poetry the sun is described as the 'Bride of the World', and is likened to a Golden Egg, or a Golden Lamp, and to a Cock with Golden Wings.

Going back to ancient Iran, we find ourselves in quite a different world. Sun and Moon are divine entities to whom are dedicated hymns of praise and adoration. Epithets such as shining, radiant, immortal and 'possessing swift horses' are attributed to the Sun. Sacred horses and chariots, even temples were dedicated to the Sun, and the rising sun was worshipped. The solar deity presides over the eleventh day of the month and is celebrated in the first Niyayesh (or hymn of praise) in the Avesta. Among Iranian Scythians sacred horses were sacrificed to the Sun. The sacred character of the two luminaries is further indicated in the oath formula in the *Book of Kings*: "By the Sun and the Moon, by the Crown and the Throne!"

The lunar deity presides over the twelfth day of the month, and is praised as the giver of reward, wealth and cattle, with the epithets wealth-possessing, the bestower, skilful and healing, and with the chief epithet 'having the seed of the kine' (the kine symbolizing all living beings). On coins he is represented as a male deity, wearing a diadem, girded with a sword, holding a scepters with a crescent behind his shoulders. The Moon is thus celebrated in the third Niyayesh in the Avesta:

Homage to the Moon that keeps in it the seed of the kine!
Homage to thee when we look at thee!
Homage to thee when thou lookest at us!
Give us strength and victory!
Give us welfare in cattle and in bread!
Give us a multitude of children, Steadfast and chiefs in assemblies,
Who vanquish and are not vanquished,
Who smite at one stroke their adversaries,
Who smite at one stroke their foes,
Ever in joy and ready to help!

The prominence of heavenly bodies and phenomena led to many superstitions some of which persist to the present day. In connection with astrological beliefs and superstitions, certain hours, days, months and even years (in the twelve-year cycles) are considered lucky or unlucky. Instructions to take up an enterprise or to avoid embarking on one on certain days of the week, or in certain months (particularly lunar months), or predictions of conditions and events (specially ominous ones) were given in old-fashioned calendars which are still published. Of special concern is the time when the moon enters the constellation of Scorpion. Instructions are also given as to the objects one must look at when one sees the new moon for the first time each month. According to one account the following twelve objects are recommended for the twelve lunar months: gold, a mirror, water, cattle, silver, a respectable man, a holy book, a rose, a sword, greens, a child, and a beautiful girl, and commonly a horse and turquoise. After looking at the object one asks God a favour.

The relation of the heavenly bodies with time-reckoning and the calendar is of course universal. From very ancient times the Iranians used both the lunar and the solar calendars. The solar year of 365 days was used for religious purposes so that the auspicious days may revolve around the natural seasons to bless every day of the astronomical year. On the other hand, for astronomical purposes, to catch up with the natural seasons, one day was intercalated in every four years, or one month in every 120 years.

To return to the ancient worship of the pantheon of heavenly bodies, we should take notice of the reforms of Zoroaster in the eighteenth century BC (as indicated by recent research). Zoroaster with his spiritual religion and Ahura Mazda, the Wise Lord, as the supreme God, left no room for the ancient deities. He no longer pays religious homage to the Sun and the Moon as divine objects. He reveres the sun and its earthly counterpart Fire which he recognizes as the symbol of purity and as offspring of the Wise Lord. But after Zoroaster the ancient gods gradually crept in, and the new syncretism revived their cults, albeit in subordination to Ahura Mazda. Sasanian emperors (AD third to seventh century) who promoted Zoroastrianism to state religion and proclaimed themselves Mazda worshippers, continued to pay homage to the gods of the ancient pantheon. They even claimed descent from the gods and placed their royal rank on a level with the sun. The disc of the sun and the crescent moon were adopted as the imperial insignia. This insignia was the sacred symbol of the secular power and at the same time had a religious significance. The sun or the crescent moon was set on the top of the domes of temples and shrines and on the crowns of the arches of religious monuments. The tradition was so deep-rooted that it has persisted to the present day. The disc of the sun with rays, or the crescent moon appear on the top of the spires of domes on Islamic shrines and mosques.

On the crown of the archivolt of Taq-e-Bostan near Kermanshah we see the crescent moon set in an undulating scarf, the ends of which flutter like the fillets seen in portraits of Sasanian emperors. The motif represents the diadem of the emperors where both the fluttering scarf and the crescent are portrayed. Sasanian coins also show the emperor wearing a crown which consisted of a diadem with the fluttering ribbons and the crescent moon. The addition of a star in the crescent on the crown, with crescents and stars on the rims of the coins is significant. The symbol of crescent and star also appears on early Islamic coinage which imitates the Sasanian coins and has since been adopted as a badge on flags of Moslem countries such as Turkey and Pakistan. The Iranian flag carries the disc of the sun with rays rising behind the back of a lion. The lion was the insignia of the Achaemenian emperors, although the emblem on the Iranian flag may represent an astronomical date: the sun in the constellation Leo.

It is interesting that the moon has played a role as an instrument of miracles. One such instance is the case of the miracle-monger Hashem the Moqanna (the veiled), known as the 'Veiled Prophet of Khorasan' and celebrated by Moore in *Lalla Rookh*. This heresiarch revolted against Islam and the Caliph in Merv, in northeastern Iran, during the third quarter of the eighth century AD He used to veil himself in green silk or a mask of gold, as his enemies claimed, to cover his hideous aspect with one eye, or as his followers believed, to cover the dazzling effulgence of his divine countenance. He had proclaimed himself the incarnation of God, and had gathered around himself large crowds of believers. He defeated several armies of the Caliph and ruled large areas in Kharazm and Soghd during fourteen years. He killed those who opposed him and delivered their property and women to his followers. As narrated by Moslem historians, he had revived the communist Mazdakite movement and made his laws obligatory for his followers.

Finally, he was besieged in his castle with his companions and defeated. When he found himself surrounded on all sides and saw that death was inevitable, he burned himself in fire so that his body might be annihilated as a confirmation of his claim to be God as well as to convince his followers that he had disappeared and would return again.

His claim was supported by a false moon which he caused to rise from a well in Nakhshab — hence its name in literature as the 'Moon of Nakhshab'. The moon was visible for miles around. As the fame of the miracle was spread abroad multitudes of people flocked to Nakhshab to see the moon. Men were thus deceived and thought they were looking at the image of a real moon. After his defeat and death it was rumoured that a great bowl had been discovered at the bottom of the well, filled with quicksilver, from which he succeeded through his knowledge of magic and incantations to make the false moon rise night after night.

So we bring our survey of the story of the moon to a close with the magical moon of the veiled Prophet of Khorasan.

Deities of Sun and Moon in Indian Mythology

The Sun and the Moon as two of the Nine Planets as well as individual deities govern almost all the aspects of life of the Indians since times immemorial. The best form of blessing among the Hindus is to say 'May your life and glory be as permanent as the Sun and the Moon'. From early times the routine of life was governed by the solar and lunar positions, movements, phases and interplanetary conjunctions. The Hindu calendar is basically lunar but incorporates the important solar movements as well. Since both the luminaries enjoy strong individual positions in the mythology, art and rituals of the Indians, separate sections are being devoted to each.

The sun

Considering the cultic significance, the centrality of worship at all levels of the population, the antiquity and continuity of iconography and ritual, the multiple shrines devoted to him and the variety and bulk of mythology that exists about him, the Sun receives perhaps the highest honour in Indian culture. Already prehistoric man in India had started to recognise the power of mystery behind the Sun and had started to venerate this vital source of creation and all energy. One of the earliest and most interesting depictions of the Sun is found on a neolithic stone slab excavated from Burzahom in Kashmir. The scene consists of two hunters hunting a stag under two suns shining in the sky. The two suns are interpreted by mythologists as representing the day of the hunt and the day of successful return. The Sun was also considered, by early man, to be the Great Hunter and the Great Spirit. The imagination of the Aryan sage poets of the Rig Veda (c. 1800 BC) was so dazzled by this luminary that they described him as the soul of this world, all knowing god, illuminator of worlds, god of gods. They prayed to him: 'Let us meditate on that excellent glory of the divine vivifier; May he enlighten our understanding'.

In the Vedic period (c. 1800 to 600 BC) the Sun was called by different names depending upon his functions. When in visible form he was called Surya and when invisible he was Savitr. The Sun is also known as Aditya since his mother was called 'Aditi', the 'primordial vastness'. Already in the Vedic period mention is made of twelve Adityas or twelve forms of the Sun which are also twelve solar deities corresponding to the twelve months of the year. The twelve Adityas are variously named in different literary traditions. According to the tradition of the *Purana* literature (c. 400 BC to AD 500) as preserved in Brahma Purana, in his Indra form the Sun is the lord of the gods, in his Dhata form he creates material things, in his Parjanya form he is the rains, in his Tvstr form he pervades the living bodies, in Pushan form he provides nutrition, in Aryaman form he provides merit to sacrifices, in his seventh form he is the alms giver, in his Vivasvan form he ensures digestion, in his Vishnu form he destroys demons, in his Anshuman form he protects the vital organs, in his Varuna form he resides in waters and in his Mitra form he lives in the orb of the moon and protects the three worlds. In addition to being a presiding deity of each of the twelve months, the Sun is also one of the Nine Planets which are Ravi (Sun), Soma (Moon), Mangala (Mars), Budha (Mercury), Brihaspati (Jupiter), Shukra (Venus), Shani (Saturn), Rahu and Ketu (waxing and waning phases of the Moon).

According to a legend found in Vishnu Purana, the Sun was married to Sangna, the daughter of the maker of this Universe. After a long period of living together Sangna left him as she could not bear his brilliance. When she left, her shadow Chhaya was left behind whom the Sun mistook for his wife Sangna. One day the truth dawned on the Sun that Chhaya was not his real wife. By using his divine powers the Sun found out that his wife had become a mare. Upon making this discovery he became a horse and lived with her. Finally the father of Sangna reduced the brilliance of the Sun, and fashioned from the detached piece weapons of different gods. The couple lived happily together ever after.

Chandogya Upanishad beautifully explains the reason why the birds and other creatures sing in joy at sunrise and sunset. It says that at the time of creation the primordial 'world-egg' was divided into two parts, namely the silver part and the golden part. The silver part became the earth and the golden part heaven. The egg shells became the mountains. The inner part of the shells became the clouds, The veins formed the rivers and streams. The egg liquid became the oceans. But it was deadly cold everywhere. As soon as the Sun appeared, for the first time, there was warmth and pleasure and all creatures cried and sang out of joy. Since then the birds cry and sing at every sunrise and sunset.

Already in the Rig Veda the Sun is described as travelling in a chariot dragged by seven horses or mares. Inside the chariot the Sun sits on a lotus pedestal. The chariot is said to be driven by Aruna, the Dawn. His chariot has only one wheel. From early times the image of Surya or the Sun was conceived in anthropomorphic form. Many features of his appearance contained in literary descriptions have contributed to the development of his iconography. He is portrayed as the golden being having a golden beard and golden hair. His body colour is brown-red and his stature dwarfish. He has a lotus in each hand and wears armour and carries a shield. He wears a crown and has a halo of light behind his head.

The south Indian anthropomorphic images of the Sun show him with both his hands lifted up to the shoulders carrying half blossomed lotuses. In the north Indian images the hands are shown hanging straight or folded only at right angles and holding fully blossomed lotuses. In some images he is shown seated, whereas in others he is standing. In many images his chariot of seven horses is also depicted.

Temples exclusively devoted to the Sun are found all over India. The most famous Sun temples include the temple at Modhera in Gujarat (eleventh century), the temple at Martand in Kashmir (eighth century), the temple at Suryanarkoyil at Tanjore (twelfth century) and the temple at Konarak in Orissa (thirteenth century). Of these the most formidable, elaborate, famous and beautiful is the Sun Temple at Konarak in Orissa. The stone temple is in the form of a large chariot of the Sun god having twelve pairs of wheels which in all probability represent the twelve Adityas (corresponding to the twelve months of the Hindu calendar). Seven galloping horses are carved on the sides of the temple in groups of three and four respectively. The outer walls of the temple are richly carved. The Sun god Surya has been allotted a high status in Buddhist mythology and art too. In the Bhaja Cave Monasteries of the Buddhists (second century BC) in the Western Ghats, south of Bombay, the Sun god is shown driving across the sky in his horse-driven chariot. The Sun god here does not represent the Vedic deity but is a symbol of Buddha who removed the darkness of ignorance by the brilliance of his knowledge. Another example of Surya representing Buddha is found in a relief sculpture of a railing pillar at Bodh Gaya (c. 100 BC). Here the god is shown driving in a chariot with horses and accompanied by Ushas, the goddesses of dawn who are shown shooting arrows at the demons of darkness. It is difficult to say whether the pre-existing concept of the Sun travelling in a horse-drawn chariot from Babylon and Iran was straightaway adopted here or whether it grew out of the Vedic tradition.

In Buddhism the Vedic deities were either assimilated as forms of Buddha himself or as subsidiary attendants to Buddha. The Sun god, the remover of darkness, became the most apt symbol of Buddha who was the remover of the darkness of ignorance and bringer of the light of enlightenment and knowledge. For the same reason lions appear on the pedestals of the early Buddha images. The lion is the solar animal by virtue of his appearance on the banner of the Sun.

In popular religious beliefs and practices too the Sun and the Moon are considered to be symbols of permanent glory. In the memorial stones raised in honour of the dead, the image of the deceased is often shown under the Sun and the Moon. Ganesha, the elephant-headed god, is often shown flanked by the Sun and the Moon. The significance is that the glory of the image will last as long as the Sun and the Moon shine in the sky.

In Multan, now in Pakistan, there was an ancient village shrine of Aditya wherein a wooden image of the deity covered with leather and embellished with two rubies representing his eyes had existed. This was most probably a remnant of the ancient Iranian cult rather than an offshoot of the Vedic belief. In India, perhaps, the Vedic cult of the Sun, and that of Central Asia which came to India along with the Hunas and the Gujars, merged to grow into an indigenous cult. Perhaps due to this reason, in the Huna and the Gujar areas of India, i.e. Gujarat and Rajasthan, there are many old temples dedicated to this deity.

Sun worship continues to this day. The great ruler Harsha Vardhana (seventh century) worshipped the Sun in the following manner: 'Every morning after bath he wrapped himself in white silk and kneeling eastwards on the ground in a circle smeared with saffron paste, offered red lotuses placed in a vessel of ruby.' The Kshatriyas, the ancient warrior class and the Rajput rulers of medieval times, offered a horse as sacrifice to the Sun. Many hill and forest tribes worship the Sun even today as a symbol of fertility. The people belonging to the Brahmin and other higher castes worship the Sun with Gayatri Mantra, a magical stanza while venerating the Sun.

The solar year of the Hindus is divided into two parts, namely the Uttarayana, when the Sun moves from south to north, a phase auspicious for all activities, and the Dakshinayana, when he moves southwards, the unlucky phase. The south is also considered the direction of the god of death. On the day of 14th January, when the Sun starts to move towards the north, a festival in his honour is celebrated in many parts of India.

The moon

The personality of the Moon as portrayed in early Indian mythology is rather complex, multi-facetted and mysterious. The Moon does not enjoy such tremendous importance in the life and rituals of the Indians as does the Sun. There are no separate temples devoted to this heavenly body. But still the Hindu calendar remains a lunar one and all the events of daily life as well as the annual ritual cycle depend on the lunar calendar.

In the poetry of the early Vedas the Moon was identified with the Sacrificial Offering. In later Vedic mythology the Moon became known as Soma, the mysterious beverage or the intoxicating ambrosia of life used in the Brahmanical sacrifices.

The Moon is also described as the cup of the Soma drink consumed by the gods. The drink is divided into 15 portions and each day the gods drink up one portion. Due to constantly being consumed by the gods it wanes till it is filled up again by the Sun.

It is believed that the demon Rahu once disguised himself as a god and joined other gods in drinking Soma, the drink of immortality. The Moon recognised the demon Rahu and chopped off his head out of anger. But since the demon had already consumed some nectar, he could not be killed. Since then Rahu, who is also one of the planets, is depicted in art and iconography with a severed head. To avenge his grievance, Rahu always tries to grab the full cup of nectar (full Moon) and when he succeeds in doing so it is known as a lunar eclipse.

In yogic practices, Soma is identified with the substance of the Moon as well as the semen or the seed. The Moon and sexual energy are also equivalent to the substance of the mind. The Yogis try to bring their mind under control and thereby control their creative energies.

The Moon is also described as the deity of plants and vegetation in general, not only because she is the Soma plant, but also because she governs the high and low tides and therefore the elements of water. She is also the lake of rain water and governs fertility and the growth of herbs and health-giving plants. For this reason Indian farmers select the days of important farming activities such as ploughing, sowing, etc. from days during the brighter half of their lunar month.

One of the stories of the origin of the Moon is described as follows in the Puranas: Due to the curse of the sage Durvasa, Indra, the god of gods, lost all his strength. Now the gods were afraid that without Indra's strength they would be defeated by the demons. God Vishnu suggested that with the help of the demons the gods should churn the ocean. As the outcome of this cosmic churning of the ocean, the Moon also came out along with the other divine objects.

In the books of iconography, the Moon is described as an anthropomorphic deity having white complexion, wearing white clothes, and riding a chariot drawn by ten horses. In one of his hands he holds the mace and with the other he bestows protection. His chariot is driven by two chariotteers. His emblem is the antelope.

As one of the Nine Planets he is often depicted in art, in standing posture, holding two lotuses. He is known as Indu (drop of Soma), Chandra (the brilliant one) and Shashi (having a rabbit).

In the ritual cycle of the Hindus there is not much importance ascribed to the Moon except that their ritual calendar is a lunar one. The brighter half of the lunar month is supposed to be auspicious and therefore weddings and other festivals take place during the brighter half. On the other hand, the darker half is connected more with death and disease and therefore tantric or magical practices related to ghosts and spirits, including the annual appeasement of dead ancestors, occur during the darker half.

Eclipses of the Sun and the Moon are considered highly inauspicious. No new venture is started during an eclipse and all activities come to a standstill while an eclipse lasts.

Chinese Myths and Symbols of the Two Heavenly Bodies

The morning sun sheds its rays in all directions every day, dispelling darkness and illuminating every corner of the earth. At night, the bright and clear moon radiates its poetic and soft silver lights over the world. The sun and moon bring the people warmth and brightness, flowers, fruits and food crops, thus becoming the long-standing intimate companions of human beings in their lives. The Chinese nation which has a long history and a large population has created rich and interesting tales about the sun and moon, adding a glorious page to the history of Oriental culture.

From times immemorial, the sun and moon have affected people's lives in every way. Myths, legends, paintings, sculptures, world outlook, social customs, religious beliefs, national festivals, calendars and seasons — all are associated with the sun and moon.

Myths about the sun and moon

There are myths and folk tales about the origins of the sun and moon in most of the over fifty Chinese nationalities. They can be summed up as follows:

(1) Birth by Transformation. There was a tale spread far and wide among the Han people about a hero called Pan Gun who separated heaven and earth. After his death, he changed from one shape to another. His breath became wind and cloud, his voice thunderbolt; his left eye was the sun and his right eye the moon.

(2) Divine Transformation. The sun was begot by goddess Xi He and the moon by goddess Chang Xi.

(3) Manufacture. According to an old song of the Miao nationality, the sun was forged by Bao Gong and Xiong Gong; the sun was cast with gold, the moon with silver. This is a simple explanation of the fact that the sun gives out golden light and the moon silver light. Among the diverse legends about the source of the sun and moon, the She nationality's tale about Gao Xinshi creating the sun and moon is especially impressive. Ancient books recorded that Gao Xinshi was the forbear and king of many Chinese nationalities. As the She nationality's tale had it, giant Gao Xinshi created the sun and moon. He wove pine branches into a ball, lighted it and hung it in mid air and that became the sun. He used willow branches to weave a ball, ignited it and threw it into the sky and that was the moon.

Movement of the sun and the moon. Let's deal with the revolution of the sun first. The sun is the "God's favoured one," the source of the life of everything and the symbol of happiness and joy. Therefore, the Yin nationality in ancient times created out of rich imagination the myth of the sun goddess with her sons. Goddess Xi He begot 10 sons. At a place called Ganyuan outside the southeast sea, she bathed her sons with spring water every morning so that they could give out bright red rays for mankind when they were on duty by turns. After the baths, she drove a six-dragon carriage over the sky in company with her sons.

The descriptions in the "Nine Songs-Dong Jun" in Chu Ci about the movement of the sun goddess were even more mystical and wondrous. The sun goddess rose every morning in the east, and sped along in a dragon carriage, the rolling wheels of which rumbled past. Flags which were made with pink clouds fluttered in the breeze. The sun goddess, wearing a blue-sky jacket and white-rainbow trousers and a bow of the God in hand, shot down the disastrous stars and the destructive wolves, rid the people of scourge and brought them happiness. Then the Sun God ladled with the Big Dipper wine fermented with osmanthus flowers to celebrate victory. After this, he flew eastward via the other side of the earth, rising in the east the next morning.

With regard to the movement of the moon, the folk tale of the Tong nationality, "The Sun, the Moon and the Stars," is quite a relish. It said that the sun, the moon and the stars were members of the same family, related to each other as husband, wife and children. Cruel as the father was, he ate his children every morning. So, when the sun rose in the east, the sky was crimsoned with the blood of the stars. The moon, being a kind mother, moved around in the absence of the sun, She roamed the sky with her children every night.

"Kua Fu Pursues the Sun" and "Chang Ngo Goes to the Moon" are well-known myths in China. Kua Fu was a giant, a step of his equals 1,000-*li*. In a race with the sun, he exhibited the spirit that can conquer mountains and rivers. This may be an ideal of ancient people of subduing the sun and eliminating drought. When he reached the solar halo, he felt very hot and extremely thirsty. At one gulp he drank up the Weihe River water. Still, he died of thirst. His stick turned into a peach grove to entertain people of later generations with shade and sweet peaches. This demonstrated Kua Fu's lofty spirit of benefiting the people.

Chang Ngo was a beauty and wife of the legendary hero Yi. Yi asked the Queen Mother of the West for an elixir, but before he could take it, his wife took it on the sly. Then she flew with a rabbit and a bay tree to the moon where she became a fairy and the moon goddess. An old man in the moon said to her: "You've come just in time. A lamp holder is needed here". So Chang Ngo took over the job every night. The moon thenceforth became brighter and clearer.

Shooting down suns and looking for the sun have been the myths of many nationalities in China. "Yi Shoots Ten Suns" is representative of this type of myth. In the twenty-sixth century BC under the reign of Emperor Yao, ten suns were said to have appeared in the sky, scorching the crops and killing trees and plants. This brought a famine upon the people, and centaurs, wild boars, huge serpents and other monsters began to wreak havoc. Hence the story about Yi shooting down the suns. As a matter of fact, this demonstrated ancient labouring people's determination and will to conquer natural disasters. Parallel to this myth is the tale about looking for the sun.

As there were many scorching suns, it became necessary to shoot them down. Succumbing to the incomparable bravery of the hero, the last sun dared not make its appearance. But nothing on earth could live without the sun. So those with noble aspirations took great pains to find the sun and entreated him to benefit the people.

There is also an interesting story about the sun coming out at the crow of the cocks. "Why the Sun Comes out at the Crow of the Cock" was the folk tale of the Hani nationality in Yunnan Province. It was said that in ancient times nine suns came out at the same time and eight were brought down by a hero. The last one was so scared that he hid himself behind a mountain. Though orioles, skylarks and thrushes tried to invite him out by their sweet songs, they failed. Then the cocks came in, crowing with great sincerity, warmth and frankness. Moved, the sun popped out his head from behind the mountain in the east. It was only then that the world was flooded with brightness and warmth.

The sun and moon in Chinese culture and life

In Chinese custom, the sun and moon are regarded as propitious signs. In myths, epics and popular legends, the mother of a hero often dreamed of the sun and moon entering into her womb, became pregnant and gave birth to the national hero. With the development of society, the primitive worship of the sun and moon was stamped with the brand of the class. Whoever had a red naevus on his shoulder, would become an aristocrat in the future. And the naevus was named the "phase of the sun and moon". The flags of ancient emperors' guards of honour with the designs of the sun and moon were called "flags of the sun and moon." The 15th day of the 8th lunar month is the traditional Mid-Autumn Festival in China. Every household worships the moon with moon cakes as if to pray for the reunion of the family. Solar and lunar eclipses are considered by the Hand nationality as the sun or the moon being swallowed up by the Heavenly Dog. The Hans, therefore, toll bells and beat gongs to scare away the Heavenly Dog.

There were also pictures of the sun and moon painted on ancient artifacts which were buried with the dead. On the "divine part" of the silk painting excavated in No. 1 Han grave in Mawangdui, in Chang-sha, China's Hunan Province, there are nine suns on the upper right part of the painting. One sun is conspicuous. There is a crow with two feet on the painting. The crow is probably a totem in the clan society which then gradually evolves into a golden bird, representing the sun. The golden bird becomes a synonym alluding to the sun. On the upper left part of the drawing is a crescent moon in which there is also a toad and a rabbit. Under the moon sits a woman on the wing of a dragon, indicating that the soul of the grave's master has "gone to heaven".

Most of the tales of various nationalities in China venerated the sun or the moon as god. But the names for the sun and moon varied from place to place. In Taian, east China's Shandong Province, people respectfully called the sun the venerable "Grandpa", the moon the venerable "Grandma moon". People in other places called the sun "Grandad Sun" or "Grandma Sun". In Mongolian tales, people called the sun and moon "King Sun" or "King Moon." Since the time of King Yao (legendary monarch in ancient China), there already existed religious beliefs of offering sacrifices to the Sun God. Ancient books recorded that there were special officials in charge of offering sacrifices to the sun. Temples were built by feudal emperors for the Sun God and the Moon God. The Solar Palace, the Temple of Heaven, the Temple of the Sun and the Temple of the Moon in Beijing are famous arenas where sacrifices were consecrated to the Sun God and the Moon God. The religious paintings called "water-land drawings" in ancient China were used mainly for ceremonies held by Buddhists and Taoists. Most of the drawings used by Taoists contained the sun, the moon and the stars. The sun and moon are closely related to farming. Emperor Yan was called Sun God in "Baihutong-Wuxing" written by Ban Gu of the Han Dynasty. Like the Sun God in charge of the arts and medicine in Greek mythology, Emperor Yan was revered as a god in charge of farming and medicine. This is probably because the sun symbolizes an abundant harvest of all food crops and represents good health. In the meantime, the myth about Emperor Yan marked the change from the fishery and hunting period of primitive society to the period of farming in human history. The lunar calendar emerged as required by farming. As far back as the Xia Dynasty (c. twenty-first — sixteenth BC), China already had a calendar. Hence, the traditional Chinese calendar was also called the "Xia calendar." The Shang Dynasty (c. sixteenth — eleventh century BC) continued to use the Xia calendar, which was also called a lunar calendar. The lunar calendar was mainly formulated according to changes of the phase of the moon. A day is calculated by sunrise and sunset and a month by the waxing and waning of the moon. A solar month has 30 days and a lunar month 29 days. Twelve months make a year and the intercalary year has 13 months.

In Chinese myths and folk stories, the images of the sun and the moon artistically reflect the development of the socio-economic life and the people's world outlook from the age of barbarism to that of civilization. They have left indelible traces in the history of the cultural development of the Chinese nation.

The Sun and Moon in Thai Folk Belief

There are very few records of traditional Thai folktales which feature the sun and the moon in a complete and coherent manner. Thai poets, however, are in the habit of associating the moon with the fair sex-not unlike the Chinese belief in which the moon is imagined to be the wife of the sun. Most Thai myths about the sun and the moon were influenced by Hinduistic beliefs. In such myths, both the sun and the moon are considered male.

A Thai legend, "Triloka Vinicchaya" describes the sun and the moon as mere self-luminous objects. The legend tells of deities blessed with self-luminosity descending to the earth. By ingesting the food that was raised upon the earth, they lost the light which once radiated from their bodies. The world was thus plunged into total darkness and all earthlings were gripped in awesome fear. It was not long before a large fire-ball appeared in the heaven and darkness was subsequently dispelled. Realizing that their fears had vanished in the advent of the object which gave them back light, they called it "suriya" which is a Pali word for "one who inspires bravery". The sun or "Suriya" constitutes a deity in Thai myth.

The confidence of the earth-bound people was soon shattered when the sun, having traversed the sky, disappeared over the horizon, and darkness reigned over the whole earth. Again another bright object, although not as bright as the sun, showed up in the sky. The people rejoiced at seeing its light and named it "chanda", a Sanskrit word for "that which gives joy". The word "chanda" later degenerated into "Chandra" which is the current word for the moon in the Thai language. Like Suriya, Chandra ranks as a deity in Thai mythology.

One ancient Thai chronicle makes reference to two Thai princes, Khun Lu and Khun Lai who, according to a legend, were born of a supreme deity lording the heavens. Both princes were accompanied upon their descendance to the earth by Khun Tun and Khun Pun who hailed from the sun and the moon respectively.

What ancient Thai folk belief sees on the moon

Fascinated by the beauty of the moon, the ancient Thais formed an impression of what they saw there in the form of two different image patterns depending on the imagination of the moment. The first one was that of a couple of elderly persons pounding away rice seeds in a mortar with a long wooden pestle. The second one was that of a rabbit.

Indeed one of the Buddhist jataka tales links the rabbit with the moon. It is related in this tale that Boddhisattva (the Buddha-to-be) was born a rabbit living in a forest. Besides being a vegetarian (a matter of necessity for all herbivorous animals), the rabbit also observed 'dhamma' or the principle of selflessness and was therefore worthy of being reincarnated later as Buddha. It dawned on the poor rabbit that he had nothing at all in his possession to give away. If a hungry pauper should ask him for a simple meal, he could not very well offer grass which he normally ate. The rabbit finally resolved that should such a situation arise, he would offer his own flesh.

The resolution of the noble rabbit soon came to the notice of the god 'Indra' who decided in earnest to test the steadfastness of the rabbit. Disguised as a Brahmin, (a holy man), Indra came face to face with the rabbit and begged for a meal. The rabbit thus promised his guest food which he had never provided for anyone before. This was to be his own carcass. Recognizing the fact that no Brahmin had ever taken life, the rabbit persuaded his guest to prepare a fire which he would use to dispatch himself.

Indra made a magic fire and then urged his host to fulfil the pledge. Unhesitatingly the rabbit threw himself into the burning pyre. To his utmost surprise, the flame appeared to be as cool as ice. The rabbit felt that all he could do was to tell the waiting Brahmin that the fire did not do the trick. At this point Indra revealed his true self and the purpose of the whole ordeal to the rabbit. To ensure that the honour and virtue of the rabbit would be forever remembered, Indra caused the likeness of the rabbit to be etched on a stone slab which he placed on the surface of the moon.

Eclipses in folk belief

One Thai folktale tells a story of three brothers, Aditya, Candra and Rahu. Their father was Hasavisai, and their mother, Sundra. Hasavisai died of old age. The family invited the Buddhist priests to perform a merit-making rite. In the process, each brother was required to dish out rice from a traditional rice bowl and offer it to the priests. Aditya, the eldest of the three brothers took a golden bowl, while Candra who was the second eldest took a silver one. Rahy, the youngest brother, seeing that nothing was left for him picked a wicker container and used it as though it were a proper bowl.

It is the custom for a Buddhist to lift the bowl over his head and make a wish before offering rice to the priests. Aditya wished that he be reborn as the sun to reign over day. Candra made a similar wish by asking to be reborn as the moon to reign over night. Rahu became very enraged. He thought he was badly dealt with by his two brothers who, after taking gold and silver, left him with no decent wish. Through sheer wrath, he wished that he be reborn with a body large enough to blot the light of the sun and the moon.

The wishes of the three brothers were granted.

Rahu has his sweet revenge by seizing the sun or the moon during a solar or lunar eclipse.

Of the two kinds of eclipses, the lunar one is more common. Whenever there is a lunar eclipse, the Thai people will beat out loud noises on traditional bamboo gongs, or else fire volleys. The idea is to frighten Rahu into releasing the moon.

The northeastern people of Thailand refer to the lunar eclipse as "Frog eating the moon phenomenon". This reference is similar to that of the Lawa, a Thai ethnic group who believe that Rahu is a frog. During the Songkran festival, (a traditional new year day which falls on 13 April) the Lawa will be seen tossing frogs into a river. This is thought to appease Rahu the frog. Otherwise he will not free the moon after a lunar eclipse.

Important rites and practices during eclipses

In early times, a court astronomer was expected to inform the King of the time and date on which a lunar eclipse was to take place, so that all necessary preparations could be made. As soon as a lunar eclipse began, the King would proceed to receive a ceremonial bath. At the same time, conch shells and victorious gongs were sounded, and the traditional pi-phart orchestra played auspicious tunes.

The common folk also have traditional beliefs which they follow or used to follow during eclipses. For instance, as soon as a lunar eclipse begins, a pregnant woman should stick a sewing needle to the skirt at the position where a buckle is. This was believed to prevent a baby from being born with defects.

Seals bearing engravings of the sun and the moon

It is not very surprising that many official great seals in Thailand bear symbols and signs either representing or relating to the sun and the moon. Some of the well-known great seals are:

1. *The Large Phra Suriya Mandhala Seal* which depicts the deity Suriya driving a chariot pulled by mythical lions (singha). This great seal was once reserved for Lord Treasurer.
2. *The Small Phra Suriya Mandhala Seal* which consists of a circle and a peacock in the circle. The peacock in this case is the symbol for the sun.
3. *Large Candra Mandhala Seal* which shows a rabbit inside the moon.

The sun and the moon in the names of noblemen

Thai noblemen and high court officials were granted illustrious names by the King. Many of their names contain the words that mean the sun or the moon. They are for examples: Somdej Chao Phraya Sri *Suriyawongse*, Phra *Candramatya*, Phra *Candra Suriyawongse*, Phra *Candraditya*, Chao *Candradewa Suriyawongse* Tamrong Rath Sima Muktathibodi.

Taboos

Profanity or even small pungent references against the sun or the moon are tabooed for traditional Thais. This is probably due to the fact that the sun and the moon are useful to mankind and that they constitute deities in the minds of most people. It is also in the character of the Thai people to refrain from acts which may be construed as expressing ingratitude to their bona fide benefactors.

The Life-Giving Sun and Symbolic Moon of Pakistani Folk Tradition

In Pakistan, like elsewhere in the world, the sun and the moon are believed to be two immortal phenomena of nature. The sun is the grandest of all heavenly bodies, as it is endowed with most indispensably constructive and awe-inspiring destructive characteristics, on which only Nature can prevail. As Pakistan is an under-developed country, a major part of its land and population is totally at the mercy of the sun. Pakistan's masses constituting the rural society, the country's true representatives, are still untouched by modern civilization and therefore have no means to harness the sun's energy. Hence today, the masses continue to hold traditional beliefs that define ominous and glorious aspects of the sun.

In terms of religion, as Islam markedly dominates Pakistan's population, the sun's presence is considered imperative for human existence, but it is not worshipped. Only a few segments of heathen society in Kafristan/Kalash or in the other remote regions alienated from the country due to geographical factors, tend to hold the sun as supreme. Pakistan being an agricultural country where modern farm technology is used to a very limited extent, a large section of the farming community totally relies on two major life-giving natural factors — sunshine and rain.

In Tharparkar, once an island sea (an extension of the Arabian sea), now a vast inhabited desert with its own distinct character and vegetation, a farmer sings *hermerchoo* (a call-song) in the local dialect in his fields summoning the villagers to help him weed-out the grass. In a *hermerchoo* all objects of nature around — the birds, bees, animals, plants, and heavenly bodies are praised. But the sun is the most lavishly praised object. "Let us work so hard under the watchful sun that it rewards our labour" or, "Let us not fail him (the sun) which bestows us with unending energy and light."

From songs of the rustic to the world of literature is not a far cry. The sun and the moon are regarded as two positive symbols of life. The sun is considered a symbol of rejuvenation of nature and man — a life-giving element, whereas the moon symbolises beauty and love. If the modern scientist of Pakistan looks at the sun as a source of energy that increases the physical dimensions, gives texture and hue to an animate or inanimate object, all that we call the normal natural processes of growth, a litterateur places the sun as an absolute immortal essential of the universe that stands for light, hope and guidance.

If the sun has been attributed life-giving qualities, the moon stands for beauty and love. A little baby, even a grown-up, is usually referred to as "chand" or "chanda" by its mother — for a child to a mother is the ultimate of beauty to whom she gives herself totally, imparting perpetually boundless and unconditional love.

Though the moon symbolises beauty, it does not represent perfection of beauty, as the scars on its face are never forgiven — hence the proverb, *"chand ke chihre pe bhi dagh hai:*, (even the moon has scars on its face). This light-hearted proverb tends to dismiss any flaws in an ingenious piece of fine or performing arts, or any other thing of life recalling the imperfections of nature's works.

References are made to the moon by a poet, even a common man, in relation to the physical beauty of his beloved. The lovers moods that take their complexion from the beloved's attitude towards him are compared to the ebb and flow of tides that depends upon the movement of the moon.

The sun and the moon have often inspired names of places, people and flowers. *Sooraj mukhi* (Sunlike face, the Sunflower) because of its bright yellow colour and its floral pattern resembling the sun has been named after the sun. The moon has inspired the name of one of the famous rivers of the Punjab, Chenab (moon-water), because of its breath-taking beauty during moon-lit nights. Chand Bibi and Channa are Muslim names popular in all parts of Pakistan. In Punjabi the lover is always referred as "chan mahi". A most popular and expressive metaphor declaring the lover is "as dear as the moon".

Save for the regions in which the five rivers Indus, Jhelum, Chenab, Ravi and Sutlaj and Bias flow, the barrage and the well-irrigated areas, more than half of Pakistan constitutes arid land or desert — Rajistan, Tharparkar and Thal being the most famous. In the folklore of these waterless barren lands the sun more often than not is depicted as a villain.

In "Sassi Punnu", a famous folk tale of Sind, Sassi searches her husband Punnu, kidnapped by his brothers, in the desert while the burning sun beats mercilessly upon her. The scorching heat is followed by a fatal storm which buries Sassi under the sand. The sun plays a powerful, cruel and heartless sadist in most folklore and ballads, in which occasionally the quest for some material, physical or spiritual gain leads the major character to undertake a journey. Here no journey is complete without mentioning the intensity of heat that becomes a big hurdle in the major character's journey.

The sun and the moon yet again form recurrent images in the country's mystic poetry — past and present. In the mystic poetry too, the poet's quest, fear and love of God is expressed and reiterated by different approaches to the images of the sun and moon and their attributes. The sun and moon lend richness and depth to the mystic poetic expressions. Nationally the rising moon symbolises progress and a promise of better times and dominates the green of Pakistan's flag along with a star that stands for guidance. The full moon represents the climax, the fulfilment of a promise, after which begins a decline. Hence generally even marriage dates in Pakistan synchronise with the rising moon period. Marriage on the nights when the moon begins to decline/descend are superstitiously avoided. Interestingly enough even during "Andhiari", a period when the moon rise has not been ascertained due to clouds or other cosmic delusions, a marriage ceremony is avoided.

As for the sun, the Holy Quran recitation in Pakistan must cease at 12 noon, the peak hour of the sun, which is considered the hour of the devil. Scripture recitation, however, resumes when the climax solar hour is over.

If a pregnant woman encounters a mishap during a solar or lunar eclipse, the incident, they say, can influence the new born. An expectant mother, it is generally believed, may give birth to a baby born with a scar, if she receive a knife bruise. There are certain interesting common folk beliefs, prevailing in contemporary Pakistan regarding the sun's role in a marriage. For example, the elders advise the would-be groom not to lick the *degchee* (cooking utensil) because of a superstition that the sun would not shine on his marriage day.

As marriage is an elaborate festivity in our society in which neighbours, friends and relatives all participate, for both the rich and the poor, bright sunshine is a blessing from heaven. If the threatening clouds loom large in the skies prophesying a rainy day, a would-be bride in a Punjabi society is advised by the elders to make a clay puppet carrying a sack of belongings on its back and leave it under the open sky. Here, the puppet represents a traveller heading for his destinations on a rainy day. It is generally believed that the sun pities the poor traveller and blows the clouds asunder for the bright sunshine to descend on the festivity.

Special congregation prayers are offered in mosques to stop a constant downpour of rains flooding the plains and destroying the summer crops and threatening with a famine. It is a trusted Muslim belief that such mass prayers are answered with bright sunshine that saves the nation from a major catastrophe. This is the most practical of all the beliefs mentioned so far. Every year, in Pakistan at one time or the other, the Head of the State may request the nation to offer a special congregation prayer either for sunshine or for rain.

If the position of the sun in relation to the earth determines the Christian calendar, the position of the moon in relation to the earth marks the months of the Islamic year.

As Pakistan is a Muslim country the importance of the moon here is evident. The first Islamic month is Muharram, the month of the great tragedy of Kerbala, when in the first century of the dawn of Islam, a grandson of the Prophet Mohammad (peace be upon him), Imam Hussain, laid down his life for the glory of Islam. Whereas the Christian New Year (1st January) is celebrated with great enthusiasm, the Islamic New Year as heralded by the first moon, the Muharram, is observed with great solemnity and reverence.

All holy festivals are held only after the new moon is sighted. The new moon announcing Eid-ul-Fitr and Eid-ul-Azha, the two major celebrations, is always received enthusiastically with fire works and crackers. Eid-ul-Fitr marks the end of the Ramzan, the holy month of fasting, while Eid-ul-Azha marks the end of rituals of pilgrims in Mecca, Saudi Arabia, who gather there from all over the world to perform Haj. The new moon introducing the Ramzan, which ushers in 30 days of fasting, is received with great reverence.

So marked is the new moon's significance in folk life that people in Pakistan mostly raise hands in a prayer for a peaceful and prosperous month ahead. As a matter of fact a girl praying before the new moon is a typical traditional subject of an Eid greeting card.

Because of their prominence, the sun and the moon have never escaped the artist's eye. Lunar and solar motifs therefore, have been frequently used in modern and ancient times in all works demanding artistic expression. The patterns were and are still used in embroidery of various kinds, floor, roof and wall tile work, mosaic, wood and metal carvings, engraving, ornamental decorations, and on pottery. The pottery excavated from the ruins of Kot Diji (located in southern Sind, Pakistan), a civilization that dominated the Indus valley about 3,500 BC, has solar motifs of various kinds. Any non-geometrical pattern with a spread of more than six leaves emerging from a definite disc is actually a solar motif often mistaken for a floral pattern.

The Sun and Moon in Melanesian Folklore

ur star and our satellite feature prominently in Melanesian folklore and many stories have been collected on them for the Folklore Archive stored at the Institute of Papua New Guinea Studies in Port Moresby. From these archives, Ulli Beier and Prithvindra Chakravarti have compiled their book *Sun and Moon in Papua New Guinea Folklore*, published by the Institute in 1974. The stories are drawn from coast, highlands and islands, and well illustrate the Melanesian world view of separate tiers of existence (i.e. underground, ground and sky).

Occasionally there is interaction between any of the inhabitants of these levels — for example, people come out of or go into the ground, or the moon is reached; there might be marriage between sky-people or land-people; or a tragic figure might become the moon or run away to live in the sky. In a highlands story the sun and moon are described as visiting the humans via ascent in the East, then the underground or "earthquake" people via descent in the West. Thus the sun and moon provide links between the inhabitants of the various layers of existence, and we might add, between the living and the dead.

By contrast, a coastal story tells of the sun-figure descending to earth each day and helping to provide good crops. Unfortunately he also steals one child every evening when he returns to the sky. The angry parents attack him and damage his ladder, causing the sun and sky to become more remote but allowing the population to increase.

The widespread explanation of the origin of the language group as lying in the behaviour of a heroic ancestor also involves the sun and the moon. This almost always involves the figure on a journey and in conflict. In one coastal story, the hero tries to kill the moon because of adultery with his wife. It is made apparent in the story that the earthly wives are truly married to the moon because of monthly menstruation. Once the hero accepts this fact he progresses well on earth because he and his male-followers accept the fact that they are only the secondary husbands of the women.

In a coastal story which appears to have been borrowed from non-Austronesian trading-partners, the hero goes through various trials on a journey to find out if the moon is male or female, but discovers at last that the moon is a male whose age waxes and wanes.

In another coastal story (but of people who probably migrated thence from inland) the hero admires his own long hair, which is rather puzzling because the people of the area have short-tight hair, and remarks that his hair is like a thread joining him to the moon. When he finally locates the moon's house he also finds the resplendent sun and a room full of stars and is sent back with the yam as a staple food. The agricultural calendar linked to the annual thirteen moons is relevant here. But also in this and other stories above we should bear in mind the important facts that many traditions are borrowed and that oral evidence is the result of complicated migrations and even of radical changes of language as well as derivation from the supposed proto-language. In other words, even the early ethnographers could not be sure whose story they were listening to, and this is so much truer in the collection of stories today when even foreign elements, e.g. from the Bible, have crept in. It does, however, serve to remind us that the oft-quoted fact of Papua New Guinea having over seven-hundred languages (based on statistics compiled long ago in only one part of the world) does not mean, as once thought, that Melanesia had hundreds of different "cultures". The more that is collected, the more are the similarities rather than differences seen. And "Sun and Moon" stories lend added support to this. This does not, of course, rule out many variations in sun and moon stories and although one language group might tell a story of a cruel sun, for example, and another language group talk of a kind sun, the delineations are not exclusive. Other stories will partly contradict the first told. The sun may be good and the moon evil, and of course this is very convenient for the men to hear if they think of female functions as bad. Sunstroke is referred to in one story as a deliberate act of the sun. In some stories there are different suns appearing at different times, e.g. a grandfather sun and a granddaughter sun. This obviously could be a seasonal reference. One ancestress is impregnated by the sun and one ancestor marries the sun's granddaughter. One sun is killed by a man; in another story is a giant which vomits it out every morning. Another sun is portable until released by the ancestor so that it can shine on all. In a highlands story sunshine is caused by a man rubbing his forehead with a leaf. In another, both sun and moon are suns but to reduce the excessive heat, the moon is rubbed with mud and dimmed. The link between sunlight and plant growth is referred to in a number of stories.

A highlands group claims to fight only by day, not because it is easier to see by daylight, but because of the cooling effect of the moon on the brain. One island story claims that the moon and her star family rise in the west and set in the east! A story from the largest language group in Papua New Guinea (Enga) sees the moon's phases as a series of smiles because the moon is happy to have separated from the sun after a quarrel. The authors of *Sun and Moon* claim that moon stories are much more frequently found than sun stories and it will be interesting to see if this trend continues as more oral collection takes place. Sometimes the markings on the moon are explained — it is visited, settled in, or in one case used as a taro-scraper. It may be a piece of vegetable which begins to shine, it may be kept in pot, it often possesses magical properties or has some human origin. In its evil aspect it may be a thief, rapist, cannibal, child-stealer or a dismembered sun. Children fall in love with the moon and go there or a man experiencing great shame escapes to the moon.

An eclipse is explained by the story in which the grandmother becomes a sacrifice to a giant monster while her grandsons climb a tree and "spear" the moon to escape.

The sun and moon are used in Melanesian carvings and modern painting and are referred to in songs and poems. Not surprisingly, the very romantic lyrics of the Central Province of Papua New Guinea use the moon as a symbol of love and there is no reason to believe that this is a post-contact introduction.

What the authors of *Sun and Moon* do not tell us is how the sun and moon played their part in Melanesian life and social control; although they do suggest another structure in the book which claims to explain the Papua New Guinea world view. Unfortunately, the theory is not developed enough to examine for fault or further support from other oral evidence. The stories, however, surely had fairly obvious functions. First of all, as the authors point out, they help to explain where we came from and how we got here in timeless and non-geographical terms. Secondly they were great stories for entertainment; many of them slanted towards children. Then they attempt scientific explanation of observed phenomena in nature and in human behaviour. Hidden in them probably are glimpses of history, e.g. the highlands ocean-crossing story, or the cannibal moon or sun which might represent a hostile tribe now defeated or co-existed with. Then there is the important functions of saying, "look what happens if you do not behave in accordance with our mores", or "see how men are superior to women", or "men must not maltreat their wives". They are related to necessary agricultural knowledge and almost certainly, to religious beliefs.

That sun and moon are seen as species of supernatural entities can hardly be denied, although often acting in a wonderful human fashion as did the gods on Olympus. An important aspect of this are the fears and hopes which link the living to the dead-ancestor's spirit world. Sun and moon are heavenly bodies and the dead may be in the sky, or they may be under the world where the sun and moon make frequent journeys. If we don't obey the ancestors' wishes, they may punish us by some behaviour of the sun and moon or their extensions, e.g. weather and crops. Or the moon may kill the fish in the rivers or cause a man to die in some inexplicable way by sorcery or sunstroke. In the foreword to John Kasaipwalova's poetic drama, *Sail the Midnight Sun*, Greg Murphy writes of this modern interpretation of a Trobriands legend that the "midnight sun" has elements of the sea, carving, magic and the stars. One of the characters in the drama is the Woman of the Moons. Perhaps as he becomes aware of the many other ways in which Melanesians have viewed the sun and the moon, he will reflect this in celebrating other folklore from Papua New Guinea.

Religion and Literature in Indonesia

What is Indonesian literature?

What is regarded as Indonesian literature is modern literature written in the national language of Indonesia. This needs special mention here, since before the beginning of modern literature that took place about the turn of the twentieth century, there were quite a few forms of literature in the different ethnic and cultural regions of Indonesia. They were the Javanese, Sundanese, Balinese, Batak, Mingkabau and other literatures written in their respective regional languages. These regional languages are numerous. Their total number is not known for certain vet, but a figure around for hundred may be a good guess (that does not include the hundreds of local languages spoken in remote and sparsely inhabited areas like Irian Jaya, which haven't been thoroughly researched yet).

The national language, Bahasa Indonesia, is a new outgrowth of one of the regional languages, that is, Malay. It is originally a regional language, chosen and adapted to the needs of modern times and used for communication at the national level between the different communities of the Indonesian archipelago. Malay as a regional language is used locally in many coastal areas of the Moluccas, the island of Ternate, Kalimantan, the Jakarta area and North Sumatra. The Indonesian language is based on this Malay, a fact which has been unanimously acknowledged and upheld by the Indonesian people since 1928.

Influx of great religions in the world

A study on the link between religion and literature in Indonesia on the basis of our knowledge of modern Indonesian literature may yield some interesting points which have hitherto been paid little attention to. This may be due to insufficient data and opportunities to follow the recent development of literature. However, a firmer ground for discussion can be obtained by looking back to the time when there was not yet any national literature, and when literature was written in the diverse local languages throughout the vast area of Indonesia. Proceeding from the every historical periods towards the present time one can find a clearer picture of religion as it is reflected in the development of Indonesian literature.

Perhaps it would be more appropriate to mention religions rather than religion, since throughout the ages Indonesia has experienced an influx of almost all the great religions of the world. First, it was Buddhism, followed by Hinduism in the special form of Shaivism, then Islam, and lastly Christianity, which came together with the process of modernization and westernization of the country. They left their imprint on Indonesian cultural life and they constitute layer upon layer of civilization in the general lifestyle of the people. On the other hand, the original beliefs, which have been kept alive by local customs and traditions, persistently penetrate the newly adopted religions. As a result, everywhere syncretism occurs, and the imported religions in Indonesia have undergone a local colouring and different directions of thinking.

The syncretism as mentioned above is already apparent in the tenth century in Java wherein an ancient script Hinduism and Buddhism tended to be regarded as identical. Shiva and Buddha were glorified as one and the same god.

It can also be discerned in an old story in Old Javanese about the fat Bubuksah and the thin Gangak Aking. Both were hermits, the former a follower of Buddhism, the latter of Shaivism. Bubuksah eats everything, while Gagak Aking avoids every enjoyment and becomes thin. A deity appearing in the form of a white tiger wants to eat them up. Gagak Aking shows his thinness and points to the fat Bubuksah. The latter is willing to be devoured and be carried away by the tiger.

Unexpectedly the deity in tiger form gives Bubukshah a place in the highest heaven. Whereas Gagak Aking has to be content with a place in a lower one. The story indicates this blend of Buddhism and Shaivism, and the higher degree accorded to the former religion compared to the latter one.

How religious life is reflected

To limit the scope of our discussion, we will focus our attention on two regional literatures, the Javanese and the Malay ones, while touching briefly on modern Indonesian literature. In so doing, we hope that we can use these literatures as samples to preset a picture of the link between religion and literature in Indonesia, particularly to show how religious life is reflected in literature.

Reference to Javanese literature cannot be avoided, since it is on the island of Java that one finds the oldest evidence of written literature. It was around AD 900 that a beautiful adaptation in Old Javanese was made of the Indian epic *Ramayana,* which was made accessible to the common reader who was not acquainted with Sanskrit. The oldest literary work in Old Javanese, *Arjuna Wiwaha,* although derived from the *Mahabharata,* is an original work written in the eleventh century to celebrate the wedding of a ruling king.

In other parts of Indonesia, regional literature, such as that in Malay, was not written before the sixteenth century.

Literature in Java has undergone changes which can be identified by the successive development of the language used as its vehicle; from Old Javanese to Middle Javanese and modern Javanese. Works in the Old Javanese employ themes which mostly derive from the Indian epics *Mahabharata and Ramayana.* Literature written in Middle Javanese deals mainly with events in Javanese history, whereas modern Javanese relates happenings in the twentieth century.

Apart from the experts, present-day readers in Java are not able to understand stories written in the Old Javanese language. Nevertheless, the ancient literature still exerts a fresh influence on the mind of the people, due to the *wayang* or leather puppet performances which are still popular among the people, regardless of their differences of class and environment. The religious philosophy of the Indian epics, although not in its purely original form, continues to guide people's world views and ethical conduct. The figures in the stories of *Mahabharata* and *Ramayana* provide the Javanese public with exemplary attitudes and behaviour in their daily life. A courageous man, for example, should not brag about his strength and power, he should be restrained and self-possessed like the hero Arjuna. On the other hand, a devious and sly politician would be identified as Durna, the deceitful and scheming advisor of the bad Kaurawas.

The wisdom of governing a country

The *wayang* stories are so well-known to the public that a coalescence and mixture of the two epics does not cause any confusion to the Javanese audience. In the peculiar combination of *Mahabharata* and *Ramayana,* such as in the story of *Wahyu Makuta Rama* (The King's Ruling Principles), in which figures of the *Ramayana* enter the scene of the story of *Mahabharata,* no one evidently cared about the mix-up, which is purposefully done to present the religio-philosophical theme of the wisdom of governing a country.

This kind of literature in Old Javanese and Middle Javanese, whether kept in books or performed as puppet shows, fulfils the need of an active cultural life in Bali, more so than in Java. This is due to the preservation of the habit of reading together this classical literature, and to the survival and continuation of the Hindu religion.

Early Malay literature was written in Arabic script in the sixteenth century when Islam became the new religion in Indonesia. In Malay literary life the Indian epics — although there is a sufficient number of Malay versions of the *Mahabharata* and *Ramayana* — have not received an appreciation as high as in Java and Bali. The stories have no real impact on the moral and social behaviour of the people.

More interest is directed towards works with historical intent like the *Sejarah Melayu* (Malay History) and the exploits of the courageous figures as in *Hang Tuah.*

Also the life of the prophets and the struggle for the victory of Islam are themes which very much attract the Malay reader, as they provide guidance towards a virtuous religious life.

Literature inciting controversy

However, it would not be out of context to point to an important incident in Malay literary life that is quite relevant to our interest in the link between religion and literature. It is the contention between two mystical views which occurred in the middle of the seventeenth century in the region of Aceh. Hamzah Fansuri, who is known as the first Malay poet, and Syamsuddin Pasai in his religious treatises, believed in the identity of man and God. Opposing them were Nuruddin Al-Raniri and Abdul Rauf Singkel who contended that although man and God are one, they are not alike. God is eternal truth, whereas man is transitory. These two latter mystics regarded Hamzah Fansuri and Syamsuddin as heretics who would lead the masses astray. Finally the Sultan, who sided with the orthodoxy, ordered most of Hamzah Fansuri's and Syamsuddin's books be burnt.

This tendency of literature to contain religious and mystical beliefs and thereby incite controversy was already apparent in the sixteenth century in Javanese literature. Well-known are the several versions of the manuscript on the Moslem saint Siti Jenar who taught and propagated the mystical belief in the identity of man with God. He incited the animosity of other saints who considered his activity to be a violation of Islamic law. They were of the opinion that his mystical view should be kept secret for fear that the masses might become confused and arrogant. But despite their warnings, Siti Jenar persisted in his heretical teachings. Therefore he was condemned to death and was decapitated.

According to another literary text, the *Serat Cabolek,* the mystic Sunan Panggung neglected to observe the religious rituals of praying and fasting, convinced as he was that in the mystical union with God such rituals were not necessary.

For this neglect he was condemned to be burnt at stake by the orthodoxy. In the same writing two other mystics were mentioned, Ki Bebeluk of the region of Pajang and Among Raga of Mataram, who were sentenced to death by drowning.

The authors of the writings on the Javanese mystics were either sympathetic or critical to their conviction and behaviour. But the important fact that should be noted here is that mysticism, as an expression of religious beliefs, has been a frequently recurring theme in Indonesian literature, which attracts the readers' attention. Containing this religious theme, literature is not regarded as an entertainment and a pastime, but a cultural engagement with the seriousness of life.

Mysticism in modern Indonesian literature

In the modern period of Indonesian literature, where there is more freedom in the expression of mysticism, one finds the same tendency in the writing by Amir Hamzah, Soetardji Calzoum Bachri, Abdul Hadi, Danarto and other authors who yearn for the presence of the closeness to God, whether they put their thoughts and feelings in Islamic or Christian symbols and metaphors. This tendency proves that literature and religion, particularly as a mystical experience, basically emerge from the same creative impulse.

In this connection the description given by Prof. P.J. Zoetmulder in his book *Kalangwan* of the creative process in Old Javanese poetry may be cited. The *kakawin* poems are created by the poet in his meditation and in his union with the god of beauty. By writing his poetry the poet also attempts to attain the final liberation in this union, the freedom from the bonds of his earthly existence. This religious implication of literature which is also found in the writing of the Japanese *haiku,* which, according to Alam Watts on *The Way of Zen,* emerges from the deep meditation of the poet when he reaches the "full emptiness" of *satori.*

The Magic Mantra of Literature and the People of India

A mantra is an incantation that is supposed to summon up beneficial forces from another dimension. Every writer aspires to that perfect concatenation of words, a spell that will conjure with the world and "remould it closer to the heart's desire". At the very least, literature is a dip deep into the well of the universal subconscious in the hope of snaring a pattern that will make more comprehensible and bewildering complexity of the world.

Both the search for a sacred Reality and the hunt for a secular inspiration have a common origin. Just as the first thespians in ancient Greece were the outcome of conscious aberrations in the practice of ritual, the creators of literature are the cultural descendants and extensions of priests. They are the new Brahmins. Not because they have power but because they seek it beyond the temporal pale.

This is a universal phenomenon. In England, in the first half of the nineteenth century, after many discussions with William Wordsworth, Thomas De Quincy wrote, "All that is literature seeks to communicate power; all that is not literature, to communicate knowledge."

To understand the people of India and their literature, it is necessary to quickly go back in time and trace the foundations of both.

The people of India

India has been for 5000 years what America is today — a melting-pot of many races and traditions. In spite of temporary conflicts and upheavals, it has gradually evolved ways to successfully accommodate, adjust to and absorb every new stream of settlers.

Some of these have poured down from the north as invaders, plundering and pillaging their way through the Himalayan passes; but eventually their roiling progress has been dissipated on the vast expanse of the Indian plains, their turmoil has been stilled into peaceful activity and creative endeavour.

Others have arrived by other routes — overland or overseas — as adventurers, traders, mendicants, monks, students, pilgrims, scholars; there have been hordes of trudging refugees and shiploads of asylum-seekers who have been welcomed when they promised to "mix like sugar in milk" with the earlier inhabitants of their new homeland.

As Chopra, Puri and Das, the authors of *A Social, Cultural and Economic History of India* note, "India — with its vast collection of people differing from one another in physical characteristics, in language and their way of life — represents primarily all the ethnographical divisions of mankind. The white type constituting the Caucasian, the yellow one signifying the Mongolian, and the black one of the Ethiopian group are all to be found in different parts of the country."

The earliest known major influx was that of the Aryans who, it is deduced, came from a shared Indo-European heritage based in Central Asia, one branch moving westwards to populate Persia and Europe while the other moved down into India, displacing the autochthonous Indus Valley civilization and pushing the darker Dravidian races further south into the peninsula.

The first book

The earliest literary work known to mankind, the *Rig Veda*, was compiled by the Indo-Aryans around the year 2000 BC in Northwest India. It consists of 1017 poems or hymns divided into ten books and seems to represent the best outpourings of the vedic civilization at its zenith. The work is an accretion of the output of many minds and is shot through with a healthy, robust, intellectual sophistication which in today's terminology would be called agnosticism. The spirit of enquiry overrides all dogmatism and permeates even its magnificent *Ode* to *Genesis* wherein the origin of the universe is beautifully evoked. But then, suddenly, there is a wry, refreshing twist into what can only be called cosmic humour for the author says, "Only the One who began it all knows how it happened. Or perhaps even the Creator knows it not!"

The oral tradition in Sanskrit

Historically, India's experience with learning and literature has been unique in that, in the earliest recorded days when the Indo-Aryan language, Sanskrit, was the predominant medium of cultural expression, the greatest (and, indeed, the lengthiest) works were not written down — as they could have been — but composed in the mind, transmitted orally from guru to shishya (from master to disciple) and committed to memory for onward transmission to succeeding generations of the initiate. Literature was power; and it was guarded.

Though the centuries, an increasingly rigid class and caste system based on the division of social function and the strengthening of genetic lines came into being. Literature and the arts became the preserve of the highest caste, the Brahmins. Most of the rest of India, especially the lower castes, remained illiterate and their pursuit of knowledge was limited to the furtherance of the trades and crafts by which they earned their livelihood.

The position of women too underwent a change for the worse. Whereas earlier they had participated equally with men in literary composition and philosophic debate, they were now restricted from participation in sacred ritual or attending to the sacrificial fire.

The advent of Pali and Prakrit

In the sixth century BC, Buddhism and Jainism sought to reform the structure and thought of Indian society by challenging the efficacy and esoterically of Brahmanical ritual. Buddhist literature came to be preserved not only in Sanskrit but also in Pali. The Buddha and Mahavira, the founder of Jainism, preached in the language of the masses, Prakrit.

The result of these tugs at the status quo was a great cascade of literature, both sacred and secular, in a variety of languages. The classical stream of Sanskrit, rich with voluminous versified treatises on philosophy, metaphysics, grammar, mathematics, law, economics, statecraft, medicine, yoga, surgery, astronomy, art, architecture, etymology, prosody, rhetoric, music, dance and drama and adorned with vast collections of poetry, legend, fable and the great epics *Mahabharata* and *Ramayana*, was now augmented by works in the vernaculars. Among the most important of these new works were those based on the life of the Buddha, commentaries on his sermons and the Jataka stories which deal with the Buddha's previous incarnations.

Centres of learning

By AD fifth century India was renowned throughout the East for its many centres of advanced learning. The most famous of these universities was Nalanda which was visited, in the seventh century by the Chinese traveller Hiun-tsang who noted that this lofty place had 10,000 residents of whom 1500 were teachers. Another visitor, I-tsing remarks that students came here from as far away as Mongolia, China, Korea, Tibet and Indonesia; only 20% of applicants got through the different entrance examination.

Other literary and linguistic influences

Between 500 BC and AD 500 three Sangams (Confluences) of academics took place which sought to amalgamate into the mainstream the Dravidian literature of the south. The Dravidian group of languages includes Tamil, Kannada, Telegu and Malayalam. Malayalam is spoken in Kerala which today has the highest literacy rate among the different states in India. Perhaps this is because Kerala has an undisturbed inheritance of literature coupled with a dynamic tradition of the mimetic arts. Dance-drama forms, such as Kathakali, communicate the lore; and the people turn to literature to know more.

With the advent of Islam, which came to India on the back of fresh invasions from Central Asia, also came the contribution to India of Persian literature and its sources of inspiration. Arabic too exerted an influence though it was marginal compared to Persian. The result of all these when married to Hindi, the daughter of Sanskrit, was Hindustani, a popular polyglot which, much later, Mahatma Gandhi was to recommend, unsuccessfully, to the nation as a viable link-language for the country.

Hindustani is a close sister of a language that was born in the Mongol war-camp known as the ord; the new language came to be called Ordu. Over the years the word Mongol came to be pronounced Mughal and Ordu became Urdu, but the preferred language of the Mughal court was chaste Persian.

Like other demotic growths, Urdu had to find acceptance through popular usage and vibrant body of dynamic literature. Today it is used quite widely on both sides of the border though it is the national language of Pakistan.

The British impact on the subcontinent was considerable, both during the Raj and in its wake. English became the language of the courts and administration, and remains so to this day. The *de facto* link-language of the administrative elite, north and south, east and west, is English. Newspapers and magazines of nation-wide standing are published in English. Higher education and the language of advancement in English. There is an awesome body of effective literature written by Indians in English in India today. It reaches out to the world, and has made an impact abroad as well.

In a sense, English has slid into the position of Sanskrit. More and more publishing houses are coming up, or coming in from abroad, to caster to this sizeable intelligentsia that constitutes a growing market of between 40 to 80 million. And this figure will increase as literacy increases among India's 800 million.

Despite the fact that India has 16 major languages and more than 400 dialects, about 40% of the books published each year are in English. Increasingly, many of these are translations from the other languages. Or they are textbooks. Literacy and learning lead to literature and the continuing search for the elusive magic mantra — that powerful set of perfect words in a perfect book.

Large Thai seal showing a rabbit inside the moon.

Part 13

The Wonder That is Asia — Glorious Monuments

Wat Mahathat, the central temple of Sukhothai, Thailand.

Afghanistan — Bamiyan

History of Afghanistan

For centuries life in Afghanistan has been affected by turbulent empires, expanding cultures and great world religions. The country has always been a cross-roads of civilizations, absorbing what it could, initiating some cultures, preserving others. The result is that, today, Afghanistan can take pride in its role of safeguarding the remnants of early cultures — prehistoric, classical, Buddhist, Islamic — that have left their abiding mark.

Excavations have identified remains dating back to Middle Palaeolithic, 30,000 to 50,000 years ago. Northern Afghanistan may have been one of the transitional zones where man developed physically and began to revolutionize Stone Age technology. Sites in southern Afghanistan have thrown light on rural and urban communities that arose five millenniums ago in major river valleys from the Nile to the Indus.

Ancient Afghanistan, then known as Bactria, is first mentioned in history in Rig Veda hymns (2000 BC) which make abundant geographic references to this area. Among the rivers mentioned are the Khuba (Kabul) and the Suvastu (Swat). Balkh and the Helmand river are mentioned in the sacred texts of the Avesta as being part of Aryana, whence came the Aryans, common ancestors of the Iranians and Indians.

Various world religions were nurtured on Afghan soil. Mazdaism involved the worship of Ahura Mazda as a supreme deity and a cosmic struggle between a spirit of good and a spirit of evil. Zoroaster, the great religious teacher of the sixth century BC, is thought to have lived in northern Afghanistan. He transformed many of the Mazda beliefs into ethical precepts and made abstract entities of the autonomous gods of mythology, so approaching the concepts of a monotheistic religion. Around the thirteenth century BC, Aryan tribes poured into India through the Afghan passes and subjugated and then slowly reorganized the structural character of the sub-continent. Even in the southern Deccan, Aryan India imposed its religion and social system and achieved linguistic dominance in the world of the Indus and the Ganges. Remnants of a pre-Dravidian language are still spoken today by some 20,000 Brahuis in the remote southern deserts of present-day Afghanistan,.

Alexander passed through Central Asia and north-west India like a meteor (330-325 BC). He left behind in Bactria, between the Oxus and the Hindu Kush, tenacious Greek settlements whose customs, mythology, government and art influenced the culture of this Aryan region for over 200 years. Recent excavations reveal the extent to which Hellenistic culture had taken root in Afghanistan.

From Bactria, Greek kings expanded their empire over the lands south of the Hindu Kush down to northern India, from Kapisa near Kabul to Texila in the Punjab and further east. Hellenism moved east along the ancient roads which led into the heart of the Indian world. At the same time, Indian culture was moving west and came face to face with Hellenism. Buddhism, the first universal religion which mankind has known, was carried north to the now declining Greek kingdoms and produced an astounding new Indo-Greek culture that mingled Greek realism with Buddhist abstractionism.

In the middle of the third century BC, the great Indian emperor Ashoka, returning sick at heart from the fighting and bloodshed in eastern India, was converted to Buddhism and henceforward renounced all conquest but spiritual. Some two centuries after the death of its founder, Buddhism discovered in the person of this remarkable Maurian king a most fervent propagandist. To every part of his empire, even to the Greek monarchs of the west, he sent messengers to explain the new faith and to establish moral order. Ashoka had the rules of Buddhism engraved on rock and stone pillars, two of which, inscribed in Aramaic and Greek, were found in Kandahar, south of Kabul. Another stone inscription in Aramaic which was found in Laghman mentions the old trade route from India to Tadmor (Palmyra) in present-day Syria.

The adoption of Buddhism in the Gandhara plain and the valleys of the Indus at the time of Ashoka and the Indo-Greeks was favoured by political circumstances. However, retarded in its progress by Scythian and Parthian invasions, it did not take hold in central Afghanistan until AD second century.

It then still had a third stride to take northward in order to cross the Hindu Kush and establish itself in Bactria. All in all, Buddhism took nearly six hundred years to spread over the entire eastern part of Afghanistan.

Around the beginning of AD first century, Turkik or Scythia Scythian invaders drove down from the far eastern borders of the Oxus, reaching as far as Kabul. This energetic Kushan dynasty held power for some five hundred years, from the decline of the Indo-Greek empire to the invasion of the Ephthalites, or White Huns, in the fifth century.

The Kushans united Bactria and Sogdiana, defeated the Parthians and Scythiams in the west, extended their rule over the Kabul Valley and Kashmir to the east and later expanded their domains as far as Benares.

Between AD first and third century, the Kushans played an important role in the expansion of Buddhist culture. The great Kanishka himself was influential in establishing the reformed Mahayana doctrine of Buddhism which is today that of the major Buddhist sect.

The Kushan Empire traded with all neighbouring States, controlled the various arteries of the great Silk Route through the Middle East to Europe and served as a transit point in commercial exchanges between Rome and India. During Kanishka's reign, the Middle East continued to be open to the influence of Greek Civilization and art and to commercial relations with the Roman Empire. One of the capitals of the Kushan Empire was Kapisa, today's Begram, north of Kabul. Afghanistan thus provided a meeting-place for religious and artistic as well as commercial exchange.

Between the second and the seventh century, Afghanistan was a dynamic propagator of Buddhist literature and art in Chinese Turkestan and in China itself. Chinese annals tell of missionaries crossing the Gobi desert from oasis to oasis to found monasteries, or crossing the seas to reach Annam. There were monks whose point of departure was Balkh, Begram or present-day Jalalabad. From the valleys of Afghanistan, the ideas and artforms of the Indo-European world spread throughout the Far East. the influence of the frescos of Bamiyan reached to Kyzil and Turfan in Chinese Turkestan and indeed as far as Korea and Japan. In the seventh century, Arab invaders, carried on the tide of Islam, reached Afghanistan. Abu Bakr, the first Caliph after the Prophet Mohammad and Omar, the second Caliph and the great architect of Moslem expansion, had completed the conquest of Persia only a few years after the Prophet's death.

Mass conversions took place, the simplicity and nobility of the Islamic faith contrasting favourably with the already decadent dogmatism of Zoroastrian Priests in Persia and Buddhist monks in Afghanistan. No other religion has entered into the Afghan soul in so penetrating and permanent a fashion as has Islam. In 712, while Tariq was invading Spain and Qotaiba was entering Transoxiana, a young Arab general, Mohammad Quasm, reversing Alexander's route but unconsciously following his style, undertook the conquest of the Indus Valley from its delta northward. The intrigues of the court and civil wars among the Arab dynasties — already beginning to forget the commandments of Islam — were among the causes which contributed to the foundering of this expedition, which menaced the domains of the Shah of Kabul.

Soon the Caliph's governors began to proclaim autonomy in the name of Islam for the different provinces of the Arab Empire. The first principality to be formed within the Abassid Empire was that of the Tahirids (814-973) in Khorasan in west Afghanistan. Yaqub-bin-Laith, a Safarid, made himself master of Seistan in the second half of the ninth century, wrested Khorasan from the Tahirid emirs, annexed Bamiyan and then Kabul. The three cities which marked his route of conquest — Kandahar, Ghazni and Kabul — were destined to assume ever-increasing importance.

The emirs of the Samanid dynasty, who had received Transoxiana, Bukhara and Samarkand from Caliph Ma'mun, became the guardians of the Realm of Islam and of Moslem civilization against invasions from Central Asia. They annexed the former Safarid emirate of Khorasan and Seistan and soon had incorporated into their realm the most brilliant centres of Persian letters and science: Bukhara, Samarkand, Merv, Balkh, Nishapur.

The Ghaznavid dynasty, outstanding in Afghan history, was founded in Ghazni in 962. Mahmoud of Ghazni, one of the most inspiring epic figures in eastern history and the driving force of this new dynasty, came to the throne of Ghazni in 993. At that time the Samanid Empire had foundered. Mahmoud took Khorasan and then turned east, towards India. His main opponent, the Raj of Punjab, succumbed in the year 1000. Following that victory, he assumed the title of Sultan. A decade later he conquered a coalition of Hindu potentates of the Indo-Ganges world and thereafter, scarcely a year passed without a victorious expedition into the Indus Valley or the western basin of the Ganges. In 1021 he carried the torch of Islam into Kashmir and five years later the Temple of Shiva at Somnath in Gujarat, fell into his hands.

To the north, the Sultan carried his arms into Transoxiana, which in 1024 recognized him as suzerain. Shortly afterwards, he took the province of Rayy, near today's Teheran and Isfahan. Sultan Mahmoud found himself at the head of an immense empire, comprising the territories of present-day Iran and north-west India, with its capital in Afghanistan.

The Ghaznavid Empire survived for over a hundred years after Mahmoud's death. From the uncharted mountain heartland of Afghanistan came the people of Ghor, led by Jahan-Soz, the 'World Burner', avenging, sacking and destroying the marble palaces of Ghazni. The Ghorids carried the faith of Islam to north India and made Delhi the capital of their empire until the thirteenth century.

All remaining splendours perished in the Mongol invasion of Genghis Khan, who exceeded even Japan-Soz in his ability to reduce to rubble and wilderness the lands he entered. Bukhara, Samarkand, Balkh, Kabul and Ghazni were obliterated. Over a million Heratis were massacred and the great karaz system of underground irrigation was destroyed, leaving barren and deserted the lushly cultivated southern provinces of Afghanistan. This single wave of destruction left the country depopulated for centuries, its economic and spiritual structure broken.

Two hundred years later, Tamerlane swept across Afghanistan on his way to Delhi, sparing only one city,

Samarkand, which he made his capital. He subjugated all of Central Asia, brutally decimating the various provincial dynasties which had sprung up after the disappearance of the Mongol Khans. His vast empire did not survive him — it was broken into fragments by numerous offsprings all claiming the right of succession. Later, on the ruins of Herat, one of his sons built a city of beauty equal to his father's capital of Samarkand.

Shah-Rukh, founder of this Timurid dynasty of Herat, displayed exceptional capacity as a ruler. He made his son, Ulugh Beg, viceroy of Samarkand. Under their enlightened administration, Khorasan and Transoxiana attained a high degree of prosperity. Fifteenth-century Herat produced monuments of architectural, artistic and intellectual grandeur that made this period one of the most brilliant in Afghan history.

In the north, the Uzbeks had dethroned the last member of the Timurid dynasty. Baur, a young descendant of both Genghts Khan and Tamerlane, fled south to Balkh, capturing Kabul in 1504 and some twenty years later Delhi, thereby establishing himself as the first ruler of the great Moghul Empire in India. While eastern Afghanistan became a distant province of the Moghul Empire, the Afghans, under the leadership of Mir Weis Hotaki, succeeded in liberating the western part of their country from the Safavids, whose empire in Iran was brought to an end in 1722 by Afghan occupation. The expansion of the Afghan State was temporarily stopped by Nadir Afshar, who ranged as far as Delhi and there received the submission of the Moghul court.

Nadir Afshar was assassinated by a Persian officer. Ahmad Shah of the Sadozai tribe was elected sovereign of the Afghans at a gathering of tribal chieftains, where a holy man crowned him with a wreath of wheat, one of the symbols displayed on today's Afghan flag. Ahmad Shah founded a powerful empire, stretching from the northern-most boundaries of Khorasan to the Ganges plain. He excelled in battle and politics and, by consolidating the fractious tribes around him, he laid the foundation of a unified State with Kandahar as the first capital of modern Afghanistan.

Following Ahmad Shah's death in 1773, his son Timur Shah tried to strengthen the centre, transferring the capital to Kabul. His efforts were unsuccessful, however and in the following decades the outer provinces of Kashmir and the Punjab were lost and the feudal potentates of northern Afghanistan proclaimed their independence, as did the Sinds in the south. The Sikhs, allied with the British since 1806, then took Peshawar in the east. Amir Dost Mohammad, chief of the powerful Mohammadzai tribe, finally re-established Afghan unity in 1934. A few years later, the British Government sent Sir Alexander Burnes from India to Kabul to 'test the friendship the British might form in the region'. As a result of lagging and uncertain negotiations, the British gathered their famous army of India and without great difficulty, captured Kabul, putting a pro-British puppet on the throne. Within a year, tribal rebellion was galvanized into open revolt. The British envoys were assassinated, as was their figure-head ruler; 17,000 retreating British troops and camp-followers were annihilated in the mountain passes leading to Jalalabad. Dost Mohammad returned to power and set out once again to unite his people.

The political unity achieved by Dost Mohammad was shattered after his death. Amir Sher Ali, an enlightened monarch, refused to agree to British ultimatums and chose the only course left open: negotiations with czarist Russia. This led to the Second Anglo-Afghan war, with Afghanistan becoming virtually a British protectorate, acting as a buffer State between Russia and British India. The British arbitrarily established Afghanistan's borders and with the Durand Line of 1893, cut the Pashtoon tribal areas literally in half.

Nationalist sentiments were effectively expressed at this time by Sayed Jamaluddin (1838-97), venerated under the name of al-Afghani, a prominent scholar of Islam and anti-colonialist. He clashed with Moslem leaders in his own country as well as in Turkey and Iran. In an exchange with the French scholar Ernest Renan, he refuted the latter's views on the incompatibility of Islam with modern science and progress.

Modern Afghanistan took shape between 1884 and 1919. Consolidation of the central power was accomplished by the political genius of Amir Adbur Rahman, who reigned from 1880 to 1901. Amir Habibullah continued his father's efforts at reform and, during his reign, modern ideas began to enter the country. During the Third Anglo-Afghan War in 1919, Great Britain agreed officially to surrender its control of Afghan foreign policy and to recognize Afghanistan's complete independence.

Habibullah's son, Amanullah, who reigned for ten years, launched major and far-reaching reforms. He ordered the emancipation of women, established compulsory education for both sexes and sent young Afghans to study abroad. With King Amanullah's social, economic and military reforms, the foundation of modern Afghanistan had been laid.

A brief but serious uprising interrupted this progress in 1928-29 and Amanullah was forced to abdicate. Mohammad Nadir Shah restored order and ruled from 1929-33. His son, Mohammad Zahir Shah, ruled until 17 July 1973, when Mohammad Daoud in a bloodless coup abolished the monarchy and proclaimed the first Republic in the history of Afghanistan. During recent years, the government took serious measures to reform the administrative, fiscal, commercial and industrial sectors. Hospitals and schools were built, foreign advisers were brought in, programmes for the development of educational institutions were increased and the women of Afghanistan began to assume a more active role in public life. During Mohammad Daoud's years as prime minister, the country's first five-year plan was initiated.

Preservation and Conservation of Bamiyan

The monuments at Bamiyan, though fairly well-known to the scholarly world, do not appear to have received the due attention in matters of preservation. The only major structural conservation work done, some forty years back, is represented by the enormous masonry buttress wall, faced with brickwork, to support the cracked and fractured portion of the west wall of the main shrine of the small Buddha. The old photographs of the rock-cut wall, taken in the middle of the twenties, show the bottom portion of the wall with steps missing and the upper part overhanging. This area of Afghanistan being in a seismic zone, is subjected to spasmodic earthquake shocks; apparently an earthquake shock caused the wide crack which ran across the shrine. The butters wall, therefore, in spite of its incongruity was considered necessary and helped to some extent to prevent the severed portion of the rock from likely collapse. The shrine at the bottom of the east wall, which had lost its roof, presumably was walled up about this time. In respect to the big Buddha, no structural repair seems to have been carried out.

Some elementary work of filleting the broken edges of plaster of murals was however, done also at the big Buddha and in an octagonal shrine to the west of the small Buddha, by using lime-gypsum. No attempt was made to tint the lime-gypsum to tone down its natural whiteness.

Before taking up the conservation work, the shrines were found to have vestiges of modern additions. In 1956, an Indian Mission while visiting Bamiyan saw a mud wall built up in front of the small Buddha and the Shrine was under occupation; the one to the right of the central shrine had an over in the floor for baking bread. Similarly, the front of the big Buddha was walled up and rooms constructed, by erecting cross and short walls, as a granary. During clearance work, wheat and clay seals bearing the storekeeper's name, were found. But the additional constructions were demolished subsequently and the shrines vacated. After the clearance of the debris, the damaged feet of both statues were exposed. A check of their heights revealed that the 35m small Buddha measured 38m and 53m big Buddha was 55 m.

The walls and the ceiling of these shrines had extensive remains of paintings. These paintings suffered considerably owing to both physical and chemical weathering. The pigment became loose and flaky; the plaster carrying the paintings was found to be very weak and at places had come off the rock surface. Deposits of sooty and tarry matter, dust and dirt, nests of insects, etc., caused much damage to the paintings. In certain cases the murals were covered with a layer of mud plaster. the murals within reach of the occupants of the shrines were mostly defaced. The paintings on the curvilinear ceiling of the main Buddha shrine which were beyond reach, seem to have served as targets for shooting, as scores of bullets and a few iron arrow-heads were found lodged in the plaster and rock. However, with the growing awareness of the value of this cultural heritage and the eagerness to preserved it, all acts of human vandalism were checked.

But the natural process of disintegration remained unabated. As already mentioned above, due to earthquake shocks in the past, cracks had appeared in the ceiling of the main niche and on the facade of the rock-cut wall. Those on the ceiling were plastered over and the surface was painted, indicating that the cracks were of an earlier origin. The greatest damage, however, was caused by one which ran along the cliff and travelled beyond the caves in Group D, through the west wall of the main niche. In course of time, the cracked portion of the west wall was separated from the parent body and several cracks had appeared on its inner face, giving it a shattered look. The spiral staircase inside was disrupted and at places the steps came away with the separated chunk. Annual deposits of snow inside these cracks and fissures had widened them and made the condition of the west wall still worse and more alarming. The gaping staircase could swallow a visitor and spelt danger!

The Afghan Government was anxious to save the monuments from further deterioration and sought the co-operation of India in this difficult task. In June 1969 the Prime Minister of India, Mrs. Indira Gandhi, visited Afghanistan at its invitation. When visiting Banyan she shared their concern that urgent steps to preserve the statues and shrines were called for and a team of experts was immediately sent to take up the work. Of the two images, the small Buddha, being in a worse condition, was taken up first for preservation in July 1969.

In the joint project of preservation, the first of its kind in Afghanistan, the Afghan side came forward to provide the required building materials, tools and workshops available locally, labourers' conveyance and residential accommodation for the Indians participating in the work. The Indian side, in turn, took with them the necessary expertise and technicians, like engineers, chemists, artist modellers and photographer as well as chemicals, photographic materials and machinery and procured a steel scaffolding to reach the great heights of the Buddha "colossis".

The purpose of the Indian team working at Banyan was to conserve the monument, arrest its further deterioration and to render it aesthetically presentable without altering its original look and character. No missing portion was to be renewed unless it was absolutely necessary for preservation or structural stability; nor were the murals to be retouched in any form with colour. These are the principles followed by Archaeological Survey of India, even before it was enunciated in the Venice Charter in 1964 by the International Council of Monuments and Sites.

The conglomerate rock of Banyan is a mixture of heterogeneous materials like gravel of various sizes, clay and layers of sand deposited alternatively. The rock is damaged by the snow-water flowing from the top, as such drains are constructed at the top to divert the flow of water away from the facade. Such constructional works, stabilization of structures of the shrines and also securing the loose or cracked portions by rock-bolting and filling of the cracks and fissures are done by the engineers. The modellers attend to the repairs of the sculptures, as they have done to the damaged feet of both the Buddhas, without attempting any reconstruction. The murals are cleaned, the pigments secured and then a coat of preservative applied by the chemists. All these operations are documented at various stages by the artist and photographer so that the condition of the monument can be studied before, during and after its preservation. Working for seven seasons (May-September, till the end of September, 1975), the small Buddha along with its surrounding shrines have been conserved and the murals there preserved. At the big Buddha, the buried portion of the feet has been exposed and preserved, the passage to the gallery summit conserved and the overhanging portion of the fractured right leg secured by rock-bolting.

It was proposed to take about three more seasons to complete the preservation work at the big Buddha. During that period the shrines at the ground level — the back and side walls of the main niche — were freed from modern accretions and conserved. A portion of the eastern wall along with the approach to the shrine at a higher level has been eroded by the flow of snow-water. The missing portion was to be restored to provide access to the shrine as well as to give support to the overhanging portion of the wall above. In respect to the image proper, the cracks in the body were to be filled in, the disrupted folds of the upper garment in plaster secured and stabilized. In effect the general character of the damaged statue was to remain the same and yet to impart a feeling of all pervading solidity. The extant murals on the ceiling of the main niche were to be cleaned and preserved, after the defective filleting replaced and matched with the colour scheme of the paintings.

In repairing the various members of the rock-cut shrines, rubble masonry has been used largely to make up the volume of the disintegrated or missing mass of the rock, then the surface of the masonry finished, to match the rock surface with a coat of cement-concrete plaster varying in thickness from 3cm. to 5 cm. The plaster tinted with the local sandy soil has been applied mainly for aesthetic considerations, but its composition shows a difference to the discernible eye. Lest the conservator is unduly blamed for what is not done by him, The part played by nature in effecting 'falsification' must be made clear here. The facade receives a 'clay-wash', due to the annual snow-water washing down the soft clay of the rock. New constructions against the facade also, in course of time, became merged with the rock and looks like part of it, having a similar clay wash spread uniformly. The restored surface, till its merger with the rock surface, stands out as an alien feature and an incongruity; as such the conservator imitates Nature and applies the 'clay wash' that it would have naturally received in due course of time. The aesthetic effect of the finished work, one must admit, is quite pleasant.

The main task at the small Buddha was to secure the severed piece of rock in position and to save the image from being exposed to the actions of weather. This was done by filling in the entire length of the fissure with cement concrete duly reinforced with a network of mild steel rods. The reinforcement steel rods, anchored well inside the rock, were intended to hold the severed portion in position. Around this chunk, belts of flat-iron bars were further introduced as additional grip, with tie-rods duly embedded in the compact rock of the back wall.

Having secured the fractured mass of rock in position, the buttress wall was treated. The wall was found to be resting on a shallow base laid on disintegrated soft rock. The foundation, therefore, had to be strengthened by adding a masonry toe-wall. The recess between the flanks of the buttress wall was then filled in with rubble masonry upto the base of the fractured rock. Inside the masonry filling, reinforcement steel rods were provided with concrete, from the base of the toe-wall, to act as a columnar support and to establish a bond between the new work and the old. The wall was trimmed and the entire surface covered with cement-concrete plaster, in a manner so as to simulate the undulated rock surface. The use of 'cut blocks' of rock in the support was suggested by one conservator, but masonry with cement-concrete plaster was used, in preference to cut blocks of rock, mainly for the reason that by its strength, homogeneity and mass, it was more durable and suitable to match the irregular surface and contour of the rock. In the case of the Nurbian monuments in Egypt, the precious stone-carvings along with the shrines were to be preserved, so the entire mass of rock was sawed into blocks which were transported to the new site and reassembled there. While at Bamiyan the main job was to secure the detached mass of rock by providing a 'suitably fashioned' support that would not interfere with the general disposition of the rock-facade, either in shape or in fabric, yet it would remain separated from the original rock.

The original entrance to the staircase which was blocked, was opened up and the decayed steps were reconditioned. At a higher level, the rock-cut steps for a height of about two metres were missing and so the staircase could not be used. A visitor was required to take a circuitous route from the eastern side to reach the painted shrines on the west. A new series of steps was, therefore, constructed at that place by scooping out the masonry of the buttress wall. The old staircase was thereby restored for ascent right up to the top.

At the ground floor, the shrines in the walls of the three sides have been reconditioned by removing the modern accretions and repairing the damaged portions. The central shrine, shown in earlier publications as circular on plan, turned out to be octagonal. The topless shrine in the east wall, on the outer edge, has been restored to utilize the roof-top to support the overhanging portion of the rock above it.

The preservation work executed to the murals included elaborate physical and chemical cleaning, fixing and consolidation of the plaster and general strengthening of the painted surface. The broken edge of the plaster has been filleted with "quch" tinted with a lighter colour than that of the painting, so that the portions treated are indistinguishable. Careful and diligent cleaning work has laid bare many interesting paintings which remained so long under a layer of soot. Paintings were also exposed after removing a layer of modern mud-plaster applied by later occupants. Among these new paintings special mention may be made of the figure of Buddha with flames issuing form the shoulders in, a scene depicting the miracle of Sravasi and of a cherub with lotus-buds in its hands.

The image of the small Buddha has been carved out of the rock in 'alto-releivo', but the arms appear to have been built up with wooden armatures. In the grooves of the arms were found, during repairs, remains of the wood in a charred condition. The image was plastered with layers of stucco which was damaged at places, especially in the area above the chest which was affected by snow-drifts. The exposed rock surface of the chest was covered with a layer of plaster mixed with cement and a water-proofing compound. In doing so, the folds of the garment were also repaired with a rough surface, as it would look without its finishing coat of plaster. The contrast is well demonstrated in the area between the neck and the right breast. Even in mending the patches, the repaired surfaces have been finished to look weathered. On the other hand, the portions of the chin and the neck where the stucco is missing, no attempt has been made to replaster the surface, but only the broken edge of the stucco has been filleted to halt any further disintegration. Such restraints were exercised mainly with a view to respecting the 'traditional look' of the weathered and damaged image. Similarly, only the barest minimum repairs have been carried out to the damaged feet without effecting any material change in the general look. The fractured portion of the right leg, above the ankle, has been secured by fixing steel bolts concealed in the rock and the feet have been finished rough after consolidation.

With the damages repaired in an aesthetic manner and the unsightly buttress wall treated to merge with the rock, the entire look of the surroundings of the small Buddha has been immensely improved. The image of the Buddha, duly preserved now looks much better. Regarded in this part of Asia as a solar deity and also the earthly reflection of the heavenly prototype, here signified by the painting of the Sun-god on top, the Buddha will continue to be a beacon for posterity. The patrimony is being handed over to posterity in a much better condition, to cherish for many years to come.

The Art of Bamiyan

Bamiyan lies in the valley between the Hindu Kush mountain range which cuts diagonally across central Afghanistan and Koh-i-Baba range and occupies an important position on the ancient trade routes that link India and Central Asia. Caravans and pilgrim monks followed the route, stretching from Balkh through Bamiyan and Kapisa and then onto Gandhara and the valley of Bamiyan no doubt offered these travellers welcome respite from their journeys across deserts and through rugged mountains.

This narrow valley is not so abundantly blessed by nature but here, amazingly, were constructed two gigantic Buddhas and a host of caves and in its day, this small oasis saw the flourishing of Buddhist art. There are no records, no inscriptions revealing during what age and through what process these great Buddhas were created and we must rely for all our information about Bamiyan on a few passing remarks in the chronicles of pilgrim monks. In 632, the monk Hiuen Tsang passed through Bamiyan on a journey from Balkh and recorded that here there were "tens of convents and monks in the thousands following the school of Lokottaravadin of Hinayana Buddhism". Huei Tch'ao, who visited Bamiyan in 727, related that here, "the king, the chieftains and the farmers all revere the Three Treasures of Buddhism; monasteries and monks are plentiful, they practice both Mahayana and Hinayana Buddhism", thus testifying to the prosperity of Buddhism there at that time.

Today, however, the capital and the former convents witnessed by Hiuen Tsang have disappeared from Bamiyan. Today, the magnificent past of Bamiyan is revealed only through the two great Buddhas, gazing out to the south from the sheer cliff across the valley floor, several seated Buddhas and the caves that honeycomb the face of the cliff — all marred by the destruction of vandals. Caves of great interest may also be found in the cliffs of Kakrak and Foladi near Bamiyan valley. Among the ruins remaining in Bamiyan, the items which are of particular interest in terms of art history are the two great Buddhas, the structures of the caves, wall paintings remaining in the niches and caves, and a small number of plastic images and ornaments that have survived in caves.

The first sight to strike the viewer's eyes is the pair of gigantic Buddhas towering near the east and west ends of the kilometer-long cliff. The eastern Buddha stands 37 meters tall, while the one to the west is 55 meters in height and each occupies a niche in the cliff. The faces of both Buddhas have been destroyed and only the mouths and chins remain and the arms and legs also badly marred. The niche housing the eastern Buddha is somewhat perverted in that the Buddha itself has an exaggeratedly large head and severely squared shoulders so that the overall proportions are fairly inaccurate. The pleats in the Buddha's robes are represented by parallel grooves.

In contrast, the western Buddha presents a balanced, dignified figure in a niche of regular trefoil form. The pleats are expressed by rows of wooden stakes and linking ropes which are finished with stucco, thus delineating the folds of the robes in string-like lines. The two Buddhas each have different methods of representing pleats but both robes are draped in the same manner, still following the Gandharan style. Little of the hair remains, but in both cases this too takes on a wavy pattern after the Gandharan style. In overall styling, there are few great differences between the two, implying that the period between their construction was not extremely long.

However, even though the Buddhas follow the Gandharan style in the drapery of the pleats and the hair, the rather solemn, powerful form of the torsos and the schematic representation of the folds of the robes are quite apart from the usual form taken by Gandharan Buddhas. Some scholars point to strong influences of the Gupta style as evinced in the schematic style of the pleats and the stately composure of the body of the western Buddha, but such resemblances are not extremely strong. The great Buddhas of Bamiyan could most likely be compared to the great Buddhas of Yun Kang, built under the T'o-panomad tribe and evincing their own particular vigorous style.

Bamiyan's beautiful wall paintings in particular attract the attention of scholars and visitors. Although they have been greatly defaced over the centuries and only fragments remain, such wall paintings may still be found in the niches of the great Buddhas and the seated Buddhas and in some of the cave temples.

In the niche of the western Buddha are paintings of Buddhist subjects indicating that the huge, well-ordered composition followed the trefoil shape of the alcove. Much of the surface above the head of the Buddha has peeled away from the ceiling of the alcove, but the remaining portions seem to indicate that once this spot was occupied by a huge painting of a bodhisattva. Below it, two lovely female musicians play harp and flute and around the great bodhisattva appear many other beautiful bodhisattvas. These bodhisattvas are interspersed with fascinating figures of gods and goddesses, some scattering flowers, some playing musical instruments and others in attitudes of worship. These figures, both bodhisattvas and gods, are depicted in light brown forms against a dark blue background with yellow ocher shading the bodies, arms and legs.

This heavenly world depicted on the ceiling of the niche is bordered by an ornamental canopy, of lotus flowers and curtain-like designs. Below this canopy seated Buddhas appear beneath bodhi trees. The representations of these Buddhas indicate a trend toward 'manierisme'. At the level of the great Buddha's shoulders, the projection portion of the trefoil niche carries beautiful pictures of gods and goddesses soaring about the heavens and facing towards the Buddha as they scatter flowers and worship him. A skilful use of colour and line has produced a work of outstanding and highly lifelike quality. The paintings on both walls below these projecting portions have largely been destroyed but the pattern from above has continued here also; namely these walls bore seated Buddhas.

The paintings in the niche of the western Buddha are of slightly differing styles according to the ceiling, side walls and projecting portions, but overall they do present an ordered, cohesive development of one main theme. Most likely, this entire work was conducted by various groups of artists under the inspired direction of one leader. These paintings do convey an echo of traditional Gandharan artistic style in the decorative elements and form given to the torso of figures but one can also see the influence of Indian art, in particular Gupta art, in the tribhanga form of Bodhisattvas, the shading of the arms, legs, body and the alluring unclothed female forms. These paintings however, are even more closely related to the art of Central Asia. On the one hand, they have several elements in common with wall paintings of Kizil Style No.1 (particularly the treasure cave), such as the use of colours centering on browns and understanding of the human body which draws on classical style, delicate shading and details of decorative designs. On the other hand, the sharp yet smoothed line especially used to delineate facial expressions, are extremely close to the wall paintings of Balalik-Tepe near Termez and Farhad-Beg-yailaki near Khotan. The wall paintings surrounding the western great Buddha are the most classical and naturalistic examples to be found at Bamiyan, and may be termed as Bamiyan Style No. 1.

The niche paintings of the seated Buddha H have approximately the same composition as those of the western great Buddha — a bodhisattva on the ceiling with seated Buddhas aligned below it and flying gods arranged on the projecting portion of the trefoil alcove. The flying gods use only a limited range of colours and yet they project subtle nuances. The face, bodies, hands and feet are drawn in vital, powerful lines that easily attract and hold the eye. While these wall paintings of cave H do belong to Style No. 1, they already show the transition to Style No. 2.

The paintings of cave E, I,N,B,S,G and F may be given as examples of Style No. 2. Here the classicism and naturalism of Style No. 1 have been absorbed and changed under the influence of new concepts and techniques to produce a qualitative shift in overall style. For example, a bodhisattva painting on the ceiling of the second seated Buddha E's alcove is oriented strictly to the front and firm lines, strong shading and resolutely spread elbows of the body have captured the majesty of "the lord of the cosmos". The ribbons and shawls of the bodhisattva are schematically portrayed and the long flowing hair are given in painstaking detail. The lotus figures used in the painting are also schematically designed. Here in the wall paintings of cave E, the classical nature of Style No. 1 gives way to a new sensualistic style which features sharp lining, painstaking detail, schematical design, sensual shading and gradation and "deformation".

The wall painting of cave N, a small square chapel discovered a few years ago by a team from Nagoya University, represents one of the pinnacles of Style No. 2. The eastern wall is fairly well preserved, presenting two seated Buddhas (one of which is a decorated Buddha) attended by monks and heavenly nymphs in attitudes of adoration. In this painting, the artists have surpassed the naturalism of Style No. 1 and the elements of painting, namely, line and colour are now independent of each other. The painting has got an effect of dazzling form by the use of luxurious colours. The facial expressions and the folds of the robes are accomplished by skilful sharp lines. The graduation of vermillion used in the face produces a mysterious effect of animation. Although Style No. 2 seems to reflect stylistic features seen in Central Asian paintings such as those of Kizil and Khotan, it also displays its own striking independent development at Bamiyan.

In contrast, the wall paintings in the niche enclosing the eastern great Buddha which typify Style No. 3, seem to be rather isolated. On the ceiling of the niche there is a god, seemingly the god of the sun, on a four horse chariot, appearing with cape flying in the midst of a circular aureole and holding a spear in his right hand and a sword in his left. This god floats against a sky of lapis blue. On both sides above the chariot are winged goddesses bearing shields and bows. This highly interesting picture has a few similarities with the Sasanian iconography but it is difficult to find any examples that exactly correspond to that at Bamiyan.

The stylistic feature of this painting is its exclusion of gradation and shading in favour of graphic art lines using light flat colours and accomplishing a thorough two-dimensionality through contrast with each light colour. This style is diametrically opposed to the classical Style No. 1 and seems to have descended from the Sasanian style.

A series of people encompasses the large ceiling painting at each side. Here appear six seated Buddhas (of which four are decorated Buddhas) and several royal families. The crowns worn by these figures have frequently been cited as examples of the Sasanian style but they do not conform to those actually used during the Sasanian dynasty. This painting does descend from Sasanian art but it may be imagined that it has undergone considerable change. This wall painting can be compared to the painting of Dokhtar-i-Noshirwan, but in Bamiyan's case, the ceiling painting of the vestibule of cave D is merely an example of Style No. 3.

There is also a fourth Style to be found in the wall paintings of caves A, B1, J, M and East-III. This Style No. 4 could be called pseudo-naturalistic or ornamentalistic and primarily uses rough, flat colours and even the outlines do not have a sharp, clear-cut quality. This style appears to be the most retrogressive of the paintings found at Bamiyan.

Let us now turn from the wall paintings to the cave-temples. The caves, numbering over 1,000, are scattered here and there throughout the cliff. Unlike India, where Buddhist caves can be readily labelled as Chaitya or Vihara, it is difficult to apply a clear classification to the caves of Bamiyan.

They may, however, be categorized by their structure as, for example, extremely simple caves which appear to have been monks' cells or storerooms, or more elaborate caves which seem to have been sanctuaries or monasteries. Monks' cells and storerooms are very simple and small. Monasteries are frequently laid out in a rectangular large plan but the interior decorations are comparatively plain. The caves used as sanctuaries were constructed with great care and are carefully decorated.

So the structure of the sanctuaries provides a theme of great interest in terms of the history of architecture. A large number of the plans of the sanctuaries are centralized halls, namely, square, octagonal and round, of which the former two are most common.

The ceilings generally take the form of a dome or 'Laternendecke' and a complicated course of development can be seen in the various combinations of that plan with this ceiling. When a dome is used with a square chamber, the corners of the ceiling are sometimes left flat and at other times arched squinch may be used. The style of arched squinch has its roots in the Sasanian period but brick buildings constructed in such a manner are common in Central Asia and these may have been copied for the caves at Bamiyan. The structural nature of the dome caves using arched squinches is clear and they usually have no series of niches, centering instead on decoration provided by wall paintings. On the other hand, the structural form of the dome caves using plain squinches is unclear and in many cases the work itself is rather roughly done. One point deserving of attention is that the square caves with domed ceilings are concentrated in the eastern section of the cliff.

In the square caves using a 'Laternendecke' ceiling, there is a comparatively large sanctuary and a small attached chapel. In many cases the section of the larger chamber is trapezoidal, containing pilasters or an arcade around the sides of which provides niches. Carved and sculptured decoration is found in the latter case. The smaller chapels are generally rich in wall paintings and 'Laternendecke' is frequently used not so much functionally as decoratively. The 'Laternendecke' is originally formed by two pairs of parallel wooden beams placed perpendicularly, with this same pattern repeated in the resultant centre space and with the centre square resulting from a further repetition being left open to serve both as a skylight and as a smoke outlet.

Such a style of ceiling construction seems to have been developed in the region at the foot of the Pamir mountains and it has frequently been applied to the ceilings of the square and the octagonal chambers at Bamiyan, testifying to its popularity.

Octagonal chambers using domed ceilings are mostly found near the western great Buddha and they include niches set into all the walls except that of the entrance. Archades encircle the bases of the domes and one contained Buddhist statuary and reliefs of Buddha were also affixed to the domes as well; such composition may be said to be kind of "mandala". Here, the carved and sculptured ornamentation is abundant and the structural nature is clear, but there are no known structures having just this particular form outside of caves. Rather than imitating or reproducing some actual buildings, the aim here seems to have been to create some kind of symbolic space. Among the octagonal caves, there are some with distinctive cross-vault ceilings and these seems to be the height of such a development of symbolic space. One might even think that this form was suggested by the shape of a nomadic people's tents, but here such a shape has taken on an extremely symbolic, schematized form.

It is difficult to find any examples of octagonal plan among building from the Sasanian period and there are few examples in India as well. The source of Bamiyan's octagonal caves is thus unclear, but this style may have originally developed in Syria or northern Iran.

As mentioned above, Buddhist caves of Bamiyan are closely linked to a wide variety of Central Asian architecture and one may imagine that they were the result of a complex development and interaction of cultures. Moreover, there seems to be many cases in which the creators of the structures at Bamiyan received some inspiration for their creations from existing structures and styles, but even in such cases, there frequently seems to have been no strong conscious attempt to exactly duplicate these existing buildings; rather, the attempt appears to have been to create a type of symbolic space that exploits the specific nature of the caves themselves. Anyone who enters the cave-temples of Bamiyan is struck by a type of illusionary feeling of being emotionally pressed and appealed to by the Buddhas of these caves. Within these dimly lit caves the monks found places for their meditation and other religious practices in strongly symbolic spaces.

In Bamiyan's cave-temples, there are practically no didactic decorations such as illustrations depicting the life of Buddha or Jataka (such being limited to the scenes of nirvana) and there are also few sanctuary caves centering on main images or stupas; a lack of such cave-temples is probably related to the emphasis given to the concept of symbolic space as a place of religious practice.

Before concluding about the art of Bamiyan, a word must be added about the sculptures and carved decorations. The vast number of Buddhist images revered in the caves have been destroyed by the people of later generations, so that few remain today. The few figures which have survived in caves G and V, are made of clay and although their style is descendent from the Gandharan art, there are also indications of a trend toward "manierisme". Viewed as a whole, these figures were no doubt created later than stucco works of Hadda. The ornamentation of the arcades and borders used in the caves is relatively intact and these too are moulded of clay and take on wavy arabesque patterns such as octopus' arms, thus resembling similar works from Fondukistan, Adzhina-Tepe and Tapa-Sardar. Other themes used in the ornamentation include faces of mysterious beings, winged beasts and rows of birds, each of them interesting in its own right.

It is extremely difficult to arrange the arts of Bamiyan in chronological order. However, judging from the styles of the extant wall paintings and carved and sculpted ornamentation, they are most likely products of the sixth to eighth centuries. The caves themselves probably date from approximately the same period. The two great Buddhas were probably created during earlier period, but it may be impossible to say just how much earlier they were constructed.

Even though it may well be assumed that the Buddhist arts of Bamiyan developed against the background of Gupta and Sasanian civilizations, they are not a direct fusion of the two. Most likely the art of Bamiyan was generated by an independent Buddhist culture of Central Asia that grew up in a small kingdom established by Iranian nomads, skilfully absorbing the broad and varied arts then existing in Central Asia. Here blossomed arts which differed greatly both in style and basic concept from the Buddhist arts flourishing in central India and Gandhara. The deeply rooted orientation toward the stupa found in India here was replaced by the systematic conception of the great Buddha. Such a development carries with it a strong reminder of national Buddhism and this approach can easily be compared to that seen in the great Buddhas of Yun Kang in China and Todai-Ji in Japan. In fact, there are certain characteristic Buddhist figures which support this idea of state Buddhism, the 'decorated Buddhas' draped in the robes of kings, illustrating the coming of the sacred and the secular worlds. However, we do not know the name of the kings of the name of the dynasty-instead, all that remains are the many cave-temples that stood as places of meditation.

No doubt the king, many monks and many common people were among the fervent believers who dreamed of the ideal land in which the country was united in belief in Buddhism. In his writings, Huei Tch'ao recorded that 'the king of this country is an Iranian and the country belongs to no other land. It is strong in soldiers and horses, thus preventing other countries from invading The king, the chieftains and the farmers all revere the Three Treasures'. It is interesting to wonder whether the efforts made by the people of Bamiyan to create their own particular Buddhist culture faded and disappeared within the boundaries of their small country, or whether they were conveyed in some manner to Central or East Asia.

Bamiyan and its Surroundings

The highly-developed cultures of the East and the West have throughout history met and interacted and Central Asia has most often served as the stage for such cultural interchange. The Buddhist culture that grew up in India was also passed on the East through the medium of Central Asia, experiencing in the process the influences of Greco-Roman and Sasanian cultures. Through these and other contacts with western-derived cultures, Indian Buddhism was endowed with new and different elements before its passage into China. Afghanistan in particular stands as the scene of Buddhism's first extended exposure to the influences of Central Asia.

It is no wonder, then, that here in Afghanistan can be found ruins and remains which call to mind the parent body of culture that eventually gave birth to the Buddhist cultures of East Asia, including China, Korea and Japan.

1. The caves of Bamiyan

Bamiyan lies amidst the Hindu Kush, the range of rugged mountains stretching from east to west across the centre of Afghanistan. Here, at the high elevation of 2,500 meters above sea level, is the small Bamiyan valley where flows the River from east to west. In the ancient past, the route from India to the Western countries passed through Bamiyan and this caravanserai flourished as it welcomed and housed both commercial caravans and private and religious travellers. The flow of travellers was also fostered by the pass in this region cutting through the Hindu Kush from south to north. Running along the northern edge of this caravanserai is a cliff of magnificent proportions, facing to the south along its 1.5 kilometer length and rising up to 100 meters. The cliff is also honeycombed with a variety of large and small caves. Although the actual number of such caves is not precisely known, well over 1,000 exist in the face of the cliff alone and many more may found in the general vicinity. During the early part of the seventh century, the Chinese pilgrim monk Hsuan tsang visited Bamiyan and recorded the Buddhism that thrived there then.

The most famous of the landmarks of Bamiyan are the two colossal Buddhas located near the east and west ends of the cliff. Both are large standing Buddhas set back in trilobed niches carved into the face of the cliff. The eastern Buddha is the smaller of the two at 37 meters, while the western Buddha is 55 meters in height. Roughly carved from the living stone, the Buddhas are finished with plaster and ornamented in detail. The faces of these two great Buddhas have been almost totally destroyed, so that only the small part of the hair and ears remain and it also appears that there were holes which a beard was attached.

The drapery of the cloaks employs heavy ropes driven into grooves in the stone with wooden pegs and finished with plaster.

Around the base of the great Buddhas have been dug seven or eight ancillary caves.

It is possible to climb up above the heads of the Buddhas and a tunnel has been hollowed out of the rock around the upper portion of the niche. Originally, balconies were also provided on either side of the Buddhas' heads.

Paintings covered the wall of the alcoves and the wall paintings of the 37-meter alcove are stylistically older. In the centre of the vault is a painting of a number of figures grouped around Surya riding in a four-house chariot. Surya stands in the middle, backed by the halo of the sun, draped in robes after the fashion of Iran and bearing a sword and spear. Around him are clustered wind gods, half-human, half-animal Kinnaras, winged warriors carrying bows, arrows and shields and winged drivers.

Around the walls below this huge vault paintings are the royal family, in front of which are a Buddha and seated bodhisattvas and in turn below these are rows of figures of seated Buddhas. These wall and ceiling paintings present a strong Iranian flavour and are considered to date from the third or fourth century.

The central portion of the vault painting of the 55-meter Buddha has flaked away to a great extent, but we can make an attempt at reconstructing its original form. The large central figure is a Bodhisattva seated beneath a Bodhi tree. Below and on both sides of this figure are Bodhisattvas in the middle of gables and the forms of lovely females in sensual poses in an Indian style.

On both side walls are ranks of seated Buddhas and this portion is well known for the triple angels shown in the medallions between the Buddhas.

The wall paintings here relate strongly to the Indian Gupta style and are seen as having been created during the fifth or sixth century.

In addition to the alcoves housing the two large standing Buddhas, there are two or three niche-grottos of seated Buddhas. These seated Buddhas, carved out of the living rock, are in a state of severe disrepair, but tunnels have been opened in the rock behind their pedestals to permit a complete round of the Buddhas in the pradaksina ritual. The cave paintings in these niche-grottos consist of decorative Bodhisattvas on the centre of the vaults and rows of seated Buddhas at each side. With the exception of the above-mentioned types of alcoves and niche-grottos, most of the caves found here are grottos. They are variously constructed on rectangular, square, octagonal and circular plans and are appropriately provided with flat, vault, cross-vault, dome, dome and squinch-arch, or laternendecke ceilings.

These grottos have common vestibules or art at times linked by tunnels and they served as halls for worship or congregation, priests' cells and the like.

Many of these caves possess niches of their own, but all of the holy figures contained by these have been lost. Plaster and wall paintings adorned the inner surfaces of these niches, often depicting Buddhas, Bodhisattvas, donors, monks, stupas and the like. Illustrations of the legend of Buddha in the form of parinirvana pictures are found in only two or three cases. As described above, Bamiyan thus represents one flourishing of Buddhism on its movements to the east through Central Asia. Both the style of ornamentation and the architecture place Bamiyan between the third or fourth century and the seventh century and here the arts of the Kushans of Turkestan, the Sasanians of Iran and the Guptas of India have been fused into a treasure house of Buddhist art found in Bamiyan alone. One feature worthy or particular comment is that the construction of great Buddhas began here in Bamiyan and spread to tun Huang, of Yun Kang and eventually to Nara in Japan.

2. The Buddhist caves of Kakrak and Foladi

At the east and west ends of the Bamiyan valley lie two valleys running north and south and these, too, have their share of Buddhist caves. Those to the east are the Kakrak caves and of the statuary which originally adorned the caves, only a small standing Buddha in one niche remains today. These caves were also decorated with wall paintings, with the figure of Buddha enclosed in circular pattern standing as the oldest extant example of the mandala form. Another noted illustration here is that of king-hunter in Kushano-Sasanian style.

The valley to the west is called Foladi Valley. There are a large number of caves here, of which five or six are Buddhist caves in which wall paintings may still be found. These caves have already collapsed and crumbled to a considerable extent, but the ceilings featured combinations of laternendeckes and domes. The ceilings also bore ranks of Buddhas and stupas in mandala fashion and there is one extremely interesting black-skinned Buddha.

3. Fondukistan

The ancient route from Bamiyan to Gandhara crossed the Shidar Pass, followed around the southern foothills of the Hindu Kush, descended the Ghorband Valley and finally led the traveller out onto the plains at Begram. When one turns south at the village of Siagird in the middle of the Ghorband Valley and proceeds about five kilometers up the Fondukistan Valley, one will come upon the hamlet of Fondukistan. Here, near the hamlet, is a conical hill topped by a Buddhist temple site.

The square stupa-court remains and the walls of the various structures are of mud bricks. In the centre of the court stands a stupa and each of the four enclosure walls holds three niches, in which a large number of clay statues and wall paintings have been discovered. The unbaked clay figures are coloured very appealingly and all of the Buddhas, Bodhisattvas and royal donors are depicted in particularly slender and elegant form in the later Gupta style of India. Some features of part of the figures, however, such as the clothing of some of the figures of gods, have an Iranian flavour to them. This temple and its ornamentation date from the seventh century.

4. Begram

Along the southern slopes of the Hindu Kush flow two rivers, the Ghoband running from west to east and the Panjshir, flowing from east to west. These rivers converge and flow out onto the plains at Begram, the site of the ancient city of Kapisa. According to writings of the Chinese monk Hsuan–tsang, this was the summer capital of King Kanishka of the Kushan Dynasty and the records left by Hsuan–tsang describe the great walled city and the numerous nearby temples.

The fortified city stood on the plateau to the south of the point where the rivers converge and the excavations of a French archeological team have disclosed a large volume of treasures in one room of the site.

Here were gathered objects of outstanding quality from both east and west: Roman style bronze objects and plaster reliefs; glass and pottery seemingly from Syria and Egypt; Indian craftsmanship in bone and ivory; and Chinese lacquer objects. This room has also disclosed coins of Kanishka and Vasudeva and all this testifies to the important role played by the Kushan people in the history of east-west cultural exchange. There are number of Buddhist temple sites in the vicinity, at such places as Shotorak, Paitava, Qal-i-Nader, Khamzargar and Tepe-Kalan and these are very similar to the Buddhist temples of the Gandhara region of Pakistan. They have schist stone stupas and viharas and number of schist carvings as well, all in a style that approaches that of the Gandharan school.

In this region there are also ruins of large stupas at Topedara, Qaleh-Surkh, Kafir-Qaleh and the like. Sixty kilometers to the south of Begram lies Kabul, the capital of Afghanistan. This city is also surrounded by quite a number of ruins, such as the remains of castle at Tapa-i-Skandar and the Buddhist stupas of Burji-Kafir Shevaki and Guldara.

5. Hadda

About half way along the road from Kabul east to Gandhara is Jalalabad, the ancient town of Nagarahara. this site has the ruins of the ancient town as well as a number of Buddhist stupas and caves.

Some 7-8 miles SSE of Jalalabad may be found the ruins of Hadda. Among the remains atop the broad plateau are such Buddhist temple sites as Tapa-Kalan, Tapa-i-Kafariha, Baghgai, chakhil-i-Gundi, Deh-Ghundi and Gar-Nao. From the stupa-centered structures have been unearthed a large number of stucco figures and stone sculptures.

At the ruins of Tapa-Shutur outside the northern edge of this plateau, excavation of a large and well-preserved temple is currently being carried on by an Afghan archeological team. Here, quite a few stucco figures remain in the wall of the stupas and in the shrines and various notable figures dating from the first to fifth centuries have been unearthed, such as that of the Naga King in the fish Porch and a realistic figure of Heracles in a shrine.

6. Surkh Kotal

Across the Hindu Kush to the north of Bamiyan is the town of Puri Khumli. Atop the mountain of the northwestern outskirts of the town is a large temple site from the Kushan period. A number of terraces have been set into the face of the mountain and steep steps in the centre of these terraces lead up to a broad, square plaza with an altar and temple in its centre. This seems to have been a Zoroastrian temple and limestone carvings and Greek inscriptions have been found therein. The ruins have also revealed carved figures of a Kanishka king, Kushan nobles, eagles and the like, as well as acanthus and pilasters with figured capitals. These are non-Buddhist remains from the Kushan Dynasty.

7. Haibak

The ancient town of Samangan — today's Haibak — lies on the road from Puki Khumri to Balkh. to the southwest of this town are caves sites collectively called Takhti-i-Rustam. There are five caves around the foot of a solitary hill, the first being a chapel with the Lotus Sutra carved in its domed ceiling, the second cave stretching horizontally below the face of the hill and provided with many monks, cells. Among the other caves, there were those serving as kitchens, toilets and the like.

On the top of a hill facing these caves are the hemispherical body and harmika of a large stupa set down in the soil of the hill.

Memories of Bamiyan

My first visit to Bamiyan was in September 1939, as the Second World War was beginning in Europe. It was just at this time that Joseph Hackin, under whom I had studied and who was both Director of the Guimet Museum in Paris and Chief of the French Archeological Delegation in Afghanistan, was setting out with a small group to conduct a study in northern Afghanistan and he kindly gave permission for me to travel part of the way with the party. At seven o'clock in the morning, the group set out from Kabul in two large six-wheeled trucks loaded with the mission's equipment and stores. First following the Garband River Valley to the source of the river, then mounting a cliff, we came to the pass that marks the divide between the watersheds of the Indian Ocean and the Caspian Sea. As it grew dark, we passed out onto the high tableland and at last arrived at the Afghan Government's hilltop hostelry at ten o'clock at night. The trucks themselves were slow, of course and the poor condition and difficult course of the roads made the day's journey even harder.

During our trip, we had our middle meal in a beautiful valley a short distance beyond the gorge of the Garband. Here at this door to Central Asia, we sat in the shade and gathered around Mr. and Mrs. Hackin-two members of the party, Mr. Meunter and Mr. Carl, a driver named Bonigace, the other driver and Afghani and myself — and talked about the various expectations for the group's survey. As I sat and listened to the others, I found myself thinking that the utopian land of beauty imagined by the ancient Chinese must have been like this peaceful, lovely valley. The sparkling sunshine, the clear fresh air and the pure waters did indeed give an impression of other-worldly perfection.

After lunch, we again took to the road, following the river upstream to its source. Here, too, the scenery was unusual but superb. In the centre of a limestone cliff was a large, pale

Moenjodaro, Pakistan

1

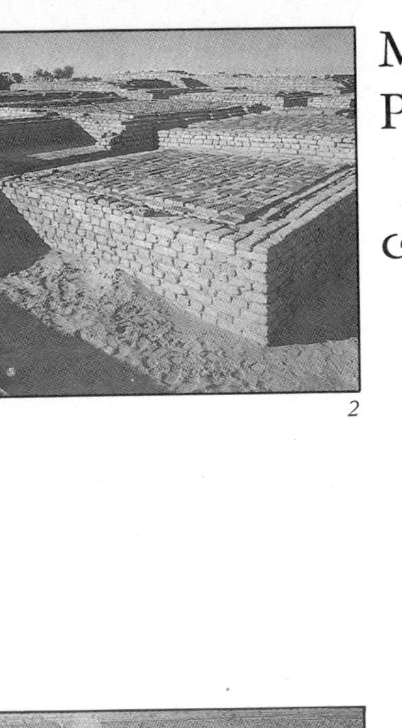

2

3

1. *General view of a Kushan period stupa.*
2. *Close-up view of brick architecture*
3. *General view of the well-planned city of Moenjodaro.*

Herat, Afghanistan

4

5

4. *Minarets in the desert.*
5. *Fortress of Ikhtiaruddin, rebuilt in* AD *1305, where Alexander is reputed to have earlier built a fortress town.*

Paharpur, Bangladesh

1. *The cruciform terraced temple in the centre of the Somapurimaha Vihara monastery.*
2. *Terracotta figure.*

Ajanta and Ellora, India

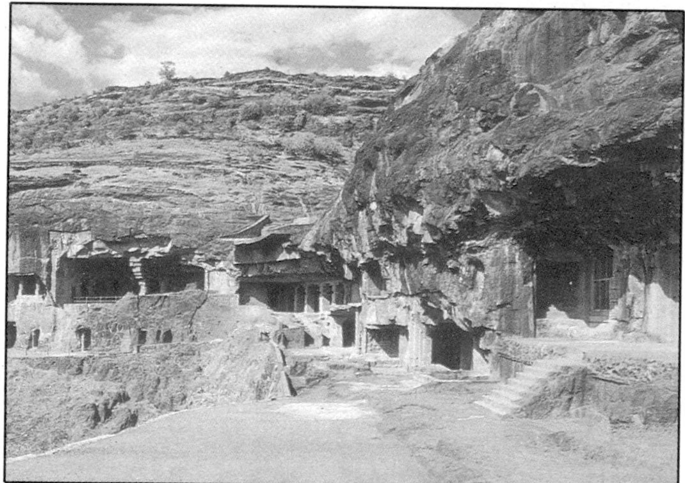

3. *Rock temples of Ellora.*
4. *Cave No. 10 (Chaitya), Ellora.*
5. *Cave No. 26 (Chaitya), Ajanta.*

1

2

Kathmandu Valley, Nepal

1. *Swayambhunath Stupa, the oldest temple in the Kathmandu Valley.*
2. *Nyatapola Temple, Bhadgaon.*

3

4

Bhutan

5

3. *Procession from the main temple of Paro Dzong; Paro Tshechu Festival.*
4. Tungma, *Dance of Terrifying Deities, Paro Tshechu Festival.*
5. *(Left)* Durdag, *Dance of the Lords of the Cremation Grounds.*
   (Centre) Rinya dance, Paro Tshechu Festival.
   (Right) Shanag, *Black Hat dance.*

Pagan, Burma

1

2

3

1. *Ananda Temple, the largest and best preserved temple in Pagan.*
2. *Grass-covered pagodas.*
3. *Sulamani Temple.*

Angkor Wat, Cambodia

4

5

6

4. *Pillars inside Bayon bearing bass-relief of Apsaras dancing on lotus (around* AD *1200).*
5. *Relief of the First Gallery of Bayon, "Marching Khmer soldiers".*
6. *Front view of Angkor Wat.*

Hue, Vietnam

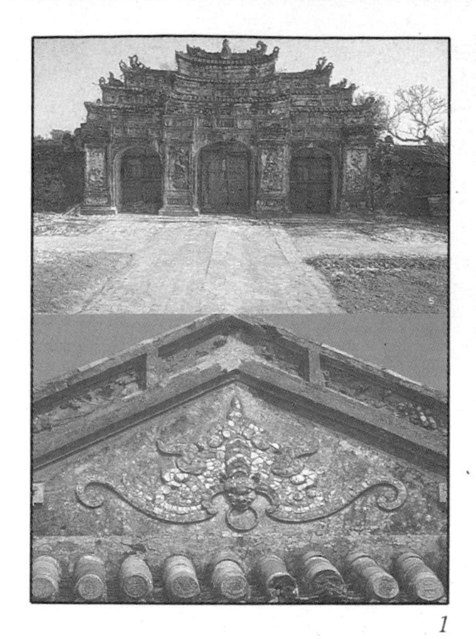

1

2

1. *(Above) Entrance gate to the Royal City and (below) design carved on a gate.*
2. *Soul Porch in the Imperial tomb of Khai Dinh.*

Sukhothai, Thailand

3 4

3. *A large seated Buddha called Pra Achana at Wat Sri Chum in the attitude of subduing Mara.*
4. *(Above) Great image of Buddha of Wat Mahathat and (below) ruins of the central chedi of Wat Phraphai Luang.*

Xian, China

1

2

1. *Interior of the Gu Lou situated in the centre of Xian, Ming dynasty.*
2. *Xiaoyan-ta (Small Wild Goose Pagoda) situated in the Daqianfu Temple, built in* AD *707.*

Mongolia

3

5

4

3. *Festivities at a co-operative, painted by Ts. Dawahuu, Museum of Revolution.*
4. *Old warrior, painted by D. Manibadar.*
5. *Heavenly residence of Amitabha in wood, by Balgan, Choijin Lama Temple Museum.*

Kyongju, Korea

1

2

1. *Tomb of King Muyol, the 29th king of Silla.*
2. *Pulguksa Temple. From left, Blue Cloud Bridge and White Cloud Bridge, Lotus Bridge and Seven Treasures Bridge (Great Silla Dynasty, mid-8th century).*

Nara, Japan

3

3. *Kondo (the main hall) and five-storeyed pagoda of Haryuji.*

Sri Lanka

1. *The recumbent Buddha at the Gal Vihara, Polonnaruwa.*
2. *Rock fortress of Sigiriya with carved rock claws of a lion at the entrance.*
3. *Jetavana Stupa at Anuradhapura, the tallest stupa in the world.*

Borobudur, Indonesia

4. *Bas-reliefs of the First Gallery.*
5. *Chandi Plaosan, a neighbouring site of Borobudur.*

green cave, out of which flowed a broad rush of water, falling down the cliff and giving birth to the Garband River. When I contemplated that this stream grew into a river, first flowing into the Kabul River and eventually into the Indus, I was struck by the marvelously structured way in which the continent and its mountains, watercourses and rivers were organized. The water flowing forth from this cave was a translucent green and as I watched its ripples and the flickering play light on its surface, I could well imagine how the people of long ago had seen in it the shape of a huge snake or dragon. For a moment I was so taken by wonder and mystery of the world's workings that I awoke with a start when the mechanical motion of the trucks working their way up the cliff brought me back to reality. when we reached the top of the cliff, I was told that the reddish -brown sands of these broad highlands marked the divide of water drainage between the Indian Ocean and the Caspian Sea. In the far distant past, this land had once been under the sea and it was startling to see how this area had risen from sea bottom to mountain highlands. Signs of such great geological change can be found throughout Afghanistan and every time one was pointed out to me, I felt how brief aloof mankind's history has been compared to that of the earth. And that this perfectly ordinary-looking highland should be a great divide was itself quite an unexpected revelation.

As we moved along into the sunset, I watched the cloud of sand thrown into the air by the lead truck and I recalled a painting by Delacroxi depicting mounted Arabs fighting in the desert. Other thoughts also came to mind while our trucks descended ceaselessly across these tablelands and I reflected that over the centuries, armies and caravans of Greeks from Bactirana, those Parthians and Kushans had passed along this same way.

The manager of the government hotel at Bamiyan seemed to be an old acquaintance of Dr. Hackin and his party. A number of small oil lamps were placed here and there in the hotel and after being shown to a room on the second floor where I left my baggage on a simple steel bed, I joined the others for a simple meal in a large central room. During the meal we listened to an English broadcast, mostly likely from India, on the shortwave radio we had brought along. There we heard the news of the German army's invasion of Poland. Mr. Hackin impatiently wondered about the French army's response to an attack on the Siegfried Line. In the dim light of the oil lamps, I could see the expressions of tension and apprehension graven on their faces. At last, Mr. Hackin turned to another subject, that of the opposition and rebellion sparked by reforms carried out by former king Aman'ullah Khan of Afghanistan. He related how during the nine-month rule of the rebel army he alone with his wife had travelled from Iran to Herat and then moved on to Kabul on horseback and he described for us the situation that had existed then.

Soon after crossing the Afghanistan border, they had been arrested and taken before the regional rebellion camp commander. When the chief of this band, however, learned that Mr. Hackin had been an officer who had twice been wounded at Verdun but had still returned to the battlefield time and again, his attitude suddenly changed. He asked many questions about the First World War and at last allowed them to continue on to Kabul, wishing them safety in their travels. One point that Mrs. Hackin remarked she remembered particularly well was the large barrack hall where they questioned. It had been filled with soldiers dressed in rags resting around the walls and the chief had been sitting at a simple table in a corner of the room. In the middle of the table, she said, there was only one red apple. In his talk with Mr. Hackin, the chief had been especially interested in Marshall Foch — What did he look like? What was his attitude and what habits did he have? In battle, did he lead his troops or did he command them from behind? When Mr. Hackin replied that Marshall Foch remained behind the lines to take overall command of the army, the Afghani rebel chief commented that on the contrary he always led his own troops into battle.

Mr. Hackin later learned that this was indeed true. When the forces of the king's father, Nadir Shah attacked the rebel army, this chief was at the head of a troop of cavalry and died a hero's death in battle.

From the border camp, Mr. and Mrs. Hackin travelled almost ten days by horseback to reach Kabul, then in the ands of the rebels. There they met with the leader of the rebel army and negotiated for the rebel forces' guarantee of the interests of France and other countries. The couple resided in Kabul for several months until the defeat of the rebel army by Nadir Shah's forces. Just before I left Paris to travel to Afghanistan, I had met the Afghan ambassador to France to receive a visa. The ambassador, said Mr. Hackin, was a member of the royal family and had served with distinction as a general in the army, playing an important role in the recapture of Kabul. This gentleman was the very picture of a military man: tall and slender, sharp-nosed, with piercing glance and swarthy complexion. On his chest he wore medals, awarded to him when he surprised the enemy during the siege of Kabul by leading a small cavalry unit in a plunge down a hard, steep mountain slope, attacking the fortified government quarter from the rear and defeating the rebel forces there.

The following morning, I was awakened by the sunlight splashing into my room. As I returned to the large room of the night before, I saw the reddish-brown face of Bamiyan's gigantic cliff unfolded in the slanted rays of the early sun. The hotel, on a slight rise, provided a striking view of this deeply furrowed wall of rocks and I let out a gasp in spite of myself. On the right, was the 35-meter Buddha set into the face of the cliff and on the left the 53-meter Buddha stood staring out of its niche. Near the 35-meter Buddha I could also see the vertical white projection of a large buttress that had just been built and the whole face of the cliff was pierced by seemingly infinite number of caves.

I was already generally familiar with this sight, having seen photographs of Bamiyan for several years, but I was still not prepared for the emotional intensity of first seeing this magnificent panorama for myself.

Soon after breakfast we descended the small rise, passed through the small village on the green floor of the Bamiyan Valley and sat about exploring the site. From 1931 to 1933, while Mr. Hackin was serving as French director of scientific studies at the invitation of the Japanese Foundation "Masion Franco-Japonaise" in Tokyo, he had directed my studies of French medieval arts and at the same time he taught me about archeological research in Afghanistan. This dealt with the Buddhist arts of Bamiyan and in particular I studied the relationship between these Buddhist arts and the early Christian art of the Mediterranean world and this topic attracted my strong interest. I went to study in France from the autumn of 1933 until the summer of 1939 and around the time that I finished my doctoral thesis on my studies of medieval French arts, Mr. Hackin recommended me to the Japanese Foreign Ministry's Culture Division, headed by Mr. Hikozaburo Ichikawa. That division provided me with a grant of travel expenses, allowing me to stop in Afghanistan on my way back to Japan in the Summer of 1939. Just at that time, Mr. Hackin was directing excavations at Begram near Kabul and it was decided that I should meet him and the survey team in Kabul.

We began our inspection of Bamiyan with the remains around the foot of the 35-meter Buddha, under Mr. Hackin's guidance. We had already been joined by the curator of Bamiyan artifacts, an elderly Afghani gentleman who had been waiting there for our party. I had been surprised by the close friendship evident in the embrace of greeting that he and Mr. Hackin had exchanged and was even more surprised by the fluent Persian in which Mr. Hackin had spoken. The great stone Buddhas of Bamiyan present a picture of noble humanity filled with a universal concept of beauty. In their heroic representation of the reality of this concept, they are seemingly trying to surmount all differences of time and race to convey a noble message of salvation to all mankind and in this they stand as a perfect embodiment of the traditional ideals of classical Greek art. As Islam, which forbids the portrayal of the divine in human form, later became the principal religion of Afghanistan, the people of this country chipped away the faces of the great Buddhas, but even this act probably derived from religious and spiritual puritanism which prohibits any attempt to portray the essence of the absolute God, the ruler of the cosmos, in human form as being a sacrilegious act which limited and diminished God by making him too human, too humanly congenial. The Buddhists of Bamiyan, however, had embraced the image of the Buddha brought in from the south but had expanded this image from that of a mere holy man who had once lived on this earth to that of the magnificent lord of all mankind and all the cosmos, and they had created these huge and stately stone Buddhas as a fitting representation of that enlarged ideal. Historically, there has been no large portrayal of the absolute being in sublime human form, and as such, the Buddhas of Bamiyan stand as the foremost examples of anthropomorphism. The great Buddhas of Nara and Kamakura in Japan are of course the descendants of those at Bamiyan, not only in form but also in the essence they portray.

No other creation has surpassed this triumphal expression of the classical conception of human beings. Moreover, as ultimate level of classicism, applied through a universal ideal, has been able to move above and beyond the personal history and legends surrounding Shakyamuni in a manner that reminds one strongly of the new rise of Platonism and Neo-Platonism. With only a few exceptions from later periods, the stupa construction found at Gandhara was rejected by the Buddhist art of Bamiyan, and the kind of paintings and carvings of the legend of Buddha which flourished farther to the south are nowhere to be found at Bamiyan. Here, the main ornamental elements of the wall paintings are different figures of the Buddha and literally countless ranks of smaller Buddhist figures. Nowhere else has the arrangement of the "Thousand Buddhas" been developed in such number and variety of forms. There are, admittedly, some compositions of Nirvana among the extant wall paintings, but these are exceptions dating from the later period of Bamiyan art, and compared to the arts of the philosophical cosmology which combines both a macrocosm and a microcosm represented by the "Great Buddhas" and the "Thousand Buddhas", these are no more that a nostalgic recollection of the southern ethnic legends.

It is precisely this conception of the "Great Buddhas" and the "Thousand Buddhas" that stands as Bamiyan's greatest contribution to Buddhist art. When one considers the dimensions of this legacy, one cannot help but suppose that here at Bamiyan one of the ancient centres of there must have been Buddhist philosophy.

During the several days that Mr. Hackin's survey team spent here, I worked with them in inspecting the ruins and remains and studied a great number of the Buddhist caves at Bamiyan. These Buddhist caves in many cases drew on a variety of actual Buddhist temples, once built on earth in the valley, and reproducing their forms in the caves cut into the living stone, finishing the surfaces with stucco, and duplicating even the smallest details of the form of classical temple structures. Judging from the small portions remaining, the architectural ornamentation must have been impressive indeed, in many cases fully rivalling the best of ancient Roman or early Christian architecture.

This Buddhist cave architecture has a number of unique, characteristic features. Most of the caves are sanctuaries constructed on circular, octagonal, or square plans with cupolas, some of the caves even containing wooden structures in the "laternendeck" style. In these ways, the caves reflect the folk architecture of ethnic groups of this region. The circular caves echo the classical form of the Grecian circular memorial monuments of the "tholos" style, and the octagonal sanctuaries, as a variation on the circular plan, also reflect classical traditions. The octagonal plan is an important architectural form frequently applied in Christian sanctuaries of the Mediterranean world and even in the sanctuaries of Ravenna and Aachen also in the East appearing in the well-known Yumedono Octagon, Nanyendo Octagon, and Hokuyendo Octagon of Japan. The square sanctuaries with cupolas represent an architectural form particular to Iran, where this plan was developed during the Parthian and Sassan Dynasties, and this form was also used in Islamic mosques of later ages on a larger, more highly developed scale. Even earlier than mosques it also became a mainstay of Byzantine Christian church architecture. Joseph Srzygowski, who focused his attention on the development of the multifarious central plans used in Armenian churches, argued that such various forms had arisen solely from Armenian folk architectural patterns and pointed to the "laternendeck" style used in such folk architecture as their source. Had he been acquainted with styles used in the Buddhist cave architecture of Bamiyan he would no doubt have recognized that the same phenomena had appeared here as well. Indeed, the very fact that the Buddhist cave architecture of Bamiyan was both more varied and simpler than even that of the Armenian churches, and further that wooden laternendeck styles of folk architecture here converged, would have provided him with valuable backing for his own theory.

The ornamentation of the round ceilings of the circular sanctuaries generally consisted of a large central medallion focusing on the figure of a central Buddha surrounded by eight smaller medallions, each containing a Buddhist figure of its own. On the walls below this design are ranks of medium-sized and small Buddhas in a type of Thousand Buddhas composition. Mr. Hackin pointed out that here could be seen the first appearances of the mandala formula, and through the combination of this mandala formula and the conceptual trends described above, Bamiyan opened up a great new field for Buddhist arts. Today, the world of Bamiyan is apt to be overlooked, but through this central location on the Silk Road passed goods going north and south, east and west, and with them went an exchange of ideas. As Buddhist culture passed through Bamiyan on its gradual move to the east, it met with and absorbed a variety of new and old cultural elements from the west and north which spurred its even greater development. We cannot ignore the fact that this region provided Buddhist art with a number of totally new elements, such as the great Buddhas, a characteristic Buddhist architecture, and symbolic ornamentation based on the human form.

After Mr. Hackin and his party had moved on to the north, Japanese Ambassador Mr. Kazuro Moriya graciously sent his own car near to Bamiyan to meet me, and thereafter I spent three weeks living in the embassy compound while continuing my studies, visiting museums and such nearby ruins as those at Begram. All this was due to the kindness of Ambassador Moriya.

On the day before my final departure from Bamiyan, I went in an embassy car to see the famous lakes of Band-i-Amir, accompanied by agricultural technician Mr. Indo and his wife. This magnificent scenery, along with the cliff of Bamiyan and the fantastic ruins of the city of Shar-i-Golgora which stood on a nearby plateau and which was entirely destroyed by Genghis Khan, remains particularly clear in my memory. From the Kushan period to the twelfth century, this valley of the Bamiyan River and the plateau overlooking it held a succession of flourishing cities that was once an important centre of human activity. After lying silent for centuries, life here was again beginning to bud, and visiting here in 1939 as a young student; I could see the promise of a peaceful blooming ahead. Rows of tall, thin trees stood everywhere, and while trees and shrubbery would not grow here naturally, they could be planted and irrigated by the constant care of man. The greenery growing in this land was a symbol of good and peaceful governments. The bazaar, small and simple though it was, offered a wide variety of goods, and it provided a gathering place for caravans and the people of the village. But what was even more impressive to me was the newly built elementary school, in whose rooms the local children could be seen studying.

Herat — A Crossroad of Peoples and Cultures

When Alexander of Macedon set foot in Herat in 330 BC there may already have been an urban establishment, perhaps from the ninth century BC when Aryan tribes moved to settle in fertile plains of Heri Rud (Herat River). Alexander is credited with building a new city that became known as Aria. The Greek writers referred to Herat as 'Artocoana', but in the Avesta it is mentioned as 'Haraiva' and after the advent of Islam in the seventh century it became popularized as 'Heri' and finally as it is known today, 'Herat'. Except for sites of archaeological interest, not much of the pre-Islamic Herat exists today; instead, we find an Islamic town with a unique urban character and a collection of fine monuments representing the different epoches of Islamic civilization in

Afghanistan. On approaching Herat one finds a densely woven town of low minarets piercing the skyline here and there. Herat has not only been the urban centre for the fertile region which is irrigated by the Heri Rud, but it was also the crossroads on the widely travelled ancient silk route that brought together the ancient civilizations of East and West, thus forming an important commercial centre whose influence covered a large territory in Central Asia and the Near East.

Markings of this long and heterogeneous history are felt in the configuration of present-day Herat. What the historic sources refer to as the fort of Shamiran, the oldest construction in town, was in all likelihood located on the site where the fortress of Ikhtyaruddin, rebuilt in 1305, is nov located. The raised platform on which this fortress stands, in itself speaks for the successive construction on this site, including the fortress town Alexander built. Adjacent to the north wall of the city, another construction that played an important role in the successive history of Herat, Kuhandazh or Masrakh, is located; but, it is the squarely layed out Islamic town of Herat that more than anything else reflects the cultural identity of Herat. It has only been since the establishment of the new quarters in the 1930's that this identity has been threatened with uncontrolled growth.

The old Islamic town that is laid out on a square, measuring 1.6 km by 1.6 km, has largely retained its pre-industrial form and structure. Its configuration, that bears a similarity to the Arabic 'medina', is uniquely developed according to Islamic values and wisely responds to human needs and comforts. From the choice of materials for durability, insulation and structural systems, to carefully planned streets, bazaars, houses, mosques, madrases, caravansaries and water reservoirs, the town has been moulded to a unified and intricate network. Within the urban network, the Masjid-i-Jami, one of the oldest mosques in the country dating from the twelfth century, dominates the urban profile and constitutes the religious and congregational focus of the town. Two axial streets that divide the town into four quarters, make the commercial spines of the town and their crossing known as Chahar Suq, forms its commercial and social heart. Near this centre the town's largest cistern is located, a masonry structure with a 20m span, which is a genuine example of construction technology of the seventeenth century.

Within the region of which the town forms the urban centre, lie a great number of monuments that represent the rich array of art and architecture of Central Asia from the tenth to the nineteenth century. At least forty outstanding monuments and hundreds of lesser importance but not yet systematically investigated, are scattered in the area. Among the outstanding periods that these monuments represent we can mention the Ghorids (twelfth to thirteenth century), the Karts (thirteenth to fourteenth century) and the Timurids (fourteenth to sixteenth century).

The most flourishing period in the history of Herat was the Timurid Period when, after the devastating conquests of the Mongols in the thirteenth century, an artistic and literary renaissance was blooming in Herat that enhanced most of Central Asia. Architects, builders, craftsmen, writers, poets, painters, calligraphers, book-binders and musicians gathered in Herat to nourish this cultural movement. The standing monuments of this period enhance the charms of the region while its rare books and miniature paintings enrich the collection of Islamic art in museums. Rarely in the history of the region were so vast resources dedicated to man's cultural and artistic aspirations and ambitions.

To cite an example, immediately north of the town lie the remains of a fifteenth century madrasa/musalla, complex of buildings for religious worship and teaching as well as public welfare, whose six lofty minarets and an imposing mausoleum proudly reflect the glory of the time that was described by a nineteenth century French traveller as the most elegant and imposing structures to be seen in all of Asia.

Another example is the complex of buildings known as Gazaragah that were built in the fifteenth century for the shrine of the eleventh century mystical writer, Abdullah Ansari. Here from the appropriateness of form, delicacy of tilework and harmony of colours one can still get the feeling of the excellence to which Timurid art was elevated at the time. Apart from the many refined examples of Timurid architecture there are marvels of the Ghorid style as well. These buildings, whose decorations and inscriptions are executed in three-dimensional plain brickwork, stand with grandeur and opulence. An outstanding example is the 63 m Minaret of Jam whose location on a river bank within the mountains rivals the majesty of the surrounding landscape. Built in the twelfth century, the minaret is a masterpiece of Islamic art and engineering construction.

No doubt Herat, which developed over many centuries and has seen so many upheavals, glories and tragedies, will be a challenge to visitors and investigators. It will require a patient search to appreciate its charms and elegance and feel sympathy for its tragedies. Here and now in the twentieth century Herat reflects the same pride that it was boasting in the fifteenth century or, as described by a sixteenth century poet:

The universe being a boundless sea,
Khorasan is an oyster prosperous.
In which the city of Herat as you see,
Is a dear pearl ever luxurious.

(Khorasan was the name referred to Afghanistan after the advent of Islam.)

Facts about Herat

Original name: Haraiva, Artocoana, Aria, Heri and finally Herat

Literal meaning: The old name Artocoana means "Royal Town of the people of Aria"

Race/nation that constructed Herat: Aryans

Purpose of construction: Urban settlement

History of construction: Settlements in Herat existed as far back as the Ninth Century BC Alexander, capturing Herat in 330 BC, built a new city probably in the same location where the Ikhtyaruddin Fortress stands now. After the Arab conquest the city became known as Heri from which the name Herat is derived.

Location: 34°21' north, 24°11' east; 964 m above sea level; 1,162 km from Kabul (14 hours by bus)

Size of Old Town area: 1,560 m long, 1,530 m wide, 239 hectare

Representative architecture: Masjid-i-Jami, Gazaragh, Minaret of Jam

Style of architecture: Islamic

Building materials: Mostly brick

Famous objects of fine art: Miniature wall and ceiling paintings

Reasons for destruction: The city was destroyed and deserted more than once as a result of plundering conquests and natural disasters.

Causes of present collapsing: Lack of financial capability, conservation measures and proper publicity.

Plans of preservation: The Ministry of Information and Culture of the Afghanistan Government has restoration plans, but not very effective due to limited financial means. Unesco has begun to help the government in its conservation programmes.

Present population: 175,000 people.

Life and culture in Herat's golden period

Flourished during: Fourteenth — sixteenth centuries

Population: Probably 80,000 people

Social system: Feudalism mixed with monarchy and theocracy

Religion: Islam

Economical foundation: Agriculture, crafts and trade

Staple food: Grains and meat

Housing: Interior-looking court houses

Costume: Turban and long clothes

Marital system: Polygamy

Calendar: Islamic Calendar

Festivals: Mostly on religious occasions

Currency: Darham and Dinar

Writing system: Arabic script

Tools of writing: Pen, reed, paper and leather

Means of transportation: Horse, donkey and carriages

Entertainment: Music.

Painted inscription frieze, Herat.

Bangladesh

Paharpur — Once Asia's Largest Monastery

Bangladesh, geographically occupying a strategic area between South Asia and the Far East, has been a crossroad of peoples of diverse origin and civilization. From the dawn of history it has played an important role in absorbing and defusing various cultures between these two cultural zones.

In the third century BC, Bangladesh formed a part of the extensive Maurya kingdom, comprising roughly the entire triangular delta from the snow-capped Himalaya in the north to the Bay of Bengal in the south. From the third century BC to the end of AD twelfth century, the northern and western part of the delta was successively ruled by the great Mauryas, the Guptas, the Palas and the Sena kings until the Sena's rule was overthrown by the Muslims in AD 1204 However, the trans-Meghna region in the south and east was ruled independently since the seventh century by the Buddhist Deva and Chandra rules of Sematata kingdom. During more than two millennia of its eventful history, a large number of prosperous cities, fortified palaces, magnificent temples, stupas, monumental gateways, mosques and mausoleums were built by various rulers of the country. Many of these noble monuments have perished with the passage of time and have been obliterated by various destructive forces of nature and man. Among the surviving pre-Muslim monuments in Bangladesh, the most spectacular monument discovered during the excavation between 1922 and 1934 is the gigantic monument at Paharpur in Rajshahi district. Architecturally and historically, the monument of Paharpur is a treasured heritage of the world which set for the first time in ancient Asia, striking new style of temple building on a grandiose scale followed later in Southeast Asia, especially at the Pagan temples in Burma and at Chandi Loro Jongrang and Chandi Sewu temples in central Java.

The monument of Paharpur has been identified, from an inscription, as the famous Somapura Maha Vihara of the great Pala emperor, Dharmapala (AD 770-810). The ruins of this extensive monument, covering an area of about 21 acres of land is now known to be the biggest single monastery in Asia. This vast rectangular monastery, enclosed by a massive brick wall into which a single elaborate gateway complex is built on the north side, looks more like a fortress than a religious establishment. The ruins comprise 177 living cells for the hermits arranged in regular rows of the quadrangular monastery, numerous votive stupas, minor chapels, tank, well, a multitude of other ancillary buildings inside the courtyard and most dominantly, a cruciform lofty central temple which rises in receding three pyramidal terraces. This immense temple is conspicuous for its complicated scheme of adornment of its basement walls with carved brick cornices, friezes of terracotta plaques and stone sculptures. In plan it is a gigantic square cross with angles of projection between the arms. Each receding terrace has an ambulatory passage around the monument.

Access to the first and the second terraces was provided by a grand staircase on the north. The whole scheme of the temple pivots round a square hollow shaft shooting high up above the three terraces and appears to be the result of a pre-meditated development of a single central unit in which future expansion was pre-determined in a vertical plane.

The basement wall of the temple is adorned with 63 elegant stone images, placed in specially built niches, most of which belong to the Brahmanical pantheon and above this runs a single row of terracotta plaques, depicting faithfully the prevailing folk art of Bengal. The monotony of the walls in the first and the second terraces is relieved, on the outer face, by unbroken bands of terracotta sculptures, set in recessed panels; each terrace having double rows and the rows being separated from one another by projecting cornice of ornamental friezes. Three distinct groups of stone sculptures, embellishing the base of the temple, are distinguishable from their variation of style and artistic excellence. The first group, mostly depicting scenes from the life of Krishna or portraying popular themes of the great Hindu epics, the Ramayana and the Mahabharata, is characterised by intensely human and vivacious nature. The second group appears to be the product of a transitional period between the eastern Gupta classicism and later Pala art. It is distinguished by a general heaviness of forms, except in few panels marked by the classical Gupta idioms. The third group manifests soft and refined modelling of forms, delicacy of features and ornaments typical of peoples of the royal court of upper stratum of society.

The terracotta art, embellishing the base of the temple, however, plays the most prominent part in the scheme of decoration. There are about 2,000 plaques still fixed in their original position on the faces of walls and about 800 were pecked up loose from the site during excavation. The richness, variety and exuberance of this rather technically archaic terracotta art are unrivalled. It faithfully portrays the contemporary folk art of Bengal as distinct from the more sophisticated art of the royal court. It included in the repertoire, besides divinities of Hindu-Buddhist pantheon and popular folktales, all conceivable subjects which peopled the simple mind of the rural artists: Human and animal life in various movements, floral and geometric motifs; semi-divine beings and decorations from the plant kingdom.

Since the main fabric of the gigantic temple was completely exposed in 1934 after more than a decade of excavation, it has steadily deteriorated in nearly half-a-century. The vast inner courtyard of the monument, enclosed by the heavily fortified monastery walls, is now a depressed reservoir basin of monsoon rain where the central temple seems to float on a vast sheet of trapped water in high season. This is the result of removing immense quantity of earth from the courtyard during excavation, accumulated in last twelve centuries. This extremely dismal situation is likely to further aggravate with the removal of another 4/5 feet of earth from the courtyard in order to expose the lower basement wall of the temple, embellished with numerous stone sculptures in specially built recessed niches, originally intended to be exposed to view. Even now at the present level, lower bands of the terracotta friezes, decorating the upper base of the shrine, goes under water during copious rains. The waterlogging of the base of the temple for virtually half of the year over a long period of time has already undermined its foundation alarmingly. Combined with this, the salinity in the rising sub-soil water poses a great threat to the preservation of the monument and its decorative art.

Facts about Paharpur

Original name: Somapura Vihara

Purpose of construction: Important centre of Buddhist learning and pilgrimage.

History of construction: Pala emperor, Dharmapala constructed the monument between AD 770-810

Location: 25°2'north, 89°3' east; 255 km from Dacca (10 hours by car)

Size: 73 feet (about 22.3 m) high, 922 feet (about 281.2 m) long, 919 feet (about 280.3 m) wide.

Representative architecture: Buddhist Monastery and Temple

Style of architecture: Cruciform ground plan with pyramidal terraced temple occupying the centre of vast quadrangular monastery.

Building material: Brick laid in mud mortar

Famous objects of fine art: Stone sculptures and terracotta plaques.

Reasons for destruction: Partly Human being's destruction and natural erosion.

Causes of present collapsing: The weak cementing material, natural process of decay over a thousand years, excessive monsoon rain, rank vegetation growth. Now the two principal factors are salinity and waterlogging.

Plans of preservation/presentation: Unesco terms of experts are investigating and carrying on field-tests of various factors with a view to drawing up a Master Plan for its preservation, restoration and presentation.

Present population: The monument is uninhabited; surrounding villages are sparsely populated.

Life and culture in Paharpur's golden period

Flourished during: Eighth — twelfth centuries

Population: Unknown

Social system: Monarchy

Religion: Hinduism, Jainism and Buddhism

Economical foundation: Agriculture, trade and some industry.

Staple food: Rice, fish, meat, fruits, vegetable and milk

Housing: Thatched cottages

Costume: Dhoti (male), Saris (female), Chauli (bodice) and Utariya (scarf)

Marital system: Unknown

Calendar: No definite single calendar; chronology is based on reignal year of kings recorded on inscription.

Currency: Metallic coins as medium of exchange (Gandaka, Kakanika, etc.)

Writing system: Sanskrit (proto-Bengali)

Tools of writing: Copper plate and Palmyra leaf

Means of transportation: Bullock cart, horse, carriage, elephants and boats.

Entertainment: Chess, music, dancing, wrestling and acrobatics.

Bhutan

Land of the Peaceful Dragon: Past and Present — A Brief History

Of the pre-history of Bhutan, little is known. The number of stone stools and megaliths found in the country suggest that Bhutan was populated from a relatively early date, probably around 2000-1500 BC. It is difficult, however, to draw firm conclusion on the pre-history of Bhutan because almost no archeological survey has yet been conducted. There are several traditional names for Bhutan. They are Lon-Mon Khasi "The Southern Mon Country of Four Approaches", Lho-Mon Tsenden Jong "The Southern Mon Country of Sandalwood" and Lho Jong Menjong "The Southern Country of Medicinal Herbs". (*Mon* is a general term to denote all non-Tibetan, non-Indian groups through the Himalayas).

The origin of the present name "Bhutan" remains obscure. It is thought that it was derived from the Indian term *bhotanta* meaning 'end of Tibet".

The history of Bhutan begins with the advent of Buddhism in the country in the middle AD seventh century at which time the Jampa Lhakhang in Bumthang and the Kichu Lhakhang in Paro were constructed. They are considered as the oldest Buddhist temples in the country and are regarded very holy even today. Since then the Buddhist faith has played such a large part in shaping the course of Bhutan's history that the very name of the country and its inhabitants derives from that of the Buddhist school, the Drukpa Kagyupa, which has been dominant in the country since the seventeenth century. In Dzongkha (the official language of Bhutan), Bhutanese call themselves Drukpa and the country Drukyul "Land of the Drukpas". The etymology of Drukyul, which also means the "Land of the Dragon", is explained by the following anecdote: while Tsangpa Gyarey Yeshey Dorji (1161-1211) was consecrating a monastery in central Tibet at the end of the twelfth century, he heard the thunderbolt, the voice of the dragon (*druk*), according to the popular belief. He decided therefore to name the monastery "Druk" and the religious school he founded was called consequently "Drukpa".

In the history of Bhutan up until the end of the nineteenth century, some of the principal religious figures of the period when religious and secular powers were almost always interlocked, who not only played important roles in their respective times but also remain alive in the memory of the people, will be briefly introduced.

According to the Bhutanese tradition, an Indian saint named Padmasambhava alias Pema Jungney "One who was born from a lotus flower", more popularly known as Guru Rimpoche "Precious Teacher", arrived in Bhutan around 800 AD He is the founder of the Nyingmapa "Old" school of Himalayan Buddhism and considered as the Second Buddha. As in Tibet, he introduced in Bhutan the tantric Buddhism (highly esoteric form of the Mahayana Buddhism "Great Vehicle").

All the places he visited are now places of pilgrimage for the Bhutanese who revere this saint and his Eight Manifestations (Guru Tshengye) in almost all the temples throughout the country. One of the most famous exploits of Guru Rimpoche in Bhutan is the conversion of the King Sindhu Raja of Chakhar in Bumthang. The famous Taktshang "Tiger's Nest" Monastery in Paro is founded on the place where Guru Rimpoche visited in the form of Dorje Droloe (one of his Eight Manifestations) mounted on a flying tiger. The historical records of the ninth and tenth centuries which follow this first introduction of Buddhism are obscure. In fact, after the assassination of the anti-Buddhist Tibetan King Langdarma in 842, Tibet itself underwent a period of political turmoil and Buddhism almost disappeared except in the remote areas. The situation of Bhutan during this troubled period is little known but it is supposed that numerous emigrants escaped from Tibet to settle in the Bhutanese valleys. The eleventh century marks the revival of Buddhism which is manifested in Bhutan by the activity of *tertons* ("treasure discoverers") at Paro and Bumthang. The treasures are in general sacred texts which Padmasambhava and other saints had concealed and that the *tertons* were predestined to discover at favourable moments.

The end of the eleventh century and the beginning of the twelfth century were, in Tibet, a flourishing period for Buddhism and several schools, for example, Kadampa, Kagyupa and Sakyapa were founded. The missionary activities of these new schools were equally directed towards the "Southern Valleys". Thus towards the end of the twelfth century, Gyelwa Lhanangpa (1164-1224) arrived in western Bhutan. He was the founder of the Lhapa school, a branch of the Kagyupa. Gyelwa Lhanangpa inherited some land from his great grandfather in the fertile valley of Paro and established there the Lhapa school.

In the first half of the thirteenth century, Phajo Drugom Shigpo (1208-1276) arrived in Bhutan. He belonged to the Drukpa school, another branch of the Kagyupa, which was founded, as already mentioned, by Tsangpa Gyarey Yeshey Dorji. He came to Bhutan following the prophecy of Tsangpa Gyarey who had ordered him to go to the south. Soon after his arrival, Phajo Drugom Shigpo was confronted with the Lhapa school which was already firmly established in western Bhutan. The school of Phajo Drugom Shigpo was finally victorious over the Lhapa and being with a lady of Thimphu valley, Phajo Drugom Shigpo founded the first Drukpa monasteries at Phajoding and Tango. However, the Lhapa school continued to exist until the seventeenth century at which date it was definitively ousted by Shabdrung Ngawang Namgyal.

Between the twelfth and seventeenth centuries, numerous monks, not all belonging to the Drukpa school, came to Bhutan almost continuously. Thus, Barawa (1320-1391) who founded a subsect of the Drukpa constructed a monastery of Brangyekha in Paro valley and in the same way the Nenyingpa school constructed several monasteries in western Bhutan like Dzongdrakha in Paro valley.

The great philosopher of the Nyingmapa school Longchen Rabjampa (1308-1363) came to Bumthang where he founded Tharpaling and Samtenling monasteries.

In the fifteenth century arrived in western Bhutan the one who has become without doubt the most popular man of religion in Bhutan: the "Divine Mad Man" Drukpa Kunley (1455-1529). Every Bhutanese knows his life and anecdotes. He belonged to the Drukpa school and to the princely family of Gya which provided successive abbots of the Ralung monastery, one of the principal monasteries of the Drukpa. His wandering life style, his extravagant and shocking behaviour ensured him a special place in the history of tantric Buddhism. Some of his descendants also became famous in Bhutan, especially Tenzin Rabgye (1638-1696) who occupied the post of the 4th temporal ruler (Desi/Deb) of Bhutan.

Up to now, only the teachers who came from Tibet to Bhutan have been mentioned, but one should not forget that from the fourteenth century eminent masters were born on the Bhutanese soil. Among them, Dorji Lingpa (1346-1405), famous Nyingmapa "treasure discoverer" of the Bumthang valley who also founded a number of monasteries and Pema Lingpa, descendant of Gyelwa Lhanangpa, who was born in Bumthang in 1450 and died there in 1521. The latter, however, did not belong to the Lhapa school but to that of Nyingmapa, very popular in central Bhutan.

Pema Lingpa was the reincarnation of not only Guru Rimpoche but also of the great Nyingmapa scholar Longchen Rabjampa. In addition to his activities as *terton* "treasure discoverer", Pema Lingpa founded the temples of Petsheling, Tamshing and Kunzangdra in Bumthang, left important writings and created numerous dances based upon a vision. He is closely linked with the history of Bumtang valley, where one finds his traces everywhere. His descendants also played an important role in the development of the Nyingmapa school and one of them founded Gantey Gompa (monastery) near Pele-la Pass in the Black Mountains which separate western Bhutan from central Bhutan.

The above account shows that between the twelfth century and the beginning of the seventeenth century, Bhutan was an important domain of missionary activities for different Buddhist schools but it also indicates the lack of political unity which characterized Bhutan during these centuries.

It was only in the seventeenth century that Bhutan became unified, this under the political and religious charisma of Ngawang Namgyal (1594-1651) of the Drukpa school who took as honorific title the Shabdrung "At whose feet one submits". In 1616, Shabdrung Ngawang Namgyal arrived from Tibet in western Bhutan. He was born in the princely family of Gya and was the 18th abbot of Ralung, an important Drukpa monastery. He was recognized as the reincarnation of the famous Drukpa scholar Pema Karpa (1527-1592) but this recognition was objected to by the chief of Tsang province, Tsang Desi, who supported his own candidate. Under these circumstances, the Shabdrung escaped from Tibet and came to western Bhutan where, as we have already seen, the Drukpa school had become well established.

The Shabdrung founded in 1620 Cheri monastery in the upper valley of Thimphu and in 1629 his first dzong at Simtokha, several kilometers down the river from the present capital Thimphu. Dzongs, or fortress-cum-monasteries, were subsequently constructed in all the main valleys of western Bhutan. However before the unification of Bhutan, the Shabdrung had to struggle with both external and internal enemies. The external enemies were the Tibetan armies who repeatedly tried to invade Bhutan after the arrival of the Shabdrung in the country. The Shabdrung, however, successfully repulsed the Tibetan attempts of invasion. Internally, the Shabdrung consolidated his position over the other schools which had long been established in Bhutan.

In this way the Shabdrung established himself as the ruler of Bhutan both temporal and religious. He founded a State clergy headed by the spiritual leader, the Je Khempo (Head Abbot) and a theocracy of monk-functionaries at the head of which he placed the temporal ruler the Desi/Deb (Regent). This dual system of government called choesi was unified and sublimed in the person of Shabdrung Ngawang Namgyal. In 1651, the Shabdrung entered into a retreat in Punakha Dzong and passed away during the course of this retreat. His death was, however, kept secret for more than half a century, the purpose of which deception was most probably to avoid any trouble resulting from the death of the Shabdrung in the newly unified nation until a suitable successor to the Shabdrung had been found.

It is during the first half of the eighteenth century that the theory of triple reincarnation (physical, verbal and mental) was finally established. However it is the mental reincarnations who were considered as successors to the Shabdrung as head of State. Hierarchically speaking, under the incarnations of the Shabdrung (or Dharma Rajas as called by the British), the Je Khempo as head of the clergy and the Desi/Deb or (Deb Rajas as called by the British) as temporal ruler, continued the dual system of government which lasted until the emergence of the hereditary monarchy at the beginning of the twentieth century.

The regional administration was headed by Dzongpons ("Masters of Dzong", Lt. Governors) of which three collectively called Chilasum (Daga, Tongsa, Paro) who had the title of Penlop (Governors) were most important. During the eighteenth and nineteenth centuries, these regional governors increased their power at the expense of the Central government who lost their firm hold on the country. Instability and internal strifes resulted from the combination of these factors and more and more of these led to civil wars. Further, beyond its southern frontiers Bhutan was facing to a new element: the British hegemony in Assam and its apparent desire of colonial expansion throughout the Himalayas. The British missions of the eighteenth century which tried to establish privileged commercial links with Tibet and Bhutan succeeded in establishing good relations between the Bhutanese and the British, without, however, materializing any concrete result as expected by the latter. Because of the divergence of interests concerning the Duars (narrow tract of land extending along the foot of the lower range of the Himalayan mountains), their good relations deteriorated rapidly, numerous conflicts in the border areas attained such proportion that in 1864 the Duar War started. This ended in November 1865 when the Sinchula Treaty was signed and the previous state of good neighbourhood was restored. By this treaty Bhutan ceded the right over the Duars against the payment of the annual indemnity from the British. This compensation continues today by the terms of the 1949 treaty with newly independent India.

Meanwhile the process of weakening of the Central government progressed towards the end of the nineteenth century and coincided with the emergence to the power of provincial governors, Penlops of Paro and Tongsa who controlled de facto western and central Bhutan respectively. The struggle for power between these two governors culminated in 1904 on the occasion of the British Younghusband expedition to Tibet. While the Paro Penlop was rather inclined to side with the Tibetans, already under the zone of Chinese influence, Tongsa Penlop Ugyen Wangchuck, following the advice of Kazi Ugyen Dorji, decided to cooperate with the British. Ugyen Wangchuck played an important role of mediator for the negotiation between the Tibetans and the British and thus gained the respect and confidence of the latter. He emerged as the strong man who Bhutan needed after a long period of instability.

On 17 December 1907, Ugyen Wangchuck was unanimously elected the first hereditary king of Bhutan by an assembly consisting of representatives of the clergy, the government and the people. That day marked the end of the dual system of government and the beginning of a hereditary monarchy which is the guaranty of the stability, unity and prosperity of the country.

Ugyen Wangchuck died in 1926 and was succeeded by his son Jigme Wangchuck who reigned over the country until his death in 1952. The twenty years reign (1952-1972) of the third King, Jigme Dorji Wangchuck, was marked by the progressive opening of the country to the outside world: in 1963 Bhutan joined the Colombo Plan and in 1971 Bhutan became a member of the United Nations. Internally, the restructuring of the country's social, economic, political and institutional setups was carried out under his enlightened leadership and earned him the well-deserved title of "Father of Modern Bhutan".

His son, His Majesty Jigme Singye Wangchuck who ascended the Golden Throne in 1972, actively pursues the policy of socio-economic and cultural progress started by his late father. New roads and telecommunication facilities, hydroelectric projects, modern educational facilities, expanding townships, improved agriculture, rising incomes, fresh avenues for trade and industry and increasing participation in regional cooperation and international affairs, including the Non-Aligned Movement — these constitute some of the many revolutionary elements in the make-up of present-day Bhutan. The country has strived judiciously to keep in step with the times without falling prey to the ulcers of modernization. As His Majesty has observed, "In these times, we hear of strife, wars, disease, floods and famine in other countries, but in the midst of all this turmoil we here are enjoying peace and prosperity. There are two reasons for this. Firstly, we have kept firm faith in Konchogsum (Three Jewels) and we have been blessed with peace and prosperity. Secondly, we have maintained strong unity between the Government and the people".

In addition, the preservation and promotion of the rich cultural and religious heritage of the country amidst growing modernization is one of the corner-stones of the Royal Government's dynamic, perspective and progressive national policy.

In statistical terms, Bhutan may be regarded as undeveloped, but if account is taken of the contentment of its people, their relative freedom from wants, their self-sufficient way of life and the lack of poverty as it exists elsewhere and if one compares the Bhutan of today with that of even ten years ago, then the conclusion is inescapable that the country's progress has been nothing short of phenomenal.

Ravaged Treasures of the Past — Preservation of Cultural Heritage

The term "culture" connotes a distinct and specific type of civilization. Bhutanese culture may be broadly divided under three main categories:

a) The religious and literary heritage of the country;
b) Arts and crafts;
c) The way of life of Bhutan's people.

In view of the fact that the last two topics have been dealt with at some length elsewhere in this issue, here the first aspect of Bhutanese culture mentioned above is largely dealt with.

Religion may justifiably be called the fountain-head of Bhutanese culture. Not only does it exert a pervasive influence in Bhutanese society, but almost every single facets of life in the country draws inspiration from it. From archery contests to the painting of murals, from the phenomenon of birth to that of sickness and death, almost each significant moment in the life of a Bhutanese is, in one way or another, linked with religion.

Before proceeding to an account of the determined steps being taken to preserve and promote the Bhutanese religious and literary heritage, it will be instructive to briefly review its main components.

The first Buddhist temples in Bhutan

During the seventh century AD the 33rd Tibetan King Srongtsan Gampo took upon himself as atonement for a sin, the task of constructing 108 temples in important places in Tibet and in the neighbouring countries. Bumthang Jampa Lhakhang in central and Paro Kichu Lhakhang in western Bhutan are two of them and are the oldest temples in the country.

At a later time of history, Kichu Lhakhang was burnt down by fire and destroyed by other external forces. It is believed that *terton* Pemalingpa excavated the temple from underground. However, no harm was done to the inner valuable statues. At the centre of the temple is a remarkably life-like Buddha statue and one is led to imagine that it is the Buddha Himself, in flesh and blood, sitting serenely in enlightened bliss. Belief has it that through this statue, the Buddha has spoken to many holy people in this temple. The beauty and splendour of the Paro valley, the progress the region has made and the well-being of its inhabitants are attributed to the blessings of the Buddha of the Kichu.

Jampa Lhakhang is situated at the Upper Chhokhor in Bumthang. Upper Chhokhor is considered one of the most important holy places among the four divisions of Bumthang. The coming Buddha "Jampa" is set up in the temple and this was the only temple which had not been destroyed by fire, water or earthquake till AD 1300. It is said that Guru Rimpoche blessed King Sindhu Raja in this temple. This magnificent temple is surrounded by *chortens* of four colours, pointed in the four directions of the temple. It is believed that these *chortens* were also erected at the time the Tibetan King Srongtsan Gampo built the 108 temples.

Other temples and their architecture

Most of the great *dzongs* and monasteries in the country dates back to the time of Shabdrung Ngawang Namgyal, the builder of medieval Bhutan, who was a prodigious builder. Simtokha is the oldest *dzong* built in the early years of the seventeenth century, by the first Shabdrung Rimpoche (Ngawang Namgyal). It has now been converted into a school of Buddhist studies and literature known as Rigney School. Its ancient wall frescoes, time-worn floorboards and steep step-ladders, its old, Chinese-style carved slate panels and scrolls provide inspiration to approximately 200 lamas and lay students who live there. These students specialize in the study of Buddhism and literature including Dzongkha, the national language of Bhutan.

The *dzongs* or fortified castles of Bhutan are a characteristic architectural feature of the country's landscape. They were built in medieval times at strategic locations — towering over valleys or at the confluence of rivers — and served as secular as well as religious centres of the area. The *dzongs* generally house the main temple, a square-based tall structure that dominates the cluster of buildings and is surrounded by monastery buildings which house the monks and the administrative wings. They are still the seat of governmental and ecclesiastical functions in the provinces. Like other old structures in the country, *dzongs* are usually constructed of pounded mud and rubble, with sloping, whitewashed walls and an ornamental timber superstructure that is richly carved, gilded and painted. Their inner courtyards, halls, temples and monasteries are sumptuous repositories of age-old Bhutanese arts and crafts; wall paintings, sculpture, wood and slate carvings, *thankas* or painted and appliqued silk and brocade hangings, masks, calligraphy, manuscripts, icons and silver and gold work.

A striking example of the preservation of ancient skills in Bhutan is the rebuilding of the Tashichho Dzong in Thimphu. The 400 year old Tashichho Dzong was largely demolished in 1963 and around the core of the old temple a magnificent new *dzong* was built. It was built in the traditional style of nail-less framework architecture, exactly the same way that *dzongs* were built centuries ago. It was decorated by hereditary craftsmen who used traditional motifs, employed age-old methods and worked in soft earth and vegetable colours.

The literary language

The introduction of the script in Bhutan is closely related to the spread of Buddhism, Padmasambhava, known in Bhutan as Guru Rimpoche, came to Bumthang in central Bhutan in the eighth century. He taught the Dharma to the King of Bumthang and his subjects. At that time there was no written language among the Bhutanese. Therefore, Denma Tsemang, who was among the retinue of Guru Rimpoche, wrote down certain important scriptures for the King of Bumthang. He also taught the Bhutanese how to read and write. Denma Tsemang was a famous scribe who legends claim could write innumerable texts in a moment. He is the scribe for the majority of the concealed texts recorded in Bhutanese script, which is different from the Tibetan script. One name for this cursive form is Lhoyig. This literally means "southern script" and is so named because Bhutan is situated to the south of Tibet. The other name is Juying which refers to the use of this script for ordinary correspondence. The origin of the Bhutanese script can thus be traced back to the eighth century. The contemporary manuscripts found at Tunhuang appear to bear the same similarity to the Bhutanese scripts of today, as those of Denma Tsemang.

After the creation of the Tibetan alphabet, the Tibetans started a vast project of translating Buddhist literature from Sanskrit, Pali, Chinese and other languages into Tibetan. Under the patronage of the Tibetan kings beginning from Srongtsan Gampo, the translation project was carried out by Indian pandits and Tibetan lotsavas. The most famous among them are Padmasambhava, Vimalamitra, Shantaraksita, Jinamitra, Vaironcana and Kawa Paltshek. In order to ascertain an exact and faithful translation, the orthography, grammar and terminology were revised and unified and the Kesar-ce, or so called "newly fixed language" was worked out in the first half of the ninth century. Thus the standard classical Tibetan was fixed and it became the religious language (Choekay) for all Buddhists in the vast region which included Tibet, Mongolia, Bhutan and other Himalayan regions. The Kanjur of 108 volumes and the Tanjur of more than 200 volumes written in Choekay are still used in Bhutan today and they form the foundation of Buddhist teachings and practice. Thus, the Bhutanese Buddhist tradition goes back to India through the intermediary of Tibet and its Buddhist Canon in Choekay. Bhutan thus shares a common religious and literary heritage with all Asian Buddhists.

The linguistic situation of Bhutan is complex and there are many dialects. To mention the most important, these are Ngalonggikha of western Bhutan, Tsangla or Sharchopikha of eastern Bhutan, Bumthangpikha of central Bhutan. Kurteypikha of north-eastern Bhutan, Khenkha of central-south Bhutan and Nepali of southern Bhutan.

In the past, as mentioned earlier, written communications in Bhutan, both of an official and private nature, had always been in Choekay, the classical religious language written in Juyig, the Bhutanese cursive script. Because of its classical nature, Choekay can only be understood by those persons who have received a traditional education. Its meaning has to be interpreted into the local language or dialect, in order to make it intelligible to the common man. Despite this, Choekay is still widely in use among educated persons both in ordinary correspondence and in the broader context of religious teachings and practice.

In addition to Choekay, which exists only in written form, there has long existed in Bhutan an official form of speech known as Dzongkha (language of the fortress). Dzongkha is based on the major language group of Ngalonggikha prevailing in western Bhutan, but closely resembles the vernacular speech of Punakha, the valley where the ancient winter capital was situated. From the seventeenth century onwards, Dzongkha was used throughout the country as the language of government in each of the *dzongkhag*, the administrative units of local government centred in the fortress of *dzong* of each district. It is against this linguistic background that when the five-year economic and social development plans were launched to modernize the country in 1960, the Royal Government decided to develop Dzongkha as a modern language. For this purpose, the Dzongkha Division in the Department of Education was established in 1961.

The principal reason for adopting Dzongkha as the national language was that, except for a few differences of accent, spelling and grammar, Dzongkha maintains the basic standard set by Choekay and lends itself readily towards a written standardization. Textbooks written to Dzongkha are now used by students in schools and colleges throughout the country. The subjects of these textbooks in Dzongkha cover the history of Bhutan, history of religion, poetry, literature and so on. Religious subjects which have usually been treated only in Choekay, will also gradually be translated into Dzongkha, with the hope that in this way the full heritage of Buddhist culture, formerly the preserve largely of monks, will be brought within the reach of the common man.

A weekly news bulletin and a quarterly magazine are also published in Dzongkha. In order that Dzongkha can fulfil the functions of a modern language in a period of rapid economic, social and technological development in Bhutan, Dzongkha has to develop a sufficient range of terminology, especially with regard to science and technology. For this reason, the Department of Education is compiling a dictionary of Dzongkha containing a fundamental vocabulary of scientific and technical words. It is hoped that soon a sufficient Dzongkha vocabulary will be built up to meet the needs of both traditional and modern usage.

Historical records

The origin of Bhutan is lost in obscurity. The historical beginning of Bhutan and of the Bhutanese people is shrouded in mystery. There is not much reliable writing about the early history of Bhutan, most of the official annals having been destroyed by fire, floods, or earthquakes. The burning of the historical Dzong in Punakha, the ancient capital of the country in 1832 and the widespread destruction by the earthquake of 1897 were responsible for the destruction of almost all of Bhutanese historical documents.

A meagre collection of manuscripts and official annals survive and it is possible to piece together from them an impression of the primitive Kingdom. It would appear that, even before the eighth century, Bhutan was more than merely a geographical expression. Though it lacked internal political unity, it was an independent and self-contained state.

Religious order

The State religion of Bhutan is Buddhism of Mahayans tradition, including Vajrayana. It was introduced into Bhutan by the great Indian saint Padmasambhava, towards the second half of the eighth century. The Buddhism taught by this great teacher is known as Nyingma (pa). Most of the Bhutanese people belong to the Drukpa sect, which was introduced into the country from Tibet by Phajo Drugom Shingpo sometime in the early part of the thirteenth century. This was further consolidated by Shabdrung Ngawang Namgyal in the seventeenth century. The first monastic centre was established at Tango Monastery with 30 monks under the head abbotship of Khenchen Pekar Jungney. It was then shifted to Punakha with 600 monks. Gradually monastic centres were established throughout the country. At one stage, the number of monks increased to about 6000. The Central Monastic Body was housed alternately in Punakha and Thimphu.

The monks spent the six months of winter in Punakha and the six months of summer in Thimphu. The number of monks in the Central Monastic Body at present is about 1660 and the total number of monks, including those in the provincial monastic centres, is about 3000. The supreme head of the Central Monastic Body is known as Je Khempo and the provincial monastic centres as Netens.

Preservation of heritage

a) The fight against natural calamities

There are four major elements against which the Royal Government of Bhutan has been fighting — fire, water, earthquake and insects.

Fire: Throughout its history, Bhutan has witnessed innumerable cases of fire which have caused wide-spread destruction to the country's cultural and religious heritage. In traditional Bhutanese architecture, wood is used abundantly for the roof, ceiling, floor, window, etc. Any traditional building is, therefore, perpetually exposed to the danger of destruction by fire. A minimum security measure (fire alarm system, fire extinguisher unit, etc.) is hoped to be installed in each and every building of historical importance.

Water-Floods and Rain: The Punakha Dzong, one of the most important in Bhutan, has been damaged by previous floods because it stands at a low negligible elevation at the junction of the Mo Chu and Pho Chu rivers. The Dzong still faces the danger of floods to come. Therefore scheme has been drawn up for the elevation and reinforcement of the banks surrounding the Dzong.

Earthquake: As is the case with the majority of traditional buildings in the world, Bhutanese monuments and houses are not earthquake-resistant. Unfortunately, earthquakes have been frequent in Bhutan and many monuments have suffered from them. The Royal Government is undertaking the task of restoring the damaged buildings and reinforcing the structure of others in poor condition.

Insects: Insects cause damage to the wooden portion of buildings and to other objects made of wood or paper. In this respect, the most severely affected items are precious manuscripts (some of them richly illustrated), xylographic prints and xylographic blocks.

An attempt is now being made to protect these national treasures by disinfecting them or, in the case of movable objects, transferring them to the National Library or the National Museum, where they can be restored and be kept properly and safely.

b) Religious/cultural organizations

With the establishment of hereditary monarch in 1907, Bhutan entered a grand new era of political unity and peace. Ugyen Wangchuck, Bhutan's man of destiny, restored order and set up a Government of distinct national character. Among his numerous sterling qualities, he was a devout Buddhist. He built and repaired many temples and monasteries and encouraged the training of lamas and monks.

His descendants followed in his noble and illustrious footsteps and their munificence to the monk communities, along with their zeal in the upkeep and promotion of religious centres, gave a strong impetus to the development of Buddhism in Bhutan. This process of development has further accelerated under the dynamic leadership of the present monarch, His Majesty Jigme Singye Wangchuck. The contributions of His Majesty towards the growth of Buddhist culture in the country include the setting up of a National Religious Committee, the first of its kind in the country and through it, the establishment of a school of Buddhist studies at Tango and Cheri. Bhutan also began to send its scholars to participate in international Buddhist seminars and conferences. The National Library was upgraded and a National Council for Social and Cultural Promotion was established. These events constitute, as it were, notable and towering landmarks in the preservation, promotion and propagation of the country's rich cultural and religious heritage.

The National Religious Committee

The National Religious Committee or Druk Choedon Lhentshok (D.C.L.) is a non-political and non-sectarian organization whose aims and objectives are:

a) To understand, practise and propagate the sacred Doctrine of Lord Buddha.
b) To observe and celebrate the important and sacred Buddhist Duchens (important events).
c) To initiate and educate younger brothers and sisters in the field of religion.
d) To organize lectures, talks, discussions on various aspects of Buddhism and conduct advanced courses in Choe (Dharma), where and when the organization is prepared.
e) To arrange classes in Dzongkha and other languages in order to encourage and promote higher studies in Buddhist culture.
f) To conduct religious, cultural, social activities and other services to promote happier and more peaceful community life.
g) To translate Buddhist texts and publish pamphlet journals of Buddhism and reports on the activities of the Lhentshok whenever possible, dependent upon the availability of funds.
h) To establish and maintain a library of Buddhist literature in various languages to provide facilities of study to its members and to the general public.
i) To establish contact with other Buddhist Associations, Organizations, Centres and other academic institutions abroad in order to promote co-operations and to obtain publications through exchanges.

National Council for Social and Cultural Promotion (NCSCP)

The NCSCP was set up in 1980 in pursuance of the command of His Majesty the King. Among its primary aims are the harmonizing of different cultural, religious and social interests of the people and the consolidation and strengthening of faith in and loyalty to the King and country. Its projections for the period 1982-86 include the nurturing of the younger generation to understand, appreciate and appropriate the social goals and cultural values of our nation and, by the inevitable process of filtration, to implement the mandate for the entire population.

The NCSCP is currently headed by Her Royal Highness Ashi Pema Lhaden Wangchuck.

The National Library

The National Library of Bhutan was established in 1967 with the object of collecting and preserving ancient Bhutanese and Tibetan literatures and scriptures depicting religion, culture, history and traditions. Since then, the activities of the National Library have been greatly diversified and include publication, research and acquisition of pertinent materials. At the same time, in the course of the current Five Year Plans, the library intends to offer a variety of public services so as to make its collection more accessible.

National Service

On completing education, a Bhutanese student is exposed to a carefully-planned orientation course on the country's rich heritage. Thereafter, he or she lives in close contact with the local community. In this way it is ensured that those acquiring modern education do not become alienated from the mainstream of national life, but become, instead, bulwarks of its preservation and growth.

Conclusion

Although closely linked to Tibet and India culturally, Bhutan has maintained its independence and individuality over the centuries by deliberately following a systematic policy of isolationism which earned for the country the reputation of being the world's last forbidden kingdom. This policy was pursued until as recently as 1952, when the third hereditary monarch, King Jigme Dorji Wangchuck, ascended the throne. He quickly realized that the old policy of isolation was causing Bhutan to remain socially, economically and politically backwards. Gradually, so as not to upset old traditions, but firmly in accordance with modern needs, King Jigme Dorji Wangchuck introduced administrative reforms and launched the Five Year Plan. Today, the country, under the dynamic leadership of the world's youngest monarch His Majesty Jigme Singye Wangchuck, is all set to achieve a happy co-existence of tradition and progress in the best interests of its particular genius in the midst of the comity of nations.

Burma

Pagan — Where Pagodas Numbered Thousands

On the left bank of the Irrawaddy River is the ruins of the capital of Pagan, the first unified Burmese Kingdom which flourished for approximately 250 years from the middle of the eleventh century to the end of the thirteenth century.

According to various chronicles and records, the citadel kingdom's of the Pyu tribe, the predecessor of the Burmese people, were destroyed in the 830s. The royal city of Pagan, which might have been the centre of the nineteen Pyu villages on the eastern bank of the Irrawaddy River, was built in the 850s. The Burmese chronicle, Hmannan Maha Yawazin, says that 42 kings succeeded to the throne between Thamudarit who constructed Pagan and Anawrahta. However, from what can be ascertained from the existing Burmese inscriptions, King Anawrahta (1044-77) seems to have essentially been the founder of Pagan. He accomplished the political unification of Burma with Pagan as its centre and the highlight of all this was the campaign against Thaton in 1057. This campaign had the effect of bringing Mon culture to Pagan via Mon prisoners taken back to Pagan. The esoteric (Tantric) Mahayana Buddhism practised by the Pagan people up to then was replaced by the Theravada Buddhism brought from Thaton.

According to the Burmese chronicles, before the application of Theravada Buddhism, a group of priests called Ari enjoyed the reigning authority. Their authority was not simply religious, for they carried spears, rode horses and were solidly protected by some sixty thousand monk soldiers who had the best mobile power of the time. Anawrahta, who changed his faith to the Theravada Buddhism after hearing the teachings of a Mon monk named Shin Ahahan, forced all the Ari priests and their followers who denied the teachings of Gautama to return to a secular life and become spearmen, lancers and elephant keepers. Anawrahta devised severe measures against them in order to expel the existing authority and to establish new order with a royal power base. Along with the expansion of Theravada Buddhism, the sculpting of Buddhist status and the construction of temples and monasteries came to be carried out vigorously in Pagan. Even today over 2,200 Buddhist temples may still be seen in the ruins of Pagan stretching out for about sixty square kilometers along the Irrawaddy. All of them are brick constructions. Their structure is divided into the two types of solid pagodas and hollow temples. The former is something which developed from the stupa and it is either a cylindrical or bell-shaped structure. The latter is a square-shaped building having on its roof a four-sided pinnacle or a spiral-shaped obelisk whose tip gradually gets narrower.

A pagoda symbolizes the Parinirvana of Buddha. Though there are structures like the Shwezigon Pagoda, in which sacred relics such as the frontal bone, collar bone and tooth of Gautama are enshrined, pagodas usually just have unglazed terracotta votive tablets dedicated as the relic bones of a saint. Temples were originally patterned after the cave temples of India, having inside sanctum with a huge seated statue of the Buddha made of brick and covered with consecrated whitewash. Structurally they were divided into large and medium sized temples using a pile of solid brick work in the middle to support the weight of the building and small-sized temples, with a cavity created inside by building the surrounding walls to converge with a point in the centre of the ceiling. Small-sized temples have only one entrance; a Buddhist statue is enshrined in the front interior. The temples with a main block are sub-divided into the large kind with four entrances and the medium-sized kind which has a mandapa protruding out from the paulownia hall toward the singular entrance and with its interior serving as the chapel. A narrow corridor surrounding the main block with an image of the Buddha has been set up in medium-sized temples.

Among the Buddhist pagodas and temples of Pagan, a considerable number have scenes from the Jataka inserted on glazed or unglazed terracotta plaques around the terraces. Jataka reliefs can be found at pagodas such as Shwezigon, Mingalazedi, East and West Petleik and Dhammayazika as well as at temple like Ananda built by Kyansittha. They all have the Pali Jataka name and number carved in Burmese letters above or below each figure.

The plaster carvings outside and the wall paintings inside make for one special feature of the brick temples of Pagan. The arch pediments, the upper parts of windows, friezes and plaster mouldings, etc. have been painted with whitewash. Their designs consist of decorations in stone and stucco carvings in the form of ogre-heads called kirtimukha, floral patterns and so on. They are noted for being extremely delicate and graceful.

Aside from the large temples, where repainting was conducted several times in later ages, wall paintings can be found in most of the medium and small-sized temples. Ceilings and walls, the four corners of the walls, the borders between the ceilings and the walls, the boundaries between sanctum and hall, archway, window frames, in other words, all places with flat surfaces were painted. The wall paintings contain the Eight Scenes including Buddha's Birth, his Enlightenment, his First Sermon, his Twin Miracles and Parinirvana; the Scenes from the Buddha's life, which depict the major events during his lifetime; the Scenes from the Jataka, which show the figure of the Buddha in a previous existence; the Boddhisattva, the guardian deity of the gate to praise Buddha and to protect him from the instruction of outside enemies; semi-gods like Kinnara, Gandharva, Apsaras, Naga and Yaksa; animals such as elephant, horses, birds and fish, etc.; figurised botanical patterns like lotus flowers or leaves, stalk, buds, etc.; various geometric designs and so on.

How wealthy Pagan was and the degree to which it prospered can be understood from the following passages from King Kyansitta's Mon Inscription written in the eleventh century: During his reign, mushrooms, bamboo shoots, flowers and the fruit of the trees shall abound. Poor people who find it hard to get rice and clothing shall wear gold ornaments and fine apparel... Throughout the King's realm, a hundred and twenty times a year the rain shall fall. Always the paddy shall be full in the year. There shall be plenty of elephant, horses, water buffaloes, cattle, pigs, goats and fowls... Farmers who excel in planting and burrowing shall fill their barns and granaries with paddy, millet and all manner of grain. (Epigraphia Birmanica I. Part II, Inscription I, Face D)

A vast expense was procured to construct Buddhist pagodas and temples. Besides the obvious cost of the construction itself, it was common to dedicate lands and slaves to Three Gems. The donated lands were tax exempt and the donated slaves outside the jurisdiction of worldly authority. Therefore, the more the construction of Buddhist edifices increased, the greater amount of national finances consumed and the more exhausted the country's power became. In addition to such a collapsing budget within the Kingdom of Pagan, a physical shock was received from the outside in the late thirteenth century when Yuan Dynasty of China demanded tribute and claimed suzerainty. Pagan refused the demand and it was attacked four times, in 1277, 1283, 1286 and 1287. King Narathihapate eventually agreed to subordination to the Yuan and the hegemony of Burma was soon transferred in the hands of the Shan tribe, which had advanced from the Shan Plateau. That spelled the collapse of Pagan, the first unified kingdom of the Burmese people.

Facts about Pagan

Original name: Pugam or Pukam (Corruption of Pyu game)

Literal meaning: Probably the village of Pyu

Race/nation that constructed Pagan: Burmese

Purpose of construction: Capital of Pagan Kingdom

History of construction: Legend asserts its construction to King Thamudarit in 108 AD But the Burmese chronicle *Zatadawbon Yazawin* tells us that present walled city of Pagan had been built by King Pyinbya in AD 850 It is said that Pagan was originally a cluster of 19 villages of Pyu refugees.

Location: 21° north, 94°, 52' east; about 700 km from Rangoon (1½ hour by plane)

Size: The ruin of Pagan is about 16 square miles, but the whole area covers some 25 square miles including Nyaung-oo, Pagan, Wetkyi-in, Myinkaba, Thiripyitsaya, Myinnanthu villages.

Representative architecture: Shwezigon pagoda built by King Anawrahta and completed by King Kyansittha; Thatbyinnyu Temple built in the twelfth century by King Alaungsithu.

Style of architecture: Pagan style.

Building materials: Mostly brick.

Famous objects of fine art: Four colossal standing images of the Previous Buddhas in the Ananda Temple; Frescoes illustrating scenes from life of Buddha and the Jatakas in Wetkyi-in Kubyank-gyi Temple

Style/features: Pagan style.

Reasons for destruction: Pagan was deserted mainly due to abandonment by King Narathihapate in 1287 and secondly removal of the capital from Pagan to Pinya and Sagain in the late half of the thirteenth century by three brothers of Shan.

Causes of present collapsing: Mainly due to hot weather and scarcity of rain during the past 700 years.

Plans of preservation/presentation: Archaeological Department, Ministry of Culture, Government of Burma is carrying out the repairs and maintenance of the ancient buildings and surveys of the historical remains.

Present population: Roughly 150,000 in Nyaung-oo township.

Life and culture in Pagan's golden period

Flourished during: Eleventh — thirteenth centuries

Population: Unknown

Social system: Monarchy

Religion: Theravada Buddhism mixed with Brahmanism and Mahayana Buddhism

Economical foundation: Agriculture (Foodstuffs were supplied mainly from the two irrigated rice-planting areas, Kyaukse and Minbu)

Staple food: Rice

Housing: Houses made of wood and bamboo

Costume: Textile and various ornaments

Marital system: Basically monogamy

Calendar: Buddhist Era and Burmese Era starting from AD 638

Festivals: Buddhist festivals and Traditional festival of Nat worship.

Currency: Weight of gold, silver and copper

Writing system: Burmese adopted from the Mon scripts

Tools of writing: Stones and probably palm leaves

Means of transportation: Cow, horse, elephant and cart with two wheels

Entertainment: Singing, dancing and playing the musical instruments.

Cambodia

Angkor Wat — Vishnu-Raja's Crowning Glory

Angkor: A glorious castle town

One of Southeast Asia's great ruins, Angkor Wat, is located in the Siem Reap district of northwest Cambodia. In the Khmer language the words "Angkor Wat" mean "town of temples". The town was formerly known as Yasodharapura, being named after Yasovarman I who built the first royal city there at the end of the 9th century. Many of the kings who ruled the city continued to build castle towns and temples one after another, until the city finally fell in 1432. Among the hundreds of ruins that remain at the present site of Angkor, Angkor Wat is the largest stone-built temple.

In 1113 however, Suryavarman II defeated the former King, his great uncle, by means of a *coup d'etat.* On succeeding to the throne, he immediately commenced work on Angkor Wat which was brought to near completion about thirty years later. As pictured in the reliefs along the corridor, Suryavarman II was a dauntless, imposing man. He enforced measures to enrich and strengthen the country and was continually engaged in the gaining of territory and in construction of all kinds. However, thirty years of intermittent war coupled with this excessive temple building was to deplete national funds and impoverish the people. So with the country in a state of chaos and Angkor Wat still unfinished, the King went into hiding.

Angkor Wat: A great stone temple

Angkor Wat was built on an enormous scale. The circumference of its surrounding moat is 5.4 km and it is 700 m from the entrance along the approach to the main shrine. The tower of the central temple soars above several kilometres of three-tiered corridors, banking and the stone foundations. The front approach faces west. On walking along the stone-paved approach with its railings decorated with carvings of *Naga* (the Serpent god), one slowly rises from the level of the first corridor to that of the second. Then on passing through the second corridor, one enters the inner courtyard to find a steep, grand stairway right before one's eyes. At the top of the stairs is the first corridor connecting five towers. The constructor of Angkor Wat ingeniously worked with the illusionary capability of man's eye to make it seem as though the building led up to a grand world.

On the average, it takes an adult a good thirty minutes to walk from the entrance to the pinnacle of the main temple.

Khmer architecture had undergone about ten transitions in styles before Angkor Wat was erected. Therefore this great temple is the culmination of the mastery and experience of these many building techniques. For example, one of these traditionally fundamental techniques, that of linking the tower to the foundation with corridors is a distinct feature of Angkor Wat. This remarkable structure not only adopts a three-dimensional arrangement of tower, temple and corridor passages, but at the same time is part of a bisymmetrically geometric plane. In constructing this temple, the Khmers were endeavoring to express realistically on earth their unique sense of the universe. For example, the central temple and the pinnacles of its four towers represent Meru, the sacred mountain at the centre of the earth, while the surrounding walls represent the majestic Himalayas. The arterial roads running north-south and east-west along with the Buddhist sutra library and the position of the temple are said to be the actualization of god. The surrounding moat symbolizes the deep endless ocean.

Angkor Wat is the temple that Suryavarman II had devoted to Vishnu. A special image of Vishnu-raja (a union of the King and Vishnu) was worshipped in the central temple where the god is said to have always descended. Then having received a posthumous name, the King went to live in the world of both men and gods. This was thought to be the incarnation of god according to the Devaraja faith.

Grand funerary temple

Angkor Wat is thought to have been a funerary temple so it was a matter of great interest to find out what lay buried under the central temple where special festivals were said to have been held. Excavations revealed a well at what would have been the surface of the earth. At the bottom of the well was found a circular gold casket. This further clarifies the fact that Angkor Wat was erected as a funerary temple. The hypothesis that Angkor Wat was a funerary temple also stems from the fact that the front approach to the temple faces west, the direction the deceased took to reach the Western Paradise. As well, the third corridor runs in an anti-clockwise direction which is the same as that taken by pilgrims in funeral marches. After death, one could communicate with god from the high tower above the grave, the same position as that of the funeral style.

High artistic worth

Apart from the immense scale on which Angkor Wat was built, it is also highly valued for its artistic worth. To begin with, elaborate scenes depicted in bas-relief, in the frescos along the several kilometres of corridor reliefs, give the appearance of a three-dimensional picture scroll. Spaces in the wall are filled with the charming figure of the goddess Devata; the sculpture of the lintels and gables is unsurpassed; the circular windows and pinnacles shaped like artillery shells: Whichever feature is discussed, they all reveal the creative modelling and artistic sense of the Khmer architects.

Since this temple was dedicated to Vishnu, related themes abound in the artistic designs, e.g. his incarnation Krishna, Prince Rama, the united Vishnu and Suryavarman II. For instance, in one of the sketches from the corridor relief, there is the scene from the Creation of Heaven and Earth, Myth of Churning the Sea of Milk, where Vishnu is shown leading the two gods Deva and Ashura. There is also the brave figure of Vishnu climbing onto Garuda's shoulders to overthrow the enemy. Another scene shows the incarnated Krishna beating the monster Bana and the battle plan for the bitter struggle on Lanka island as is recounted in the Ramayana tales.

The will to create has left no blanks on the several hundred metre long wall reliefs. It's almost as if the more was carved, the more filled with fervour and life the carvings become. Certainly anyone would realize that the workmanship of the methods used is unsurpassable. The charm, influence and power of Khmer art and the skill and craftsmanship of the artists are exquisitely expressed in the relief.

Several thousand stone masons, stone cutters and watchmen were called on for the construction of Angkor Wat. Skilled groups of craftsmen, carvers, Buddhist image sculptors and paper hangers were also commissioned. Labourers, carriers, village folk and other such war slaves were hunted out and shipped. The latest techniques of the time were freely employed and within a thirty-year period, immense resources were poured into the construction of Angkor Wat. Hence this terrific operation was begun. Angkor Wat embodies the sweat and hard toil of the Khmer: the wonderful fruit of Khmer energy.

Save Angkor ruins

After the capital was transferred, Angkor Wat underwent a change and was converted into a Theravada Buddhist Temple where lights were continually burnt as offerings to Buddha. In the central temple, Buddhist images were brought in to replace the images of god.

Angkor Wat was known in the neighbouring areas for its majestic appearance and so was often visited by pilgrims. They followed the Mekong River upstream from Phnom Penh to the Tonle Sap Lake, taking the route up the Siem Reap River by river boat.

Since 1907 the Ecole Francaise d'Extreme Orient and the Cambodian government have promoted restoration work on the ruins. However, since 1970 the operations have remained suspended due to civil war.

Results of a survey in 1980 confirmed the fact that natural destruction due to water, bacteria and vegetation along with human destruction caused by the country's internal chaos are in considerably advanced stage. The ruins of Angkor Wat represent the cultural heritage of the Khmer and yet at the same time they are treasures of all mankind and have to be saved from further destruction.

Facts about Angkor Wat

Original name: Angkor Wat

Literal meaning: Temple of the Royal Castle

Race/nation that constructed Angkor Wat: Khmers

Purpose of construction: To dedicate a shrine to Vishnu (Vishnu-raja) and to build an imperial tomb.

History of construction: Suryavarman II constructed Angkor Wat between 1113 and 1145.

Location: 13°49' north, 103°81' east; 20 m above sea level; 315 km from Phnom Penh (5 or 6 hours by car)

Size: 65 m high (central tower), 1,300 m long, 1,500 m wide; 200 ha

Style of architecture: Angkor Wat

Building materials: Laterite and sandstone

Famous objects of fine art: Reliefs on the galleries; statues of Devata.

Important sites in the neighbourhood: Angkor Thorn, Bayon, West Baray, West Mebon, Phimeanakas Baphuon, Phnom Bakheng, Neak Pean, Ta Prohm, Banteay Kdei, Srah Srang, East Baray, East Mebon, Pre Rup, Ta Som, Preah Khan, Ta Keo, Banteay Srei, Banteay Samre, Bakong, Lolei, Preah Ko, etc.

Reasons for destruction: Invasion of the Siams (14-15c), transfer of capitals, change of religion from Vishnu worship to Theravada Buddhism, and civil war.

Causes of present collapsing: Vandalism, natural destruction by tropical plants and weeds, rain and strong sunshine.

Plans of preservation/presentation: Conservation Programme of Angkor Monuments organized by the Ministry of Information and Culture was resumed in September, 1979.

Life and culture in Angkor Wat's golden period

Flourished during: twelfth century

Population: About 200,000 people including inhabitants in the neighbourhood

Social system: Monarchy (unity of religion and state)

Religion: Hinduism (Vishnu sect), spirit worship

Economical foundation: Agriculture

Staple food: Rice, cereals and fresh-water fish

Housing: High-floored houses made of wood, bamboo and palm leaves

Costume: Sampot (folk dress)

Calendar: Lunar calendar

Festivals: Rituals/festivals worshipping the Vishnu-raja
Currency: Barter system
Writing system: Old Khmer and Sanskrit
Tools of writing: Stone and shell

Means of transportation: Boat (river), buffalo, horse, elephant
Entertainment: Cockfight, pigfight, circus, musical instrument, gambling (seen from the reliefs)

Devata of Ta Prohm (12th/13th century), Angkor Wat.

China

Xian — Seat of Ancient Internationalism

Xian, called Changan in ancient times, is one of the famous ancient capitals of China. It is centrally located in the Weihe-river Plain in China's Shaanxi province. To the south is Mt. Qinling, to the north are the Jin and Wei Rivers. Xian, with fertile land, favourable physical features and a beautiful scenery, was the first place of communication between China and Asian, European and African countries in ancient times. Eleven dynasties established their capitals in Xian, namely the Western Zhou, Qin, Western Han, Western Jin, Former Zhao, Former Qin, Later Qin, Western Wei, Northern Zhou, Sui and Tang, spanning over 1,100 years.

As early as 500,000-600,000 years ago, Gong Wang Ling on the south bank of the Ba River (about 60 km southeast of Xian, but now in Lantian County) was the hometown of the Paleolithic Lantian Ape-men. The Banpo site in the eastern suburbs of Xian, a 6,000 year-old matriarchal clan community village, is the remains of Yangshao Culture in the neolithic age. Emperor Wenwang and Wuwang of the Zhou dynasty made their capitals Fengjing and Haojing on the west and east banks of the Feng River (in the northwest of present-day Xian) respectively. In about the eleventh century BC Emperor Wuwang dispatched his troops from Haojing, destroyed the Shang dynasty and established China's third ancient slave state. Thus the capital of Feng and Hao became the nationwide metropolitan city. Since the founding of New China, about 3,000 pieces of bronze wares of the Zhou dynasty have been found in Shaanxi province. Such a large number, the superb craftsmanship, the exquisite designs and the inscriptions covering so many contents are quite rare in other countries. The highly developed bronze culture casts a brilliant light on the world's ancient civilization.

After making its capital in Xianyang in 350 BC the Qin dynasty fulfilled the great cause of unifying the other six powers and established the first feudal autocratic centralized state power. Since 1974, the terra-cotta army vaults attached to the first emperor of the Qin dynasty's mausoleum in the Lintong County of Shaanxi province have been excavated. The clay figures unearthed vividly portray the heroic warriors of the Qin dynasty; clay horses reproduce the finebred Hequ horses for drawing chariots and the shiny chromium-coated bronze swords indicate the high achievements of the metallurgical technique during the Qin dynasty. These cultural relics are valuable data for the study of the histories of military affairs, sculpture and metallurgy of the Qin dynasty. Changan was the name of a village in the Qin dynasty. In 202 BC Emperor Gaozu of the Han dynasty decided to make Changan his capital. In 194 BC Emperor Weidi of the Han dynasty (Liu Ying) began to have the city of Changan built. The city was 25,100 m in circumference while its plan was an irregular square, symbolizing the Dipper in the sky. Hence it was also called "Dipper City". The city was divided into a palatial area, 2 city gates, 17 streets, 9 eastern and western markets and 100 residential quarters, having a population of about 260,000. Changan and Rome in the west were the largest and most important cities in the world at that time, like two glittering stars in the sky shining on the east and west of the world. Changan of the Han dynasty was the starting point of the Silk Road. In 138 and 119 BC Zhang Qian went to many countries of the Western Regions from here on diplomatic missions, made significant contributions to the development of cultural exchanges between China and other countries. It was a great event in the history of friendship along the Silk Road.

Towards the end of the sixth century, a large-scale and magnificent capital, Daxing of the Sui which later became Changan of the Tang, was set up in the urban districts of the present-day Xian. Changan of the Tang dynasty was 35.5 km in circumference with the imperial city and palatial city in its northern centre. Inside the city there were 11 streets running from north to south and 14 from east to west. The whole city, with Zhuque (ostrich) Street as its axle line, could be divided into eastern and western parts comprising 108 Fang (residential quarters) in the form of a chessboard with a population of about one million. Based on the previous architecture, the city of Changan was laid out with thoroughfares, central markets and dwelling areas. It surpassed the predecessors' achievements, and was a milestone in the architectural history of China's ancient cities. As an international city, Changan and Constantinople (the capital of the Eastern Empire, the present-day Istanbul in Turkey) were the starting and terminal points of the Silk Road. The Tang dynasty had a friendly relationship with over 70 countries and regions. On the mural of "Courtiers and Guests" inside Prince Zhang Hui's tomb envoys from the Eastern Empire, Arab countries and Japan, and of China's national minorities are portrayed. The "Daqin Nestorian Stele", gold coins from the Eastern Empire, silver coins from

Persia, the silver coins of "Wado Kaiho" from Japan and a wealth of pottery, tricoloured camels and Hu figurines add a brilliant splendour to the Silk Road sounded with jingling camel-rings.

Xian ended its historic mission as a capital after the Tang dynasty. In 1369 Feng Yuan Road was changed into Xian Fu (prefecture). It was the first time the name of Xian appeared in history. Between 1370-1378 the city of Xian was built, and its name has been used until now. In 1949, the centuries-old city of Xian was reborn. It has radiated its youth and become a new rising industrial city which attracts friends both from home and abroad to visit.

Facts about Xian

Original name: Changan in ancient times

Literal meaning: Ever-lasting peace

Race/nation that constructed Changan: Han nationality

Purpose of construction: To build a centre of politics, economy and culture as well as to consolidate the reign of the feudal ruling class

History of construction: The city of Changan of the Han dynasty was built in AD 190 and the city of Changan of the Tang dynasty was built in the early seventh century on the site of Daxing city of the Sui dynasty which was built in AD 590

Location: 34°15' north, 108°55' east; 410-450m above sea level; 1,200 km from Beijing (21 hours by train)

Size: The city of Changan of the Han was over 30 km in circumference (65,318 square km). The city of Changan of the Tang dynasty was 35.5 km in circumference (78,573 square km).

Representative architecture (existent): Dayan Pagoda (AD 652) and Xiaoyan Pagoda (AD 707) of the Tang dynasty

Style of architecture: Dayan Pagoda in a chamber-pavilion style and Xiaoyan Pagoda in a multi-eaves style.

Building material: Brick

Famous objects of fine art: The typical works of the Western Han dynasty are the stone sculptures of the galloping horse, the crouching ox, the freak, etc. The typical ones of the Tang dynasty are the six bass-relief horses at Zhaoling mausoleum.

Other important sites: The remains of Feng-Hao, the capital of the Western Zhou dynasty; the remains of Zhouyuan, the capital of the early Western Zhou dynasty; the remains of Xianyang, the capital of the Qin dynasty; Qin Shihuang's mausoleum; the eleven emperors' mausoleums of the Han dynasty; the eighteen emperors' mausoleums of the Tang dynasty.

Reasons for destruction: Human being's destruction and natural erosion.

Plans of preservation/presentation: Only 20 places in this province are under the state government's protection. Having special signs, scopes, files and protection departments, they are open to the public at present.

Present population: The remains of Changan of the Han has an agricultural population of 100,000. The present urban area of Xian has a population of 1,42 million.

Life and culture in Xian's golden period

Flourished during: Second century BC — AD first century (Han dynasty); AD seventh-tenth century (Tang dynasty)

Population: 246,200 people (Han dynasty); one million (Tang dynasty)

Social system: Feudal monarchic system

Religion: Confucianism, Menciuism, Huangciuism and Laociuism during the Han; Taoism, Buddhism, Nestorism, Islam during the Tang.

Economical foundation: Agriculture, handicrafts, foreign trade.

Staple food: Millet and cereals during the Han; wheat and cereals during the Tang

Housing: Brick-wood structured houses. Most of them were compounds with houses around a courtyard.

Costume: Shirts, robes, skirts and trousers.

Marital system: Monogamy

Calendar: Lunar calendar

Festivals: The New year's Day, the Lantern Festival, the Pure Brightness Festival, the Dragon Boat Festival, the Double Ninth Festival, the Mid-autumn Festival and the Cold-food Festival.

Currency: Copper coins

Writing system: Chinese characters

Tools of writing: Chinese brush, bamboo slip, wooden slip and silk during the Han; Chinese brush and paper during the Tang.

Means of transportation: Carriages, horses and boats.

Entertainment: Songs, dances and acrobatic shows.

India

Sanchi, Ajanta & Ellora — Ancient Monuments of Indian Culture

The great stupa at Sanchi

On a hill some 45 km away from Bhopal in Madhya Pradesh State stands the great Sanchi Stupa. In the early years of the Christian era when Buddhism was spreading throughout India, Sanchi was situated on an important trade route. It is at Sanchi that the evolution of the Stupa can be traced as there are numerous ruins of smaller stupas and monasteries for Buddhist monks and other buildings at this site. The philosophy of Buddha taught of the concern of man for nature, of the perpetual cycle of life and death which is fundamental to nature. These concepts of Buddhism were symbolized in the hemispheric shape of the stupa. For the stupa is raised on a circular ground plan, and forms a hemispheric dome presenting the earth that gives life. The stupa is also a funeral mound venerated by the Buddhists in which the mortal remains of Buddha or his disciples are encased. It is thus the cycle of life and death are represented in the shape and form of the stupa. The round plan of the stupa is circular and in elevation has a hemispheric shape. The rubble mound was faced with stone. Plaster and mortar was applied and later carved and painted. From sculptures we know that during festivals and ceremonies the stupa was often decorated with flower garlands and flags. An ambulatory in the form of a terrace, reached by a double staircase, runs round the whole structure, enabling pilgrims to perform the ritual circumambulation; an ambulatory was also provided at ground level between the stupa and the outer railing.

The outer railing is an exact reproduction of a timber fence: this imitation of the carpenter's technique by stone-cutters is a special feature of ancient Indian art of this period. The railing consists of a series of uprights 3.10 m high, linked by three tiers of horizontal members and a top rail (height 0.68 m) and is without ornament of any kind. The four gateways on the cardinal points are profusely decorated with carvings depicting the life and times of Buddha. Free standing statues of the Buddha in meditation were erected opposite the four entrances in the fifth century.

The sculptures panels on the gateways are carved in low relief and depict the life of Buddha. Since the Sanchi stupa was constructed during the Hinayana period no figures of Buddha can be found, yet these sculptured reliefs give a vivid account of the previous incarnations of Buddha. There is a great exuberance in the depiction of nature; plant life, animal life and bird life. The respect for nature is symbolized in the worship of the Bodhi tree which represents Buddha. As Buddhism spread through South East Asia, the original hemispherical shape of the stupa was transformed into loftier domes and pagodas. However, it is at Sanchi that the first breath of Buddhist philosophy gave life to a joyous artistic expression in which all of nature was seen in its abundance, coexisting with human beings.

Ajanta

The 29 rock-hewn caves at Ajanta, cut into the scarp of a cliff, are either *chaityas* (temples) or *viharas* (monasteries). Most of these are carved so that a flood of natural lights pours into them at given times of the day. Both the facade and the inside of the chambers faithfully reproduce the structural patterns known to those ancient builders. On the walls are paintings, many still glowing with their original colours. On the outer walls are brilliantly executed sculptures. Here ancient Indian art attained the zenith of its development and revealed a dynamic rhythm of life.

The antiquity of these caves and paintings ranges between the second century BC and AD seventh century The work was completed in two phases, the first lasting between the second century BC and AD second century and the second commencing in about AD fifth century.

Six of these caves — caves No. 9, 10, 16, 17, 2, and 1 contain considerable fragmentary remains of paintings of what were once a lavish and colourful decorative scheme. But even in this ruinous state after centuries of neglect and vandalism, these wall paintings of Buddhist caves represent a comprehensive record of religious, social and cultural life of India at that time, her people and their attitude towards life.

The subject matter of these paintings is almost exclusively Buddhist excepting decorative patterns on the ceilings and the pillars. They are mostly associated with the Jatakas — a collection of stories recording the previous births of the Lord Buddha. The contours of the Ajanta figures are superb and reveal a keen perception of beauty and form. The drawing is spontaneous and unrestrained. The painters of Ajanta had realised the true glory of the Buddha, whose life story was employed here as a motif to explain the eternal pattern of human life. The stories illustrated here are continuous and elaborate, presenting the drama of Ancient India enacted in the palaces of the kings and in the hamlets of the common people equally engaged in the quest for the beautiful and spiritual values of life.

Ellora

The 34 caves, all hewn out of the sloping side of another sickle shaped hill Ellora, date back from the fifth to the twelfth century. Besides being masterpieces of sculpture, the Ellora caves indicate the religious tolerance of the three faiths in the early medieval period, Buddhist, Hindu and Jain. The Buddhist shrines are the earliest, relatively simple and austere. The Hindu temples are comparatively more elaborate. We see in these an attempt to surpass earlier Buddhist achievements in architecture and sculpture.

The most remarkable of the carved shrines at Ellora is the Kailasa temple dedicated to the Hindu God Siva. This temple was constructed by king Krishna during the reign of the Rashtrakuta in the middle of the eighth century. This fantastic edifice was chiselled out by hand from a single rock with gateway, pavilion, courtyard, assembly hall, vestibule, sanctum and tower — all these out of the same enormous rock. The Kailasa temple is approximately twice the area of the Parthenon and one and a half times its height. It is truly sculpture on a grand scale. Both inside and outside the temple, there are beautiful, graceful and dignified sculptural decorations, largely pertaining to the theme of Siva and Parvati.

The beautiful architectural rock sculpture from Cave No. 29 shows the marriage of Siva and Parvati. Siva holding the head of the bashful Parvati occupies the centre of the composition. To the right Brahma, the creator, is actively engaged in stirring up the flames of the sacrificial fire. The parents of Parvati stand behind her to offer their daughter to the great God. A number of gods assembled to witness the function are shown hovering above the principal figures. The dignified grace of the divine couple and the gentle solemnity of the occasion have been portrayed by the sculptor with a masterly skill.

Another magnificent sculpture at Ellora is a panel depicting Ravana, shaking Mt. Kailasa. In this remarkable scene the quivering of the mountain can be felt and Parvati is shown greatly agitated, turning to Siva, grasping his arm in fear, while her maid takes to flight: but the Great God is unmoved and holds on fast by pressing down the mountain with his foot. The lower half of the composition exhibits Ravana exerting all the force of his twenty arms against the mountain

There are also several fragments of paintings on the ceilings of the different parts of the Kailasa temple and on the walls of some Jain cave temples. The flying figures from the Jain temple (Cave No. 32) belonging to mid-ninth century AD are beautiful examples of swift movement through clouds. The rounded plasticity of the classical period Ajanta modelling on the face and the medieval tendency of portraying angular bends of the arms are well marked here.

Facts about Sanchi

Race/nation that constructed Sanchi: Indian

Purpose of construction: Religious building for Buddhist. Stupa is a funeral mould containing mortal remains of Buddha and his disciples.

History of construction: Constructed between second century BC and AD second century

Location: 23° north, 77° east; 500-2,000 m above sea level; 50 km from Bhopal in Madhya Pradesh

Size: Stupa No. 1: 23.8 m in diameter and 12.8 m in height

Representative architecture: Stupa Nos. 1,2, and 3

Style of architecture: Hinayana Buddhist

Building materials: Mound filled with rubble and faced with stone.

Famous objects of fine art: Sculptured reliefs on Toranas

Reasons for destruction: Abandoned as religious communities no longer live there.

Causes of present collapsing: Wind erosion of sculptured reliefs.

Plans of preservation/presentation: Preserved as a national monument.

Present population: None

Facts about Ajanta/Ellora

Race/nation that constructed Ajanta/Ellora: Indian

Purpose of construction: Monastic residence and religious buildings for Buddhist, Jain and Hindu religious communities.

History of construction: Ajanta caves were constructed between second century BC and AD seventh century; Ellora caves were constructed between 5th and 12th century AD

Location: Ajanta: 20° north, 75° east; 500-2,000 m above sea level; 66 km from Aurangabad

Ellora: 20° north, 75° east; 500-2,000 m above sea level; 18 km from Aurangabad.

Representative architecture: Ajanta caves Nos. 1,2,17 and 19; Ellora caves No. 10 and Kailasa Temple

Building materials: Rock cut

Famous object of fine art: Mural painting and sculpture

Reasons for destruction: Abandoned as religious communities no longer live there.

Causes of present collapsing: Murals of Ajanta are fading due to exposure to light.

Plans of preservation/presentation: Unesco undertook the preservation of Ajanta murals.

Present population: None

Life and culture in the golden period of Sanchi, Ajanta & Ellora

Flourished during: Second century BC — AD tenth century

Population: Not more than 500 monks at a time.

Social system: Monarchy

Religion: Sanchi & Ajanta — Buddhism; Ellora — Buddhism, Jainism and Hinduism.

Economical foundation: Agriculture and trade of textiles to China and of gems, spices and ivory to West Europe

Staple Food: Rice, wheat, barley, fruit.

Housing: Houses made of wood, thatch, and brick

Costume: Loin cloth and turban with jewellery accessories (Both male and female)

Marital system: Religion and caste began to determine relationships between families.

Calendar: Solar

Festivals: Buddhist and Hindu religious festivals

Currency: Coins

Writing system: Brahmi script (Sanchi); Sanskrit Pali (Ajanta/Ellora)

Tools of writing: On stone with chisel; brush with bamboo for murals.

Means of transportation: Bullock cart, horse, camel, elephant and boats

Entertainment: Music, dance, theatre mainly.

Jagannath Temple at Puri: Its History, Significance, and Architectural Beauty

The Jagannath Temple at Puri is famous in the world as the largest Hindu temple. It is one of the four main pilgrim centres in India, attracting thousands of pilgrims daily and millions from different parts of the world for the annual Car-festival. This 65 metre high temple, built in the twelfth century by King Chodaganga Dev of the Ganga dynasty, represents all the richness and plasticity of the Kalinga style of architecture. In its exuberance of sculptures, the archaic iconography of the cult images mingled and interspersed with the highest Hindu iconology reflects a splendid synthesis for an all-Indian tradition.

History

How old is the cult of Jagannath or the concept of the Jagannath triad? Answers to these are yet to be determined with any specificity. Though its historical antiquity is still shrouded in mystery, the Puranas and ancient texts make ample references to it. The Rig Veda (10/155/3) alludes to the wooden form of Purusottama by which name Jagannath is mentioned till eighth century. The *Ramayana*, the *Mahabharata*, *Vishnu Dharma* (c. fourth century), as well as the Vishnu, Skanda and Bamana Puranas, etc. make mention of it. The Chinese traveller I-tsing speaks of its phenomenal popularity in South East Asia and Sumatra, in particular, by seventh century. Indrabhuti's prayer to Jagannath (c. eighth century) is the first explicit mention of 'Jagannath'. Murari's play *Anargharaghav* (c. tenth century) alludes to the Car-festival. Many other works like *Mukti Chintamani* and Jaimini's account of Puri in *Purusottama Mahatmyam* make profuse mention of it. There is reason enough to suppose therefore that the cult and the triad are older than the present temple. Ample literary references are there, pertaining to the legendary King Indradyumna setting up the temple in pre-Chirstian era. King Yayati II's construction of temple and its consecration to Jagannath long before the trip of Shankaracharya to Puri is a historical fact. The present temple was probably built on the ruins of the old one.

Paleographic references to Jagannath are traceable from the Maihar (tenth century) and Govindpur (early twelfth century) inscriptions in Madhya Pradesh and Bihar respectively. Iconographic antiquity of the Jagannath Triad is evident from a Mathura relief of the Kushana period (c second century). as attested by the one at the Bindusagara Tank in Bhubaneswar (c seventh century) and innumerable epigraphic evidences from the temple-precincts itself.

The Madala Panji, the palm-leaf chronicle of the Temple, wrongfully speak of Anangabhimadev as the builder of the temple. The inscription of Chodagangadev in the adjacent Nrsimha temple (AD 1113) is a categorical proof that the construction of the modern temple was in progress by then. The latter ruled upto 1147. The temple was completed before that and Chodaganga consecrated it to Lord Purusottama, all the while regarding himself as a servant of the Lord. Subsequently King Anangabhima Dev II of the same dynasty dedicated the empire to Lord Jagannath (AD 1230-31). Henceforward, Jagannath became the State-Deity and the King, His first servitor. As such, the cult became a symbol of unity, a focus of pan-Indian influence and secular or sectarian loyalty.

The Lord of the Universe (Jagannath) is not a mere log of wood. He is 'Darubrahman', identical with 'OM' the pranava. He is 'Bhairav' for Saivites, Rama, Krishna, and Vishnu for the Vaisnavites, 'Ganesh' for the followers of the Ganapatya cult, the 'Tri-Ratna' for the Buddhists, the 'Nath' for the Jainas, 'Vitthal' for the Marathas, and of no exclusive alienism to the Muslims during their rule of Orissa. Even the British were content to play second fiddle to it, not daring to infringe upon its ecclesiastical intricacies. The cult of Jagannath is a composite one.

Significance

From modest beginnings of tribal village in the pre-historic era, Puri grew into a centre of culture, literature, and art including music, dance, and painting, in a typically original way. The supreme artistic merits of the Jagannath Temple are overshadowed by its sacredness. Jagannath, the Lord of the Universe, is the principal deity. Seated to his right and on the raised platform (ratnavedi) in the 'sanctum sanctorum' are sister Subhadra and elder brother Balabhadra. There is also Sudarshan, the symbolic disc of Vishnu, alongside the triad. The triad is in consonance with deep Upanishadic philosophy. Balabhadra represents the purity of Advaita (non-dualism) and is thus, monism exemplified. Subhadra embodies the phenomenal plurality or 'Sakti'. Jagannath is the apotheosised epitome of *Jnana* (wisdom), *Karma* (work), *Bhakti* (devotion) and *Prema* (love). Sudarshan symbolises the formless form of non-dualistic philosophy.

The Jagannath cult is a striking interaction of diverse faiths and a synthetic compendium of Hindu philosophy. Purusottama Jagannath is the composite God assimilating diverse features belonging to different sects, and, as such, in a comprehensive theological perspective transcends the doctrinal particularism of any single philosophy, from the Rig Veda to Vishnu Sahasra Nama, from the Ramayana to the Mahabharata, From Buddhist philosophy to Jaina concepts, from Shankaracharya and Ramanuja to Vallabhacharya and Ramananda, from Nimbarka to Sankardev, and from Nanak and Kabir to Chaitanya and Totapuri.

The cult has been the spring-board of various cultural tenets originating out of it. The Odissi dance and music evolved from the labyrinths of ecstatic and trance-like devotion to the deities. The nuances of Odissi songs and the mystic rhythms of the accompanying dance were climaxed by Jayadeva's 'Gitagovindam' and the 'devadasi' cult of virgin dancers consecrated to the triad. 'Patta' painting is another rich legacy, as also is the development of different 'Silpa Shastras' associated with architecture, sculpture and carpentry. The egalitarianism of the 'Mahaprasad' brotherhood is the capstone point of the cultural growth. The Lord as the saviour of the down-trodden (Patitapawana) is a magnanimous growth of humanism as evident from micro-empirical analysis of the temple services that reflect an Aryan-Dravidian synthesis to the macro-structural perspectives of its rich philosophical traditions. The cult gleans a composite cosmopolitan culture. Other associated cults and institutions grew under its wide expanse. Among them mention may be made of the Mahavira, the Madhav, the Naga and the Tree cults and the 'Jaga's and 'Akhada's (community centres of martial arts).

Architecture

Perhaps the single greatest monument of Hindu architecture, the Jagannath Temple, though squat and gigantic, majestically rises to soaring heights from inside its rectangular compound wall that is 665 x 644 feet and invariably 24 feet high. The temple conforms in architectural style to the canons of Kalinga school of temple architecture comprising of Vimana, Jagamohana, Nata Mandir and Bhoga Mandap in a symmetrical alignment. The Vimana is a curvilinear tower of vertical sections rising from the sides of an 80 feet square plinth to a height of nearly 215 feet.

According to the temple chronicle, Madala Panji, about five million grams of gold were spent in the construction of the temple and an additional 1.25 million grams of gold were set aside for ornaments of the deities. Jaya and Vijaya, the two celestial guards, are custodians of the Nata Mandir. The Nata Mandir (dancing hall) and the Bhoga Mandap or refectory are conical in shape. These were added to the main temple, in a unique style, during the fifteenth century. The main temple is of a circular-conical shape capped by a flute disc crowning the spire atop which are the Kalasa and the Vaishnavite symbol of 'Nilachakra', a gigantic and rust-proof iron disc. Extensive use of iron slabs in the construction of the temple gave it ample room for density and scope for innovative conicalities that are symbolic of the predilection for archaising.

There are many smaller temples inside the temple complex consecrated to the side-deities (Parsvadevatas). The most important of these are the temples of a four-armed Vishnu (Nilamadhab), Kasi Viswanath and Patalesvara Siva, and goddesses Laxmi and Vimala. A 16-pillared Mukti Mandap with exquisite sculptures stands by the right side of the temple, constructed by one of the consorts of Raja Mansingh. Another irresistible point of attraction is the Anand Bazar, where people of all walks of life and irrespective of caste, creed or sectarian affiliation take the Mahaprasad (food offered to the Jagannath triad). It is the biggest food market in the world. The Lion's Gate on the eastern side is the principal of the four points of entrance to the main temple. In front of it stands, in majestic grace, the Aruna Pillar, a monolithic sixteen-sided polygonal colomn that is 25'.2" tall. It was brought over from Konark and placed here during the Maratha rule of Orissa. The recent de-plastering of the temple by the Archaeological Survey of India is constantly bringing to light new marvels of architectural splendour that speak profusely of the wonder that was Orissa.

Taj Mahal

The mausoleum of Mumtaz Mahal, the empress of Shah Jahan, is called the Taj Mahal and was built by Shah Jahan to enshrine her mortal remains. It is also known as Taj Bibi-ka-rauza (the mausoleum of Taj Bibi) and is often called just the Taj. Shan Jahan loved Mumtaz Mahal with devotion and never liked to be separated from her and she accompanied him even on his difficult military expeditions. It was on one of these trips that she died in 1630 in Burhanpur. Her body was conveyed to Agra after six months where it was interred in a garden of Raja Man Singh till a fitting mausoleum could be erected for it, the beauty of which the emperor desired no other edifice in the world should excel. When it was built it became the pride of Agra and has been adjudged by many to be the most beautiful building in the world. Shah Jahan, who wanted in life as in death to be near the woman he loved so well, lies buried beside her in this glorious last resting place to which he followed her thirty-five years after her death. It was his wish "to make imperishable a tear-drop of love" and his love "is wrought in the perpetual silence of stone and has crowned formless death" with "fadeless form". "Though empires crumble to dust and centuries are lost in shadows, the marble still sighs to the stars 'I remember'."

This poem in marble stands on the right bank of the Yamuna, a mile and a half east of the fort. The authorship of the design is disputed. According to Spanish friar, Manrique, who was in Agra in 1641, the work was entrusted to a Venetian named Geronimo Verroneo, who died before its completion: another tradition ascribes the decoration of the mausoleum to a French artist, Austin de Bordeaux, who was in the emperor's employ but in support of the purely oriental style and construction of the building, is the character of the monument itself, which shows in all its aspects the logical evolution of the art of architecture as practised by the Mughals, true to tradition and entirely free from any external influence. There is no mention of any foreign architects of artists having had a hand in the execution of this building in any Indian record nor do the European travellers. Tavernier (who was here when the Taj was begun and when it was completed) and Bernier (who visited it only five years after the completion)mention anything about its having been built by European architects. On the basis of a manuscript, Diwan-i-Ajridi, the names of the main artisans employed possibly were Amanat Khan Shirazi (a Persian and the writer of Tughra inscriptions), Ustad Isa, a master mason and Ismail Khan Rumi (a Turk from Asia Minor and the maker of the dome) and that of the designer of the garden was Ran Mal, the Kashmiri. But a recently discovered epigraph mentions Ustad Ahmad Lahori as the designer. According to a contemporary document, the *Badshahnama* of Abdul Hamid Lahori, the mausoleum and its subsidiary buildings were constructed under the superintendence of Makramat Khan and Mir Abdul Karim at a cost of about fifty lakhs of rupees (reckoned in the coin of the day) and the work took twelve years to complete. Tavernier, however, assigns a much longer duration of this period. He says, "I witnessed the commencement and accomplishment of this great work, on which twenty-two years have been spent, during which twenty thousand men worked incessantly; this is sufficient to enable one to realise that the cost of it has been enormous." It is likely that many of those who contributed to the planning and designing of these buildings were from Iran and other Asian countries, but the actual execution seems to have been carried out by Indian artisans who were famous for their faultless workmanship.

The precious and semi-precious stones which are inlaid in the Taj were collected from many parts of the world: carnelian was brought from Baghdad, lapis lazuli from Ceylon, corel from the Atlantic ocean, *musai* (stone of Moses) from Mount Sinai, jasper from Persia, marble from Makrana (in Jaipur), red sandstone from the neighbourhood of Agra and a number of other precious stones from far-off lands. These sources being unlimited, the exquisite matching of colours could be ensured in the inlaid work, even to the minutest detail.

The entrance gateway — Rising to a height of about a hundred feet — is by itself a monumental composition resembling the famous Buland Darwaza at Fatehpur Sikri to some extent and has been called a worthy pendant to the Taj itself. Along the frame of the central alcove are inscribed Quranic texts in letters of black marble inlaid on a white marble background with such mathematical precision that the letters appear to be the same size throughout their distance from the ground, a feature repeated above the entrance arch of the mausoleum itself. The gateway is built on a raised platform which descends to a formal garden. The long water channel leading to the mausoleum has a row of fountains in the middle and is flanked on either side by stone-flagged paths. The garden has avenues of cypress trees (a characteristic Mughal feature). Edwin Arnold has said "The garden helps the Tomb, as the Tomb dignifies the garden."

The mausoleum rises from the middle of a white marble platform 313 feet square, standing twenty-two feet high over the garden level and paved with squares of black and white marble. At each corner stands a slender marble minaret tapering into an airy kiosk carried on four pillars capped with a cupola rising on eaves. The mausoleum itself is a square of 186 feet, truncated at the corners to the extent of 33 feet 9 inches and thus forming an irregular octagon. On each principal side there is an archway 66½ feet high flanking which, on either side, there are two arched windows one upon the other, the shorter faces also having a similar arrangement of windows. There are four domed cupolas surrounding the huge central dome, an arrangement which (according to Havel) is known in Hindu architecture as the *panchratna* (five-jewel) pattern, symbolising the five elements. The central dome is 58 feet in diameter and grows from the base with exquisite subtlety, its summit being 213½ feet above the ground, the gilt pinnacle which rises from it with its crescent being thirty feet in height. The dome has for its neck a belt of inlaid ornamentation and an inverted lotus motif, from the summit of which the elaborately gilded pinnacle rises which is reminiscent of the *kalasha* (water-pot) — an ancient traditional and auspicious symbol of the Hindus, all features typical of Hindu architecture.

The central chamber, which is below the dome, contains the cenotaphs of the royal pair, Mumtaz Mahal's being in the centre alongside which is that of Shah Jahan (who had intended to build a tomb in black marble for himself opposite the Taj, on the other side of Yamuna). Each is inscribed with the relevant date of death and is of finest white marble exquisitely inlaid with a great variety of gems in the form of flowers. Both are enclosed by a screen of beautiful tracery in floral-arabesque design of great intricacy. The *Badshahnama* says that originally there was a gold screen, studded with jewels, surrounding the cenotaphs which for fear of theft was replaced in 1642 by the present marble one. It is said that in 1784 the Jats of Bharatpur picked out a number of precious stones and carried off the silver doors of the entrance which were set up by Shah Jahan at a cost of Rs. 1,27,000. The pall of pearls which he had placed over his wife's tomb was taken away by the Barha Saiyids. The real graves are immediately below the cenotaphs in a crypt which is approachable through a subterranean passage, which has its opening on the south. The sarcophagi are plainer than those above but bear similar inscriptions. The interior of the Taj is a central octagonal hall with subsidiary chambers in the angles, all connected by radiating passages; the main hall is also in two stories of arcades, over which there is a semi-circular vault forming the inner shell of the double dome, the other apartments being each contrived in an angle, with a second story immediately above it. The acoustics of the central chamber is such that a remarkable echo is produced inside the chamber when the voice is raised.

The calligraphic decoration on the frames of the external arches consists of passages from the *Quran* which are inlaid in black marble, some being twenty-five feet in length. The most exquisite example of inlaid work with precious and semi-precious stones, called *pietra-dura* (which had become the characteristic of the decorative style of Mughal buildings from the time of Jahangir) is the perfectly executed ornamentation in the Taj. It is said that the *pietra-dura* work was in the charge of Chiranji Lal, a Hindu master craftsman. "All the spandrels of the Taj, all the angles and more important architectural details, are heightened by being inlaid with precious stones, such as agates, blood-stones, jaspers and the like. These are combined in wreaths, scroll and frets, as exquisite in design as beautiful in colour; and relieved by the pure white marble in which they are inlaid they form the most beautiful and precious style of ornament ever adopted in architecture — it certainly stands first among the purely decorative forms of architectural design." This mode of ornamentation conveys an idea of the taste and skill of the Indian architects of that age.

The Taj is the most well-finished example of Mughal architecture and symmetry is its keynote. Structurally it is dominated by elements of Persian derivation but a few of its features are also of Indian origin. Perfect in its entirety and superb in conception, it is also most sound organically.

The chief beauty of the building is in the complete lucidity and coherence of its external architectural effect. The marble of Makrana is of such a nature that it takes on incredibly subtle variations of tint and tone, according to the changes in the light, thus picturing the passing colour of the moment. For every hour of the day and for every atmospheric condition the Taj has its own colour values, from the soft dreaminess at dawn and the *dazzling* whiteness at midday to its cold splendour in the moonlight, when the dome, thin of substance as the air, hangs among the stars like a great pearl, and then there are those few fleeting moments when, softly illuminated by the brief after glow, it assumes the enchanting tint of some pale and lovely rose. On every full-moon day crowds visit it and on the Sharada Purnima in the month of Asvina a fair is held nearby when people in large numbers visit the mausoleum and stay by it late into the night to see it by the light of the full moon.

On either side of the Taj, on a lower platform, stand two identical buildings, that to the west being a mosque and the other its architectural counterpart of *jawab* (answer) but which was never intended for a mosque. Faced with red sandstone, each of these edifices consists of an arcaded hall with three marble domes and a facade having a large central apse and two flanking arches of small size. The quoins of each structure and surmounted by kiosks with marble cupolas. In the frames of the earches and spandrel the white marble has been used as facing material and has been decorated with inlaid work. The interiors of these buildings are profusely painted. An enclosure to the south of the mosque is said to be the place where Mumtaz Mahal's embalmed body was deposited when the mausoleum was being erected. In front of the *jawab*, on the open terrace, is inlaid the representation in black stone of the spike crowning the Taj. From the inscriptions on the western and eastern arches, it may be presumed that these two parts were completed in 1016 Hijri (AD 1637) and 1018 Hijri (AD 1639) respectively. That on the front of the entrance gateway states that it was completed in 1057 Hijri (AD 1648) and ends with an invitation to the pure in heart to enter the garden of paradise. Executed by

Amanat Khan Shirazi, these inscriptions are in Tughra characters and have been taken from the suras of the *Quran*.

These buildings are well preserved on the whole and have been kept in repair through the centuries and are now the responsibility of the Archaeological Survey of India as are the gardens and the precincts. In view of the national importance of this edifice, extensive repairs to conserve it were carried out in 1911-12 at a cost of Rs. 92,000 and again from 1917 to 1949 at a cost of Rs. 1,17,577. Further repairs to the facade of the mausoleum were started in February, 1953, and were completed during 1956-57. Minor repairs are also taken up from time to time.

Temple of Madurai

The temple of Madurai is in the middle of the town of the same name. It is dedicated to goddess Minakshi and is famous all over India. According to the local legend, Minakshi was the daughter of a Pandyan King who, to the consternation of her parents, was born with three breasts. A fairy, however, told the King that the third breast would disappear as soon as she met her future husband; and it did so when she first encountered Siva. They were wedded accordingly and later on enshrined in the temple.

Except the inner shrines, probably, none of it is older than the sixteenth century. The original building of the days of the Pandyan Kings was almost entirely destroyed by the Muslim troops of Malik Kafur in the invasion of 1310. The temple was known in olden times as Velliambalam or the "hall of silver" in contradistinction to Ponnambalam or the "hall of gold", the name of the Chindambaram temple. Four high stone walls in the middle of each of which is a gateway surmounted by huge pyramidal gopurams, enclose a nearly rectangular space about 830 feet by 730 feet within which are several cloisters, mantapams and lesser shrines and the sacred tank, and in the centre, surrounded by the other walls with more gateways and towers, the inner shrines of the god and goddess. Round about the temple, outside the high outer walls, is a neat garden fenced in with iron railings. The gopurams are of the ordinary pattern, the lowest storey consisting of sculptured stone and the upper ones of brick work profusely ornamented with figures made of brightly painted plaster and representing the puranic gods and legends. They are usually lofty and are a landmark for miles around. The highest of them is the southern gopuram which is about 150 feet high. The northern gopuram originally consisted of only the brick and stonework storeys and was in consequence known as the "mottai (bald) gopuram". But about 50 years ago it was completed by a devotee by the provision of the usual plaster top.

Visitors generally enter the temple by what is called the "Ashta Sakti Mantapam" (so called from the images of these goddesses on the pillars inside it) which juts out of the eastern wall. At the further end of this mantapam is a doorway on either side of which are images of Ganesa and Shanmukha. Passing through the doorway one enters the mantapam of Minakshi Nayaka who is said to have been one of the Ministers of Tirumala Nayaka who is said to have been one of the Ministers of Tirumala Nayaka. This is supported on six rows of tall carved pillars each of which consists of a single stone. At the further end of the mantapam is a doorway surrounded with a brass frame containing numerous small oil lamps which are lighted daily. Beyond it is the Mudali Pillai mantapam or the "dark mantapam". This is supported by several large stone figures executed with great spirit. Passing through this one reaches the tank of the golden lily which is considered to be a holy bathing place. It is surrounded by a pillared colonnade from one corner of which the golden tops of the two inner shrines can be seen. Its walls are decorated with representations of puranic stories. On the western side of the tank is the Kilikatti mantapam, so called from the screaming parrots which are kept in cages in it. It is upheld by pillars formed of excellent statues of Yalis and the Pancha Pandavas, each cut out of a single block of granite. They are believed to have been brought from a temple of Kariyamanicka Perumal which formerly stood immediately south-west of the Chinna Mottai gopuram but was demolished. Leading out of this mantapam is Minakshi's shrine within which are several smaller shrines dedicated to Ganesa and Subrahmanya.

Passing northwards, the visitor goes towards Sundareswara's shrine through a gateway under the Nadukkattu (middle) gopuram. This shrine contains the statues of the 63 Saivite saints and a stump which is said to be all that now remains of the legendary forest of Kadamba trees which is formerly supposed to have covered all this part of the country. In the covered colonnade surrounding the shrine are little shrines sacred to the Sangattar or members of the famous Third Sangam, to the nine planets and to the saint Tirugnanasambandhar. In one corner of it is the Mantapanayaka mantapam or the king mantapam among mantapams. It is, however, quite eclipsed by the Kambattadi (foot of the flagstaff) mantapam which adjoins it and surrounds the gilded flagstaff which directly faces the entrance to Sundareswarar's shrine. This was built in the seventies of the last century by Nattukottai Chettiars and is supported by high monolithic pillars which are elaborately chiselled. Behind the flagstaff are huge images of Nataraja, Kali and Virabhadra, all cut out of single blocks of stone and all executed with great vigour and skill. Eastward of these images is the great Viravasantaraya mantapam which is said to have been built by Muttu Virappa, the predecessor of Tirumala Nayaka. It is supported on pillars cut from single rocks of granite and is roofed with slabs of stone. South of it is the Kalyana (marriage) mantapam. In it is conducted the marriage of the god and goddess at the time of the great annual Chittrai festival.

North of the Viravasantaraya mantapam is the "thousand pillared" mantapam. Two shrines built within it reduce the actual number of pillars (all of which are monolithic) to 985 but it is not their number but their marvellous elaboration that makes it the wonder of the place. The sculptures are also of a superior quality. The mantapam is supposed to have been built by the famous Arya Natha Mudali and an equestrian statue of him flanks one side of steps leading up to it.

Passing through the gateway in the eastern tower and crossing the street, one enters the Pudu (new) mantapam, otherwise called Tirumala Nayaka's choultry. It was built by Tirumala Nayaka as a summer retreat for the god and being formerly surrounded by a narrow stone water course designed to cool the air in it, is sometimes called the Vasanta (spring) mantapam. It consists of a rectangular porch 333 feet long and 105 feet wide roofed with long slabs of granite which are supported by four parallel rows of 124 sculptured stone pillars about 20 feet high. Some of the pillars are decorated with life-size figures of Tirumala Nayaka (with his wives) and his predecessors. At one end is a porch made of polished black granite. The facade is adorned with yalis or groups representing a warrior seated on a rearing horse, the fore feet of which are supported by the shields of foot-soldiers slaying tigers or men. "As works exhibiting difficulties over patient labour", says Fergusson, the well-known archaeologist, "they are unrivalled so far as I know, by anything found elsewhere". The whole building is perhaps the most remarkable of its kind in South India.

East of it is the unfinished Rayagopuram (King tower) which Tirumala Nayaka began and never completed. It is said that he began no less than 64 other mantapams, all at one and the same auspicious time, but that many of them were never completed. Unfinished examples very similar to that at Madurai can be seen at Alagar Kovil and Periyakulam. Beginning a Rayagopuram is a saying now applied in Madurai to the commencement of any hopelessly ambitious undertaking. The lowest storey of this tower occupies more than twice the space occupied by any of the existing gopurams and the sculpture on it is richer and cleaner cut than that on any other. The doorposts of the gateway through it are formed of monoliths over 50 feet high and 3 feet wide, carved with exquisite scrolls of foliage. Had it been finished, it would have been the finest gopuram in Southern India.

The temple is so vast that there is no point from which more than a small portion of it can be seen and the chief impression it leaves is wonder at the enormous amount of labour spent upon the immense quantity of elaborate carving which it contains. This granite is supposed to have come from Tirupparankunram. It is not known where the fine grained black stone which appears here and there in it and in Tirumula Nayaka's palace was quarried.

The chief festivals are the Chittrai, Teppakulam and Avanimulam feasts. The first occurs in April-May and celebrates the marriage of Sundaresa and Minakshi. The great event in it is the dragging of the temple car through the four Masi streets so called because this originally took place in the month of Masi (February-March). A very large cattle-fair is held at the same time and the Alagar Kovil god comes to the town. The Teppakulam festival takes place in Thai (January-February). The images of the god and goddess are taken on a raft round the Teppakulam which is lit with thousands of little lamps for the occasion. This festival was originated by Tirumula Nayaka after he had built the Teppakulam and is fixed for the anniversary of his birthday. The Avanimulam festival occurs in August-September and at it are commemorated the legends of Siva.

Indonesia (Java)

Borobudur — The Ultimate Truth in Stone

Chandi Borobudur, situated in the very heart of the Island of Java, is only one of the hundreds of monumental stone structures that witnessed the glorious past of the Indonesian people. Nevertheless its complete difference from any other Chandi, both in design and in meaning, justifies its unique position in Indonesia's cultural heritage.

Built around and over the top of a hill, using a considerable amount of fill to provide the structure with an adequate core, Chandi Borobudur rises from the landscape in successive stages. It is constructed like a stepped pyramid, consisting of nine superimposing square terraces, and crowned by a huge bell-shaped stupa which is supported by a three-fold circular base. Consequently the general design of the chandi, being an edifice erected on a flat horizontal base while leaving an inner space for the enthronement of a statue, is not to be found. The structural design of Chandi Borobudur is somewhat complicated, but a main vertical division into parts (base, body and top) is evident.

The base forms a square, measuring 113 x 113 metres against the height of 4 metres. The body, that is the middle part of the monument, is composed of 5 terraces, which diminish in size with height. As if to emphasize the changes from one part to another, the first of these terraces stands back some 7 metres from the sides of the base, thus creating a broad platform right around the monument. The other terraces retreat only some 2 metres at each stage, and balustrades at the outer sides convert the narrow galleries into corridors.

The superstructure is again clearly distinguished from the terraces. It consists of three re-entrant circular platform, each of which support a row of perforated stupas. Surmounting the rows of stupas, which are arranged in concentric circles, the central dome on top of the whole structure soars into the sky to a height of 35 metres above ground-level.

Access of the upper part of the monument is provided by stairways in the middle of each side of the pyramid. Through a series of gates, (most of which have been lost) a stair leads directly to the circular platforms, at the same time intersecting the corridors of square terraces. The main entrance is to be found at the eastern side.

The vertical division of Chandi Borobudur into base, body and superstructure perfectly accords with the idea of Chandi as representing the Cosmic Mountain. The three superimposed parts of such a chandi depict the three spheres of Universe, viz. the *bhurloka* or the sphere of the Mortals, the *bhuvarloka* or the Sphere of the Purified, and the *svarloka* or the Sphere of the Gods. It is in the middle part of the *bhuvarloka* that Man meets his God, that the worshipper meets the worshipped. And it is for this purpose that the chandi is provided with an inner space and furthermore with an object of worship, either a statue or any other symbol representing the deity. Since Chandi Borbudur has no inner space, it cannot function fully as a chandi. It is a place of pilgrimage rather than a place of worship. The system of staircases and corridors guides the pilgrim gradually to the uppermost platform through perambulations along the successive terraces. Spiritually the pilgrim follows in silent meditation the stages of mental preparation before attaining the ultimate goal in Buddhism, i.e. the definitive liberation from all earthly bonds and the absolute exclusion from being reborn. The three spheres of the Universe are consequently designated in similar terms. The lowest sphere is the *Kamadhatu* or the Sphere of Desires. At this stage man is bound to his desires. The second sphere is the *rupadhatu* or the Sphere of Forms, where man has abandoned his desires but is still bound to name and form. The highest sphere is the *arupadhatu* or the Sphere of Formlessness. In this sphere there is no longer either name or form. Man is once and forever freed from all bonds with the phenomenal world.

At Chandi Borobudur the *kamadhatu* is represented by the base, the *rupadhatu* by the five square terraces, and the *arupadhatu* by the three circular platforms plus the big dome on top of the monument. The three stages are distinguished from each other not only by the architectural features but also by the treatment of the architectural components.

The broad base of the monument is actually an additional construction to encase the real support of the edifice, hiding a series of 160 reliefs that depict the operation of *karma* or the law of cause and effect. The stories visualized in the reliefs are derived from the holy script "*Mahakarmavibhangga*". And since this law of *karma* is fundamentally based on the predominance of desire, the designation *kamadhatu* for the base plus the "hidden foot" of Chandi Borobudur is undoubtedly correct.

The *rupadhatu* is at first sight bewildering. The walls are full of reliefs, and so are the balustrades. No less than 1300 panels of narrative reliefs, for a total length of 2500 metres, flank the corridors. The reliefs on the first gallery depict the biography of historical Buddha, derived from the *Lalitavistara* text, and also the former lives and incarnations of the Buddha before he was born as Prince Siddhartha. These stories are known as *jataka*-stories. The reliefs on the second and the following stages deal with the tireless wanderings of Sudhanakumara in search of the Ultimate Truth, as told in the *Gandavyuha* text.

The endless row of narrative reliefs in the *rupadhatu* has its counterpart in the varied decorative elements. Over the reliefs on the walls is carved a continuous frieze that stretches over 1500 metres, while the cornices above it are beautified by 1416 antefixes. The upper part of the walls, corresponding to the outer facades of the balustrades, consists of niches alternating with decorative reliefs. There are 432 niches around the five terraces, each containing a seated life-size Buddha statue. Over and above the niches small solid stupas, amounting to a number of 1400, soar into the sky forming a rugged skyline of the balustrades.

In striking contrast to the square terraces representing the Sphere of Forms, the circular platforms of the *arupadhatu* are plain: no carvings, no ornaments, no embellishments. The only break in the complete plainness is offered by the 72 stupas that encircle the big central dome, arranged in three concentric circles corresponding to the three circular platforms. Each of 72 stupas shows a latticed surface, disclosing partly the seated Buddha statue inside.

The central stupa rising to a height of 7 metres above the huge lotus cushion of 9 metres diameter, has an inner space, but no entrance is possible. Though empty when investigated, it is quite plausible that the inner space was meant to be the depository for the relics.

The builders of Chandi Borobudur apparently did not overlook the necessity of having an adequate drainage system in view of the heavy rains peculiar to the area. No less than one hundred beautifully carved spouts at the corners of the mounting square terraces were to drain off rain water from the galleries. The construction around and over a terraced hill-top, however, could not prevent the rain water from penetrating the porous stones and eroding the earthen core of the monument, thus weakening the very foundations. Subsidence of the walls and the gallery floors, and leaning of the walls and balustrades, endangered Chandi Borobudur with complete collapse and total loss. Moreover, the porous building material not only absorbed rainwater but also functioned as a filter for the seepage water from behind the walls, so that many of the reliefs are practically wet throughout the year, thus inviting the growth of moss and other kinds of micro-organisms. Furthermore, after the evaporation of the seepage water all kinds of chemical elements brought from the earthen core are left behind on the surface of the reliefs, enhancing the degree of decay.

Alarmed by the technical and physical aspects of the process of degradation of the monument, and also by the accelerated physico-chemical and biological process of the stone weathering, a bold plan of anastylosis was evolved since 1960. A reexamination of earlier studies and researches, continued by new and more thorough investigations, carried out in close cooperation with international experts commissioned by Unesco from 1968 on, indicated that there was no other alternative if the projected restoration was intended to be final. And since the Indonesian people are determined to pass on the best of their cultural heritage to forthcoming generations, drastic but deliberate action was called for in the form of the present gigantic restoration project.

The work to be carried out, comprising the dismantling and subsequent rebuilding of the monument, is confined to the five terraces of the *rupadhàtu*, since the upper structure and the base proved to be stable and strong enough. The international efforts to safeguard it ensures its being a monument for all mankind.

Facts about Borobudur

Original name: Borobudur

Literal meaning: Unknown (many interpretations)

Race/nation that constructed Borobudur: Indonesians

Purpose of construction: To glorify the defined forefather who was identified with the Buddha.

History of construction: Chandi Borobudur was constructed around AD 800 when Central Java was reigned by the Mahayana Buddhistic dynasty of the Caliendras.

Location: 7°59' south, 110°23' east; 276 m above sea level; About 500 km from Jakarta (one hour by plane)

Size: 113 m long, 113 m wide, 35 m high; 15,000 square metre

Important sites in the neighbourhood: Dieng, Gedong Songo, Prambanan, Sewu, Plaosan, Majapahit, Singosari, Panataran, Gunung Kawi, Padang Lawas, Muara Takus, Muara Jambi.

Reasons for destruction of Borobudur: Deserted because of shift of Government of East-Java in the middle of the tenth century.

Causes of present collapsing: Sagging and leaning of the walls; weathering process of building material.

Plans of preservation/presentation: Dismantling and subsequent rebuilding of middle part of monument; international co-operation and funds through Unesco; seven years work costing US$20 million.

Present population: About 13,000.

Life and culture in Borobudur's golden period

Flourished during: Eighth-tenth centuries

Social system: Monarchy

Religion: Mahayana Buddhism

Economical foundation: Agriculture

Staple food: Rice

Calendar: Caka era

Writing system: Ancient Javanese

Tools of writing: Leaves of lontar tree.

Japan

Nara — Monument to Japan's Classic Past

Nara is one of Japan's ancient capital cities. The mere mention of such words as "ancient capital" is enough to bring to mind thoughts of bygone days. Although Kyoto and Kamakura were also once capitals and each city in its own way is rich in appeal, Nara was capital in the era when perfection of ancient Japan was foremost and is, so to speak, a symbol of Japan's classic period.

Japan emerged as a unified country in the fifth century. In the sixth century it adopted Buddhism and assimilated culture from the Asian mainland. In the seventh century it made considerable political development and two or three cities were also built. The capital of Nara was built to embody the final attainment of the development of Japan and was named Heijokyo in 710. For the next seventy odd years Heijokyo flourished as the capital of Japan. During this Nara period, cultural exchange with China thrived and the civilization of lands as far as the region west of China was introduced. In fact Heijokyo could quite appropriately be called the terminus of the Silk Road. However, after the capital was transferred to Heiankyo (present-day Kyoto), the once prosperous Heijokyo rapidly fell into decline. The impermanence of life shown by these changes gave rise to a deep emotional sensitivity to the fleeting nature of things, which heightened the charm of Nara all the more. More than a thousand years have passed since Nara was the centre of political activity. Yet even while it was not a political centre its attributes as an ancient capital were increasingly refined. This is to say, it did neither fall into complete oblivion in the country nor undergo any transformation at all. As a "religious town" centred around many Buddhist temples and Shinto shrines, Nara has fostered the atmosphere appropriate to that of an ancient capital. Recently, once buried ruins have been excavated and thanks to maintenance work, the number of places reminiscent of the past has increased.

Heijokyo

Heijokyo was constructed in the northern extremity of the basin known as the Yamato Plain. To the Japanese of old, this oval-shaped plain that stretches for about 30 km from north to south and 15 km from east to west was a stage for political activity. The mountains encircling the plain were low, blanketed with a rich green verdure and form a picture frame for the beautiful Yamato landscape. Of these Mt. Mikasa and Mt. Miwa are revered as holy places. It was here in an area measuring 4.7 km from north to south and 4.2 km from east to west and with a projected area in the east that a capital city was planned. Following the layout of Chinese capitals, an Imperial Palace was erected in the central northern area. A main road, Suzaku Oji was extended to the south dividing the capital into two parts, Sakyo in the east and Ukyo in the west. The projecting area was known as Gekyo or the outer part of the capital. Present-day Nara is centred in the Gekyo district.

The Imperial Palace is the only part of the vanished vestige of Heijokyo being restored now as part of a national park. Each side of the Imperial Palace measures about one km and together with the eastern projection, the complex occupies an area of 130 hectares.

Architecture and Art

Horyuji is the oldest Buddhist temple in the vicinity of Nara. The Main Hall, the five-storied pagoda, the middle gate and parts of the corridor standing in the Western Precinct were founded before Heijokyo was, and are the oldest wooden structures in the world. The style, inherited from that of the Chinese six dynasties is dynamic and awe-inspiring. In contrast, the Eastern Precinct was constructed during the Nara Period. Yumedono, the main structure in the Eastern Precinct is octagonal in shape and is truly worthy of its beautiful name meaning "dream palace". Together with notable architecture of the Heian and Kamakura period, Horyuji is like a museum of Japanese architecture. It is also rich in *objects d'art.* The rustic flavour of long ago effuses from such statues as those of *Shaka Nyorai* (Buddha), *Yakushi Nyorai* (Bhaisajyaguru) and the Four Devas enshrined in the Main Hall and the statue of *Kannon Bosatsu* (Avalokitesvara, Goddess of Mercy) in the Yumedono building.

Of those temples in the original Heijokyo, Yakushiji and Kofukuji temples were transferred from the old capital. The *Yakushi* Triad (Bhaisajyaguru and two attendants) in the main building of Yakushiji, the main image of Avalokitesvara in the east building and the architecture of the east pagoda all show the style prevalent in Heijokyo just prior to its transfer. Each statue is said to convey the style of the early Tang dynasty and radiates a timeless beauty.

The compound of Kofukuji temple with its five-storied pagoda standing near the Sarusawa pond is preserved in what is now called Nara Park. Having been burnt during war in the twelfth century, this temple is consequently in the style of the middle ages. Apart from the works of the Nara Period to be admired such as that of the *Judai-deshi* (Ten Great Disciples of the Buddha), there are also many excellent works from the Kamakura Period.

Nara's most prominent place of interest is the Todaiji Temple. The temple was burnt twice in war in 1180 and 1567 and both times the colossal image of Buddha, Vairocana, underwent large scale repairs. One could imagine the majestic appearance it showed when first built in 752. The 1709 reconstruction of the Main Hall enshrining the Great Buddha is considerably smaller than the original. But even so, it is the world's largest wooden construction still standing today. Shosoin Repository of Imperial Treasures has preserved numerous treasures dedicated at the time of Todaiji's construction. These can be thought of as having come from the Western Region which reminds us of the international nature of Japan at that time. Toshodaiji is the temple founded by the Chinese monk, Ganjin (Jian Jhen) in 759 and it has some superb examples of architecture and sculpture in the Main Hall and in the Lecture Hall.

Events in Nara

A variety of events are held at the temples and shrines throughout Nara. First of all there is the traditional water-drawing ceremony, Shunie, at Todaiji's Nigatsudo temple. Since its origin in the Nara Period, many factors have been gradually interwoven to produce an event of substantial interest. Without a doubt it demonstrates the breadth and depth of Buddhist culture in Japan. The highlights continue for two weeks from 1st March when large torchlights are held aloft to shed a feast of light.

Shunie ceremonies are usually held in February and are also commonly known as festivals to drive away evil spirits. Shunie at Horyuji and Kofukuji are held at the beginning of February. At Yakushiji a similar event called Hanae ceremony takes place in April.

Typical Japanese temples and shrines abound in Nara. Along with this man-made beauty, nature itself helps to calm people's hearts; the round hillside of Mt. Wakakusa with its rich green carpet, wisteria flowers of Kasuga Shrine hanging in all their glory from the trellises, and the deer, the most popular of all, which have been preserved and tamed for centuries in Kasuga Shrine.

Facts about Nara

Original name: Heijokyo

Race/nation that constructed Nara: Japanese

Purpose of construction: To build a capital

History of construction: In 710, during the reign of the Empress Gemmei, the capital was moved to Nara, where it remained for seventy years, covering seven reigns. A magnificent palace called the Heijo-kyu and the imperial city was constructed modelled after Changan, the capital of the Tang Empire.

Location (Site of the Heijo-kyu): 34°41'20" north, 135°48' east; 72 m above sea level; about 520 km from Tokyo (3½ hours by special express train)

Representative architecture: Main hall of Todaiji temple; Main Hall and pagoda of Horyuji Temple; Pagoda of Yakushiji Temple; Main Hall of Toshodaiji Temple

Style of architecture: Japanese (Japanese style absorbing the influence of the Tang Empire.)

Building materials: Wood

Famous objects of fine art: The Great Buddha Statue (16 m high) of Todaiji Temple; the Shaka Triad (Sakyamuni and two attendants) of Horyuji Temple; the Yakushi Triad (Bhaisajyaguru and two attendants) of Yakushiji Temple; the Statue of Chinese Monk Ganjin of Toshodaiji Temple.

Reasons for destruction/desolation of Nara: After the capital was transferred to Heiankyo (present Kyoto) in 794, Nara gradually declined.

Plans of preservation/presentation: The historical sites and monuments in Nara have been carefully protected and restored when necessary under the Law for the Protection of Cultural Properties and Special Measures Law for the Preservation of Historical Climate in Ancient Capital.

Present Population: 303,000 people

Life and culture in Nara's golden period

Flourished during: Eighth century

Population: 200,000 people

Social system: Ritsuryo system (society governed by penal code and civil code) under the reign of Tenno (Emperor or Empress)

Religion: Buddhism, Shintoism

Economical foundation: Agriculture, industry (mining of gold, silver & copper)

Staple food: Rice and cereals

Housing: High-floored and tile-roofed houses for high-ranking nobles; Thatched huts without floors for common people.

Costume: High-ranking nobles in the fashion of the Tang Empire; common people clad in simple clothes of cotton or linen.

Marital system: Principally monogamy

Calendar: Lunar Calendar

Festivals: Festivals in accordance with agricultural cycles; Court and temples festivals of *Bugaku* (court dance and music)

Currency: Copper coin (rice, cloth, thread were also used for money by common people)

Writing system: Chinese character

Tools of writing: Paper and wooden tablet

Means of transportation: Palanquin, bullock cart, boat, horse

Entertainment: Court performance, Japanese chess.

Korea

Kyongju — The Silla Kingdom's Heart

The mountains and fields, which roughly constitute the Kyongju area were from early times inhabited by tribesmen whose six villages achieved confederation and unanimously agreed to enthrone Pak Hyok-kose as chieftain. That was 57 years before the time of Christ. After that, three families, the Paks, Suks and Kims ruled the kingdom in turn until AD 936 As the political and the cultural center of the kingdom, Kyongju came to take on the characteristics of the whole of Korea itself. Because of this Kyongju still remains the focal point of yearning for the old glory as well as the spiritual home of the nation.

The longer the life of a kingdom, the more tombs she leaves. Royal tombs and those of the aristocrats abound in and around Kyongju. These round tombs, small and large, can still be seen on the way to the city. There were 56 Silla kings, but there is a considerably larger number of tombs.

It has become evident from excavations that tombs in the beginning were built on flat fields around the city and then were moved to the hills as the city grew in size.

This change of tomb site is also manifest in the style of tomb construction. The earlier ones, built in fields, contain wooden chambers, on which stones were piled and then the whole was covered with earth; while the later tombs consist of a stone chamber with the outside of the tomb ringed with a stone balustrade more often than not engraved with the twelve Oriental signs of the zodiac. Human and animal figures in stone stand at the entrance to the tombs.

All the capitals of ancient Korea were fortified by a fortress-wall to defend the city from enemies. Kyongju is no exception. Only fragmentary remains are to be found here and there around Kyongju.

Wolsong (Moon Castle) in Kyongju is the traditional site of the royal palace, the crescent castle wall and the foundation stones which remain to this day, give an idea of the size of the castle but the excavation of this site has not yet been initiated. Adjoining Moon Castle, a water mass called Anapchi, Duck Lake, still remains.

Posok-jong is famous as a detached palace, of which the skeleton that remains is sufficient for us to reconstruct the outline of the palace. It is here that King Kyongae was killed by invaders. Moon Castle, Duck Lake and Posok-jong are historic spots that tell of the rise and fall of the Silla dynasty. On the way to Moon Castle, one comes to the Chomsongdae observatory standing beside the road. This observatory was built in 647 AD and stands 9.8 meters high. Although the wooden top of the structure has disappeared, the bottle-shaped stone structure erected on a round foundation still stands only slightly inclined. The oldest in the Orient, this observatory stands as a symbol of agricultural Silla and is a fine example of the stone structures of the time.

Buddhism was not recognized in Silla until the reign of King Pobhung in the sixth century and following that time this religion became the national phenomenon which was accompanied by the increased construction of Buddhist temples, small and large, throughout the country. The temples, some of which were built by the state, others by aristocrats and still others by important families, are innumerable. Kyongju thus became one of the most important capitals in the Orient. An ancient document records the splendour of the city: "Buddhist temples dotted the country like stars in the sky and pagodas were lined up like ducks heading for water." The most popular of these was Hwangyong-sa Temple, which stood on the flat not far from Duck Lake and east of Moon Castle. It was constructed over a period of 90 years from 552 AD The temple possessed two of the three Silla treasures: one statue of three Buddha images made of gold and bronze which was enshrined in the main hall, and the nine-story wooden pagoda These were masterpieces representing the apex of pagoda and Buddha art. The temple was repaired many times after the fall of the Silla Dynasty but it was completely destroyed by the invading Mongols. The majestic splendour of the pagoda has disappeared except for the huge foundation stone which suggests the scale of the pagoda.

Punhwang-sa was built in 634 and within its grounds stands the oldest stone pagoda. The first story of the three-story pagoda is a square stone chamber, on both sides of which were engraved images of the Inwang Buddha.

Many other temple sites have been found not only on the plain around the city but also in the hills and in the valleys, and especially on Mt. Namsan, which was truly the holy mountain of Silla.

Mt. Toham-san about 10 miles south-east of Kyongju was also highly respected by the people and after the introduction of Buddhism it became a place of worship. Pulguk-sa and Sokkulam, among others, have preserved the glory of this mountain to this day.

Pulguk-sa Temple stands on stone foundations erected at the southern foot of Mt. Toham-san. Two stone bridges lead to the elevated temple grounds: the one to the east is called the Bridge of Blue Cloud and White Cloud and the other to the west is the Bridge of the Lotus Flower and the Seven Treasures. Between the bridges was Lotus Lake in which the temple was reflected. Crossing either bridge one stands before the main temple, in the front yard of which stand two pagodas, one on either side: Tapo-tap on the right and Sokka-t'ap on the left. This arrangement of Pagodas is in accordance with the custom of the unified Silla period.

Mt. Toham-san commands a superb view of the ocean to the east and gives a bird's-eye view of downtown Kyongju. Sokkulam is hidden in pine woods near the top of the mountain, facing the eastern sea.

It is a Buddhist grotto, which originated in India and came to Korea through Central Asia and northern China, but the style of construction and the arrangement of the figures of Buddha are characteristically in accord with Silla tradition. The main chamber, in which is enshrined the main Buddha image, is a stone structure with a dome, different from the rock-hewn cave temples in India and China. It is round and has a short fan-like corridor leading to it, in front of which is a small rectangular anteroom.

Two Bodhisattvas stand on each side of the threshold and five figures of disciples face the eleven Kwanum images standing right behind the main Buddha. The figures around the wall, numbering fifteen in all, stand, carved in life-size relief, on rectangular stone slabs.

The grotto faces east and the main Buddha's hand is posed in the so-called "signal to the devil" patterned after Indian temples. That the grotto faces east implies the national mission to defend the eastern sea and also to pray for bliss for heroic kind Munmu who unified the three kingdoms and whose ashes were scattered on the eastern sea.

Pulguk-sa Temple and the grotto are not only the embodiments of Silla's sculpture and craftsmanship, but also concrete expressions of the very essence of the spirit of Silla. All in all, the spiritual as well as the material glory of Silla is evidenced in Mt. Toham.

The Kyongju National Museum should be visited since it is, in a sense, a miniature of the ancient city. It houses, besides what has been excavated from the tombs, sculptures in gold and bronze, stone lanterns and pagodas and stone tortoises, the last named being used as foundation stones for pagodas and statues. However, the most precious item housed in the museum is no doubt the Pongdok-sa Temple Bell. The mere existence of this huge bell attests to the high technical skill achieved by Korea's ancient metal craft, which represents, along with the stone pagodas and Koryo celadons, the ancient civilization of Korea.

Facts about Kyongju

Original name: Sorabol

Literal meaning: "Town" later developed into "capital city"

Race/nation that constructed Kyongju: Saro Kingdom

Purpose of construction: A centre of government

Location: 35°40' north, 129°20' east; 70 m above sea level; 410 km from Seoul (5 hours by express train)

Size: 10 km long (from north to south), 8 km wide (from east to west), 214.29 square km

Representative architecture: Pulguk-sa (AD 535), Sokkul-am Grotto (AD 751) Ch'omsongdae Observatory (AD 647), Wolsong (Moon Castle) (AD 101), Anapchi Pond (AD 674), P'osok-jong Pavillion, Royal tombs

Style of architecture: Oriental style

Building materials: Wood, stone, mud, etc.

Famous objects of fine art:

1) Gold: Crowns, Buddhist images, earrings, buckles, bracelets, etc.
2) Bronze: Buddhist images, bells, buckles, bracelets, etc.
3) Stone: Buddhist images, pagodas, gravestones, reliefs, and stone lamps
4) Others: Wall paintings, Buddhist paintings, etc.

Other important sites: King Muyol's tomb and its stone tortoise base, King Munmu the Great's underwater tomb, Chonmach'ong tomb, General Kim Yu-sin's tomb and its twelve zodiacal figures.

Reasons for destruction: 1) The downfall of Sill in AD 935, 2) The Mongolian Invasion of Koryo in the 13th century, 3) Toyotomi Hideyoshi's Invasion of Korea in 1592-7, 4) The Manchurian Invasion of 1636.

Causes of present collapsing: Pollution, natural eroding

Plans of preservation/presentation: The 10-year Comprehensive Plan for the Development of Kyongju (1972-1981) costing 300 million dollars (Preservation and conservation of the historical sites, relics and landmarks; Excavation and restoration of major temples and pagodas for construction of an international, cultural sightseeing city.)

Present population: 122,038 people

Life and culture in Kyongju's golden period

Flourished during: Eighth century.

Population: About one million (178,000 families)

Social system: Monarchy

Religion: Buddhism

Economical foundation: Agriculture

Staple food: Rice

Housings: Tile-roofed houses

Marital system: Monogamy

Calendar: Lunar Calendar

Festivals: The Lotus-lamp Festival, the May Festival on the 15th of May, the harvest moon festival on the 15th of August, New Year's Day by the lunar calendar.

Currency: Nonexistent

Writing system: Chinese character and "Idu", a writing system with which to transliterate the native spoken language into Chinese characters

Tools of writing: Paper, bamboo and stone

Means of transportation: Oxcart, horse

Entertainment: Dance.

Mongolia

Looking through the History of the Mongolian State

It would be no exaggeration to say that Mongolia is the only one of the ancient nomad states to retain the tenets of its original nomadic civilization, including the classic migration of livestock and closeness to nature. If you visit Mongolia you will feel the beauty of nature, where forest-covered mountain ranges and hills meet desert and steppe. You will also meet Mongols just like those who have been building traditional 'Yurts' since olden times, hospitable cattle-breeders breeding throughout four seasons traditional kinds of livestock (horse, camel, cow sheep, goat), as well as the half-settled inhabitants of cities, who develop the industry and culture of the country. Specialists in the history of Mongolia from many countries have proved that it goes back over 2000 years. In 1991 the MPR celebrated the anniversary of the establishment of the first Hun State in 209 BC

Mongolian archaeologists have discovered 500,000 year-old stone implements that are the remains of Mongolia's earliest inhabitants. Since the early primitive communal era, Mongols had lived independently in the neighbourhood of such nomadic tribes as Turk and Khamnigan.

In 209 BC, the Huns, who were by origin from ancient nomadic tribes such as Xianyu, Xianyung, Hun yi and Di, set up the first state in Central Asia. The Hun State was equal in power to the Chinese states of Tsin and Han. Khan, the sovereign of the State of Han Xiao Wendi wrote to Shan Yu of the Hun State in Laoshan: "In accordance with the decree of his Majesty, the state situated to the north of the Great Wall shall be governed by the decrees of Shah Yu, and the territory situated to the south of the Great Wall, peopled by those who wear tushmed belts and caps, shall be governed by me. Both the State of the Huns and the State of Han are powerful neighbour states". This message proves the aforesaid.

The territory of the Huns was vast and extended to the Great Wall in the South, the Lake of Baikal in the North, Hingan Hills in the East and Erchis river in the West. The State maintained wide diplomatic, cultural and trade relations with the neighbouring countries. In the middle of AD first century the Hun State split into North and South. The Southern Huns established within the Great Wall the states of Han and Xia, which existed until the tenth century, while Northern Huns migrated to East Europe and settled down there by the fourth-fifth centuries AD.

Between the third-sixth centuries the territory of the Hun State was occupied successively by the states of Xianbi and Jhou Jhan, and Chinese historians noted the power of these states was equal to that of the Huns.

During the seventh-tenth centuries, the present Mongolian territory was inhabited by the Turkic, Uighur and Kirghiz tribes. But there is little information historic documents about the life of the Mongols at this period.

During ninth-tenth centuries the Kidans, who were a Mongolian speaking tribe, established in the north of China a Great Liao State. At this time of the Kidans (Liao), the Chinese tribal states for the first time submitted to foreign supremacy, and the Chinese Khan officially recognized the Kidan Khan as "his father", and thus himself as "a son".

During the eleventh-twelfth centuries the Mongol tribes came into history under the names Whole Mongolia, Tatar, Kerait, Jalair. These neighbouring tribes had their own rulers and were constantly fighting with each other. At this time of intertribal struggle, a Mongol chieftain called Temudjin gathered various tribes under his leadership, named his state "Mongolia", and renamed himself "Genghis Khan". The difficult process of establishing the Mongolian State was finely described in the famous Mongolian document "Noots Tovchoo" (*Secret History of the Mongols*). In the thirteenth century Mongolia was one of the most powerful states in the world. All major world trade and political relations went through the capital of Mongolia of that time, Kara Khorino (which is situated in the present territory of the MPR), and the flow of ambassadors from France, sons of Georgian and Armenian sovereigns, Russian princes, and Chinese officials was unceasing. After having established the state, following the custom of the ancient nomads, Genghis Khan undertook campaigns against the neighbouring states. As a result of the wars undertaken by Genghis Khan and his successors with the purpose of "conquering the whole world" Mongolia became a powerful empire, extending from the East China Sea to Western Europe, covering vast areas of Europe and Asia. After the death of the last Mongolian emperor, Mongke, in 1259 the Mongolian empire broke up into the Golden Horde of Batuu Khan (Genghis Khan's grandson), inhabiting the Russian Kipchak steppe, the Kingdom of Tsagadai (Genghis Khan's son), who had conquered East Turkestan and Uzbek, and the Yuan State of Khubilai Khan, which included the Mongolian and Chinese territories.

The wars waged by the Mongols resulted in the dispersal of the Mongolian tribes, a considerable reduction in the size of the Mongolian population, and the destruction of a lot of cities and villages in the conquered countries. But on the other hand, these wars precipitated the process of unification of various Asian and European tribes, and drew East and West nearer together, something that had never been done before.

After the defeat in 1367 of the Mongolian Yuan State by the Chinese Min State, the Mongolian Khans returned from Beijing to their native territory. At this time Mongolia ceased to be the centre of world trade and culture, but the Mongols retained their home territory.

During the fourteenth and fifteenth centuries the Mongols lost their previous unity and were divided into Eastern Mongols and Western Mongols (Oi rat Mongols). Then in the sixteenth century the Eastern Mongols split up into Outer Mongolia (Khalh Mongolia) and Inner Mongolia. The Mongols waged war on each other, and dominance went first to Oi rat Mongolia and then to East Mongolia. East Mongolia was the more powerful. At the beginning of the seventeenth century, the Zurchid tribe of Manchurians became powerful and established the State of Chin. The Manchurians subdued Inner Mongolia in the 1630s, Khalh Mongolia in 1691 and Oi rat Mongolia in 1757.

The seventeenth-twentieth century period was the most tragic for the Mongols. In fact the Manchurians cut off the Mongolian State from world civilization for many centuries, and the Mongols remained as if on the inside of an inverted copper pot. At the beginning of the twentieth century the movement for the renascence of the Mongolian State led by Bogdoo Khan, which spread widely like a fire, was suppressed in 1911 by the Manchurian colonial domination. The Mongolian People led by Khalh Mongolian Javzandamba Khutagt (Bogdoo Khan) established the Khanate uniting religion and state, and intended to unite all Mongolian-speaking people. But this aim remained unfulfilled because of Tsarist Russian and Chinese expansionist policy. In 1919 the Chinese government grossly violated the Russian, Chinese and Mongolian tripartite treaty of 1915, and with the aid of armed forces conquered the Mongolian State. This precipitated again the upsurge of the national liberation movement in the country, and so in 1921 Khalh Mongols under the direction of S.Danzan, D. Bodoo, and D. Sukhbaatar liberated our territory from the foreign conquerors and won our freedom. In this struggle the assistance of Soviet Russia played a considerable role.

From 1921-1924 Mongolia was a republic which joined religion and state and then, in 1924, became a republic with a one-party system. From 1921-1990 the MPR successfully developed with Soviet assistance the social life, culture science and national intellect. In 1961 the MPR became a member of the UN, and its prestige rose. The MPR established diplomatic, trade, and cultural relations with about 200 countries of the world. The domination of a one-party system and Soviet Stalinist regime had bad consequences for Mongolia. As result of this influence, over 750 temples and churches were destroyed, and more then 100,000 monks and many thousands of intellectuals and patriots were repressed.

The wind of the European democratic changes of 1990 also came to our country. The Mongolian Democratic Union, New Progressive Union and Socialist Democratic movement were created, and the democratic revolution in the MPR was realised in a peaceful way. In July of 1990 the first democratic general election took place in the MPR and the MPR became a parliamentary republic with a president and a multi-party system. At present, the MPR is in the period of transition from a centralized economy to a free market system.

Cultural Heritage of Mongolia

The broad land of Mongolia has a history and a culture that have been built up during the course of several thousand years of human habitation, and it is one of the cradles of civilisation. It is, therefore, very rich in relics dating from Paleolithic times to the late middle ages. In many ways, the territory of Mongolia has been a bridge between east and west since the earliest times and therefore the study of those relics not only enriches Mongolia's history but is also of great relevance to the study of the history and culture of all mankind. Stone tools 500,000 years old have been found in Mongolia, proving that Man was settled in the area at that time, and that it was from Central Asia that he went on to the American continent. Early Man took the stones provided by nature and from them fashioned stone tools; as he began to acquire finer skills in the working of stone, he made not only weapons but also all kinds of jewellery, implements and stone monuments, and began to learn how to construct towns and villages.

The earliest stone monuments that are most commonly found in Mongolia today date from the bronze age. The nomadic herdsmen of those times constructed stone mounds and stone -flagged graves of great size, and used great skill in the beautiful execution of carved 'reindeer stones'. Such stone monuments were placed on the steppe, in valleys, in gullies or on the tops of small hills either singly or in groups of up to twenty stones, either as graves or markers of dedicatory sites, and some of them still remain in their original positions. The 'reindeer stones' are between one and four metres high. The four sides of a long oblong stone are nicely trimmed and the total surface is divided vertically into three bands. All around the stone in the upper section are images of the sun and moon, and in the middle section are many deer, leaping and flying. The lower section is decorated with carvings of knives, swords, bows and quivers, battle axes, whetstones, hooks, mirrors and so on. The deer themselves are executed according to a very precise formula, with long narrow limbs like those of birds, graceful necks, majestic curving many-branched antlers, but most especially the full flight of their leap is shown with consummate skill. Some particular examples of these 'reindeer stones' have, carved in the upper section of the stone, a human head and face. The skill with which these animals, widespread among the nomadic peoples of Central Asia, are represented is everywhere plain. 'Reindeer stones' have been found over an exceptionally wide area; of the 500 so far brought to light, 450 have been discovered in this country and the remainder in southern Baikalia, Tuva, the Russian Altai — from Central Asia in fact to the Danube basin. Scholars of these stone monuments estimate that they range in age from the second millennium to the third century BC.

Other examples of the stone monuments of Central Asia are the statues which are to be found right across Mongolia from east to west. Those that have been found on Mongolian territory fall into two basic categories and the most common date from the sixth to eighth centuries. These stone statues are skilfully carved to show the clothes that these ancient people made and wore, hats, belts, weapons, jewellery and sometimes the tools of their trades. Scholars research and categorise the carvings on the statues and, by them with other archaeological finds and with written records, can establish their date and tribe. A large group of statues was found in the eastern part of the country from the Turk period but these are quite different, and it is thought that they are from the Mongol state of the thirteenth and fourteenth centuries. What is particular about these examples is that the figures are carved seated on backed chairs not associated with other kinds of stone statue, and their clothes, hats, hairstyles and utensils are very different from those on the Turk stones. The purpose of these stones was probably the same as that of the Turk monuments — they were erected as part of a cult dedicated to the memory of the great Khans, and thus are descended from the early reindeer stones. Study of the stone statues and research into the customs, religious beliefs, and social relations of those people not only serves to enrich the science of history, it is also very important in that it shows the level of skill that these early artists attained.

It has become a truism widespread in many places that because the Mongols adopted a nomadic pastoral economy they did not build towns or villages. And yet we know from archaeological research and from written documents that peoples of Mongol origin were establishing towns about 2000 years ago and that they were erecting buildings of a very distinctive architecture. Archaeological evidence of more than 200 ancient towns has so far been discovered on Mongolian territory.

The thirteenth century capital of the Mongolian Empire, Karakorum, is a special example of Mongolia's early towns and is attracting attention from scholars in many countries. The city was built in 1220 on the orders of Genghis Khan and was founded on the site of a city previously occupied during the Uighur period. It is said that the work went on until the time of Ogodei Khan when, in 1235, the outer wall was built and the great 'Myriad Peace' palace was erected. Not only was Karakorum the administrative, industrial and cultural capital of the Mongol Empire, it was also an important crossroads between the eastern and western worlds.

Around the city was a large square wall, in the middle of each side of which was a gate, beside which all kinds of goods and livestock were bartered, bought and sold. Within the city were separate districts occupied by artisans and craftsmen, traders, administrators and private citizens. Because the Khans of Mongolia in those days honoured all religious faiths, a total of 12 worshipping places of the Christian, Buddhist and Islam faiths actively held services. We know from archeological research that Karakorum was a great centre for metalwork and other handicrafts. The city had an iron and steel foundry well advanced for its time.

The most beautiful part of the city was the palace in the south-western sector. Within the city wall and inside a wall of its own was the 'Myriad Peace' palace of Ogodei Khan; surrounded by the residences of the princes and noblemen. The main building of the palace was founded upon a specially landscaped dais; its main hall was floored with green enamelled flat bricks; and the roof covered with red and green enamel tiles. In the southern section of the main hall was a silver tree-fountain, crowned with a silver figure of a man blowing a trumpet. At festival times a beautiful sound would be heard as four kinds of delicious drink poured from four dragons' heads facing in four directions from the trunk of the tree, and flowed down into silver vessels placed there to receive them. The layout of the city of Karakorum and the architecture of the buildings combine the very best of city planning of the nomadic Mongols and of eastern and western architecture. Evidence of other early Mongolian cities of this time is still being discovered and researched.

Although Buddhism has a 2000 year-old history of propagation in Mongolia, it was not until the sixteenth century that it was widely spread among the people and brought together their minds and their everyday lives. From this time there was a tremendous growth in monastery and temple building in Mongolia, and a great development in the combination of traditional nomadic architecture with temple building skills. At the beginning of the twentieth century there were more than 700 temples and monasteries in

Mongolia. Every single one of these had its own particularities and all were exceptional examples of oriental architecture. In Mongolian architecture the frame of the building is made of wood but other materials are also used, such as felt, bricks and stone, and the main wooden props are set in stone foundations. The influence of the nomadic lifestyle is plain to see in the architecture of Buddhist religious structures and dwelling places. This is why it is so convenient to use the 'Mongol gher' (dwelling of Mongolian nomads), which can be taken down and re-erected, as a temple hall. The trellis walls, roof poles and layers of felt were replaced by stone, brick, beams and planks, and became permanent. As parts were added to the upper and side parts of the 'gher' so architecture acquired new material. As the 'gher' changed in this way, gher-shaped buildings emerged. From early times Mongolian architecture has shown the influence of the architecture of those countries with which it has closest cultural relations; India, Tibet and China. The science of architecture appeared with the teachings of Buddhism and eighteenth and nineteenth century writings contain a wealth of theoretical information on architectural ways and means, principles and measurements. There were highly specialised religious schools in operation training architects, artists, and sculptors. Of the monasteries left in Mongolia, Erdene Zuu in Ovorkhanggai, Amarbayasgalangt in Selengge and Gandang in Ulaanbaatar deserve particular mention.

A Mongolian winter cap.

Nepal

Kathmandu Valley — Where Gods and People Converge

Once a lake and now a bowl-shaped valley, the Kathmandu Valley is surrounded by Chanda Giri, Nargarjun, Sivapuri, Phulchoki and other foothills to the Himalayas, and drained by the holy Bagmati river. What makes the Kathmandu Valley unique is the combination of its magnificent natural environment with its man-made environment — its towns, settlements and cultural sites which are still part of the living culture, not just fossils of a bygone civilization. While constituting only a small part of Nepal with regard to its territory or people, the Valley has nevertheless been both politically and culturally the dominant part of the country throughout its history.

According to legends and some literary sources, the Kiratis ruled the Valley before the beginning of the Christian Era. Later the Lichchavis ruled the Valley during its golden period of history. After the twelfth century up to the arrival of the Shahs in the middle of the eighteenth century, the Mallas ruled the valley, during which time Kathmandu was one of the principal towns, a dreamland of poets and artists in the Valley. Its scenic beauty, history and cultural richness has been attracting visitors, pilgrims, traders and scholars since time immemorial. Its origin, however, is obscure. The first settlement took place in Kathmandu city during the Lichchavi period. According to tradition, Kantipur — one of the original names of Kathmandu — was founded in the tenth century by King Guna Kama Deva. In Kathmandu the main developments of the palace of Darbar Square (Hanuman Dhoka) temples and domestic architecture of the city seem to have occurred during the sixteenth-eighteenth centuries under the Malla rulers. After the unification conquest of the Valley by King Prithivi Narayan Shah the great, Kathmandu was proclaimed capital of the newly founded kingdom of Nepal. Since then it became the seat of power, politics and centre of arts and culture. The establishment of the Shah Dynasty saw the introduction of new forms of art and gave new impetus to the development of the city.

Lalitpur popularly known as Patan is the oldest city in the valley. Tradition claims that the city was founded by the Kiratis before the Christian Era. Likewise during the Malla Period almost all of the celebrated palaces and temples in the city were erected as well as many of the older religious buildings reconstructed or refurbished. It has remained a great centre of Mahayana Buddhism and Buddhist arts and crafts as shown by the large number of surviving bahals or monasteries.

Of the three main cities of the Valley, Bhaktapur is the youngest. Though smaller in size, it became prominent only after the fourteenth century, when under the Mallas it became a seat of power and a centre of arts, learning and culture. Its claim to distinctive architecture derives from that time although the main temples and palaces date from the late sixteenth century onwards. The process of development seems largely to have been arrested with the growing importance of Kathmandu, which some two hundred years later became the sole capital under Prithivi Narayan Shah.

The Kathmandu Valley is undoubtedly a unique treasure house of art and culture added to which its tremendous scenic appeal. The writings of the seventh century Chinese travellers report well-built towns and settlements with splendid palaces and temples already established in the Valley. Inter-relationship and a tolerance between Buddhism and Hinduism as well as the liberal mindedness of the Nepalese have created a congenial atmosphere for the development of arts and culture. Each object of art is not only a wonderful creation of human endeavour but is also remarkable in that it has always some history to reveal. The Kathmandu Valley, a unique open air museum of outstanding universal value is in fact one of the richest cultural treasures of mankind. People of the valley have not only a deep and sentimental attachment to their cultural assets but they also live and breathe them.

Pakistan

Moenjodaro — Five Thousand Years in the Desert

On the banks of the mighty Indus river, destroyed by the recurrent fury of its floods, lie the ruins of a city known the world over as the largest remains of the world — Moenjodaro, "the mound of the dead".

The Moenjodaren were an agrarian people growing wheat, barley dates and cotton and depending on annual rains and floods for irrigation of their fields. In antiquity the civilisation resembles Mesopotamia and Egypt in being an alluvial plain watered jointly by the Indus river and its five tributaries. But in area it is more extensive than the civilisation of the Tigres-Euphrates valley, being roughly 1,000 miles in length from north to south and more than 800 miles wide.

The existence of brick-lined street drains, the universal use of burnt-brick, excavation of art objects such as burnt clay figurines and models of birds, figural art illustrated by steatite seals bearing life-like representations of short-horned bull, buffalo, tiger, rhinoceros, crocodile, beautifully bedecked gold ornaments such as amulets, bangles, finger-rings, pendants of beads and semi-precious stones and the existence of a pictographic script, reveal a high level of civilisation attained by Moenjodaro.

The cradle of Moenjodaro civilisation lies in the south-west of Pakistan in the plateau of Baluchistan. Here lived a hive of hidden tribal and village society. By the year 3000 BC their pottery was of good quality, wheel turned, well-baked, often thin and attractively painted with geometrical motifs. They made stone implements and little ornaments of copper and bronze. It was not however till these semi-nomadic hordes came in contact with the fertile coastal settlements of the Indus river that the great civilisation proliferated. The agricultural produce of cotton and availability of easy means of communication, trade and transportation through the river spread the civilisation to neighbouring countries. The architecture of Moenjodaro is plain but utilitarian. It seems that the aim of the city builders was to make life comfortable rather than luxurious. The houses are well planned. Drains are well-laid and amongst the principal glories of the city. The system is certainly the most elaborate ancient system yet discovered and might almost be termed modern in character.

The most striking building at Moenjodaro is the "Great Bath" used for religious or ceremonial bathing as many of the dwellings at Moenjodaro possessed their own bath rooms and walls.

Various objects of art have been found in the ancient city of Moenjodaro. It appears that the plastic arts were well-developed as can be seen in the cutting of the steatite seals, figural art on the ornaments and terracotta female figurines bedecked with jewellery. These figurines represent the ancient "Great Mother Goddess" whose cult was also wide-spread in the Near Middle East in ancient times. There is evidence that tree and animal worship was also practised. Later religious influences include Buddhism evidenced by the mound-stupa of the Kushana period and Hinduism from the Siva Lingam. Amongst the artifacts excavated from the ruins are a toy replica of a bullock cart, the figure of dancing girl and a musical instrument — a small clay ball with four holes called Borendo. It is said that we do not so much outgrow the past as we grow out of it. Moenjodaro, the mound of the dead, is not so dead. 5,000 years later, a few miles from the ruined city, farmers still use the same bullock cart and stray shepherds still blow the baneful melody of the Borendo during their lonesome wanderings in search for green pasture. The houses, streets and drainage system of nearby towns still bear a marked resemblance to Moenjodaro architecture.

Cotton still forms a main crop of the valley and like the Moenjodarens the Sindhis still wear a long printed cloth around their bodies. Through the ages, the Sindhis have been known for bright and richly coloured cotton textiles and a highly developed sense of colour combination. Ajrak is still one of the most fascinating block printing techniques in Sindhi fabrics.

The bible mentions that when Christ was born, he was wrapped in a cloth called "Sindon". It is said that this cloth was being exported from Sind which had trade relations with other countries. The carpets in the courts of the Pharoah's likewise came from Sind or the Indus valley.

Thus antiquity and continuity go together in the land of the Indus river — a many faceted land of a thousand doors each different from the other.

Facts about Moenjodaro

Original name: Moenjo-daro

Literal meaning: Mound of the dead.

Race/nation that constructed Moenjodaro: Skeletons found in the remains of the city, identified by archaeologist are the following four racial types: 1) Proto-Australoid, 2) Mediterranean, 3) Mongoloid, and 4) Alpine.

Purpose of construction: Human settlement

History of construction: Between the years of 2500 and 1500 BC, one of the most well-developed urban civilisations of the ancient world, namely the Indus Valley Civilization having two metropolitan cities, Moenjodaro and Harrapa flourished.

Location: 27°32' north, 68° east; about 45m above sea level; 618 km from Karachi (8 hours by the new Super Highway)

Size: Original dimensions of the city unknown, the Indus valley civilization is spread over an area roughly 1,000 miles in length, from north to south and is more than 800 miles wide.

Representative architecture: Great Bath (with a flight of steps at either end, it has a large tank with verandas at all four sides), Granary, and Pillared Hall (80 feet square with twenty rectangular pillars to support the roof.)

Building materials: Fired bricks of English and Flemish bonds.

Famous objects of fine art: Terracotta figures of male, female and bird; (The female figurines are bedecked with jewellery and represent cult of great Mother Goddess.) Seals bearing life-like representation of animals such as the Brahamani Bull, the short-horned bull, buffalo, tiger, and also mythological animals like the unicorn and a horned tiger; Dancing girl in bronze; Gold necklaces, pendants of beads of semi-precious stones, and other ornaments.

Reasons for destruction: Various opinions are raised such as adverse climatic changes and recurrent floods plus increasing pressure on population which weakened the economic resources until the city suffered a sudden and complete eclipse about 1500 BC by the invasion of a barbarian people identified as Aryans.

Causes of present collapsing: Soon after the excavations, these remains were afflicted by the plaque of waterlogging and the leprosy of salinity. These two diseases combined with the threat of erosion by the Indus river.

Plans of preservation: A master plan was prepared at the International Symposium in 1973 in Pakistan for preservation of Moenjodaro. Unesco has mobilized the world opinion to raise the sum of US$5 million. Pakistan government, on the other hand, is implementing a number of short-term measures to arrest further decay of the remains.

Present population: No habitation or settlement within the excavations of remains of the city.

Life and culture in Moenjodaro's golden period

Flourished during: 2500 to 1500 BC

Population: Not ascertainable

Social system: Probably theocracy

Religion: There is evidence of a cult of water bath as ceremonial medium, the cult of Great Mother Goddess, and animal and tree worship.

Economical foundation: Agriculture, ocean trade with Mesopotamia and Egypt

Staple food: Wheat, barely, dates, sesame.

Housing: Mostly double-storeyed houses with drainage system. They varied only in size, from 2 to 10 or more rooms. A single passage-way from the exterior to inner court. Wooden staircase leading to the upper store was steep and narrow. Roofs of the houses were flat and rested on wooden rafter. Very few examples of windows were found. Very simple, comfortable and utilitarian.

Costume: The indication of the dyers workshop in the remains of city and certain patterns depicted on short dresses worn by sculptured figures suggested that they liked colour clothing, often embroidered or printed and they wore peculiar kind of headdress.

Marital system: Not ascertainable.

Calendar and festivals: The public festivals may have corresponded with seasonal changes, and therefore there must have existed some kind of primitive calendar based upon observation of the sun, the moon and certain constellations.

Currency: Nonexistent

Writing system: Pictographic script on seals stamps. A close study of South Indian scripts such as Tamil, Telegu and Malyalam, suggested that all these Dravidian scripts are most probably the by-products of the Indus writing.

Tools of writing: Steatite seals of steatite stone & stamps.

Means of Transportation: Bullock cart, boat.

Sri Lanka

Cultural Triangle of Sri Lanka — Buddhist Capitals of the Sinhala Dynasty

Sri Lanka, the home of Theravada Buddhism, a country steeped in the tradition exemplified in the texts written in an old Indian dialect Pali, has also an unbroken tradition of written history. Its outstanding monuments, though now mostly in ruin, affirm the validity of these past records. Buddhist culture as confirmed in these chronicles has flourished in the island of Sri Lanka for well over two thousand years in spite of internal conflicts and invasions from outside. The people of Sri Lanka are now trying to restore and preserve their cultural heritage that have faced rapid destructive forces especially during the last four centuries. To supplement this national effort, Unesco has undertaken the task of mobilizing international solidarity and co-operation to assist Sri Lanka in her requirements as are not obtainable in the country itself. An international campaign has been launched for this purpose stressing the historical and cultural significance of monuments within the area now identified as the Cultural Triangle.

Monuments and sites selected for preservation and restoration under the Project of the Cultural Triangle are scattered within an area stretching between the present towns of Anuradhapura, Polonnaruwa and Kandy.

Anuradhapura

The capital of Sri Lanka from the fifth century BC until the AD tenth century was Anuradhapura. It has seen not only the introduction of Buddhism to Sri Lanka but also its many upheavals and predicaments under various rulers throughout this long period. Numerous buildings erected and razed down to earth; inscriptions short and long, well preserved or weather-beaten, artistic creations extant or destroyed at various points of time have in numerous ways left their indelible marks for us to be reminded of a highly developed civilization with a remarkable aesthetic sense and artistic refinement that existed in Sri Lanka in the past. The walled city of Anuradhapura housed the oldest Buddhist establishment Mahavihara and its rival institution Abhayagiriya. Among its monasteries the priority for restoration has been placed on Jetavana, supposed to be the tallest stupa in the world when it was completed. Founded by King Mahasen in AD fourth century, it was completed by his successor Sirimeghavanna. It had been restored a number of times until Parakrama Bahu I in the twelfth century raised it to a height of 140 cubits (400 feet). The second major stupa to be conserved in Anuradhapura is the Abhayagiri situated to the north of the capital city. Much older than Jetavana, this Vihara was founded by Vattagamani Abhaya in the second century BC and later became the seat of a heterodox sect of Mahayana monks who were in constant ideological conflict with the Mahavihara bhikkhus. Mahayana monks were growing in numbers and when the famous Chinese traveller Fa-Hsien visited Sri Lanka in AD fifth century he found 5,000 of them in residence at Abhayagiri.

Polonnaruwa

The capital of Sri Lanka was shifted to Polonnaruwa by about the tenth century, but it gained fame only in the twelfth and thirteenth centuries after the colossal work done by its greatest ruler and one of the foremost men in Sri Lanka's history, Parakrama Bahu the Great. The eight mile long bund of the giant irrigation work he constructed called the Sea of Parakrama extends from the east side of the capital and its water is tapped from a river 15 miles away. Most of the historic buildings at Polonnaruwa, except those in the Alahana Parivena group are comparatively in a better conserved state than the monuments at Anuradhapura. Among the remaining structures at Polonnaruwa one finds numerous Hindu temples dedicated to Siva and Vishnu from where valuable bronzes of some Hindu gods have been recovered. The main buildings dominating the landscape of Alahana Parivena complex are the Buddhasimapasada, Lankatilaka Image House and Kirivehera all founded by Parakrama Bahu the Great. Buddhasimapasada is said to have been twelve storeys high while the Lankatilaka Image House was originally five storeys in height. On the facade of the Lankatilaka Image House there are rows of lions in relief and dwarfs as ornamentation. Paintings and images of celestial beings found here are of special interest. Kirivehera also known in the past as Rupavati, is the best preserved stupa in this complex. Edifices in the Alahana Parivena complex stand out among other monuments as they are situated on terraced ground covering a large acreage.

Dambulla Vihara attracts not only tourists but every pilgrim on his way to the sacred places in Anuradhapura and

Polonnaruwa for it is situated midway between Kandy and the other two old cities. Founded in the second century BC, Dambulla Vihara contains numerous caves and pre-Christian inscriptions. The natural caves of Dambulla were refashioned at a later period to house a series of shrines. It was renovated in the eleventh century and rebuilt and embellished in the twelfth century. King Nissankawalla who was responsible for the rebuilding in the twelfth century states in his inscription that he gilded 73 images in the cave temple. Some of the old paintings there belong to the Anuradhapura period while most of the other murals could be traced to the eighteenth century which saw the last phase of its restoration.

Not far away from Dambulla, we come across a rock rising to a height of 600 feet from the ground containing a royal palace and a garden on its summit. It is believed that Kassapa, a ruler who lived in the fifth century, built his palace on Sigiri in imitation of the residence of the god Kuvera and lived there as a god-king. A series of paintings of beautiful damsels adorn its precipitous Rockwell and the graffiti on the gallery wall has provided an excellent collection of folk verse.

Kandy

The last Sinhala kingdom had its capital at Kandy, a greenclad town nestling in the central hills of the island of Sri Lanka. Its monuments include the Temple of the Tooth, the two Viharas of Malwatta and Asgiriya and the four Devales, or four shrines Natha, Maha Vishnu, Pattini and Kataragama. The Tooth Relic of the Buddha from the medieval period of the country's history has been the palladium of the sovereignty of the people and the insignia of royalty. Dalada Maligawa, the repository of the Tooth Relic, exhibits some unique architectural designs and contains exquisite works of craftsmanship.

The spectacular annual festival held in Kandy to parade the guardian deities of the country represents one of the oldest festivals known to man. The practice of carrying the Tooth Relic in this procession started in the time of Kirthi Sri Rajasingha in the eighteenth century. A popular festival to invoke the blessings of gods to bestow life giving water (rain) has from this time changed over to a religious festival without losing its original ritual form.

Facts about cultural triangle (Anuradhapura, Polonnaruwa & Kandy)

Race/nation that constructed Anuradhapura, Polonnaruwa & Kandy: Sinhalese.

Purpose of construction: To establish cities and monastic establishments.

History of construction: Anuradhapura was the first capital built in the fifth century BC. Polonnaruwa was the second capital built in AD tenth century. Kandy was the capital of the Central region in the fourteenth-eighteenth century.

Location: 7°23'-8°36' north, 80°36'-81°04' east

Representative architecture: In Anuradhapura: Mahavihara (the oldest monastery of Anuradhapura); the Jetavana, the Abayagiri & the Ruvanvalisaya (colossal Buddhist stupas)

In Polonnaruwa: the Buddhasim pasada, Lankatilaka Image House and Kirivehera in the Alahana Parivena complex founded by Parakrama Bahu the Great.

In Kandy: The Temple of the Tooth, two viharas of Malwatta and Asgiriya.

Style of architecture: Sinhalese Buddhist Style.

Building materials: Mud, lime, brick, stone, wood.

Famous objects of fine art: The colossal Buddha image at Avukana; stone reliefs at the Issruminiya in Anuradhapura.

Wall paintings of beautiful maidens in the rock fortress of Sigiriya. The Buddha statues at the Gal-vihara and many other statues of the Buddha and Hindu gods in Polonnaruwa.

Frescoes in the Tivanka Pilimage in Polonnaruwa.

Statues and wall paintings in the Dambulla rock temple.

Style of art: Sinhalese, Gupta, Amaravati and Dravidian.

Reasons for destruction : Foreign invasion

Causes of present collapsing: Natural and climatic forces

Plans of preservation/presentation: Unesco-Sri Lanka Cultural Project costing 600 million rupees and taking five years.

Present population: No inhabitants in the old cities of Anuradhapura and Polonnaruwa; no inhabitants in the area declared as sacred city in Kandy.

Life and culture in the golden periods of Anuradhapura and Polonnaruwa

Flourished during: Anuradhapura from the fifth to tenth century; Polonnaruwa in the twelfth century

Population: Unknown

Social system: Monarchical democracy

Religion: Buddhism

Economical foundation: Agriculture and trade

Staple food: Rice

Housing: Houses made of wattle, daub and brick

Costume: Sinhalese dress

Marital system: Unknown

Calendar: Lunar calendar

Festival: Mainly religious festivals

Currency: Coins (gold, silver and copper)

Writing system: Brahmi and Sinhala

Tools of writing: Stone, ola leaves.

Means of transportation: Carts and animals.

Entertainment: Music, dancing and singing.

Thailand

Sukhothai — Where Ancient Silent Buddhas Reigned

Sukhothai, literally meaning "the dawn of happiness" is evidently one of the oldest cities of the Thai race. About seven and a half centuries ago, the history of Sukhothai began. The great man of Sukhothai whose name was Pohkhun Bang Klang Hao led the Thai to drive away the Khmers who had occupied this small Thai town, and became the first king of the Sukhothai Dynasty.

Sukhothai soon became a mighty kingdom of Southeast Asia. It extended its territory from year to year till the end of the period of King Ramkamhaeng the great. King Ramkamhaeng, the third king of Sukhothai, was not only one of the greatest warriors but is also considered the greatest man Thailand has ever produced. He succeeded his elder brother in 1279 AD and his reign lasted until 1299. It was Ramkamhaeng himself who devised the Thai alphabet which has been used ever since. King Ramkamhaeng also started to write Thai history, which was inscribed in stone. So far, more than twenty stone inscriptions have been found around the area of the original city of Sukhothai.

The old Sukhothai is now dead. There now remain only the relics of the past, yet this mighty civilization can be traced back. The ruins left over seven hundred years ago scattered throughout the great city of Sukhothai are almost three hundred in number. A great many more ruins remain in nearby towns once also called royal towns, and what has been left speaks to us today, telling us how prosperous the Sukhothai kingdom once was!

The glorious past can even be pictured more clearly if we read through the inscriptions, some examples of which are as follows:

"In my father's time, I served my father, I served my mother. Whenever I got animals and fish, I brought them to my father. When I had fruits which were delicious, I brought them to my father. When I caught elephants, I brought them to my father. When I conquered a town and captured elephants, men or women, silver or gold, I gave them all to my father. When my father died, then came my elder brother's time. I served my brother just as I served my father. My brother died and I got the whole kingdom for myself."

These words were, no doubt, the King's himself. The following, however, is believed to have been added by his men. It tells us something of what life in Sukhothai was like in the thirteenth century. It reads as follows: "Muang Sukhothai is wonderful. There are fish in the streams, and rice in the fields. The King does not levy tolls on his subjects for the roads. People take cattle and horses to trade. Whoever wants to trade in elephants may do so. Whoever wants to trade in horses may do so. Whoever wants to trade in silver or gold may do so. People are happy. If anyone, son of the royal family, or son of lords, passes away, he leaves for his sons all properties including his elephants, wives, children, granaries, stores of rice and groves of areca and betel. When commoners, sons of the royal family, or sons of lords disagree, the King examines the cases to find the truth and then settles it justly for them".

These words not only give us an idea of how life was in Sukhothai politically, economically and traditionally, but also confirm that Sukhothai was once very civilized indeed. Ruins of temples as well as images of Buddha lying here and there and all other valuable objects found within the city give an indication of the civilization and prosperity of the Sukhothai period.

The Sukhothai period is very well-known among artists as well as those who appreciate works of art. Around the thirteenth century, a completely new approach appeared. Instead of emphasizing volume, which is typical of the Khmer style adopted at the very beginning, the Thais developed ethereal and linear qualities. The large images of Buddha of the period both in bronze and carved from stone, considered master-pieces, are characterised by oval faces, long noses and impart a feeling of serenity.

Sukhothai is also well-known for its pottery. There are a few indications that the Thais of that time were so advanced that they even exported some of their celadon, known by the name Sung-galok. Although the Thais received instruction from the Chinese on techniques of making fine ceramics, the style was quite different.

There were also some mural paintings in certain temples in Sukhothai. It is a pity, however, that they could not be well preserved in Thailand's hot climate and high humidity. The study of Sukhothai has indicated that the Sukhothai Kingdom was unable to maintain its power and prosperity for very long because of the problems of political geography and economics, both of which hampered the development of the city.

For visitors today, Sukhothai represents one of the most fascinating archeological centres in Asia. The ancient temples which now stand as a romantic reminder of the town's past glory are many and varied and spread over a vast area of land. Some of these shrines have been badly damaged by the ravages of weather and time but most of them are still in remarkably good condition, considering their age. The weather-bitten appearance of these ruins gives them a charm and beauty which the original structures could never have had. Each shrine is different, or at least there are general distinctive architectural styles to be seen, and the setting is beautiful. While most of the temples are located on flat ground, some are set deep in the jungle, where the monks of that time presumably were able to enjoy the peace and serenity that they sought for their temple. Others are to be found on open ground. The setting for these temples is often made more beautiful by the range of mountains some distance away, which forms an attractive backdrop to these already serene and peaceful ruins. Others are located beside large man-made ponds which were designed to hold water to supply the city needed during the dry season. To quote the author Archilles Clarac, "The detail, balance and harmony of the proportions and decorations... and the beauty of the area where it stands, bear witness to the unusual and refined aesthetic sense of the architects of the Sukhothai period".

Sukhothai ruins certainly are not monuments to commemorate the achievement of any single person in history. Every single building was constructed with a pure faith and firm belief in Buddhism, which at that time was beginning to spread through the country. That is why there are no signs of bitterness, either from forced labour by the citizens or as the result of destruction by the enemy. They can only be the symbols of art — pure art that has been ruined only by nature, and is waiting to be appreciated by all interested travellers and art lovers.

Facts about Sukhothai

Original name: Sukhothai

Literal meaning: Dawn of happiness

Race/nation that constructed Sukhothai: Thai

Purpose of construction: Kingdom

History of construction: In 1238, Pokhun Bang Klang Hao led the Thai to drive away the Khmers who had occupied this small Thai town, and became the first king of the Sukhothai dynasty.

Location: 17°01' north, 99°42' east; 65 m above sea level; 452 km from Bangkok (6 hours by bus)

Size: 70 square km

Representative architecture: Wat Mahathat; the lotus bud stupa in Wat Trapang Ngoen; the round stupa in Wat Sra Sri.

Style of architecture: Sukhothai

Building materials: Mostly brick

Famous objects of fine art: Pra Sri Sakyamuni (Buddha image) in Wat Suthat, Bangkok; Walking Buddha Image in Wat Benjamabopit, Bangkok.

Style/features: Sokhothai

Other important sites: Turiang kiln site; Aranyik area

Reasons for destruction: In 1584 when King Naresuan of Ayudhya proclaimed independence from Burma, he ordered all the populations of the northern cities to migrate to Ayudhya. Sukhothai was thus deserted and had since been destroyed by time and nature.

Causes of present collapsing: Vandalism and the ravage of weather

Plans of preservation/presentation: Construction of National Historical Park by restoring the environment of the ancient city of Sukhothai as described in the stone inscriptions of the era by means of planting historical trees, clearing the sand out of dikes and ponds, and strengthening some of the monuments to prevent them from further destruction.

Unesco film "Save Sukhothai" already produced.

Present population: 521,361

Life and culture in Sukhothai's golden period

Flourished during: Thirteenth-fifteenth centuries

Population: Over 300,000 people

Social system: Monarchy

Religion: Buddhism

Economical foundation: Agriculture, "Sung-galok" ceramic ware

Staple Food: Rice

Housing: Houses made of wood

Costume: Textile and ornament

Marital system: Polygamy

Calendar: Lunar calendar

Festivals: Candle-burning, Fireworks (Loy Krathong festival at present.)

Currency: Unknown

Writing system: Thai alphabet

Tools of writing: Stone

Means of transportation: Cow, buffalo, horse and elephant

Entertainment: Singing and playing the musical instruments such as drum, xylophone and harp.

Vietnam

Hue — The Imperial City of Poetry

Hue was once the capital of Vietnam. Everyone still remembers it as a poetic epic, a huge architectural work built in harmony with the majestic environment of perennial green vegetation. Hue boasts 99 palaces, tombs, shrines, pagodas and temples interlacing with one another. The main palaces were built with the support of over one hundred long columns of precious wood lacquered in red and gold or laid bare as if to challenge the power of time. The Thai Hoa palace, Ngo Mon gate, The Mieu (chapel), Hung Mieu (temple devoted to the cult of King Gia Long's parents), Hien Lam Cac (Soul Porch), Phu Van Lau (Pavilion of Phu Van), Cung Dien Tho (the mother-queen's apartments) were built with cornered roofs covered with yellow and green enamelled tiles. The roofs are often decorated with a sun, moon, or dragons, phoenixes, wine and calabashes. Everywhere we see skilfully carved statues and engravings of great aesthetic value representing deified men, and the four-animal set of dragon, giraffe, tortoise and phoenix.

The Perfume river

The Perfume River (the Huong Giang), which has witnessed the ups and downs of the city, meanders in an immense forest pervaded with the fragrancy of medicinal plants. It is closely linked to the pagodas and temples such as Confucius temple, Hon Chen shrine, Elephant temple, and the seven-story Thien Mu pagoda. The tombs of Nguen Emperors were built near its course to the south of the Citadel.

The boatmen and passengers sing merrily with each other when they meet on the river. They recite satirical poems and sing folksongs. At Dong Ba market place or Thuong Dao railway station near the river, people throng to hear a 3000-verse satire about the "surrender of the imperial city" with the accompaniment of a mono-string instrument.

Historical sites

The Citadel, having a square shape, 2.6 km each side, was built from 1805 to 1825. The Royal City — a square enclosed by a wall with four gates — is inside this citadel and the Forbidden Purple City is inside the Royal City. In this huge working site, 50,000 to 80,000 people did forced labour everyday. The court arrogated to itself the right to make use of the most precious materials, to import valuable articles from abroad and to mobilize the most skilful workmen and artisans in the country to work for it.

Before the Mieu chapel, there are nine big copper urns (the one in the middle was cast in 1835) representing nine Nguyen Kings. Each urn weighing about 2.6 tons relates the history of the reign of a king and its elaborate sculpture depicts the events of the remote past. Each urn has an open mouth to receive the favours from Heaven and stands on three feet symbolizing the stability and prosperity of the empire.

Thien Mu pagoda, built in 1601, stands on top of a vast hill hemmed in between the Perfume River and a mountain range. It is a seven-story tower (22 metres) built on the foundation of a demolished pagoda. On both sides are four smaller pagodas, one of which has a bell weighing 2.6 tons. At the rear of Thien Mu pagoda is the Dai Hung temple adorned with statues of a protecting genie and generals coming from Heaven. The pagoda is wrapped in a clam, serene and ethereal atmosphere.

Life at court

Built on a 2-metre high foundation, Thai Hoa palace has about 135 red and gold painted columns. There stood the throne hall and the audience hall. The monarch lived in Truong Sinh palace; he read books and heard book commentaries in Kham Van (royal library) in Co Ha garden. The forbidden purple enceinte with seven gates each having a special function was reserved for the Royal family. The King's harem occupied five palaces. In the forbidden precinct there were also the royal theatre, royal kitchen, the rest home and living quarter of the guards and physicians. Ngo Mon gate was opened only on grand occasions when the monarch received high-ranking dignitaries.

The royal band played the traditional music with such instruments as 16-string zither, 36-string dulcimer, two-string violin, flute, trumpet, cymbals, drum, gong, tocsin, castanets and mono-string zither. It usually performed on festive days, on the occasion of a wedding or funeral. Of the traditional dances only the principal ones are performed at present: flower dance, candle-dance, twin phoenix dance, unicorn dance and sword dance. Today, we still meet a living witness in the person of Mr. Duong Van Lam, 76 years old, who was the conductor of the royal band. He returned to his function in 1975 to direct a group of musicians and to collect old musical treasures.

Imperial tombs

The tombs of the Nguyen Kings concentrated in a spacious area and encircled by walls are built in a particular style and surrounded by gardens, lakes, shrines, palaces, statues of tiger, dragon, phoenix and china vases.

Gia Long's tomb, built in 1814 when the monarch was still alive, is characterized by majestic simplicity harmonizing with picturesque pine-clad hills.

Minh Mang's tomb (built in 1841) and Tu Duc's tomb (1864) contain in their precincts lakes, angling pavilion, "pleasure" pavilion, temples, theatre, royal bathing-place, shrines and even palaces reserved for the King's harem.

King Tu Duc personally watched the construction of his palaces and tomb for which he spent a lot of money and forced the inhabitants to do a gruesome corvee. This construction was started in 1864 with the participation of tens of thousands of soldiers, artisans, artists and peasants. The work was completed after thirteen years of hard labour.

Destruction

In this tropical country, everything — pagodas, temples, shrines and roofs of houses — is worn out by humidity. The mortared parts of buildings are destroyed by moss and roots of trees though this mortar was made of the famous Long Tho lime, mixed with treacle, pulp and sand and had great solidity. Hue has frequently suffered from flood. Sometimes the water of the Perfume River rose so high that it caused the death of many people and threatened Minh Mang's tomb. The fire in 1947 destroyed many monuments and their sumptuous decorations such as Dai Kim Mon, Can Chanh Palace, the private apartment of the King and Queen.

Since ancient times, people have been captivated by beautiful Hue, a city lying among gently-sloping hills and watered by the calm Perfume River. This beautiful city, however, has weathered terrible trails caused by fire and warfare, and shared the same fate as other cultural ruins, worn out by time and climate. Now, Hue has the secret and captivating beauty of an ancient imperial capital, with nature and man, the new and the old, merging harmoniously with each other.

Facts about Hue

Race/nation that constructed Hue: Vietnamese

Purpose of construction: To build a capital

History of construction: Hue was the site of the capital of Champa Kingdom constructed by the Chams (twelfth-fourteenth century). After destruction of Champa Kingdom by Vietnamese in the early 14th century, Vietnamese dynasties were established. The existing imperial city was constructed by Nguyen Dynasty (1802-1945).

Location: 16°45' north, 107°52' east; 654 km from Hanoi

Representative architecture: Royal residence in the Imperial City; Khai Dinh Museum; Seven tombs of the Nguyen rulers consisting of temples, palaces and reflecting pools; Thien Mu Pagoda.

Style of architecture: Nguyen style

Building materials: Brick, wood & Laterite

Famous objects of fine art: Lacquer paintings, potteries, Vietnamese tapestries, statues of Buddha and Emperors.

Reasons for destruction: After Nguyen royal families fled to France in 1945, Hue was under the protection of the government of South Vietnam at that time. Monuments of Hue were then gradually destroyed due to the absence of any maintenance for more than thirty years, air raids and gunfire during the war, especially the 1947 fire.

Causes of present collapsing: Abundant rainfall and humidity (roofs are almost all leaky and the timbers are deteriorating as a result of water coming through.)

Plans of preservation/presentation: In 1976, the Vietnamese government empowered the Hue Historical Monuments Service to take urgent protective measures. Unesco, in co-operation with the Vietnamese government, has drawn up an aid project. The first phase of the restoration programme concerns 17 monuments including two tombs and runs from 1981 to 1986, costing US$4 million of which Vietnam would contribute US$757,000.

Present population: Over 200,000.

Life and culture in Hue's golden period

Flourished during: Former half of the nineteenth century

Social system: Monarchy

Religion: Confucianism, Buddhism

Economical foundation: Agriculture and Trade

Staple food: Rice

Housing: Wooden houses without floors

Costume: Vietnamese dress

Marital system: Monogamy

Calendar: Lunar Calendar

Festivals: Festival (every three years) related to Royal ceremony where Emperor himself offers prayers to Gods, Heaven and Earth and ancestral spirits for the happiness and welfare.

Writing system: Vietnamese Chinese characters, Chu'Nom

Tools of writing: Paper, Vietnamese handmade paper

Means of transportation: Bullock cart, horse, jinrikisha

Entertainment: Singing and dancing.

Contributors

Part 1: The Way of Life

A.D.T.E. Perera; A.K. Bhattacharyya; Abdul Hamid bin Abdul Shukor; Abhi Subedi; Ashr F. Malek-Madani; Assad Behrouzan; Asutosh Bhattacharyya; Atsuhiko Bekki; Bandula Jayawardhana; Behruz Mussavi; Chalermsri Dhamabutra; Chamrieng Bhavichitra; Christopher Hooi; Crystyn Cech; Dendeviin Sandagdorj; Dovdoin Bayar; Du-hyun Lee; Farooq Hossain; Fr. Pedro Walpole; Francoise Pommaret Imaeda; Hae Young Lee; Hamdam bin Yahya; Hidesaburo Hagiwara; Htin Fatt; Ine Istanto; James Danandjaja; Junichi Hayashi; K.M. Chadha; Kapila Vatsyan; Kaushalya Ramdas; Kay Thi Kyi Win; Kazuo Inoue; Khunying Pa-ob Poshakrishna; Koh Bou-Ja; L.K. Karunaratne; M. Hanif Raza; Machiko Aoyagi; Madhuri Madhok; Mah Para Zaidi; Manu Bangdel; Masuda Akhtar; Mayuree Veraprasert; Mien Ahmad Rifai; Mohammed Hassan Abrishami; Muna Salam; Myank R. Rimpoche; Naomichi Isige; Nguyen Thi Anh; Nhok Thaisith; Niched Suntornpithug; Pranee Wongdes; Premlata Puri; R. Acosta; Ramani Fernando; Ramon Arevalo Obusan; Rigzin Dorji; Samrith Buasisvath; Seki Yoko; Shigeru Ikuta; Shigeru Makita; Sombat Plainoi; Takenori Noguchi; Takeo Nakamatsu; Tseeliin Ayush; Tulasi Diwasa Joshi; U Htin Gyi; Vijay Parmer; Virgilia P. Talaboc; Wang Yangle; Wen Yuan; Whang Hae Sung; Yasmin Rauf Khan; Yoshiro Imaeda.

Part 2: Folk Dances in Asian Villages

Du-Hyun Lee; Hisashi Hata; I.M.S. Sinnya; Jiryo Miyao; Kapila Vatsyan; Keiji Iwata; Kullasap Gesmankit; M. Hanif Raza; M.H. Goonatilleka; Pairote Gesmankit; Shigeko Nakamura; Suwandono; U Htin Gyi.

Part 3: Asian Music Scene

Charles Lazaroo; Commission National de Mongolie pour l', Unesco; Exequiel S. Molina; Maki Okada; Sumati Mutatkar.

Part 4: Animals and Folk Culture

Asutosh Bhattacharyya; Han Meilin; John Kolia; Meena Vaidya; Muhammad Haji Salleh; Pranee Wongdes; Taryo Obayashi; Tulasi Diwasa Joshi.

Part 5: Bamboo Culture

A.Y. Tating; Hiroshi Muroi; I.M.S. Sinnya; Ismail Zain.

Part 6: Performing Arts

Chung Byung-ho; Grace Morley; Jacob Simet; Misumi Haruo; Premlata Puri.

Part 7: Puppet Theatre

J. Tilakasiri; Jiryo Miyao; Kapila Vatsyan; Lin Kun; Michael Creighton; Pandam Guritno; Taiji Kawajiri.

Part 8: Cinema in Asia

Film Centre of the University of the Philippines; Osamu Takizawa; Shanta Serbjeet Singh; Tadao Sato; Wen Yuan.

Part 9: The *Ramayana* in Asia

G. Sankara Pillai; I. Made Bandem; Kapila Vatsyan; Mattani M. Rutnin; Tulasi Diwasa Joshi; Yoshihiro Matsunami.

Part 10: Games and Pastimes

A.M. Paktiawal; Abdul G. Dershen; Anwar Enayetullah; Cao Er-si; Chaleo Manilero; Fumio Koizumi; Gesmankit Kullasap; Haku Shah; Harumi Koshiba; Iqbal Jatoi; Ismail Zain; Kitade Seigoro; Kwak Joon; Leticia G. Del Valle; Madhuri Madhok; Mahmud Shah Qureshi; Nonoy Marcelo; Pairote Park Kijoon; Raza Hamadani; Sadao Yamane; Shan Peng; Tadao Saito; Teodulo Lugtu; Tseeliin Ayuoh; Wen Yuan.

Part 11: Embroidery, Textiles and Batik

Anupa Lal; Apolinario Y. Tating; Dorji Nyima; Douangdeuane Bounyavong; Huh Dong-hwa; Iran Ala Firouz; Ismail Zain; M. Hanif Raza; Prabha Panwar; Shobita Punja; Suwati Kartiwa; Tirta Amidjaja; Violet Oon; Vipula Dharmawardena; Zhang Chang Ban; Zhang Wen Bin; Zohreh Rouhfar.

---

* The various chapters in this book are largely based on articles contributed to *Asian Pacific Culture,* a cross-cultural magazine of the Asian Cultural Centre for UNESCO. In spite of our best efforts we could not trace the names of some of the contributors to whom we express our apologies — Editors.

Part 12: Myths, Superstitions and Heavenly Bodies

John Kolia; Jyotindra Jain; M. Moghdam; Nighat N Malik; Partap Sharma; Sombat Plainoi; Subagio Sastrowardoyo; Wen Yuan.

Part 13: The Wonder That is Asia — Glorious Monuments

[Afghanistan (Bamiyan), Bangladesh, Bhutan, Burma, Cambodia, China, India, Indonesia (Java), Japan, Korea, Mongolia, Nepal, Pakistan, Sri Lanka, Thailand, Vietnam]

Akira Miyaji; Centre for Cultural Resources & Training, India; Dejo Savanananda; Dovdoin Bayer; H.S. Patnaik; Itsuji Yoshikawa; Jamijang Ganbold; Lopon Pemala; Ly Khac Cung; Nazimuddin Ahmed; Nobuo Ito; Paik Syeung-gil; R. Sengupta; R. Soekmono; Rafi Samizay; Rigzin Dorji; S.J. Sumanasekera Banda; Shafie Rahel; Shaphalya Amatya; Takayasu Higuchi; Toru Ono; Uxi Mufti; Wang Renbo; Yoshiaki Ishizawa.